The American Business Cycle

Studies in Business Cycles
Volume 25

National Bureau of Economic Research
Conference on Research in Business Cycles

The American Business Cycle

Continuity and Change

Edited by Robert J. Gordon

 The University of Chicago Press

Chicago and London

Robert J. Gordon, professor of economics at Northwestern University and research associate at the NBER, is the editor of *Milton Friedman's Monetary Framework,* also published by the University of Chicago Press.

The University of Chicago Press, Chicago 60637
The University of Chicago Press, Ltd., London

Library of Congress Cataloging in Publication Data

Main entry under title:

The American business cycle.

    Includes bibliographies and index.
    1. Business cycles—United States—Addresses, essays, lectures.   I. Gordon, Robert J. (Robert James), 1940– .
HB3743.A47 1986   338.5'42'0973   85-29026
ISBN 0-226-30452-3

Relation of the Directors to the
Work and Publications of the
National Bureau of Economic Research

1. The object of the National Bureau of Economic Research is to ascertain and to present to the public important economic facts and their interpretation in a scientific and impartial manner. The Board of Directors is charged with the responsibility of ensuring that the work of the National Bureau is carried on in strict conformity with this object.

2. The President of the National Bureau shall submit to the Board of Directors, or to its Executive Committee, for their formal adoption all specific proposals for research to be instituted.

3. No research report shall be published by the National Bureau until the President has sent each member of the Board a notice that a manuscript is recommended for publication and that in the President's opinion it is suitable for publication in accordance with the principles of the National Bureau. Such notification will include an abstract or summary of the manuscript's content and a response form for use by those Directors who desire a copy of the manuscript for review. Each manuscript shall contain a summary drawing attention to the nature and treatment of the problem studied, the character of the data and their utilization in the report, and the main conclusions reached.

4. For each manuscript so submitted, a special committee of the Directors (including Directors Emeriti) shall be appointed by majority agreement of the President and Vice Presidents (or by the Executive Committee in case of inability to decide on the part of the President and Vice Presidents), consisting of three Directors selected as nearly as may be one from each general division of the Board. The names of the special manuscript committee shall be stated to each Director when notice of the proposed publication is submitted to him. It shall be the duty of each member of the special manuscript committee to read the manuscript. If each member of the manuscript committee signifies his approval within thirty days of the transmittal of the manuscript, the report may be published. If at the end of that period any member of the manuscript committee withholds his approval, the President shall then notify each member of the Board, requesting approval or disapproval of publication, and thirty days additional shall be granted for this purpose. The manuscript shall then not be published unless at least a majority of the entire Board who shall have voted on the proposal within the time fixed for the receipt of votes shall have approved.

5. No manuscript may be published, though approved by each member of the special manuscript committee, until forty-five days have elapsed from the transmittal of the report in manuscript form. The interval is allowed for the receipt of any memorandum of dissent or reservation, together with a brief statement of his reasons, that any member may wish to express; and such memorandum of dissent or reservation shall be published with the manuscript if he so desires. Publication does not, however, imply that each member of the Board has read the manuscript, or that either members of the Board in general or the special committee have passed on its validity in every detail.

6. Publications of the National Bureau issued for informational purposes concerning the work of the Bureau and its staff, or issued to inform the public of activities of Bureau staff, and volumes issued as a result of various conferences involving the National Bureau shall contain a specific disclaimer noting that such publication has not passed through the normal review procedures required in this resolution. The Executive Committee of the Board is charged with review of all such publications from time to time to ensure that they do not take on the character of formal research reports of the National Bureau, requiring formal Board approval.

7. Unless otherwise determined by the Board or exempted by the terms of paragraph 6, a copy of this resolution shall be printed in each National Bureau publication.

(Resolution adopted October 25, 1926, as revised through September 30, 1974)

To
OTTO ECKSTEIN (1927–84)
AND
ROBERT AARON GORDON (1908–78)

Both of whom devoted most of their professional lifetimes to the study and understanding of the American business cycle, and both of whom served the National Bureau of Economic Research as long-standing members of its board of directors.*

*Eckstein served on the NBER board of directors from 1968 to 1984, and Gordon from 1961 to 1976.

Contents

Prefatory Note

This volume contains the proceedings of the National Bureau of Economic Research Conference on Business Cycles, held at the Dorado Beach Hotel, Puerto Rico, 22–25 March 1984. Authors were given the opportunity to revise their papers after the conference, and in turn the discussants' comments were revised to take account of these revisions. At the conference itself, one of the two discussants for each paper was responsible for the oral summary and in some cases did not write out in full the critical comments that followed the summary; in these cases the commentators have subsequently rewritten their contributions to exclude their summarizations and extend their critiques. All authors were given a chance to contribute a rejoinder to their critics and also to correct factual errors that may have infiltrated the discussants' comments and the floor discussion summary.

Preparing the summaries of the floor discussion at each session was a task shared equally by Stephen R. King and John M. Veitch, both of whom worked from their own handwritten notes rather than a formal transcript. If in some cases the discussion summaries seem somewhat brief, it is because relatively little time was available for floor discussion and because they exclude floor remarks that were later taken into account by authors in their final revisions.

A unique feature of the volume is an extensive data appendix, compiled as a project independent of the conference in collaboration with Nathan S. Balke.

The idea of a conference on the topic Has the Business Cycle Changed? originated early in 1982 with Martin Feldstein, president of the National Bureau of Economic Research (NBER), before his two-year leave to serve as chairman of the Council of Economic Advisers. Although there was no program committee, helpful suggestions on the format of the conference and on candidates for participation came from Feldstein, Eli Shapiro (president of the NBER during 1982–84), and Robert Hall (head of the NBER's Research Program in Economic Fluctuations). Those chosen early as authors also were helpful in guiding my choice of other authors and of some discussants. Further remarks on the participants are contained in the last section of the Introduction.

My secretary Joan Robinson acted as administrative assistant in charge of local arrangements at the conference, which she handled with her customary efficiency and good cheer. Joan has also expedited publication of the volume, in cooperation with Mark Fitz-Patrick of the NBER's publications department. Invaluable aid in site selection, local arrangements for the February "preconference," and lots of expert advice on how to run a conference were contributed by Kirsten Foss of the NBER.

A final and special note of thanks goes to Martin Feldstein for his conception of the conference, his encouragement to select a pleasant site, and his provision of the NBER's financial support and to Eli Shapiro and David Hartman for their consistent encouragement and aid in seeing the conference through to its realization.

On the morning of 22 March 1984, the day conference participants were to travel to Puerto Rico and convene, came the sad news of Otto Eckstein's death. Otto, as a coauthor of the paper that appears first in this volume, had participated in our preconference. Allen Sinai, Otto's coauthor, graciously agreed to present the elegant and moving tribute that appears here. The conference session at which Allen read his tribute and participated in discussion of the Eckstein/Sinai paper had been scheduled, by coincidence, for the very hour when the memorial service for Otto was taking place in Lexington, Massachusetts. This volume is dedicated to the memory of Otto Eckstein and of my late father, R. A. Gordon, both of whom devoted much of their professional lives to the study and understanding of American business cycles.

Robert J. Gordon
March 1986

Introduction: Continuity and Change in Theory, Behavior, and Methodology

Robert J. Gordon

> For well over a century business cycles have run an unceasing round. They have persisted through vast economic and social changes; they have withstood countless experiments in industry, agriculture, banking, industrial relations, and public policy; they have confounded forecasters without number, belied repeated prophecies of a "new era of prosperity" and outlived repeated forebodings of "chronic depression."
>
> Arthur F. Burns (1947, 27)

> Analyzing business cycles means neither more nor less than analyzing the economic process of the capitalist era. . . . Cycles are not like tonsils, separable things that might be treated by themselves, but are, like the beat of the heart, of the essence of the organism that displays them.
>
> Joseph A. Schumpeter (1939, 5)

The postwar era has not surprised Arthur Burns, for business cycles have continued their "unceasing round." Although the United States recession of 1981–82 was the eighth since World War II and the deepest postwar slump by almost any measure, the 1983–84 recovery displayed an upward momentum sufficient to befuddle forecasters and delight incumbent politicians. Nor would a reincarnated Joseph Schumpeter be disappointed in the current status of business cycle research in the economics profession. To be sure, interest in business cycles decayed during the prosperity of the 1960s, as symbolized in the 1969 conference volume, *Is the Business Cycle Obsolete?* and in Paul Samuelson's re-

Robert J. Gordon is professor of economics at Northwestern University.

I am grateful to Moses Abramowitz, Solomon Fabricant, Milton Friedman, Allen Sinai, and Lawrence Summers for helpful comments on the first draft of this introduction.

mark the same year that the National Bureau of Economic Research "has worked itself out of one of its first jobs, namely, the business cycle."[1] But business cycles as a subject for study have enjoyed a revival for at least a decade now, stimulated in part by the severity of the 1974–75 and 1981–82 recessions and in part by the intellectual ferment surrounding the development of the "equilibrium business cycle model" and the attention paid to the seminal work of Robert E. Lucas, Jr., contained in his book *Studies in Business Cycle Theory* (1981). Indeed, there is no longer any need to lament the passing of economics courses explicitly carrying the title "Business Cycles," since the topic of business cycle behavior and analysis has so infiltrated courses carrying the title "Macroeconomics" that the two subjects have become almost interchangeable.[2] In this light it is fitting that the major research program of the NBER in this area is called "Economic Fluctuations" rather than "Macroeconomics."

During the relatively brief period in the late 1960s when economists were pondering the possible obsolescence of business cycles, the scholarly discipline of macroeconomics showed signs of becoming fragmented into speciality areas devoted to components of the then popular large-scale econometric models—for example, consumption, investment, money demand, and the Phillips curve. But more recently the revival of severe real world business cycles, together with the revolutions associated with Milton Friedman's monetarism and Lucas's classical equilibrium models, has brought about a revival of interest in economic analysis that focuses on a few broad aggregates summarizing activity in the economy as a whole—nominal and real income, the inflation rate, and the unemployment rate. There seems now to be little dispute that "Understanding Business Cycles," to use the title of a famous Lucas article, is the central preoccupation of theoretical and applied macroeconomics in the mid-1980s. We seem to be experiencing just the latest in "the cycle of interest in cycles," with troughs in the 1920s and 1960s and peaks in the 1930–40s and 1980s.

Definition of Cycles and Scope of the Volume

The best definition of business cycles is still that of Burns and Wesley Mitchell:

1. The 1969 conference volume is listed in the references as Bronfenbrenner 1969. The Samuelson quotation is from a 1969 conference remark that appears in Zarnowitz 1972, 167.
2. Michael Lovell's comment in this volume recalls a course in business cycles given at Harvard in 1955 by Otto Eckstein and Gottfried Haberler as being "one of the last of its breed."

Business cycles are a type of fluctuation found in the aggregate activity of nations that organize their work mainly in business enterprises: a cycle consists of expansions occurring at about the same time in many economic activities, followed by similarly general recessions, contractions, and revivals which merge into the expansion phase of the next cycle; this sequence of changes is recurrent but not periodic; in duration business cycles vary from more than one year to ten or twelve years; they are not divisible into shorter cycles of similar character with amplitudes approximating their own. (Burns and Mitchell 1946, 3)

This definition encapsulates several of the basic features of business cycles that make them so intriguing an object for economists to study, and yet so elusive a phenomenon to capture in a simple economic model. First, the economy spends most of its time in recessions, recoveries, or expansions rather than in the steady-state condition of "full-employment equilibrium" favored by economic theorists. Subject to cycles lasting as long as ten years, with an average length of about four years, neither workers nor firms can realistically adopt the convenient competitive assumption that they will be able to sell all the labor or commodities they desire at the existing vector of wages and prices. That cycles are "recurrent but not periodic" makes decisions risky and creates an exposure to unemployment and bankruptcy, since workers cannot predict when a layoff may eliminate the extra income needed to pay a consumer loan or mortgage, and firms cannot predict whether the needed extra sales to support a plant expansion will be forthcoming through continued prosperity or will evaporate through the onset of another recession. Finally, the pervasive character of business cycles, "occurring at about the same time in many economic activities," means, even neglecting the fixity of labor skills and physical capital, that workers and firms cannot effortlessly shift into another occupation or industry when business in their own turns sour.

Confronted by the difficulty of developing a single theory that encompasses major features of business cycles, including their irregular timing and varying amplitudes, economists usually find it fruitful to apportion the study of cycles among smaller and more digestible units. These include research on particular components of expenditure—for example, consumption and investment—and their relation to aggregate economic activity, monetary and fiscal policy, and institutional aspects of the economy. Some studies focus only on aggregate activity—that is, real or nominal income—and relate this empirically to a small subset of the factors that might be involved in the generation of business cycles, such as changes in the growth rate of the money supply. Others limit their concern to a particular phase of the business cycle during a relatively limited period of time, such as the role of "disintermediation" and "credit crunch" in the upper turning point of postwar cycles between 1957 and 1979.

This volume contains twelve papers by distinguished economists on substantive aspects of business cycle behavior, and a thirteenth paper by Geoffrey Moore and Victor Zarnowitz (appendix A) that presents the history and role of the NBER business cycle chronology as well as a rich assemblage of tables tracing the timing of business cycles back to the year 1700.[3] The last element of the volume is a data appendix containing a wide variety of historical time series, including a newly created set of quarterly data on components of expenditure for 1919–41 and new quarterly data series on nominal and real GNP extending back to 1875.

The substantive papers were commissioned to address separate and well-defined topics within the framework of the common theme "Has the Business Cycle Changed?" Seven of the twelve papers address specific components of economic activity—consumption, investment, inventory change, fiscal policy, monetary behavior, open-economy issues, and aspects of labor-market behavior. The remaining five focus on aggregate economic activity. Two of these, by Otto Eckstein and Allen Sinai and by Oliver Blanchard and Mark Watson, attempt to identify the "impulses" or "shocks" that give rise to business cycles. The other three, by Victor Zarnowitz and Geoffrey Moore, by John Taylor, and by J. Bradford DeLong and Lawrence Summers, take a broad view of the overall conference theme, changes in cyclical behavior. All the authors of the twelve papers were asked to investigate a longer historical horizon than the overworked post-1946 data so frequently studied by time series econometricians. As a result the coverage of every paper but two extends before World War II, and for several it extends before World War I.[4]

Several limitations of coverage and treatment were imposed to control the size and scope of the volume. The papers are exclusively concerned with the business cycle in the United States and not (excepting a few tables in the Moore/Zarnowitz chronology appendix) with other countries. Some topics receive scant coverage because no paper was commissioned to cover them, including theories of the political business cycle and theories of "real cycles" originating in productivity shocks or in the process of technological advance. No paper is purely theoretical in nature, though most use theory in the development and interpretation of the empirical investigation. Thus the volume does not

---

3. Solomon Fabricant has pointed out that the cycles recorded for the United Kingdom before 1800 may be mainly agricultural cycles rather than business cycles.

4. Of the two exceptions, the Eckstein/Sinai paper works with a large-scale quarterly econometric model that cannot by its nature by extended before 1947. The Blanchard/Watson paper also is limited to postwar quarterly data.

contribute a new theory of the business cycle, but rather offers a set of tests of old theories, applying a variety of modern frameworks of analysis and econometric techniques to a wide variety of United States data covering the period from 1890 to 1983.

Rather than summarizing the papers in turn, this introduction explores broader themes and their relation to results contained in the conference papers. It examines continuity and change in economic ideas about the sources of business cycles, in the behavior of the economy itself, and in the methodology and style of research on business cycles. The discussion of continuity and change in economic ideas focuses on a few central themes that are echoed in the content of several of the conference papers; it is deliberately not a full-fledged survey of business-cycle theory, that task having been admirably accomplished very recently by Victor Zarnowitz (1985). The treatment of continuity and change in economic behavior pulls together results from several conference papers and concentrates on changes in the nature of the business cycle before and after World War II. The interest in continuity and change in methodology and style is stimulated by the contrasts between this conference and a previous NBER conference on business cycles held in 1949, with proceedings published in 1951, and by the fact that several participants attended both conferences.[5]

Continuity and Change in the Analysis of Business Cycles

Development of Business Cycle Theory

The distinction between impulses and propagation mechanisms, introduced into economic analysis by Ragnar Frisch (1933) and Eugen Slutsky (1927), is accepted as a common analytical framework by the authors in this volume and can serve to classify earlier and more recent contributions to the theory of business cycles. Pre-Keynesian theories were primarily concerned with the propagation mechanism and focused on the internal dynamics of the economic system. Recurrent fluctuations were viewed as an outcome of these dynamic elements, with a strong tendency to repeat themselves even in the absence of exogenous influences, and such external impulses were viewed as of secondary importance, mainly accounting for the varying amplitudes and nonperiodic character of cycles.[6]

The endogenous processes might be primarily monetary or real. Monetary elements included R. G. Hawtrey's induced changes in the supply

5. See National Bureau of Economic Research 1951.
6. For supporting quotes and further detail, see Haberler 1958, 10, and Zarnowitz 1985.

of bank credit, Knut Wicksell's discrepancy between market and equilibrium rates of interest, and Friedrich Hayek's overinvestment financed by excessive bank credit creation. Real elements focused on particular aspects of long-lived durable goods, including the "Austrian" emphasis on "vertical maladjustments" or imbalances between the production of capital and consumer goods and J. M. Clark's early version of the acceleration principle. The studies by Mitchell (e.g., 1927) stressed the cyclical evolution of relative prices, particularly changes in unit labor costs relative to output prices, which lead to profit and investment fluctuations. Schumpeter's waves of innovation, opening up and then exhausting opportunities for profitable new investment, could be viewed as impulses from a short-run perspective or as a dynamic process from a longer-run perspective. Similarly, impulses in the form of unpredictable shifts in demand or supply schedules for particular products, Dennis Robertson's so-called horizontal maladjustments, could lead to temporary recessions if the costs of moving factors of production between industries were high.

The first mathematical theories of the business cycle excluded shocks and were based entirely on a dynamic propagation mechanism, as in Paul Samuelson's (1939) multiplier/accelerator model. Theories of this type, while a staple of classroom teaching for instructors eager to display their ability to solve difference equation systems, have long been recognized as incapable of explaining the irregular nonperiodic timing of cycles, and as generating cycles that are implausibly explosive or damped into extinction, depending on the value of an accelerator coefficient that could generate recurrent cycles only at a single knife-edge value.

The inadequacy of Samuelson's purely linear dynamic model led in two directions in the postwar development of business cycle theory. Some writers, especially John R. Hicks (1950) and Richard Goodwin (1955), attempted to salvage the theory of a self-generating no-shock business cycle by imposing capacity ceilings and capital replacement floors to limit the amplitude of an otherwise explosive Samuelson-type cycle. However, early attempts to build realistic dynamic cycle models with econometrically estimated parameters, for example, by Lawrence Klein and Arthur Goldberger (1955), soon showed that such systems were highly damped, even when private investment was allowed to be fully endogenous, and could not generate recurrent cycles in the absence of exogenous shocks.[7] This evidence naturally helped to shift the attention of economists from propagation mechanisms to the sources of impulses, and soon the profession lost interest in business cycle theory per se as it became caught up in the emerging debate regarding

7. See Adelman and Adelman 1959.

the relative role of monetary and fiscal shocks.[8] Since that time the business cycle has been viewed as resulting from irregular impulses whose effect on economic activity is transmitted by a complex dynamic propagation mechanism.

The aftermath of the early 1960s monetary/fiscal policy debates was a growing dichotomy im empirical studies of business cycle phenomena. The main thrust of research by "Keynesian" economists was to try to understand the propagation mechanism itself, the "black box" through which monetary and fiscal influences altered spending. This involved the construction of large "structural" econometric models and spawned growing subliteratures on the components of these models—consumption function, investment function, money demand function, Phillips curve, and others. Monetarist economists (an adjective coined in 1968) were less interested in probing the black box and were content to develop reduced-form single-equation models that linked fluctuations in economic activity directly to prior fluctuations in the growth of the money supply, although in fairness one must acknowledge Milton Friedman's earlier research on elements of the black box that yielded his permanent income theories of consumption expenditures and the demand for money. By the early 1970s debates between monetarists and their Keynesian critics had come to center on successive techniques for relating business cycles to monetary impulses, including the much discussed work of Anderson and Jordan (1968) and of Sims (1972, 1980).

The "oil shocks" of 1973–74 and 1979–80 reinforced the interest in external impulses as sources of business cycle fluctuations and recalled Robertson's "horizontal maladjustments." Now, however, the source of the aggregate disturbance was not the immobility of factors of production, but rather the stickiness of prices in the nonoil part of the economy that prevented the overall price level, and hence aggregate real balances and real aggregate demand, from remaining unaffected by the relative oil price shock.[9] A "macroeconomic externality" developed, with an ensuing recession and recovery transmitted through the economy's dynamic propagation mechanism. As a result of the experience of the 1970s, it is now common to extend the earlier dichotomy between monetary and real shocks to a three-way distinction between monetary shocks, real demand, and real supply shocks, with real demand impulses further subdivided among private investment and consumption shocks, fiscal disturbances (particularly in connection with

8. In the early 1960s this debate centered on the monetary history of Friedman and Schwartz 1963 and the statistical "contest" between autonomous spending and monetary impulses developed by Friedman and Meiselman 1963.

9. Analysis of the critical effects of external price shocks was developed by Gordon 1975 and Phelps 1978 and is reviewed in Gordon 1984.

tax rates and defense expenditures), and portfolio or "money demand" shifts (often induced by changes in financial regulations).

Another effect of the supply shocks of the 1970s was to shift the blame away from government as the sole source of shocks. The monetary/fiscal controversy of the 1960s had tended to locate the source of economic fluctuations in the vagaries of the Federal Reserve Board and the spending and tax decisions of successive federal administrations. But the oil shocks of the 1970s clearly seemed to be an external phenomenon that forced upon the Fed a decision whether to accommodate. In turn this led to a broader perspective on the nature at monetary shocks, which could be viewed not as truly exogenous, but at least in part as representing the passive role of the monetary authority in reacting to supply shocks and in financing deficits that arise from politicians' unwillingness or inability to finance expenditures through increases in conventional taxes. When the monetary authority reacts to changes in interest rates, inflation and/or unemployment with a stable set of response coefficients, it is said to have a stable "monetary reaction function." A shift from one set of responses to another in today's terminology is designated a "change in monetary regime" and may bring with it a change in behavior in the private sector, such as a greater reliance on escalator clauses in wage contracts if the monetary authority is believed to have shifted to a more accommodative or less inflation resistant reaction function.

At the same time that some economists were developing an analysis of "macroeconomic externalities" that depended on sticky prices in part of the economy, a completely different direction was taken by Lucas and his disciples, who developed a theory of the business cycle within the context of a central norm of continuous market clearing equilibrium that had not been taken seriously in macroeconomics since the publication of Keynes's *General Theory* four decades earlier. The underlying impulse generating the Lucas business cycle could be either a monetary or a real ("productivity") shock, and this created a response in output for the length of time that agents, with their rational expectations based on knowledge of the underlying economic model, were assumed to need to acquire information on the value of the aggregate shock. Although this approach has been given the label of "rational expectations macroeconomics," it could more accurately be called "classical equilibrium macroeconomics" or "stale information macroeconomics," since the aggregate shock could cause a business fluctuation away from the classical equilibrium solution only in the presence of an information barrier.

The Lucas approach spawned an explosion of sometimes fertile model-building exercises on particular aspects of labor, product, and financial markets, but it remained unconvincing to most of the macroeconomics profession and never took hold in the policymaking community as had Keynesian economics in the 1940s and 1950s and monetarism in the late 1970s and early 1980s. Classical equilibrium macroeconomics suffered from two Achilles' heels. First was its inability to explain how an information barrier of a month or two could generate the output persistence observed in the typical four-year business cycle, much less the twelve-year Great Depression. Models that combine rational expectations with multiyear labor contracts, like those developed by John Taylor and others, maintain the attractive elements of rational expectations but yield dynamic behavior closer to traditional Keynesian models than to the pure Lucas market-clearing models. The second Achilles' heel was the internal inconsistency of stale information itself, which should, if solely responsible for the phenomenon of business cycles, have led to the development of an "information market" with newsboys on every street corner peddling instant reports on the latest aggregate monetary and inflation shocks. A possible additional reason for the lack of widespread acceptance of the market-clearing Lucas models was the deep-seated belief of many economists and policymakers that a significant fraction of unemployment in recessions is "involuntary."

The Sources of Postwar Business Cycles

Two different methodological approaches are used by the conference papers to isolate and measure impulses that contribute to business cycles. The Eckstein/Sinai paper, the first in this volume, uses as its tool of analysis the Data Resources, Incorporated (DRI), large-scale econometric model of the United States economy. This model contains five hundred equations that relate endogenous economic variables to each other and to a small set of exogenous variables, which are treated as the impulses that generate a substantial fraction of business-cycle variability. The central results of the paper consist of an attribution of the postwar variation of real GNP to specific supply and demand shocks. The oil shocks of 1973–74 and 1979–80 are the most important sources of supply disturbances. Demand shocks are primarily monetary, resulting from the tendency of the Federal Reserve Board to pursue a procyclical monetary policy that aggravated cyclical swings. A second aspect of demand impulses is the "credit crunch" or "financial factor" emphasized by the authors. This involves three elements: (1) the institutional element of deposit rate ceilings and loan rate ceilings that aggravate the impact of endogenous swings in interest rates on the demand for housing and some categories of consumer spending; (2) the propagation mechanism that produces fluctuations in interest rates and loan demand as a side effect of output cycles; and (3) increasingly risky balance sheet configurations late in the business cycle, leading to the possibility of abrupt cutbacks in production and employment following a downturn in sales or profits. It may seem surprising that the authors attribute just one-third of the amplitude of postwar business cycles to the oil shock, monetary policy, and credit crunch phenomena combined, indicating that a substantial business cycle remains after purging the economy of these elements.

The remaining two-thirds of business cycle volatility is attributed to a combination of additional supply and demand shocks, together with the underlying propagation mechanism that generates cycles in the absence of impulses. Additional supply shocks included isolated large strikes in the steel and auto industries, as well as the Nixon-era wage and price control program that tended to stimulate the economy during the boom of 1972–73 and to aggravate the decline in output during the 1974–75 recession. Another more subtle supply factor was the influence on the underlying growth of capacity (and indirectly on the demand for investment goods) exerted by changes in the demographic structure of the labor force and by the much discussed productivity growth slowdown of the 1970s. Of the demand elements that are isolated in the paper, the most important contributions to business cycle volatility are made by consumer durable and residential housing expenditures, and the smallest contribution is made by business fixed investment.

The latter finding is consistent with the conference paper by myself and John Veitch, which shows that consumer durable and residential housing expenditures have been the most volatile components of investment in the postwar period, whereas in the interwar interval (1919–41) producers' durable equipment and nonresidential construction were relatively greater sources of volatility. In the end the Eckstein/Sinai paper leaves about one-third of the variability of real GNP unexplained, "reflecting the propagation mechanisms in the system," although at least part of their "variance-stripping" exercise that reaches the one-third residual involves removing variations in real investment expenditures that result from the propagation mechanism linking investment to income. And at least a part of the residual portion of variation identified with the propagation mechanism should be viewed as a result of autonomous impulses in government defense and nondefense spending, as well as in exports.

A second method of identifying shocks is carried out by several of the other conference papers, which estimate equations that relate a few economic aggregates (e.g., real GNP) to their own lagged values and also to lagged values of other economic aggregates (e.g., money, interest rates). The "residual" in each equation is identified as the relevant economic impulse or "innovation." The Blanchard/Watson paper uses this method to answer much the same question as the Eckstein/Sinai paper—that is, What was the nature of the impulses that generated postwar business cycles? They conclude that postwar fluctuations were due neither to an accumulation of small shocks nor to infrequent large shocks, but rather to a mixture of large and small shocks. Further, no one source of shocks was dominant. Blanchard and Watson find demand, supply, fiscal, and monetary shocks to have been equally important, but at different times, and conclude that "postwar recessions appear to be due to the combination of two or three shocks."

An examination of the time series of the Blanchard/Watson shocks allows us to link their shocks with particular historical episodes. By far the dominant fiscal impulse was the upsurge of defense spending during the Korean War period, 1951–53, and the sharp decline thereafter in 1953–55. A smaller positive fiscal impulse occurred during the Vietnam War period, 1966–68. The authors find that monetary shocks were relatively small but frequently destabilizing, aggravating the recessions of 1953–54, 1957–58, 1960–61, and 1981–82 and amplifying the boom of 1972–73. Supply shocks were particularly important in the period 1974–75. The impulse they identify as the "demand shock" was larger in magnitude in several episodes than the monetary shocks and any but the Korean War fiscal shocks. The timing of the demand shocks duplicates that of the economywide business cycle itself and can be interpreted as the residual variation that cannot be explained by the other three shocks, just as the Eckstein/Sinai exercise also yields a residual component.

Overall, we emerge from the Eckstein/Sinai and Blanchard/Watson papers with a very different view of the underlying sources of business cycles than is contained in pre-Keynesian classical theory or in Keynesian theory itself. The pre-Keynesians, with their attention to financial and real aspects of the propagation mechanism, treated business cycles as a self-generating and recurrent aspect of the uncoordinated interaction among economic agents in the private sector. Keynesian theory also attributed the origin of cycles to private behavior and emphasized one particular aspect, the instability of business expectations that gave rise to fluctuations of fixed investment. But Eckstein/Sinai and Blanchard/Watson follow the shift in the intellectual tide that can be dated back to the Friedman/Schwartz *Monetary History* by attributing to government rather than private actions a substantial fraction of the blame for postwar cycles. Part of the government contribution to instability, measured by the Blanchard/Watson fiscal impulse variable, result from wartime fluctuations in defense expenditures and may be regarded as unavoidable.

The monetary impulse is interpreted differently in the two papers. Eckstein and Sinai attribute instability mainly to interest rate fluctuations, deposit rate and loan rate ceilings, and balance sheet instability, while Blanchard and Watson adhere to the monetarist interpretation that treats monetary instability as equivalent to innovations in the money supply. Thus a Milton Friedman–like monetary rule would eliminate instability as measured by Blanchard and Watson but might aggravate instability as measured by Eckstein and Sinai, insofar as more steady monetary growth would allow shifts in private sector commodity demand and portfolio choice to be communicated directly to variations in interest rates. That both papers attribute a residual portion of business cycles to these private sector commodity and portfolio demand shifts establishes continuity with the earlier business cycle literature and sustains our motivation to study the private sector investment process and to investigate the feasibility of countercyclical stabilization policy.

Continuity and Change in Cyclical Behavior

General Characteristics

Zarnowitz and Moore's paper documents elements of continuity in American business cycle behavior since 1846 as well as changes in the postwar period as compared with the century before 1945. They find both continuity and change in the most basic measures of the cycle, with an unchanged frequency of about 3.5 years but with a major change in the diminished amplitude of cycles after 1945. For instance, the average increase of both industrial production and employment in pre-1945 expansions was roughly double that in post-1945 expansions. As for contractions, the pre-1945 decline in industrial production was roughly double that in the postwar period, while the decline in employment was more than four time as great. There was continuity, however, in the timing relationships of the major groups of indicators (leading, coincident, and lagging), an indication that the reduced amplitude of postwar business cycles did not cause much change in the sequence of events occurring in a typical cycle.[10]

Not only were postwar recessions much shallower, they were shorter; from 1846 to 1945 recessions were two-thirds as long as expansions, but from 1945 to 1982 they were only one-fourth as long. Another major change was in the cyclical behavior of inflation. Average inflation rates were similar in expansions before and after 1945 but were much higher in the postwar than in the prewar contractions. Thus a novel element

---

10. A revisionist view has been developed in Christina Romer 1984a, b, two recent papers that argue that the greater stability of the postwar economy is a figment of changes in data measurement techniques and that the use of prewar measurement techniques on postwar data makes the postwar economy appear more volatile than in the official data.

in the postwar business cycle has been the persistence of upward price pressures in contractions.

Sources of Greater Postwar Stability

It took only a decade of postwar experience to make private agents aware that there had been a major improvement in economic stability compared with the pre-1945 era. The dating of this recognition can be established as occurring during the interval 1953–59, when stock market investors reacted to the shallowness of the 1953–54 and 1957–58 recessions by bidding up the Standard and Poor's composite stock market index by 124% over that six-year interval. It was just at the end of this period, in late 1959, that Arthur Burns delivered his presidential address to the American Economic Association that is cited and taken as a point of departure by several papers in this volume.[11] To what extent do the papers in this volume affirm, contradict, or go beyond Burns's analysis of the sources of greater stability and reduced amplitude of the postwar business cycle?

The following sections begin with the factor that Burns stressed most heavily, the stabilizing role of government through the sheer increase in the size of its tax and transfer system. Next I turn to the effects of discretionary stabilization policy in general and then to specific aspects of fiscal and monetary policy highlighted in the conference papers. Then I examine briefly some of the postwar structural changes Burns emphasized and the rather different evaluation contained in this volume. The most controversial issue tackled in this volume is one that Burns neglected entirely, the causes and consequences of the greater persistence of wage and price changes evident in the postwar data. The analysis of changes in behavior concludes by reviewing the main findings of four papers devoted to the analysis of components of spending— inventory change, consumption, investment, and the foreign sector.

The Size of Government and Its Role as a Buffer

Of central importance to Burns was the increased size of the federal government, particularly the stabilizing role of government transfer payments and the government's much greater participation in the ebb and flow of private incomes through the enlargement of the personal income tax system. He pointed out that personal disposable income did not decline during the 1957–58 recession, and I may update this point, as do DeLong and Summers in their paper, by contrasting the mere $2 billion decline in real disposable personal income over the five quarters of the 1981–82 recession with the much greater $45 billion decline in real GNP.

11. See Burns 1960.

The increased size of government and the "buffering" of the fluctuations of disposable personal income show up in several types of quantitative evidence. The role of government is largely responsible for the decline in dynamic multipliers implied by large-scale econometric multipliers, from multipliers of four or five in prewar data to two or less in postwar data.[12] The DeLong/Summers paper shows that the dollar response of disposable income to a dollar change in GNP was 0.76 in 1898–1916, 0.95 in 1923–40, but a much smaller 0.39 after 1949. Hall's conference paper finds that innovations or shocks to consumption spending fell by a factor of three from the period 1920–42 to 1947–82, and this must reflect in part the greater stability of disposable income relative to total income.[13]

DeLong and Summers note that the "buffer" role of government in stabilizing the postwar economy should not be taken at face value, for an additional assumption is required. The increased stability of disposable income implies increased stability of consumption expenditures "only if liquidity constraints are an important factor in the determination of aggregate consumption." By this they mean that prewar consumers, if not liquidity constrained, should have been able to sustain a permanent level of consumption by borrowing during recessions and repaying loans during expansions. One may doubt that this theoretical possibility was of any practical relevance in prewar business cycles, given their large amplitude and nonperiodic character noted above in the discussion of the Burns/Mitchell definition. Smoothing of consumption during the Great Depression of the 1930s would have required consumers to borrow sums equal to several years' income, with only the promise of uncertain future income available as collateral. DeLong and Summers define "liquidity constrained" as *any* sensitivity of consumption to disposable income beyond the effect of changes in current disposable income on permanent income and find, not surprisingly, that by this definition almost all prewar consumers were liquidity constrained. Hence they accept that the reduction in the elasticity of disposable income to total income did have the stabilizing effect that is usually accepted in the literature.

The Full Employment Commitment and the Role of Stabilization Policy

Burns also emphasized a second aspect of government's role, not only its increased size, but also its new commitment to full employment. He pointed not just to the stabilizing role of monetary policy in achieving a prompt decline in long-term interest rates shortly after postwar

12. See Hickman and Coen 1976, table 9.6, 194.
13. Here the size of the innovations is taken to be the standard error of estimate in Hall's equations that regress the change in consumption on the change in total income.

business cycle peaks (in contrast to the long lags that were prevalent before the war, documented in the Zarnowitz/Moore paper), but also fiscal policy, with its well-timed tax reduction achieved midway through the 1953–54 recession. Burns felt, however, that more important than any specific actions of monetary and fiscal policy was a general change in attitude, as consumers and businessmen gained confidence that a business cycle contraction would not be allowed to go too far and thus avoided the sharp cutbacks of spending plans that had heretofore typified the contraction phase. Burns gave less emphasis to other government measures, for example, price supports that eliminated the sharp declines in farm prices that were so important in 1920–21 and 1929–33 and the insurance of bank deposits by the Federal Deposit Insurance Corporation (FDIC). In the aftermath of the monetarist tilt in business cycle analysis associated with the Friedman/Schwartz monetary history and its emphasis on the destruction of bank deposits during the 1929–33 Great Contraction, we tend now to rank FDIC higher than Burns did on the list of reforms contributing to postwar economic stability.

The conference paper by DeLong and Summer does not accept Burns's view that discretionary stabilization policy made a contribution to the smaller amplitude of postwar business cycles. Rather than examining specific aspects of monetary and fiscal policy, they propose an indirect test. Turning again to the impulse propagation framework, they assume that all impulses originated in the private sector and that the presumed role of government stabilization policy was to influence the propagation mechanism, "reducing the persistence of shocks to GNP, not by limiting the size of the initial shocks." In other words, prompt action by discretionary government stabilization policy following a negative shock in year one would return real GNP to its normal value in year two rather than allowing the shock to persist.

One may question the usefulness of this test, however. First, it seems to associate all impulses with private sector activity. However, we have noted the Blanchard/Watson analysis that identifies not just private sector demand and supply shocks, but also shocks originating in fiscal and monetary policy. The "political branch" of government may have increased instability by starting and stopping wars during the period 1950–75, and the "stabilization branch" of government may have attempted to reduce the impact of instability originating not just in the private sector but also in the "political branch." Second, the increased persistence of output fluctuations in the postwar period does not necessarily mean that stabilization policy was less effective, but could imply that the impulses themselves had more serial correlation in the postwar period. We all know that the Korean War lasted three years and the Vietnam War for more than a decade. Third, supply shocks of the 1970s identified by Blanchard and Watson not only persisted over several years but also had a negative influence on real output that could not be offset by monetary policy without an inflationary response that fully accommodated the shocks. Most characterizations of the postwar monetary reaction function, including that in John Taylor's paper, imply that the Federal Reserve reacted against both output and inflation shocks.

Herschel Grossman, in his discussion of the DeLong/Summers paper, also points to the decreased volatility of monetary aggregates in the postwar period. It is hard to believe that the Fed's success in avoiding anything like the 1929–33 collapse in the money supply did not contribute to postwar stability, though as a semantic point this achievement might be attributed as much to the FDIC as to discretionary Federal Reserve actions. And as we have seen, both the Eckstein/Sinai and the Blanchard/Watson papers attribute a modest portion of postwar instability to monetary policy. As for fiscal policy, the record is mixed when we abstract from fluctuations in defense expenditures. Some fiscal actions have aided stabilization, including tax reductions during the recessions of 1954 and 1975 and the countercyclical pattern of nondefense expenditures achieved by the Eisenhower administration in 1958. Destabilizing episodes include the failure to raise taxes to pay for the Vietnam War in 1966–67 and the expansion of government purchases in the overheated economy of 1972–73.

Additional Empirical Evidence on Fiscal and Monetary Policy

The conference paper by Robert Barro, like the DeLong/Summers paper, conflicts with Burns's view that fiscal policy has contributed to the postwar stabilization of the American economy. Barro's analysis of fiscal policy is limited to a particular question, the determinants of changes in the United States public debt over the period 1920–82. Barro finds that the equation he estimates for changes in the debt is stable before and after World War II, and this implies that there is no "support for the idea that there has been a shift toward a fiscal policy that generates either more real public debt on average or that generates larger deficits in response to recessions." The support for the first proposition is that there is very little change between 1920–40 and 1948–82 in the constant term in the debt change equation, indicating a similar "normal" creation of real debt in the absence of temporary government expenditures and when the economy is operating at a stable unemployment rate. The support for the second proposition is that the extra debt creation in business cycle recessions per extra point of unemployment was similar before 1940 and after 1948. Since Barro's test does not distinguish between cyclical deficits created by automatic stabilization (i.e., tax progressivity) and discretionary fiscal policy changes, it leaves open the source of its surprising result that the cyclical responsiveness of the debt has not changed since 1920.

Just as changes in the impact of fiscal policy can be divided in principle between the role of automatic stabilization working through changes in the size of government and in tax rates and the role of discretionary destabilization policy, so changes in the impact of monetary policy can be divided among the roles of changing government regulations, private institutions and practices, and discretionary monetary policy. The conference paper by Benjamin Friedman documents the many regulatory changes that have altered the interrelationships between the financial and real sectors in the United States economy. In addition to insurance for deposits in commercial banks and savings intermediaries, Friedman points to deposit rate ceilings (introduced in 1933 and phased out gradually in the 1980s), which caused the brunt of monetary restriction in most postwar recessions to fall disproportionately on the housing industry. Changes in private practices have included greater integration across regions and nations and the growth of pension funds relative to insurance companies and mutual savings banks.

Has the net influence of these changes in the monetary sector been to make the real sector more stable since World War II? Friedman's evidence finds important strands of continuity between the prewar and postwar eras. In particular, the growth of money and credit and the levels of interest rates continue to display procyclical patterns. And as shown in the comment by Allan Meltzer, the lead of the growth rate of the money supply in advance of business cycle turning points in the postwar period was about eleven months at troughs and fifteen months at peaks, only a month or two shorter than the estimates of Milton Friedman and Anna Schwartz for the period 1870–1960. Benjamin Friedman distinguishes between continuity in the qualitative relationships of financial and real variables and the absence of stability in specific quantitative relationships. "These monetary and financial aspects of U.S. economic fluctuations exhibit few quantitative regularities that have persisted unchanged across spans of time in which the nation's financial markets have undergone profound and far reaching changes."

Despite these quantitative changes, however, Friedman's paper does not conflict with the widely accepted ideas that financial and monetary factors made a major contribution to postwar stability, particularly in the role of deposit insurance in eliminating the danger of a deposit drain such as occurred in 1929–33 and the role of less variable monetary growth (achieved both directly by discretionary monetary policy and indirectly by deposit insurance) in contributing to the reduced amplitude of postwar business cycles. And as DeLong and Summers emphasize, the much greater role of consumer credit in the postwar era has helped to loosen the connection between fluctuations of income and consumption and thus to reduce the fraction of consumers who are "liquidity constrained." That monetary growth continued to exhibit procyclical fluctuations after World War II can be given the monetarist interpretation that a constant growth rate rule for the money supply would have improved economic performance or the Keynesian-activist interpretation that countercyclical swings in monetary growth would have been even better.

Structural Changes

In addition to structural changes involving financial markets and the size of government, Burns emphasized other changes in the private sector, including the increasing concentration of business enterprise and the role of corporations, as well as the shift of employment away from the most cyclically sensitive industries. The role of corporate concentration attracts virtually no attention in the conference papers (except for a brief mention by DeLong and Summers), probably because the degree of concentration was already substantial in 1929 and did not appear to mitigate or dampen the Great Contraction.[14]

The shifting structure of labor markets may have been more important in contributing to cyclical stability. Burns stresses that the "broad effect of economic evolution until about 1920 was to increase the concentration of jobs in the cyclically volatile industries, and this was a major force tending to intensify declines in employment during business contraction." However, after 1919 the tide turned, and the share of employees in the most volatile industries stabilized and henceforth, since the time of Burns address, has declined rapidly.

The extent of this shift is highlighted by the official data shown in table I.1, which includes both government employees and farm managers and workers. The most dramatic changes from 1920 to 1981 were the decline by half in the "blue collar" operative and laborer categories, and the virtual doubling of the "white collar" sales, clerical, and service occupations. This shift has resulted partly from the greater growth of the demand for services than for goods, and partly from the more rapid growth of productivity in farming and manufacturing than in the nonfarm nonmanufacturing sector (a gap that has widened since 1970). However, the timing shown in table I.1 does not support a major role for this structural shift in explaining the smaller amplitude of postwar business cycles, since the shift was greater from 1950 to 1981 than from 1920 to 1950. The conference paper by Zarnowitz and Moore concurs that shifts in the structure of employment were more important after 1959, and particularly after 1969, than they were from 1929 to 1959.

---

14. The share of total manufacturing assets held by the one hundred largest corporations was already 35% in 1918 and reached 49% by 1970.

Table I.1

	Percentage of Total Employment		
	1920	1950	1981
Cyclically sensitive	*52.0*	*45.5*	*32.4*
Craftsmen and foremen	13.0	14.2	12.6
Operatives and laborers	39.0	31.3	19.8
Cyclically insensitive	*48.0*	*54.5*	*67.6*
Professional, technical, and managerial, including farmers and farm managers	27.3	24.8	29.3
Sales, clerical, and service	20.7	29.7	38.3

Further evidence on changes between interwar and postwar labor markets is provided in the conference paper by Bernanke and Powell. They find important elements of continuity in labor market behavior within the manufacturing sector that appear to leave little room for labor market elements to explain the greater stability of the postwar economy. First, procyclical labor productivity fluctuations appears to be present in every industry in both their periods, 1923–39 and 1954–82. This means that even before World War II it was common for hours of labor input to fluctuate less than output, thus dampening the impact of output fluctuations on personal income. Labor market variables are more stable in the postwar period, but this may simply reflect the greater stability of output. Otherwise the main postwar change has been a greater reliance on layoffs rather than short workweeks as a means of reducing labor input, at least in part owing to the greater generosity and availability of unemployment benefits. To the extent that laid-off workers perceive a greater reduction in their "permanent income" or a greater liquidity constraint than workers experiencing a reduction in hours, this shift may have contributed to a greater cyclical sensitivity of consumption in the postwar period, partly mitigating other factors contributing to greater stability.

Greater Wage and Price Stickiness: Causes and Consequences

A major change in the postwar business cycle that was neglected in Burns's 1959 address, perhaps because it was not yet evident, was the shift to a greater degree of wage and price stickiness. Here it is necessary to distinguish "price flexibility" from "price persistence." As documented in recent years by Charles Schultze, myself, and others, the postwar period has combined continuity with the pre-1929 period in the short-run *flexibility* of prices, that is, the division of a nominal GNP change between price and quantity in the first year after the change, but a shift toward much greater *persistence* in the form of a dependence of this year's inflation rate on last year's rate. Taylor's conference paper confirms the greater persistence of postwar wage and price behavior: "wages and prices have developed more rigidities, in the sense that past values of wages and prices influence their current values. . . . In comparison, during the period before World War I wage inflation fluctuated up and down much more rapidly."

The greater postwar persistence of wages and prices is generally attributed to two factors. First, the increased importance of labor unions since the late 1930s has led to centralized wage bargaining, and high perceived costs of negotiation have made it economical to establish three-year contracts in many industries. That today's wage changes were in many cases agreed upon last year or the year before tends to insulate wage changes from current market forces and to increase their dependence on what has happened previously. Second, the greater confidence of private agents in the willingness of monetary and fiscal policy to reduce the severity of recessions lessens their need to reduce wages and prices quickly and increases their incentive to wait for the expected prompt return of prosperity. An additional third factor in wage stability may be the structural shift in the occupational mix of employment documented in the table I.1, with a major shift from operatives and laborers in the cyclically volatile manufacturing and construction industries to less volatile sales, clerical, and service occupations. Another related shift has been toward lower quit rates and a greater importance of lifetime job attachment.[15]

This characterization of postwar behavior, with continuity from earlier periods in the short-run response of prices to demand disturbances but much greater year-to-year persistence, is not disputed by any of the papers in the volume. However, the *consequences* of greater wage and price persistence is a matter of lively debate between Taylor and DeLong/Summers in an exchange that appears at the end of the volume. Did postwar wage and price stickiness contribute to more (Taylor) or less (DeLong/Summers) amplitude in fluctuations of output?

The issue in dispute can be understood within the context of conventional aggregate supply and demand analysis, in which price stickiness is represented by a relatively flat aggregate supply curve and price flexibility by a relatively steep aggregate supply curve. Clearly, any exogenous shift in nominal GNP, which changes the position of the aggregate demand curve, will cause a greater response of output along a flat aggregate supply curve than along a steep aggregate supply curve. John Taylor's main conclusion can be interpreted in this context, that

---

15. Data on quit rates are discussed in the conference paper by DeLong and Summers. Lifetime job attachments are emphasized by Hall 1982.

given the smaller nominal GNP shocks that occurred in the postwar era (owing to the many factors discussed above, e.g., the FDIC), stickier wages and prices implied more pronounced output fluctuations than in the alternative hypothetical case where the more flexible prewar wage and price response had been maintained. "But the dynamics, or *propagation mechanisms,* of the economic system are much slower and more drawn out in the postwar period. This tends to translate the smaller shocks into larger and more prolonged movements in output and inflation than would occur if the prewar dynamics were applicable in the later period. In other words, the change in the dynamics of the system offset some of the gains from the smaller impulses."

DeLong and Summers contend, however, that the crucial step of taking the smaller size of postwar demand impulses as given is unwarranted. The main conclusion of their paper is that the greater persistence of wage and price changes is directly responsible for the smaller fluctuations in nominal aggregate demand. The theoretical background of the DeLong/Summers argument was set out a decade ago by James Tobin (1975), who shows that there are conflicting effects of a decline in prices in a recession. Through the conventional wealth or Pigou effect, price flexibility raises real balances and helps to stabilize the economy. But there is a countervailing destabilizing effect of price flexibility, owing to the "expectations effect" and the "distribution effect." The first is the tendency of consumers and firms to postpone purchases if they expect deflation to continue, and the second is the tendency of debtors with nominal fixed obligations that rise in real value during a deflation to have a higher propensity to consume, that is, to cut back consumption more than the increase in consumption by the creditors whose assets increase in real value at the same time. If the destabilizing effects of price flexibility offset the stabilizing effects, this would confirm the DeLong/Summers argument that less wage and price flexibility has reduced the amplitude of postwar demand impulses.

In their theoretical discussion DeLong and Summers place less emphasis on the "distribution effect" channel than on an "expectation effect" channel operating through real interest rates: "changes in the aggregate price level produce changes in the real cost of capital that have effects on the level of expenditures on items that have a high interest elasticity of present value." The evidence provided in support of this channel is a reduced-form vector autoregression model containing the inflation rate, the ratio of real GNP to "natural" real GNP, and the nominal commercial paper rate. Their striking finding is that price innovations have a positive effect on future output both in 1893–1915 and in 1949–82. The implication is that nominal GNP shocks cannot be taken as exogenous, but rather vary in the same direction as price shocks. This evidence of an accommodative demand policy is consistent with Taylor's empirical finding for the period before World War I but inconsistent with his conclusion that policy was nonaccommodative after World War II.

Further discussion of the Taylor and DeLong/Summers results is carried out in the exchange between the authors at the end of the volume. Here it is appropriate to note a conflict between the DeLong/Summers results and the study of investment behavior in the Gordon/Veitch conference paper. If DeLong and Summers were correct that real interest rates represent the channel by which price innovations influence expenditures, then we would expect to find a significant influence of the real interest rate in equations for household and business expenditures on structures and equipment. Yet Gordon and Veitch find no significant real interest rate effects on these expenditures at all for the interwar period and only modest effects on these expenditures at all for the interwar period and only modest effects in the postwar period that are concentrated on household investment (consumer durables and residential housing) rather than on business investment. In contrast to these weak real interest rate effects, they find a strong and consistent impact of the real money supply on all forms of investment in both the interwar and the postwar periods. Since the real balance effect makes a price innovation push investment spending in the opposite direction, it represents the stabilizing channel in the Tobin (1975) framework described above. At least we can agree that the effects of price flexibility on output stability are opened up by the Taylor and DeLong/Summers papers as key issues that for a full resolution will require additional future research.

Impulse and Propagation in Components of Spending

Four conference papers examine components of spending: Alan Blinder and Douglas Holtz-Eakin on inventory behavior, Robert Hall on consumption spending, Gordon and Veitch on investment spending, and Rudiger Dornbusch and Stanley Fischer on the foreign sector. There is modest overlap in this division of labor, since consumer durables expenditures are included in the spending components studied by both Hall and Gordon/Veitch, while all components of spending include the traded goods of interest to Dornbusch and Fischer.

Of all the conference papers that examine changes before and after World War II, the Blinder/Holtz-Eakin paper finds the most evidence of continuity and the least evidence of change. In both periods inventory changes have played a major role in business cycles, especially around turning points and during cyclical downswings, and they have been strongly procyclical. If the World War II years are omitted, the correlation of nominal final sales and inventory changes remained similar when 1929–41 and 1947–83 are compared. But whereas the variance of nominal final sales decreases substantially after World War II, the variability of inventory investment actually increases. The paper also shows that certain features of inventory data, "annoying" because they conflict with standard theories of inventory adjustment, characterize the prewar as well as the postwar data. In particular, the fact that production is more variable than sales and that sales and inventory change covary positively tends to contradict the production smoothing/buffer stock model equally in both periods.

Hall's study of consumption behavior contrasts the Keynesian and equilibrium business cycle models. In Keynesian models, the consumption function slopes upward; when the public earns more income, it consumes more. But in the equilibrium theory households choose their desired level of work—that is, income—by moving along a negatively sloped consumption function representing the trade-off between work and consumption. Hall's estimates imply a "draw" between the two models, with the estimated consumption function essentially flat and a marginal propensity to consume of roughly zero. Because this phenomenon equally characterizes the periods 1920–42 and 1947–82, it reveals no change in behavior that would explain greater economic stability in the postwar period. The residual terms in Hall's equations, the implied consumption impulses, are moderately more variable in the interwar period, and this is dominated by a negative innovation in 1930–32. Overall, however, the size of the impulses is small relative to the magnitude of overall changes in real GNP, and Hall concludes that shifts in consumption behavior are "an important, but not dominant, source of overall fluctuations in the aggregate economy."

The Gordon/Veitch study of investment behavior includes consumer durables as well as the usual components of fixed investment—producers' durable equipment and residential and nonresidential construction. The paper finds that the covariance of investment with noninvestment GNP was large and positive in the interwar period and that changes in interwar structures investment were largely autonomous; that is, they can be treated as a primary impulse responsible for the interwar business cycle. Interwar expenditures on durable goods (both consumer and producer), however, appear to have been part of the economy's propagation mechanism rather than an independent source of shocks.

An important change in the postwar era has been that investment contributed much less to the overall business cycle than in the interwar period. The variance of investment, together with the covariance of investment with noninvestment GNP, together account for fully 71% of the variance of real GNP during 1919–41 but only 7% during 1947–83. The covariance of investment and noninvestment spending is actually negative during the full postwar period, possibly as a result of "crowding out" of investment in periods of high defense expenditures. This phenomenon is one more indication of the destabilizing role of the "political branch" of government, in contrast to earlier periods when a larger share of instability originated in the private sector.

However, more can be said about the investment process than simply that "structures investment was autonomous" and "durables investment was induced as part of the propagation mechanism." In addition to the real impulse embodied in the structures innovation, there was also a financial impulse. Both structures and equipment investment have been influenced by changes in the real monetary base in the postwar period, as was equipment investment in the interwar period. Further, both types of investment have been influenced by changes in the money multiplier (that is, the money supply M1 divided by the monetary base) in both the interwar and the postwar periods. In the earlier period, the multiplier change may convey the effect of the destruction of bank deposits in the Great Depression, and in the postwar period it may be related to the periods of credit crunch and disintermediation emphasized by Eckstein and Sinai.

The Dornbusch/Fischer paper on the open economy is not oriented around changes in the business cycle before and after World War II. Indeed, it is difficult to see how open economy issues could explain the greater stability of the economy in the early postwar years, since the authors show that the ratio of both imports and exports to GNP was lower in 1950–69 than in any period before 1929 or after 1970. Thus when Burns was examining the sources of postwar economic stability, the United States was virtually a closed economy, and we must search within rather than outside it to gain an understanding of that period. In fact the main influence of the foreign sector on the domestic economy in the period 1947–60 was destabilizing, including the contribution of declining exports to the 1949 recession after their 1947 Marshall Plan peak and to the 1957–58 recession after their 1956–57 Suez peak.

Nevertheless, other aspects of business cycle behavior are illuminated by the Dornbusch/Fischer treatment. Their analysis of the pre-1914 gold standard era stresses the greater international synchronization of business cycles than in the postwar period, suggesting that foreign shocks were a more important source of American cycles in that period. They are skeptical that the Smoot-Hawley tariff of 1930 could have played any major role in explaining the severity of the Great Depression.[16] They stress the impact of foreign price innovations, in

16. Their treatment of the interwar period exhibits a surprising neglect of the "great pyramiding of international credits" in 1927–29, stressed by Burns 1968 and Kindleberger 1973.

the form of jumping oil and raw materials prices, on the United States business cycle in the 1970s and early 1980s. Finally, they point out the implications of flexible exchange rates in altering the effectiveness of monetary and fiscal policy. In particular, flexible rates steepen the economy's aggregate supply or Phillips curve and imply that a period of monetary tightness will achieve a faster and less costly disinflation than under fixed rates. The opposite (a flatter Phillips curve) occurs when disinflation is attempted through tight fiscal policy.

Concluding Comments on Changes in Behavior

We emerge from the conference papers with an updated version of Burns's (1960) analysis of the sources of postwar stability. Burns is supported in his emphasis on the greater size of government, with the concomitant growth in the personal income tax system and buffering of changes in disposable personal income from changes in total income. But other changes Burns stressed receive less support in this volume. There is doubt in several papers that discretionary stabilization policy did more good than harm, as Burns claimed, and considerable evidence that fiscal policy (primarily through variations in defense spending) and monetary policy contributed their own set of destabilizing influences that aggravated the postwar business cycle. Also receiving little support is Burns's emphasis on structural changes; for instance, most of the shift in the structure of employment out of the cyclically volatile industries came after 1970 and hence cannot explain the period of relative stability between 1950 and 1970. There is no dissent in this volume, however, to the suggestion that the creation of the FDIC in 1934, which Burns treated as only a secondary factor, deserves elevation to first rank among structural changes dampening the postwar cycle.

Another major structural change emphasized here but neglected by Burns was the role of labor unions in the development of staggered three-year wage contracts, and the resulting increase in the postwar persistence of wage and price changes. What remains unsettled is whether greater price persistence contributed to economic instability by offsetting the postwar decline in the size of economic impulses or whether it could have played a major role in reducing the size of the impulses themselves. We are left with a chicken/egg interaction, in which greater output stability may have contributed to price persistence while greater price persistence may have contributed to output stability. Perhaps the underlying causes of both chicken and egg were the simultaneous emergence in 1946 of the larger personal tax system and the symbolic role of the Full Employment Act, together with the growing evidence throughout the 1940s and 1950s that the FDIC, together with changed Federal Reserve attitudes, had converted a collapse in the banking system from an ever-present danger into a remote historical relic.

Continuity and Change in Methodology and Style

This volume is the second that reports on the proceedings of a major NBER conference devoted entirely to the subject of business cycles. The proceedings of the 1949 conference were published in 1951. Contrasts between the two conferences provide some illumination on changes that have occurred in the study of business cycle phenomena over the past thirty years, a contrast that received insufficient attention at the conference itself (a complaint made at the end of Fabricant's conference comment).[17]

As at our conference, participants in the 1949 conference spanned several generations. Wesley Mitchell had agreed to open the conference and to unveil for the first time in public some of the results of his forthcoming book (1951), but he died just before the conference began. Another major figure of the older generation, Joseph Schumpeter, presented a defense of the historical approach to the analysis of business cycles but died before he could revise his paper for the conference volume. Among the participants were economists who have since won the Nobel Prize for their pioneering work, much of it related to the study of business cycles (Jan Tinbergen, Milton Friedman, Lawrence Klein, Simon Kuznets, and Wassily Leontief). And some continuity is achieved by Moses Abramowitz, Solomon Fabricant, and Geoffrey Moore, who were present at both the 1949 and the 1984 conferences.

The most striking difference between the two conferences lies in the much greater domination in 1949 of methodological development and disputes and the much smaller role of substantive analysis of the sources of business cycles and changes in their nature. One symbol of the difference in emphasis is that the earlier conference volume contains four times as many index entries to "Econometrics" as it does to "Depression." Perhaps it is natural that some economists in 1949 should have been as excited to be in on the ground floor of econometric modeling as others in the mid-1970s were about the development of equilibrium business cycle models.

In a sense the 1949 conference can be viewed in retrospect as a confrontation between the NBER, a long-established organization devoted to a descriptive style of empirical research intended to provide a basis for hypothesis formation, and the new Cowles Commission, devoted to the still novel econometric approach in which theory and empirical testing were, in principle, integrated. Some of the econometricians came to the 1949 conference not so much to talk about

17. Correspondence with three participants in the 1949 conference (Moses Abramowitz, Solomon Fabricant, and Milton Friedman) has been immensely helpful in developing the interpretation in this section, and some sentences here are drawn directly from their letters.

whatever substantive work might be presented as, full of the belief that they had found the truth, to convert and obtain disciples while exposing the dead end that the older work had reached. Perhaps the reason this confrontation occurred was that indeed the technical development of econometrics was proceeding rapidly and the time had come to apply a new standard of evaluation to the past wholly speculative theorizing on business cycles of people like Robertson, Pigou, and J. M. Clark, together with the reluctance of Burns and Mitchell at the NBER to go very far beyond their "natural history" technique of observation, classification, and description and enter the realm of hypothesis formation and testing.

The main methodological tension in 1949 was between the econometric method, which at that time involved specification of many behavioral relationships as part of what we now call "large scale" econometric models, and the "historical" or "historical-quantitative" method, represented both by the NBER approach and by the descriptive historical method as practiced and defended by R. A. Gordon and Schumpeter. One dimension of the dispute was whether business cycles could be treated as a stable process, as required by an econometric model with fixed parameters. Schumpeter's defense of the historical method started from the proposition that the differences between cycles were more important than the similarities: "that the darkest hues of cyclical depressions and most of the facts that make of business cycles a bogey for all classes are not essential to business cycles per se but are due to adventitious circumstances" (National Bureau of Economic Research 1951, 150). But Schumpeter was more charitable to the econometric method than econometricians were to the historical. In a perceptive conclusion that recognized the importance of the Frisch/Slutsky distinction between impulses and propagation mechanisms, Schumpeter thought the historical method most suitable for studying impulses and the econometric method for studying propagation mechanisms: "historical analysis gives information as regards impulses and dynamic models as regards the mechanisms by which these impulses are propagated through the system or, to put it differently, as regards the manner in which the economic resonator reacts when 'irritated' by the impulses" (p. 153). However, econometricians were not so ready to accept a role for the historical method. In the words of one critic of a historical paper, "Facts, especially statistical facts, do not by themselves prove a relationship between cause and effect," and in another comment Tinbergen stressed the importance of developing refutable hypotheses.[18]

In the first two decades after the 1949 conference, growing armies of econometricians advanced toward the methodological frontier with

---

18. The quotation is from National Bureau of Economic Research 1951, 215.

their ever-larger models, now estimated on quarterly rather than annual data. But the advance of the armies was slowed and then halted in the late 1960s and early 1970s by the unexpected difficulty of the terrain, which sent the inflation, productivity, stock market, and money demand regiments into retreat. Then the remaining regiments were defeated in a "last stand" by small opposing forces led by Lucas and Sims. Lucas's critique undermined the use of econometric models (either large or small scale) for policy simulation experiments, since private behavior could not be assumed to remain unchanged in the face of arbitrary changes in policy parameters. Sims's critique struck a blow at the "incredible" exclusion restrictions assumed in the specification of structural equations of large-scale models and in addition introduced into common usage the small-scale reduced-form vector autoregression (VAR) models, distinguished by their symmetry in treating all variables of interest as endogenous and in entering every variable into every equation. As a result large-scale models were cast out of academic research to the Siberia of commercial forecasting firms.

The methodological uniformity of the papers at this conference attests to the victory of Lucas and Sims and the demise of large-scale models containing many separate behavioral equations. Just one paper (Eckstein/Sinai) reports simulations with a large-scale model. Four others test particular structural theories and estimate equations for inventory change, consumption, federal debt, and Phillips curves that can be viewed, at least in principle, as components of large-scale models. But this leaves six papers that base some or all of their main conclusions on small-scale VAR models.

One reason for the current popularity of small models is that their workings can be understood and compactly displayed, in contrast to large-scale models where (as Singleton notes in his comment) so many of the specification decisions are made "behind the scenes." Interestingly, at the 1949 conference Tinbergen was already aware that "most economists when criticizing econometric models were pressing toward including many variables. This very inclusion, however, makes the model unintelligible" (National Bureau of Economic Research 1951, 140). Tinbergen's solution was to build small "inner circle" models of key variables that could be "backed" by detailed equations for components of spending, income, and financial markets. The papers at this conference attest to the powerful attraction of building such "inner circle" (i.e., small) models and the unwillingness of contemporary economists to become enmeshed in secondary details until a consensus has been reached on primary issues.

An important contribution of the VAR technique is to formalize the distinction between impulses and propagation mechanisms. Impulses ("innovations") are simply the residual variation that remains net of the contribution of a variable's lagged values, as well as the other lagged values in the model. Taylor's decomposition of output and price impulses and Blanchard and Watson's decomposition of fiscal, monetary, demand, and supply impulses are examples of this technique (although these authors also develop small structural models to explain the same data). In some papers the VAR technique is used not to identify innovations but to establish direction of causation (Friedman) or the sign of a response (DeLong and Summers's positive response of output to price innovations).

This reliance on small-scale VAR models creates in some of our conference discussants the feeling that the methodological counterrevolution has gone too far. In Allan Meltzer's words, "perhaps a principal conclusion to be drawn is that you cannot get something for nothing. If we are unwilling to impose a structure on the data, by stating testable hypotheses, the data may mislead us into accepting that the world is as lacking in structure as this approach." One can argue, however, that imposing structure on a small VAR model by omitting some variables to achieve identification does not in most cases lead to much change in the estimated decomposition of variance. What is needed, following Schumpeter, may be a greater application of the historical method to the estimated impulses. In which episodes was the "economic reasonator irritated" by special and nonrecurrent impulses, such as the influence of war and the aftermath of war, speculation and the breakdown of the banking system, temporary institutions like deposit rate ceilings, and external supply shocks? More attention to the nature and origin of impulses may lead to increased clarity in discussions of policy, with shocks that can be offset by a policy reaction distinguished from those that cannot.

The tendency in some contemporary papers is to practice the historical method by default. In the development of a VAR model, any extension beyond the standard core variables (prices, output, money, interest rates) must be guided by the characteristics of the historical period to be studied. For instance, inclusion of import prices might be required in the 1970s, but a distinction between exogenous and endogenous changes in the money supply (as in the Gordon/Veitch split of money between the base and multiplier) might be more appropriate in assessing the role of deposit destruction in the Great Depression. In the present conference an implicit historical judgment is made in several papers that the Great Depression is so special an episode that the interwar data should be excluded entirely (Taylor) or that an attempt to estimate a small model for interwar data leads to implausible results (DeLong/Summers). An example of the historical method applied to an understanding of econometrically estimated impulses is provided in the Gordon/Veitch paper, where a serially correlated negative impulse to investment spending in 1929–30 is related to the historical circumstances of overbuilding and immigration legislation in the 1920s.

A final methodological question concerns the influence of the Burns/Mitchell NBER methodology on the course of business cycle research since 1949. Some research conducted after that data by associates of the NBER continued to use the Burns/Mitchell methodology, most notably the recent volume by Milton Friedman and Anna Schwartz, *Monetary Trends* (1982). The Zarnowitz/Moore paper in this volume continues the NBER tradition. But in the rest of the profession there is little residual use of reference cycles as a method of organizing data and analysis, with the important exception involved in the continued use of the NBER chronology for dating peaks and troughs of business cycles and the continuing role of the NBER as the official arbiter of these dates.

One reason the NBER reference cycle methodology has fallen into disuse is set forth in the short contribution by DeLong and Summers on asymmetries in business cycles, which the reference cycle technique was designed to investigate. They find little evidence of asymmetries of behavior in expansions and contractions, and they write off asymmetric behavior as a first-order problem in business cycle research. Another contribution to the demise of the NBER methodology has been the role of the computer in encouraging individual rather than team research. Individuals can now sit at home with their terminals or personal computers and carry out analyses that before the 1960s would have required a large number of research assistants and background research—the institutional base that the NBER provided. In fact, in the past decade the NBER has changed its role almost completely, becoming a clearinghouse for individual researchers rather than a central location where full-time employees are engaged in empirical research.

Immersion in the volumes from the 1949 and 1984 conferences stimulates a few reflections on changes in academic style. One finds the 1949 conference papers less interesting, inconclusive, and often immersed in unimportant details, in contrast to most of the papers here. But the 1949 remarks by discussants are often livelier, more interesting, and more antagonistic. Perhaps today we are more polite because air travel and the expansion of our profession brings us together at conferences so often, and today's discussion of A's paper by B may be followed in six months by an assignment of A to discuss a paper by B. There is a sense in the earlier volume that participants were more distant and saw each other less often. They also much less often read each other's work before publication, for we should not neglect the contribution to communication and understanding made by the Xerox machine and low-cost photo-offset printing available to economists and at least partly made possible by an infusion of government research funds. Today we tend to "work things out" by revising papers and discussions to eliminate blatant errors and misunderstandings. There is nothing in this volume to match a discussant's remark in 1949: "I shall argue that his time series data contain an obvious gross error, that he has not chosen a desirable postwar revision of my prewar econometric model, and that his forecasting technique is both wrong and inefficient" (National Bureau of Economic Research 1951, 115). Part of the lack of friction evident in this volume may simply reflect the narrower range of disagreement in 1984, despite the fact that in several conference sessions authors of a mainstream or "Keynesian" background have their papers discussed by developers and practitioners of monetarism and of the equilibrium business cycle approach, and vice versa.

A final difference in academic style worth noting is the shift from book-length research projects in the old days to the production of short and discrete research papers today. Many authors at this conference have combined the business cycle research reported here with papers on one or more other topics given at other conferences in the same year, and perhaps a journal article or two on the side. Naturally this frenetic pace inhibits cleaning up loose ends and unsettled issues and encourages the frequent finesse that a particular interesting question is "beyond the scope" of the current paper. In contrast the activity of Burns, Mitchell, Schumpeter, Kuznets, and others tended to be concentrated on book-length projects that took years to complete. While those earlier economists sometimes lost the forest for the many trees they studied in detail, it is hard to avoid the conclusion that their work gained some of its originality and depth from concentrated immersion.

All of us can benefit from the study of these earlier works, and we may ponder why contemporary economists have just begun to extend their quarterly econometric studies to the long business cycle experience of 1890–1947 when the requisite data, long assumed to be unavailable, has been resting all this time on dusty library shelves in books written by Mitchell and many other pioneering associates of the National Bureau of Economic Research.[19]

References

Adelman, Irma, and Frank L. Adelman 1959. The dynamic properties of the Klein-Goldberger model. *Econometrica* 27 (October): 596–625.

19. A notable exception are the two papers by Romer (1984a,b) cited earlier.

Andersen, Leonall A., and Jerry L. Jordan. 1968. Monetary and fiscal actions: A test of their relative importance in economic stabilization. [Federal Reserve Bank of Saint Louis] *Review* 50 (November): 11–23.

Bronfenbrenner, Martin, ed. 1969. *Is the business cycle obsolete?* New York: John Wiley.

Burns, Arthur F. 1947. *Stepping stones towards the future.* Annual Report 27. New York: National Bureau of Economic Research.

———. 1960. Progress toward economic stability. *American Economic Review* 50 (March): 1–19.

———. 1968. Business cycles, I. General. In *International encyclopedia of the social sciences,* 2:226–45. New York: Macmillan.

Burns, Arthur F., and Wesley C. Mitchell. 1946. *Measuring business cycles.* New York: National Bureau of Economic Research.

Friedman, Milton, and David Meiselman. 1963. *The relative stability of monetary velocity and the investment multiplier in the United States, 1897–1958.* Stabilization policies, ed. E. C. Brown et al. (a series of research studies). Englewood Cliffs, N.J.: Commission on Money and Credit.

Friedman, Milton, and Anna Schwartz. 1963. *A monetary history of the United States, 1867–1960.* Princeton: Princeton University Press.

———. 1982. *Monetary trends in the United States and the United Kingdom: Their relation to income, prices, and interest rates, 1867–1975.* Chicago: University of Chicago Press.

Frisch, R. 1933. Propagation problems and impulse problems in dynamic economics. In *Economic essays in honor of Gustav Cassel.* London: George Allen.

Goodwin Richard M. 1955. A model of cyclical growth. In *The business cycle on the post-war world,* ed. E. Lundberg, 203–21. London: Macmillan.

Gordon, Robert J. 1975. Alternative responses of policy to external supply shocks. *Brookings Papers on Economic Activity* 6, no. 1: 183–206.

———. 1984. Supply shocks and monetary policy revisited. *American Economic Review* 74 (May): 38–43.

Haberler, Gottfried. 1958. *Prosperity and depression.* Harvard Economic Studies 105. Cambridge: Harvard University Press.

Hall, Robert E. 1982. The importance of lifetime jobs in the United States economy. *American Economic Review* 72 (September): 716–24.

Hickman, Bert G., and Robert M. Coen. 1976. *An annual growth model of the United States economy.* Amsterdam: North-Holland.

Hicks, John R. 1950. *A contribution to the theory of the trade cycle.* Oxford: Clarendon Press.

Kindleberger, Charles P. 1973. *The world in depression, 1929–39.* Berkeley: University of California Press.

Klein, Lawrence R., and Arthur S. Goldberger. 1955. *An econometric model of the United States, 1929–1952.* Amsterdam: North-Holland.

Lucas, Robert E., Jr. 1981. *Studies in business cycle theory.* Cambridge: MIT Press.

Mitchell, Wesley C. 1927. *Business cycles: The problem and its setting.* New York: National Bureau of Economic Research.

———. 1951. *What happens during business cycles: a progress report.* New York: National Bureau of Economic Research.

National Bureau of Economic Research. 1951. *Conference on business cycles.* Universities–National Bureau Committee for Economic Research. New York: National Bureau of Economic Research.

Phelps, Edmund S. 1978. Commodity-supply shock and full-employment monetary policy. *Journal of Money, Credit and Banking* 10 (May): 206–21.

Romer, Christina. 1984a. Spurious volatility in historical unemployment data. Working Paper, Massachusetts Institute of Technology.

———. 1984b. Is the stabilization of the postwar economy a figment of the data? Evidence from industrial production. Working Paper, Massachusetts Institute of Technology.

Samuelson, Paul A. 1939. A synthesis of the principle of acceleration and the multiplier. *Journal of Political Economy* 47 (December): 786–97.

Schumpeter, Joseph A. 1939. *Business cycles.* New York: McGraw-Hill.

Sims, Christopher A. 1972. Money, income and causality. *American Economic Review* 62 (September): 540–52.

———. 1980. Macroeconomics and reality. *Econometrica* 48 (January): 1–48.

Slutsky, Eugen. 1927. *The summation of random causes as the source of cyclic processes* 3, no. 1. Moscow: Conjuncture Institute. Russian with English summary.

Tobin, James R. 1975. Keynesian models of recession and depression, *American Economic Review* 65 (May): 195–202.

Zarnowitz, Victor. 1972. *The business cycle today.* New York: Columbia University Press.

———. 1985. Recent work on business cycles in historical perspective: Review of theories and evidence. *Journal of Economic Literature* 23 (June): 523–80.

Tribute to Otto Eckstein

Allen Sinai

Otto Eckstein passed away yesterday morning. At about this time, funeral services are being conducted in Lexington, Massachusetts.

It is a strange coincidence of timing, perhaps, but a fitting tribute to Otto that his last paper be presented as scheduled.

Otto was a man who met all his commitments. He was a prodigious and prolific worker and felt particularly good when, at the end of a day, he could point to something tangible he had accomplished.

This conference is about business cycles.

Otto was a longtime student of business fluctuations, spending a good portion of his time analyzing, forecasting, writing, publishing articles, teaching, speaking about, and developing models of the business cycle.

He was the principal creator of a new industry concerned with the business cycle and its implications for decision makers; establishing, motivating, and transmitting, through Data Resources, Incorporated, systems and methods for the use of data, macroeconomic analyses, and econometrics that could be used in applications by large numbers of organizations and individuals. Macroeconomics is a household subject today as an outgrowth of this activity.

Time and timing are essential elements in the business cycle. For Otto, time was not to be wasted.

The range and breadth of his activities was astounding—enough to fill many lifetimes—as a successful businessman, academic, and public servant. He was an active and strong chief executive officer, president and chief economist in his years at DRI, a productive member of the academic community, and dedicated to his family.

He was a quick study, to the point, and taught everyone around him the value of substantive content in limited space or time.

He worked right up to the end of his illness, organizing and using his time wisely, producing several books and articles in recent years, spending his last months and days visiting and talking with his family, friends, and colleagues, lifting their spirits even as he knew his time was running out.

For those of us fortunate enough to know Otto well, most striking was his uncommon degree of common sense—an ability to see the forest rather than the trees, humility and a sense of perspective, accessibility, and above all a marvelous sense of humor.

Otto's passing is a great loss to the economics profession, to his family, friends, and colleagues, and to the public at large for what might yet have been and all that was his to give. But just as Otto felt particularly good when at the end of a day he could point to something tangible he had accomplished, he undoubtedly must have felt particularly satisfied at the end of his life for having accomplished so much in so short a time.

May he rest in peace.

23 March 1984

I   The Sources of Cyclical Behavior

1 The Mechanisms of the Business Cycle in the Postwar Era

Otto Eckstein and Allen Sinai

1.1 Introduction

The business cycle has persisted in the postwar period, producing eight separate episodes of systematic fluctuations. Although a depression of the 1930s variety has been avoided, more severe and frequent recessions have occurred in recent years, and the hope of cycleless prosperity generated in the long expansion of the 1960s has been disappointed by the record of the 1970s and early 1980s.

The experience of recent years has revived the scientific study of the business cycle. In this paper the point of departure is an analysis of historical events and processes, applying the ideas of the business cycle literature to draw what generalizations can legitimately be made about phenomena common to most or all cycles. First, the eight postwar cycles are surveyed for their key elements. Second, a set of business cycle phases are derived from this survey. Third, the types of mechanisms that can trigger cycles are summarized. Fourth, particular attention is paid to the financial side of the business cycle and its systematic patterns since the mid-1950s. Fifth, we run a set of large-

Otto Eckstein was chairman of Data Resources, Incorporated and Paul M. Warburg Professor of Economics, Harvard University. Allen Sinai is chief economist with Shearson Lehman Brothers, Incorporated, and adjunct professor of economics, Graduate School of Business, New York University. He was at Data Resources from 1971 to September, 1983.

We gratefully acknowledge the work of Russell Robins, of Data Resources, Incorporated, and Shearson Lehman Brothers, and Peter Rathjens, of Shearson Lehman Brothers, in performing the computer simulations and in related support. We are also grateful to Robert Gross, of Data Resources, Incorporated, for his research assistance and to Kathleen Chapman and Debra Jenkins for producing the manuscript. Robert E. Hall, Robert J. Gordon, and Lawrence R. Klein made helpful suggestions on an earlier draft. The discussants of this paper, Michael Lovell and Kenneth Singleton, made valuable suggestions, and we thank Cary Leahey and Victor Zarnowitz for their comments.

scale econometric model simulations to estimate more precisely the relative role of several possible business cycle mechanisms. Finally, we draw some conclusions from our work on the main causes of cyclicality in the postwar period and the nature of any changes that have occurred. Throughout, the exposition focuses on the cycle both in real activity and in financial conditions, emphasizing the interactions.

1.2   An Overview of the Eight Postwar Business Cycles

There appear to have been five distinct phases of business cycle behavior in the postwar era: (1) from the end of World War II to the outbreak of the Korean War; (2) from the Korean War to 1961; (3) from 1961 to 1969; (4) from 1969 to 1979; and (5) from 1979 to 1983. The first phase was a period of adjustment from an economy in wartime mobilization to peacetime normality. The second phase contained several cycles and ended with considerable slack in the economy. In particular, three recessions occurred in the eight years from 1953 to 1961, a by-product of the boom in the mid-1950s and concern over inflation on the part of the Federal Reserve and the administration. From 1961 to 1969 there was a sustained business expansion, the longest in history, though two extended pauses in growth occurred in 1962 and 1967. Inflation rates were very low in the early 1960s, but in 1965 inflation began to accelerate. Between 1966 and 1979 the economy was characterized by a severe upward spiraling of inflation, with wide fluctuations in economic activity. In part these resulted from a series of demand, supply, and policy shocks and a worldwide boom. Then, between 1979 and 1982, two deep downturns occurred, primarily as the result of severely restrictive turns in monetary and fiscal policy to achieve lower inflation.

1.2.1   Business Cycle Events and Mechanisms

Without attempting to provide a complete historical account of the eight postwar business cycles, tables 1.1 and 1.2 highlight the events particular to each episode and summarize the major dimensions. Table 1.1 stresses the clearly identifiable special features, thereby allowing some common mechanisms to become visible as well. Table 1.2 provides the dimensions of length and amplitude for key parameters of performance in the postwar expansions and recessions.

The business cycle events can be classified into five types: (1) booms—periods in which aggregate demand rises much more rapidly than a balanced growth path and/or pushes the economy close to its productive ceiling; (2) negative demand shocks—sudden declines in aggregate demand that are a primary cause of cycle movements; (3) supply shocks—sudden curtailments in the supply of key materials or other disruptions

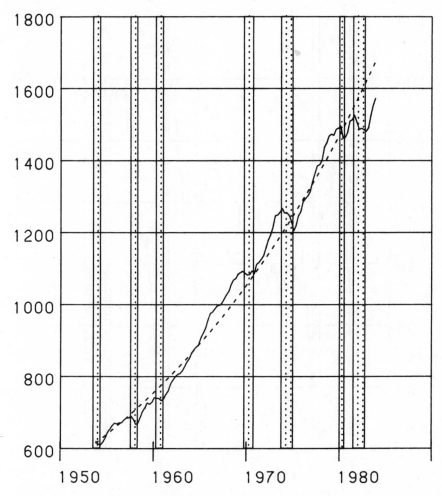

Fig. 1.1   Real GNP relative to trend: postwar period (billions of 1972
dollars). Shaded areas are NBER recessions.

to production; (4) price shocks—sudden exogenous movements in the
price level (such as the imposition and the ending of price controls);
and (5) credit crunches—periods when financial distress produces sharp
discontinuities in flows of funds and spending and when the financial
strains include tight monetary policy, much lessened availability of
money and credit, sharp rises of interest rates, and deteriorating balance sheets for households, businesses, and financial institutions.

It can be seen that six of the recessions were preceded by booms.
The causes of these booms were varied: two involved wars, in Korea

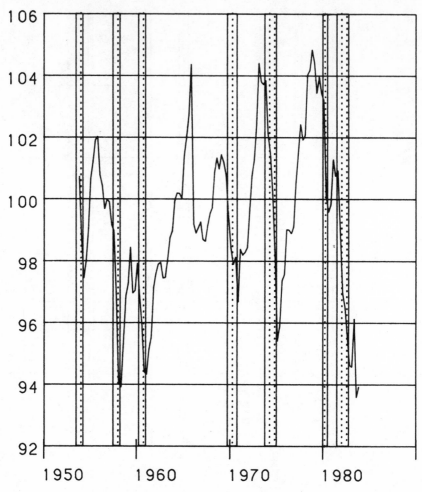

Fig. 1.2   Changing cyclicality of real GNP in the postwar period (percentage of trend). Shaded areas are NBER recessions.

and Vietnam, two involved stock-flow adjustments of consumer durable goods, and one involved an unsustainable capital goods boom. One boom was worldwide, following the collapse of the fixed exchange rate regime in 1971. The most recent brief boom, in late 1978 and early 1979, was the result of excessively stimulative monetary and fiscal policies, negative real interest rates, and a sharp, if short-lived, decline of the dollar.

There were at least two exogenous negative demand shocks, both of which originated in the federal budget. The recession of 1948 was

Table 1.1   Summary of Business Cycle Events in the Postwar Era

Date of Onset of Recession	Preceding Booms	Demand Shocks	Supply Shocks	Price Shocks	Crunch, Including Precrunch Period	Recession Depth and Duration
November 1948	Consumer durables boom	End of war economy				Mild, brief
July 1953	Korean War 6/50–3/51, 10/52–7/53					Mild, brief
August 1957	Auto boom Investment boom 3/55–12/55			Break in raw materials prices	1955:4 to 1957:4	Severe, brief
April 1960		Swing to balanced federal budget, FY 1960	Steel strike		1959:2 to 1960:2	Mild, brief
December 1969	Vietnam War 12/64–12/66, 12/67–11/69		Auto strike General Electric strike	Vietnam War inflation	1966:1 to 1966:3 1969:1 to 1970:1	Mild, brief
November 1973	World boom, wage price controls and easier money 8/71–9/72; collapse of fixed exchange rate regime 6/72–4/73		OPEC I—fourfold oil price hike; world food supply shortages	OPEC I—fourfold oil price hike; end of price controls	1973:1 to 1974:3	Severe, extended
January 1980	Small domestic boom 8/78–3/79		OPEC II—doubling crude oil prices; New Fed Policy 10/79	OPEC II—doubling crude oil prices	1978:2 to 1980:1	Mild, brief
July 1981					1981:1 to 1981:4	Severe, extended

Table 1.2   Dimensions of Postwar Business Cycles

Trough to Peak or Peak to Trough	Length of Expansion (months)	Length of Contraction (months)	Industrial Production (% change)	Real GNP (% change)	Amplitude Inflation[a] (% change)	Unemployment Rate (%)
October 1945 (T) to November 1948 (P)	37		n.a.[b]	n.a.	0.0 (T); 6.9 (P)	3.1 (T); 3.8 (P)
November 1948 (P) to October 1949 (T)		11	−8.5	−1.4	−6.9 (P); −4.1 (T)	3.8 (P); 7.9 (T)
October 1949 (T) to July 1953 (P)	45		50.1	27.2	−4.1 (T); 0.6 (P)	7.9 (T); 2.6 (P)
July 1953 (P) to May 1954 (T)		10	−8.9	−2.6	0.6 (P); 3.3 (T)	2.6 (P); 5.9 (T)
May 1954 (T) to August 1957 (P)	40		21.8	13.2	3.3 (T); 3.9 (P)	5.9 (T); 4.1 (P)
August 1957 (P) to April 1958 (T)		8	−12.6	−2.7	3.9 (P); 2.8 (T)	4.1 (P); 7.4 (T)
April 1958 (T) to April 1960 (P)	24		22.7	10.2	2.8 (T); 5.7 (P)	7.4 (T); 5.2 (P)
April 1960 (P) to February 1961 (T)		10	−6.1	−0.1	5.7 (P); 0.0 (T)	5.2 (P); 6.9 (T)
February 1961 (T) to December 1969 (P)	106		76.8	47.2	0.0 (T); 7.7 (P)	6.9 (T); 3.5 (P)
December 1969 (P) to November 1970 (T)		11	−5.8	−0.1	7.7 (P); 5.2 (T)	3.5 (P); 5.9 (T)
November 1970 (T) to November 1973 (P)	36		25.6	16.7	5.2 (T); 10.1 (P)	5.9 (T); 4.8 (P)
November 1973 (P) to March 1975 (T)		16	−15.1	−4.9	10.1 (P); 3.9 (T)	4.8 (P); 8.6 (T)
March 1975 (T) to January 1980 (P)	58		37.0	24.3	3.9 (T); 19.2 (P)	8.6 (T); 6.3 (P)

January 1980 (P) to July 1980 (T)	6	−8.3	−2.2	19.2 (P); 1.0 (T)	6.3 (P); 7.8 (T)
July 1980 (T) to July 1981 (P)	12	9.7	4.2	1.0 (T); 14.6 (P)	7.8 (T); 7.3 (P)
July 1981 (P) to November 1982 (T)	16	−12.3	−3.0	14.6 (P); 0.0 (T)	7.3 (P); 10.7 (T)

Recessions:
  Average length: 11.0 months
  Median length: 10.5 months
  Industrial production
    Average decline: 9.7%
    Median decline: 8.7%
    (peak to trough)
  Real GNP
    Average decline: 2.1%
    Median decline: 2.4%
    (peak to trough)
  Inflation (change in percentage points)
    (peak to trough)
    Average: −5.4
    Median: −4.8
  Unemployment rate (change in percentage points)
    (peak to trough)
    Average: 2.9
    Median: 3.3

Expansions:
  Average length: 44.8 months
  Median length: 38.5 months
  Industrial production
    Average rise: 34.8%
    Median rise: 25.6%
    (trough to peak)
  Real GNP
    Average rise: 20.4%
    Median rise: 16.7%
    (trough to peak)
  Inflation (change in percentage points)
    (trough to peak)
    Average: 5.4
    Median: 4.1
  Unemployment rate (change in percentage points)
    (trough to peak)
    Average: −2.0
    Median: −2.0

[a]Consumer price index—all urban; annual rate at peak or trough.
[b]n.a. = not available.

an inevitable concomitant of the conversion of the American economy from war to a peacetime footing. The swing in the federal budget was so great that even though there was an early boom in civilian demand, industrial production declined sharply and an "official" recession did occur. The other shock of this type was President Eisenhower's achievement of a balanced federal budget in 1960, when the largest swing of the postwar period was registered in the full employment budget.

At least four supply shocks can be identified as having played a major contributing role in particular business cycles. The steel strike of 1959 was a major cause of the 1960 recession (and the auto strike of 1970 came close to aborting that recovery in its early stages). The two supply disruptions of world oil, in 1973 and again in 1979–80, the agricultural crisis created by the extraordinarily poor crops of 1972, and the United States–Russia wheat deal also had broad cyclical implications.

All but the first two of the recessions were preceded by credit crunches. In each case interest rates shot up to high, usually unfamiliar levels late in the upswing and began the process of diffusing recessionary forces through the entire economy. In all but the most recent two cases, the credit crunches also were characterized by sharply increased credit rationing created by the presence of interest rate ceilings that produced gross distortions in the flow of funds of the financial system. And in every situation, balance sheets deteriorated to the point where risks of bankruptcy and failure became costly. Sharp cutbacks in spending and borrowing were the consequence.

As a result of these events and the underlying business cycle mechanisms, the economy experienced six recessions that can be safely characterized as brief and mild, though they did not always feel that way at the time. Three of the recessions were more serious: the 1957–58, 1973–75, and 1981–82 episodes. The 1957–58 recession, which followed a major boom and prolonged period of a worsening credit crunch, was severe, with the unemployment rate rising from 4.1% to 7.4%. A worsening inflation, reaching 5.9% at the peak and largely caused by "wage-push" and bottleneck excess demands, made the Federal Reserve prolong its period of tightness and made the government reluctant to aid the economy with fiscal stimulus. The recovery from this recession was rather weak and ultimately proved incomplete.

The other severe recessions were longer and in each case represented a complicated interaction of supply shocks that first triggered double-digit inflation and then severe credit crunches. The recession of 1973–75 was complicated by the collapse of price controls that had been instituted in 1971–72 and by the synchronization of the business cycle across the industrial world. The recessions of 1980 and 1981–82 were worsened by the policy decision to accomplish a massive disinflation by maintaining a condition of severe credit restraint deep into the recession.

This very brief survey of business cycle events makes clear that no single, simple feature of the economy's behavior can be the cause of the business cycle. Some ideas from the recent literature, such as asymmetric information, the misreading of absolute price changes as relative price changes, the serial correlation introduced by buffer inventory stocks in production, and lags in the wage/price process, may be part of reality, but even the most cursory look at actual history shows that they can be no more than a small part of it.

1.2.2   Has the Business Cycle Changed in the Postwar Era?

Tables 1.1 and 1.2 and figure 1.2 indicate some changing characteristics of the postwar business cycle, especially in recent years. First, the cyclicality of real GNP has increased. Real GNP underwent swings from 104% of trend in 1953 to just under 94% in 1958, from a little over 94% to 106% between the early 1960s and 1969, and then from over 106% in 1973 to under 92% in November 1982. Second, cyclical downturns have become more frequent and severe since 1969 (table 1.2, fig. 1.2). Three recessions have occurred in the past ten years, and two of them were the longest in the postwar period. Third, the business cycle in general has become increasingly volatile in the postwar era. Swings of industrial production, inflation, and the unemployment rate have exceeded the average for the complete postwar period, both in expansions and downturns, since the mid-1970s.

1.3   Stages of the Business Cycle in the Postwar Period

In a descriptive sense, there has been general agreement on the stages of the business cycle, as chronicled by the National Bureau of Economic Research.[1] These have been variously named the peak or upper turning point, contraction or downturn, trough or lower turning point, recovery, and expansion. The timing of these stages has been identified on the basis of the systematic behavior of numerous statistical series that primarily describe the real economic behavior of the United States economy. These stages do no more than separate periods of expansion from periods of contraction, however, and attach precise dates to the turning points.

The actual events of the postwar business cycles, real and financial, suggest a more elaborate set of "stages" in greater recognition of the processes that are intrinsic to the fluctuations in economic activity. The simultaneous and interrelated behavior of real and financial markets

1. See Burns and Mitchell 1946 and Mitchell 1927.

produces real and financial sides to the business cycle that should be described by the nomenclature.[2]

Thus, we propose the following stages: (1) recovery/expansion; (2) boom; (3) precrunch period/credit crunch; (4) recession/decline; and (5) reliquefication. This nomenclature recognizes and suggests that the business cycle is more than just an occasional reversal of direction, instead consisting of systematic real-sector movements as well as associated financial phenomena.[3] An occasional cycle may omit one or another of the stages, and there will be some overlap in their timing. But the typical cycle seems to run through all five stages. Table 1.3 shows the chronology of these five stages in the eight business cycle episodes since 1950.

1.3.1   Recovery/Expansion

The lower turning point marks the beginning of recovery. The forces of contraction having run their course, or improvements being made in final demands, will cause an expansion to begin. Since the United States enjoys continuous technological progress, positive capital accumulation, and a continued increase of the working-age population, the normal condition for the economy is growth. No special theory, therefore, is required to "explain" expansion; indeed, only significant disruptive events can avoid it. Typically, however, certain catalytic events have helped to initiate the expansion, most often changes in policy that were designed to arrest and reverse the downturn.

In common usage, the recovery phase is usually defined to stretch from the lower turning point to the time when aggregate measures of physical activity such as real GNP or industrial production have returned to their previous peak levels. Once the economy is on new ground, recovery is said to be complete, though a more demanding set of definitions would call for a return to prerecession unemployment levels or a return to the neighborhood of the natural rate of operation of the economy. The expansion phase continues from the end of recovery until the upper turning point is reached. In the business cycle

2. Most theories of the business cycle have paid little attention to the financial factor, probably because of the difficulty of integrating "financial" with "real" theory. The Keynesian tradition spawned a host of real theories (multiplier/accelerator) of business fluctuations. Yet, clearly, events that are financial have played a major role in most cycles.

3. The notion here is that each stage in the "real" business cycle is accompanied by a stage in a "financial" or "flow of funds" cycle. A flow of funds cycle has been described as having stages named the precrunch period, crunch, reliquefication, and accumulation (Sinai 1978). The precrunch period overlaps with the expansion stage of standard business cycle nomenclature. The crunch corresponds to the upper turning point. Reliquefication occurs in recession and recovery. And the accumulation stage overlaps the expansion, especially the early stage. Since the accumulation phase essentially is the expansion, it was not separately identified in table 1.3.

Table 1.3   Stages of Postwar Business Cycles

Episode	Recovery/Expansion	Boom	Recession	Precrunch Period/Crunch	Reliquefication
I	1945:4 to 1948:4	—	1948:4 to 1949:4	—	—
II	1949:4 to 1953:2	1952:4 to 1953:2	1953:2 to 1954:2	—	—
III	1954:2 to 1957:3	1955:1 to 1955:4	1957:3 to 1958:2	1955:4 to 1957:4	1958:1 to 1958:2
IV	1958:2 to 1960:2	—	1960:2 to 1961:1	1959:2 to 1960:2	1960:3 to 1964:3
V	1961:1 to 1969:4	1964:4 to 1966:4	—	1966:1 to 1966:3	1966:4 to 1967:3
			1969:4 to 1970:4	1969:1 to 1970:1	1970:2 to 1971:2
VI	1970:4 to 1973:4	1972:2 to 1973:4	1973:4 to 1975:1	1973:1 to 1974:3	1974:4 to 1976:2
VII	1975:1 to 1980:1	1978:3 to 1979:1	1980:1 to 1980:3	1978:2 to 1980:1	1980:2 to 1980:3
VIII	1980:3 to 1981:3	—	1981:3 to 1982:4	1981:1 to 1981:4	1982:1 to 1983:2
IX	1982:4–	—	—	—	—

Sources: National Bureau of Economic Research; Eckstein 1976; Conner and Eckstein 1978; "Boom Monitor," *Data Resources Review*, various issues; Sinai 1978.

timing of table 1.3, we accept the National Bureau of Economic Research approach and the United States Bureau of the Census implementation of the definitions of this stage in each business cycle.

1.3.2   Boom

A boom is a period of an unsustainable rapid rate of advance of economic activity, with the major sectors growing at rates that are clearly temporary. In this stage the economy as a whole is often significantly above its trend growth path and usually is near its ceiling of potential output. There have been six booms since 1945, with five of them soon succeeded by recessions and one (1964 to 1966) followed by a growth recession. Only two of the recessions were not preceded by booms, and both are easily explained by other circumstances. The recession of 1960 was due to the negative demand shock of a suddenly balanced budget and credit crunch, with recovery kept incomplete by restrictive demand management policies. The recession of 1981–82 was part of a longer downturn that began in 1980. The brief expansion of 1980–81 can be viewed as little more than a short disruption of a recession caused by a severely restrictive monetary policy, in a temporary deviation from the basic goal of disinflation. Industrial production only briefly surpassed its previous peak, but by enough for the National Bureau of Economic Research to declare a business cycle expansion.

The boom episodes are defined by the Data Resources, Incorporated (DRI) composite boom index, a list of eight time series analogous to the NBER leading indicator indexes but designed to identify the presence of a boom rather than the imminence of a downturn (fig. 1.3 and table 1.4). This index was originally constructed because recessions usually develop so quickly that even the best leading indicator indexes barely give warning. If the boom could be identified instead, then advance notice with longer, though imprecisely known lead times should become possible. The eight series are: (1) change in the ratio of consumer credit outstanding to disposable income, (2) ratio of car sales to driving-age population, (3) ratio of housing starts to population age twenty years and older, (4) the DRI index of labor market tightness, (5) eighteen-month growth in the real monetary base, (6) Federal Reserve Board capacity utilization rate for materials industries, (7) ratio of capital spending to real trend line GNP, and (8) vendor performance.

The eight series fall into two types. Items 1, 2, 3, and 7 are measures of sectoral final demands that show disequilibrium from sustainable trend values. Items 4, 6, and 8 measure the degree of resource utilization, that is, the tightness of markets. Item 5 measures deviations of monetary policy from its sustainable trend: when the real monetary base has grown too fast for eighteen months, a boom is likely to be under way.

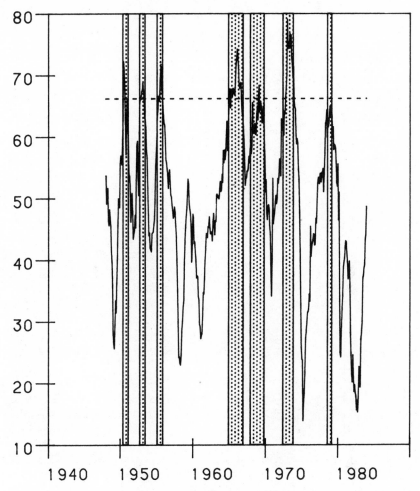

Fig. 1.3   The DRI composite boom index. Horizontal line denotes boom average; shaded areas indicate boom periods.

1.3.3   Precrunch Period/Credit Crunch

Because every recession since the mid-1950s was preceded and triggered by a credit crunch, this experience can be included in the standard stages of the business cycle. Late in the expansion, the demand for credit expands beyond the ability of businesses, households, and governments to finance still expanding commitments out of internally generated funds. Accelerating inflation may also intensify the demand for credit. At some point the supply of credit ceases to keep pace, usually because the central bank becomes increasingly perturbed by visible signs of a boom. As the Federal Reserve curtails the growth of bank

Table 1.4 The DRI Boom Monitor

	Three Boom Periods, Average Values			All Boom Periods, Average	Historical Average	Third Quarter 1983	October 1983	November 1983	December 1983
	67:12 to 69:11	72:6 to 73:11	78:8 to 79:3						
The DRI composite boom index	62.65	70.69	63.19	66.210	50.00	38.31	42.03	43.57	45.34
Ratio of change in consumer credit to disposable income	0.015	0.023	0.028	0.018	0.013	0.018	0.024	0.023	
Index[a] (weight = 0.107)	52.08	67.67	74.63	60.29	50.00	52.30	65.57	62.94	
Per capita car sales	0.072	0.078	0.069	0.070	0.059	0.053	0.056	0.054	0.060
Index[a] (weight = 0.107)	72.19	79.25	57.99	70.87	50.00	24.75	30.22	27.02	37.36
Ratio of housing starts to adult population	0.013	0.017	0.013	0.014	0.013	0.011	0.010	0.011	0.010
Index (weight = 0.098)	47.82	76.41	49.84	58.81	50.00	39.12	33.29	37.36	33.64
DRI index of labor market tightness	70.49	64.69	62.24	66.320	50.06	30.11	34.26	35.50	37.00
Index (weight = 0.152)	75.34	68.14	65.11	70.17	50.00	25.27	30.42	31.95	33.82
Real monetary base growth	2.674	4.399	1.793	2.494	0.922	6.379	6.645	6.695	6.130
Index (weight = 0.096)	61.64	73.09	55.78	60.44	50.00	86.24	88.01	88.34	84.59
Capacity utilizations/materials	0.878	0.904	0.880	0.887	0.830	0.775	0.794	0.798	0.801
Index (weight = 0.147)	66.68	75.68	67.40	69.86	50.00	31.12	37.70	39.09	40.12
Ratio of capital spending to trend GNP	0.108	0.106	0.108	0.111	0.104	0.090	0.089	0.093	
Index (weight = 0.191)	60.27	54.43	60.67	66.30	50.00	18.81	16.78	26.67	
Vendor performance	0.58	0.80	0.70	0.671	0.51	0.58	0.64	0.59	0.67
Index (weight = 0.102)	58.74	84.21	72.12	69.12	50.00	58.10	65.52	59.66	69.04

[a]Index reflects trend adjustment of base series.

reserves and seeks to limit the money supply, interest rates rise sharply and credit rationing becomes widespread. The period over which these processes occur can be identified as the precrunch period, when the preconditions of a financial crisis are laid.

More recently, with the deregulation of deposit and loan rates at financial institutions and new deposit innovations, rising interest rates have become the focus of adjustment through affordability and debt service effects. Excessive monthly loan payments on big-ticket items and onerous debt service charges relative to income or cash flows were a principal mechanism of financial restraint in 1980 and 1981–82, although some traditional credit strains also occurred.

In the credit crunch itself, households, businesses, and financial institutions find that the expectations upon which spending plans are based become falsified as balance sheets deteriorate, with loan repayments, debt burdens, and costs of financing all becoming surprisingly burdensome. Interest rates move sharply higher, rising in nonlinear fashion from a combination of strong private sector credit demands, reduced liquidity in the commercial banking system, sales of financial assets to raise funds or prevent large capital losses, and a monetary squeeze by the Federal Reserve. As rising interest rates, credit rationing, and the financial risk associated with deteriorated balance sheets reduce the total level of spending, market activities grow less than expected, curtailing internal cash flows and adding further to the needs for external financing. Households reduce outlays and become extremely cautious. Firms cease to hire new workers and attempt to reduce inventories. Business plant and equipment outlays are sharply cut. As a new perception of the state of the economy spreads, business demand for the factors of production shrinks. Changes in inventory policy amplify the production cutbacks of the more basic industries.

The crunch is at the heart of the business cycle mechanism, particularly the upper turning point, and is discussed more fully in section 1.5. The timing of both the precrunch period and crunches since the mid-1950s is shown in table 1.3.

1.3.4 Contraction/Recession

According to the NBER methodology, a recession covers the period beginning with the upper turning point and continuing through the interval of absolute decline in physical activity. Once the decline begins, business has to adjust its inventories to the lower current volume of sales and curtail its total spending commitments to reflect the reduced availability of internal capital. Depending on the extent of revision of business expectations between the months before the upper turning point and the period of recession, the adjustment will be large or small.

The severity of the financial disturbance associated with the credit crunch and the speed with which fiscal and monetary policies switch from restraint to stimulus also affects the length and severity of the recession.

The lower turning point is reached when business spending commitments have moved closer to the new, lower equilibrium and stock adjustment processes set up for a reversal. Exogenous forces, such as stimulative changes in monetary and fiscal policy, also can accelerate or delay the lower turning point.

1.3.5   Reliquefication

Reliquefication is a stage of financial restructuring that occurs during recession and early recovery. During the period leading up to a crunch, business and household balance sheets become more and more strained, remaining troublesome through the crunch itself and even in the early stages of recession. Financial commitments can be reduced only so fast, and sources of funds usually shrink even more quickly when the economy turns down. Business adjusts to this situation by an "undershoot" on spending commitments, including hiring freezes or even layoffs, drastic deferrals on capital budgets, and a dumping of inventories through sales at distress prices, all in order to quickly improve cash flow and strengthen balance sheets. A rebuilding of balance sheets through the accumulation of financial assets, other than transactions money, and a decumulation of liabilities then takes place to help set the stage for further expansion.

The process of reliquefication has taken anywhere from two to sixteen quarters, according to table 1.5. Until a minimum degree of reliquefication is accomplished, a business cycle upturn is difficult to achieve or sustain.

1.4   The Generic Cyclical Mechanisms

The analytical minimum requirements of a macro model capable of producing cycles have long been understood.[4] The cycles can originate in a two-period, second-order linear difference equation model in which the parameters on the endogenous variables are of sufficiently destabilizing magnitudes. If the coefficients are very large and destabilizing, the economy takes on an explosive character. If the coefficients are smaller, the cycles are quickly damped. Intervening values will generate a self-sustaining cycle in linear systems, without random shocks.

4. For an exposition of this business cycle mechanism, see Samuelson 1939, and Baumol 1959.

A model with intrinsically damped properties can generate cycles if it is combined with a shock mechanism that reinforces the cyclical movements. Such shocks can be systematic, with their own periodicity—for example, a cyclicality in fiscal or monetary policy that is created by politics or lagged responses to business conditions in the private sector. Or the shocks can appear to be random in nature—occasional strikes, droughts, or even events such as the OPEC oil price hikes.

The business cycle literature has proposed many mechanisms that stem from the analytics of the basic dynamic second-order linear difference equation. The multiplier/accelerator model is the best known, with its linear consumption function and an investment equation based on the rate of change of output one quarter earlier. Hicks (1950) concluded that the accelerator coefficient in such a system was sufficiently large to make the cycle intrinsically explosive. A ceiling and a floor therefore were used to contain the economy to a stable cyclical path.

The accelerator model, or its more flexible variant the capital stock adjustment model, has been applied to various components of final demands. The stock of business fixed capital is the archetypal example, of course. Adjustment of the inventory stock to expected sales was proposed by Metzler (1941). Consumer durable goods purchases can be governed by a stock adjustment mechanism, with changes in permanent income producing changes in the desired stock of consumer durables.

Financial behavior also contains a large element of stock adjustment mechanisms. Individuals and businesses desire certain portfolios of assets and liabilities. If there are changes in the target stocks, the flows necessary to accomplish the desired stock adjustments can be highly volatile and cyclical.

The dynamics of adjustments in wages and prices can reinforce the cyclical mechanisms, or provide an impetus of their own, so long as they are not of the market clearing type. If it takes a considerable interval for wages to fully adjust to changes in the inflation rate, whether for reasons of contracts or gradual learning processes, cyclical mechanisms may be reinforced because the inflationary effects of a strong expansion will not be fully felt for some time. Consequently, the reaction of policy or of consumers may coincide in timing with the downturn in the real cycle.

The dynamics of the production process accentuate cycles.[5] Producers often misperceive the strength of final demand because they are removed by several stages of production from end markets; they find

5. See Zarnowitz 1973.

it difficult to distinguish inventory changes at intermediate stages of production from swings in final demands. Optimal buying policy responds to actual delivery periods and short-term price behavior, and these buying policies in turn lengthen order books, thereby intensifying supply shortages, triggering further inventory buying, and raising prices of factors and intermediate goods.

The business cycle mechanism also can be reinforced by external developments. Whereas foreign markets and foreign sources of supply usually serve as stabilizers of the business cycle, the international monetary system and changes in such factors as world oil prices can help create a synchronization of cycles in real demands that intensify the instability of material and product markets of internationally traded goods.

Expectations have long been recognized as a source of potential instability and fluctuations in economic activity (see appendix 1.2). Keynes stressed the importance of expectations as a source of instability in the investment and liquidity preference functions. Autonomous shifts in investment demand and in the demand for money provided impulses for cyclical movements, affecting the amplitudes of expansions and declines. The consumption function also was subject to autonomous shifts.

Subsequently, there was a general acceptance of expectations phenomena as a determinant of economic behavior. Stock adjustment and adaptive expectations models became widespread, though characterized by a backward look at actual behavior. In Hicks (1950), distributed lags in the adjustment of consumption and investment contributed to the dynamics of the trade cycle that was analyzed. In more recent years, surveys of expectations and notions of rationally formed expectations have replaced extrapolative or adaptive expectations in much of theory, as a more forward looking means of incorporating expectations into the analysis of economic behavior.

As a generic mechanism, expectations can affect the business cycle in several ways. First, the manner by which expected values are formed can have an impact—in particular on business cycle dynamics through the lags involved in expectations formation. Second, deviations of actual from expected behavior in the form of surprises or disappointments affect economic and financial market behavior. Third, expectations of movements toward equilibrium are based on notions that derive from theoretical constructs or practical knowledge of processes and affect behavior. Finally, waves of optimism or pessimism influence both the amplitude and the time lags of economic activities.

Expectations are formed rationally, through adaptive behavior or learning from past errors or by extrapolation of past behavior. Financial markets generally come closest to exhibiting rationally formed expectations. There is an early discounting of potential future events and, in particular, expectations on policy. Information is used efficiently, and decisions are made quickly. One exception is in the formation of expected inflation, where a slow process of adjustment seems to characterize the reactions of fixed income investors to changes in the actual rate of inflation.

Other markets, whether for reasons of adjustment lags, slow changes in perceptions, delivery lags, contractual time lags, surprises, or unexpected shocks, exhibit extrapolative or adaptive expectations. The labor market is characterized by slower reactions in expectations through instances of money illusion and considerable extrapolative behavior based on past inflation. Cost-of-living agreements, for example, perpetuate past changes of inflation into wages, which in turn affect future inflation through unit labor costs.

Finally, the element of surprise or disappointment can be important for the business cycle. When the sales expectations of business are disappointed on more than a random basis, capital outlays and inventories are cut back, imparting cyclicality to the economy. Tighter than expected Federal Reserve policy can bring worse than expected debt service charges and unexpected reductions in spending and borrowing. The quantification of expectations in models of the United States economy remains fairly primitive but still contributes to explaining cyclical behavior.[6]

The list of generic business cycle mechanisms can be extended and presented in a more elaborate classification (table 1.5). There are factors that principally affect the amplitude of the business cycle: the impulse mechanisms. Impulses can stem from autonomous shifts in exogenous variables having to do with stabilization policy, wars, strikes, new institutional arrangements, financial deregulation, and technological advances. "Endogenous" contributions to the amplitude of the business cycle include shifts in sentiment, swings of inflation and interest rates, and deviations of actual events from expectations, among others. These factors have seemed to affect the amplitude of the business cycle but themselves occur in response to other inputs.

Propagation mechanisms affect the oscillations, phase, and duration characteristics of the business cycle. The internal diffusion of business cycle responses often occurs through the signal mechanisms (prices, wages, interest rates, etc.) of the economic system and distributed lag reactions to them. Adjustment lags, in both real and financial processes, propagate various impulses through the system. Stock adjustments and expectations formation are major generic propagation mechanisms, oc-

6. See Eckstein 1983, 40–49, and Brimmer and Sinai 1981 for a discussion of how expectations influence the economy in the DRI model.

Table 1.5   The Mechanisms of the Business Cycle

Impulse Mechanisms (amplitude)	Propagation Mechanisms (oscillations, phase, duration)

"Exogenous"
  Policy/monetary and fiscal
  Rest of the world
  "Autonomous" spending
    Sentiment
    Wealth
  "Shocks"
    Wars
    Strikes
    OPEC
  Legislation/taxes, spending,
    financial
  Institutional change
  Technological change
"Endogenous"
  Inflation
  Interest rates
  Balance sheets and liquidity
  Availability of funds
  Stock prices
  Expectations
  Surprises or disappointments
    relative to expectations
	Flow-stock adjustments: real
	  Consumer durables—autos,
	    furniture, etc.
	  Investment
	    Residential construction
	    Inventories
	    Business fixed investment
	    Public construction
	Flow-stock adjustments: financial
	  and balance sheet
	  Debt and financial asset
	    accumulation
	  Debt service burdens
	  Loan deposit ratios
	  Financial risk
	  Failure, bankruptcy, and default
	Expectations formation
	  Consumption
	  Investment
	    Residential construction
	    Plant and equipment
	    Inventories
	    Inflation—wages and prices
	Policy responses to the economy,
	  inflation, unemployment, and
	  monetary growth

Note: Many of the mechanisms are not mutually exclusive, overlapping between providing an impulse to the system and acting as a propagation mechanism.

curring in durable goods spending by households and business, inventory accumulation, debt and financial asset accumulation, and derivative factors such as debt service relative to cash flow, loan repayment burdens, and even cataclysmic disturbances like bankruptcies or default. Finally, certain elements of policy enter into the propagation of impulses, for example, the response of monetary policy to changes in inflation engendered by the quadrupling of crude oil prices in October 1973. Though the endogenous response of policy may operate only with long lags, it must be regarded as an essential part of the propagation mechanism.

The postwar period has seen instances when each of the mechanisms in table 1.5 played a role. How important have these mechanisms been, on average? Which of them are really central to the persistence of the business cycle? And, have they changed over the postwar era? In section 1.6 below, the results of some simulations with the large-scale

DRI econometric model of the United States economy provide some perspective on these questions. But since many of the mechanisms of the business cycle are financial, we present a more detailed examination of the role for money and finance in the business cycle before turning to these results.

1.5 The Financial Factor in the Postwar Business Cycle

In the 1930s, 1940s, and 1950s, formal theories of the business cycle typically paid scant attention to the role of money, credit, and interest rates, concentrating instead on "real" explanations, principally multiplier/accelerator interactions.[7] The availability of finance was recognized as a constraint and critical ingredient in the upper turning point. Interest rates were thought to have only a minor role, operating through the cost of finance and with inelastic response coefficients for spending.

These limited views did not capture the essence of how financial factors condition the pattern of business fluctuations, however. Virtually every major recession or depression has contained financial events as critical ingredients.[8] And expansions and booms have been affected by the financial factor as well—in particular through a high elasticity of supply.

In the postwar era a newer phenomenon, although having many characteristics similar to other episodes throughout history, has emerged as a systematic element in the business cycle. This is the credit crunch experience.[9] The financial events of the crunch and interactions with housing activity, consumer spending, business outlays, and state and local government spending have served as both impulse and propagation mechanisms. Periods of major financial disturbances are generally agreed to have occurred in the form of credit crunches in 1966, 1970, 1974, 1980, and 1982.[10] Less obvious has been the expansiveness of the financial system during the early stages of business expansions. All of this suggests a financial side to the business cycle, just as systematic in its effects as real phenomena but not widely analyzed.

The financial side of fluctuations in business activity can be termed a "flow of funds" or "credit" cycle.[11] The notion of a flow of funds

7. Haberler 1937 provides a discussion of the place of the monetary factor in the overinvestment theories of the business cycle.

8. See the various discussions in Hawtrey 1926, Fisher 1933, Haberler 1936, Hicks 1950, Minsky 1977, and Sinai 1976, who highlight the "financial factor" as a key element in the mechanism of the business cycle.

9. Credit crunches or financial crises have been discussed and analyzed in Fisher 1933, Minsky 1977, Sinai 1976, 1978, 1980, and Wojnilower 1980. To Fisher, Minsky, and Sinai the process is endogenous, a by-product of the real cycle that simultaneously occurs.

10. The Great Depression also has been viewed as arising from financial processes. See Friedman and Schwartz 1963 and Bernanke 1981.

11. Sinai 1976, 1978, 1980; Eckstein 1983, chap. 4.

cycle is based on the fully simultaneous nature of "real" and "financial" activities and the feedback effects on spending of balance sheet positions and the liquidity of various sectors as the business cycle evolves.

Changes in spending and employment are accompanied by financial activities such as borrowing or debt repayment and sales or purchases of financial assets that affect interest rates, balance sheets, and liquidity. This in turn brings fluctuations in spending through both flow and stock adjustment effects. Since every expenditure or use of funds must be financed by a source of funds, systematic patterns of financial behavior accompany the real outlays for households, businesses, and government.[12] Financial institutions such as banks and thrifts show analogous patterns of behavior, except they use funds to make loans and investments and obtain funds from deposits and loan repayments. In addition to the flows of money, credit, and assets that accompany real side activities, flow-stock cumulations and decumulations of debts and assets occur, altering the state of sectoral balance sheets.

Along with interest rates and cash flows, the balance sheets determine the financial risk associated with each sector. At the crunch stage of the business cycle, the degree of financial risk that is present constrains sectoral spending, limits the availability of credit, can result in bankruptcies, default, and failures, and intensifies the downturn in the economy. Monetary policy and interest rates play an important role in this process, setting limits on the availability of funds, affecting debt service burdens, and acting as determinants of financial risk.

Most prominent in the flow of funds cycle is the crunch, which has appeared late in expansion to help bring about a turning point and to intensify the ensuing downturn. Less well documented and not so obvious has been the processes of repair and rebuilding of balance sheets and liquidity that have systematically occurred in recovery and expansion, along with the real side characteristics of the business cycle. These, in fact, have been every bit as systematic as the financial crisis or crunches. This stage is called reliquefication.

12. In a flow of funds cycle, uses of funds include acquisitions of financial or physical assets. Sources of funds comprise the borrowing necessary to finance acquisitions of physical assets and the "new money" flows that become available to each sector period by period. These new money flows are current sources of funds such as disposable income (households): cash flow (corporations); deposit inflows, adjusted for reserve requirements, and loan repayments (financial institutions); and tax receipts (federal, state, and local governments). The new money flows can be used for spending on goods and services, accumulating financial assets, or reducing outstanding liabilities. When they are insufficient to at least cover the uses of funds, external financing is necessary. The balance sheet and liquidity positions of different sectors of the economy change and evolve during the flow of funds cycle as well, providing yet another source of fluctuations in the business cycle.

1.5.1   The Flow of Funds Cycle

The "flow of funds" or "credit cycle" can be divided into phases of accumulation, developing financial instability or the precrunch period, crunch, and reliquefication.[13]

In the *accumulation* stage, there is an upturn in the acquisitions of physical and financial assets corresponding to the expansion phase of the business cycle. Financial constraints are minimal, and previously restored liquidity is dissipated only slowly. Funds are available, affordability is not a major limiting factor, and the institutions that supply finance are eager to make funds available. A boom often develops during the accumulation phase and is an important ingredient in the crunch process that follows. New money flows rise most rapidly during accumulation, helping to keep sectoral external financing requirements to a minimum.

The *precrunch period* is characterized by an intensifying squeeze on liquidity where the credit demands of households, businesses, and government progressively outstrip the ability of the financial system to provide sufficient funding at affordable interest rates. Both internal and external sources of finance slowly, but continuously, diminish for each sector or become available only at high costs. New money flows become insufficient to finance the planned uses of funds and to cover rising debt burdens. During this stage, rising interest rates and increased debt worsen the balance sheets of the private sector, although not sufficiently to fully discourage spending.

The ensuing liquidity squeeze takes effect sector by sector until the uses of funds are curtailed, whether for expenditures on physical assets (households, business, and government), for hiring of labor (business and government), for the production of loans (financial institutions), or for the accumulation of financial assets (households, business, financial institutions). A sustained and increasingly tighter monetary policy also is an important characteristic of the precrunch period. Free reserves become highly negative, interest rates begin to rise sharply, and monetary growth eventually shows a decided slowing.

The *crunch* is the financial crisis that culminates a precrunch period. A crunch may be defined as a credit crisis stemming from the collision of an expanding economy with a financial system that has been depleted of liquidity. The crunch is characterized by extremely depressed li-

---

13. Sinai 1978. The accumulation stage corresponds to the expansion phase of the traditional business cycle. The precrunch period occurs in late expansion and boom. The crunch overlaps with the upper turning point or peak, and very early stages of a downturn. Reliquefication is at the same time as the downturn and early recovery. In recent years there has been more of an "open" side to the flow of funds cycle as the effects of United States financial phenomena spread to the rest of the world through flexible exchange rates and policy reactions to protect domestic currencies, with subsequent feedback effects on the United States economy.

quidity and deteriorated balance sheet positions for households, corporations, and financial institutions; sharply increased interest rates as all sectors scramble for remaining available funds; rising yield differentials as investors sell risky investments and switch to safe assets; a severely depressed stock market; and the inability of many borrowers to obtain funds at any cost. Increased failures of business and financial institutions are part of the picture, though only occasionally exceptionally severe. Rising delinquencies on loans and defaults also characterize the process. The crunch or crisis itself occurs as these factors reach a breaking point and are often accompanied by some cataclysmic financial event such as the bankruptcy of a major company or the surprising failure of a financial institution. With one exception during the Vietnam War, the outcome of each crunch has been a recession or pause in economic growth near or at the end of the episode.

No single factor has ever been solely responsible for the onset of a full-blown credit crunch. It has been caused by the prolonged presence of (1) the pressure from a strongly expanding real economy and the demand for funds, often a boom; (2) the shortage of lendable funds stemming from reduced savings flows, weak deposit inflows, diminished cash flows, and tighter bank reserves; and (3) a restrictive monetary policy.

The financial factor has affected the length, depth, amplitude, and intensity of the cyclical process. Indeed, along with evidence from the 1930s, the postwar experience suggests that the financial factor is a critical ingredient in the business cycle. Since, over time, monetary policy reactions are endogenous to the economy, their role as an integral part of the business cycle mechanism should be expected. But it is not just monetary policy that influences the business cycle process; the feedback effects from borrowing, lending, flow-stock processes in finance, balance sheets, changes in liquidity, and financial risk affect cyclical behavior as well.

1.5.2 The Crunch

The most salient financial events in the postwar business cycle have been the crunch and its aftermath, reliquefication. Four ingredients have typically characterized the credit crunch episodes: boom, inflation, tight money and disintermediation, and financial instability.[14] Sharply rising interest rates and depressed asset prices also have been characteristic. These factors have varied in their intensity and changed over the years with new legislation, evolving institutions, and changes in the practice of monetary policy.

---

14. Sinai 1978, 9–10.

Boom

The boom has been described (section 1.3.2) as a major stage in the generalized business cycle. Its role in the financial or flow of funds cycle is to drain liquidity from households and business as new money flows become inadequate to support a strong pace of spending and as financial assets are sold to provide funds. In the boom, savings rates decline and business cash flow diminishes relative to capital outlays. Loan demands rise sharply, first by consumers and then by business. The rising loan demands and declining savings flows squeeze banks and financial intermediaries into tight liquidity situations. The boom has usually preceded a precrunch period but also has overlapped the early stages of the crunch process (table 1.3).

Inflation

High and accelerating rates of inflation tend to intensify the crunch process. Household disposable income may not keep pace with the rising prices of goods and services, and the personal savings rate may fall. During an initial burst of inflation, the cash flow of business may actually be enhanced, but as rising inflation becomes increasingly cost based, nominal spending on plant, equipment, and inventories outpaces internally generated funds, and firms must borrow heavily. Inflation also erodes the value of outstanding financial assets, reducing the proceeds from any liquidation. Because of inflation, a greater volume of external financing is necessary to fill the gap between spending and internally available funds, both for households and for business. Borrowing requirements increase for these sectors, and deposit inflows to financial institutions are reduced as a result. The lessened new savings flows to financial institutions, in turn, restrict the availability of mortgage money, adding upward pressure to interest rates, limiting affordability, and restraining housing. Inflation may also raise the financing requirements of the government sector, since the rising costs of goods and services and higher interest rates may exceed tax receipts from higher prices. Finally, rising inflation increases long-term interest rates, through premiums related to expectations. The result is considerably increased pressure on the financial markets.

Tight Money and Disintermediation

Tight money and disintermediation have been essential ingredients of every credit crunch. A severely restrictive monetary policy has limited the reserves of the banking system and caused short-term interest rates to rise sharply. The commercial banking system has transmitted the changes in the policy related federal funds and treasury bill rates to other money market rates. Before 1980, as these rates moved above the ceiling-constrained returns on deposits at banks and nonbank financial intermediaries, disintermediation became prevalent. Depleted bank liquidity from weakened inflows of deposits, and tight reserve positions caused banks to seek funds aggressively by issuing large CDs and Eurodollars and by borrowing at the Federal Reserve, bidding money market interest rates higher. Pressure exerted through increased borrowing at banks and issues of commercial paper also added to the upward thrust of interest rates. In these circumstances short-term interest rates rose at an accelerating rate, accompanied by credit rationing to channel bank lending to the more profitable commercial and industrial loan area.

With sharply rising interest rates, stock market declines occurred and the confidence of households and business weakened. The higher interest rates and lower stock prices increased borrowing costs to corporations and households and made existing debt service burdens more onerous. Savings and cash flows diminished further, extending the period of disintermediation and greatly reducing the supply of mortgage money. Typically an ongoing tight monetary policy intensified these effects. With some lags, significant effects on the real final demands of the economy have eventually caused sharp reductions in aggregate demand, production, and employment.

In the most recent episodes of 1980:2 and 1981:1 to 1981:4, a new approach to monetary policy instituted in October 1979 permitted interest rates to reach unprecedented levels. With the lifting of ceilings on deposit and loan rates in 1980, the disintermediation of funds from financial intermediaries was delayed, and extraordinarily high interest rates were required to price out most homebuyers. The tight money and disintermediation factor worked more through interest rates and debt burdens in recent years than previously.

The duration of monetary tightness has always been a critical element in the crunch process. In virtually every precrunch period, the Federal Reserve overstayed a restrictive monetary policy for longer than was necessary. Similarly, periods of reliquefication often have been characterized by a prolonged period of excessively stimulative monetary policy.

Financial Instability

Financial instability refers to progressively weakening balance sheets and the development of more risky financial positions for households, business, financial institutions, and government during a credit crunch period. Deteriorating liquidity and weakened balance sheets arise from endogenous developments in the economy or from external shocks. The endogenous developments include a spending boom on the part of households and business, which causes loan demand and debt burdens to become excessive. External shocks, such as the commodity and oil price shock inflation of 1973-74, can lead to large needs for finance in every sector of the economy. The financial instability takes the form of a shortage in liquidity, overwhelming debt service or debt repayment burdens, or an undesired liability structure. The development of exceptionally risky financial positions for each sector in the economy has characterized every crunch. Indeed, an increased frequency of bankruptcies, defaults, and failures has been induced by this process, sometimes leading to further apparently "autonomous" reductions in spending.

Reliquefication

The stage during which sectoral balance sheet strength and liquidity are restored is called reliquefication. In setting a base for future expansion, the process of reliquefication plays a key role in the financial cycle. The outlays of the household and corporate sectors are drastically reduced. Borrowing proceeds more slowly, outstanding liabilities are reduced, and the demand for financial assets rises sharply. New money flows are well in excess of the depressed outlays, providing ample funds to "reliquefy." Financial institutions benefit from the increased savings and cash flows of the private sector, through substantially higher deposit inflows. The financial institutions repay debts and accumulate financial assets in the face of weak loan demand. Monetary policy eases during this stage as the central bank strives to stimulate the economy. The reserves position of the banking system is enhanced, and interest rates decline or stay low.

During reliquefication, federal budget deficits and treasury financing are high but do little harm. The large deficits principally arise from the reduced tax receipts and higher government outlays of recession, corresponding to lower spending and increased financial saving by households and businesses. In a period of rebuilding balance sheets, the increased savings flows are used to strengthen the asset side of balance sheets—in particular through purchasing large amounts of the treasury financing associated with the deficits. The flows of funds from commercial banks and nonbank thrift institutions are directed toward absorbing a large volume of treasury securities. The Federal Reserve, before October 1979, also absorbed much of the treasury debt, as part of its monetary easing. And often the rest of the world sector has purchased a considerable volume of treasury securities. Interest rates stay low longer because of the phenomenon of reliquefication, with its strongly rising demands for high-quality assets to reduce the financial risk that has arisen during the crunch.

In the most recent episode of 1979 to 1982, the crunch process was somewhat different. This is because of the change in approach to monetary policy by the Federal Reserve in October 1979. Increases in the demand for money, whether from strong sectoral spending, shock inflation, or some interaction of both, put increasing pressure on interest rates with no attempt by the central bank to restrain the rises. Flows of funds were sustained through the deregulation of deposit and loan rate ceilings and new depository instruments, so that funds availability was less affected. Because scarce credit was almost entirely allocated through higher interest rates, affordability and debt service burdens played a greater role in the crunch process, eventually bringing a downturn just as in prior episodes.

The role of monetary policy in reliquefication has been the reverse of that in the crunch process, generally following a stimulative posture to aid the rebuilding of sector balance sheets.

1.5.3   Measures of Sectoral Financial Behavior in the Flow of Funds Cycle

Figures 1.4 to 1.10 show several summary measures that reflect the systematic behavior in the liquidity and balance sheet positions of households, businesses, and depository institutions. The precrunch period/crunch episodes are shaded in each. The clear areas represent the reliquefication and accumulation phases. The various measures show similar patterns of behavior across most flow of funds cycles, reflecting the stages of the financial cycle. The various balance sheet ratios also serve as an indicator of the financial strain that eventually induces restrained spending and borrowing in risk averse sectors.

For households, the mortgage loan repayment burden relative to disposable income and the ratio of financial assets to liabilities indicate strain or ease in the balance sheet. The higher the proportion of loan repayments to income, the less spending and borrowing will take place. The greater the quick ratio, the more room exists for new commitments. Other measures, such as wealth and net worth or the growth in financial assets, reflect the state of household liquidity.

For business, the "quick" ratio, proportion of debt service to cash flow, the ratio of short to total outstanding liabilities, and leverage are indicators of balance sheet strength and liquidity. These measures show the greatest deterioration near or in the crunch.

For financial institutions, loan-to-deposit ratios aptly characterize the state of liquidity. When high, depository institutions aggressively seek funds in the open market, pushing interest rates up sharply. The capital position of depository institutions also generally weakens at these times.

1.6   Sources of the Business Cycle: Some Simulation Results

The empirical significance of the various potential sources of the cycle has not been studied much, and doing so is an elaborate and difficult undertaking. Yet if the business cycle is to be a serious subject of scientific study, such investigation must be performed.

The following simulations represent some initial research in that direction. The DRI model of the United States economy has been used in a series of counterfactual simulation exercises designed to identify and quantify the impact of some causes of the business cycle. The results are model-specific and thus must be viewed cautiously. Further, econometric model simulations provide only approximations, with each simulation one of a possible large distribution of outcomes.

However, though the model is inevitably imperfect, it is an elaborate representation of the United States economy. Since it is built on quarterly data and heavily used for short-term forecasting, the successful representation of the economy's short-run dynamics was high on the list of criteria in determining the model's design. Therefore it is probably at least as good as any other device for exercises designed to analyze business cycle cyclicality on a quantitative basis.

1.6.1   An Index of Cyclicality

To assess the contributions of different factors and mechanisms in the business cycle, an index of cyclicality is defined. Such a quantitative index is inevitably somewhat arbitrary. For the present set of exercises, we define the index as the sum of the absolute values of the differences of the simulated values from their own trend values, divided by the trend values. This division was done to weight the index by the relative magnitude of the series.[15] Since the deviations are strongly serially correlated, this statistic corresponds closely to cyclicality. The percentage deviations from trend are also plotted over time in numerous figures, to indicate how much and when a particular factor contributed to cyclicality during the simulation cycles.

1.6.2   The Tracking Simulation

The tracking simulation (Track Sim) is a full dynamic simulation of real GNP, conducted from 1966 to 1983:2, using actual values for ex-

---

15. The formula used was

$$\sum_{t=66:1}^{83:2} \frac{|X_{sim_t} - X_{simtrend_t}|}{X_{simtrend_t}},$$

which provided a measure of deviations from trend, normalized for the position of X relative to the trend at various points in the period 1966:1–1983:2. X_{sim} was the simulated value of real GNP, and $X_{simtrend}$ was the trend value generated by the simulation of real GNP values in a given simulation. As particular causal factors in the cycle were removed, a simulation of the result produced a new pattern relative to a new trend. The calculations were repeated, and a summary statistic for reductions or increases in the cyclicality index was used to measure the effects of the various factors on cyclical amplitude and duration.

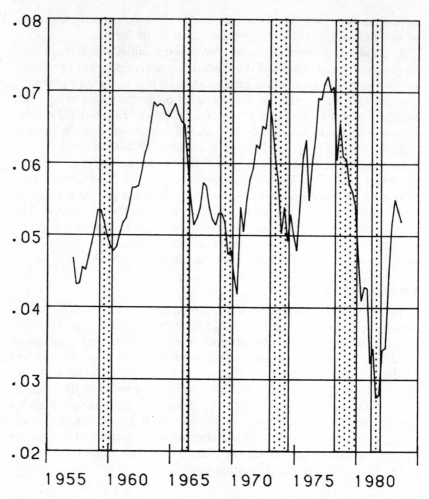

Fig. 1.4   Mortgage repayments relative to disposable income: households, 1955:3 to 1983:4 (ratio). Shaded areas, precrunch/
crunch periods; clear area, accumulation and reliquefication.

ogenous variables and inputting all individual equation errors as add
factors into the solution.[16] As a result, the tracking simulation reproduces history quite precisely. Given this baseline, it becomes possible
to show how removing certain causes of instability from history as
modeled reduces the recorded cyclicality. Both the direct and the prop-

16. Appendix 1.1 provides a fuller discussion of the experimental conditions underlying
each simulation. Tables showing the cyclicality index calculations for inflation and the
unemployment rate also are provided.

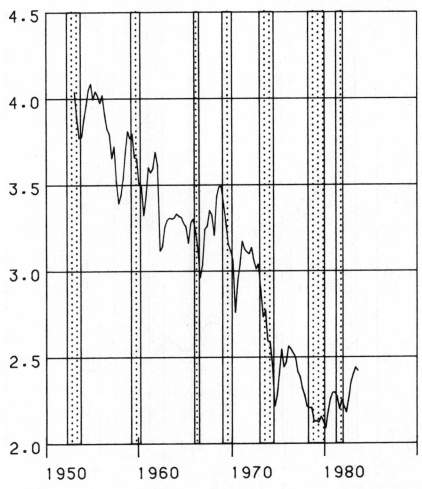

Fig. 1.5   "Quick" ratio: household sector, 1953:2 to 1983:4 (ratio of household financial assets to total liabilities). Shaded areas, precrunch/crunch periods; clear area, accumulation and reliquefication.

agation effects of a particular factor can be removed from the model, and the resulting path of behavior for real GNP and other variables can then be compared with the historical baseline.

This method of analysis assumes that the observed error terms are not correlated with the sources of instability, an assumption that probably understates the effects of removing various sources of instability. Error terms most likely are positively correlated with measured sources of instability.

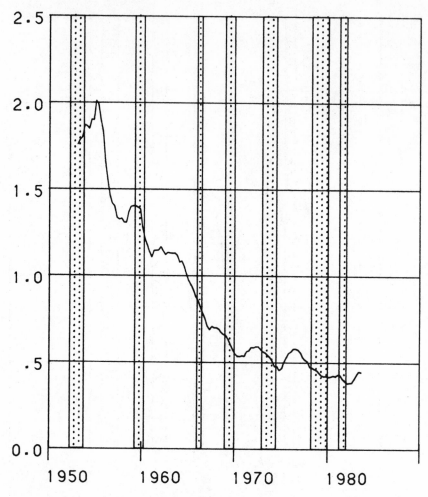

Fig. 1.6   "Quick" ratio: nonfinancial corporations, 1953:4 to 1983:4.
Shaded areas, precrunch/crunch periods; clear area, accumulation and reliquefication.

1.6.3   The Role of Noise in Creating Cyclicality

Frisch (1933) showed that an otherwise damped system can become
cyclical by the addition of random noise. The testing of this idea requires a definition of "noise": it could be specified to include not only
the random errors of the equations, but also certain categories of exogenous shocks, including policies and coefficient uncertainty.

In the present exercise, in order to come closer to a taxonomy of
causes of cyclicality, "noise" was defined very narrowly: only equation

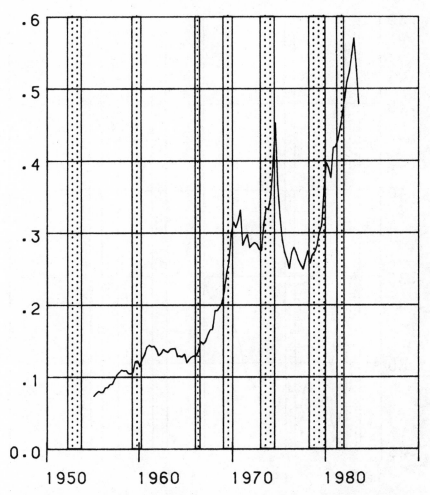

Fig. 1.7   Debt service burden of nonfinancial corporations, 1953:2 to 1983:4 (estimated interest charges on outstanding short- and long-term debt divided by cash flow). Shaded areas, pre-crunch/crunch periods; clear area, accumulation and reliquefication.

errors were included, with exogenous shocks and policies left unchanged. Although this is an impure measure of noise, since the residuals of individual equations can reflect both systematic and random elements, the high degree of fit of most model equations suggests that "approximate randomness" probably was an appropriate assumption.

In order to identify the contribution of "noise" to the fluctuations of real GNP, a full historical dynamic simulation was run in which the

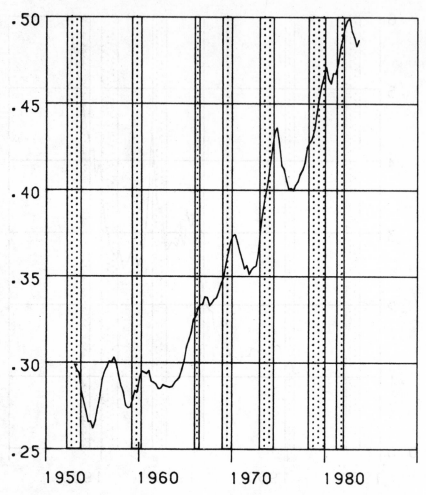

Fig. 1.8   Ratio of short-term to total outstanding debt: nonfinancial corporations, 1953:2 to 1983:4. Shaded areas, precrunch/crunch periods; clear area, accumulation and reliquefication.

equation errors were included and permitted to interact in the model simulation. The contribution of "noise" was then identified by comparing the results of this simulation with the tracking simulation that did not include the equation errors. Whereas the tracking simulation showed a cyclicality index value of 1.449, the "no noise" simulation indicated a comparable index value of 1.342, a reduction of 7.4%. Noise, defined in this way, seems to have contributed significantly to the recession of 1975; at other times the effect was small. Although the overall effect was small, it is a useful reminder that "noise" is part

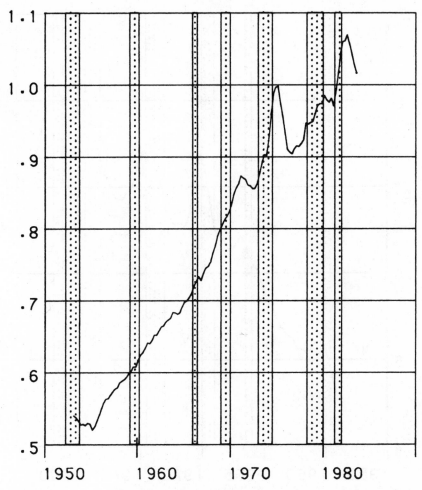

Fig. 1.9   "Leverage" of nonfinancial corporations, 1953:2 to 1983:4 (total outstanding debt relative to assets, physical and financial, less total liabilities). Shaded areas, precrunch/crunch periods; clear area, accumulation and reliquefication.

of reality, and it also sets the Frisch hypothesis in quantitative perspective (fig. 1.11 and table 1.6). The reduction in cyclicality may well have been limited because of interactions in the full model simulation that were not random.

1.6.4 The Oil Price Shocks

The business cycles since 1973 were partly triggered by the two jumps in the world price of oil during 1973–74 and 1979–80, which interacted

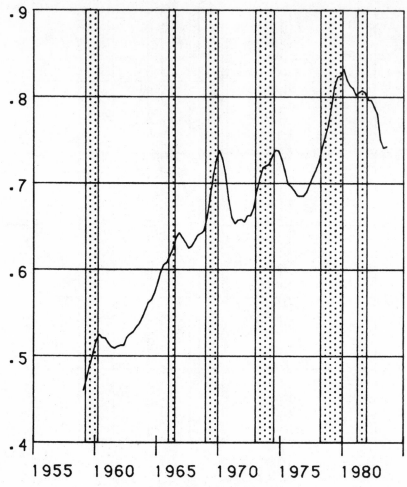

Fig. 1.10   Loan/deposit ratio: commercial banks, 1959:1 to 1983:4 (total of outstanding commercial and industrial, mortgage, and personal loans relative to demand and time deposits). Shaded areas, precrunch/crunch periods; clear area, accumulation and reliquefication.

with other destabilizing forces in the economy and with economic policies. A model solution removed the oil price shocks by replacing the exogenous values for world crude oil prices by a steady 7.1% rate of increase, a figure that left the terminal value for the oil price equal to the actual result but removed any other variation from this shock variable. Monetary policy was made to hold the path of the money supply (M1) essentially unchanged, creating easier financial conditions. The result was a reduction in the cyclicality index from 1.449 to 1.219, for a drop of 15.9% (fig. 1.12 and table 1.6).

The modesty of this result can partly be explained by the fact that oil became a cyclical problem only in the second half of the simulation period. As might be expected, the fluctuations in real GNP over 1973 to 1980 were reduced the most. If the cyclicality index is calculated from 1974 on, its reduction is from 0.935 in the baseline to 0.688 under no oil price shocks, or 26.4%. The experiment also was limited to the price side of the oil problem; the supply disruptions, with their gasoline shortages and damage to consumer confidence, created additional cyclicality but were not removed.

1.6.5 Stable Money Policy

One major potential source of instability is monetary policy, a key impulse mechanism in the business cycle. Throughout the postwar era, there has been controversy over whether monetary policy has stabilized or destabilized the business cycle. There has been considerable opinion that monetary policy was too "stop/go," adding a large amount of instability to the cycle.

Defining a stable monetary policy is difficult for a large-scale, structural econometric model that contains a full complement of policy instruments. The reserve components of the monetary aggregates, reserve requirements, regulatory ceilings on deposit and loan interest rates, the discount rate, and selective controls on margin requirements and loan down payments all have formed part of policy.[17] For example, to simply impose a smooth growth of nonborrowed bank reserves on history would still leave a highly unstable financial system, because interest rate ceilings, reserve requirements, and selective controls could still be operative. Variations in the growth of potential GNP, inflation, and other factors would convert smooth reserve growth into highly unstable paths for the various monetary aggregates and interest rates, probably for GNP, and would still leave business and household balance sheets buffeted by disturbances.[18]

A simulation was developed that dealt at least partially with these problems. In "stable money policy," all deposit rate ceilings were removed, extreme changes of reserve requirements over the simulation period were eliminated, and open market operations on reserves were eased when monetary policy was tight and tightened when monetary policy was easy. The monetarist policy after 6 October 1979 was mit-

---

17. There has been one instance of outright credit controls, in spring 1980. For some analysis of this episode, see Brimmer and Sinai 1981.

18. Such a simulation actually produced a higher cyclicality index than for the Track Sim, 1.727, or a 19.1% increase.

igated by limiting the range of interest rate volatility between 1979:4 and 1982:4.

The result was a reduction in the cyclicality index from 1.449 to 1.127 for a relatively large drop of 22.2%, offering support for the notion that monetary policy was destabilizing from 1966 to 1983 (fig. 1.13 and table 1.6). The biggest improvements occurred in 1966, between 1976 and 1980, and in 1981–82, periods generally recognized as having been characterized by a too tight or over expansive monetary policy.

1.6.6   No Oil Shocks, Stable Money Policy

Removing both the cyclicality induced by the oil price shocks and the variations in monetary policy led to an even larger reduction in the cyclicality index, to 1.055, or 27.2% (fig. 1.14 and table 1.6). It was surprising that there was not a stronger interaction effect. Removing both sources of instability added little to removing only one. This result was probably due to a less complete adjustment of the assumed monetary policy rather than to the different oil price assumptions. The combination of the two did limit the swings in almost all the cycles, however.

1.6.7   Simulating the Financial Factor

To examine some effects on postwar business cycles of the factors that characterize the crunch and reliquefication stages, a component by component removal of some major ingredients in the flow of funds cycle was attempted.

First, a critical factor in all the crunches and subsequent upturns, tight money and disintermediation, was eliminated from the Track Sim. This was accomplished in the stable money policy simulation (described in section 1.6.5 and fig. 1.13). The greatest improvement occurs between 1976 and 1983 because an over expansive monetary policy, then extremely restrictive policy, and wide swings in interest rates are attenuated. The lifting of deposit rate ceilings prevented the disintermediation of funds that characterized periods of boom and financial strain. The brief expansion of 1980–81 was more pronounced than in actual history, since interest rates were prevented from rising as high as actually occurred.

A second ingredient in the experiment was the removal of excessive loan demands by both households and businesses, thus toning down the boom ingredient of crunches as it affected the financial system and limiting the pressure on banks that is a major source of rapidly accelerating interest rates. The resulting behavior of real GNP with stable monetary policy, limited disintermediation, and less fluctuation in loans is shown in figure 1.15. Here the cyclicality index is a low 0.994, for a 31.4% drop in cyclical behavior relative to the Track Sim.

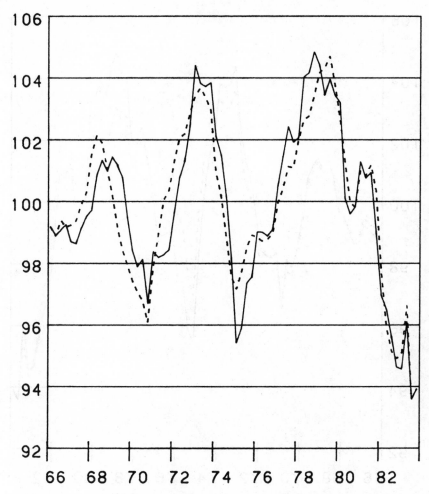

Fig. 1.11   No "noise" simulation compared with Track Sim (percentage of trend). Track Sim ——; no noise------.

Finally, the oil price shocks also were removed (stable money policy, no oil shocks, no crunch), thus mitigating the inflation ingredient of the crunch periods in 1973–74 and beyond. Although not fully eliminating the accelerating inflation of these episodes, limiting the pace of increases in OPEC prices to 7.1% per annum served to show the effects of lesser inflation rates interacting with financial phenomena. The cyclicality index was only 0.960 in this simulation (fig. 1.16 and table 1.6).

Thus, with stable money policy, no disintermediation, lessened boom effects on private sector loan demands, and lower inflation because of

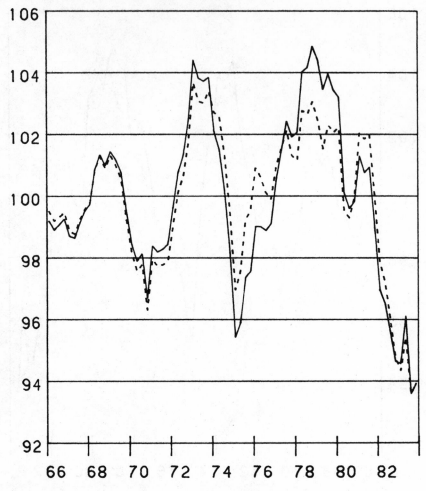

Fig. 1.12   No oil shocks simulation compared with Track Sim (percentage of trend). Track Sim ——; no oil shocks ------.

no oil price shocks, fully 33.7% of the original deviations in real GNP from trend were eliminated. Figures 1.17 to 1.23 also show that removing these factors greatly reduced the interest rate fluctuations and financial instability that actually occurred, as indicated by various summary measures of sectoral balance sheets and liquidity. It was inevitable that interest rates would be better behaved with monetary policy smoother, not exhibiting the large swings of actual history.

Figure 1.16 reveals that an oscillation mechanism remained, but without the severity of the late 1970s. Inflation was also less severe in the

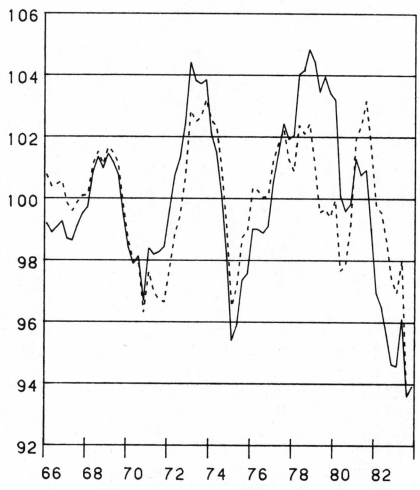

Fig. 1.13   Stable money policy simulation compared with Track Sim
(percentage of trend). Track Sim ——; stable money ------.

simulations of figures 1.14 to 1.16, as an endogenous response, suggesting that the series of interrelated shocks portrayed in these simulations were themselves a kind of propagation mechanism.

The flow of funds cycle and its ingredients thus appear to have operated as both an impulse and a propagation mechanism. In the model,
the impulse comes mostly from changes in nonborrowed reserves and
the resulting fluctuations of interest rates. Interest rates affect asset
allocation, spending, and borrowing behavior. Reactions in stock prices,
household net worth, debt service, and the flows of funds to housing

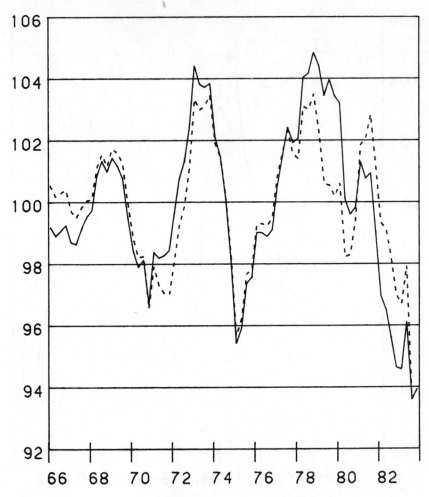

Fig. 1.14   No oil shocks, stable money policy simulation compared with Track Sim (percentage of trend). Track Sim ———; no oil shocks, stable money ------.

follow. Prices and wages, then interest rates, react further, imparting additional motion to the system. As real and financial stocks are altered, the numerous stock adjustment or multiplier/accelerator mechanisms that permeate the financial and real systems of the United States economy are activated.

1.6.8   A Simple Cycle Exercise on the Propagation Mechanism

To gain some insight into the dominant features of the cyclical mechanism in the economy as depicted in the DRI model, a simple multiplier exercise was run. Nonmilitary federal purchases of goods and services

Table 1.6   Sources of Cyclicality in Postwar Business Cycles
Results of DRI Model Simulations, 1966 to 1983:2

Simulation	Cyclicality Index	Percentage Reduction from History	Trend Growth[a]
Historical Track Sim	1.449	—	2.8
No "noise"	1.342	−7.4	2.8
No oil shocks	1.219	−15.9	3.0
Stable money policy	1.127	−22.2	3.0
No oil shocks, stable money policy	1.055	−27.2	3.1
Stable money policy, no crunch	0.994	−31.4	3.2
Stable money policy, no oil shocks, no crunch	0.960	−33.7	3.3
Autonomous real final demands	0.571	−60.6	2.9
Durables consumption	0.985	−32.0	2.8
Business fixed investment	1.149	−20.7	2.8
Inventories	1.223	−15.6	2.9
Residential construction	1.032	−28.8	2.7
Autonomous real final demands, no oil shocks, stable money policy, no crunch	0.482	−66.7	2.9

Note: Calculated for fluctuations in real gross national product.
[a]The trend growth for each was calculated from a regression for an exponential trend.

were boosted by $10 billion and set to grow at the growth rate of potential GNP thereafter. How does the economy absorb such a stimulus? Does it lead to explosive growth, a stable multiplier, or a temporary multiplier portraying a business cycle? Figure 1.24 shows the multiplier, holding the money supply unchanged, peaking at 1.25 during the first year, dropping to 0.5 in year five, and reaching zero in year eight.

Table 1.7 shows that consumption reacts in the conventional Keynesian fashion, responding to the increased income created by the fiscal stimulus. Interest rates rise promptly, immediately producing the beginnings of a reduction in residential construction. In part, this is due to reductions of nonborrowed reserves in order to maintain a fixed money supply (nonaccommodating money). Business fixed investment initially is boosted slightly, as sales expectations are revised upward along with expectations on capacity utilization rates, inducing extra investment. By the second year, the higher interest rates begin to crowd out business fixed investment, and after three years the reduction is substantial. Under an accommodating monetary policy, defined as unchanged nonborrowed reserves, the crowding out would be mitigated.

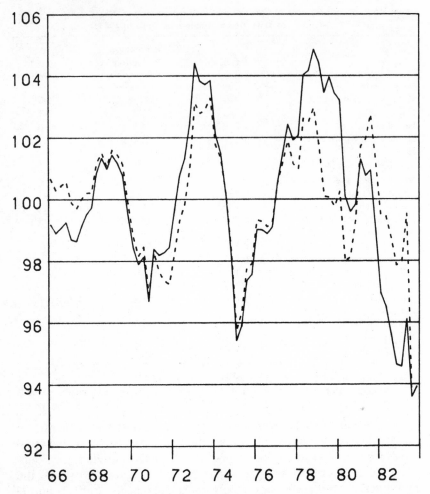

Fig. 1.15   Stable money policy, no crunch simulation compared with Track Sim (percentage of trend). Track Sim ——; stable money policy, no crunch ------.

The crowding out occurs not only because interest rates are higher, but also because the stronger economy gradually converts the larger nominal GNP into higher prices. Figure 1.25 shows the output/inflation transform, a plot of the percentage of the increase in nominal GNP that represents increased real activity. In year one, when the output/inflation transform (OIT) is equal to or near unity, nearly all the gain in gross national product is real. But after eight quarters it is down to 0.7, and after twelve quarters it is 0.5. By year seven the OIT is zero, so that the entire stimulus is converted into higher prices.

The results of this solution are largely, but not entirely, due to the assumption of an unchanged money supply that guarantees crowding

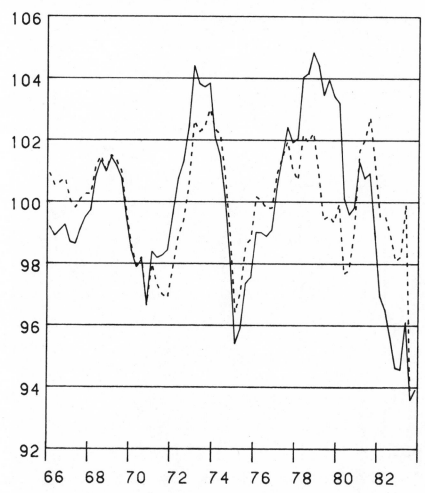

Fig. 1.16   Stable money policy, no crunch, no oil shocks, no crunch simulation compared with Track Sim (percentage of trend). Track Sim ———; stable money, no crunch, no oil shocks ------.

out. If nonborrowed reserves are left unchanged, the multiplier is initially larger, equal to 1.48, and remains above unity for over five years. Nonetheless, there is a gradual reduction of the multiplier from its peak value, mainly owing to increased inflation, higher interest rates, and a using up of the financial base of the economy as measured by household and business balance sheets.

The traditional cyclical mechanisms, the stock flow adjustments of business and household fixed capital, play a rather minor role. The stock of business capital enters the investment equation with a small but positive sign. Apparently the increased opportunity for investment

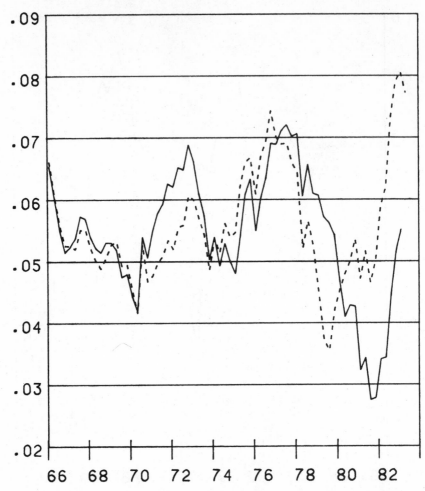

Fig. 1.17   Mortgage repayments relative to disposable income: households, 1966:1 to 1983:1 (before and after removing unstable
Fed policy, crunch, and oil shocks). Track Sim ———; stable
money, no crunch, no oil shocks ------.

created by replacement and modernization outweighs the negative accelerator effect. Inventory investment does follow the stock adjustment
mechanism, but the coefficients are not large and the adjustments are
quick. Household capital stocks, both for cars and homes, do have an
impact through negative feedback, but their overall importance is small
in comparison to the financial and inflationary reactions.

When money is not accommodating, much greater rises of interest
rates create negative feedbacks to housing and other finance-sensitive

Fig. 1.18   "Quick" ratio: household sector, 1966:1 to 1983:2 (before and after removing unstable Fed policy, crunch, and oil shocks). Track Sim ——; stable money, no crunch, no oil shocks ------.

final demands through reduced flows of funds and negative balance sheet effects. Increased debt service cuts business fixed investment, and reduced household net worth lowers consumption. Even the outlays of state and local governments are cut by reduced revenues and higher interest rates. When money is accommodating, the negative feedback originates in the output/inflation transform. As the initial stimulus converts into higher prices, real income gains are lost, and the extra inflation may adversely affect various demands, including net

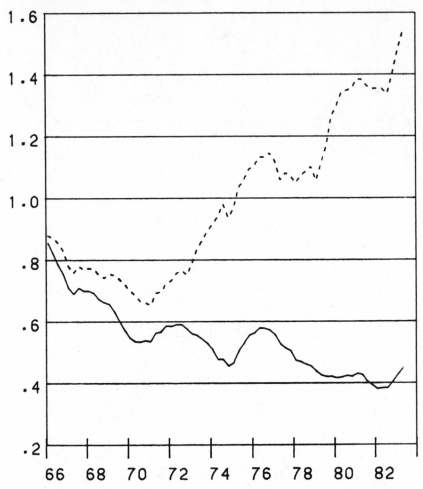

Fig. 1.19 "Quick" ratio: nonfinancial corporations, 1966:1 to 1983:2 (before and after removing unstable Fed policy, crunch, and oil shocks). Track Sim ——; stable money, no crunch, no oil shocks ------.

exports, housing, consumption (via consumer confidence), and investment. In any event, monetary policy never has retained a fully accommodative stance in the face of increasing inflation.

1.6.9 Remaining Sources of Cyclicality

The simulations show some effect on the trend growth rate of real GNP. Whereas the historical growth rate was 2.8% per annum from 1966 to 1983:2 and the no noise simulation left that figure unchanged,

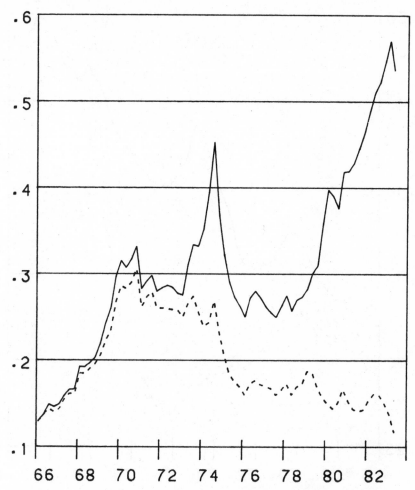

Fig. 1.20   Debt service burden of nonfinancial corporations, 1966:1 to 1983:2 (before and after removing unstable Fed policy, crunch, and oil shocks). Track Sim ———; stable money, no crunch, no oil shocks ------.

removing the variability of the increase in the world price of oil boosted trend GNP growth to 3.0%, and adding stable money policy raised it to 3.1%. Thus instability does appear to reduce trend growth, partly by leaving unemployment high and partly by reducing the rate of capital formation and therefore the growth of aggregate supply.

The cyclicality that remains after the removal of the oil price shocks, stop/go monetary policy, and certain elements of the crunch is consid-

Fig. 1.21   Ratio of short-term to total outstanding debt: nonfinancial corporations, 1966:1 to 1983:2 (before and after removing unstable Fed policy, crunch, and oil shocks). Track Sim ———; stable money, no crunch, no oil shocks ------.

erable, however—still 66.3% of the total experience. The possible sources of cyclicality that remain are extensive (table 1.5).

The United States government budget and fiscal policies may well have been destabilizing, particularly during the buildup for the Vietnam War and as a result of Reaganomics. The price controls of 1971–74 contributed to peak inflation, which in turn was a major factor contributing to the large 1974–75 recession. The world food price explosion of 1972–73 was a serious disturbance. The General Motors strike of

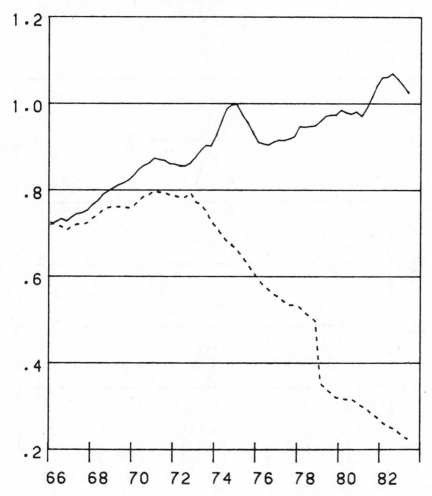

Fig. 1.22   "Leverage" of nonfinancial corporations: nonfinancial corporations, 1966:1 to 1983:2 (before and after removing unstable Fed policy, crunch, and oil shocks). Track Sim ——; stable money, no crunch, no oil shocks ------.

1970 affected the macro data. The two disruptions in the availability of gasoline supplies caused consumer sentiment to collapse, shifting the consumption function downward and worsening the recessions of 1974–75 and 1980.[19]

Variations in aggregate supply also contribute to the large residual cyclicality. Our index was calculated on the basis of an exponential

19. For the 1974–75 recession, these matters were pursued in Eckstein 1978.

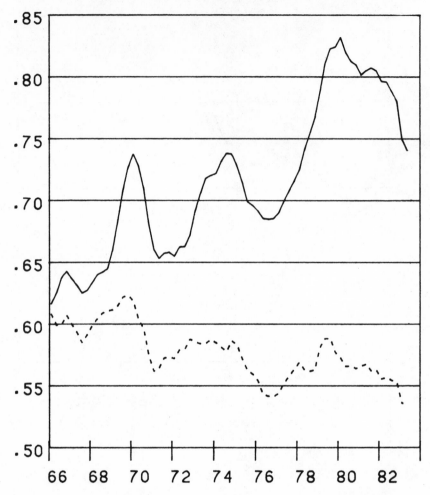

Fig. 1.23   Loan/deposit ratio: commercial banks, 1966:1 to 1983:2 (before and after removing unstable Fed policy, crunch, and oil shocks). Track Sim ———; stable money, no crunch, no oil shocks ------.

trend. Aggregate supply did not grow so smoothly, however, because of demographic variations and changes in the productivity trend. Indeed, a cyclicality index calculation for aggregate supply, as measured by potential GNP, had a value of 0.649, or 45% of the cyclicality of actual real GNP. Although the timing of the supply variations does not coincide perfectly with the business cycle, there was sufficient coincidence to make the supply variations account for a significant portion of the residual cyclicality.

Table 1.7 The Multiplier and Related Measures ($10 Billion Increase in Real Government Spending)

Quarters after Shock	Real GNP[a]	Investment in Residential Structures[a]	Total Consumption[a]	Implicit Price Nonresidential Fixed Investment[a]	Deflator (% difference in levels)	Change in T-Bill Rate (basis points)
			Fixed Money Supply (M1)			
4	1.26	−0.15	0.41	0.01	0.2	+77
8	0.94	−0.35	0.28	−0.02	0.4	+87
12	0.81	−0.32	0.18	−0.07	0.6	+135
16	0.64	−0.34	0.10	−0.13	0.7	+142
24	0.56	−0.34	0.10	−0.21	1.0	+186
			Accommodating Money Supply[b]			
4	1.48	−0.04	0.37	0.03	0.4	+20
8	1.45	−0.06	0.36	0.07	1.0	+30
12	1.38	−0.08	0.31	0.08	1.6	+17
16	1.30	−0.06	0.27	0.05	2.1	+27
24	1.10	−0.06	0.22	−0.03	2.7	+36

[a]Ratio of change in final demand category to autonomous change in spending.
[b]Unchanged nonborrowed reserves—in the fixed money supply case, nonborrowed reserves were reduced to keep M1 at its original values.

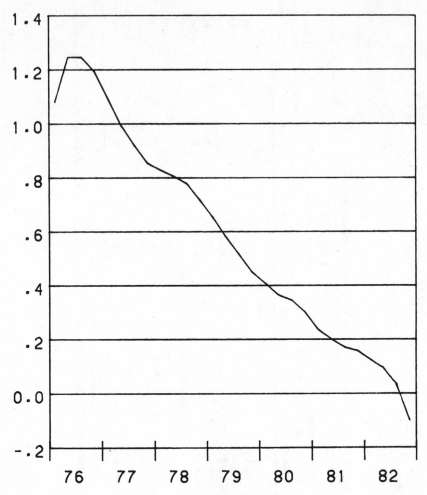

Fig. 1.24   Multiplier, civilian federal purchases. Sustained $10 billion rise, unchanged money supply.

To test further the sources of cyclicality, simulations were performed that set each of the major volatile components of private sector aggregate demands equal to their trend growth paths.[20] These included (1) consumption of durable goods, (2) business fixed investment, and (3) inventory outlays, all in real terms, and (4) housing starts. Another simulation set all the growth paths at trend. Finally, a combined sim-

20. Values of add factors, the intercept terms in the key behavioral equations, were selected to set the various spending components on their trend growth paths. There was no trend in housing starts, which were set at their mean value.

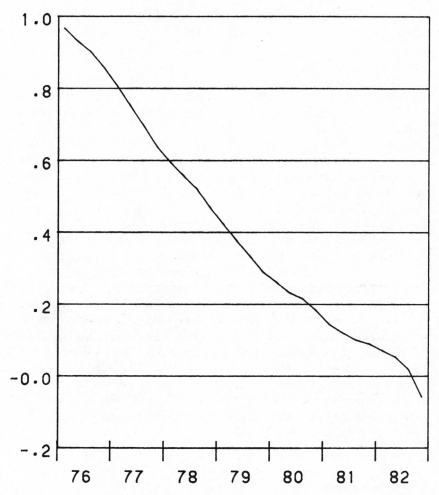

Fig. 1.25   Output/inflation transform, civilian federal purchases up $10 billion (fixed money supply).

ulation of the final demand trend growth paths with the stable money policy, no oil shocks, and no crunch case was performed. The intent here was to identify the real final demands that were major sources of cyclicality over 1966 to 1983. The results are summarized in table 1.6.

From the table, it can be seen that of the real final demands that were considered, durable consumption spending was the major source of cyclicality. Setting the growth in durable consumption at trend reduced the cyclicality index to 0.985, a reduction of 32% from the Track Sim value. The multiplier/accelerator impacts of smoothing this major component of final demand, more even impacts on the financial markets through consumer loans and deposit flows, and a more stable performance for household balance sheets contributed to the lessened cyclicality.

Setting housing starts at its mean value resulted in the next largest reduction in cyclicality, with the cyclicality index falling from 1.449 to 1.032, a reduction of 28.8%. While somewhat surprising in that it was a lesser factor than durable consumption in cyclical behavior, this result supports the highly cyclical role of housing indicated in earlier experiments and most of the literature. In a sense, housing starts can be thought of as related to consumption spending. Surprisingly, business fixed investment and fluctuations in inventories accounted for the least amount of cyclicality.

With all the more volatile elements of real final demands set at trend, the cyclicality index was 0.571, down 60.6% from the value of the historical Track Sim. Of course such an exercise begs the question of the "causes" for the fluctuations, but it does permit an assessment of the domestic private, nonpolicy sources of cyclical behavior.

Finally, in addition to stabilizing the real final demands, removing the oil price shocks, stabilizing monetary policy, and eliminating the volatility of loans stemming from the crunch and reliquefication stages in the flow of funds cycle, produced a cyclicality index value of 0.482. Figure 1.26 shows the resulting behavior of real GNP relative to trend, where the cyclicality is 66.7% less than in the Track Sim. Again, however, considerable volatility remains, reflecting the propagation mechanisms in the system and suggesting that a full removal of cyclicality is not possible in the real world.

1.7 Conclusions

What are the causes of the business cycle in the postwar era? It is very clear that impulse mechanisms have been crucial. Large shocks, ranging from OPEC oil price changes to shifts in monetary policy and credit crunches, were responsible for up to one-third of the cyclicality of the United States economy from 1966 to 1983:2, using a very conservative measure. Of the various components of aggregate demand, changes in durable consumption spending and residential construction accounted for a large amount of cyclicality. Small shocks, on the other hand, as measured by the equation errors of the DRI model, seemed to be of minor significance. Our examination of the internal propagation mechanisms was very incomplete. Calculated as a residual, after removing a large number of impulse mechanisms, it is about one-third of the cyclicality from 1966 to 1983 (table 1.6, fig. 1.26). A core of

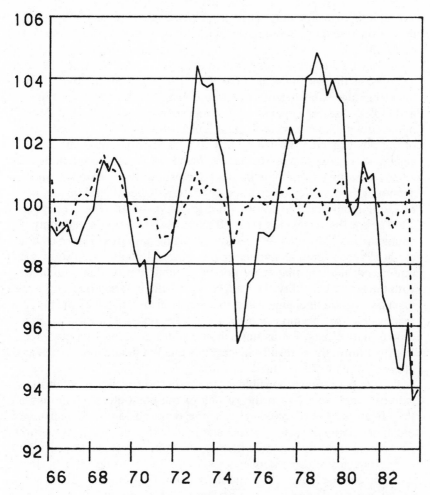

Fig. 1.26   Autonomous final demands at trend, stable money policy, no oil shocks, no crunch simulation compared with Track Sim (percentage of trend). Track Sim ——; autonomous real final demands, stable money, no oil shocks, no crunch ------.

cyclicality thus remains, suggesting that a balanced growth path for the economy was and is not attainable.

One essential business cycle mechanism appears to have been financial, especially since a near-monetarist approach has been taken to monetary policy, and was estimated to provide a 31.4% reduction in cyclicality over 1966 to 1983:2 (table 1.6; stable money policy, no crunch). If a boom in real activity or an unacceptable rate of inflation develops, the central bank causes these phenomena of the upswing to be converted into crowding out, credit crunches, and recessions. Other stock flow adjustments are numerous but do not seem to add much to cyclicality.

Has the business cycle changed in the postwar era? Have there been changes in the mechanisms? On the surface, an affirmative answer might be suggested to both of these questions. As figure 1.1 and 1.2 and table 1.2 show, expansions and recessions have become more pronounced with severe, volatile, and longer recessions in the later years of the postwar era. But from our experiments it is not clear that any significant changes really occurred. From the model simulations, the apparent result is that shocks matter most, whether external shocks stemming from policy or inflation or "internal shocks" taking the form of autonomous shifts in consumption and investment. The propagation mechanism that transmits their effects to the rest of the economy remains intact. The simulations show changing amplitudes from a series of shocks that acted as impulses. But figures 1.16 and 1.26 show continuing oscillations that were not fully eliminated in the simulations with the least cyclicality. This suggests that the inherent business cycle mechanisms are unchanged and that a greater frequency of shocks was responsible for the more violent recent episodes. Also, if a balanced growth path exists, it was not achieved during the past twenty years. For the future, these results suggest it is highly unlikely that a balanced growth path can be attained.

The factors most responsible for the increasing cyclicality of business activity were revealed in the results of the computer simulations on the effects of OPEC price shocks, the extremes and mechanisms of monetary policy, financial crises and instability, and their interaction. Smoothing or removing these factors substantially reduced the severity of the business cycles between 1966 and 1983 through the business cycle mechanisms that are structured in the DRI model. The business cycles did not disappear but were mitigated in severity, duration, and the extreme behavior that actually occurred, suggesting that, despite appearances to the contrary, an intrinsic cyclical mechanism remained.

While the factors associated most with greater cyclicality generally would be classed as exogenous, the monetary policy responses of 1966 to 1983 certainly were greatly conditioned by the presence of worsening inflation. Supply side cost shocks, particularly from OPEC oil price increases, reverberated through the price/wage mechanism in the United States economy to raise inflation and alter inflation expectations to a large degree, eventually requiring a strong response by the central bank to limit the inflation. And even these shocks had an endogenous element, of course.

One surprising result is that autonomous changes in real durable consumption were found to be a greater source of cyclicality than either housing, business fixed investment, or inventory fluctuations.[21] The latter components of real final demands are most often considered the key elements in short-run business fluctuations. But durable consumption has taken a larger share of total aggregate demand over the postwar years. And given its large absolute size, the derived real and financial effects from shifts in this category of spending are now considerable.

As for the propagation mechanisms, several factors underlying the business cycle have been altered in the postwar period and do suggest some changes. The changed approach to monetary policy over the 1970s and early 1980s has altered the propagation mechanism and is surely the single most identifiable change. Monetary policy changed from free reserves and interest rate targeting in the 1960s to monetary growth targeting vis-à-vis the federal funds rate in the 1970s, and then quite radically in the period 1979–82 to reserve growth and freely fluctuating interest rates. The predominant change in structure occurred with the New Fed Policy of October 1979 and has been demonstrated here to be a major source of cyclical instability since then.

In the DRI model, wide fluctuations of interest rates induce wide swings in spending and borrowing behavior that in turn feed back to sustain the volatility of interest rates. The change in monetary policy that unhinged interest rates from Federal Reserve control inevitably had to create substantial instability in both financial and real markets. The simulation (stable money policy) that had Federal Reserve policy return to stabilizing interest rates over 1979:4 to 1983:2 produced a much more damped performance in the economy than actually occurred. Some interest rate effects of the unanticipated monetary policy shock of the New Fed Policy also were removed in other simulations with similar results.[22]

Second, the housing cycle, though just as volatile as in previous years, has been affected by changing patterns in mortgage finance and interest rates. Simulations of a less volatile monetary policy with more stable interest rates worked, in part, through the housing cycle as a major component of business cycles. Tight monetary policy, high interest rates, and disintermediation have always been major causes of instability in housing and construction as an impulse mechanism to shorter-run fluctuations. Whereas the periods from the mid-1950s to the late 1970s were characterized principally by availability of funds constraints on housing activity, the deregulation of financial institutions and the removal of interest rate ceilings now has thrown the burden of adjustment on demand and affordability. Much greater fluctuations

---

21. This result provides empirical support for the hypotheses of Hall, discussed in chapter 4.

22. See Brimmer and Sinai 1981 for an attempt to quantify the effects from the New Fed Policy in simulations with the DRI model.

in interest rates now seem to be required for a given cyclical movement in housing, throwing the rest of the interest rate sensitive areas of the economy into a more volatile cyclical pattern.

Finally, also important in recent years have been the globalization of economic activity and the effect on the dollar of fluctuating exchange rates. Increased trade, interest rate, and capital linkages are transmitting the business cycle, though the adoption of flexible exchange rates may serve as a partial buffer. More fundamentally, the worldwide boom of 1971–73 and the post-OPEC experience suggest that the business cycle is becoming more of an interrelated global phenomenon.

Appendix 1.1
Descriptions of Simulations

1. Track Sim

The historical tracking simulation was obtained by removing the errors of a dynamic historical simulation through offsetting equation add factors. In each quarter, an add factor equal to the simulated error of each behavioral equation and opposite in sign was inserted (about five hundred behavioral equations were involved). After several iterations, the solution converged on the actual historical data, producing a model-based tracking of history on which other simulation exercises could be performed.

2. No Noise

The "no noise" simulation represented an attempt to simulate the effects of random shocks on the cyclicality of the United States economy from 1966:1 to 1983:2. A full solution of the model over this period was run, with actual historical values inserted for all exogenous variables and the solved values for each endogenous variable fed back into the right-hand side of the equations in current and subsequent periods. No add factors were used in the behavior equations for this simulation.

The resulting residuals comprised two components: individual equation and interactive model simulation errors. In a properly specified model, with appropriate properties for the estimated parameters, both the equation and model simulation errors would be random and could be assumed to reflect "noise." The reduction in cyclicality from the Track Sim of this simulation thus represents an approximation, defined in this way, of the effects from noise over the simulation period. To the extent that the equation or model simulation errors contain non-random components, certainly likely in a large-scale macroeconometric model simulation, the reduction in cyclicality from history would be understated.

3. No Oil Shocks

The overall purpose of this simulation was to remove the variability of inflation created by the OPEC oil price shocks. The DRI model has a well-defined energy sector (Eckstein 1983, 234–45) that serves three functions: "to trace the effects of exogenous prices to the retail stage, to provide a supply-demand check to see if available supplies can sustain particular levels of economic activity, and to determine the effects on potential GNP and productivity."

One way to examine the effect of the severe OPEC inflation on the business cycle was to create a new more stable time path for oil prices and to have the model endogenously trace the implications.

Therefore in this simulation the only change made was in the series for crude oil prices, the key exogenous input to oil and energy prices. The prices of both domestic and foreign crude oil were lowered. Although part of the OPEC disruption was through effects on supply and production, no attempt was made to include them except through endogenous reactions in the model. The only other change was in the path of nonborrowed reserves, the key exogenous variable for monetary policy, which was raised to produce an unchanged M1 from the Track Sim over the simulation period. In effect this amounted to an easing of monetary policy, since inflation rates generally were lower. Interest rates were permitted to respond endogenously in this simulation.

4. Stable Money Policy

In this simulation, the objective was to remove from the business cycle the variability stemming from the wide swings in monetary policy over 1966 to 1983. The Federal Reserve is generally agreed upon as having been "tight" in 1966, "easy" in 1968, "tight" in 1969–70, "easier" in 1971–72 with the advent of a wage/price freeze, "tight" in 1973–74, "easy" in 1975–76, perhaps too easy in 1977–78, and exceedingly tight in 1980–81.

The modeling of monetary policy is a complicated matter in a large-scale macroeconometric model, involving not only movements in the money supply but also variables like bank reserves, legal reserve requirements, deposit rate interest ceilings, and loan down payment conditions. Since the money supply, whether measured as M1, M2, or M3, is an endogenous variable, monetary policy is not implemented by controlling the growth in the money supply. Instead, changes in the pattern of nonborrowed reserves, reserve requirements and required reserves on demand and time deposits, deposit and loan interest rate ceilings, the discount rate and sometimes loan-to-value ratios are the mechanisms.

The general approach was to impose more stability on the path of monetary policy, as measured by the exogenous policy instruments. Large shifts in monetary policy, as measured by the growth in non-borrowed reserves and changes in reserve requirements, were reduced in those periods of known easy or tight monetary policy by smoothing the growth of nonborrowed reserves and raising reserve requirements when the Federal Reserve had lowered them and lowering reserve requirements when the Federal Reserve had raised them. Monetary policy thus was tightened when it had been easy and eased when it had been tightened. The timing of these historical changes also was altered, with the undoing of the historical changes in monetary policy implemented early rather than late, given the lags between changes in monetary policy and the effects on the economy. Regulation Q deposit rate ceilings were removed during the historical period, thus eliminating a major distortion in relative interest rates that was responsible for much of the disintermediation that occurred from 1966 to 1980.

The first major policy lever considered was legal reserve requirements. The DRI model has two legal reserve requirement variables—one for demand deposits and one for time deposits. For the sake of simplicity, total required reserves was smoothed, using legal reserve requirements on demand deposits, the more erratic of the two variables.

This change had a significant impact on the interest rate block of the model, both through a free reserves equation and also directly in individual interest rate equations. These equations include the federal funds rate equation, the three-month treasury bill rate equation, the prime interest rate equation, and the consumer installment rate equation. These in turn have a simultaneous impact on other short-term interest rates, on yield curves, and to a lesser extent on longer-term interest rates.

Another policy instrument altered was deposit interest rate ceilings. The historical ceilings on rates for large certificates of deposits, deposits at commercial banks, deposits at savings and loan associations, and deposits at mutual savings banks were all removed. Deposit interest rates thus rose above historical ceilings during tight money periods and prevented the massive disintermediation that actually occurred. There was some simultaneous impact upon other short-term interest rates as well.

Nonborrowed reserves also were changed directly, made to grow more rapidly in periods when growth was very low or negative and limited in growth during times of rapid increase to tone down the periods of aggressively easier monetary policy.

To mitigate the effects of the New Fed Policy after 1979:4; nonborrowed reserves were altered to limit the swings in key short-term interest rates. This variable has a strong impact on short-term interest rates, especially the federal funds and treasury bill rates, and operates by altering free reserves. There is also a smaller impact on longer-term rates through a liquidity variable in the key long-term corporate bond rate equation.

5. No Oil Shocks, Stable Money Policy

This simulation was constructed by combining the changes made in the no oil shocks and stable money policy simulations. The one alteration was to eliminate the change in the no oil shock simulation by adjusting nonborrowed bank reserves to retain M1 at its baseline path. Otherwise, all changes were as described in simulations (3) and (4).

6. Stable Money Policy, No Crunch

This simulation used the stable money policy exercise as a base and included all the changes in it. Tight money and disintermediation was essentially eliminated as a crunch ingredient in this exercise. But in addition several elements of the credit crunch and reliquefication experienced during this simulation period were removed.

The growth patterns of certain loan and asset variables were smoothed throughout the simulation interval to remove the effects on interest rates and real final demands brought by volatile credit growth and asset accumulation and decumulation. Those variables smoothed were commercial and industrial loans at all large weekly reporting banks, loans to individuals, outstanding mortgage loans and commitments, borrowing by nonfinancial corporations at banks, and issues of commercial paper by nonfinancial corporations, all of which exert considerable upward pressure on interest rates late in expansions and put downward pressure on interest rates in recessions. Household and business balance sheets also were made more stable as a result, as asset/debt ratios were less volatile. The rate of growth in these categories of borrowing was reduced during the credit crunch periods. The loan variables directly influence short-term interest rates and indirectly affect the deposit flows and balance sheets of households, nonfinancial corporations, and state and local government.

A financial variable that was adjusted was household financial assets, which consists of household holdings of money, deposits, bonds, and equity. In credit crunches, the growth of household financial assets is considerably diminished. Instead, the growth in this variable was increased during credit crunches, easing one of the major negative household balance sheet inputs to the business cycle. Household financial assets influence household net worth, the performance of the stock market, and also the final demands of real personal consumption.

7. Stable Money Policy, No Oil Shocks, No Crunch

This simulation combined the changes and features of the stable money policy, no oil shocks, and no crunch simulations, removing the cyclicality brought about by "stop/go" monetary policy, the oil price shock inflation, and several elements of the crunch process. In essence, almost all the ingredients of the "financial factor" in the business cycle were smoothed as a result.

8. Autonomous Real Final Demands

In this simulation, the more volatile components of final demands were exogenized at trend values one by one, then all together. These were, specifically, personal consumption expenditures of durable goods in real terms, gross fixed private nonresidential investment in real terms, the total change in real business inventories, and housing starts. These variables were constrained to grow at their historical levels over the entire simulation interval; housing starts were set at their mean value for the period.

In the DRI model, most of these variables enter directly into real gross national product. However, feedback effects influenced some other variables, with endogenous reactions permitted elsewhere, except back on the final demand category that was exogenized.

9. Autonomous Real Final Demands, No Oil Shocks, Stable Money Policy, No Crunch

This simulation combined the exogenizing of the various components of real final demands at trend growth rates and the characteristics and underlying features of the no oil shocks, stable money policy, and no crunch solutions to remove most of the suspected major sources of volatility during the simulation period. All the changes described in the relevant simulations above were combined for this exercise.

Appendix 1.2
Expectations and Econometric Models

The role of expectations in the business cycle has not yet been fully and systematically explicated or empirically determined. The "new macroeconomics" provides an equilibrium theory of business cycles, stressing the impact of unanticipated shocks as a source of cyclical

Table 1.A.1   **Sources of Cyclicality: Results of DRI Model Simulations, 1966 to 1983:2 (Inflation, GNP Deflator)**

Simulation	Cyclicality Index	Percentage Reduction from History
Historical Track Sim	18.964	—
No "noise"	16.003	−15.06
No oil shocks	17.064	−10.0
Stable money policy	18.709	−1.3
No oil shocks, stable money policy	17.462	−7.9
Stable money policy, no crunch	18.116	−4.5
Stable money policy, no oil shocks, no crunch	16.792	−11.5
Autonomous real final demands	n.m.[b]	n.m.
Durable consumption	n.m.	n.m.
Business fixed investment	n.m.	n.m.
Inventories	n.m.	n.m.
Residential construction	n.m.	n.m.
Autonomous real final demands, no oil shocks, stable money policy, no crunch	n.m.	n.m.

[a]Since the historical dynamic simulation gave a less cyclical result than the Track Sim, the "gap" between potential and real GNP in the simulation did not widen as much as in history, especially in downturns, producing a more cyclical result. Setting the final demand components exogenously at trend growth values eliminated certain model feedback mechanisms on inflation that limit the usefulness of these results.
[b]n.m. = not meaningful.

movements and rationally formed expectations in making anticipated changes in policy ineffective (Lucas 1975).

In the new theory, expectations affect the business cycle through "disappointment" or "surprise" over monetary and fiscal policy actions. Unanticipated changes in monetary and fiscal policies perturb the amplitude of the cycle, with the propagation of these shocks depending on internal mechanisms.

The new expectations theory challenges econometric models on several counts. First, conventional macroeconomic models have often been devoid of expectations phenomena and, where existing, derived from historical data of the same series rather than "rationally" formed. Specification errors may exist on both grounds, biasing the results in the dynamic simulations of these models. Second, to the extent that parameters (the structure) vary in response to policy changes, the predictions of econometric models that are conditional on assumed policies may be invalid or biased. More important for the business

Table 1.A.2   Sources of Cyclicality: Results of DRI Model Simulations, 1966 to 1983:2 (Unemployment Rate)

Simulation	Cyclicality Index	Percentage Reduction from History
Historical Track Sim	9.560	—
No "noise"	9.483	−0.8
No oil shocks	8.349	−12.7
Stable money policy	8.827	−7.7
No oil shocks, stable money policy	8.143	−14.8
Stable money policy, no crunch	8.328	−12.9
Stable money policy, no oil shocks, no crunch	7.795	−18.5
Autonomous real final demands	6.159	−35.6
Durables consumption	8.820	−13.4
Business fixed investment	7.060	−26.2
Inventories	9.924	3.9
Residential construction	8.591	−10.1
Autonomous real final demands, no oil shocks, stable money policy, no crunch	7.853	−17.9

cycle, anticipated changes in policy are believed to have no impact on real variables or inflation, since the economic structure adjusts to offset them. Third, the activity may really be equilibrium paths in a world where information is rationally used, since markets have quickly adjusted and learned in an efficient manner. These arguments, though valid in certain circumstances, nevertheless must themselves be questioned. Expectations formation is not necessarily rational, but at times can be adaptive and slow, depending upon the markets in question. It is not clear that the errors potentially introduced by using a formulation of expectations different from rational expectations are large enough to perturb equation parameters sufficiently to render invalid the approximate conclusions of econometric model simulations. It is an empirical question whether significant variation occurs in structural coefficients when policy is changed. Many policy changes are not different enough from history to alter structural parameters by a large amount.

Further, the notion that economic agents perceive and use the correct structure in forming expectations is difficult to accept. A homogeneity of views across decision makers on the determinants of the economy, interest rates, and responses to policy is very unlikely. Equilibriums are not instantaneous: the real world is characterized by quarter-to-quarter adjustments. Finally, only few economic markets are characterized by quick, inexpensive, full information flows on those activities relative to decisions. The flow of information and reactions of decision makers might be near perfect in the financial markets, but reactions in labor and other markets are much less efficient.

Comment   Michael C. Lovell

I think I have an advantage in reading Eckstein and Sinai's paper, for whereas courses in the business cycle are no longer offered at most institutions, I was well trained; in the fall of 1955—six recessions ago—it was my pleasure to take a graduate course about business cycles that was team taught by Gottfried Haberler and Otto Eckstein. That was a precomputer course; it was not until the following summer that the dawn of modern computers at Littauer was marked by the arrival of the Burroughs E101. That machine was the wonder of its day, for it had 110 words of storage. Eckstein and Haberler taught a great course, one of the last of its breed; at the time it was obvious to everyone that Otto would go far, but I suspect that few of us in the class anticipated that he would pass the market test so well, entrepreneuring business cycle forecasting on time-sharing computers.

The six recessions suffered by the American economy since Eckstein and Haberler taught their course provide additional evidence on the nature of business cycle phenomena. But in the interim the very existence of the business cycle came to be questioned: it was suggested at one time that the business cycle was a topic that could be relegated to economic historians; more than a decade ago a former colleague of mine, Martin Bronfenbrenner, edited a Social Science Research Council volume entitled *Is the Business Cycle Obsolete?* and successful macro texts avoid even a chapter on the business cycle. This conference gives testimony that the business cycle is alive and sick. And we have much to learn about business cycle phenomena from Eckstein and Sinai's contribution.

Key Points

Let me begin by saying that to my mind the most surprising thing about the contribution is that so much of it is so familiar. With the exception of the simulation results of section 1.6, the Eckstein/Sinai

Michael C. Lovell is professor of economics at Wesleyan University.

paper closely resembles the Eckstein/Haberler course. Indeed, the business cycle mechanism described is not that different from the one discussed by Joseph Schumpeter in his *Theory of Economic Development* and his two-volume *Business Cycles*; and much that is in the paper would offer no surprise to readers of Burns and Mitchell. In particular, Eckstein and Sinai follow Burns and Mitchell in stressing the sheer complexity and irregularities of business cycle phenomena. Let me mention some of the most striking features of their contribution:

1. They augment in a rather interesting way the standard NBER business cycle chronology, as is most easily seen from table 1.3, which chronicles five types of cyclical phenomena. The recovery expansion dates and the recession dates are those of the NBER (in contrast to Blinder's contribution to this volume, they stick to the official chronology). Eckstein and Sinai have superimposed on this standard chronology three types of "stages." The first of these are "booms." In addition there is the "precrunch period/crunch" and the "reliquefication" stage. Reliquefication is a process that usually takes place near the end of the recession but may be continuing while the recovery phase is getting under way. The boom usually precedes the onset of recession. Observe, however, that there is considerable irregularity, testifying to the complexity of the phenomena under study; in particular, the precrunch period/crunch of 1966 was not followed by recession (though at one point the authors refer to a "growth recession"). And the downturn of 1960 was not preceded by a boom, which they attribute to Eisenhower's efforts at balancing the budget.

2. Eckstein and Sinai present the "DRI boom monitor," which may be a close cousin of the NBER coincident indicators; by identifying periods of boom, they hope to determine more precisely the upper turning point. It is plotted on figure 1.3, and its components are listed on table 1.4. Note that it is a weighted average of eight components; six are real indicators; one is a measure of credit conditions; the one with smallest weight is the monetary base growth index, but in real terms, which means it is not considered a policy instrument by monetarists. It is interesting that in terms of their boom index the 1972:6 to 1973:11 boom is the biggest bang since World War II—perhaps the magnitude of the Korean War boom is artificially downplayed because of the cutback in new car sales.

3. While Eckstein and Sinai do not focus on any single measure of monetary conditions, they do emphasize the importance of the financial factor in referring to the "flow of funds cycle." To briefly summarize, they explain that the precrunch period culminates in the *crunch,* which they define "as a credit crisis stemming from the collision of an expanding economy with a financial system that has been depleted of liquidity." It is characterized by deteriorating balance sheets, sharply

increased interest rates, a scramble for available funds, depressed stock markets, and the inability of many borrowers to obtain funds at any cost. "The financial factor is a critical ingredient of the business cycle. . . . But it is not just monetary policy that influences the business cycle process; the feedback effects from borrowing, lending, stock-flow processes in finance, balance sheets, changes in liquidity, and financial risk affect cyclical behavior as well." If my memory serves me right, there is not much in this description that would surprise either John Maynard Keynes or Joseph Schumpeter.

4. While their paper does not blame the cycle on any single factor, they do cast a few stones at the policymakers—Eisenhower for shifting so abruptly toward the balanced budget in 1960 and the Fed for being too contractionary in downturns and too expansionary in revivals. Thus they state: "In virtually every precrunch period, the Federal Reserve retained a restrictive monetary policy for longer than was necessary. Similarly, periods of reliquefication often have been characterized by a prolonged period of excessively stimulative monetary policy." They argue that the October 1979 shift in Fed policy was a mistake, causing the subsequent crunches to become more intense; also, the shift to flexible exchange rates contributed to the globalization of cyclical phenomena in the 1970s.

Kindleberger

5. Simulation results focusing on the sources of the business cycle are conveniently summarized in section 1.6. They compare a variety of alternative counterfactual simulations using an "index of cyclicality," defined as the sum of the absolute value of deviations from trend over the period 1966 to 1983:2. The results are conveniently summarized on table 1.6, the middle column of that table being most informative. In the absence of random shocks (no noise), the cycle in real output would have been 7.4% less severe. No oil *price* shocks would have removed 15.9% of the cycle, and a stable money policy would have smoothed out 22.2%. And table 1.7 shows the multiplier effect of a $10 billion increase in real government spending, contrasting a fixed money supply with unchanged nonborrowed reserves.

Critique

1. I suspect many readers of this paper will be upset; but I am sure those sections that are most upsetting to some readers are likely to receive strong applause from others.

Some will be upset because Eckstein and Sinai do not focus on any single simple indicator of what the central bank is about—if they do mention the rate of M1 growth once or twice, they also refer more than a few times to free reserves.

Some readers may be upset because they do not advance a straightforward statement as to what *causes* cyclical phenomena. My own inclination is to applaud Eckstein and Sinai for following Burns and Mitchell in stressing the complexity of the business cycle; they explicitly reject monocausal explanations.

Others will be upset by the things they leave out. They have little to say about the slowdown in productivity growth or rational expectations. And I am sure many will dissent from their proclivity to downplay much that is new in the literature: "Some ideas from the recent literature, such as asymmetric information, the misreading of absolute price changes as relative price changes, the serial correlation introduced by buffer inventory stocks into production, and lags in the wage/price process, may be part of reality, but even the most cursory look at actual history shows that they can be no more than a small part of it." Because I believe the jury is still out on these issues, I myself am not upset on these points. I am an agnostic, and I believe the pendulum of professional wisdom will be swinging back toward Eckstein and Sinai.

2. I think Eckstein and Sinai may not have adequately qualified the results of their simulation runs. True, they do provide the following cautionary note concerning the precision of their simulation results: "This method of analysis assumes that the observed error terms are not correlated with the sources of instability, an assumption that probably understates the effects of removing various sources of instability, because error terms most likely are positively correlated with measured sources of instability." I believe this is an inadequate qualification; in particular, readers must be cautioned about the problem of specification error. And it would be useful to know how sensitive their simulation results and multiplier estimates are to perturbing their parameter estimates within the indicated range of sampling error. No argument is presented as to why the multiplier response profile presented in table 1.7 is any more creditable than any of the wide-ranging candidates plotted for alternative models by Carl Christ in his article "Judging the Performance of Econometric Models of the U.S. Economy" (Christ 1976). Some readers may suspect that the simulation results reported in this contribution may be telling us more about the characteristics of the DRI model than about the United States economy.

3. I also believe that their simulations do not constitute a definitive exercise in counterfactual history. To illustrate, consider the "no oil shocks" simulation reported in table 1.6. Potentially this is the most interesting of simulations, not only for academic economists but also for Detroit autoworkers who lost their jobs and New Englanders who heat their homes with oil. According to their analysis, their cyclicality index for the period 1973–80 would have been 26.4% lower if the world price of oil had climbed at a steady 7.1% rate over this period. While removing the erratic jerks, this simulation leaves the price of oil at its historical high by the terminal year of the simulation. Thus the reduc-

tion in cyclicality is entirely due to the erratic nature of the price shocks, leaving out the consequence of supply disruptions; and the simulation does not purport to show how productivity and prices would have behaved in the absence of OPEC price hikes.

In thinking about this exercise in counterfactual history, it seems obvious that it should make a difference whether the experimental effect was achieved through an increase in oil imports or by the imposition of price ceilings, with accompanying shortages—the Eckstein/ Sinai simulation focuses only on the price effects. The consequence would also depend upon whether the lower price for gasoline would have prevented the shift away from Detroit's "gas guzzlers" to Japanese minis. Research by Ohta and Griliches, as reported in the *NBER Digest* (February/March 1984), reveals that tastes were stable but consumers responded to changes in the price of gasoline and the associated changes in the implicit prices based on weight and size of cars. Unfortunately, Eckstein and Sinai do not explore the effect of stable petroleum import prices on car sales and so forth; and they do not tell us whether energy conservation expenditures by public utilities and households are appropriately netted out; they do not tell us whether they assume that the elimination of the petroleum price hikes would influence the direction of investment spending and the rate of productivity growth.

In the oil price shock simulation they held the historical time path of the money supply (M1) unchanged, which meant the interest rates were made much lower. This simulation is not without interest, but it is of greatest interest to those who believe the money supply is exogenous—some may believe that the problems of the 1970s arose because the Fed spontaneously ran amok with the money supply; the Eckstein/Sinai simulations suggest that, even so, elimination of price shocks would have reduced the real-output cyclicality index by about 15.9%; it would have cut fluctuations in the rate of inflation by 10% and achieved a 12.7% reduction in fluctuations in the unemployment rate.

For those of us who believe that Fed policy was responsive, rightly or wrongly, to what was happening at the moment, an alternative set of simulations is required in which monetary policy is treated as an endogenous variable. The "stable money policy" simulations are a step in this direction. For these simulations Eckstein and Sinai specify that deposit ceilings are removed, extreme changes in reserve requirements are eliminated, and open market operations on reserves are eased when monetary policy was tight and tightened when monetary policy was easy; the range of interest rate volatility was limited after 1979:4. This is a very complex specification; and while I sympathize with their statement that the definition of a stable monetary policy is complex, I for one would find it interesting to have supplemental information on the resulting time path of interest rates and the money supply.

They do report on a simulation simultaneously eliminating oil price shocks and invoking a stable money policy. If I interpret their brief discussion of this simulation correctly, they are having reserves and interest rates follow the same time path as in the second simulation, which means that the path of M1 departs substantially from its historical path.

4. I think what is needed are *more* DRI simulations better described! It would be useful to simulate within the DRI model environment the implications of alternative assumptions (rules) about the determination of monetary and fiscal policy. A number of years ago Edward Prescott and I (*Southern Economic Journal,* 1968) modeled alternative monetary rules within a simple analytical framework—because which policy rule worked best depended on the relative magnitude of the system's parameters, the basic questions of which policy was most appropriate could not be resolved analytically. Appropriate simulations with the DRI model would provide one set of answers to these fundamental policy issues. One set of simulations would introduce monetary rules attempting to model as closely as possible the actual decision rules of the authorities. These would be contrasted with normative policy rules— for example, constant money supply growth, leaning against the wind, or stable interest rates. The relative success of alternative policy rules in coping with various types of large shocks, such as OPEC price hikes, should be explored by simulation.

Comment   Kenneth J. Singleton

The paper by Otto Eckstein and Allen Sinai focuses on the role of the financial sector in both the generation and the propagation of cyclical fluctuations in aggregate variables. I shall begin my comments by placing the analysis in this paper in a somewhat different light than the authors have. Then I shall discuss the different phases of the business cycle set forth by Eckstein and Sinai, as well as their taxonomy of the mechanisms underlying the cycles, examining the theoretical underpinnings of the DRI model in relation to modern theories of portfolio choice and consumption. Finally, I shall present some comments on the simulations. Consistent with the focus of the paper, most of my comments will address the specification of the financial sector in macroeconomic models.

Kenneth J. Singleton is professor of economics at Carnegie-Mellon University.

The optimal decisions of consumers, firms, and governments embody the structure of financial markets through the budget constraints faced by these agents. Thus the cyclical behavior of such aggregates as GNP, unemployment, and inflation is intimately related to the nature of the financial instruments available for financing expenditures and for saving. In a frictionless world with complete contingent claims markets, there would be many equivalent ways of arranging financing to achieve the optimal level and rate of growth of expenditures. Indeed, non-interest-bearing money is typically a dominated asset in such an economy, in which case fiat money would not circulate in equilibrium.

Of course there are in fact many restrictions in the United States and other countries that preclude certain types of financial contracts or the provision of certain types of insurance and that limit the forms of the contractual arrangements that can be achieved with the available instruments. The time series properties of aggregate variables are affected in important ways by these restrictions, so economies with and without such restrictions imposed, though otherwise identical, may behave very differently. Furthermore, changes in the types of contracts and in communications technologies over time will in general alter both the amplitude and the periodicity of macroeconomic time series.[1] The important role of financial arrangements in the business cycle process is the central theme of this paper.

Historically, the emphasis on the financial sector in models of business cycles has varied. Fluctuation in interest rates has long been recognized as a central factor in the determination of aggregate real economic activity. However, as Eckstein and Sinai emphasize, much less attention has been given to developing formal models of the business cycle that account explicitly for disintermediation, bankruptcy risk, and considerations of "liquidity."[2] In sections 1.3 and 1.5, Eckstein and Sinai provide a useful and informative description of the evolution of several financial aggregates during the postwar business cycles, giving particular attention to the changes in the composition of the balance sheets of firms, consumers, and financial intermediaries. Both the magnitude and the timing of the changes in these financial aggregates lead the authors to conclude that financial factors were important for shaping the business cycle.

While these sections present clear evidence of a "flow of funds" cycle, a detailed description of the mechanisms by which changes in

1. Some properties of the equilibria of monetary economies have been discussed recently by Townsend 1982, Lucas 1983, and Bewley 1984, among others, under different assumptions about borrowing and insurance markets.

2. Many authors have, of course, argued that these financial factors play an important role in generating cycles. For instance, illiquidity and the bankruptcy of firms was a key feature of Irving Fisher's (1930) theory of the business cycle. These considerations have not, for the most part, been incorporated into recent analytical models of aggregate behavior.

credit variables affect real economic variables is not provided, beyond several informal observations. Throughout their discussion they use such terms as liquidity, credit availability, and insufficient financing, but without providing precise definitions of these terms or giving precise reasons why these conditions obtain. It seems clear, however, that they are implicitly making assumptions about the existence of legal restrictions and transactions costs and about the nature of the contingent claims markets that are excluded from their model. For instance, the authors note that there has been substantial fluctuation in durable goods purchases during the postwar period, but they do not provide a formal description of the mechanisms that produced the fluctuation. Instead, only a brief outline of the "mechanisms" of the business cycle is displayed in table 1.5. Several of these mechanisms seem to refer implicitly to the consequences of incomplete contingent claims markets, but the links between the inability to insure against certain types of risks, illiquidity and bankruptcy, and durable goods purchases over the cycle are not formalized. The imprecision here is unfortunate, since precisely which markets are excluded and which legal restrictions are imposed in an economic model have important implications for how policies affect real economic activity through financial markets and hence for the design and analysis of monetary and fiscal policies.[3]

Furthermore, if liquidity and bankruptcy are as important as Eckstein and Sinai suggest, then different types of consumers and firms may be affected differentially by economic events. Hence a distinction should be made between those who are wealthy and less likely to be affected by a financial crunch and those in the lower and middle income groups who are most likely to be affected. By making this distinction, very different time series properties for consumption and output in the presence of a given monetary and fiscal environment may emerge, compared with the time series properties of a model with representative agents. In particular, individual consumption may be much more volatile and may exhibit quite different patterns of comovements with interest rates than aggregate consumption. Some qualitative evidence about the different time series properties of individual and aggregate consumption in the presence of borrowing constraints is provided by the simulations in Scheinkman and Weiss (1983). Their findings suggest that substantially more insights into the financial factor in the business cycle may be obtained by disaggregating by types of individuals (e.g., constrained and unconstrained) in the presence of restrictions on financial contracting.

3. More generally, the assumptions about informational asymmetries on the part of agents and the nature of the legal restrictions affect the nature of the financial contracts that will be observed. For instance, Townsend 1984 shows that the type of communication technologies available affects the structure of financial markets.

The way expectations are introduced into a model also has important implications for both the magnitude and the cyclicality of the responses of GNP to monetary and real shocks. The role of expectations in the DRI model is described briefly in this paper and more extensively in Brimmer and Sinai (1981) and Eckstein (1983). In light of the evidence that the credit crunch experience has been a systematic element in the postwar business cycle and the general perception that expectations are important determinants of the behavior of financial variables, an evaluation of the expectational assumptions underlying the Eckstein/ Sinai analysis seems warranted.

For the most part, Eckstein and Sinai assume that agents form expectations adaptively according to a long distributed lag. The reasons given for choosing this specification seem to represent misconceptions about the properties of dynamic economic models. First, Eckstein and Sinai (appendix 1.2) argue that the assumption of rational expectations implies that anticipated changes in policy have no effect on real variables. This interpretation of the rational expectations assumption is incorrect. The assumption of rational expectations per se has no implications for the effectiveness of systematic policy. Rather, it is the underlying structural model, together with the expectational assumption, that determines whether anticipated policy has real effects. In a monetary model in which markets are incomplete and there are legal restrictions on financial contracting, it seems likely that anticipated monetary policy will have real effects under rational expectations.

Second, they argue that adaptive expectations processes are incorporated into the equations of the financial sector of the DRI model in part because rational expectations requires a "quick adjustment" of the economy to shocks. In fact, the assumption of rational expectations does not restrict the speed by which the economy adjusts to exogenous shocks or how far into the past a rational agent looks when forming expectations about the future. Such properties of a model are determined jointly by the structure of the model and the assumptions about the expectations formation process.

Furthermore, such rigidities as long-term contracts are not incompatible with the assumption of rational expectations. Recent studies of price setting under asymmetric information have shown that wages and prices may appear to be relatively unresponsive to economic events, even though agents have rational expectations conditioned on their own information.[4] An implication of this literature on optimal contracting is that standard pricing formulas derived under symmetric information do not apply. Eckstein and Sinai study labor market relations derived under the assumption of symmetric information among workers and

4. See, for example, Hall and Lilien 1979 and Stiglitz and Weiss 1981.

firms. If long-term contracts are a consequence of imperfect information, then it may be that, by studying a misspecified model, the authors are led to the conclusion that expectations are formed extrapolatively when they are in fact rational.

Before discussing in more detail the specification of the financial sector in the DRI model, it will be helpful to digress briefly and comment on the specification of the consumption sector described in Eckstein (1983). The theory underlying the consumption equation in the DRI model is one in which a representative household maximizes the expected value of a two-period utility function. While not formally deduced from a complete specification of the economy, this relation embodies a key feature of modern consumption theory. Namely, consumption decisions today are affected by the returns on alternative assets and the uncertainty about future consumption opportunities. This risk is captured by the probability of a contingency's arising, and this probability is in turn a function of the current inflation and unemployment rates and the variability of income.

The equations describing interest rates are based on a static theory of portfolio selection, augmented by the introduction of adjustment costs. This formulation virtually ignores the dynamic considerations underlying the specification of the consumption equation. Modern theories of portfolio choice and asset price determination proposed by Merton (1971), Lucas (1978), Breeden (1979), and others have forward looking investors considering all moments of the distributions of the variables in the models.[5] Additionally, Eckstein and Sinai assume that the yields on long-term bonds are determined separately from the yields on short-term securities, as in the model proposed by Feldstein and Eckstein (1970). Their interest rate equation has long rates depending principally on long-term price expectations formed according to an adaptive learning process, and a measure of the policy controlled liquidity of the economy. Sargent (1971) has argued previously that this "mongrel" equation, which represents an attempt to merge Fisher's theory of interest with the liquidity preference theory, is not identified as a structural equation. Thus there is little reason to expect that the parameter estimates for this equation will bear any simple relation to the true parameters of agents' expectations of inflation. Like the short-rate equations, this relation is also not linked in an economically consistent way to the real sectors of the economy.

The motivation for the introduction of adjustment costs is that businesses cannot adapt their balance sheet portfolios fully in response to

5. In practice, it is often assumed that agents have quadratic objective functions and face linear constraints, so that decision rules are linear (e.g., Hansen and Sargent 1980). This is one rationalization for restricting attention to conditional first moments in models with rational expectations.

changing market conditions. The "need" for the introduction of adjustment costs in the financial sector in order to "fit the data" may well be a consequence of the following features of the model. First, the model is based on a static theory. In a dynamic, uncertain environment, the portfolio decisions of consumers and firms will in general depend nonlinearly on the current and past values of variables summarizing market conditions. Agents will typically adjust their portfolios gradually over time as the optimal response to disturbances, even when there are small transaction costs associated with portfolio adjustments.

Second, the equations for the long-term bond rates use yields to maturity as the dependent variables. It is well known that yields obscure the links between nominal interest rates and movements in expected inflation or real interest rates. It is the pure discount bond returns that convey information about the value of money in future periods, not yields to maturity. The latter are a confounding of the discount rates for all periods over the life of the security.

These observations are not intended to suggest that there are no adjustment costs associated with financial transactions. There may be adjustment costs induced, for instance, by such restrictions on financing as those mentioned at the outset of this discussion. However, if such restrictions are present, then the static portfolio theory underlying the analysis in this paper does not hold. The specification of the consumers' optimum problems should explicitly incorporate these restrictions through the specification of the budget constraints.

For the purpose of discussing the role of the financial factor in the business cycle, Eckstein and Sinai take the constructs of a representative consumer and a representative firm as given. They argue that the financial factor manifests itself most strongly during two stages of the business cycle that heretofore were not considered explicitly as part of the NBER business cycle stages: the credit crunch and reliquefication stages. Here again their discussion leaves several important questions unanswered. In particular, the basic issue of what exogenous and endogenous factors induce a credit crunch at the peak of a cycle and the stage of "reliquefication" at the trough is not resolved. In section 1.5.1 it is noted that no single factor is responsible for the onset of a credit crunch, and that a combination of several factors "causes" a crunch. A restrictive monetary policy is clearly an important ingredient in generating a credit crunch. What is not clear is whether it is a necessary ingredient. Will, for example, a crunch emerge whenever certain legal restrictions and borrowing constraints become binding? That is, can this stage of the business cycle be induced by both real and nominal disturbances in the absence of a restrictive monetary policy? Another question raised by this analysis in whether the monetary authorities could prevent a credit crunch by acting differently in the expansion phase of a business cycle.

The answers to these questions are likely to be model specific, which further underscores the importance of being precise about the structure of financial markets. Of course, institutional and legal restrictions on financial contracting are not easily modeled at a formal level. The implied nonlinearities and inequality restrictions typically preclude closed-form relations for the optimal consumption decisions or asset prices. Similarly, the implications for economic behavior of moral hazard and adverse selection under asymmetric information have to date been analyzed only in the context of fairly simple models. Finally, throughout the postwar period there have been changes in the operating procedures of the Federal Reserve and important revisions in the tax codes, and markets for new financial instruments have been established. Accounting for all of these considerations in models of the business cycle specified at the level of the objective functions of economic agents is currently not feasible. Therefore, large-scale models that introduce explicitly "frictions" in financial markets but have hybrid expectations schemes may provide some insights into the implications of such frictions for the business cycle.

The DRI model represents in part the product of an ambitious attempt at incorporating some of the many institutional and legal restrictions on financial contracting into a macroeconomic model. Unfortunately, no catalog of the restrictions or description of the way they are imposed on the decision rules of agents in the DRI model is provided by Eckstein and Sinai. This omission limits the potential insights about the role of financial markets in the business cycle process that can be obtained from the simulations reported in the final section of the paper.

Turning to the simulations, the effect of removing a particular source of shocks from the model is measure by a "cyclicality index," defined as the normalized absolute deviations in real GNP from a trend growth path. The index was calculated first with all sources of shocks included in the model and then with a particular source of shocks removed. The difference between the two values of the index is a measure of the importance of the omitted source of shocks in the business cycle process. There are, as I am sure the authors realize, numerous problems with such a measure when shocks are removed stepwise as in some of the simulations—most notably, the results will in general not be insensitive to the order in which the shocks are removed. In addition, the results may be sensitive to the measure of the trend growth path for output, so a description of the trend used in the simulations would be useful.

These simulations are also based on the assumption that the residuals in the equations of the DRI model are not correlated with the sources of instability. Errors in asset and commodity demand equations typically arise for one or more of the following reasons: shocks to utility or production functions (e.g., random elements in tastes), surprises in the behavior of the policy authorities, measurement errors, and shocks that originate externally to the United States. Measurement errors may well be uncorrelated with the other sources of shocks. On the other hand, the remaining shocks may be correlated owing, for example, to various types of automatic stabilizers built into the economic system. Moreover, the errors that appear in the demand equations that constitute the DRI model are themselves complicated functions of all of these "primitive" shocks. Thus, not only will the residual typically be correlated with exogenous shocks, but the signs of these correlations seem difficult to predict a priori. Consequently, I am less sure than Eckstein and Sinai that their presupposition leads to an understatement of the effects of removing sources of instability. For the same reasons, I find it difficult to interpret the results from the first simulation in which the errors in the equations were set to zero, while the shocks to the exogenous variables and the policy variables remained unchanged.

Consider first the simulation of a stable monetary growth. A stable monetary environment was taken to be one in which deposit ceilings were removed, extreme changes in reserve requirements were removed, and open market operations were eased when policy was tight and tightened when policy was easy. As a result, the cyclicality index decreased by 22.2%. The reason given for removing such restrictions as interest rate ceilings and selective credit controls was that simply imposing a smooth growth path for nonborrowed reserves would still leave a highly unstable financial system. But this seems to be one of the key issues that would be interesting to address with the DRI model. That is, by how much does the cyclicality of GNP decrease in the presence of a stable monetary growth path and in the presence of legal restrictions on financial contracts? Although the results from such a simulation would have to be interpreted with caution for the reasons outlined above, they would provide some information about the severity of credit crunches that arise owing to nonmonetary shocks.

Turning to the analysis of oil price shocks, the structure of this simulation presumes (no doubt correctly) that there was a strong response by the monetary authorities to be oil price increases. Thus the simulation amounts to the analysis of the combined effects of removing the oil price increase and holding the path of monetary policy unchanged. Interestingly, the results from this analysis were very similar to those from the simulation in which both the oil price shocks were removed and a stable monetary path (as broadly defined above) was imposed. As Eckstein and Sinai note, this result may be a consequence of a less than complete adjustment of the assumed monetary policy to the different oil price assumptions. Put somewhat differently, since the monetary authorities respond to exogenous shocks, to analyze the consequences of eliminating a shock it is necessary to alter the structure of the time series on all of the policy variables. Accurate adjustments to the policy variables is in general feasible only when the decision rules of the private agents and policy rules of the governments are solved for simultaneously from the model.

The final simulations reported were designed to examine the effects on postwar business cycles of the flow of funds cycle. Here again no attempt was made to assess the importance of certain "structural" restrictions in financial markets on the cyclical behavior of output. First, the stable money policy considered previously was imposed. Then additional limitations were placed on the endogenous responses of consumers and firms to economic developments. Specifically, in a way not described in the paper, limited fluctuation in loan demand and disintermediation was allowed. Limiting the behavior of endogenous variables in this manner provides little information about the role of the financial sector in economic activity. Experiments designed to determine the importance of different features of the financial sector should involve direct changes in the assumed structure of the financial sector.

In sum, it seems indisputable that a better understanding of how financial arrangements affect economic decisions is critical for a better understanding of business cycles. As in-depth analysis of the implications for economic activity of different contractural arrangements in financial markets will probably require simulating a closed model specified at the level of individual agents objective functions, with the limitations on financing introduced explicitly into the budget constraints. The analysis in section 1.5 of this paper could have provided some information about which limitations on financing are likely to be most important quantitatively. Overall, however, Eckstein and Sinai did not provide enough detail about the structure of the DRI model or conduct sufficiently focused experiments with the model for the potential gains from their analysis to be realized.

Discussion Summary   Stephen R. King and John M. Veitch

Robert Hall drew attention to the fact that table 1.6 implied that almost no economic variation was attributable to residuals in equations, im-

Stephen R. King is assistant professor of economics at Stanford University. John M. Veitch is assistant professor of economics at the University of Southern California.
    The discussion summaries for all the chapters were written by Professor King and Professor Veitch.

plying that the DRI model had been constructed with special factors to dummy out otherwise inexplicable variation in time series. The analysis of the table showed that exogenous shifts to demand for consumer durables were responsible for most cyclical variation. Robert Gordon also drew attention to the overlap between this paper and those by Hall and by Gordon and Veitch. All had noted the increased importance of shocks to consumer demand for durable goods in the postwar period, whereas before the war much of the variation had been in demand for nonresidential structures.

Benjamin Friedman noted that the paper drew an unusual distinction between accommodative and nonaccommodative monetary policies, the former being used to signify a constant nonborrowed reserve aggregate and the latter signifying constant M1. He noted that a more natural use of the term would have led "accommodative" to mean keeping an interest rate constant, while "nonaccommodative" would imply keeping a monetary aggregate fixed. Stanley Black felt that the paper's finding that cycles were due to fluctuations in autonomous spending was reminiscent of Adelman and Adelman's findings (1959). He consequently felt that the benefits of a large model compared with a small one were yet to be demonstrated.

Allen Sinai defended the use of special variables to capture variation in equations that other variables could not account for. He stressed that they were not included in the equations arbitrarily but were meant to capture special events such as automobile strikes whose effects could not be expected to be captured by equations estimated for the entire sample period. Merely treating such events as residuals would not identify why the schedule shifted. He also defended the use of large models over small ones, emphasizing that which one is appropriate depends on the purposes for which they are required.

References

Adelman, Irma, and Frank L. Adelman. 1959. The dynamic properties of the Klein-Goldberger model. *Econometrica* 27 (October): 596–625.

Baumol, William J. 1959. *Economic dynamics*. New York: Macmillan.

Bernanke, Ben S. 1983. Non-monetary effects of the financial crisis in the propagation of the Great Depression. *American Economic Review* 73 (May): 257–63.

Bewley, T. 1984. Fiscal and monetary policy in a general equilibrium model. Manuscript, Yale University.

Breeden, D. T. 1979. An intertemporal asset pricing model with stochastic consumption and investment opportunities. *Journal of Financial Economics* 7:265–96.

Brimmer, Andrew F., and Allen Sinai. 1981. Rational expectations and the conduct of monetary policy. *American Economic Review* 71 (May): 259–67.

Burns, Arthur F., and Wesley C. Mitchell. 1946. *Measuring business cycles.* New York: National Bureau of Economic Research.

Christ, Carl. 1976. Judging the performance of econometric models of the U.S. economy. In *Econometric model performance: Comparative simulation studies of the U.S. economy,* ed. Lawrence R. Klein and Edwin Burmeister. Philadelphia: University of Pennsylvania Press.

Conner, James, and Otto Eckstein. 1978. DRI boom monitor. *Data Resources Review* (August), 20–26.

Eckstein, Otto. 1976. The boom monitor. *Data Resources Review* (April), 5–14.

———. 1978. *The great recession.* Amsterdam: North-Holland.

———. 1983. *The DRI model of the U.S. economy.* New York: McGraw-Hill.

Eckstein, Otto, and Allen Sinai. 1973. Crunch monitor. *Data Resources Review* (August), 47–50.

Feldstein, Martin S., and Otto Eckstein. 1970. The fundamental determinants of the interest rate. *Review of Economics and Statistics* 52 (November): 363–75.

Fisher, Irving. 1930. *The theory of interest.* New York: Macmillan.

———. 1933. The debt-deflation theory of great depressions. *Econometrica* 1 (October): 337–57.

Friedman, Milton, and Anna J. Schwartz. 1963. *A monetary history of the United States, 1867–1960.* Princeton: Princeton University Press.

Frisch, Ragnar. 1933. Propagation problems and impulse problems in dynamic economics. In *Economic essays in honor of Gustav Cassel.* London: George Allen.

Gordon, Robert A. 1974. *Economic instability and growth: The American record.* New York: Harper and Row.

Haberler, Gottfried. 1936. Monetary and real factors affecting economic stability: A critique of certain tendencies in modern economic theory. *Banca Nazionale Del Lavoro Quarterly Review,* September.

———. 1937. *Prosperity and depression: A theoretical analysis of cyclical movements.* Geneva: League of Nations.

Hall, R. E., and D. M. Lilien. 1979. Efficient wage bargains under uncertain supply and demand. *American Economic Review* 69:868–79.

Hansen, L. P., and T. J. Sargent. 1980. Formulating and estimating dynamic linear rational expectations models. *Journal of Economic Dynamics and Control* 2:7–46.

Hawtrey, Ralph G. 1926. The trade cycle. *Economist* (Rotterdam). Reprinted in *Readings in business cycle theory,* 330–49. Homewood, Ill.: Irwin, 1951.

Hicks, John R. 1950. *A contribution to the theory of the trade cycle.* Oxford: Oxford University Press.

Kindleberger, Charles. 1978. *Manias, panics, and crashes.* New York: Basic Books.

Lucas, Robert E. 1975. An equilibrium model of the business cycle. *Journal of Political Economy* 83 (December): 1113–46.

———. 1978. Asset prices in an exchange economy. *Econometrica* 46:1345–70.

———. 1983. Money in a theory of finance. Manuscript, University of Chicago.

Merton, R. 1971. Optimum consumption and portfolio rules in a continuous-time model. *Journal of Economic Theory* 3:373–413.

Metzler, Lloyd A. 1941. The nature and stability of inventory cycles. *Review of Economics and Statistics* 23 (August): 113–29.

Minsky, Hyman P. 1977. A theory of systemic financial instability. In *Financial crises: Institutions and markets in a fragile environment,* ed. E. I. Altman and A. W. Sametz, 138–52. New York: Wiley.

Mitchell, Wesley C. 1927. *Business cycles: The problem and its setting.* New York: National Bureau of Economic Research.

Samuelson, Paul A. 1939. Interactions between the multiplier analysis and the principle of acceleration. *Review of Economics and Statistics* 21 (May): 75–78.

Sargent, Thomas J. 1971. A Note on the "Accelerationist" Controversy. *Journal of Money, Credit, and Banking* (August) 3:721–25.

Scheinkman, J. A., and L. Weiss. 1983. Borrowing constraints and aggregate economic activity. Manuscript, University of Chicago.

Sinai, Allen. 1976. Credit crunches: An analysis of the postwar experience. In *Parameters and policies of the U.S. economy,* 244–74. ed. Otto Eckstein, Amsterdam: North-Holland.

———. 1978. Credit crunch possibilities and the crunch barometer. *Data Resources Review* (June): 9–18.

———. 1980. Crunch impacts and the aftermath. *Data Resources Review* (June): 37–60.

———. 1977. Financial instability: A discussion. In *Financial crises: Institutions and markets in a fragile environment,* ed. E. I. Altman and A. W. Sametz, 187–203. New York: Wiley.

Stiglitz, J., and A. Weiss. 1981. Credit rationing in markets with imperfect information. *American Economic Review* 71:393–410.

Townsend, R. 1982. Asset prices in a monetary economy. Manuscript, Carnegie-Mellon University.

———. 1984. Financial structures as communication devices. Manuscript, Carnegie-Mellon University.

Wojnilower, Albert. 1980. The central role of credit crunches in recent financial history. *Brookings Papers on Economic Activity* 2:277–340.

Zarnowitz, Victor. 1973. *Orders, production and investment: A cyclical and structural analysis*. New York: Columbia University Press.

2 Are Business Cycles All Alike?

Olivier J. Blanchard and Mark W. Watson

2.1 Introduction

The propagation impulse framework, which was introduced in economics by Frisch (1933) and Slutsky (1937) has come to dominate the analysis of economic fluctuations. Fluctuations in economic activity are seen as the result of small, white noise shocks—impulses—that affect the economy through a complex dynamic propagation system.[1] Much, if not most, empirical macroeconomic investigation has focused on the propagation mechanism. In this paper we focus on the characteristics of the impulses and the implications of these characteristics for business cycles.

It is convenient, if not completely accurate, to summarize existing research on impulses as centered on two independent but related ques-

Olivier J. Blanchard is professor of economics at Massachusetts Institute of Technology. Mark W. Watson is associate professor of economics at Harvard University.

We thank Rudiger Dornbusch, Stanley Fischer, Robert Hall, Pok-sang Lam, Lawrence Summers, Victor Zarnovitz, and participants in the Monetary and Fiscal Policy Seminar at Harvard University for discussions and suggestions. We also thank Pok-sang Lam for careful research assistance, and the National Bureau of Economic Research and the National Science Foundation for financial support.

1. This framework is only one of many that can generate fluctuations. Another one, which clearly underlies much of the early NBER work on cycles, is based on floor/ceiling dynamics, with a much smaller role for impulses. There are probably two reasons why the white noise impulse-linear propagation framework is now widely used. It is convenient to use both analytically and empirically, because of its close relation to linear time series analysis. Statistical evidence that would allow us to choose between the different frameworks has been hard to come by.

In the standard dynamic simultaneous equation model, impulses arise from the exogenous variables and the noise in the system. In the model we employ we do not distinguish between endogenous and exogenous variables. The entire system is driven by the innovations (the one step ahead forecast errors) in the variables. A portion of what we call "innovations" would be explained by current movements of exogenous variables in large macroeconomic models. For example, we find large negative "supply" innovations in late 1974. In a larger model these would be explained by oil import prices.

tions. The first question concerns the number of sources of impulses: Is there only one source of shocks to the economy, or are there many? Monetarists often single out monetary shocks as the main source of fluctuations;[2] this theme has been echoed recently by Lucas (1977) and examined empirically by the estimation of index or dynamic factor analysis models. The alternative view, that there are many, equally important, sources of shocks, seems to dominate most of the day-to-day discussions of economic fluctuations.

The second question concerns the way the shocks lead to large fluctuations. Are fluctuations in economic activity caused by an accumulation of small shocks, where each shock is unimportant if viewed in isolation, or are fluctuations due to infrequent large shocks? The first view derives theoretical support from Slutsky, who demonstrated that the accumulation of small shocks could generate data that mimicked the behavior of macroeconomic time series. It has been forcefully restated by Lucas (1977). The alternative view is less often articulated but clearly underlies many descriptions and policy discussions—that there are infrequent, large, identifiable shocks that dominate all others. Particular economic fluctuations can be ascribed to particular large shocks followed by periods during which the economy returns to equilibrium. Such a view is implicit in the description of specific periods such as the Vietnam War expansion, the oil price recession, or the Volcker disinflation.

The answers to both questions have important implications for economic theory, economic policy, and econometric practice. We cite three examples. The role of monetary policy is quite different if shocks are predominantly monetary or arise partly from policy and partly from the behavior of private agents. The discussion of rules versus discretion is also affected by the nature of shocks. If shocks are small and frequent, policy rules are clearly appropriate. If shocks are instead one of a kind, discretion appears more reasonable.[3] Finally, if infrequent large shocks are present in economic time series, then standard asymptotic approximations to the distribution of estimators may be poor, and robust methods of estimation may be useful.

This paper examines both questions, using two approaches to analyze the empirical evidence. The first is the natural, direct approach, in which we specify and estimate a structural model. This allows us to examine the characteristics of the shocks and to calculate their contributions to economic fluctuations. In section 2.2 we discuss the struc-

2. A supplement to the *Journal of Monetary Economics* was devoted to the analysis of the sources of impulses in different countries, using the Brunner/Meltzer approach. Conclusions vary somewhat across countries, but "measures expressing an unanticipated or accelerating monetary impulse figure foremost" (Brunner and Meltzer 1978, 14).

3. A good example of the importance of the nature of the shocks for the rules versus discretion debate is given by the answers of Lucas and Solow to the question, What should policy have been in 1973–75? in Fischer 1980.

tural model, the data, and the methodology in detail. In section 2.3 we present the empirical results. We conclude that fluctuations are due, in roughly equal proportions, to fiscal, money, demand, and supply shocks. We find substantial evidence against the small-shock hypothesis. What emerges, however, is not an economy characterized by large shocks and a gradual return to equilibrium, but rather an economy with a mixture of large and small shocks.

Our second approach to analyzing the data is an indirect one, which tests one of the implications of the small-shock hypothesis. If economic fluctuations arise from an accumulation of small shocks, business cycles must then be, in some precise sense, alike. We therefore look at how "alike" they are. The comparative advantage of the indirect approach is that it does not require specification of the structural model; its comparative disadvantage is that it may have low power against the large-shock hypothesis. It is very similar to the study by Burns and Mitchell (1946) of commonality and differences of business cycles. Instead of focusing on graphs, we focus on correlation coefficients between variables and an aggregate activity index. Although these correlation coefficients are less revealing than the Burns and Mitchell graphs, they do allow us to state hypotheses precisely and to carry out statistical tests. Our conclusions are somewhat surprising: business cycles are not at all alike. This, however, is not inconsistent with the small-shock hypothesis, and it provides only mild support in favor of the view that large specific events dominate individual cycles. These results cast doubt on the usefulness of making "the business cycle" a reference frame in the analysis of economic time series. These results are developed in section 2.4.

2.2 The Direct Approach: Methodology

2.2.1 The Structural Model

Let X_t be the vector of variables of interest. We assume that the dynamic behavior of X_t is given by the structural model:[4]

$$(1) \qquad X_t = \sum_{i=0}^{n} A_i X_{t-i} + \epsilon_t$$

$$E(\epsilon_t \epsilon_\tau) = D \text{ if } t = \tau$$

$$0 \text{ otherwise}$$

where D is a diagonal matrix.

---

4. We assume that the propagation mechanism is linear and time invariant. Violation of either of these assumptions would probably lead to estimated shocks whose distributions have tails thicker than the distribution of the true shocks.

Our vector X_t includes four variables. Two are the basic macroeconomic variables, the variables of ultimate interest—output and the price level. The other two are policy variables. The first is a monetary aggregate, M_1, the second is an index of fiscal policy. We shall describe them more precisely below.

The structural model is composed of four equations. The first two are aggregate demand and aggregate supply. The other two are equations describing policy; they are policy feedback rules. The vector ϵ_t is the vector of four structural disturbances. It includes aggregate supply and demand disturbances as well as the disturbances in fiscal and monetary policy. The matrices A_i, $i = 0, \ldots, n$ represent the propagation mechanism.

We assume that the structural disturbances are contemporaneously uncorrelated and that their covariance matrix, D, is diagonal. However, we do allow the matrix A_0 to differ from zero, so that each structural disturbance is allowed to affect all four variables contemporaneously.

Leaving aside for the movement the issue of identification and estimation of equation (1), we now see how we can formalize the different hypotheses about the nature of the disturbances.

2.2.2   Is There a Dominant Source of Disturbances?

There may be no single yes or no answer to this question. A specific source may dominate short-run movements in output but have little effect on medium- and long-run movements. One source may dominate prices movements, another may dominate output movements.

Variance decompositions are a natural set of statistics to use for shedding light on these questions. These decompositions show the proportion of the K-step ahead forecast error variance of each variable that can be attributed to each of the four shocks. By choosing different values of K, we can look at the effects of each structural disturbance on each variable in the short, medium, and long run.

2.2.3   Are There Infrequent Large Shocks?

A first, straightforward way of answering this question is to look at the distribution of disturbances—or more precisely the distribution of estimated residuals. The statement that there are infrequent large shocks can be interpreted as meaning that the probability density function of each shock has thick tails. A convenient measure of the thickness of tails is the kurtosis coefficient of the marginal distribution of each disturbance, $E[(\epsilon_{jt}/\sigma_j)^4]$. We shall compute these kurtosis coefficients. In addition we shall see whether we can relate the large realizations to specific historical events and fluctuations.

This first approach may, however, be too crude, for at least two reasons. The first is that a particular source of shocks may dominate a given time period, not because of a particular large realization but because of a sequence of medium-sized realizations of the same sign. The second reason is similar but more subtle. The system characterized by equation (1) is highly aggregated. Unless it can be derived by exact aggregation—and this is unlikely—it should be thought of as a low-dimensional representation of the joint behavior of the four variables X_t. In this case the "structural" disturbances ϵ will be linear combinations of current and lagged values of the underlying disturbances. An underlying "oil shock" may therefore appear as a sequence of negative realizations of the supply disturbance in equation (1). For both reasons, we go beyond the computation of kurtosis coefficients. For each time period we decompose the difference between each variable and its forecast constructed K periods before, into components due to realizations of each structural disturbance. If we choose K large enough, forecast errors mirror major fluctuations in output as identified by NBER. We can then see whether each of these fluctuations can be attributed to realizations of a specific structural disturbance, for example, whether the 1973–75 recession is mostly due to adverse supply shocks.

2.2.4 Identification and Estimation

Our approach to identification is to avoid as much as possible over-identifying but controversial restrictions. We impose no restrictions on the lag structure, that is, on $A_i, i = 1, \ldots, n$. We achieve identification by restrictions on A_0, the matrix characterizing contemporaneous relations between variables, and by assuming that the covariance matrix of structural disturbances, D, is diagonal. We now describe our approach and the data in more detail.

Choice of Variables

We use quarterly data for the period 1947:1 to 1982:4. Output, the price level, and monetary and fiscal variables are denoted Y, P, M, and G, respectively. Output, the price level and the monetary variable are the logarithms of real GNP, of the GNP deflator and of nominal M_1. The price and money variables are multiplied by four so that all structural disturbances have the interpretations of rates of change, at annual rates. The fiscal variable G, is an index that attempts to measure the effect of fiscal policy—that is, of government spending, deficits, and debt, on aggregate demand. It is derived from other work (Blanchard 1985) and is described in detail in appendix 2.2.

Reduced-Form Estimation

Since we impose no restrictions on the lag structure, A_i, $i = 1, \ldots, n$, we can proceed in two steps. The reduced form associated with equation (1) is given by:

$$(2) \qquad X_t = \sum_{i=1}^{n} B_i X_{t-i} + x_t$$

$$E(x_t x_y') = \Omega \qquad \text{if } t = \tau$$

$$= 0 \qquad \text{if } t \neq \tau$$

$$B_i = (I - A_0)^{-1} A_i \; ; \; \Omega = [(I - A_0)^{-1}] D [(I - A_0)^{-1}]'.$$

We first estimate the unconstrained reduced form (2). Under the large-shock hypothesis, some of the realizations of the ϵ_t and thus x_t may be large; we therefore use a method of estimation that may be more efficient than ordinary least squares (OLS) in this case. We use the bounded influence method developed by Krasker and Welsch (1982), which in effect decreases the weight given to observations with large realizations.[5] We choose a lag length, n, equal to 4.[6]

The vector x_t is the vector of unexpected movements in Y, P, M, and G. Let lower-case letters denote unexpected movements in these variables, so that this first step in estimation gives us estimated time series for y, p, m, and g.

Structural Estimation

The second step takes us from x to ϵ. Note that equations (1) and (2) imply:

$$(3) \qquad x = A_0 x + \epsilon.$$

Thus, to go from x to ϵ we need to specify and estimate A_0, the set of contemporaneous relations between the variables. We specify the following set of relations:

$$(4) \qquad y = b_1 p \qquad\qquad\quad + \epsilon^s \text{ (aggregate supply)}$$

$$(5) \qquad y = b_2 m - b_3 p + b_4 g + \epsilon^d \text{ (aggregate demand)}$$

$$(6) \qquad g = c_1 y + c_2 p \qquad\quad + \epsilon^g \text{ (fiscal rule)}$$

$$(7) \qquad m = c_3 y + c_4 p \qquad\quad + \epsilon^m \text{ (money rule)}$$

5. LAD or other robust M estimators could also have been used. In some circumstances OLS may be more efficient than the robust estimators because of the presence of lagged values.

6. Each equation in the vector autoregression included a constant and a linear time trend. When the vector autoregression was estimated without a time trend, the estimated residuals, x, were essentially unchanged.

We have chosen standard specifications for aggregate supply and demand. Output supplied is a function of the price level.[7] Output demanded is a function of nominal money, the price level, and fiscal policy; this should be viewed as the reduced form of an IS-LM model, so that ε^d is a linear combination of the IS and LM disturbances. The last two equations are policy rules, which allow the fiscal index and money to respond contemporaneously to output and the price level.[8]

Even with the zero restrictions on A_0 implicit in the equations above, the system of equations (4) to (7) is not identified. The model contains eight coefficients and four variances that must be estimated from the ten unique elements in Ω. To achieve identification, we use a priori information on two of the parameters.

Within a quarter, there is little or no discretionary response of fiscal policy to changes in prices and output. Most of the response depends on institutional arrangements, such as the structure of income tax rates, the degree and timing of indexation of transfer payments, and so on. Thus the coefficients c_1 and c_2 can be constructed directly; the details of the computations are given in appendix 2.2. Using these coefficients, we obtain $\hat{\varepsilon}^g$ from equation (6).

Given the two constructed coefficients c_1 and c_2, we now have six unknown coefficients and four variances to estimate using the ten unique elements in Ω. The model is just identified. Estimation proceeds as follows: $\hat{\varepsilon}^g$ is used as an instrument in equation (4) to obtain $\hat{\varepsilon}^s$; $\hat{\varepsilon}^g$ and $\hat{\varepsilon}^s$ are used as instruments in equation (7) to obtain $\hat{\varepsilon}^m$. Finally, $\hat{\varepsilon}^g$, $\hat{\varepsilon}^s$, and $\hat{\varepsilon}^m$ are used as instruments in equation (5) to obtain $\hat{\varepsilon}_d$.

The validity of these instruments at each stage depends on the plausibility of the assumption that the relevant disturbances are not correlated. Although we do not believe this is exactly the case, we find it plausible that they have a low correlation, so that our identification is approximately correct.

It may be useful to compare our method for identifying and estimating shocks with the more common method used in the vector autoregres-

---

7. A more detailed specification of aggregate supply, recognizing the effects of the price of materials would be:

$$y = d_1 p - d_2(p_m - p) + \epsilon^{ys}$$
$$p_m = d_3 p + d_4 y + \epsilon^{pm},$$

where supply depends on the price of materials, p_m, and the price level, and where in turn the nominal price of materials depends on the price level and the level of output. The two equations have, however, the same specification, and it is therefore impossible to identify separately the shocks to the price of materials and to supply ϵ^{pm} and ϵ^{ys}. Equation (4) is therefore the solved-out version of this two-equation system, and ϵ^s is a linear combination of these two shocks.

8. If money supply responds to interest rates directly rather than to output and prices, ϵ^m and ϵ^d will both depend partly on money demand shocks and thus will be correlated. Our estimation method will then attribute as much of the variance as possible to ϵ^m and incorporate the residual in ϵ^d.

sion literature. A common practice in that literature is to decompose, as we do, the forecast errors into a set of uncorrelated shocks. There the identification problem is solved by assuming that the matrix $(I - A_0)$ is triangular or can be made triangular by rearranging its rows. This yields a recursive structure that is efficiently estimated by OLS. We do not assume a recursive structure but rather impose four zero restrictions in addition to constructing two coefficients c_1 and c_2. Our method produces estimated disturbances much closer to true structural disturbances than would be obtained by imposing a recursive structure on the model.

2.3   The Direct Approach: Results

2.3.1   Reduced-Form Evidence

The first step is the estimation of the reduced form given by equation (2). The estimated B_i, $i = 1, \ldots, 4$ are of no particular interest. The estimated time series corresponding to unexpected movements of x— that is of y, m, p, and g—are of more interest. Table 2.1 gives, for y, m, p, and g, the value of residuals larger than 1.5 standard deviations in absolute value, as well as the associated standard deviation and estimated kurtosis.

The kurtosis coefficient of a normally distributed random variable is equal to 3. The 99% significance level of the kurtosis coefficient, for a sample of 120 observations drawn from a normal distribution, is 4.34. Thus, ignoring the fact that these are estimated residuals rather than actual realizations, three of the four disturbances have significantly fat tails. Since linear combinations of independent random variables have kurtosis smaller than the maximum kurtosis of the variables themselves, this strongly suggests large kurtosis of the structural disturbances.[9] We now turn to structural estimation.

2.3.2   The Structural Coefficients

The second step is estimation of A_0, from equations (4) to (7). We use constructed values for c_1 and c_2 of -0.34 and -1.1 respectively. Unexpected increases in output increase taxes more than expenditures and lead to fiscal contraction. Unexpected inflation increases real taxes but decreases real expenditures, leading also to fiscal contraction. We are less confident of c_2, the effect of inflation, than we are of c_1. In

9. A more precise statement is the following: Let X_1 and X_2 be independent variables with kurtosis K_1 and K_2, one of which is greater than or equal to 3. Then if Z is a linear combination of X_1 and X_2, $K_Z \leq \max (K_1, K_2)$. We do not, however, assume independence but only assume zero correlation of the structural disturbances.

Table 2.1   **Large Reduced-Form Disturbances**

Date	y	g	m	p
1948:4				−2.6
1949:1				−2.2
1949:4	−2.4			
1950:1	3.2	2.6		
1950:2		−5.1		1.6
1950:3	1.8	−1.6		5.1
1951:1				3.7
1951:2		4.2		−2.8
1951:3		2.2		−1.6
1951:4			1.6	
1952:2		1.6		
1952:3		1.7		
1952:4	1.6			
1953:1		1.6		
1953:4				−1.6
1954:1	−1.7			2.1
1958:1	−2.2			
1959:1		−1.8		
1959:3	−2.7			
1959:4			−2.9	
1960:1	2.2	−2.7		
1960:4	−1.9			
1962:3			−1.5	
1965:4	1.6			
1966:3			−2.2	
1967:3			1.8	
1970:4	−1.8			
1971:3	−1.6			
1972:2				−1.5
1972:4		1.7		
1974:4	−1.6			1.7
1975:1	−3.1			
1975:2		3.6		−1.7
1975:3		−3.1		
1975:4			−1.6	
1978:2	2.2			2.1
1979:2			1.7	
1980:2	−2.5		−4.2	
1980:3	2.4		4.7	
1981:3			−3.5	
1982:4			3.0	
Standard error	.0085	.0431	.0244	.0182
Kurtosis	4.0	10.2	8.6	8.2

Note: Ratios of residuals to standard errors are reported.

appendix 2.1 we report alternative structural coefficient estimates based on $c_2 = -1.3$ and $c_2 = -1.0$.

The results of estimating equations (4) to (7) are reported in table 2.2. All coefficients except one are of the expected sign. Nominal money has a negative contemporaneous effect on output; this is consistent with a positive correlation between unexpected movements in money and output because of the positive effect of output on money supply. Indeed the correlation m and y is .32. (Anticipating results below, we find that the effect of nominal money on output is positive after one quarter.) Aggregate supply is upward sloping; a comparison with the results of table 2.A.1 suggests that the slope of aggregate supply is sensitive to the value of c_2.

Given our estimates of the reduced form and of A_0, we can now decompose each variable (Y, P, M, G) as the sum of four distributed lags of each of the structural disturbances ϵ^d, ϵ^s, ϵ^m, and ϵ^g. Technically, we can compute the structural moving average representation of the system characterized by equation (1).

2.3.3   One or Many Sources of Shocks? Variance Decomposition

Does one source of shocks dominate? We have seen that a natural way of answering this question is to characterize the contribution of each disturbance to the unexpected movement in each variable. We define unexpected movement as the difference between the actual value of a variable and the forecast constructed K periods earlier using equation (1). We use three values of K. The first case, $K = 1$, decomposes the variance of y, p, m, and g into their four components, the variances of ϵ^d, ϵ^s, ϵ^m and ϵ^g. The other two values, $K = 4$ and $K = 20$, correspond to the medium run and the long run respectively.

The results are reported in table 2.3. Demand shocks dominate output in the short run; supply shocks dominate price in the short run. In the

Table 2.2   Structural Estimates

Fiscal[a]	$g = -.34y - 1.1p$	$+ \epsilon^g$
Money supply	$m = 1.40y + .19p$	$+ \epsilon^m$
	$\quad\;\;(1.4)^{[b]}\quad (.7)$	
Aggregate supply	$y = .81p$	$+ \epsilon^s$
	$\quad\;(1.1)$	
Aggregate demand	$y = -.10p - .20m + .06g$	$+ \epsilon^d$
	$\quad\;(-3.1)\quad (-2.2)\;(2.4)$	

Standard deviations

	ϵ^g	ϵ^m	ϵ^s	ϵ^d
	.041	.024	.017	.011

[a]Coefficients constructed, not estimated.
[b]t-statistics in parentheses.

Table 2.3   **Variance Decompositions**

	Structural Disturbance			
	ϵ^g	ϵ^s	ϵ^m	ϵ^d
Contemporaneously				
$Y - E_{-1}Y$	.03	.19	.04	.74
$G - E_{-1}G$	.78	.14	.00	.08
$M - E_{-1}M$	.01	.01	.74	.25
$P - E_{-1}P$	.01	.74	.01	.24
Four quarters ahead				
$Y - E_{-4}Y$	.15	.16	.16	.54
$G - E_{-4}G$	.70	.13	.00	.16
$M - E_{-4}M$	.13	.03	.67	.17
$P - E_{-4}P$	.01	.65	.01	.33
Twenty quarters ahead				
$Y - E_{-20}Y$	.27	.20	.17	.37
$G - E_{-20}G$	.66	.12	.05	.17
$M - E_{-20}M$	.28	.04	.64	.05
$P - E_{-20}P$	.15	.22	.36	.26

medium and long run, however, *all four shocks are important in explaining the behavior of output and prices.* There is no evidence in support of the one dominant source of shocks theory.

2.3.4 Are There Infrequent Large Shocks? I

Table 2.4 reports values and dates for all estimated realizations of $\epsilon^d, \epsilon^s, \epsilon^m$ and ϵ^g larger than 1.5 times their respective standard deviation. We can compare these with traditional, informal accounts of the history of economic fluctuations since 1948 and see whether specific events that have been emphasized there correspond to large realizations. A useful, concise summary of the events associated with large postwar fluctuations is contained in table 1.1 in the paper by Eckstein and Sinai in this volume (chap. 1).

The first major expansion in our sample, from 1949:4 to 1953:2, is usually explained both by fiscal shocks associated with the Korean War and by a sharp increase in private spending. We find evidence of both in 1951 and in 1952. From 1955 to the early 1970s, large shocks are few and not easily interpretable. There are, for example, no large shocks to either fiscal policy or private spending corresponding to either the Kennedy tax cut or the Vietnam War. In the 1970s, major fluctuations are usually explained by the two oil shocks. There is some evidence in favor of this description. We find two large supply shocks in 1974:4 and 1975:1; we also find large fiscal and large demand shocks during

Table 2.4   **Large Structural Disturbances**

Date	Fiscal	Supply	Money	Demand
1948:3	1.9			
1948:4		2.5		
1949:1	−1.5			−1.9
1949:4				−1.8
1950:1	3.0	1.8		2.0
1950:2	−4.6	−1.6		
1950:3		−3.7		3.6
1951:1	1.7	−3.6		
1951:2	3.1	3.2		
1951:3	1.6	1.8		
1951:4			1.6	
1952:2	1.5			
1952:3	2.0			
1952:4				1.7
1953:4				−1.6
1954:1		−2.8		
1954:3		1.8		
1957:4				−1.7
1958:1		−1.5		−1.7
1958:3	1.7			
1959:1		−1.6		
1959:3				−2.3
1959:4			−2.6	
1960:1	−2.6			2.4
1960:3			1.5	
1960:4				−2.0
1966:3			−2.2	
1968:4			1.5	
1971:2			2.1	
1971:3				−1.8
1972:2		1.6		
1972:4	1.7			
1974:4		−2.4		
1975:1		−2.5		−2.4
1975:2	3.1	1.9		
1975:3	−3.1			
1975:4			−1.8	
1978:2				2.7
1979:2			1.6	
1980:2		−2.1	−3.2	−2.7
1980:3			3.4	3.4
1981:2			1.6	
1981:3			−3.8	
1982:1			1.6	
1982:4			3.7	

the same period. The two recessions of the early 1980s are usually ascribed to monetary policy. We find substantial evidence in favor of this description. There are large shocks to money supply for most of the period 1979:2 to 1982:4 and two very large negative shocks in 1980:2 and 1981:3.

The overall impression is therefore one of infrequent large shocks, but not so large as to dominate all others and the behavior of aggregate variables for long periods. To confirm this impression, we report the kurtosis coefficients of the structural disturbances in table 2.5A; in all cases we can reject normality with high confidence. In table 2.5B we use another descriptive device. We assume that each structural disturbance is an independent draw from a mixed normal distribution, that is for $x = g, d, s,$ or m:

$$\epsilon^x = \epsilon_1^x \qquad \text{with probability } 1 - P_x$$
$$\epsilon^x = \epsilon_2^x \qquad \text{with probability } P_x$$

where

$$\epsilon_1^x \sim N(0,\sigma_{1x}^2) \,, \; \epsilon_2^x \sim N(0,\sigma_{2x}^2) \,.$$
$$\sigma_{1x}^2 < \sigma_{2x}^2$$

The realization of each disturbance is drawn either from a normal distribution with large variance, with probability P, or from a normal distribution with small variance, with probability $1 - P$. The estimated values of $\sigma_{1x}, \sigma_{2x}, P_x,$ estimated by maximum likelihood, are reported in table 2.5B. The results suggest large, but not very large, ratios of the standard deviation of large to the standard deviation of small shocks; they also suggest infrequent, but not very infrequent, large shocks. The estimated probabilities imply that one out of six fiscal or money shocks and one out of three supply or demand shocks came from the large variance distributions.

Table 2.5   Characteristics of Structural Disturbances

	ϵ^g	ϵ^s	ϵ^m	ϵ^d
A. Estimated kurtosis				
K	7.0	5.4	5.9	4.6
B. Disturbances as mixed normals				
σ_1	.68	.63	.72	.68
	(.08)[a]	(.10)	(.09)	(.13)
σ_2	2.01	1.62	1.97	1.50
	(.64)	(.41)	(1.03)	(.41)
Ratio	2.95	2.57	2.73	2.21
Probability	.15	.27	.14	.30
	(.09)	(.15)	(.15)	(.22)

[a]Standard errors in parentheses.

The dating of the large shocks in table 2.4 suggests two more characteristics of shocks. First, large shocks tend to be followed by large shocks, suggesting some form of autoregressive conditional heteroskedasticity as discussed in Engle (1982). Second, there seems to be some tendency for large shocks to happen in unison. In 1950:1, for example, we find large fiscal, supply, and demand shocks, whereas in 1980:3 we find large supply, money, and demand shocks. To confirm these impressions we present in table 2.6 the correlations and first autocorrelations between the squares of the structural shocks.[10] The table shows a large positive contemporaneous correlation between the square of the supply shock and the square of the demand shock. A weaker contemporaneous relationship between supply and the fiscal shock is present. The squares of all shocks are positively correlated with their own lagged values; there is also significant correlation between demand, the lagged fiscal and supply shocks, and the fiscal shock and lagged supply shock. All in all, these results suggest an economy characterized by active, volatile periods followed by quiet, calm periods, both of varied duration.

2.3.5 Are There Infrequent Large Shocks? II

We discussed in section 2.2 the possibility that a specific source of shocks may dominate some episode of economic fluctuations, even if there are no large realizations of the shock. To explore this possibility, we construct an unexpected output series, where the expectations are the forecasts of output based on the estimated model corresponding to equation (1), eight quarters before. We chose eight quarters because the troughs and peaks in this unexpected output series correspond closely to NBER troughs and peaks. We then decompose this forecast

Table 2.6   **Correlations between Squares of Structural Disturbances**

	$(\epsilon^g)^2$	$(\epsilon^s)^2$	$(\epsilon^m)^2$	$(\epsilon^d)^2$
$(\epsilon^g)^2$	—	.27	−.05	.08
$(\epsilon^s)^2$		—	−.01	.36
$(\epsilon^m)^2$			—	.28
$(\epsilon^d)^2$				—
$(\epsilon^g_{-1})^2$	.33	.43	.00	.33
$(\epsilon^s_{-1})^2$	.35	.38	.03	.13
$(\epsilon^m_{-1})^2$	.02	−.09	.23	.21
$(\epsilon^d_{-1})^2$	.15	.08	.13	.16

10. Although the contemporaneous correlation between the levels of the shock is zero by construction, the same is not true of the squares of the shocks.

error for GNP into components due to each of the four structural disturbances. This decomposition is represented graphically in figure 2.1; the corresponding time series are given in table 2.A.2 in appendix 2.1.

No single recession can be attributed to only one source of shock. Post-war recessions appear to be due to the combination of two or three shocks. The 1960:4 trough, for example, where the GNP forecast error is -6.7%, is attributed to a fiscal shock component (-2.4%), a supply shock component (-1.1%), a money shock component (-1.7%), and a demand shock component (-1.4%). The 1975:1 trough, where the GNP forecast error is also -6.7%, seems to have a large supply shock component (-3.6%) and a demand shock component (-2.9%). The 1982:4 trough, where the GNP forecast error is -4.5%, is decomposed as -1.4% (fiscal), 1.1% (supply), -1.4% (money), and -2.8% (demand).

To summarize the results of this section, we find substantial evidence against the single source of shock hypothesis. We find some evidence of large infrequent shocks; however, they do not seem to dominate economic fluctuations.

2.4   The Indirect Approach

If economic fluctuations are due to an accumulation of small shocks, then in some sense business cycles should all be alike. In this section we make precise the sense in which cycles should be alike and examine the empirical evidence.

The most influential contribution to the position that cycles are alike is the empirical work carried out by Burns and Mitchell (1946) on pre–World War II data. Their work focused not only on the characteristic cyclical behavior of many economic variables but also on how, in specific cycles, the behavior of these variables differed from their characteristic cyclical behavior. Looking at their graphs, one is impressed at how similar the behavior of most variables is across different cycles; this is true not only of quantities, for which it may not be too surprising, but also, for example, of interest rates.

We considered extending the Burns/Mitchell graph method to the eight postwar cycles but decided against it. Many steps of the method, and in particular their time deformation, are judgmental rather than mechanical. As a result, it is impossible to derive the statistical properties of their results. When comparing the graphs of short rates across two cycles, for example, we have no statistical yardstick to decide whether they are similar or significantly different. As a result also, we do not know which details, in the wealth of details provided in these graphs, should be thought of as significant.

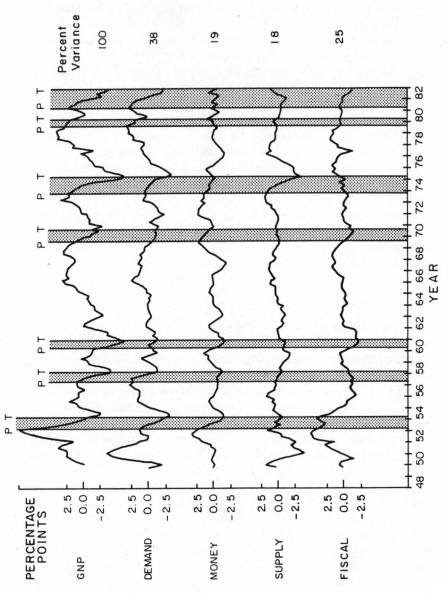

Fig. 2.1   Components of GNP forecast error.

Therefore we use an approach that is in the spirit of Burns and Mitchell but allows us to derive the statistical properties of the estimators we use. The trade-off is that the statistics we give are much less revealing than the Burns/Mitchell graphs. Our approach is to compute the cross-correlations at different leads and lags between various variables and a reference variable such as GNP, across different cycles.

2.4.1   The Construction of Correlation Coefficients

The first step is to divide the sample into subsamples. We adopt the standard division into cycles, with trough points determined by the NBER chronology. This division may not be, under the large-shock hypothesis, the most appropriate, since a large shock may well dominate parts of two cycles. It is, however, the least controversial. Defining the trough-to-trough period as a cycle, there are seven complete cycles for which we have data; their dates are given in table 2.7. This gives us seven subsamples.

For each subsample, we compute cross-correlations at various leads and lags between the reference variable and the variable considered. Deterministic seasonality is removed from all variables before the calculation of the correlations. A more difficult issue is that of the time trend: the series may be generated either by a deterministic time trend or by a stochastic time trend or by both. In the previous two sections, this issue was unimportant in the sense that inclusion or exclusion of a deterministic trend together with unconstrained lag structures in the reduced form made little difference to estimated realizations of the disturbances. Here the issue is much more important. Computing deviations from a single deterministic trend for the whole sample may be very misleading if the trend is stochastic. On the other hand, taking first or second differences of the time series probably removes nonstationarities associated with a stochastic trend, but correlations between first or second differences of the time series are difficult to interpret.

In their work, Burns and Mitchell adopt an agnostic and flexible solution to that problem: they compute deviations of the variables from subsample means. Thus they proxy the time trend by a step function. Although this does not capture the time trend within each subsample, it does imply that across subsamples, the estimated time trend will track the underlying one. We initially followed Burns and Mitchell in their formalization but found this procedure to be misleading for variables with strong time trends. During each subsample, both the reference and the other variable are below their means at the beginning and above their means at the end; this generates spuriously high correlation between the variables. We modify the Burns/Mitchell procedure as follows: for each subsample, we allow for both a level and a time trend; the time trend is given by the slope of the line going from trough to trough. This should be thought of as a flexible (perhaps too flexible) parameterization of the time trend, allowing for six level and slope changes over the complete sample.

The cross-correlations are then computed for deviations of each of the two series from its trend. We compute correlations of the reference variable and of the other variable, up to two leads and lags.

2.4.2   The Construction of Confidence Levels

For each variable we calculate cross-correlations with our reference variable, GNP, for each of the seven cycles. We then want to answer the following questions: Should we be surprised by the differences in estimated correlation across cycles? More precisely, under the null hypothesis that fluctuations are due to the accumulation of small shocks, how large are these differences in the correlation coefficients likely to be? Thus, we must derive the distribution of the differences between the largest and smallest correlation coefficients, at each lag or lead for each variable. This distribution is far too difficult to derive analytically; instead we rely on Monte Carlo simulations.

The first step is to estimate, for each variable, the bivariate process generating the reference variable and the variable under consideration. We allow for four lags of each variable and a linear time trend, for the period 1947:1 to 1982:4. The method of estimation is, for the same reasons as in section 2.2, Krasker-Welsch.

The second step is to simulate the bivariate process, using disturbances drawn from a *normal* distribution for disturbances. (Thus we implicitly characterize the "small-shock" hypothesis as a hypothesis that this joint distribution is normal.) We generate 1,000 samples of 147 observations each. We then divide each sample into cycles by identifying troughs in the GNP series. Let x_t denote the log of real GNP at time t. Time t is a trough if two conditions are satisfied. The first is that $x_{t-1} > x_t < x_{t+1} < x_{t+2} < x_{t+3}$, and the second that x_t be at least 0.5 % below the previous peak value of x. The first ensures that expansions are longer than three periods, and the second eliminates minor downturns. (When applied to the actual sample, this rule correctly identifies NBER troughs, except for two that differ from the NBER trough by one quarter.) Given this division into cycles, we compute, as in the actual sample, cycle-specific correlations and obtain, for each of the 1,000 samples, the difference between the largest and the smallest correlation. Finally, by looking at the 1,000 samples, we get an empirical distribution for the differences.

What we report in table 2.7 for each variable and for correlations at each lead and lag are probabilities that in the corresponding empirical distributions the difference between the largest and smallest correlation exceeds the value of this difference in the actual sample. This probability is denoted *p*. *A very small value of p indicates that the difference observed in the actual sample is surprisingly large under the small-shock hypothesis.* It would therefore be evidence against the small-shock hypothesis.

2.4.3   The Choice of Variables

Most quantity variables, such as consumption or investment, appear highly correlated with real GNP. Most of the models we have imply that it should be so, nearly irrespective of the source of shocks. Most models imply that correlations of prices and interest rates with GNP will be of different signs depending on the source of shocks. We report results for various prices, interest rates, policy variables, and quantities.

We look at *three real wages*. In all three cases, the numerator is the same, the index of average hourly earnings of production and nonsupervisory workers, adjusted for overtime and interindustry shifts, in manufacturing. In table 2.7A, the wage is deflated by the GNP deflator. In table 2.7B, it is deflated by the CPI and is therefore a consumption real wage. In table 2.7C, it is deflated by the producer price index for manufacturers and is therefore a product wage. In all three cases, we take the logarithm of the real wage so constructed.

We then look at *two relative prices*. Both are relative prices of materials in terms of finished goods. Because of the two oil shocks, we consider two different prices. The first is the ratio of the price of crude fuel to the producer price index for finished goods and is studied in table 2.7D. Table 2.7E gives the behavior of the price of nonfood, nonfuel materials in terms of finished goods.

We then look at the behavior of *interest rates*. Table 2.7F characterizes the behavior of the nominal three month treasury bill rate. Table 2.7G gives the behavior of Moody's AAA corporate bond yield.

We consider the two *policy variables:* the fiscal index defined in the first section, and nominal M_1. The results are given in tables 2.7H and I.

Finally, we consider three quantity variables. Table 2.7J shows the behavior of real consumption expenditures. Table 2.7K and L shows the behavior of nonresidential and residential investment.

2.4.4   General Results

In looking at table 2.7, there are two types of questions we want to answer. The first is not directly the subject of the paper but is clearly of interest. It is about the typical behavior of each variable in the cycle. The answer is given for each variable by the sequence of average correlation coefficients at the different lags and leads.

Table 2.7   **Correlations**

Cycle	Trough to Trough	Peak
1	1949:4 to 1954:2	1953:2
2	1954:2 to 1958:2	1957:3
3	1958:2 to 1961:1	1960:2
4	1961:1 to 1970:4	1969:4
5	1970:4 to 1975:1	1973:4
6	1975:1 to 1980:2	1979:4
7	1980:2 to 1982:4	1981:2

ρ_i = correlation between the reference variable, logarithm of real GNP at time t, and the other variable at time $t + i$.

Real Wages

A. Real wage in terms of the GNP deflator (in log)

Cycle	ρ_{-2}	ρ_{-1}	ρ_0	ρ_{+1}	ρ_{+2}
1	−.81	−.70	−.36	−.25	.09
2	−.06	−.41	−.48	−.18	.44
3	−.17	.02	.03	−.35	−.59
4	−.11	−.13	−.01	−.04	−.00
5	.85	.90	.90	.65	.37
6	.75	.84	.84	.75	.63
7	.62	.61	.06	−.29	−.38
Average	−.15	−.16	.14	.04	.08
Difference	1.67	1.61	1.38	1.10	1.22
p	.04	.07	.27	.65	.52

B. Real wage in terms of the CPI (in log)

Cycle	ρ_{-2}	ρ_{-1}	ρ_0	ρ_{+1}	ρ_{+2}
1	−.53	−.58	−.57	−.64	−.57
2	.09	.44	.79	.85	.76
3	−.15	.29	.75	.47	−.07
4	.56	.57	.63	.56	.49
5	.84	.67	.47	.02	−.31
6	.78	.89	.88	.78	.65
7	.57	.32	−.31	−.53	−.24
Average	.30	.37	.37	.21	.10
Difference	1.37	1.47	1.45	1.49	1.34
p	.48	.31	.32	.22	.49

C. Real wage in terms of the PPI (in log)

Cycle	ρ_{-2}	ρ_{-1}	ρ_0	ρ_{+1}	ρ_{+2}
1	−.68	−.71	−.63	−.55	−.28
2	.17	.60	.91	.88	.63
3	−.29	.45	.87	.62	.27
4	−.46	−.56	−.62	−.72	−.76
5	.88	.74	.52	.08	−.27
6	.78	.86	.82	.71	.59
7	−.42	−.70	−.72	−.60	.01
Average	−.02	.09	.16	.06	.02
Difference	1.57	1.57	1.62	1.61	1.40
p	.17	.18	.13	.11	.44

Table 2.7   (continued)

Relative Prices

D. Relative price of crude fuels in terms of finished goods (in log)

Cycle	ρ_{-2}	ρ_{-1}	ρ_0	ρ_{+1}	ρ_{+2}
1	−.65	−.61	−.45	−.43	−.19
2	−.25	−.04	.09	.31	.41
3	−.07	.45	.42	.46	.17
4	−.61	−.75	−.86	−.91	−.91
5	−.66	−.86	−.91	−.81	−.63
6	.47	.46	.35	.34	.44
7	−.56	−.39	−.23	−.16	−.01
Average	−.33	−.24	−.22	−.17	−.10
Difference	1.13	1.33	1.33	1.37	1.35
p	.56	.39	.39	.30	.38

E. Relative price of nonfood/nonfuel materials in terms of finished goods (in log)

Cycle	ρ_{-2}	ρ_{-1}	ρ_0	ρ_{+1}	ρ_{+2}
1	.62	.66	.56	.30	−.12
2	.17	.69	.92	.78	.51
3	.32	.75	.89	.64	.24
4	.09	.06	.02	−.16	−.35
5	−.06	.28	.62	.82	.89
6	−.75	−.77	−.58	−.40	−.23
7	−.02	.59	.92	.82	.32
Average	.05	.32	.47	.40	.18
Difference	1.38	1.53	1.51	1.22	1.24
p	.32	.16	.15	.37	.56

Interest Rates

F. Three-month treasury bill rate

Cycle	ρ_{-2}	ρ_{-1}	ρ_0	ρ_{+1}	ρ_{+2}
1	−.20	.22	.68	.86	.88
2	−.30	.02	.56	.83	.84
3	−.29	.33	.71	.83	.67
4	−.15	−.01	.20	.36	.49
5	−.26	.05	.40	.69	.84
6	−.56	−.42	−.07	−.23	.39
7	−.42	.41	.71	−.58	−.46
Average	−.31	.60	.45	.62	.65
Difference	.41	.83	.79	.62	.49
p	.94	.64	.70	.77	.88

G. AAA corporate bonds yield

Cycle	ρ_{-2}	ρ_{-1}	ρ_0	ρ_{+1}	ρ_{+2}
1	−.54	−.03	.44	.66	.70
2	−.65	−.35	.16	.32	.38
3	.12	.69	.90	.69	.29
4	−.79	−.71	−.62	−.48	−.30
5	−.88	−.73	−.52	−.08	.19
6	−.82	−.87	−.68	−.48	−.29
7	−.72	−.10	.42	.62	.80
Average	−.61	−.30	.01	.17	.25
Difference	1.00	1.56	1.58	1.17	1.11
p	.55	.13	.25	.63	.67

(continued)

Table 2.7   (continued)

Policy Variables

H. Fiscal index

Cycle	ρ_{-2}	ρ_{-1}	ρ_0	ρ_{+1}	ρ_{+2}
1					
2	−.49	−.31	−.03	.12	.58
3	−.43	−.74	−.89	−.67	−.32
4	.73	.45	−.01	−.46	−.74
5	.40	.36	.28	.14	.04
6	−.10	−.20	−.35	−.67	−.63
7	.51	−.08	−.55	−.54	−.47
Average	.09	−.07	−.22	−.29	−.22
Difference	1.22	1.19	1.17	.81	1.32
p	.56	.61	.70	.92	.51

I. Nominal money, log of Ml

Cycle	ρ_{-2}	ρ_{-1}	ρ_0	ρ_{+1}	ρ_{+2}
1	.07	.44	.71	.76	.67
2	.59	.94	.92	.53	.02
3	.68	.73	.69	.40	−.08
4	−.46	−.38	−.31	−.17	−.05
5	.71	.88	.94	.80	.50
6	.08	.23	.53	.64	.74
7	.83	.87	.43	.11	−.16
Average	.35	.53	.56	.44	.23
Difference	1.29	1.32	1.25	.97	.90
p	.23	.14	.21	.65	.89

Quantity Variables

J. Logarithm of real consumption expenditures

Cycle	ρ_{-2}	ρ_{-1}	ρ_0	ρ_{+1}	ρ_{+2}
1	.22	.35	.32	−.02	−.46
2	.47	.78	.97	.72	.23
3	−.03	.61	.90	.84	.33
4	.69	.78	.88	.91	.90
5	.87	.96	.88	.59	.26
6	.69	.83	.96	.76	.60
7	.39	.86	.91	.40	−.03
Average	.47	.74	.83	.60	.26
Difference	.90	.61	.65	.93	1.36
p	.73	.69	.42	.54	.35

K. Logarithm of real residential investment expenditures

Cycle	ρ_{-2}	ρ_{-1}	ρ_0	ρ_{+1}	ρ_{+2}
1	.34	.18	−.09	−.49	−.82
2	.77	.71	.55	−.00	−.50
3	.31	.78	.92	.65	.08
4	.02	−.01	−.11	−.29	−.47
5	.91	.88	.78	.43	−.01
6	.73	.86	.94	.73	.52
7	.72	.93	.68	.16	−.37
Average	.54	.62	.52	.17	−.22
Difference	.91	.94	1.05	1.21	1.34
p	.58	.38	.28	.22	.17

Table 2.7   (continued)

L. Logarithm of real nonresidential investment expenditures

Cycle	ρ_{-2}	ρ_{-1}	ρ_0	ρ_1	ρ_2
1	.30	.50	.63	.39	−.19
2	.02	.45	.86	.90	.75
3	−.65	−.23	.28	.81	.84
4	.75	.83	.89	.91	.87
5	.38	.68	.92	.97	.89
6	.39	.53	.77	.88	.89
7	−.58	.08	.64	.88	.84
Average	.09	.41	.71	.82	.70
Difference	1.40	1.06	.64	.58	1.08
p	.15	.41	.52	.53	.39

How do these sequences relate to Burns/Mitchell graphs? The relation is roughly the following: if the sequence is flat and close to zero, the variable has little cyclical behavior. If the sequence is flat and positive, the variable is procyclical, peaking at the cycle peak; if flat and negative, it is countercyclical, reaching its trough at the cycle peak.

If the sequence is not flat, the variable has cyclical behavior but reaches its peak, or its trough if countercyclical, before or after the cyclical peak. If, for example, ρ_{-1} is large and negative, this suggests that the variable is countercyclical, reaching its trough one quarter before the cyclical peak. As expected, the quantity variables are procyclical; there seems to be a tendency for nonresidential investment to lag GNP by one quarter and residential investment to lead GNP by one quarter. We find little average cyclical behavior of real wages. Relative fuel prices and long-term interest rates are countercyclical and lead GNP by at least two quarters. Relative nonfood/ nonfuel materials and short-term rates appear to be procyclical. We now turn to the second question, which is one of the subjects of this paper. How different are the correlations, and are these differences surprising?

The first part of the answer is that *correlations are very different across cycles*. This is true both for variables with little cyclical behavior, such as the real wage, and for variables that vary cyclically, such as nominal rates. These differences suggest that business cycles are indeed not all alike. The second part of the answer may, however, also be surprising: it is that *under the small-shock hypothesis, such differences are not unusual*. For most correlations and most variables, the p values are not particularly small. Thus the tentative conclusion of this section is that, although business cycles are not very much alike, their differences are not inconsistent with the hypothesis of the accumulation of small shocks through an invariant propagation mechanism.

2.5 Conclusions

In sections 2.2 and 2.4 we specified and estimated a structural model that allowed us to directly investigate the properties of shocks and their role in economic fluctuations. From this analysis we conclude that fluctuations are due, in roughly equal proportions, to fiscal, money, demand, and supply shocks. We find substantial evidence against the small-shock hypothesis. What emerges, however, is not an economy characterized by large shocks and a gradual return to equilibrium, but rather an economy with a mixture of large and small shocks.

In section 2.4 we investigated the influence of shocks on economic fluctuations in an indirect way by examining stability of correlations between different economic variables across all of the postwar business cycles. Here we found that correlations were very unstable—that business cycles were not at all alike. This, however, is not inconsistent wtih the small-shock hypothesis and provides only mild support for the view that large specific events dominate the characteristics of individual cycles. These results cast doubt on the usefulness of using "the business cycle" as a reference frame in the analysis of economic time series.

Appendix 2.1

Table 2.A.1   **Alternative Structural Estimates**

$c_2 = 1.3$

Fiscal	$g =$	$-.34y - 1.3p$		$+ \epsilon^g$
Money supply	$m =$	$1.20y + .22p$		$+ \epsilon^m$
Aggregate supply	$y =$	$.45y$		$+ \epsilon^s$
Aggregate demand	$y =$	$.09g - .10m - .40p$		$+ \epsilon^d$
Standard deviations	ϵ^g	ϵ^m	ϵ^s	ϵ^d
	.041	.024	.011	.014

$c_1 = 1.0$

Fiscal	$g =$	$-.34y - 1.0p$		$+ \epsilon^g$
Money supply	$m =$	$1.52y + .14p$		$+ \epsilon^m$
Aggregate supply	$y =$	$1.40p$		$+ \epsilon^s$
Aggregate demand	$y =$	$.05g - .10m - .09p$		$+ \epsilon^d$
Standard deviations	ϵ^g	ϵ^m	ϵ^s	ϵ^d
	.040	.029	.027	.010

Table 2.A.2   Decomposition of Eight-Quarter Forecast Errors for GNP

Date	GNP	Eg	Es	Em	Ed
1950:1	−0.31	0.53	1.72	−0.17	−2.40
1950:2	1.09	0.29	1.12	0.11	−0.43
1950:3	1.99	−1.68	−0.30	0.16	3.81
1950:4	2.56	−0.76	−2.15	0.01	5.46
1951:1	2.44	0.41	−4.10	−0.27	6.41
1951:2	2.52	1.31	−3.59	−0.39	5.19
1951:3	3.65	2.07	−2.37	0.29	3.66
1951:4	3.05	2.83	−2.06	0.40	1.88
1952:1	1.33	1.39	−2.74	1.55	1.13
1952:2	4.47	4.55	−1.99	2.02	−0.12
1952:3	7.00	4.82	−0.62	2.97	−0.17
1952:4	8.85	5.16	−0.27	3.14	0.81
1953:1	9.98	4.65	1.51	2.70	1.12
1953:2	6.31	3.47	0.44	1.46	0.94
1953:3	2.81	2.85	−0.39	0.47	−0.12
1953:4	1.10	3.09	0.50	−0.85	−1.64
1954:1	−0.39	4.14	−0.56	−1.41	−2.56
1954:2	−2.66	3.27	−0.66	−1.64	−3.62
1954:3	−2.76	1.79	0.25	−1.53	−3.26
1954:4	−0.75	1.17	0.75	−0.70	−1.96
1955:1	0.44	0.03	0.54	0.00	−0.14
1955:2	0.83	−0.55	0.37	0.31	0.70
1955:3	2.08	−0.64	0.75	0.55	1.42
1955:4	1.12	−1.24	0.57	0.32	1.48
1956:1	0.64	−2.01	1.62	−0.21	1.24
1956:2	0.76	−1.60	1.44	−0.34	1.27
1956:3	−0.21	−1.26	0.47	−0.59	1.18
1956:4	0.78	−1.04	0.47	−0.70	2.04
1957:1	0.85	−1.37	0.24	−0.69	2.67
1957:2	0.74	−1.04	0.45	−0.80	2.13
1957:3	0.25	−1.55	0.04	−0.70	2.45
1957:4	−1.44	−1.13	−0.13	−0.86	0.69
1958:1	−4.20	−0.86	−0.54	−1.44	−1.35
1958:2	−4.48	−0.86	−0.55	−1.38	−1.69
1958:3	−2.85	−0.57	−0.25	−0.57	−1.46
1958:4	−1.07	0.30	−0.58	−0.11	−0.68
1959:1	−0.78	−0.14	−1.07	0.30	0.13
1959:2	0.09	0.08	−1.68	0.69	1.00
1959:3	−1.04	0.29	−1.85	0.66	−0.13
1959:4	−1.58	0.42	−1.92	1.46	−1.54
1960:1	−1.60	−0.51	−0.92	0.71	−0.89
1960:2	−3.47	−1.06	−0.78	−0.67	−0.96
1960:3	−5.34	−2.28	−1.06	−1.69	−0.30
1960:4	−6.69	−2.39	−1.14	−1.72	−1.44
1961:1	−5.33	−1.93	−0.20	−1.65	−1.55
1961:2	−3.84	−1.95	−0.05	−0.92	−0.93
1961:3	−4.10	−2.13	0.12	−0.88	−1.21
1961:4	−1.95	−1.84	0.22	0.23	−0.56
1962:1	−0.09	−0.17	−0.59	0.54	0.13

(*continued*)

Table 2.A.2   (continued)

Date	GNP	Eg	Es	Em	Ed
1962:2	-0.33	0.10	-0.99	0.38	0.17
1962:3	-1.15	-0.11	-0.66	-0.29	-0.10
1962:4	-2.39	0.08	-0.90	-1.02	-0.56
1963:1	-3.32	0.26	-1.36	-1.60	-0.62
1963:2	-2.71	0.06	-0.91	-1.42	-0.43
1963:3	-1.95	-0.03	-0.46	-1.20	-0.26
1963:4	-1.92	-0.03	-0.97	-0.76	-0.17
1964:1	-1.25	-0.70	-0.21	-0.18	-0.15
1964:2	-0.99	-0.38	0.01	-0.12	-0.50
1964:3	-0.76	-0.17	-0.15	-0.07	-0.37
1964:4	-1.01	-0.40	0.20	-0.05	-0.76
1965:1	0.34	-0.31	0.25	0.41	-0.01
1965:2	0.83	0.11	0.27	0.40	0.04
1965:3	1.16	0.22	0.34	0.05	0.55
1965:4	2.55	0.21	1.11	-0.28	1.51
1966:1	2.97	-0.09	0.85	-0.17	2.38
1966:2	2.06	-0.14	0.34	-0.16	2.02
1966:3	2.43	0.61	0.71	-0.08	1.19
1966:4	2.33	1.04	0.92	-0.71	1.08
1967:1	2.22	1.44	1.28	-1.36	0.85
1967:2	1.79	1.72	1.21	-1.88	0.74
1967:3	1.32	1.21	1.09	-2.22	1.24
1967:4	1.07	1.31	0.42	-1.77	1.10
1968:1	1.43	1.47	0.15	-1.09	0.90
1968:2	2.75	1.60	0.67	-0.50	0.98
1968:3	3.00	1.48	0.60	0.50	0.42
1968:4	2.57	1.13	0.20	0.97	0.27
1969:1	2.22	0.66	-0.10	1.51	0.14
1969:2	1.39	0.36	-0.35	1.98	-0.60
1969:3	0.44	-0.19	-0.44	1.82	-0.76
1969:4	-0.90	-0.79	-0.17	1.42	-1.35
1970:1	-1.76	-1.28	0.06	0.99	-1.52
1970:2	-2.69	-1.83	-0.05	0.63	-1.44
1970:3	-1.89	-1.09	0.19	0.28	-1.26
1970:4	-3.37	-1.32	0.14	-0.39	-1.79
1971:1	-1.04	-0.55	-0.01	0.04	-0.52
1971:2	-1.16	-0.22	-0.24	0.26	-0.95
1971:3	-0.94	-0.24	-0.15	1.38	-1.93
1971:4	-0.84	0.03	-0.02	2.07	-2.92
1972:1	0.08	-0.14	0.29	1.91	-1.98
1972:2	0.28	-0.65	0.86	1.84	-1.78
1972:3	0.57	-0.26	0.74	1.50	-1.40
1972:4	1.45	-0.30	1.53	1.05	-0.83
1973:1	3.28	-0.47	1.71	1.57	0.48
1973:2	1.98	-1.00	1.75	1.09	0.14
1973:3	2.00	-0.66	1.55	1.11	0.00
1973:4	2.19	-0.38	1.35	1.08	0.14
1974:1	0.96	0.00	1.03	0.16	-0.23

Table 2.A.2   (continued)

Date	GNP	Eg	Es	Em	Ed
1974:2	−0.46	−0.41	−0.18	0.44	−0.31
1974:3	−1.53	0.41	−1.05	−0.09	−0.81
1974:4	−4.78	−0.63	−2.35	−0.51	−1.30
1975:1	−6.75	0.13	−3.65	−0.30	−2.93
1975:2	−5.90	0.84	−2.88	0.00	−3.87
1975:3	−3.68	1.52	−2.63	0.60	−3.17
1975:4	−3.41	0.84	−2.71	0.88	−2.43
1976:1	−1.96	1.49	−2.14	−0.28	−1.02
1976:2	−1.68	0.80	−1.14	−0.78	−0.56
1976:3	−1.23	0.91	−0.51	−1.19	−0.44
1976:4	−0.92	0.65	0.33	−1.87	−0.04
1977:1	0.10	0.14	1.61	−2.01	0.36
1977:2	−2.03	−1.64	0.90	−1.75	0.46
1977:3	1.31	0.66	1.12	−1.21	0.74
1977:4	1.20	0.68	1.07	−0.81	0.27
1978:1	1.72	1.16	0.81	−0.49	0.23
1978:2	3.65	1.77	0.20	−0.23	1.90
1978:3	3.54	1.66	0.16	−0.11	1.83
1978:4	3.68	1.19	0.25	−0.29	2.53
1979:1	3.65	1.53	−0.01	−0.41	2.54
1979:2	2.47	0.73	0.00	−1.02	2.75
1979:3	2.55	0.17	0.04	−0.61	2.95
1979:4	2.10	0.26	0.52	−0.28	1.60
1980:1	1.83	0.29	0.10	−0.19	1.62
1980:2	−0.42	0.05	−0.45	0.42	−0.44
1980:3	−0.53	0.04	−0.53	−1.30	1.26
1980:4	0.25	−0.09	−0.66	−0.77	1.78
1981:1	2.05	0.27	−0.88	0.08	2.59
1981:2	1.00	0.36	−0.64	−1.05	2.32
1981:3	0.47	−0.21	−1.10	0.07	1.71
1981:4	−1.68	−0.03	−1.51	−0.76	0.61
1982:1	−3.30	−0.37	−1.04	−1.29	−0.58
1982:2	−2.69	−1.11	0.27	0.46	−2.30
1982:3	−4.26	−1.50	0.61	−0.69	−2.68
1982:4	−4.47	−1.41	1.14	−1.40	−2.80

Appendix 2.2
Construction of the Fiscal Index G

The index is derived and discussed in Blanchard (1985). Its empirical counterpart is derived and discussed in Blanchard (1983). This is a short summary.

The Theoretical Index

The index measures the effect of fiscal policy on aggregate demand at given interest rates. It is given by:

$$\tilde{G}_t \equiv \lambda(B_t - \int_t^\infty T_{t,s}\, e^{-(r+p)(s-t)}ds) + Z_t \,,$$

where Z_t, B_t, T_t are government spending, debt, and taxes; $x_{t,s}$ denotes the anticipation, as of t, of a variable x at time s.

The first term measures the effect of fiscal policy on consumption; λ is the propensity to consume out of wealth. B_t is part of wealth and increases consumption. The present value of taxes, however, decreases human wealth and consumption; taxes are discounted at a rate $(r + p)$, higher than the interest rate r. The second term captures the direct effect of government spending.

The index can be rewritten as:

$$\tilde{G}_t = (Z_t - \lambda \int_t^\infty Z_{t,s}e^{-(r+p)(t-s)}ds)$$

$$+ \lambda(B_t - \int_t^\infty (T_{t,s} - Z_{t,s})e^{-(r+p)(t-s)}ds).$$

This shows that fiscal policy affects aggregate demand through the deviation of spending from "normal" spending (first line), through the level of debt and the sequence of anticipated deficits, net of interest payments, $D_{t,s} \equiv (Z_{t,s} - T_{t,s})$.

The Empirical Counterpart

We assume that any time t, D and Z are anticipated to return at rate ξ to their full employment values D^*, Z^* respectively. More precisely:

$$dZ_{t,s}/ds = \xi(Z_t^* - Z_{t,s})$$

$$dD_{t,s}/ds = \xi(D_t^* - D_{t,s}).$$

The index becomes:

$$\tilde{G}_t = Z_t - \lambda\left(\frac{1}{r+p} Z_t^* + \frac{1}{r+p+\xi}(Z_t - Z_t^*)\right)$$

$$+ \lambda\left(B_t + \frac{1}{r+p} D_t^* + \frac{1}{r+p+\xi}(D_t - D_t^*)\right).$$

From the study of aggregate consumption by Hayashi (1982), we choose $\lambda = .08$, $p = .05$, $r = .03$. We choose $\xi = .30$ (all at annual rates). This gives:

$$\tilde{G}_t = .79(Z_t - Z_t^*) + .08B_t + .21D_t + .79D_t^*.$$

Let $\bar{Z}_t$ be the exponentially fitted trend for government spending. The index used in the paper is $G_t = \tilde{G}_t/\bar{Z}_t$. Time series for G_t and its components $(Z_t - Z_t^*)/\bar{Z}_t, B_t/\bar{Z}_t, D_t/\bar{Z}_t, D_t^*/\bar{Z}_t$ are given in table 2.A.3.

Construction of the Fiscal Feedback Rule

Let g, z, z^*, d, d*, t, and t^* be the unexpected components of G, $(Z/\bar{Z})$, $(Z^*/\bar{Z})$, $(D/\bar{Z})$, $(D^*/\bar{Z})$, $(T/\bar{Z})$, and $(T^*/\bar{Z})$. They satisfy, therefore:

$$g = .79(z - z^*) + .08b + .21d + .79d^*.$$

Using $d = z - t$, $d^* = z^* - t^*$ gives:

$$g = z - (.21t + .79t^*) + .08b.$$

Let y and p be, as in the text, the unexpected components of the logarithms of GNP and of the price level. Then

$$\frac{dg}{dy} = \frac{dz}{dy} - .21\frac{dt}{dy},$$

as by definition $\dfrac{dt^*}{dy} = 0$ and by construction, B being beginning of quarter debt, $\dfrac{db}{dy} = 0$:

$$\frac{dg}{dp} = \frac{dz}{dp} - .21\frac{dt}{dp} - .79\frac{dt^*}{dp} \approx \frac{dz}{dp} - \frac{dt}{dp},$$

since the effect of unexpected price movements on actual and full employment taxes is approximately the same.

Let σ_1, σ_2 be the elasticities of movements in government spending with respect to unexpected movements in the level of output and in the price level respectively. Let θ_1, θ_2 be similar elasticities for taxes. Then:

$$dg = (\sigma_1 - .21\theta_1)dy$$

$$dg = (\sigma_2 - \theta_2)dp.$$

We assume that, within a quarter, there is no discretionary response of g to either y or p. The response depends only on institutional arrangements. We therefore use the results of deLeeuw et al. (1980) and deLeeuw and Holloway (1982) to construct σ_1, σ_2, θ_1, and θ_2.

σ_1: From table 19 of deLeeuw et al. (1980), a one percentage point increase in the unemployment rate increases spending in the first quarter by 0.6% at an annual rate. From Okun's law it is reasonable to assume that a 1% innovation in output reduces unemployment by roughly 0.1 percentage point in the first quarter. Putting these together we have σ_1 = −0.06.

σ_2: G is composed of (1) purchases of goods and services, (2) wage payments to government employees, and (3) transfer payments. There is little or no effect of unexpected inflation on nominal purchases within a quarter. Although parts of (2) and (3) are indexed, indexing is not contemporaneous. Nominal payments for some transfer programs (Medicare, Medicaid) increase with inflation. A plausible range for σ_2 is −0.8 to −1.0. We choose −0.9 for the computations in the text.

θ_1: We considered four categories of taxes and income tax bases:(1) personal income tax; (2) corporate income tax; (3) indirect business taxes; (4) social security and other taxes.

We have

$$\theta_1 = \sum_{i=1}^{4} \frac{T_i}{T} \eta_{T_i Y_i} \, \eta_{Y_i Y}$$

$\dfrac{T_i}{T}$ is available in deLeeuw et al. (1980), table 6, for selected years.

$\eta_{Y_i Y}$ is available in ibid., table 8.

$\eta_{T_i Y_i}$ is available in ibid., table 10.

$\eta_{T_2 Y_2}$ is available in ibid., 38, col. 1.

$\eta_{T_3 Y_3}$ is available in ibid., table 15.

$\eta_{T_4 Y_4}$ is available in ibid., table 18.

We calculated θ_1 using elasticities and tax proportions for 1959 and 1979. The results were very close and yielded $\theta_1 = 1.4$.

θ_2: We considered the same four categories of taxes. In the same way as before, we have

$$\theta_2 = \sum_{i=1}^{4} \frac{T_i}{T} \eta_{T_i Y_i} \, \eta_{Y_i P}$$

$\dfrac{T_i}{T}$ is available in deLeeuw et al. (1980), table 6.

$\eta_{T_i Y_i}$ are given in deLeeuw and Holloway (1982), table 8. (They are lower than the $\eta_{T_i Y_i}$ reported above for the computations of θ_1.)

$\eta_{Y_i P}$ are given in ibid., table 7.

We calculated θ_2 using elasticities and tax proportions for 1959, 1969, and 1979. The results were very close. A plausible range for θ_2 (de-

Table 2.A.3   Fiscal Index and Its Components

Date	G	$(Z-Z^*)/\bar{Z}$	$B/\bar{Z}$	$D/\bar{Z}$	$D^*/\bar{Z}$
1947:1	0.238	−0.003	7.788	−0.560	−0.533
1947:2	0.225	−0.003	7.521	−0.515	−0.527
1947:3	0.280	−0.003	7.216	−0.396	−0.450
1947:4	0.141	−0.003	6.877	−0.523	−0.550
1948:1	0.165	−0.003	6.654	−0.466	−0.506
1948:2	0.253	−0.003	6.472	−0.373	−0.397
1948:3	0.354	−0.003	6.257	−0.248	−0.275
1948:4	0.408	−0.002	6.219	−0.186	−0.219
1949:1	0.447	0.002	6.212	−0.119	−0.191
1949:2	0.501	0.012	6.201	−0.030	−0.153
1949:3	0.513	0.020	6.144	−0.005	−0.145
1949:4	0.486	0.024	6.099	−0.007	−0.177
1950:1	0.582	0.017	6.071	0.007	−0.050
1950:2	0.347	0.009	5.976	−0.285	−0.252
1950:3	0.218	0.002	5.762	−0.474	−0.332
1950:4	0.171	0.000	5.596	−0.477	−0.367
1951:1	0.156	−0.002	5.353	−0.478	−0.352
1951:2	0.318	−0.006	5.258	−0.265	−0.187
1951:3	0.459	−0.006	5.187	−0.111	−0.041
1951:4	0.466	−0.004	5.095	−0.056	−0.036
1952:1	0.424	−0.006	5.057	−0.093	−0.073
1952:2	0.490	−0.006	5.020	−0.014	−0.006
1952:3	0.551	−0.006	4.951	0.058	0.062
1952:4	0.505	−0.008	4.872	−0.015	0.034
1953:1	0.535	−0.009	4.834	0.000	0.074
1953:2	0.555	−0.009	4.808	0.033	0.094
1953:3	0.513	−0.009	4.768	0.022	0.049
1953:4	0.539	−0.002	4.757	0.129	0.048
1954:1	0.504	0.009	4.674	0.105	0.011
1954:2	0.431	0.012	4.626	0.035	−0.060
1954:3	0.409	0.014	4.605	0.009	−0.080
1954:4	0.361	0.010	4.539	−0.045	−0.114
1955:1	0.325	0.008	4.462	−0.104	−0.134
1955:2	0.276	0.003	4.394	−0.151	−0.170
1955:3	0.285	0.002	4.328	−0.148	−0.150
1955:4	0.250	0.002	4.246	−0.177	−0.175
1956:1	0.225	0.000	4.156	−0.175	−0.195
1956:2	0.225	0.002	4.067	−0.162	−0.188
1956:3	0.216	0.001	3.969	−0.151	−0.190
1956:4	0.194	0.001	3.884	−0.170	−0.202
1957:1	0.215	0.000	3.793	−0.139	−0.170
1957:2	0.224	0.000	3.730	−0.114	−0.158
1957:3	0.214	0.001	3.647	−0.114	−0.162
1957:4	0.236	0.008	3.621	−0.059	−0.152
1958:1	0.288	0.022	3.586	0.030	−0.119
1958:2	0.298	0.035	3.556	0.090	−0.130
1958:3	0.361	0.032	3.515	0.088	−0.042
1958:4	0.349	0.023	3.481	0.058	−0.037
1959:1	0.258	0.016	3.434	−0.033	−0.115

(*continued*)

Table 2.A.3 (continued)

Date	G	$(Z-Z^*)/\bar{Z}$	$B/\bar{Z}$	$D/\bar{Z}$	$D^*/\bar{Z}$
1959:2	0.208	0.010	3.391	−0.092	−0.150
1959:3	0.220	0.011	3.360	−0.056	−0.142
1959:4	0.211	0.013	3.317	−0.061	−0.148
1960:1	0.106	0.009	3.261	−0.171	−0.241
1960:2	0.132	0.010	3.222	−0.126	−0.216
1960:3	0.150	0.012	3.176	−0.091	−0.198
1960:4	0.160	0.019	3.142	−0.059	−0.197
1961:1	0.195	0.023	3.116	−0.021	−0.163
1961:2	0.212	0.025	3.072	−0.012	−0.141
1961:3	0.201	0.021	3.029	−0.025	−0.142
1961:4	0.204	0.016	3.013	−0.042	−0.127
1962:1	0.241	0.012	2.976	−0.007	−0.081
1962:2	0.224	0.011	2.954	−0.025	−0.094
1962:3	0.210	0.011	2.936	−0.037	−0.107
1962:4	0.205	0.011	2.902	−0.030	−0.110
1963:1	0.181	0.012	2.874	−0.050	−0.132
1963:2	0.150	0.011	2.857	−0.087	−0.159
1963:3	0.162	0.009	2.834	−0.081	−0.141
1963:4	0.172	0.009	2.794	−0.068	−0.126
1964:1	0.206	0.008	2.767	−0.045	−0.085
1964:2	0.240	0.007	2.740	−0.011	−0.047
1964:3	0.196	0.005	2.705	−0.049	−0.086
1964:4	0.175	0.004	2.680	−0.063	−0.104
1965:1	0.142	0.003	2.639	−0.107	−0.128
1965:2	0.149	0.002	2.608	−0.103	−0.115
1965:3	0.212	0.000	2.575	−0.044	−0.046
1965:4	0.227	−0.001	2.537	−0.044	−0.022
1966:1	0.202	−0.002	2.488	−0.074	−0.037
1966:2	0.184	−0.002	2.436	−0.080	−0.052
1966:3	0.213	−0.003	2.399	−0.046	−0.019
1966:4	0.227	−0.004	2.361	−0.028	−0.001
1967:1	0.263	−0.003	2.332	0.022	0.035
1967:2	0.263	−0.004	2.310	0.027	0.037
1967:3	0.264	−0.004	2.274	0.028	0.042
1967:4	0.259	−0.003	2.279	0.019	0.037
1968:1	0.235	−0.003	2.278	−0.005	0.013
1968:2	0.257	−0.005	2.277	0.005	0.040
1968:3	0.195	−0.005	2.220	−0.057	−0.015
1968:4	0.166	−0.006	2.210	−0.077	−0.044
1969:1	0.100	−0.006	2.181	−0.144	−0.106
1969:2	0.091	−0.005	2.143	−0.143	−0.113
1969:3	0.104	−0.005	2.050	−0.112	−0.093
1969:4	0.095	−0.005	2.041	−0.101	−0.106
1970:1	0.110	−0.005	2.031	−0.070	−0.094
1970:2	0.164	−0.003	2.002	−0.004	−0.041
1970:3	0.169	0.002	1.958	0.003	−0.036
1970:4	0.179	0.006	1.950	0.032	−0.035
1971:1	0.188	0.011	1.953	0.021	−0.025
1971:2	0.210	0.013	1.917	0.050	−0.003

Table 2.A.3   (continued)

Date	G	$(Z\text{-}Z^*)/\bar{Z}$	$B/\bar{Z}$	$D/\bar{Z}$	$D^*/\bar{Z}$
1971:3	0.206	0.013	1.910	0.048	−0.007
1971:4	0.201	0.014	1.938	0.040	−0.015
1972:1	0.166	0.013	1.944	−0.006	−0.047
1972:2	0.207	0.012	1.923	0.025	0.000
1972:3	0.164	0.009	1.885	−0.017	−0.035
1972:4	0.230	0.007	1.869	0.040	0.038
1973:1	0.180	0.005	1.886	−0.032	−0.008
1973:2	0.159	0.004	1.871	−0.042	−0.028
1973:3	0.127	0.002	1.817	−0.065	−0.054
1973:4	0.128	0.001	1.772	−0.060	−0.048
1974:1	0.109	0.000	1.751	−0.056	−0.070
1974:2	0.118	0.001	1.707	−0.034	−0.059
1974:3	0.086	0.002	1.647	−0.044	−0.089
1974:4	0.106	0.006	1.605	0.003	−0.075
1975:1	0.146	0.019	1.584	0.076	−0.054
1975:2	0.327	0.037	1.599	0.242	0.112
1975:3	0.226	0.038	1.625	0.132	0.007
1975:4	0.218	0.037	1.638	0.122	0.000
1976:1	0.200	0.036	1.673	0.088	−0.017
1976:2	0.176	0.033	1.706	0.062	−0.042
1976:3	0.182	0.030	1.722	0.068	−0.035
1976:4	0.191	0.027	1.714	0.077	−0.022
1977:1	0.153	0.026	1.722	0.026	−0.056
1977:2	0.170	0.022	1.716	0.034	−0.032
1977:3	0.200	0.019	1.685	0.058	0.005
1977:4	0.188	0.018	1.699	0.051	−0.008
1978:1	0.175	0.014	1.699	0.037	−0.016
1978:2	0.139	0.010	1.687	−0.016	−0.043
1978:3	0.124	0.010	1.658	−0.028	−0.055
1978:4	0.118	0.008	1.644	−0.039	−0.057
1979:1	0.089	0.007	1.624	−0.062	−0.084
1979:2	0.068	0.005	1.593	−0.070	−0.101
1979:3	0.091	0.005	1.559	−0.048	−0.074
1979:4	0.103	0.006	1.550	−0.030	−0.063
1980:1	0.106	0.006	1.540	−0.022	−0.060
1980:2	0.117	0.013	1.518	0.019	−0.062
1980:3	0.125	0.019	1.491	0.035	−0.058
1980:4	0.110	0.018	1.487	0.020	−0.071
1981:1	0.062	0.021	1.468	−0.039	−0.117
1981:2	0.063	0.027	1.480	−0.035	−0.124
1981:3	0.078	0.025	1.442	−0.019	−0.102
1981:4	0.099	0.020	1.434	0.024	−0.081
1982:1	0.099	0.028	1.446	0.041	−0.094
1982:2	0.099	0.035	1.458	0.043	−0.104
1982:3	0.146	0.046	1.449	0.094	−0.068
1982:4	0.204	0.051	1.502	0.157	−0.022

pending on which $\eta_{T_i Y_i}$ are used) is 0.1 to 0.3. We choose 0.2 for computations in the text.

Our fiscal policy rule is therefore: $g = -.34y - 1.1p + \epsilon^g$.

Comment   Robert J. Shiller

These are intriguing questions: Is the macroeconomy disturbed by very large shocks occasionally or by small shocks regularly? Is there a single source of shocks to the economy, or are there many? Is the pattern of behavior constant through time or changing? These questions are not stated in terms of an explicit model and seem to call for some sort of exploratory data analysis. The authors have done this in an imaginative and careful manner, showing thoughtful attention to methods. They took the trouble to do Monte Carlo work to get empirical distributions for statistics for which no distribution theory is available, to use modern robust regression techniques instead of the usual ordinary least squares, and even to create new formal techniques that capture some motivation of popular exploratory techniques.

They rightly perceive that to answer the questions posed here one really would like to have a model of the propagation mechanism for the shocks. Part of their work involves constructing such a model. The model, however, is not used throughout the paper, and some techniques used here are really in the nature of data description.

The authors refer to a "common framework of analysis" in modern macroeconomics that uses stochastic difference or differential equations to model the propagation of shocks. This framework is not enough by itself to suggest any way of studying the kurtosis of the extraneous shocks that strike the economy. We need to know more; we need to know the structure of the model. We can, of course, observe the residuals in an autoregression, as are shown in the authors' table 2.1. But what do these residuals mean? Suppose the true model is a continuous time stochastic differential equation of the form $dX_t/X_t = dW_t + .5dt$, where W_t is a unit Wiener process. Then $X_t = c^* \exp(W_t)$ is a lognormal variable whose kurtosis increases with t. Here the underlying shocks are all normal, but the propagation mechanism creates a variable X_t with an arbitrarily high kurtosis. (The kurtosis of a lognormal variable goes to infinity as the variance of the underlying normal variable is increased to infinity.)

Nor is there any way in the absence of a model to study whether the economy is dominated by a single shock or by many shocks. Even

Robert J. Shiller is professor of economics at Yale University.

if we knew that the vector X_t is determined by a first-order vector autoregression model, we might have problems. Suppose all components of the vector error term were in fact zero except for the first; that is, the economy is driven by a single shock. That is, $X_t = BX_{t-1} + u_t$, where B is a matrix and $u_t = [u_{1t}, 0]$. We could discover that u_t has this special form by regressing X_t on X_{t-1} and looking at the variance matrix of residuals. However, if the special model holds for quarterly data but we had semiannual data for estimation, we would not observe this special structure for the error term. With data for every other quarter we would observe $X_t = B^2X_{t-2} + v_t$, where $v_t = u_t + Bu_{t-1}$. In general, none of the elements of v_t will have zero variance.

The model presented here is therefore of primary importance to the paper. The model is described not inappropriately as a "standard macroeconomic model," though not all the coefficient restrictions are "standard." The equations look something like standard textbook equations with lagged endogenous variables and error terms added. The policy variables are represented by fiscal and monetary reaction functions. The fiscal policy index g is unusual; it is a mixture of government expenditure, the national debt, and the deficit.

How are the equations identified? The identifying restrictions are almost those of the standard recursive model in which the matrix of coefficients is triangular and the variance matrix diagonal. Recall that in that system the diagonality of the variance matrix is necessary for identification of all equations in the model. Also, in the recursive system all equations can be estimated consistently by ordinary least squares. This system differs from the recursive system only in that the equation that in the recursive system would contain only one endogenous variable is an equation with three endogenous variables but with all of the coefficients assumed known a priori. This equation is the fiscal policy reaction function, the equation that determines g. The coefficients are specified before estimation by a clever use of some institutional data on government reactions. Now the model is identified, but the equations cannot be estimated by ordinary least squares. Since the matrix of coefficients of the endogenous variables is not triangular, we must instrument the regressions.

Even so, the assumption that the error terms are uncorrelated across equations is necessary for identification. I wonder if that is a reasonable assumption. Where did the assumption come from? One way of appreciating the arbitrariness of such an assumption is to note that if the model holds for monthly data, say, with error terms uncorrelated across equations, then the quarterly data will not generally have a representation with error terms uncorrelated across equations.

Since lack of correlation of residuals across equations was used to identify the model, it follows that if we doubt these restrictions we can take linear combinations of these equations as we please so long as these combinations do not violate zero restrictions on the coefficients. The authors are concerned that the coefficient of M in the aggregate demand equation has the wrong sign. One might, for example, add the money supply equation to this equation, thereby rectifying the wrong sign.

Another identifying assumption is that monetary policy does not depend on the contemporary fiscal policy variable. Why is this omitted? Does the Fed always ignore fiscal policy? How much trust do we wish to place in the high kurtosis of the monetary policy error term shown in table 2.4? Without the identifying assumptions above, the error term in the monetary policy equation could be any linear combination of the error terms in the other equations.

The assumptions used here for estimation might be compared with those of Hall in this volume (chap. 4). Hall felt that he could find no more than one truly exogenous variable for estimation of such a model, this variable being his military expenditure variable. The discussion of his paper questioned whether even this variable was exogenous. The assumed exogeneity here of residuals of equations lower in the hierarchy is certainly even more questionable than the assumption made by Hall.

The authors, inspired by the methods of Burns and Mitchell for describing business cycles, offer a formalization of their approach. As an exploratory technique, the Burns and Mitchell reference cycle approach has apparently had a wide appeal. It was a dominant theme in empirical macroeconomics for at least a decade after their book appeared in 1946, and the calculation of the reference cycle dates continues to be a widely publicized activity of the NBER. Like most statistical methods belonging in the realm of exploratory methods it is controversial, and the motivations for the techniques are only intuitive. Blanchard and Watson borrowed from the Burns and Mitchell approach and also modified it.

It is interesting to see a formalization of the reference cycle dating itself. It has sometimes been claimed that, while no simple formula is used to date the reference cycle, in fact a recession is declared whenever real GNP shows two consecutive quarters of decline. Blanchard and Watson have found that the quarter of a trough can be identified instead as any quarter in which real GNP declined from the previous quarter so that it is at least 0.5% below the previous peak and then increased for the each of the next three consecutive quarters.

Rather than present the Burns/Mitchell charts of cyclical patterns that were used to judge the business cycle pattern of series, the authors offer a summary measure. This measure is rather different from Burns and Mitchell's own "index of conformity," which relied on a sort of time deformation that in effect reduced all cycles to the same length and that depended only on the directions of change at various phases of the cycle and not on their magnitude. The authors instead present for each variable in each cycle five correlation coefficients: cross-correlations between the variable and real GNP contemporaneously and for two leads and lags. By fixing the leads and lags in terms of quarters rather than fractions of cycles, Blanchard and Watson's lead or lag may be a much higher proportion of the cycle for short cycles, such as that between 1960:2 and 1982:4, which was only ten quarters long. The authors' interpretation of the correlation coefficients relies on a sort of approximation whose validity is not independent of the length of the cycle. A procyclical variable will tend to show a correlation pattern that is not quite flat. There is probably a tendency for the peak of the specific cycle to occur, relative to the reference cycle, as indicated by these leads or lags, but that is not necessarily so. There is a fundamental difference between such correlation coefficients and methods involving identification of peaks and troughs. For example, all these correlations would be about zero for any series that was ninety degrees out of phase with the business cycle. These correlations would stay zero if the series were to switch sign in another business cycle, and so a dramatic change in the cyclical behavior would not be revealed by a change in correlations.

The correlations seem to serve well enough, however, to show to what extent the behaviors of the various series are directly "procyclical" or "countercyclical." What is immediately apparent in looking at the correlation coefficients is that there are not a lot of regular patterns to be seen. There is no series that shows a simple procyclical or countercyclical pattern in all seven cycles.

The authors characterize Burns and Mitchell (who studied cycles between 1854 and 1933) as having found substantially less variation in the cyclical pattern across cycles. That conclusion may be overstated. In looking at the Burns and Mitchell pictures one usually finds for any specific series at least one business cycle with an anomalous pattern. Only two of the Blanchard/Watson series appear to correspond approximately to series studied by Burns and Mitchell: these are the long-term and short-term interest rates. Plots very similar to those of Burns and Mitchell appear in the Zarnowitz/Moore paper, "Major Changes in Cyclical Behavior" in this volume (chap. 9). Comparing their tables 9.3 and 9.6 with their tables 9.4 and 9.7 suggests that conformity to the cycle has declined since World War II only for the short rate.

Both Blanchard and Watson and Zarnowitz and Moore find that short rates are procyclical, show good conformity to the cycle, and lag the reference cycle somewhat. Both papers find less conformity of long rates to the cycle. However, Blanchard and Watson find that the long rate is countercyclical and tends to lead the business cycle by at least two quarters. This last conclusion is not in Zarnowitz and Moore. One might note that it hardly seems likely that the short rate should be procyclical and the long rate countercyclical, since the two series are fairly positively correlated. This points up some of the rather important differences between the Zarnowitz/Moore and Blanchard/Watson approaches. The correlation patterns shown in Blanchard and Watson's table 2.7 are not totally dissimilar for long and short rates, but their identification of leads or lags or procyclical or countercyclical behavior depends on which correlation coefficient is biggest in absolute value. Of course, a procyclical variable that leads the cycle by x degrees can always be described as countercyclical and as leading the cycle by $180 - x$ degrees. With an average duration of postwar cycles of about four years, such calculations suggest that the long rate leads by over a year, which is beyond the range for which they computed correlation coefficients. (They could not have computed correlation coefficients out much further on all cycles, since one postwar cycle is only eleven quarters long.)

The summary statistics provided by Blanchard and Watson, the difference between the maximum and minimum correlation coefficient over the seven cycles, are generally above one for all series but the short rate. This documents the observation that for most variables there is at least one business cycle where the variable shows anomalous behavior.

The authors rightly felt that some sort of significance test for the statistic was desirable. They wanted to know whether differences of this magnitude should be "surprising." They then computed for each series an empirical distribution for this statistic for data generated according to the estimated fourth-order bivariate autoregression representation for the series and real GNP. Since the null hypothesis for this test allows a bivariate autoregression process for which the pattern of cycles may be either usually very similar across cycles or usually very different across cycles, it is not clear in what sense we could expect the power function for this test to divide important alternative hypotheses.

Comment   Peter Temin

The paper by Blanchard and Watson is extremely interesting. The authors deserve our thanks for their efforts to take an informal con-

Peter Temin is professor of economics at Massachusetts Institute of Technology.

troversy in the literature and endow it with enough shape to be testable. As any historian knows, there are pitfalls in that process. But the effort itself is necessary, even if it only provides a forum for others to disagree. By moving the discussion out of the realm of slogans into the arena of testable hypotheses, the authors have done a great service.

The question in the title turns out to have two (related) meanings. The obvious meaning, whether all business cycles look alike as they develop, is treated in the second part of the paper. A more subtle formulation, whether all business cycles have the same cause, is the concern of the first part. After a brief comment on the former topic, I will concentrate on the latter.

Postwar business cycles, according to Blanchard and Watson, are not all alike. But, they continue, little information is contained in their differences. These differences do not indicate that business cycles are caused by identifiable, discrete large shocks. It is just that the economy is not a tight enough system to force all fluctuations into a single fixed mold. This result then poses a further question for us to ponder— namely, whether the variance Blanchard and Watson found is truly random or the result of a regular process more complex than their model can capture.

Causation of business cycles is treated in an elegant way. The authors distinguish between proponents of so-called large-shock theories and small-shock theories of business cycles. Large shocks by their nature are identifiable and different one from another; they are the stuff of economic history. Small shocks, by contrast, are nameless and individually uninteresting. It is only their distribution over time that matters for the origin of cycles, which are then produced by the interaction of the economy's internal dynamics and the accumulation of small shocks. The shocks that we observe are themselves, the authors imply, the sum of many smaller shocks that we cannot even see in the data, much less describe or verify from other sources.

My comments will deal both with the authors' methods and with their conclusions. I will start with methodology and work toward substance.

The first point follows from Blanchard and Watson's interpretation of the imprecise distinction between large and small shocks. A discovery that the distribution of innovations has fatter tails than a normal distribution provides evidence of large shocks, in their parlance, but it may not capture the earlier discussion. Disturbances large and infrequent enough not to be captured by a normal distribution may still be too small and frequent to be noted by the proponents of large shocks. In fact, independent one-quarter shocks may be too limited in time to be counted as large. A different error structure and a different definition of large might well produce a different answer.

The factual basis of this investigation consists of precisely four quarterly time series. There are casual references to the rest of the world, but this is an exercise undertaken with strict rules. It is like classical geometry, in which the student is limited to what he or she can prove with straightedge and compass. Or like black-and-white photography in which the drama of color is eschewed in favor of a concentration on light and form. But since, unlike these two examples, there are no generally accepted guidelines to indicate which "stylized facts" should be included and which omitted, it is appropriate to ask if the use of four series seems attractive.

One alternative can be rejected immediately. The use of a large forecasting model would hopelessly complicate the issue without much anticipation of gain. There are so many errors in those models, with so many special properties, that a simple characterization of them as coming from a simple, stationary distribution would be impossible. Another alternative, though, appears more attractive. Why not five series, or six? The gains are not as impressive as those claimed by Bob Solow in the transition from one-sector to two-sector growth models, but they may not be negligible either. The authors provide us with one cautionary tale along these lines. They say that they cannot decompose prices into raw materials prices and other prices in order to examine more closely oil price shocks and related phenomena, because the errors relating to those shocks cannot be disentangled from other price shocks. The gain in information is only apparent, not real.

This argument does not seem, at least on its face, to be applicable to the omission of an interest rate, q, or other series reflecting the cost of capital. I am prepared to hear that there are good statistical reasons for omitting this kind of variable, but it gives me pause. True, the aggregate demand equation is derived from IS and LM curves, and its errors (innovations) are linear combinations of the errors in the underlying IS and LM curves. If errors in these two relationships are uncorrelated, little is lost. But if, as the authors suggest, there is a tendency for innovations to cluster in time, the aggregate demand innovations will miss offsetting innovations in the fiscal and monetary areas.

Blanchard and Watson, then, limit themselves to a simple aggregate demand/aggregate supply model. There are two other equations, but they do not provide additional detail about the functioning of the private economy. They are policy feedback rules. So if we compare this model with, say, Klein's simple models of the economy in the infancy of modern econometrics, we discover two differences. First, as already noted, it gives explicit attention to both fiscal and monetary innovations, even if information about them is limited. And second, it incorporates rules for government policy formation.

The second differences affects the identification of shocks no less than the first. Monetary and fiscal shocks are deviations from the assumed rules of behavior, not from constancy or some smooth path over time.

The policy rules are themselves of interest. The fiscal rule is calculated, not estimated. It reveals a countercyclical fiscal policy: automatic stabilizers. The fiscal policy variable was constructed to show various effects of government spending and debt. It contains a cyclical component, and the fiscal policy equation can be thought of as cleansing it. That is, the equation for g separates the normal cyclical movements of fiscal policy variables from "true shocks." This seems like an awkward process in which the cyclical components of fiscal policy are first built into g by construction and then removed again by calculation. It was indicated, apparently, to distinguish changes in discretionary fiscal policy from cyclical movements in the government budget while allowing both to influence subsequent events.

The monetary policy rule, by contrast, is estimated. It shows exactly the opposite pattern. Whereas fiscal policy was "normally" countercyclical, monetary policy was procyclical. It was, in other words, accomodating. This is in itself an important conclusion. It may be an accurate description of monetary policy in the immediate postwar years, but it hardly seems to describe the role of the Fed in recent years. The use of a single model for the entire period from 1947 through 1982 cannot uncover such a shift. It would be interesting to see what would happen if the sample was broken at some point in time.

This procedure would provide information about changes both in policy rules and in shocks. (Were the 1970s really worse than the 1960s?) If there was a structural shift midway through the sample, its absence would tend to magnify the apparent shocks, particularly at the ends of the period. An informal look at table 2.4 suggests that something like this may indeed be going on.

Examining table 2.4 moves us from methodology to substance. As Blanchard and Watson comment, the most striking feature of table 2.4 (which shows the structural disturbances) is its lack of intuitive appeal. Despite considerable ingenuity, the authors succeed in making only one positive identification between their calculated innovations and the economic history of the postwar years (in 1974–75). I do not count large disturbances of one sign followed immediately by equally large disturbances of the opposite sign or disturbances that can be assigned to a known cause only by Procrustean tailoring of the date. There are sixty large disturbances shown in table 2.4, and it would be surprising if chance alone did not place a few of them on the dates of historical events. There does not seem to be much correlation between the calculated disturbances and our historical memory.

This is due partly, no doubt, to the matter of definition and procedure mentioned earlier. But to the extent that it is not, this result forces us to choose between the formal history of Blanchard and Watson and the more informal history of Eckstein and Sinai. How should one choose?

To aid this choice, I compared the structural disturbances in table 2.4 with deviations of the four variables from simple time trends. The differences are striking. The large disturbances of table 2.4 do not look autocorrelated. And the distributions of the four disturbances do not appear very different. Compared with a time trend, however, the variables divide into two clear groups. M1 and the GNP deflator (m and p) have highly autocorrelated disturbances, with little variation from one quarter to the next. GNP and the fiscal index (y and g), by contrast, have far less autocorrelation and far more quarter-to-quarter variation.

M1 and the GNP deflator grew slower than trend until the late 1960s and faster thereafter. (If one were to break the sample into two, as suggested earlier, the turning point of the later 1960s would be the obvious break point.) Neither of the other variables seems to show a break in trend at that time, although the fiscal variable appears to have much larger (relative) variation than GNP.

This pattern can be discerned in Blanchard and Watson's table 2.3, which decomposes forecast errors of their model. First, it is worth noting that the policy innovations seem to have little effect on the rest of the economy. Fiscal shocks affect the fiscal shock and nothing else in the next quarter. Even after a year, they have almost no effect on the other variables. And after five years, the effect of past fiscal shocks on current fiscal shocks is over twice as large as its effect on any of the other variables. Monetary shocks have exactly the same pattern. After five years, there is some effect of monetary shocks on prices, but the effect is only about half as strong as the effect on money itself.

Second, there is a sharp separation between the effect of supply and demand shocks. Supply shocks affect prices, and demand shocks affect output. This is true in the next quarter and remains largely true after a year. (Demand shocks have noticeable effects on prices by then, although supply shocks still dominate.) Only after five years do prices and income appear to be affected by a mixture of influences.

In the short run, therefore, Blanchard and Watson's economy has a roughly horizontal aggregate supply curve and a roughly vertical aggregate demand curve. As the authors note, this conclusion is strongly affected by their derivation from the fiscal equation. They present alternative structural estimates of their model in appendix 2.1, based on different calculated values of the price responsiveness of the fiscal stimulus. They allow the coefficient of p in the fiscal equation to vary from 1.0 to 1.3. This makes the price coefficient in the supply equation vary from 0.45 to 1.40—a threefold variation. It follows that the particular short-run characterization of the economy given by Blanchard and Watson may not be the only reasonable description. This in turn implies that the pattern of variances shown in table 2.3 may not be the only one generated by reasonable constructions of the economy.

In the long run this model appears to give more conventional results, showing the joint effect of all the shocks cited. A note of caution may be injected, however, in the use of a very simple model like this one to project the effect of errors over fifty years. The last section of table 2.3 may only be telling us that the relations estimated in table 2.2 are too simple to use in projecting an economy over five years. The authors use this kind of model to look at the short-run errors; there is no reason to think it is the best way to approach problems of longer-run forecasting.

Blanchard and Watson therefore seem to be presenting us with an economy that, at least in the short run, decomposes into several rather independent subeconomies. This surely is different from the economy described by Eckstein and Sinai. It also may well depend on the particular derivation used, as suggested by the alternatives furnished in appendix 2.1. The principal issue they raise, therefore, may not be whether shocks to the economy are generated by a normal distribution, but rather whether the short-run responsiveness of the economy has the simple structure they have attributed to it.

Discussion Summary

The discussion began with a response by Sims to Shiller's comments regarding identification and exogeneity. Sims stated that the identification of any stochastic model requires that restrictions be placed on the model's error process. Usually investigators make assumptions about the exogeneity of certain variables entering the model. Blanchard and Watson's approach, however, is to regard nothing as totally exogenous. This forces them to turn to exclusion restrictions and explicit assumptions on the error terms, in particular a diagonal covariance matrix for the contemporaneous shocks, to achieve identification. Shiller's point that the use of the wrong sampling period can induce contemporaneously correlated errors applies equally to incorrect identifying restrictions. Such a criticism does not mean that identification should not be attempted; it means only that identifying restrictions should be used wisely, as Blanchard and Watson have done. Finally Sims drew attention to the sophisticated extension of VAR methodology used by this paper. A vector autoregression was first used to generate "reduced form" residuals. Robust simultaneous equation estimation techniques were then used to transform the reduced-form shocks into shocks arising from a structural model.

Although McCallum felt that the large-shock versus small-shock view of impulses was valuable, he questioned the authors' statements on the associated policy implications. McCallum said he could see no reason why the presence of small shocks necessarily supported policy rules or why large shocks necessarily led to a need for discretionary policy. In reply, Blanchard referred McCallum to the debate between Robert Lucas and Robert Solow in *Rational Expectations and Economic Policy* (Fischer 1980, 249–64). Blanchard felt that the prevailing view of the profession, as espoused by Solow, seemed to be that large shocks were unique events whose source could be readily identified and counterbalanced with specific policies. The sources of small perturbations were harder to isolate, and this argued for built-in automatic stabilizers to offset their effects. Finally, several participants remarked that there might be difficulties in differentiating between true small shocks and a large shock that came in as a succession of small shocks because of the choice of the sampling interval. Blanchard conceded that this was a potential problem, but held that the eight-quarter forecast decompositions of GNP presented in table 2.A.2 did not seem to indicate that this was the case here.

Additional Contribution
Are Business Cycles Symmetrical?
J. Bradford DeLong and Lawrence H. Summers

1. Introduction

The dating of peaks and troughs and the concomitant emphasis on the different qualitative mechanisms involved in cyclical expansions and contractions have been major features of the NBER program on business cycle research. Asymmetry between expansions and contractions has long been a focus of such research. Thus Wesley Mitchell wrote (1927), "the most violent declines exceed the most considerable advances . . . . Business contractions appear to be a briefer and more violent process than business expansions." Keynes wrote in the *General Theory* (1936) that "the substitution of a downward for an upward tendency often takes place suddenly and violently . . . no such sharp

J. Bradford DeLong is a graduate student in the Department of Economics at Harvard University. Lawrence H. Summers is professor of economics at Harvard University.

We wish to thank the National Science Foundation for financial support.

turning point occurs when an upward is substituted for a downward tendency." Indeed Neftci (1984) states that "the claim that major economic time series are asymmetric over different time phases of the business cycle arises in almost all major works on business cycles."

In many respects the techniques of modern statistics and econometrics surely supersede earlier methods of cyclical analysis. They make possible the application of techniques of statistical estimation and inference. They remove the need for judgment in data description. And they provide a rigorous basis for nonjudgmental forecasting. Yet statistical models of the sort used in economics—whether built in the structural spirit of the Cowles Commission or in the modern time series tradition—are entirely unable to capture cyclical asymmetries. If, as Keynes, Mitchell, and others belived, cyclical asymmetries are of fundamental importance, then standard statistical techniques are seriously deficient. Something like traditional business cycle analysis may then be necessary to provide an adequate empirical basis for theorizing about cyclical behavior.

Hence the question of the magnitude of cyclical asymmetries seems to be of substantial methodological importance. Yet with the exception of the work of Neftci (1984), it appears to have attracted relatively little attention. This paper examines the extent of cyclical asymmetries using American data for the prewar and postwar periods and data on five other major OECD nations for the postwar period. We find no evidence of asymmetry in the behavior of GNP or industrial production. For the United States only, we find evidence of some asymmetry in the behavior of unemployment. We conclude that asymmetry is probably not a phenomenon of first-order importance in understanding business cycles. It appears that there is not much basis for preferring some version of traditional cyclical techniques of analysis and forecasting to more statistical methods.

Section 2 of this note describes our methods and presents the results of our analysis of GNP and industrial production. Section 3 follows Neftci (1984) in considering unemployment. We note some methodological problems we have with his analysis and then show that his conclusions about the behavior of unemployment appear to be invalid outside the United States. Section 4 provides some brief conclusions.

2. Asymmetries in Output?

The essence of the claims of Keynes and Mitchell quoted in the previous section was that economic downturns are brief and severe relative to trend, whereas upturns are longer and more gradual. This hypothesis has a clear implication: there should be significant skewness in a frequency distribution of periodic growth rates of output. That is, the distribution should have significantly fewer than half its observations below the mean; and the average deviation from the mean of the observations below the mean should be significantly more than the average deviation of the observations above the mean. The median output growth rate should exceed the mean by a significant amount. Figure C2.1 depicts the predicted frequency distribution of output growth under the null hypothesis of symmetry and under the alternative hypothesis of Keynes and Mitchell.

Our procedure is simple: it is to calculate the coefficient of skewness of the distribution of output growth rates for a variety of output measures and time intervals. The coefficient of skewness is defined as the ratio of the third centered moment to the cube of the standard deviation. For a symmetric distribution, the coefficient of skewness is zero, and the mean equals the median.

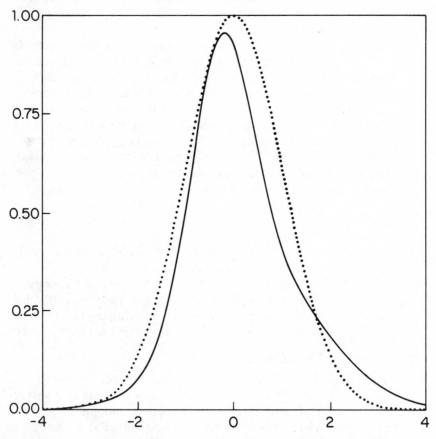

Fig. C2.1   Standardized (zero mean and unit variance) distribution with zero and unit skewness, respectively.

Evaluation of the statistical significance of any measured deviations from symmetry clearly requires an estimate of the sampling variability in our estimates of skewness. Standard statistical works such as Kendall and Stuart (1969) note that under the null hypothesis of zero skewness, the estimated skewness of a set of n independent random normal observations is normally distributed with a standard error of $(6/n)^{1/2}$. Unfortunately, the observations on growth rates considered here are highly serially correlated, and so this formula is inapplicable. We therefore used the following Monte Carlo procedure for each series and sample period considered. First, a third-order autoregression process was estimated for the time series of growth rates. It was then used to generate three-hundred artificial series for the sample period under the assumption that the shocks to the autoregression process were normally distributed. The standard deviation of the estimated skewness under the null hypothesis was then used calculated as the standard deviation of the skewnesses of the artificially generated series.[1]

Table C2.1 presents some evidence on skewness in quarterly and annual growth rates of United States GNP and industrial production

Table C2.1   **Skewness of United States GNP and Industrial Production Growth Rates**

Variable	Period	Annual Data		Quarterly Data	
		Skewness	Standard Error	Skewness	Standard Error
GNP	1891–1915	− .47	.73	.55	.29
GNP	1923–40	− .70	1.12	.04	.42
GnP	1949–83	− 1.37	.74	− .33	.29
IP	1949–83	− .55	.68	− .58	.40

Source: Data from Gordon 1982 and from the 1984 *Business Conditions Digest*.

1. We verified that the estimated skewnesses were approximately normally distributed. Coefficients of kurtosis were less than 10% away from their value of three under the null hypothesis. Note that our test of asymmetry is appropriate if output is stationary either when detrended or when differenced. Our standard errors are calculated under the second assumption, which is weakly supported by Nelson and Plosser 1982. Because they include periods in their analysis like the Great Depression and World War II, during which no one would expect the underlying rate of growth of the economy to stay constant, it is hard to interpret how their warnings against the practice of detrending apply to analyses that deal only with periods for which one has good reason to suspect that the underlying growth of potential output has been approximately constant.

For the United States industrial production index, estimated skewnesses for subperiods of the post–World War II period are highly variable—more variable than the stochastic errors calculated under the assumption of an AR(3) generating process would suggest. Apparently, modeling the generating process as an AR(3) does not capture all the serial dependence in the series and leads to estimated standard errors that are presumably too low. Therefore the standard errors reported in this paper are probably below their actual values.

for various sample periods. We use industrial production as well as GNP because the latter contains a greater number of imputed series, and because cyclicality is most apparent in the manufacturing sector of the economy. Because using quarterly data is complicated by the need for seasonal adjustment and by high-frequency movements that might render existing skewness undectable, both annual and quarterly data are examined.

Very little evidence of significant asymmetries emerges. Before World War II, quarterly GNP growth rates exhibit *positive* skewness, the opposite of that implied by the hypotheses of Keynes and Mitchell. The failure of the steep 1929–33 decline to dominate the interwar period is somewhat surprising. We expected significant skewness to be most apparent around the Great Depression. Similar conclusions are obtained with annual GNP data and with data on annual industrial production for the prewar period. Asymmetries do not appear to be substantial enough to be important. The difference between the median and mean growth rates reaches a maximum of 0.3% using quarterly data on industrial production for the postwar period. This difference is only 2% of the interquartile range of the distribution of quarterly growth rates: it is a very small number.

There is a little bit of evidence in favor of skewness in postwar data. All the estimated skewnesses are negative, as predicted by Keynes and Mitchell. In the case of annual GNP data, the estimated skewness approaches statistical significance. However, no equivalent result is found with either quarterly GNP or annual industrial production data. Hence we are inclined to discount its significance. It is of course possible that with longer time series significant asymmetries would emerge—the estimate of skewness would become sharper. But as figure C2.2 reveals, the observed skewness does not appear to be substantively important. The naked eye cannot easily judge the direction of asymmetry.

As a further check, table C2.2 reports estimated skewnesses of quarterly GNP and industrial production for other major OECD countries for the postwar period. Skewness is noticeably negative for only two of the five countries—Canada and Japan—using either industrial production or GNP data. There is no significant evidence of asymmetry for any country. The only natural grouping suggested by the data is a possible division into the United States, Canada, and Japan on the one hand and the United Kingdom, France, and West Germany on the other. But this possible difference between "non-European" and "European" business cycles is not strongly enough present in the data to give us any confidence that it is anything more than the workings of chance.

How has the picture of recessions as short violent interruptions of the process of economic growth emerged? Part of the answer lies in

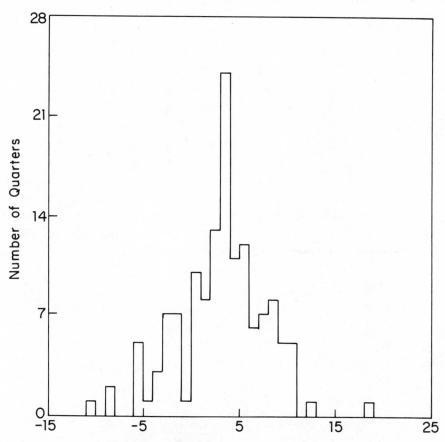

Fig. C2.2   Histogram of quarterly GNP growth rates, 1949–82.

Table C2.2   **Skewness of Quarterly Changes in GNP and Industrial Production, 1950–79**

Country	Industrial Production		GNP	
	Skewness	Standard Error	Skewness	Standard Error
United States	− .61	.42	− .33	.29
Japan	− .66	.40	− .43	.29
Canada	− .52	.39	− .42	.30
West Germany	− .01	.34	− .11	.26
United Kingdom	.13	.35	.61	.27
France	.27	.33	− .03	.24

Source: Data from the OECD *Historical Statistics* and from the 1984 *Business Conditions Digest.*

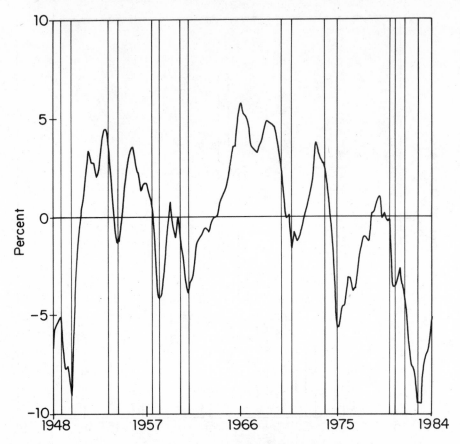

Fig. C2.3   Deviation of United States GNP from its natural rate. NBER reference cycle recessions shaded.

the way economic data are frequently analyzed. Figures C2.3 and C2.4 depict the NBER reference cycles, contractions are definitely shorter than expansions, confirming the judgments of Keynes and Mitchell. But this is a statistical artifact. The superposition of the business cycle upon a trend of economic growth implies that only the most severe portions of the declines relative to trend will appear as absolute declines and thus as reference cycle contractions. Even a symmetric business cycle superimposed on a rising trend would generate reference cycles for which the recessions would be short and severe relative to trend, even though the growth cycles—the cycles in detrended indexes— would be symmetric. As this argument suggests, there is little difference between the lengths of growth cycle expansions and contractions. The difference in length between expansions and contractions for the nine

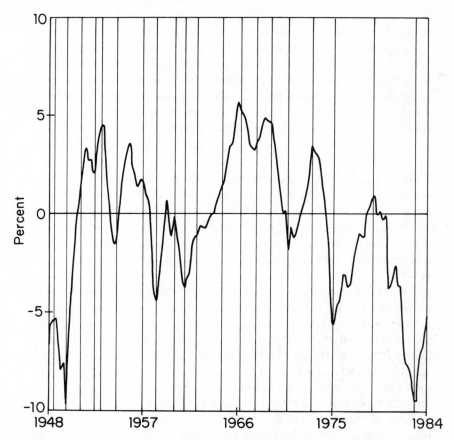

Fig. C2.4   Deviation of United States GNP from its natural rate. NBER growth cycle recessions shaded.

growth cycles averaged 0.9 quarters; the standard deviation of this estimate of the average is 1.4 quarters.[2] By contrast, the average length of the seven reference cycle expansions was 11.4 quarters longer than the length of the subsequent contractions.[3]

We conclude from this investigation that once one takes proper account of trend growth—using either our skewness-based approach or

2. We are assuming that each postwar business cycle is an independent draw from a population characterized partly by the difference in length between the expansion and the recession phase. Cycle dates are taken from Moore and Zarnowitz's "The Development and Role of the National Bureau of Economic Research's Business Cycle Chronologies" (appendix A to this Volume). Note that, as Moore and Zarnowitz report, it was not always the case that expansions were as a rule longer than contractions.

3. With a standard error of the mean of 3.3 quarters. Excluding the highly anomalous 1961–70 reference cycle, the mean difference is 8.1 quarters, and its standard error is 1.8 quarters.

the traditional NBER cycle dating approach—little evidence remains of cyclical asymmetry in the behavior of output. The impression to the contrary that we used to hold seems to result from a failure to take account either imrpessionistically or quantitatively of the effects of long-run economic growth. Few extant theories suggest that business cycles should depend on the rate of underlying growth of either productivity or population.[4] The next section considers whether similar conclusions are obtained using data on unemployment.

3.   Asymmetries in Unemployment?

Our conclusions so far contradict those of Neftci (1984), who examines the behavior of the unemployment rate and finds evidence against the null of symmetry at the .80 level. Neftci's statistical procedure seems inappropriate to us: eliminating the quantitative information in the data by reducing it to a series of ones (unemployment increasing) and zeros (unemployment decreasing) cannot lead to a test of maximum power.

Table C2.3 presents estimates of the skewness in detrended unemployment rates for the United States and other major OECD countries for the postwar period. We examine only the postwar data because earlier unemployment estimates are in general not derived independently from output data. For the United States, we confirm Neftci's conclusion. Indeed, we are able to reject the null hypothesis of symmetry at the .95 level. Annual data suggest as much skewness as quarterly data, but the skewness in annual data is not statistically significant.

None of the other OECD countries, however, have statistically significant skewnesses in their detrended unemployment rates.[5] This suggests that skewness in the United States is either a statistical accident or a result of a peculiarity in the United States labor market. Asymmetry in changes in unemployment rates is not a strong general feature of business cycles.

We have briefly attempted to examine the reasons for asymmetry in American unemployment rates. Skewness does not arise from the behavior of labor force participation: labor force participation rates exhibit no noticeable skewness, and skewness is present in detrended

4. But see Schumpeter 1939 for arguments that the cyclical variance of output is itself positively related to the rate of long-run growth.

5. Detrending European unemployment rates is not easy: there appears to have been an enormous rise in structural unemployment rates all over Europe in the past ten years. The results reported used a second-degreee polynomial to detrend the data. The results were effectively unchanged when a third- or a fourth-degree polynomial was used or when a piecewise linear trend with a breakpoint in 1973 was used. If the rise in unemployment is attributed entirely to cyclical factors—if the skewness of raw changes is calculated—then changes in European unemployment rates since 1970 appear strongly skewed.

Table C2.3	Skewness of Quarterly Changes in Unemployment Rates, 1950–79	
Country	Skewness	Standard Error
United States	1.03	.30
Japan	.40	.28
Canada	.55	.29
West Germany	− .13	.27
United Kingdom	.27	.30
France	.14	.33

Source: Data from the 1984 *Business Conditions Digest.*

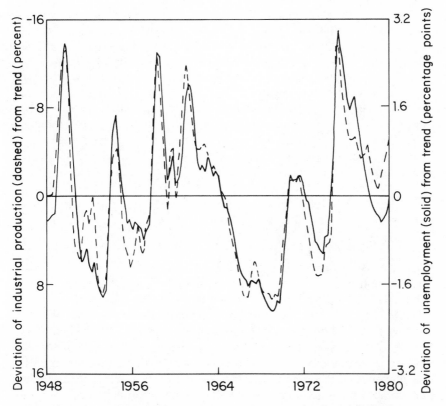

Fig. C2.5   United States industrial production and unemployment, 1948–80.

unemployment numbers as strongly as in detrended unemployment rates. Moreover, quarterly changes in employment over the period 1949–82 exhibit a skewness coefficient of − 1.90, significant at the .95 level. Skewness in employment and unemployment but not in GNP clearly indicates a breakdown in Okun's law. In figure C2.5, inverted deviations of industrial production from trend are plotted alongside the detrended unemployment rate. At business cycle peaks—unemployment troughs—the unemployment rate lags behind output measures. Output measures start to decline relative to trend before unemployment starts to rise. There is a period of time, after the growth cycle peak and before the reference cycle peak, during which output is falling relative to trend and employment is still rising relative to trend. This discrepancy in timing appears only near business cycle peaks. At business cycle troughs, the unemployment rate peaks within one quarter of the trough of output measures.

The significant coefficient of skewness found in the United States unemployment rate is apparently another manifestation of the "end of expansion" productivity effect documented in Gordon (1979). According to Gordon, normal equations for raw labor productivity go awry in the quarters after output reaches its maximum relative to trend. The magnitude of this effect can be seen in Gordon's figure 1 (reprinted as fig. C2.6). Output has begun to fall relative to trend; employment is still rising relative to trend; and so raw labor productivity naturally declines sharply. Firms are able to expand their work forces rapidly after business cycle troughs in order to keep pace with rising aggregate demand. Why don't they contract their work forces relative to trend after growth cycle peaks? We suspect that there is an explanation related to the burgeoning literature on labor hoarding (see Medoff and Fay 1983 or Fair 1984, for example), but it is beyond our competence to suggest here what the explanation might be.

4.   Conclusion

Our investigation into the possible asymmetry of the business cycle has, in our estimation, failed to turn up significant evidence that the econometric model building approach to business cycles is misguided. We could not find the skewness coefficients we thought we would find; and we therefore conclude that it is reasonable in a first approximation, to model business cycles as symmetric oscillations about a rising trend. GNP growth rates and industrial production growth rates do not provide significant evidence of asymmetry. We therefore think that the main advantage of the econometric model building approach—the body of statistical theory behind it—makes it the methodology of choice for analyzing macroeconomic fluctuations.

Our results call into question at least one possible justification for using reference cycles in studying macroeconomic fluctuations. An alternative justification for the reference cycle approach stresses the commonality of the patterns of comovements in variables across different business cycles. Blanchard and Watson's paper challenges this proposition. Studies of macroeconomic fluctuations using the reference

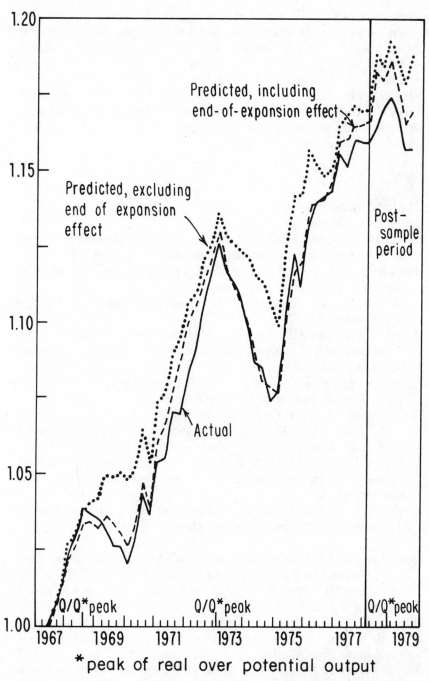

Predicted, including
end-of-expansion effect

Predicted, excluding
end of expansion
effect

Actual

Post-
sample
period

Q/Q*peak

Q/Q*peak

Q/Q*peak

1967 1969 1971 1973 1975 1977 1979

*peak of real over potential output

Fig. C2.6   Output per hour in the nonfarm business sector, actual and
predicted from alternative equations, 1969:2 to 1979:3. Reprinted from Gordon 1979.

cycle approach are the foundation of empirical macroeconomics. But given the availability of modern statistical methods, there appears to be no scientific basis for the use of reference cycles in either macroeconomic analysis or forecasting. As yet, no phenomenon or regularity has been adduced that can be studied using the reference cycle approach but is inconsistent with the assumptions of standard time series methods. Until such a demonstration is provided, there is little justification for the continued use of reference cycles in studying or forecasting macroeconomic fluctuations.

References

Adelman, Irma, and Frank L. Adelman. 1959. The dynamic properties of the Klein-Goldberger model. *Econometrica* 27: 598–625.

Blanchard, O. J. 1983. An index of fiscal policy. Mimeographed, Massachusetts Institute of Technology.

———. 1985. Debt, deficits and finite horizons. *Journal of Political Economy* 93:223–47.

Brunner, Karl, and Allan Meltzer. 1978. *The problem of inflation.* Carnegie-Rochester Conference Series on Public Policy 8. Amsterdam: North-Holland.

Burns, A., and W. C. Mitchell. 1946. *Measuring business cycles.* New York: National Bureau of Economic Research.

deLeeuw, F., T. M. Holloway, D. G. Johnson, D. S. McClain, and C. A. Waite. 1980. The high-employment budget: New estimates, 1955–1980. *Survey of Current Business* 60 (November): 13–43.

deLeeuw, F., and T. M. Holloway. 1982. The high employment budget: Revised estimates and automatic inflation effects. *Survey of Current Business* 62 (April): 21–33.

Engle, R. F. 1982. Autoregressive heteroskedasticity with estimates of the variance of United Kingdom inflation. *Econometrica* 50: 987–1008.

Fair, Ray C. 1984. Excess labor and the business cycle. Working Paper 1292, National Bureau of Economic Research.

Fischer, Stanley. 1980. *Rational expectations and economic policy.* Chicago: University of Chicago Press.

Frisch, R. 1933. Propagation problems and impulse problems in dynamic economics. In *economic essays in honor of Gustav Cassel.* London: George Allen.

Gordon, Robert J. 1979. The " end-of expansion" phenomenon in short-run productivity behavior. *Brookings Papers on Economic Activity* 10: 447–62.

————. 1982. Price intertia and policy ineffectiveness in the U.S., 1890–1980. *Journal of Political Economy* 90:6.

Hansen, A. H. 1951. *Business cycles and national income*. New York: Norton.

Hayashi, F. 1982. The permanent income hypothesis: Estimation and testing by instrumental variables. *Journal of Political Economy* 90 (October): 895–916.

Kendall, Maurice, and Alan Stuart. 1969. *The advanced theory of statistics*. 3 vols. London: McGraw-Hill.

Keynes, J. Maynard. 1936. *The general theory of employment, interest and money*. London: Macmillan.

Krasker, W. A., and R. E. Welsch. 1982. Efficient bounded-influence regression estimation. *Journal of the American Statistical Association* 77: 595–604.

Lucas, Robert E. 1977. Understanding business cycles. In *Stabilization of the domestic and international economy*, 7–29. Carnegie-Rochester Conference Series on Public Policy 1. Amsterdam: North-Holland.

Mitchell, Wesley C. 1927. *Business cycles: The problem and its setting*. New York: National Bureau of Economic Research.

Medoff, James L., and John A. Fay. 1983. Labor and output over the business cycle: Some direct evidence. Mimeographed.

Moore, Geoffrey, ed. 1961. *Business cycle indicators*. New York: National Bureau of Economic Research.

Neftci, Salih N. 1984. Are economic time-series asymmetric over the business cycle? *Journal of Political Economy* 92:21.

Nelson, C. R., and C. I. Plosser. 1982. Trends and random walks in macroeconomic time-series. *Journal of Monetary Economics* 10:2.

Schumpeter, Joseph A. 1939. *Business cycles*. New York: McGraw-Hill.

Slutsky, E. 1937. The summation of random causes as the sources of cyclic processes. *Econometrica* 5: 105–46.

II   Components of Expenditure

3　Inventory Fluctuations in the United States since 1929

Alan S. Blinder and Douglas Holtz-Eakin

3.1 Introduction

Inventory fluctuations are of great importance in business cycles. Indeed, to a surprisingly large extent, business cycles *are* inventory fluctuations—especially during recessions and in the early stages of recoveries. This basic feature of business cycles has been known for a long time, at least since the seminal work of Abramovitz (1950).

But inventory fluctuations are fundamentally a short-period phenomenon. Stocks of all types of inventories typically amount to about three months' sales, and even large changes in inventories amount to only a week's sales or less. Consequently, annual data may shed relatively little light on the nature of inventory fluctuations; most of the "action" may be played out within the year. For this reason, economists know precious little about inventory behavior before World War II.

This paper seeks to lift this veil of ignorance in two ways. First, we create—from some admittedly incomplete and imperfect data—monthly time series on inventory holdings in manufacturing, durables manufacturing, and nondurables manufacturing. To our knowledge, these are the first such series ever made available. We offer these data in the data appendix to this volume (appendix B) in the hope that others will find them useful. Second, we apply to the prewar data certain statistical

Alan S. Blinder is professor of economics at Princeton University. Douglas Holtz-Eakin is assistant professor in the Department of Economics at Columbia University.

We thank Ben Bernanke and Bruce Lehmann for alerting us to useful sources of historical data, Robert Gordon for providing his data on "natural" GNP, and Owen Irvine, Michael Lovell, Louis Maccini, Carl Walsh, Kenneth West, our discussants, and several conference participants for helpful comments on earlier drafts. Research support from the National Science Foundation and the Social Science Research Council is gratefully acknowledged.

procedures and models that are in common use with postwar data. In this way we can address the central issue of this conference: Has the business cycle changed?

While we do not wish to overstate the case, we were struck more by the similarities in inventory behavior between the prewar and postwar periods than by the differences. Considering the tremendous changes in the nature of American industry, in inventory management practices, in forecasting, and in the amplitude of business cycles, we found the degree of similarity surprising. But the relevant stylized facts are displayed below, and each reader can make up his or her own mind.

The rest of the paper is organized into three main sections. Section 3.2 documents the dominant role of inventories in recessions. Here the facts are fairly well known. Section 3.3 investigates some less well known aspects of the variances of production, sales, and inventory investment that Blinder (1981b, 1984) has recently emphasized using postwar data. In section 3.4, stock adjustment models similar to those popularized by Lovell (1961) are fit to data covering 1929–83 and subperiods. At least qualitatively, the results are rather similar in the prewar and postwar periods. Section 3.5 is a brief conclusion.

3.2   Inventories in Recessions

In a previous paper, Blinder (1981b) documented the dominant role of inventory swings in cyclical contractions. The data presented there are repeated and extended in table 3.1. Panel A shows the peak-to-trough movements in real GNP and real inventory investment in the eight postwar recessions, using quarterly data.[1] With the single exception of the "minirecession" of 1980, which some people think should never have been designated a recession, the important role of inventory movements is evident. Taking each recession as one observation, inventory changes have accounted, on average, for 101% of the total peak-to-trough change in real GNP. Or keeping score in a different way, the mean peak-to-trough change in inventory investment is 68% of the mean peak-to-trough change in GNP.[2]

Panel B, which is restricted to annual data, shows that a similar pattern prevailed in prewar recessions. In fact, the dominance of inventory fluctuations looks even more dramatic here. However, this

---

1. Peaks and troughs are defined by movements in real GNP, which sometimes differ a bit from NBER reference cycle peaks and troughs.

2. Naturally, trough-to-peak movements, which generally cover far longer periods, show no such dominance by inventory behavior. Hence these data are not shown. However, it is well known that GNP movements in the first few quarters of recoveries are dominated by inventory movements.

Table 3.1   **Changes in GNP and in Inventory Investment during Recessions**

Period	Change in Real GNP[a]	Change in Inventory Investment[a]	Change in Inventory Investment as Percentage of Change in Real GNP	Change in Inventory Investment as Percentage of GNP Gap at Trough[b]
A. Postwar Recessions (peak and trough)[c]				
1948:4 to 1949:4	−7.1	−13.0	183	71
1953:2 to 1954:2	−20.2	−9.2	46	90
1957:3 to 1958:1	−23.0	−10.5	46	41
1960:1 to 1960:4	−8.6	−18.0	209	68
1969:3 to 1970:4	−7.3	−12.3	168	60
1973:4 to 1975:1	−60.7	−38.0	63	52
1980:1 to 1980:2	−35.0	−1.6	5	3
1981:3 to 1982:4	−45.1	−38.8	86	25
B. Interwar Recessions				
1920–21	−3.6	−4.2	117	30
1923–24	1.5	−3.7	—[d]	336
1926–27	1.0	−0.8	—[d]	—[e]
1929–32	−32.0	−5.6	18	17
1937–38	−3.1	−2.9	94	11
C. Postwar Recessions (peak and trough)[c]				
1953–54	−7.5	−3.7	49	71
1957–58	−2.9	−3.3	114	14
1969–70	−2.0	−7.3	365	365
1973–75	−22.7	−23.9	105	37
1979–80	−4.4	−11.7	266	23
1981–82	−28.4	−17.9	63	13

Source: Postwar data are from the national income and product accounts; interwar data are adapted from Abramovitz (1950, table 84, 476–77).
[a]Billions of 1972 dollars for postwar data, billions of 1929 dollars for interwar data.
[b]GNP gaps are based on Gordon's (1984) natural GNP series.
[c]Peaks and troughs of real GNP, not official dates of the National Bureau of Economic Research.
[d]Real GNP rose during this recession.
[e]No GNP gap in "trough" year.

may be an artifact of using annual data. As can be seen in panel B, several "recessions" display no decline in GNP on an annual basis. To get a cleaner prewar/postwar comparison, panel C puts the postwar data on an annual basis. (Two of the eight recessions disappear in the process.) Comparing panels A and C shows that annual data make inventory fluctuations look even more important than quarterly data, as we suspected. Comparing panels B and C suggests that inventory fluctuations played a more predominant role in postwar than in prewar recessions.

But in any case the main conclusion is obvious: there is really no hope of understanding the dynamics of recessions without analyzing inventory behavior. Lest we be accused of false advertising, we hasten to point out that inventories play their main role in *propagating* business cycles, not in *causing* them. We do not claim, and we do not believe, that business cycles are typically initiated by autonomous movements in inventory investment. In fact, as we shall show later, a crude measure of the impulses originating in the inventory sector suggests that they are rather small.

Another well-known fact about business cycles is that much of the cyclical action comes in the manufacturing sector, and more particularly in the durables manufacturing subsector. For this reason we tried to use our more detailed monthly data on manufacturing to conduct a peak-to-trough analysis of inventory investment in manufacturing and in the durables and nondurables subsectors.

This, however, proved impossible to do in any systematic way. One minor problem was that monthly data on manufacturing output display so much volatility that picking out peaks and troughs was no easy matter. But the major problem was that month-to-month gyrations in inventory investment are so large that—for most recessions—a strategic choice of endpoints can make inventory change appear to be either a large or a small fraction of the decline in production. Though it is hard to quantify, we did cull one basic impression from this effort: inventory swings seems to be a less dominant force in contractions in the manufacturing sector than in the whole economy. This observation underscores the importance of retail inventory movements—a point emphasized in Blinder (1981b).

3.3 Decomposing the Variance of Output

So far we have considered only periods of recession, which are, almost by definition, special cases. A more general impression of the importance of inventory movements in business cycles can be obtained by asking how much of the variance of output is attributable to changes in inventory investment.

3.3.1 The Whole Economy

An identity relates production, sales, and inventory investment. For the whole economy, if Y is GNP, X is final sales, and ΔN is inventory investment, the identity is:

(1) $$Y_t = X_t + \Delta N_t.$$

If we then detrend each time series and take the variances of both sides, we obtain:

(2) $$\text{var}(y) = \text{var}(x) + \text{var}(\Delta n) + 2\text{cov}(x, \Delta n),$$

which is a convenient way to decompose the variance of GNP around trend.

Estimates of the elements of equation (2) invariably lead to the conclusion that var(y) exceeds var(x); in this sense, inventory fluctuations are "destabilizing." This is well known. But to go further, or to be more precise, a serious data problem must be confronted. The period 1929–46 contains nothing but aberrant observations—the Great Depression followed by World War II. While the precise procedure used to detrend postwar data has little effect on equation (2), quite different results can be obtained by applying different detrending procedures to the momentous ups and downs of the earlier data. Thus we really must decide how to "detrend" the depression and the war.

We experimented with two procedures and ultimately settled on one. We first developed a purely statistical definition of trend by regressing the log of each time series in (1) on a constant, time, and time squared—omitting the years 1930–39 and 1941–46 on the grounds that they were obviously far from trend. Two problems quickly became apparent. First, the choice of which years to omit from the regression is somewhat arbitrary. Second, since each time series is detrended separately, and in logs, the identity (1) does not add up in the detrended data, and so (2) does not hold exactly. This discrepancy never amounted to much in previous work on postwar data by Blinder (1981b, 1984). But in this application, the left-hand side of equation (2) turned out to be 16% smaller than the right-hand side. That is quite a discrepancy.

So we rejected the purely statistical approach. Instead, we defined trend GNP as Robert Gordon's (1984) "natural" GNP, which he computes by applying an Okun's law conversion to a series for the natural rate of unemployment. "Natural" final sales and "natural" inventory investment were defined, essentially, by assuming that the mean value of X/Y observed in the sample was the "natural" ratio of final sales to GNP. (Details are in appendix 3.3.)

Table 3.2 shows the elements of equation (2), plus some related statistics, for the whole period and for several subperiods. Several dramatic differences between the periods 1947–83 and 1929–46 can be observed.

First, notice that the variance of detrended GNP in the postwar period is less than one-third as large as it was in the earlier period (col. 1), and the variance of detrended final sales is less than one-fourth as

Table 3.2   Decomposition of the Variance of Real GNP (Annual Data, in Billions of 1972 Dollars)

Period	Var (y)	Var (x)	Var (Δ n)	2Cov (x, Δ n) (Corr (x, Δ n))	$\frac{\text{Var (y)}}{\text{Var (x)}}$	$\frac{\text{Var (Δ n)}}{\text{Var (x)}}$
	(1)	(2)	(3)	(4)	(5)	(6)
1929–83	3123.7	2821.7	41.8	260.2 (.38)	1.11	.015
1947–83	1746.3	1327.1	48.7	370.5 (.73)	1.32	.037
1929–46	5992.9	5935.3	29.5	28.0 (.03)	1.01	.005
1929–41	1355.1	1109.6	28.0	217.6 (.62)	1.22	.025

Note: Entries are the *variances* of the differences between the actual and "natural" times series, not merely the squared deviations of actual from natural.

large (col. 2). In contrast, the postwar variance of inventory investment is actually larger than its value in the earlier period (col. 3). Thus the remarkably more stable postwar economy did not have more stable inventory behavior. In consequence, inventory fluctuation played a much more important role in the postwar economy than it had previously (col. 6).

Since the covariance between inventory investment and final sales rises tremendously after the war (col. 4, top number of each row), x and Δn are much more positively correlated in the postwar period (col. 4, bottom number). With cov$(x,\Delta n)$ and var(Δn) both growing larger relative to var(x), the ratio var(y)/var(x) increased from 1.01 before 1947 to 1.32 after—a large increase.

A natural question to ask is, How much of these differences can be attributed to the war years? And the answer, as table 3.2 shows, is most of it. Naturally the variances of GNP and final sales are much smaller when the war years are excluded. What is striking, however, is that the variance of inventory investment hardly changes. If we compare the period 1929–41 with the period 1947–83, we find that both the ratio var(y)/var(x) the correlation between sales and inventory change are quite similar in the two periods (see cols. 4 and 5).

Thus, if we exclude the war years, a clear picture of continuity in the stylized facts emerges between the prewar and postwar periods. This is an important link to earlier work with postwar data. Blinder (1981b, 1984) called attention to two salient features of the variance decomposition that seem to cast doubt on the major prevailing theory of inventory behavior: the production smoothing/buffer stock model. These features are: (*a*) The variance of production exceeds the variance of sales, in apparent contradiction of the idea that inventories are used to smooth production in the face of fluctuating sales. (*b*) Final sales and inventory change actually covary positively (or not at all), not negatively, in contrast to the alleged role of inventories as a buffer stock.

Blinder (1984) shows that these two facts are not literally inconsistent with an elaborate version of the production smoothing model that includes cost shocks and allows for a complicated structure of demand disturbances. Specifically, cost shocks lead to intertemporal substitution possibilities in production that can make it optimal for var(y) to be greater than var(x) for a value-maximizing firm. And a particular type of persistence in demand shocks can make it optimal for a firm to build inventories when it experiences a positive sales shock.

Nonetheless, the facts do suggest that the theory is barking up the wrong empirical tree in that these appendages, not the basic theory itself, carry all the explanatory power. The central idea of the theory is that a firm with a concave production function and sales that vary over time (either deterministically or stochastically) will find it optimal to smooth production relative to sales. Yet, in fact, output is more variable than sales. The buffer stock motive emphasizes the role of inventories in cushioning the effects of sales "shocks" on output. Yet inventories rise, rather than fall, when sales rise.[3]

Table 3.2 shows that these two troublesome features of the postwar data also characterize the earlier data, and to a remarkably similar degree if the war years are excluded. Thus the problems with conventional inventory theory emphasized by Blinder (1981b, 1984) did not originate in the postwar period.

3.3.2   The Manufacturing Sector

Manufacturing output is the most volatile component of GNP, so it is worth seeing how a variance decomposition like equation (2) looks using monthly data for manufacturing. Before looking at the results, we should say something about how the prewar data on manufacturing output, shipments, and inventories were constructed, although the details are reserved for appendixes 3.1 and 3.2.

In this context it is important to note that when the identity (1) is applied to the manufacturing sector, Y denotes production, X denotes shipments, and N denotes the stock of finished goods plus works in progress. Inventories of materials and supplies are excluded.[4] Unfor-

---

3. Deviations of sales from trend include both anticipated and unanticipated components. Thus the observed covariance between inventory investment and deviations of sales from trend is a composite of two effects that presumably differ in sign. The evidence suggests that the anticipated component of sales fluctuations is dominant, whereas the buffer stock model stresses the unanticipated component.

4. Let y_t be goods that are fully produced within the period, z_t be goods that are started, and q_t be works in progress that are completed. Then the change in finished goods inventories is $y_t + q_t - X_t$, while the change in works in progress is $z_t - q_t$. Adding these up and noting that $Y_t = y_t + z_t$ gives the conclusion stated in the text.

tunately, the data available to us did not distinguish among finished goods, works in progress, and raw materials, but lumped all inventories together. Consequently, our inventory data are not quite appropriate. Because our general procedure was to piece together two of the three time series needed for equation (1) and then use the identity to infer the third,[5] this data problem introduced some unavoidable errors into our constructed series.

For the whole manufacturing sector, we used the Federal Reserve Board index of industrial production to create a monthly series on output (Y) in 1929 dollars. Then we combined annual end-of-year inventory data from Abramovitz (1950) with monthly index numbers from the *Conference Board Economic Record* to create a monthly inventory stock series (N). (Details are in appendix 3.1.) From these, X was created by using equation (1). Thus our synthetic series on shipments is actually "true" shipments minus the change in raw materials inventories (which is unobserved). Our constructed series on production is displayed in figure 3.1. The underlying data, as well as corresponding data on shipments and inventories, are in the data appendix to this volume.

For the durable and nondurable subsectors, the situation was just the reverse. Conference Board data on monthly shipments and inventory stocks were used to create a synthetic "production" series from equation (1). (Details are in appendix 3.2, and the data are in the data appendix to the volume, appendix B.) Thus our series on Y_t is actually the "true" Y_t plus the change in raw materials inventories.

With these provisos understood, let us look at the data. Because our prewar inventory data include changes in raw material inventories (ΔM) even though (1) excludes them, our measured series for manufacturing are related to the conceptually "true" series by:

$$\hat{\Delta N} = \Delta N + \Delta M$$

$$\hat{X} = X - \Delta M,$$

where "hats" denote measured time series. Hence our measured series will almost certainly overstate var(Δn)[6] and can overstate or understate var(x) and cov($x,\Delta n$) depending on how strongly X and ΔM covary.[7] The output series (Y) is constructed independently and hence is not

5. This is actually what is done with the postwar data as well. The Bureau of Economic Analysis provides data on inventories and shipments, from which we create production data to satisfy equation (1).

6. Only if ΔM and ΔN were strongly negatively correlated, which is emphatically untrue in the postwar data, could measured inventory change display less variation than true inventory change.

7. With the magnitudes that characterize the postwar period, var(x) and cov($x,\Delta n$) might actually both be biased down by the measurement error. But we cannot be sure.

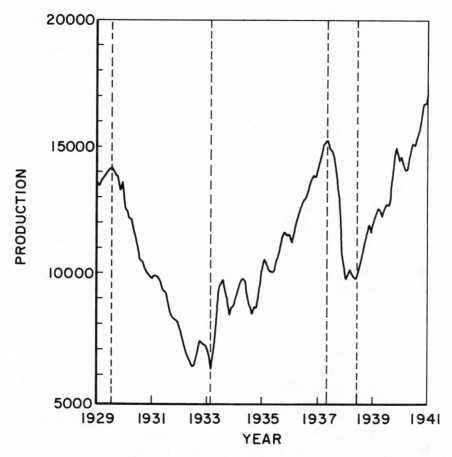

Fig. 3.1   Total manufacturing production, 1929–41. Vertical lines mark
turning points.

affected by this particular measurement problem. Some evidence presented in appendix 3.1 suggests that these measurement errors are not
too severe if we stick to the levels of the variables rather than the first
differences. So that is what we do.

But there remains the problem of "detrending" the Great Depression
and World War II, a period in which manufacturing output first sank
like a stone and then rose like a rocket (see fig. 3.1). For manufacturing
we have no "natural output" series, analogous to Gordon's natural
GNP, to fall back on. So a statistical procedure was imperative. We
tried three alternatives: (a) peak-to-peak interpolation (in logs), using
1929 and either 1940 or 1941 as "peak" years; (b) estimating the 1929–
41 trend by fitting a log-linear regression line to the monthly data.

Notice that either version of procedure (*a*) treats essentially the whole period as "below trend." (The monthly data end in 1941.) This is a strange way to define a trend, but it is conceptually close to Gordon's "natural GNP." By contrast, a regression line must pass through the point of means, so procedure (*b*) labels half the period 1929–41 as "above trend" and half as "below trend." Neither procedure is particularly appealing. Fortunately, as appendix 3.3 shows, although the choice of detrending procedure greatly affects the estimated variances, *ratios* of variances are relatively insensitive. Hence the tables that follow use one particular detrending procedure (peak-to-peak interpolation between 1929 and 1941) and report only the statistics that are "scale free."

Detrending the postwar data (1959–82) was easier. Each time series was detrended by the following model of the trend component:

$$\log Z_t = a + bt + cD_t + dA_t + e_t,$$

where t is time, D_t is a second time trend (for OPEC) beginning at 1 in October 1973, A_t is zero until January 1966 and 1 thereafter, and e_t is a white noise disturbance. (The variable A_t—used because the Bureau of Economic Analysis (BEA) has revised the data since 1966, but not before—is unimportant in practice.)

Finally, we are ready to look at the results. Panel A of table 3.3 shows that the prewar data share with the postwar manufacturing inventory and sales data the two outstanding characteristics emphasized above:

1. The ratio var(y)/var(x) is greater than one, in apparent contradiction of the idea that firms want to smooth production. This ratio is a bit smaller in the prewar period (1.08 versus 1.15) but still greater than one. As noted above, the model is not literally contradicted by the finding that var(y) exceeds var(x) because cost shocks can rationalize such a variance ratio. Nonetheless, some statement about the nature of shocks is part and parcel of any stochastic model of economic behavior, and there is no doubt that the traditional production smoothing model emphasizes demand shocks, not cost shocks.[8]

2. Cov($x,\Delta n$) is not negative, as suggested by the buffer stock motive for holding inventories. In fact, the covariance is slightly more positive in the prewar period than in the postwar period.

8. McCallum's comment offers a numerical example in which demand shocks and cost shocks apparently have equal variances, and yet the optimal value of var(y)/var(x) for the firm is 18.7! This example is misleading, however. By picking numerical values that make the marginal revenue curve ten times as steep as the marginal cost curve, McCallum makes the Lagrange multiplier (the shadow value of inventories) ten times as sensitive to shifts in the MC curve as to shifts in the MR curve. Thus his choice of parameter values renders demand shocks totally unimportant, as can be seen in his equations (13). The tremendous coefficient of the cost shock (u) in the output (y) equation dominates all the others when variances are computed.

Table 3.3   **Analysis of the Variance of Manufacturing Output (Monthly Data)**

Period	Var (y)/Var (x) (1)	Corr (x, Δn) (2)	Var (Δn)/Var (x) (3)
A. Total Manufacturing			
Prewar (1929–41)	1.08	0.25	0.012
Postwar (1959–82)	1.15	0.20	0.063
Postwar (with errors)	1.26	0.23	0.056
B. Durables Manufacturing			
Prewar (1929–41)	1.11	0.46	0.014
Postwar (1959–82)	1.43	0.22	0.089
Postwar (with errors)	1.61	0.27	0.067
C. Nondurables Manufacturing			
Prewar (1929–41)	1.05	0.12	0.035
Postwar (1959–82)	1.06	0.05	0.046
Postwar (with errors)	1.16	0.12	0.040

One noticeable difference between the two periods is the relatively greater role of inventory variability in the (more stable) postwar period. The variance of inventory investment is only about 1% of the variance of shipments in the prewar period, but it rises to 6% in the postwar period. This finding in the monthly manufacturing data echoes what we saw earlier in the annual economywide data for 1929–46, but not for 1929–41.

The third line in each panel of table 3.3 requires some explanation. Our postwar data have been corrected (by us, not by the BEA) to account for the facts that one 1972 dollar of finished goods in inventory represents more physical units than one 1972 dollar of shipments and, similarly, one 1972 dollar of works in progress represents more physical units than one 1972 dollar of finished goods.[9] These adjustments cannot be made to the prewar data. Also, the aforementioned problem with raw material inventories does not afflict the postwar data. To put the two time periods on a more equal footing, we created an ''incorrect'' set of postwar data in which we deliberately introduced the wrong

9. For a full explanation of the problem and an explanation of our corrections, see West 1983 and Blinder and Holtz-Eakin 1983.

treatment of raw material inventories (and calculated shipments incorrectly from the identity) and failed to make the corrections for physical units just mentioned.

Results with these erroneous data are presented in the third line of each panel of table 3.3. In general they suggest that the data errors are not of enormous import.

3.3.3 Durables and Nondurables Manufacturing

Data problems are a little different in the durables and nondurables sectors because here we have data on sales and inventories (including, once again, raw material inventories) and need to construct output. Hence our measured series are related to the "true" series by:

$$\hat{Y} = Y + \Delta M$$

$$\hat{\Delta N} = N + \Delta M.$$

This creates different statistical biases from those present in the data for manufacturing as a whole.

Results from decomposing the variance of output in durables and nondurables manufacturing are presented in panels B and C of table 3.3. The results for durables are rather similar to those for all manufacturing, except that the ratio var(y)/var(x) in the postwar period is much larger in durables than in manufacturing as a whole. Results for nondurables show a smaller var(y)/var(x) ratio and less covariance between sales and inventory change but are qualitatively similar.

Thus the findings of this section seem quite robust. Like the postwar data, the prewar data are characterized by a ratio of var(y)/var(x) that exceeds unity, a positive cov($x,\Delta n$), and a small ratio of var(Δn)/var(x). The major difference between the two periods seems to be that var(y)/var(x) is higher after the war.

3.4 A Simple Characterization of the Inventory Cycle

How can we characterize the cyclical behavior of inventory investment in a simple way? The stock adjustment model pioneered by Lovell (1961) seems a good place to start, since it has become the workhorse of empirical research on inventories.

The model consists of two equations. The first states that inventory investment is some fraction of the gap between actual and desired inventories, minus a fraction of unanticipated sales; the latter represents the buffer stock role of inventories. Thus

(3) $N_{t+1} - N_t = b(N^*_{t+1} - N_t) - c(X_t - {}_{t-1}X^e{}_t) + e_t,$

where N^*_{t+1} is desired inventories, ${}_{t-1}X^e{}_t$ is expected sales, and e_t is a stochastic error. The second equation is a specification of desired inventories, which are commonly taken to be a linear function of expected sales:

$$(4) \qquad\qquad N^*_{t+1} = A + a_{t-1}X^e_{t+1}.$$

This model of inventory behavior has many defects, some of which have already been mentioned.[10] In addition, several other problems have emerged when equations like (3) and (4) have been estimated. One persistent problem is that the estimated speed of adjustment, b, usually turns out to be too slow to be believed.[11] Despite this apparently slow adjustment, the estimate of c normally turns out to be near zero (and is sometimes negative!), suggesting that production moves almost one to one with sales.[12] In addition, when such obvious "cost" variables as wages and interest rates are added to (4) as determinants of desired inventories, they often get the wrong sign. Finally, except for manufacturers' inventories of finished goods, the theoretical motivation for partial adjustment is not clear.[13]

Despite all these reservations, the stock adjustment model is a simple way of putting some structure on the data, summarizing the time series in a way that is more meaningful than an unrestricted vector autoregression. Obviously, the stock adjustment model is a vector autoregression that has been constrained in a particular way suggested by economic theory—which has the advantage of giving economic interpretations to the estimated coefficients.

Note, however, that the stock adjustment model is incomplete in that it tells us nothing about the path of final sales. Since the X_t process is autonomous, the model only describes how inventories (and implicitly output) fluctuate given autonomous fluctuations in sales. Explaining fluctuations in sales goes well beyond the purview of this paper; indeed, this volume contains several papers devoted to this task.

10. For a discussion of these defects, see Blinder 1981b, 1984.

11. Maccini and Rossana 1984 appears to be a prominent exception. But we believe their rapid adjustment speeds are artifacts of their estimation technique. Blinder 1984, using essentially the same data as Maccini and Rossana, reports that the likelihood function implied by the stock adjustment model with first-order serial correlation in the disturbance has two local maxima: one with rapid adjustment and high serial correlation, the other with slow adjustment and little serial correlation. Maccini and Rosanna use a two-step procedure that, in practice, selects the former. But Blinder 1984 finds that the latter is the global maximum in most industries.

12. Slow adjustment and low c have often been thought to be contradictory. However, Blinder 1984 shows that there is no necessary contradiction. He also shows that a negative value of c can be rationalized if the econometrician knows less about the firm's sales than the firm does and if demand shocks have a particular form of persistence.

13. For manufacturers' inventories of finished goods, Holt et al. 1960 and Blinder 1982 show that the model can be derived by maximizing discounted profits subject to quadratic revenue and cost functions.

3.4.1 Stock Adjustment Estimates for the Whole Economy

We begin with annual data for the whole economy. To "close" the model, we assume that expectations are formed rationally. There are several ways to estimate rational expectations models like this one.

One way, a limited information method suggested by McCallum (1976, 1979), is to substitute equation (4) into (3) and use an instrumental variable procedure to deal with the unobserved expectation. But as McCallum (1979) notes, this technique may not be very promising when both the actual and the expected value of sales appear in the equation—which is the case in (3).

Another way, a full information procedure suggested by Sargent (1978), is to posit an explicit stochastic process generating sales and then estimate the parameters of the stochastic process jointly with the parameters of (3) and (4), imposing the cross-equation restrictions implied by rational expectations. This paper is not an appropriate place to discuss the merits and demerits of limited versus full information econometric procedures. Suffice it to say that both have both.

We adopted the full information technique under the assumptions that the disturbance e_t in equation (3) is AR(1) and that final sales are generated by an autonomous AR(2) time series process around a quadratic time trend:

$$(5) \qquad X_t = a_0 + a_1 t + a_2 t^2 + pX_{t-1} + qX_{t-2} + u_t:$$

As a check, we also estimated the system without the cross-equation constraints. Much to our surprise, the constrained estimates hardly differed from the unconstrained estimates, so we report only the constrained estimates (with asymptotic t-ratios in parentheses) for the whole period 1929–83 below:

$$N_{t+1} - N_t = .19 \, (N^*_{t+1} - N_t) + .075 \, (X_t - {}_{t-1}X^e_t)$$
$$(2.1) \qquad\qquad\qquad (2.1)$$

$$N^*_{t+1} = 44.1 + .235 \, {}_{t-1}X^e_{t+1}$$
$$(0.8) \quad (1.9)$$

$$R^2 = .35, \, \rho = .23, \, DW = 1.96$$
$$(1.8)$$

$$X_t = \text{time trend} + 1.44 \, X_{t-1} - .44 \, X_{t-2}.$$
$$(11.3) \qquad\qquad (3.3)$$

$$R^2 = .996 \qquad DW = 1.86$$

These estimates share the problems that are familiar from studies of less aggregative postwar data. The estimated speed of adjustment is quite low—only 19% per year. The coefficient of "unexpected sales" gets the wrong sign, indicating that unexpectedly high sales lead to inventory accumulation. More probably, this coefficient indicates that our unexpected sales proxy is not unexpected by firms, which is hardly surprising when using annual data.[14]

Since the constant in the desired inventory equation is small, the estimated marginal inventory/sales ratio is close to the historical average inventory/sales ratio, which is .25. The AR(2) process for final sales takes a familiar form: the coefficient of lagged sales exceeds unity, and the coefficient of X_{t-2} is negative.[15]

These results are less than awe inspiring. One possibility is that the stock adjustment model should be applied only to the sales of goods—or perhaps only to durable goods—rather than to all final sales, because there are no inventories in the service sector. However, when we did this, the only parameter estimate that changed much was "a"—which increased to reflect the rising inventory/sales ratio as we moved from goods and services to goods and then to durable goods. The parameter estimates may be unreasonable from a theoretical point of view, but they are robust.

The simple stock adjustment model tracks history surprisingly well, even during the Great Depression and World War II. The reason, of course, is that our simple AR(2) model of final sales fits the data quite well. The model underestimates sales at the start of World War II and overestimates them by more at the end. But considering that no special allowances were made for either the war or the depression, the tracking performance was good.

Since stock adjustment models have been estimated many times on postwar data, but never to our knowledge on prewar data, it is of interest to split the data and estimate the model on 1929–46 and 1947–83 subsamples. In splitting the sample, the number of degrees of freedom drops precipitously—especially in the prewar period. So we eliminated the quadratic time trend. Table 3.4 reports the results for the whole period and for the two subperiods.[16]

14. Monthly regressions with manufacturing data produce the correct (positive) sign for c, as will be seen shortly.

15. Unfortunately, this particular AR(2) model has a root that is almost exactly unity.

16. Notice that the earlier sample is 1929–45, not 1929–46. At first we included 1946, but we discovered that this one year had an extraordinary effect on all the regression estimates. It happens that inventory investment shot up to an unusually high level in 1946, even though final sales plunged. Though this may sound like normal behavior, it is not. When 1946 is added to the regression reported in table 3.4, the coefficient of unexpected sales falls from .12 to .02, the speed of adjustment falls from .32 to .05, the marginal inventory/sales ratio falls from .17 to .04, and the R^2 of the equation drops from .71 to .19.

Table 3.4   Estimates of Stock Adjustment Model: Whole Economy

Parameter	1929–83	1929–45	1947–83
Inventory equation			
a (inventory			
accelerator)*	.23	.17	.21
	(18.4)	(3.0)	(7.0)
b (adjustment			
speed)	.15	.32	.10
	(2.4)	(2.4)	(1.0)
c (unexpected sales)	−.093	−.123	−.230
	(3.1)	(2.4)	(6.6)
Autoregression			
for sales			
p	1.44	1.91	1.23
	(11.4)	(8.8)	(11.5)
q	−.43	−1.06	−.23
	(3.3)	(3.9)	(2.1)
R^{2a}	.34, .996	.71, .98	.66, .996
ρ^b	.22	.37	.28
	(2.0)	(2.2)	(3.7)
DW^a	1.97, 1.86	2.01, 1.71	2.14, 1.85
σ_e^2	30.3	8.51	16.2
σ_u^2	645.1	328.0	383.8

Note: The model is:
(3) $N_{t+1} - N_t = b(N^*_{t+1} - N_t) - c(X_t - {}_{t-1}X^e) + e_t$
(4) $N^*_{t+1} = A + a_{t-1}X^e$
(5) $X_t = \text{const.} + pX_{t-1} + qX_{t-2} + u_t$.

[a]The first number is for the inventory investment equation; the second number is for the final sales equation.

[b]For the inventory investment equation.

The results for the whole period are given only to provide a basis for comparison with the subsample results. They differ insubstantially from those given above, reflecting the fact that the best AR(2) sales model hardly changes when the time trend is omitted.

Despite the topsy-turvy nature of the economy during 1929–45, the estimates differ only moderately from those for the whole sample and the postwar subperiod. The main difference is that the estimated speed of adjustment is much faster in the period 1929–45 (32% per year) than in the period 1947–83 (10%). The marginal inventory/sales ratio is quite similar in the two periods, and the incorrectly signed buffer stock coefficient is smaller in the earlier period. In general, however, the 1929–45 and 1947–83 estimates of the stock adjustment are qualitatively similar.

Finally, and not surprisingly, the estimated AR(2) processes for final sales are quite different in the two subperiods. (Remember: no special allowances were made for the Great Depression or World War II.) Figure 3.2 shows how the simple AR(2) model of final sales copes with the Great Depression and World War II. Notice in particular that the beginning of the war comes as a large positive sales surprise to the model. Nevertheless, the fit is surprisingly good.

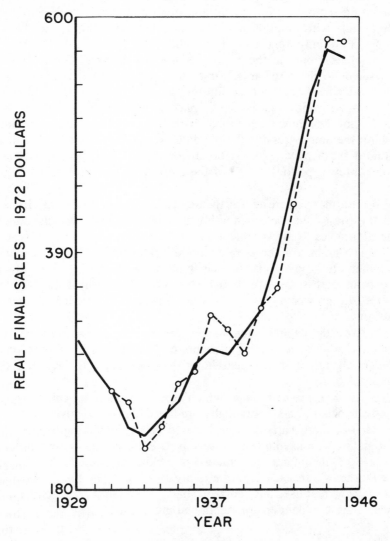

Fig. 3.2   Stock adjustment model, 1929–45. Actual, solid line; predicted, broken line.

One interesting observation can be added here. Notice that the variance of the disturbance term in the inventory equation—σ_e^2—is estimated to be almost twice as large in 1947–83 as in 1929–45. By this simple measure, then, business cycle *impulses* originating in the inventory sector have been almost twice as important since the war ended.

3.4.2 Stock Adjustment Estimates for Manufacturing

The same stock adjustment model can be estimated for the manufacturing sector and for the durables and nondurables subsectors. In doing this with monthly data, we modeled shipments as an AR(12) process around a quadratic time trend, rather than an AR(2). We do not bother reporting the many AR coefficients, but simply confine ourselves to three remarks. First, the coefficients in the prewar and postwar periods are not as different as might be expected. Second, the cross-equation restrictions implied by rational expectations were again imposed in all equations, with little effect on the estimates. Third, the autoregression fits the data on shipments so well that there is no point displaying its performance graphically. Even in the tumultuous prewar period, the R^2 of the autoregressions never falls below .92.

We are more interested in the stock adjustment equations. In estimating these equations on monthly manufacturing data, we added three new variables to the specification:

1. The nominal interest rate. Interest rates play an obvious role in all theoretical inventory models but rarely "work" empirically in postwar regressions. We thought it worth finding out if they do any better in prewar regressions. The theoretically predicted sign is negative.

2. Expected capital gains, as generated by an autoregression. This variable allows the two components of the real interest rate to enter separately rather than constraining the coefficients to be equal and opposite.

3. The real product wage, which serves as an empirical proxy for "cost shocks."³ The theoretically predicted sign is negative.

Each of these variables was entered in distributed lag form.[17] The estimates, with asymptotic t-ratios in parentheses, are shown in table 3.5 (for all manufacturing), table 3.6 (for durables), and table 3.7 (for nondurables). In each table there are two equations for the postwar period: the first uses the "correct" data, while the second deliberately makes the two data errors mentioned previously.

---

17. These were all quadratic Almon lags running from t to $t - 11$ with no endpoint constraints.

Table 3.5   **Estimates of Augmented Stock Adjustment Model: Manufacturing**

Parameter	Prewar	Postwar Good Data	Postwar Bad Data
a (inventory accelerator)	.50	3.06	1.85
	(5.8)	(2.5)	(6.7)
b (adjustment speed)	.43	.01	.02
	(8.2)	(1.1)	(3.6)
c (unexpected sales)	.11	.02	.03
	(4.0)	(1.8)	(1.3)
Nominal interest rate	683.8	−68.4	−18.8
(sum of lag coefficients)	(3.7)	(2.7)	(10.0)
Expected capital gains	−4.9	.16	.44
(sum of lag coefficients)	(4.1)	(0.5)	(1.6)
Real wages	1.9	−.012	−.004
(sum of lag coefficients)	(1.2)	(1.4)	(0.7)
Variance of residuals[a]	0.11, .298	.133, .769	.088, .770
R^{2}[a]	.86, .96	.297, .995	.49, .995
DW[a]	1.73, 1.74	2.06, 1.98	2.08, 1.95
ρ[b]	.85	.08	.23
	(22.0)	(1.2)	(3.7)

[a]The first number pertains to the inventory investment equation, the second to the sales equation.
[b]A first-order serial corrrelation correction was made to the inventory investment equation.

There are both differences and similarities between the prewar and postwar estimates. And where notable differences emerge, the fact that the postwar estimates with the deliberate data errors are close to the postwar estimates with the "correct" data suggests that the differences are genuine, not artifacts of the data. As in the economywide data, we once again find an indication that business cycle impulses originating in the inventory sector have been larger since the war. In each case, the variance of the residual in the inventory investment equation is larger in 1959–83 than it was in 1929–41.

It is probably best to deal with the individual coefficients variable by variable.

Adjustment speeds: With one exception (all manufacturing in the prewar period), monthly adjustment speeds are very low.[18] Interestingly, there is a clear tendency to find faster adjustment in the prewar

18. Notice that, in conformity with note 11, the one equation with rapid adjustment also has high estimated serial correlation in the disturbance term.

Table 3.6   Estimates of Augmented Stock Adjustment Model: Durables Manufacturing

Parameter	Prewar	Postwar Good Data	Bad Data
a (inventory accelerator)	2.19	3.38	2.33
	(3.3)	(3.5)	(9.0)
b (adjustment speed)	.06	.02	.04
	(2.8)	(2.8)	(6.0)
c (unexpected sales)	.07	.01	.01
	(2.0)	(0.4)	(0.5)
Nominal interest rate	18.2	−30.1	7.8
(sum of lag coefficients)	(0.4)	(1.5)	(0.5)
Expected capital gains	−.08	−.10	.33
(sum of lag coefficients)	(0.4)	(0.5)	(1.9)
Real wages	−.15	−.11	−.003
(sum of lag coefficients)	(0.7)	(1.2)	(0.5)
Variance of residuals[a]	.0022, .0134	.101, .449	.059, .451
R^{2a}	.68, .97	.35, .991	.53, .991
DW[a]	1.96, 1.98	2.04, 1.97	2.09, 1.92
ρ[b]	.34	.07	.12
	(3.7)	(1.1)	(2.0)

[a]The first number pertains to the inventory investment equation, the second to the sales equation.
[b]A first-order serial correlation correction was made to the inventory investment equation.

period than in the postwar period—just as we found with economywide annual data.

Inventory accelerator: In all manufacturing and in nondurables, the marginal inventory/sales ratio is much lower in the prewar period. In durables, this tendency is obscured by the data problems in the prewar period.

Unexpected sales: Unlike the economywide results, the proxy for unexpected sales gets the correct (positive) sign in all equations and is even significantly positive in several cases. However, all the coefficients are small in magnitude. So the basic finding of a weak buffer stock motive is maintained.

In sum, as compared with the postwar period, the inventory adjustment mechanism in the prewar period in manufacturing seems to have been characterized by more rapid (but still slow) adjustment, a correctly signed but small effect of unanticipated sales on inventory investment,

Table 3.7 **Estimates of Augmented Stock Adjustment Model: Nondurables Manufacturing**

Parameter	Prewar	Postwar Good Data	Postwar Bad Data
a (inventory accelerator)	0.61	1.83	1.58
	(2.1)	(0.9)	(4.9)
b (adjustment speed)	.14	.01	.03
	(3.1)	(0.5)	(1.7)
c (unexpected sales)	.05	.07	.07
	(1.3)	(1.8)	(2.2)
Nominal interest rate	57.2	− 13.4	− 7.0
(sum of lag coefficients)	(2.3)	(1.5)	(0.9)
Expected capital gains	.50	− .15	− .17
(sum of lag coefficients)	(2.2)	(1.1)	(1.2)
Real wages	.65	− .003	− .002
(sum of lag coefficents)	(1.8)	(1.0)	(0.9)
Variance of residuals[a]	.0032, .021	.031, .095	.022, .095
R^{2a}	.54, .88	.08, .996	.23, .996
DW[a]	1.93, 1.86	1.99, 1.97	1.95, 1.98
ρ^b	.43	.09	.24
	(4.0)	(1.4)	(3.8)

[a]The first number pertains to the inventory investment equation, the second to the sales equation.
[b]A first-order serial correlation correction was made to the inventory investment equation.

and a lower marginal inventory/sales ratio (and hence a weaker inventory accelerator).

Interest rates: The nominal interest rate variable gets the correct sign in all three postwar regressions (using good data).[19] But it is significant only in total manufacturing, not in either subsector—which raises suspicions about aggregation. Furthermore, the expected capital gains term is correctly signed in only one of the three postwar regressions, and the signs of the two interest rate variables are systematically wrong in the prewar regressions. In general, the interest rate variables

19. To interpret the magnitudes of the coefficients, it is necessary to know the units of measurement. In the prewar regressions, inventories and sales are in billions of 1929 dollars at monthly rates; in the postwar regressions, inventories and sales are in billions of 1972 dollars at monthly rates. In both cases the interest rate variables are monthly rates in decimal form (that is, .01 means roughly a 12% annual rate of interest).

do not perform well—which echoes the findings of most investigators of this issue.

Wage rates: Real wages get the wrong sign in two of the three prewar regressions. They get the correct sign in the postwar regressions but are far from significant.[20]

In general, then, neither the prewar nor the postwar data embrace the stock adjustment model—a matter not improved by the addition of some basic cost variables suggested by economic theory. Again, however, we find the prewar and postwar estimates quite similar, even if they fail to accord with the theory.

3.5 Summary and Conclusions

Inventory investment is the most volatile component of GNP. It plays a major role in business cycles, especially around turning points and during cyclical downswings, and is strongly procyclical. These facts are all well established for the postwar United States economy. And everything we know from prewar data—including annual national income data and monthly data on the manufacturing sector—suggests that the same stylized facts held in the prewar period as well.

Although the variability of the other 99% or so of GNP fell drastically between 1929–46 and 1947–83, most of this can be attributed to the wartime gyrations of final sales. The variability of inventory investment actually increased after the war. Furthermore, though inventory investment and final sales are essentially uncorrelated over 1929–46 and strongly positively correlated over 1947–83, most of this difference is also attributable to the war years. In fact, if the periods 1929–41 and 1947–83 are compared, the basic stylized facts about inventories and final sales for the whole economy look quite similar.

These stylized facts, for both the whole economy and the manufacturing sector in both the prewar and postwar periods, appear to contain bad news for the dominant empirical model of inventory behavior— the production smoothing/buffer stock model. In particular, while the fact that production is more variable than sales does not literally contradict the model, it certainly does move production smoothing off center stage. And the fact that sales and inventory change covary positively rather than negatively casts serious doubt on the empirical importance of the buffer stock motive.

Besides this circumstantial evidence, conventional stock adjustment equations do not perform at all well when estimated econometrically:

20. In the postwar regressions, real wages are an index number (1972 = 100); in the prewar regressions, real wages are in real 1929 dollars per hour. Hence the coefficients are not comparable across periods.

speeds of adjustment turn out to be implausibly low, the effect of "unanticipated" sales is rarely important and sometimes incorrectly signed, and such cost variables as interest rates and wages often (but not always) get the wrong sign. These annoying features of the inventory data are by now well known in postwar data. This paper shows that they more or less characterize the prewar data as well and that estimated stock adjustment models for inventory investment in the prewar period look moderately similar to their postwar counterparts.

The emphasis of this paper, therefore, unlike many of the others at this conference, is on continuity rather than on change. While other aspects of the business cycle were undergoing a virtual transformation, changes in the nature of inventory behavior were surprisingly small.

Appendix 3.1
Construction of Total Manufacturing Data

This study employs new data on production, shipments, and inventory holdings in constant dollars for the manufacturing sector of the United States economy monthly from 1929 to 1942. We constructed these data using a variety of sources; the details are presented in this appendix.

1. Production

The primary source is the monthly Federal Reserve Board (FRB) index of industrial production (1957–59 = 100) obtained from the Mitchell data base.[1] This index number was converted into a (seasonally adjusted) series on real output measured in 1929 dollars in the following steps:

1. From the *Economic Report of the President*, real GNP originating in manufacturing was obtained for the years 1957, 1958, 1959.
2. The average monthly output (the sum of the three annual outputs divided by thirty-six) was converted from 1972 to 1929 dollars using the implicit price deflator for total goods. In addition, the units were changed from billions to millions of dollars to be conformable with shipments and inventory data (see below).
3. A monthly real output series was created by using this benchmark and the monthly percentage changes from the FRB index.
4. The real output series was seasonally adjusted using the Census Bureau's X-11 program.

1. A computerized data base containing most of the time series used by Mitchell, available from the Inter-University Consortium for Political and Social Research.

2. Inventories

Two basic data sources are available. From the Mitchell data base, and ultimately from Abramovitz (1950), annual observations on the value of inventory holdings at the end of December of each year are available from 1929 to 1942. To create a monthly time series we used a monthly, seasonally adjusted index of the value of inventory holdings of the end of each month from the *Conference Board Economic Record* of 26 December 1940 (henceforth, *CBER*). Several observations are in order.

First, the inventory data from both sources include finished goods, works in progress, *and* raw materials. The inclusion of the latter presents a problem when the inventory data are used in the production-shipments-inventory investment identity:

$$Y_t = X_t + (N_{t+1} - N_t).$$

Here the conceptually appropriate inventory concept is the sum of finished goods and works in progress. Since the identity is used extensively, the inclusion of materials stocks in inventories is strictly incorrect, certainly unfortunate, but unavoidable. An effort will be made below to judge the importance of this on all critical calculations.

Second, the series created by deflating the nominal value of inventories by an (index of) output prices does not accurately reflect physical quantities. This is because inventory values are book values, which depend on the type of accounting (LIFO vs. FIFO), composition of inventory, and whether the inventories are valued at cost or market value. Typically, they are entered at the lower of the two choices. These problems are not restricted to interwar data but also are important in postwar inventory analysis (see West 1983 and Blinder and Holtz-Eakin 1983).

Finally, the *CBER* index is not a comprehensive index of manufacturing inventories. It is based on industries that account for only about one-eighth of inventory and shipment values, and it deliberately excludes data covering "food products, tobacco, liquors and petroleum, and certain lumber products" (*CBER*, 2).

The data used in this paper were derived in the following steps:
1. Consider the two series N_1 and N_2. N_1 is created by benchmarking the *CBER* index to the beginning-of-year inventory values given by Abramovitz (actually the 31 December value from the previous year), and N_2 is created by using the end-of-year values. The nominal, monthly series we use is a linear combination of N_1 and N_2 given by:

$$N_t = a_k N_{1t} + (1 - a_k)N_{2t},$$

where the weight in month k is a decreasing function of the distance

from the start of the year. Specifically, the weight (a_k) for January is 1, February 10/11, March 9/11, and so forth until a_k for December is equal to 0.
2. This series was converted to a real inventory series using the index (1929 = 100) of manufacturing prices described above. As noted above, that inventories are often valued at cost implies that this procedure will not exactly mimic movements in physical quantities of inventories.

3. Shipments

Real monthly shipments (in millions of 1929 dollars) were created using the identity

$$X_t = Y_t - (N_{t+1} - N_t),$$

and a corresponding nominal output series was created by multiplying the real series by the price index described below. As mentioned above, the inclusion of raw materials in the inventory stocks induces an error into the constructed shipments series. If X_t is the "true" shipments and $\hat{X}_t$ our estimate:

$$X_t - \hat{X}_t = M_{t+1} - M_t,$$

where M_t is the raw material inventory at the start of month t.

4. Price Index

The data from Mitchell contain a Bureau of Labor Statistics index of manufacturers' prices (1926 = 100). The price index was first converted to a 1929 = 100 base and then seasonally adjusted using the Census X-11 program.

5. A Check on Data Construction

There is one possible check on the accuracy of the data construction used above. The *CBER* data include a monthly, seasonally adjusted index of the value of manufacturers' shipments. Since our method of deriving shipments understates true shipments by the amount of raw material inventory investment (see above), it is of interest to see how well it resembles the movements in the direct measure of shipments given by the *CBER* index. In *levels*, the two measures are in close accord; the simple correlation between them is .989. However, the correlation between *percentage changes* in the *CBER* index and percentage changes in the constructed shipments series is less satisfactory—.511.

Because of this, we investigated alternative methods of constructing the data series.

6. Alternative Construction of Manufacturing Data

The alternative methods of data construction all involve measuring two of three variables—production, shipments, and inventories—and then using the identity linking them to impute the third. Earlier, we described a method that computes benchmarks for the production and inventory indexes and then constructs shipments as the residual. Below, we present the results of three variants of the following procedure: find benchmarks for shipments and production, and construct inventory investment using the identity. There is a catch. We are unable to locate a source containing estimates of the level of manufacturing shipments in the interwar period to use in converting the *CBER* index number into real 1929 dollars. Instead, we use various years from our basic series, above, as benchmarks to the *CBER* shipments index and then compute inventories accordingly. By doing this we include in the benchmark shipments the amount of raw materials inventory disinvestment during the benchmark month. However, the remaining monthly movements in raw materials inventory will be included in the inventory series via the identity. Ideally, the behavior of our basic series and the alternative will be quite similar. In practice they are not similar, and the behavior of the alternative is highly dependent upon the benchmark month chosen. We computed three variants of this alternative method:

	Benchmark Month
Variant I	February 1929
Variant II	January 1932
Variant III	December 1942

The relationships among the basic series and our three variants are summarized by the simple correlations:

	Shipments			
	Basic	*Variant 1*	*Variant 2*	*Variant 3*
Basic	1.0	—	—	—
Variant 1	.981	1.0	—	—
Variant 2	.981	1.0	1.0	—
Variant 3	.981	1.0	1.0	1.0

	Inventories			
	Basic	*Variant 1*	*Variant 2*	*Variant 3*
Basic	1.0	—	—	—
Variant 1	.457	1.0	—	—
Variant 2	−.207	−.402	1.0	—
Variant 3	.382	.864	.114	1.0

	Inventory Investment			
	Basic	*Variant 1*	*Variant 2*	*Variant 3*
Basic	1.0	—	—	—
Variant 1	−.030	1.0	—	—
Variant 2	−.180	.897	1.0	—
Variant 3	−.150	.936	.995	1.0

7. Effect of Construction Method on Variance Decomposition

The variance decomposition is the workhorse summary measure in this paper. We wish to determine the size and direction of the bias induced into the variance measures by the alternative methods of constructing the data.

Method 1

This is the method used to derive our "basic" series. First production and inventory data are derived, and then shipments are computed using the identity. *Assuming* that the indexes accurately reflect physical production and the value of inventory *and* that we may deflate using our price index (both are probably wrong):

$$X_t^1 = X_t - \Delta M_t,$$

where ΔM_t is raw materials inventory *investment* in month t, X^1 is the constructed series, and X is actual shipments. Accordingly:

$$\sigma_{x^1}^2 = \sigma_x^2 + \sigma_{\Delta M}^2 - 2\rho\sigma_x\,\sigma_{\Delta M}\,.$$

We know that $\rho > 0$ in postwar data. Similarly, we can show:

$$\text{cov}(x^1,\hat{\Delta N}) = \text{cov}(x,\Delta N) + \text{cov}(x,\Delta M)$$
$$- \text{cov}(\Delta M,\Delta F + \Delta W) - \sigma_{\Delta M}^2\,,$$

where ΔF is finished goods inventory investment and ΔW is investment in inventories of work in process. Thus:

$$\sigma_{x^1}^2 > \sigma_x^2 \text{ iff } 2\rho < \sigma_{\Delta M}/\sigma_x\,,$$

and

$$\text{cov}(x^1,\Delta\hat{N}) > \text{cov}(x,\Delta N) \text{ iff } \text{cov}(x,\Delta M) > \sigma_{\Delta M}^2 + \text{cov}(\Delta M,\Delta F + \Delta W).$$

Neither of these conditions is satisfied in the postwar data. Thus it seems likely that the variance of shipments is *biased down* and the covariance of shipments with inventory investment is *biased upward*.

Method 2

In this method we use the production series derived above and benchmark the *CBER* index of the value of shipments using a shipments value from our basic series. Assuming the same things as above, this method implies:

$$X_t^2 = X_t - X_t \left(\Delta M_B / X_B\right),$$

where X^2 is the constructed shipments series, ΔM_B is the investment in raw materials inventory in the base year, and X_B is shipments in the base period. Clearly, the behavior of this series is highly dependent upon the base period chosen. In particular

$$\sigma_{x^2}^2 = \sigma_x^2 \left[1 - \frac{\Delta M_B}{\Delta X_B} \right]^2,$$

which is biased either up or down depending upon the (unobserved) movement of raw materials inventory in the base period. Similarly:

$$\text{cov}(x^2, \Delta \hat{N}) = \left(1 - \frac{\Delta M_B}{\Delta X_B} \right) \left\{ \text{cov}(X, \Delta N) + \sigma_x^2 \left(\frac{\Delta M_B}{X_B} \right) \right\}.$$

Again the direction of the bias in the constructed series is unclear.

Appendix 3.2
Construction of Data for the Durables and Nondurables Sectors

This appendix describes the construction of data on manufacturers' production, shipments, inventory, and prices for durable and nondurable goods. It is worth emphasizing at the outset that different basic data series and different benchmarks were used to construct these data then were used to construct the data for all manufacturing described in appendix 3.1. Hence our data for durables and nondurables manufacturing in the paper do not add up to our data for all manufacturing.

1. Inventories

Indexes of the value of end-of-month inventories, seasonally adjusted, are available from the *CBER* for both durables and nondurables. These indexes are not ideal. (See the discussion in appendix 3.1.) The indexes were converted into a series on the nominal value (in millions of dollars) of inventories by benchmarking the indexes in December 1937, using information in the *1937 Census of Manufactures*[1] (in particular, 2:121). The nominal value of inventories in the durables and

---

1. 1937 was chosen because this census was used by *CBER* to weight its indexes.

nondurables sectors was computed as the sum of the end-of-year inventories in the appropriate (see below) industries from the census. Note that this includes raw materials and hence is subject to the same problems as the basic total manufacturing series.

Durable Goods Industries	*Nondurable Goods Industries*
Forest products	Food
Stone, clay, glass	Textiles
Iron and steel	Paper
Nonferrous metals	Printing and publishing
Machinery	Chemicals
Transportation equipment	Petroleum and coal
Miscellaneous	Rubber products
	Leather products

This division was chosen so as to conform as closely as possible with the categorization used by the BEA on postwar data.

The nominal series were converted to real (1929) dollars using a (common) price index for total manufacturing. This index was described in appendix 3.1.

2. Shipments

The *CBER* data provide indexes of the value of shipments, monthly and seasonally adjusted, for both types of goods. A direct benchmark to convert this index number into dollars was not available. Instead, the 1937 Census of Manufactures was employed to derive an average value of shipments in 1937, which was equated with the average value of the index in 1937. To do so, it was necessary to assume that the identity

$$y_t = x_t + (n_{t+1} - n_t)$$

held in value terms for 1937. That is, the value of shipments for 1937 was estimated by:

value of shipments = value of production − value of end of year
    inventory + value of beginning of year inventory,

where data for the value of production and value of inventory are taken from the census.

Then the value of shipments series constructed in this manner was deflated using the total manufacturing price index, resulting in a series on real shipments for both durables and nondurables.

3. Production

Real production was computed using the shipments-inventory-production identity. A nominal series was computed by multiplying the real series by the total manufacturing price index.

4. A Check on Data Construction

Ideally, the sum of the data on, say, production for durables manufacturing and nondurables manufacturing should exactly match the data for total manufacturing. Because of the methods employed here, however, this is far from true. Below are mean values (in millions of 1929 dollars) of shipments, inventories, and production for both total manufacturing as derived above and the sum of durables and nondurables manufacturing as derived above and the sum of durables and nondurables manufacturing as derived for this paper.

	Total Manufacturing	Sum of Durables plus Nondurables	Ratio
Production	13,216.3	4,669.7	.392
Shipments	12,858.7	4,646.8	.392
Inventory	13,405.8	9,275.7	.713

However, though the levels differ substantially, the movements in the two measures of manufacturing behavior are closely related. Below are correlations between the two:

Production	.983
Shipments	.979
Inventory	.932

Thus, while estimates of the behavior of levels of manufacturing shipments, production, and inventory will vary depending upon which method is chosen, the overall response to business cycle conditions will likely be similar.

Appendix 3.3
Detrending Procedures

1. Whole Economy

Method Used in Text

We take Gordon's natural GNP series as the starting point, extending it to 1983 by assuming (as he did for 1981–82) a 3% natural growth rate. We then compute "natural final sales" as

$$X^T = \theta y^T,$$

where y^T is natural GNP and θ is the mean ratio of final sales to GNP over the period 1929–83 (excluding 1932 and 1933). Although the ratio is quite stable over time, these two years are obvious outliers and were removed for that reason. In practice it makes little difference; our computed θ is .994, and including 1932 and 1933 changes this only to .996.

The process is completed by computing natural inventory investment via the identity $y^T = x^T + \Delta N^T$. Using deviations from this series gives the variance decomposition in the text (reproduced in the top row of table 3.A.1.)

Alternative (Statistical) Trend

Here we simply fit the trend model

$$\log(z_t) = \alpha_0 + \alpha_1 t + \alpha_2 t^2 + \epsilon_t$$

to each of GNP, final sales, and inventories, dropping the years 1930–39 and 1941–46 as aberrant. For reasons described in the text, this procedure is not entirely satisfactory. Nevertheless, the variance decomposition derived by detrending in this manner is shown for comparison in the second row of table 3.A.1.

2. Total Manufacturing

The method used in the text was method A, log-linear interpolation between 1929 and 1941. We also experimented with method B, log-linear interpolation using 1929 and 1940, and method C, log-linear trend line fitted to all months in 1929–41.

Table 3.A.1

	σ_y^2	σ_x^2	$\sigma_{\Delta N}^2$	Cov $(x, \Delta N)$	σ_y^2/σ_x^2	$\sigma_x^2/\sigma_{\Delta N}^2$	Corr $(x, \Delta N)$
Total economy (ECONOMIC)	1309.9	1210.4	20.9	43.2	1.082	57.9	.271
Total economy (STATISTICAL)	951.4	965.6	23.9	70.5	.985	40.4	.464
Manufacturing (Method A)	7.39	6.85	.084	.270	1.079	81.8	.250
Manufacturing (Method B)	10.35	9.73	.084	.371	1.063	116.1	.318
Manufacturing (Method C)	7.29	6.77	.084	.276	1.076	80.8	.259

Note: In billions of 1929 dollars for manufacturing and billions of 1972 dollars for total economy.

The variance decomposition for each type of detrending is shown in table 3.A.1.

Comment   Moses Abramovitz

Blinder and Holtz-Eakin have given us a stimulating and useful paper. Besides developing new data, their survey confirms the existence of certain broad similarities in inventory behavior between prewar and postwar years. At the same time, their data and findings raise questions about both the observed relations between output and inventory investment and the adequacy of our working model of inventory behavior. My remarks are intended mainly to supplement the authors' argument and to suggest directions for future work.

The Variances of Production and Sales

Early in the paper, the authors make a calculation decomposing the variance of GNP in the years 1929–83 into the variances of final sales and inventory accumulation and the covariance of the two. They find that the variance of GNP is larger than that of final sales and, of course, that the covariance of inventory investment and final sales is positive. They point out that their finding "appears to contain bad news for the dominant empirical model of inventory behavior—the production smoothing/buffer stock model."

As the authors suggest, this finding is a generalization of what is already implicit in a familiar observation—that for the interwar years inventory investment rose and fell in perfect, synchronous conformity with business cycles, at least annually. But the authors' result has several virtues. It extends the finding to postwar years; it bases it on an analysis of monthly data; and it derives it from an analysis of data in all units of the entire period and not merely an analysis of cyclical troughs and peaks.

I think there is some interest in pointing out that the results represent a notable bit of continuity in business cycles work connected with the NBER. A finding with similar implications (but, of course, derived from much less satisfactory data) was made by Simon Kuznets in his second publication—his first in English. This was his Columbia University doctoral dissertation, prepared under Wesley Mitchell's supervision. It was published as *Cyclical Fluctuations: Retail and Wholesale Trade* in 1926, fifty-eight years ago. Here Kuznets found that retail

Moses Abramovitz is professor of economics at Stanford University and editor of the *Journal of Economic Literature*.

sales, wholesale sales, and production in manufacturing moved together during business fluctuations, but the amplitude of wholesale sales was wider than that of retail sales and the amplitude of manufacturing production was wider than that of wholesale sales. By comparing sales and production of similar products at the three stages, Kuznets satisfied himself that the amplitude difference was due only in part to the presence of capital formation items that were produced at the manufacturers' level but that did not move through wholesale and retail trade channels.

Kuznets's explanation of the magnification of cyclical amplitude as one progresses from the consumer to the manufacturer was inventory investment. His model was derived from J. M. Clark's acceleration principle as published three years earlier in *The Economics of Overhead Costs*. Kuznets's adaptation of Clark to the inventory case, however, is exactly the stock adjustment model on which contemporary students rely. Purchases at any level are the sum of expected sales—assumed, by way of illustration, to be equal to last period's sales—plus desired inventory investment. Desired investment has two parts. One is a multiple of the change in expected sales, a multiple that reflects the desired inventory/sales ratio. The second is the amount needed to reverse last period's unintended investment. And unintended investment is the difference between actual sales last period and expected sales.

In developing his argument, Kuznets is fully conscious of the feedback from desired inventory investment to income and retail sales. Only the absence of a definite consumption function prevents him from taking the subject as far as Metzler and Nurkse eventually did in their well-known papers. In certain other respects, however, he went further than these writers, and further than most contemporary treatments go today. I want to return to that somewhat later.

Next—I go on to the question Blinder and Holtz-Eakin's paper poses: Why indeed do inventories serve to destabilize production rather than to stabilize it, as the micro theory of inventories would have it? A minor part of the answer lies in the technical lock between output and goods that are truly in the process of production or in the process of transportation. I believe that a major part of the answer, however, is connected with the fact that by far the greatest part of total stocks consists of inventories of firms who are the purchasers, not the producers, of the goods. They have an interest in supporting their own production or marketing activities, not in stabilizing their suppliers' operations. Since supporting their own activities—given their uncertainty about the delivery of supplies and about their own customers' requirements—usually means carrying larger, not smaller, stocks of purchased materials when the volume of sales or production is high, an expansion of sales is passed back to suppliers in earlier stages with magnified force.

Needless to say, that is no more than a partial answer. It assumes there are good reasons, still to be spelled out quantitatively, that explain why manufacturers' stocks of goods *for sale* do not move inversely with sufficient force and weight to protect their production fully from fluctuations in their sales or that explain why suppliers do not when business falls off, offer price concessions big enough to induce customers to build up rather than liquidate stocks. I do not have a tested answer, but I imagine many of us share the same hunch. Plant capacity is expensive to hold idle, but it has the virtue of flexibility. It permits a manufacturer to adapt the specifications of the goods he makes to the varied and changing technical requirements of customers or to the styles that may rule when the goods are finally to be sold. In that respect, excess plant capacity reduces risk. Inventories, on the other hand, carry the heavy risks associated with predetermining the characteristics of goods, whether in technical matters like chemical composition, speed, hardness, specialized function, and so on, or in matters of color, style, and fashion. And that is why it is only for inventories of durable staples made to stock that one finds the inverse behavior implied by the buffer stock model.

This judgment again is dependent on a set of institutional arrangements that makes fixed capital an overhead cost but permits most labor to remain a variable cost. If labor became more largely an overhead cost than it now is in this country, one might see changes in the kinds of goods produced and used that would make business safer for countercyclical inventory policy. It might be useful to see whether such changes have been taking place in Western Europe now that those countries have made it harder to lay off workers.

Comparisons between the Interwar and Postwar Periods

The Blinder/Holtz-Eakin variance analysis generally confirms earlier ideas that inventory investment fluctuations are positively associated with those of output and final sales.[1] Inventory investment has mostly acted to magnify the cyclical impact of sales movements on output rather than to cushion them. Nevertheless, the results of the variance analyses do present some features that call for comment.

In their analysis of the whole economy (annual data: 1929–41 vs. 1947–83), our authors find that the covariance between inventory investment and final sales and the correlation between these variables rise between the prewar and postwar periods. This finding is generally

---

1. In saying this, I disregard findings for periods including the World War II years when extreme pressures of demand on capacity constrained inventory accumulation in the face of rapidly rising output and even required some inventory liquidation.

consistent with the familiar notion that inventories have been more tightly controlled since the war and more sensitively adjusted to movements of sales. On the other hand, when they turn to an analysis of activity in manufacturing (monthly data 1929–41 vs. 1959–82), they find that the correlation coefficients between inventory investment and final sales, besides being much lower in both periods than they are for the whole economy, appear to decline between the prewar and postwar periods. The decline is small for total manufacturing, substantial for durables manufacturing (table 3.3).

Why these differences? Is it a difference between manufacturing and trade? A vagary of the methods of data estimation our authors had to resort to in order to build up their data for manufacturing? Or is it a quirk of monthly data? It does seem likely that the adjustment of inventories to sales would be quite rough from month to month and more nearly parallel over somewhat longer intervals. Experiments with quarterly and annual data would be revealing.

For both the whole economy and manufacturing, the ratio of the variance of inventory investment to the variance of final sales rises considerably between the prewar and postwar periods. For the whole economy, the increase is about 50% (1929–41 vs. 1947–83). For manufacturing the percentage increase in the ratio is about eight times as great.[2] The same questions arise.

What should we make of these numbers? Although Blinder and Holtz-Eakin point to an apparent increase in the variance of inventory investment, they conclude: "if we exclude the war years, a clear picture of continuity in the stylized facts emerges between prewar and postwar periods." They seem to refer mainly to the ratios between the variances of GNP and final sales and to the covariances (or correlations) between inventory investment and final sales. Their interpretation may be right. It is unfortunate, however, that data problems required them to confine their analyses to a prewar period running from 1929 to 1941 (or including the war years, to 1946). In that period, fluctuations of output and final sales were, of course, dominated by great contractions and expansions in fixed investment and consumer purchases. By contrast, postwar business cycles can be more nearly characterized as inventory cycles. On that account, it seems important to compare the postwar years with the predepression period, say 1919–29, when consumption and fixed investment were also more stable.

I have not followed our authors in making a variance analysis, and I confine my attention to comparisons between the postwar period and

2. The increase is concentrated in durables. For nondurables, the ratio rises by only 31%.

the 1920s in just one respect: the contributions of changes in inventory investment to the changes of GNP between cyclical peaks and troughs. There are two matters to consider:

1. Although the share of inventory investment in the postwar GNP *contractions* was larger than in 1919–29, as our authors say, its share in postwar GNP *expansions* was smaller. The average share in the four expansions of the 1920s was 43%. The average share in seven postwar expansions was under 10%.

2. Inventory investment and GNP reached cyclical troughs together (in annual data) both before the war and after. In expansions, however, there was a change. Inventory investment turned synchronously with GNP before the war.[3] After the war, however, there were repeated long and significant leads of inventory investment compared with GNP, which I shall describe presently.

We can make a first, somewhat superficial approach to the change in the inventory investment share of GNP fluctuations by considering the differences between the durations of prewar and postwar expansions. We expect the inventory investment share of GNP change to vary inversely with the duration of the cyclical phase. The underlying reason is that the change in the volume of inventory investment between expansion and contraction (or vice versa) will be strongly influenced by the interphase difference in the growth rate of GNP or final sales. But the change in GNP itself during a contraction or expansion will depend on both the average growth rate and the duration of the phase. On that account, we expect the inventory investment share to be larger in contractions than in expansions. It is a notable fact, however, that from the 1920s to the postwar period, contractions became shorter and expansions longer.[4] And these changes are consistent with the larger postwar inventory investment contribution to GNP contractions and its smaller postwar contribution to expansions.ˊ

The reduced postwar share of inventory investment in expansions, however, reflects more than the longer durations of those phases. In the postwar period, inventory investment often reached its peak level

3. That is not literally true. Total inventory investment reached a peak in 1925. The reference peak was 1926. The lead, however, was due entirely to stocks on the farms. Nonfarm inventory investment peaked in the reference peak year without exception.

4. The figures for the average durations of reference contractions and expansions run as follows:

	Durations (in months)	
	1919–29	*1948–82*
Contractions	(3) 16.0	(8) 10.0
Expansions	(4) 19.5	(7) 45.9

Figures in parentheses are the number of phases.
Computed from the NBER Quarterly Reference Cycle Chronology.

long before GNP and declined a great deal before the reference cycle peak.[5] Measured between GNP turns, therefore, the contribution of inventory investment change to GNP change is reduced.

These are, in a sense, preliminary considerations. To push the matter further, we should ask why the durations of expansions and contractions changed the way they did and why inventory investment, which reached its peaks, as well as its troughs, more or less synchronously with GNP before the war, has tended to exhibit a long lead at cycle peaks in the postwar period. There are a number of possibilities, which may share responsibility for the outcome.

An obvious consideration is autonomous spending. Subject as it is to a rising trend, such spending tends to stretch out expansions even in the face of a decline of inventory investment, a decline that is itself induced by retardation in the rate of increase of final sales. Inventory investment then tends to turn ahead of total spending. Just the opposite happens in contractions. The general contraction is cut short by the rising trend of autonomous expenditures. The GNP trough is therefore brought closer to the low point in the rate of decline of output and thus to the trough of inventory investment. Autonomous spending was probably more important after the war than before. The increased importance of government outlays is the most obvious matter, but its effect may have been supported by larger elements of fixed capital formation sustained by confident anticipations of long-term growth and so rendered less responsive to short and mild contractions of current output.

Next there are lessons we can take from Ragnar Nurkse (1954). Both the inventory investment share in output changes and the duration of cyclical phases are under the combined influence of the marginal propensity to save and the trend of autonomous spending. Suppose we follow Nurkse and divide total spending into autonomous spending, inventory investment, and other income-induced spending. Then it emerges that if autonomous spending were a constant, the inventory investment share in GNP growth or decline would equal the marginal propensity to save, if that were constant. And that points to a reason the inventory investment share tends to be smaller in expansions than in contractions—the standard finding. The reason is that the Duesenberry/Modigliani ratchet effect makes the marginal propensity to save lower and the multiplier higher in the latter portions of expansions than it is in contractions (or during the initial recovery segment of expan-

---

5. Inventory investment turned down before GNP at five out of eight postwar turning points (annual data). There was one lead of three years, two leads of two years, and two of one year. On the average, inventory investment in the GNP peak years was only 61% as large as it was at its own specific cycle peaks. (Cf. Stanback 1962, who had already stressed this point in his early postwar study.)

sions). If we now allow for autonomous spending that follows a rising trend, than the difference between the inventory investment shares in expansions and contractions is made all the larger.[6]

Our main concern, however, lies in the prewar/postwar change of marginal spending propensities in contractions and expansions separately. For representative contractions in each period (I set aside the Great Depression), I suggest that the postwar marginal propensity to save out of GNP was probably higher than before the war. I am thinking about the postwar built-in stabilizers. If that is right, it would help explain the larger postwar contribution of inventory investment during contractions. It would also help explain the shorter duration of contractions. If the feedback from inventory investment to spending is weaker, it permits faster liquidation of unwanted stocks and therefore an earlier reversal of orders and production.

The situation for expansions is less clear. Built-in stabilizers act in expansions as well as contractions. On the other hand, the long and vigorous postwar expansions may have worked to lift people's expectations and so to have strengthened the responses of spending to income change as growth continued. If that is right, then by analogy with my contraction argument, we have a consideration that helps to explain both the reduced contribution of inventory investment to the postwar expansions of GNP and the longer duration of such expansions. And all these considerations, speculative as some of them may be, are strengthened if, as seems likely, the rising trend of autonomous spending was more pronounced after the war than before.

Finally, there is a question about the proper lag structure in a model of inventory investment. It bears on the observed postwar leads of inventory investment before the upper turning points of GNP. We know

---

6. Nurkse employs a simple Keynesian model. Adapting and simplifying his notation, we may write the value of realized inventory investment (ΔN) at the peaks and troughs of GNP (or indeed in any period) as follows:

$$\Delta N_p = (1 - c) Y_p - Z_p$$
$$\Delta N_t = (1 - c) Y_t - Z_t,$$

where c is the marginal propensity to spend, Z is autonomous spending, and p and t are indexes for peaks and troughs. Subtracting values for troughs from those for following peaks and expressing the change in ΔN as a ratio to the change in Y gives us (for expansions):

$$\frac{\Delta N_p - N_t}{Y_p - Y_t} = (1 - c) - \frac{Z_p - Z_t}{Y_p - Y_t}.$$

If autonomous spending is constant, the last term disappears. The inventory investment share equals the marginal propensity to save. And (remembering to subtract peaks from following troughs) the same is true for contractions. Allowing for a rising trend in Z makes the inventory investment share smaller than $(1 - c)$ in expansions and larger than $(1 - c)$ in contractions.

that in stock adjustment models the existence and importance of un-intended inventory investment arise from the presumption that the lag of planned output behind final sales is longer than the lag of final sales behind income. And Metzler and Nurkse have taught us that given a relatively long output lag, it is the rise of unintended investment as the growth rate of sales declines that keeps total realized investment in-creasing after planned investment begins to fall. In a pure inventory cycle, this ensures that inventory investment and GNP reach cyclical turns together. But if the output lag is short relative to the expenditure lag, unintended investment disappears. On the other hand, as Nurkse shows, output continues to increase after planned investment turns down because of the lag of expenditures—and therefore of output to meet sales—behind income produced (1954, 219–20). Realized inven-tory investment then tends to lead turns of output.

Nurkse (1954) and others—for example, Ackley (1951) and Metzler (1947)—have argued persuasively that the output lag is longer than the expenditure lag. There *is* unintended investment. What we do not know—at least I do not know—is whether there has been a change in the relative size of these lags that might make unintended investment less important and might enter, together with other factors, into an explanation for the current long leads of inventory investment ahead of the postwar peaks of GNP.

These comments suggest several considerations likely to be useful in the continuing work on inventory investment and business cycles:

1. The possible importance of changes in the composition of inven-tory holdings in explaining changes in the behavior of the aggregate. The differences, noted above, between durables and nondurables man-ufacturing in the relations of inventory investment and final sales are suggestive. So are the differences between inventory investment in manufacturing and in the whole economy (tables 3.2 and 3.3).

2. The need to distinguish between contractions and expansions—because of interphase differences in the marginal propensity to spend; because of the differential impact of autonomous expenditure; and because inventory responses to income change may be different in expansions and contractions.

3. The need to consider the comparative durations of output and expenditure lags because of what these mean for unintended investment and for the roles of inventory investment and other spending near turning points. Here again there may be differences between expan-sions and contractions.

The Stock Adjustment Model

I turn now to Blinder and Holtz-Eakin's attempt to compare the prewar and postwar behavior of inventory investment in terms of the stock adjustment model familiar in comtemporary studies. Their estimates of the coefficients of the model appear to replicate the unsatisfactory outcome of earlier work and to show that the defects characteristic of work with postwar data also emerge in estimates based on their own new prewar data. I cannot add anything substantive to their findings, but I think it useful to raise a question that bears on the structure of a satisfactory model. I can do little more than indicate the nature of the problem.

The standard stock adjustment models are usually, perhaps uniformly, evaluated empirically on the presumption that the coefficients on the various elements of inventory change are cyclically stable. There are three coefficients to consider:

The desired ratio of inventories to expected sales.

The rate at which firms try to reduce the difference between desired and actual stocks.

The relation between unintended investment and firms' misjudgment of sales.

Each of these relations, however, is influenced by supply conditions—by what is usually called "vendor performance" and "expected vendor performance." Such performance varies with the state of business, and one only has to look at each month's report of the survey of purchasing agents to see the interest such agents take in the changing state of vendor performance. When capacity utilization rises, delivery periods begin to lengthen and to become less assured. Firms then want to hold larger stocks to support an expected volume of sales. When supply conditions become still tighter, there are more vigorous efforts to meet their higher stock objectives and to correct inventory deficiencies. Orders are placed further ahead and in larger volume than would be required to meet objectives if firms were confident that everything ordered would be actually delivered or accepted. In spite of magnified orders, firms may be disappointed by deliveries. The unintended investment equation changes. Unintended investment is no longer correctly portrayed as the difference between actual and expected sales. There must be an allowance for a difference between deliveries and orders.

It is in this respect that Kuznets's early book went further than Metzler did and perhaps further than many contemporary studies go. He tried to take account, at least in a verbal treatment, of the effect of changing supply conditions. And as we all know, Ruth Mack seized on the same idea and developed it both theoretically and empirically in her 1956 study *Consumption and Business Cycles*. And then Mack and Victor Zarnowitz carried it still further (Mack and Zarnowitz 1958; Zarnowitz 1961). Perhaps I am raising issues here that adequate tests already show are of little significance. I suspect, however, that we shall have to return to the themes and problems of these earlier NBER studies if we are to get a good understanding of the changing role of inventories in business cycles.

Comment   Bennett T. McCallum

Introduction

In its original conference version, the paper by Blinder and Holtz-Eakin filled me with enthusiasm, for what a discussant likes most in a paper is something of significance with which he can wholeheartedly disagree. Now the most objectionable portion of the paper—a genuine, full-fledged Keynesian multiplier model of the business cycle[1]—has been deleted, taking with it a substantial part of my discussion. In addition, other arguments have been modified and the language has been adjusted in several ways. Nevertheless, there are a few items remaining that call for qualification or partial disagreement. In all cases, it should be said, my objections are directed not at the explicit conclusions of section 3.5, but at statements and suggestions that are scattered through the body of the paper. My remarks presume, furthermore, that the basic rationale for the study is the possibility of shedding light on macroeconomic fluctuations, not the analysis of inventory behavior per se.

There is little possibility for disagreement in sections 3.1 and 3.2, which include (respectively) a short introduction and a tabulation showing that the peak-to-trough declines in inventory investment are nearly as large as those for GNP itself in both postwar and prewar business cycles. But I would like to emphasize the restrictive nature of the authors' statement that "there is really no hope of understanding the dynamics of recessions without analyzing inventory behavior." It is indeed likely that good models of inventory fluctuations are needed to account for the details of month-to-month or quarter-to-quarter movements in aggregate output. But such models may nevertheless be unnecessary for understanding business cycles in the sense of knowing

Bennett T. McCallum is a professor in the Graduate School of Industrial Administration at Carnegie-Mellon University.

I am indebted to Martin Eichenbaum for helpful suggestions, to Kun-Hong Kim for research assistance, and to the National Science Foundation (SES 82–08151) for financial support.

1. The inclusion of this model provided a contribution, in a sense, by serving as a reminder of what hard-core Keynesian macroeconomics was actually like. The model implied, for example, that real GNP could be controlled (subject to random errors) by manipulation of real government purchases, with a steady state multiplier of 4.5.

what are the sources of the initiating shocks and why—in the case of monetary shocks—they have (apparently) major effects on real aggregates. Nor is it clear that such knowledge is crucial to learning whether the nature of recessions is such that activist demand management would be socially beneficial.

Variance Decompositions and Prevailing Theory

In section 3.3, the first of those that constitute the heart of the paper, Blinder and Holtz-Eakin present a large quantity of data concerning the variability of production, sales, and inventory changes. The discussion begins with the identity

$$(1) \qquad y_t = x_t + \Delta n_t,$$

where y_t is production and x_t the quantity of sales during period t, with n_t denoting the inventory stock at the end of period t and $\Delta n_t = n_t - n_{t-1}$. The variance of production is then decomposed as

$$(2) \qquad \text{var}(y) = \text{var}(x) + \text{var}(\Delta n) + 2\text{cov}(x,\Delta n)$$

where var(.) and cov(.,.) denote variance and covariance magnitudes for the indicated series. Throughout, this decomposition is applied to *detrended* versions of the basic variables. Since one of the subperiods examined is 1929–46, the authors have some difficulty in deciding how to detrend. Accordingly, they experiment with different methods and report only figures that are reasonably insensitive to the method utilized. This strategy is commendable, but the discussion would be improved by some explicit recognition of the reason detrending is desired. Apparently their reason has only to do with the concept of "fluctuations" they have in mind rather than a desire to obtain series that could be viewed as resulting from covariance stationary stochastic processes.[2]

In their table 3.2, Blinder and Holtz-Eakin report sample variances pertaining to the decomposition (2) using annual GNP data. For postwar, prewar, and combined sample periods they find that var(y) exceeds var(x) and that cov(x,Δn) is nonnegative. These inequalities also hold, they show in table 3.3, if one uses monthly rather than annual data for total manufacturing and its two main subdivisions (i.e., durable and nondurable products). This finding reinforces similar ones previously reported by Blinder (1981a, 1984) for various postwar data sets and suggests that var(y) > var(x) and cov(x,Δn) $\geq$ 0 should be regarded as empirical regularities that a satisfactory theory must accommodate. This demonstration is quite useful, as is their construction and reporting of monthly series for y, x, and n during the prewar period.

2. There seems to be, in other words, no concern for issues of the type discussed by Plosser and Schwert 1978.

The authors go on, however, to suggest that these two empirical regularities "seem to cast doubt on the major prevailing theory of inventory behavior." Elsewhere, Blinder has stated that "these facts add up to a stunning indictment of the production smoothing/buffer stock model" (1984, 4). Now, to evaluate these statements we have to specify what model or models they refer to. But there appears to be ample reason to say that "the prevailing theory" is well represented by the models utilized in Blinder (1981a) and Blinder and Fischer (1981)— which are essentially the same as those in Brennan (1959), Muth (1961), McCallum (1972), and many other papers. That Blinder himself shares this judgment is evidenced by section 3 of his 1984 paper, in which he considers the issue within precisely this framework.[3] Let us, then, consider whether this "standard prevailing" model is inconsistent with the findings var(y) > var(x) and cov($x,\Delta n$) $\geq$ 0.

The model in question pertains to a monopolistic firm[4] that at t chooses sequences of x_t, y_t, and n_t values to maximize the objective function

$$(3) \qquad E_t \sum_{j=0}^{\infty} (1 + r)^{-j} [R(x_{t+j}, v_{t+j}) - C(y_{t+j}, u_{t+j}) - B(n_{t+j-1})]$$

subject to the sequence of constraints

$$(4) \qquad y_{t+j} + n_{t+j-1} - x_{t+j} - n_{t+j} = 0, \qquad j = 0,1,2, \ldots$$

Taking the disturbance processes $\{u_t\}$ and $\{v_t\}$ to be white noise and pretending that certainty-equivalence prevails, we obtain first-order conditions that for $j = 0$ we write as

$$(5) \qquad R_1(x_t, v_t) - \lambda_t = 0$$

$$(6) \qquad -C_1(y_t, u_t) + \lambda_t = 0$$

$$(7) \qquad -B'(n_t) - (1 + r)\lambda_t + E_t\lambda_{t+1} = 0$$

$$(8) \qquad y_t + n_{t-1} - x_t - n_t = 0,$$

where λ_t is of course the relevant Lagrange multiplier.

---

3. It should be noted that a slightly (but crucially) more general framework—involving a more general specification of the firm's cost structure—was proposed in a managerial-economics context by Holt et al. 1960. The most satisfactory empirical studies I am familiar with, namely, those of Blanchard 1983 and Eichenbaum 1984, provide results that indicate these generalizations are important. That does not contradict the argument to be developed in the remainder of the present section, which is adapted from McCallum 1981.

4. Eichenbaum 1983 has shown that it is not necessary to give the firm monopoly power, as several analysts have claimed, but doing so simplifies the present discussion.

To render these expressions operational, let us suppose that the R, C, and B functions are quadratic. Then (5), (6), and (7) can be written as

(5') $a_1 + a_2 x_t + v_t = \lambda_t$ $a_2 < 0$
(6') $c_1 + c_2 y_t + u_t = \lambda_t$ $c_2 > 0$
(7') $b_1 + b_2 n_t + (1 + r)\lambda_t = E_t \lambda_{t+1}.$ $b_2 > 0$

Reduced-form "solution" equations will then be of the form

$$(9) \qquad y_t = \pi_{10} + \pi_{11} n_{t-1} + \pi_{12} u_t + \pi_{13} v_t$$

$$(10) \qquad x_t = \pi_{20} + \pi_{21} n_{t-1} + \pi_{22} u_t + \pi_{23} v_t$$

$$(11) \qquad n_t = \pi_{30} + \pi_{31} n_{t-1} + \pi_{32} u_t + \pi_{33} v_t$$

$$(12) \qquad \lambda_t = \pi_{40} + \pi_{41} n_{t-1} + \pi_{42} u_t + \pi_{43} v_t,$$

and the π values can be found by the familiar undetermined coefficients procedure. The only complication involved is that there are two possible sets of solutions, these arising because π_{31} is found from a quadratic equation. The approach developed in McCallum (1983) can be used, however, to pick out the unique bubble-free solution.

To avoid entanglement in tedious algebraic expressions, let us consider a numerical example that will suffice to make the relevant point. In particular, suppose that $a_2 = -1.0$, $b_2 = 0.1$, $c_2 = 0.1$, and $r = 0.01$. Then simple calculations reveal that production, sales, and inventory stocks obey

$$y_t = -.574 n_{t-1} - 4.26 u_t + .574 v_t$$

$$(13) \qquad x_t = .057 n_{t-1} - .574 u_t + .943 v_t$$

$$n_t = .368 n_{t-1} - 3.68 u_t - .368 v_t,$$

where constant terms are ignored. Furthermore, let us suppose that the variances of u_t and v_t are equal in magnitude, and in particular that $\sigma_u^2 = \sigma_v^2 = 1.0$. Also, suppose that $E(u_t v_t) = 0$. Then it is easily found that

$$(14) \qquad \text{var}(y_t) = 23.7, \ \text{var}(x_t) = 1.27, \ \text{var}(n_t) = 15.8.$$

But these values demonstrate that the model at hand—the "prevailing" model—is consistent with much larger fluctuations in production than in sales. In addition, the example yields $\text{cov}(x_t, \Delta n_t) = 1.72$ and thus also shows that the model under consideration does not imply a negative correlation between sales and inventory change. Thus the two empirical regularities stressed by Blinder and Holtz-Eakin may in some sense spell bad news for "buffer stock" or "production smoothing" *notions,* but they do not discredit the prevailing model in any fundamental way. That they appear to do so in the early parts of Blinder (1984) is because the analysis there proceeds under the assumption that supply-side shocks are nonexistent.[5]

We now ask if this conclusion continues to hold if one modifies the foregoing model in the ways that the Blanchard (1983) and Eichenbaum (1984) results suggest. The first of these is to add to the firm's objective function a term that reflects costs of *changing* production rates, namely, $0.5c_3(y_{t+j} - y_{t+j-1})^2$ with $c_3 > 0$. The second is to replace the inventory cost function implied by (7'), which is $b_0 + b_1 n_{t+j-1} + 0.5b_2 n_{t+j-1}^2$, with one of the form $0.5\, b_3(n_{t+j-1} - n_{t+j-1}^*)^2$, where the "desired" or "target" level n_{t+j-1}^* depends upon the rate of sales in period $t + j$, $n_{t+j-1}^* = \alpha x_{t+j}$.[6] With those two changes in specification, the relevant set of first-order optimality conditions for the firm becomes

(5") $$a_1 + a_2 x_t + \alpha b_3(n_{t-1} - \alpha x_t) + v_t = \lambda_t$$

(6") $$c_1 + c_2 y_t + c_3(y_t - y_{t-1}) + u_t = \lambda_t$$

(7") $$b_3(n_t - \alpha E_t x_{t+1}) + (1 + r)\lambda_t = E_t \lambda_{t+1}$$

plus the constraint (8), which we for convenience also refer to as (8").

(8") $$y_t + n_{t-1} - x_t - n_t = 0.$$

But from these conditions we see that the previous system can be regarded as a special case of this one, the special case that obtains as c_3 and α approach zero. So at the present level of analysis the two empirical regularities do not suffice to contradict this model either.

The foregoing does not, it might be added, constitute a claim that either of the two models under discussion is in fact thoroughly satisfactory. But to discredit them apparently requires more evidence than is provided by the findings that $\mathrm{var}(y) > \mathrm{var}(x)$ and $\mathrm{cov}(x, \Delta n) \geq 0$.

Estimates of Stock Adjustment Speeds

In their section 3.4, Blinder and Holtz-Eakin characterize some features of the relation between inventories and sales by reporting estimates of the "stock adjustment" model that has been prominent in

---

5. This is recognized in a later section of Blinder 1984, which also shows that nontransitory components in the demand disturbance v_t will tend to increase the ratio of $\mathrm{var}(y)$ to $\mathrm{var}(x)$.

6. There is a related possibility, namely, that $n_{t+j-1}^* = \alpha E_{t+j-1} x_{t+j}$. This specification leads to equations (6") and (7") below but implies that (5') prevails instead of (5"). The difference between this specification and the one in the body of the paper appears to correspond to the difference between "precautionary" and "transaction" motives for holding inventories. Blanchard 1983, 378, uses the latter specification but offers a rationalization that seems more applicable to the former. That he—like Eichenbaum—avoids the "precautionary" specification may reflect recognition that it implies dynamic inconsistency on the part of the firm.

empirical work on inventory movements.[7] In my notation, this model focuses on the adjustment relation

(15) $$n_t - n_{t-1} = b(n_t^* - n_{t-1}) - c(x_t - {}_{t-1}x_t) + \eta_t,$$

where n_t^* is the stock of inventories "desired" at the end of t and where ${}_{t-1}x_t$ is the value of sales during t anticipated at the end of $t - 1$. An essential component of this model is, of course, the specification of n_t^*. The ones utilized by Blinder and Holtz-Eakin are variants of

(16) $$n_t^* = \alpha_0 + \alpha_1 {}_{t-1}x_{t+1}.$$

In addition, hypotheses concerning expectation formation and the generation of x_t are needed to complete the system. The authors assume that expectations are rational, that is, that ${}_{t-1}x_t = E_{t-1}x_t$, and that x_t is generated by a second-order autoregression process[8] that is exogenous to n_t:

(17) $$x_t = \emptyset_1 x_{t-1} + \emptyset_2 x_{t-2} + \zeta_t.$$

Prewar, postwar, and full-period estimates of this system are reported by Blinder and Holtz-Eakin based on annual aggregate data and monthly data for manufacturing and its two major subdivisions. In all cases the results conform to the usual finding[9] that the estimated adjustment speed, represented by b, is implausibly low. In several cases, furthermore, the estimated values of c are negative and thus inconsistent with the theoretical presumptions of the model.

One possible reaction to this "empirical regularity" is to claim that the stock adjustment model is without rigorous theoretical content and so the findings should be of little or no interest. In my opinion it would be wrong to take that line, for the reduced-form equation (11), obtained above from a coherent theory, can obviously be expressed in stock adjustment form, with $1 - b = \pi_{31}$ and with $n_t^* = \alpha_0 + \alpha_1 E_{t-1}x_{t+1} = \alpha_0 + \alpha_1[\pi_{20} + \pi_{21}(\pi_{30} + \pi_{31}n_{t-1})]$. Instead, attention should be directed toward understanding what it is that the estimates are saying in terms of the models described above.

My attempt to do this will proceed in terms of the Blanchard/Eichenbaum specification summarized above in equations (5″) to (8″). To simplify the exposition, suppose that c_2 and c_3 are small enough that we will not be misled if we approximate λ_t as $c_1 + u_t$. Putting that expression in (5″) and rearranging gives

7. The model is usually attributed to Lovell 1961. For a sizable number of references to other applications, see Feldstein and Auerbach 1976, 352–53.

8. In the cases using monthly data, the autoregression is of order 12.

9. This finding gained prominence from the study of Feldstein and Auerbach 1976. It had been noted earlier by Orr 1967 and by Carlson and Wehrs 1974.

(18) $$x_t = \emptyset^{-1}[c_1 - a_1 - \alpha bn_{t-1} + u_t - v_t],$$

where $\emptyset = a_2 - \alpha^2 b_3 < 0$, while doing the same for (7″) yields

(19) $$b_3 n_t - \alpha b_3 E_t x_{t+1} + (1 + r)(c_1 + u_t) = c_1 + E_t u_{t+1}.$$

But from (18) we can find $E_t x_{t+1}$; substitution in (19) then yields an equation that relates n_t to u_t, $E_t u_{t+1}$, and $E_t v_{t+1}$:

(20) $$(b_3 + \alpha^2 b_3^2 \emptyset^{-1})n_t = (1 + \alpha b_3 \emptyset^{-1})E_t u_{t+1}$$
$$- \alpha b_3 \emptyset^{-1} E_t v_{t+1} - (1 + r)u_t + \text{const.}$$

Now suppose that u_t is not white noise but is instead first-order autoregressive:

(21) $$u_t = \rho u_{t-1} + e_t, \qquad e_t \text{ white noise.}$$

Then (20) can be put in the form

(22) $$n_t = \zeta_0 + \zeta_1 u_t,$$

where ζ_0 and ζ_1 are composite parameters involving $\alpha, b_3, \emptyset$, and ρ. In terms of the white noise disturbance e_t this can be written as

(23) $$n_t = \rho n_{t-1} + \zeta_0 (1 - \rho) + \zeta_1 e_t.$$

But the coefficient on n_{t-1} in this equation corresponds to $1 - b$ in the stock adjustment expression (15). Consequently, if this model is a good approximation to reality, the estimates usually interpreted as adjustment-speed parameters will actually be estimates of $1 - \rho$. Thus the finding that these estimates are close to zero may simply be a finding that shocks to technology—supply shocks—are highly serially correlated; that the process generating these shocks is close to a random walk.[10] Thinking about the nature of technological progress, and other cost shocks, that seems to me a highly plausible interpretation.

Now most of the estimates reported by Blinder and Holtz-Eakin in their tables 3.4 to 3.7 utilize a Cochrane/Orcutt correction designed to take account of first-order autoregression disturbances, and the same is true for stock adjustment estimates reported in Blinder (1984, table 4) for various two-digit industries (monthly postwar data). For the most part these estimates continue to suggest that reaction speeds (b values) are very low even when the existence of autoregression disturbances is taken into account.

Interestingly, though, Blinder (1984, 34) mentions that:

in several cases, two local minima of the sum of squared residuals function were found. In such cases, one of the minima always had

---

10. Blinder has himself pointed out this possibility in a nice discussion that is less complicated than mine, but also less theoretically explicit (1984, 33–34).

high ρ and rapid adjustment while the other had low ρ and slow adjustment. . . . This point is important because the extremely high adjustment speeds recently found by Maccini and Rosanna (1984) result from an estimation technique that, I [i.e., Blinder] believe, settles on the local minimum with high ρ. The estimation method used here [i.e., Blinder 1984] typically shows that the low ρ solution is the global maximum.

What this discussion—together with the Maccini/Rosanna results—indicates is that the data can be "explained" either by slow adjustment speeds in combination with low ρ values *or* by fast adjustment speeds in combination with large ρ values.[11] Blinder's case for the first combination relies on the empirical finding that it fits the data slightly better than the second combination, and that the Maccini/Rosanna estimates are obtained by an inappropriate estimation technique.[12]

But reflection upon the nature of the estimation problem suggests that Blinder (1984) and the present authors are at least as guilty as Maccini and Rosanna of using inappropriate estimators. In particular, Blinder's procedure involves a serial correlation "correction" applied after inserting fitted values from an autoregression on x_t to "proxy" for rationally anticipated sales (Blinder 1984, 32). But that is precisely the sort of procedure that involves the "pitfall" described by Flood and Garber (1980),[13] so Blinder's and the present authors' estimators are inconsistent, and their sums of squared residuals are consequently unreliable indicators of which ρ, b combination provides a better fit to the data.[14]

Furthermore, the instrumental variable procedure used by Maccini and Rosanna (1984) bears some resemblance to the one developed in McCallum (1979, 67–68), which is designed to be consistent in situations with autoregression disturbances. In particular, the Maccini/Rosanna procedure first estimates by instrumental variables[15] an equation in which the residual is serially correlated, then uses the residuals from that equation to estimate the serial correlation parameter. I do not believe that their procedure is actually appropriate, for they treat as

11. See Blinder 1984, 33–34. Also note the first column of Blinder and Holtz-Eakin's table 3.5.

12. This claim is cited by Blinder and Holtz-Eakin, note 11.

13. The point is also discussed in McCallum 1979, 68.

14. This statement presumes that the econometrician possesses fewer data than the agents whose behavior is being modeled. In that situation, use of "full information" (i.e., simultaneous estimation) econometric techniques will not escape the problems discussed in McCallum 1979. With sales treated as exogenous, it seems clear that this situation obtains in both of the studies under discussion.

15. With the instruments created by regressions on lagged values of (supposedly) exogenous variables.

exogenous variables that the theory says are jointly dependent, but it does not seem less appropriate than Blinder's.[16]

In short, I would conjecture that the data are trying to tell us that, in a representation of the form

$$(24) \qquad n_t - n_{t-1} = b[n_t^* - n_{t-1}] + (1 - \rho L)^{-1} e_t,$$

both b and ρ are very close to 1.0. Adjustment is essentially complete within each period, even when these refer to monthly observations.

To complete the discussion, something needs to be said about the tendency for estimates of c in expression (15) to be negative. A likely reason for this finding is that it is unreasonable—and inconsistent with the prevailing theory described above—to treat x_t (sales) as exogenous to n_t. The point is that if x_t is in fact jointly determined with n_t, then it will be almost impossible to *identify* the parameter attached to the "surprise" term $x_t - E_{t-1} x_t$. Several writers have made analogous arguments in the course of debates over the nature of aggregate supply behavior; for a more general but technically elementary treatment see McCallum (1979, 68).

Conclusion

In sum, there are several ways Blinder and Holtz-Eakin's paper makes a useful contribution. One of these, clearly, is by compiling and reporting monthly data on manufacturing sales, output, and inventories for the prewar period. Another is by cataloging some empirical regularities and providing prewar/postwar comparisons for several series. But the paper's main *analytical* suggestions seem to be that the empirical regularity var(y) > var(x) serves to discredit prevailing inventory theories[17] and that econometric evidence implies very slow adjustment speeds for stock adjustment models. For the reasons developed above, I think both these suggestions should be viewed with considerable skepticism.

Reply   Alan S. Blinder and Douglas Holtz-Eakin

The reader of Bennett McCallum's comment may be puzzled because most of the items at which McCallum directs his fire are neither said

---

16. My interpretation of these results is consistent with Eichenbaum's (1984) finding of strong serial correlation in his inventory cost disturbance $\psi(t)$. He also found two local minima (i.e., likelihood function maxima) with high and low values of the serial correlation parameter, but his maximum likelihood procedure settled on the former.

17. This suggestion has been substantially qualified in the published version.

nor done in the paper he is allegedly discussing. In part this is because the two of us took his criticisms of our original draft to heart and revised the paper substantially. Rather than being flattered by this, McCallum appears chagrined that we have deprived him of target practice. That is a shame, but we thought intellectual exchange was the purpose of a conference.

Nonetheless, at least two points need rebuttal. The primary disagreement is over the nature of the major prevailing inventory theory—the production smoothing/buffer stock model. McCallum seems to view it as a model in which it is quite plausible that cost shocks dominate, leading production to be more variable than sales. This is a strange interpretation of a model that was designed to highlight the way production is smoothed in the face of demand shocks. It is, after all, pretty clear that supply shocks tend to make supply more variable than demand, while demand shocks tend to make demand more variable than supply. As we noted in note 8, his choice of numerical values makes cost shocks dominate all the variances and covariances. While it is true (see the text p. 189 and notes 10 and 12) that the empirical findings (production is more variable than sales, slow adjustment speeds, etc.) do not literally lead one to reject the theory, they do suggest that there is a problem. (The major points in this debate were all anticipated in Blinder 1984, as evidenced by McCallum's numerous references to it.)

McCallum's interpretation of the estimated adjustment speed leaves something to be desired as well. To analyze this parameter using his model, he assumes that "c_2 and c_3 are small" (despite earlier claims that costs of changing production rates (c_3) are too important to be ignored). In doing so, he creates a linear cost structure in which there is no incentive for either production smoothing or partial adjustment. As evidence of this, notice that lagged inventories do not appear in his equation (22); they show up in his equation (23) only after quasi-differencing to eliminate serial correlation in the disturbance term.

Our final remark concerns the methods used to estimate the stock adjustment models. McCallum takes Blinder (1984) to task for not following econometric procedures recommended in McCallum (1979), even though McCallum (1979, 68) notes that these procedures are unlikely to work in an equation containing both x_t and x^e_t. The reader should realize that the full-information procedure used in the present paper jointly estimates expectations formation, serial correlation, and the parameters of the model. It avoids, therefore, the Flood/Garber problem resulting from the use of separately fitted residuals. Any problems that remain are shared by much of the empirical literature using rational expectations (for example Sargent 1978). Although McCallum *asserts* a preference for the "high ρ rapid adjustment" estimate, we have in fact examined the likelihood functions and found that the "low ρ slow adjustment" estimate achieves a higher value in most cases— sometimes by a narrow margin, to be sure, but sometimes by quite a large margin. We prefer to let the data, not our priors, decide the issue.

Discussion Summary

Some of the discussion was directed to the absence of an interest rate variable in the conference version of the paper, and these suggestions led the authors to include the interest rate in table 3.5 in the final version. Among those suggesting that the interest rate variable be tested were Michael Lovell and Benjamin Friedman. Stanley Fischer pointed out that the fact that interest rate effects had not been detected until recently was consistent with the limited variation of real interest rates in much of the postwar era, when as the Eckstein/Sinai paper describes, financial disturbances influenced the real economy via credit rationing, not interest rate variation. Recent fluctuations in real interest rates, however, may well have caused inventory fluctuations. Fischer was also concerned that the data used for the prewar period may have been subject to considerable, possibly nonrandom, measurement errors.

Alan Auerbach drew attention to the model's inability to distinguish empirically between serial correlation and the partial adjustment coefficient estimated. He felt that this "weak identifiability" was a serious drawback in interpreting the results. Robert Barro questioned how much of the variation in inventories was for goods in progress and how much was in final goods inventories, and Moses Abramovitz stated that for individual firms, almost all inventory variation was in final sales, whereas for industry as a whole the variation was in work in progress. Barro continued that table 3.1 overstated the role of inventories by tabulating changes in inventories with respect to GNP, not relative to normal inventories.

Alan Blinder agreed that it was difficult to distinguish serial correlation from partial adjustment and that this was a serious drawback to the stock adjustment model. But, he added, there are some industrial sectors in which such a distinction is possible. He also noted that for the whole economy, most of the variation in postwar inventories was in finished goods, not work in progress. In manufacturing, work in progress and finished goods are roughly of equal importance. Unfortunately, there are no data for the interwar period to distinguish among the types of inventories.

References

Abramovitz, Moses. 1950. *Inventories and business cycles.* New York: National Bureau of Economic Research.

Ackley, Gardner. 1951. The multiplier time period: Money, inventories and flexibility. *American Economic Review* 41 (June): 350–68.

Blanchard, Olivier J. 1983. The production and inventory behavior of the American automobile industry. *Journal of Political Economy* 91:365–400.

Blinder, Alan S. 1981a. Inventories and the structure of macro models. *American Economic Review* 71:11–16.

————. 1981b. Retail inventory behavior and business fluctuations. *Brookings Papers on Economic Activity* 2:443–505.

————. 1982. Inventories and sticky prices. *American Economic Review* 72 (June):334–48.

————. 1984. Can the production smoothing model of inventory behavior be saved? Working Paper 1257, National Bureau of Economic Research.

Blinder, Alan S., and Stanley Fischer. 1981. Inventories, rational expectations, and the business cycle. *Journal of Monetary Economics* 8:277–304.

Blinder, Alan S., and Douglas Holtz-Eakin. 1983. Constant dollar manufacturers' inventories: A note. Mimeographed. Princeton University.

Brennan, Michael J. 1959. A model of seasonal inventories. *Econometrica* 27:228–44.

Carlson, John A., and William E. Wehrs. 1974. Aggregate inventory behavior. In *Trade, stability, and macroeconomics: Essays in honor of L. A. Metzler,* ed. G. Horwich and P. A. Samuelson. New York: Academic Press.

Eichenbaum, Martin S. 1983. A rational expectations model of the cyclical behavior of inventories of finished goods and employment. *Journal of Monetary Economics* 12:259–78.

————. 1984. Rational expectations and the smoothing properties of inventories of finished goods. *Journal of Monetary Economics* 14:71–96.

Feldstein, Martin S., and Alan Auerbach. 1976. Inventory behavior in durable goods manufacturing: The target adjustment model. *Brookings Papers on Economic Activity* 2:351–96.

Flood, Robert P., and Peter M. Garber. 1980. A pitfall in estimation of models with rational expectations. *Journal of Monetary Economics* 6:433–36.

Gordon, Robert J. 1984. *Macroeconomics.* 3d ed. Boston: Little, Brown.

Holt, Charles C., Franco Modigliani, John Muth, and Herbert A. Simon. 1960. *Planning production, inventories and work force.* Englewood Cliffs, N.J.: Prentice-Hall.

Irvine, Owen F. 1981. Specification errors and the stock-adjustment model: Why estimated speeds-of-adjustment are too slow in inventory equations. Working Paper, Federal Reserve Board.

Kuznets, Simon S. 1926. *Cyclical fluctuations: Retail and wholesale trade, United States, 1919–1925.* New York: Adelphi.

Lovell, Michael C. 1961. Manufacturers' inventories, sales expectations, and the acceleration principle. *Econometrica* 29 (July):293–314.

McCallum, Bennett T. 1972. Inventory holdings, rational expectations, and the law of supply and demand. *Journal of Political Economy* 80:386–93.

———. 1976. Rational expectations and the natural rate hypothesis: Some consistent estimates. *Econometrica* 44 (January):43–52.

———. 1979. Topics concerning the formulation, estimation, and use of macroeconometric models with rational expectations. In *Proceedings of the Business and Economics Statistics Section,* 65–72. Washington, D.C.: American Statistical Association.

———. 1981. Alternative inventory models. Manuscript presented at National Bureau of Economic Research Summer Institute.

———. 1983. On non-uniqueness in rational expectations models: An attempt at perspective. *Journal of Monetary Economics* 11:139–68.

Maccini, Louis J., and Robert J. Rossana, 1984. Joint production, quasi-fixed factors of production, and investment in finished goods inventories. *Journal of Money, Credit, and Banking* 16 (May):218–36.

Mack, Ruth P. 1956. *Consumption and business cycles.* New York: National Bureau of Economic Research.

Mack, Ruth P., and Victor Zarnowitz. 1958. Cause and consequence of changes in retailers' buying. *American Economic Review* 48 (March):18–49.

Metzler, Lloyd A. 1941. The nature and stability of inventory cycles. *Review of Economics and Statistics* 23 (August):113–29.

———. 1947. Factors governing the length of inventory cycles. *Review of Economics and Statistics* 29 (February):1–15.

Muth, John F. 1961. Rational expectations and the theory of price movements. *Econometrica* 29:315–35.

Nurkse, Ragner. 1954. Period analysis and inventory cycles. *Oxford Economic Papers,* n.s., 6 (September): 203–25.

Orr, Lloyd. 1967. A comment on sales anticipations and inventory investment. *International Economic Review* 8:368–73.

Plosser, Charles I., and G. William Schwert. 1978. Money, income, and sunspots: Measuring economic relationships and the effects of differencing. *Journal of Monetary Economics* 4:637–60.

Sargent, T. 1978. Estimation of dynamic labor demand schedules under rational expectations. In *Rational expectations and econometric practice,* ed. R. Lucas and T. Sargent, 463–99. Minneapolis: University of Minnesota Press.

Stanback, Thomas M., Jr. 1962. *Postwar cycles in manufacturers' inventories*. New York: National Bureau of Economic Research.

West, Kenneth D. 1983. A note on the econometric use of constant dollar inventory series. *Economic Letters*, 337–41.

Zarnowitz, Victor. 1961. The timing of manufacturers' orders during business cycles. In *Business cycle indicators,* ed. Geoffrey H. Moore, vol. 1. Princeton: Princeton University Press.

4   The Role of Consumption in Economic Fluctuations

Robert E. Hall

4.1 The Issues

Consumption is the dominant component of GNP. A 1% change in consumption is five times the size of a 1% change in investment. This paper investigates whether the behavior of consumers is an independent source of macroeconomic fluctuations or whether most disturbances come from other sectors.

Informal commentaries on the business cycle put considerable weight on the independent behavior of consumption. It is commonplace to hear of a business revival sparked by consumers. On the other hand, all modern theories of fluctuations make the consumer a reactor to economic events, not a cause of them. Random shocks in technology are generally the driving force in fully articulated models.

This paper develops a framework where the distinction between a movement along a consumption schedule and a shift of the schedule is well defined. Application of the framework to twentieth-century American data shows that shifts of the consumption schedule have probably been an important cause of fluctuations but have probably not been the dominant source of them.

I consider three sources of disturbances to the economy: (1) shifts of the consumption schedule; (2) shifts of the schedule relating spending in categories other than consumption and military spending; and (3) shifts in military spending. The reason for the explicit examination of military spending is that such spending is the only plainly exogenous

Robert E. Hall is professor of economics at Stanford University.

I am grateful to Olivier Blanchard and Ben Bernanke for comments and to Valerie Ramey for expert assistance.

major influence on the economy. Movements in military spending reveal the slopes of the consumption schedule and other spending schedules.

My basic strategy is the following. Fluctuations in military spending reveal the slope of the consumption/GNP schedule. GNP rises with military spending—quite stably, GNP has risen by about sixty-two cents for every dollar increase in military spending. This conclusion is supported by data from years other than those of major wars, when resource allocation by command may have made the consumption schedule irrelevant. But when GNP rises under the stimulus of increased military spending, consumption actually falls a little—the same dollar of military spending has depressed consumption by about seven cents.

Under the reasonable assumption that higher military spending does not shift the consumption schedule but only moves consumers along the schedule, we can infer the slope of the schedule from the ratio of the consumption change to the GNP change. The slope is essentially zero.

Equipped with this knowledge, we can measure the shift of the consumption schedule as the departure of consumption from a schedule with the estimated slope. My main concern is the absolute and relative importance of these shifts.

The effect of a consumption shift on GNP depends on the slope of the consumption schedule and also upon the slope of the schedule relating other spending to GNP. For this reason it is necessary to carry out a similar exercise for other spending. Again, the way other spending changes when military spending absorbs added resources is the way the slope can be inferred. Historically, other spending has declined when military spending has risen; investment, net exports, and non-military government purchases are crowded out by military spending. For each dollar of added military spending, other spending declines by about thirty cents. The inference is that the schedule relating other spending to GNP has an important negative slope.

Over the period studied here, the correlation of the change in consumption and the change in GNP has been strong; the correlation coefficient is .59. Similarly, the correlation of the change in other spending and the change in GNP is strongly positive at .61. The results of this paper explain *all* of the correlation of consumption and GNP in terms of the unexplained shifts in the two schedules and *none* as the result of movements along the consumption function. Even more strikingly, the results explain the strong *positive* correlation of other spending and GNP in spite of the *negative* slope of the schedule relating the two.

Stated in terms of the scale of the economy in 1982, the standard deviation of the annual first difference of GNP for the period was $90 billion. The standard deviation of the component associated with the shift of the consumption function was $28 billion; for other spending including military, $72 billion. The decomposition between the two schedule shifts is ambiguous because they are highly correlated, but by assumption both are uncorrelated with the shift in military spending.

Because the slightly negative slope found for the consumption function in this work contradicts the thinking of many macroeconomists on this subject, I have repeated the exercise for two assumed values for the slope of the consumption/GNP schedule. One, which I think of as Keynesian, assumes a value of 0.3. The standard deviation of the consumption shift effect on GNP is $26 billion. The shifts in the consumption function are estimated to be smaller in this case, but their contribution to movements in GNP is larger because the multiplier is larger.

A second case derives from equilibrium models of the business cycle. It interprets the consumption/GNP schedule as the expansion path of the consumption/labor supply decision of the household. The slope of the schedule should be *negative,* since presumably both consumption and leisure are normal goods. Any events that make people feel it is a good idea to consume more should also cause them to take more leisure and therefore work less. A reasonable value for the slope of the consumption/GNP schedule under this interpretation is − 1. When this is imposed on the problem, the consumption shifts appear much larger, since this is a long step away from the regression relation. The standard deviation of the effect of consumption on GNP is $47 billion, comparable to the effect of shifts in other spending, $46 billion.

4.2   Earlier Research

Modern thinking about the possible role of shifts in the consumption function in overall macro fluctuations began with Milton Friedman and Gary Becker's "A Statistical Illusion in Judging Keynesian Models" (1957). They pointed out that random shifts in the consumption function could induce a positive correlation between consumption and income, which in turn could make the consumption look more responsive to income than it really was and also make the consumption function more reliable than it really was. However, neither Friedman and Becker nor other workers on the consumption function pursued the idea that shifts in the consumption function might be an important element of the business cycle.

More recently, Peter Temin's *Did Monetary Forces Cause the Great Depression?* (1976) argued forcefully for a role for shifts of the consumption function in explaining the contraction from 1929 to 1933. Temin focuses particularly on the residual from a consumption function in the year 1930 and suggests that the shift in consumption in that year was an important factor in setting off the contraction. His results are strongly supported in this paper, which finds large shifts in the consumption/GNP relation in all the years of the contraction.

Temin's critics, Thomas Mayer (1980) and Barry Anderson and James Butkiewicz (1980), confirm that consumption functions of various types had important negative residuals in 1930. It is a curious feature of Temin's work and that of his critics that no attention has been paid to the issue of finding the true slope of the consumption/income schedule. If the history of the United States is full of episodes where consumption shifts affected GNP, then the observed correlation of consumption and income is no guide at all to the slope of the consumption function. Temin considerably understates the power of his case by looking for departures from the historical relation between consumption and income, which is not at all the same thing as the slope of the structural relation. The historical relation summarizes numerous other episodes where a spontaneous shift in consumption had important macro effects. Temin looks only at the excess in 1930 over the usual amount of a shift, when his argument logically involves the whole amount of the shift.

Because of my use of military spending as the exogenous instrument that identifies the structural consumption function, I spend some effort here in understanding how a burst of military purchases influences the economy. Robert Barro (1981) has examined the theory of the effect of government purchases in an equilibrium framework and has studied United States data on the effect on GNP. He found a robust positive effect of all types of government purchases, with an especially large coefficient for temporary military spending. My results here are in line with Barro's, though I do not attempt to distinguish permanent and temporary purchases. Barro notes that higher government purchases should *depress* consumption as a matter of theory (p. 1094) but does not examine the actual behavior of consumption. Barro and Robert King (1982) point out the difficulties of creating a theoretical equilibrium model in which the covariance of consumption and work effort is anything but sharply negative.

Joseph Altonji (1982) and N. Gregory Mankiw, Julio Rotemberg, and Lawrence Summers (1982) use the observed positive covariation of consumption and hours of work to cast doubt on the empirical validity of equilibrium models. However, neither paper considers the possibility that feedback from shifts in household behavior creates an econometric identification problem. The results of this paper give partial support to their conclusion. With a serious treatment of the identification problem, the structural relation between work and consumption appears to be flat or slightly negatively sloped, but not nearly enough negatively sloped to fit the predictions of the equilibrium model.

Here I examine the importance of fluctuations in consumption as an interesting question in its own right. My finding of important shifts in the consumption function is also important for recent research on consumption and related issues in finance. As Peter Garber and Robert King (1983) point out, shifts in preferences or other sources of unexplained fluctuations in consumption behavior invalidate the Euler equation approach I and others have used in studying the reaction of consumers to surprises in income and to changes in expected real interest rates. The hope that the Euler equation is identified econometrically without the use of exogenous variables depends critically on the absence of the type of shift found in this paper. My findings suggest that the Euler equation is identified only through the use of exogenous instruments, just as are most other macroeconomic structural relations.

4.3   A Simple Structural Relation between GNP and Consumption

Keynesian theory denies consumers choice about the level of work effort. The effective demand process dictates the amount of work and the corresponding level of earnings. Consumers choose consumption so as to maximize satisfaction given actual and expected earnings. In general, the resulting relationship between earnings and consumption can be complicated—consumers will use the information contained in current and lagged earnings to infer likely future earnings and thus the appropriate level of consumption. Traditional Keynesian thought has emphasized the strength of the contemporaneous relation between income and consumption. Liquidity constraints probably contribute to the strength. Recent tests by Hall and Mishkin (1982) and by Marjorie Flavin (1981) have rejected the optimal response of consumption in favor of excess sensitivity to current income (however, these tests are likely to be contaminated by shifts in consumer behavior of the type investigated in this paper).

Otto Eckstein and Allen Sinai's paper in this volume (chap. 1) provides a reasonable estimate for the slope of the GNP/consumption schedule in a Keynesian framework. In their table 1.7, they estimate the effects on GNP and consumption of an exogenous increase in government purchases. The ratio of the change in consumption to the change in GNP is an estimate of the slope of exactly the schedule considered in this paper. The ratio is

Quarters after Increase	GNP	Consumption	Ratio
4	1.26	0.41	0.32
8	0.94	0.28	0.30
12	0.81	0.18	0.22
16	0.64	0.10	0.16
24	0.56	0.10	0.18

I will use an estimate for the year-to-year marginal propensity to consume of 0.3 on the basis of this evidence about the overall behavior of a fully developed Keynesian model.

4.3.1   Equilibrium Thinking about the Consumption/GNP Schedule

In an equilibrium model consumers are free to choose the most satisfying combination of hours of work and consumption of goods, subject to the market trade-off between the two:

$$\max_{\{c_t, y_t\}} \Sigma \, D^t u(c_t, y_t)$$

$$\text{subject to } \Sigma \, R_t \, (p_t c_t - w_t y_t) = W.$$

My notation is:

D: time preference factor
$u(\ )$:   one-year utility function
c_t: consumption in year t
y_t: employment in year t
R_t: discount factor
p_t: price of consumption goods in year t
w_t: wage in year t
W: initial wealth

I will work with one aspect of the overall problem, the consumption/work choice in year t. The first-order condition for that choice is:

$$\text{Marginal rate of substitution} = \text{real wage}$$

or

$$-\frac{\partial u/\partial y_t}{\partial u/\partial c_t} = \frac{w_t}{p_t} = \omega_t$$

Define the expansion path, $f(y_t, \omega_t)$, by

$$-\frac{\partial u(f(y,\omega),y)/\partial y}{\partial u(f(y,\omega),y)/\partial c} = \omega.$$

Other aspects of the overall choice problem determine the point the consumer chooses on the expansion path. These include wealth and the timing of consumption and work. With the real wage held constant, higher wealth moves the consumer to a point of higher consumption and lower work. Again with the real wage held constant, a higher real interest rate moves the consumer to a point of lower consumption and more work. Altonji (1982) pointed out the usefulness of examining the joint behavior of work effort, consumption, and the real wage;

his paper presents many more details on the derivation of their relationship.

It should be apparent that the expansion path slopes downward as long as consumption and leisure are normal goods.

The expansion path shifts downward if the real wage declines. Consequently, a higher tax rate depresses consumption given the level of

CONSUMPTION

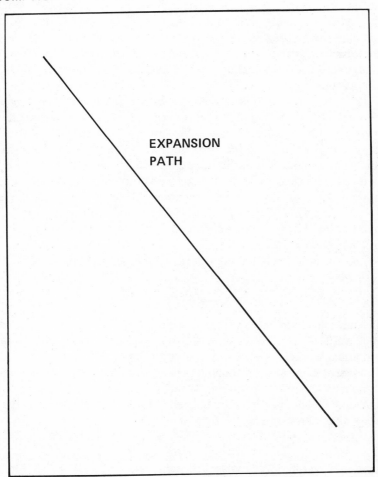

WORK

Fig. 4.1   The expansion path. For a given real wage, consumption and work occur in combinations given by the path. The real interest rate and the level of wealth determine the position on the expansion path chosen by the consumer.

work effort. On the other hand, the expansion path is unaffected by an increase in government purchases of goods and services or by lump-sum transfers or taxes. These latter influences will move the consumer along the expansion path but will not shift the path.

The slope of the expansion path can be estimated as the negative of the ratio of the income effect in the demand for consumption goods to the income effect in the labor supply function. Estimated income effects for labor supply run on the order of fifty cents less in earnings for each dollar in increased nonlabor income. That is, an increase in nonlabor income of one dollar raises total income by only fifty cents. If all of the increase in total income sooner or later is applied to goods consumption, then the income effect for goods consumption is also fifty cents per dollar of nonlabor income. The resulting slope of the expansion path is -1.

The structural relation in the equilibrium model refers to consumption and work effort. For the purposes of this paper, I think the best measure of the change in work effort from one year to the next is the change in real GNP. In the short run, the amount of capital available for use in production hardly changes, though of course the intensity of its use changes. Almost all changes in output correspond to changes in hours of labor input and in the amount of effort per hour spent on the job (see Hall 1980 for an elaboration and empirical study of this point). Real GNP is the best available measure of all the dimensions of changes in work effort in the short run.

The structural relation suggested by the equilibrium model has the form

$$c_t = \beta y_t + \gamma \omega_t.$$

In addition to the level of work effort, measured by y_t, the after-tax real wage, ω_t, shifts consumption up relative to work effort. In the empirical work carried out here, it is not possible to estimate the coefficients of two different endogenous variables. The best that can be done is to estimate the coefficient of y_t, *net* of the part of a real wage movement that is systematically related to y. For example, if the real wage is countercyclical, so that

$$\omega_t = -\delta y_t,$$

then it is possible to estimate the net relation,

$$c_t = (\beta - \gamma\delta)y_t.$$

Because β is negative, the countercyclical wage movements makes the consumption/GNP relation even more negatively sloped. It seems unlikely that procyclical movements of after-tax real wages are anywhere near large enough to explain my finding here of a zero net slope of the consumption/GNP relation. That finding is probably evidence against a pure equilibrium model.

4.3.2 Synthesis

Equilibrium and Keynesian models agree on a structural relation between consumption and income or work of the form

$$c_t = \beta y_t + \epsilon_t.$$

Here,

β: slope of the structural relation, negative for the equilibrium model (say -1), positive for the Keynesian model (say 0.3);

ϵ_t: random shift in the c-y relation.

4.4 Other Components of GNP

I will assume that military purchases of goods and services, g_t, is an exogenous variable.

I will define x_t as the remainder of GNP, that is, investment plus net exports plus nonmilitary government purchases of goods and services (the latter is largely state and local). x_t has a structural relation to GNP; fluctuations in this relation are a source of fluctuations in almost all theories of the business cycle.

It is not possible to estimate a detailed structural model for x_t for the reason just mentioned—a single exogenous variable limits estimation to a single endogenous variable. Basically, what can be estimated is the net effect of an increase in GNP on investment, net exports, and nonmilitary government purchases. On the one hand, considerations of the accelerator (particularly important for inventory investment) suggest a positive relation between GNP and x. On the other hand, increases in interest rates that accompany an increase in GNP bring decreases in x. For investment, especially in housing, the negative response to interest rates is well documented. For net exports, an increase in GNP raises imports directly. In addition, under floating exchange rates, the higher interest rates brought by higher GNP cause the dollar to appreciate, making imports cheaper to the United States and exports more expensive to the rest of the world. It is perfectly reasonable that the overall net effect of higher GNP on investment, net exports, and nonmilitary purchases should be negative.

The following simple relation summarizes these considerations:

$$x_t = \mu y_t + v_t.$$

The coefficient μ may well be negative, if crowding out through interest rates is an important phenomenon.

4.5 The Complete Model

The model comprises three equations:

$$c_t = \beta y_t + \epsilon_t$$

$$x_t = \mu y_t + v_t$$

$$y_t = c_t + x_t + g_t.$$

The solution for GNP is

$$y_t = \frac{1}{1 - \beta - \mu} (g_t + \epsilon_t + v_t).$$

This equation gives a precise accounting for the sources of fluctuations in output. The three driving forces for the economy are military purchases of goods and services, g_t, the random shift in the consumption schedule, ϵ_t, and the random shift in other spending, v_t.

4.6 Identification and Estimation

The goals of estimation in this work are threefold:
1. Estimate the multiplier,

$$\frac{1}{1 - \beta - \mu},$$

which applies to each of the three components in the decomposition in the last section.

2. Estimate the "propensity to consume," β, in order to compute the residuals, ϵ_t, in the consumption function.

3. Estimate the "propensity to spend," μ, in order to compute the residuals, v_t, in the function for other spending.

The solution to the first problem is perfectly straightforward. In the equation for the movement in GNP, military spending appears as a right-hand variable along with two disturbances assumed to be uncorrelated with military spending. Hence the regression of GNP on military spending should estimate the multiplier directly. Again, the interpretation of the estimated multiplier is net of feedback effects through interest rates.

To estimate the slope of the consumption/GNP schedule, β, note that c and g have the regression relation,

$$c_t = \frac{\beta}{1 - \beta - \mu} (g_t + v_t) + \frac{1 - \mu}{1 - \beta - \mu} \epsilon_t.$$

An estimate of β can be computed as the ratio of this coefficient to the multiplier. Alternatively, exactly the same estimate can be computed with two-stage least squares applied to the c-y relation with g as the instrument.

The slope of the x-y relation can be computed analogously either by the ratio of the regression coefficient of x on g to the multiplier, or by applying two-stage least squares to the x-y equation with g as instrument.

The relationships estimated in this paper are approximations to more complicated equations. For example, the complete model does not do justice to the modern Keynesian notion that gradual wage and price adjustment gives the model a tendency toward full employment in the long run. The results are likely to look somewhat different with an estimation technique that gives heavy weight to lower frequencies from those based more on higher frequencies. Because cyclical fluctuations are the focus here, I want to exclude the lower frequencies from the estimation. I have accomplished the exclusion in two ways. First, I have detrended all the data in a consistent fashion. Second, I have used first differences in all of the basic estimation. With annual data, using first differences puts strong weight on the cyclical frequencies and no weight at all on the lowest frequencies.

4.7 Data

The data on real GNP in 1972 dollars for 1919–82 and real personal consumption expenditures for 1929–82 are from the United States national income and product accounts (NIPA). For 1919–28, data on real consumption are taken from John Kendrick (1961).

I used data on real military purchases of goods and services from the NIPA for 1972 through 1982 and from Kendrick for 1919–53. For 1954 through 1971, nominal military spending is taken from the NIPA and deflated by the implicit deflator for national security spending from the Office of Management and Budget (1983), converted to a calendar year basis.

For some additional results described at the end of the paper, I used the number of full-time equivalent employees in all industries, including military, from the NIPA.

To eliminate the noncyclical frequencies from the data, I started by fitting a trend to real GNP:

$$\log y_t = 5.14 + .0206\, t + .00014\, t^2.$$
(t is one in 1909)

Then I detrended real GNP, real consumption, and real military purchases with this real GNP trend. I preserved the 1982 values of each of the three variables, so the effect of detrending was to raise the earlier levels. For employment, I detrended with a log-linear trend of 1.96% per year and rebased the series so that it equals real GNP in 1982.

All of the estimates used the first differences of the detrended series.

4.8 Results

All of the regressions reported here include intercepts, but the values of the intercepts are not reported because detrending makes them almost meaningless.

Estimation of the multiplier by regressing the change in GNP on the change in military spending for the years 1920–42 and 1947–82 gives the following results:

$$\Delta y_t = .62 \ \Delta g_t.$$
$$(.16)$$
$$\text{SE:} \quad \$81 \text{ billion;} \quad \text{DW:} \quad 1.48$$

Because the multiplier is less than one, it is clear that a certain amount of crowding out took place, on the average. Each dollar of military purchases raises GNP by sixty-two cents, so nonmilitary uses of output decline by thirty-eight cents.

The regression of consumption on military spending is:

$$\Delta c_t = -0.07 \ \Delta g_t$$
$$(.08)$$
$$\text{SE:} \quad \$38 \text{ billion;} \quad \text{DW:} \quad 1.50$$

Because the coefficient is close to zero, with a small standard error, it is clear that the implied slope of the c - y relation will be close to zero as well. Even though periods of wartime controls on consumption have been omitted from this regression, there is strong evidence against the proposition that those increases in GNP that can be associated with exogenous increases in military spending stimulated any important increases in consumption. Similarly, the strong *negative* response of consumption to military spending predicted by the equilibrium model has also been shown to be absent.

The ratio of the two regression coefficients is $-.12$; this is the estimate of the slope of the consumption/GNP schedule. The same estimate can be obtained by two-stage least squares, together with the standard error of β and the standard error of the residuals:

$$\Delta c_t = -0.12 \ \Delta y_t.$$
$$(.15)$$
$$\text{SE:} \quad \$46 \text{ billion;} \quad \text{DW:} \quad 1.39$$

The confidence interval on the slope of the c - y relation includes a range of values but excludes the Keynesian value of 0.3 and the equilibrium value of -1 as well. Neither theory is able to explain the lack of a structural association of consumption and GNP.

In the next section I will make use of consumption equations with two different assumed values of the slope:

Keynesian, $\qquad\qquad\quad$ $\beta = 0.3$

$$\Delta c_t = 0.3\Delta y_t$$

$$\text{SE:} \quad \$31 \text{ billion}$$

Equilibrium, $\qquad\qquad\quad$ $\beta = -1$

$$\Delta c_t = -\Delta y_t$$

$$\text{SE:} \quad \$117 \text{ billion.}$$

The basic results of the paper can be guessed from these results. The residuals in the Keynesian consumption relation are smaller than those for the estimated relation (standard errors of $31 billion against $46 billion) and are very much smaller than are those for the equilibrium case ($117 billion). Even the smaller Keynesian residuals turn out to be important in the overall determination of GNP. GNP and consumption are positively correlated both because the consumption relation slopes upward and because shifts in the relation are an important determinant of both variables.

On the other hand, the equilibrium model sees very large shifts in the c - y relation. When the relation shifts upward, both c and y rise. Because most of the variation in both variables comes from the shifts in the relation, the two are highly positively correlated, even though the relation has a negative slope. That a positive slope gives a better fit in the consumption equation is not evidence against the equilibrium view at all.

4.8.1   Results for Other Spending, x

The regression of Δx on Δg gives:

$$\Delta x_t = -0.30 \, \Delta g_t.$$
$$(.12)$$
$$\text{SE:} \quad \$58 \text{ billion;} \quad \text{DW:} \quad 2.03$$

Investment, net exports, and nonmilitary government spending are quite strongly *negatively* influenced by military spending, again during years when wartime controls on private spending were not in effect. The estimate of the slope of the x - y schedule inferred by dividing by the multiplier is -0.48. The same estimate is available from two-stage least squares:

$$\Delta x_t = -0.48 \, \Delta y_t.$$
$$(.30)$$

SE: \$95 billion;   DW: 1.79

Plainly, the negative effects operating through interest rates dominate the positive effects of the accelerator. Higher GNP depresses nonconsumption, nonmilitary spending along this structural schedule.

4.9   Estimates of the Importance of the Consumption Shift

Because neither of the major schools of business cycle theory is consistent with my estimates of the slope of the c - y relation, I will proceed by making estimates for three different cases:

1. *Estimated.* The slope of the c - y relation is $-.12$, the value inferred from the fact that, historically, higher military purchases have raised GNP but not consumption. Consumption is virtually an exogenous variable. It influences GNP but is not influenced by GNP.

2. *Keynesian.* The slope of the c - y relation is 0.3. When more work is available, people consume more as well.

3. *Equilibrium.* The slope of the c - y relation is -1. Events that move consumers along their expansion paths leave the sum of GNP and consumption unchanged. Departures of the sum of GNP and consumption are a signal of a shift in the expansion path, possibly associated with a change in the after-tax real wage, but usually a random, unexplained shift.

Though the movements of GNP can be decomposed into three components for the three driving forces listed in the model in section 4.4 (military purchases, the random shift in the consumption schedule, and the random shift in the investment/exports schedule), I will concentrate on the consumption shift on the one hand and the sum of the two other components on the other hand. The consumption component is

$$\frac{1}{1 - \beta - \mu} \, \epsilon_t,$$

where ϵ_t is the residual from the consumption equation. Note that the magnitude of the consumption component depends on the magnitude of the residual and on the magnitude of the multiplier. The other component is just Δy_t less the consumption component.

Figure 4.2 shows the total change in real GNP and the consumption components for the three cases. As a general matter, the consumption component is most important for the equilibrium case and least im-

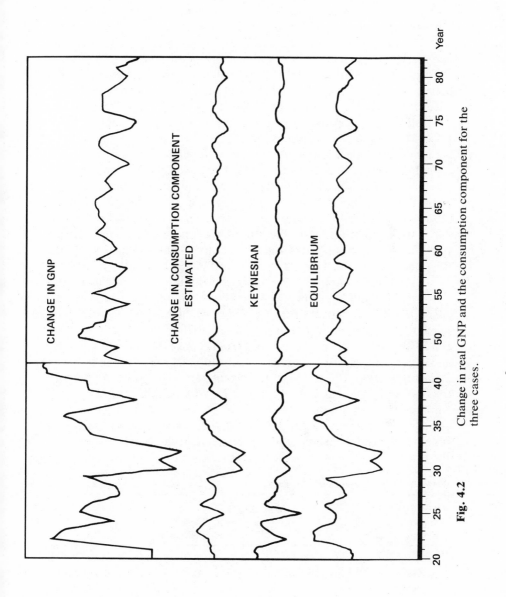

Fig. 4.2   Change in real GNP and the consumption component for the three cases.

portant for the Keynesian case. However, it is a significant contributor to GNP fluctuations in all three cases.

Under the estimated results where consumption is effectively exogenous, shifts in the consumption schedule are important, but so are shifts in the other determinants of GNP, especially in the interwar period. Responsibility for the Great Contraction is shared between shifts in the c-y relation and the other sources. However, in the postwar period, shifts in other spending account for the bulk of the movement of GNP. The two large drops of GNP in 1973–74 and 1974–75 are partly the result of drops in consumption. Some of the long contraction since 1978 is the result of a consumption shift as well.

In the Keynesian view, shifts in the consumption function are bound to be less important than in the other two cases. When consumption and GNP drop together, all or part of the decline in consumption can be attributed to the drop in GNP. Still, shifts in consumption are a part of the story of total fluctuations.

For the equilibrium case, the story about the Great Contraction in 1929–32 told by these results will help clarify what the theory is saying. Rescaled real GNP fell by $227 billion in 1929–30, $171 billion in 1930–31, and $243 billion in 1931–32. Of this, $140 billion came from a random shift in household behavior toward less work and less consumption in 1929–30, $97 billion in 1930–31, and $148 billion in 1931–32. The remaining $87 billion in the first year, $74 billion in the second year, and $95 billion in the third year came from changes in military spending and shifts in the investment/exports schedule. Of the two, the first was almost negligible. But the most important part of the story of the contraction was a sudden lack of interest in working and consuming, according to the equilibrium model.

Table 4.1 summarizes the findings for the three cases in terms of simple statistical measures. It is interesting that the standard deviation

Table 4.1	Statistical Summary		
Standard Deviation of Change	Keynesian	Case Estimated	Equilibrium
Real GNP	90	93	93
Consumption component	26	28	47
Other component	97	72	46
Correlation of two components	−.40	.53	.86

Note: Standard deviations are in billions of 1972 dollars, with quantities rescaled to 1982 magnitudes.

of the consumption component for the Keynesian case is about the same as for the estimated case. Although the residuals in the Keynesian consumption function are smaller than the residuals in the other case, the multiplier is quite a bit higher (0.85 as against 0.62). The big difference between the two cases is in the size of the other component. Again, because the multiplier is lower for the estimated case and higher for the Keynesian case, the other component is larger for the Keynesian case. The Keynesian case reconciles a larger other component with a consumption component of about the same size by invoking a lower correlation of the two components. The negative correlation permits the sum to have the same standard deviation (the known standard deviation of the change in real GNP) even though one of the components is more variable.

4.10   Other Estimates

Estimates for other time periods and other specifications have convinced me that the basic findings of this paper are robust. First, estimates for the entire period, the interwar period, and the postwar period are

Entire period, 1920–82

$$\Delta c_t = -.16 \, \Delta y_t$$
$$(.09)$$

SE: $47 billion;   DW: 1.37

$$\Delta x_t = -.54 \, \Delta y_t.$$
$$(.18)$$

SE: $96 billion;   DW: 1.78

For both equations, the considerable extra variance from the extraordinary level of military spending during World War II helps to reduce the sampling variation without changing the coefficients much.

Interwar period, 1920–42

$$\Delta c_t = -0.13 \Delta y_t$$
$$(.24)$$

SE: $70 billion;   DW: 1.31

$$\Delta x_t = -.50 \, \Delta y_t$$
$$(.50)$$

SE: $144 billion;   DW: 1.75

Postwar period, 1947–82

$$\Delta c_t = -.11 \, \Delta y_t$$
$$(.20)$$

SE: \$23 billion; *DW:* 1.78

$$\Delta x_t = -.36 \, \Delta y_t.$$
$$(.41)$$

SE: \$46 billion; *DW:* 1.94

4.10.1 Results for a Direct Measure of Work Effort

In his comment on the version of this paper presented at the conference, Angus Deaton suggested that the negative findings for the equilibrium model might be the result of the use of GNP as a measure of work effort. Because GNP might measure the result of other productive factors, including pure good luck, and these other factors reasonably might be positively correlated with consumption, the consumption/GNP relation might be more positively sloped than is the consumption/work effort relation.

To check this possibility, I repeated the analysis with full-time equivalent employment in place of real GNP. I detrended the series by its own exponential trend and rescaled it to equal real GNP in 1982. Application of two-stage least squares to the relation of the first difference of consumption to the first difference of employment, with the change in military spending as the instrument, for the periods 1930–42 and 1947–82, is

$$\Delta c_t = -0.10 \, \Delta y_t.$$
$$(.18)$$

SE: \$41 billion; *DW:* 0.91

Again, the structural slope is slightly negative, but not nearly negative enough to fit the equilibrium hypothesis. The hypothetical value of -1 is strongly rejected.

4.11 Conclusions

A simple structural relation between GNP and consumption is a feature of two major theories of economic fluctuations, though the theories differ dramatically in most other respects.

In the Keynesian analysis, the consumption function slopes upward, so in principle the positive correlation of GNP and consumption could be explained purely by forces other than shifts in consumption behavior. Nonetheless, my results show that shifts in the consumption function are a source of overall fluctuations in a Keynesian analysis. In the first place, even the Keynesian consumption function has residuals, though they are smaller than the residuals from the equilibrium or estimated c - y relationships. In the second place, exactly because of the Keynesian multiplier process operating through a positively sloped consumption function, the consumption disturbances are much more strongly amplified than they are in the equilibrium or estimated models.

In the equilibrium theory, the relation is the expansion path of the work/consumption choice. The public is free to pick a point along the path in response to economic conditions. Shifts in government tax and spending policies and shifts in investment and net exports will move the economy along its negatively sloped c - y schedule. If ever GNP and consumption move together, it is the result of a shift in the consumption schedule. Because consumption and GNP frequently move together, random shifts of the consumption/work schedule must be a *dominant* part of the equilibrium explanation of cyclical fluctuations.

In the Keynesian model, an increase in military purchases should raise GNP and raise consumption. In the equilibrium model, an increase in military purchases should raise GNP and lower consumption. The data for the past six decades examined in this paper seem to split the difference—consumption is unaffected by military purchases, whereas GNP rises. Hence the estimate of the slope of the c - y relation inferred through the use of military purchases as an instrument is about zero. In the compromise economy (which does not have a theory to go with it), random shifts in consumption are an important source of overall fluctuations.

Comment   Angus Deaton

In these comments I discuss a number of both theoretical and empirical issues. First I take up the question of the theoretical equilibrium relationship between consumption and income. While Hall interprets observed fluctuations with respect to two models of consumption, and while the first, Keynesian, formulation with its coefficient of 0.3 is clearly arbitrary, I shall not quarrel with it but shall concentrate rather on the equilibrium story. I argue that it is the relation between consumption and wage income, not between consumption and GNP, that ought to have a negative slope, and that even this result depends on asset shocks dominating wage shocks in affecting consumer behavior. I also dispute Hall's reading of the empirical evidence; if his model is taken seriously, then his equilibrium consumption function should have

Angus Deaton is a professor in the Department of Economics and the Woodrow Wilson School at Princeton University.

a slope not of -1, but of somewhere between -5 and -9. These large negative slopes suggest an even more exaggerated role for consumption in the genesis of economic fluctuations, one that I for one do not find in the least plausible. In fact Hall finds that, using either GNP or full-time equivalent employment as a measure of work effort, the *actual* slope of the consumption function is essentially zero, a result that, if credible, would challenge a good deal more than Hall's version of the equilibrium story. Fortunately, I do not yet believe that it is necessary to discard the findings of the past four decades of research; the second section explains why.

Theoretical Considerations

I use the intertemporal linear expenditure system as a simple framework to illustrate the issues. The maximand is

$$(1) \qquad \sum_t D^t\{\beta \log (c_t - \gamma_1) + (1 - \beta) \log (l_t - \gamma_2)\}$$

for discount factors D^t, consumption c_t and leisure l_t. Maximization *under certainty* yields

$$(2) \qquad\qquad c_t = \gamma_1 + \beta D_t r_t$$

$$(3) \qquad\qquad w_t h_t = (T - \gamma_2) - (1 - \beta) D_t r_t$$

for work effort (hours) h_t, *real* wage w_t, and parameters γ_1, $(T - \gamma_2)$ and β. The quantity r_t is written

$$(4) \qquad r_t = \delta\{A_0 - \sum_0^L \bar{p}_t\gamma_1 + \sum_0^L \bar{w}_t (T - \gamma_2)\}/\bar{p}_t$$

for discounted present values at 0 of prices, $\bar{p}_t$ and wage rate $\bar{w}_t$, initial assets A_0 and $\delta = \Sigma D_t$. r_t is the real price of utility in t, or reciprocal of the marginal utility of money. Under *uncertainty*, the *expected value* of (1) is maximized. Following through the standard stochastic control problem yields (2) and (3) unchanged, with r_t governed by

$$(5) \qquad\qquad E_t \{(1 + i_{t+1})/r_{t+1}\} = 1/r_t$$

for real interest rate i.

To simplify further discussion, I assume that real interest rates are known and constant and equal to the rate of time preference. There are therefore two sources of uncertainty, real wage shocks and asset shocks. I can then write $\theta_t = D_t r_t$ and the system is

$$(6) \qquad\qquad c_t = \gamma_1 + \beta\theta_t$$

$$(7) \qquad\qquad w_t h_t = (T - \gamma_2)w_t - (1 - \beta)\theta_t$$

$$(8) \qquad\qquad E_t(\theta_t/\theta_{t+1}) = 1.$$

Write u_t for $\Delta\theta_t$, and assume that (8) allows us to assume $E_t(u_{t+1}) = 0$ in the usual way. Detrending of (6), (7) removes wage growth, so after first-differencing we get

(9) $$\Delta c_t = \beta u_t$$

(10) $$\Delta(w_t h_t) = (T - \gamma_2) u_t^w - (1 - \beta)u_t.$$

With no wage shocks, u_t^w can be deleted, so that

(11) $$E(\Delta c_t, \Delta(w_t h_t)) = -\beta(1 - \beta)\sigma^2$$

(12) $$E[\{\Delta(w_t h_t)\}^2] = (1 - \beta)^2\sigma^2.$$

Hence the slope of the consumption function, b, is given by

(13) $$b = -\beta/(1 - \beta),$$

which is Hall's result. With $\beta = \frac{1}{2}$, $b = -1$, but my reading of the empirical evidence suggests a much larger value for β. By far the most up to date and authoritative survey of empirical studies of male labor supply is that by Pencavel for the forthcoming *Handbook of Labor Economics*. Pencavel discusses twenty-three studies using American data, nine based on experimental data and fourteen on nonexperimental data. Without making any attempt to exclude estimates that are of doubtful experimental status, the mean value of $1 - \beta$ from the experimental studies is 0.12, while that of the nonexperimental studies is 0.20. Of the latter, two studies produce estimates that Pencavel dismisses as very unlikely; if these are excluded, the mean is again 0.12. This is certainly a more likely figure than that of 0.5 as assumed by Hall, in which case the equilibrium slope would be -7.3, not -1. But the former only *seems* more absurd than the latter; given the truth of the theory, it is the more plausible number of the two.

But there are other, theoretical difficulties: (*a*) consumers experience real wage shocks, not only asset shocks; (*b*) GNP does not consist only of wage income, but also includes income from capital. Allowing for (*a*) and (*b*) produces a quite different picture. Take point (*a*) first and note that u_t^w and u_t will typically be correlated, since new information about real wages will also change the marginal utility of money. In view of (4), a likely formula is

(14) $$u_t = \delta u_t^A + \delta L(T - \gamma_2)u_t^w,$$

where u_t^A is the asset shock and L is the time horizon. Substituting in (9) and (10), assuming that u_t^A and u_t^w are uncorrelated, and evaluating the variance and covariance gives a consumption function with slope

(15) $$b = \frac{\beta\delta L - \beta(1 - \beta)\rho}{\{1 - (1 - \beta)\delta L\} + (1 - \beta)^2\rho},$$

with

(16) $\rho = \sigma_A^2 \delta^2 \{\sigma_w^2 \{\sigma_w^2(T - \delta_2)^2 (1 - (1 - \beta)\delta L)\}^{-1}.$

This is much more likely to be positive than is the previous expression (13), to which it reduces if $\sigma_w^2 = 0$. Indeed, if δ^2 is small or σ_A^2 is small, $b = 1$ if $\delta L = 1$, and values of b between 0 and 1 are easily generated for smaller values of δL.

Even this is not the correct expression for the slope between consumption and GNP. The latter includes asset income that can be allowed for in a number of ways. The simplest is to write y_t for GNP and to assume

(17) $\Delta y_t = (w_t h_t) + \delta \Delta A_t$

(remember that $\delta \simeq$ rate of time preference and is taken to be equal to the real rate of interest). Recalculating b gives (finally)

(18) $b = \dfrac{\beta \delta L + \beta^2 \rho}{\{1 - (1 - \beta)\delta L\} + \beta^2 \rho} .$

All traces of Hall's negative coefficient have now gone, and we have once again that $\delta L = 1$ implies $b = 1$ with $b < 1$ for lower values. The equilibrium story is clearly consistent with a fairly wide range of *positive* coefficients; it is certainly consistent with Hall's evidence.

The Empirical Results

Turning now to Hall's empirical results, I should like first to protest the extraordinarily sparse reporting style. While I too am a great believer in economic theory, that is no reason to suppress or omit reasonable diagnostic statistics. The key equations are presented with standard errors and Durbin-Watson statistics only. The latter are low enough to suggest *substantial* positive autocorrelation, even after detrending and differencing, so that if conventional formulas were used to calculate them, the standard errors as presented are not consistent estimates of the true standard errors. This is hardly the way to win friends and influence people! Hall's procedure here is based on the assumption that military expenditure is exogenous to the process of income determination, so that it is a valid instrument, indeed the *only* valid instrument, for estimating the relation between consumption and income, both of which are endogenous. Old-fashioned empirical macroeconomics used to be careful to exclude wars. Modern analysis has discovered the mistake, and we know now that nothing can be known *without* the wars! But why should military expenditure be singled out for such special attention? There are many theories, of no greater implausiblity than the equilibrium theory considered here, in which wars and military buildups are endogenous, and standard expressions such as "arms race" implicitly suppose so. It seem to me that either we accept more conventional instrumentation procedures for the consumption function together with their more conventional estimates of the consumption/income slope, or we admit that everything depends on everything else, throw up our hands, and go home. If instrumentation by quadratically detrended first-differenced military expenditure is the only way of identifying macroeconomic relationships, then macroeconomic relationships are not identified.

Even so, it seems churlish to refuse to admit the exogeneity of military expenditure, at least as a starting point, so that, even if the standard errors are ignored (as they ought to be, except possibly as lower bounds), Hall's parameter estimates still require explanation. Three dollars of differenced detrended military expenditures generate two dollars of differenced detrended GNP, none of which is differenced detrended consumption. The results are qualitatively similar if full-time equivalent employment is substituted for GNP. In my original comments, I indicated such results did not seem at all surprising, given that we are told nothing about the measurement and timing of recorded military expenditure in relation to actual military procurement or about the *type* of income generated. For example, as Robert Gordon has pointed out to me, if military expenditure is recorded as such at the moment when the tanks and planes are physically transferred from private manufacturers' stocks to government installations, then there is no reason to predict any relationship with consumption no matter what is believed about the consumption function. The relationship with income is likely to be more complex, and it seems to me that the current aggregate model, without clear distinctions between profits and wages, is not a good vehicle for uncovering what is really going on. While the result that changes in income are typically *not* accompanied by changes in consumption requires explanation, there are many possible candidates, and until they are examined, it still seems to me that Hall is most likely exaggerating the role that consumption disturbances play in economic fluctuations.

Comment   Robert G. King

In this provocative paper, Robert Hall argues that shifts in consumption behavior play a major role in business fluctuations. A corollary is that a major revision is necessary in thinking about fluctuations from either

Robert G. King is associate professor of economics at the University of Rochester.

the Keynesian or the equilibrium perspective, since each of these strands of thought generally views the main business cycle impulses as originating outside the consumption sector.

Hall's analysis is based on two simple theoretical elements: (*a*) a static Keynesian consumption function; and (*b*) a static efficiency condition relating consumption and effort, which is a necessary condition for optimal intertemporal consumption and labor supply decisions of an agent with time-separable preferences and thus forms a component of most equilibrium theories of fluctuations. These conditions are manipulated so each becomes a parameter restriction on "a simple structural relation between GNP and consumption," with the residuals from this relation taken to be shifts in consumption behavior.

Generally, my bias is in favor of simple and revealing empirical work; I rank two of Hall's previous consumption studies (1978, 1981) highly according to that metric. But the simplicity of the present analysis strikes me as providing misleading directions to research. That is, the role of behavioral shifts is probably *overstated* by the simple framework Hall employs.

The Consumption/GNP Relation

The centerpiece of Hall's analysis is the following "simple structural relation between GNP and consumption."

$$(1) \qquad\qquad c_t = \beta y_t + \epsilon_t,$$

where c_t is consumption, y_t is gross national product, and ϵ_t is a random shift in the c-y relation. Interpretation of the error term is the main focus of this discussion because Hall views it as representing purely behavioral shifts.

For the purpose of discussing the consumption/GNP relationship in Keynesian and equilibrium models, it is useful to systematically discuss the sort of intertemporal problem under certainty posed by Hall. (For the sake of clarity, however, I use n_t to denote hours worked in year t and reserve y_t for income/product in year t.) That is, the household is viewed as choosing sequences of consumption and effort so as to maximize the lifetime utility function (2),

$$(2) \qquad\qquad U_t = \sum_{j=0}^{\infty} D^j \, u(c_{t+j}, n_{t+j}),$$

subject to the lifetime budget constraint,

$$(3) \qquad\qquad \sum_{j=0}^{\infty} R_{t,j} \, (p_{t+j} c_{t+j} - w_{t+j} n_{t+j}) = A_t,$$

where $R_{t,j}$ is the date t discount factor applicable to cash flows at $t + j$ and A_t is initial wealth.

The Keynesian Relation

Since quantities are demand determined in a pure Keynesian regime, the household faces a sequence of maximum labor quantities that can be supplied, $n_t \leq \bar{n}_t$.[1] This constraint is taken to be binding on the household's choice in each period, so that the sole nontrivial decision is the intertemporal allocation of consumption. If $u(c,n)$ is additively separable in its two arguments, then date t consumption is a function of "lifetime wealth" and real discount factors, without any direct effect of the constrained level of hours worked $(\bar{n}_t)$. For example, if $u(c_t, n_t) = \{c_t^{1-\sigma}\}/(1 - \sigma) + v(n)$, then the consumption function takes the form

$$(4) \qquad c_t^k = g(\{\rho_{t,j}\}_{j=0}^{\infty}) \left[\frac{A_t}{p_t} + \sum_{j=0}^{\infty} \rho_{t,j}\omega_{t+j}\bar{n}_{t+j} \right],$$

where $\qquad \rho_{t,j} = p_{t+j}R_{t,j}/p_o$; ω_t/P_t; and

$$g(\{\rho_{t,j}\}_{j=0}^{\infty}) = \left[\sum_{j=0}^{\infty} \rho_{t,j}^{1-\frac{1}{\sigma}} \beta^{\frac{j}{\sigma}} \right]^{-1}.$$

If some portion (λ_t) of the population is fully liquidity constrained[2] in period t, then its consumption will just be initial wealth plus current labor income, $c_t^l = [W_t^l/p_t + \omega_t^l \, \bar{n}_t^l]$.

Thus the aggregate structural consumption relation will be given by

$$(5) \qquad c_t = \lambda_t c_t^l + (1 - \lambda_t)c_t^k.$$

Suppose that (5) is the true structural consumption relationship, which is exact in the sense that there are no preference shifts in the household's objective (2). Nevertheless, the error term in (1) would not be zero, but would reflect omitted variables such as wealth, (expected) future income, and discount factors.

The Equilibrium Relation

Under the equilibrium regime, consumption and effort are both nontrivial intertemporal choices. Time-separable preferences, however, deliver strong restrictions on the cyclical comovements of consumption and effort (see Barro and King 1982 for a detailed discussion). If the date t wage is held fixed, then consumption and leisure move in the

---

1. I abstract here from temporary constraints on factor supply. Barro and Grossman 1976, chap. 2, discuss such hybrid situations.

2. Again I abstract from the potential that the liquidity constraint will be binding in future periods but is not at present. Again, Barro and Grossman 1976, chap. 2, analyze this case.

same direction in response to changes in all relevant variables (initial wealth, real interest rates, future wages, etc.), so long as consumption and leisure are normal goods. This is readily seen from the data t intratemporal efficiency condition

$$(6) \qquad \frac{\partial U_t/\partial n_t}{\partial U_t/\partial c_t} = \frac{u_1(c_t,n_t)}{u_2(c_t,n_t)} = \omega_t \, (1 \, - \, z_t),$$

where $u_i\,(c_t,u_t)$ is the partial derivative of momentary utility with respect to its ith argument. Nonseparabilities in preferences typically imply that the marginal rate of substitution depends on actions at dates other than t, so avoiding the implication about the correlation of consumption and effort discussed above.

From my perspective, the key implication of (6) is that consumption and effort cannot be positively correlated—as they are in business cycles—unless the real wage is procyclical or taste shifts toward consumption and away from leisure take place. In this analysis, the real wage refers to the shadow value of an individual's time and is not necessarily well represented by aggregate series.

To discuss the relation between consumption and GNP, let us adopt one of MaCurdy's (1981) specifications of the momentary utility function

$$(7) \qquad u(c_t,n_t,\theta_t) = \frac{\theta_t}{1 \, - \, \sigma} \, c_t^{\ 1-\sigma} - \frac{1}{1 \, + \, \gamma} \, n_t^{\ 1+\gamma} \, ,$$

where the parameters σ and γ are positive. The positive stochastic process θ_t represents behavioral shifts that induce more consumption in period t. Taking logarithms of the associated first-order condition, the following log-linear specification is derived.

$$(8) \qquad \log c_t \, = \, \frac{1}{\sigma} \log \omega_t \, \frac{\gamma}{\sigma} \log n_t \, + \, \frac{1}{\sigma} \log \theta_t.$$

Suppose that one knows (or consistently estimates) γ and σ, then the Hall procedure would compute the error term as the term $\{\ \}$ in (9):

$$(9) \quad \log c_t \, = \, - \frac{\gamma}{\sigma} \log y_t \, + \, \left\{ \frac{1}{\sigma} \log \omega_t \, + \, \frac{\gamma}{\sigma} \log \left(\frac{y_t}{n_t} \right) \, + \, \frac{1}{\sigma} \log \theta_t \right\}.^3$$

That is, in this equilibrium version of the model, the regression error

3. This relationship may readily be linearized to conform more closely to the specification (1). If one defines $\bar{c}_t, \bar{y}_t$ as the trend values of consumption and GNP, then

$$\frac{c_t \, - \, \bar{c}_t}{\bar{c}_t} \, \cong \, - \frac{\gamma}{\sigma} \frac{y_t \, - \, \bar{y}_t}{\bar{y}_t} \, + \, \epsilon_t.$$

term would be an agglomeration of movements in real wages, productivity, and true behavioral shifts.

Thus the error term in specification (1) does not capture simply behavioral shifts in either the Keynesian or the equilibrium versions of the model.

Implications

Based on the theoretical analysis above, it is impossible for me to rationalize treating the error terms in Hall's consumption functions as a purely behavioral disturbance. Thus the historical decompositions for the three models—equilibrium, estimated, and Keynesian—do not aid me in interpreting either specific episodes (such as the Great Depression) or the sectoral origins of economic fluctuations in general.

A specific example may be helpful in this regard. Following Temin (1976), Hall notes that there are major negative consumption function residuals in the early years of the Great Depression. The Temin/Hall interpretation is old-fashioned Keynesian, viewing these, as autonomous shifts, as independent causes of the depression. But suppose the true Keynesian consumption function is of the permanent income variety—for example, (4) above—so that Hall's error term includes expected future income as an omitted variable. Further, in the early years of the depression, let consumers adjust their expected future income downward. Then a negative residual will occur in the static consumption function (1), but it need not be autonomous or causal.

That is not to say that elements that Hall would view as "taste shocks" are not an important component of business fluctuations. It is true that most fully articulated business cycle models (e.g., Long and Plosser 1983) view random shocks to technology as the central driving variables in economic fluctuations, with individuals having stable preferences over consumption of final market produced goods. The assumption of stable preferences highlights the two factors that lead to rich dynamics in real business cycle theories: agents' desire to spread wealth increments across time and goods; and rich intra- and intertemporal substitution possibilities in production that permit them to accomplish that goal. But if one adopts a Beckerian view of household activities, then there is no special reason to view household production technology as less subject to technical shocks than market production technology. With variations in home production technology, derived preferences over market inputs would fluctuate, even if preferences over ultimate consumption goods were stable. But my own research preference is to push equilibrium analysis as far as possible without relying too heavily on such fluctuations in basic tastes or home production technology.

Discussion Summary

Several of the participants felt the Keynesian view had been given short shrift in this paper. Eisner pointed out that a Keynesian model should contain two regimes: one when the economy was away from full employment and another when it was at full employment. Ignoring this change of behavior and estimating a single regime would lead to Hall's downward biased estimate of the marginal propensity to consume. Gordon echoed this view and pointed to the 1941–42 military buildup and the Korean conflict, when output rose but consumption fell, as the main forces driving the estimated coefficient downward. In regard to the equilibrium model, Robert Barro claimed that the "puzzling" comovement of consumption and work effort found by Hall could be arrived at easily in a model where shocks to the economy came through technology that affected labor productivity.

The exogeneity of the government defense spending instrument used by Hall was called into question by several participants. In addition DeLong noted that this instrument had power only at low frequencies, since it came in discrete chunks from the Korean and Vietnam wars, and hence it was not clear why it should bear on the high frequency consumption/income relation. Singleton argued that even if this instrument were taken to be exogenous, Hall's multiequation model was unlikely to be identified as estimated. To achieve such identification would entail imposing a priori restrictions on the error structure of the model. However, economists have priors about coefficients rather than about covariances, and as the examples of Angus Deaton and Robert King made clear, it is not possible to arrive at unique restrictions on covariances from restrictions on coefficients. It seemed then that there was little justification for Hall's claim that the errors from the estimated consumption equation represented random shifts in consumption behavior.

Hall responded to several of the points made in the discussion. He dismissed Eisner's remark about the two regimes by pointing out that in almost all recent empirical work the aggregate supply curve is found to be a straight line. He agreed with Gordon's observation about the role of the 1941–42 and Korean observations in leading to his result, and added that the Vietnam period has the same effect. The failure of consumption to rise in such periods was precisely the point of the paper. He agreed with Barro's comment as a matter of theory but had been unable to find any evidence in the data for the twentieth-century American economy suggesting that shocks in technology were an important driving force in economic fluctuations. As for DeLong's comment about the low frequency power of the defense spending variable, Hall replied that the bulk of the power of the military spending variable is in middle frequencies, corresponding to the three major buildups during the period. Finally, Hall claimed that Singleton was mistaken in his belief that the model in the paper was not identified. It could not have been estimated by two-stage least squares. Furthermore, Hall stressed that he had not made any restrictions on error covariances, nor were any needed for identification.

References

Altonji, Joseph G. 1982. The intertemporal substitution model of labour market fluctuations: An empirical analysis. *Review of Economic Studies* 49:783–824.

Anderson, Barry L., and James L. Butkiewicz. 1980. Money, spending, and the Great Depression. *Southern Economic Journal* 47:388–403.

Barro, Robert J. 1981. Output effects of government purchases. *Journal of Political Economy* 89:1086–1121.

Barro, Robert J., and H. I. Grossman. 1976. *Money, employment and inflation*. London: Cambridge University Press.

Barro, Robert J., and Robert G. King. 1982. Time-separable preferences and intertemporal-substitution models of business cycles. Working Paper 888, National Bureau of Economic Research.

Flavin, Marjorie A. 1981. The adjustment of consumption to changing expectations about future income. *Journal of Political Economy* 89:974–1009.

Friedman, Milton, and Gary S. Becker. 1957. A statistical illusion in judging Keynesian consumption functions. *Journal of Political Economy* 65:64–75.

Garber, Peter M., and Robert G. King. 1983. Deep structural excavation? A critique of Euler equation methods. Technical Paper 31, National Bureau of Economic Research.

Hall, Robert E. 1978. Stochastic implications of the life cycle—permanent income hypothesis: Theory and evidence. *Journal of Political Economy* 86:971–88.

———. 1980. Employment fluctuations and wage rigidity. *Brookings Papers on Economic Activity* 1:91–123.

———. 1981. Intertemporal substitution in consumption. Working Paper 720, National Bureau of Economic Research.

Hall, Robert E., and Frederic S. Mishkin. 1982. The sensitivity of consumption to transitory income: Estimates from panel data on households. *Econometrica* 50:461–81.

Kendrick, John. 1961. *Productivity trends in the United States.* New York: National Bureau of Economic Research.

Long, J. B., and C. I. Plosser. 1983. Real business cycles. *Journal of Political Economy* 91:39–69.

MaCurdy, T. 1981. An empirical model of labor supply in a life cycle setting. *Journal of Political Economy* 89:1059–85.

Mankiw, N. Gregory, Julio J. Rotemberg, and Lawrence H. Summers. 1982. Intertemporal substitution in macroeconomics. Working Paper 898, National Bureau of Economic Research.

Mayer, Thomas. 1980. Consumption in the Great Depression. *Journal of Political Economy* 86:139–45.

Office of Management and Budget. 1983. *Federal government finances: 1984 budget data.* Washington, D.C.: Office of Management and Budget.

Temin, Peter. 1976. *Did monetary forces cause the Great Depression?* New York: Norton.

5 Fixed Investment in the American Business Cycle, 1919–83

Robert J. Gordon and John M. Veitch

All induction is blind, so long as the deduction of causal connections is left out of account; and all deduction is barren, so long as it does not start from observation.

John Neville Keynes 1890, 164

5.1 Introduction

The behavior of fixed investment is one of the four core topics (along with consumption, money demand, and the Phillips curve) that have dominated theoretical and empirical research in macroeconomics during the postwar era. An understanding of the sources of persistent swings in investment spending seems to be a key ingredient in any satisfactory explanation of business cycles. This paper develops a new data set and uses a new methodology to investigate the behavior of household and business fixed investment in the United States since 1919. Its results have implications for at least four partly overlapping groups of economists who have strong views about the nature of the fixed investment process and, indirectly, about the sources of business cycles.

Robert J. Gordon is professor of economics at Northwestern University. John M. Veitch is assistant professor of economics at the University of Southern California.

Gordon's research is supported by the National Science Foundation and the Sloan Foundation. Veitch acknowledges support from the Social Sciences and Humanities Research Council of Canada. We both are indebted to Ben Bernanke, Robert Chirinko, Thomas Doan, Robert Eisner, John Geweke, Fumio Hayashi, Andrew Rose, Allen Sinai, Larry Summers, Mark Watson, and members of the Northwestern University Macro-Labor workshop for helpful comments. We would also like to thank Nathan Balke for his help with the data and econometric estimation and Joan Robinson for preparing a long and complex manuscript so efficiently.

Keynesians, following the *General Theory*, regard investment behavior as containing a substantial autonomous component; investment responds to the state of business confidence and incorporates the effect of episodes of speculation and overbuilding. The instability and unpredictability of fixed investment behavior, of course, forms the basis of Keynesian support for an activist and interventionist role for government fiscal policy. A crucial and often unstated component of the Keynesian view is that these autonomous investment movements exhibit *positive serial correlation* and last long enough for government action to be effective.

In contrast, monetarists do not single out investment for special attention. Changes in aggregate private spending, consumption and investment alike, are attributed to prior fluctuations in the supply of money. Since monetarists are usually reluctant to provide detailed structural interpretations of what happens inside the black box through which the influence of money is channeled to economic activity, they are not concerned whether the primary channel runs through consumption, investment, or both. But monetarists would expect (if forced uncharacteristically to devote special attention to fixed investment behavior) to find a strong role for the money supply as a primary determinant of investment behavior.

In addition to the general approaches to macroeconomic analysis advocated by Keynesians and monetarists, two additional groups of economists have made a special effort to understand investment behavior. The "neoclassical" school, represented by the work of Jorgenson and his collaborators, emphasizes changes in the relative price or "user cost" of capital as a dominant influence, together with changes in output, on fluctuations in fixed investment. The user cost of capital is the primary channel by which both monetary policy (working through interest rates) and fiscal policy (working through investment tax incentives) influence the flow of investment spending. The final group consists of advocates of Tobin's "Q" approach, in which the influence on investment of forward-looking expectations regarding output and capital costs is captured by a single variable, Q, the ratio of the market value of capital to its reproduction cost. Since the dominant portion of fluctuations in Q is accounted for by changes in stock market prices, proponents of this approach expect econometric work to single out the stock market as an important (or dominant) factor explaining investment behavior.

Because of the long time span of data covered in the empirical portion of this paper, its results have implications for the sources of business cycles in general and of the Great Depression in particular. Keynesians view business cycles as the inevitable reflection of the instability of investment spending, which in turn justifies government intervention to reduce the amplitude of cycles. Keynesian interpretations of the Great Depression, especially Temin (1976), minimize the role of monetary factors in the first two years of the 1929–33 contraction. Monetarists reverse the roles of the government and private sector and view the basic source of business cycles as autonomous and largely unexplained fluctuations in the money supply that lead to fluctuations in private spending. A reduction in the amplitude of business cycles requires a reduction in the instability originating in government management of the money supply.

The neoclassical and Q approaches to the explanation of investment behavior are explicitly partial equilibrium in nature and have not been developed into broader theories of the business cycle. The neoclassical approach is compatible with some aspects of monetarism, since instability in investment can originate from government control over interest rates and investment tax incentives. But the policy implications differ from those of monetarism; to the extent that the monetarist recommendation of a constant monetary growth rate rule would increase the volatility of interest rates, then the neoclassicists would predict the consequence to be greater rather than lesser fluctuations in investment spending. The Q advocates have not addressed themselves to business cycle implications, but their approach creates a natural link to those (like Mishkin 1978) who emphasize the role of the 1929 stock market crash in the Great Depression.

The conflict between the Keynesian and monetarist approaches can be related to the distinction in business cycle analysis between "impulses" and "propagation mechanisms." Keynesians argue for activist monetary and fiscal policy responses to counter serially correlated investment *impulses*, while monetarists view investment as part of the *propagation mechanism* that carries the influence of autonomous money supply impulses from their origin in the government sector to their effect on private sector spending.[1] The Keynesian/monetarist debate can be translated into the modern econometric language of Granger causality and innovation accounting. Keynesians would expect to find a large role for "own innovations" in the empirical explanation of investment spending, with a relatively small role for feedback from monetary variables. An extreme Keynesian would expect investment to be exogenous in the Granger sense to prior changes in the money supply, and the same expectation would be held by neoclassicists and Q advocates, none of whom (to our knowledge) has ever entered the money supply directly as an explanatory variable in an empirical in-

---

1. Recall the famous debate of the mid-1960s set off by the attempt by Milton Friedman and David Meiselman (1963) to characterize "autonomous spending" and "the money supply," respectively, as the driving forces in the Keynesian model and their own model of income determination.

vestment equation. Monetarists, of course, would expect to find that the money supply is Granger causally prior to fixed investment.

This paper reopens the question of exogeneity in investment behavior by inquiring whether the standard approach to the estimation of "structural" investment equations leads to an overstatement of the endogeneity of investment spending. Its primary objective is to decompose fluctuations in fixed investment into three components: (a) feedback from policy variables and from noninvestment spending; (b) the propagation mechanism imparted by the investment process itself, which displays a high degree of positive serial correlation; and (c) "own innovations" or "shocks" in fixed investment expenditures that remain after accounting for (a) and (b). The main contributions of the paper can be divided into three categories—methodological, data creation, and empirical.

The methodological section finds that, while structural model building exercises may be useful in suggesting lists of variables that might play an explanatory role in investment equations, they generally achieve identification of structural parameters only by imposing arbitrary and unbelievable simplifying assumptions and exclusion restrictions. Consideration of real world decision making suggests that economic aggregates play "multiple roles" in investment behavior, which implies that the observed coefficients on explanatory variables in equations describing investment behavior represent a convolution of numerous structural parameters that cannot be separately identified. As a result it is possible only to estimate reduced forms.

The estimation methodology suggested here is the same as that proposed in a previous paper on inflation (Gordon and King 1982). It starts with guidance from traditional structural models on the choice and form of explanatory variables to be included. Then estimation is carried out in a format similar to that of the unconstrained "Simsian" vector autoregression (VAR) models. Explanatory variables are typically entered with unconstrained lags of the same length, and the list of explanatory variables typically includes a mixture of those suggested by several structural models, together with those that may not be suggested by any structural model but might in principle play a role through real wealth effects, credit constraints, or expectation formation (e.g., the real money supply). The approach differs from the usual VAR model building exercise by focusing mainly on equations for the variable of primary interest (inflation in Gordon and King and investment expenditures in this paper) rather than by giving "equal time" to all the variables in the model. It is less "atheoretical" than most VAR research, because structural models retain a usefulness in suggesting lists of candidate variables to be included in reduced-form equations and the form in which those variables should be entered (in this paper, for instance, stock market prices enter in the form of Tobin's Q variable), even if the underlying structural parameters cannot be identified.

The second contribution is the use of a new set of quarterly data for major expenditure categories of GNP extending back to 1919. The data file also contains quarterly data back to 1919 for other variables that have been suggested as explanatory "candidates" in investment equations. These include the capital stock, interest rates, the cost of capital including tax incentive effects, a proxy for Tobin's Q, and the real money supply.

Equipped with its hybrid methodology and its extended data set, the paper then proceeds to empirical estimation. The empirical section differs from the usual research on investment that typically attempts to measure response parameters within the context of a single structural theory, for example, neoclassical or Q. Instead, our skepticism that structural parameters can be estimated leads us to estimate reduced-form equations. These include explanatory variables suggested by several theories and can be used to decompose the variance of investment within particular historical periods among the contribution of lagged values of explanatory variables (output, interest rates, money, Q), the contribution of lagged investment, and "own innovations" to investment. The analysis of shocks to investment links this paper to the debate between Temin (1976), Thomas Mayer (1980), and others on the role of an autonomous shock to consumption in 1930, and to papers in this volume by Hall on shifts in the consumption function and by Blanchard and Watson on "shocks in general." Our extended data set also allows us to investigate changes in investment behavior between the interwar and postwar periods.

The discussion begins (section 5.2) with a review of the central issues that lead to our choice of a reduced-form rather than a structural approach. This is not a full-blown survey of the literature, but rather a selective analysis of problems with structural estimation that have emerged over the past twenty years. Then section 5.3 introduces the data set and describes the behavior of the major variables in each of the fourteen business cycles since 1919, as well as over longer subperiods. Section 5.4 presents the estimated equations for four categories of investment (producers' durable equipment, nonresidential and residential structures, and consumer durables expenditures), and section 5.5 offers a study of multivariate causality and exogeneity, innovation accounting, and a historical decomposition of the sources of investment spending. Section 5.6 summarizes the main results and implications.

5.2 Pitfalls in Structural Estimation of Investment Equations

Most of the investment literature is concerned solely with business investment. This orientation reflects the influence of Keynes's *General Theory*, especially its preoccupation with the state of business confidence as a determinant of investment plans. However, business investment constitutes less than half of total private investment in the United States economy. Consumer expenditures on durable goods have been larger than producers' durable equipment expenditures since 1920, and residential structures expenditures have exceeded those on nonresidential investment in at least half the years since 1929.

One might expect household investment behavior to respond to different variables than does business investment. For instance, if a substantial proportion of consumers are credit constrained, then episodes of "credit crunches" are liable to produce a greater response in the investment outlays of consumers than of businessmen.[2] A systematic exploration of household investment behavior may need to explore factors that matter in household decision making; for example, it may be disposable income that matters for households but total GNP for businessmen, and the various tax incentive terms conventionally included in measures of the user cost of capital may matter for businessmen but not for households. Here we begin with a critique of the more familiar literature on business investment and subsequently apply our analysis to the determinants of household investment.

Chirinko's (1983a) systematic review of assumptions and results distinguishes four classes of econometric models describing business investment behavior—Jorgenson's neoclassical approach, Tobin's Q, the "general forward-looking" approach based on explicit modeling of expectations, and Feldstein's "return-over-cost" and "effective tax rate" models. Because they have accounted for the vast majority of empirical studies completed to date, we concentrate only on the neoclassical and Q frameworks for investment research. Extended surveys are presented by Eisner and Strotz (1963), Jorgenson (1971), Helliwell (1976), and Chirinko (1983a), whereas here we treat only a few selected issues that lead to our skepticism that traditional structural parameters can be identified.

5.2.1 The Neoclassical Paradigm

As of the mid-1970s, the neoclassical paradigm was so dominant (at least outside New Haven) that Helliwell's (1976) survey makes no mention of any other framework. Before the mid-1960s, investment equations had been dominated by the accelerator approach and had

---

2. The quantitative importance of the credit crunch phenomenon is explored in the paper by Eckstein and Sinai in this volume (chap. 1).

added interest rates, profits, or other variables as determinants of investment without explicit constraints based on optimizing behavior. The studies initiated by Jorgenson and collaborators, particularly Jorgenson (1963, 1967), Hall and Jorgenson (1967, 1971), and Jorgenson and Stephenson (1967, 1969), are distinguished by their derivation of the desired capital/output ratio from specific assumptions about behavior and about the form of the production function. The centerpiece in the determination of the desired capital stock is the expected real rental price of capital services, which is equated with the expected marginal product of capital. If factors are paid their marginal products and the production function is of the Cobb-Douglas form, the desired capital stock at a given point in time (K_t^d) is a linear function of expected output (X_t^e) divided by the expected real price of capital services (C_t^e/P_t^e):

$$(1) \qquad K_t^d = \frac{\gamma P_t^e X_t^e}{C_t^e} \, ,$$

where γ is the income share of capital in output. Decision and delivery lags make actual net investment a distributed lag on past changes in the desired capital stock:

$$(2) \qquad I_t^N = \sum_{j=0}^{J} \alpha_j \Delta K_{t-j}^d.$$

When the expected variables $(P^e, X^e, \text{ and } C^e)$ are replaced by current actual values (an unjustified assumption discussed below), and when the demand for replacement capital is represented by a fixed geometric depreciation factor (δ) times the lagged capital stock (K_{t-1}), the neoclassical investment model becomes:

$$(3) \qquad I_t = \alpha_0 + \sum_{j=0}^{J} \beta_j \Delta (PX/C)_{t-j} + \delta K_{t-1} + \epsilon_t.$$

Equation (3) embodies a number of strong assumptions and restrictions, and a large "counterrevolution" literature has developed to explore the consequences of loosening them. The "pure" Jorgensonian neoclassical approach assumes a "putty/putty" technology without adjustment costs; the capital stock can be adjusted instantly, transformed, bought, or sold as needed to bring a firm's actual capital stock into line with its desired capital stock. As long as expectations are assumed to be static, the only justification for the lag distribution included in (3) is the technological gestation lag. Another interpretation is that investment expenditures involve adjustment costs. Without adjustment costs or gestation lags, the Jorgenson model is subject to the criticism that whenever a gap exists between K_t^d and K_t, the rate of investment will be infinitely large and the gap will be eliminated instantaneously. However, with either of these assumptions "tacked on," the Jorgensonian K_t^d is not derived from a complete cost minimization problem and is probably not optimal.[3]

Another peculiarity of the approach is apparent in equation (1), which allows the desired capital stock to be a function only of the relative price of capital rather than the relative price of all inputs. Yellen (1980) has shown that (1) can be derived only by assuming that real wages are inversely related to C/P and respond fully and instantaneously to any changes in C/P. As a result, all factor price changes must be assumed to leave the profitability of the firm unaffected, even in the short run. Thus the neoclassical approach leaves no room for theories that predict a profit squeeze, investment slump, and growth slowdown following a period of excessive real wage growth (see Malinvaud 1982).

However, even if one were to accept the formulation in (1) with the single relative price variable, the measurement of capital's user cost is fraught with ambiguity. As shown recently in Auerbach's (1983) survey, taxes and inflation may not change the cost of capital in the same way for all firms, leaving the feasibility of aggregation an open question. Simple formulas for C/P are also elusive when markets are incomplete and when managers use financial leverage and dividend policy to influence market perceptions.

The empirical "counterrevolution" begins with Eisner and Nadiri (1968), an article that takes particular exception to the multiplicative specification in (3) that forces both the short-run and long-run responses to X and C/P to be identical. Eisner and Nadiri find that the elasticities with respect to output are considerably higher than those with respect to relative prices, and Bischoff (1971) finds that lags are shorter on output than on relative prices. Chirinko and Eisner (1983) find in experiments with the Data Resources, Incorporated (DRI) and MIT–Penn–Social Science Research Council (MPS) econometric models that splitting apart the X and C/P variables can cause the implicit relative price elasticity to fall by more than half, and together with minor redefinitions of the C/P variable can cause a reduction in that elasticity by a factor of four. However, even by loosening restrictions in this way they find that response coefficients to changes in the investment tax credit in six models still vary by a factor of four (or a factor of about two for the four most extensively used models—Chase, DRI, MPS, and Wharton).

5.2.2   Expectations and Identification

An even more serious problem in equations (1) through (3) is the cavalier treatment of expectations, which are included in (1) but as-

---

3. This paragraph reflects an oral history provided to us by Fumio Hayashi.

sumed to be static in the transition from (1) to (3). In Helliwell's words, "This important issue has been dealt with principally by the handy assumption that the future will be like the present" (1976, 15). At best, expectations of future output are allowed to depend on a distributed lag of past values of output, but generally lagged values of other variables that might be relevant for expectations formation (e.g., the money supply) have been excluded as an identification restriction. Since investment is a forward looking activity, not only must the X and C/P variables be represented by expectations that in principle should depend on an information set containing past values of all relevant macroeconomic aggregates, but also the functional parameters entering the investment model should depend on the same general information set.

This point can be illustrated in a generalization of a simple model set forth recently by Andrew Abel and Olivier Blanchard (1983) that falls into the class of "general forward looking models." In place of (1) we allow the desired capital stock to depend on a sequence of expected future sales, with a discount factor σ; unlike Abel and Blanchard, we also allow the desired capital stock to depend on the sequence of expected future rental rates (C/P):[4]

$$(4) \qquad K_{t+n}^d = \alpha(1 - \sigma) \sum_{i=0}^{\infty} \sigma^i E\{F[X_{t+n+i},(C/P)_{t+n+i}]|\Omega_t\}.$$

Here t is the time an investment order is placed for delivery at $t + n$, with n the length of the delivery or gestation lag. The parameter α is the steady-state ratio of capital to output, and Ω_t is the information set relevant at time t to the formation of expectations about all future variables. The relevant information set might, for instance, include past values of output, the interest rate, and the money supply.

It has been an almost universal practice in the empirical literature to express the depreciation rate of capital as a fixed exponential constant. In contrast Eisner (1972), Feldstein and Foot (1971), and Feldstein and Rothschild (1974) have argued that the timing of replacement investment is an economic decision and is motivated by economic considerations. In particular, fixed proportions in building or machine construction create an enormous incentive for net investment and replacement investment to be considered as part of the same economic decision making process.[5] Accordingly we replace the fixed replace-

---

4. Even if a project is financed by issuing a long-term bond on the day of its completion, time periods after the date of completion are relevant both for the taxation of earnings and for any capital gains that may accrue.

5. Students of United States twentieth-century architecture know that there was virtually no central city office building construction between 1930 and 1955; that is, there was *neither* any expansion in the number of square feet *nor* any replacement of old buildings, both for the same set of reasons.

ment rate in the Abel/Blanchard model by an expected rate (θ) that depends on the information set:

(5) $$K_{t+n} = [1 - E(\theta|\Omega_t)]K_{t+n-1} + I_{t+n},$$

where I_{t+n} represents investment expenditures made at time $t + n$ (strictly speaking this should be an expectation—see note 6 below).

Investment orders depend on the gap between desired and actual capital that is expected to occur at time $t + n$ and the present expectation of the fraction of the capital stock that will be replaced at that time. Although the fraction of the gap to be closed is decided at time t and is not an expected value, today's decision regarding the fraction depends on the expected cost of adjustment during the period of the gestation lag, for example, expected interest rates on short-term construction loans, r_t:[6]

(6) $$0_t = \lambda[E(r_{t+1}|\Omega_t)][K^d_{t+n} - K_{t+n-1}] + E(\theta|\Omega_t)K_{t+n-1} + \xi_t,$$

where ξ_t is a disturbance term.

Finally, actual investment expenditures (I_t) are a sum of past orders, with a distributed lag indicating that projects have heterogeneous gestation lags:

(7) $$I_t = \sum_{j=0}^{n} \omega_j(\Omega_t)0_{t-j}.$$

Here in (7) for completeness we allow the ω_j coefficients to depend on the information set, thus introducing the possibility that orders may be canceled before delivery or that the gestation lag is influenced by the evolution of the economy between time periods $t - j$ and t.[7] Thus it appears that the Abel/Blanchard assumption that $\sum_{j=0}^{n} \omega_j = 1$ is unrealistically restrictive.

It is obvious from inspection of equations (4) through (7) that in principle it is not possible to identify structural coefficients on current and lagged economic aggregates in an aggregate investment equation, because any of those aggregates could be playing double, triple, or even more complex roles as ingredients in the information sets Ω_t. The reduced form involves complicated convolutions of the variables en-

6. To be consistent with the rest of the formulation, the term "K_{t+n-1}" in equation (6) should be an expectation, not an actual value. This approximation is adopted to simplify the reduced-form equation in (8) below.

7. As an example, airlines that ordered the Boeing 757 and 767 aircraft in 1978 reacted to the previously unexpected period of poor profits that occurred during 1980–82 both by canceling part or all of their orders and by "stretching out" the delivery period. American Airlines initially ordered both the 757 and the 767, but it canceled its entire order for 757 aircraft. United Airlines has stretched the delivery dates on half of its 767 order by up to five years and has finally canceled that half.

tering the information set, which appears in five places in the reduced form:

(8) $I_t = \sum_{j=0}^{n} \omega_j(\Omega_t)\{\lambda[E[r_{t+1}|\Omega_t)][\alpha(1 - \sigma)$

$\sum_{i=0}^{\infty} \sigma^i E(F[X_{t+n+i},(C/P)_{t+n+i}]|\Omega_t) - (1 - E(\theta|\Omega_{t-j-1}))K_{t+n-j-2}$

$- I_{t+n-j-1}] + E(\theta|\Omega_{t-j})K_{t+n-j-1} + \xi_{t-j}\}.$

The research by Abel and Blanchard (1983) provides a good example of the arbitrary assumptions and simplifications needed to achieve identification in a model like equations (4) through (7). Their problems occur despite a much simpler framework that differs by (a) excluding the rental price from any appearance, even in determining the desired capital stock; (b) allowing expectations based on an information set only with regard to the sequence of expected future output; (c) allowing only past values of sales to be included in that information set; and (d) assuming fixed values of all other parameters. Further, Abel and Blanchard have two additional types of data not available in this historical study of aggregate expenditures: (e) separate data on orders and expenditures and (f) sectoral data that allow a distinction between aggregate and sectoral sales. Despite these differences, Abel and Blanchard achieve identification of a structural model only by assuming arbitrary fixed values of several parameters, and they find no conclusive evidence for preferring the resulting structural model to the corresponding reduced form.[8]

In our application to a set of aggregate data, the more general model in equations (4) through (7) does not appear to allow the identification of structural parameters. For instance, consider the role of interest rates and stock prices. Both seem to be relevant information for economic agents forming expectations about future output, not to mention future interest rates and stock prices (both components of the Jorgensonian rental price). Yet how is the estimated coefficient on a lagged interest rate variable to be disentangled to allow identification of separate roles that this variable plays in forming expectations in different places in the model in affecting the desired capital stock, in affecting the desired rate of replacement of old capital, and in affecting the desired rate of closing the gap between desired and actual capital?

---

8. "For the information set containing also aggregate sales, the structural model performed poorly, being unable to explain the relation—or the lack of relation—between investment in a sector and aggregate sales. . . . The model . . . is clearly not structural; some of its maintained assumptions . . . are rejected by the data. Some of the additional assumptions made in estimation . . . are rejected for some of the sectors. Nor are the econometric results overwhelmingly supportive" (Abel and Blanchard 1983, 44).

5.2.3 The Q Approach

The expectations quagmire is inherent in the neoclassical approach, with its identification of key parameters requiring ad hoc exclusion restrictions in the set of variables allowed into the information set influencing expectations. The "pure" Q approach differs from the usual investment accelerator by explaining investment activity on the basis of deviations from portfolio balance, and by assuming from the start that there is no "time to build," that is, that there are no gestation lags, so that $I_t = 0_t$. Net investment activity takes place when marginal Q, the ratio of the increase in the value of the firm from acquiring an additional unit of capital to its marginal purchase cost, exceeds unity. Numerous authors, including Abel (1979) and Hayashi (1982), have derived Q investment functions in the following form that adds lags to allow for delivery or gestation lags:[9]

$$(9) \qquad \frac{I_t}{K_t} = \psi_0 + \sum_{s=0}^{S} \mu_s(Q_{t-s} - 1) + e_t.$$

The theoretical derivation involves "marginal Q," which is forward looking and hence unobservable. Actual estimation of (9) involves replacing marginal Q with average Q, the ratio of the market value of firms to the replacement cost of their assets. (Hayashi 1982 has shown that actual and marginal Q are equal under specified assumptions but does not test whether these assumptions are empirically supported.) If (9) is estimated for data on net investment, then the constant term ψ_0 should be zero, since net investment should be zero in the steady state when Q is unity. When data on gross investment are used, then the constant term implicitly measures the depreciation rate. At a Q ratio of unity, the firm should just replace its old capital but should not buy any new capital. More generally, the constant term ψ_0 reflects the mean value of any omitted variables.

Much of the discussion of possible problems in the Q approach relates to measurement errors in either the numerator (market value) or the denominator (replacement cost) of the Q ratio. For instance, firms may not pay attention to every quarterly movement in securities prices, given the possibility of excess volatility in financial markets (Shiller 1981). In addition Hall (1977) and Chirinko (1983b) have emphasized the likelihood of errors owing to the indirect measurement of the value of stocks and bonds and to the fact that the value of a firm's shares depends on everything owned by the corporations—not just their physical capital but also intangible capital, natural resources, goodwill, mo-

---

9. Hall (1977, 88) shows that with a geometric delivery lag, only the current value of Q enters. In the basic analysis of Abel and Hayashi, only current Q enters, and gestation lags are a special case.

nopoly position, and firm specific human capital. The denominator of the Q ratio is likely to be measured with error because of the absence of a complete inventory of the capital actually in place and the need for approximations that may ignore premature retirements (owing, for instance, to changes in energy prices), and because of mismeasurement of the replacement price of capital owing to inadequate adjustment for quality change.

To date empirical results with the Q model have been disappointing. It does not perform as well in the 1970s as other alternatives (Clark 1979) and yields a relatively low R^2 even when carefully adjusted for tax effects (Summers 1981).[10] One possible problem is illustrated by the increases in energy prices after the two oil shocks of the 1980s. These were followed by a sharp decline in the stock market and in measured average Q, but not by a marked decline in investment. This might reflect a production relation in which capital and energy are substitutes, so that a higher relative price of energy induces new capital investment.

Similarly, an episode of "wage push" that increases the share of labor semipermanently could well reduce the Q ratio for a long time by depressing the numerator much faster than the denominator can adjust. Recall that the denominator is the replacement cost of capital, measured as today's capital goods price index times a perpetual inventory measure of the real capital stock. If the inflation rate is larger than the retirement rate, the denominator of the Q ratio can grow while the numerator is falling. A decline in the stock market can occur when higher prices of labor or energy eliminate the profit earned by old plants, but nevertheless firms may keep operating these plants as long as they contribute more to cash flow than to variable cost (recent examples include dinosaur steel plants recently closed by United States Steel or the Boeing 707s finally grounded by TWA four years after the second oil shock.)

Even if Q could somehow be measured accurately, with a correct measure of capital actually in place used to calculate the denominator of the Q ratio, empirical tests of the theory would run aground on a basic asymmetry in adjustment costs and gestation lags that seems to have been ignored. An increase in Q above unity should induce positive net investment limited only by the size of adjustment costs and delivery lags, but a decrease in Q below unity induces negative net investment subject to a quite different set of adjustment costs. Firms may not retire capital until its cash flow falls to its variable cost, and there may be a

10. The poor postsample performance of the Q approach is illustrated by Clark (1979, 93). Since his article was written, a national accounts revision has substantially raised the level of actual investment for the later 1970s, thus implying an even poorer performance of the Q approach.

long transition period that brings with it the danger of bankruptcy before this variable cost point is actually reached. Firms with little profit making potential and with a near zero value on the stock market may nonetheless have sufficient residual goodwill or monopoly power to be able to keep themselves afloat by issuing debt, as has been so evident in the airline industry. An implication is that a revival of industry fortunes (owing, for instance, to a decline in energy prices) may cause stock prices to soar without setting off an investment boom, as firms concentrate on paying off debt and restructuring their balance sheets.

Such portfolio arrangements can create considerable looseness between stock market movements and investment decisions. The same looseness may occur in part because the evaluation of a company's future formed by firm management differs from that formed by the market. In graduate school we were first exposed to Paul Samuelson's joke that "the stock market has predicted nine out of the last five recessions," and we also have heard much from Modigliani and Cohn (1979) and others about irrationality in market valuations. So it seems no wonder that management should be as skeptical of the market's verdict in making valuations as we economists have been. In a recent survey of six hundred companies, *Business Week* found that 60% of executives responding felt that the "real value" of their company was underestimated by the stock market.[11]

Our criticism of the Q theory has been based on asymmetric adjustment costs and possible irrationality or differences in opinion in market valuations. It is related to the critique by Bosworth (1975), which stresses that firms will pay little attention to Q because the stock market fluctuates excessively whereas investment projects take time to plan and construct. Bosworth's argument is criticized by Fischer and Merton (1984), who deny that managers would ignore the stock market even when granting Bosworth the extreme assumptions that (*a*) there occurs a completely exogenous and irrational decline in the stock market (with an accompanying increase in the expected return on the stock market from 15% to 20%) while (*b*) firm managers' assessments are "completely unaffected by such animal spirits and they know with certainty the true objective probabilities" (that the expected equilibrium real return is 15%; p. 39). Even in such a situation, Fischer and Merton argue, the stockmarket would influence investment, since rational managers would use retained earnings to purchase their own or other firms' shares. Similarly, they would be reluctant to finance new investments by issuing equity at the depressed stock market prices.

No doubt some firms are influenced by such considerations, but others may forge ahead with new investment projects, for at least two

11. See "Companies Feel Underrated by Street," *Business Week*, 20 February 1984, 14.

reasons. First, animal spirits may influence the stock and bond markets differently. The 1973–75 episode of collapsing stock market was accompanied by negative short-term ex post real interest rates and by long-term real bond rates that were relatively low, judged either in terms of the high contemporaneous inflation rate of 1974–75 or by the average inflation rate of the period 1974–81 viewed retrospectively. Thus firms may simply have switched from equity to debt issue. Fischer and Merton would contend that rational managers should have borrowed short term to buy back their shares instead of planning new investment projects, but their view seems to ignore the potentially large costs of postponing investment projects.

Managers face a trade-off between the uncertain capital gains to be made on purchase and subsequent resale of their own shares or those of other firms and the less uncertain losses that would be incurred if (given long lead times and gestation lags) new capacity were not constructed *now* in anticipation of the next period of prosperity and high capacity utilization. The planning and implementation of investment in new plant and equipment may be an ongoing bureaucratic process involving high costs of delay or postponement.

Surely the real world is characterized by both responses, with some firms responding to a stock market slump that they believe is temporary by choosing the buy-back route while others engage in friendly or hostile takeover bids and still others continue with previously planned investment projects. Fischer and Merton may argue correctly that the stock market must make *some* difference to investment expenditures, while we put forth the compatible argument that the stock market may be used as just *one piece of information*, in addition to the traditional factors (expected output, rental prices, etc.). If this is a correct interpretation, then the Q model, by including only the single Q variable, as in equation (9), incorporates arbitrary exclusion restrictions just as does the neoclassical paradigm. When we incorporate looser restrictions into both approaches, they melt together into a generalized reduced form in which output, interest rates, stock prices, the money supply, tax rates, and other variables enter a model like equations (4) through (7) in multiple roles, influencing desired capital, expectations, desired adjustment speeds, and replacement rates.

5.2.4 Household Investment

Household investment is durable goods and residential structures has received much less attention than business investment in equipment and structures.[12] This neglect cannot be justified by the share of household fixed investment in GNP, since this share has been at least as large

---

12. There are exceptions, however, particularly for residential housing. See deLeeuw (1971), Feldstein (1981), and Polinsky (1977).

as that of business investment throughout the period 1919–83 and has become relatively larger in the past two decades. Perhaps it is the perception that household investment is passive rather than a driving force in business cycles that has kept it in the background. Expenditures on consumer durables and residential structures, rather than being treated on a par with business investment, enter into macroeconomic model building mainly as a channel of transmission of monetary policy episodes of disintermediation and credit controls.

There are many parallels between the models used for consumer expenditure and those used to explain business investment. Both the simple Keynesian consumption/income relation and Friedman's permanent income hypothesis are close analogues to certain variants of the accelerator hypothesis of business investment behavior. Lagged or expected GNP is replaced as an explanatory variable by lagged or expected disposable income in moving from business to consumer investment, but the mechanism remains the same. More recent attempts at modeling the consumer's decision, such as Bernanke (1982), treat optimal durable goods investment within the framework of intertemporal utility maximization under uncertainty. The resulting model closely parallels the "business investment in the presence of adjustment costs" literature that originated with Lucas (1967). All models like Bernanke's either implicitly or explicitly require consumers to form expectations of future values of relevant variables, leading to the same complications (delivery lags, replacement timing) that occur for business investment above in equation (8). As is the case in (8), the estimated coefficients of the relevant time series variables are underidentified convolutions of many structural parameters.

5.2.5 Relation to Other Critiques

Christopher Sims (1980a) presented a critique of traditional econometric models and urged the profession to shift from structural estimation to his atheoretical VARs. In a sense the preceding critique of structural investment equations represents a special case of Sims's more general critique. Both place particular emphasis on the fact that any set of lagged variables may in principle influence expectations of a variable, and that thus there is little justification for many of the exclusion restrictions that are incorporated in traditional econometric models. For instance, there is ample evidence that it is suboptimal to form expectations of real output using only a univariate autoregression, as in most empirical implementations of the neoclassical investment model and in such recent papers as Abel and Blanchard (1983).[13] In

13. Unrealistically restrictive assumptions regarding the set of variables admissible into the information set pervade theoretical papers, not just empirical tests. In a related

contrast, our own recent work (Gordon 1983b) shows that nominal GNP growth is associated with past changes in interest rates, the monetary base, and the money multiplier, with different weights in each postwar decade. And in another paper (Gordon 1982) we showed that, for a given nominal GNP change, real output depends among other things on its own lagged value, lagged inflation, lagged changes in real energy prices, and variables to capture the effects of government price control programs.

Despite the preceding critique of traditional investment equations and its similarity to Sims's general critique, there is no need to go as far as Sims in endorsing completely atheoretical VAR models. Consideration of a reduced-form equation like (8), together with the long list of candidate variables that might influence expectations, suggests that degrees of freedom are likely to be exhausted even in a relatively large data set like that used in this paper. VAR models estimated to date usually involve short lists of aggregate variables without including individual categories of expenditure—for example, investment—or special variables that might be important for a particular category.

Gordon and King (1982) recommend an econometric approach that combines the VAR approach with the estimation of reduced-form equations suggested by traditional theory. Both the reduced-form and VAR approaches can be viewed as selecting different methods of allocating zero restrictions in the face of scarce degrees of freedom. As with any trade-off in economics, the best way to allocate these restrictions depends on an assessment of benefits and costs. The VAR technique, in which every variable is included on the right-hand side of every equation with lag distributions of equal length, is a useful tool for checking traditional specifications and determining, for instance, whether stock prices or the money supply "belong" in an investment equation. To repeat a phrase frequently used in oral discussions by Sims, Shiller, and others, the VAR technique is an efficient way to conduct "exploratory data analysis."

But reduced-form econometrics must be guided by prior structural analysis. Excessive pursuit of symmetry in the VAR approach can lead an investigator to omit particular variables that may matter for one equation but not others, for example, variables to measure the effect

---

paper John Taylor (1983) derives a model of investment with gestation lags that shares with equations (4) and (6) the feature that current investment orders depend on expectations of both future output and capital costs. Taylor is not concerned with the identification issues under discussion here, but he does choose to simplify his model, as do Abel and Blanchard, by making expectations of future output depend only on past output, and in addition he makes future capital cost depend only on future and past output. By omitting the multiple roles for past financial variables in determining expectations of all future variables, Taylor thus introduces prior simplifying restrictions that have no empirical justification.

of the wartime price controls in a study of inflation or the investment tax credit in a study of investment behavior. Gordon and King (1982; and in more detail King 1983) have concluded that specifications used in some VAR applications have been cavalier about detrending and have tended to yield estimates that mix secular and cyclical effects and can result in biased coefficients.

The general Simsian critique, and our particular critique of the investment literature, seems to point to estimation of highly unrestricted and unconstrained specifications. Both appear to move in the opposite direction from econometric work set in motion by the Lucas (1976) critique, which has embarked on the task of estimating parameters "at deep levels of choice—for example, parameters of utility and production functions—that remain invariant in the face of changes in policy rules. As yet this line of research, represented, for instance, by Hansen and Singleton (1982), has not yet provided convincing time series characterizations of the major macroeconomic variables that might be compared with traditional explanations. Further, applications of the Hansen/Singleton methodology appear to achieve "identification via an 'incredible' disturbance assumption," according to a recent critique by Peter Garber and Robert King (1983).

5.2.6 The Hybrid Methodology: Blending Structure with VAR Reduced Forms

The central role of investment fluctuations in business cycles has spawned an enormous number of papers that estimate structural investment equations in which unconvincing simplifications and exclusion restrictions have been introduced to achieve identification. Often the focus is on persuading the reader that the author's favorite explanatory variable is statistically significant, or that some other author's favorite variable is insignificant. Our skepticism regarding the multiple roles played by aggregate time series variables, and our doubt that any proxy for Tobin's Q can adequately summarize all the influences on investment appropriations and expenditures, leads us to estimate reduced-form equations. Our point of departure is a list of "candidate" explanatory variables that has been suggested in previous theoretical research. Our basic emphasis is on determining which variables play an important role in the investment process and how much of the variance of investment remains to be attributed to "innovations."

The methodological approach adopted here is similar to that previously applied to the econometric explanation of inflation behavior. This line of research has proved fruitful in developing an inflation equation that over the postwar period appears to remain relatively stable and that, when estimated for the period before 1981, seems able to track reasonably well the sharp disinflation that has occurred since then.[14] Insights of previous structural models are used to develop the list of explanatory variables and to emerge with a specification that introduces a few more constraints than typically appear in "pure" VAR models. The equation can be used to test for the exogeneity of particular sets of lagged variables in the inflation process, for temporal stability, and for biases in one set of coefficients that result from the omission of another variable. They can be used to identify significant shifts in sets of lagged coefficients between one period and another. However, what has been lost in the inflation equation literature, and cannot be regained, is the ability to use particular coefficients to identify specific aspects of the behavior of labor markets as opposed to product markets.[15]

The specification of the investment equation in this paper begins with the lagged dependent variable. Just as we are interested in "inflation inertia," we are interested in "investment inertia." The serial correlation properties of the investment process, which result at least in part from aggregation over heterogeneous projects having different gestation lags, are part of the basic "propagation mechanism" by which random shocks in the demand for investment goods are translated into business cycles displaying persistence in the deviation of output from trend. Most previous econometric work on investment, whether based on a neoclassical specification like equation (3) or a Q specification like (9), has omitted the lagged dependent variable. If the "true" investment process exhibits a high degree of positive serial correlation, then estimated coefficients are likely to be biased when the lagged dependent variable is omitted. Although we exhibit evidence of the effects of this misspecification below, the nature of the bias can be illustrated in the following simple model. Imagine that the true model of investment spending (I_t) involves both an accelerator effect on the lagged change in output (ΔX_{t-1}) and dependence on the lagged dependent variable (I_{t-1}):

$$(10) \qquad I_t = \beta \Delta X_{t-1} + \rho I_{t-1} + e_t,$$

while the misspecified regression that is actually estimated is:

$$(11) \qquad I_t = b \Delta X_{t-1} + u_t.$$

By the usual analysis of specification error in the case of a left-out variable, we can write the expectation of the estimated accelerator coefficient as:

$$(12) \qquad E(\hat{b}) = \beta + \gamma \rho,$$

14. An assessment of the 1981–83 "disinflation experiment" using the DRI model and a reduced-form approach is presented in papers by Eckstein (1983) and Gordon (1983a, 1984b). A detailed quantitative review of the performance of my equation in postsample dynamic simulations is provided by Perry (1983).

15. See Gordon (1977) and Sims's comments in the printed discussion of that paper.

where γ is the coefficient of the "auxiliary" regression of lagged investment on the lagged change in output. Since investment is *part* of output, there is a presumption that γ is positive, although a precise expression for γ requires a more complete specification of the time series process generating noninvestment output. A full analysis of this problem would also need to take account of the fact that most empirical accelerator equations include a set of current and several lagged ΔX terms. It is sufficient here to note simply that tests of the accelerator hypothesis may yield biased coefficients, as in (12), and that the error term in (11) is quite likely to exhibit serial correlation, since it is related to the "true" error term e_t as follows:

(13) $\qquad u_t = e_t + \rho[(1 - \gamma)I_{t-1} + \gamma I_{t-2} - \gamma \Delta N_{t-1}],$

where N is noninvestment output.

The list of regressors for our investment equations, in addition to the lagged dependent variable, begins with the two central variables in the neoclassical approach, the change in output and in the real price of capital services (C/P). Tobin's Q is included as well, in combination with the neoclassical variables rather than alone as in equation (9). Because changes in the money stock may be relevant for the formation of expectations and/or as a proxy for the effect of credit rationing, these are included as well. The most important variables that are omitted are the prices of other inputs besides capital, for example, the real wage and real energy prices. This omission is justified by the need to control the scale of this empirical investigation, which tends to grow with the square of the explanatory variables considered as candidates.

The empirical equations share with the VAR approach the use of unconstrained and relatively short lag distributions and the inclusion of the same number of lags for each explanatory variable, including the lagged dependent variable. In our initial research, as in much other recent VAR research, lag distributions were limited to four quarters. Later we adjusted the lag length to eight quarters for the postwar period, in light of the evidence that the coefficient on the price of capital services for the postwar period is sensitive to an extension of lag length. Contemporaneous values of variables are excluded from the estimated regressions. Subsequently we examine correlations among contemporaneous orthogonalized innovations in a VAR model containing equations for investment and for each of our final set of explanatory variables. At that stage we carry out several "innovation accounting" exercises for two alternative choices of the ordering of contemporaneous errors in the VAR system. As shown by Gordon and King (1982, 212–14), such choices amount to decisions about admitting current variables into the estimating equations.

The specification of the investment equations in this paper differs from most applications of the VAR technique in its correction for heteroskedasticity and in its attention to the form of variables. All real expenditure series are normalized by "natural real GNP" (X^N). The money supply is expressed in *real* terms, since it is entered into an equation for *real* investment expenditures, and it is also normalized by X^N. Our empirical tests also examine shifts in coefficients over time. The precise values of the individual lag coefficients are of no particular interest. Instead, we emphasize exclusion tests on the contribution of all lags of a given right-hand variable, running these tests for both the interwar and the postwar periods. This technique allows us to determine whether the relative contribution of different sets of variables has changed over time. There is no analogy in the paper to the usual search for significant coefficients, since positive and negative results in the exclusion tests are equally interesting.

5.3   Data and Descriptive Statistics

5.3.1   Development of the Basic Variables

This paper investigates the historical behavior of four categories of fixed investment: producers' durable equipment (*PDE*), nonresidential structures (*NRS*), residential structures (*RS*), and consumer durables expenditures (*CD*). Whereas in the previous literature some of these categories have been analyzed with different theories in separate papers, here they all seem amenable to analysis within the same reduced-form methodology. Our inclusion of consumer durables expenditures as part of "investment" creates an overlap in coverage with Hall's paper in this volume (chap. 4).

Quarterly data on the four investment categories for 1947–83 come from the national income and product accounts. Investment and real GNP data for 1919–41 are created by the Chow and Lin (1971) method of interpolation from a variety of sources, as described in the appendix to this chapter. We have been careful to interpolate each component of real GNP on the basis of separate data sources, in order to avoid a spurious correlation between dependent and explanatory variables in this study. The Chow/Lin method is an iterative procedure in which a regression is run to explain a data series available only annually (e.g., real GNP), using as explanatory variables the annual average of one or more series available monthly (e.g., industrial production and real retail sales). In this example the coefficients from the regression are used to create monthly (or in our case quarterly) values for real GNP.

Some investigators have carried out historical studies with raw monthly data rather than interpolated data. Examples include Bernanke (1983b), Sims (1980b), and the papers in this volume by Bernanke and Powell (chap. 10) and Blinder and Holtz-Eakin (chap. 3). This makes sense when comparable monthly data are available for both the interwar and the postwar periods. However, investigators of postwar investment behavior have uniformly used national accounts quarterly data, not monthly data on the industrial production of producer durables and on square feet of nonresidential construction. To achieve comparability in a study of investment, interpolated quarterly data for the interwar period are preferable. Further, to use the raw monthly data would involve discarding the information available in the annual averages for components of réal GNP. It seems clear from the literature that the previous absence of quarterly investment expenditure data for the interwar period has caused investigators to limit themselves to the postwar period, and we hope that the availability of the new data set will spur further historical research on investment and other components of real GNP.

All expenditure series, real GNP, the real capital stock, and the real money supply are deflated by the "natural real GNP" (X^N) series, whose the creation is described in Gordon (1984a, appendix C). The basic procedure is to establish a constant "natural rate of unemployment" for the portion of the labor force not engaged as self-employed farmers and proprietors—this natural rate is arbitrarily set equal to the rate estimated for 1954 in a study of inflation dynamics covering the period 1954–80. Then, adjusting for the shrinking share of self-employed proprietors (who are not counted among the unemployed), the corresponding total natural unemployment rate series is used to establish the level of X^N in selected benchmark years (1901, 1912, 1923, 1929, 1949, and 1954). Since actual and natural unemployment are not equal in the benchmark years, an assumed "Okun's law" coefficient of 2.0 was used in calculating X^N for those years, and the values for intervening years were interpolated using logarithms. The deflation by X^N is introduced to avoid heteroskedasticity—the level of X^N rises from $229 billion in 1919 to $1,667 billion in 1983. Use of the X^N series is superior to detrending in a study of business cycles, since detrending for a period like 1929–41 yields an unrealistically low estimate of "normal" conditions.

In addition to data on investment expenditures, this study has developed five other series as possible explanatory variables. All are from original sources, and only the capital stock is interpolated. The others are available monthly.

1. *Capital stock.* This is available as an annual series from the Commerce Department capital stock study for both producers' durable equipment and nonresidential structures. Four concepts are available, gross and net, in current and constant dollars. In this study the net real stock is interpolated quarterly (as described in the appendix). It is used and subsequently rejected as an explanatory variable, and the

net real stock times the current investment price deflator is used as an estimate of the replacement cost of capital for construction of the "Q proxy" described below.

2. *Real money supply and real monetary base.* The "high powered money" series is from Friedman and Schwartz (1970), divided by the interpolated GNP deflator and linked to the corresponding postwar series. The M1 series has been created by Benjamin Friedman back to 1915 on a basis that is consistent with the current (early 1980s) definition.

3. *"Average Q."* First a "Q proxy" series is calculated as an index number, with 1972:2 = 1.0, since the numerator and denominator are in different units. The numerator is the Standard and Poor's 500 stock price index, and the denominator is the replacement-cost net capital stock index described above. This quarterly series is used to interpolate Summers's annual average "conventional Q" series (1981, table 3, col. 1) for the period 1931–79. Data for 1919–30 and 1980–83 are obtained by linking "Q proxy" to the interpolated Summers series in 1931 and 1980.

4. *Real interest rate.* The expected inflation rate used to calculate the real interest rate is typically computed as the predicted value from a simple time series regression including lagged inflation and a few other lagged variables. Invariably this leads to a predicted series in which the main weight is carried by the first lag on inflation, and the result is a highly volatile estimate of the expected inflation rate and the corresponding expected real interest rate relevant for investment decisions. In this study the volatile series produced by this procedure is ignored, and in its place we use a twelve-quarter "rectangular" weighted average of past inflation. Even this arbitrary approximation is flawed, however, because it gives unreasonable values in periods for the first few years after both World War I and World War II. As Gordon has argued previously (1973), rational agents would have treated wars and immediate postwar periods as special episodes, in light of a long history of wartime inflation and postwar deflation. Since there was no trend in prices over the century before World War I, an expected inflation rate of zero is imposed for the interval 1919–24, and the twelve-quarter average is introduced beginning in 1925:1. After World War II the same procedure is used for 1947–49, except that the constant value is set equal to 2.6%, the value of the twelve-quarter average in 1950:1. This series on expected inflation is subtracted from the Baa rate, to reflect the presumed relevance of a less than highest grade interest rate for the average investment decision.

5. *The real price of capital services* (C/P). Standard formulas, shown in the appendix, are used to calculate the real price of capital services from a variety of data sources. The before-tax real borrowing rate is taken to be the real Baa rate, from series 4 above. This facilitates

comparisons of the effects of the full C/P variable as contrasted with that of the real Baa rate, one of the major components of C/P. The depreciation rate included in the estimate of C/P is that which is yielded by an iterative search for the rate that makes the quarterly interpolated capital stock series in (1) above consistent with the published annual capital stock series and our new interpolated quarterly investment series. Tax rates are obtained from published sources, as described in the appendix.

5.3.2   Fixed Investment in Recessions, 1920–82

Descriptive statistics on the variables used in this paper are provided in tables 5.1, 5.2, and 5.3. The first of these calculates the percentage decline in three ratios to X^N over the thirteen recessions in our sample period, five in the interwar period and eight in the postwar period. NBER reference cycles are used throughout, and this creates an inconsistency between the cycle dating procedure actually used (see the chronology paper by Moore and Zarnowitz in this volume, appendix A) and the "growth cycle" concept that would be more relevant given our deflation of real variables by X^N.

Column 1 of table 5.1 shows the percentage decline in the "output ratio" X/X^N, ranging from 40.2% in 1929–33 to only 2.7% in 1960–61. The next three columns exhibit recession declines in the ratio of three different investment magnitudes to X^N—all four types of expenditure, the two "business" types ($PDE + NRS$), and the two "household" types ($RS + CD$), respectively. Leaving aside the mammoth numbers for 1929–33, the largest absolute declines in total investment were in the recessions of 1920–21, 1937–38, and 1973–75, in that order.

The remaining columns of table 5.1 establish the importance of fixed investment behavior as a contributing factor in business cycles. Shown for each cycle is the percentage of the total decline in the X/X^N ratio accounted for by the decline in the ratio of total investment to X^N. While these percentages are quite small for the first two postwar recessions, in other recessions they range from 30% to 78%, with the recessions in which investment played the largest role ranked as 1920–21, 1960–61, and 1980. Interestingly, the relative contribution of investment to the Great Contraction of 1929–33 was less than in all five of the postwar recessions between 1957–58 and 1980. There seems to be no systematic difference between the interwar and postwar recessions in the division of the investment decline betweeen the two business types and the two household types. The two business types accounted for a larger contribution in eight of the thirteen recessions, and the two household types did so in the remainder.

The three right-hand columns display an elasticity concept, measured as the percentage change in the ratios shown in columns 5 through 7

Table 5.1   Peak-to-Trough Decline in Percentage Ratios to Natural Real GNP: Thirteen Business Cycles, 1920–82

	Percentage Decline				Share of Total			Elasticities		
Cycle	Real GNP (1)	Four I Types (2)	PDE + NRS (3)	CD + RS (4)	Four I Types (5)	PDE + NRS (6)	CD + RS (7)	Four I Types (8)	PDE + NRS (9)	CD + RS (10)
Interwar										
1920:1 to 1921:2	9.0	7.0	3.3	3.7	77.8	36.7	41.1	3.4	3.4	3.4
1923:1 to 1924:3	4.1	2.1	0.9	1.2	51.2	22.0	29.2	2.1	1.6	2.6
1926:4 to 1927:4	5.5	1.7	1.1	0.6	30.9	20.0	10.9	1.3	1.6	1.0
1929:3 to 1933:1	40.2	16.6	9.4	7.2	41.3	23.4	17.9	1.8	2.0	1.6
1937:2 to 1938:2	11.9	6.5	4.2	2.3	54.6	35.3	19.3	3.0	3.7	2.3
Postwar										
1948:4 to 1949:4	5.3	1.0	2.1	−1.1	18.8	39.8	−21.0	0.8	3.6	−1.7
1953:2 to 1954:2	7.2	0.9	0.6	0.3	12.7	7.8	4.9	0.6	0.8	0.4
1957:3 to 1958:2	5.0	2.3	1.4	0.9	45.8	29.0	16.8	2.2	2.9	1.6
1960:2 to 1961:1	2.7	1.7	0.6	1.1	61.4	20.6	40.8	3.0	2.2	3.7
1969:4 to 1970:4	4.2	1.8	1.1	0.7	43.1	25.2	17.9	1.9	2.2	1.6
1973:4 to 1975:1	8.5	4.7	2.0	2.7	55.2	23.4	31.8	2.2	2.0	2.4
1980:1 to 1980:3	3.6	2.1	0.8	1.3	59.2	22.2	37.0	2.4	1.9	2.9
1981:3 to 1982:4	6.3	2.1	1.4	0.7	34.0	22.8	11.2	1.5	2.0	1.0

divided by the average value of each ratio in the peak quarter of each cycle. An elasticity of unity would indicate that the decline in investment was proportional to its peak-quarter share, that is, that the percentage responses of investment and noninvestment were equal. An elasticity above unity indicates that the contribution of investment to the decline in real GNP was larger than its peak-quarter share in real GNP, and that the contribution of noninvestment must have been smaller. For all four types of investment (col. 8), the elasticities range from 0.6 to 3.7. The elasticity for the Great Contraction is a middle-ranked 1.8, less than in the 1920–21, 1923–24, and 1937–38 interwar recessions and in all five of the recessions between 1957–58 and 1980. At least one example with a low elasticity can be easily explained, the 1953–54 recession in which the dominant depressing influence on real GNP was the post-Korea decline in defense spending. And the relatively high elasticity of household investment in 1980 may reflect the influence of the Carter credit controls.

5.3.3   Means and Standard Deviations

Table 5.2 displays means and standard deviations of the variables used in this paper over thirteen complete trough-to-trough business cycles between 1919 and 1982 and one incomplete cycle between 1938 and 1941. Also shown are averages for the entire interwar period and postwar period. Each cell shows the mean, with the associated standard deviation displayed immediately below in parentheses. The first column shows that on average the X/X^N ratio was considerably higher in the postwar period than the interwar period, and of this 10.3 percentage point difference, 5.2 points are accounted for by the four investment types taken together. Also evident is the much higher standard deviation of the X/X^N and the total real investment series during the interwar period over individual cycles. The regression equations in the subsequent tables of results cover several business cycles in each subsample period, and this implies that regression coefficients depend not just on the quarter-to-quarter variance of the investment series, but also on changes in means across cycles.

In this light it is interesting to note the high means for both types of structures investment that reflect the construction boom of the 1920s, which plays a large role in some nonmonetary explanations of the Great Depresson (see Gordon and Wilcox 1981) and in our analysis below in section 5.5. The ratios to X^N of nonresidential structures were higher in the 1921, 1924, and 1927 cycles than in any postwar cycle. The mean for the 1924 cycle was highest for residential construction, followed by 1949 and a tie between 1921 and 1954. The ratios to X^N of producers' durable equipment and consumer durables show quite a different pattern, with all three of the highest ratios achieved during the period 1971–82.

Table 5.2   Means and Standard Deviations of Basic Variables

Cycle Beginning in Trough[a]	Real GNP (1)	Four I Types (2)	PDE (3)	NRS (4)	RS (5)	CD (6)	Real M1 (7)	Service Price C/P (8)	Q (9)	Real Corporate Baa Rate (10)
Interwar (1919–41)	89.8 (12.5)[c]	17.2 (6.2)	4.1 (1.4)	4.4 (2.4)	3.3 (1.6)	5.4 (1.3)	28.0 (3.3)	14.9 (0.4)	147 (48)	6.6 (3.8)
1919:1	96.4 (4.2)	19.1 (3.1)	5.7 (1.1)	3.1 (0.5)	4.4 (0.7)	6.0 (1.3)	28.7 (2.0)	15.0 (0.4)	104 (14)	7.8 (0.6)
1921:2	99.1 (6.1)	22.0 (3.3)	4.8 (0.9)	6.5 (1.3)	4.6 (0.5)	6.1 (0.8)	28.5 (0.9)	15.1 (0.3)	115 (10)	7.3 (0.6)
1924:3	103.4 (1.9)	25.5 (1.3)	5.3 (0.3)	8.0 (9.5)	5.4 (0.5)	6.9 (0.5)	28.7 (0.7)	12.5 (0.8)	156 (19)	4.8 (0.8)
1927:4	87.8 (13.8)	16.6 (6.7)	3.7 (1.6)	4.9 (2.1)	2.9 (1.7)	5.2 (1.4)	25.5 (1.2)	16.9 (0.5)	186 (71)	9.1 (4.6)
1933:1	75.8 (6.7)	10.8 (2.7)	2.9 (0.9)	2.1 (0.6)	1.4 (0.4)	4.3 (0.8)	26.1 (2.7)	14.8 (0.5)	153 (40)	6.2 (5.4)
1938:2[b]	87.0 (7.3)	14.5 (2.3)	3.7 (0.7)	2.8 (0.7)	2.8 (0.5)	5.2 (0.6)	32.6 (3.2)	14.0 (0.9)	133 (17)	4.2 (0.9)

(*continued*)

Table 5.2 (continued)

Cycle Beginning in Trough[a]	Real GNP (1)	Four I Types (2)	PDE (3)	NRS (4)	RS (5)	CD (6)	Real M1 (7)	Service Price C/P (8)	Q (9)	Real Corporate Baa Rate (10)
					Percentage Ratio to Natural Real GNP					
Postwar (1947–82)	100.1 (3.4)	22.4 (1.8)	6.3 (0.9)	3.9 (0.5)	4.2 (0.8)	8.0 (1.1)	26.0 (9.0)	15.8 (2.7)	91 (24)	3.1 (2.1)
1947:1	99.5 (1.4)	21.5 (0.8)	6.4 (0.6)	4.0 (0.2)	4.5 (0.5)	6.7 (0.4)	43.9 (2.5)	11.2 (0.6)	84 (12)	0.8 (0.1)
1949:4	103.6 (2.6)	21.6 (1.7)	5.7 (0.4)	3.9 (0.1)	4.8 (0.7)	7.1 (0.7)	37.3 (1.8)	13.1 (0.9)	67 (2)	0.7 (0.6)
1954:2	100.7 (2.3)	21.6 (1.3)	5.5 (0.4)	4.2 (0.2)	4.6 (0.5)	7.3 (0.5)	32.2 (1.9)	15.3 (0.6)	85 (6)	1.9 (0.1)
1958:2	98.4 (1.8)	20.2 (0.9)	4.9 (0.3)	4.0 (0.2)	4.5 (0.4)	6.8 (0.3)	28.2 (0.9)	16.4 (0.5)	102 (6)	2.7 (0.6)
1961:1	101.9 (2.5)	22.4 (1.5)	6.1 (0.8)	4.3 (0.3)	4.2 (0.5)	7.8 (0.8)	24.2 (1.6)	16.0 (1.0)	124 (12)	3.6 (0.4)
1970:4	100.2 (2.5)	24.4 (1.9)	7.0 (0.6)	3.7 (0.3)	4.5 (0.8)	9.2 (0.6)	20.0 (1.0)	16.3 (0.4)	95 (12)	3.6 (0.2)
1975:1	98.0 (2.0)	23.7 (1.5)	7.3 (0.7)	3.1 (0.2)	3.7 (0.5)	9.6 (0.6)	16.3 (0.8)	16.4 (0.2)	70 (4)	3.2 (1.2)
1980:3	94.3 (2.5)	22.2 (1.0)	7.5 (0.5)	3.3 (0.1)	2.5 (0.4)	8.8 (0.3)	13.9 (0.3)	22.5 (1.3)	63 (3)	7.6 (1.0)

[a]Statistics cover quarters from first quarter after trough to next trough.
[b]Through 1941:3 only.
[c]Standard deviations in parentheses.

Another difference between the two structures types and the two equipment types concerns the difference between the interwar and postwar standard deviations. The standard deviations of nonresidential and residential structures fell from 2.4 to 0.5 and 1.6 to 0.8 points, respectively. The standard deviations of producer and consumer durables fell much less, from 1.4 to 0.9 and 1.3 to 1.1, respectively. While nonresidential structures had by far the highest standard deviation in the interwar years, consumer durables had the highest standard deviation in the postwar years.

Additional insight into the behavior of investment spending is provided by figures 5.1 and 5.2. The former displays real GNP (X), total investment (I), and noninvestment GNP (N), each expressed as a ratio to X^N. Here we note the contrast between the volatility of I in the 1920–21 recession and subsequent recovery, and its relative stability during 1923–29. Evident throughout the interwar period is the high positive covariance between I and N; this covariance appears to occur at annual and lower frequencies and is not an artifact of our interpolation procedure. The postwar period is dominated by the large bulge in N during the Korean War, though there is a less pronounced hump in I in 1972–74. Also evident is the downward drift in both X and N relative to I after 1966. The robust health of the I/X^N ratio in the second half of the 1970s suggests the possibility that our average Q variable may perform poorly, in light of its collapse after 1973.

Figure 5.2 exhibits each of the four categories of investment, also expressed as a ratio to X^N. The investment boom of the 1920s and the unusual share of boom contributed by nonresidential structures are clearly visible. The 1930s are characterized by a simultaneous collapse in all four categories, as well as by a milder slump of consumer durables spending. By 1939–40, the two equipment categories had each recovered to within a percentage point of the 1926–29 average, but residential structures had recovered only to about half of the 1926–29 level, and nonresidential structures to less than one-third. Postwar business cycles exhibit a continuing shift from structures to equipment, together with a general tendency for booms in residential structures to lead booms in PDE, with consumer durables in between. Cycles in nonresidential structures do not coincide with those in the other four categories, with the appearance of a process involving much longer lags.

Table 5.2 exhibits the means and standard deviations of the major explanatory variables—the real money stock expressed as a ratio to X^N, the price of capital services, average Q, and the real Baa rate. The behavior of these variables is illustrated in figure 5.3, where each is expressed as an index with 1919:1 = 1.0. The most stable variable in both the interwar and postwar periods was real M1, the variation of

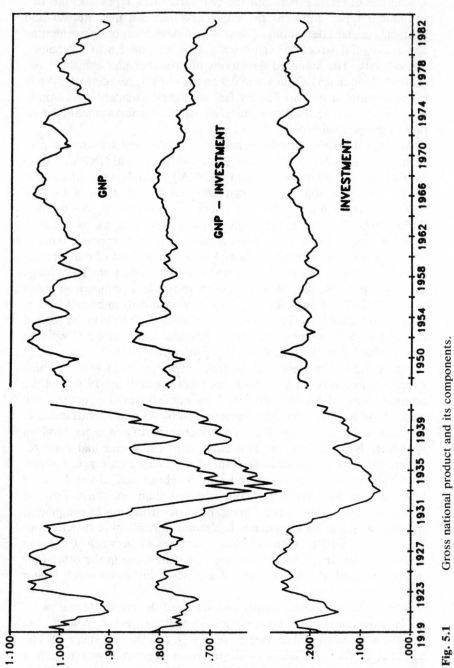

Fig. 5.1   Gross national product and its components.

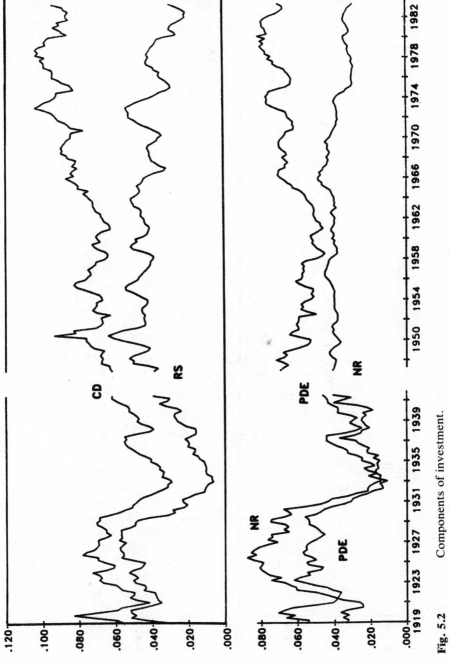

Fig. 5.2   Components of investment.

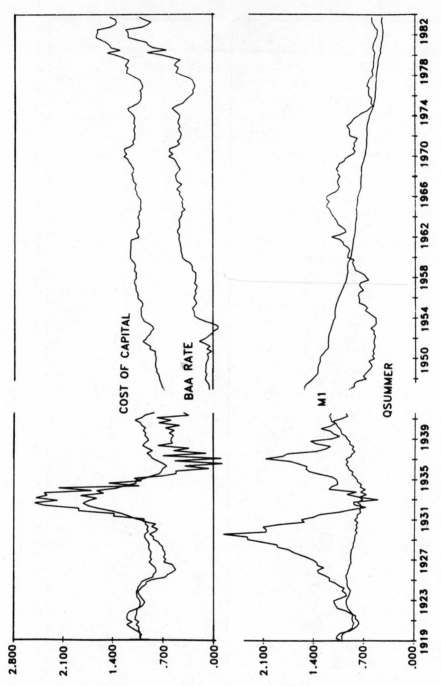

Fig. 5.3   Normalized monetary and financial variables.

which consists of a slight uptrend at the end of the 1930s and a consistent downtrend during the postwar period. The standard deviation of real M1 is smaller than that of total investment within most interwar cycles and is about the same order of magnitude during postwar cycles.

The capital service price has a small standard deviation and little drift. It exhibits two major humps, in response to high real interest rates in 1930–34 and 1980–83. The smaller degree of volatility in the capital service price than in the real interest rate reflects the dominant role in the former variable of a fixed depreciation rate. Both the service price and the real interest rate exhibit minima in 1936–37, 1952–53, and 1975–77, reflecting price increases that are subtracted from the nominal Baa rate. The average Q variable (expressed as a percentage in table 5.2) has a much higher mean in the interwar period than in the postwar. The standard deviation of Q averaged over the interwar period was double that in the postwar, and the average for individual cycles in the interwar period was more than four times higher than the average for individual postwar cycles.

The regression analysis in the next part of the paper compares the differing relative contributions of lagged investment and lagged GNP in explaining current investment. As a preliminary, we present a decomposition of variance of the ratios to X^N of real GNP (X), real investment (I), and real noninvestment GNP (N). A familiar formula linking the variances of these three variables is:

$$(14) \qquad \text{var}(X) = \text{var}(I) + \text{var}(N) + 2\text{cov}(I,N).$$

The top half of table 5.3 presents a decomposition of variance as in (12) for the interwar and postwar periods, and for the two halves of the postwar. The bottom half of the table exhibits a parallel decomposition for the four components of total investment.

The enormous decline in the variance of all components in the postwar period is immediately apparent. There is no decline, however, in the ratio var(I)/var(X), which is slightly higher in 1947–65 and 1947–83 than in 1919–41. The most interesting contrast between the interwar and postwar periods is in the covariance term. The positive covariance between I and N contributes almost half of the total variance of real GNP in 1919–41, whereas it contributes a negligible fraction in 1947–65 and is actually negative in the postwar period taken as a whole. One may conjecture that whereas the interwar period was dominated by the cyclical behavior of private spending, much of the variance of noninvestment in the postwar period was contributed by government spending. The negative covariance of I and N in the postwar period may suggest that investment was "crowded out" by major increases in government spending.

The bottom half of the table shows that about two-thirds of the total variance of investment in the interwar period was contributed by the

Table 5.3   Decomposition of Variance: Real GNP, Investment, and
             Noninvestment, Percentage Ratios to Natural Real GNP

	1919:1 to 1941:3	1947:1 to 1965:4	1966:1 to 1983:4	1947:1 to 1983:4
Total real GNP				
Variance (X)	157.4	7.3	15.8	12.0
Variance (I)	38.9	2.0	2.2	3.2
Variance (N)	45.7	4.9	10.6	11.2
2 covariance (I, N)	72.8	0.4	3.0	−2.4
Variance (I)/variance (X)	0.25	0.27	0.14	0.27
Variance (N)/variance (X)	0.29	0.67	0.67	0.93
Four types of investment				
Variance (I)	38.9	2.0	2.2	3.2
Variance (PDE)	2.0	0.4	0.3	0.9
Variance (RS)	2.7	0.3	0.6	0.6
Variance (NRS)	5.7	0.1	0.3	0.2
Variance (CD)	1.6	0.4	0.4	1.4
Residual covariance terms	26.9	0.8	0.6	0.1

covariance term, that is, a shock common to all investment types rather than to only one. In the two halves of the postwar period the covariance terms contribute less than half, and they contribute virtually nothing for the postwar period taken as a whole. The largest "own variance" in the full postwar period is for consumer durables, but the smaller value of this term for the two separate halves of the postwar period indicates the dominance of a trend effect. Nonresidential structures shifted from contributing the largest own variance in the interwar period to the smallest in the postwar period.

5.4   Regression Equations Explaining Total Investment Expenditures

5.4.1   Will the Real Accelerator Please Stand Up?

The starting point of our hybrid methodology is to determine the specification for a reduced-form investment equation that seems "reasonable" a priori. Our goal is then to use the estimated reduced-form equations to suggest "data coherent" ways of moving to more structural models and interpretations. In arriving at such interpretations, we recognize the conventional wisdom that many structural models may imply the same reduced form. However, there is a similar problem with structural models. Quite dissimilar "structural" models may result when the same general economic phenomenon is interpreted by different authors.

For example, a starting point in many studies of investment behavior, and an ending point in some, is the accelerator hypothesis. In its simplest form, dating back to Clark (1917), it explains the level of real investment as a function of the change in real GNP. But this apparently straightforward idea does not imply a single "structural" specification. The change in real GNP may enter only as a current value or as a combination of current and lagged values. Or the investigation may start from the "flexible accelerator" hypothesis, in which investment depends on the current level of output and one lagged value of the capital stock. Or one might adopt a more general dynamic specification, as in table 5.4 below, that allows several lagged values of investment to enter as well as current and lagged changes in output. Since the coefficient on lagged investment turns out to be roughly unity, this last alternative amounts to a regression explaining the *change* of investment spending, in which case the accelerator hypothesis would call for the output variable to enter as a *second* difference. A rational expectations approach to the accelerator, as in Abel and Blanchard (1983), would imply a reduced form in which levels of *expected* future output appear, rather than lagged values. These expectations may be functions of many variables in addition to lagged output. An extreme version of the expectational approach to investment behavior might lead to the conclusion that investment is a random walk, parallel to Hall's (1978) interpretation of consumption as a random walk.

All these models are merely alternative formulations of a single underlying structure, the accelerator mechanism. However, each model results in a different specification for the appropriate reduced-form equation. This proliferation of structural models is also a problem with the other mechanisms that are claimed to be important for explaining investment, for example, the Q approach. To avoid losing sight of our objectives by examining a multitude of different formulations, we choose to set up "straw man" reduced forms that are relatively unrestricted and allow alternative explanatory variables suggested by alternative theories to enter on equal terms.

5.4.2 Contribution of the Accelerator and the Cost of Capital

We begin by examining reduced-form regressions for each of the four individual categories of total investment: consumer durables, residential structures, producers' durable equipment, and nonresidential structures. We begin at a disaggregated level and subsequently study the consequences of alternative aggregation schemes. In table 5.4 and later tables, the full sample period of available quarterly data is divided into 1919–41 and 1947–83. In preliminary work a break was allowed in the middle of the postwar period at 1965, but Chow tests rejected the hypothesis of a structural change for most equations, and so here the postwar period is treated as a single entity. There are insufficient degrees of freedom available to test for a structural break within the interwar period at 1929. Chow tests indicate a decisive break in structure at World War II.[16]

Our reduced-form equations omit the lagged capital stock (K_{t-1}) term, which appears in (3), for two reasons. First, an identity links the lagged capital stock and lagged investment, precluding an investment equation containing several lagged values of investment from also including several lagged values of the capital stock. Second, although a single lagged value of the capital stock may appear, preliminary tests indicated statistical insignificance in every sample period.

Tables 5.4 and 5.5 are each arranged in two sections, corresponding to the two sample periods (interwar and postwar). Each cell in the tables contains results for each of the four categories of investment spending in the following format: the first line of each section gives the sum of coefficients with its significance level, and the second line exhibits the significance level for an F-test on the exclusion of all lags of that explanatory variable. A blank on the second line indicates that the .10 level of statistical significance was not attained.

The first line for each investment type in tables 5.4 and 5.5 presents the regression results for what might be termed a "naive accelerator/cost of capital" specification of the investment equation. The log level of investment spending (I/X^N) is regressed on eight lagged first differences of real noninvestment GNP, $\Delta N/X^N$, and eight lagged values of first differences of the appropriate real cost of capital series ($\Delta C/P$). In the regressions involving household investment in table 5.5, real personal disposable income, $\Delta Y^D/X^N$, replaces real GNP, and eight lags of the first difference of the real Baa interest rate are used as a proxy for the price of investment. In line 1 both the $\bar{R}^2$ and Durbin-Watson statistic are very low for all categories over all periods, indicating a poor fit and serially correlated errors. The "accelerator" variable passes the exclusion test only for producers' durable equipment in the interwar period and for residential structures in the postwar. An even poorer showing is exhibited by the "cost of capital," which passes the exclusion test only for postwar residential structures.

Line 2 in each block is identical to line 1, except that four lags of the dependent variable are included as additional regressors. The results from these regressions further weaken the case for the accelerator and the price of investment. For all categories and all sample periods the lagged dependent variables terms enter significantly at the .01 level.

---

16. Recall that quantitative controls during World War II preclude a meaningful analysis of investment behavior during that period. Further, some of the series used for our data interpolation are not available after 1941; thus our data series have not been created for the 1942–46 interval.

Both the accelerator and the price of investment become insignificant for most types and sample periods. While the accelerator variable has explanatory power for postwar producer durables, and for consumer durables in both periods, the sums of the coefficients are insignificantly different from zero in every equation. Overall this formulation of the two traditionally dominant explanations of investment behavior fares poorly in both the interwar and the postwar periods.

5.4.3   Contribution of Q and Real M1

Since the sum of coefficients on lagged investment in line 2 of each block is close to unity, the equation amounts to an explanation of the behavior of the first difference of investment. To be consistent with the first difference format, in line 3 the accelerator is expressed as the first difference of the first difference of real noninvestment GNP, $\Delta\Delta N/X^N$, and the remaining explanatory variables are entered as lagged values of their first differences. Noninvestment GNP and the cost of capital or interest rate terms enter with eight lags, while the remaining explanatory variables enter with four lags. Our measure for Tobin's average Q has no significant explanatory power, except for postwar nonresidential structures, and as often as not enters with the wrong sign. The change in C/P continues to be insignificant in the exclusion tests, although the sum of coefficients is significantly negative for the two durables categories in the postwar period.

Previous research by King (1983) and Sims (1983) has emphasized a distinction between the role of inside and outside money as a determinant of real output. In the work of King this distinction is implemented by entering the two multiplicative components of M1, the money multiplier and monetary base $(M1/P = m(B/P))$, separately in VAR models for total output. We can investigate the same issue here and inquire whether the effect of monetary changes on investment occurs through the multiplier, the base, or a mixture of the two. The first difference specification for the explanatory variables suggests that we should split the change in M1 into the level of the multiplier times the first difference in the base $(m\Delta B/P)$, and the level of the base times the first difference in the multiplier $(B/P\Delta m)$. Both components enter significantly into the equations for producer and consumer durables, interwar and postwar. The change in the money multiplier has moderate explanatory power for both structures categories in the postwar period, as well as for nonresidential structures in the interwar period.

5.4.4   Other Specifications

The final reduced-form specification appears in line 3 or 4 of each block. The specification in line 4 differs from that in line 3 only in

Table 5.4   Equations for Business Investment: Interwar and Postwar Sample Periods

			Explanatory Lagged Variables						
I (1)	ΔN (2)	$\Delta\Delta N$ (3)	$\Delta C/P$ (4)	ΔQ (5)	$m\Delta B/P$ (6)	$B/P\Delta m$ (7)	$\bar{R}^2$ (8)	SEE (9)	DW (10)
1921:2 to 1941:3									
Producer durables									
1.	.95*** *		.16				.08	1.26	.181
2. .96*** ***	−.06		−.09				.93	0.34	
3. .92*** ***		−.03	.14**	.01**	.36*** ***	.57*** ***	.96	0.28	
4. .93*** ***		−.14 *		.01*	.27*** ***	.34*** ***	.95	0.29	
Nonresidential structures									
1.	.56		.09				−.19	2.70	.048
2. .98*** ***	.09		−.07				.96	0.51	
3. .93*** ***		.30	.17	−.00	.12	.82**	.96	0.48	
4. .95*** ***		.19		−.00	.05	.46**	.96	0.47	

1949:2 to 1983:4

Producer durables

1.		.07		−.25			−.11	1.03	.057
2.	.98***	.08		−.27***			.95	0.21	
	***	***							
3.	1.00***	.51***	−.22**	.39**	.55***		.96	0.19	
	***	***		**	***				

Nonresidential structures

1.		.30**		−.30*			−.02	0.486	.066
2.	.97***	.01		−.04			.96		
	***								
3.	.98***	.02	−.01	.01***	.06	.20***	.97	0.085	
	***			***		*			

Note: Numbers shown in each cell are sums of coefficients, and asterisks next to these numbers indicate significance levels of the sums (* for .10, ** for .05, and *** for .01). Asterisks below the numbers indicate with the same notation the joint significance of all lags in an exclusion test. All equations include, in addition to the listed variables, a constant term. Durbin-Watson statistics are now shown for equations containing lagged dependent variables.

Table 5.5   Equations for Household Investment: Interwar and Postwar Sample Periods

		Explanatory Lagged Variables								
	I (1)	ΔY^D (2)	$\Delta\Delta Y^D$ (3)	Δr (4)	ΔQ (5)	$m\Delta B/P$ (6)	$B/P\Delta m$ (7)	$\bar{R}^2$ (8)	SEE (9)	DW (10)
1921:2 to 1941:3										
Consumer durables										
1.		.64***		.12				.08	1.22	.102
2.	.97*** ***	.04 **		−.09 *				.95	0.28	
3.	.94*** ***		.00	.08 *	.002	.23** *	.46** *	.96	0.26	
4.	.96*** ***		.07		.002	.21** *	.34** *	.95	0.28	
Residential structures										
1.		.48*		.21				−.16	1.79	.072
2.	.98*** ***	−.00		−.08				.96	0.31	
3.	.98*** ***		−.11	−.06	−.12**	.11	.33	.97	0.31	
4.	.96*** ***		−.21	.05		.15	.34	.96	0.31	

1949:2 to 1983:4

Consumer durables

1.		.91*		.17				−.06	1.18	.098
2.	.97***	−.13**		−.31				.92	0.33	
3.	.95***		.56	−.46**	−.00	.86***	1.27***	.93	0.30	
4.	.96***		.60*	−.47**		.83***	1.23***	.93	0.30	

Residential structures

1.		.84***		−2.24***				.22	0.72	.231
2.	.94***	−.08*		−.20*				.95	0.18	
3.	.93***		−.03	−.22*	−.004*	.02	.22	.96	0.16	
4.	.92***		−.05	.22*		−.05	.12	.96	0.16	

Note: See note to table 5.4.

excluding variables that are significant but have the wrong signs. Both the accelerator and the price of investment are included along with average Q and the monetary variables. The accelerator variable is significant only for postwar producers' durable equipment. We experimented with alternative specifications of the final reduced form in order to check the robustness of our results. In these tests the cost of capital term in the business investment equations was replaced by the real Baa rate, but this rate was never significant and as often as not carried the wrong sign.

A variant of the "expectational accelerator" was also estimated by a two-stage procedure. Time series models for noninvestment GNP and personal disposable income were estimated and used to generate k-step ahead forecasts. Eight leads of these forecasts, in various transformations, were used as explanatory variables but were always insignificant, often with the wrong sign, for all but postwar producers' durable equipment. This set of results implies that the significant monetary variables in tables 5.4 and 5.5 enter *directly* into the determination of investment spending, rather than *indirectly* through an effect on expectations of future output.

5.4.5   Summary of Disaggregated Results

Perhaps the most surprising result of these initial reduced-form estimates is the small explanatory role accorded conventional variables and the large role given to unconventional variables like the real money supply. The poor showing of the interest rate and cost of capital, combined with the singular importance of average Q for nonresidential structures, leads one to suspect that the financing decision is an important determinant of investment expenditures. The broad role played by the money multiplier may indicate that credit rationing, rather than interest rate changes, is the primary constraint in the financing decision. This view is consistent with that expressed in Roosa (1951) as to the dominant channel through which monetary policy affects the economy.

The similarities in the behavior of the two structures and the two durable goods categories suggest that aggregation by asset type rather than by decision maker is preferable. This approach to disaggregation would also be in accord with Tobin's asset approach, insofar as durable goods are normally shorter lived than structures. However, this approach is at odds with the conventional structural approach to investment. With its focus on the investment decision, the traditional approach has always aggregated by decision maker (i.e., household vs. business) rather than by character of the asset (i.e., structures vs. equipment).

5.4.6   Aggregation Schemes

Table 5.6 displays our basic equation for two alternative aggregation schemes, household/business and durables/structures. The household/business aggregation scheme is not particularly successful. In the interwar period both categories appear to be autonomous, with only lagged "own values" passing the exclusion test (as well as the money multiplier in the business equation). Both real monetary variables become highly significant for the two categories in the postwar period. The only difference in behavior between household and business investment appears in the postwar period, when business investment exhibits a strong accelerator effect. If we were to ignore real balance effects, as does most of the literature, then aggregation by decision maker would result in a pair of highly autonomous investment series in the interwar period. Stated another way, this aggregation scheme would indicate that the decision maker does not respond to relevant economic variables.

Aggregation by the asset character of investment leads to more illuminating results. Durable equipment and structures exhibit marked differences in behavior in both sample periods. Structures investment for 1919–41 is quite autonomous, but durables expenditures exhibit sensitivity to interest rates (with the wrong sign) and to real monetary variables. More important is the finding that real money balances are highly significant in explaining both investment categories in the postwar period. Durable goods are sensitive to the accelerator and interest rates (with the correct sign), whereas structures depend significantly on the average Q variable. This result may indicate the importance of the different financing methods that are used for equipment and structures. One might think of short-lived assets as financed to a large extent by internally generated funds, that is, retained earnings and disposable income, while investment in structures may depend heavily on conditions in the bond and security markets.

Using the alternative aggregation criterion of asset durability produces the most sensible results in table 5.6. Investment behavior is found to differ between short- and long-lived assets in a way that is statistically significant. The accelerator and the Baa rate are both important for investment in durables, while structures (dominated by the nonresidential category) respond to average Q. These results provide evidence supporting the importance of financial conditions for investment decisions. What is surprising is the way the conventional investment literature, with its emphasis on the business investment decision, has overemphasized disaggregation by decision maker and has glossed over the importance of the asset characteristics of investment and the role of real monetary variables.

Table 5.6   Equations for Alternative Aggregation Schemes: Interwar and Postwar Sample Periods

	I (1)	$\Delta\Delta N$ (2)	$\Delta\Delta Y^D$ (3)	Δr (4)	$\Delta C/P$ (5)	ΔQ (6)	$m\Delta B/P$ (7)	$B/P\Delta m$ (8)	$\bar{R}^2$ (9)	SEE (10)
				Explanatory Lagged Variables						
1921:3 to 1941:3										
Household	.96*** ***		−.18	.07		−.01	0.27*	0.75**	.98	.442
Business	.95*** ***	.26			.23	.01	0.41	1.11** *	.97	.647
Durables	.91*** ***	−.22		.32** **		.01	0.48*** ***	1.07*** ***	.97	.430
Structures	.94*** ***	.43		.14		−.01	0.27	1.36**	.97	.754
1949:1 to 1983:4										
Household	.86*** ***		.31	−.77***		−.02 *	1.16*** ***	1.96*** ***	.89	.399
Business	1.01*** ***	.46** ***			−.24**	.03** ***	0.45 ***	0.74*** ***	.94	.222
Durables	.98*** ***	.81** ***		−.97*** **		.02	1.67*** ***	2.23*** ***	.96	.401
Structures	.97*** ***	−.16		−.24		.01 ***	0.16 ***	0.60*** ***	.97	.198

Note: See note to table 5.4.

5.5   Investment in a Vector Autoregression Model

5.5.1   Correlations among Contemporaneous Innovations

The equations estimated in tables 5.4 to 5.6 investigate the feedback from the various lagged explanatory variables to components of investment, but they say nothing about the relationships among contemporaneous innovations in the variables, or about the feedback from investment to the explanatory variables. These issues can be addressed by analyzing a vector autoregression (VAR) system that contains the primary variables of interest. We economize on space by restricting attention to a VAR model containing six variables—real investment in structures (*ISTR*), real investment in durable goods (*IDG*), real non-investment GNP (*N*), the real money base (*B/P*), the M1 money multiplier (*m*), and the real Baa interest rate (*r*). For the interwar period the interest rate variable in table 5.6 has the incorrect (positive) sign in the equations for both *ISTR* and *IDG*, leading us to choose a five-variable system omitting the interest rate for 1920–41.

All variables (except *m* and *r*) are once again expressed as ratios to natural real GNP (X^N). To maintain the symmetry required for the VAR system, all variables are expressed as first differences, in contrast to tables 5.4 to 5.6, where investment is expressed as a ratio, output as a second difference, and the other variables as first differences. Extra degrees of freedom allow the inclusion of eight lags on all variables in the postwar period, as opposed to four lags in the interwar period.

Columns in table 5.7 correspond to each of the six variables in the VAR system. A slash (/) divides the interwar result from the postwar result in both the top and bottom sections of the table. The dashes (—) indicate the exclusion of the interest rate in the interwar model. The top section shows correlations among contemporaneous innovations. There is a uniformly high correlation between the two components of investment, *ISTR* and *IDG*. Another similarity between the interwar and postwar periods is the positive correlation between the money multiplier (*m*) and both *ISTR* and *IDG*, the negative correlation between *IDG* and the monetary base (*B/P*), and the high negative correlation between the base and the multiplier. Perhaps the most important difference between the interwar and postwar periods is the sharp decline in the correlation of durable goods investment (*IDG*) with noninvestment GNP (*N*). This is similar to the decomposition of variance in table 5.3 above and may indicate that *N* in the interwar period is dominated by a common impulse to private spending that also influenced *IDG*, whereas in the postwar period *N* was more affected by defense expenditures in the Korea and Vietnam periods that had no impact or even a negative impact on *IDG*.

Table 5.7   Correlation Coefficients and Exogeneity Tests in Basic VAR Models (Interwar/Postwar)

	ΔISTR (1)	ΔIDG (2)	ΔN (3)	ΔB/P (4)	Δm (5)	Δr (6)
Correlations						
ΔIDG	.35/ .35					
ΔN	−.04/ .09	.51/ .04				
ΔB/P	.09/ .18	−.17/−.17	−.29/ .17			
Δm	.19/ .25	.24/ .28	.30/−.07	−.54/−.39		
Δr	—/−.26	—/−.15	—/−.00	—/−.30	—/−.21	
Exogeneity Test						
ΔISTR	—/	—/	*/	—/	/**	—/
ΔIDG	/**	**/***	/***	***/**	**/**	/*
ΔN	—/	—/	/*	**/***	—/	—/***
ΔB/P	—/	—/	—/	***/***	***/**	—/
Δm	/*	—/	—/	/**	*/**	—/
Δr	—/	—/	—/	—/	—/*	—/

Note: Asterisks designate significance levels of .10 (*), .05 (**), and .01 (***). Blanks indicate that the interest rate is excluded from the model for the interwar period.

The correlations of the base and the multiplier with noninvestment GNP change signs in the postwar period. This is suggestive of a change in the behavior of monetary policy between the two periods. Another "structural" shift is suggested by the change of the coefficient of the interest rate on *IDG* from positive (shown in table 5.6 but not table 5.7) to negative. This should be interpreted in conjunction with the sharp decline in the correlation of *N* and *IDG* in the postwar period. These facts may indicate that durable goods expenditures in the interwar tended to be more constrained by income or retained earnings, whereas in the postwar period the availability and price of credit was relatively more important.

5.5.2 Multivariate Exogeneity Tests

The bottom section of table 5.7 displays significance levels for the contribution of each explanatory variable in each equation. Explanatory variables are represented by the six columns, and dependent variables by the six lines. Asterisks denote the same significance levels as in tables 5.4 to 5.6 and are calculated from *F*-ratios on the joint exclusion of all lags of a particular variable. Often such tables reveal a highly significant set of diagonal elements, reflecting highly significant lagged dependent variables in the VAR equations. This occurs here only for *IDG*, *B/P*, and *m*. The insignificance of the other diagonal elements may reflect the fact that all variables in the model are expressed as first differences.

Investment in structures appears to be relatively exogenous in both periods, with modest feedback from noninvestment GNP in the interwar and the money multiplier in the postwar. Durable goods investment exhibits substantial feedback from several variables in either period or both, and in this sense is much less "autonomous" than investment in structures. The pattern of monetary influences on *IDG* and *N* differs. While *IDG* reflects significant feedback from the base and the multiplier in both periods, *N* reflects feedback from the base in both periods, the interest rate in the postwar period, and the multiplier in neither. A notable feature of the pattern of exogeneity is the independence of the money multiplier and the interest rate from almost all the other variables. In the postwar period the interest rate is totally independent of all the remaining variables, feeding into only *IDG* and *N*. The channel of influence from the interest rate to investment, if any, appears to be indirect, running through noninvestment GNP, with only a weak direct effect in the postwar period. The pattern of these exogeneity results may suggest the existence of two impulse sources in the business cycle, one financial (interest rates and money multiplier) and the other real (investment in structures), whose effects interact through the propagation mechanism represented here by the remaining variables.

5.5.3 Innovation Accounting

VAR modeling techniques are often criticized for the ambiguity inherent in the a priori ordering of the variables necessary to carry out the usual "innovation accounting" exercise. However, the allocation of the variance of the investment categories between "own" innovations and innovations in other explanatory variables is of interest in any investigation of the role played by investment in business cycles. As with our choice of aggregation schemes, we allow our earlier empirical results to suggest "appropriate" orderings of the variables. The equations estimated in table 5.6 suggest that investment in structures is quite autonomous, a result reinforced by the exogeneity tests of table 5.7. Our basic model, as it appears in the top half of table 5.8, places structures (ISTR) first in the ordering, followed by investment in durables (IDG). Gestation lags in both types of investment make it plausible that at least one quarter is required before investment spending can be influenced by changes in noninvestment real GNP (N), the real base (B/P), the multiplier (m), or interest rate (r). Although our empirical results cast doubt on other ordering schemes, a priori notions about the importance of autonomous government spending in the postwar period might suggest an ordering with noninvestment real GNP first, followed by investment in structures, then durables. Results for this ordering appear in the bottom half of table 5.8. The interest rate

Table 5.8   **Innovation Accounting at Sixteen-Quarter Forecast Horizon in Two VAR Models (Interwar/Postwar)**

Dependent Variable	$\Delta ISTR$ (1)	ΔIDG (2)	ΔN (3)	$\Delta B/P$ (4)	Δm (5)	Δr (6)
$\Delta ISTR$	76.8/58.0	4.4/ 4.2	7.7/ 5.6	3.3/ 2.8	7.8/22.5	—/ 7.0
ΔIDG	13.2/15.8	44.4/45.4	10.0/ 8.1	8.3/ 5.2	24.1/11.7	—/13.7
ΔN	7.8/10.0	20.9/ 3.3	47.6/56.6	10.5/ 6.7	13.2/10.4	—/13.0
$\Delta B/P$	6.7/ 4.8	4.9/ 7.3	11.7/ 7.1	63.0/68.6	13.7/ 8.3	—/ 3.9
Δm	13.2/ 7.4	8.6/ 5.4	13.5/ 6.5	24.7/20.5	40.0/49.4	—/10.8
Δr	—/10.3	—/ 7.1	—/ 2.2	—/ 7.4	—/11.0	—/62.0

Dependent Variable	ΔN (1)	$\Delta ISTR$ (2)	ΔIDG (3)	$\Delta B/P$ (4)	Δm (5)	Δr (6)
ΔN	64.8/57.5	7.7/ 9.1	3.8/ 3.3	10.5/ 6.7	13.2/10.4	—/13.0
$\Delta ISTR$	5.3/ 6.6	76.9/57.1	6.7/ 4.1	3.3/ 2.8	7.8/22.5	—/ 7.0
ΔIDG	19.6/ 8.8	13.7/15.0	34.3/45.5	8.3/ 5.2	24.1/11.7	—/13.7
$\Delta B/P$	13.5/ 7.8	7.0/ 4.1	2.8/ 7.4	63.0/68.6	13.7/ 8.3	—/ 3.9
Δm	16.1/ 6.5	13.8/ 7.4	5.4/ 5.4	24.7/20.5	40.0/49.4	—/10.8
Δr	—/ 2.1	—/10.5	—/ 7.0	—/11.0	—/ 7.4	—/62.0

Note: As in table 5.7, dashes indicate that the interest rate is excluded from the model for the interwar period.

is placed last in both orderings, since the theory of efficient markets suggests an instantaneous response to innovations in other variables. B/P and m are intermediate variables but are capable of moving quickly, particularly if the Federal Reserve is operating to stabilize the interest rate.

In the ordering with structures first, the own innovation of structures accounts for most its variance at the sixteen-quarter forecast horizon in both sample periods. This own contribution is not altered in the slightest by placing N first in the ordering. Structures appear to be virtually autonomous, with a highly significant influence only from the money multiplier in the postwar period. $ISTR$ acounts for more than 10% of the variance of IDG in both periods, N and r in the postwar, and m in the interwar. In an alternative version of the model in which the variables are expressed in levels (not shown in table 5.8), the role of $ISTR$ is substantially greater, accounting for at least one-third of the variance of almost all the other variables in both periods.

Innovations in IDG account for more of the variance of N than vice versa in the interwar period, which might be interpreted as indicating that the multiplier was a stronger influence than the accelerator during that interval. Investment in durables displays substantial feedback both from investment in structures and from the money multiplier in both periods. That the money multiplier has a larger effect on the three categories of spending ($ISTR$, IDG, and N) than the two other financial variables (B/P and r) may indicate that the collapse of the banking system in 1929–33 and disintermediation in the postwar period were important channels of influence, proxied by the money multiplier, of the financial system on real expenditures. As mentioned above, the ordering in the bottom of table 5.8 that places N first does not change these results significantly, and this seems to support our argument for the exogeneity of investment in structures.

5.5.4 Historical Decomposition of Variance in Both Investment Types

A more revealing display of the implications of the VAR model is contained in the historical decomposition of each series in the system over each of the sample periods. The ordering used in arriving at these decompositions was that of our basic VAR model that places the explanatory variables in the order shown in the top half of table 5.8 ($ISTR$, IDG, N, B/P, m, and r). To limit the number of diagrams, we present only the decomposition of the two categories of investment—interwar structures in figure 5.4 and durable goods in figure 5.5, followed by postwar structures in figure 5.6 and durable goods in figure 5.7.

The top frame in each diagram compares the actual time path of investment with a ''projection'' that summarizes the net effect of the constant terms in all of the equations. The contribution of each of the other variables in the system then appears below. These contributions refer not just to the lagged values times the estimated coefficients in the *IDG* equation alone, but rather to the contributions of the inno-vations in each variable to investment behavior, taking account of *all* channels of feedback working through the six-equation model (recall that interest rates are excluded in the interwar period).

The predominant role of own innovations in the structures invest-ment (*ISTR*) process is evident in figure 5.4. There is a high plateau in the own innovations series in 1926–27, a gradual downward movement in 1928–29, and a sharp plunge beginning in 1929:3, before the fourth-quarter stock market debacle. Equally interesting is that the own in-

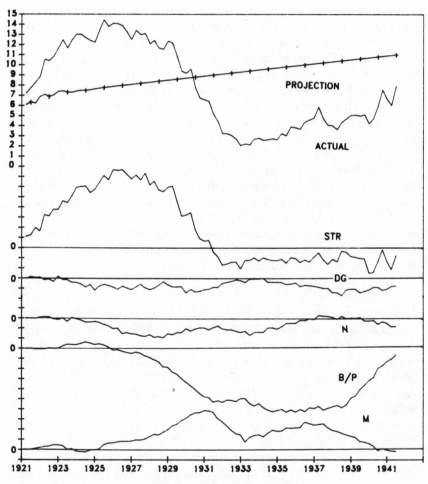

Fig. 5.4   Decomposition of structures, 1921–41.

novation series remains negative throughout 1931–41, supporting the interpretation of "overbuilding" in the 1920s that required a long period of subsequent adjustment in the 1930s.

Two other variables display interesting patterns in figure 5.4. The real monetary base (B/P) makes a major negative contribution in 1927–31 and a positive contribution in 1938–41. The latter episode is easy to understand in light of the large inflow of gold to the United States during this period. However, the decline in the contribution in B/P in 1927–31 may seem puzzling, since nominal B varied little in the Great Contraction of 1929–33, while the price level (P) declined substantially. The behavior of the B/P contribution can be explained in terms of the "projection" for B/P (not shown), which displays a sharp upward trend during the entire period 1920–41 in response to the doubling of B/P between 1920 and 1941. The actual value of B/P is below this "projection" continuously from 1920 to 1938 and then above it from 1939 to 1941. Thus the VAR historical decomposition algorithm interprets the slow increase in the real base in 1927–31 as being an actual decline relative to trend, and this is reflected in the contribution of base innovations to structures investment in figure 5.4. The other variable making an important contribution is the money multiplier, which exhibits a sharp decline during the period of monetary contraction and bank failures between 1931 and 1933, as well as after the increase in reserve requirements in 1936–37. The role of the multiplier makes our analysis compatible with the emphasis on the financial crisis in Bernanke (1983b).

Figure 5.5 shows the interwar historical decomposition of innovations to equipment investment. Compared with figure 5.4 for interwar structures, the own innovations in *IDG* are relatively less important and the innovations in the monetary base and money multiplier are more important. To some extent the innovations in the base and multiplier are offsetting, and this reflects in part the upward trend of the base and downward trend of the multiplier in the interwar period. However, we recall from tables 5.4 to 5.6 that both the base and the multiplier have consistently positive coefficients in the interwar regression equations for expenditures on durables.

Figures 5.6 and 5.7 decompose the variance of *ISTR* and *IDG* for the postwar years. Note that in these figures the scale is compressed horizontally and expanded vertically, since the ratio of investment to natural output varied over so much smaller a range in the postwar period. Figure 5.6 for postwar structures shares with the interwar figure 5.4 a predominant role for own innovations. However, figure 5.7 for durables is quite different from the other historical decompositions. Structures innovations play a much more important role in explaining postwar durables expenditure fluctuations than the own innovations in

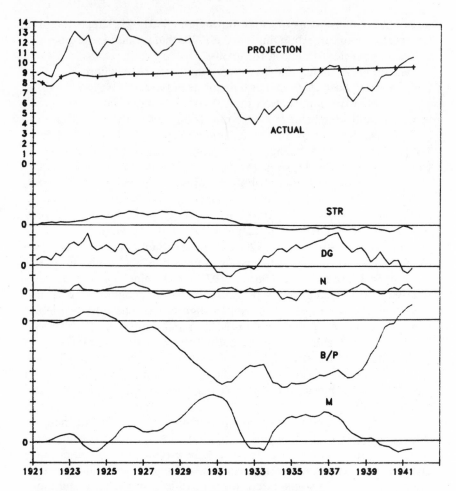

Fig. 5.5   Decomposition of equipment, 1921–41.

durables. Further, there is a substantial role for real interest rate innovations in figure 5.7, supporting the highly significant negative coefficients on the real interest rate variable in tables 5.4 to 5.6. The effect
of high real interest rates in 1981–83 in reducing investment expenditures is particularly noticeable.

   Thus any conclusion in this paper that investment contains a large
autonomous component must refer mainly to structures, whereas durable equipment investment displays substantial feedback both from
structures investment and from financial variables. It does not seem
surprising that there should be feedback from structures investment to
equipment investment, since the two activities are complementary.
Construction of a new factory, office building, or shopping center re-

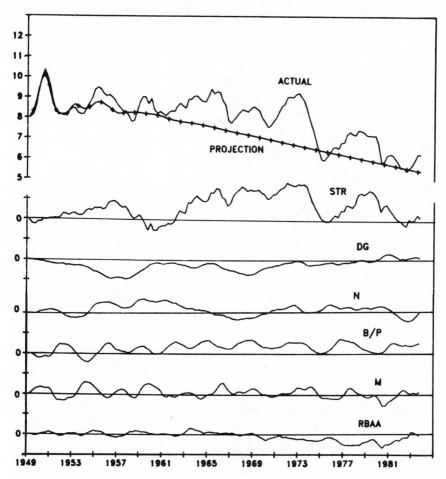

Fig. 5.6   Decomposition of structures, 1949–83.

quires investment in equipment, just as residential construction stimulates investment in furniture, appliances, and other components of consumer durables expenditures.

5.5.5   The Temin "Autonomous Shift" in 1930

An important part of Temin's (1976) interpretation of the first stage of the Great Contraction of 1929–33 is an autonomous shift in consumption in 1930, which he identified by estimating an annual consumption function. Our purpose here is not to review the controversy stirred up by Temin's result (see Mayer 1980), but rather to reexamine his hypothesis using the more definitive microscope provided by our quarterly data set. Table 5.9 exhibits quarter-by-quarter residuals from

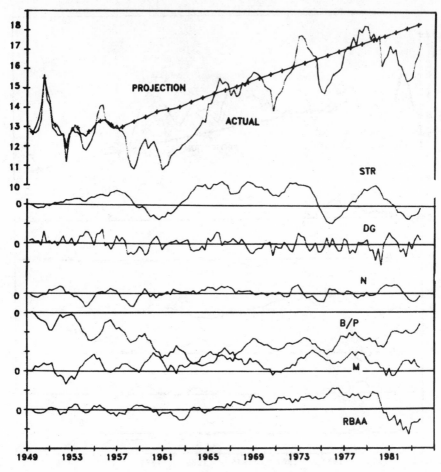

Fig. 5.7   Decomposition of equipment, 1949–83.

our interwar VAR models for the sixteen quarters covering 1929–32. Asterisks are used to mark off residuals greater in size than 1.0 times the standard error of estimate (see note to table 5.9).

The five variables of the model are the first differences of, respectively, investment in structures (*ISTR*), investment in durables (*IDG*), noninvestment real GNP (*N*), the real monetary base (*B/P*), and the money multiplier. All variables (except *m*) are expressed as percentage ratios to natural real GNP, and beneath the residuals the table shows the level of these ratios in 1929:2, ranging from 5.6% for the monetary base to 77.6% for noninvestment real GNP. Here we treat the behavior of noninvestment real GNP as representing "consumption," actually nondurable consumption, since in 1929 nondurable consumption made

Table 5.9   **Residuals ("Innovations") in Interwar VAR Model: 1929:1 to 1932:4**

Cycle	$\Delta ISTR$ (1)	ΔIDG (2)	ΔN (3)	$\Delta B/P$ (4)	Δm (5)
1929:1	0.77*	0.05	1.10	−0.38*	0.12*
1929:2	0.10	−0.29	−0.89	−0.10	−0.04
1929:3	−1.29**	0.41	3.10**	−0.08	0.02
1929:4	−1.20**	−1.11**	−1.07	−0.21	−0.03
1930:1	−0.14	−0.13	−1.45	−0.08	0.04
1930:2	−0.03	−0.48	−1.35	−0.11	0.02
1930:3	−1.17**	−0.36	−0.11	−0.22	−0.05
1930:4	−0.12	−0.19	−0.55	−0.01	0.01
1931:1	−0.21	−0.46	0.81	0.34*	−0.07
1931:2	−0.21	0.04	1.27	−0.14	−0.09*
1931:3	−0.54	−0.45	−2.01*	0.40*	−0.21**
1931:4	0.10	0.09	−0.65	0.04	−0.09*
1932:1	−0.69	0.32	0.10	0.21	−0.04
1932:2	0.08	0.10	−0.35	0.07	−0.01
1932:3	0.63	0.15	−1.42	−0.35*	0.06
1932:4	0.34	0.02	0.67	0.29	0.03
Level in					
1929:2	12.2	12.2	77.6	5.6	4.4
Cumulative residuals					
1929–30	−3.08	−2.10	−1.22	−1.19	0.17
1931–32	−0.46	−0.23	−1.58	0.86	−0.42
Cumulative residuals as percentage of 1929:2 level					
1929–30	−25.2	−17.2	−1.6	−20.5	3.9
1931–32	−3.8	−1.9	−2.0	14.8	−9.5

Note: Asterisks are used to denote residuals as follows: (*) indicates between 1.0 and 1.5 times the sample period standard error, and (**) indicates more than 1.5 times the standard error.

up 85.2% of N, and it accounted for 74.6% of the decline in N from 1929 to 1930.

The emphasis in this paper on autonomous movements in investment, particularly structures investment, is supported in table 5.9. There were three large negative innovations in 1929–30 to *ISTR*, including one in 1929:3, one quarter before the business downturn and stock market crash. There was a large negative innovation in *IDG* in 1929:4. The cumulative residuals of *ISTR* and *IDG* in 1929–30 amount, respectively, to −25.2% and −17.2% of their *levels* in 1929:2. In contrast, the only large N residual for 1929–30 is *positive* in 1929:3. The cumulative N residuals in 1929–30 amount to only −1.6% of its level in 1929:2. Thus we find no evidence that negative residuals for nondurables consumption played a key role in the initial stages of the Great Contraction.

Two other interesting results are evident in table 5.9. First, there are substantial negative innovations in the real monetary base beginning as early as 1929:1 and cumulating to −20.5% of the 1929:2 level in 1929–30. Second, the largest cumulative negative residuals in the period 1931–32 are contributed by the money multiplier, supporting a role for bank failures and the credit contraction in aggravating the contraction. Especially interesting is the large negative multiplier innovation in 1931:3, the quarter when the Fed tightened its policy following Britain's departure from the gold standard.

Overall, these results are consistent with our interpretation of two sources of the business cycle, real and financial, with the negative innovations in real investment playing a dominant role in 1929–30, and with the nature of the negative financial innovations shifting from a contribution of the monetary base in 1929–30 to one by the money multiplier in 1931–32.

5.6 Summary and Conclusion

5.6.1 Methodology and Data Description

Most of the tests of "structural" investment equations that have been carried out in the literature embody what Sims (1980a) calls "incredible" exclusion restrictions. The literature on the neoclassical investment paradigm embodies prior assumptions about the form of the production function. In its putty/putty version it neglects expectations entirely, and in its putty/clay version it fails to allow time series aggregate variables to play multiple roles in the formation of expectations in different phases of the investment process. As a result, coefficients on variables like lagged output and interest rates cannot be interpreted in the structural way that has been typical in the literature.

The Tobin Q theory starts from a plausible point of departure but then takes itself too seriously, allowing *only* Q to influence investment. There seems to be no reason the single Q variable, whether or not it is measured with error, should embody all influences of other variables on the investment process. Our discussion emphasizes in particular the role of asymmetric adjustment costs, as well as the trade-off firms face between costly alternatives when the stock market gives one set of signals and output or other variables give a conflicting set.

We conclude that the difficulties of structural equation building are irremediable. As a substitute we carry out a hybrid methodology, in which theory is used to suggest sets of variables and their form but empirical estimation is carried out by estimating equations in the symmetric VAR format, with all explanatory variables entering the investment equation and with the dependent variable included with the same number of lags. Our hybrid approach thus combines insights from structural models with the unconstrained approach to testing and data exploration that typifies investigations using VAR models.

Our first empirical task is to establish the importance of fixed investment in historical business cycles. Using procedures described in the appendix, we have created a new set of quarterly data on major expenditure components of GNP extending back to 1919:1. We include four types of real investment expenditures in our study—producers' durable equipment, nonresidential structures, residential structures, and consumer durables expenditures. The decline in the sum of these four components (I) contributes between one-third and one-half of the decline in real GNP in recessions, even though the share of I in GNP at the typical business cycle peak is about one-quarter. Total investment actually was relatively more important in postwar recessions between 1957 and 1980 than it was during the Great Contraction of 1929–33.

A decomposition of variance allows a description of the relation between investment (I) and noninvestment real GNP (N) in major episodes. The interwar years were characterized by a high own variance of investment, particularly in 1919–29, and after 1929 by a high covariance between I and N. The own variance of N was more important in the postwar period and was dominated by the Korean War episode. Of the four components of investment, the own variance of nonresidential structures was the largest in the interwar period, while the own variance of consumer durables expenditures was largest in the postwar period.

5.6.2 Implications for Four Schools of Thought

Keynesians, monetarists, neoclassicists, and Q advocates all have an interest in the results of this investigation. Members of each group will be disappointed with our results if they are seeking support of "monocausal" or "one factor" hypotheses of investment behavior. Yet ironically the empirical findings offer some solace to each group, because they provide substantial support for an eclectic view of investment that blends elements of each approach while providing evidence against opponents of each who insist on some alternative monocausal explanation.

Keynesians view investment behavior as containing a substantial autonomous component. Our empirical investment equations summarized in table 5.6, together with the historical decompositions in figures 5.4 to 5.7, support the view that autonomous innovations in *structures* investment are an important driving force in the business cycle. In table 5.8 the effect of innovations in structures investment on durable equipment expenditures, as well as on noninvestment GNP, is greater than the reverse feedback from equipment and noninvestment GNP innovations to structures investment, in both the interwar and the postwar periods. The boom in structures investment between 1923 and 1929, the subsequent slump in the 1930s, and the smaller negative innovations in the early 1960s and boom in 1971–73 all can be viewed mainly as autonomous events rather than as a passive reaction to other economic variables.

While monetarists would doubtless be unhappy with a view that treats major swings in structures investment as autonomous, they nevertheless have the consolation of learning that the response of both structures and equipment investment to the real money supply is significantly greater than to the "traditional" variables in investment equations, the accelerator (output change), the user cost of capital, and Q. The effect of money, split here between the real monetary base and the M1 money multiplier, is substantial in both the interwar and the postwar periods. The regression results in table 5.6 find a strong impact of both the base and multiplier on equipment investment in the interwar period, and on both structures and equipment investment in the postwar. The historical decompositions in figures 5.4 to 5.7 indicate that base innovations had an important impact on both structures and equipment investment, as well as on noninvestment GNP, in the interwar period, whereas the multiplier played a role in both the interwar and the postwar periods.

It seems ironic that this study of investment behavior provides more support for the general views of the economy represented by Keynesians and monetarists than it does for the views of specialists in the investment process, the neoclassicists and Q advocates. In tables 5.4 and 5.5 the user cost of capital for businesses and the real interest rate for households are insignificant or have the wrong signs in every equation for the interwar years. The equations for consumer and producer durables spending exhibit a significant and correctly signed (negative) sum of coefficients for the postwar period, but in every postwar equation the user cost or interest rate variable fails an "exclusion test" on the joint significance of all lagged values in the explanation of investment spending. The verdict on the Q approach is even more negative. In the aggregated regression equations of table 5.6, the Q variable passes the exclusion test only in one equation, for postwar structures investment. This appears in table 5.4 to be attributable to the nonresidential component of structures investment. Such results pose a new task for Q theorists, that is, to determine what factors would make investment in structures more responsive to Q than investment in producers' durable equipment.

Our empirical work casts doubt on the importance of the accelerator hypothesis of investment behavior that has been supported by some past work, for example, Clark (1979). The simple device of including four lags on the dependent variable in equations explaining total I eliminates the significant explanatory contribution of lagged values of real GNP, except in the equipment equations for the postwar period. However, we find that it is possible to obtain significant sums of coefficients for an accelerator effect in a postwar durable equipment equation only when real GNP is entered as a second rather than a first difference. These findings support our basic interpretation that there is a sharp difference between the behavior of structures and equipment investment, with the former behaving mainly in an autonomous fashion, whereas the latter reflects feedback both from investment in structures and from financial and monetary variables.

5.6.3   Deeper Issues and Unsettled Questions for Future Research

In a recent paper Blanchard (1981, 154) reached the conclusion that "the multiplier is dead and the accelerator alive." This paper reaches the opposite conclusion, particularly for the structures component of investment. The accelerator mechanism, interpreted as the feedback from autonomous movements in noninvestment GNP to investment in structures, seems to be considerably weaker than the multiplier mechanism, interpreted in the elementary textbook fashion as the effect on total GNP of autonomous movements of investment, particularly the structures component. Although there is a substantial effect of monetary and financial variables on investment, nevertheless there are major and persistent movements in investment that occur in both the interwar and the postwar periods that cannot be explained by prior changes in output, money, stock prices, or interest rates.

That we label major movements in structures investment "autonomous" does not mean we leave them unexplained. Rather, this basic interpretation of the paper treats structures investment as exogenous *with respect to the explanatory variables included in our statistical analysis.* This does not rule out other explanations, and in fact we can offer three complementary explanations of the behavior of structures investment in the interwar period. First, the residential structures boom of the 1920s and subsequent slump of the 1930s can be explained in part by demographic factors that lie outside the scope of this paper. While the rapid population growth of 1900–1920, together with the postponement of construction during World War I and the 1920–21 recession, may provide a partial explanation of the intensity of the

1920s residential construction boom, the restrictive immigration law of 1924 and subsequent deceleration in population growth may help to account for the decline in residential construction after 1926.

Hickman (1973) has documented both the effect of the decline in population growth on the desired housing stock and also the extent of overbuilding in the mid-1920s. Hickman's work treats the rate of population growth as endogenous, with the rate of household formation responding to the growth rate of income, and he is able to decompose the observed decline in the rate of population growth between the early 1920s and mid-1930s into two components—that due to the effect of declining income, and a remaining exogenous decline due primarily to the decline in immigration. To isolate the effect of the exogenous component of the decline in household formation, Hickman calculated two dynamic simulations of his model, one in which standardized households are assumed to increase steadily at the 1924–25 rate of growth and another in which income and other economic variables are identical but in which standardized households follow their actual declining path after 1925. The impact of the actual demographic slump gradually becomes more important as the 1930s progress, accounting for a decline in housing starts between the two simulations of 28.3% for 1933 and 39.1% for 1940. His result is consistent with our figure 5.4 above, in which the own innovation in structures investment is negative throughout the 1930s.

A second factor, more relevant for investment in structures than in equipment, is the element of speculation. The Florida land boom of the 1920s, the stock market "bubble" of 1928–29, and earlier investment excesses like the "South Seas Bubble" of the early eighteenth century all have some similarity to the construction boom of the 1920s. For six years (1923–28) real residential construction achieved a level more than double the average of the entire decade before World War I, and in four successive years (1924–27) the ratio of real residential construction investment to GNP reached by far its highest level of the twentieth century. Hickman estimates that even with a continuation of population growth at the 1924–25 rate rather than a post-1925 decline, housing starts would have fallen by 35% between 1925 and 1930 (as a ratio to natural real GNP, real residential investment actually fell by 57%).

Nor is the phenomenon of overbuilding confined to the interwar period. Figure 5.6 shows that the postwar own innovation to structures investment peaked in 1972–73. Several years later contemporary accounts recognized the phenomenon of overbuilding: "In Chicago, new apartment construction has just about ceased. In Atlanta, where there is at least a three-year supply of unsold condominiums overhanging the market, mortgage companies are auctioning off high-rise units to the public at two-thirds their original asking price. . . . The current problems stem fromm overbuilding in the early 1970s" ("The Great High-Rise Bust," *Newsweek*, 30 August 1976, 5).

The third factor that may be an important explanation behind the apparently "autonomous" structures investment boom of the 1920s and slump of the 1930s is the "Schumpeterian" bunching of innovations. This hypothesis is developed by R. A. Gordon (1951), who argued that the buoyancy of both residential and nonresidential construction in the 1920s reflected in large part the influence of the automobile in expanding the boundaries of urban areas:

> Between 1923 and 1929 the growing *use* of automobiles and trucks had a more important impact on total investment and employment than did the expansion of motor vehicle output. Motor vehicle registrations in 1929 were about 75 percent greater than in 1923 and nearly three times the number in 1920. . . . large scale investment was necessary for roads and bridges, oil wells, pipe lines, garages and service stations, and tire and automobile supply stores, as well as for oil refining and tire manufacture. In addition, the automobile accelerated the trends toward urbanization and "suburbanization," stimulating thereby residential and commercial building.

Other industries were also involved in the bunching of investment opportunities in the 1920s. Among these were electric power—well over half the installation of electric generating capacity during 1902–40 occurred during the decade of the 1920s. Other important new industries were radio, telephone, and chemicals.

The results in this paper support the view that there are two basic impulses in the business cycle, real and financial. The real impulse appears in our statistical evidence as an autonomous innovation to investment in structures. This concluding section has suggested three factors that may underlie the cycle in structures investment. We choose to emphasize this element of investment behavior here because it has received relatively little attention in recent research, however familiar it may seem to experts on the earlier literature on business cycles. The financial impulse works through the effect on investment of changes in the monetary base and money multiplier, as well as the real interest rate for postwar investment in durable equipment. In these results the money multiplier may be acting as a proxy for such phenomena as the banking contraction of 1929–33 and the episodes of credit crunches and disintermediation in the postwar years.

Many avenues for future research are opened up by these results. Past studies of structures investment need to be reviewed for problems of identification and simultaneity that may have led to a misleading emphasis on the investment accelerator, rather than autonomous movements, as the driving force behind structures investment. Our inability to find a strong influence of the stock market (working through our Q variable) on investment, except for postwar nonresidential structures, needs to be reconciled with the recent findings of Fischer and Merton (1984), who find a stronger connection between economic activity and prior movements in the stock market. Finally, we hope that our new quarterly interwar data on components of expenditures will stimulate further research into the interrelations of real and financial variables during the Great Depression.

Appendix

General Description

This appendix investigates the behavior of investment in the United States economy over both the interwar (1919–41) and the postwar (1947–1983) periods. Annual nominal and real expenditures and deflator series are available as far back as 1929 using *Survey of Current Business* supplements (hereafter *SCB*). Before 1929, however, one must resort to a number of sources to collect annual data that can be matched up to the 1929 Commerce Department figures. Swanson and Williamson (1971) contains nominal series for all the major national account categories for the period 1919 to 1928, which have been adjusted from Kuznets's figures to conform to the *SCB* definitions. These annual nominal series are used here for all the national accounts categories except for investment in structures and foreign trade. The desired division of investment into residential and nonresidential structures uses figures from Grebler, Blank, and Winnick (1956) and adjusts nominal GNP accordingly. Net exports are broken down into the two nominal components, exports and imports, using index available in the *Statistical History of the United States*, which are then linked to the 1929 *SCB* values.

This provides us with a complete set of annual nominal national income accounts. The next task is to find implicit deflators for these nominal series. Our starting point is the set of *SCB* implicit deflators for all the national income categories for the period 1929 to 1941. Annual figures for the GNP deflator, 1919–28, are obtained by linking Kuznets's GNP deflator to the *SCB* 1929 implicit GNP deflator. Since both current and constant dollar index are available for exports and imports, it is possible to construct implicit deflators for both series from 1919 to 1928 that can be matched to the *SCB* 1929 deflators. For the remaining categories, such as consumption and investment, deflators are not available for the period 1919–28. To obtain figures for this period, our interpolation program is run over the available annual price series, 1929–41, to produce quarterly figures. The final regression is used to "back forecast" the quarterly values over the period 1919–28. These quarterly values are then averaged to yield annual price series for 1919–28. With the complete set of price deflators it is possible to convert the nominal national accounts into real series covering the full period 1919–41. The real annual national account series are interpolated to arrive at a complete set of real quarterly accounts and a corresponding set of deflators.

An interpolation procedure following that of Chow and Lin (1971) is used in converting the annual series to quarterly observations. A more complicated procedure, such as that suggested by Litterman (1981), is deemed too costly compared with the possible gain in accuracy. The procedure itself is fairly simple. Since our annual series are annual averages of quarterly variables, the procedure we use is that termed "distribution" by Chow and Lin. In what follows upper-case letters represent annual series, and lower-case letters represent the associated quarterly series. To each annual series to be interpolated (Y_{it}) is associated a number of quarterly series (x_{it}) that a priori information suggests move within the year the way quarterly observations on the annual dependent variable would. These quarterly explanatory variables are annualized (X_{it}), and a regression against the annual dependent variable is run:

(A1) $$Y_{it} = X_{it}\beta + U_t.$$

It is assumed in each interpolation that the *quarterly* errors follow an AR(1) process, which induces a complicated covariance structure on the annual error, U_t. The first autocorrelation of U_t, ρ_A, is related to the quarterly autocorrelation coefficient, ρ_Q, by the nonlinear formula:

(A2) $$\rho_A = \frac{\rho_Q^7 + 2\rho_Q^6 + 3\rho_Q^5 + 4\rho_Q^4 + 3\rho_Q^3 + 2\rho_Q^2 + \rho_Q}{2\rho_Q^3 + 4\rho_Q^2 + 6\rho_Q^2 + 4}.$$

Estimating ρ_A as the first autocorrelation of the residuals from the regression in (A1), we can obtain an estimate of ρ_Q by solving (A2), and this is used in an iterative GLS procedure to obtain estimates of β and ρ_Q. The final estimates from this procedure are then used to generate quarterly observations for the dependent variable as:

(A3) $$\hat{y}_{it} = x_{it}\hat{\beta} + \hat{\rho}_Q\hat{u}_{t-1}.$$

The assumption of AR(1) errors in the quarterly equation overcomes the artificial choppiness induced if u_t is assumed to be white noise.

This procedure is used to derive the quarterly series for the implicit deflators and real series of the national accounts as well as Summers's Q and some components of the cost of capital.

Sources of Annual Interwar and Postwar Quarterly Variables

1. GNP

    1919–28 (annual): Implicit deflator constructed from a nominal and a real GNP series available on NBER tape, dataset 08A Income

Table 5.A.1

Annual National Account Category	Time Period Interpolated	Independent Series in Interpolation
1. GNP (*Q*)		
Deflator—*QD*	Derived as residual	
Real GNP—*Q*	1919:1, 1941:4	*C T IIPTT DPTSLS*
2. Consumer durables (*CDG*)		
Deflator—*PDCDG*	1929:1, 1941:4	*C T CPINF*
Real—*QCDG*	1919:1, 1941:4	*C T IIPDCG*
3. Consumer Nondurables and services (*CNDSV*)		
Deflator—*PDCNDSV*	1929:1, 1941:4	*C T CPI*
Real—*QCNDSV*	1919:1, 1941:4	*C T IIPNDCG DPTSLS*
4. Investment, producers' durable equipment (*IPDE*)		
Deflator—*PDIPDE*	1929:1, 1941:4	*C T WPI CPWGE*
Real—*QIPDE*	1919:1, 1941:4	*C T IIPPG*
5. Investment, residential structures (*IRSTR*)		
Deflator—*PDIRSTR*	1929:1, 1941:4	*C T WPI CPWGE*
Real—*QIRSTR*	1919:1, 1941:4	*C T CONSTR QRSTR*
6. Investment, nonresidential structures (*NRSTR*)		
Deflator—*PDINRSTR*	1929:1, 1941:4	*C T WPI CPWGE*
Real—*QINRSTR*	1919:1, 1941:4	*C T CONSTR QNRSTR*
7. Investment, change in inventories (*IBINV*)		
Real—*QIBINV*	Derived as residual	
8. Government purchases (*G*)		
Deflator—*PDG*	1929:1, 1941:4	*C T CPWGE*
Real—*QG*	1919:1, 1941:4	*C T*
9. Exports (*X*)		
Deflator—*PDX*	1919:1, 1941:4	*C T WPI*
Real—*QX*	1919:1, 1941:4	*C T QXPROXY*
Imports (*M*)		
Deflator—*PDM*	1919:1, 1941:4	*C T WPI*
Real—*QM*	1919:1, 1941:4	*C T QMPROXY*

and Employment. Nominal GNP taken from Swanson and Williamson (1971, table B-1), adjusted for the use of the investment in structures series taken from Grebler, Blank, and Winnick (1956).

1919–41 (quarterly): The quarterly series for the GNP deflator was calculated by adding up the real and nominal interpolated account categories, except inventories, and dividing the nominal sum by the real sum.

1929–41 (annual); 1947–83 (quarterly): Nominal GNP series from *SCB* table 1.1. Implicit deflator from *SCB* table 7.1. All references to *SCB* figures are updated through June 1984.

2. Consumer Durables Expenditures

1919–28 (annual): Nominal expenditures from Swanson and Williamson (1971, table B-2). Implicit deflator constructed from interpolation.

1929–41 (annual); 1947–83 (quarterly): Nominal series from *SCB* table 1.1, deflator from *SCB* table 7.1.

3. Consumer Nondurables and Services

1919–28 (annual): Implicit deflator constructed from interpolation. Nominal series is the sum of consumer semidurables, perishables, and services from Swanson and Williamson (1971, table B-2).

1929–41 (annual); 1947–83 (quarterly): Nominal and real series are the sum of consumer durables and services from *SCB* tables 1.1 and 1.2 with the implicit deflator defined as the ratio of the nominal sum to the real sum.

4. Investment in Producers' Durable Equipment

1919–28 (annual): Implicit price deflator from interpolation, nominal series from Swanson and Williamson (1971, table B-3).

1929–41 (annual); 1947–83 (quarterly): Nominal and real series are the sum of the corresponding residential and nonresidential investment in producers' durable equipment from *SCB* tables 1.1 and 1.2. Implicit deflator is the ratio of the nominal sum to the real sum.

5. Investment in Residential Structures

1919–28 (annual): Implicit deflator from interpolation. Nominal series taken from Grebler, Blank, and Winnick (1956, table K-4, col. 4), does not include residential investment in farm structures.

1929–41 (annual); 1947–83 (quarterly): Nominal series for residential construction, nonfarm taken from *SCB* table 1.1, implicit deflator taken from *SCB* table 7.1.

6. Investment in Nonresidential Structures

1919–28 (annual): Implicit deflator from interpolation. Nominal series from Grebler, Blank, and Winnick (1956, table K-4, col. 5), includes farm investment in structures.

1929–41 (annual); 1947–83 (quarterly): Real and nominal series are the sum of nonresidential and residential farm investment in structures, *SCB* tables 1.1 and 1.2. Implicit deflator is arrived at by dividing the nominal sum by the real sum.

7. Change in Business Inventories

1919–41 (quarterly): Both real and nominal series were arrived at as residuals by subtracting from total real (nominal) GNP the real (nominal) sum of all other account categories.

1947–83 (quarterly): Both real and nominal series taken from *SCB* tables 1.1 and 1.2.

8. Government Purchases of Goods and Services

1919–28 (annual): Price deflator from the interpolation, nominal purchases from Swanson and Williamson (1971, table B-1).

1929–41 (annual); 1947–83 (quarterly): Deflator from *SCB* table 7.1 and nominal series from *SCB* table 1.1.

9. Exports

1919–28 (annual): Real and nominal series constructed by matching constant and current dollar index from the *Statistical History of the United States*, series U21 and U22, to the *SCB* export series in 1929. The deflator was then defined as the ratio for the real and nominal series.

1929–41 (annual); 1947–83 (quarterly): Deflator from *SCB* table 7.1 and nominal series from *SCB* table 1.1.

10. Imports

1919–28 (annual): Real and nominal series constructed by matching constant and current dollar index from the *Statistical History*, series U33 and U34, to the *SCB* import series in 1929. The deflator is then defined as the ratio of the real and nominal series.

1929–41 (annual); 1947–83 (quarterly): Deflator from *SCB* table 7.1 and nominal series from *SCB* table 1.1.

11. Capital Stock, Equipment and Structures

1925–83 (annual): Nominal and real series for the two types of capital stock, equipment and structures, was taken from various issues of *SCB*. Nominal and real series for the capital stock of consumer durables was taken from Musgrave (1979). To utilize the information available from our associated quarterly investment series in constructing each quarterly capital stock series, we followed the iterative procedure: (*a*) the annual series provide a beginning and ending value for the capital stock; (*b*) assuming a fixed exponential rate of depreciation, the quarterly series must satisfy $K_t = I_t + (1 - \delta)K_{t-1}$. The procedure uses the starting value of the capital stock and the associated quarterly I_t series, iterating on δ until the value of the quarterly capital stock at the end of the period is "close" to the specified ending value. Below we present the estimated annual depreciation rate for each type of capital stock in each of the subperiods.

Nonresidential structures	1919–41	$\hat{}$ = 6.396
	1947–83	= 6.036
Consumer durable goods	1919–41	$\hat{\delta}$ = 20.40
	1947–83	= 20.63
Producers' durable equipment	1919–41	$\hat{\delta}$ = 14.88
	1947–61	= 13.80
	1962–83	= 14.96

Rental Price of Capital Services

The rental price of capital services, for equipment and for structures, was constructed using for equipment:

$$C_E = \frac{P_E(\delta_E + r)(1 - RITC_E - DUM \cdot Z_E \cdot TAX \cdot RITC_E - Z_E \cdot TAX)}{(1 - TAX)}$$

and for structures:

$$C_S = \frac{P_S(\delta_S + r)(1 - RITC_S - Z_S \cdot TAX)}{(1 - TAX)}.$$

A composite cost of capital series was constructed by weighting each of C_E and C_S by their share in the sum of the capital stock of equipment and structures. Individual components of the cost of capital services are:

δ_E = Depreciation rate of the net stock of producers' durable equipment estimated iteratively as explained above.

δ_S = Depreciation rate of the net stock of nonresidential structure estimated iteratively as above.

DUM = Dummy variable, set equal to 1.0 for the duration of the Long amendment to the Revenue Act of 1962 and set equal to zero in all other periods.

P_E = Implicit deflator for investment in producers' durable equipment, as explained above.

P_I = Implicit deflator for investment in nonresidential structures, as explained above.

$RITC_E$ = Rate of investment tax credit on equipment investment, from Jorgenson and Sullivan (1981).

$RITC_S$ = Rate of investment tax credit on nonresidential structures investment, from Jorgenson and Sullivan (1981).

TAX = Highest marginal tax rate on corporate income from Tax Foundation (1979).

r = Discount rate, which is calculated as the Moody's Baa corporate bond yield minus the expected rate of inflation. The construction of the expected inflation rate is discussed in the text.

Z_E = Present value of one dollar's worth of depreciation on equipment. Figures for 1947–83 are from Jorgenson and Sullivan (1981), while figures for 1919–41 are calculated using straight-line depreciation, average asset life for the period from Jorgenson and Sullivan and the Baa corporate bond rate.

Z_S = Present value of one dollar's worth of depreciation on non-residential structures. Figures for 1947–83 are from Jorgenson and Sullivan (1981), while figures for 1919–41 are calculated using straight-line depreciation, average asset life for the period from Jorgenson and Sullivan, and the Baa corporate bond rate.

Sources of Interwar Quarterly Variables

The data utilized in this section were made available, in part, by the Inter-University Consortium for Political and Social Research. The data for macroeconomic time series were originally collected by the National Bureau of Economic Research.

C = Constant term used in the regression.

CONSTR = Index of total construction, s.a. Monthly observations from NBER tape, dataset 02A Construction: data originally collected for *Engineering News-Record Yearbook*.

CPI = Consumer price index, all items, s.a.

CPINF = Consumer price index, less food, s.a. Monthly observations for both taken from NBER tape, datasest 04A Prices: data originally collected by the Bureau of Labor Statistics.

CPWGE = Index of composite wages, s.a. Monthly observations from NBER tape, dataset 08A Income and Employment: data originally collected by the Federal Reserve Board and the Federal Reserve Bank of New York.

DPTSLS = Physical volume of department store sales, s.a. Monthly observations taken from NBER tape, dataset 06A Distribution of Commodities: data originally collected by the Federal Reserve Board.

IIPTT = Index of industrial production, total, s.a.

IIPDCG = Index of industrial production, durable consumer goods, s.a.

IIPNDCG = Index of industrial production, durable consumer goods, s.a.

IIPPG = Index of industrial production, producers' goods, s.a. Monthly observations on the four variables above taken from NBER tape, dataset 01A Production of Commodities: data originally collected by the Federal Reserve Board and the Federal Reserve Bank of New York.

QNRSTR   = Real value of contracts for industrial buildings, s.a. Quarterly observations arrived at by deflating the value of contracts for industrial buildings (from NBER tape, dataset 02B Construction: data originally collected by the Federal Reserve Board) by the interpolated deflator for nonresidential structures.

QRSTR   = Real value of residential construction contracts, s.a. Quarterly observations arrived at by deflating value of residential contracts (from NBER tape, dataset 02B Construction: data originally collected by *Engineering News-Record*) by the interpolated deflator for residential structures.

QMPROXY = Constructed variable for real imports, s.a. A quarterly nominal series on imports, which did not match the *SCB* definition, was deflated by the interpolated *WPI*. The nominal import series was taken from NBER tape, dataset 07A Foreign Trade: data originally appeared in the *Monthly Summary of Foreign Commerce,* various issues.

QXPROXY = Constructed variable for real exports, s.a. A quarterly nominal series on exports, which did not match the *SCB* definition, was deflated by the interpolated *WPI*. The nominal export series was taken from NBER tape, dataset 07A Foreign Trade: data originally appeared in the *Monthly Summary of Foreign Commerce,* various issues.

RBAA   = Yield on corporate bonds, Moody's Baa rating. Monthly observations originally collected by Moody's Investors Service, taken from Federal Reserve Board and various issues of the *Federal Reserve Bulletin.*

RHCPBD   = Yield on corporate bonds, highest rating. Monthly observations from NBER tape, dataset 13A Interest Rates: data originally collected by the United States Department of Commerce.

STKPRCE   = Index of all common stock prices, New York Stock Exchange. Monthly observations from NBER tape, dataset 11A Security Markets: data originally collected by Standard and Poor's.

T   = Trend term appearing in the regression.

WPI   = Wholesale price index, all items, s.a. Monthly observations taken from NBER tape, dataset 04A Prices: data originally collected by Babson Statistical Organization.

Comment   John Geweke

In their paper Gordon and Veitch have made a commendable and intellectually honest effort to compare the relationship between fixed investment and other important macroeconomic variables during the interwar period and in two postwar periods. Their strongest empirical finding is a sharp difference between the interwar and postwar periods, fixed investment being more nearly autonomous before the war than after. By contrast, there is little evidence of shifts since World War II. In common with many other researchers, they conclude that measurable variants of Tobin's Q have little explanatory power in an equation for aggregate fixed investment. In contrast with some other empirical work using aggregate data, they find no evidence for an accelerator, at least a limited role for a cost of capital variable in the postwar era, and substantial feedback from the monetary base, the monetary multiplier, or both, to fixed investment.

In reaching these conclusions the authors employ an econometric model with many fewer prior constraints than are typically found in the empirical aggregate investment literature. They point out that a reduced-form equation for aggregate investment, like their (8), is hopelessly underidentified without restrictions for which there are no sound theoretical arguments. While I find this argument persuasive, I think there is a more fundamental criticism of the use of "representative agent" models to achieve identification of parameters estimated from aggregate data, to which I shall return. The authors abandon the conventional approach in favor of a methodology described as a combination of the vector autoregression (VAR) approach with the estimation of reduced-form equations suggested by traditional theory. Experience suggests that evaluation of the paper's empirical results is likely to be overshadowed by an effort to delineate economic interpretations that are admissible from those that are inadmissible on the basis of this "hybrid" methodology. It may therefore be useful to provide an interpretation of this methodology complementary to the authors'.

Prior considerations—from economic theory or at any rate from professional common sense—are used at two points in the formulation of the model. The first is in the choice of the variables that will appear; short of the most blatant data mining imaginable, this use of "theory" is indispensable. The second use of prior considerations is the (identifying) restriction that the relevant structural econometric model is block recursive, in the classical sense, with the investment equation

John Geweke is professor of economics at Duke University.

Financial support from the National Science Foundation and the Sloan Foundation is gratefully acknowledged.

being the sole occupant of its block. The position of the investment block within the system determines which contemporaneous variables appear on the right-hand side of this equation. The authors argue, very much in the spirit of Herman Wold, that the investment equation comes first, with no contemporaneous variables on the right-hand side. Given the restriction to block causal chain models, that further restriction seems quite reasonable, but table 5.8 suggests the decision does matter. The assertion that a causal chain model of this form is structural is necessary for the interpretations of the estimates made throughout the latter part of the paper: without it, for example, the coefficients on output have no direct bearing on the accelerator hypothesis, and coefficients on the cost of capital cannot be associated with the supply of capital.

The hypothesis that the relevant structural model involves a specified list of variables in a specified causal chain is structure of a minimal sort. Whether one calls the model theoretical or atheoretical is a matter of taste; "minimally structural" seems more precise. What is much more important is to delineate the kinds of conceptual experiments that can be conducted and the kinds of hypotheses that can be tested in the context of such a model. The vector of disturbances for each block of equations is identified, and so one can ask about the effects on endogenous variables of certain kinds of variation in these disturbances. (We seem to learn most about such systems when examining the effects of very artificial movements in the disturbances, such as one-time shocks [Sims 1980a] or sine and cosine waves [Geweke 1983].) This point is a rather simple one; confusion usually arises if the notion that the ordering of the variables in the system is merely a normalization is paired with subsequent reference to a disturbance as a shock to a particular variable. The latter interpretation presumes a causal chain structure. The true assumptions and legitimate applications of the VAR models in this paper, and in the earlier work of Sims, are the same. The preeminent hypothesis that can be tested using this methodology is that of no structural change in one or more blocks from one regime to another. The methodology employed here is therefore one approach well suited to the theme of the conference.

Nothing else in the model is identified. As the authors have pointed out, what appears on the right-hand side is a confounding of determinants of desired capital stock, gestation lags, and variables that enter through the information set employed in the formation of expectations. It is precisely in this sense that the investment equation is a reduced form. This fact must be employed carefully in interpreting the empirical findings in the paper. The presence of money and capital costs in the postwar investment equation and the absence of output effects when the investment block appears first rather than second are interesting food for thought. But the joint insignificance of coefficients on output in the investment equation is only circumstantial evidence that the accelerator is dead: the accelerator could simply be hiding behind an expectations mechanism and a monetary authority that tightens credit during booms. "Missing and presumed dead" might be a better appellation. Certainly either is preferred to "dead on arrival" in an arbitrarily overidentified ambulance.

I would like to return now to the predicament described in the first part of the paper, which provided the justification for applying a minimally structural model to aggregate data. The authors develop a model in which gross investment is a function of the expected price of capital services, expected output, decision lags, delivery lags, gestation lags, the current capital stock, the price of all other inputs, and (certainly not least) the variables upon which expectations are conditioned. They conclude that these functional relationships cannot be disentangled from an estimable equation without some heroic and entirely unjustified assumptions about each relationship. The model they set forth is not a "deep parameter" model, in that it is not derived from engineering technology and the preference functions of firm managers, but that is probably beside the point. I suspect that any deep parameter model would have been more prone to the identification problems posed. Their argument persuasively illustrates the incredibility of common overidentifying restrictions on investment equations. That alone should make us skeptical of reported estimates and their interpretation. In this sense, no more is needed. However, greater megatonnage could have been brought to bear in the attack; the stronger attack would in turn suggest some approaches complementary to the estimation of minimally structural aggregate models.

Observe first of all that the problems cited in section 5.2 are not peculiar to macroeconomic models or aggregate data. They exist even for a single firm producing a single homogeneous output from capital alone in a stationary stochastic state. Even for such a firm, the assumptions made would most likely be inappropriate and unrealistic in a model intended to be genuinely structural in an interesting variety of circumstances. Much capital is in fact indivisible, and most investment is in fact irreversible: log linear production functions may be reasonable, but smooth delivery and gestation lags are not. Key investment decisions typically revolve around "whether, when, and how much" rather than taking the form of smooth adjustment to changing output and prices. Economies and diseconomies of scale are critical in deciding whether to enter new markets. These inconvenient facts are not cited by way of attacking the method of analysis per se: smooth problems are tractable and have closed-form solutions, whereas realistic ones generally do not. But if one is really trying to obtain reliable estimates of technological parameters invariant under some kinds of policy changes, this sort of objection is very much to the point. In formal terms, if a true technology involving lumpy capital and irreversible decisions is projected onto a smooth adjustment space, then we should not expect that projection to remain undisturbed when nontechnological dimensions of the environment are changed. Investment models with closed-form solutions could not be applied seriously to firms accounting for the majority of business fixed investment in the United States. This observation is supported by the dearth of such applications in the literature, especially at the deep parameter level.

The argument is even stronger when applied to investment in consumer durables and owner-occupied residential structures. Competitive pressures may assure optimization and a homogeneous technology in long-run industrial equilibrium, but the assumption that households maximize homogeneous utility functions is much weaker.

Even if these problems were surmounted, industry by industry, the problem of aggregation would remain. Necessary conditions for the existence of capital aggregates and aggregate production functions have been known for a long time (see the surveys by Fisher 1969 and Muellbauer 1975). American Telephone and Telegraph, as newly constituted, can produce long distance telephone service with capital alone—as the next AT&T "strike" will remind us—and that precludes the existence of capital aggregates (Fisher 1969, 558). In the art of macroeconometric modeling it may be wise, for many purposes, to sweep the aggregation problem under the rug. In explaining quarterly investment, however, it is difficult to conclude that the problem is anything but central. To take one example, consider the response of business fixed investment, as defined in the national accounts, to alternative, fully specified paths for monetary policy. Because of very great differences in gestation lags and provisions for cancellation of orders in different industries, this response must be presumed to depend to a large degree on the distribution of orders and states of completion of projects across industries. To the extent that these distributions, and other relevant factors, cannot be inferred from aggregate data alone, we should observe very different behavior of fixed investment in different business cycles. This the authors have documented, most vividly in their table 5.1.

To focus on the capital aggregation problem is, perhaps, to beat a dead horse in polite company. In a quarterly macroeconometric model of investment, however, it is difficult to conclude that the problem is anything but central. We would expect the aggregation issue to pose larger problems in modeling changes in levels of capital stocks, defined broadly as "immobile factors of production," than in any other kind of macroeconomic modeling. To the extent that aggregation is the *dominant* difficulty in short-run macroeconometric modeling—and I am not arguing here that this is necessarily the case—we should expect that efforts to nail down tightly "structural" relationships with aggregate data and to elucidate common behavior across business cycles will be more futile for the investment sector than for any other. In any event, the aggregation argument implies that there cannot exist structural representative agent models of investment demand over the business cycle. The frustrations of various empirical investigators cited in this paper, and the poor performance of investment models generally, probably are deeply rooted.

Considerations of these kinds ought to receive more weight in modeling investment demand. They provide an argument against the application of optimizing models that is complementary to the one in the present paper in the case of aggregate data, and they suggest that even if the numerous identification problems could somehow be solved, models would still be unstable and predict poorly from one business cycle to the next. They suggest that "deep parameter" models are a waste of intellectual energy if the goal is to provide better predictions of the behavior of aggregate time series and that they will not prove structural if the representative firm assumption is taken literally.

On the positive side, there emerges a more productive agenda for future research. The modeling of short-run investment demand ought to proceed at a level at which the conditions for capital aggregation are more plausible, or at which the aggregation problem reasonably appears to be second order. At this level it might also be possible to use engineering and institutional considerations to produce credible models of the technology and identifying restrictions that would sort out the multiple roles of variables. Realistic models are not likely to be of the linear quadratic variety with closed-form solutions, but the advance of computing technology is rapidly removing this constraint. Such a model with predictive power significantly beyond mechanical extrapolation would be a very important advance. Aggregate fixed investment would, in this approach, be attacked sector by sector. In the interim, minimally structural approachs like the one taken here are useful in organizing statistical information and developing stylized facts of aggregate behavior. Acceptance of either the authors' identification argument or the aggregation argument advanced here implies that the minimally structural approach dominates representative agent models with arbitrary identifying restrictions.

Comment   Christopher A. Sims

Gordon and Veitch approach the analysis of investment in the business cycle in a style that, as they point out, is close to that employed by

Christopher A. Sims is professor of economics at the University of Minnesota.

Gordon and others in analyzing inflation using price equations and wage equations. The data are treated carefully, with the complexities of their dynamics drawn out and discussed in some detail. Interpretations are explored both for the regularities persistent enough to affect equation parameters and for the special episodes that show up as residuals. But the interpretation is largely informal, with no attempt to construct an explicit mapping from the empirical estimated parameters to a set of "deeper" parameters.

I share Gordon and Veitch's skepticism toward empirical studies that interpret data under a narrow set of ad hoc maintained hypotheses. The combination of careful statistical treatment of the data with informal interpretation of the statistical models is far more useful than the reverse—elaborate formal interpretation of models that do not fit or that have not seriously confronted the data in all their complexity. Once one moves away from a style of research in which a single overidentified model is treated as a maintained hypothesis, results are likely to emerge in the form of degrees of plausibility for various classes of interpretations, and expressing such results formally will often, maybe even usually, be impractical.

Nonetheless, informality in discussion of scientific research is only an occasional practical necessity, not a virtue in itself. It carries with it some pitfalls of its own. Interpretation of a statistical model, that is, translation of the numerical properties of the data into conclusions about the way people behave, necessarily involves making assumptions. Formal modeling makes these assumptions explicit. While it may seem at times that in economics formality carried to enough of an extreme gives professional license to make explicitly ridiculous assumptions, informal interpretation of models may allow assumptions to remain hidden.

Gordon and Veitch find implications in their results for Keynesian theory, monetarist theory, "neoclassical" theory, and Q theory. They also interpret some of their results as casting light on the relative strength of the multiplier and the accelerator. All of this is done without explicit fitting of models embodying these theories or explicitly identifying multiplier and accelerator with parameters in fitted statistical models. I think it is worthwhile to examine more closely how these implications are arrived at, not because I think most of them are wrong, but because in the long run those that are correct will carry more weight if the assumptions they are based on are more explicit.

The authors point out that the "theories" in conventional theoretical discussions often are empty, having no implications for data without auxiliary assumptions that their proponents leave implicit or indeterminate. This does make it frustrating to try to use formal models in interpreting data. The econometrician is forced to make explicit the assumptions that give business cycle theories content, and especially if he does this clearly in a context where he treats more than one theory as retaining plausibility, he is likely to be accused of not formulating the theories "correctly." In fact, these implicit assumptions often exist in many versions, with each "monetarist," "Keynesian," or "Q theorist" having his own.

Nonetheless I think more formal modeling would have been possible and helpful in this paper and would not necessarily have compromised realistic assessment of the data. One can construct formal models exemplifying various theories and discuss how far they are, in what dimensions, from fitting the data. Even where it is not practical to generate formal models that fit well, the qualitative character of such models may be important in guiding our interpretations.

Old-Fashioned Keynesian Theory

The old-fashioned Keynesian theory is implicit in much of Gordon and Veitch's discussion, as, for example, when they cite the size of feedbacks found in a VAR model as relevant to the size of multiplier (for feedback from investment) effects. Keynesian theory emphasizes that investment is volatile and that consumption responds to it, via the multiplier, so that investment fluctuations engender larger income fluctuations. Accelerator theory in its original forms emphasizes the response of investment to the rate of growth of income without, usually, much emphasis on the notion that noninvestment expenditure has substantial volatility. Multiplier theory is usually presented with a dynamic component—the idea of rounds of expenditure propagating across sectors, with "leakages." Accelerator theory has been presented with various dynamic appendages to its basic notion that there is an instantaneous equilibrium relation between the rate of growth of income and the level of the capital stock.

Multiplier theory by itself, combining an assertion about where unpredictable variation arises with a description of how it propagates, is a theory with content. It gains policy relevance if one makes the further identifying assumption that deliberately induced changes in government expenditure or taxation will propagate in consumption with the same dynamics as do the volatile shifts in investment expenditure. It can be made testable by identifying the notion of "volatility" in investment with the notion that investment should have substantial unpredictable variance. Then unpredicted disturbances to investment should be followed with some delay by increases in consumption, probably larger than the increase in investment itself.

Samuelson's classic multiplier/accelerator paper showed how an accelerator, with an arbitrary delay introduced into it, could strongly affect the dynamics of a multiplier model. His model was not stochastic, and he did not argue for a relocation of the source of volatility. One might take a pure Keynesian multiplier/accelerator to be one in which volatility in investment is the main generator of the business cycle, with propagation through both multiplier and accelerator dynamics. I know of no example of anyone's arguing strongly for the opposite, a model in which shifts in consumption behavior are the main source of volatility, with multiplier/accelerator dynamics still generating the cycle. Such a model is clearly a logical possibility, however. More generally, both consumer and investor behavior might be independent sources of volatility.

If we estimate reduced-form regressions of consumption and investment on lagged investment and lagged consumption, that is, a two-by-two VAR, we might then interpret the consumption regression as reflecting consumer behavior, with its residual representing shifts in such behavior and the investment equation as correspondingly representing investor behavior. Multiplier dynamics and accelerator dynamics could then be read off from the MAR (moving average response) representation of the VAR.

In this framework, the size and pattern of the MAR responses are important to the interpretation. If the multiplier mechanism is at work, any shock, whether in consumption residuals, investment residuals, or both, should lead to a sustained rise in consumption, probably larger than the rise in investment, if it leads to a sustained rise in investment. It is therefore regrettable that, in giving us neither the VAR coefficients nor plots of the MARs, Gordon and Veitch choose not to present the information that would allow us to assess whether shocks really get "multiplied," and if so by what multiplier. They give us only statistical significance on blocks of coefficients and variance-explained accounting. Neither tells us what we need to know to find the point estimates of the dynamic multiplier.

The identifying assumptions we are using to distinguish consumption disturbances from investment disturbances here rely on delays in responses. If the two sorts of disturbances are distinct and responses are delayed, we ought also to expect the VAR residuals to show little correlation. (We are relying for identification of ideas close to those put forth years ago by Herman Wold, as I pointed out in Sims 1981). Investment and noninvestment innovations do not show small correlation in all of the periods and categories Gordon and Veitch explore, and in fact the strongest feedbacks occur precisely when contemporaneous correlations are strongest.

When identifying "multiplier" and "accelerator" with MAR feedbacks, the notion that reduced-form residuals (innovations) in the two equations can be identified with shifts in consumption and investment behavior is critical. Gordon and Veitch do not make the connection between this point and their choice of aggregation scheme—household versus business or durable goods versus structures. They focus on equation parameters as the basis for choice. But the degree of orthogonality of the disturbances is at least equally important. It is hard to see a priori why there should be distinct durable goods and structures shocks to household behavior, with delays in propagation of the shock from one category to the other. The Keynesian notion that business decisions may change for reasons not much related to consumer behavior, and that the results propagate into consumer decisions with a delay, may be wrong, but at least it is supported by a plausible story— consumers are credit constrained, or for other reasons they react directly to income flows with a transactions lag. If Gordon and Veitch mean for us to take seriously the idea that household durable goods consumption is subject to shocks distinct from household nondurable goods consumption, and that these propagate with a delay into nondurable consumption, a simple model showing how the notion works would have been helpful.

The Expectational Accelerator

Gordon and Veitch point out that expectational accelerator models are likely to be consistent with a variety of dynamic behavior patterns and hence to be underidentified. Such models do nonetheless provide a possible framework for interpreting results like those in this paper. In such a model, multiplier effects might still be read off from MAR response patterns, but the idea that shocks to investment and consumption equations separately represent consumption and investment behavioral disturbances no longer holds. If shocks to consumption behavior are persistent, small disturbances in it might generate large changes in expected future output, hence large, and undelayed, changes in investment. Investment innovations might be a better index of shifts in consumption behavior than consumption innovations.

Here is a simple example of a multiplier/expectational accelerator model:

(1) $$C(t) = a + bY(t - 1) + u(t)$$

(2) $$K_t = c(1 - h) \sum_{i=0}^{\infty} h^i E_t[Y(t + i)] + v_t$$

(3) $$Y(t) = C(t) + K(t) - K(t - 1).$$

Equation (1) is the consumption function and (2) is the expectational accelerator. In (2) it is asserted that the current capital stock is kept at a fixed ratio to an exponentially weighted average of future output levels. For some ranges of its parameter values, the system has stationary solutions. Assuming, say, $b = .94$, $c = 3.33$, and $h = .90$, that at t investors know the values of current and past K and C, and that u and v are each serially uncorrelated yields as autoregressive representation

$$(4) \qquad C(t) = .94 \, C(t - 1) + .94 \, I(t - 1) + u(t)$$

$$(5) \quad K(t) = 4.37 \, C(t - 1) - .28 \, K(t - 1) - 4.37 \, K(t - 2) + e_I(t),$$

where e_I is a linear combination of the original u and v. (Note that, though the operator applied to K in [5] is not invertible, the system as a whole is stable. Also note that to derive [4] and [5] we assume that self-perpetuating exponential explosions in the capital stock are known by investors not to be sustainable.)

Gordon and Veitch give us the analog of (5) in isolation. But in the system (4) and (5), (5) cannot be interpreted in isolation. If we were to treat (5) as an "accelerator equation" describing the response of capital stock to consumption, in attempting to use it to generate a distributed lag determining K from current and past C we would find it implied explosive behavior for K. The usual trick for measuring "long-run response" of K to C (dividing the coefficient on lagged C by one minus the sum of coefficients on lagged Ks) produces a negative number. Furthermore, though the coefficients in (4) and (5) are invariant to the variances of the disturbances in (1) through (3), the explanatory power of each variable, and hence significance tests for blocks of variables, is sensitive to those variances.

The moving average representation implied by (4) and (5), with the variance of u about twice that of the "investment schedule" disturbance v, gives the following variance decomposition at the sixteen-quarter horizon, with I first in the orthogonalization:

	Explained by	
% Variance in	I	C
I	92.8	7.2
C	91.3	8.7

Investment appears as driving variation in consumption in the model, even though consumption schedule disturbances are larger. It does so because an innovation in the consumption schedule generates an expectation of sustained higher income and is therefore accompanied by an immediate expansion of investment. In fact, the proportion of variance in investment explained by consumption innovations is lowest when *either* investment or consumption shocks have relatively large variance. Investment innovations tend to pick up the dominant source of disturbance to the system. When the two underlying shocks have about equal variance, the proportion of variance in investment explained by consumption shocks rises to about 15%.

Using the kind of interpretation Gordon and Veitch apply at some points in their paper, this model seems to show a strong multiplier and little accelerator. It is a model Keynesian in spirit—volatile investment, driven by shifts in expectations, has large multiplier effects on consumption—but it has an accelerator mechanism as an important part of its transmission dynamics, and the consumption schedule in it is more volatile than the investment schedule.

Cost of Capital Models

None of the foregoing models includes prices of any kind as an explicit variable. They do not deny, however, that prices exist and are likely to be correlated with real business cycle fluctuations. Multiplier theory asserts that disturbances in investment expenditure propagate into other components of GNP. It is quite consistent with this theory that an investment disturbance should be associated with an interest rate disturbance, either through financial market reactions or through the reaction of investment to policy or foreign sector shifts. Thus multiplier theory does not deny the possible explanatory power of financial variables in a regression model of investment and noninvestment spending. It does, however, suggest that if such financial variables are included in the model its interpretation will become much more complicated.

In all their reported results, except for a few regressions of investment on lagged investment and noninvestment, financial variables are mixed in with real variables in a single system. This makes interpretation of the results in the light of "real theories" like the multiplier/accelerator difficult. Multiplier/accelerator theory does not say anything about how much predictive power price and financial variables should have. It does suggest likely patterns for the joint behavior of investment and noninvestment MAR response paths even when prices are in the model, but these are not discussed by Gordon and Veitch.

Gordon and Veitch interpret neoclassical and Q theory as predicting that cost of capital variables should have a lot of predictive value for investment. They also point out that these theories are partial equilibrium theories and really make no statement about how data should behave. My view is that the question of how much predictive power such variables have (and whether high cost of capital is predictive of lower or higher investment) is interesting and important. It affects the interpretation and plausibility for many theoretical approaches to business cycles. However, it is not reasonable to think of the relative predictive powers of such variables and lagged noninvestment as relating to a horse race between accelerator, Q, and neoclassical theories. It is an interesting race, but these are not the horses performing—in fact, these are not even horses.

Monetarist Theory

The comments of the preceding section apply here as well. That monetary variables should have predictive value is not at all inconsistent with multiplier/accelerator theory. The difference is that monetarist theory, unlike Q and neoclassical investment theories, is seriously put forward as a complete theory with implications for data, at least by some of its proponents. That is, monetarists argue not only that there is an equilibrium relation between money and real activity, but that disturbances to monetary variables propagate into real variables with a delay, are not explainable as systematic reaction to the real variables themselves, and account for much of the observed business cycle.

Monetarist theory is therefore confirmed in Gordon and Veitch's finding that monetary aggregates have substantial explanatory power for investment. On the other hand, as I pointed out in the *American Economic Review* paper Gordon and Veitch cite (Sims 1983), this confirmation is analogous to confirming the existence of an exploitable trade-off between inflation and unemployment by regressing unemployment on inflation: even in a model where monetary policy is totally ineffective, a policy authority aiming at stabilizing the price level would generate a path for money aggregates that would have great predictive value for real variables. And this result applies both to the money stock itself and to the base.

Conclusion

Gordon and Veitch have cleanly displayed the empirical regularities that are the focus of their discussion. They have isolated some interesting phenomena and given sensible interpretations of at least some of them. Multiplier and monetarist theories each show some degree of consistency with the data. Financial variables show substantial predictive power for investment. Investment contains a lot of unpredictable variation. For reasons they have laid out themselves, they have had difficulty connecting these results to much of the conventional "theory of investment," but this reflects defects in that theory.

The criticisms in this comment arise from holding the authors to an idealized standard. We have little in the way of formal theory capable of making predictions about observed data on investment and other aggregate variables, particularly when some of the variables are price variables. If Gordon and Veitch had gone some way toward providing such theories, even if only simple models whose quantitative properties could be compared with the data, their paper would have been better.

I think they would have in this case been led to give us a more detailed look at their regression and VAR data analysis. But good models in this area will involve at least some elements of modeling dynamic optimization under uncertainty, and such models, even apparently simple ones, are challenging to solve and understand. It will probably take many economists, working over some years, to develop practically fruitful ways of combining sophisticated, honest data analysis with stochastic theory.

Reply   Robert J. Gordon and John M. Veitch

Christopher Sims has contributed a constructive set of comments. We agree with his characterization of our paper as achieving a clean display of interesting empirical regularities, as well as with his criticism that, holding us to an "idealized standard," he would have preferred that some part had been devoted to developing simple models whose qualitative properties could have been compared with the data. Sims contributes one example that he calls a "multiplier/expectational accelerator model" and discusses its implications for the decomposition of variance in a hypothetical two-variable VAR model that includes only consumption and investment. A related criticism is that our paper estimates only equations for investment rather than equations for both investment and consumption.

In urging us to carry out a parallel study of consumption and investment, Sims can be interpreted as making a suggestion for future research rather than a serious criticism of the present paper. In focusing on the four components of investment (which include consumer durables expenditures), we were attempting to limit the scope of a long and ambitious paper that was primarily intended to provide an empirical contrast between existing postwar quarterly data and our newly created set of quarterly expenditures data for the interwar period. To have carried out a serious study of consumer expenditures on nondurable goods and services would have poached on the turf of Robert Hall, who has contributed a paper on that subject to this volume (chap. 4). The systems properties of small VAR models for the whole economy, including not only consumption expenditures but also the nature of policy feedbacks from expenditures to government spending and the money supply (alluded to by Sims in his section "Monetarist Theory"), could be usefully studied in a sequel to this paper.

The purpose of this rejoinder is to provide some quantitative evidence to clothe the bare bones of Sims's conjectures regarding the implications for multiplier/accelerator theory of a small two-by-two VAR model containing equations only for aggregate investment and consumption. Before proceeding with the exercise we must demur that limiting a VAR model to just investment and consumption, without any separate role for monetary variables, is inconsistent with the findings in our paper that monetary shocks were important in both the interwar and the postwar periods.

In what follows we shall maintain definitions that are consistent with those in our paper, including consumer durables expenditures in "investment" and treating "consumption" as including only consumer expenditures on nondurable goods and services. In the interpretation that Sims suggests, evidence in support of the multiplier mechanism would be based on an inspection of the MAR (moving average response) representation of the VAR model. We should expect to find a sustained rise in consumption, probably larger than the rise in investment, following any shock to consumption residuals or investment residuals.

The results, shown in table C5.1, provide a partial confirmation of Sims's conjectures for the interwar but not for the postwar period. In the interwar two-by-two VAR model, a shock to either consumption or investment generates a sustained response of consumption, confirming the multiplier mechanism, but also a response of investment. However, in contrast to Sims's prediction, the response of consumption is in no case appreciably larger than that of investment. Behavior in the

Table C5.1   Moving Average Responses in Two-by-Two Investment Consumption Model

Quarters after Shock	Investment Innovation		Consumption Innovation	
	Interwar	Postwar	Interwar	Postwar
Investment response				
4	1.55	0.71	0.89	0.08
8	1.31	0.29	1.12	−0.04
12	0.92	0.10	0.99	−0.06
16	0.65	0.06	0.80	−0.05
Consumption response				
4	0.31	0.18	1.15	0.22
8	0.72	0.05	1.07	0.17
12	0.76	−0.05	0.98	0.11
16	0.67	−0.07	0.85	0.08

Innovation Accounting at Sixteen-Quarter Horizon (Interwar/Postwar)		
	Investment	Consumption
Investment	79/98	45/26
Consumption	21/2	55/74

postwar period is completely different, with very small responses except for the response of investment to its own innovations. A possible reason for the difference between the interwar and postwar responses involves the omitted monetary variables, which in the Great Depression acted to amplify expenditure shocks but, at least in the second half of the postwar period, acted to counteract expenditure shocks.

The bottom section of table C5.1 displays the decomposition of variance ("innovation accounting") for the two-by-two model in the same format as table 5.8 in the paper. Here we see that, as in the larger models discussed in the paper, the investment innovation accounts for most of the variance of investment and a substantial fraction of the variance of consumption, 45% in the interwar and 26% in the postwar period. Sims may doubt the relevance of this result in light of his multiplier/expectational accelerator model that makes investment appear to be driving consumption when in fact consumption disturbances are the dominant source of variance. But we in turn may doubt the relevance of his model, in which investment is free to jump instantaneously within the current quarter in response to a consumption shock (allowing the investment innovation to "mask" the consumption shock), in contrast to the real world, in which there are substantial gestation lags in the investment process.

Finally, Sims is skeptical of our preference for aggregating the four categories of investment along the structures/equipment dimension rather than along the household/business dimension. We have examined the pattern of orthogonality of the disturbances in a four-variable VAR model containing only the four components of investment. These results are displayed in table C5.2, which is in the same format as the bottom part of table 5.7 in the paper. The results are mixed. In addition to the significant diagonal elements, we find examples of strong feedback from consumer durables (CD) to producers' durable equipment (PDE) in the postwar period and from residential structures (RS) to nonresidential structures (NRS) in the interwar period. These confirm the structures/equipment pattern of aggregation. But there are other elements that support the household/business pattern of aggregation, including feedback from RS to DG in the postwar period and DG to

Table C5.2	**Exogeneity Tests**			
	DG	*PDE*	*RS*	*NRS*
DG	***/***	/	/***	/
PDE	/***	***/***	/***	*/
RS	**/		***/***	/*
NRS	***/		***/	***/***

RS in the interwar, and weak feedback from *NRS* to *PDE* in the interwar. The ambiguity of these results may suggest that investment should be studied either with all four categories lumped together or with each studied separately, with little justification for either two-way aggregation scheme.

Discussion Summary

Allen Sinai suggested that the bulk of the analysis was at too aggregated a level, and this comment led the authors to devote much more attention in the final version to the four components of investment and to alternative aggregation schemes. Sinai also found the role played by real balances interesting. Robert Eisner felt that the analysis confused output expectations with a fixed distributed lag on past output. He argued that such an expectational proxy was inadequate because the weights on past output were likely to change over time. Olivier Blanchard felt that the structural interpretation, given the results, was too strong and would be valid only if investment were independent of contemporaneous variables. Robert Hall believed that more structural information on the investment process would be interesting but that identification of the structure would require that additional exogenous variables be found. He noted how hard it was to find such variables.

Mark Watson questioned the use of interpolated data in the prewar and not the postwar period. He noted that the interpolated series were essentially conditional expectations of the actual interpolated variables and that consequently the second moments of the data were not the same as the second moments of the conditional expectations. However, he observed that explicit corrections could be made in the estimation procedure.

John Veitch reported that to check the consistency between the prewar and postwar samples, he and Gordon had also used data for the postwar period interpolated in the same manner as the prewar data and found that the results (not reported in the conference version of the paper) were not sensitive to this change. In regard to the issue of contemporaneous correlations, Veitch suggested that the accounting conventions of the Bureau of Economic Analysis made it much more likely that investment in structures might be contemporaneously uncorrelated with other variables. As an example, he noted that current housing starts inevitably appear in the income accounts as residential investment for future quarters.

References

Abel, Andrew B. 1979. *Investment and the value of capital*. New York: Garland.

Abel, Andrew B., and Olivier Blanchard. 1983. Investment and sales: An empirical study. Paper presented at National Bureau of Economic Research Macro Conference, July.

Auerbach, Alan J. 1983. Taxation, corporate financial policy, and the cost of capital. *Journal of Economic Literature* 21 (September): 905–40.

Bernanke, Ben S. 1982. Adjustment costs, durables, and aggregate consumption. Working Paper 1038, National Bureau of Economic Research.

————. 1983a. Nonmonetary effects of the financial crisis in the propagation of the Great Depression. *American Economic Review* 73 (June): 257–76.

————. 1983b. An equilibrium model of industrial employment, hours, and earnings, 1923–1939. Working Papers in Economics E-83-19, Hoover Institution.

Bischoff, Charles W. 1971. The effect of alternative lag distributions. In *Tax incentives and capital Spending*, ed. Gary Fromm, 61–130. Washington, D.C.: Brookings Institution.

Blanchard, Olivier J. 1981. What is left of the multiplier accelerator? *American Economic Review* 71 (May): 150–54.

Bosworth, Barry. 1975. The stock market and the economy. *Brookings Papers on Economic Activity* 6(2): 257–300.

Chirinko, Robert S. 1983a. Investment and tax policy: A survey of existing models and empirical results with applications to the high-technology sector. Report for the National Science Foundation, Division of Policy Research and Analysis.

————. 1983b. Investment, Tobin's Q, and multiple capital inputs. Paper presented to the Econometric Society winter meetings, December.

Chirinko, Robert S., and Robert Eisner. 1983. Tax policy and investment in major U.S. econometric models. *Journal of Public Economics* 20 (March): 139–66.

Chow, Gregory C., and An-loh Lin. 1971. Best linear unbiased interpolation distribution and extrapolation of time series by related series. *Review of Economics and Statistics* 53 (November): 372–76.

Clark, J. Maurice. 1917. Business acceleration and the law of demand: A technical factor in business cycles. *Journal of Political Economy* 25 (March): 217–35.

Clark, Peter K. 1979. Investment in the 1970s: Theory, performance, and prediction. *Brookings Papers on Economic Activity* 10(1): 73–124.

deLeeuw, Frank. 1971. The demand for housing: A review of cross-section evidence. *Review of Economics and Statistics* 53 (February): 1–10.

Eckstein, Otto. 1983. Disinflation. In *Inflation: Prospects and remedies*, ed. W. D. Nordhaus. Alternatives for the 1980s, no. 10. Washington, D.C.: Center for National Policy.

Eisner, Robert. 1972. Components of capital expenditures: Replacement and modernization versus expansion. *Review of Economics and Statistics* 54 (August): 297–305.

Eisner, Robert, and M. I. Nadiri. 1968. Investment behavior and neoclassical theory: A comment. *Review of Economics and Statistics* 50 (August): 369–82.

Eisner, Robert, and Robert H. Strotz. 1963. Determinants of business investment. In *Impacts of monetary policy*, ed. Commission on Money and Credit, 60–337. Englewood Cliffs, N.J.: Prentice-Hall.

Feldstein, Martin S. 1981. The distribution of the U.S. capital stock between residential and industrial uses. *Economic Inquiry* 19 (January): 26–37.

Feldstein, Martin S., and David K. Foot. 1971. The other half of gross investment: Replacement and modernization expenditures. *Review of Economics and Statistics* 53 (February): 49–58.

Feldstein, Martin S., and Michael Rothschild. 1974. Towards an economic theory of replacement investment. *Econometrica* 42 (May): 393–424.

Fischer, Stanley, and Robert C. Merton. 1984. Macroeconomics and finance: The role of the stock market. Working Paper 1291, National Bureau of Economic Research.

Fisher, F. M. 1969. The existence of aggregate production functions. *Econometrica* 37:553–77.

Friedman, Milton, and David Meiselman. 1963. The relative stability of monetary velocity and the investment multiplier in the United States, 1897–1958, In *Stabilization policies*, ed. Commission on Money and Credit. Englewood Cliffs, N.J.: Prentice-Hall.

Friedman, Milton, and Anna J. Schwartz. 1963. *A monetary history of the United States*, 1867–1960. Princeton: Princeton University Press.

———. 1970. *Monetary statistics of the United States: Estimates, sources, and methods*. New York: Columbia University Press.

Garber, Peter M., and Robert G. King. 1983. Deep structural excavation? A critique of Euler equation methods, Technical Paper 31, National Bureau of Economic Research.

Geweke, J. F. 1983. The superneutrality of money in the United States: An interpretation of the evidence. Working Paper, Duke University.

Gordon, Robert A. 1951. Cyclical experience in the interwar period: The investment boom of the twenties. In *Conference on Business Cycles*, 163–214. New York: National Bureau of Economic Research.

Gordon, Robert J. 1973. Interest rates and prices in the long run: A comment. *Journal of Money, Credit, and Banking* 5 (February): 460–63.

———. 1977. Can the inflation of the 1970s be explained? *Brookings Papers on Economic Activity* 8(1): 253–77.

———. 1982. Price inertia and policy ineffectiveness in the United States, 1890–1980. *Journal of Political Economy* 90 (December): 1087–1117.

———. 1983a. "Credibility" vs. "Mainstream": Two views of the inflation process. In *Inflation: Prospects and remedies*, ed. W. D. Nordhaus, 25–34. Alternatives for the 1980s, no. 10. Washington, D.C.: Center for National Policy.

———. 1983b. The conduct of domestic monetary policy. Working Paper 1221, National Bureau of Economic Research.

———. 1984a. *Macroeconomics*. 3d ed. Boston: Little, Brown.

———. 1984b. Inflation in the recovery. Paper presented to a meeting of academic consultants with the Board of Governors of the Federal Reserve System, May.

Gordon, Robert J., and Stephen R. King. 1982. The output cost of disinflation in traditional and vector autoregressive models. *Brookings Papers on Economic Activity* 13(1): 205–42.

Gordon, Robert J., and James A. Wilcox. 1981. Monetarist interpretations of the Great Depression: Evaluation and critique. In *The Great Depression revisited*, ed. Karl Brunner, 49–107. Boston: Martinus Nijhoff.

Grebler, Leo, David M. Blank, and Louis Winnick. 1956. *Capital formation in residential real estate: Trends and prospects*. Princeton: Princeton University Press.

Hall, Robert E. 1977. Investment, interest rates, and the effects of stabilization policies. *Brookings Papers on Economic Activity* 8(1): 61–103.

———. 1978. Stochastic implications of the life cycle–permanent income hypothesis: Theory and evidence. *Journal of Political Economy* 86:971–88.

Hall, Robert E., and Dale W. Jorgenson. 1967. Tax policy and investment behavior. *American Economic Review* 57 (June): 391–414.

———. 1971. Application of the theory of optimum capital accumulation. In *Tax incentives and capital spending*, ed. G. Fromm, 9–60. Washington, D.C.: Brookings Institution.

Hansen, Lars P., and Kenneth J. Singleton. 1982. Generalized instrumental variables estimation of nonlinear rational expectations models. *Econometrica* 50 (September): 1269–86.

Hayashi, Fumio. 1982. Tobin's marginal q and average q. *Econometrica* 50 (January): 213–24.

Helliwell, John F. 1976. Aggregate investment equations: A survey of issues. In *Aggregate investment: Selected issues*, ed. J. Helliwell, 13–53. London: Penguin Education.

Hickman, Bert G. 1973. What became of the building cycle? In *Nations and households in economic growth: Essays in honor of Moses Abramovitz*, ed. Paul David and Melvin Reder. New York: Academic Press.

Jorgenson, Dale W. 1963. Capital theory and investment behavior. *American Economic Review* 53 (May): 247–59.

———. 1967. The theory of investment behavior. In *Determinants of investment behaviour*, ed. R. Ferber, 129–55. Universities–National Bureau Conference Series no. 18. New York: Columbia University Press.

———. 1971. Econometric studies of investment behavior: A survey. *Journal of Economic Literature* 9 (December): 1111–47.

Jorgenson, Dale W., and James A. Stephenson. 1967. The time structure of investment behavior in U.S. manufacturing, 1947–1960. *Review of Economics and Statistics* 49 (February): 16–27.

———. 1969. Issues in the development of the neoclassical theory of investment behavior. *Review of Economics and Statistics* 51 (August): 346–53.

Jorgenson, Dale W., and Martin Sullivan. 1981. Inflation and corporate capital recovery. In *Depreciation, inflation, and the taxation of income from capital*, ed. Charles R. Hulten, 171–237. Washington, D.C.: Urban Institute Press.

Keynes, John Neville. 1890. *The scope and method of political economy*. London: Macmillan.

King, Stephen R. 1983. Macroeconomic activity and the real rate of interest. Ph.D. diss., Northwestern University.

Litterman, Robert A. 1981. A random walk, Markov model for the interpolation of time series. Working Paper 190, Federal Reserve Bank of Minneapolis.

Lucas, Robert E., Jr. 1967. Adjustent costs and the theory of supply. *Journal of Political Economy* 75 (August): 321–34.

———. 1976. Econometric policy evaluation: A critique. In *The Phillips curve and labor markets*, ed. Karl Brunner and Allan Meltzer, 19–46. Carnegie-Rochester Conference Series on Public Policy 1. Amsterdam: North-Holland.

Malinvaud, Edmond. 1982. Wages and unemployment. *Economic Journal* 92 (March): 1–12.

Mayer, Thomas. 1980. Consumption in the Great Depression. *Journal of Political Economy* 86 (January): 139–45.

Mishkin, Frederic S. 1978. The household balance sheet and the Great Depression. *Journal of Economic History* 38:918–37.

Modigliani, Franco, and Richard A. Cohn. 1979. Inflation, rational valuation and the market. *Financial Analysts Journal* (March/April), 3–23.

Muellbauer, J. 1975. Aggregation, income distribution and consumer demand. *Review of Economic Studies* 42 525–43.

Musgrave, John C. 1979. Durable goods owned by consumers in the United States, 1925–77. *Survey of Current Business* 59 (March): 17–25.

Perry, George L. 1983. What have we learned about disinflation? *Brookings Papers on Economic Activity* 14(2): 587–602.

Polinsky, A. Mitchell. 1977. The demand for housing: A study in specification and grouping, *Econometrica* 45 (March): 447–61.

Roosa, Robert. 1951. Interest rates and the central bank. In *Money, trade, and economic Growth: Essays in Honor of John H. Williams*, 270–95. New York: Macmillan.

Samuelson, Paul. 1939. A synthesis of the principle of acceleration and the multiplier. *Journal of Political Economy* 47 (December): 786–97.

Shiller, Robert. 1981. Do stock prices move too much to be justified by subsequent changes in dividends? *American Economic Review* 71(3): 421–36.

Sims, Christopher A. 1980a. Macroeconomics and reality. *Econometrica* 48 (January): 1–48.

———. 1980b. Comparison of interwar and postwar business cycles: Monetarism reconsidered. *American Economic Review, Papers and Proceedings* 70(2): 250–57.

———. 1981. An autoregression index model for the U.S., 1948–1975. In *Large-scale macro-econometric models*, ed. J. Kmenta and J. B. Ramsey. Amsterdam: North-Holland.

———. 1982. Policy analysis with econometric models. *Brookings Papers on Economic Activity* 13(1): 107–64.

———. 1983. Is there a monetary business cycle? *American Economic Review* 73 (May): 228–33.

Summers, Lawrence H. 1981. Taxation and corporate investment: A *q*-theory approach. *Brookings Papers on Economic Activity* 12(1): 67–127.

Swanson, J., and S. Williamson. 1971. Estimates of national product and income for the U.S. economy, 1919–41. Working Paper 71–32, Department of Economics, University of Iowa.

Tax Foundation. 1979. *Facts and figures on government finance*. Washington, D.C.: Tax Foundation.

Taylor, John. 1983. Optimal stabilization rules in a stochastic model of investment with gestation lags. Working Paper 1225, National Bureau of Economic Research.

Temin, Peter. 1976. *Did monetary forces cause the Great Depression?* New York: Norton.

U.S. Bureau of the Census. 1965. *The statistical history of the United States from colonial times to the present.* Stamford, Conn.: Fairfield.

U.S. Department of Commerce. 1981. *The national income and product accounts of the U.S., 1929–76.* Supplement to the *Survey of Current Business*, September.

Wilcox, James A. 1983. Disaggregating data using related series. *Journal of Business and Economic Statistics* (July), 187–91.

Yellen, Janet, 1980. Jorgensonian investment theory: The case of the missing wage rate. Working Paper, University of California at Berkeley.

III   Fiscal and Monetary Policy

6   The Behavior of United States Deficits

Robert J. Barro

Much recent attention has focused on the large values of actual and projected federal deficits. To evaluate this discussion we must know whether these deficits represent a shift in the structure of the government's fiscal policy or are just the usual reaction to other influences, such as recession, inflation, and government spending. A related, but broader, question is whether the process that generates deficits in the post–World War II period differs systematically from that in place earlier—say, during the interwar period 1920–40. For example, has there been a change in the average deficit or in the magnitude of the countercyclical response of deficits?

I begin by describing the tax-smoothing theory of deficits that I developed earlier. Then I estimate this model on United States data since 1920. Basically, the results are consistent with an unchanged structure of deficits since that time. Specifically, the recent deficits and the near-term projections of deficits reflect mainly the usual responses to recession and, it turns out, to anticipated inflation.

6.1 The Tax-Smoothing Model of Deficits

I analyze the determination of deficits within the framework of the tax-smoothing model that I developed in an earlier paper (Barro 1979).[1]

Robert J. Barro is professor of economics at the University of Rochester.

This research was supported by the National Science Foundation. I have benefited from comments at the International Seminar in Public Economics Conference on Public Debt in Santa Cruz, February 1984, a seminar at the University of California at Los Angeles, and the preconference for the National Bureau of Economic Research meeting.

1. Some related work is Kydland and Prescott 1980 and Lucas and Stokey 1983. The general idea of the implications of tax smoothing for the behavior of deficits appears also in Pigou 1928, chap. 6.

In this approach the government faces the exogenous, deterministic stream of real expenditures other than interest payments, as given by $g(t)$. The base of real taxable income is the deterministic amount $y(t)$, which generally depends on the path of tax rates. I think of $y(t)$ as a fixed fraction of the economy's real GNP for period t. Let $\tau(t)$ be the average tax rate at date t, so that the amount of real income tax revenue is $\tau(t)y(t)$. Then, if the real interest rate is the constant r and the initial real public debt is $b(0)$, the government's budget constraint in terms of present values is[2]

(1)
$$\int_0^\infty \tau(t)y(t)e^{-rt}dt = \int_0^\infty g(t)e^{-rt}dt + b(0).$$

In the present formulation I do not separate the revenue from money creation from the government's other revenues. Rather, I think of inflationary finance as a tax on the holdings of money. Then, in order to focus on taxes in one period versus those in another, I combine the inflation tax with the variety of other levies (on income, sales, property, etc.) that apply at the same date. In particular, there seems to be no reason to give special treatment to the inflation tax.[3]

Suppose that the allocative effects from taxation depend on the "average marginal tax rate," $\tau^m(t)$, for each period. That is, the time path of average marginal tax rates, $\tau^m(1)$, $\tau^m(2)$, . . . , influences people's incentives to work, produce, and consume in the various periods. Here I take a Ramsey-like optimal taxation perspective in order to formulate a testable positive theory of the government's choices of tax rates over time.[4] In particular, if each period is similar in terms of elasticities of labor supply, and so on, then the Ramsey formulation dictates roughly equal tax rates, $\tau^m(t)$, for each period.[5] More generally, this approach would allow the tax rate to depend on time-varying features of the economy such as war or peace and boom or recession. But to bring out the main implications of the approach, I assume to begin with that the government plans for equal average marginal tax rates, $\tau^m(t)$, in each period. Then I examine later some perturbations from this path of uniform taxation.

2. This formulation assumes that the real interest rate exceeds the economy's steady-state growth rate. For a discussion, see McCallum 1984.
3. Anticipated inflation amounts to a form of excise tax. But unanticipated inflation entails a capital levy, which has different implications for the excess burden of taxation (see, for example, Barro 1983). However, changes in other kinds of taxes can also imply capital levies.
4. For discussions of Ramsey taxation, see Atkinson and Stiglitz 1980, chap. 12, and Ramsey 1927.
5. Kydland and Prescott 1980, 185–86, suggest that this rule will be close to optimal if intertemporal substitution effects are strong.

I assume that the average marginal tax rate for any period bears a stable relation to that period's average tax rate, $\tau(t)$—that is,

(2) $$\tau^m(t) = f[\tau(t)],$$

where the function f is invariant over time. In this case the stabilization of average marginal tax rates entails stabilization of average tax rates. If τ denotes the constant value of the average tax rate, then the government's intertemporal budget constraint in equation (1) implies that this tax rate is

(3) $$\tau = [\int_0^\infty g(t)e^{-rt}dt + b(0)]/\int_0^\infty y(t)e^{-rt}dt.$$

Suppose that real government spending, $g(t)$, and the real tax base, $y(t)$, are fluctuating around trend values that grow at the common rate n. That is, the time paths, $g^*(t) = g^*(0)e^{nt}$ and $y^*(t) = y^*(0)e^{nt}$, have the same present values as the respective actual time paths, $g(t)$ and $y(t)$.[6] Then the current "normal" values, $g^*(0)$ and $y^*(0)$, satisfy the conditions

(4)
$$g^*(0) = (r - n)\int_0^\infty g(t)e^{-rt}dt,$$

$$y^*(0) = (r - n)\int_0^\infty y(t)e^{-rt}dt.$$

Dropping the time subscripts and substituting back into equation (3) yields the formula for the (stabilized) average tax rate,

(5) $$\tau = [g^* + (r - n)b]/y^*.$$

Hence the tax rate equals the ratio of normal real spending to normal real income, where normal real spending includes the real interest payments on the outstanding public debt, rb, less the amount financed by the usual growth of the real debt, nb. I discuss this last item further below.

The current deficit—which I think of as the change in the real quantity of interest-bearing public debt, db/dt—is given at any date by

$$db/dt = g + rb - \tau y = g + rb - y[g^* + (r - n)b]/y^*.$$

After rearranging terms, this expression becomes

(6) $$db/dt = (1 - y/y^*)[g^* + (r - n)b] + g - g^* + nb.$$

The first term on the right side of equation (6) indicates that the real debt rises when output is below "normal"—that is, when $y/y^* < 1$.

---

6. These assumptions rule out any drift in the ratio, g/y. In the long run this drift would be subject to the bounds, $0 < g/y < 1$.

Effectively, tax revenues fall in proportion to the fall in output (in order for the average tax rate not to change). Hence, the amount of revenue lost is the proportional shortfall of output $(1 - y/y^*)$ multiplied by the normal amount of real government spending (and revenues), $g^* + (r - n)b$. Note that, when tax rates are stabilized over time, the coefficient of the cyclical variable, $(1 - y/y^*)[g^* + (r - n)b]$, is unity in equation (6). Alternatively, if the government were to set relatively low tax rates during recessions, then it would have to engineer a more dramatic countercyclical response of deficits. In this case the coefficient of the cyclical variable would be greater than one. In any case, the present analysis does not distinguish the automatic cyclical response of tax revenues under a given tax law (which people sometimes try to filter out in the construction of a "full-employment deficit") from that effected through "discretionary" fiscal policy. For example, under a proportional income tax, average tax rates tend automatically to be stabilized over the business cycle, whereas under a graduated rate setup the average tax rate tends to be below normal during recessions and above normal for booms. Thus a well-designed tax system may make it unnecessary to change the tax laws frequently in order to achieve the desired cyclical pattern of tax rates. If the analysis included adjustment costs for altering the tax laws, then it would be possible to study the optimal design of these laws. But for the present analysis I assume that some combination of automatic response within the tax system plus discretionary changes in the laws achieves the desired behavior of deficits.

The second term on the right side of equation (6), $g - g^*$, indicates that the real debt rises by the amount of temporarily high real government spending. Thereby the government avoids abnormally high tax rates during periods when its expenditures are unusually high. Empirically, my measure of temporary spending focuses on the unusually high levels of military spending during wartime. Thus the unitary coefficient on the $(g - g^*)$ variable in equation (6) reflects the government's desire to equalize tax rates during wartime and peacetime periods. Alternatively, if the tax rates were above normal during wars, then the coefficient on the $(g - g^*)$ variable would be less than one.

Finally, other things equal, the last term in equation (6) says that the real debt grows at the rate n, which is the trend growth rate of the economy. If the debt did not grow along with the economy, then interest payments would fall over time relative to GNP, which would be inconsistent with stabilizing the average tax rate.

Note that the present formulation deals with the conventional concept of the funded real public debt, b. Sometimes people suggest adding the implicit debt that corresponds to the anticipated present value of social social security benefits or of other government obligations. In fact, the pertinent variable for the government's decisions on taxes is g^* (plus the amount, $(r - n)b$), which is the anticipated flow of normal real spending. Aside from differences in the degree of uncertainty attached to various categories of expenditures, it is clear that future social security benefits play no special role—rather, they enter the analysis in a manner analogous to future defense spending, and so forth. However, the debt could be redefined if desired to include either the present value of social security benefits or of other expenditures. This change in definition would not alter the central economic problem, which concerns the government's choice of tax rates at different dates. But different concepts of deficits would behave in different manners.

Suppose, for example, that people expect a bulge in social security benefits to occur five years from now and to last for ten years. On this count, current spending g would be below the normal flow g^*, which calls for a surplus ($db/dt < 0$) in equation (6). Correspondingly, the government raises taxes currently in order to prepare for the eventual bulge in spending. However, if the debt included the present value of social security benefits, then the rise over time in this present value (as the bulge in spending approaches) would offset the surplus in the funded debt. That is, the broader concept of public debt—which included social security—would not tend to decline over time. But no matter how one defines the debt, the important point is that the prediction for tax rates is identical. Namely, the expectation of a bulge in future spending calls for a rise in current tax rates. (Unfortunately, I have not yet isolated this type of effect empirically for prospective government spending, whether for social security or for other types of spending.)

Dividing through in equation (6) by the level of real debt, b, the results can be written in terms of the proportionate growth rate of the real debt:

$$(7) \quad (1/b)db/dt = (1 - y/y^*)(g^*/b + r - n) + (g - g^*)/b + n.$$

Empirically, the term $r - n$ is small relative to g^*/b. (That is, normal real spending g^* is large relative to real interest payments, rb, less the growth term, nb.) Hence I neglect the term $r - n$ in the subsequent analysis. Then it is appropriate to measure g^* as the normal amount of real government expenditures exclusive of interest payments.

When the time paths $g(t)$ and $y(t)$ are uncertain, the values g^* and y^* are also uncertain. I interpret these magnitudes in equation (7) as corresponding to anticipated present values of real government spending and GNP, assuming a known value of the real interest rate r. Possibly some further results could be obtained by modeling explicitly the uncertainty for future government spending and private endowments.[7]

---

7. See Lucas and Stokey 1983 for a treatment of uncertainty.

The main point is that new information about the long-run values of spending, g^*, and income, y^*, lead to corresponding changes in the average tax rate, τ, as shown in equation (5). Thus the tax rate adjusts for surprise changes in spending and income, but the sign or magnitude of the necessary adjustments cannot be predicted in advance. In other words, the tax rate follows a martingale. However, some predictable changes in tax rates may appear if—as mentioned before—the tax rate depends on the state of the economy. For example, if tax rates were lower than normal during recessions, then predictable increases in tax rates would occur along with the (predictable) ends of recessions. Similarly, if tax rates were higher than normal during wars, then predictable declines in tax rates would show up at the (predictable) ends of wars. Thus, the martingale property for tax rates is not central to the approach followed in this paper.[8]

Another property of the theory is that it prescribes no target value for the level of public debt or for the ratio of debt to income. A higher initial value of debt is "undesirable" in the sense that it requires a higher tax rate at each date (equation 5), which then entails a larger excess burden from taxation. But (with default ruled out) it is not worthwhile for the government systematically to run surpluses in order to pay off the debt.[9] Such a policy implies temporarily high tax rates, which violates the tax-smoothing criterion. Thus, given the right-side variables in equation (7), there is no independent effect on the growth rate of debt from the starting value of the debt/income ratio. (This conclusion would still follow even if the government varied the tax rate with the business cycle or with conditions of war and peace.)

The argument above is consistent with the marked tendency of the ratio of public debt to GNP to fall during peacetime, nonrecession years. (See Barro 1984, chap. 15, for the long-term evidence on this behavior from the United States and the United Kingdom.) The variable g^* incorporates a country's propensity to experience infrequent but possibly large wars. Therefore temporary spending, $g - g^*$, is negative rather than zero during the typical peacetime year. Hence the debt/income ratio tends to fall during peacetime and to rise sharply during the infrequent large wars.

If the price level follows a known path, then equation (7) describes the time path of the real debt. Hence, the nominal debt—denoted by

8. In a previous study (Barro 1981a) I accepted the random walk hypothesis for average tax rates, although the statistical tests were not very powerful. Subsequently I have rejected the random walk hypothesis for some revised systems. Sahasakul 1983 finds evidence that average marginal tax rates are lower than normal during recessions and higher than normal during wars.

9. If an increase in the debt/income ratio raises the required real interest rate payable on public debt (perhaps because of an increasing probability of the government's default), then there would be a force that deters the government from amassing very high debt/income ratios.

B—grows at the rate of inflation, π, plus the amount shown on the right side of equation (7). That is (neglecting the term, $r - n$, in equation 7),

$$(8) \quad (1/B)dB/dt = n + \pi + (1 - y/y^*)(g^*/b) + (g - g^*)/b.$$

Note that the inflation rate, π, has a one-to-one effect on the growth rate of the nominal debt.

A one-time surprise jump in the price level would shift the real debt, b, by a discrete amount in the opposite direction. Then, except for the shift in b on the right side of equation (8), there would be no alteration to the subsequent path of growth rates of the debt—in particular, there is no tendency to adjust the nominal debt in order to compensate for the unexpected inflation (and thereby to restore some target value of the real debt). It follows in equation (8) that the variable π should be replaced by the expected rate of inflation, π^e. (In the presence of indexed public debt, the actual rate of inflation would be appropriate.) The main point is that the planned growth rate of the real debt, $(1/B)$ $(dB/dt) - \pi^e$, depends on the real variables (other than π) that appear on the right side of equation (8). Hence, the government's deficit policy is specified in real terms, rather than being subject to some form of money illusion.

Given the expected real interest rate r, a higher value of anticipated inflation shows up as a higher nominal interest rate. Hence the previous result says that the government finances the (expected) inflation part of its nominal interest payments by issuing new nominal debt rather than by levying taxes. Although this interpretation is suggestive, it turns out that the results do not depend on a one-to-one relation between expected inflation and nominal interest rates. Any discrepancy here appears as a different value for the expected real interest rate. But a different level for the real interest rate does not affect the growth rate of the debt in equation (8) (assuming a given real growth rate, n, and neglecting the effect from the $r - n$ term in equation 7). A permanently higher real interest rate induces a once-and-for-all adjustment of the tax rate (equation 5), but no response of the deficit. On the other hand, if the expected real interest were temporarily high or low, then the deficit would adjust accordingly. Thus far I have not investigated this possibility empirically.

When the debt is long term there are also changes in the real market value from changes in long-term nominal interest rates. A one-time jump in the nominal interest rate shifts the current market value of the debt by a discrete amount in the opposite direction. For example, Butkiewicz (1983) shows that the market value of the debt (B^m) can be well approximated empirically from the par value (B^p) by using the formula

$$(9) \quad B^m \simeq B^p(1 + hc)/(1 + hR),$$

where c is the average coupon rate on the outstanding bonds, R is the overall market yield, and h is the average maturity of the bonds. For given values of c and h, the effect of a change in market yield on the market value of debt is approximately

$$(10) \qquad dB^m/B^m \simeq -dR \cdot h/(1 + hR).$$

Equations (7) and (8) describe the paths of the market value of the real and nominal debt, respectively, subsequent to the initial discrete shift in market value at the moment of the one-time shift in yield. In particular, this discrete shift affects subsequent growth rates of the debt only through the change in b on the right side of the equations (and by any change in expected inflation that accompanies the shift in the long-term nominal interest rate). As with a surprise change in the price level, there is no tendency to return to a normal real market value of the debt. But in order to explain the overall movements in the market value of the debt, it is necessary to include an additional variable—such as that shown in equation (10)—in order to measure the effect of surprise changes in interest rates. In practice, I assume that all changes in the yield on government bonds, R, are unanticipated.

When considering the public debt, most researchers deal with the par value rather than the market value. (However, some reliable estimates of market value are now available for the post–World War II period, as discussed below.) A surprise jump in nominal interest rates has no immediate effect on the debt when measured at par value. But as the old debt matures the government effectively replaces it with new debt, which bears, say, a higher coupon. (I assume that all debt is issued at par.) Thus, if nothing else changes the government would face a rising path of real interest payments—that is, current real payments would be low relative to the average of anticipated future real payments. As with any path of rising real expenditures, the government's policy of tax smoothing requires a rise in the current tax rate, which means a smaller current deficit. In other words, a surprise increase in nominal interest rates leads to a gradual reduction over time in the real debt when measured at par value. In fact, if there are no further surprises in interest rates (and the debt has finite maturity), then the real par value gradually approaches the real market value, which fell in a discrete fashion at the moment of the one-time shift in interest rates.

Using equation (9), the effect on the par value of the debt from a change in the average coupon rate is

$$(11) \qquad dB^p/B^p \simeq -dc \cdot h/(1 + hc).$$

Suppose that the retirement of old debt means that the coupon rate, c, approaches the market yield, R, gradually, with the speed of adjustment depending inversely on the average maturity, h—that is,

$$dc/dt \simeq (1/h)(R - c).$$

Then, using equation (11), the effect on the par value of the debt is

(12) $$(1/B^p)dB^p/dt \simeq -(R - c)/(1 + hc).$$

I add the right-side variable (unsuccessfully) to some of the equations that I estimate below. (I have data on R, c, and h only for the period since 1946.)

6.2 Setup of the Empirical Analysis

The equation that I estimate with annual United States data over subsamples of the period 1920–82 takes the form

(13) $$\log(B_t/B_{t-1}) = a_0 + a_1\pi_t^e + a_2 YVAR_t$$
$$+ a_3 GVAR_t + a_4 RVAR_t + u_t,$$

where u_t is an error term with the usual properties and the other variables are as follows:

- B: end-of-calendar year (par or market) value of the United States government's interest-bearing public debt, exclusive of holdings at federal agencies and trust funds or the Federal Reserve. Market value figures are based on Seater (1981) and Butkiewicz (1983).

- π_t^e: expected rate of inflation (for the CPI),[10] generated as a forecasting relation based on the following: two annual lags of inflation, π_{t-1} and π_{t-2}; two annual lags of monetary growth (based on annual averages of M1), μ_{t-1} and μ_{t-1}; and the interest rate on four- to six-month commercial paper at the end of the previous year, RC_{t-1}.[11] That is, the equation for inflation is

(14) $$\pi_t = b_0 + b_1\pi_{t-1} + b_2\pi_{t-2} + b_3 \mu_{t-1}$$
$$+ b_4\mu_{t-2} + b_5 RC_{t-1} + \text{error term.}$$

10. These inflation rates are January-to-January values, using the consumer price index less shelter since 1947. For 1943–47, the data are strongly affected by price controls. Instead of using the reported price levels, I substituted values based on the extrapolation of an estimated price-level equation from some previous research (Barro 1981c, 157). This adjustment shifts the inflation rates as follows: from 2.9% to 25.8% for 1943, from 2.3% to 13.0% for 1944, from 2.2% to 3.2% for 1945, from 16.7% to −4.8% for 1946, and from 10.2% to −2.9% for 1947. This procedure affects the subsequent results mainly for the samples that include the World War II years. (There are also some effects of lagged inflation rates on the estimates for 1948–49.)

11. Theoretically, the annual average of π_t^e would matter, which means that some updating of expectations for current-period information comes into play. The present procedure excludes current-period information (and thereby avoids some econometric problems). I used the commercial paper rate, rather than, say, a one-year treasury bill rate, in order to have a consistent variable for the full sample. The difference between a four- to six-month maturity and a one-year maturity would not be of major significance for the results.

This equation for inflation is estimated jointly with the debt equation (13).

The behavior of inflation in the post–World War II period differs markedly from that before the war. First, there is positive persistence in inflation rates from year to year, which is not true earlier; second, lagged monetary growth is a positive predictor of inflation, which also does not apply earlier; and third, the variance of the inflation rate—conditioned on information from the previous year—is much smaller now than before. Some experimentation indicated that the main break in the structure of the inflation equation occurred around the Korean War—possibly with the accords between the Fed and the Treasury, which relieved the Fed from strict stabilization of interest rates. In any event, I estimate separate coefficients of the inflation equation (14) for the period up to 1953 and for the recent period, 1954–82. (It turns out that, in order to maximize the overall value of the likelihood function, it would be slightly preferable to break the sample at 1955/56. But I have retained the break at 1953/54, which has some rationale a priori.) Note that in equation (13) the hypothesized coefficient of the π^e variable is $a_1 = 1$.

Returning to the specification of variables in equation (13),

$$\text{YVAR}_t \equiv (1 - y_t/y_t^*) \cdot (g_t^*/\bar{b}_t),$$

$$\text{GVAR}_t \equiv (g_t - g_t^*)/\bar{b}_t,$$

where $\bar{b}_t$ is a geometric average of the year-end values, B_t and B_{t-1}, divided by the GNP deflator for year t.[12]

I base the measure of temporary real federal spending, $g_t - g_t^*$, on the variable I used previously (Barro 1981b) to explain fluctuations in real GNP. In that approach I isolated mainly the temporary parts of military spending that accompanied wars. Shifts in the ratio of federal nondefense expenditures to GNP and shifts during peacetime in the ratio of military spending to GNP were treated as predominantly permanent (in the sense that the ratios followed random walks). Sahasakul (1983) finds additional components of temporary real federal spending from the following: (1) a drift since the 1930s in the ratio of federal transfers to GNP; (2) the tendency since the 1930s of real federal transfers to move countercyclically; and (3) the tendency of wars to crowd out the nonmilitary components of federal spending. However, these influences do not introduce variables that are independent of those that

---

12. The forms of the *YVAR* and *GVAR* variables in equation (13) arise as an approximation for discrete-time data to the continuous-time formulation in equation (8). The approximation seems to be satisfactory except for the very large values of $(g_t - g_t^*)/\bar{b}_t$ that arise at the start of World War I.

I include anyway in the equation to explain the growth rate of debt. Mainly, there are implications for the interpretations of coefficients—for example, the variable GVAR will measure the impact of temporary wartime spending net of the typical transitory decline in the other components of real federal spending during wartime. Recall that the tax-smoothing model predicts that the coefficient of $GVAR_t$ in equation (13) is $a_3 = 1$. But the crowding out of other federal spending during wars implies $a_3 < 1$. In addition, if tax rates are somewhat above normal during wartime, then the coefficient a_3 would be reduced further below one.

For the cyclical variable YVAR in equation (13), I need a measure of the temporary shortfall of output, $(1 - y_t/y_t^*)$. In my previous study (Barro 1979), I used the deviation of current real GNP, which measured y_t, from trend real GNP, which measured y_t^*.[13] I again report results with this construct, although it deals incorrectly with permanent shifts to the level of output. In these cases the variable indicates a permanent departure of output from normal. The results improve if I use instead the unemployment rate, U_t, to proxy for the shortfall in output, $(1 - y_t/y_t^*)$. As long as the unemployment rate is stationary in levels, this variable will work satisfactorily even when there are permanent shifts to the level of output.

My main results use the total unemployment rate (including the military in the labor force).[14] Then I assume a stable relation between percentage shortfalls in output and the departure of the unemployment rate from a fixed natural rate:

(15) $$(1 - y_t/y_t^*) = \lambda(U_t - .054).$$

I take the natural unemployment rate in this formulation to be 5.4%, which is the median rate over the sample 1890–1982. (The value 5.4% is also close to the median and mean over the period 1948–82.) For the post–World War II period (for which data are available), I obtain similar results if I use instead the prime-age male unemployment rate, U_t^m. Some people argue that this variable is more stable over long periods than the overall unemployment rate. Note that in equation (15) the parameter λ is an Okun's law type of coefficient, which is likely to lie between two and three.

As a general statement it would be preferable to construct normal output, y_t^*, as an explicit time series representation for "permanent income." (My measure for $g_t - g_t^*$ does take this approach, although

13. For trend real GNP, the growth rate was 3.4% per year since 1946 and before 1914. From 1915 to 1945, the two trend lines were connected, implying an average growth rate of 2.5% per year.
14. I also adjust the values from 1933 to 1943 as suggested by Darby 1976 to include New Deal workers as employed.

only for military spending.) But I have thus far been unsuccessful along these lines in the construction of the variable y_t^*.

The variable $YVAR_t$ depends also on normal real federal spending, g_t^*. I use here Sahasakul's (1983) concept of normal real federal spending, which combines normal military spending (which entered above into the construction of the $GVAR$ variable) with measures of normal real federal spending for transfers and nondefense purchases. In this context the results are relatively insensitive to the precise measure of g_t^*, as long as the variable picks up the longer-term movements in the size of the federal government. But when making comparisons over long periods, it is important to recall that the growth rate of the debt in equation (13) depends on the $YVAR$ variable, which equals the percentage shortfall in output, $(1 - y_t/y_t^*)$, multiplied by the ratio $g_t^*/\bar{b}_t$. For example, in 1982 this last variable is 0.83, while in 1933 it is 0.17. Hence—because of the high value of normal real federal spending in recent years—a one-percentage-point shortfall in output has five times as much effect on the growth rate of debt as it would have in 1933 (where the percentage shortfall in output was much larger).[15]

The tax-smoothing model suggests that the coefficient of $YVAR_t$ in equation (13) would be $a_2 = 1$. However, the countercyclical behavior of transfers and any tendency to lower tax rates during recessions lead to $a_2 > 1$. When the unemployment rate proxies for the shortfall in output (equation 15), the estimated coefficient on $YVAR_t$ is also multiplied by the Okun's law coefficient, λ.

The variable $RVAR_t$ in equation (13) accounts for the effects of changes in interest rates. With the debt measured at par value, the interest rate variable (available since 1946) is $RVAR_t = (\bar{R}_t - \bar{c}_t)/(1 + \bar{h}_t \bar{c}_t)$, where R is the yield, h is average maturity, c is the average coupon rate, and overbars signify averages over the year. When the debt is measured at market value (available accurately since 1941), the interest rate variable is $RVAR_t = \bar{h}_t(R_t - R_{t-1})/(1 + \bar{h}_t\bar{R}_t)$. In both cases the hypothesized coefficient in equation (13) is $a_4 = -1$.

6.3   Empirical Results

Table 6.1 shows joint, maximum-likelihood estimates for the debt equation (13) and the inflation equation (14). For the debt equations in this table, the $RVAR$ variable is omitted and the $YVAR$ variable is based on the overall unemployment rate. The first six sets of results refer to the sample 1920–40, 1948–82, which excludes the years associated

---

15. The ratio of the real deficit to real GNP, $(db/dt)/y_t$, depends on g_t^*/y_t. This last variable is .21 in 1982 and .06 in 1933.

with World War II. The inflation equations report separate coefficients for the two subperiods 1920–40, 48–53 and 1954–82. Also, the observations in the inflation equation for the first subperiod, 1920–40/48–53, are weighted by .40 in order to correct for heteroskedasticity (that is, for a higher error variance in the earlier sample).

For set 1 in table 6.1, the coefficients of the inflation equation in the earlier subperiod are insignificant except for *negative* effects of the lagged interest rate (coefficient of -1.2; $SE = 0.2$) and of the second lag of monetary growth (-0.29; $SE = 0.09$). The first effect probably reflects the tendency for (real) interest rates to be high during financial crises, which were also times of deflation. The second effect picks up the tendency for reversals in monetary growth under the earlier monetary regime. By contrast, for the later subperiod 1954–82, the coefficients of the first lags of inflation and monetary growth are each strongly positive (0.81; $SE = 0.18$ and 0.67; $SE = 0.15$, respectively). Surprisingly, the coefficient of the nominal interest rate is still negative (-0.37; $SE = 0.14$). The results for the inflation equation remain basically similar in the specifications discussed later.

Expected inflation, π_t^e, is calculated from the coefficients in the inflation equation. In set 1 of table 6.1, the coefficient of π_t^e in the debt equation is constrained to equal one, while in set 2 this coefficient is left free. Note that the unconstrained estimate for this coefficient is 0.97; $SE = 0.12$, which is consistent with the theoretical value of unity. Therefore I focus on the constrained results, which appear in set 1.

The estimated coefficient of *GVAR* (0.27; $SE = 0.09$) is significantly positive, but well below the value of unity that is suggested by the tax-smoothing model. The results in Sahasakul (1983) indicate that a small part of this discrepancy reflects the crowding out of other components of federal spending during wartime. But the main element is the tendency for average tax rates to be above normal during wars. I discuss these results further when the observations for World War II are included.

The estimated coefficient of *YVAR* (3.88; $SE = 0.26$) is positive and highly significant, which shows the strong countercyclical behavior of deficits. Dividing by an Okun's law coefficient of 2.5 (see equation 15) suggests that the reaction of debt growth to shortfalls in output involves a coefficient of about 1.5. The excess of this coefficient above one reflects the tendency during recessions for average tax rates to be below normal and for real federal transfers to be above normal (see Sahasakul 1983 for a detailed breakdown between these two elements). To see the quantitative effect of unemployment on the deficit, recall that the pertinent variable is $YVAR_t = (U_t - .054) \cdot (g_t^*/b_t)$, which has an estimated coefficient of 3.9. In 1982 the variable g_t^*/b_t equals 0.83, which means that a one-percentage point increase in the unemployment rate

Table 6.1   **Basic Regression Results for Debt Growth and Inflation**

Set	Sample	ℒ	Constant	π^e	GVAR	YVAR	$\hat{\sigma}$/DW
					Equation for DB_t		
(1)	1920–40,	289.0	.009	1	.27	3.88	.023
	1948–82		(.006)		(.09)	(.26)	2.2
(2)	1920–40,	289.0	.010	.97	.27	3.90	.023
	1948–82		(.007)	(.12)	(.09)	(.26)	2.2
	For DB_t	290.6	.013	1	.26	3.48	.022
(3) I:	1920–40		(.017)		(.20)	(.45)	2.2
II:	1948–82		.013	1	.38	4.54	
			(.006)		(.12)	(.45)	
	For DB_t	293.1	.026	1.65	.30	3.21	.021
(4) I:	1920–40		(.021)	(.58)	(.21)	(.50)	2.1
II:	1948–82		.024	.71	.38	4.85	
			(.007)	(.15)	(.12)	(.42)	
	For DB_t	290.9	.009	1	.24	3.54	.022
(5) I:	1920–40,		(.010)		(.12)	(.32)	2.2
	1948–53		.014	1	.40	4.63	
II:	1954–82		(.007)		(.14)	(.45)	
	For DB_t	293.1	.011	1.32	.22	3.56	.022
(6) I:	1920–40,		(.011)	(.42)	(.12)	(.33)	2.1
	1948–53		.029	.64	.42	5.03	
II:	1954–82		(.009)	(.15)	(.14)	(.42)	
(7)	1920–82	288.7	.023	1	.76	4.90	.045
			(.006)		(.05)	(.41)	1.7
(8)	1920–82	288.7	.024	.97	.76	4.91	.045
			(.007)	(.15)	(.05)	(.41)	1.7

Note: For the debt equation, the dependent variable, DB_t, is the growth rate from end December to end December of the privately held, interest-bearing public debt. The figures are par value except for sets 13–14 in table 6.2, which use market values. For the inflation equation, the dependent variable, π_t, is the growth rate (January to January) of the consumer price index (measured without the shelter component since 1947).

The inflation equation (in sets 1–8 and sets 19–24 in table 6.3) allows for separate coefficients for the subperiod up to 1953 and for the later subperiod 1954–82. The earlier observations are weighted by .40 (the maximum likelihood estimate from set 1) to correct for heteroskedasticity. In sets 7–8, which include World War II, the observations for 1943–47 are deleted from the inflation equation.

For the debt equation, there are separate coefficients over two subperiods in the cases indicated (sets 3–6 and 21–24). Otherwise a single set of coefficients applies for the full sample. In any event, the variance of the error term is assumed to be constant for the full sample.

ℒ is the log of the value of the likelihood function. The independent variable π^e is calculated as a forecast of π_t from the coefficients of the inflation equation. The value

Table 6.1   (continued)

Equation for π_t (I. Sample up to 1953   II. Sample 1954–82)

Constant	π_{t-1}	π_{t-2}	μ_{t-1}	μ_{t-2}	RC_{t-1}	$\hat{\sigma}$/DW
0.33	.06	.14	.04	−.29	−1.16	.015
(.010)	(.12)	(.11)	(.10)	(.09)	(.23)	1.6
.002	.81	−.02	.67	.05	−.37	
(.006)	(.18)	(.12)	(.15)	(.20)	(.14)	
.033	.06	.14	.04	−.29	−1.18	.015
(.010)	(.12)	(.11)	(.10)	(.09)	(.25)	1.6
.002	.82	−.03	.68	.05	−.37	
(.006)	(.18)	(.12)	(.16)	(.20)	(.14)	
.037	.01	.17	.05	−.31	−1.26	.015
(.010)	(.12)	(.11)	(.11)	(.09)	(.24)	1.5
.004	.81	−.06	.71	.05	−.40	
(.006)	(.18)	(.13)	(.16)	(.20)	(.14)	
.025	−.01	.16	.01	−.24	−.94	.015
(.012)	(.10)	(.09)	(.08)	(.09)	(.30)	1.6
.000	.89	−.15	.81	.03	−.40	
(.006)	(.19)	(.14)	(.17)	(.21)	(.15)	
.037	.01	.17	.05	−.32	−1.25	.015
(.011)	(.12)	(.11)	(.10)	(.09)	(.23)	1.5
.004	.81	−.07	.71	.05	−.41	
(.006)	(.18)	(.13)	(.16)	(.20)	(.14)	
.030	−.01	.16	.04	−.27	−1.04	.014
(.013)	(.10)	(.10)	(.08)	(.10)	(.31)	1.7
−.002	.91	−.20	.84	.02	−.37	
(.007)	(.20)	(.14)	(.18)	(.22)	(.15)	
.005	.13	−.41	.19	−.04	−.55	.015
(.014)	(.16)	(.14)	(.15)	(.13)	(.32)	2.0
−.004	.91	−.34	.85	−.06	−.21	
(.007)	(.21)	(.14)	(.18)	(.24)	(.16)	
.005	.13	−.41	.19	−.04	−.55	.015
(.014)	(.16)	(.15)	(.15)	(.13)	(.33)	2.0
−.004	.91	−.35	.85	−.06	−.20	
(.007)	(.21)	(.14)	(.18)	(.24)	(.16)	

1 indicates that the coefficient of this variable is constrained to unity. The variable GVAR, based on temporary military spending, is discussed in the text.

The cyclical variable YVAR, described in the text, is based on the overall unemployment rate, U_t − .054, for sets 1–10 and 13–18. Sets 11 and 12 use the prime-age male unemployment rate, U^m − .041. Sets 19–24 use real GNP relative to trend.

In sets 13–14 of table 6.2 (which use the market value of debt), the variable $RVAR_t$ = $\bar{h}_t(R_t − R_{t-1}) / (1 + \bar{h}_t R_t)$, where R is the average yield on government debt and h is the average maturity. Overbars indicate estimates of averages over the year. For sets 15–16 the variable is $RVAR_t = (\bar{R}_t − \bar{c}_t) / (1 + \bar{h}_t \bar{c}_t)$, where c is the average coupon rate on government debt. Sets 17–18 use the lagged value of this last measure of RVAR.

$\hat{\sigma}$ is the standard error of estimate; DW (shown below $\hat{\sigma}$) is the Durbin-Watson statistic.

In the inflation equation, π_{t-1} and π_{t-2} are lagged values of the dependent variable, μ_{t-1} and μ_{t-2} are lagged values of monetary growth (based on annual averages of M1), and RC_{t-1} is the value from the previous December of the four-to six-month rate on commercial paper.

raises the estimated growth of the debt by $3.9 \cdot (0.83) = 3.2$ percentage points per year. For a debt level of $850 billion (December 1982), the corresponding increase in the deficit is by $3.2\% \cdot 850 = \$27$ billion.

The standard error of estimate for the debt equation is $\hat{\sigma} = 0.023$ (that is, ± 2.3 percentage points per year). This result corresponds to an R^2 of .91, although the maximization of R^2 is not the criterion for the estimation. The Durbin-Watson statistic of 2.2 suggests that serial correlation of residuals is not a problem.

The results in sets 3–6 of table 6.1 check whether the debt equation is stable over various subperiods. Sets 3 and 4 allow the coefficients for 1920–40 to differ from those for 1948–82. Sets 5 and 6 specify the first subperiod as 1920–40, 48–53 and the second as 1954–82. Also, sets 3 and 5 constrain the coefficient of the π^e variable to unity, while sets 4 and 6 relax this constraint. In all cases the hypothesis of stable coefficients over the two subperiods is accepted at conventional significance levels by likelihood-ratio tests. For example, for set 3 (where the samples are 1920–40 and 1948–82, and where the coefficient of π^e is fixed at one), the value of $-2 \cdot \log$ (likelihood ratio) is 3.2, which is below the 5% critical value for the χ^2 distribution with three degrees of freedom of 7.8. For set 4 (where the π^e coefficients are unrestricted), the test statistic is 8.2, with a 5% critical value with four degrees of freedom of 9.5. The results are basically similar in sets 5 and 6, where the break in the sample is at 1953–54.

These findings are important, since they indicate that the process for generating deficits in the interwar period, 1920–40 (or the period 1920–40, 1948–53) is broadly similar to that in the post–World War II period, 1948–82 (or 1954–82). In particular, the statistical evidence does not support the idea that there has been a shift toward a fiscal policy that generates more real public debt on average or that generates larger deficits in response to recessions. (In set 3 of table 6.1, the estimated coefficients of the *YVAR* variable are 3.48; $SE = 0.45$ for 1920–40; and 4.54, $SE = 0.45$ for 1948–82. However, even this pattern of higher point estimates in the later period reverses later when I consider an alternative measure of the *YVAR* variable.)

Sets 7 and 8 of table 6.1 deal with the full sample, 1920–82, which adds the years associated with World War II, 1941–47, to the previous sample.[16] Aside from the deterioration in fit—as measured by the standard error of estimate, $\hat{\sigma}$—the most striking change is the increase in the coefficient of the *GVAR* variable. Naturally this variable is the principal source of deficits during World War II. The estimated coef-

---

16. Because of the problems with price controls (note 10 above), I exclude the years 1943–47 from the inflation equation. The values of π_t^e for these years are those implied by the estimated coefficients for the earlier subperiod, 1920–40, 1948–53.

ficient is now 0.76; $SE = 0.05$, which is highly significant and closer to the hypothesized value of unity. But it is also clear that the present formulation does not satisfactorily include the observations from World War II into the specification that works satisfactorily for the other years. One of the problems is that the estimated inflation equation (using the coefficients from the earlier subperiod, 1920–40, 1948–53—see note 16 above) generates implausibly low values of anticipated inflation during World War II. Specifically, these values are close to zero throughout the period 1941–45. The specification has to be changed to allow the earlier monetary regime to generate high values of monetary growth and inflation during wartime. (Similar problems arise when I attempt to add the observations from World War I, 1917–19.) It is also clear that the measure of temporary wartime spending, $GVAR$, is subject to substantial measurement error during the major wars, which accounts for some of the increase in the standard error of estimate. This problem can probably be handled by estimating the $GVAR$ variable (as I did in Barro 1981b) jointly with the debt and inflation equations.

Table 6.2 shows some additional results for the recent sample, 1954–82. Sets 9 and 10 (with the π^e coefficient restricted to one and unrestricted, respectively) are similar to those for the longer sample (with World War II excluded), as shown in sets 1 and 2 of table 6.1. Sets 11 and 12 of table 6.2 change the $YVAR$ variable to use the prime-age male unemployment rate, $U_t^m - .041$, where 0.041 is the mean value of U^m over the period 1954–82. Although the fit of the equation for debt growth in sets 11 and 12 is slightly worse than that in sets 9 and 10, the general nature of the results is similar.

Sets 13 and 14 of table 6.2 use the estimated market value of the public debt, rather than the par value, in the construction of the dependent variable. The equation for debt growth now includes an interest rate variable, $RVAR_t$, which picks up the effect on the market value of debt from changes in interest rates. For set 13 (where the coefficient of π^e is fixed at one), the estimated coefficient of $RVAR_t$ is -0.83; $SE = 0.13$, which differs insignificantly from the hypothesized value of -1. The other results are broadly similar to those found in sets 9 and 10, which are based on the par value of public debt.

In sets 15–18 of table 6.2 I attempt to find an effect from changes in interest rates on the growth in debt when measured at par value. (The variable $RVAR_t$ is now based on the difference between the yield and the coupon rate—see the notes to table 6.2.) Although the hypothesized coefficient of $RVAR_t$ is -1, the estimated values in sets 15 and 16 are positive, but with very high standard errors. Since the $RVAR_t$ variable may be proxying for within-period revisions of expected inflation, I used instead the lagged value, $RVAR_{t-1}$, in sets 17 and 18. The estimated coefficients do decrease—for example, to -0.13; $SE =$

Table 6.2   Regression Results for 1954–82 Sample

Set	Sample	$\mathscr{L}$	Constant	π^e	GVAR	YVAR	RVAR	$\hat{\sigma}$/DW
(9)		156.0	.011 (.007)	1	.31 (.12)	4.21 (.42)		.019 2.2
(10)		156.8	.024 (.009)	.71 (.16)	.35 (.12)	4.67 (.41)		.019 2.0
(11)	YVAR uses U^m	152.5	.004 (.008)	1	.19 (.13)	3.73 (.44)		.022 1.8
(12)	YVAR uses U^m	152.8	−.003 (.012)	1.18 (.23)	.20 (.12)	3.57 (.46)		.022 2.0
(13)	DB from market value	151.6	.022 (.008)	1	.39 (.15)	4.72 (.49)	−.83 (.13)	.023 2.3
(14)	DB from market value	153.2	.038 (.009)	.66 (.16)	.46 (.14)	5.31 (.47)	−.81 (.13)	.023 2.1
(15)	Add $RVAR_t$ to (9)	156.3	.007 (.009)	1	.30 (.11)	4.18 (.42)	.45 (.59)	.019 2.2
(16)	Add $RVAR_t$ to (10)	157.2	.020 (.010)	.68 (.17)	.32 (.12)	4.63 (.14)	.57 (.62)	.019 2.1
(17)	Add $RVAR_{t-1}$ to (9)	156.0	.012 (.009)	1	.32 (.12)	4.23 (.44)	−.13 (.60)	.019 2.2
(18)	Add $RVAR_{t-1}$ to (10)	156.9	.024 (.010)	.70 (.16)	.35 (.12)	4.68 (.42)	.11 (.65)	.019 2.1

Note: See notes to table 6.1.

0.60, in set 17. These results are consistent with the theoretical value of −1, although the estimates are very imprecise.

Table 6.3, which refers to the sample 1920–40, 1948–82, uses output relative to trend rather than the unemployment rate in the construction of the cyclical variable, YVAR. The fits for the debt equation are substantially worse than those achieved with the unemployment rate—compare, for example, sets 19 and 20 in table 6.3 with sets 1 and 2 in table 6.1. It turns out that the main differences arise in the post–World War II sample, especially during the 1974–76 recession. In any event the results based on output relative to trend are still consistent with an unchanged structure of the debt equation over either the subperiods, 1920–40 and 1948–82 (sets 21 and 22 of table 6.3) or 1920–40/48–53 and 1954–82 (sets 23 and 24).

One advantage of the results in table 6.3 is that the estimated coefficient of the YVAR variable reveals directly the effect on debt growth from shortfalls in output. For example, in set 19, the estimated coefficient is 1.35; $SE = 0.13$. This estimate is significantly above the value of unity that comes from the tax-smoothing model, though some of this

Table 6.2   (continued)

			Equation for π_t			
Constant	π_{t-1}	π_{t-2}	μ_{t-1}	μ_{t-2}	RC_{t-1}	$\hat{\sigma}/DW$
.005	.77	.05	.63	.08	−.44	.015
(.005)	(.14)	(.11)	(.13)	(.15)	(.11)	1.5
.000	.88	−.08	.79	.06	−.45	.014
(.006)	(.17)	(.12)	(.16)	(.18)	(.13)	1.7
.000	.84	.08	.72	.12	−.52	.016
(.005)	(.14)	(.11)	(.13)	(.16)	(.11)	1.6
.003	.78	.13	.64	.12	−.50	.016
(.006)	(.15)	(.10)	(.14)	(.15)	(.12)	1.5
.001	.77	−.10	.70	.02	−.29	.014
(.006)	(.17)	(.12)	(.15)	(.19)	(.13)	1.7
−.003	.88	−.25	.84	−.02	−.27	.013
(.006)	(.19)	(.13)	(.17)	(.21)	(.14)	2.0
.006	.78	.06	.62	.09	−.47	.016
(.005)	(.14)	(.10)	(.12)	(.15)	(.11)	1.5
.001	.90	−.07	.78	.07	−.49	.014
(.006)	(.17)	(.12)	(.16)	(.18)	(.14)	1.7
.004	.77	.05	.64	.08	−.44	.015
(.005)	(.14)	(.11)	(.13)	(.15)	(.11)	1.6
.000	.88	−.09	.79	.06	−.45	.014
(.006)	(.17)	(.12)	(.16)	(.18)	(.13)	1.8

excess reflects the countercyclical behavior of federal transfers. (Sets 21–24 show that the point estimates of the YVAR coefficients from the earlier subperiods exceed those from the later subperiods, which reverses the pattern found before with the unemployment rate. However, these differences across subperiods are statistically insignificant.)

6.4   Some Episodes of United States Debt Issue

Table 6.4 shows actual and estimated values for the growth rate of nominal debt, DB_t, and the inflation rate, π_t, over the sample 1920–40, 1948–82. The estimated values come from the regressions shown in set 1 of table 6.1 (where the coefficient of π^e is constrained to unity). Table 6.5 shows the values of the explanatory variables GVAR and YVAR (based on the overall unemployment rate), as well as the ratio $g^*/\hat{b}$, which enters into the construction of the YVAR variable.

Note first the negative values of DB and $\hat{DB}$ (i.e., "surpluses") throughout the 1920s. These derive, first, from negative values of anticipated inflation, especially for 1921–22; second, from the economic boom (negative values of the cyclical variable, YVAR) for most of 1923–

Table 6.3   **Regression Results Using Output Relative to Trend**

Set	Sample	$\mathscr{L}$	Constant	π^e	GVAR	YVAR	$\hat{\sigma}$/DW
			\multicolumn{5}{c}{Equation for DB_t}				
(19)	1920–40, 1948–82	277.1	.004 (.008)	1	.08 (.10)	1.35 (.13)	.029 1.7
(20)	1920–40, 1948–82	281.4	−.011 (.011)	1.56 (.22)	.13 (.09)	1.41 (.13)	.025 2.1
(21)	For DB_t 1920–40	278.0	−.005 (.024)	1	.12 (.25)	1.51 (.28)	.029 1.8
	1948–82		.003 (.008)	1	−.02 (.13)	1.17 (.23)	
(22) I:	For DB_t 1920–40	282.1	−.007 (.026)	1.85 (.74)	.14 (.23)	1.41 (.28)	.025 2.1
II:	1948–82		−.013 (.012)	1.58 (.26)	.12 (.13)	1.22 (.23)	
(23) I:	For DB_t 1920–40,	278.5	−.002 (.014)	1	.20 (.13)	1.44 (.17)	.028 1.8
	1948–53		.002 (.009)	1	−.06 (.15)	1.21 (.23)	
II:	1954–82						
(24) I:	For DB_t 1920–40,	282.4	.003 (.020)	1.80 (.86)	.18 (.13)	1.44 (.16)	.025 2.1
	1948–53		−.023 (.016)	1.69 (.32)	.04 (.14)	1.21 (.24)	
II:	1954–82						

Note: See notes to table 6.1.

29; and third, from relatively low values of the *GVAR* variable. From 1931 to 1940 the values of debt growth are all positive (i.e., "deficits"). This behavior reflects the countercyclical response of deficits to the Great Depression (that is, to the positive values of the cyclical variable, *YVAR,* particularly for 1931–35). There are large increases in real federal spending during the New Deal period after 1932, but not in the wartime spending that is the basis for my measure of temporary spending, *GVAR.* Therefore, higher federal spending is not a major element in my estimates of debt growth during the 1930s. (The variable *GVAR* equals $(g - g^*)/\bar{b}$, which is negative but declining in magnitude during the 1930s because of the substantial rise in the real debt, $\bar{b}$.) However, the higher real spending on nondefense items—which I implicitly treat as permanent—would account for the large increases in tax rates that occurred under Hoover and Roosevelt from 1932 to 1936. (See Barro

Table 6.3   (continued)

		Equation for π_t	(I. Sample up to 1953	II. Sample up to 1954–82)		
Constant	π_{t-1}	π_{t-2}	μ_{t-1}	μ_{t-2}	RC_{t-1}	$\hat{\sigma}$/DW
.040	−.10	.26	−.02	−.37	−1.42	.017
(.009)	(.11)	(.10)	(.09)	(.08)	(.20)	1.3
−.005	.81	.23	.78	.23	−.62	
(.005)	(.15)	(.11)	(.14)	(.17)	(.12)	
.036	−.10	.21	−.01	−.29	−1.02	.017
(.007)	(.08)	(.07)	(.06)	(.06)	(.19)	1.3
.002	.65	.28	.64	.24	−.58	
(.005)	(.14)	(.09)	(.13)	(.15)	(.11)	
.039	−.08	.24	−.02	−.36	−1.30	.017
(.010)	(.11)	(.10)	(.10)	(.08)	(.23)	1.3
−.006	.80	.25	.72	.22	−.56	
(.005)	(.15)	(.11)	(.15)	(.17)	(.13)	
.032	−.08	.19	−.02	−.25	−.92	.017
(.011)	(.08)	(.08)	(.06)	(.08)	(.29)	1.4
.002	.65	.31	.57	.21	−.55	
(.006)	(.14)	(.09)	(.14)	(.15)	(.12)	
.041	−.08	.23	−.02	−.36	−1.29	.017
(.011)	(.11)	(.10)	(.09)	(.08)	(.21)	1.3
−.006	.79	.23	.73	.23	−.56	
(.005)	(.15)	(.11)	(.15)	(.17)	(.13)	
.025	−.09	.18	−.01	−.25	−.87	.017
(.016)	(.08)	(.09)	(.05)	(.11)	(.35)	1.4
.004	.61	.29	.55	.21	−.51	
(.006)	(.14)	(.09)	(.14)	(.14)	(.12)	

and Sahasakul 1983, for further discussion.) In any event, the actual debt growth, DB, is reasonably in line with the estimated values, $\hat{DB}$, throughout the 1930s.

I have already mentioned that the dramatic increases in public debt during World War II derive primarily from the high values of temporary federal spending, as reflected in the $GVAR$ variable. In fact, the average growth rate of the nominal debt from the end of 1940 until the end of 1945 is 34% per year. (From the end of 1916 until the end of 1919 it is over 100% per year.) However, since my detailed results for the periods of the world wars are at present unsatisfactory, I cannot say much more about these episodes.

For the post–World War II period, note first that neither the actual nor the estimated values of debt growth are very high during the Korean War, say, 1950–53. The values of $GVAR$ are high, but those for the cyclical variable, $YVAR$, are low. Also, the calculated values of expected inflation, π^e, are relatively low at this time. The response of deficits to recessions shows up, for example, in 1949, 1954, 1958, and

Table 6.4   Values of Debt Growth and Inflation

Year	DB	$\hat{DB}$	$DB - \hat{DB}$	π	$\hat{\pi}$	$\pi - \hat{\pi}$
1920	− .038	− .026	− .012	− .014	− .021	.007
1921	− .039	− .030	− .009	− .117	− .091	− .026
1922	− .036	− .054	.018	− .008	− .062	.054
1923	− .038	− .045	.007	.027	− .010	.038
1924	− .049	− .036	− .014	.002	− .028	.030
1925	.000	− .049	.049	.036	− .018	.054
1926	− .112	− .073	− .039	− .023	− .022	.000
1927	− .064	− .072	.008	− .015	− .038	.023
1928	− .049	− .048	− .001	− .010	− .023	.013
1929	− .059	− .072	.013	.000	− .031	.031
1930	− .007	.009	− .016	− .073	− .030	− .043
1931	.084	.132	− .048	− .106	− .008	− .098
1932	.123	.116	.007	− .103	− .021	− .082
1933	.162	.147	.015	.026	.010	.016
1934	.167	.172	− .005	.030	.040	− .011
1935	.177	.135	.042	.015	.036	− .022
1936	.104	.082	.022	.019	.016	.003
1937	.029	.032	− .002	.009	− .014	.023
1938	.043	.064	− .021	− .019	− .011	− .008
1939	.070	.081	− .011	− .002	.015	− .018
1940	.072	.090	− .018	.012	.030	− .018
1948	− .038	− .018	− .019	.008	− .008	.016
1949	.035	.006	.029	− .030	.002	− .032
1950	− .014	.019	− .033	.082	.015	.067
1951	− .018	.013	− .031	.041	.017	.023
1952	.019	.003	.016	.002	.014	− .012
1953	.019	− .022	.041	.007	.001	.006
1954	.013	.027	− .014	− .012	.018	− .031
1955	.000	− .019	.018	.000	− .001	.001
1956	− .029	− .010	− .019	.033	.013	.020
1957	− .011	.001	− .012	.034	.025	.010
1958	.033	.038	− .005	.013	.019	− .006
1959	.035	.001	.034	.011	.008	.004
1960	− .014	.011	− .025	.016	.018	− .002
1961	.022	.022	.000	.007	.005	.002
1962	.018	.002	.016	.014	.009	.005
1963	.006	.014	− .009	.015	.018	− .003
1964	.008	.004	.004	.010	.020	− .011
1965	− .009	− .005	− .004	.020	.023	− .003
1966	− .005	− .011	.005	.030	.031	− .001
1967	.018	.007	.012	.035	.035	.000
1968	.030	.000	.030	.040	.037	.004
1969	− .025	.012	− .037	.053	.058	− .005
1970	.036	.036	.000	.044	.052	− .019
1971	.076	.048	.028	.033	.043	− .010
1972	.057	.049	.008	.036	.055	− .020
1973	− .003	.016	− .020	.095	.059	.036

Table 6.4   (continued)

Year	DB	$\hat{DB}$	$DB - \hat{DB}$	π	$\hat{\pi}$	$\pi - \hat{\pi}$
1974	.039	.080	−.041	.112	.094	.018
1975	.255	.206	.050	.065	.093	−.028
1976	.159	.133	.027	.052	.062	−.011
1977	.114	.110	.003	.060	.064	−.004
1978	.092	.087	.005	.082	.076	.006
1979	.072	.089	−.016	.113	.084	.029
1980	.131	.154	−.022	.103	.097	.006
1981	.119	.137	−.018	.077	.065	.012
1982	.201	.189	.012	.041	.058	−.018

Note: $DB_t \equiv \log(B_t/B_{t-1})$, where B_t is the value from the end of December of the privately held part of the interest-bearing public debt—that is, the gross public debt less holdings by federal agencies and trust funds and the Federal Reserve. (See Barro 1979 for details.) $\hat{DB}_t$ is the estimated value from set 1 of table 6.1.
$\pi_t \equiv \log(P_{t+1}/P_t)$, where P_t is the January value of the seasonally adjusted CPI (less shelter since 1947). $\hat{\pi}_t$ is the estimated value from set 1 of table 6.1.

1961. The Kennedy-Johnson tax cuts for 1964–65 do not correspond to notable residuals in the equation for debt growth.

For the Vietnam War—say 1966–68—the positive residuals for debt growth support the common view that taxes were raised insufficiently at this time. But perhaps because of the surcharge on the income tax, a substantial negative residual does show up for 1969.

Since 1969 expected inflation has become an important influence on the deficit, as measured by the growth in the nominal debt. In particular, the values of π^e (which have a one-to-one effect on the estimates of debt growth, $\hat{DB}$) are between 4% and 6% for 1969–73, increase to 9% for 1974–75, fall to between 6% and 8% for 1976–79, reach 10% in 1980, and then decline to 6% for 1981–82.

The debt equation underpredicts the deficits during the recession years 1975–76. (However, the error is much greater if the $YVAR$ variable is based on real GNP relative to trend rather than the unemployment rate.) But the debt equation is basically on track for the 1980–82 recession. For 1982 the actual growth rate of the nominal debt is 20% (corresponding to an increase by $155 billion in the nominal, privately held, interest-bearing debt), while the estimated value is 19%. This estimate breaks down into six percentage points owing to anticipated inflation ($\pi_t^e = 6\%$, although $\pi_t = 4\%$) and thirteen percentage points owing to the recession ($YVAR_t = .034$, based on the unemployment rate of 9.5%). Because nothing special is going on with the constructed measure of temporary federal spending, $GVAR$, it turns out that the constant and the contribution from the $GVAR$ variable essentially cancel out.

Table 6.5   Values of Explanatory Variables

Year	GVAR	YVAR	$g^*/\bar{b}$
1917	1.203	− .004	1.12
1918	1.067	− .036	.89
1919	.284	− .014	.37
1920	− .072	.001	.31
1921	.015	.012	.16
1922	− .067	.004	.20
1923	− .071	− .006	.24
1924	− .070	.000	.22
1925	− .083	− .005	.25
1926	− .088	− .009	.28
1927	− .089	− .005	.29
1928	− .096	− .002	.32
1929	− .101	− .006	.34
1930	− .092	.014	.31
1931	− .069	.039	.31
1932	− .048	.036	.17
1933	− .045	.036	.17
1934	− .045	.035	.25
1935	− .037	.026	.22
1936	− .034	.017	.30
1937	− .035	.012	.24
1938	− .029	.019	.22
1939	− .029	.017	.23
1940	.008	.013	.24
1941	.147	.003	.35
1942	.476	− .008	.41
1943	.571	− .010	.27
1944	.494	− .008	.19
1945	.345	− .005	.14
1946	.039	− .002	.15
1947	− .016	− .003	.18
1948	− .022	− .004	.22
1949	− .034	.001	.25
1950	− .012	− .001	.23
1951	.044	− .007	.30
1952	.053	− .009	.36
1953	.029	− .010	.40
1954	.002	.000	.36
1955	− .033	− .005	.39
1956	− .036	− .006	.41
1957	− .038	− .006	.46
1958	− .041	.005	.47
1959	− .052	.000	.48
1960	− .054	.000	.49
1961	− .053	.006	.52
1962	− .053	− .001	.57
1963	− .058	.001	.57
1964	− .062	− .002	.59

Table 6.5 (continued)

Year	GVAR	YVAR	$g^*/\bar{b}$
1965	−.051	−.006	.62
1966	−.007	−.013	.70
1967	.041	−.013	.74
1968	.055	−.016	.78
1969	.038	−.017	.85
1970	−.018	−.005	.91
1971	−.055	.003	.94
1972	−.061	.000	.98
1973	−.087	−.007	1.06
1974	−.087	.000	1.16
1975	−.076	.032	1.10
1976	−.073	.021	.99
1977	−.067	.014	.95
1978	−.063	.005	.96
1979	−.060	.003	.97
1980	−.050	.016	.98
1981	−.049	.020	.94
1982	−.040	.034	.83

Note: $GVAR_t \equiv (g_t - g_t^*)/\bar{b}_t$, where $(g_t - g_t^*)$ is temporary real defense spending (based on Barro 1981b), and $\bar{b}_t \equiv \sqrt{B_t \cdot B_{t-1}}/P_t$, where B_t is the privately held public debt at the end of year t (table 6.4) and P_t is the GNP deflator for year t.
$YVAR_t \equiv (U_t - .054 \cdot g_t^*/\bar{b}_t$, where U_t is the unemployment rate in the total labor force (adjusted as suggested by Darby 1976 for 1933–43) and g_t^* is normal real federal spending, based on Sahasakul 1983.

I also use the estimated equation to forecast deficits for 1983 and 1984. The inflation equation implies the value $\pi_t^e = 4.8\%$ for 1983. (The actual value of the inflation rate for 1983 is about 3.5%.) The main element in the decline of inflationary expectations from 1982 to 1983 is the low actual rate of inflation, $\pi_t = 4.1\%$, for 1982. Using the actual unemployment rate of 9.5% for 1983, the resulting estimate for debt growth, $\hat{DB}_t$, for 1983 is 16.6%. Note that 4.8 percentage points of this total come from expected inflation, while 11.8 percentage points derive from the continuing effect of the recession. (The combined effect of the constant and the GVAR variable is near zero.) The projected value for debt growth implies that the level of debt would increase from $848 billion at the end of December 1982 to $1,001 billion at the end of December 1983. Thus the predicted nominal deficit—in the sense of the change in the privately held, interest-bearing public debt—for calendar 1983 is $153 billion. (To get closer to conventional measures of the deficit, one should add the increase in high-powered money, which is roughly $15 billion for calendar 1983.) The data I have at this writing (kindly supplied to me by Eric Hanushek) indicate that the actual value of privately held public debt at the end of December 1983 is about

$1,018 billion. This figure implies an actual growth rate of the debt, DB_t, of 18.3% for 1983, compared with my projected value of 16.6%. The gap of 0.017 between actual and estimated values is not out of line with the fitted equation, for which the standard error of estimate was $\hat{\sigma} = 0.023$. The actual deficit—in the sense of the change in the nominal, privately held debt for calendar 1983 is about $170 billion, compared with my forecast of $153 billion.

For 1984 the value of π_t^e turns out to be 6.6%. The main reason for the rise from 1983 (where $\pi_t^e = 4.8\%$) is the increase in the annual average rate of monetary growth from 6.3% in 1982 to 10.3% in 1983. Assuming an unemployment rate of 7.8% for 1984 (see, for example, Litterman 1984), the projected value of debt growth, $\hat{DB}_t$, for 1984 turns out to be 13.3%. This forecast breaks up into 6.6 percentage points from expected inflation and 6.7 percentage points from the cyclical variable, $YVAR_t$. The forecast implies that the level of debt would rise from about $1,018 billion at the end of 1983 to $1,163 billion at the end of 1984, or by $145 billion during calendar 1984. (Again, one should add about $15 billion for the creation of high-powered money to get closer to the standard concept of the nominal deficit.) This forecast seems to be roughly in line with other near-term projections of deficits. It also turns out that my forecasts for 1983–84 are basically similar if I use either the equation where the $YVAR$ variable is based on output relative to trend (table 6.3, set 19) or the one based on the prime-age male unemployment rate (table 6.2, set 11).

The main point is that the actual behavior of public debt through 1983—as well as popular forecasts for 1984—is reasonably well in line with the experience of debt issue since at least the end of World War I. The main things that are out of line with the previous structure are projections of longer-term deficits on the order of $300 billion, conditioned on relatively low values of the unemployment rate and expected inflation. Since there is nothing yet in the data to suggest this type of structural break, I view these forecasts of deficits as amounting to predictions that either taxes will be increased or spending will be decreased. Standard projections of deficits should not be regarded as forecasts, once the endogeneity of taxes and spending is taken into account.

For recent years, where the effects of the constant term and the $GVAR$ variable turn out to cancel, the forecasts of debt growth—and hence deficits—emerge from a remarkably simple equation. Namely,

$$\hat{DB}_t = \pi_t^e + 3.9 \cdot YVAR_t = \pi_t^e + 3.9 \cdot (U_t - .054) \cdot g_t^*/b_t.$$

The values for g_t^*/b_t until 1982 appear in table 6.5, while the values for

1983 and 1984 are 0.75 and (roughly) 0.71, respectively. Using the value 0.71 in the expression above, the forecasting equation becomes

$$(16) \qquad \hat{DB}_t = -.15 + \pi_t^e + 2.8 \cdot U_t.$$

Equation (16) provides a close approximation to the previously mentioned forecasts of debt growth for 1983–84. The equation would also apply satisfactorily to projections further out, subject to the absence of major changes in the ratio of normal federal spending to the debt, g_t^*/b_t. (Recall that this ratio rose by a factor of five from 1933 to 1982.)[17] Notably, equation (16) implies that the planned growth rate of the real debt, $\hat{DB}_t - \pi_t^e$, would approach zero if the unemployment rate were to decline to about 5.5%. It implies further that the projected growth rate of the nominal debt, DB_t—which determines the conventional nominal deficit (aside from changes in high-powered money)—would approach zero if, in addition, the expected rate of inflation were to approach zero. The point is that there is nothing in the experience of actual deficits through 1983 that conflicts in any major way with these propositions.

Comment   Martin J. Bailey

I will concentrate my remarks mainly on the descriptive aspects of the paper, after a few words on the theory. Barro's first maintained hypothesis posits a long-range rational plan that produces tax smoothing. Contrary to initial appearances, his second is that nonwar government expenditures represent a random walk, exogenous to the government decision process. I am surprised that Barro takes these hypotheses seriously, either on their a priori merits or after seeing the results his data provide. On the merits, I see no basis for believing that it is even a fair approximation to say that Congress operates on a long-range rational plan, no basis for thinking that the congressional appropriations process is a mindless random walk, and especially no basis for claiming both simultaneously. Besides John Shoven's point on the history of

---

17. If one plugs in the 1933 unemployment rate of 27% into equation (16), then (with $\pi_t^e = 6\%$) the projected growth rate of debt is a remarkable 67%. The actual growth rate of debt for 1933 was only 16%, which I attribute primarily to the smaller size of the federal government, as measured by the ratio g_t^*/b_t. My assessment is that if the United States encounters a much more serious recession than that in 1982, then (with no change in structure) we will observe numbers for deficits that dwarf those experienced recently. The main element that generates high real deficits is the interaction between recession (high unemployment) and big government.

Martin J. Bailey is professor of economics at the University of Maryland.

marginal tax rates, we have direct evidence on tax smoothing through long-range planning in the history of the social security program. On this, as Barro delicately put it, "I have not yet isolated empirically this type of effect . . . for social security." Indeed not. Tax smoothing for social security purely and simply means full actuarial funding of the expected program of benefits. Further, the data for World War II fit neither the regressions based on other years nor the maintained hypothesis. So much for the theoretical framework.

The empirical results viewed as pure description, however, merit attention. The equations for expected inflation are reasonable versions of the Feige/Pierce concept of economically rational expectations: they use a small, reasonably efficient set of lagged variables. Their change in coefficients after the period break at the end of 1953 roughly confirm Gordon's (1980) findings on Phillips curves and the Sargent (1973) argument on the dependence of the appropriate lag structure on the policy regime. However, the best time for a period break was about 1970. Before that, inflation decayed rapidly or reversed itself; afterward, it persisted.

The deficit regressions provide a provocative characterization of the way our political system has on the average worked out. The main findings are the following, as I interpret them.

1. The portion of nominal federal interest costs that compensate for expected inflation is either partly, wholly, or more than wholly financed by new debt, depending on which regression you prefer. The regressions I prefer include an interest rate variable; they show the compensation for inflation to be about two-thirds financed by nominal bond issues and one-third financed by tax and seigniorage (money printing) revenues.

2. The budgeted costs of small wars were about two-thirds financed by taxes and seigniorage, and the remaining third by net new bond issues. The difference between this allocation and the preceding one for expected inflation does not appear to be statistically significant.

3. Debt issues increase in recessions as revenues net of transfers fall more than proportionately to income and decrease in recovery and boom periods. That's reassuring; any regression with such an implication can't be all bad.

4. The question whether recent deficits are out of line with past experience is not answered conclusively. In the regressions that contain an interest-rate variable, the question was not tested (as it could have been by including a dummy for the pertinent period, say that after 1971). However, there are indications of a shift, contrary to Barro's claim. Equation (6), which breaks the periods at the end of 1953, has a higher constant term for the post-1953 period than that for the pre-1954 period; the difference exceeds its standard error but is short of

significance. The poorer fitting but parallel equation (24), which uses output instead of employment as the output variable, has a coefficient for expected inflation significantly greater than one. Inasmuch as both inflation and real deficits had uptrends, this otherwise surprising coefficient probably is a proxy for an uptrend of deficits since 1953. The question is still open.

5. In the regressions that included World War II, the coefficient for wartime expenditures, no doubt driven by the extreme points given by that war, shows the war to have been financed three-fourths by debt held by the private sector. Even apart from the poor fit of these regressions, the World War II experience cannot possibly help the tax-smoothing hypothesis, because the government allowed the allocation of financing between debt financing and money printing to be decided by the private sector. Acceding to the Treasury preference of the day, the Federal Reserve System stood ready to buy all treasury bonds offered at prices low enough to yield 2.5% nominal interest; it pegged the treasury bill yield even lower. (It is amazing to me that households and firms were willing to hold such huge amounts of government debt on such unattractive terms.)

In summary, if we dismiss Barro's maintained hypotheses, we can nevertheless read his results with some instruction and profit. I think we could learn even more from a study that tried alternative, more plausible specifications and that tested the popular hypothesis of increasing budget indiscipline more directly. I would want the test to be imbedded in a regression that allows the data to determine how nonwar spending changes are financed. Besides that one, other systematic tendencies of fiscal behavior are worth investigating and describing. For most issues, I would want to see a different breakdown of periods. For all that, Barro's work is a useful, and in some ways original and surprising, contribution.

Comment   John B. Shoven

This is an interesting and thought-provoking paper, along the same lines as Barro's 1979 *Journal of Political Economy* article. Frankly, though, it is not clear at all that it is successful. It presents Barro's earlier tax-smoothing model of deficits. The argument is that under certain restrictive assumptions regarding separability of utility between goods and leisure and the like, it can be shown that a constant marginal tax rate on commodities is Pareto optimal. Under these conditions, the

John B. Shoven is professor of economics at Stanford University.

tax rate should be constant both across commodities and through time. The time constancy prevents people from inefficiently allocating market activity toward those periods with temporarily low tax rates. The conclusion of this model is that tax rates should not follow the uneven pattern of government expenditures, and that deficits are the vehicle that allows the government to separate the timing of expenditures and taxes.

Taken literally, the theory provides strong predictions about the size of the government deficit as a function of the deviations of aggregate output and government expenditure from their "normal" path. The theory, of course, is not very plausible. How is it that policymakers in Washington figured out the Ramsey optimal tax rule fifty years before public finance economists? Does anyone really believe that the projected 1984–88 deficits are what they are owing to tax smoothing?

The theory, though, is clear in its predictions. However, the empirical results of the paper do not lend support to the theory. The paper finds that the deficit generating process has been more or less stable, but that it has not followed a pattern consistent with tax-smoothing principles. First, Barro ran twenty-four sets of aggregate time series regressions in tables 6.1 through 6.3, and in none of them did the temporary government spending variable have a coefficient approximating unity, which the theory predicts. In fact, the results of table 6.3, which use output relative to trend for the economic activity variable, show the coefficient of temporary government spending as being not significantly different from zero. Second, and more disturbing, in almost all of his regressions Barro has had to throw out the World War II years. This is particularly destructive to the theory, since these years provide, in some sense, "the real test" of the theory, especially when one notices that battle casualties are the primary proxy for temporary government expenditures. When Barro does include the World War II years, the fit of his regressions seriously deteriorates and produces very large residuals for the World War II years.

Another approach to investigating the tax-smoothing theory would be to look at the tax rates themselves. The broadest measure of average tax rates is the ratio of total federal tax collections to GNP. This ratio has been relatively stable, at least in the post–World War II period. However, constant average tax rates do not imply fixed average marginal tax rates. Barro and Sahasakul (1983) have calculated average marginal tax rates for the federal personal income tax. The rates they find certainly are not constant. I have not done any statistical analysis of the series, and it is hard to recognize a random walker when you see one, but this series certainly looks as though it is headed toward higher average marginal tax rates. Even if the average marginal tax rate were constant, we know the composition of tax rates has changed. For instance, the highest rate has fallen from roughly 90% to 50%. Further, we know that the marginal income tax rate changes in predictable ways for individuals facing a typical age/earnings or experience/earnings profile. Certainly medical students do not believe their marginal tax rates are going to follow a random walk; they know that their tax rate is going to rise, and they can and will retime economic activity on this account. The point is that the optimal tax literature Barro invokes calls not for constant average marginal tax rates, but rather for a flat marginal tax rate.

What have we learned after Barro's analysis? Well, not much that we did not know before. First, average tax rates tend to rise in wars; on the other hand, wars are partially financed with debt. Some would argue that this spreads the burden of the war onto future generations, but that is not an argument I want to get into here. Second, deficits are countercyclical—even more so than a constant average tax rate suggests. This either means that we have a progressive tax system (which we clearly do, since the elasticity of tax receipts to nominal income is about 1.5) or that an active countercyclical tax policy was pursued—probably a little of both. The final conclusion of the paper that I will mention, and perhaps the one I find most interesting, is that the current deficits, even those projected for 1984, are not far off the usual pattern. The assertion is that if "normal" unemployment is taken as 5.4% (which is lower than the consensus today for NAIRU [non-accelerating rate of unemployment]) and if 1984 unemployment comes in at 7.8% (which is higher than the consensus), and if inflation is 6.6% (again, higher than the consensus), then Barro's operation predicts a $145 billion deficit for 1984, lower than other projections, but in the ballpark. It is clear that the historical deficit generating process can almost account for the current deficit, but it requires several assumptions, each shaded relative to consensus in a direction that will generate higher deficit forecasts.

Let me conclude by saying that I think Barro is conducting an interesting and important line of research despite the fact that the data did not come through in this paper in support of the posited theory. More work is required for us to gain a better picture of the deficit generating process.

Discussion Summary

Alan Auerbach pointed out that the Ramsey tax-smoothing model predicts that there should be no capital taxes but simply levies on labor or consumption. The existence of capital taxes in the United States system, and the progressivity of income taxes, was, he felt, inconsistent with the thrust of the paper. Robert Hall noted that upward drift of tax rates was not at all inconsistent with the Ramsey model in a world with real growth—the optimal tax rate would rise. A problem that both he and Lawrence Summers saw with the paper was the "positive versus normative" issue; he suggested that World War II exemplified bad policy in that it was financed by increases in marginal tax rates, and this fact made him doubt the relevance of the analysis. Christopher Sims received some comfort from the accuracy of the predictions but felt that the use of future values of anticipated inflation could rationalize any deficit projection. Stanley Fischer also believed that the "unrealistic" inflation projections used for 1983 and 1984 adversely affected the interpretation of the results.

Both Fischer and Herschel Grossman felt that the temporary nature of wars was overdone, since many of the costs of wars are paid long after they have ended on the battlefield, and Grossman gave as an example the permanent change in the defense posture of the United States following Pearl Harbor. Summers also noted that wartime expenditures were mismeasured in conventional accounts, since they ignore the "draft tax" imposed on the economy.

Grossman suggested that the analysis should have been conducted for the consolidated federal and state and local government sectors, and he suspected that there was substantial crowding out of state and local spending by federal expenditures, especially in wartime. Summers suggested that modeling government expenditures as a random walk was misleading, since random walks not only rise but also fall—unlike government spending; he felt a model with irreversibility was necessary. He also noted that economists' advice was endogenous, hence when deficits rise, economists provide pressure for these deficits to be reduced.

Alan Blinder noted that a major reason the model was incapable of explaining the events of the World War II was that it generated excessively high inflation expectations. To test the substantive part of the model, he believed that an alternative expectational assumption such as perfect foresight should have been attempted. Second, he suggested that aggregating money and taxes was inadequate; he felt that money, taxes, and bonds deserved separate treatment. Robert Gordon suggested that an incorrect place had been selected for the regime breaks. He felt that a more natural break occurred in the 1960s when the decision was made to finance the Vietnam War with money, not bonds. Rudiger Dornbusch questioned making expenditures independent of tax rates, since he felt the two were interdependent. He also believed that including unanticipated tax collections in the empirical analysis was inadvisable, since the model purported to account for the planning behavior of the government. Finally, he observed that the real interest rate used in the paper should be posttax, and that this might influence the results.

In response to the concerns about the appropriateness of the inflation predictions used, Robert Barro pointed out that the predictions were implicit in the estimated model, not picked from an outside source. He also noted that the ratio of government purchases to GNP did both rise and fall, so modeling it as a random walk was not obviously at variance with the facts. He also defended the aggregation of money and taxes by drawing attention to the similarity of the inflation taxes and other taxes.

References

Atkinson, A. B., and J. E. Stiglitz. 1980. *Lectures on public economics.* New York: McGraw-Hill.

Barro, Robert J. 1979. On the determination of the public debt. *Journal of Political Economy* 87 (October):940–71.

———. 1981a. On the predictability of tax-rate changes. Manuscript, University of Rochester.

———. 1981b. Output effects of government purchases. *Journal of Political Economy* 89 (December):1086–1121.

———. 1981c. *Money, expectations and business cycles.* New York: Academic Press.

———. 1983. Inflationary finance under discretion and rules. *Canadian Journal of Economics* 16 (February):1–16.

———. 1984. *Macroeconomics.* New York: Wiley.

Barro, Robert J., and Chaipat Sahasakul. 1983. Measuring the average marginal tax rate from the individual income tax. *Journal of Business* 56 (October): 419–52.

Butkiewicz, J. 1983. The market value of outstanding government debt: Comment. *Journal of Monetary Economics* 11 (May):373–79.

Darby, M. R. 1976. Three-and-a-half million U.S. employees have been mislaid; or, An explanation of unemployment, 1934–1941. *Journal of Political Economy* 84 (February):1–16.

Gordon, Robert J. 1980. A consistent characterization of a near-century of price behavior. *American Economic Review* 70 (May):243–49.

Kydland, F., and E. Prescott. 1980. A competitive theory of fluctuations and the feasibility and desirability of stabilization policy. In *Rational expectations and economic policy,* ed. Stanley Fischer. Chicago: University of Chicago Press.

Litterman, R. 1984. Economic forecasts from a vector autoregression. Federal Reserve Bank of Minneapolis.

Lucas, R., and N. Stokey. 1983. Optimal fiscal and monetary policy in an economy without capital. *Journal of Monetary Economics* 12 (July):55–93.

McCallum, B. 1984. Bond-financed deficits and inflation: A Ricardian analysis. *Journal of Political Economy* 92 (February):123–35.

Pigou, A. C. 1928. *A study in public finance.* London: Macmillan.

Ramsey, F. P. 1927. A contribution to the theory of taxation. *Economic Journal* 37 (March):47–61.

Sahasakul, C. 1983. Are marginal tax-rate changes predictable? Manuscript, University of Rochester.

Sargent, Thomas J. 1973. Rational expectations: A correction. *Brookings Papers on Economic Activity* 3:799–800.

Seater, J. 1981. The market value of outstanding government debt, 1919–1975. *Journal of Monetary Economics* 8 (July):85–96.

7   Money, Credit, and Interest Rates in the Business Cycle

Benjamin M. Friedman

The monetary and financial aspects of fluctuations in economic activity have long attracted the attention of economists and other observers of the business cycle. Throughout the nineteenth century and into the early years of the twentieth, business downturns in the United States were typically associated in a quite obvious way with "panics" or other sharp discontinuities in the financial markets. Such readily visible events have all but vanished since the establishment of the Federal Reserve System in 1914 and especially the Federal Deposit Insurance Corporation in 1934, but the pace of activity in the financial markets has continued to vary closely with that in many of the economy's nonfinancial markets. Much of this covariation is by now highly familiar, if not necessarily well understood. The regularities on which macroeconomists have focused most intensively in this context are those involving money (including either high-powered money or deposit money), credit (including public debt, private debt, or the sum of the two), and interest rates.[1] In large part because of the availability of data extending back to the early years of this century, and in some cases still earlier, the documentation of these regularities over fairly long time periods is now broadly familiar.

One factor motivating the long history of interest in this subject is, of course, simply the desire to understand more fully the underlying

Benjamin M. Friedman is professor of economics at Harvard University.

I am grateful to Diane Coyle and Ken Weiller for research assistance and helpful discussions; to them as well as Stephen Goldfeld, Allan Meltzer, Robert Gordon, and other participants in the NBER business cycles conference for useful comments on an earlier draft; and to the National Science Foundation and the Alfred P. Sloan Foundation for research support.

1. Stock prices have also attracted substantial attention in a business cycle context, but less so than have money, credit, and interest rates.

causes and internal dynamics of business fluctuations. Implications for public policy have also been important in this regard, however. A common thread running through decades of literature on the monetary and financial aspects of business cycles has been the actual or potential role of monetary policy in affecting either real economic outcomes or price stability, or both. Indeed, even those strands of literature that have argued vigorously against the existence of any possibility that monetary policy can improve real outcomes have heavily emphasized the negative results to follow, typically via the speed or variability of price inflation, from an ill-chosen (according to that view) policy regime.

The basic theme of this paper, in contrast to much of the extensive literature of the subject to date, is that the quantitative relationships connecting monetary and financial variables to the business cycle exhibit few if any strongly persistent regularities that have remained even approximately invariant in the context of the widespread and, in some instances, dramatic changes undergone by the United States financial markets over familiar time periods both long and short. At a *qualitative* level, of course, broadly familiar regularities have characterized many monetary and financial aspects of United States business fluctuations. The procyclical behavior of money, credit, and interest rates is well known, as is the tendency of money and credit growth to "lead" real economic growth at major business cycle turning points. Nevertheless, these characteristic qualitative features of most business fluctuations have not corresponded to persistent regularities in the *quantitative* relationships that constitute the main focus of modern business cycle analysis.

The finding that stable quantitative relationships to monetary and financial variables have been absent from the United States business cycle experience does not mean that monetary and financial phenomena are unimportant elements of business fluctuations, or that there is no consistent basis for seeking to understand or explain them. The basic monetary and financial elements of economic behavior have no doubt persisted in some fundamental sense. The problem is instead that these basic elements of economic behavior do not correspond straightforwardly in theory or closely in practice to the specific quantities that economists can typically measure. In addition, the relevant behavior is probably far too complex to be readily represented in simple linear relationships limited to very few variables.

From the perspective of positive economics based on familiar and available data, therefore, the main message of this paper is that simple relationships usually taken to be central to monetary and financial aspects of business cycles have in the past changed often and much. From the perspective of inferences about monetary policy, the chief implication is a warning against proceeding as if any one, or a few, of these simple relationships will reliably remain immutable.

Changes in the working of the United States financial markets that are potentially important for monetary and financial aspects of business fluctuations are not difficult to identify. Within the twentieth century the entire apparatus and orientation of United States monetary policy have undergone several dramatic shifts. In addition to monetary policy, major changes in government regulation and the expansion of government intermediation have been potentially important and often shifting influences. Moreover, the nation's private financial institutions and practices have also undergone profound and far-reaching changes over these years, partly in response to changing patterns of government regulation and monetary policy, but also as a result of private institutions' taking advantage of new developments elsewhere in the economy.

Any attempt to see whether the monetary and financial aspects of United States economic fluctuations have remained invariant, or nearly so, in the face of these financial market changes must at the outset confront the methodological choice between structural and reduced-form approaches to this question. A structural framework imposes potentially valuable restrictions on the way the corresponding empirically estimated model summarizes the quantitative relationships exhibited by the prior experience in question. Whatever analysis is grounded in a specific structural model is therefore conditional on those restrictions. Restrictions that are valid reflections of actual economic behavior will enable the model to extract the relevant behavioral relationships from the available data more efficiently, but incorrect or arbitrary restrictions will distort the representation of those relationships. Either kind of error can introduce the appearance of change where in fact there has been continuity, or of continuity where there has been change.

The subject of monetary and financial influences on economic fluctuations is not lacking for suggested structural frameworks. One long-familiar strand of thinking along these lines, which has emphasized interest rate, asset price, and credit rationing effects on specific kinds of spending, is the expanded IS-LM aggregate demand model typical of the post-Keynesian neoclassical synthesis, perhaps best exemplified empirically by the MIT–Penn–Social Science Research Council (MPS) model.[2] A closely related line of structural analysis, which has placed more emphasis on portfolio substitutions and asset valuations, is the disaggregated asset market approach of Tobin (1961, 1969) and of Brunner and Meltzer (1972, 1976). A third line of analysis, which in its structural components is related to these two but has more narrowly emphasized the role of monetary assets in affecting aggregate demand,

---

2. See, for example, de Leeuw and Gramlich 1968, 1969; Ando 1974; and Modigliani and Ando 1976.

is the monetarist model of Friedman (1956, 1971), as exemplified empirically by the Saint Louis model.[3] A more different line of structural analysis is the rational expectations model of aggregate supply developed by Lucas (1972, 1973), and exemplified empirically by Sargent (1976). A still more recent line of analysis has been the explicit banking sector model of Fama (1980a, b).[4] Moreover, each of these different structural approaches essentially refers to a closed economy. To the extent that the United States economy's increasing openness may also be important for monetary and financial aspects of economic fluctuations, the range of choice—and, consequently, of potential disagreement—is only greater.

The approach taken in this paper is to sidestep the choice among, or synthesis of, these disparate structural models and to employ instead only a reduced-form empirical approach that in principle is compatible with any of them. The basic advantage in this approach is to avoid making the analysis conditional on explicit structural restrictions that would attract sharp disagreement from the outset, and that could indeed be incorrect. The key disadvantages are the loss of efficiency in the extraction of the relevant quantitative relationships from the data and, correspondingly, the loss of explicit connection between the estimated relationships and more specific elements of monetary and financial behavior.

Section 7.1 sets the stage for the empirical analysis by briefly reviewing the major twentieth-century changes in the United States financial markets that would make it surprising if there had been no significant changes in the monetary and financial aspects of United States economic fluctuations during this period—at least under the view that the prevailing institutions, including government structures as well as private business practices, importantly affect economic behavior. Section 7.2 documents at a qualitative level the familiar interrelatedness of money, credit, interest rates, and nonfinancial economic activity in a business cycle context, but it then goes on to point out some changes in these relationships over time that are apparent even at a very simple level of analysis. Section 7.3 digresses to consider the relationships connecting money, credit, and their respective "velocities" to the fluctuations of both nominal and real income during the economy's seven and one-half recognized business cycles since World War II. Section 7.4 applies formal time series and frequency domain methods to examine at a quantitative level, and in an explicitly dynamic context, the

3. See, for example, Anderson and Jordan 1968 and Anderson and Carlson 1970. These models are really reduced-form in spirit, however. See Jonson 1976 for an example of an attempt at a more structural rendering of the same ideas.

4. Empirical work to date among these lines has mostly adopted a reduced-form approach. See, for example, King and Plosser 1981.

familiar relationships introduced in section 7.2. Section 7.5 pursues this line of analysis further, to determine whether differences in these familiar relationships from one time period to another are significant not just in a statistical sense but economically as well. Section 7.6 digresses again to consider the postwar evidence on the economy's "credit cycle." Section 7.7 concludes by summarizing the principal empirical findings presented throughout the paper.

7.1   Changes in the United States Economy's Financial Structure

Whether or not the monetary and financial aspects of economic fluctuations in the United States have changed their character over any specific period of time—within the twentieth century, for example, or since World War II, or since October 1979—is an empirical issue. Before examining the evidence on this question, however, it is appropriate to ask whether during the relevant time period there have been changes in the economy's underlying financial structure that, at least in principle, could have effected changes in the cyclical relationships between monetary and financial variables and nonfinancial economy activity. Three broad categories of changes in the United States economy's financial structure stand out in this regard.

First, within the time period spanned by available data (and studied in this paper), the entire apparatus and orientation of United States monetary policy have undergone dramatic shifts. Before 1914 the United States had no central bank as such but relied instead on a largely unregulated national banking system anchored by a gold standard.[5] Prompted by a recurrent series of financial crises and panics, especially in 1901, 1907, and 1913, Congress created a new Federal Reserve System charged with the basic task of preserving stability in the financial markets—more specifically, instructed "to furnish an elastic currency." The macroeconomic objectives almost universally associated with monetary policy in the post–World War II era, including especially the objective of price stability, received no mention in the original Federal Reserve Act.

Between 1914 and World War II, monetary policy evolved in a variety of ways, as Federal Reserve decision makers gradually came to understand what effects the system's open market purchases and sales

5. Much earlier on the Bank of the United States had constituted a rudimentary form of central bank, but it passed out of existence when Andrew Jackson declined to renew its charter in 1832. From then until the passage of the National Banking Act in 1864, private commercial banks were chartered exclusively by the individual states. Thereafter, until 1914, federally chartered banks enjoyed a monopoly over the note-issuing power but continued (as they do today) to share other banking functions, like deposit taking, with state-chartered banks.

of government securities had in the new world of fractional reserve banking directly based on central bank liabilities. The establishment in 1923 of what subsequently evolved into today's Federal Open Market Committee led temporarily to an increasing emphasis on open market operations in a monetary policy context, but in the 1930s the confusions of the depression and the associated international monetary crisis, including the abandonment of the gold standard in 1934, arrested the development of the monetary policy mechanism. Then, during World War II and thereafter until 1951, this evolution effectively ceased as the Federal Reserve assumed an obligation to support the open market price of the government's outstanding debt (which was then almost entirely a war loan).

In 1951 the Treasury/Federal Reserve Accord relieved the central bank of this obligation, and monetary policy assumed the quasi-independent macroeconomic role it has played ever since. Even so, there have been several major changes in monetary policy orientation and procedures since then. In the early post-Accord years, the Federal Reserve keyed its operations to the net free reserve position of the commercial banking system. By the late 1960s the principal policy focus had changed to setting interest rates on short-term debt instruments, sometimes treasury bills and later on federal funds. From 1970 onward, quantity targets for the growth of various aggregative measures of money and credit, including especially the narrowly defined money stock (M1), played a generally increasing albeit sporadic role in the formulation and implementation of monetary policy. In 1979 the Federal Reserve announced a renewed emphasis on these quantity growth targets and adopted new operating procedures for achieving them, based on the growth rate of nonborrowed bank reserves. In 1982 the M1 target was publicly suspended, however, and the weight placed on even the broader money and credit targets in 1982 and 1983 was uncertain. At present, the role of quantity growth targets in United States monetary policy may be central, irrelevant, or more likely, somewhere in between.

Second, the often shifting evolution of monetary policy has hardly been the only way actions of the federal government (not to mention those of state governments) have effected structural changes that may well have altered, perhaps importantly, how the economy's financial and nonfinancial markets interact in a business cycle context.[6] Government regulatory actions have also been a potentially important and often changing influence. The three most dramatic changes—the in-

6. The discussion that follows focuses narrowly on the financial markets and therefore omits such important elements of the changing role of government as taxes, government spending, bankruptcy arrangements, and so on—all of which could importantly affect the relationships between monetary and financial varibles and levels of economic activity.

surance of private bank deposits, the prohibition of interest on demand deposits, and the separation of the commercial banking and securities industries—all took effect in the 1930s. Further potentially important changes in bank regulation and supervision have occurred from time to time since then, including most prominently the key legislation governing bank holding companies in the late 1960s and the deregulation of banks and other depository institutions in the early 1980s. Moreover, in several further complete turns of the wheel, the prohibition of interest on demand deposits has become effectively inoperative within the past decade, and long-standing prohibitions on interstate banking and on banking firms engaging in the securities business (and vice versa) are even now becoming fictional. Perhaps most important, in recent years the entire distinction between transactions balances and savings balances has become blurred to the point of meaninglessness.

Changes in government financial regulation have also extended well beyond the banking system and other depository institutions. The securities legislation of the 1930s created a whole separate industry, and subsequent regulation has continued to affect how it works. Key regulatory changes effected by the Securities and Exchange Commission have ranged from requiring competitive bidding in most public utility company underwritings beginning in the 1950s, to allowing the spread of open-end mutual funds beginning in the 1960s, to prohibiting fixed minimum commissions on stock exchange brokerage beginning in the 1970s, to permitting "shelf" offerings of corporate securities beginning in the 1980s. As a result of these and many other regulatory actions over the years, the securities markets in the United States function differently today than they did in earlier times.

The National Banking Act of 1933 introduced deposit interest rate ceilings, in part as a response to banks' alleged overaggressive bidding for interbank demand deposits during the 1920s. The ceilings have also applied to time and savings deposits, however, and in this context they have at times had enormous impact on the workings of the financial markets and on the financing of economic activity. Specific episodes of disintermediation during the 1960s and 1970s, owing to regulation Q ceiling rates that remained low in comparison to sharply rising market interest rates, led to the rise of whole new patterns of portfolio behavior and to periodic depression in the homebuilding industry. The Federal Reserve System first moved to eliminate these adverse effects in 1970 by suspending the ceiling on interest paid on most large bank certificates of deposit. As of this time, these ceilings appear to be on the way out altogether as a result of the Depository Institutions Deregulation and Monetary Control Act of 1980.

A related development in the government's role in the credit market, which came about partly in response to the distortions caused by deposit interest ceilings, has been the great increase in government intermediation. The Federal Home Loan Bank System and the Federal Intermediate Credit Bank began operations before World War II, but the scale of their activity was small at first, and their initial focus was on agricultural credit. The Federal National Mortgage Association began its lending operations in 1955. Only in the 1960s and 1970s, however, as periodic disintermediation became severe, did the scope and size of government financial intermediation expand greatly. In recent years the government-sponsored credit agencies have been joined by pools issuing mortgage-backed securities that are not only government sponsored but in some cases formally guaranteed. As of the late 1960s, and as recently as 1982, it was not atypical for these quasi-government institutions to account for half or more of all home mortgage lending in the United States in high disintermediation years. Moreover, in recent years the federal government has extended its direct loan and loan guarantee operations far beyond housing- and agriculture-related credits, to the benefit of such diverse borrowers as college students, New York City, and the Lockheed and Chrysler corporations.

Third, the nation's private financial institutions and practices have undergone profound and far-reaching changes over these years, partly in response to changing patterns of government regulation and monetary policy but also in large part as a result of private initiatives taking advantage of new developments elsewhere in the economy, including especially the rapidly changing technology of communications and data processing. New forms of deposits (for example, negotiable time certificates, Eurodollar credits, and money market deposit accounts) and new securities (for example, variable rate mortgages, floating rate notes, interest rate futures, and listed stock options) have come and in some cases gone. So have new kinds of financial institutions (for example, money market mutual funds and mortgage pass-through pools).

Other forms of change in private financial practices have been more gradual, but potentially just as important. The nation's financial markets have steadily become less segmented and presumably more efficient in the classic sense. Diverse regional markets have become more integrated, though they are still far from entirely so, and barriers separating different kinds of borrowers from different kinds of depositors or lenders have steadily eroded. Meanwhile, some institutions like pension funds and credit unions have grown rapidly in relative terms, while others like insurance companies and mutual savings banks have done the opposite. In a further series of developments of potentially very great importance for the questions at issue here, the United States financial markets as a whole have at times become less open to foreign participation, and more recently more so, as capital controls have come and gone, while most (though not all) foreign markets have become more accessible from here. Indeed, during large parts of the period under study in this paper, many key foreign currencies simply were not convertible.

Although adequately summarizing the elements of these private financial market changes that are of greatest potential importance in a business cycle context is probably impossible in the space available here, several basic trends that are relevant in this context stand out. One is that transactions costs have fallen, irregularly but persistently nonetheless, over the period under study in this paper. Another is that financial assets have increasingly become negotiable, and those that have always been negotiable have become more liquid. A third is that, despite the potentially very important episodes of retrogression, financial markets around the world have in fact become more closely integrated.

In light of these changes in the role of monetary policy, in government regulations and intermediation, and in private financial institutions and practices, it would be astonishing if there had been no changes at all in the relationships connecting money, credit, and interest rates to United States economic fluctuations. In the context of business cycles, however, as opposed to a study of financial markets per se, what matters is whether these (or still other) changes have brought about significant, and economically important, changes in such relationships at the macroeconomic level.

7.2   Basic Cyclical Relationships in Monetary and Financial Data

The four panels of figure 7.1 give an overview of the basic relationships of four key monetary and financial variables to United States economic fluctuations by showing these variables' annual variation from either 1891 or 1919 to 1982. The figure does not explicitly include any measure of nonfinancial economic activity, but the conventional shadings indicate business contractions as designated by the NBER.

The top panel of the figure shows the annual percentage change in the money stock, measured both by the Friedman/Schwartz "old M2" concept for 1891–1975 and by the "new M1" concept for 1919–82. The "old M2" measure includes currency held by the public plus "adjusted" total deposits at commercial banks but not at nonbank depository institutions (and also, since 1961, excluding large certificates of deposit).[7] The "new M1" measure is that adopted in 1980 (as "M1-B") by the Federal Reserve System, including currency held by

7. The underying data are annual averages centered on 30 June. From 1890 to 1907 the annual data are averages of quarterly figures. From 1908 to 1945 they are averages of end-of-month data. From 1947 to 1975 they are averages of daily-average monthly data.

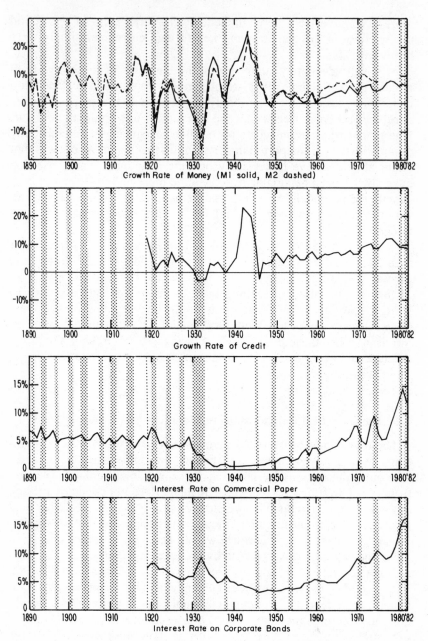

Fig. 7.1   Money, credit, and interest rates in the business cycle.

the public plus all checkable deposits other than those held by foreign commercial banks and official institutions, and as amended in 1982 to include traveler's checks.[8] As is well known from the work of Friedman and Schwartz (1963a, 1970, 1982) and others, the major historical fluctuations in United States nonfinancial economic activity have been accompanied by often sharp fluctuations in the rate of money growth. Prominent examples that stand out in the figure include the episodes of negative money growth in 1921, 1931, and 1949 and the sharp slowing of money growth in 1938. Especially during the post–World War II period, however, fluctuations in economic activity and variations in money growth have both been more modest. The comovement of money growth and real economic growth has been less pronounced also, though it is still readily visible.

The second panel of figure 7.1 shows the annual percentage change in domestic nonfinancial credit, including the total outstanding credit market indebtedness of all United States public and private sector borrowers other than financial intermediaries.[9] As is documented in Friedman (1981, 1983b), domestic nonfinancial credit has also borne a close relationship to United States nonfinancial economic activity, especially in the postwar period. Even before World War II, however, several major episodes of reduced credit growth, including those in 1921, 1931, and 1938, stand out as having occurred in conjunction with recognized economic fluctuations.

The bottom two panels of figure 7.1 show the annual average levels of interest rates on prime four- to six-month commercial paper offered in New York, and on Baa-rated corporate bonds, respectively.[10] The main features that stand out immediately in the interest rate data are the great volatility of both short- and long-term rates before 1930 and after 1970, the extraordinarily low level of both rates during the late 1930s and early 1940s, and the persistent upward trend since World War II. As is thoroughly familiar, however, interest rates also fluctuate cyclically, and many of the recognized business cycle episodes during this period also coincide with readily visible interest rate movements.

Table 7.1 focuses more closely on the comovements of both the M1 money stock and domestic nonfinancial credit with economic activity by arranging seasonally adjusted quarterly data in the context of the seven and one-half complete episodes since World War II designated as contractions and expansions by the NBER.[11] For each designated

8. The underlying data, constructed for this paper, are annual averages of monthly data, including end-of-month data through 1946 and daily-average data since 1947. (The Federal Reserve has constructed the official new M1 series back only to 1959.)

9. The underlying data are end-of-year data. The domestic nonfinancial credit concept is roughly analogous to "primary securities" in the sense of Gurley and Shaw 1960.

10. The data are annual averages of daily-average monthly data.

11. The expansion ending in 1948:4 officially began in 1945:4, but the analysis here and below excludes it so as to avoid any remaining effects due to the wartime economy.

Table 7.1   Postwar Cyclical Movements of Money and Credit

Business Cycles		Average Growth Rate of Money (M1)		Average Growth Rate of Credit	
Peaks	Troughs	Contractions	Expansions	Contractions	Expansions
1948:4					
		−0.75%		—	
	1949:4				
			3.90%		—
1953:2					
		1.16		5.28%	
	1954:2				
			1.69		5.67%
1957:3					
		0.64		5.42	
	1958:2				
			2.30		6.77
1960:2					
		1.43		4.65	
	1961:1				
			4.14		6.89
1969:4					
		4.53		6.71	
	1970:4				
			6.72		9.61
1973:4					
		4.38		8.48	
	1975:1				
			6.65		10.90
1980:1					
		6.60		8.81	
	1980:3				
			7.89		9.44
1981:3					
		6.69		8.71	
	1982:4				
Mean for all contractions		3.08%		6.86%	
Mean for all expansions			4.76%		8.21%

Note: Values shown are in percent per annum.

contraction or expansion, the table shows the average per annum growth rate of money and credit, respectively.[12] Despite the secular postwar trend toward faster growth of money and credit, the strongly cyclical aspect of both money growth and credit growth stands out clearly in

12. The table excludes credit growth for the first contraction and expansion because quarterly credit data are available only from 1952:1 onward.

these summary data. Money growth in expansions has exceeded money growth in contractions by 1.68% per annum on average, while credit growth in expansions has exceeded credit growth in contractions by 1.35% per annum on average. The basic cyclical regularity is much more striking than these average differences suggest, however. Money growth in each expansion was faster than in the preceding contraction, and money growth was slower in each contraction than in the preceding expansion. Similarly, credit growth in each expansion was faster than credit growth in the preceding contraction, and credit growth in each contraction was slower than in the preceding expansion.

Table 7.2 presents analogous data (not seasonally adjusted) for the postwar cyclical levels and movements of short- and long-term interest rates. Once again a secular postwar trend, toward higher interest rates and larger (absolute) interest rate changes, stands out immediately. Interest rates have also exhibited strong cyclical regularities, but they are not so striking as in the case of money and credit growth. Interest rate levels have been lower in expansions than in contractions by about 0.75% on average, but there has hardly been uniformity in this respect. In only two expansions were short-term interest rates lower than in the previous contraction, and in only one expansion was the long-term rate lower (by more than a single basis point).[13]

By contrast, the chief cyclical regularity that does stand out in table 7.2 is the rise of the short-term interest rate in every expansion and the corresponding decline in every contraction. The 6.72% (algebraic) difference between the average short-term rate *change* in expansions and in contractions, respectively, dwarfs the small difference in the corresponding average levels. The long-term interest rate has also risen in all seven postwar expansions and declined in six of the eight contractions, though here the (algebraic) difference for the respective average changes has been much smaller, as most familiar theories of the pricing of long-term versus short-term assets would imply.

In summary, both the annual data plotted in figure 7.1 and the cycle-specific averages of quarterly data shown in tables 7.1 and 7.2 give the impression of strong and persistent regularities in the monetary and financial aspects of United States economic fluctuations. On closer inspection, however, many of these regularities turn out not to be so regular or so persistent after all. Although the investigation of these relationships in a dynamic context is the subject of sections 7.4 and 7.5 below, table 7.3 provides a quick overview by showing simple correlation coefficients relating the annual movements of the monetary

13. It is at first tempting to suggest that, given the upward secular trend, the lower average levels for expansions are simply due to the omission of the expansion that began in 1982:4; but any such claim would of course be merely a forecast.

Table 7.2   Postwar Cyclical Movements of Interest Rates

Business Cycles		Average Level of Short Rate		Average Level of Long Rate		Change in Short Rate		Change in Long Rate	
Peaks	Troughs	Contractions	Expansions	Contractions	Expansions	Contractions	Expansions	Contractions	Expansions
1948:4		1.50%		3.43%		−0.20%		−0.19%	
	1949:4		2.00%		3.42%		1.25%		0.47%
1953:2		2.28		3.69		−0.99		−0.31	
	1954:2		2.68		3.87		2.32		1.38
1957:3		3.12		4.79		−2.24		−0.28	
	1958:2		3.52		5.00		2.36		0.65
1960:2		3.43		5.12		−1.06		−0.19	
	1961:1		4.72		5.72		5.61		3.44
1969:4		7.89		8.97		−2.32		0.65	
	1970:4		6.02		8.38		2.69		0.70
1973:4		9.15		9.58		−2.42		2.18	
	1975:1		7.57		10.10		7.69		3.04
1980:1		11.55		13.42		−4.61		−0.23	
	1980:3		14.05		15.20		6.57		3.20
1981:3		12.78		16.22		−7.40		−2.36	
	1982:4								
Mean for all contractions		6.46%		8.15%		−2.65%		−0.09%	
Mean for all expansions			5.79%		7.38%		4.07%		1.64%

and financial variables plotted in figure 7.1 to the annual percentage change in real gross national product.[14] For the monetary and credit aggregates, the table also shows analogous correlations for the corresponding aggregates deflated by the gross national product price deflator.

To highlight changes in these relationships over time, table 7.3 presents correlation coefficients separately for the pre–World War I (1891–1916), interwar (1919–40), and post–World War II (1947–82) periods, and also for two subperiods (1947–65 and 1966–82) within the postwar period. Especially from the perspective of changes in monetary policy, other possible breaks in the postwar period would also be logical, including 1951 when the Treasury/Federal Reserve Accord took effect, 1970 when the Federal Reserve System first began to employ explicit monetary aggregate targets and also first began to suspend regulation Q ceilings, and 1979 when the Federal Reserve (temporarily) adopted new operating procedures. The break at 1966 roughly separates the early postwar years of low price inflation, stable real economic growth, and few apparent "supply shocks" from the subsequent years of rapid and accelerating price inflation, less stable and on average slower real growth, and occasional large supply-side disturbances.

For each monetary or financial variable among the eight considered, and for each separate time period, table 7.3 reports the simple correlation of the variable's annual percentage change (for interest rates, the absolute change) with the annual percentage change of real gross national product for three lead/lag relationships: first with the monetary or financial variable leading real growth by one year, next contemporaneously, and last with that variable lagging real growth by one year.

In contrast to the appearance of strong regularities in figure 7.1 and in tables 7.1 and 7.2, the dominant impression given by these correlations is the absence of systematic relationships that have persisted across the different time periods under consideration.[15] The only two consistently significant relationships are the tendency of real M2 growth to be rapid (slow) contemporaneously with rapid (slow) real growth, and of long-term interest rates to fall (rise) in the year before a year of rapid (slow) real growth. Nominal M1 growth was strongly positively correlated with contemporaneous real growth during the interwar period, but less so during either half of the postwar period considered separately and not at all for the postwar period overall. Real M1 growth

---

14. From 1929 to 1982 the underlying GNP data are the standard national income and product accounts (NIPA) estimates. From 1909 to 1928 the data are United States Department of Commerce estimates, which (in principle) are analogous to the subsequent NIPA estimates at the aggregate level. From 1890 to 1908 the data are Department of Commerce estimates based on Kendrick 1961.

15. In addition, because the underlying variables are serially correlated, the conventional statistical confidence levels indicated in table 7.3 are overstated.

Table 7.3   Simple Annual Correlations With Real Economic Growth

Variable	1891–1916	1919–40	1947–82	1947–65	1965–82
Money growth (M1)	—	.20	-.22	-.02	-.18
	—	.69***	.17	.46**	.43*
	—	.43*	.05	.19	.13
Real balances growth (M1)	—	.28	-.04	.11	-.06
	—	.77***	.42***	.56**	.36
	—	.19	.12	.13	.05
Money growth (M2)	-.02	.09	—	.04	—
	.65***	.64***	—	.22	—
	-.18	.56**	—	.12	—
Real balances growth (M2)	-.08	.22	—	.13	—
	.58***	.85***	—	.44**	—
	-.29	.34	—	.10	—
Credit growth	—	.25	-.17	.01	.04
	—	.69***	.13	.54***	.31
	—	.50**	-.20	-.54***	.12
Real credit growth	—	-.00	-.07	-.01	.01
	—	.34	.49***	.52**	.67***
	—	-.31	.15	-.38	.56**
Short rate growth	-.21	.22	-.34**	-.03	-.48**
	-.39*	-.24	-.65***	-.49**	-.79***
	.56***	.19	.26	.55***	.20
Long rate growth	—	-.59***	-.52***	-.74***	-.52**
	—	-.65***	-.38**	-.05	-.52**
	—	.03	-.02	-.04	-.01

*Significant at .10 level.
**Significant at .05 level.
***Significant at .01 level.

was strongly correlated with contemporaneous real economic growth earlier on, but not during the later postwar period. Neither nominal nor real M1 growth has shown a significant lead or lag relationship to real economic growth on an annual basis. Nominal M2 growth was strongly positively correlated with contemporaneous real growth during the prewar and interwar periods, but not since World War II.

Nominal credit growth resembles nominal M1 growth in being strongly positively correlated with contemporaneous real economic growth during the interwar period and the early postwar period, but not for the later postwar period or for the postwar period as a whole. For the interwar and early postwar periods, lagged credit growth has been significantly correlated with real economic growth, although positively in the former years and negatively in the latter. Real credit growth has been positively correlated with real economic growth on a contemporaneous basis throughout the postwar period, but it was not so earlier on.

Finally, both short- and long-term interest rate changes have been negatively correlated with contemporaneous real economic growth, and (except for short-term rates in the interwar period) with the following year's real growth, throughout the period under study here. Many of these correlations are not significant, however. The contemporaneous relationship for short-term rates is significant except for the interwar years, and for long-term rates it is so except for the early postwar period. The change in short-term rates has been positively correlated with the prior year's real growth, but significantly so only during the prewar and early postwar periods.

Simple correlations based on annual data are a crude way of summarizing economic relationships, of course, even when they allow for modest leads or lags. Nevertheless, if the regularities connecting monetary and financial variables to business cycles were sufficiently powerful and persistent, they would be likely to show up more strongly even in these simple correlations. That they do not is hardly the end of the story, but the fact that it is necessary to look harder in order to find them is itself suggestive.

7.3 Money, Credit, and "Velocity" in Postwar Business Cycles

A subject that has run throughout the long-standing literature of monetary and financial aspects of economic fluctuations is the respective roles in this context of money (or credit) and the associated "velocity" defined simply as the ratio of nominal income to money (or, again, to credit). Before examining the United States experience in this regard, it is useful to point out the absence of any economic meaning of "velocity" as so defined—other than, by definition, the income-to-money ratio. Because the "velocity" label may seem to connote deposit or currency turnover rates, there is often a tendency to infer that "velocity" defined in this way does in fact correspond to some physical aspect of economic behavior. When the numerator of the ratio is income rather than transactions or bank debits, however, "velocity" is simply a numerical ratio.[16]

As table 7.1 shows for the postwar period, both money and credit grow faster on average during economic expansions than during contractions. The issue of money or credit movements versus their respective "velocities," in a business cycle context, is just the distinction between movements of nominal income that match movements of money or credit and movements of income that do not, and hence that imply movements in the income-to-money or income-to-credit ratio.

Table 7.4, using quarterly data for postwar cyclical episodes exactly analogous to the money and credit growth averages in table 7.1, shows that the "velocity" associated with each aggregate has also exhibited strong cyclical properties. Monetary velocity, which has had an upward secular trend since World War II, has risen on average in each expansion and has declined on average in six of eight contractions. The average growth of monetary velocity in expansions has exceeded that in contractions by 4.76% per annum, a much greater difference than the 1.68% per annum shown in table 7.1 for money growth itself. Credit velocity, which has been trendless on average since World War II, has risen on average in four of six expansions and declined on average in each contraction. The average growth of credit velocity in expansions has exceeded that in contractions by 4.31% per annum, again a much larger difference than the 1.35% per annum difference shown in table 7.1 for credit growth.

Because the numerator of the "velocity" ratio is nominal income, while business cycle expansions and contractions typically refer to fluctuations of real economic activity, it is difficult to go much further in considering money, credit, and their respective "velocities" in a business cycle context without allowing for cyclical variation in price inflation. As table 7.5 shows, however, during the postwar period price inflation has apparently followed the business cycle with a sufficient lag that the movements of real and nominal gross national product during expansions and contractions have almost exactly corresponded on average. Real income, of course, has grown on average in each expansion and declined on average in each contraction, with an (algebraic) difference of 5.83% per annum between the mean for all expansions and the mean for all contractions. By contrast, because of

---

16. See Cramer 1983, for example, for evidence on the different respective movements of income and total transactions.

Table 7.4   **Postwar Cyclical Movements of Money and Credit "Velocities"**

Business Cycles		Average Growth Rate of Money "Velocity"		Average Growth Rate of Credit "Velocity"	
Peaks	Troughs	Contractions	Expansions	Contractions	Expansions
1948:4		−1.61%		—	
	1949:4		5.57%		—
1953:2		−2.00		−6.12%	
	1954:2		4.46		0.47%
1957:3		−1.00		−5.78	
	1958:2		4.26		−0.21
1960:2		−1.17		−4.39	
	1961:1		3.03		0.27
1969:4		−0.16		−2.34	
	1970:4		3.01		0.12
1973:4		2.35		−1.75	
	1975:1		3.95		−0.29
1980:1		0.47		−1.74	
	1980:3		4.34		2.79
1981:3		−2.33		−4.35	
	1982:4				
Mean for all contractions		−0.68%		−3.78%	
Mean for all expansions			4.08%		0.53%

Note: Values shown are in percent per annum.

the upward secular trend in price inflation, nominal income declined in the first three postwar contractions but increased in the subsequent five. Even so, the difference between the average growth of nominal income in expansions and contractions, respectively, has been 6.44% per annum—almost identical to the corresponding difference for real income. At least for averages across business cycle expansions and contractions, therefore, relationships to nominal income (like those

Table 7.5   **Postwar Cyclical Movements of Real and Nominal Income**

Business Cycles		Average Growth Rate of Real income		Average Growth Rate of Nominal Income	
Peaks	Throughs	Contractions	Expansions	Contractions	Expansions
1948:4					
	1949:4	− 0.37%		− 2.36%	
			6.36%		9.47%
1953:2					
	1954:2	− 1.94		− 0.84	
			3.43		6.15
1957:3					
	1958:2	− 2.11		− 0.36	
			4.62		6.56
1960:2					
	1961:1	− 0.38		0.26	
			4.38		7.17
1969:4					
	1970:4	− 0.54		4.37	
			4.51		9.73
1973:4					
	1975:1	− 2.79		6.73	
			3.73		10.60
1980:1					
	1980:3	− 2.27		7.07	
			3.45		12.23
1981:3					
	1982:4	− 1.42		4.36	
Mean for all contractions		− 1.48%		2.40%	
Mean for all expansions			4.35%		8.84%

Note: Values shown are in percent per annum.

based on "velocity" ratios) approximately carry over to relationships to real income, and hence to economic fluctuations in the ordinary business cycle sense. Table 7.6 summarizes these relationships by collecting the means from tables 7.1, 7.4, and 7.5 and the corresponding implied means of price inflation.[17]

17. The reason for calculating the relationships among the nonfinancial variables a second time in the lower half of the table is that quarterly credit data are not available for the first postwar contraction and expansion. The same point applies to table 7.7.

Table 7.6   **Cyclical Means for Income, Money, Credit, and "Velocity"**

	1948:4 to 1982:4		
Variable	Eight Contractions	Seven Expansions	Difference
Mean X	−1.48%	4.35%	5.83%
Mean Y	2.40	8.84	6.44
− Mean P	−3.89	−4.51	− .62
Mean Y	2.40%	8.84%	6.44%
Mean M	3.08	4.76	1.68
Mean Vm	− .68	4.08	4.76

	1953:2 to 1982:4		
Variable	Seven Contractions	Six Expansions	Difference
Mean X	−1.64%	4.02%	5.66%
Mean Y	3.08	8.74	5.66
− Mean P	−4.72	−4.72	.00
Mean Y	3.08%	8.74%	5.66%
Mean C	6.86	8.21	1.35
Mean Vc	−3.78	.53	4.31

Note: Values are in percent per annum; detail may not add to totals because of rounding.
Definitions of variable symbols:
X = growth rate of real GNP;
Y = growth rate of nominal GNP;
P = growth rate of GNP price deflator;
M = growth rate of Ml money stock;
Vm = growth rate of Y/M;
C = growth rate of domestic nonfinancial credit;
Vc = growth rate of Y/C.

Table 7.7 pursues further the distinction of money and credit growth versus "velocity" growth by showing an analysis of variance for the respective real and nominal income identities summarized in terms of means in table 7.6. The upper half of the table first decomposes the variation of real income growth into components representing nominal growth, price inflation, and their covariance and then decomposes the variation of nominal income growth into components representing money growth, "velocity" growth (that is, nominal income growth that does not correspond to money growth), and the associated covariance term.

The first column of the table applies this decomposition only to contractions, treating each one as a simple observation—in other words, asking what role money growth, "velocity" growth, and price inflation have played in accounting for differences between one business contraction and another. The average (negative) real growth rate has varied little among successive contraction episodes, so that the differences here are almost entirely differences among respective contractions' rates of price inflation and hence of nominal growth.

Table 7.7   Cyclical Variance Decompositions for Money, Credit, and
                   "Velocity"

| | 1948:4 to 1982:4 | | |
Variable	Eight Contractions	Seven Expansions	Fifteen Periods
Var (X)	.89	1.03	9.96
Var (Y)	13.38	5.17	19.96
Var (P)	17.66	6.56	11.74
-2 cov (Y, P)	-30.15	-10.70	-21.76
Var (Y)	13.38	5.17	19.96
Var (M)	8.04	5.64	7.18
Var (Vm)	2.30	.79	7.52
$+2$ cov (M, Vm)	3.04	-1.26	5.25

| | 1953:2 to 1982:4 | | |
Variable	Seven Contractions	Six Expansions	Thirteen Periods
Var (X)	.81	.30	9.14
Var (Y)	11.28	6.11	16.80
Var (P)	14.04	7.42	10.11
-2 cov (Y, P)	-24.51	-13.23	-17.77
Var (Y)	11.28	6.11	16.80
Var (C)	3.22	4.20	3.85
Var (Vc)	3.42	1.31	7.25
$+2$ cov (C, Vc)	4.64	.60	5.70

Note: Values are in percent per annum squared. See table 7.6 for definitions of variable symbols.

The results show that money growth variations have dominated velocity growth variations in accounting for these differences. Analogous results presented in the second column show an even greater predominance of money growth variations over velocity growth variations in accounting for nominal income growth differences across expansions. The final column of the table presents the results of an analogous decomposition applied to all contractions and all expansions, again treating each as a single observation—in other words, asking what role money growth, velocity growth, and price inflation have played in accounting for differences not just among contractions or among expansions but also between contractions and expansions. In this context the respective variations of money growth and velocity growth have been more nearly coequal, and also importantly correlated.

The lower half of table 7.7 presents the analogous three sets of decompositions including credit and credit "velocity." The results are similar to those for money and money velocity shown above, but in each case with a smaller role for the aggregate, and consequently a greater role for velocity. Variations in credit growth have predominated over velocity growth variations only in accounting for differences among expansions. For differences among contractions, the two have been approximately coequal and importantly correlated. Variations in credit velocity, and its correlation with credit growth variations, have been more important than variations in credit growth per se in the broader cyclical context of accounting also for differences between expansions and contractions.

7.4 Dynamic Relationships

Simple annual correlations like those shown in table 7.3 fail to convey what it is important to know about the comovement of economic time series in a business cycle context for at least three reasons. First, the relevant lead/lag relationships may be distributed over either more or less than one year. The work of Friedman and Schwartz (1963a), for example, concluded that variations in money growth typically lead variations in income growth by less than a year. Second, even highly significant lead correlations may merely reflect the interaction of contemporaneous (or even lagged) relationships among time series that are individually autocorrelated. In contrast to the propositions that characterized much of the earlier literature on monetary and financial aspects of economic fluctuations, which typically referred simply to the comovement among two or more variables, the modern analysis of business cycles focuses instead on whether movements in one variable are systematically related to those parts of the movements in another that are not purely autoregressive. Third, the relationship of one variable to another may depend on what further variables the analysis includes. The proposition that two variables exhibit a stable relationship to one another without allowance for further variables implies either that other variables are unimportant to that relationship or that whatever other variables are relevant have not varied (will not vary) significantly during the period under study. The results presented in this section of the paper extend the simple overview provided in table 7.3 so as to take account of each of these potentially important considerations.

Table 7.8 presents F-statistics for conventional exogeneity ("causality") tests of bivariate annual relationships connecting nominal income growth respectively to the growth of M1, M2, and credit, and the change in short- and long-term interest rates, for the same time periods used in table 7.1. Table 7.9 presents analogous results for bivariate re-

Table 7.8   Summary of Bivariate Annual Relationships: Financial Variables and Nominal Income

Variable	1891–1916	1919–40	1947–82	1947–65	1966–82
Equation for Y					
F (Y)	—	0.21	1.97	1.21	1.20
F (M1)	—	1.39	6.87***	6.38**	0.32
Equation for M1					
F (Y)	—	1.13	1.64	0.93	0.17
F (M1)	—	4.77**	13.77***	2.83*	4.10**
Equation for Y					
F (Y)	4.01**	0.08	—	1.68	—
F (M2)	4.07**	1.01	—	0.19	—
Equation for M2					
F (Y)	2.11	0.54	—	1.11	—
F (M2)	3.29*	2.20	—	1.38	—
Equation for Y					
F (Y)	—	0.16	2.12	0.64	5.82**
F (C)	—	3.14*	9.83***	0.40	11.18***
Equation for C					
F (Y)	—	0.03	18.21***	18.17***	1.98
F (C)	—	1.08	64.11***	2.59	11.89***
Equation for Y					
F (Y)	0.34	2.92*	0.28	1.01	5.75**
F (Rs)	4.09**	1.42	1.03	0.67	8.82***
Equation for Rs					
F (Y)	1.70	0.88	0.51	0.21	0.77
F (Rs)	9.86***	0.95	4.29**	3.38*	1.88
Equation for Y					
F (Y)	—	0.15	0.09	1.12	0.37
F (Rl)	—	6.23**	0.31	4.32**	1.91
Equation for Rl					
F (Y)	—	0.18	1.48	0.06	1.48
F (Rl)	—	1.27	8.49***	0.23	1.71

Note: Values shown are F-statistics.
Definitions of variable symbols:
   Y = growth rate of nominal GNP;
   M = growth rate of money stock (M1 or M2);
   C = growth rate of domestic nonfinancial credit;
   Rs = change in prime commercial paper rate;
   Rl = change in Baa bond rate.
Significance levels:
    *Significant at .10 level.
    **Significant at .05 level.
    ***Significant at .01 level.

Table 7.9	Summary of Bivariate Annual Relationships: Financial Variables and Real Income				
Variable	1891–1916	1919–40	1947–82	1947–65	1966–82
Equation for X					
$F(X)$	—	0.14	0.85	1.69	0.17
$F(M1)$	—	0.19	7.73***	5.57**	2.42
Equation for $M1$					
$F(X)$	—	0.19	2.39	4.20**	0.74
$F(M1)$	—	2.53	22.57***	4.40**	1.10
Equation for X					
$F(X)$	2.56	0.78	—	0.47	—
$F(M2)$	0.70	0.06	—	2.40	—
Equation for $M2$					
$F(X)$	5.12**	0.64	—	3.48*	—
$F(M2)$	5.53**	1.91	—	4.98**	—
Equation for X					
$F(X)$	—	0.13	0.42	0.73	0.02
$F(C)$	—	0.79	2.42	0.81	1.82
Equation for C					
$F(X)$	—	0.58	7.94***	8.08***	2.20
$F(C)$	—	0.78	42.64***	3.92**	14.23***
Equation for X					
$F(X)$	0.71	1.98	2.74*	1.68	2.83*
$F(Rs)$	3.65**	1.51	14.91***	3.52*	25.11***
Equation for Rs					
$F(X)$	2.48	0.58	0.50	0.02	1.15
$F(Rs)$	10.90***	1.22	3.69**	3.35*	0.48
Equation for X					
$F(X)$	—	0.07	.35	2.64	1.21
$F(R1)$	—	3.57*	4.84**	8.32***	3.13*
Equation for $R1$					
$F(X)$	—	0.04	0.83	0.13	1.99
$F(R1)$	—	0.94	9.89***	0.37	2.75

Note: X = growth rate of real GNP. See also table 7.8.

lationships to real economic growth.[18] Such exogeneity tests constitute the modern formal analogue to the investigation of leads and lags that has been central to the more traditional business cycle literature. Once again, however, the chief impression given by these results is the absence of persistence over time in familiar simple quantitative relationships.

18. The underlying vector autoregressions include a constant term and two lags on each variable in each equation. The results for analogous autoregressions also including a linear time trend are broadly similar. (The most interesting difference to emerge on the introduction of a time trend is that M1 no longer helps explain nominal income.) Two lags appear to be sufficient to eliminate most, if not all, of the serial correlation in the residuals of the equations based on these annual data. Because each equation includes lags on *both* variables, and therefore a rational distributed lag, there is no limitation on the length of lag in the economic process represented.

The often-assumed relationship by which M1 growth helps explain either nominal or real economic growth, but not vice versa, appears in the results in tables 7.8 and 7.9 only since World War II, and only when the first half of the postwar period is included. Growth in M2 helps explain nominal economic growth only before World War I, and it does not help explain real economic growth in this sense in any of the three periods studied. Credit growth helps explain nominal income growth both in the interwar period and in the postwar period as long as the more recent postwar years are included, but for the postwar period as a whole nominal income growth also helps explain credit growth. Credit growth does not help explain real income growth in this sense in any period. The change in short-term interest rates helps explain both nominal and real income growth, but not vice versa, in the prewar period and in the second half of the postwar period. The change in long-term interest rates helps explain both nominal and real income growth, but not vice versa, in the interwar period and the first half of the postwar period.

It is important to distinguish these generally negative findings from the more traditional propositions, noted and in some cases documented above, about the comovement in a simple sense, including lead and lag relationships, connecting income with familiar monetary and financial variables. As figure 7.1 and tables 7.1 to 7.3 show, each of the five monetary and financial variables considered here has exhibited distinctly cyclical movements, at least during some time periods. What the tests in tables 7.8 and 7.9 seek to establish, however, is not just whether a variable has fluctuated in conjunction with movements in income, but whether it has shown a relationship to that part of the movement in income that is not explainable in purely autoregressive terms. Even a readily visible simple relationship to income fluctuations need not—indeed, evidently often does not—imply a corresponding relationship to the elements of income fluctuations that are not purely autoregressive.

More important, the basic theme of this paper focuses less on what helps explain what than on which, if any, quantitative relationships have persisted across spans of time during which the United States financial markets have undergone changes like those reviewed in section 7.1, which at least in principle could have importantly affected the monetary and financial aspects of economic fluctuations. Table 7.10 presents further F-statistics testing the null hypothesis of absence of structural change in the bivariate relationships summarized in tables 7.8 and 7.9 against the alternative hypothesis of breaks at World War II and at the midpoint of the postwar period to date (and also, for relationships involving M2 and the short-term interest rate, at World

Table 7.10   Test Statistics for Stability in Bivariate Annual Relationships

	Break at 1916	Break at 1940	Break at 1965
Equation for Y	—	6.15***	9.34***
Equation for $M1$	—	6.80***	8.07***
Equation for Y	22.92***	5.01***	—
Equation for $M2$	12.45***	24.24***	—
Equation for Y	—	2.12**	34.49***
Equation for C	—	15.45***	5.59***
Equation for Y	13.90***	2.56**	5.23***
Equation for Rs	4.26***	24.16***	52.23***
Equation for Y	—	5.12***	10.93***
Equation for $R1$	—	4.68***	52.91***
Equation for X	—	8.23***	7.92***
Equation for $M1$	—	6.64***	13.26***
Equation for X	20.24***	4.26***	—
Equation for $M2$	24.58***	15.49***	—
Equation for X	—	1.72	9.42***
Equation for C	—	18.97***	10.79***
Equation for X	10.76***	2.49**	2.16
Equation for Rs	6.43***	22.66***	50.77***
Equation for X	—	3.87***	10.91***
Equation for $R1$	—	4.79***	55.82***

Note: See tables 7.8 and 7.9.

War I). In all but two isolated cases, the data indicate significant structural change. What is especially striking in the results of these stability tests is that even sets of coefficients that tables 7.8 and 7.9 report to be not significantly different from zero are nonetheless significantly different from one another.

Annual data, of course, may simply be too coarse to capture the relevant behavior connecting these aspects of aggregative economic activity. Tables 7.11 and 7.12 therefore present F-statistics for analogous bivariate exogeneity tests for the respective relationships of nominal and real income growth to the growth of money (M1) and credit and the change in short- and long-term interest rates, based on quarterly data for the post–World War II period.[19] Money growth consistently helps explain both nominal and real economic growth, as is familiar from previous work, but these results show that either nominal or real income growth also typically helps explain money growth (so that money does not "cause" income in the Granger sense). Credit growth helps

19. The underlying vector autoregression systems include a constant term and four lags on each variable in each equation. (The discussion of lag length in footnote 18 applies here too.) Once again, the results for analogous autoregressions also including a linear time trend are broadly similar.

Table 7.11   **Summary of Bivariate Quarterly Relationships: Financial Variables and Nominal Income**

Variable	1952:1 to 1982:4	1952:1 to 1965:4	1966:1 to 1982:4
Equation for Y			
$F(Y)$	3.84***	2.23*	0.28
$F(M)$	10.28***	2.13*	2.80**
Equation for M			
$F(Y)$	4.09***	2.30*	1.01
$F(M)$	14.42***	8.31***	1.69
Equation for Y			
$F(Y)$	2.95**	2.61**	2.23*
$F(C)$	13.52***	1.69	9.04***
Equation for C			
$F(Y)$	2.17*	1.21	1.69
$F(C)$	45.41***	2.50*	28.22***
Equation for Y			
$F(Y)$	3.93***	2.94**	0.30
$F(Rs)$	5.43***	5.75***	4.03***
Equation for Rs			
$F(Y)$	0.68	1.42	1.02
$F(Rs)$	5.99***	6.71***	2.65**
Equation for Y			
$F(Y)$	6.33***	8.39***	0.32
$F(Rl)$	0.94	1.42	0.69
Equation for Rl			
$F(Y)$	0.88	1.36	0.81
$F(Rl)$	2.04*	1.10	3.39**

Note: Values shown are F-statistics.

Definitions of variable symbols:
   Y = growth rate of nominal GNP;
   M = growth rate of M1 money stock;
   C = growth rate of domestic nonfinancial credit;
   Rs = change in prime commercial paper rate;
   Rl = change in Baa bond rate.

Significance levels:
   *Significant at .10 level.
   **Significant at .05 level.
   ***Significant at .01 level.

explain nominal income, but not vice versa, in the second half of the postwar period. For the postwar period as a whole, credit growth again helps explain nominal income growth, while the reverse effect is only marginally significant. Changes in short-term interest rates consistently help explain nominal income growth, but not vice versa, and the same is true with respect to real income growth in the later postwar years. Changes in long-term interest rates never help explain income at all in this context. Finally, table 7.13 shows that most of these quarterly results also fail to exhibit stability across the earlier and later halves

Table 7.12   **Summary of Bivariate Quarterly Relationships: Financial Variables and Real Income**

Variable	1952:1 to 1982:4	1952:1 to 1965:4	1966:1 to 1982:4
Equation for X			
$F(X)$	3.91***	3.43**	1.35
$F(M)$	3.81***	3.72**	3.32**
Equation for M			
$F(X)$	2.71**	2.30*	0.97
$F(M)$	21.02***	7.24***	2.05*
Equation for X			
$F(X)$	3.16**	6.83***	0.89
$F(C)$	0.69	3.12**	0.54
Equation for C			
$F(X)$	4.94***	4.39***	0.84
$F(C)$	58.09***	1.49	24.15***
Equation for X			
$F(X)$	4.61***	3.57**	2.63**
$F(Rs)$	5.44***	1.20	5.81***
Equation for Rs			
$F(X)$	3.70***	3.46**	1.95
$F(Rs)$	7.40***	4.30***	3.90***
Equation for X			
$F(X)$	5.47***	4.90***	1.91
$F(Rl)$	1.00	0.88	0.75
Equation for Rl			
$F(X)$	1.31	2.18*	1.73
$F(Rl)$	2.35*	1.39	3.10**

Note: X = growth rate of real GNP. See table 7.11.

of the postwar period. Further results (not shown) are also broadly similar for other logical break points like those suggested in section 7.2.

One reason relationships like these may appear to be unstable, of course, is that they are misspecified—for example, by the omission of other relevant variables. Given the results for the bivariate relationships in tables 7.8 and 7.9 and tables 7.11 and 7.12, in which several monetary and financial variables each appear to be related to either nominal or real income growth at least in some periods, it is difficult to justify the use of only bivariate relationships. Table 7.14 presents F-statistics for analogous exogeneity tests based on a five-variable annual system including real income growth, price inflation, money (M1) growth, credit growth, and the change in the short-term interest rate, for the same interwar and postwar periods studied earlier.

Even with only three monetary and financial variables in the system, however, it is difficult to draw any solid conclusions from this expanded analysis. Among the three, only money growth significantly helps ex-

Table 7.13   Test Statistics for Stability in Bivariate Quarterly Relationships

	Break at 1965:4
Equation for Y	1.24
Equation for M	1.70*
Equation for Y	2.29**
Equation for C	2.94***
Equation for Y	5.58***
Equation for Rs	0.79
Equation for Y	3.90***
Equation for Rl	1.77*
Equation for X	2.12**
Equation for M	2.30**
Equation for X	1.81*
Equation for C	2.76***
Equation for X	1.63
Equation for Rs	0.31
Equation for X	.83
Equation for Rl	2.51***

Note: See tables 7.11 and 7.12.

plain real income growth—given the presence of the other included variables—in any period examined, and even this effect is evident only for samples including the first half of the postwar period.[20] At the same time, real income growth helps explain both money growth and credit growth during the full postwar period, and it also helps explain money growth during the later postwar years. Real income growth only marginally helps explain the short-term interest rate change. Once again, what significant regularities do appear have not been regular enough to persist across different time periods.

The same generalization also characterizes analogous results for multivariate systems estimated for the post–World War II period using quarterly data. There is little point in displaying vast quantities of empirical results along these lines, since the basic lack of consistency is readily apparent just from a summary of what does and does not help explain real income growth in quarterly systems based on different subperiods. For the quarterly version of the same *five*-variable system shown in table 7.14, neither money growth nor credit growth nor the short-term interest rate change significantly helps explain real income growth, even at the .10 level—again, given the presence of one another—for 1952:1 to 1982:4, 1952:1 to 1965:4, or 1966:1 to 1982:4. By

---

20. In this system the most interesting difference to appear on the introduction of a time trend is that the one variable that helps explain real income growth is not money growth but the change in short-term interest rates.

Table 7.14 Summary of Annual Relationships: Five-Variable System

Variable	1919–40	1947–82	1947–65	1966–82
Equation for X				
$F(X)$	0.40	3.95**	1.50	1.42
$F(P)$	0.82	1.13	1.46	1.51
$F(M)$	0.59	5.17**	4.11*	2.44
$F(C)$	0.44	0.85	0.40	3.18
$F(Rs)$	2.43	2.49	0.09	3.43
Equation for P				
$F(X)$	4.51**	4.46**	3.67*	1.64
$F(P)$	5.61***	3.50**	0.67	0.83
$F(M)$	8.59***	0.52	1.07	1.10
$F(C)$	2.86	2.75*	0.01	1.74
$F(Rs)$	2.59	6.57***	0.40	3.08
Equation for M				
$F(X)$	1.06	6.15***	2.04	5.04***
$F(P)$	0.82	1.04	0.22	9.35***
$F(M)$	2.18	0.38	1.19	1.95
$F(C)$	1.64	4.58**	0.85	10.41**
$F(Rs)$	2.56	2.74*	0.29	10.66**
Equation for C				
$F(X)$	1.11	11.57***	3.69*	0.88
$F(P)$	0.68	3.25*	0.28	1.00
$F(M)$	1.69	0.34	0.89	1.29
$F(C)$	1.66	11.62***	0.94	4.87*
$F(Rs)$	3.81*	3.44**	0.46	1.39
Equation for Rs				
$F(X)$	0.99	2.74*	0.64	3.70*
$F(P)$	0.54	1.62	0.07	0.35
$F(M)$	0.41	1.12	0.07	2.15
$F(C)$	2.15	2.38	0.12	1.51
$F(Rs)$	0.27	2.24	0.29	2.16

Note: Variables shown are F-statistics.

Definitions of variable symbols:

X = growth rate of real GNP;
P = growth rate of GNP price deflator;
M = growth rate of M1 money stock;
C = growth rate of domestic nonfinancial credit;
Rs = change in prime commercial paper rate.

Significance levels:

*Significant at .10 level.
**Significant at .05 level.
***Significant at .01 level.

contrast, for the *four*-variable system estimated for 1953:1 to 1978:4 in Friedman (1983c), including all of the same variables as in table 7.14 except the interest rate change, money growth and credit growth each significantly help explain real income growth at the .05 level.[21] Similarly, for the *six*-variable system estimated for 1962:3 to 1979:3 in Clar-

21. In this system real growth in turn helps explain money growth but not credit growth.

ida and Friedman (1984), including all the same variables as in table 7.14 plus the change in the federal government budget deficit, credit growth significantly helps explain real income growth at the .01 level, money growth does so at the .05 level, and the short-term interest rate change does so at the .10 level.[22]

Moreover, these multivariate relationships too show significant evidence of instability from one time period to another, thereby revealing that the instability of the bivariate systems documented in table 7.10 is not due to anything so simple as merely omitting a small number of familiar variables. Table 7.15 presents F-statistics testing the null hypothesis of absence of structural change in the five-variable annual relationships summarized in table 7.14, and in the corresponding quarterly relationships, against the alternative hypothesis of a break between the interwar and postwar periods or between the first and second halves of the postwar period. The annual data indicate significant structural change in each relationship at World War II, though only for the interest rate equation at 1965. The appearance of stability between the first and second halves of the postwar period is probably just due to lack of degrees of freedom, however, since the corresponding quarterly data indicate highly significant structural change in each relationship at 1965:4. In sum, neither using quarterly data in place of annual, nor using multivariate systems in place of bivariate, nor doing both at once overturns the general finding of heterogeneity from one period to another in the monetary and financial aspects of economic fluctuations.

Finally, because the very notion of business "cycles" suggest the possibility of comovements that recur at possibly regular intervals, it is interesting to see whether the frequency domain properties of the comovements studied here can provide further information to supplement the time-domain properties reported above. In particular, what

Table 7.15   **Test Statistics for Stability in Five-Variable System**

	Annual Relationships		Quarterly Relationships
	Break at 1940	Break at 1965	Break at 1965:4
Equation for X	2.42**	2.15	10.82***
Equation for P	17.35***	1.15	11.00***
Equation for M	6.34***	2.18	14.67***
Equation for C	39.82***	2.05	8.32***
Equation for Rs	44.09***	7.13***	121.79***

Note: See table 7.14.

22. In this system real growth in turn helps explain money growth but not credit growth or the interest rate change.

light can the associated frequency domain properties of these data shed on familiar questions like the "leads and lags" of monetary and financial aspects of economic fluctuations?

As would be expected, frequency domain methods immediately confirm the presence of strong cyclical comovements along the lines reported in section 7.2. The top two panels of figure 7.2 show the respective power spectra of money growth and credit growth, estimated using the full sets of available postwar quarterly data spanning 1947:1 to 1982:4 for money and 1952:1 to 1982:4 for credit.[23] Both

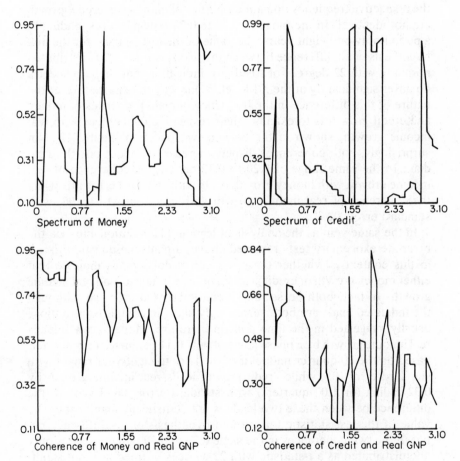

Fig. 7.2   Money and credit: spectra and coherences with real GNP.

23. This exercise relies on data for the full postwar period, despite the time domain evidence of structural change within that period, so as to provide enough observations to make the frequency domain analysis sensible. Both spectra, as well as the coherences displayed below, were estimated using a triangular window with bandwidth eleven.

spectra display substantial "noise" at high frequencies—say, 1.5 radians and above. More important from the perspective of the questions addressed here, both also display significant power at or near frequencies plausibly related to recognized business cycles. The record of seven complete cycles from the peak in 1948:4 to that in 1981:3 implies a mean cycle length of just under nineteen calendar quarters, equivalent to a frequency of almost exactly one-third radian. The spectra of both money growth and credit growth display sharp spikes at just that point.

Closer analysis of these two power spectra indicates, however, that the respective frequency domain properties of money and credit growth are not identical. In the range of 0.20 to 0.79 radian, corresponding to a period of two to eight years, the value of the test statistic for the null hypothesis of no difference between the two spectra is 3.90 (distributed normally with 22 degrees of freedom), indicating that the two spectra do differ significantly at the .01 level.[24] One way to explore further the nature of this difference in the frequency domain properties of money and credit growth is to examine their respective coherences with real income growth, shown in the bottom two panels of figure 7.2. Not surprisingly, both coherences display increases at about one-third radian. In the same range of 0.20 to 0.79 radian, the coherence of real income growth with money growth is .98 with standard error .01, while the coherence of real income growth with credit growth is .96, with standard error .02.[25]

In the same vein as the analysis of lead and lag relationships via the bivariate exogeneity tests reported above, a plausible question to ask in this context is whether these respective coherences indicate that either money growth or credit growth, or both, tends to lead real income growth. In fact, both do so, and credit somewhat more so, although the indicated leads are both surprisingly short in comparison to those usually suggested in the time domain literature. Money growth leads real income growth by a phase angle of only 0.11 radian (or 0.35 quarter, based on the 20-quarter midpoint of the two- to eight-year range) with standard error .05, while credit growth leads real income growth by 0.32 radian (or 1.02 quarters) with standard error .06. Even so, the difference between these two leads is not statistically significant. The value of the test statistic for the null hypothesis of no difference between the two coherences in the same 0.20 to 0.79 radian range is only .39 (distributed as a *t*-statistic with 22 degrees of freedom), not significant at any reasonable level.

24. I am grateful to Jim Powell for assistance in constructing the tests and for calculating the test statistics and their distributions reported here and in section 7.6 below.

25. With the estimated coherences so close to unity, the calculated standard errors are not well behaved.

In addition, in the same vein as the analysis of partial relationships via the multivariate exogeneity tests reported above, a further plausible question to ask in this context is whether the *partial* coherence of either money growth or credit growth with real income growth is significantly different from zero—in other words, whether either adds significantly to explaining the frequency domain properties of real income growth—given the presence of the other. As is largely consistent with the time domain results, the answer is no in both cases. For the same range of 0.20 to 0.79 radian, the values of the relevant test statistic (distributed as an F-statistic with 2 and 20 degrees of freedom) are .04 for the additional role of money growth and .42 for the additional role of credit growth. Neither value is significant at any reasonable level.

7.5 Statistical Significance and Economic Significance

The results of the stability tests reported in tables 7.10 and 7.15 indicate strong evidence of statistically significant differences, between one time period and another, in both bivariate and multivariate relationships summarizing the monetary and financial aspects of United States economic fluctuations. For many purposes, however, the statistical significance of such differences does not necessarily mean they are significant in a broader economic sense. After all, two corresponding coefficients, estimated for different time periods, can differ by an amount that is statistically significant but economically trivial if each is individually measured with sufficient precision. In addition, in dynamic relationships involving several coefficients, offsetting shifts in different coefficients can leave important properties of the resulting overall relationship unaffected.

The structural shifts in the monetary and financial aspects of the United States business cycle experience reported above are significant not just statistically but economically as well. Table 7.16 shows the full sets of estimation results for the bivariate annual relationship between real income growth and money growth summarized in the top section of table 7.9, for 1919–40, 1947–65, and 1966–82, respectively. As table 7.10 shows, the data indicate statistically significant shifts in these two estimated relationships. Comparison of the three full sets of results shown in table 7.16 confirms that these significant differences are typically due not to small changes in a few precisely measured coefficients but to one or even several quite large changes, sometimes even involving switches of sign.

Figure 7.3 shows the implications of the differences among these respective sets of estimated coefficients for the overall relationship between real income growth and money growth by tracing out the first ten years of the dynamic response pattern exhibited by the solved-out

Table 7.16   Bivariate Relationships between Real Income and Money

1919–40
$$X_t = .019 + .190X_{t-1} - .106X_{t-2} + .277M_{t-1} - .157M_{t-2}$$
$$(.9) \quad (.5) \quad\quad (-.3) \quad\quad (.6) \quad\quad (-.4)$$
$$\bar{R}^2 = .00 \quad\quad SE = .089 \quad\quad\quad DW = 2.02$$

$$M_t = .022 + .024X_{t-1} + .156X_{t-2} + .702M_{t-1} - .581M_{t-2}$$
$$(1.3) \quad (.1) \quad\quad (.6) \quad\quad (1.9) \quad\quad (-1.9)$$
$$\bar{R}^2 = .28 \quad\quad SE = .071 \quad\quad\quad DW = 1.66$$

1947–65
$$X_t = .060 - .156X_{t-1} + .351X_{t-2} + .142M_{t-1} - 1.21M_{t-2}$$
$$(4.1) \quad (-.5) \quad\quad (1.5) \quad\quad (.3) \quad\quad (-3.3)$$
$$\bar{R}^2 = .32 \quad\quad SE = .023 \quad\quad\quad DW = 1.46$$

$$M_t = .020 + .018X_{t-1} + .365X_{t-2} + .216M_{t-1} - .596M_{t-2}$$
$$(2.6) \quad (.1) \quad\quad (2.8) \quad\quad (.8) \quad\quad (-2.9)$$
$$\bar{R}^2 = .38 \quad\quad SE = .013 \quad\quad\quad DW = 2.13$$

1966–82
$$X_t = .089 + .211X_{t-1} - .164X_{t-2} + .269M_{t-1} - .837M_{t-2}$$
$$(3.0) \quad (.5) \quad\quad (-.5) \quad\quad (-.4) \quad\quad (-1.2)$$
$$\bar{R}^2 = .19 \quad\quad SE = .024 \quad\quad\quad DW = 2.01$$

$$M_t = .045 - .034X_{t-1} - .147X_{t-2} + .429M_{t-1} - .071M_{t-2}$$
$$(2.8) \quad (-.2) \quad\quad (-.9) \quad\quad (1.1) \quad\quad (-.2)$$
$$\bar{R}^2 = .02 \quad\quad SE = .013 \quad\quad\quad DW = 2.17$$

Note: X = growth rate of real GNP; M = growth rate of M1 money stock; $\bar{R}^2$ = adjusted coefficient of determination; SE = standard error of estimate; DW = Durbin-Watson statistic. Numbers in parentheses are t-statistics.

(but not orthogonalized) moving average representation of each of the three estimated bivariate autoregressions. The implied own-disturbance responses shown in the upper left and lower right panels of the figure are roughly similar among the three systems, but the implied cross-disturbance responses shown in the upper right and lower left panels diverge sharply and even include differences in the direction of the initial responses.

Table 7.17 and figure 7.4 present analogous sets of estimation results and associated dynamic response patterns for the bivariate annual relationship between real income growth and credit growth summarized in the middle section of table 7.9. Here again, large differences appear among corresponding coefficients estimated for different time periods, as do readily visible differences among the implied response patterns, especially for the respective cross-responses. In addition, further results (not shown) indicate similar large differences for systems relating the growth of either money or credit to nominal income growth, as well as for systems relating either real or nominal income growth to the change in short-term interest rates. Finally, still further results (also not shown) indicate large differences in the results for analogous sys-

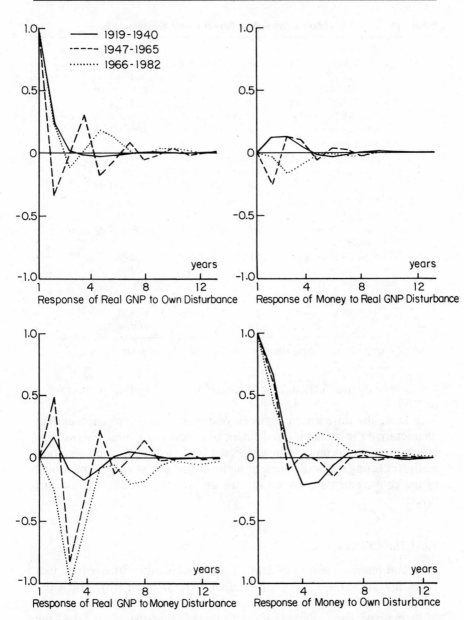

Fig. 7.3   Responses of money and real GNP to unit disturbances.

Table 7.17   **Bivariate Relationships between Real Income and Credit**

1919–40

$X_t = .027 + .161X_{t-1} - .063X_{t-2} + .959C_{t-1} - .962C_{t-2}$
$\quad\quad\;(1.1)\quad\;(.5)\quad\quad\;(-.2)\quad\quad\;(.8)\quad\quad\;(-1.3)$
$\quad\;\bar{R}^2 = .00 \quad\quad\quad\quad SE = .086 \quad\quad\quad\quad DW = 2.00$

$C_t = .012 + .109X_{t-1} - .027X_{t-2} + .350C_{t-1} - .117C_{t-2}$
$\quad\quad\;(1.5)\quad\;(1.1)\quad\quad\;(-.3)\quad\quad\;(1.0)\quad\quad\;(-.1)$
$\quad\;\bar{R}^2 = .16 \quad\quad\quad\quad SE = .026 \quad\quad\quad\quad DW = 1.30$

1947–1965

$X_t = .015 - .235X_{t-1} + .355X_{t-2} + .896C_{t-1} - .563C_{t-2}$
$\quad\quad\;(.4)\quad\;(-.8)\quad\quad\;(1.0)\quad\quad\;(1.3)\quad\quad\;(-.8)$
$\quad\;\bar{R}^2 = -.16 \quad\quad\quad\quad SE = .029 \quad\quad\quad\quad DW = 1.95$

$C_t = .045 - .389X_{t-1} + .135X_{t-2} + .647C_{t-1} - .242C_{t-2}$
$\quad\quad\;(3.7)\quad\;(-3.9)\quad\quad\;(1.2)\quad\quad\;(2.8)\quad\quad\;(-1.1)$
$\quad\;\bar{R}^2 = .45 \quad\quad\quad\quad SE = .009 \quad\quad\quad\quad DW = 2.05$

1966–82

$X_t = .055 - .009X_{t-1} - .052X_{t-2} + 1.01C_{t-1} - 1.32C_{t-2}$
$\quad\quad\;(1.7)\quad\;(-.0)\quad\quad\;(-.2)\quad\quad\;(1.4)\quad\quad\;(-1.8)$
$\quad\;\bar{R}^2 = .13 \quad\quad\quad\quad SE = .025 \quad\quad\quad\quad DW = 2.08$

$C_t = .035 - .195X_{t-1} - .086X_{t-2} + 1.16C_{t-1} - .439C_{t-2}$
$\quad\quad\;(2.5)\quad\;(-1.4)\quad\quad\;(-.7)\quad\quad\;(3.7)\quad\quad\;(-1.5)$
$\quad\;\bar{R}^2 = .65 \quad\quad\quad\quad SE = .010 \quad\quad\quad\quad DW = 2.27$

Note: C = growth rate of domestic nonfinancial credit. See also table 7.16.

tems based on quarterly data, estimated for 1947:1 to 1965:4 and 1966:1 to 1982:4.

In sum, the differences between one time period and another that characterize the monetary and financial aspects of United States economic fluctuations have been significant both statistically and economically, reflecting major differences in the magnitude as well as the timing of the comovements between income and money, credit, and interest rates.

7.6 The Credit Cycle

A final financial aspect of United States economic fluctuations that bears investigation here is the familiar "credit cycle" by which the economy's public and private sectors alternate over the business cycle in their respective volumes of credit-market borrowing. In brief, the basic idea behind this familiar notion is that the federal government's reliance on the credit market typically bulges when weakness in the economy enlarges the government's budget deficit, whereas the private sector's borrowing does just the opposite as a consequence of the cyclical variation of typically debt-financed spending. As a result, federal government borrowing is greater in economic contractions than in

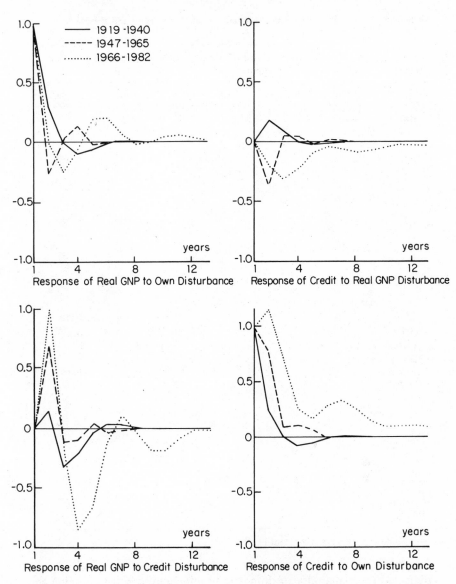

Fig. 7.4   Responses of credit and real GNP to unit disturbances.

expansions, whereas private sector borrowing is greater in expansions than in contractions. This cyclical regularity is broadly familiar in somewhat general terms, although to date little if any formal analysis of it has appeared.

Table 7.18 summarizes the main outlines of this regularity by showing the respective quarterly average growth rates of federal government

Table 7.18   **Postwar Cyclical Movements of Government and Private Sector Debt**

Business Cycles		Average Growth Rate of Government Debt		Average Growth Rate of Private Debt	
Peaks	Troughs	Contractions	Expansions	Contractions	Expansions
1953:2					
		2.50%		7.86%	
	1954:2				
			−0.74%		10.49%
1957:3					
		2.71		7.08	
	1958:2				
			2.49		9.14
1960:2					
		−0.41		7.21	
	1961:1				
			2.23		8.63
1969:4					
		3.40		7.62	
	1970:4				
			5.01		10.74
1973:4					
		5.20		9.21	
	1975:1				
			11.92		10.69
1980:1					
		11.02		8.31	
	1980:4				
			10.88		9.11
1981:3					
		15.42		7.03	
	1982:4				
Mean for all contractions		5.69%		7.76%	
Mean for all expansions			5.30%		9.80%

Note: Values shown are in percent per annum.

debt and the remainder of domestic nonfinancial credit (including the debt of state and local governments) during the six and one-half recognized business cycles since 1953. In part because of the lag of federal tax receipts behind fluctuations in economic activity, but also in part because of the upward secular trend in the growth rate of federal debt outstanding (as budget deficits have grown, while the level of federal debt outstanding has shrunk, relative to nonfinancial economic activity), the basic regularity of the "credit cycle" is more uniformly descriptive of private than of public borrowing.[26] In four contractions out of six, average federal debt growth was faster than in the preceding expansion, but the mean difference in growth rates between contractions and expansions has been only 0.39% per annum. By contrast, private debt growth in each expansion has been faster than in the preceding contraction, and private debt growth in each contraction has been slower than in the preceding expansion, resulting in a mean growth rate in expansions 2.04% per annum greater than in contractions.

Attempts to analyze the dynamic aspects of these regularities using the same time-domain results applied in section 7.4 yielded few interesting results, but the corresponding frequency domain results do bear inspection. The top two panels of figure 7.5 show the respective power spectra of federal and private sector debt growth, estimated using quarterly data for 1952:1 to 1982:4. The spectrum for federal debt growth displays an obvious spike at almost exactly the mean cyclical frequency of one-third radian, while that for private debt growth exhibits a large spike at a frequency only moderately higher. In contrast to the results reported in section 7.4 for the growth of money and credit, the respective frequency domain properties of federal and private debt growth do not exhibit significant differences. In the range of 0.20–0.79 radian, the value of the test statistic for the null hypothesis of no difference between these two spectra is only .44 (distributed normally with 22 degrees of freedom), not significant at any reasonable level. The bottom two panels of figure 7.5 show the respective coherences of federal debt growth and private debt growth with real income growth. Both show increases at about one-third radian, although the coherences are smaller than those reported above for the growth of money and credit. In the same range of 0.20–0.79 radian, the coherence of real income growth with federal debt growth is .36 with standard error .19, while the coherence between private debt growth and real income growth is .77 with standard error .09.

In addition to this evidence of regular comovements of federal and private debt growth with real income growth at cyclical frequencies, the associated phase relationships (corresponding to leads and lags in the time domain) provide some support for the idea that private borrowing helps in part to determine real income while the federal government's budget posture reacts passively.[27] Federal debt growth *lags*

---

26. See Friedman 1983a for a discussion of the divergent trends in federal deficits and federal debt outstanding in relation to economic activity.

27. This idea is consistent with a cyclical role for "credit crunches." It is also consistent with the fact that only about one-fourth of the cumulative federal budget deficit incurred during the period under study here would have emerged had the economy remained at "high employment" throughout; see again, for example, Friedman 1983a.

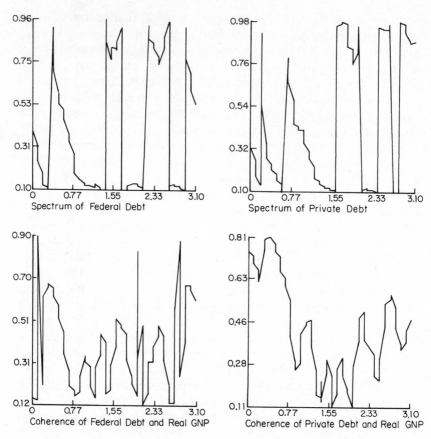

Fig. 7.5   Federal debt and private debt: spectra and coherences with real GNP.

real income growth by a phase angle of 1.47 radians (or 4.7 quarters) with standard error .55, while private debt growth *leads* real income growth by a phase angle of 0.97 radians (or 3.1 quarters) with a standard error of .18. Despite the small standard errors, however, these apparent differences are not statistically significant. The value of the test statistic for the null hypothesis of no difference between the two coherences in the same 0.20–0.79 radian range is only 0.002 (distributed as a *t*-statistic with 22 degrees of freedom).

Similar negative results emerge from asking whether either federal debt growth or private debt growth significantly contributes to explaining the frequency domain properties of real income growth in the presence of the other.[28] In the range of 0.20–0.79 radian, the values of the

28. The lack of significance here parallels the results of time domain exogeneity tests.

test statistic (distributed as an F-statistic with 2 and 20 degrees of freedom) for the partial coherence of real income growth with federal debt growth and with private debt growth—in each case taking the other as given—are respectively 1.49 and 0.17. Neither is significant at the .10 level.

In sum, there is evidence of a "credit cycle" in the sense of regular movements of federal and private sector debt growth, and regular co-movements of each with real income growth, at cyclical frequencies. In addition, there is some indication that private debt growth leads real income growth while federal debt growth lags, but the differences between these respective comovements are not statistically significant, nor does either federal or private debt growth contain significant information about real income growth beyond what is also in the other.

7.7 Summary of Conclusions

There can be no doubt that economic fluctuations in the United States have their monetary and financial side. The comovements among money, credit, interest rates, and nonfinancial economic activity are evident enough at the crudest eyeball level of inspection, as well as in the results of more sophisticated time and frequency domain exercises. Moreover, many of these comovements have coincided with major historical business cycle episodes.

On closer inspection, however, these monetary and financial aspects of United States economic fluctuations exhibit few quantitative regularities that have persisted unchanged across spans of time in which the nation's financial markets have undergone profound and far-reaching changes. The evidence for the absence of such persistent quantitative regularities assembled in this paper shows major differences among the pre–World War I, interwar, and post–World War II periods, and between the first and second halves of the postwar period. Evidence suggesting changes from one period to another repeatedly emerges, regardless of whether the method of analysis is simple or sophisticated, whether the underlying data are annual or quarterly, and whether the relationships under study are bivariate or multivariate. Moreover, the differences between one period and another reported here are significant not just statistically but economically as well, in the sense of major differences in the magnitude and timing of cyclical comovements.

The paper's main message, therefore, is a warning against accepting too readily—either as a matter of positive economics or for policy purposes—the appearance of simple and eternal verities in much of the existing literature of monetary and financial aspects of business fluctuations. More complicated models involving many variables and/or nonlinear relationships may have remained stable, but the evidence clearly shows that simple linear relationships among only a few such variables have not.

Comment   Stephen M. Goldfeld

Benjamin Friedman has given us an extensive empirical analysis of the behavior of monetary and financial variables over the businesss cycle. One aim of this paper seems to be engendering humility regarding what we as economists think we know about the world. More specifically, by a range of alternative procedures, Friedman seeks to establish the proposition that the cyclical behavior of monetary and financial variables does not exhibit persistent regularities. Put in somewhat over-simplified terms, movements in both nominal and real GNP do not seem to be related in a stable fashion to a conventional set of monetary and financial variables. Or to put it more crudely still, the great ratios of economics are not so great.

A second aim of the paper, and perhaps the major one, is to impart the message that this humble view of what we know should condition our policy prescriptions. That is, we should avoid making monetary policy on the presumption of any assumed statistical regularity, let alone on the presumption that this regularity will persist for long periods. Although not so identified, this is clearly the intergenerational battle of the Friedmans, and while my heart lies with the younger generation, I'm not sure the evidence presented is ultimately as persuasive as young Friedman suggests.

Friedman begins by characterizing the dramatic changes in the financial structure of the United States economy over the past seventy years. He considers three classes of change—in the role of monetary policy, in government regulations and intermediation, and in private financial institutions and practices—and amply documents each. The list provided is impressive, so impressive, in fact, that Friedman says it would be astonishing if the cyclical behavior of monetary and financial variables had not been altered. One almost senses that Friedman is ready to declare victory at this point, but he wisely recognizes that the negative-thinking approach to positive economics is not particularly persuasive and turns to the evidence.

The evidence presented is diverse in terms of technique, ranging from the pictorial and arithmetic to relatively sophisticated techniques for analyzing time series. To begin with, the long-term behavior of a number of monetary and financial variables is displayed visually. The

Stephen M. Goldfeld is professor of economics at Princeton University.

basic cyclical relationships are then quantified for the postwar period. These apparent regularities are then subjected to closer scrutiny. This is first done by computing simple annual correlations between real economic growth and a substantial number of variables, measuring changes in money, credit, and interest rates for various leads and lags and for alternative sample periods. On the whole, these calculations show substantial variations, in terms both of magnitude and of statistical significance, across time periods.

However, the lack of stability of simple correlation coefficients is rather weak evidence of any more fundamental structural change. These correlation coefficients are merely summary statistics of a complex multivariate stochastic process, and these is no reason, even if the underlying process remains the same, for these bivariate correlations to remain "stable" across time periods. For example, in a conventional simultaneous equations model, we know that the correlation between any two endogenous variables will depend on all the exogenous variables in the system. The finding that two endogenous variables have different sample correlations for different time periods may simply reflect the behavior of the exogenous variables in the two time periods. Friedman, of course, is well aware of these potential difficulties and consequently presents an alternative analysis of the same data using the more sophisticated vector autoregression technique (VAR).

Friedman first estimates bivariate VARs with annual data using either real or nominal GNP growth and a measure of money or credit growth. Overall summary measures of statistical significance are reported for various time periods, and inspection suggests that persistent regularities are few and far between. Friedman confirms this impression with an extensive set of tests for structural stability that generally indicate widespread structural change. With the recognition that annual data may be incapable of capturing the relevant dynamics, Friedman repeats a similar exercise with postwar quarterly data and an expanded set of financial measures. Structural instability is once again evident and widespread.

Finally, the robustness of these results is examined with reference to larger VAR models. Selected results are presented for a five-variable annual model, suggesting that structural change is again present. Formal stability tests with this model, for both annual and quarterly data, confirm these impressions.

The punchline, then, is that monetary and financial variables do not bear a stable relationship to changes in real and nominal GNP. Moreover, Friedman examines dynamic response patterns and suggests that these instabilities have economic as well as statistical significance. As a consequence, policies based on a presumed stability are to be avoided. As noted earlier, I have considerable sympathy for both parts of the punchline, but I wonder whether those not so inclined will find the evidence persuasive.

My doubts on this score stem from the fundamental difficulty of "proving" that instabilities exist. The standard retort to such exhibitions of instability is that one is simply working with the wrong specification. This was certainly the response of the vast hordes, myself included, who attempted to fix up an apparently errant money demand function in the 1970s. In the present case, the skepticism of those who are not willing to accept Friedman's results is bolstered by the seeming sensitivity of the VAR technique to the size of the model used.

In discussing his reasons for using a reduced-form approach such as a VAR technique, Friedman cites the benefits of being able to sidestep the inevitably controversial specification issues inherent in a structural approach. Although these same issues may appear less controversial in a VAR approach, they are nonetheless of equal substance. For example, Friedman briefly reports comparative results for four-, five-, and 6-variable VAR systems, suggesting, as others have similarly found, that adding a single variable to a VAR system can often reverse conclusions. When one adds to this all the other conventional specification issues (e.g., lag length, use of differencing to achieve stationarity), one can see why it is tricky to establish the presence of instability. These difficulties are further compounded in the present case by an implicit assumption made in the tests, namely that the variances in the several subperiods considered are identical. This assumption is somewhat suspect in the light of the well-established differences in variability for many economic variables between the prewar and postwar periods. Given this, it might be desirable to test the hypothesis of coefficient stability without maintaining the constancy of variances across subperiods. Standard methods for doing this are available.

Overall, then, in the face of these specification and technical issues, it is difficult to know what degree of confidence one can have in the tests of stability reported. Indeed, some may feel there remains substantial room for indulging one's prior beliefs. Nevertheless, let us suppose we are fully comfortable with the notion that the instabilities of the sort Friedman reports are truly genuine. Does it necessarily follow that something like a constant money growth policy is necessarily worse than it would be in a world where the VAR models had passed stability tests? Put another way, while I am perfectly willing to believe that a constant growth rule is not optimal even in a world that passes stability tests, does such a rule become more suboptimal when structural stability tests fail? Friedman strongly implies this is the case, and this view does have some intuitive appeal. However, on closer examination I am not sure how one would establish this case.

The problem in evaluating a particular monetary policy proposal is, as in most things, Compared to what? One must be prepared to specify such an alternative and see how it performs in the face of presumed instabilities. This in turn would require a more complete characterization of the nature of the instabilities and the learning process whereby the authorities discover the presence of structural shifts. Furthermore, to be fair to a constant money growth rule, one would not have to restrict this to a single number to be followed no matter what the emerging evidence. The only feature necessary to capture the spirit of this idea is that the constant growth be maintained for some substantial period. I do not know how the results of such an exercise would turn out, but as a matter of logic it does not seem that the sorts of instabilities Friedman found necessarily add to the case against a constant growth rule.

To reiterate, I am neither surprised nor disappointed with Friedman's findings of instability and his policy bias. I would be surprised, however, if the battle did not go on.

Comment   Allan H. Meltzer

Near the start of his paper, Benjamin Friedman writes: "The basic theme of this paper . . . is that the quantitative relationships connecting monetary and financial variables to the business cycle exhibit few if any strongly persistent regularities that have remained even approximately invariant in the context of the widespread and, in some instances, dramatic changes undergone by the United States financial markets." In the conclusion, he repeats this theme: "economic fluctuations exhibit few quantitative regularities that have persisted unchanged across spans of time in which the nation's financial markets have undergone profound and far-reaching changes." And he warns us not to accept "the appearance of simple and eternal verities in much of the previous literature of monetary and financial aspects of business fluctuations."

I find these conclusions misleading for at least two reasons. First, even if we accept Friedman's evidence, it is not clear that it rejects any well-established proposition. Friedman does not give any clues about the particular "simple and eternal verities" that should not now be accepted. Economists have known that *numerical* estimates of structural parameters and reduced-form coefficients are subject to change whenever there are changes in behavior. (This is a principal implication of the early Cowles Commission work on identification that has been more fully developed in Lucas 1976.) Second, Friedman's paper is

Allan H. Meltzer is a professor in the Graduate School of Industrial Administration at Carnegie-Mellon University.

atheoretical, and much of his evidence comes from two-way comparisons of financial and real variables. Failure at this level of testing is informative but not alarming. Vector autoregressions (VARs) using five or six variables are more informative, but this technique has well-known limitations that Friedman (1983b) recognizes.

My comment is in three parts. First, I reconsider some of the propositions on the role of money in business cycles developed in the sixties by Milton Friedman and Anna J. Schwartz (1963a, b), Phillip Cagan (1965), and Karl Brunner and Allan H. Meltzer (1964). I report some of the evidence on these relations I find in the paper. Second, I comment on some reasons that Friedman and I draw different conclusions from his data and suggest that his work is most usefully interpreted as a test of the quantitative significance of the well-known Lucas critique of econometric practice. Third, I comment briefly on his discussion of the credit variable during business cycles.

Money and Business Cycles

G. L. Bach (1963, 3) summarized Friedman and Schwartz's contribution at a previous NBER conference as follows: "The Friedman and Schwartz paper, together with Friedman's other published works, provide the strongest empirical foundation for the proposition that the supply of money is a—probably the—dominant variable in determining the level of total spending on current output. . . . there was a general willingness to admit that the supply of money does now appear to be an important variable in explaining the level of aggregate spending."

Friedman and Schwartz (1963b) offered a number of propositions about the stock of money and its rate of change during business cycles, measured according to NBER chronology, and about the relation of changes in money growth to business cycles. They investigated cyclical patterns of velocity and demonstrated the procyclical conformity of velocity—the finding that velocity rises relative to trend during expansions and declines relative to trend during contractions. They summarized their principal findings as showing "beyond any reasonable doubt that the stock of money displays a systematic cyclical behavior. The rate of change in the money stock regularly reaches a peak before the reference peak and a trough before the reference trough, *though the lead is rather variable*" (1963b, 63; italics added).

These and other conclusions were extended in a study of the Federal Reserve system by Brunner and Meltzer (1964), in a study of the cyclical and secular behavior of the money stock by Cagan (1965), and in Friedman and Schwartz's (1963a) *Monetary History of the United States*. One or more of these studies presented evidence for the following propositions that, together, constituted a major part of the foundations for "monetarism": (1) money growth rises and falls procyclically; (2) accelerations and decelerations of money are frequently followed after a lag by cyclical expansions and contractions of real output;[1] (3) sustained money growth relative to the growth of output is a sufficient condition for inflation; (4) market interest rates typically rise in periods of cyclical expansion and fall in contractions; and (5) velocity growth is procyclical.

Benjamin Friedman's study of postwar data supports several of these propositions. His table 7.1 shows, as he notes, that money growth is higher in each expansion than in the preceding or following contraction.[2] This finding supports proposition 1.

For each peak and trough beginning with the fourth quarter 1949, I chose the peak and trough in the quarterly rate of money growth nearest to the quarterly reference peaks or troughs recorded by the NBER. Friedman and Schwartz (1963b, 37) used peaks and troughs in monthly rates of money growth as one means of dating specific cycles in money and computing the leads of money growth at business cycle turning points. There are now more sophisticated methods of computing leads and lags, but my method permits replication of Friedman and Schwartz's work on an extended sample. Multiplying the average lead of money growth measured in quarters by three to compare to Friedman and Schwartz's monthly data shows that the average lead of money growth is 10.5 months at reference cycle troughs and 15.4 months at reference cycle peaks. This lead is one to two months shorter than the earlier estimates. Given the relatively high variability of the leads that Friedman and Schwartz note, the difference is not impressive.[3] This *quantitative* proposition stands up well.

Table C7.1   **Computed Average Lead of Specific Cycles in Money Growth (*M1*) before Reference Cycle Turning Points**

Peaks	
Average at peaks 1953–81	− 15.4 months
Average all peaks 1870–1960	− 17.6 months
Average all mild cycles 1870–1960	− 16.4 months
Troughs	
Average at troughs 1949–82	− 10.5 months
Average all troughs 1870–1960	− 12.0 months
Average all mild cycles 1870–1960	− 11.8 months

1. Economists would now substitute "unanticipated money growth" for "accelerations and decelerations of money." It is not clear that the more precise restatement makes a major difference for United States data.

2. There is one minor exception. Money growth is higher on average during the 1969–70 contraction than in the preceding expansion. The lengthy expansion includes a period of relatively low money growth and low inflation.

3. Dating for each peak and trough is shown in the appendix. Friedman and Schwartz used M2; I used M1. Where the two series overlap, differences in dating are small.

These data, and econometric studies by Barro (1978), Korteweg (1978), and others support proposition 2 on the role of changes in money growth as a dominant impulse in business cycles. Proposition 3 on the central role of money growth for inflation is now accepted by economists with many fewer reservations or disclaimers than twenty years ago. Friedman's comparison of average rates of growth of nominal and real GNP during expansions and contractions casts doubt on the relationship, however. He reports that the differences between the average rate of change in expansion and the average rate of change in contraction is the same (6.5%) for nominal and real GNP. Taken literally, this implies that the average rate of inflation has been the same for expansions as for contractions. Since average money growth is procyclical, money growth differs systematically between half-cycles.

Comparing cyclical average rates of growth of money with inflation using Friedman's data shows a persistent effect of money growth on inflation. The comparative size of money growth and inflation is positively associated without any allowance for lags, supply shocks, or the effects of real output growth. Rank correlations of half-cycle average rates of money growth and inflation are .74 for the eight contractions and .89 for the seven expansions. These rank correlations are significant at better than the .05 and at the .01 level respectively.

Friedman's table 7.2 shows that the average change in short-term rates is negative in each contraction and positive in each expansion, as required by proposition 4. The average change in long-term rates is positive in two of the eight contractions, however, contrary to the proposition. One of the exceptions includes the first oil shock, when interest rates were raised by the effects of the supply shock.

Friedman's discussion of table 7.4 notes that monetary velocity rises in every expansion and falls in every contraction. This supports a strong form of proposition 5, since no allowance has to be made for trend. Velocity growth, like money growth, is higher in each expansion than in either the preceding or the following contraction.

The five propositions of monetary economics are supported by Friedman's study. Among other propositions, one is of particular interest for policy. In a recent paper, Brunner and Meltzer (1983) pointed out that covariances of money growth and velocity growth computed from quarterly data are positively correlated at times. Friedman shows that the positive correlation of money growth and velocity growth is found also for the eight cyclical contractions and for the combined contractions and expansions. Further, Friedman finds that the variance of nominal GNP growth is dominated by the variance of money growth in both contractions and expansions. These findings imply that constant money growth would lower the variability of GNP growth by reducing or eliminating the variability of money growth and by removing the covariance of money growth and velocity growth found during expansions.

If households are risk averse, welfare increases as the variability of GNP growth declines. Friedman's estimates suggest that the static effect of constant money growth on nominal GNP growth is a reduction of more than 80% of measured variability in the cyclical averages. Or to put the same point another way, the data in his table 7.7 imply that the variability of velocity growth would have to rise by an average of 570% in contractions and 650% in expansions to raise the variability of GNP growth following the adoption of a rule mandating constant money growth. This suggests again, that the Federal Reserve's discretionary policy has lowered welfare by adding more variability to GNP growth than it removed and, at times, by maintaining positive correlation of money growth and velocity growth.

Differences in Interpretation

Friedman reports and comments on several of the relations discussed in the preceding section. In addition, he analyzes some power spectra and reports evidence of coherence that is consistent with propositions relating money growth to the fluctuations we call business cycles. Why, then, is his principal conclusion a warning against accepting these regularities as a reliable basis for theory or policy?

One reason is that Friedman may have been misled by the data he presents. He recognizes that the bivariate relationships can be misleading because they omit relevant variables and replace partial responses with total responses. The vector autoregressions (VAR) have been the subject of many recent criticisms, and it is now well known that this method is sensitive to changes in the ordering of variables and the number of variables included in the VAR, and that the results are subject to the Lucas critique. Elsewhere, Friedman (1983b, 33) has recognized these criticisms and makes only modest claims about what can be learned from VARs.

The bivariate relationships are subject to other, no less trenchant criticisms. Correlations between annual data are unlikely to yield useful information about business contractions that last less than four quarters or are spread over parts of two calendar years. Four of the eight postwar contractions are of this kind. Quarterly relations are not subject to this criticism, but they are open to two others.

First, some of Friedman's tests are not tests of plausible economic relations. Included here are bivariate tests of a relation between money growth and the growth of real income. As tests of a relation running from money to income, the tests either fail to distinguish between anticipated and unanticipated money growth or, in the case of the VARs, impose tight restrictions on anticipations. As tests of a relation running from income to money, they fail to hold prices and interest rates constant, as required for the demand for money, and fail to take account of relevant foreign variables and exchange regimes as required for the supply of money. Other tests also have problems. Economic theory does not imply that interest rates are related in a simple way to the growth of real or nominal income or to the growth rate of money. Tests of the relation between growth of income, money growth, and interest rates shed no light, and Friedman does not attempt to interpret them or provide an analytic foundation to help the reader interpret them.

Second, work on monetary relations published in the sixties, and cited above, made no claims that lags are constant or that numerical values are fixed. Typically, the emphasis was on the variability of lags.

The five propositions discussed in the previous section do not require constant coefficients. Earlier work using the NBER's business cycle method encouraged a search for common features of business cycles but did not impose uniform leads or lags or other constant coefficients on the data. The basic unit of time in these studies is not a year or a quarter; it is a cyclical phase of varying length when measured in calendar time but assumed to be comparable to similar phases of other cycles. The NBER also distinguished, at times, between wartime and peacetime cycles, between mild and severe recessions, and between the recoveries from mild and severe recessions. While I have not found the NBER's method attractive, I find it more useful *for bivariate comparisons* than Friedman's use of years or calendar quarters as units of observation.

One reason is that the seven expansions studied by Friedman vary in length from 12 to 106 months, roughly four to thirty five quarters. The eight contractions vary from 6 to 16 months, or from two to more than five quarters. It would be surprising if the forces (including policy) influencing the length of expansions and contractions had no influence on the measured length of lags and other parameters.

An additional reason for believing that Friedman's null conclusion is misleading is that economic theory gives no reason for assuming that lags are constant. The variability of the lead of money growth at business cycle turning points has frequently been remarked upon. Recent work shows that the length of leads or lags varies directly with the ratio of the variance of permanent to the variance of transitory changes. See Brunner, Cukierman, and Meltzer (1980).

Current research on policy rules or regimes, recognizing the so-called Lucas effect, makes no claim that the parameters of economic models are invariant to changes in policy rules. At times during this century, the United States has followed the rules of the gold standard, the gold exchange standard, the Bretton Woods system, the system of fluctuating exchange, and the 1942–51 system of pegged interest rates. Other countries have experienced as many changes, and often more violent ones, in monetary regime. Each of these regimes, in principle, changes the path through which money influences economic activity or the timing of the responses of income to the stock of money or the responses of demand for money to income and other variables.

Friedman's findings are not inconsistent with this view. Although he does not mention the particular changes in policy regimes, in principle the same conclusion applies to the introduction of federal deposit insurance that changed the risk of banks' deposit liabilities, the development of substitutes for money, or changes in the effective ceilings on interest rates arising from the combination of regulation and increased rates of anticipated inflation.

Friedman's findings are part of the accumulating analysis and evidence on the problems faced by policymakers who seek to control or modify economic activity using either econometric models and sophisticated feedback, control procedures or fully discretionary policies based on judgment about average responses, or the many mixtures of these control techniques.[4] The results that he calls "qualitative," and the evidence I summarized in the preceding section, do not rule out the relevance of economic research and economic theory for economic policy. Nothing in Friedman's work rejects such *quantitative* relations as: (1) the so-called Fisher equation relating nominal rates of interest to anticipated inflation; (2) approximate long-run proportionality between growth of nominal income and money growth; and (3) long-run purchasing power parity.

The Role of Credit

A considerable part of Friedman's paper compares cyclical properties of credit and money and studies cyclical relations between credit and other variables. I ignored these sections in the previous comments because I do not know how to interpret the findings, and Friedman offers little guidance. A section on the credit cycle discusses some regular features of cyclical changes in public and private debt but concludes that movements of private debt provide no information about the growth of real income that is not contained in the growth of public debt. In an earlier section, Friedman concludes that the growth rate of credit or of money provides no useful information once the other growth rate is known.

This last comparison and Friedman's parallel treatment of credit and money throughout the paper suggest that he finds little basis for choos-

---

4. His finding of an absence of any effect of money on real income—other than those reported in table 7.9 that are purely autoregressive—is consistent with rational expectations.

ing between the two measures. Although I am convinced that the study of intermediation is useful, I am as skeptical about Friedman's parallel treatment of credit and money as I am about his procedure for studying the role of credit or intermediation during business cycles.

Friedman defines credit as the total liabilities of nonfinancial borrowers—private and public—that have been issued in the financial markets. He computes a measure of credit velocity, defined as the ratio of GNP to credit, and compares this measure of velocity with monetary velocity, the ratio of GNP to money.

It is always possible to analyze a stock flow relation by multiplying a particular stock by its velocity, measured in units per time, so that the product is equal to the flow. The quantity equation shows that this tradition is as old as systematic thinking about money. The initial appeal of the quantity equation, and its persistence through time, owed much to the (quantitative) empirical observation that prices and other nominal values move over time in direct proportion to money, although the correspondence may not be close during a particular year or quarter.

The relation of money to nominal GNP has been formalized in the quantity theory. Whatever reservations one may have about the content of this hypothesis, there can be no doubt about its survival or its usefulness in explaining differences in rates of inflation between countries and in the same country at different times.

There is no comparable hypothesis about domestic nonfinancial credit. Is there more than arithmetic behind Friedman's idea that the growth rate of credit plus the growth of credit velocity equals the growth of nominal GNP? Is the growth of nominal GNP independent of the growth of money and dependent on credit? How dependent is the postwar growth of credit relative to money on the effects of prohibitions on interest payments and regulation Q in the presence of inflationary monetary policy? How dependent is the growth of the private component of credit on the growth of the public component—the growth of the public debt?

Although Friedman does not pursue these issues, his data provide some answers. Rank correlation of his measures of the growth of public and private debt show very little relation between the two during either expansions or contractions, contrary to the complete crowding out hypothesis. The difference between the growth of private debt and money is negatively related to the short-term rate of interest. This difference is a measure of the growth of intermediation, since M1 and the monetary base grow at approximately parallel rates during half-cycles. The measure declined in both expansions and contractions as interest rates rose. The decline is dramatic, more than 50% on average, between half-cycles during which short-term market rates are below regulation Q ceilings and the half-cycles in which short-term rates are substantially above the ceilings. A smaller and less uniform decline in the growth of intermediation is shown by the comparison of interest rates and the difference in the growth rate of total credit and money.

The introduction suggests that the paper will explore relationships of this kind. Regrettably, it does not do so. Friedman is too eager to dismiss what is known and too reluctant to use his data to extend existing theories of the relation of credit and money, or the theory of intermediation, during business cycles.[5]

Conclusion

This conference has produced a large number of null results, and Friedman's paper is of this kind. I am not persuaded that the null conclusions tell us as much about business cycles as they do about the method common to many of the papers. Perhaps a principal conclusion to be drawn is that you cannot get something for nothing. If we are unwilling to impose a structure on the data by stating testable hypotheses, the data may mislead us into accepting that the world is as lacking in structure as this approach.

Benjamin Friedman has ably summarized the data for main financial variables. I find in his null results additional information about the errors that are likely to be made when policymakers rely on estimates from quarterly equations or models. The results are far less damaging—and often supportive—of well-known qualitative and quantitative relations between monetary and other variables. My comments try to make this distinction and to suggest the limits to the scope of reliable quantitative knowledge that economists and policymakers face.

At least since the time of Lucas's (1976) critique of econometric practice and policy simulation, economists have been aware that parameter estimates of economic models are subject to change when private or public policies change. The quantitative significance of Lucas's results has been left largely to individual judgment, and judgments differ. Friedman's work, summarized in tables 7.10 and 7.15 and in his discussion of the *economic* significance of his findings, can be interpreted as evidence of the quantitative significance of the Lucas's critique. Although Friedman avoids this interpretation, I find it appealing and suggestive of the way his study can be a useful start on the quantitative analysis of an important topic.

5. One surprising claim is that financial panics "have all but vanished since the establishment of the Federal Reserve System in 1914 and especially the Federal Deposit Insurance Corporation in 1934." This statement neglects the experience from 1929 to 1933 and particularly the waves of banking failures from 1930 until the bank holiday in March 1933.

Appendix

Leads of Money Growth at NBER Turning Points

Reference Cycle Dates (Quarters)		Money Growth Specific Cycle		Lead in Quarters	
Peak	Trough	Peak	Trough	Peak	Trough
	1949:4		1948:4		4
1953:2		1951:4		6	
	1954:2		1953:3		3
1957:3		1954:4		11	
	1958:2		1957:4		2
1960:2		1959:1		5	
	1961:1		1959:4		5
1969:4		1968:4		4	
	1970:4		1969:3		5
1973:4		1972:3		5	
	1975:1		1973:3		6
1980:1		1979:2		3	
	1980:3		1980:2		1
1981:3		1981:1		2	
	1982:4		1982:2		2
Mean lead in quarters				5.14	3.50
Mean lead in months				16.4	10.5

Reply   Benjamin M. Friedman

Allan Meltzer asks what familiar proposition the empirical evidence assembled in my paper contradicts. Meltzer's question is a useful one, and it deserves a serious answer.

This book is about business cycles. The focus of my contribution to it is the behavior, in a business cycle context, of money, credit, and interest rates. Like the book's other papers, mine follows conventional understanding in taking "business cycles" to mean aggregate-level fluctuations in real economic activity, typically lasting more than a year (for the full cycle) but well under a decade. At the same time, because money and credit are nominal variables and so may bear a stronger connection to nominal economic activity, much of the analysis in the paper focuses on both real and nominal activity measures in parallel.

Of the five *qualitative* propositions Meltzer lists on pages 442–43 of his comment, therefore, all but the third involve business cycles and hence are of at least some interest here. Indeed, as he points out, my paper presents evidence corroborating each of them. By contrast, of the three *quantitative* relationships he lists on page 447 of his comment, none is of interest here (although the Fisher equation certainly could be).

What familiar proposition, then, does the evidence presented in my paper contradict? It is, in Meltzer's wording, "the role of changes in money growth as a dominant impulse in business cycles"—or, in Bach's even stronger wording, which Meltzer quotes, "the proposition that the supply of money is a—probably the—dominant variable in determining the level of total spending on current output."[1] This proposition has become as familiar an idea as any that macroeconomics has to offer. Although it is far from universally believed, there can be little doubt that acceptance of it—by economists, by policymakers, and by the general public—has grown enormously in the twenty years since the publication of the work Meltzer cites by Friedman and Schwartz, himself and Brunner, and others.

In his reference to his own table C7.1 and to work by Barro and by Korteweg, Meltzer treats this *quantitative* proposition about what is a (or the) driving force underlying business cycles as equivalent to the *qualitative* proposition that changes in money growth "are frequently followed" by fluctuations of real output. But the two are not the same. The issue is not whether it is possible to replicate the mean lag findings of Friedman and Schwartz, as Meltzer does, but whether the evidence warrants singling out money as playing some special, dominant role in the initiation or propagation of cyclical movements in economic activity.

In short, is there anything special about the role of money in business cycles? Given that there is no dispute about Meltzer's first and second qualitative propositions—that money growth varies procyclically and that it frequently leads cyclical variations of output growth—my paper addresses this question in three ways. The first is to go beyond the documentation of whether movements in money growth tell anything about movements in income growth by asking whether movements in money growth tell anything about movements in income growth that prior movements in income growth itself cannot say equally well. The second is to examine the importance of other variables in this context, either indirectly by asking whether what movements in money growth have to say about movements in income growth varies from one time period to another, or more directly by asking what movements in several variables (including money growth) have to say together. The third

1. The part of Bach's statement Meltzer quotes could, of course, be taken to refer only to nominal spending without any implications at all for real economic activity and hence business cycles. A reading of Bach's introduction makes clear that this is not the case, however, so that Meltzer's citation is apt in the business cycle context.

is to undertake comparisons, by asking whether what movements in money growth tell about movements in income growth differs from what movements in credit and interest rates tell.

The conclusion indicated in my paper is that the evidence does not identify anything special, or dominant, about the role of money in the business cycle context. First, although for some time periods there is evidence that movements in money growth tell something about movements in income growth that prior movements in income growth do not already say, that evidence is hardly overwhelming, and for other time periods there is no such evidence. Second, just what it is that movements in money growth tell about movements in income growth varies substantially from one time period to another,[2] and movements in money growth do not stand out in this context in a multivariate setting. Third, movements in other financial variables—specifically, interest rates and credit—tell about as much about movements in income growth as do movements in money growth.

No, of course these findings do not contradict the *qualitative* propositions that money growth varies procyclically and that it frequently leads real income growth. But they do cast doubt on the *quantitative* proposition that the impulse to business cycles from money growth is dominant in any ordinary sense.

Meltzer's criticism of the use of two-variable relationships to address such questions—including in part relationships between nominal money and real income—has merit, as my paper should also make clear.[3] But his brusque treatment of the subject does not get to the fundamental underlying tension it involves.

At one level, what is being asserted is indeed a relationship between two variables, one nominal and one real: nominal money growth varies procyclically, nominal money growth leads real income growth, nominal money growth is a (the) dominant impulse driving real income growth, and so on. Meltzer's own table C7.1 is itself one way of examining just this bivariate relationship between nominal money and

2. It is difficult to understand Meltzer's claim that my paper does not acknowledge "changes in policy regimes" as a source of these differences. Of the three categories of change in the economy's financial structure that section 7.1 sets forth as reasons for not expecting to find unchanging business cycle relationships, the first one discussed is monetary policy and the second is financial regulation. It is also ironic in this context that Meltzer's detailed discussion of what some of my paper's findings imply for a constant money growth rule simply assumes that the variability of the velocity ratio would remain invariant to that specific regime change.

3. Meltzer also criticizes the use of natural time units rather than business cycle phases in examining these relationships, but this criticism seems misplaced. If money growth is dominant in determining income growth, why take the length of a business expansion or contraction as exogenous? Regression or vector autoregression relationships based on natural time units allow the length of each movement in income growth to be determined by the length of each movement in money growth if the data so indicate.

real income. Yet Meltzer wants to disallow evidence from bivariate relationships in addressing the three questions posed above. Why is it admissible to ask if money growth leads real income growth but not to ask if money growth leads the part of real income growth that is not already predictable from past real income growth itself? Why is it legitimate to examine the relationship of real income growth to money growth but not to credit growth or interest rates?

The tension here arises because, if other things beside money growth matter for business cycles, then a simple two-variable relationship between money growth and real income growth is fundamentally misspecified. This misspecification has significant implications both for the use of simple money/income relationships in economic forecasting and policymaking and for the investigation of hypotheses like those in question here. In both settings it is then necessary to admit that the world is more complicated, and to advance to richer representations importantly featuring variables other than money. In the research context, my paper shows that simply moving to nonstructural systems of modestly higher order does not satisfactorily represent this complexity (nor does it indicate any special role for money growth), and here I fully agree with Meltzer about the need for structural analysis. As most readers of this volume surely know, however, it is hardly the case that the evidence from structural models clearly points toward money growth as the driving force behind business cycles either.

In sum, the thrust of Meltzer's comment is that somehow economists know, presumably from the work of Friedman and Schwartz and their followers, that money growth is what matters most for business fluctuations, and that efforts to question whether this is so, or to examine the role of other variables, must accept the burden of proof. That position is untenable. One cannot simultaneously embrace the long tradition of nonstructural investigation of the relation between money growth and the business cycle—including simple lead/lag analysis early on, then straightforward regression analysis, and more recently bi- or even multivariate autoregression analysis—but ignore parallel investigations showing comparable results for other variables. One cannot accept the conclusions of whatever structural analyses indicate a unique role for money yet discard all those that do not.

Nowhere is this schizophrenic view more apparent than in Meltzer's concluding section remarking on the approach maintained throughout my paper of examining, in a way parallel to that applied to money, the role of credit—that is, of a nominal financial quantity other than money. Meltzer acknowledges that the results provide little or no empirical basis for choosing between money and credit as a (the) dominant impulse underlying business cycles if one wants to make such a claim. Instead, he says he is "skeptical" about the entire parallel treatment of money and credit, arguing that empirical examination of business cycle relationships is somehow legitimate for money but not for credit. Meltzer motivates this presumption in favor of money by appealing to the quantity theory.

But what quantity? And what theory? The mere statement that the growth of "money" bears a relation to income growth is no more than a hypothesis subject to empirical testing. That people have believed in it for many years would not make it so if the available empirical evidence systematically contradicted it. Similarly, that people have believed in this relation for a long time does not, in the absence of evidence, make it more valid than any other relation. A long tradition of belief that money growth bears such-and-such a relation to income growth also does not make it a "theory" in the sense of a behavioral explanation that is applicable to one observed relationship but not to others.

To be sure, the theoretical literature provides many models of the demand for money for transactions purposes, as well as of the demand for asset holding. To justify Meltzer's presumption, however, it is necessary to connect the theory to the quantity in question and also to show that the theory does not connect to other quantities as well. In an earlier era, Milton Friedman's "Restatement" of the quantity theory explicitly defined money as claims "that are generally accepted in payment of debts,"[4] yet Friedman and Schwartz's empirical work focused on an aggregate also importantly including savings balances. Today, neither M1 nor M2 readily corresponds with either the transactions or the savings models of money demand, respectively. The deposits included in M1 often serve a savings function, and these deposits and currency are hardly the only way to make payments anyway. The more comprehensive M2 certainly does not represent total financial assets, or even total liquid assets.

Failing these conditions, the theory that is needed to relate any of the familiar Ms to the business cycle is a more general theory describing *inside* asset holding, and in particular a theory relating the holding of inside assets to the determination of nonfinancial economic activity.[5]

---

4. Popular usage of the "quantity theory" idea notwithstanding, Friedman's "Restatement" in no way provided a rationale for describing movements of income growth in terms of movements of money growth alone. Even after all of the simplifying assumptions Friedman imposed, his final equation related nominal income not only to money but also to interest rates, equity returns, the rate of price inflation, the ratio of human to nonhuman wealth, and real income, in addition to any variables affecting tastes and preferences.

5. Models in which all assets are outside assets and (inside) liabilities do not exist have been a staple of monetary economics for decades, and they have provided valuable theoretical insights. But the world they describe corresponds to a modern economy only if the inside assets and liabilities that obviously exist do not matter much. The empirical evidence relating the monetary base to nonfinancial economic activity suggests that that is not so in this context. The base does not show relationships to income that M1 and M2 do not, and often the base shows weaker relationships than either M1 or M2.

As Tobin and others have shown, however, theories of inside asset holding are inseparable from theories of inside liability issuing. Regardless of whether credit is viewed as an aggregate of debt assets held or an aggregate of debt liabilities issued, there is no reason to presume that a satisfactory theory exists for M1 or M2 in isolation from other inside assets and liabilities, or that a comprehensive theory of inside asset holding and liability issuing would somehow point to a special role for M1 or M2.

Whether there is something special about "money" in initiating or propagating business cycles is an empirical question. The evidence presented in my paper indicates that there is not.

Discussion Summary

Christopher Sims took issue with Allan Meltzer's claim that VARs are particularly unrobust to specification changes by noting that, first, a fortiori the same could be said of structural models. Second, while it was true that time series relationships change through time, the changes were not enormous. Third, a standard of comparison was needed before one could claim that the relationships estimated were poorly captured.

Phillip Cagan observed that the NBER research on the relation between output and money had found that from the Civil War to the end of the 1950s the qualitative evidence favored the view that variations in the supply of money from various sources did affect output and prices subsequently. This was not necessarily the case recently, since Federal Reserve behavior might have shifted, but there remained the question whether these changes affected the relationship between money and GNP in an economically significant way.

Geoffrey Moore drew attention to the fact that money and credit behavior is very different at the peaks and troughs of the cycle and that one should not expect simple time series methods necessarily to show stability over time. Stanley Fischer suggested a more general hypothesis than the one in the paper, that persistent monetary expansion is eventually followed by inflation. This, he said, seemed to be a consistent qualitative result. Anna Schwartz took exception to Friedman's assertion in the paper that velocity is "only a ratio," which has no relevance beyond that.

Benjamin Friedman stressed that what was important for the conduct of monetary policy along "monetarist" lines was that relationships should remain *quantitatively* stable and said he had shown that such stability does not exist. While qualitative features of the money/nominal income relationship might persist, these are of limited use for policymakers.

References

Anderson, Leonall C., and Keith M. Carlson. 1970. A monetarist model for economic stabilization. [Federal Reserve Bank of Saint Louis] *Review* 52:7–25.

Anderson, Leonall C., and Jerry L. Jordan. 1968. Monetary and fiscal actions: A test of their relative importance in economic stabilization. [Federal Reserve Bank of Saint Louis] *Review* 50:1–24.

Ando, Albert. 1974. Some aspects of stabilization policies, the monetarist controversy and the MPS model. *International Economic Review* 15:541–71.

Bach, G. L. 1963. Introduction. *The state of monetary economics. Review of Economics and Statistics,* suppl. 45 (February): 3–5.

Barro, R. J. 1978. Unanticipated money, output and the price level in the United States. *Journal of Political Economy* 86: 549–80.

Brunner, K., A. Cukierman, and Allan H. Meltzer. 1980. Stagflation, persistent unemployment and the permanence of economic shocks. *Journal of Monetary Economics* 6 (October): 467–93.

Brunner, K., and Allan H. Meltzer. 1964. *The Federal Reserve's attachment to the free reserve concept.* Washington, D.C.: House of Representatives, Subcommittee on Domestic Finance, Committee on Banking and Currency.

———. 1972. Money, debt, and economic activity. *Journal of Political Economy* 80:951–77.

———. 1976. An aggregative theory for a closed economy. In *Monetarism,* ed. Jerome Stein. Amsterdam: North-Holland.

———. 1983. Strategies and tactics for monetary control. In *Money, monetary policy, and financial institutions,* 59–103. Carnegie-Rochester Conference Series on Public Policy 18. Amsterdam: North-Holland.

Cagan, P. 1965. *Determinants and effects of changes in the stock of money, 1875–1960.* New York: Columbia University.

Clarida, Richard H., and Benjamin M. Friedman. 1984. The behavior of U.S. short-term interest rates since October 1979. *Journal of Finance* 39 (July): 671–82.

Cramer, J. S. 1983. Transactions demand and the circulation of money in the United States, 1950–1979. Mimeographed, University of Amsterdam.

de Leeuw, Frank, and Edward Gramlich. 1968. The Federal Reserve–M.I.T. econometric model. *Federal Reserve Bulletin* 54:11–40.

———. 1969. The channels of monetary policy: A further report on the Federal Reserve–M.I.T. model. *Journal of Finance* 24:265–90.

Fama, Eugene F. 1980a. Banking in the theory of finance. *Journal of Monetary Economics* 6:39–57.

———. 1980b. Inflation, output and money. Mimeographed, University of Chicago.

Friedman, Benjamin M. 1981. The relative stability of money and credit "velocities" in the United States. Mimeographed, National Bureau of Economic Research.

———. 1983a. Implications of the government deficit for U. S. capital formation. In *The economics of large government deficits*. Boston: Federal Reserve Bank of Boston.

———. 1983b. Money, credit and Federal Reserve policy: Reply to Porter and Offenbacher. [Federal Reserve Bank of Richmond] *Economic Review* 69 (November): 30–34.

———. 1983c. The roles of money and credit in macroeconomic analysis. In *Macroeconomics, prices and quantities: Essays in memory of Arthur M. Okun*, ed. James Tobin. Washington, D.C.: Brookings Institution.

Friedman, Milton. 1956. The quantity theory of money—A restatement. In *Essays in the quantity theory of money*, ed. Milton Friedman. Chicago: University of Chicago Press.

———. 1971. A monetary theory of nominal income. *Journal of Political Economy* 79:323–37.

Friedman, Milton, and Anna J. Schwartz. 1963a. *A monetary history of the United States, 1867–1960*. Princeton: Princeton University Press.

———. 1963b. Money and business cycles. In *The state of monetary economics. Review of Economics and Statistics,* suppl. 45 (February): 32–64.

———. 1970. *Monetary statistics of the United States: Estimates, sources and methods*. New York: National Bureau of Economic Research.

———. 1982. *Monetary trends in the United States and the United Kingdom: Their relation to income, prices, and interest rates, 1867–1976*. Chicago: University of Chicago Press.

Gurley, John G., and Edward S. Shaw. 1960. *Money in a theory of finance*. Washington, D.C.: Brookings Institution.

Jonson, P. D. 1976. Money and economic activity in the open economy: The United Kingdom, 1880–1970. *Journal of Political Economy* 84:979–1012.

Kendrick, John W. 1961. *Productivity trends in the United States*. Princeton: Princeton University Press.

King, Robert G., and Charles I. Plosser. 1981. The behavior of money, credit and prices in a real business cycle. Mimeographed, National Bureau of Economic Research.

Korteweg, P. 1978. The economics of inflation and output fluctuations in the Netherlands, 1954–1975. In *The problem of inflation*, 17–68. Carnegie-Rochester Conference Series 8. Amsterdam: North-Holland.

Lucas, Robert E. 1972. Expectations and the neutrality of money. *Journal of Economic Theory* 4:103–24.

————. 1973. Some international evidence on output-inflation trade-offs. *American Economic Review* 63:326–34.

————. 1976. Econometric policy evaluation: A critique. In *The Phillips curve and labor markets,* ed. Karl Brunner and Allan Meltzer, 19–46. Carnegie-Rochester Conference Series on Public Policy 1. Amsterdam: North-Holland.

Modigliani, Franco, and Albert Ando. 1976. Impacts of fiscal actions on aggregate income and the monetarist controversy: Theory and evidence. In *Monetarism,* ed. Jerome Stein. Amsterdam: North-Holland.

Sargent, Thomas J. 1976. A classical macroeconometric model for the United States. *Journal of Political Economy* 84:207–37.

Tobin, James. 1961. Money, capital and other stores of value. *American Economic Review* 51:26–37.

————. 1969. A general equilibrium approach to monetary theory. *Journal of Money, Credit, and Banking* 1:15–29.

8 The Open Economy: Implications for Monetary and Fiscal Policy

Rudiger Dornbusch and Stanley Fischer

The exchange rate has by the mid-1980s become as central in United States economic policy discussions as it has long been in the rest of the world. Economists argue that the rapid dollar appreciation in the current disinflation has contributed powerfully to the speed of the disinflation. The 1984 *Economic Report of the President* fears that the "overvalued" dollar creates an unbalanced recovery by curtailing export growth and fears also that large current account deficits will lead to a depreciation of the exchange rate that will contribute to a resurgence of inflation.

As the Bretton Woods system came under increasing pressure in the 1960s, economic policymaking became more constrained by balance of payments and exchange rate considerations. Supporters of a shift to flexible exchange rates—and by the end this included most economists—believed that a shift to floating rates would enable countries to insulate themselves from foreign disturbances. That did not happen. One reason is that the dominance of supply shocks in the 1970s was certainly not foreseen: real shocks will be transmitted between countries under both fixed and flexible rates. A second reason is that with different speeds of adjustment of assets and goods markets, shifts in monetary policy produce *real* rather than merely nominal exchange rate changes.

We start by describing trends and cycles in United States international linkages, in goods, factor, and asset markets. We then develop

Rudiger Dornbusch and Stanley Fischer are professors in the Department of Economics, Massachusetts Institute of Technology.

We thank Stanley Black, Allan Meltzer, and Anna Schwartz for comments, David Wilcox for research assistance, and the National Science Foundation for financial support.

the analysis of the operation of fiscal and monetary policy in the current flexible rate environment.

8.1   The External Linkages: Trends and Cycles

The United States economy is linked to the rest of the world through goods, factor, and assets markets. The linkages are reflected in the flows of goods and services in international trade; in the relationships between goods and factor prices at home and abroad; and in the asset pricing and capital flow relationships between domestic and foreign assets markets. This section documents trends and cycles in these linkages.

We start with summary measures of the degree of coordination of business cycles in different periods. Morgenstern (1959) calculated the percentage of months when business cycles in the United States, France, Germany, and the United Kingdom were in the same phase in the periods 1879–1914 and 1919–32. In the pre–World War I period business cycles in the four countries were in the same phase 54% of the time; in the interwar period the phases coincided only 36% of the time. Working with the same four countries, over the period 1953 to 1980 we find business cycle phases coinciding 35% of the time.[1] There is no substantial difference in the measure of coincidence between the fixed and flexible exchange rate periods after World War II.[2] Thus business cycles seem to have been more coordinated internationally during the vintage gold standard period than subsequently. But the data are too crude and the differences too small to provide strong support for the view that the truly fixed exchange rates provided by the gold standard linked countries together more closely than the less reliable exchange rate arrangements of subsequent periods.

8.1.1   Trade in Goods and Services

Table 8.1 presents summary data on trade in goods and services for over a century. Data are expressed as a percentage of GNP. The table shows exports and imports of goods and net exports of services: net exports of goods plus net services exports constitute net exports in the national income accounts, shown as the fourth column in table 8.1. The current account is not shown in the table. The main difference between net exports (NIPA) and the current account is the inclusion

1. Calculations are based on growth cycle chronologies reported in Klein and Moore 1983.
2. However, including the years 1981–83 might tilt the balance to the conclusion that business cycles have been more coordinated in the flexible rate period than in the fixed rate period.

Table 8.1   **United States Trade and Tariffs, 1869–1983**

Period	IMG/GNP	EXG/GNP	NSER/GNP	NX/GNP	TAR/IMG
1869–76	7.7	6.6	−0.8	−2.0	35.1
1877–86	5.9	7.4	−0.9	0.7	29.8
1887–96	6.0	6.5	−1.3	−0.8	25.5
1897–1906	4.4	6.8	−0.8	1.7	26.3
1907–14	4.5	5.9	−0.8	0.7	19.7
1915–19	4.7	9.6	0.2	5.1	8.1
1920–29	4.4	5.6	0.4	1.6	13.0
1930–39	2.9	3.5	0.2	0.8	17.0
1940–49	2.3	3.8	0.0	1.5	9.7
1950–69	3.1	3.8	0.3	1.0	6.6
1970–73	4.6	4.5	0.7	0.5	5.9
1974–77	7.1	6.7	1.3	0.8	3.8
1978–83	8.4	7.2	1.7	0.4	3.5

Note: Data are expressed as a percentage of GNP for imports of goods (*IMG*), exports of goods (*EXG*), net exports of services (*NSER*), and net exports (*NX*). The last column shows tariff proceeds as a percentage of total imports of goods.

Sources: For the years to 1929, *Historical Statistics of the United States,* part 2, series U201, U202, U211, U1, U2, U8, U9.

in the latter of unilateral transfers and of government interest payments to the rest of the world.

The most striking point is the extent to which the United States economy has, from the viewpoint of trade in goods and services, been closed. Even back into the nineteenth century, neither exports nor imports exceeded 10% of GNP for any substantial period. Merchandise exports peaked as a percentage of GNP during World War I, falling in the 1920s to lower levels than ever before, and then in the 1930s and well into the 1960s remaining even below 4% of GNP. The merchandise trade balance was in surplus for a long time, but in the past decade it has moved into a large and growing deficit. Despite the doubling in the shares of both imports and exports in GNP since the 1950s, the United States remains the most closed of all industrialized countries.

The average rate of tariffs has fallen substantially over the past century. But the decline was not monotonic: tariff acts punctuated the generally declining trend, notably in this century the Fordney-McCumber tariff of 1922 and the Smoot-Hawley tariff of 1930.[3] The effect of the Smoot-Hawley tariff on the domestic economy will be discussed below.

3. Column 5 of table 8.1 gives the ratio of tariff revenues to imports of goods, dutiable and nondutiable. Such measures are imperfect indicators of the level of tariffs, as exemplified by the fact that a prohibitive tariff would have no weight in an index of this type.

The cyclical behavior of imports and exports (goods and services) is summarized in table 8.2, which presents correlations among the growth rate of real GNP, the growth rates of (real) exports and imports, and the change in the share of net exports in GNP over different periods. The consistent result is that imports are, as would be expected from the effects of aggregate demand on imports, procyclical. The cyclical behavior of exports varies over the different periods shown in table 8.2. There is no expectation of a consistent cyclical pattern in the case of exports: the correlation depends on the coordination of domestic and foreign business cycles and on whether a particular expansion is domestically led or export led. Net exports tend to move in an anticyclical direction, driven by the positive relationship between imports and the cycle. However, in periods in which export growth is positively correlated with GNP growth, as for 1954–83, net exports can on balance move procyclically.

The correlation results of table 8.2 agree with the findings of Mintz, who examined the cyclical behavior of exports, imports, and the trade balance over periods extending back to 1879. Mintz shows imports peaking at business cycles peaks and at their lowest at the trough.[4] Exports, by contrast, she shows not to have a consistent cyclical pattern, being strongly procyclical in the interwar period but peaking well after the business cycle peak in the pre–World War I era. The trade balance was on average countercyclical.

Figure 8.1 shows the trade balance and the current account as a percentage of GNP over the period since 1946. The eye may see a generally deteriorating current account in figure 8.1, but more careful examination suggests that the enormous surpluses of the World War II era had been worked off by the end of the Korean War and that the current account then fluctuated around a basic surplus of about 1% of GNP until a marked deterioration took place at the end of the period. The absence of any strong cyclical behavior of net exports in table 8.2

Table 8.2   Cyclical Behavior of Imports and Exports

	1930–83		1946–73		1954–83	
	GNP72GR	*M72GR*	*GNP72GR*	*M72GR*	*GNP72GR*	*M72GR*
M72GR	.586		.611		.492	
EX72GR	.063	− .093	− .215	− .696	.359	.164
DNXSH	− .162		− .276		.052	

Note: Data are correlation coefficients. Variables are year-to-year growth rates of real GNP (*GNP72GR*), real imports (*M72GR*), and exports (*EX72GR*) and the change in the share of net exports in GNP (*DNXSH*).

4. See Mintz 1959 and 1967. Mintz 1959 presents the cyclical pattern of imports.

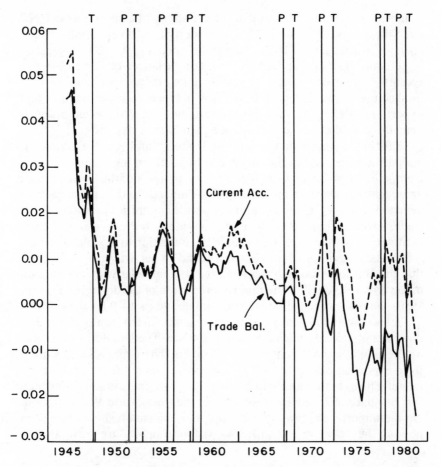

Fig. 8.1   The trade balance and the current account (relative to GNP).

is reflected in the differing behavior of the trade balance (and the current account) from cycle to cycle. The trade balance improved during the recessions in 1954, 1960, 1970, and 1980 and worsened during the recessions of 1957, 1973–75, and 1982.

Although the United States is, by the criterion of the shares of exports and imports in GNP, the most closed of the Western economies, it is not closed at the margin. Tariffs have declined to very low levels and leave only a few areas in which domestic industries are sheltered from foreign competition, except where quotas or their equivalent in the form of voluntary export restraints (automobiles, steel, textiles, etc.) have been imposed. Estimates of the income elasticity of aggregate imports are typically in the range of 1.5 to 2. Export shares in GNP have also fluctuated substantially.

Table 8.3 presents a measure of the variability of components of GNP over the period 1954 to 1983. The underlying data are year-to-year changes in the ratio of each category of spending to GNP, expressed in percent.[5] The data in table 8.3 are the variances of those changes. Exports and imports each vary less than the other components of GNP in absolute terms, but despite the low average ratios of imports and exports to GNP, their year-to-year variability is of the same order of magnitude as that of the remaining expenditure categories.

Shifts in the competitiveness of the United States relative to its trading partners are among the major determinants of merchandise trade. Competitiveness is shown in figure 8.2 by an index of the United States value-added deflator in manufacturing compared to the exchange-rate-adjusted, trade-weighted deflators of partner countries in international trade.[6] Note in figure 8.2 the large adjustment in the measure of competitiveness in the period 1971–73, in the transition to flexible exchange rates. The magnitude of the adjustment and its persistence demonstrate that the Bretton Woods system had led to a cumulative overvaluation of the dollar. Even after the rapid appreciation of the dollar in the early 1980s the real exchange rate is still well above its 1970 level.

Tables 8.4 and 8.5 show long-term shifts in the composition and direction of United States merchandise trade. The long-term shifts are, on the side of exports, entirely as expected. The United States shifted from exporting primarily food and raw materials in the past century to manufactures in the twentieth century. Even so, there is some tendency for the share of manufactures to fall in the post–World War II period. On the import side, raw materials are as significant a share of imports now as they were in the world wars; food imports are currently ex-

Table 8.3   **Variability of Components of GNP**

DCSH	DISH	DINVSH	DGSH	DEXSH	DIMSH
.589	.640	.642	.750	.540	.319

Note: Data are variances of the change in the shares (expressed as a percentage) of GNP of consumption (*DCSH*), fixed investment (*DISH*), inventory investment (*DINVSH*), government spending (*DGSH*), exports (*DEXSH*), and imports (*DIMSH*) for annual data, 1954–83.

5. We work with changes to remove possible trends in the shares of the different categories of spending in GNP.
6. The index is of manufacturing prices because the assumption is that agricultural goods prices, subsidies and tariffs aside, are equal across countries. See *International Financial Statistics* for other indexes and a discussion of the series. Exchange rates and measures of competitiveness frequently leave the reader not knowing which way is up. In this paper we adopt the convention that a depreciation of the dollar appears as an increase in the exchange rate and an increase in competitiveness.

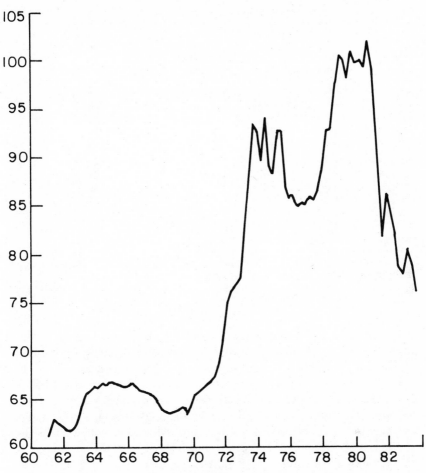

Fig. 8.2   The real exchange rate (index, 1980 = 100).

tremely low. The reorientation in the direction of trade is also simple: away from Europe, especially the United Kingdom, and toward Asia.

We conclude the review of trade patterns with a comment on the importance of the United States in world trade. The share of the United States in world trade has steadily declined over the post–World War II period. In 1951–53 the United States share of world exports was 21%, in the early 1960s and 1970s respectively 17.2% and 13.5%. By 1981–82 the United States share of world exports had declined to 12.5%, despite the increase in the share of exports in United States GNP. Germany and Japan are becoming near equals of the United States in world trade as their share of exports approaches 10% in the early 1980s.

Table 8.4   **The Composition of United States Trade**

	Exports			Imports		
Years	Raw Materials	Food	Manu-factures	Raw Materials	Food	Manu-factures
1869–76	47	33	20	15	35	49
1877–86	33	47	20	20	36	44
1887–1906	32	40	28	28	31	41
1907–14	33	23	44	35	24	42
1915–19	17	29	54	41	27	32
1920–29	26	21	53	37	25	39
1930–39	28	12	62	30	28	41
1940–49	10	15	75	33	27	39
1950–69	13	15	72	21	23	58
1970–73	14	14	72	16	14	70
1974–77	16	15	69	35	10	55
1978–82	16	15	69	35	8	57

Source: Historical Statistics of the United States, part 2, series U-214 through U-224, and *Economic Report of the President,* 1983.

Digression: The Smoot-Hawley Tariff and the Great Depression

The tariff changes shown in table 8.1 have been receiving increasing attention as a macroeconomic phenomenon. In particular, the Smoot-Hawley tariff of 1930 is argued to have played an important role in the Great Depression. This view is certainly not found in the classic Friedman/Schwartz account of the depression:[7] the Hawley-Smoot Tariff Act does not appear in the index; when it does appear, in a footnote on page 342, it is only as a contributor to the gold inflow of late 1930; and it is not featured in the discussion (359–63) of the international character of the depression. Kindleberger gives the tariff act a substantial role, but on symbolic grounds: its signing represented United States abdication of its responsibility to take charge of the world economy.[8]

The modern interest in the Smoot-Hawley tariff traces mainly to Meltzer's brief analysis.[9] The argument "assigns a large role to the

7. Friedman and Schwartz 1963. Schwartz 1981 discusses the Smoot-Hawley tariff at greater length. Although she regrets the tariff, she does not give it any greater role in the propagation of the depression than do Friedman and Schwartz.

8. See Kindleberger 1973. See, too, League of Nations 1942. In the *World Economic Survey,* the impact of the Smoot-Hawley tariff is described in terms of its effects on protection: "From the middle of 1929, the steady deepening of depression, particularly in the raw material producing countries, greatly reinforced the pressure for higher tariffs. . . . The whole movement was undoubtedly accentuated both by the alarm and resentment felt in many countries as the discussions of the new Hawley-Smoot tariff dragged on in the United States Congress from May 1929 to June 1930, and by the real effects of that tariff when it went into operation." There is no suggestion that the tariff is *the* or even a chief cause of the depression.

9. See Meltzer 1976, especially 459–61. Meltzer refers also to Haberler 1976.

Table 8.5   The Direction of United States Trade, 1869–1982 (%)

	Imports					Exports				
Years	Canada	Other America	United Kingdom	Other Europe	Rest of World	Canada	Other America	United Kingdom	Other Europe	Rest of World
1869–76	6	28	35	20	11	6	12	53	27	3
1877–86	6	28	26	27	13	5	9	53	29	4
1887–1906	5	27	20	32	16	7	10	45	32	7
1907–14	5	25	16	34	18	13	14	28	37	9
1915–19	12	36	10	12	30	12	11	32	34	10
1920–29	11	27	9	20	32	15	18	20	31	17
1930–39	14	25	7	22	33	15	17	18	28	23
1940–49	23	37	4	8	28	15	18	21	25	21
1950–69	23	27	6	20	25	20	20	6	28	26
1970–73	27	14	5	23	31	23	15	5	28	30
1974–77	22	16	4	18	41	21	15	5	26	33
1978–82	18	15	4	17	46	17	17	5	26	35

Source: Historical Statistics of the United States, part 2, pp. 903–6, and Survey of Current Business, various issues.

Hawley-Smoot tariff and subsequent tariff retaliation in explaining why the 1929 recession did not follow the path of previous monetary contractions but became the Great Depression'' (460). The detailed explanation gives considerable weight to the reductions in imports of semifinished goods and exports of agricultural goods following the tariff, suggesting that the fact that bank failures in 1930 and 1931 were concentrated in agricultural regions was in part a consequence of the tariff. But it is important to note that Meltzer is mainly discussing the onset and rapid worsening of the recession rather than the responsibility of macroeconomic policy for the depression's becoming great. There is no implication that intelligent macroeconomic, and particularly monetary, policy could not have prevented the disasters of 1932–33.

In table 8.6 we present summary data on trade and GNP in the periods 1918–23 and 1928–33. Each of these periods saw a major recession and a major increase in tariffs. Indeed, the 1922 Fordney-McCumber tariff increased tariff rates (calculated as the ratio of duties to either total imports or dutiable imports) as much as the Smoot-Hawley tariff.[10] In light of the increases in tariffs shown in table 8.5, it is difficult to accept Haberler's "skyscraper" description of Smoot-Hawley (1976, 8, 33). Fordney-McCumber would on the same scale qualify as a "rocket" tariff. Further, as a matter of arithmetic, part of the blame for the increase in tariffs between 1929 and 1933 goes to the drop in price levels, since many tariffs were specific—that is, specified in dollar terms—rather than ad valorem.[11]

Fordney-McCumber was imposed in 1921–22 and was followed by an *increase* in imports and a decrease in exports. The economic expansion was responsible for the import increase; the decrease in exports was a deflationary impulse, outweighed by the start of the expansion of the 1920s. A recession did begin in May 1923, but it was brief; 1924 real GNP was unchanged from that of 1923, and imports fell very little. Smoot-Hawley was also followed by a reduction in exports, but this time there was a reduction in imports. These were primarily the result of the recession. The decline in agricultural exports following Smoot-Hawley was large, but so was the decline following Fordney-McCumber.

From either a Keynesian or a monetarist perspective, the tariff by itself would have been an expansionary impulse in the absence of re-

10. Tariffs rose in 1921 as a result of "emergency" measures to aid agriculture and, because tariffs were partly specific, as a result of the fall in prices.

11. Taussig 1964 presents the results of a Tariff Commission calculation of what tariff revenues would have been in 1922 and 1930 for imports at the level of 1928. This index thus holds constant the composition of imports *and their prices:* tariffs increase for all categories, but the increases are small. The largest increase is from 19.9% to 33.6% for agricultural products and provisions. Other examples are chemicals, oils, and paints from 29.22% to 31.4%, metals and manufactures from 33.7% to 35.0%, and manufactures of cotton from 40.3% to 46.4%.

Table 8.6   **Tariffs and the Macroeconomy, 1918–23 and 1928–33**

Years	Real GNP (1918 = 100)	Ratio of Duties to Total Imports (%)	Ratio of Duties to Dutiable Imports (%)	Quantity of Imports (index)	Export Index	Exports of Crude Food (quantity index)
	(F3)	(U211)	(U212)	(U237)	(U225)	(U229)
1918/1928	100/126	5.8/13.3	23.7/38.8	71/115	98/128	148/98
1919/1929	97/134	6.2/13.5	21.3/40.1	81/131	120/132	174/94
1920/1930	92/121	6.4/14.8	16.4/44.7	88/111	116/109	213/69
1921/1931	84/112	11.4/17.8	29.5/53.2	74/98	97/89	269/71
1922/1932	98/95	14.7/19.6	38.1/59.1	95/79	90/69	218/59
1923/1933	109/93	15.2/19.8	36.2/53.6	99/86	91/69	122/32

Source: Historical Statistics of the United States, 1970; series numbers indicated in column headings.

taliation. In the Keynesian view, the reduction in imports diverts demand to domestic goods; in the monetarist view the gold inflow increases the domestic money stock if not sterilized. In the event, the balance of goods and services fell after the imposition of the tariff. The behavior of net exports suggests the emphasis on recession abroad and retaliation, rather than the direct effect of the tariff, as a force contributing to recession. Exports were 7% of GNP in 1929. Between 1929 and 1931, they fell by 1.5% of 1929 GNP. Attributing the entire fall to the tariff retaliation and assuming a multiplier of two, real GNP would have fallen 3% on this account. The fall in real GNP between 1929 and 1931 was over 15%, thus indicating that the tariff could not have played the major role in creating the recession by affecting the demand for goods. Further, the 3% of GNP calculation is surely a high estimate of the effects of the tariff on exports.

In addition to the tariff United States net exports were, of course, affected by the extensive competitive depreciation on the part of foreign countries. This consideration further reduces the significance to be attached to the tariff as a cause precipitating the Great Depression.

On the monetary side, gold inflows increased at the end of 1930, but 1931 saw a reduction back to close to the 1929 proportion to NNP.[12] These inflows were an inflationary force. To the extent that the tariffs, via foreign retaliation, worked by creating distress in agricultural areas and thereby setting off early bank collapses, they had an adverse monetary effect. But this only emphasizes the perversity of the Fed's bank-closing policy. Further, it is not clear that a United States tariff on agricultural imports that sheltered domestic producers from the col-

12. Data in Friedman and Schwartz 1963.

lapse of world commodity prices would adversely affect those producers. Rather, it was likely to have raised their incomes (given inelastic supply) above the free trade level.

We can summarize our argument briefly: Fordney-McCumber increased tariffs substantially when the United States economy was in a deep recession that was followed by a rapid recovery. Smoot-Hawley increased tariffs at the start of a deep recession that was followed by the Great Depression. Neither should receive prime credit or blame for what followed: macroeconomic policies are far more significant.[13]

8.1.2   Goods and Factor Price Links

The strict purchasing power parity (PPP) theory of the exchange rate holds that exchange rates move proportionately with national price levels.[14] PPP thus implies a one-for-one link between domestic and foreign prices. Figure 8.3 and much other evidence show that PPP does not hold in any relevant sense. Relative national price levels, adjusted through exchange rates, can and do move for lengthy periods.[15]

Despite the absence of any strong relationship between national price levels, exchange rate and foreign price level changes do affect domestic prices. Changes in the dollar prices of imports directly affect goods and raw material input prices in the United States and thus affect the prices of final goods. The pressure of international competition on the prices of traded goods also affects domestic prices and the wage settlements reached in the affected industries. Links of these types, to be reviewed in the next section, change the dynamics of inflation between fixed and flexible exchange rate systems.

8.1.3   Asset Market Linkages and Capital Flows

The international integration of assets markets is in the 1980s an accepted fact. Interest rates are linked internationally (adjusted for anticipated depreciation), and capital flows are highly, perhaps excessively, responsive to anticipated return differentials.

Asset market integration was of course a well-known feature of the pre–World War I and interwar world economies. The thrust of careful empirical work is, however, to suggest that the linkages were less tight than simple accounts of the gold standard imply. Morgenstern calcu-

13. It should be unnecessary to add that we are not advocating raising tariffs as a way either into or out of recessions. Exchange rate changes that can be made to stick achieve most of the same purposes.

14. For a careful review and analysis of the alternative versions of PPP, see Katseli-Papaefstratiou 1979.

15. For discussion of the failure of PPP, see Kravis and Lipsey 1983 and Frenkel 1981. This is one of the key points at which the monetary theories of the exchange rate of the early 1970s, which linked the domestic price level to the domestic money stock and then set the exchange rate as the ratio of price levels, broke down.

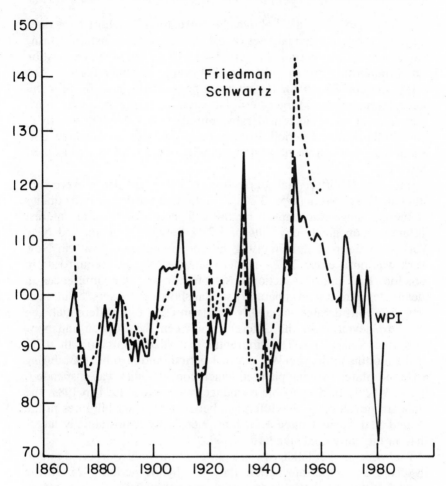

Fig. 8.3   International purchasing power comparisons: United States/
United Kingdom. *Source:* Friedman and Schwartz 1963, 769–
71 (wholesale prices).

lated correlation coefficients among short-term interest rates in London, New York, Paris, and Berlin. For the period 1876–1914 the correlation between the New York commercial paper rate and the London
private discount rate is only .45; for the period 1925–38 the correlation
is .93.[16] The correlation between monthly United Kingdom and United
States treasury bill rates for the *flexible* rate period, January 1974 to

16. Morgenstern 1959, 105. The data and sources are described on pages 119–23. The
meaning of these correlations is obscured by the fact that there are consistent and
noncoincident seasonals in the rates in different countries.

November 1983, is .583,[17] above the correlation for short-term rates for the earlier gold standard period calculated by Morgenstern. During the adjustable peg period, January 1964 to July 1971, the correlation between monthly British and United States treasury bill rates was .794, below the correlation for the interwar period calculated by Morgenstern. Although the Morgenstern data give the impression that short-term interest rates had considerable latitude to move independently in the pre–World War I period, the economic significance of the low correlation depends on the absolute variability of the rates as well as their correlation.

Interest rate differentials during the gold standard period were substantial. Morgenstern (1959, 335) calculates that the degree of flexibility of the exchange rate implied by the gold points allowed an interest differential on ninety-day bills of 3.73% between London and New York.[18] In the period 1876–1914 the commercial paper rate in New York was on average 2.17% higher than the private discount rate in London. Risk and transaction costs of course permit differences in mean rates of return on apparently similar short-term assets.[19] But there was also considerable variability in the interest rate differential: the standard deviation of the difference between the London and New York rates was 1.21%. The differential exceeded 4% in more than 7% of the months in the pre–World War I period, and in July 1893, during a United States banking panic in which convertibility was suspended, it was 9.63%. In the flexible exchange rate period, 1974 to 1983, the standard deviation of the difference between treasury bill rates in the United States and United Kingdom, 2.66%, was substantially larger than in the early gold standard period.

The asset market linkages were closer in the interwar period and in the fixed exchange rate period 1964–71. In the period 1925–38 the mean London–New York differential was only 0.24% with a standard deviation of 0.71%. The mean differential in the period 1964–71 was 1.33%, with the standard deviation of the difference, 0.72%, almost identical to that for the interwar period.

There appear to be no reliable data on the size of short-term capital flows during the gold standard periods, but the presumption is that they were both large and an essential part of the mechanism that tied capital markets together. The extent to which disturbances to United States financial markets originated abroad rather than domestically has not

17. Calculations use *International Financial Statistics* data.
18. The gold points are given as $4.845 to $4.890, a range of 0.92%. Incidentally, one of Morgenstern's findings is that the gold points were on many occasions violated by actual exchange rates.
19. In this connection it would be useful to calculate differentials between similar assets in the same national market, as a benchmark for the international comparisons.

to our knowledge been documented, although there are discussions of the national origins of international financial crises.[20] Morgenstern (1959, 548–49) shows the United States as more frequently the originator than the recipient of (stock market) panics. Of the eleven first- and second-order United States panics recorded for the period 1873–1932, the United States transmits panic abroad in nine episodes and is the recipient of foreign shocks in only two (1890 and 1907). On other occasions, including 1914, foreign disturbances are transmitted to the United States without causing a panic.

There are estimates of aggregate capital flows, long- plus short-term, that are consistent with the net export data presented in table 8.1 above.[21] These show the United States as primarily an importer of capital (averaging 0.8% of NNP) over the period until 1896; an exporter of capital (average equal to 1.1% of NNP) over the next nine years; once more an importer on a small scale until 1914; exporting capital on a large scale during World War I (average of 4.8% per year of NNP for the years 1914–19) and continuing to do so until 1933; reverting to the role of importer until 1941; and thereafter exporting capital until the most recent period.

8.1.4 Adjustment under the Gold Standard

We now briefly pull together the strands in this discussion of the mechanisms linking the United States and foreign economies under the gold standard, as background for our analysis in the next section of the operation of the current flexible exchange rate system.

The earliest analysis of the operation of the gold standard, the Hume price-specie flow mechanism, focused on the goods markets and on movements in relative national price levels. These mechanisms should be expected to produce slow adjustment to disturbances. Consider, for example, the response of the economy to an upward shift in the domestic demand for money. Under the price-specie flow mechanism, the reduced demand for goods tends to reduce domestic prices and the demand for imports. The current account goes into surplus, and gold flows increase to satisfy the increase in money demand. The mechanism can operate successfully through real balance effects on the demand for imports even if PPP holds exactly. In the event the disturbance to money demand is temporary, the process will have to be reversed when the disturbance disappears.

Subsequent analysis described a system with more rapid adjustment in which asset market linkages allowed capital flows in response to in-

---

20. Kindleberger 1978 and Morgenstern 1959, 541–55. Friedman and Schwartz 1963 typically regard American banking panics as of domestic origin. An exception is the 1890 crisis, in which the Baring failure receives mention (p. 104).

21. For the period 1869–1960, see Friedman and Schwartz 1963, 769–71.

cipient interest rate movements, perhaps caused by active central bank (or in the case of the United States, Treasury) intervention, to help equilibrate the system.[22] We continue with the example of an upward shift in the demand for money. The impact of such a shift, which might be associated with a financial panic, is to increase domestic interest rates. There is a capital inflow that equilibrates interest rates at home and abroad and helps meet the increased demand for money. If the demand shift is temporary, there need be no major disruptions to the goods markets. Thus in this case the capital markets promote more rapid adjustment to a domestic disturbance. If the demand shift is permanent, goods market adjustments are needed to pay the interest on the capital inflow.

This example is chosen as a case in which capital flows ease domestic adjustment. But of course from the viewpoint of the foreign country the asset market linkages permit transmission of a disturbance that would otherwise have been much slower in appearing. Further, as we know from the downfall of the Bretton Woods system, international capital flows in fixed exchange rate systems are not always regarded as an unmitigated blessing. There are thus two questions: How did the gold standard system survive during the period 1879–1914 when capital flows were not restricted? And did capital flows on average ease the system's adjustment to disturbances?

Bloomfield argues that because there was no serious belief, even during the silver agitation in the United States, that exchange rates would change, capital flows under the pre–World War I gold standard, though substantial and sensitive to interest rate movements, were not destabilizing. He argues also that over the period, the discount rate actions needed for external balance typically coincided with those needed for internal stabilization, so that capital flows were on balance stabilizing. The latter argument is vitiated by the well-known fact that even during the heyday of the gold standard central banks did not conform to the rules of the game and frequently sterilized gold flows.[23]

The issues of the stabilizing or destabilizing roles and relative importance of the goods market, price-specie flow, and asset market linkages, and of intervention, under the gold standard have not been settled,

---

22. Sayers 1958 describes the use of bank rate in maintaining the international financial system and includes references to earlier literature, including Clapham, Hawtrey, and Viner. See also Bloomfield 1959, 41–46. Keynes 1930, chaps. 35–38, describes the operation of the international gold standard and the role of central banks. Nurkse 1978 [1944], 98–105, also describes the adjustment mechanism.

23. Bloomfield 1959, 69, for the interwar period. It was suggested during discussion that the behavior of central banks was different in the heyday of the gold standard. Bloomfield 1959, 48–51, compares central bank behavior before 1914 with the post–World War I behavior studied by Nurkse. His conclusion on the propensity to sterilize is noteworthy (50): "By an amazing coincidence, these overall percentages [frequency of offsetting] are virtually identical to those reached in the League study for the interwar period. . . . One might even conclude, on the basis of this formula, that central banks in general played the rules of the game just as badly before 1914 as they did thereafter!"

despite the extensive literature. Friedman and Schwartz emphasize the importance of relative national price level adjustments in response to money flows.[24] Nurkse (1978) argues that adjustment was typically more rapid than the price-specie flow mechanism implies and credits multiplier effects of the trade balance for part of the speedup. The capital account tended to move procyclically, apparently offsetting the stabilizing effects on the system of the money stock movements implied by the anticyclical current account. Such capital flows might appear to have been destabilizing from the viewpoint of the cycle, but that would not be the case if they were accommodating temporary disturbances.[25] And the issue of whether central bank sterilization had and can have any real effects, and if so whether the effects are stabilizing, is still alive.

8.2 Open Economy Macroeconomic Linkages

In this section we study the ties between United States macroeconomic variables and the world economy and discuss how the openness of the economy affects stabilization policy. The analysis relies on the theoretical model sketched in the appendix to this chapter, which embodies the main channels and effects that are given emphasis in open economy macroeconomics.[26] As in the previous section, we start with goods market linkages between the United States and other economies.

8.2.1 Goods Markets

The channels of transmission in the goods market are described by equations (1) and (2) below. (For notation, and other arguments of the demand function, see the appendix; time subscripts are omitted when there is no risk of confusion.)

(1) $Y = D(eP^*/P, Yd, q, V, \ldots) + NX(eP^*/P, Yd, Y^*d, V, V^*, \ldots)$.

Equation (1), the goods market equilibrium condition, describes the contribution of net exports to aggregate demand. The demand for domestic goods is determined by real disposable income, the profitability of investment, the real exchange rate eP^*/P, and real wealth. Exports depend on the real exchange rate, and on domestic and foreign income and wealth.

24. Friedman and Schwartz 1963. Friedman and Schwartz calculate the PPP data presented in figure 8.3 in examining the role of capital flows in moving relative goods price levels.

25. Aghevli 1975 estimates an econometric model that includes both capital flows and the influence of the current account on the money stock. He concludes that though capital flows moved in a procyclical direction, thus offsetting the effects on money supply of the anticyclical current account, the current account effects dominate.

26. For recent discussions of open economy macroeconomics, see Branson 1980, Branson and Buiter 1983, Dornbusch 1982a, 1983, Frenkel 1983, Henderson 1984, Mussa 1984, and Obstfeld and Stockman 1983.

Equation (2) is the price equation:

(2) $P = C(W, Pm, eP^*, Y/K)$.

In (2) the materials price term, *Pm,* changes as the prices of imported inputs change. The term in foreign prices, eP^*, represents the effects of foreign competitiveness on domestic prices. Equation (2) can be thought of either as a markup equation or as the description of equilibrium price determination in a competitive economy.

Several channels of transmission, which can be described in aggregate supply and demand terms, emerge from equations (1) and (2).[27] We confine ourselves for the moment to impact effects, thus taking into account only short-run cyclical flexibility of prices and wages. The channels are:

1. Most familiar, a rise in foreign income and spending raises the demand for our goods, shifts the aggregate demand curve up, and thus leads to an increase in output and home goods. An example is an increase in foreign import demand as a result of expansion abroad. This channel is of course present under both fixed and flexible exchange rates. Such multipliers should be close in size to government spending multipliers.[28]

2. A rise in import prices, induced by exchange depreciation or increased foreign prices, shifts *both* aggregate demand and supply curves. On the demand side, assuming a sufficiently large price elasticity, there is a shift toward domestic goods and therefore a tendency for output and prices to rise. On the supply side, the increase in competitors' prices leads to an increase in home prices as domestic firms increase their markup.[29] Domestic prices certainly rise; we would expect output to increase.

The effects of an import price increase in practice depend on the extent to which other endogenous and policy variables react to the disturbance. In particular, it is important to know whether wages rise in response to higher import prices and whether the monetary authorities accommodate the disturbance. The more wages rise with import prices, and the more accommodating is money, the smaller the real effects, and the larger the impact of the import price change on prices.

27. To derive the aggregate demand schedule, we assume away complications in the model presented in the appendix that result from the multiplicity of assets and direct links between exchange rates and asset markets.

28. Multiplier assumptions or estimates in large-scale trade models range between one and two. For instance, the OECD international linkage model assumes a first-year government spending multiplier for the United States of 1.5. See *OECD Economic Studies* (1983). The EPA model has an implied first-year multiplier closer to one. See Amano, Sadahiro, and Sasaki 1981, 50. (Calculation based on the elasticity of United States GNP with respect to world imports in the EPA model.) However, Darby and Stockman find very weak multiplier effects in their international model. See chapters 5–7 in Darby et al. 1983.

29. Here obviously we interpret (2) as a markup equation.

Results of simulations of econometric models, such as the OECD interlink model, the Japanese Economic Planning Agency (EPA) model, or the Federal Reserve's multicountry model (MCM) will differ in their assumptions about the nominal feedbacks resulting from an import price increase, and conclusions about the effects of disturbarces are likely to differ.

Even leaving aside feedbacks from wages and money, there are effects of import price changes on aggregate demand. To the extent that higher import prices raise the price level, without there being offsetting reductions in domestic prices, the real money stock falls and the equilibrium interest rate that clears the assets markets will rise. Higher interest rates in turn imply a reduction in income and spending and reduced aggregate demand and employment.

It is well known from the literature on trade equations[30] that higher import prices can in the short run lead to increased import spending and a decline in net exports. The fall in net demand may imply a reduction in demand for domestic goods or possibly a reduction in saving.[31] If increased import spending is financed by a reduction in domestic saving, output will expand. If it has as its counterpart reduced spending on domestic goods, output will fall. Theoretical analyses show that in this context it matters whether the disturbance is permanent or transitory and whether consumers strongly prefer smooth consumption streams and do not react to changes in the intertemporal terms of trade. The case most favorable to expansion of employment occurs if a disturbance is believed to be temporary and consumption smoothing dominates effects induced by real interest rates.

3. Increased materials prices imply increased costs and therefore cause the aggregate supply curve to shift up. But there are also demand side effects. Increased prices of imported materials imply a reduction in real disposable income, since there is a reduction in value added at a given level of output. Domestic real disposable income falls because, with real output unchanged, the higher real price of imported intermediate products implies that real income available for domestic factors of production is reduced. Aggregate demand therefore declines. Bruno and Sachs (1985) have discussed the relative importance of the supply and demand shifts and the resulting ambiguity for the net effects. There is no question that output will decline, but the price level may rise or fall. We assume the net effect is an increase in prices.

Materials prices are determined by supply and demand conditions in the world market. Equation (3) describes the price of materials:

$$(3) \qquad Pm = v(Y, Y^*, \ldots, P, eP^*).$$

30. See, for example, Stern et al. 1976.
31. See Laursen and Metzler 1950 and Razin and Svensson 1983.

We assume $v(\ )$ is degree-one homogeneous in the domestic and foreign price levels. Accordingly, we can rewrite (3) as

(3a) $$Pm/P = v(Y, Y^*, \ldots, eP^*/P).$$

Equations (3) and (3a) make the important point that exchange rate disturbances unrelated to price level movements directly change commodity prices, both in dollars and in real (United States goods) terms. In addition, of course, the real price of commodities is affected by short- and long-run supply conditions, such as OPEC shocks.

. 4. The wealth and disposable income terms in equation (1) point to a further channel of international linkage. Changes in the world real interest rate redistribute wealth and income internationally between net creditors and net debtors. A rise in the real interest rate is an intertemporal terms of trade change that benefits lenders, whose real income rises, and hurts borrowers. At the same time, higher real interest rates affect the valuation of existing assets. The values of real capital and long-term debt decline, thereby reducing world wealth. The net impact of these changes on aggregate demand for United States goods is not obvious.

5. Wealth effects are also important in the context of persistent international capital movements, for instance, arising from persistent public sector deficits. With marginal spending patterns differing internationally, international redistributions of wealth associated with capital account imbalances shift the pattern of world demand toward the goods demanded by persistent lenders and away from those demanded by persistent borrowers.[32]

8.2.2   Goods and Factor Price Linkages

Equations (2) and (3) show the external sector affecting domestic prices directly, both through the effects of competitive import prices on domestic markups and because import prices affect costs and thus prices. Equation (2) also points to two indirect routes through which the foreign sector affects domestic prices. Exposure to foreign competition may affect wage settlements in industries substantially involved in the international economy. Further, demand pressures from abroad affect domestic prices through their impact on aggregate demand.

---

32. Ideally we would want to quantify each of the five channels isolated in the discussion above. However, since in practice they all operate at the same time, it is not easy to separate them. Nor are we aware of attempts to do so. Large-scale econometric models typically explicitly embody some but not all of these channels; for instance, the EPA model includes the multiplier, relative price, oil (equivalent to raw materials in our discussion), and some wealth redistribution effects.

Tables 8.7 to 8.9 report evidence on the impact of the external sector on domestic inflation.[33] For simplicity, and to avoid "overfitting," we did not allow ourselves the use of dummy variables, nor did we experiment much with lag lengths. The basic approach was to enter four lagged values of each of the right-hand-side variables, but not to restrict the shape of the lag distribution. The coefficients on the wage change variable were still increasing up to the fourth lag, so we extended that lag length to six quarters. Contemporaneous values of the right-hand-side variables are generally excluded; ordinary least squares regressions suggested that the omission was serious only in regression (3) (and 6), where a contemporaneous value of the rate of change of the import price deflator is accordingly entered.[34]

The exchange rate variables in each case affect the inflation rate in the expected direction, and for the most part significantly. Further, the mean lag by which the exchange rate affects the inflation rate is always shorter than that by which wage changes affect inflation.[35] Equation (1) gives the most direct relationship between the rate of change of the

33. Inclusion of external variables in the Phillips curve, particularly import prices, has a long tradition in open economies such as the United Kingdom. Without serious loss of generality, we confined our search of the United States literature to the *Brookings Papers on Economic Activity* (*BPEA*). Foreign variables first appeared in a United States Phillips curve in *BPEA* in Nordhaus 1972. Gordon 1973 reported on a reestimate of his basic Phillips curve to include import prices. Interestingly, at that time import prices fed through only slowly into domestic prices. Pierce and Enzler 1974 used the MPS model to examine the effects of foreign disturbances. More recent empirical work that emphasizes external effects includes Gordon 1982.

34. Here are further details of and comments on our estimation or search procedure. (*a*) We also experimented with adding the rate of change of the food price deflator, omitting that variable because of collinearity with included variables. (*b*) The theoretical specification of the markup equation in equation (2) includes the level of output, but we did not find output measures or the unemployment rate entering the regressions of table 8.6 significantly. (*c*) Given the serial correlation, the endogeneity problem remains even when the right-hand side contains only lagged variables. However, the problem is limited because the serial correlation coefficient in most of the equations is low, and because the lag coefficients in the most problematic case—that of wages—typically peak only at the third lag and are small at the first lag. Instrumental variable techniques are used in equations (3), (6), and (7) to (9). We did not use the technique more extensively because we were unable to persuade ourselves that the instruments we used—the monetary base, full employment budget surplus, and military spending—were indeed exogenous, except perhaps the last. In the cases where we used instrumental variable estimation, the ordinary least squares and two-stage least squares estimates were quite similar.

35. This is not a reflection of the fact that we allow six lags for the wage variable and only four for the exchange rate variables; when we allowed only four lags for wages, the mean lag for this variable was still longer than that for exchange rates. The mean lag is easy to interpret when all lag coefficients are of the same sign. In all but one case, the coefficients on wage change are all positive. In the case of exchange rate changes, though, either the first or the last lag coefficient is usually of a different sign (though statistically insignificant) than the remaining coefficients. To avoid prejudicing the comparison of mean lags in favor of the exchange rate, we define the mean lag as $\sum^i \frac{|a_i|}{(\Sigma a_i)}$, where the a_i are the estimated coefficients.

Table 8.7　　**Exchange Rates and the GNP Deflator, 1962:4 to 1983:3**

Regression Number	Dependent Variable	C	Exchange Rate Change	DWAGE	DPROD	DPOG	p	$\bar{R}^2$	DW	SER
1	INFDEF	.419 (0.61)	DWAX .062 (2.12) [2.15]	0.722 (6.96) [3.08]	−.107 (−1.53)	.089 (4.64)	.371 (2.71)	.81	2.04	1.18
2	INFDEF	.211 (0.33)	DEX 0.089 (3.04) [2.14]	0.745 (7.85) [3.12]	−.122 (−1.87)	.089 (4.94)	.328 (2.42)	.83	2.01	1.14
3	INFDEF	.133 (0.25)	IMP* .055 (1.74) IMPL .074 (1.72) [2.72]	0.713 (8.65) [3.57]	−.108 (−1.89)	0.11 (0.51)	.278 (2.56)	.83	1.99	1.13

Notes:

1. All variables are quarter-to-quarter changes, at an annual rate.
2. Variables are defined as follows:
   INFDEF = Inflation rate, GNP deflator
   C   = Constant
   DWAX   = Rate of change of weighted average United States exchange rate
   DEX   = Rate of change of real exchange rate, defined as relative prices of manufactured goods
   IMP   = Inflation rate of import price deflator.
   IMPL   = Lagged values of IMP
   DWAGE = Rate of change of hourly wage rate, manufacturing
   DPROD = Rate of change of output per hour, manufacturing
   DPOG   = Rate of change of price of oil and gas.
3. All variables except wage enter with four lags. DWAGE has six lags. Coefficients and t-statistics are for sums of coefficients on variables. No contemporaneous variables are included except for IMP in regression (3).
4. Equation (3) is estimated using instrumental variables for IMP; instruments are current and lagged values of the monetary base, full employment deficit, and military spending. (Asterisk indicates use of instrumental variables.)
5. Entries in [ ] are mean lags; e.g., in regression (1), mean lag of distribution of coefficients on DWAX is 2.15 quarters.

exchange rate and the inflation rate of the GNP deflator. According to (1), a 10% change in the exchange rate directly changes the GNP deflator by only 0.6%. Even the largest effect, in regression (3), would change the GNP deflator by only 1.3% in response to a 10% change in import prices.[36] The direct effects are not, however, the end of the story, because we shall see in discussing table 8.8 that changes in the exchange rate affect wages.

Comparing tables 8.7 and 8.8, we find a generally more powerful effect of the exchange rate variables on consumer prices than on the GNP deflator. The feedthrough to consumer price inflation is particularly rapid in the case of changes of import prices. Even in this case, though, the sum of the lag coefficients is only 0.14: a 10% change in import prices changes the personal consumption deflator by 1.4%, with most of the effect taking place contemporaneously.

Table 8.9 examines the impact of the exchange rate on the rate of change of wages.[37] The results across the three equations show a consistent effect of exchange rate movements on the rate of change of manufacturing wages: a 10% rate of change of the exchange rate reduces the rate of wage change by between 1% and 1.5%. The mean lags are, however, longer than in the price equations.

Taking the price and wage equations together, and at a given unemployment rate, an appreciation of the currency affects the domestic price level first through direct price effects and then through indirect effects on wages. The direct effects are relatively quick, and they imply that a 10% change in the exchange rate affects the price level within a year by about 1%. There is then a second, slower-working, effect on prices, working through wages, amounting to somewhat under 1% for each 10% change in the exchange rate. We take the latter effect to represent the impact of foreign competition on domestic wages.

The results of tables 8.7 to 8.9 thus support the argument that exchange rate changes affect the domestic price level and, during the

---

36. It is noticeable in both tables 8.7 and 8.8 that the coefficient on *DEX* is larger than that on *DWAX.* The reason is probably that *DEX,* the rate of change of the real exchange rate, is approximately equal to *DWAX* plus the foreign inflation rate minus the domestic inflation rate. Since *DEX* enters negatively, it essentially includes positive lagged values of the dependent variable. Its coefficient is therefore increased as a result of serial correlation of the dependent variable. This interpretation is strengthened because the coefficient of serial correlation in regression (2) is lower than that in (1), and similarly in regressions (5) and (4).

37. In table 8.9 we use a simple adaptive expectations formulation to generate expected inflation. We have also reestimated equation (7) using a three-period distributed lag on the predicted inflation rates from equation (4) as the expectations variable. This change reduces the coefficient on the unemployment rate and also reduces the coefficient on the exchange rate to −.11 with a *t*-statistic of 2.43. The sum of the coefficients on the expected inflation rate is .93.

Table 8.8   Exchange Rates and the Consumption Deflator, 1962:4 to 1983:3

Regression Number	Dependent Variable	C	Exchange Rate Change	DWAGE	DPROD	DPOG	p	$\bar{R}^2$	DW	SER
4	INFPCD	1.024 (1.10)	DWAX .083 (2.39) [3.38]	.601 (4.36) [3.97]	−.102 (−1.29)	.085 (3.60)	.588 (4.87)	.82	1.94	1.15
5	INFPCD	0.443 (0.57)	DEX .125 (3.72) [2.87]	.666 (5.83) [3.96]	−.099 (−1.38)	.089 (4.34)	.509 (4.13)	.84	1.96	1.09
6	INFPCD	0.198 (0.34)	IMP* .086 (2.85) IMPL .054 (1.23) [1.61]	0.658 (7.26) [3.75]	−.095 (−1.59)	.012 (0.50)	.405 (3.99)	.85	1.93	1.06

Note: INFPCD is inflation rate of personal consumption deflator. Other details are as for table 8.7.

Table 8.9   Exchange Rates and the Phillips Curve

Regression Number	Dependent Variable	C	DWAX	DEX	IMPL	LOGUMM*	EXPINF	ρ	$\bar{R}^2$	DW	SER
7	DAHM	3.757 (5.31)	.141 (3.34) [4.02]			−1.821 (−2.01)	0.966 (6.94)	.059 (0.53)	.50	1.98	1.93
8	DAHM	3.922 (5.46)		.126 (3.08 [4.03]		−2.393 (−2.76)	1.033 (7.27)	0.83 (0.76)	.49	2.00	1.96
9	DAHM	4.340 (6.68)			.108 (3.07) [4.47]	−2.096 (−2.54)	0.745 (4.54)	.044 (0.40)	.50	1.99	1.94

Notes

1. Variable definitions as in table 8.7. *EXPINF* is the expected inflation rate, calculated as a weighted average (with decay coefficient of .15 per quarter) of past PCE quarter over same quarter a year before inflation rate. *LOGUMM* is logarithm of unemployment rate for married men.

2. Exchange rate variables are entered with six lags.

3. Asterisk indicates treated as endogenous, using same instruments as in table 8.6.

adjustment period, the inflation rate.[38] To the extent that monetary and fiscal policy affects exchange rates, a flexible exchange rate regime provides an extra channel of influence of policy on prices.

Table 8.10 summarizes the channels and lags with which a 10% real depreciation translates into an increased consumption deflator. The table highlights the fact that for given unemployment and expected inflation rates, real depreciation exerts a significant impact on prices and does so quite rapidly. The exchange rate must play a part in explaining United States inflation and in assessing the impact of policy changes on the price level.

Figure 8.4 shows the actual inflation rate and also an estimate of the inflation rate purged of exchange rate effects. The latter series is constructed using the estimated coefficients of the real depreciation variable in equations (5) and (8) in table 8.8 and 8.9 respectively. The adjusted series is an estimate of what inflation would have been had there been no effect of real depreciation on prices, either directly or indirectly via wages. Figure 8.4 brings out the role of exchange rate changes in the major episodes of inflation acceleration and deceleration: 1973–74, 1978–80, and 1981–83. In the acceleration periods exchange depreciation increases inflation substantially, whereas in 1981–83 exchange appreciation strongly reinforces the deceleration of inflation. This role of exchange rates in the wage/price sector of the economy is accepted as obvious in small countries. In the United States it is already part of macroeconometric models but is not yet accepted by mainline macroeconomics.[39]

We now turn to the asset markets to explore further the effects of monetary and fiscal policy on the exchange rate.

Table 8.10   Effect of a 10% Real Depreciation on Wages and the Consumption Deflator

	Wages	Direct Effect on Prices	Total Effect on Prices
Magnitude	1.26	1.25	2.09
(% change) mean	4.03	2.87	n.a.
lag (quarters)			

Source: Tables 8.8 and 8.9, equations (5) and (8).

38. Our direct coefficients are typically smaller than those of Gordon 1982. This may be a result of our choosing not to use dummy variables to account for episodes such as wage/price controls. Nonetheless, the sum of the direct and indirect effects is quite smiliar to the coefficients obtained by Gordon, whose sample period was 1952 to 1980.

39. See, for example, Blinder 1982.

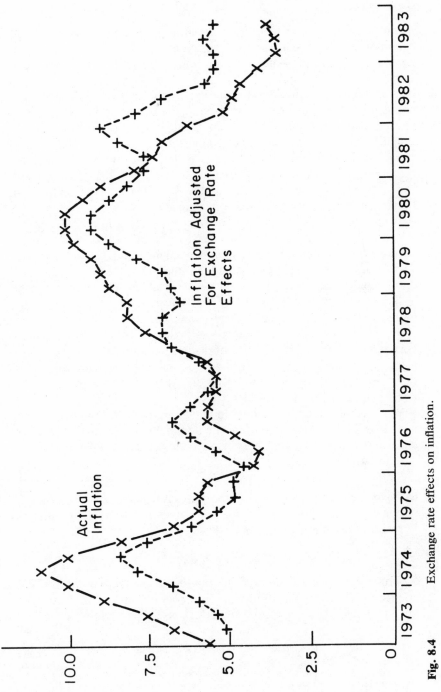

Fig. 8.4 Exchange rate effects on inflation.

8.2.3   Asset Markets

International capital mobility is a fact, but the appropriate specification of asset markets remains an open issue.[40] There are three chief questions. First, are domestic and foreign bonds perfect or imperfect substitutes? Second, should stock markets be given a prominent role in modeling international asset markets, or is the traditional money/bonds model adequate for understanding the linkages? Third, does the international redistribution of wealth through the current account play a significant role in the determination of the exchange rate and macroeconomic equilibrium? The answers to these questions help analyze the implications of sustained fiscal deficits and of long-term current account deficits—for instance, whether sustained deficits build up a "dollar overhang" that will force exchange depreciation.

We have to preface this section by noting that empirical exchange rate models perform poorly. Meese and Rogoff (1983) show that a random walk model typically predicts exchange rates as well as standard structural models, even when the forecasts of the latter are based on realized values of future explanatory variables. The exchange rate is like the stock market in that price movements are dominated by unforecastable changes; accordingly, the extraction of the systematic components of price movements is difficult in samples of the length currently available. The absence of decisive empirical evidence forces a greater reliance on theorizing, and on snippets of evidence rather than a complete empirical model, in discussing exchange rate and international economics.[41]

We start with the basic model in which foreign and domestic bonds are perfect substitutes. The domestic nominal interest rate is therefore equal to the foreign nominal rate plus the anticipated rate of depreciation:

$$(4) \qquad\qquad i = i^* + \hat{e}.$$

(A $\hat{}$ over a variable denotes its proportional rate of change.) Subtracting national inflation rates from both sides gives the equivalent equation in real interest rate form:

$$(5) \qquad\qquad r = r^* + (\hat{e} + \hat{p} - \hat{p}^*).$$

Real interest rates can diverge internationally so long as the real exchange rate is changing, but in long-run equilibrium real interest rates are equalized. The assumptions of perfect asset substitutability, in com-

---

40. See Cumby and Obstfeld 1982, Frankel 1982, Melvin 1983, chap. 13, Obstfeld 1982, and Rogoff 1983.

41. We are not certain that the situation in open economy macroeconomics is significantly different from that for the closed economy. However, discussion of that issue and its implications would take us too far afield.

bination with a specification of goods markets in which output determines demand and prices adjust slowly to excess demands and supplies, leads to the following results:[42] An increase in the money stock leads under flexible rates to an immediate depreciation of the exchange rate. The exchange rate initially overshoots its long-run equilibrium because prices are sticky, real balances increase, and output expands while the real and nominal interest rate fall. In the adjustment process following the initial overshooting, inflation is accompanied by currency appreciation as the real exchange rate returns to its long-run equilibrium value.[43]

Monetary and fiscal policy thus work in good part through the real exchange rate as well as the real interest rate channel. This was of course the fundamental insight of the Mundell/Fleming model. As Mundell (1964) noted: "It is important to notice too that budgetary policy, like monetary policy, has a different role in a flexible exchange rate system. . . . An increased budget deficit without monetary expansion would raise interest rates, attract capital, appreciate the exchange rate, and worsen the trade balance with little benefit to employment. With sufficient monetary expansion a budget deficit would be unnecessary."

8.2.4 Monetary Policy

The results of any policy change are quite sensitive to policies followed in the rest of the world. Specifically it matters whether the authorities in the rest of the world stabilize interest rates, output, or monetary aggregates. For instance, if they attempt to stabilize interest rates in the context of a foreign budget deficit, they create a monetary expansion in attempting to fight rising domestic rates.[44]

The combination of rapidly clearing assets markets and prices that adjust sluggishly implies a relation between real interest differentials and real exchange rates. In the course of adjustment to a monetary disturbance, the real exchange rate will adjust gradually to its long-run equilibrium value, $\bar{R}$. Let $R = \log(eP^*/P)$ denote the logarithm of the real exchange rate. Then the model implies that:[45]

$$(6) \qquad R_t = (1 - a)R_{t-1} + a\bar{R}.$$

---

42. See Cardoso 1983, Dornbusch 1976, and Obstfeld and Stockman 1983.

43. Overshooting is not inevitable: if dynamics are such that output initially expands sufficiently to raise the nominal interest rate when the money stock is raised, the exchange rate will not overshoot. The presumption is though that the nominal interest rate absorbs most of the initial impact of the money shock.

44. A growing theoretical literature discusses the effects of alternative policy reaction functions and coordination mechanisms. See, for example, Canzoneri and Gray 1983 and Rogoff 1984. Empirical models too may include reaction functions; e.g., chaps. 5–7 in Darby et al. 1983.

45. See Dornbusch 1983.

Combining the equation with the relation between real interest rates in (5), $r = r^* + R$, we obtain:

$$(7) \qquad R_t = \bar{R} - b(r - r^*), \qquad b = (1 - a)/a.$$

Equation (7) states that if our interest rates exceed those abroad, then the real exchange rate will be below its long-run equilibrium value. In other words, a positive real interest differential implies real appreciation. The extent of such appreciation depends on the speed of adjustment in the economy. The term b is the mean lag, which under rational expectations is a compound of the structural coefficients in the model. If the mean lag is three years, then a three-percentage-point real interest differential implies that the exchange rate deviates from its long-run equilibrium by 9%. The asymmetry in adjustment speeds between goods and assets markets thus establishes a link between tight money and significant, transitory exchange rate overvaluation.[46]

The implications of flexible exchange rates for disinflation in a sticky price world (the real world) are quite apparent: because tight monetary policy works rapidly and strongly on the exchange rate, disinflation can take place more rapidly. The Phillips curve becomes steeper under flexible exchange rates.[47]

8.2.5 Fiscal Policy

The analysis of fiscal policy under assumptions of perfect asset substitutability is straightforward: a sustained fiscal expansion raises long-run aggregate demand and therefore must bring about crowding out. The crowding out occurs through two channels. The first is a real appreciation in the expanding country owing to the relative increase in demand for that country's goods. The other is an increase in the *world* real interest rate. In a small country, crowding out will work entirely through the real exchange rate, implying that the current account deteriorates by the full amount of the fiscal expansion.

What are the implications for the exchange rate? Given the nominal money stock and full employment, higher real interest rates imply reduced real money demand and hence a higher price level in each country. For the real exchange rate to appreciate, we therefore require a nominal appreciation of the expanding country.

This analysis of the effects of a fiscal expansion is incomplete in that it does not take into account complications arising from the debt financing of the deficit in the short term and the ultimate need to raise

---

46. For an empirical implementation of this approach, see Driskill 1981. For further review of the empirical evidence, see Hacche 1983.

47. See Dornbusch and Krugman 1976, Buiter and Miller 1982, and the discussion of the Phillips curve above.

taxes to service the larger debt. Nor have we taken into consideration the implications of sustained current account imbalances that redistribute wealth away from the expanding country. What are the implications of these additional channels?

As noted above, the redistribution of wealth via current account imbalances will affect the goods markets because marginal spending patterns differ. Therefore demand for the expanding country's goods would decline over time, owing to redistribution; the need for real appreciation is therefore dampened. But this effect is offset to some extent by the stimulus due to deficit finance.[48]

The portfolio effects associated with debt finance remain an unsettled area of research. Once we depart from the assumption of perfect asset substitutability, we must reckon with the asset market implications of debt finance. These effects occur through two channels. First, there is a direct effect of debt finance on the relative supplies of assets. Debt finance implies that the relative supply of the expanding country's debt rises. Asset holders have to be compensated to hold an increasing fraction of their wealth in the form of the expanding country's debt either through an increased nominal interest differential or through anticipated appreciation. But it is also possible that a once and for all depreciation of the expanding country reduces the value of its debts in terms of foreign exchange, thus reducing the portfolio share and eliminating the need for higher interest rates or appreciation.[49]

The discussion is clarified in equation (8), where we present the international interest rate relation, taking into account the risk premium that results from imperfect asset substitution.[50] The equation states that the nominal interest differential equals the expected rate of depreciation plus a risk premium, K, which depends on the relative supply of domestic debt relative to world wealth and on the domestic share in world wealth.

$$(8) \qquad i = i^* + \hat{e} + K(B/e\bar{V}^*, V/e\bar{V}^*), \qquad K_1 > 0, K_2 < 0$$

where $\bar{V}^*$ is world wealth measured in terms of foreign exchange. Equation (8) shows that the exchange rate or the rate of depreciation must adjust to maintain portfolio balance in the face of a rise in the domestic bond supply, given interest rates. The possibility of exchange depre-

---

48. Blanchard 1983 has shown that fiscal expansion will have additional expansionary effects associated with debt issue when future taxes are discounted at more than market rates. This effect continues, though dampened, in the open economy. Unless the entire debt finance translates into current account deficits so that the rest of the world acquires all the debt, there will be some net expansion of demand from debt creation.

49. Empirical work has not clearly established that foreign and domestic bonds are imperfect substitutes. See Frankel 1982, 1983.

50. See Dornbusch 1982b for a derivation and references to the extensive literature.

ciation to clear asset markets runs counter to the analysis for the goods markets, where crowding out leads us to expect an appreciation. What then will happen? As the discussion here already makes clear, this is not an area where we expect unambiguous results.

Research on the implications of debt finance has used simulation to attempt to assess the relative importance of portfolio effects—relative asset supplies and risk premiums—and aggregate demand effects.[51] The quantitative finding that emerges is that in the long run a fiscal expansion will lead to depreciation, rather than appreciation, if the portfolio effects are relatively important. Specifically, if debt issue forces a large increase in our interest rates to maintain portfolio balance, and if demand reacts to the interest rate increase by more than full crowding out, then a real depreciation is required to restore goods market equilibrium. If, by contrast, assets are highly substitutable, then risk premiums do not play a significant role, and as a result the long run crowding out must take place via real appreciation.

In concluding the discussion of the portfolio effects of fiscal policy, we note that these effects are entirely due to the assumption that budget deficits are financed by issuing bonds denominated in terms of the expanding country's currency. The risk premium effects can be avoided by financing deficits in a way that keeps the currency composition of world outside assets unchanged. For instance, in the present circumstances, the United States would finance part of the deficit in yen and deutsche mark bonds. We also note that our analysis has not taken into account effects of fiscal policy on the stock market. These effects have not been addressed in the literature but may well turn out to be more important than the questions associated with the currency denomination of bonds.

8.2.6 Interdependence

Our discussion so far has taken as given the key foreign variables— interest rates, income, prices—that influence domestic macroeconomic equilibrium via trade in goods and assets. But of course these variables are determined jointly with those at home, and, to complicate matters, policy interdependence comes to play a role. Foreign monetary and fiscal policies respond to disturbances at home as foreign policymakers attempt to influence the movements of exchange rates, interest rates, prices, and output in a manner that optimizes their macroeconomic policy objectives. This interdependence of course influences our conclusions about the effects of monetary and fiscal policies. Tight money, for example, may not lead to appreciation if foreign governments are inflation sensitive and therefore contract their

51. See Wyplosz and Sachs 1984 and Giovannini 1982.

own money stocks in tandem with our contraction to avoid currency depreciation. In other instances "synchronized expansion" agreed upon by the governments of the major countries provides the "locomotive" for world recovery.

In view of this interdependence it is interesting to ask how closely monetary growth and discretionary fiscal policy are correlated between countries. Table 8.11 provides information on this question for the growth rates of M1 and for the discretionary fiscal policy changes.

It is interesting that there is no definite change in the money growth correlations between the fixed and flexible exchange rate periods. The qualification to that statement is the interesting shift to a negative correlation for Japan under flexible rates. For fiscal policy, taking the whole period for which data are available, the correlation is relatively low. Moreover, the correlation between fiscal policy changes in the United States and a simple average of other countries in table 8.11 is only .08.

Econometric modeling of the world macroeconomy remains at an experimental stage, but such models do exist at the Federal Reserve Board, the OECD, and the Japanese Economic Planning Agency. Comparisons of the policy multipliers from these models is rendered difficult by differing assumptions about monetary and fiscal accommodation to shocks and by differences in the simulation periods. But even so it is worthwhile to compare some results. Table 8.12 shows the multipliers of the Federal Reserve's MCM model and the EPA's world economic model (WEM) for a United States fiscal expansion under flexible exchange rates.

In looking at the effects of United States policies on the foreign countries, we note that there are spillover effects under flexible exchange rates both on output and on prices. But table 8.12 also reveals that these effects are not very sizable as long as the disturbance remains small.

Table 8.11   Correlation of Money Growth and Fiscal Policy of Major Countries with Those of the United States

	Germany	Japan	United Kingdom
Annual M1 growth			
1959–72	.16	.07	.50
1974–82	.27	−.27	.20
Fiscal policy change			
1971–82	.11	.29	−.14

Source: IMF and OECD *Occasional Studies,* June 1978, p. 19, and *Economic Outlook,* December 1983, p. 34.

Note: For definition of discretionary fiscal policy change, see the sources.

Table 8.12   **Fiscal Multipliers from Two World Macro Models (percentage increase in real GDP in the first two years)**

	United States		Japan		Germany	
Effect on real GDP						
FRB MCM[a]	1.5	0.9	0.2	0.2	0.2	0.5
EPA WEM[b]	2.02	2.01	0.17	0.56	0.17	0.59
Effect on prices						
FRB MCM	−0.0	0.3	0.0	0.1	0.0	0.2
EPA WEM	0.57	1.38	0.11	0.36	0.04	0.20

Source: See note 55.

Note: The table shows the percentage increase in real GDP and in consumer prices owing to a sustained increase in United States real government spending equal to 1% of GDP for the first two years.

[a]Federal Reserve Board multicountry model.

[b]Japanese Economic Planning Agency world economic model.

8.3   Summary

The standard macroeconomic paradigm remains the IS-LM model augmented with a Phillips curve.[52] In this paper we have shown how the model must, for the case of the United States economy, be amended to take account of international effects and interactions. What conclusions emerge?

The only key structural equation that goes unamended is the money demand equation. Even here foreign variables are often proposed, though not persuasively.[53] In the goods and assets markets, foreign prices, foreign activity, and foreign asset yields appear as important determinants of domestic activity, prices, and interest rates. The quantitative magnitude and the stability of these relations remains a topic of research, but their existence and their importance to an understanding of the United States macroeconomy are beyond question.

International interactions exert an important effect on the way monetary and fiscal policies operate. The exchange rate system determines the extent to which asynchronized policies are possible and the channels through which they exert their effects on the economy. The Mundell/Fleming model of twenty years ago introduced these ideas, and they remain valid today. For the United States economy, policy limitations became apparent in the late 1960s when capital outflows on a large scale signaled that even a large country could not set the tone for the world economy. But under flexible exchange rates these interdependence effects have become much more dramatic. They immediately affect the

52. See Board of Governors of the Federal Reserve 1983, Amano, Sadahiro, and Sasaki 1981, and Yoshitomi 1984. For further references see, too, Larsen et al. 1983.

53. See, for example, McKinnon 1982.

key trade-off—the Phillips curve. Theory suggests and empirical evidence supports the notion that under flexible rates the Phillips curve is much steeper. A tight money policy leads to appreciation and thus allows rapid disinflation. The traditional idea, appropriate to fixed rates, is that crowding out takes place chiefly via higher interest rates' depressing interest-sensitive components of spending, particularly housing. Under flexible rates the crowding out takes place also at another margin, reduced net exports owing to appreciation.

Thinking on fiscal policy, too, must be modified. Fiscal expansion via its impact on interest rates induces currency appreciation, at least in the short run. Therefore fiscal expansion is less inflationary than the closed-economy Phillips curve suggests, but it also involves more crowding out. This is because net exports decline under the impact of appreciation.

Several unsettled areas of research require attention. One is to determine the importance of relative asset supplies for risk premiums and hence for long-run interest differentials, equilibrium real exchange rates, or both. The literature as yet gives no guidance to these issues. To make the point concretely, we do not have in domestic macroeconomics any empirical evidence that the maturity of the debt affects the term structure of interest rates. Long-term and short-term debt, for macroeconomics, are much the same. Is this also true when we ask if it makes a difference whether our United States deficits are financed in deutsche mark or United States dollar bonds? If the answer is affirmative, an entire popular range of ideas about the budget and exchange rates becomes irrelevant.

The second issue on which we know very little, indeed even less, is the open economy role of the stock market. If asset markets are important via their impact on exchange rates and hence on aggregate demand and prices, then surely the stock market must take a particularly important place because it is forward looking and because of its size relative to other asset markets.

The third issue, closely linked to the previous point, concerns the open economy linkages to investment. What is the impact of real exchange rates on investment spending, and how important are long swings in real exchange rates in affecting investment and hence productivity growth and employment? This question connects, of course, with the crowding-out issue raised above. The current view expressed in policy discussions is that there is less crowding out under flexible than under fixed exchange rates. But perhaps, taking into account the open economy channels, we get as much crowding out of investment, but with real appreciation rather than increased real interest rates as the channels and with manufacturing rather than housing as the affected sector. Such effects, if they do exist, would have significant longer-run implications for the performance of the economy.

Appendix

In this appendix we set out and briefly analyze a simple model that includes the three chief links between the domestic and international economies: the demand for goods, corresponding to Keynesian multiplier analysis; asset market linkages, emphasis on which at one time led to the claim that exchange rates are determined in the assets markets; and the supply side, which has received emphasis in the recent disinflation. The model guides our discussions in the text of the effects of exchange rate changes and foreign shocks.

The Model

The Assets Markets

There are four assets: domestic money, domestic bonds, foreign bonds, and capital. Domestic money is held entirely by domestic residents. Domestic bonds and capital may be held by foreigners as well; foreign bonds may be held by domestic residents.

Equilibrium conditions in the markets for domestic assets are:

(A1) $\dfrac{M_t}{P_t} = L(Y_t, R_t^B),$ $\qquad\qquad$ $L_1 > 0, L_2 < 0.$

(A2) $\dfrac{B_t}{P_t} = H(Y_t, \gamma_t^B, \Pi_t, \gamma_t^K, \gamma_t^F, V_t, V_t^*,$ $\quad H_1 < 0, H_2 > 0,$
$\qquad\qquad\qquad\qquad\qquad\qquad\qquad\qquad H_3 \geq 0, H_4 < 0,$
$\qquad\qquad\qquad\qquad\qquad\qquad\qquad\qquad H_5 < 0, H_6 > 0, H_7 > 0.$

(A3) $q_t K_t = J(Y_t, \gamma_t^B, \Pi_t, \gamma_t^K, V_t, V_t^*),$ $\quad J_1 \leq 0, J_2 < 0,$
$\qquad\qquad\qquad\qquad\qquad\qquad\qquad\qquad J_3 \geq 0, J_4 > 0,$
$\qquad\qquad\qquad\qquad\qquad\qquad\qquad\qquad J_5 < 0, J_6 > 0, J_7 > 0.$

Symbols are defined in table 8.A.1. The expected real returns on domestic bonds, capital (equity), and foreign bonds are given by:

(A4) $\qquad\qquad (1 + \gamma_t^B) = (1 + R_t^B)_t \left(\dfrac{P_t}{P_{t+1}} \right).$

(A5) $\qquad\qquad (1 + \gamma_t^K) = \dfrac{F_K(K_t, Y_t) + {}_t q_{t+1}}{q_t}.$

(A6) $\qquad\qquad (1 + \gamma_t^F) = (1 + R_t^F)_t \left(\dfrac{e_t P_t}{e_{t+1} P_{t+1}} \right).$

The presubscript t indicates the expectation formed on the basis of information available at time t. In writing (A2) and (A3) as functions

Table 8.A.1   **Symbols**

M_t	Money stock
P_t	Price level
Y_t	Real output
R_t^B	Nominal return on domestic bonds
B_t	Stock of domestic bonds
Y_t^B	Expected real return on domestic bonds
Π_t	Expected inflation rate
γ_t^K	Expected real return on domestic equity
V_t	Wealth of domestic residents
V_t^*	Foreign wealth
q_t	Relative price of an equity claim on capital
e_t	Exchange rate
B_t^{d*}	Holdings of foreign bonds by domestic residents
B_t^d, K_t^d	Holdings of corresponding assets by domestic residents
P_t^*	Foreign price level
Y_t^d	Disposable income
G_t	Government expenditure
Y_t^*	Foreign output
P_t^m	Domestic price of material inputs
W_t	Nominal wage
δ	Rate of depreciation of capital
T_t	Real taxes minus transfers, exclusive of interest payments on government debt

not only of expected real returns but also of Π_t, the expected inflation rate, we use the first-order approximation:

(A4')
$$(1 + R_t^B) = (1 + \gamma_t^B) \frac{1}{t\left(\dfrac{P_t}{P_{t+1}}\right)}$$

$$\approx (1 + \gamma_t^B) \frac{{}_t P_{t+1}}{P_t}$$

$$= (1 + \gamma_t^B)(1 + \Pi_t).$$

A similar approximation applies for the return on foreign bonds.

Real domestic wealth, V_t, consists of holdings of the four assets by domestic residents:

(A7)
$$V_t = \frac{M_t}{P_t} + \frac{B_t^d}{P_t} + q_t K_t^d + \frac{e_t B_t^{d*}}{P_t}.$$

Because foreign residents may hold both domestic bonds and domestic equity, the amounts of these assets held by domestic residents are not usually equal to the outstanding stocks.

The assumption in (A1) is that money is held for transactions purposes, at an opportunity cost equal to the return on bonds.[54] The assets are assumed to be gross substitutes. Demand functions by domestic residents have the same general forms as $LC(\ )$, $H(\ )$, and $J(\ )$ but are not dependent on foreign wealth, V_t^*. In addition, the demand by domestic residents for foreign bonds is:

(A8) $\dfrac{e_t B_t^{d^*}}{P_t} = G(Y_t, \gamma_t^B, \Pi_t, \gamma_t^K, \gamma_t^F, V_t),$ $\begin{array}{l} G_1 \leqslant 0,\ G_2 < 0,\ G_3 \geqslant 0, \\ G_4 < 0,\ G_5 > 0,\ G_6 > 0. \end{array}$

The Goods Market

We start by specifying the demand for domestic output.

(A9) $Y_t = D\left(\dfrac{e_t P_t^*}{P_t},\ Y_t^d,\ G_t,\ V_t,\ q_t\right)$

$\qquad + NX\left(\dfrac{e_t P_t^*}{P_t},\ Y_t^d,\ Y_t^*,\ V_t\ (q, q^*, P_m/P)\right),\ D_i > 0,\ i = 1, ?,$

$\qquad NX_1 > 0,\ NX_2 < 0,\ NX_3 > 0,\ NX_4 < 0.$

Prices are based on costs and the level of output relative to capacity:

(A10) $\qquad\qquad P_t = C(W_t,\ P_t^m,\ e_t P_t^*,\ Y_t/K_t),$
$\qquad\qquad C_1 > 0,\ C_2 > 0,\ C_3 > 0,\ C_4 \geqslant 0.$

The function (A10) permits an interpretation as a supply function with output on increasing function of the price level and a decreasing function of the wage, materials prices, and the prices of imported inputs.[55]

Wages

Wages are predetermined, based on the level of output (and thus employment) and expected price level:

(A11) $\qquad W_t = \psi\left((Y/K)_{t-1},\ {}_{t-1}(Y/K)_t,\ \dfrac{{}_{t-1}P_t}{P_t},\ W_{t-1}\right),$

$\qquad\qquad \psi_1 > 0,\ \psi_2 > 0,\ \psi_3 > 0,\ \psi_4 > 0.$

---

54. The return R_t^B should therefore be thought of as applying to a short-term asset; it would be desirable to include term-structure relations in an extended version of the model.

55. We have not included cost of capital measure in (A10), though the rental rate on capital and inventory holding costs do provide a supply-side channel for interest rates to affect prices.

Accumulation Equations

The wage equation provides the first explicit dynamic equation. Asset accumulation equations add further essential dynamics.

(A12) $$K_t = (1 - \delta)K_{t-1} + I(q_{t-1}, K_{t-1}).$$

(A13) $$(M_{t+1} + B_{t+1} - M_t - B_t) = P_t(G_t - T_t) + (1 + R^B_{t-1})B_t.$$

(A14) $$\begin{aligned}(1 + R^f_{t-1})e_t B^{*f}_t &- (1 + R^b_{t-1})(B_t - B^d_t) \\ &- (1 + F_K(\ ))q_t(K_t - K^d_t) + P_t NX_t \\ &= e_t B^{*f}_{t+1} - (B_{t+1} - B^d_{t+1}) - q_t(K_{t+1} - K^d_{t+1}).\end{aligned}$$

(A12) is the capital accumulation equation, (A13) the government budget constraint, where it is implicitly assumed that all debt is one-period, and (A14) is the balance of payments constraint.

The openness of the economy is reflected in the asset market equilibrium conditions, the goods market, and the asset accumulation equations. In the assets markets, movements in foreign interest rates, or in foreign wealth, affect United States rates of return and asset prices: foreign influences appear on both the demand and supply sides in the goods market; on the supply side, external disturbances may affect both the prices of material inputs and, directly, the costs of imported inputs. Equation (A14) describes the link between the current account and net ownership of foreign assets.

We now analyze the short- and long-run equilibriums of the model, emphasizing open-economy aspects, before turning to the dynamics of adjustment.

Short-Run Equilibrium

To start we examine short-run asset market equilibrium. We wish to obtain functions:

(A15) $$\begin{aligned}R^B_t &= R(X_t) \\ q_t &= q(X_t) \\ e_t/P_t &= e(X_t),\end{aligned}$$

where

$$X_t = \left[M_t, B_t, K_t, P_t, Y_t, \frac{{}_tP_t + 1}{P_t}, \frac{{}_te_t + 1}{e_t}, \frac{{}_tq_t + 1}{q_t}, \gamma^f_t, B^d_t, K^d_t, B^{*d}_t \right].$$

Several of the variables in X_t will themselves be determined in the full equilibrium of the model. The asset holdings, B^d_t, K^d_t, B^{*d}_t are to be understood as beginning of period stocks.

The properties of the functions in (A15) are implied by the equilibrium conditions (A1)–(A3). (A1) directly implies

(A16) $$R_t^B = R\left(\frac{M_t}{P_t}, Y_t\right), \qquad R_1 < 0, R_2 > 0.$$

We are thus making the strong assumption that money market conditions alone determine the short-term interest rate. Inclusion of wealth in the demand function for money would modify this latter conclusion without affecting the signs of the derivatives indicated in (A16).

The properties of the $q(\ )$ and $e(\ )$ functions are obtained using (A2) and (A3). Suppose there is an increase in the expected real return on foreign bonds, γ_t^f, with other variables in X_t held fixed. (Thus both the nominal and real returns on foreign bonds increase.) Figure 8.A.1 shows asset market equilibrium loci, JJ representing capital market equilibrium and HH bond market equilibrium. The JJ curve is positively sloped because an increase in q creates an excess supply of capital that is offset by the wealth effect arising from an increase in

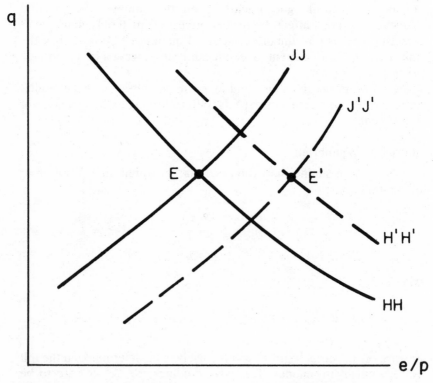

Fig. 8.A.1   Effects of an increase in the foreign interest rate.

the real exchange rate (depreciation). The HH curve slopes down because an increase in q creates excess demand for bonds through both rate of return and wealth effects, which is offset by the wealth effect of an appreciation.

An increase in the foreign interest rate creates an excess supply of both bonds and capital in the United States. The curves shift as shown in figure 8.A.1 to maintain asset market equilibrium. The real exchange rate unambiguously rises—the currency depreciates. The effects on q depend on the relative substitutability of domestic bonds and capital for foreign bonds. If the substitution is mainly between domestic and foreign bonds, then q will rise. This occurs because with the domestic interest rate given, the increase in e/P that equilibrates the bond market is large and creates excess demand in the capital market. If substitution between foreign bonds and domestic real assets is high, a rise in interest rates abroad will reduce United States stock values. An increase in the expected rate of depreciation of the dollar (i.e., a rise in $_te_{t+1}/e_t$) will have the same effects on the exchange rate and q as a change in the foreign interest rate.

An open market purchase, in figure 8.A.2, reduces the domestic interest rate, creating an excess demand for capital and—it can be shown—an excess supply of bonds. Equity prices rise, and the effects on the exchange rate are ambiguous. The more substitutable are bonds and capital, the more likely is it that the open market purchase causes the currency to depreciate.

The properties of the functions $q(\ )$ and $e(\ )$ in (A15), which can be derived using similar analysis, are:

$$(A17) \qquad \frac{\partial q}{\partial M} > 0; \frac{\partial q}{\partial B} > 0; \frac{\partial q}{\partial K} < 0; \frac{\partial q}{\partial P} < 0; \frac{\partial q}{\partial Y} \ ?; \ \frac{\partial q}{\partial_t \frac{P_{t+1}}{P_t}},$$

$$\frac{\partial q}{\partial_t \frac{e_{t+1}}{e_t}} \gtrless 0; \frac{\partial q}{\partial_t \frac{q_{t+1}}{q_t}} > 0 \ \frac{\partial q}{\partial \gamma_t^f} \gtrless 0 \ \frac{\partial e}{\partial M} > 0, \frac{\partial e}{\partial B} > 0, \frac{\partial e}{\partial K}$$

$$> 0, \frac{\partial e}{\partial P} < 0, \frac{\partial e}{\partial Y} \ ?, \ \frac{\partial e}{\partial_t \frac{P_{t+1}}{P_t}}, \frac{\partial e}{\partial_t \frac{e_{t+1}}{e_t}} > 0; \frac{\partial e}{\partial_t \frac{q_{t+1}}{q_t}} > 0 \ \frac{\partial e}{\partial \gamma_t^f} > 0.$$

Data and Definitions

1. The wage equations in table 8.5 use the following data:
   W: hourly earnings of production workers, total private nonfarm
   Wman: hourly earnings of production workers in manufacturing
   Wser: hourly earnings of production workers, services.

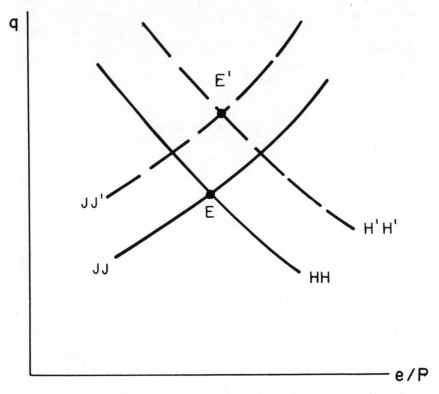

Fig. 8.A.2   Effects of an open market purchase.

Wage inflation is measured by the quarter-to-quarter change at an annual rate in each equation. The unemployment variables in the three equations are respectively the unemployment rate of wage and salary workers in manufacturing, the unemployment rate of wage and salary workers in finance and services, and the economywide unemployment rate of married men.

Expinf: expected inflation is measured by a geometrically distributed lag on the four-quarter inflation rate of the consumption expenditure deflator with a .15 decay factor so that expinf $= .15\log(P(-1)/P(-5))$ $+ .85^*$expinf(-1).

Delex denotes the twelve-quarter change in the real exchange rate. The real exchange rate variable is the relative value added deflator in manufacturing reported in the International Monetary Fund *International Financial Statistics*. With R the real exchange rate, Delex $= 100^*\log(R/R(-12))$.

2. The inflation equation in table 8.4 shows as independent variable the quarter-to-quarter change, at an annual rate, of the fixed-weight

GNP deflator. The unemployment rate is that of married men. Real exchange depreciation is defined as above. The wage inflation variable is the four-quarter change in hourly compensation in the private non-farm economy, Winf = 100*log(Wage/Wage(-4)). The dummy variable in the regression assumes a value of 0 for 1965–72 and 1 for 1973:1 to 1983:2.

3. The inflation equation for manufacturing uses as wage inflation the quarter-to-quarter change, at annual rates, of hourly compensation in manufacturing. The unemployment rate is that of wage and salary workers in manufacturing. The real depreciation variable is defined as above.

Comment   Stanley W. Black

The paper by Dornbusch and Fischer should perhaps be retitled "Linkages of the United States Economy to the Rest of the World," since that is its principal topic and theme. As such, it is a highly useful component of a domestically oriented volume such as this one.

The paper falls into two parts, of which the first examines whether the major linkages have changed in the postwar period or more recent floating exchange rate periods, as compared with prewar experience, using descriptive statistics. The second part, together with the appendix, provides an analytical model of the linkages and some estimates of price/wage linkages in the period 1962–83.

To my taste this organization of data first, theory second leaves something to be desired. To a novice in international economics, it might appear a bit like some of my ten-year-old daughter's cake-making operations: first we get out the ingredients, then we look for a recipe to combine them! Of course Dornbusch and Fischer are expert chefs, so they know which ingredients are called for. But the unwary reader might find it useful to peruse part 2 before reading part 1.

The paper begins with a perhaps surprising fact: business cycles in four major countries were more closely in phase during the gold standard era than in either the interwar or the postwar period. This result depends on comparing Morgenstern's measures of harmonization of "classical" business cycles in the prewar periods with Klein and Moore's measure of postwar "growth cycles," a comparison that involves the use of slightly different concepts.

Dornbusch and Fischer next turn to discussion of trade linkages, showing in table 8.1 that *on average* the United States economy has

Stanley W. Black is a professor in the Department of Economics, University of North Carolina.

always been relatively closed, though it reached an autarchic extreme in the 1930s. Use of the *net* service balance here is possibly misleading because of the growth in the share of services in total trade flows. However, as the authors stress, the United States economy is open *at the margin* in the sense that trade flows, though small, fluctuate as much as other components of GNP. Figure 8.2 suggests appropriately that changes in relative prices as reflected in the real exchange rate may have led to the increased importance of traded goods in the economy in the 1970s, as shown in table 8.1.

It is interesting that Dornbusch and Fischer's discussion of trade flows looks at trade in relation to income and relative prices but not, with the exception of their treatment of the gold standard period, in relation to monetary flows. I take this as a reflection of the fact that the monetary approach to the balance of payments is not particularly relevant to explaining the composition of the United States balance of payments, especially since reserve flows have usually been an unimportant component of changes in the money supply.

The digression on the Smoot-Hawley tariff argues that a tariff that is not subject to retaliation should be expansionary on both Keynesian and monetarist grounds. This argument would be more convincing if the authors could assure us that retaliation did not occur. This point is particularly worrisome in the light of current agitation to pass legislation requiring a minimum domestic content for automobiles sold in the United States.

Moving on to the discussion of asset market linkages, we note an apparent paradox in the findings: (*a*) the correlation between United States and United Kingdom monthly treasury bill rates is higher in the floating rate period 1974–83 than during the gold standard period 1876–1914; (*b*) the standard deviation of interest rate *differentials* was lower during the gold standard period than during the floating rate period. The paradox is probably due to the inflation premium in interest rates during 1974–83, which exaggerates the correlation coefficient. It might well disappear if *real* interest rates were compared rather than nominal rates.

Part 2 of the paper begins with a model of aggregate supply and demand, spelled out more explicitly in the appendix and familiar from the authors' textbook and many other places cited in a footnote. While I have no serious problems with this rather Keynesian model, Anna Schwartz and others may find things to argue with. I take it the main purpose is to describe the linkages, which is certainly accomplished.

Tables 8.7 to 8.9 offer estimates of price and wage linkages, covering 1962–83, which includes periods of both pegged and flexible exchange rates. Several questions may be raised about these estimates. Is it proper to enter the exchange rate as a predetermined variable when the exchange rate is floating? Did wage and price controls affect the relationship? Was it unchanged over such a long period? Table 8.10 estimates that a 10% depreciation of the dollar would eventually lead to a 2% rise in prices, significantly above the usual estimate of 1.5%. One should note that the larger effect of the exchange rate on the personal consumption deflator than on the GNP deflator is due to the exclusion of imports from domestic value added (i.e., GNP).

Part 2's discussion of asset markets seems disjointed, presenting the case of perfect substitutability in the text and the case of imperfect substitutability in the appendix. As the authors note, the empirical literature has in a sense rejected both cases, since random walk models forecast about as well as any standard structural model. Since the text maintains the assumption of perfect substitutability down to the section on fiscal policy, it would be helpful to the reader to understand that this implies risk-neutral investors.

The discussion of monetary and fiscal policy notes the role of movements in the real exchange rate as a key element in the transmission process in an open economy model. The familiar Dornbusch result that the nominal exchange rate overshoots its equilibrium value in a world of high asset substitutability is explained in the context of tight money leading to a temporarily overvalued exchange rate. The benefits to inflation control can be described as a steeper Phillips curve, but it should be noted that the gain to inflation control is only temporary, because the overvaluation is necessary.

Introduction of imperfect substitutability in the discussion of monetary policy would allow treatment of different monetary policy instruments such an open market operations or exchange market intervention, which cannot be distinguished in the perfect substitutes case. Recent work by Hansen and Hodrick (1980) and Loopesko (1983) rejects the perfect substitutes model when combined with the assumption of efficient markets.

The alternative approach leads to a model of a time-varying risk premium, as shown in the authors' equation (8). Among others, Dornbusch (1982b) and Black (1985) have decomposed the risk premium into factors involving a coefficient of risk aversion, the conditional variance of the exchange rate, and the relative supply of foreign currency assets. A substantial amount of current work is aimed at identifying causes of time-varying risk premiums.

This paper closes with some rather mystifying comments on the portfolio effects of fiscal policy. The authors state that fiscal expansion will lead to exchange rate depreciation if "portfolio effects are important." This presumably refers to imperfect substitutability and would be no surprise in the Mundell/Fleming model with low capital mobility. Finally, they suggest that the effects of fiscal policy on the stock market may be of major importance.

There are several issues affecting monetary and fiscal policy that do not make it into part 2 of the paper and that ought to be considered by business cycle theorists. These include Meade's (1951) analysis of the role of internal and external balance targets on the formulation of monetary and fiscal policy and more recent discussion by Sachs (1980) and others of the influence of real versus nominal wage stickiness on the effectiveness of monetary and fiscal policy. But the authors have provided a service to readers of this volume by discussing the major linkages between open economies.

Comment   Anna J. Schwartz

Let me begin by noting an error of omission and one of commission that I find in the paper. The error of omission is the absence of a money supply function. Dornbusch and Fischer state that if monetary authorities "attempt to stabilize interest rates in the context of a foreign budget deficit, they create a monetary expansion in attempting to fight rising domestic interest rates." That is the only reference to a disturbance that may arise on the supply of money side. Again, in summing up, they refer to the ways an IS-LM model must be modified to take account of international effects and interactions. They state that the only key structural equation that goes unamended is the money demand equation. If the money demand equation is the only key equation that goes unamended, why is there no amended money supply equation in the event authorities react to foreign influences in setting the target for the instrument they use in determining the money stock growth rate? The authors may respond that it is the United States economy only that they are examining, and United States monetary authorities do not react to foreign influences. That certainly has not been true of the whole period since 1962 that the second part of the paper focuses on. In any event the subject of foreign influences on the supply of money deserves discussion.

The error of commission I find in the paper is the assessment of the role of the exchange rate. Dornbusch and Fischer state, "The exchange rate must play a part in explaining United States inflation and in assessing the impact of policy changes on the price level." The exchange rate does not "explain" inflation. It is a necessary adjustment to in-

Anna J. Schwartz is a research associate of the National Bureau of Economic Research.

flation that originates in monetary actions. I shall take up this issue at a subsequent point. My comments deal with selected aspects of the paper.

Trends and Cycles

Although the first part of the paper covers trends and cycles in the external linkages, by NBER traditional standards, there is not much on cycles. The following points occur to me.

1. The measure of openness of the United States economy in table 8.1, shown in the column of tariff proceeds as a percentage of total imports of dutiable and nondutiable goods, is dubious, as the authors indicate, but not only because a tariff that excludes all imports would have no weight in an index of this type. More important, in recent years it is not the tariff but quantitative trade restraints that are the most important barriers to openness. How to express the quantitative effect of such restraints when there is no measure of the volume of trade that does *not* take place is an intractable problem.

With respect to the exchange rate regime, fixed exchange rates under the pre–World War I gold standard implied openness to foreign disturbances. It was the rejection of this condition and the consequences for domestic economic activity that led in the interwar period to the conceptions that dominated the creation of the Bretton Woods system. Fixed but adjustable exchange rates would be the new order, but international payments imbalances would not be required to affect domestic monetary policy. Although liberalization of trade would be encouraged, capital controls were acceptable. The Bretton Woods system broke down, and we now have a system with supposedly market-determined exchange rates that are periodically managed by the industrialized countries; some relaxation of capital controls among the industrialized countries, but an increasing incidence of a varied lot of protectionist measures adopted by both industrialized and developing countries; and monetary growth rates that many central banks determine by reference to foreign interest rates and exchange rate changes. Openness seems to me a concept that defies measurement.

2. Dornbusch and Fischer note that asset market linkages in the pre–World War I and interwar economies were less tight than simple accounts of the gold standard imply. I agree that the evidence does not support the instantaneous arbitrage in goods and asset markets that the doctrinaire monetary approach to the balance of payments espouses. On the other hand, I believe that debunking the linkages under the pre–World War I gold standard can be carried too far. The main reason for this belief is that the gold standard would have broken down if the countries that formally adhered to it in fact did not intend to maintain fixed exchange rates and convertibility of the domestic cur-

rency. That rules of the gold standard were flouted from time to time merely confirms that there was leeway to delay the required response. The proof is that the gold standard did not break down before World War I. So I would not agree that pre–World War I central banks "frequently sterilized gold flows." They sometimes did for periods of limited duration that did not compromise the integrity of the standard. Sterilization clearly became more generalized during the interwar period.

In this connection, the discussion in the paper of Morgenstern's findings on asset market linkages should be tempered by reference to George Borts's criticism of both Morgenstern's methodology and his data.

3. The authors argue that the effects of the Smoot-Hawley tariff of June 1930 have been substantially exaggerated. There are two views on this issue. Frank Taussig regarded the tariff as futile and the marginal increase in duties over the Fordney-McCumber tariff of 1922 as not much more damaging. The opposite view that Allan Meltzer has expressed shows that the two-year period of the slow legislative progress to enactment of the Smoot-Hawley bill enabled our trading partners to retaliate immediately on its passage. World economic welfare clearly was adversely affected. This argument and Gottfried Haberler's stress on the intensification of the world depression as a result of the imposition of the tariff and the retaliatory measures that followed seem to me valid.

Dornbusch and Fischer cite the fact that the quantity of United States imports rose smartly in 1922–23 despite the imposition of the Fordney-McCumber tariff, thanks to business expansion. Although the quantity of exports declined, that did not interrupt the expansion. The quantity both of imports and of exports declined in 1931–33 following Smoot-Hawley, but the decline in import values was much steeper than that in import quantities. The authors contend that had there been sensible macroeconomic policy after 1930, the connection that Meltzer finds between the tariff, declines in exports of agricultural goods, and bank failures in agricultural regions would not have resulted in a great depression. Moreover, even a generous allowance for a multiplier effect of the tariff-based decline in exports would account for only 3% of the 15% decline in United States real GNP between 1929 and 1931. I am in general agreement with this view, although the effects in the rest of the world probably were more severe. I do not, however, understand the statement in the paper, "In addition to the tariff, net exports were, of course, affected by the extensive competitive depreciation on the part of foreign countries." What "competitive depreciations"? Is this a reference to Britain's abandonment of gold in 1931? To the depreciation in 1936 following the United States depreciation in 1933–34? Were these "competitive"?

Open Economy Linkages

In part 2 of the paper, Dornbusch and Fischer trace open economy linkages in the goods market, between the goods market and factor prices, in asset markets, and in monetary and fiscal policies. The models presented are Keynesian. For example, the equation for the goods market equilibrium is strictly demand determined. There is no reference to the possibility that supply reacts to price changes, particularly if the changes are unexpected. The notion of transmission through a multiplier effect of foreign purchases of home goods that leads to an increase in output and employment in my view encourages the drift to protectionism. We know from the current recovery in this country that it is feasible to achieve a strong growth rate of real GNP with a balance of trade deficit. As the authors note, Darby and Stockman find very weak multiplier effects in their international model. In a Saint Louis–type equation for GNP, the evidence presented by Batten and Hafer also suggests that accounting for export activity is not statistically important for the Untied States. So emphasis on the linkages between foreign trade and aggregate demand seem to me overdrawn. International linkages are also identified in the terms for wealth and disposable income that affect the world real interest rate, but the paper admittedly does not define their impact on the aggregate demand for United States goods. A final channel mentioned is the wealth effect of "persistent international capital movements, for instance, arising from persistent public sector deficits." I shall refer to the channel in a different context later on.

The markup price equation is the basis for theorizing about the effects of a rise in import prices and materials on aggregate demand and supply: a direct route through the effects of import prices on domestic markups and on costs and thus prices, and indirect routes through the effects on wage settlements in industries involved in the international economy and the effect of demand pressures from abroad on domestic prices.

Nine quarterly regressions for 1962–83 are presented to test the theoretical impacts of the external sector on domestic inflation based on the markup equation, sets of three regressions each with the dependent variable the rate of change first of the GNP deflator, second of the personal consumption deflator, and third of wages, not otherwise identified. According to the results, exchange rate changes, the rate of change of hourly wage rates and of output per hour in manufacturing, and the rate of change of the price of oil and gas can explain about 80% of the variance of the deflators. In the regressions on the rate of change of wages, exchange rate changes, the log of unemployment for married men and expected inflation can explain about 50% of the variance of wages. The most significant variable is the expected inflation rate. Dornbusch and Fischer conclude that exchange rate changes have relatively quick direct effects on prices and a slower-working indirect effect on wages.

I believe the results of the regressions reflect how some of a necessary adjustment was worked out. The regressions do not explain why an adjustment was necessary. A price level equation can of course be obtained by equating nominal money supply and demand and solving for the price level. By opening to view the monetary source of the price rise, such an equation will demonstrate that an adjustment is necessary.

In considering the asset market, Dornbusch and Fischer indicate that answers to the questions whether domestic and foreign bonds are perfect or imperfect substitutes, whether the stock market should be accorded a role, and whether the redistribution of wealth through the current account is important for the determination of the exchange rate and macroeconomic equilibrium help analyze the implications of sustained fiscal deficits and of long-term current account deficits. The conclusion is that under flexible rates, with perfect substitutability an increase in the money stock leads to overshooting of the exchange rate because prices are sticky, real balances increase, and output expands while the real and nominal interest rates fall. The ensuing inflation returns the real exchange rate to its long-run equilibrium value. Thus monetary and fiscal policy affect the real exchange rate as well as the real interest rate channel.

Whether overshooting would in fact occur depends on whether inflationary expectations come into play when the money stock is increased. Dornbusch and Fischer agree that overshooting is not inevitable if output expands initially to raise the nominal interest rate. I would put it differently. There may be no output effects given inflationary expectations but simply higher nominal interest rates.

The asymmetry in adjustment speeds between goods and asset markets, they argue, establishes a link between tight money and significant transitory exchange rate overvaluation. Since tight money works rapidly and strongly on the exchange rate, disinflation therefore can take place more rapidly.

I do not see the close connection between money growth rates and real exchange rates in 1982 and 1983. During the four quarters of 1982 real exchange rates rose 13%. M1 rose 8.5%. Was that tight money? In the first quarter of 1983, the real exchange rate fell 3.5% while money growth accelerated from the fourth quarter 1982 annual rate of 9.9 to the first quarter 1983 annual rate of 14.3. The deceleration of money growth in the second quarter of 1983 of one-half a percentage point was accompanied by an increase in the real exchange rate of 2.9%.

To affirm a close connection between money growth rates and the exchange rate during this period, one has to appeal to the appreciation of the exchange rate as proof that double-digit money growth rates are not excessive. This is Martin Feldstein's dubious argument in the 1984 annual report of the Council of Economic Advisors: "The fact that the price of the dollar in foreign exchange markets remained high throughout 1983 is a clear signal that the market had confidence in the Federal Reserve and that the money growth rate was not excessive" (p. 62). That remains to be seen.

Turning to fiscal policy, Dornbusch and Fischer assume that sustained fiscal expansion raises long-run aggregate demand. I presume they mean budget deficits. Unless monetized, in my view, deficits have no such effect. If financed by borrowing, deficits will bring about crowding out.

While the crowding-out effect in the goods market is said to lead to appreciation, clearing asset markets in the case of debt finance requires depreciation to maintain portfolio balance. Whether appreciation or depreciation will result, the paper says, depends on the relative importance of portfolio effects versus aggregate demand effects. It seems clear that typically portfolio effects dominate, since budget deficits have usually accompanied depreciating currencies, another reason I do not believe that deficits raise aggregate demand. Dornbusch and Fischer conclude that the risk premiums in financing budget deficits by issuing bonds in the expanding country's currency can be avoided by financing in the currency of other countries so that the currency composition of world outside assets remains unchanged. I note that empirically the model of diversification has not worked very well.

Conclusion

I would like to conclude by reporting a view of the relation between fiscal and foreign sector deficits that Jan Tumlir presented at a recent Shadow Open Market Committee meeting. He noted a decline in the global savings ratio attributable to unprecedented fiscal deficits in both industrial and developing countries and the swing from a large current account surplus to a deficit of the OPEC group. Countries are competing for the limited supply of world savings. While the savings ratio in Japan is 30% of GNP, in the United States it currently is only 15%–16%. Japan, faced with intense trade discrimination abroad, cannot find investment opportunities at home to absorb its national savings. In the United States, on the other hand, investment opportunities are growing so rapidly that domestic savings cannot finance them without inflation. The United States therefore turns to foreign sources of savings. The only way to borrow capital abroad is through a current account deficit.

Tumlir remarked that the role of the real exchange rate in hurting United States exporters has been exaggerated. Despite the high exchange rate of the dollar, cyclical conditions abroad, and increased competition for export orders in the rest of the world, United States total real exports during the initial twelve-month period following the business cycle trough in November 1982 rose at a somewhat higher rate than they did in the comparable periods following the troughs of March 1975 and July 1980. Only United States real exports to oil-exporting LDCs are currently depressed. At the same time, the exchange rate helps keep domestic prices more competitive. In any event, exchange rate changes are not an independent contribution to inflation or deflation but an integral part of the mechanism by which inflation or deflation develops from the original monetary impulse.

Tumlir ended his remarks by noting possible outcomes given the current account deficit that provides the foreign capital in the absence of adequate savings to finance all attractive United States investment opportunities. Under free trade, the industries most affected by the import competition would be those with the least attractive investment opportunities. Their shrinkage would be irreversible when the investment cycle ran its course or fiscal deficits ended. When a government grants protection to selected industries, however, investment prospects improve in these industries. Industries with more promising prospects then face intensified competition from abroad, since the imports through which it would have been most economical to transfer the capital from abroad are restrained. The more promising prospects in the unprotected industries will deteriorate, and resources will be shifted to the protected industries.

The implication I draw from Tumlir's analysis is that the problem is not the current account deficit or the strong dollar. The problem is the world's low savings ratio, which fiscal deficits exacerbate. As for the level of the real interest rate, it is clearly positive now after years of negative real rates. Whether real rates are regarded as above their equilibrium level depends on an estimate of inflationary expectations. I doubt that averaging the last three years of actual inflation is an adequate measure of United States and world market expectations. We shall do more to restore real rates to whatever their equilibrium level is by eliminating once and for all the recurrence of variable and rising inflation rates.

Discussion Summary

Robert Gordon took issue with the large total effect of exchange rates on wages and prices found by the authors. He noted that the effect was much greater than he had found previously and that, in retrospect, even his coefficients had overstated the impact of exchange rate appreciation on inflation in 1981–83. He felt their finding was due to their arbitrary specification of inflation expectations and their failure to allow price markups to depend on domestic demand or to attribute some of the acceleration of inflation in 1974 to the lifting of wage and price controls.

Robert Eisner and Geoffrey Moore both expressed concern that the authors had examined the role of foreign variables on the GNP price deflator, which, they argued, would fall when import prices rose, ceteris paribus. Moore noted that the gross domestic purchases deflator did not have this defect and, in addition, was more comprehensive than the deflator for consumers' expenditure.

Allan Meltzer elaborated on his analysis of the effects of tariffs on the domestic economy. He noted that the Fordney-McCumber tariff was harder to dismiss as a contributor to the 1923 recession than was the Smoot-Hawley tariff in the Great Depression. He noted that the retaliation to the Smoot-Hawley tariff may, however, have exacerbated the Great Depression through its impact on agricultural land prices and income, and hence on bank failures in agricultural areas.

Stanley Fischer doubted that the strong impact of exchange rates on output was due to the authors' omission of a variable to capture the relaxation of price controls in 1974, since the lags in the estimated equation were too short to allow price controls to work in the manner Gordon suggested, but he did concede that the price expectations term estimated was possibly misleading. Rudiger Dornbusch noted that agricultural prices in the rest of the world fell by more than those in the United States in the Great Depression. Thus United States agricultural tariffs kept domestic prices higher than world prices and could not have caused land prices to fall by more than they would have without tariffs.

References

Aghevli, Bijan B. 1975. The balance of payments and money supply under the gold standard regime: U.S. 1879–1914. *American Economic Review* 65 (March): 40–58.

Amano, Akihiro, Akira Sadahiro, and Takahiro Sasaki. 1981. Structure and application of the EPA world econometric model. Economic Planning Agency, Tokyo.

Annual report of the Council of Economic Advisers. 1984 In *Economic report of the president.* Washington, D.C.: Government Printing Office.

Batten, Dallas S., and Rik W. Hafer. 1983. The relative impact of monetary and fiscal actions on economic activity: A cross-country comparison. [Federal Reserve Bank of Saint Louis] *Review* 65 (January): 5–12.

Black, Stanley W. 1985. The effects of alternative intervention policies on the variability of exchange rates: The Harrod effect. In *Exchange rate management under uncertainty,* ed. Jagdeep Bhandari. Cambridge: MIT Press.

Blanchard, Olivier. 1983. Debt, deficits, and finite horizons. Unpublished manuscript, MIT.

Blinder, Alan. 1982. The anatomy of double digit inflation in the 1970s. In *Inflation: Causes and effects,* ed. Robert Hall. Chicago: University of Chicago Press.

Bloomfield, Arthur I. 1959. *Monetary policy under the international gold standard: 1880–1914.* New York: Federal Reserve Bank.

Board of Governors of the Federal Reserve System. 1983. *FRB multicountry model: Version August.* Washington, D.C.: Board of Governors of the Federal Reserve System.

Borts, George H. 1964. Review of *International financial transactions and business cycles,* by Oskar Morgenstern. *Journal of the American Statistical Association* 59 (March): 223–28.

Branson, William. 1980. Trends in United States international trade and investment. In *The American economy in transition,* ed. Martin Feldstein. Chicago: University of Chicago Press.

Branson, William, and Willem Buiter. 1983. Monetary and fiscal policy with flexible exchange rates. In *Economic interdependence and flexible exchange rates,* ed. Jagdeep S. Bhandari and Bluford H. Putnam. Cambridge: MIT Press.

Bruno, Michael, and Jeffrey Sachs. 1985. *The economics of worldwide stagflation.* Cambridge: Harvard University Press.

Buiter, Willem, and Marcus Miller. 1982. Real exchange rate overshooting and the output cost of bringing down inflation. *European Economic Review* 18, 1:85–123.

Canzoneri, Matthew, and Jo Anna Gray. 1983. Monetary policy games and the consequences of non-cooperative behavior. International Finance Discussion Paper no. 219, Federal Reserve Board.

Cardoso, Eliana. 1983. Exchange rates and the stock market. Unpublished manuscript, Boston University.

Cumby, Robert E., and Maurice Obstfeld. 1982. International interest-rate and price-level linkages under flexible exchange rates: A review of recent evidence. Working Paper 921, National Bureau of Economic Research.

Darby, Michael R., James R. Lothian, Arthur E. Gandolfi, Anna J. Schwartz, and Alan C. Stockman. 1983. *The international transmission of inflation.* Chicago: University of Chicago Press.

Darby, Michael R., and Alan C. Stockman. 1983. The Mark III international transmission model: Estimates. In *The international trans-*

mission of inflation, ed. Michael R. Darby et al. Chicago: University of Chicago Press.

Dornbusch, Rudiger. 1976. Expectations and exchange rate dynamics. *Journal of Political Economy* 84 (December):1161–76.

———. 1982a. Equilibrium and disequilibrium exchange rates. *Zeitschrift fur Wirtschafts-und-Sozialwissenschaften* 102 (6):573–99.

———. 1982b. Exchange rate risk and the macroeconomics of exchange rate determination. In *The internationalization of financial markets and national economic policy,* ed. Robert Hawkins et al. Greenwich, Conn.: JAI Press.

———. 1983. Flexible exchange rates and interdependence. *IMF Staff Papers* 30 (March): 3–30.

Dornbusch, Rudiger, and Paul Krugman. 1976. Flexible exchange rates in the short run. *Brookings Papers on Economic Activity* 3:537–76.

Driskill, Robert. 1981. Exchange rate dynamics: An empirical investigation. *Journal of Political Economy* 89 (April): 357–71.

Frankel, Jeffrey. 1982. In search of the exchange rate risk premium. *Journal of International Money and Finance* 1:255–74.

———. 1983. Intervention in foreign exchange markets. *Federal Reserve Bulletin* 69 (November): 830–36.

Frenkel, Jacob. 1981. The collapse of purchasing power parity during the 1970's. *European Economic Review* 16 (May): 145–65.

———, ed. 1983. *Exchange rates and international macroeconomics.* Chicago: University of Chicago Press.

Friedman, Milton, and Anna J. Schwartz. 1963. *A monetary history of the United States, 1867–1960.* Princeton: Princeton University Press.

Giovannini, Alberto. 1982. Essays on flexible exchange rates. Ph.D. diss., Massachusetts Institute of Technology.

Gordon, Robert J. 1973. The response of wages and prices to the first two years of controls. *Brookings Papers on Economic Activity* 3: 765–78.

———. 1982. Inflation, flexible exchange rates, and the natural rate of unemployment. In *Workers, jobs, and inflation,* ed. Martin N. Baily, 89–153. Washington, D.C.: Brookings Institution.

Haberler, Gottfried. 1976. *The world economy, money, and the Great Depression, 1919–1939.* Washington, D.C.: American Enterprise Institute.

Hacche, Graham. 1983. The determinants of exchange rate movements. Working Paper, Organization for Economic Cooperation and Development.

Hansen, Lars Peter, and Robert J. Hodrick. 1980. Forward exchange rates as optimal predictors of future spot rates: An econometric analysis. *Journal of Political Economy* 88:829–53.

Henderson, Dale W. Exchange market intervention operations: Their role in financial policy and their effects. In *Exchange rate theory and practice,* ed. John F. O. Bilson and Richard C. Marston, 359–406. Chicago: University of Chicago Press.

Katseli-Papaefstratiou, Louka T. 1979. *The reemergence of the purchasing power parity doctrine in the 1970's.* Special Papers in International Economics, no. 13. Princeton: Princeton University Press.

Keynes, J. M. 1930. *A treatise on money,* vol. 2. New York: Macmillan.

Kindleberger, Charles P. 1973. *The world in depression, 1929–1939.* Berkeley: University of California Press.

———. 1978. *Manias, panics, and crashes.* New York: Basic Books.

Klein, Philip A., and Geoffrey H. Moore. 1983. The leading indicator approach to economic forecasting: Retrospect and prospect. *Journal of Forecasting* 2, no. 2:119–35.

Kravis, Irving, and Robert Lipsey. 1983. *Toward a theory of national price levels.* Princeton Studies in International Finance. Princeton: Princeton University Press.

Larsen, F., et al. 1983. International economic linkages. *OECD Economic Studies,* no. 1 (Autumn).

Laursen, S., and L. Metzler. 1950. Flexible exchange rates and the theory of employment. *Review of Economics and Statistics* 32 (February): 281–99.

League of Nations. 1942. *Commercial policy in the interwar period: International proposals and national policies.* Geneva: League of Nations.

Loopesko, Bonnie E. 1983. *Relationships among exchange rates, intervention, and interest rates: An empirical investigation. Staff Studies no. 133. Washington, D.C.: Board of Governors of the Federal Reserve System.*

McKinnon, Ronald. 1982. Currency Substitution and the world dollar standard. *American Economic Review* 72 (June): 320–33.

Meade, James. 1951. *The balance of payments.* London: Oxford University Press.

Meese, Richard A., and Kenneth Rogoff. 1983. Empirical exchange rate models of the seventies. *Journal of International Economics* 14:3–24.

Meltzer, Allan H. 1976. Monetary and other explanations of the start of the Great Depression. *Journal of Monetary Economics* (November): 455–71.

Melvin, Michael. 1983. An alternative approach to international capital flows. In *The international transmission of inflation,* ed. Michael Darby et al., chap. 13. Chicago: University of Chicago Press.

Mintz, Ilse. 1959. *Trade balances during business cycles: U.S. and Britain since 1880.* Occasional Paper 67. New York: National Bureau of Economic Research.

———. 1967. *Cyclical fluctuations in the exports of the United States since 1879.* New York: Columbia University Press.

Morgenstern, Oskar. 1955. *The validity of international gold movement statistics.* Special Papers in International Economics, no. 2. Princeton: Princeton University Press.

———. 1959. *International financial transactions and business cycles.* Princeton: Princeton University Press.

Mundell, Robert A. 1964. Problems of monetary and exchange rate management in Canada. *National Banking Review* 2 (September):85.

Mussa, Michael. 1984. The theory of exchange rate determination. In *Exchange rate theory and practice,* ed. John F. O. Bilson and Richard C. Marston, 13–78. Chicago: University of Chicago Press.

Nordhaus, William. 1972. The worldwide wage explosion. *Brookings Papers on Economic Activity* 2:431–64.

Nurkse, R. 1978. *International currency experience.* New York: Arno Press. Originally published 1944.

Obstfeld, Maurice. 1982. Can we sterilize? Theory and evidence. *American Economic Review, Papers and Proceedings* (May), 45–50.

Obstfeld, Maurice, and Alan Stockman. 1983. Exchange-rate dynamics. Manuscript, Columbia University.

Pierce, James L., and Jared J. Enzler. 1974. The effects of external inflationary shocks. *Brookings Papers on Economic Activity* 1:13–54.

Razin, Assaf, and Lars Svensson, 1983. The terms of trade and the current account: The Harberger-Laursen-Metzler effect. *Journal of Political Economy* 91 (February): 97–125.

Rogoff, Kenneth. 1983. Time series studies of the relationship between exchange rates and intervention: A review of the techniques and literature. Staff Study 132, Federal Reserve Board.

———. 1984. Productive and counterproductive cooperative monetary policies. Manuscript, International Finance Division, Federal Reserve Board.

Sachs, Jeffrey. 1980. Wages, flexible exchange rates, and macroeconomic policy. *Quarterly Journal of Economics* 64:269–319.

Sayers, R. S. 1958. *Central banking after Bagehot.* London: Oxford University Press.

Schwartz, Anna J. 1981. Understanding 1929–1933. In *The Great Depression revisited,* ed. Karl Brunner. The Hague: Martinus Nijhoff.

Stern, Robert, et al. 1976. *Price elasticities in international trade: An annotated bibliography.* London: Butterworth.

Taussig, F. W. 1964. *The tariff history of the United States.* Minneapolis: Capricorn Books.

Tumlir, Jan. 1984. Trade restrictions imposed in 1983 (report to the Shadow Open Market Committee). Mimeographed.

Wyplosz, Charles, and Jeffrey Sachs. 1984. Real exchange rate effects of fiscal policy. Working Paper, National Bureau of Economic Research.

Yoshitomi, M. 1984. The insulating and transmission mechanism of floating exchange rates analyzed by the EPA world econometric model. Economic Planning Agency, Tokyo.

IV Changes in Cyclical Behavior

9   Major Changes in Cyclical Behavior

Victor Zarnowitz and Geoffrey H. Moore

In the long stretch of time covered by business cycles, the economies of the industrialized world have undergone many profound changes of structure, institutions, and modes of operation. Business cycles have continued to have much in common as the most durable and pervasive form of short-term motion of these economies, but they have also changed significantly. This study seeks to identify and analyze some of these changes. We concentrate on the longer and relatively well-established developments in the United States.

Sections 9.1 and 9.2 review some historical facts and hypotheses concerned with types of change in cyclical behavior. Next we take a long-run view of the durations of cyclical phases, note the shifts in the relative length of expansions and contractions (9.3), and relate them to changing trends in prices (9.4). Section 9.5 examines the amplitudes of cyclical movements in production and employment during the past hundred years. There follows an analysis of structural shifts in employment and their cyclical effects (9.6); trends and cyclical changes in unemployment and labor force participation (9.7); and the consequences for the business cycles of the altered composition of personal income, reflecting the expansion of government, transfer payments, and so on (9.8). A discussion of the relationship between growth and variability of economic change (9.9) completes this part of our report.

The remaining sections deal with changes in particular categories of cyclical indicators. Of special interest here is the behavior of wholesale or producer prices (9.10) and interest rates (9.11). Also, we examine

Victor Zarnowitz is a professor in the Graduate School of Business at the University of Chicago. Geoffrey H. Moore is head of the Center for International Business Cycle Research of the Graduate School of Business at Columbia University.

the consistency of timing of the leading, coincident, and lagging indicators over as long a period as the data allow (9.12). Finally, we present our conclusions and suggestions for further research.

9.1 Business Cycles and Growth: Background and Some Hypotheses

Business cycles, defined as recurrent sequences of persistent and pervasive expansions and contractions in economic activities, are at least as old as the modern industrialization and growth processes in the principal capitalist countries. The earliest evidence of their presence, from British and United States business annals and statistics, reaches back into the eighteenth century.

The impressively high long-term growth rates of the era are well documented by the series of decade averages that reveal upward trends in employment, output, capital, productivity, and per capita consumption (see, e.g., Kuznets 1971; U.S. Department of Commerce 1973). However, over shorter periods, growth of the major private enterprise economies was very uneven. Each decade witnessed at least one contraction of aggregate economic activity in each country, but more typically there were two and sometimes three. This refers to all countries covered by the business annals (Thorp 1926) and the NBER business cycle chronologies (Burns and Mitchell 1946).[1] Most of these setbacks were mild, but some were serious. A contraction was always followed by an expansion, which as a rule consisted of recovery to the highest levels previously attained and a phase of net growth ending in a new record high ("peak") of activity. Only on a few occasions did a peak fail to exceed the preceding peak. Similarly, successive troughs usually reached higher levels, except when a particularly weak recovery or deep depression occurred. Thus overall growth was achieved through expansionary spurts punctuated every few years by mild but generalized slowdowns or recessions and at longer irregular intervals by major depressions.

During this epoch the economies, societies, and political systems involved changed profoundly in many respects. There is substantial agreement among those who have studied the subject intensively that business cycles are "a product of culture . . . found only in modern nations where economic activities are organized mainly through business enterprises and where individuals enjoy considerable freedom in

---

1. The annals begin in 1790 for England and the United States, in 1840 for France, in 1853 for Germany, in 1867 for Austria, and in 1870 for twelve other countries on four continents. They end in 1925 (Thorp 1926) and in 1931 (Thorp 1932). The NBER chronologies start in 1792, 1834, 1840, and 1866 for Great Britain, the United States, France, and Germany, respectively. See appendix A to this volume for more detail.

producing, pricing, trading, and saving or investing" (Burns 1968, 228).[2] It is therefore plausible to look for important changes in business cycles as a result of the changes in the structure of production, markets, institutions, and policies.

It is also possible to argue that the influence runs partly in the opposite direction and to see in the development of business cycles a major instrument for changes in the economy and society. Marx predicted a trend toward intensification of crises as capital/labor ratios increase, workers are displaced and pauperized, and profit rates fall, but his predictions were belied by the spread of prosperity and the capacity of capitalism and democracy first to survive and then to avoid severe depressions and bouts of high unemployment. Keynes worried about whether investment would absorb savings at full employment in countries growing in wealth, where capital accumulation lowers the return to investors. Hansen moved further, expecting weaker booms and deeper slumps to result from reduced opportunities for investment and increased propensity to save in "mature economies" with slower population growth. History dealt as harshly with these new "secular stagnation" hypotheses as it had with the earlier ones.[3] Yet they are revived in various forms whenever sluggish business conditions prevail for some time, as in the recent period of so-called stagflation.

Conversely, in times of substantial stability and growth, such as the mid-1920s and 1960s in the United States, the idea tends to gain ground that business cycles are becoming "obsolete" or are being "ironed out" by better public and business policies. In 1921–29 the Federal Reserve System "took—and perhaps even more was given—credit for the generally stable conditions that prevailed, and high hopes were placed in the potency of monetary policy as then administered" (Friedman and Schwartz 1963, 240). In the mid-1960s, many economists believed that

2. In contrast, seasonal (daily and annual) cycles, although influenced by custom—for example, the timing of holidays—are in large measure part and parcel of the natural environment of man. Centrally directed or collectivist economies suffer from various types of instability induced partly by nature (e.g., variations in harvest) and partly by government and societal actions (e.g., political purges; planning errors; imposition of, resistance to, and relaxation of price and other controls). In reaction to such disturbances, the overall growth rates of these systems can vary widely over time, but such fluctuations are very different from business cycles, just as closed centralized economies are fundamentally unlike open market or "mixed" economies.

3. Consider also the classical theories of stationary state and the law of historically diminishing returns, as well as the Malthusian population principle, in the light of the great increase in the average standard of living in the densely populated countries of Western Europe and Japan. A hundred years after Malthus, Veblen anticipated a convergence of modern economies to a chronic state of mild depression. Keynes sympathized with the intuitive underconsumption hypotheses of Malthus and Hobson as forerunners of his theory of deficient effective demand. For appraisals of current interest, see Mitchell 1927, chap. 9; Keynes 1936, chap. 23; Haberler 1964 (1937), chap. 5; and Burns and Mitchell 1946, 382–83.

the new use of discretionary fiscal policy was on its way to "dethroning the cyclical model" (Heller 1966; see also Gordon 1969, 26–29).

9.2   Three Types of Change

It is useful to distinguish three types of change in the cyclical behavior of the market-oriented economies: long-term or secular trends; discontinuous or episodic changes; and cyclical changes. The hypotheses noted in section 9.1 envisage a gradual intensification or a gradual moderation of business cycles and hence concern the first type. These are presumably irreversible changes or trends that can be projected. The second type are temporary changes observed in particular periods. They may or may not continue and may or may not be reversed.

The third type are "cycles of cycles." Here the NBER-designated business cycles are viewed as subdivisions of longer major cycles or as mixtures of several distinct types. Four patterns, named for the economists who have investigated them in detail, are found in the literature:

1. The *Kondratieff* (about forty-eight to sixty years). These "long waves" have been associated with large movements in the level of prices and perhaps also with major technological innovations, but they do not show up in the volumes of production and consumption. Too few of such swings have been observed to prove or disprove their existence conclusively.

2. The *Kuznets* (fifteen to twenty-five years). These cycles have been associated with construction of buildings and transport facilities (highways, rail lines, etc.), growth of population and labor force, urban development, and business formation. Here there is more supportive evidence of a historical nature.

3. The *Juglar* (about seven to ten years). These are the "major" business cycles, such as the Great Depression of the 1930s, that have received a great deal of attention in academic literature.

4. The *Kitchin* (about three to four years). These "minor" or "forty-month" business cycles are often related to fluctuations in inventory investment.

Schumpeter (1939, vol. 1, chap. 5) developed the much discussed scheme of three Kitchins per Juglar and six Juglars per Kondratieff. Burns and Mitchell (1946, chap. 11) reported largely negative or inconclusive results from tests of the former hypothesis for the United States. More generally, they found that long-run cyclical changes rarely had a dominant influence on the short-run cyclical behavior of a sample of United States series on general business activity, prices, production, investment in capital goods, and yields and the volume of trade in security markets.

Business cycles have certainly varied greatly in amplitude, diffusion, and duration, and important distinctions can be made between major and minor cycles—for example, with respect to the relative roles and behavior of monetary aggregates, fixed investment, and inventory investment. But these matters will not occupy us here. There is little evidence of periodicities in the occurrence of groups of major and minor cycles. However, we shall consider, in the light of currently available data, one old hypothesis related to the Kondratieff cycles, namely that business cycle expansions have tended to be longer (and larger?) and contractions shorter (and smaller?) during the upward phases of the long waves in prices than during the downward phases.

This paper, then, will focus in particular on the "secular" changes in cyclical behavior, a category that naturally seems to deserve most attention. However, the secular and the discontinuous changes are not necessarily clearly differentiated. Not all trends can be safely projected, and not all changes labeled secular may prove irreversible.

9.3   Durations of Cyclical Phases before and after World War II

Studies of business cycles in the pre–World War II era have not been able to document major changes of either secular or discontinuous type. Tests by Burns and Mitchell (1946, chap. 10) gave little or no support to the view that substantial long-term changes occurred in the durations and amplitudes of cyclical movements in the sample of long United States time series. Mills's (1926) hypothesis that the cycles tend to get shorter in stages of rapid growth also failed to be confirmed by these tests. Comparisons of cycles before and after 1914 (then often alleged to have marked a "break" in American business history) indicated more basic similarities than differences, although the fluctuations during the period between the two world wars were unusually large.

Such major changes of systematic nature as can be observed in aggregate measures and particular aspects of cyclical behavior refer principally to comparisons between the period after World War II and the earlier era. As shown in table 9.1, the eight contractions of 1945–82 were on the average much shorter, and the eight expansions much longer, than the corresponding phases in each of the three subsets with equal numbers of consecutive business cycles that together span the preceding century (lines 1–4, cols. 3 and 5). In 1846–1945, the mean duration of expansions was thirty months, that of contractions twenty months; in 1945–82, expansions averaged forty-five months and contractions eleven months.

The proportion of time that the economy spent declining dropped from 45% in 1846–1945 to 20% in 1945–82 (col. 9). These results are altered but little, to 46% and 25%, respectively, when five cycles are

Table 9.1   Duration of Business Cycles in the United States by Selected Subperiods, 1846–1982

Period (1)	Number of Business Cycles Covered (2)	Duration in Months[a]						Percentage of Time in Contraction[b]	
		Expansions		Contractions		Business Cycles			
		Mean (3)	SD (4)	Mean (5)	SD (6)	Mean (7)	SD (8)	All (9)	Peacetime[c] (10)
All Cycles									
1846–85	8	32	16	27	18	59	28	45	46
1885–1912	8	23	5	17	5	40	4	42	42
1912–45	8	33	24	17	12	51	20	34	47
1945–82	8	45	28	11	4	56	27	20	25
Excluding marginal recessions[c]									
1846–85	7	39	21	28	19	68	38	42	
1885–1912	6	36	21	18	5	53	21		33
Summary									
1846–1945	24	30	17	20	13	50	21	41	
1846–1945[c]	21	36	21	21	14	57	27	37	
1846–1982	32	33	21	18	12	51	22	35	
Peacetime cycles[d]									
1846–1982	27	28	13	19	12	46	18	41	
1846–1982[c]	24	33	18	19	13	52	25		37

Source: National Bureau of Economic Research. For individual cycle durations, annual estimates for earlier cycles (1790–1845), and specific references, see appendix A in this volume, tables A.2, A.3, and A.5.

[a]Based on the monthly NBER reference dates, except for the two earliest cycles dated in calendar years (troughs: 1846 and 1848; peaks: 1847 and 1853). Mean = mean duration; SD = standard deviation, in months. Col. (3) + col. (5) = col. (7), except for rounding.

[b]Months of business cycle contractions divided by total months covered, times 100.

[c]The following phases designated as contractions in the NBER chronology are treated as retardations rather than recessions and included, along with the preceding and following phases, in long expansions: 6/1869–12/1870; 3/1887–4/1888; 6/1899–12/1900. For detail, see Zarnowitz 1981, 494–505.

[d]Excludes five wartime cycles (trough–peak–trough dates) associated with the Civil War (6/1861–4/1865–12/1867); World War I (12/1914–8/1918–3/1919); World War II (6/1938–2/1945–10/1945); Korean War (10/1949–7/1953–5/1954); and Vietnam War (2/1961–12/1969–11/1970).

omitted that include the long wartime expansions and the relatively short postwar contractions (col. 10). The mean durations of the pre–1945 and post–1945 peacetime expansions are twenty-six and thirty-four months; contractions, twenty-one and eleven months.

A few of the mildest contractions in the NBER chronology of the nineteenth-century cycles may actually have been episodes of below-trend but still positive growth rates—pronounced retardations rather than absolute declines (Zarnowitz 1981). That is, the chronology may have (inadvertently) recognized some growth cycle slowdowns rather than recessions, which would tend to make expansions and contractions more nearly equal in length (see appendix A, sect. 8, to this volume). But allowing for this possibility would not significantly alter our conclusions. The proportions of time in contractions for peacetime cycles, recalculated on this assumption, would be 40% before 1945 and (an unchanged) 25% after 1945.

Contractions became more uniform in length after World War II (col. 6). Expansions become less uniform, but this is chiefly the effect of the wars, all but one of which occurred in the last two of our four periods (col. 4).

With regard to the total cycle durations, neither the means nor the standard deviations indicate any significant trends. Expansions lengthened and contractions shortened drastically, but cycle lengths remained about the same (cols. 7 and 8).

One of the implications of these findings is that contractions have become more predictable in length than they were in earlier times. For example, if we take two standard deviations as the likely range, this was eight months in the period 1945–82. Added to the mean of eleven months, this makes nineteen months the practical upper limit. In fact, no contraction in this period lasted more than seventeen months. Before 1945, the estimated ranges was twenty-six months, yielding an upper limit of forty-six months, which was not exceeded in the Great Depression (forty-three months).

9.4   Business Cycle Phases and Long-Term Trends in Prices

Between 1789 and 1932, wholesale and consumer prices in the United States followed alternating upward and downward trends (table 9.2). The long upswings lasted between 21 and 25 years; the long downswings varied more, from 12 to 32 years. These movements largely canceled each other over the entire stretch of more than 140 years, so that the level of prices at the bottom of the Great Depression was not much higher than when George Washington took office. The half-century since 1932, however, witnessed the longest, largest, and most continuous inflation on record. Except in the recessions of 1937–38 and 1948–

49, no significant price-level declines occurred in this period. Wholesale prices increased by a factor of almost nine, consumer prices by a factor of seven (cf. cols. 4–7 of the table).

Apart from the secular trends, the comprehensive price indexes show generally procyclical short-term movements. Before 1932, they rose during most business expansions and fell during most business contractions, conforming in this sense about three-quarters of the time.[4] In periods of upward trend, the cyclical rises in prices were on the average large and the declines small; in periods of downward trend, the opposite situation prevailed, that is, the rises tended to be small and the declines large (cols. 8 and 9). But after 1949 prices kept increasing even when the economy declined, although virtually every major slowdown and recession was associated with a temporary reduction in the inflation rate.

To be sure, the long-period averages in table 9.2 conceal a very large amount of variation over time, both between the wartime and peacetime episodes and among the latter. Nonetheless, it is important to note that over the past fifty years as a whole inflation became a grave problem not because it was unusually high during expansions but because, unlike earlier times, it was only slowed, not reversed, during contractions. The booms have not grown more inflationary, but the deflationary slumps have disappeared. Indeed, the average percentage increase per year in wholesale prices is 1.8 for the ten recessions of 1937–82, substantially higher than the 1.2 figure for the entire 193-year period covered in table 9.2.

In his introductory chapter to Thorp's *Business Annals* (1926, 65–66), Mitchell observed that the ratios of "prosperous" to "depressed" years have been systematically higher in periods of rising trends in wholesale prices than in periods of declining trends. For the United States and England, the former ratios averaged 2.7 and 2.3, the latter 0.8 and 0.6, respectively. Twenty years later, armed with better and longer chronologies, Burns and Mitchell confirmed the hypothesis that long swings in prices were associated with the relative length of business cycle expansions and contractions (1946, 437–38, 538). The results based on their data for Great Britain, France, and Germany are presented in table 9.3, sections B, C, and D. Section A shows more detailed findings for the United States, based on longer and updated records (see Moore 1983a, chap. 15).

---

4. The monthly index of wholesale prices (Warren/Pearson, 1854–91, and Bureau of Labor Statistics, 1891–1933) rose in thirteen out of twenty expansions and fell in seventeen out of twenty contractions. Snyder's monthly index of the general price level, covering a broad assortment of prices (1861–1933), rose in fifteen out of eighteen expansions and fell in thirteen out of nineteen contractions. See Burns and Mitchell 1946, 98–101. For confirming detailed evidence on the behavior of wholesale prices since 1891, see Cagan 1975, 56–57.

Table 9.2   Long-Term Trends and Average Cyclical Changes in Prices, United States, 1789–1982

Trend in Wholesale Prices[a]			First and Last Year Standings		First to Last Year Change (%/year)		Average % Change in WPI (annual rate)[f]	
Direction (1)	Dates (2)	Number of Years (3)	WPI[b] (1967 = 100) (4)	CPI[c] (1967 = 100) (5)	WPI[d] (6)	CPI[e] (7)	Business Cycle Expansions (8)	Business Cycle Contractions (9)
Rising	1789–1814	25	30–64	30–63	3.1	3.0		
Falling	1814–43	29	64–26	63–28	−3.1	−2.8		
Rising	1843–64	21	26–68	28–47	4.7	2.5		
Falling	1864–96	32	68–24	47–25	−3.2	−2.0	0.4	−2.3
Rising	1896–1920	24	24–80	25–60	5.1	3.7	9.7	−1.6
Falling	1920–32	12	80–34	60–41	−6.9	−3.1	2.1	−13.7
Rising	1932–82	50	34–299	41–289	4.4	4.0	6.5	1.8
Total or average		193			1.2	1.2		

[a]The periods of rising and falling trends in wholesale prices agree with those designated by Burns and Mitchell 1946, 432, for 1789–1932.

[b]WPI = wholesale price index. U.S. Bureau of Labor Statistics index, 1896–1982; Warren/Pearson index, 1789–1894 (spliced to the BLS index at 1890).

[c]CPI = consumer price index. Estimated by the BLS by splicing several indexes together, namely: 1800–1851, index of prices paid by Vermont farmers for family living; 1851–90, consumer price index by Ethel D. Hoover; 1890–1912, cost of living index by Albert Rees; 1913–present, BLS. See *Handbook of Labor Statistics* (1971), 253). We estimate the 1789 figure by splicing the Warren/Pearson wholesale price index to the Vermont price index at 1814 (see *Historical Statistics of the United States*, U.S. Department of Commerce 1975, 201–2). The figures for these early years are rough approximations only.

[d]Based on entries in col. 4.

[e]Based on entries in col. 5.

[f]Rates of change are computed between three-month average levels centered on business cycle peaks and troughs as dated in the NBER monthly reference chronology.

Table 9.3   Trends in Wholesale Prices and the Relative Duration of Business Cycle Expansions and Contractions, 1790–1982

Trend in Prices (direction and dates)[a]	Business Cycle Expansions (E)[b]			Business Cycle Contractions (C)[b]			Ratios (E/C)	
		Duration in Months			Duration in Months		Average	Total
	Number (1)	Average (2)	Total (3)	Number (4)	Average (5)	Total (6)	(2)/(5) (7)	(3)/(6) (8)
A. United States								
Rising								
1789–1814	5	42	210	4	22	90	1.9	2.3
1843–64[c]	6 (5)	32 (30)	194 (148)	5	15	74	2.1 (2.0)	2.6 (2.0)
1896–1920[c]	7 (6)	23 (20)	163 (119)	6	18	108	1.3 (1.1)	1.5 (1.1)
1932–82[c]	10 (7)	49 (37)	487 (256)	10	11	109	4.5 (3.4)	4.5 (2.3)
Total or average	28 (23)	36 (32)	1,054 (733)	25	16	381	2.2 (2.0)	2.8 (1.9)
Falling								
1814–43	6	27	162	7	27	186	1.0	0.9
1864–96	7	25	175	8	26	211	1.0	0.8
1920–32	3	23	70	4	22	88	1.0	0.8
Total or average	16	25	407	19	25	485	1.0	0.8

	B. Great Britain[d]							
Rising								
1854–73, 1896–1920	10	38	381	8	17	133	2.2	2.9
Falling								
1873–96, 1920–33	5	30	152	7	38	266	0.8	0.6
	C. France[d]							
Rising								
1865–73, 1896–1926	11	31	337	9	15	137	2.1	2.5
Falling								
1873–96, 1926–35	4	30	121	6	34	204	0.9	0.6
	D. Germany[d]							
Rising								
1895–1923	6	40	240	6	18	105	2.2	2.3
Falling								
1923–33	4	32	129	4	42	168	0.8	0.8

[a]Through 1932 based on Burns and Mitchell 1946, 432. Also see table 9.2 for the United States. For 1932–82, see Moore 1983 a, 240.

[b]The NBER monthly business cycle chronologies are used. From 1789 to 1843 the United States dates are based on Thorp 1926, 94, and Mitchell 1927, 444–45, with years of "revival" and "prosperity" classified as expansion, and "recession" and "depression" classified as contraction.

[c]Entries in parentheses exclude wartime expansions (Civil War, World Wars I and II, Korean War, and Vietnam War).

[d]Based on Burns and Mitchell 1946, 437.

In each period of rising trend in prices, expansions lasted on the average much longer than contractions, in most instances more than twice as long. In each period of falling trend in prices, expansions tended to be either about as long as contractions (this is so for the United States) or considerably shorter (for the other countries). These contrasts are both regular and large (table 9.3, cols. 2, 5, and 7).

In addition, the relative frequency of expansions has been greater in the long upswings of prices, that of contractions in the long downswings (cf. cols. 1 and 4). Hence the total phase durations and their ratios add further emphasis to the showing of the corresponding statistics for the average phase durations (cols. 3, 6, and 8).

Prices have risen strongly in wartime expansions, but the relationship documented above does not rely mainly on this fact. When the five major wars of United States history are excluded (as in lines 2–5 of the table), the contrast between the periods of upward and downward price trends is not much diminished.

How should the association between the price trends and the relative duration of business cycle phases be interpreted? With prices in the short run being less than fully flexible, fluctuations in aggregate demand, whatever their causes, will be met in part by output movements, in part by price adjustments. As a result, cyclical changes in output and prices will tend to be positively correlated. Beyond that, actual and expected price-level rises may temporarily stimulate economic activity if they are perceived as favorable movements in relative prices and profits, and analogously price-level declines may be discouraging if taken as signals of adverse changes in the same variables. But these can only be very short-lived effects insofar as they depend on misperceptions of general for relative price movements owing to information lags. Propagation mechanisms that may amplify and prolong the consequences of such errors have been suggested, however, and views on the matter are still divided, as reflected in the recent debates on the equilibrium models of business cycles (Zarnowitz 1984). But few have argued that *long-run trends* in the level of prices have clear and lasting effects on real activity or that secular inflation is necessary for economic growth. There is essential agreement that the long price movements reflect mainly trends in money and credit creation that have no definite, permanent effects on the evolution of the economy in real terms.

Indeed, there appears to be no association between the *rate* of inflation during each business cycle and the relative length of expansion versus contraction. The expansion/contraction ratios for the two cycles between 1953 and 1960 (3.9 and 3.0) were not unlike the ratio for the 1973–80 cycle (3.6), but inflation averaged a little over 1% per year in 1953–60 and 9% per year in 1973–80. GNP in constant dollars advanced at similar average annual rates in the two periods (2.6% and 2.8%), and unemployment increased from 4.9% in 1953–60 to 6.6% in 1973–80. As is well known, growth in the supply of money and credit accelerated sharply in the intervening twenty years; this resulted in more inflation and higher interest rates without stimulating the economy and reducing unemployment.

Prices tend to move up briskly when expansions gather steam, particularly in the boom phases at high levels of capital and labor utilization; they often used to decline and now typically rise more slowly in business contractions, particularly long slumps. This reflects both the cyclical fluctuations in aggregate demand and the typical reactions of businessmen. In a recession costs are cut, profit margins are pared, and discounts are given to move heavy inventories or prevent their costly accumulation. Failures increase, and going out of business sales at low prices multiply as well. Wages rise more slowly and are reduced here and there under the pressure of increased layoffs and unemployment. Costly overtime work is cut back or eliminated. Consumers become more economical and cautious, especially about borrowing and spending on durable goods. All of this works in the direction of lower prices or at least lower inflation rates. Thus it is not surprising that the trends are toward less inflation (or more deflation) in periods during which business contractions are relatively long and frequent and that the converse applies to periods dominated by expansions (see also Moore 1983a, chaps. 14 and 15).

Thus it is not the long inflations that should be credited with shortening recessions and lengthening expansions; rather, the opposite chain of influence deserves to be considered, in combination with the multiplicity of factors that would historically account for the shifts in the relative duration of business cycle phases. These include money and credit trends and financial innovations; changes in the structure of production, employment, and markets; changes in economic policies, institutions, and regulations; and major external shocks such as wars, financial crises, large failures, explosions and collapses of basic commodity prices, and gold discoveries. To apportion these influences to the observed shifts in the nature of business cycles would surely be an important but massive research undertaking that cannot be attempted here.

9.5 The Reduced Severity of Recessions since World War II

The limitations of the available time series data make it difficult to measure the amplitude of business cycles, particularly over long historical periods for which there are few monthly or quarterly statistics as comprehensive as such current indicators as real GNP, personal income, manufacturing and trade sales, and employment. To compare the size of recent expansions and contractions with those of the more distant past, about the best we can do is to use indexes of business activity or production and nonagricultural employment (table 9.4).

These comparisons are inevitably crude because of compositional shifts in the available measures of business activity and employment.[5] In particular, factory or manufacturing employment (used before 1929) is typically more variable over the business cycle than total nonagricultural employment, which includes a large and rising share of the relatively stable services (see next section). But such differences in the data probably account only in part for the large contrasts observed between the average percentage amplitudes in table 9.4. These measures are much smaller for 1945–82 than for 1912–45 or 1914–45. The cyclical movements in business activity and employment were also on the average smaller in 1885–1912 or 1891–1914 than in the period during and between the two world wars, but by much narrower margins.

The ranking of the three subperiods is the same for expansions and contractions, but the relative differences between the average amplitudes are greater for contractions. The exclusion of the wartime cycles does not alter the qualitative findings just summarized (its main consequence is to reduce the average expansion amplitudes for the periods concerned). When the amplitudes of expansions and contractions are added without regard to sign, the results once more confirm the shifts toward smaller movements of production and employment after 1945, for both all cycles and peacetime cycles (cols. 1, 3, and 5).

The cyclical movements in the series covered were in general less variable in 1945–82 than in the earlier periods, as indicated by the standard deviations of the individual amplitude measures (cols. 2, 4, and 6). This applies strongly and without exception to the comparisons with 1912–45 or 1914–45.

What these measures suggest, then, is that business contractions have been on the average milder in the post–World War II era and also that their depth varied less across the recent cycles than it did in

5. The Axe/Houghton index (used for the 1885–91 cycles) is based on pig iron production, imports, bank clearings outside New York City, and traffic revenue per mile for selected railroads. The Babson index (for 1891–1920) is a base-year weighted aggregate of seasonally adjusted physical volume or constant-dollar series, with coverage expanding from eleven to thirty-three components. It includes manufactures, minerals, agricultural marketings, construction, railway freight ton-miles, electric power and foreign-trade volume, weighted by value added. The Federal Reserve Board index of industrial production (1920–82) initially included about fifty series. Its coverage increased over time to more than two hundred series representing output in manufacturing, mining, and public utilities. The index of factory employment for 1891–1911 is based on data for Massachusetts, New Jersey, and New York (Jerome 1926). The Bureau of Labor Statistics (BLS) index of factory employment (1913–82) is based on a national sample of cooperating national establishments. The BLS series on nonagricultural employment (used after 1933) is based on monthly reports from a very large number of establishments (some 160,000). (For more detail, see Moore 1961a, vol. 2; U.S. Department of Commerce 1977.)

earlier times. These findings parallel those on the shorter and more uniform durations of the recent contractions as reported in section 9.3 above.

The moderation of business cycles, manifest in the relatively brief, mild, and infrequent recessions of the 1950s and 1960s, was clearly an international phenomenon. Extraordinarily long and vigorous expansions occurred in Japan, West Germany, France, and Italy. One presumed reason lies in unique initial conditions. The end of the war found Europe and the Far East economically in stages of unprecedented exhaustion. Yet the war left behind not only the ruins of much of the physical capital of industry and commerce but also huge backlogs of unutilized but skilled human resources and unsatisfied demand. What followed was an era of Great Reconstruction: first a restoration of sound currencies and free markets, then rapid growth of employment, output, investment, and trade. Cyclical setbacks assumed for some time the form of retardations of growth rather than absolute declines. The United States economy, starting after the war from so much higher levels, intact and very strong, grew more slowly than that of Japan and Western Europe (other than the United Kingdom).[6] Here mild contractions continued to recur, although the expansion in the 1960s persisted beyond all previous experience and expectations.

This record suggests the hypothesis that higher rates of real growth, which prevailed in many countries in the first quarter-century after 1945 under conditions favoring capital formation and international trade and development, tend to be associated with less cyclical instability. We shall examine the United States evidence on this point in section 9.9 below.

Another type of partial explanation relies on structural changes that make the contemporary highly developed economies less recession-prone. Trends in the industrial composition of employment illustrate such changes (sect. 9.6). Shifts in the structure of personal income provide another example (sect. 9.8). Here postdepression reforms concerning taxes and transfer payments that act as "built-in stabilizers" have played an important role.[7]

6. For example, the average annual growth rates of real GNP in 1950–69 were 3.9% for the United States, 6.8% for West Germany, and 5.3% for France. Japan's output grew 9.7% per year in 1952–69, Italy's 5.6% per year in 1951–69. The corresponding average for the United Kingdom, 1950–69, was 2.7%. See U.S. Department of Commerce 1973, 99.

7. Similarly, deposit insurance is believed to have strengthened public confidence in the financial system and prevented the runs on banks that were a major feature of the crises and some depressions in the pre–World War II era. On the other hand, there are some new sources of instability in this area, such as recurrent disintermediation, credit controls, and "credit crunches"; financial innovations and fluctuations in the demand for money and credit; and the uncertainties of current moves to relax banking and related regulations.

Table 9.4   Measures of Amplitude of Cyclical Movements in the United States, by Selected Subperiods, 1885–1982

| | Number of Business Cycles (specific cycles) Covered (1) | Percentage Changes Associated with | | | | | |
| | | Expansions[a] | | Contractions[b] | | Business Cycles[c] | |
Period		Mean (2)	SD (3)	Mean (4)	SD (5)	Mean (6)	SD (7)
		Industrial Activity or Production[d]					
All cycles							
1885–1912	8 (8)	+38.6	8.5	−15.0	6.6	53.6	8.7
1912–45	8 (8)	+68.2	61.0	−28.6	14.2	96.8	65.8
1945–82	8 (8)	+35.4	21.1	−10.6	2.9	45.9	19.2
1885–1945	16 (16)	+53.4	44.8	−21.8	12.8	75.2	50.5
1885–1982	24 (24)	+47.4	39.0	−18.1	11.8	65.5	44.5
Peacetime cycles[e]							
1912–45	6 (6)	+49.5	41.0	−27.0	16.1	76.5	44.2
1945–82	6 (6)	+25.7	9.3	−11.4	2.8	37.0	8.4
1885–1945	14 (14)	+43.2	26.8	−20.2	12.7	63.4	30.5
1885–1982	20 (20)	+38.0	24.1	−17.5	11.4	55.5	28.4

Factory or Nonfarm Employment[f]

All cycles							
1891–1914	7 (6)	+22.7	12.0	−10.5	8.4	33.2	11.7
1914–45	7 (7)	+27.5	15.4	−16.5	10.6	43.8	13.0
1945–82	8 (8)	+14.8	9.7	− 3.0	1.3	17.8	9.3
1891–1945	14 (13)	+25.3	13.6	−13.6	9.7	38.9	13.1
1891–1982	22 (21)	+21.3	13.1	− 9.6	9.2	30.8	15.6
Peacetime cycles[e]							
1914–45	5 (5)	+21.9	13.8	−18.5	12.1	40.4	13.4
1945–82	6 (6)	+11.2	6.5	− 3.2	1.4	14.4	6.6
1891–1945	12 (11)	+22.3	12.2	−14.1	10.6	36.5	12.4
1891–1982	18 (17)	+18.4	11.7	−10.3	10.0	28.7	15.1

Source: NBER business cycle files.

[a]Means and standard deviations (SD) of percentage changes measured from the trough month in the series to the peak month.

[b]Means and SD of percentage changes measured from the peak month in the series to the trough month.

[c]Percentage change in each expansion is added to that in the following contraction without regard to signs; the means and standard deviations shown are based on the resulting measures of absolute amplitudes of trough-to-trough cycles. Entries in cols. 2 and 4 add up to those in col. 6 (disregarding signs), except for rounding.

[d]1885–91: Axe/Houghton index of trade and industrial activity; 1891–1920: Babson index of physical volume of business activity; 1920–82: FRB index of industrial production.

[e]Excludes the cycles associated with the Civil War, World Wars I and II, Korean War, and Vietnam War (see table 9.1, note c for details).

[f]1891–1919: Factory employment index, Jerome; 1919–33: Factory employment index, BLS; 1933–82: Employment in nonagricultural establishments, BLS.

There are still other general hypotheses that are by no means incompatible with those noted above. Probably the one most discussed is that discretionary demand management has become more sophisticated and effective in reducing cyclical instability. This is obviously a critical issue but also one very difficult to test. Most observers would likely agree that some successes were scored by United States monetary and fiscal policies in the 1950s and 1960s but that the record was mixed and marked by increasing errors on the inflationary side. The topic will not be pursued here.

9.6   Structural Shifts in Employment and Their Cyclical Effects

The share of United States employment accounted for by agriculture dropped from 48% in 1869 to 21% in 1929 and 4% in 1970. Business cycles have contributed to major swings in food prices, but they have weak effects on the number of persons engaged in, and total output of, farming. Business cycles are to a large extent a product of industrialization. Despite the great importance of the strong downward trend in agricultural employment, we shall concentrate on shifts in the industrial composition of *nonagricultural* employment, for two reasons. (1) In recent times, the changing nature of business cycles has been strongly influenced by these shifts, and much less so by the developments in agriculture, partly because the percentage employed in farming, though still declining, has already reached very low levels. (2) Over the longer run, the huge shift away from agriculture would overshadow the trends we wish to examine.

Table 9.5 shows that in total nonagricultural employment, the combined share accounted for by manufacturing, mining, and construction and by transportation, communications, and public utilities was stable in 1869–99 at about 56% but declined steadily to 48% by 1929. In the five cycles between the peaks of 1929 and 1957, that share fluctuated in the narrow range of 43% to 46%, but in the next five cycles, 1957–81, it fell steadily from 42% to 33%. The gainers included trade, insurance, real estate, personal and business services, and government—all service industries in the broad sense. This sector as a whole employed 44% of all persons engaged in nonagricultural production in 1869, 51% in 1929, and 67% in 1979–81 (cf. cols. 9 and 10 in table 9.5).

In the present context, the importance of this strong trend in the composition of employment rests on the fact that the rising industries have been much less recession-prone than the declining industries. The net result was a substantial reduction in the sensitivity of total employment to cyclical fluctuations in aggregate demand.

Table 9.5 Trends in Industrial Composition of Nonagricultural Employment, Selected Peak Years, 1869–1929, and Business Cycle Averages, 1929–81 (percentage distribution)

| | Most Cyclical Sectors | | | | Least Cyclical Sectors | | | | Totals | |
Year or Period[a]	Mining (1)	Contract Construction (2)	Manufacturing (3)	Transportation, Communication, Public Utilities (4)	Wholesale and Retail Trade (5)	Finance, Insurance, Real Estate (6)	Other Service Industries (7)	Government (Federal, state, local) (8)	Most Cyclical Sectors[b] (9)	Least Cyclical Sectors[c] (10)
1869	2.5	9.5	34.0	9.9	15.1	0.8	21.5	6.8	55.9	44.2
1899	4.0	7.8	31.7	12.2	17.1	1.9	18.9	6.5	55.7	44.4
1929	2.8	6.2	28.5	11.0	21.1	4.2	17.5	8.6	48.5	51.4
1929–37	2.5	5.2	26.1	9.5	21.5	4.5	17.7	12.8	43.3	56.5
1937–44	2.1	4.7	28.7	7.4	19.2	3.5	14.6	19.8	42.9	57.1
1944–48	1.7	4.5	29.4	7.7	18.9	3.3	13.4	21.1	43.3	56.7
1948–53	1.8	6.3	29.9	7.7	20.2	3.8	14.7	15.5	45.7	54.3
1953–57	1.4	6.1	29.6	7.1	19.7	4.2	14.8	16.8	44.2	55.5
1957–60	1.3	6.0	28.2	6.8	20.1	4.4	16.2	16.9	42.3	57.6
1960–69	1.0	5.7	27.4	6.1	19.5	4.6	17.4	18.3	40.2	59.8
1969–73	0.8	5.0	25.7	6.0	20.6	5.0	15.8	21.0	37.5	62.4
1973–79	1.0	4.9	24.5	5.9	18.9	5.4	18.3	21.2	36.3	63.8
1979–81	1.1	4.7	22.1	5.6	22.0	5.6	19.3	19.7	33.4	66.6

Sources and notes: 1869–1929: Kendrick 1961, table A-VII, p. 308. Persons engaged are full-time-equivalent employees and proprietors and unpaid family workers. Coverage: national economy, excluding farm and agricultural services, forestry, and fisheries; government includes armed forces. 1939–69: U.S. Department of Commerce, Bureau of Economic Analysis, 1966 and 1973, part 3, table 4, p. 76. 1969–81: 1978 supplement to, and more recent issues of, *Survey of Current Business* (Department of Commerce). The employment estimates are based on establishment reports for the surveys of the U.S. Department of Labor, Bureau of Labor Statistics.

[a]The business cycle averages are from peak to peak, with peak years given half weight.

[b]Sum of corresponding entries in cols. 1–4.

[c]Sum of corresponding entries in cols. 5–8.

Table 9.6 provides the evidence. The average drop in employment during the recessions of 1948–82 varied from 10% per year for durable manufactures to 4–5% for the other sensitive industries: nondurable manufactures, mining, construction, and transportation, and so on. In trade, the declines averaged less than 1%, and in services, finance, and government, employment actually increased by about 2%, so these industries have been most resistant to cyclical declines (col. 3).

When the first four post–World War II contractions (1948–60) are separated from the last four (1970–82), some shifts in detail are observed, but the same division holds between the relatively recession-prone and recession-proof industries (cols. 1 and 2). Indeed, employment in most of the latter decreased much less or increased much more during the recessions of 1970–82 than during those of 1948–60.

If the 1959 distribution of employment among the nine major industries had prevailed in the four recessions of 1948–60, the average reduction in nonagricultural employment (other things equal) would have been 2.5%. For 1970–82 the corresponding estimate is 2%; for all eight contractions 1948–82 it is 2.3%. With the 1969 distribution, the reductions would have been 2.3%, 1.8%, and 2.0% for 1948–60, 1970–82, and 1948–82, respectively. With the 1982 distributions, the estimates are 1.7%, 1.0%, and 1.3%.

Between 1929 and 1959 shifts of this type were probably much less important, as table 9.5 suggests. Now we see that they had significant effects between 1959 and 1969 and much stronger effects between 1969 and 1982. Will they endure as a source of employment stabilization in the future? Ten years ago the United States Bureau of Labor Statistics (BLS) made projections to 1985 that assumed that the share of government and private service industries would continue to increase. Their most recent projections to 1995, however, imply a cessation (but not a reversal) of the overall shift toward the more recession-proof industries (table 9.6, col. 7). The rise in personal and business services is expected to be offset by a relative decline in government employment.

The expansion of the share of government in the economy persisted so long that even many who deplore this development regard it as nearly inevitable (''Wagner's law''). Yet it is not a natural, irreversible tendency, and forces opposed to it may be getting stronger.

The demand for services in general is often hypothesized to be more income elastic than the demand for goods, but Fuchs (1968, 3–5) noted that the proportion of services in total output was the same in 1965 as in 1929. He suggested that the shift of employment from industry to service is explained largely by the higher labor requirements in the latter sector. Output per worker grew much more slowly in the production of services than in the production of goods.[8] But real output of services, and therefore productivity, is difficult to measure and often poorly estimated. The notion of a continuing shift into less productive industries and occupations seems worrisome and hard to reconcile with competitive markets. In the current controversy on new industrial policies, proponents urge a government-supported "reindustrialization" drive that, they claim, would make the United States economy more productive and more competitive internationally. If this reverses the trend described above, however, the consequences for cyclical stability may offset some of the benefits.

9.7 Trends and Cyclical Changes in Unemployment and Labor Force Participation

Although the risk of losing a job has been reduced by the shift in the industrial composition of employment, the unemployment rate has fluctuated around a rising trend since the late 1960s. In this period shifts of product demand and derived labor demand between specific markets, industries, and occupations were accelerated by several developments, notably the intensification, fading, and end of the Vietnam War; the oil price increases; the swift spread of new products and technologies (computerization); and the decline of some old industries such as steel, prompted in part by increasing competition from imports. The unusually large intersectoral shifts contributed to the increases in unemployment (Lilien 1982). In addition, other noncyclical factors probably operated in the same direction. The composition of the labor force shifted toward greater participation by women and teenagers, groups with relatively high rates of labor market turnover and unemployment. Higher unemployment benefits and wider coverage have probably added to the average time spent in job search and hence to the average duration and rate of unemployment. At the same time, the percentage of the working-age population employed has risen, reaching a peacetime record high in 1979.

In the recession of 1981–82, the *highest* attained rate of unemployment was 10.8%, exceeded only by the maximum rate reached during the major depressions of 1920–21 (not much higher) and 1929–33 and 1937–38 (which were extraordinarily high). On the other hand, the *increase* in the unemployment rate in 1981–82 was not particularly

8. Thus the average annual rates of change in output per worker were 2.2% in industry and 1.1% in service (3.4% in agriculture). The classification here is much the same as in table 9.6, but industry includes government enterprise (service always includes general government). The corresponding statistics for 1959–82 are industry 1.9% and service 0.9% (based on BLS employment and Bureau of Economic Analysis [BEA] output data).

Table 9.6   Estimated Effects of Shifts in Industrial Composition on Cyclical Stability of Nonagricultural Employment, 1948–95

	Average Percentage Change in Number Employed[a]			Percentage of Nonagricultural Employment[b] Accounted for			
	Four Recessions, 1948–60 (1)	Four Recessions, 1970–82 (2)	Eight Recessions, 1948–82 (3)	1959 (4)	1969 (5)	1982 (6)	1995[c] (7)
Industries declining most in recessions							
Durables manufactures	−11.0	−10.0	−10.5	16.0	15.8	11.6	11.8
Contract construction	−2.4	−7.2	−5.0	6.4	5.7	5.6	6.4
Mining	−11.0	−1.4	−4.8	1.0	0.6	0.7	0.7
Nondurables manufactures	−3.3	−5.2	−4.2	12.5	11.0	8.1	7.3
Transportation, communication, public utilities	−5.4	−1.8	−3.6	7.3	6.1	5.6	5.3
All of the above	−6.8	−6.8	−6.8	43.2	39.2	31.6	31.5
Industries declining least in recessions							
Wholesale and retail trade	−1.2	−0.1	−0.7	22.2	21.8	23.0	23.1
Personal and business services	1.2	3.0	2.1	16.2	18.0	23.1	25.3

Finance, insurance, real estate	2.1	1.7	1.9	4.9	5.1	6.1	6.2
Government	1.7	2.0	1.8	13.5	15.9	16.1	13.9
All of the above	0.4	1.5	1.0	56.8	60.8	68.3	68.5
Total nonfarm employment							
Actual	−3.2	−1.6	−2.4	100.0	100.0	100.0	100.0
Estimated, using the industry composition of							
1959 (col. 4)	−2.5	−2.0	−2.3				
1969 (col. 5)	−2.3	−1.8	−2.0				
1982 (col. 6)	−1.7	−1.0	−1.3				
1995 (col. 7)	−1.7	−1.0	−1.4				

[a]The percentage changes in employment during recessions are computed from three-month standings of seasonally adjusted data centered on business cycle peak and trough months. Simple averages are used; expressing the figures on a per year basis would not alter the results significantly. (The average durations of the recessions were: 1948–60, ten months; 1970–82, twelve months; 1948–82, eleven months.) The measures are based on data from the establishment survey (jobs) of the U.S. Department of Labor, Bureau of Labor Statistics.

[b]The data used to compute these distributions are based on the establishment survey but include also self-employed and unpaid family workers (but not paid household employees). The total number of jobs represented in the distributions are (in thousands): 1959, 59,640; 1969, 76,584; 1982, 97,865; and 1955 (projected) 123,667. See Personick 1983, table 2, p.26. The "moderate growth projection" for 1995 assumes average annual growth rates of employment of 1.8% from 1982 to 1990 and 1.5% from 1990 to 1995.

[c]Projected by the U.S Bureau of Labor Statistics.

large. Jobless rates in recent contractions were generally much higher than in previous contractions of comparable size, 1923–24 and 1926–27. This can be seen clearly in table 9.7, which compares the duration, depth, and diffusion of United States business cycle contractions since 1920, using measures of production, employment, and unemployment.

The measures are highly but far from perfectly correlated (see the matrix of the correlation coefficients in table 9.7). Of course, unemployment changes and levels are inversely associated with the declines in real GNP, industrial production, and nonfarm employment. The measures of depth or amplitude (cols. 2–6) are most closely related to each other, but the correlations involving duration and diffusion (cols. 1 and 7) are also significant.

Comparisons of these and other statistics suggest that four mild recessions occurred during the sixty-two years covered in the table, one in the 1920s (1926–27), and three since 1960 (1960–61, 1969–70, and 1980). There were six sharp recessions, all but one (1923–24) in the post–World War II period (1948–49, 1953–54, 1957–58, 1973–75, and 1981–82). The three major depressions go back to 1920–21 and the 1930s: the "Great Depression" of 1929–33 was in many respects unique and was by far the most severe according to all measures. The 1945 recession was also quite particular because of its timing (end of World War II) and nature (transition back to peacetime production). It was brief and mild in terms of unemployment, sharp in terms of the decline in industrial production.

The ranks in table 9.7, column 8, based on the averages of the ranks of the entries in each of the columns 1–7, agree with the classification above. The only ambiguity refers to the sui generis 1945 reconversion episode.

An important caveat should be entered at this point, namely, that there is no way to construct a really satisfactory single measure of the severity of recessions. Cyclical movements are complex and differentiated in terms of duration, diffusion, and depth. Some are relatively short but large and pervasive, such as the business contraction of 1937–38; others are of similar length but small and less widely spread, such as the recessions of 1960–61 and 1970. The use of average ranks is a crude approximation procedure, which is further aggravated by the gaps in the data. Nevertheless, the results appear to be sensible in that they agree with much broader evidence from historical and statistical studies. We have experimented with other data without finding any good reasons to alter our conclusions.[9]

9. In particular, attempts to close the gaps in ranks run into problems of comparability. The declines in factory employment (BLS) rank the contractions of 1920–21, 1923–24, and 1926–27 in agreement with the labels MD, SR, and MR, respectively (they are −31.1%, −13.7%, and −5.3%). But factory employment has larger amplitudes than

Coming back to the unemployment rate, it is the change in, rather than the level of, this variable that deserves most attention as an indicator of relative cyclical performance. The level attained during a recession is influenced in part by the level reached during the preceding expansion—that is, it combines a measure of the weakness of the preceding expansion with the severity of the recession. Moreover, the level is influenced by trends in the age/sex composition of the labor force, as illustrated by the results from a Bureau of Labor Statistics study (table 9.8).[10]

The rise in unemployment rate between 1959 and 1977 would have been much smaller if the age/sex composition of the labor force had remained as it was in 1957 or in 1967. Over the short periods encompassed by recession, however, these demographic changes are much less consequential, hence the *change* in the rate during a recession is affected less by these shifts and more by factors related to the severity of the recession itself.

In addition, it is important to consider the sensitivity of the labor force itself to changing market conditions and the implications this has for the interpretation of the unemployment measures. In a recession, some additional workers enter the labor force to bolster declining family incomes. At the same time some unemployed workers, frustrated in their job search, withdraw from the labor market. Indeed, when the prospects for finding work at good wages appear to be poor, they may not even compensate for the expected search costs, so some would-be new entrants or reentrants will not even commence looking for jobs. Here as elsewhere, then, income and substitution effects can coexist in practice as well as in theory, and the empirical question is which one prevails. The evidence is that the civilian labor force, apart from its dominant upward trend, tends to respond positively to business cycles. That is, the "discouraged workers" effect generally outweighs the "added workers" effect.

The elasticity of the response of the labor force to cyclical changes in the demand for workers is in the aggregate not high, perhaps about 0.2 on the average (Mincer 1966, 88). Much more sensitive are those groups that are typified by relatively weak (but growing) attachment to the labor force, namely women and youth (especially working wives and students). On the other hand, the participation rate of adult men declined fairly steadily from 89% in 1948 to 78% in 1983. Among older

---

total nonagricultural employment. For example, the declines in 1929–33 were −43.0% and −31.6% respectively; in 1937–38, −21.2% and −10.8%. Real GNP also declined strongly between the years 1944 and 1946 (by some 16%), but changes in the composition of output in this period of transition from wartime to peacetime production make it difficult to interpret this development.

10. See Flaim 1979, 16–17.

Table 9.7   Selected Measures of Duration, Depth, and Diffusion of Business Cycle Contractions, 1920–82

Monthly Business Cycle Dates: Peak–Trough[a]	Duration[b] (months) (1)	Percentage Decline[c]			Unemployment Rate		Employment Diffusion (% of industries declining)[f] (7)	Severity Ranking[g] (8)
		Real GNP (2)	Industrial Production (3)	Nonfarm Employment (4)	Increase[d] (5)	Maximum[e] (6)		
1/1920–7/1921	18	−8.7	−32.4	−10.5	+10.3	11.9	97	13
5/1923–7/1924	14	−4.1	−17.9	−2.2	+2.6	5.5	94	10
10/1926–11/1927	13	−2.0	−7.0	−0.4	+2.4	4.4	71	3
8/1929–3/1933	43	−32.6	−53.4	−31.6	+21.7	24.9	100	14
5/1937–6/1938	13	−18.2	−32.4	−10.8	+9.0	20.0	97	12
2/1945–10/1945	8	n.a.	−38.3	−10.1	+3.4	4.3	n.a.	6
11/1948–10/1949	11	−1.5	−10.1	−5.2	+4.5	7.9	90	8
7/1953–5/1954	10	−3.2	−9.4	−3.5	+3.6	6.1	87	5
8/1957–4/1958	8	−3.3	−13.5	−4.3	+3.8	7.5	88	7
4/1960–2/1961	10	−1.2	−8.6	−2.2	+2.1	7.1	80	3
12/1969–11/1970	11	−1.0	−6.8	−1.5	+2.7	6.1	80	3
11/1973–3/1975	16	−4.9	−15.3	−2.9	+4.4	9.0	88	11
1/1980–7/1980	6	−2.5	−8.6	−1.4	+2.1	7.8	77	1
7/1981–11/1982	16	−3.0	−12.3	−3.1	+3.6	10.8	81	9
Averages								
Three major depressions	25	−19.8	−39.4	−17.6	+13.7	18.9	98	12–14
Six severe recessions	12	−3.3	−13.1	−3.5	+3.8	7.8	88	5–11[h]
Four mild recessions	10	−1.7	−7.8	−1.7	+2.3	6.4	77	1–3
Fourteen contractions	14	−6.6	−19.0	−6.4	+5.4	9.5	87	1–14

Correlations[i]

	(1)	(2)	(3)	(4)	(5)	(6)	(7)
Duration (1)	1.00						
Real GNP (2)	.87	1.00					
Industrial production (3)	.70	.95	1.00				
Nonfarm employment (4)	.86	.96	.91	1.00			
Unemployment increase (5)	.91	.95	.84	.96	1.00		
Unemployment maximum (6)	.78	.95	.72	.83	.90	1.00	
Employment diffusion (7)	.67	.68	.80	.69	.71	.67	1.00

[a]The monthly reference dates are determined by the National Bureau of Economic Research.

[b]Period from peak to trough according to the dates listed to the left.

[c]Percentage change from the peak month or quarter in the series to its trough month or quarter. Real (constant dollar) GNP is quarterly; the other series are monthly.

[d]From the lowest month to the highest, in percentage points.

[e]Highest figure reached during the upswing in unemployment.

[f]Before 1948 based on cyclical changes in employment in 41 industries. Since 1948 based on changes in employment over six months, centered on the fourth month of the span: 1948–59, 30 nonagricultural industries; 1960–71, 172 industries; 1972–82, 186 industries.

[g]Based on averages of the ranks of entries in cols. 1–7. Rank 1 denotes the mildest, rank 14 the most severe contraction.

[h]Excluding rank 6, the 1945 contraction. See text.

[i]Correlations across cols. 1–7, as indicated in the column and row headings, with signs disregarded.

Table 9.8   The Shifting Demographic Structure of Unemployment, 1959–77

Year	Unemployment Rate (1)	Unemployment Rate as Estimated from Constant Age/Sex Distribution of Labor Force	
		1957 Weights (2)	1967 Weights (3)
1959	5.5	5.4	5.8
1969	3.5	3.1	3.4
1973	4.8	4.1	4.5
1977	7.0	6.0	6.7

men, age forty-five to sixty-four, earlier retirement became financially more attractive and increasingly frequent in the 1960s, and the downward movement in labor force participation accelerated in the 1970s (e.g., it was 92% in 1960, 90% in 1968, and 86% in 1984; see Bednarzik and Klein 1977, 8).

It has been suggested that, when combined, all these shifts in composition "imply an over-all trend toward an increasingly sensitive, variable, and flexible labor force" (Mincer 1967, 17). As the labor force responsiveness of a group rises, the cyclical amplitude and conformity of its measured unemployment rate decline. Entries and reentries become more frequent during expansions, when search costs are low and job conditions favorable. Entry rates decline and withdrawals rise when business is sluggish, reducing the labor force. Hence the change in unemployment may understate the true loss of potential employment and output. According to some indirect estimates, based on regressions of the labor force on cyclical indicators such as the employment/population ratios, the "hidden unemployment" was large indeed under relatively adverse labor market conditions (several million people in the early 1960s). But the estimates indicate a heavy concentration of this phenomenon in the categories of "secondary" workers who spend a relatively high proportion of time outside the labor force. Many of these people make their decisions to enter or withdraw in reaction to changes in labor demand as well as in supply and other relevant factors. Still, to some extent the labor force variation also reflects the tendency for discouraged workers to disappear in business expansions and reappear in contractions (Mincer 1966, 100–105; 1967, 16–20).[11]

The percentage of the working-age population employed is affected very differently by these factors than is the unemployment rate. In

11. Over longer periods, labor force growth may respond directly to favorable economic conditions. Using the data in the form of changes in percentage points per decade, Easterlin demonstrates that the contribution to labor force growth of changes in net migration and participation rate is inversely associated with the unemployment rate. For 1880–1965, the correlation is −.83 (Easterlin 1968, 151–53, 257).

1983, for example, almost exactly the same percentage of the working-age population (sixteen years and over) was employed as in 1973, namely 58.3%. (In these calculations, employment includes resident armed forces.) Other data, such as real personal income per capita or real compensation per hour, indicate that both years were about equally prosperous, but the unemployment rate in 1983 was nearly twice as high as in 1973, 9.5% compared with 4.8%. If calculated as a percentage of the working-age population instead of the labor force, unemployment was more than twice as high, 6.1% compared with 2.9%. What happened was that a massive shift occurred in the population's disposition to seek jobs. This pushed up the unemployment rate but did not signify any great change in the availability of jobs per capita, which is measured by the employment percentage. Since the two measures do not always give the same message regarding employment conditions, it is important to consider both in evaluating the severity of recessions.

9.8   Changing Sources of Personal Income and the Business Cycle

According to annual estimates by Creamer (1956, 126), personal income in constant dollars fell during five business contractions and rose during three in the period 1910–38. The average of these changes was −5.0%. Corresponding annual measures for the eight business contractions of 1948–82, based on the present Department of Commerce data, show a reverse picture: three declines and five rises, averaging +0.7%. Hence, real income has become far more stable during business cycles since World War II than before.

The composition of personal income by major types and sources shows that several long-term shifts have contributed to this increasing stability (tables 9.9 and 9.10). Wage and salary disbursements of government rose most of the time, accounting for 5% to 6% of total income in the business cycle peak years 1913 and 1929 but more than twice as much—11% to 14%—in the peak years of 1953–81. Transfer payments rose most strongly and persistently, from less than 1% of the total in 1929 and before to 19% in 1981. The relative decline in farmers' income, from 10% in 1913 to 1% in 1981, was slow in the first half of the period covered, rapid in the second half. Nonfarm proprietors' income also fell decisively in relative terms, from 15% to 4%. Wages and salaries in the private sector, by far the largest component of personal income, increased from 48% in 1913 to 58% in 1953, then fell back again to 48% in 1981.

Of the types of property income, the shares of two show downward trends: dividends (6%–7% in 1913–17, 2%–4% thereafter) and, particularly, rent (from 11% down to 1% between 1913 and 1981). The proportion of interest income fluctuated roughly between 3% and 6% in

Table 9.9   Personal Income Distribution by Major Type, Selected Business Cycle Peak Years, 1913–81

	Percentage of Total Personal Income Accounted for							
Type of Income	1913 (1)	1929 (2)	1937 (3)	1948 (4)	1953 (5)	1960 (6)	1969 (7)	1981 (8)
	Categories Declining Most in Recessions							
Wages and salaries, private	48.0	54.9	53.5	55.8	58.2	54.2	52.5	48.0
Farm proprietors' income	10.1	6.9	7.9	8.6	4.5	2.8	3.0	1.0
Nonfarm proprietors' income	15.2	10.1	9.3	10.8	9.6	8.6	5.5	4.0
All of the above	73.3	71.9	70.7	75.2	72.3	65.8	61.0	53.0
	Categories Declining Least in Recessions							
Wages and salaries, government	4.6	5.8	10.2	8.6	11.5	11.9	13.5	11.2
Other labor income and transfer payments	0.9	1.7	3.4	6.4	6.4	9.7	12.1	18.9
Dividends	6.0	7.0	6.6	3.5	3.3	3.1	2.9	2.5
Interest	4.0	6.4	5.0	2.5	2.7	6.1	7.8	13.1
Net rent	11.2	7.0	4.3	3.7	3.8	3.5	2.5	1.3
All of the above	26.7	27.9	29.5	24.7	27.7	34.3	38.8	47.0

Source: 1913–53: Creamer 1956, pp. xxix, 9, 116–23; 1960–81: computed by Cullity 1983, tables 1 and 2, from personal income statistics of the U.S. Department of Commerce, Bureau of Economic Analysis. See also table 9.10 below.

the peak years 1913–53 but grew from 6% in 1960 to 8% in 1969, then rose rapidly to 13% in 1981 during the period of high inflation.

Table 9.10 classifies these types of income into two groups: those that have been relatively recession-proof and those that have been recession-prone. In general, the categories whose shares increased have been relatively recession-proof (interest, rental income) or even countercyclical (transfers), whereas the categories whose shares drifted mostly downward have been generally recession-prone (proprietors' incomes and wages of private workers). Income of government employees and transfer payments did not decline even in the severe depression of 1937–38 and neither did rent, while the downturn in interest income was moderate. Although dividends fell sharply in 1937–38, they often resisted the milder recessions in the post–World War II period (but note their drop in 1981–82). Labor income in the private sector typically declined at least moderately in recessions, mainly owing to wages. It should be noted that the measures for 1937–38 and 1948–49 (cols. 1 and 2) are based on data in current dollars, the measures for the 1948–80 averages and 1981–82 (cols. 3 and 4) on data in constant dollars. It was, of course, necessary to adjust the recent figures for the effects of high inflation that masked the cyclicality of the nominal income series during most of the post–World War II era.

Suppose the cyclical changes in each of the sources of personal income were as observed and taken to be independent of the shifts in the distribution of the aggregate. How would the changes in the composition of income by sources influence the movements of total income under this assumption? The answer given by the estimates in the bottom section of table 9.10 is "strongly." For example, had the relative importance of the main categories of income been the same in 1981 as in 1948, the reweighted decline of real personal income during the 1981–82 recession would have been 4.3% instead of the actual 0.7% (col. 4). Using the 1948 weights would have doubled the relative amplitude of the average decline in real personal income in the seven recessions of 1948–80, from the observed 1.1% to the estimated 2.3% (col. 3). Conversely, the 1937–38 decline, which was actually 7.7%, would have been ceteris paribus only 4.1% under the distributional conditions of 1960 and 1.2% under those of 1981 (col. 1)!

To be sure, hypothetical calculations of this type must be interpreted with great caution. The critical assumption that the amplitude of income change for each category is independent of the compositional shifts could be undermined by various factors. For example, transfer incomes may support consumption, but their strong upward trend, with its implication of rising tax burdens, may at some point damage business confidence and investment. The rising share of interest income reflects increasing and high interest rates, which again can have strong adverse

Table 9.10   **Estimated Effects of Shifts in Types of Income on Cyclical Stability of Total Personal Income, 1937–82**

	Percentage Change during Business Cycle Contractions			
	Current Dollar Incomes		Constant Dollar Incomes	
	1937–38 (1)	1948–49 (2)	Average of Seven Recessions, 1948–80 (3)	1981–82 (4)
Categories declining most in recessions				
Wages and salaries, private	−10.2	−2.2	−3.4	−3.9
Farm proprietors' income	−21.4	−27.7	−13.0	−22.1
Nonfarm proprietors' income	−4.5	−2.3	−4.7	−1.8
All of the above	−10.7	−5.1	−4.1	−4.1
Categories declining least in recessions				
Wages and salaries, government	+11.0	+9.0	+2.1	+1.8
Other labor income and transfer payments	+20.8	+10.5	+12.3	+6.5
Dividends	−31.9	+4.2	−0.5	−13.5
Interest	−2.8	+9.8	+6.2	+3.8
Net rent	+6.5	+2.7	+1.9	−5.8
All of the above	−0.5	+7.9	+5.8	+4.0
Total personal income				
Actual	−7.7	−1.9	−1.1	−0.7
Estimated, using				
1913 weights (table 9.9, col. 1)	−8.3	−2.8	−3.0	−5.5
1937 weights (table 9.9, col. 3)	−7.7	−1.4	−2.3	−4.5
1948 weights (table 9.9, col. 4)	−6.7	−1.9	−2.3	−4.3
1960 weights (table 9.9, col. 6)	−4.1	+0.7	−0.7	−2.4
1981 weights (table 9.9, col. 8)	−1.2	+3.0	+1.4	−0.6

Note: Percentage changes in 1937–38 and 1948–49 based on Creamer 1956, xxix; in 1948–80 and 1981–82 based on Cullity 1983, table 2. Also see text and table 9.9.

effects on government finance, security markets, and, most important, real capital formation by business firms and households. The expansion of government employment, in relative as well as absolute terms, contributes to the taxpayers' burden. And there are still other possible complications that the simple global estimates in table 9.10 neglect: it may be important to separate the effects of changing compensation rates and input volumes and to take account of finer distinctions, for example, the relative importance of durables, nondurables, and services in generating personal income. These qualifications were already made by Creamer and Moore in 1956.

Nevertheless, as projected in that volume nearly thirty years ago, fluctuations in income that accompany business cycles did moderate significantly, and there can be little doubt that the trends in the composition of personal income by major types and sources made a substantial contribution to this development.[12]

9.9 Growth Rates and Variability of Economic Change

Although it is true for the period since 1945 as a whole that contractions have become shorter and milder, there is nonetheless a useful distinction to be made between the first two decades and the next one. In the 1950s and 1960s high long-term growth rates prevailed in the United States economy as well as among its major trading partners. Domestically, high inflation was not yet perceived to be a persistent and grave problem with no easy, apparent solution, and neither was high unemployment so perceived. Looking back, contemporaries had little doubt about the contrast between these economically rather placid and prosperous decades and the turbulent times that followed, dominated by seemingly uncontrollable inflation, more frequent and serious recessions, energy problems, and financial instability.

To put such impressionistic comparisons on firmer ground, table 9.11 divides the United States economic record since 1903 into six periods, each covering from two to four complete business cycles measured from peak to peak. Three of these show average annual growth rates in real GNP (g) varying from 3.4% to 3.9%: 1903–13, 1923–29, and 1948–69. The other three are characterized by considerably lower long-term growth ranging from 2.4% to 2.8% per year: 1913–23, 1929–48, and 1969–81 (col. 7).[13]

To measure relatively high and low economic stability, we use standard deviations of the annual growth rates in real GNP (w). It turns out that variability in growth was generally greater in the slower growth periods (cols. 7 and 8). In addition, the more recent periods in both groups showed less variability than the earlier periods, confirming the point made above regarding the reduced severity of recessions since World War II.[14]

It is also of interest to observe that the proportion of time spent in contraction was 15% in 1948–69 and 24% in 1969–81. Even this last figure is much lower than the corresponding statistics for the earlier

12. For further evidence, particularly concerning the role of government expenditures and transfer payments, see Beck 1980 and Cullity 1983.

13. See Zarnowitz (1981, 476–80) for a discussion of how these periods were selected, references to related literature, and an attempt to push the comparison back to 1882.

14. Both 1913–23 and 1929–48 include large wartime expansions as well as major depressions (with the latter outweighing the former as regards growth effects but all contributing to high variability).

Table 9.11   Average Growth Rates and Variability of Economic Change, Selected Periods, 1903–81

Period[a] (1)	Number of Years Covered[b] (2)	Number of Business Cycles Covered[c] (3)	Number of Months[d] in		Percentage of Time in Contraction[e] (6)	Growth in Real GNP (%)	
			Contraction (4)	Expansion (5)		Average[f] (7)	SD[g] (8)
Periods of Relatively High Growth							
1903–13	10	3	60	64	48.4	3.4	6.1
1923–29	6	2	27	48	36.0	3.5	3.8
1948–69	21	4	39	214	15.4	3.9	2.6
Total	37	9	126	326	27.9	3.7	3.7
Periods of Relatively Low Growth							
1913–23	10	3	48	76	38.7	2.4	8.6
1929–48	19	3	64	167	27.7	2.5	9.4
1969–81	12	3	33	106	23.7	2.8	2.9
Total	41	9	145	349	29.4	2.6	7.2

Source: Kendrick 1961 (GNP in 1958 dollars, 1903–8); U.S. Department of Commerce, Bureau of Economic Analysis (GNP in 1958 dollars and in 1972 dollars, 1909–81). Most of the historical data and measures are taken from the U.S. Department of Commerce, Bureau of Economic Analysis 1973.

[a]For each period listed, the initial and terminal dates are business cycle peak years according to the annual reference chronology of the NBER.

[b]Number of complete years covered.

[c]Number of complete peak-to-peak cycles from the initial to the terminal year.

[d]Count based on the NBER monthly reference chronology.

[e]Entries in col. 4 are divided by the sums of entries in cols. 4 and 5 and multiplied by 100.

[f]Average annual compound growth rate between the initial peak and the terminal peak years, in percent.

[g]Standard deviation of the annual growth rates for all years in the given period (as identified in cols. 1–2).

periods (cf. cols. 4–6). These measures indicate no correspondence between the average growth rates and the relative duration of contractions. Thus in 1903–13 and 1923–29, when growth was relatively high, the percentage of time accounted for by business contractions exceeded that in 1929–48 and 1969–81, periods with lower growth rates.

Strong inflationary trends prevailed in 1913–23 and 1969–81, when monetary aggregates expanded rapidly but real growth was relatively weak. In the other periods, inflation was fairly moderate or absent. Table 9.12 shows the average annual growth rates (%) in real income, the stock of money, nominal income, and the implicit price deflator (g, m, y, and p, respectively.[15] The periods with relatively high real growth (on the left) had on the average lower m, y, and p rates than the periods with lower real growth (on the right).

9.10 Changes in the Cyclical Behavior of Prices

Reference cycle patterns provide a simple and useful device for describing the movements of a series during business cycles. The series is divided into segments, each of which covers one business cycle dated from the initial to the final trough. A pattern consists of nine averages, one for each of the consecutive stages of the cycle. Stages I, V, and IX are three-month periods centered on the initial trough, peak, and terminal trough of a business cycle, respectively. Stages II, III, and IV cover successive thirds of the expansion (trough to peak), and stages VI, VII, and VIII cover similar portions of the contraction (peak to trough). All measures are in "reference cycle relatives," that is, percentages of the average standing of the data during the given business cycle. The procedure retains the intracycle trend but eliminates the

Table 9.12   **Average Annual Growth Rates of Real and Nominal Income, the Money Supply, and the Implicit Deflator**

Years	g	m	y	p	Years	g	m	y	p
1903–13	3.4	6.1	5.4	2.0	1913–23	2.4	8.8	8.2	4.9
1923–29	3.5	4.1	3.4	−0.2	1929–48	2.5	5.3	4.2	2.0
1948–69	3.9	4.7	6.2	2.3	1969–81	2.8	9.7	10.0	7.0
Average	3.7	5.0	5.0	1.4	Average	2.6	7.9	7.5	4.6

15. The measures for 1903–48 are calculated from annual data listed in Friedman and Schwartz 1982, table 4 (following p. 121). They refer to the sum of currency held by the public plus adjusted deposits at all commercial banks; national income or net national product; and the corresponding implicit price deflator. The measures for 1969–82 are based on data on M2, GNP, and IPD as given in the Economic Report of the President, February 1984, 220, 224, and 291.

intercycle trend because the average relative for each cycle is one hundred. Note that reference cycle stages differ in duration, as do the individual business cycles. For certain purposes, therefore, such as comparisons of leads and lags at turning points, measures in fixed calendar-time units may be preferable. But an analysis of the patterns can be very revealing in some contexts. This is so in particular with respect to the identification of any major and persistent changes in broadly defined cyclical movements, which is our concern here.

We have plotted and inspected thirty reference patterns for United States wholesale prices, one for each of the complete business cycles since 1854. The first impression is one of great variability, but a closer analysis helps to explain the main differences and bring out the more persistent traits. The intracycle portions of the longer trends are often strong enough to have pronounced and readily visible effects. Thus in 1854–61 a downward local drift came to dominate the longer upswing in prices, and then between 1864 and 1896 there was a long downswing that, however, flattened temporarily in 1885–91.[16] Accordingly, the seven patterns covering the periods 1854–61, 1867–85, and 1891–97 have clear downward tilts. Between 1896 and 1920 prices tended to move up, with some leveling off in 1910–14. This left an impress upon the several corresponding patterns. The weakness of prices in 1920–32 shows up in the downward-tilted patterns for this period, and their subsequent upward trend in the upward-tilted patterns for the post–1933 cycles.

Major wars had huge effects on the behavior of prices. The patterns for 1861–67 (stages I–IV), 1914–19 (I–VI), and 1945–49 (I–IV) show the surging inflations of the Civil War and World War I and the slower, more suppressed inflation of World War II. The inflations of the Korean War and Vietnam War are much less conspicuous in the patterns for 1949–54 (III–V) and 1961–70 (III–IX). After the Civil War, a strong deflation followed immediately; after World War I, prices first stabilized and then fell sharply in the 1920–21 depression; but no strong downward movements in the price level trailed any of the later wars.

The most important findings are as follows. Virtually all business cycle contractions through 1938 were associated with some declines in prices during at least some of their stages. When the trend was down, these declines would often start during the expansions and last longer, but they would also typically accelerate after the peak stage (V). When the trend was up, the rising segments of the patterns tended to be larger and longer, frequently starting before the trough and extending beyond

16. For the chronology of the "long waves" in prices, see table 9.2. On the shorter "local" trends superimposed on these waves, see Burns and Mitchell 1946, 438–40 with chart 65.

the peak, but the contractions would still witness some significant price-level declines (mainly between stages VI and IX). The only early patterns that show very weak and irregular price movements, in the 1885–91 period, refer to two short and marginal cycles, an interlude of relative stability separating major fluctuations dominated by strong deflationary developments in the early 1880s and 1890s.

The more recent cycles present a sharply contrasting picture. The brief and peculiar end-of-the-war contraction of 1945 was accompanied by essentially flat wholesale prices. This year saw the end of wartime price controls. The last contraction during which prices fell significantly occurred in 1948–49. The Korean expansion saw new partial wage and price controls and had a phase in 1951 during which prices declined considerably, but in the ensuing contraction they merely stabilized after a new bout of wartime inflation. The stability persisted through most of the 1954–57 expansion, too, but prices started rising again moderately late in the 1957–58 contraction and during the short recovery of 1958–60, which alarmed many observers since there was little evidence of excess demand. This ended with the recession of 1960, and several years of relatively stable prices followed. With the intensification of the Vietnam War in the mid-1960s, a new and much more intensive round of inflation began, which the 1970 recession and the 1971 wage and price controls slowed down only a little and for only a short time. After the series of supply shocks in 1973–74 (sharp rises in prices of food, oil, and other raw materials worldwide, termination of United States price controls, and aftereffects of the switch to floating exchange rates), inflation accelerated strongly late in the 1973–75 recession and again in the middle stages of the 1975–80 expansion, partly owing to new supply shocks. It took a protracted period of poor business conditions in the early 1980s (two contractions separated by a weak one-year recovery) to reduce the pace of inflation substantially. As a group, the post–World War II patterns, marked by an absence of any major absolute declines in prices, are strikingly different from any comparably large subset of earlier patterns where deflation associated with business contractions was the rule.

By averaging the individual reference patterns stage by stage over some sufficiently long period, one may hope to bring out the typical features in the cyclical behavior of the variable concerned. The assumption underlying the procedure is that such persistent traits indeed exist; the more valid this premise is, the more useful the method.

The upper panel in figure 9.1 shows five average reference cycle patterns based on the measures for the overall wholesale price series used in figure 9.1. The first pattern, for the nine cycles of 1854–97, reflects weak rises during expansion and strong declines during contraction: the typical behavior in a period of long-run downward trend in prices. The second, for the five cycles of 1897–1914, when the long drift was up, shows a longer and stronger rise and weaker decline. The third, for 1919–38 (five cycles), shows very large and more symmetrical cyclical movements, with a relatively small downward tilt. The average for the nineteen cycles, 1854–1938, omitting the war-related episodes, is a nearly symmetrical, slightly downward-tilted pattern rising between each of the stages I–V and falling between each of the stages V–IX. In clear contrast, the averages for the seven cycles 1949–82 describe a steadily rising pattern, although one whose slope is definitely lower in the contraction segment V–IX than in the expansion segment I–V. In this period the contractions were associated with a lower, but not a negative, rate of inflation. Similar results for the period since 1919 are obtained from an analysis of the index of wholesale prices for industrial commodities only (omitting farm products and foods). The average reference patterns for 1919–38 and 1949–82 closely resemble their counterparts for the all-commodity index.

Cagan (1975, 90) concluded that "The failure of the aggregate index of wholesale prices to decline in the recessions of 1954 and 1958 and then again in 1961, which contrasted with the sharp declines of previous recessions, was a new phenomenon." Our results confirm this observation on the basis of longer series than those used by Cagan (his measures cover the period 1891–1970; ours cover 1854–1982).

It has been suggested that the post-1969 change in the observed behavior was due to the convergence of downward rigidities owing to the increased market power of firms over prices and of labor unions over wages. Whether such developments did in fact occur on a sufficiently large scale has been questioned by some authors but accepted by others (Cagan 1975, 90; DeLong and Summers, this volume, chap. 12). Another hypothesis is that after the Employment Act of 1946 the successive administrations demonstrated their commitment to combating unemployment so that people came to believe that contractions long or severe enough to generate any persistent deflationary movements would be effectively prevented. This explanation, which appears to be generally consistent with the evidence, is closely related to the more recent emphasis on the effect of a credible policy posture on expectations of changes in the price level (Fellner 1980).

It is difficult to measure anticipated rates of inflation, but their role is undoubtedly basic. Cagan compared the average annual rates of change in wholesale prices during the successive expansions and contractions (to be denoted E and C) and computed the differences $C - E$. This procedure amounts to using the preceding expansion rates as (admittedly rough) proxies for the anticipations. In table 9.13 we bring Cagan's results up to date. After 1949, prices ceased declining during contractions: the signs of C change from negative to positive (see cols.

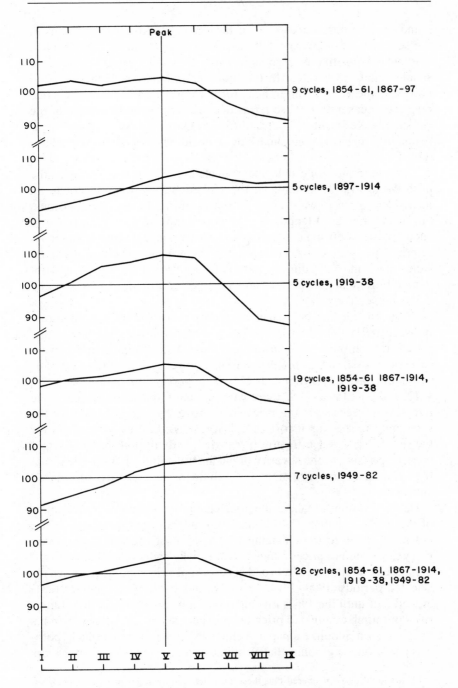

Fig. 9.1   Wholesale prices, all commodities, average reference patterns, 1854–1982. *Source*: Warren/Pearson (1854–90); U.S. Department of Labor, Bureau of Labor Statistics (1890–1982).

3 and 6). The differences $C - E$ have consistently negative signs in the seventeen cycles from 1891 to 1958 (cols. 4 and 7). The C rates, even where positive or zero as in 1945, 1953–54, and 1957–58, were smaller than the E rates. In the four cycles between 1958 and 1980, however, the $C - E$ differences turned positive as well.[17] The price response measured in these terms declined consistently in each of the six successive business cycles 1945–75. Only in 1980–82 did $C - E$ result in a negative sign, marking a decidedly disinflationary phase (col. 7).

The wholesale price data make it clear that the magnitude of the post–World War II inflation in the United States was due not to an intensification of upward price pressures during business expansions, but to the increased length of expansions and the new persistence of such pressures during contractions. The average percentage increases of prices per year were very similar in the prewar and postwar expansions (6.3% and 6.4% during 1891–1945 and 1945–82, respectively) but very different in the prewar and postwar contractions (-6.4% and 3.3%, respectively).

Prices have been very sensitive to the severity of business contractions. In 1891–1945 the wholesale price index fell at an average annual rate of 15% in the five major depressions (MD), 4% in the four severe recessions (SR), and 0.6% in the four mild recessions (MR). The corresponding average differences $C - E$, in percentage points, are -21, -12, and -6. In 1945–82 there were no major depressions, but in the five severe recessions the price index rose 2% per year, and in the three mild recessions it rose 5%. The $C - E$ differential was -6 for the five SR and $+1.6$ for the three MR. Thus in both periods prices were responsive to the severity of business declines, but it is clear that the response to recessions of comparable severity decreased substantially.

Detailed studies of wholesale price changes in the nonwar recessions of the 1920s and 1948–70 (Cagan 1975) indicate that these results are not attributable to the changing composition of the index. However, many raw materials prices retained their usually high cyclical sensitivity.

In a recent analysis of a broad spectrum of price and wage series for selected periods (1900–1914, 1923–29, and 1949–66), Schultze (1981) argued that until the 1960s low inflation "norms" in the nature of inert rules of thumb dominated price-level expectations and behavior. In his comments on Schultze's paper, Fellner (577–81) disputed this hypothesis partly on the grounds that Schultze's sample includes mainly years

---

17. It should be remembered that these measures are averages in percent per year. Taking into account the different durations of expansions and contractions and the lengthening lags in prices, it is still true that some disinflation accompanied or followed each of the recessions concerned.

Table 9.13   Rate of Change of Wholesale Prices over Business Cycles, 1891–1982

Business Cycle[a]	Severity of Contraction[b] (1)	Percent per Year[c]			Averages[d]	Percent per Year[c]		
		Expansions (E) (2)	Contractions (C) (3)	Difference, C − E (4)		Expansions (E) (5)	Contractions (C) (6)	Difference, C − E (7)
1891–93–94	MD	−0.9	−12.4	−11.5	1891–1914 (7)	4.3	−3.2	−7.5
1894–95–97	SR	1.7	−4.5	−6.2	1919–38 (5)	7.0	−13.0	−20.0
1897–99–1900	MR	6.3	5.0	−1.3	1945–61 (4)	4.8	−1.3	−6.0
1900–02–04	MR	4.6	−0.7	−5.3	1961–82 (4)	8.1	7.9	−0.2
1904–07–08	MD	3.7	−4.0	−7.7				
1908–10–12	MR	8.3	−4.0	−12.3	1891–1945			
1912–13–14	SR	6.1	−1.8	−7.9	MD (5)	6.3	−14.7	−21.0
1914–18–19	SR	18.8	−4.1	−22.9	SR (4)	7.8	−3.9	−11.7
1919–20–21	MD	19.9	−33.8	−53.7	MR (4)	5.2	−0.6	−5.8
1921–23–24	SR	4.8	−5.3	−10.1	All cycles (14)	6.3	−6.4	−12.8
1924–26–27	MR	1.6	−2.6	−4.2				
1927–29–33	MD	−0.1	−13.2	−13.1	1945–82			
1933–37–38	MD	9.0	−10.1	−19.1	MD (0)	—	—	−6.0
1938–45–45	n.c.	4.4	1.2	−3.2	SR (5)	8.3	2.3	−6.0
1945–48–49	SR	13.6	−7.1	−20.6	MR (3)	3.4	5.0	1.6
1949–53–54	SR	3.2	0.0	−3.2	All cycles (8)	6.4	3.3	−3.1
1954–57–58	SR	2.3	1.7	−0.6				
1958–60–61	MR	0.1	0.3	0.2	1891–1982			
1961–69–70	MR	1.4	2.6	1.2	MD (5)	6.3	−14.7	−21.0
1970–73–75	SR	8.0	16.4	8.4	SR (9)	8.1	−0.5	−8.5
1975–80–80	MR	8.6	12.1	3.5	MR (7)	4.4	1.8	−2.6
1980–81–82	SR	14.4	0.6	−13.8	All cycles (22)	6.4	−2.9	−9.2

[a]Identified by trough-peak-trough years of the NBER monthly reference cycle chronology.

[b]MD = major depression; SR = severe recession; MR = mild recessions; n.c. = not comparable. For the contractions 1920–82, see also table 9.7.

[c]Computed between average levels of three months surrounding business cycle peaks and troughs. Based on seasonally adjusted data for the index of wholesale (producer) prices, all commodities.

[d]Periods are identified by initial peak and terminal trough cycles. Numbers of cycles covered are given in parentheses.

in which prices had a mild upward trend (in 1923–29 there was a slight downward drift). Had longer and more continuous price series been used, they would have demonstrated more flexible behavior and supported the concept of more "rational" expectations. Indeed, the pre–1920 patterns (see fig. 9.1) seem to us to be broadly consistent with this view.

9.11 Changes in the Cyclical Behavior of Interest Rates

Short-term interest rates historically have exhibited cyclical movements varying from moderate to very large relative to their average levels. During business cycles containing major booms or slumps and affected by financial crises, large monetary disturbances, or wars, fluctuations in rates have often been huge and sudden. Financial markets are particularly sensitive to all types of factors influencing business conditions, so it is well known and not surprising that short rates are typically more volatile than most other important variables. This is well established by an analysis of twenty-seven reference cycle patterns that covers more than 120 years of United States business history.

The patterns for commercial paper rates, 1858–1932, show clear procyclical movements, consistent with the simple notion that the demand for credit tends to increase relative to supply in expansions and decrease in contractions. The single major exception was the long but slow 1933–37 recovery from the worst recorded depression, during which short rates continued to drop sharply. However, the characteristic timing of the rates was predominately lagging, particularly at peaks. Rough coincidences prevailed only at the peaks of 1860–73 and 1923–29. At troughs, the timing was on the average lagging as well but much less consistently so. A few of the patterns (1861–67 and 1888–91 in addition to those related to the depressions of 1920–21 and the 1930s) are quite different from all the others.

The patterns for the three-month treasury bill rate in the seven business cycles 1949–82 have very large amplitudes, which bespeaks heightened sensitivity to cyclical influences.[18] They rise sharply during expansions and fall sharply during contractions, but with much variability in timing. Thus their highest standings are in stages IV (for the 1958–61 cycle), V (1949–54, 1961–70, and 1980–82), VI (1954–58 and 1975–80), and VII (1970–75). Of course in the post–World War II period interest rates generally had rising long-term trends; these were mild in the 1950s and 1960s and strong thereafter, reflecting mainly the course of inflation and the corresponding adjustments of price expectations.

18. Treasury bill rates have become a particularly important and sensitive indicator of money market conditions. Commercial paper rates have somewhat different characteristics than they used to have (Selden 1963), but their reference cycle patterns since 1949 bear a fair family resemblance to the treasury bill rate patterns.

In basis points, the fluctuations in interest rates were very small until the late 1960s, then steadily increased to very large size. It is interesting that the amplitudes of the corresponding patterns do not show a similar trend. That is, relative to their average values in each cycle the movements of bill rates have been about the same in recent cycles as in the 1950s and 1960s, whereas in terms of basis points they were small in the early years when the levels of the rates were low and large in the late years when the levels of the rates were high.

The average reference cycle patterns in figure 9.2 bring out the shifts in amplitude and timing. There is a near symmetry of movement in the diagram for the four earliest cycles covered (1858–79). The averages for the eleven cycles of 1879–1919 show a rise from stage II to VI–VII and a contraction between stages VII and II, that is, lags at both peaks and troughs. The pattern for the five cycles of 1919–38 is strongly downward-tilted, with a rise between stages III and V only (a long lag at troughs). These movements have been large enough to put a strong imprint on the overall averages (compare the patterns for 1919–38 and 1858–1938). In contrast, the diagram for the treasury bill rate in seven cycles, 1949–82, shows a very large rise between stages I and VI and a somewhat smaller decline in the contraction stages VI–IX. The average swing in bill rates since 1949 has been much larger than the average swing in commercial paper rates before 1938.

It is common knowledge that long-term interest rates fluctuate much less than short-term rates; it is perhaps not so well known that they do not conform as well to business cycles. Both properties can be inferred from a comparison of the corresponding reference patterns. In 1900–1914, for example, the only large cyclical movements evident in high-grade industrial bond yields are those associated with the crisis and severe depression of 1907: first a rise in stages III–VII of the 1904–8 cycle, then a decline continuing through most of the recovery from that depression. A somewhat similar sequence occurred in connection with the depression of 1920–21 and the subsequent recovery. The large irregular movements in the great contraction of 1929–33 with a late peak in stage VIII (1931), and the long, first rapid then slow decline throughout the 1933–38 cycle are also notable episodes.

The corporate bond yield patterns for the post–World War II years contain some very large shifts, mostly upward. The timing of these movements has varied widely, with rises occurring between the following stages in each consecutive cycle:

Cycles:	1949–53	1954–58	1958–61	1961–70	1970–75	1975–80	1980–82
Stages:	I–V	I–VI	I–IV	II–VII	III–VII	III–VI	VIII–VI

Consistent with the generally rising trend in yields, lags occurred more frequently at business cycle peaks than at troughs.

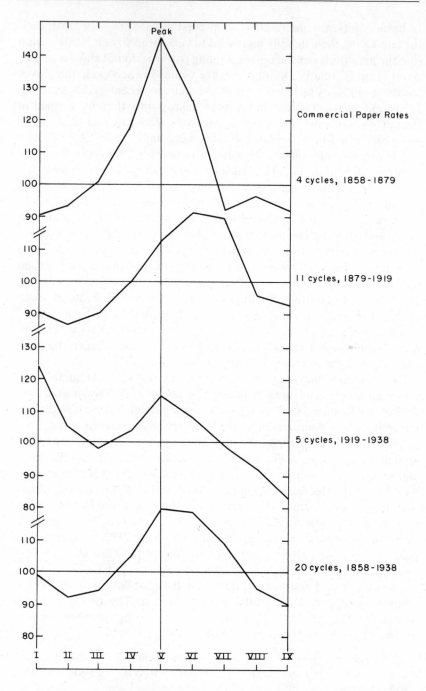

Fig. 9.2   Short-term interest rates, average reference patterns, 1858–
1982. *Source*: commercial paper rates, New York City, Ma-
caulay; treasury bill rate, Board of Governors of the Federal
Reserve System.

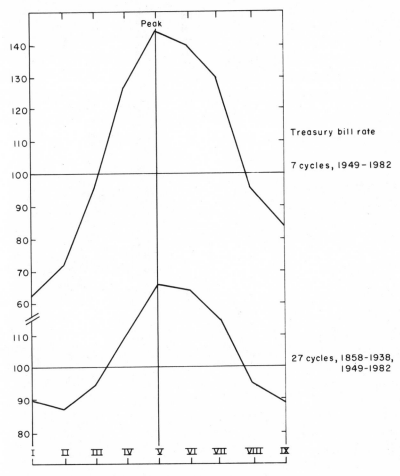

Fig. 9.2   (continued)

The average reference patterns in figure 9.3 provide a bird's-eye view. The overall amplitudes of movement in long rates have increased greatly between 1900–38 and 1954–82, but it is the strong upward trend in the recent period that dominates the average patterns. The intracycle drift tended to be down in the period between the world wars, strongly up in the past thirty years. Nevertheless, the lapping tendency can be traced throughout the twenty-seven-cycle record.

Cagan (1966), comparing the behavior of a broad group of interest rates before World War I, the 1920s, and the 1950s, noted that they may have become increasingly sensitive, conforming to moderate business cycles with larger amplitudes and shorter lags. Our reference cycle patterns are not inconsistent with this result. Table 9.14 indicates that a shift in timing toward shorter lags and more frequent leads did occur

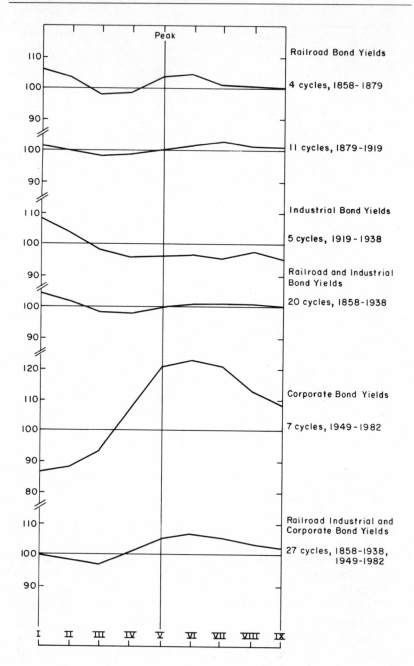

Fig. 9.3   Long-term interest rates, average references patterns, 1858–
1982. *Source*: railroad bond yields, Macaulay; industrial bond
yields, Standard and Poor's Corporation; corporate bond
yields, Citibank and U.S. Department of the Treasury.

in the early post–World War II period (1945–60), but that later the lags reasserted themselves. In 1961–82 the lags were generally longer than in 1919–29, for example. The lags of bond yields behind bill rates also increased between these two periods (compare the first and fourth lines in the "Averages" section). On the whole, lags have prevailed heavily in the timing at troughs for both bills and bonds, but at peaks bills usually led while bonds lagged. The individual timing comparisons show a high degree of dispersion.

9.12   Changes in the Timing of Leading and Lagging Indicators

Since the 1960s, a collection of economic indicators that systematically lead, coincide with, or lag business cycle turning points has become widely used in current economic analysis. The selection of these indicators has been based upon historical measures of the kind employed earlier in this paper, as well as upon hypotheses of economic behavior that yield plausible explanations of the observed leads and lags. Here we examine the historical record of two of the selected groups of indicators with respect to their timing at business cycle peaks and troughs.

The longest available record of the timing of the leading and lagging indicators during business cycles covers nearly a century. In tables 9.15 and 9.16 the median leads or lags of specific groups of indicators are shown for each business cycle turn between 1885 and 1982. The indicators in the leading group show an unbroken record of leads, while those in the lagging group lag at all except two peaks and three troughs. Moreover, when the turns in the lagging group are compared with the opposite turns in the business cycle, they lead at every turn, and by longer intervals than the leading indicators do. The economic relations between the lagging and the leading indicators are such as to make these results reasonable, according to the considerable literature that has been devoted to the subject (for a summary and list of references, see Moore 1983a, chap. 21).

From 1885 to 1938, the timing record is based upon seventy-five leading and thirty lagging indicators, the classification having been determined in 1950. Since the classification was based on the prior record, it is not surprising that the leading group led and the lagging group lagged. But the consistency over the entire period was not controlled by the method of classification, nor was the relations between the opposite turns in the lagging and leading groups. For the period 1948 to 1982, the record was based upon twelve leading and six lagging indicators selected in 1975. Again the prior record was examined in making the selection. As has been shown elsewhere, however, the behavior of a group of indicators selected in 1950, without benefit of

Table 9.14   **Timing of Turning Points in Treasury Bill Rates and Corporate Bond Yields during Business Cycles, 1919–82**

Business Cycle		Leads (−) or Lags (+), in Months					
		Treasury Bill Rate[a]		Corporate Bond Yield[b]		Bond Yield vs. Bill Rate[c]	
Trough (1)	Peak (2)	Trough (3)	Peak (4)	Trough (5)	Peak (6)	Trough (7)	Peak (8)
March 1919	January 1920		+5	−1	+5		0
July 1921	May 1923	+13	−2	+14	−1	+1	
July 1924	October 1926	+1	−11	+5	+1	+7	+4
November 1927	August 1929	−2	−3	+46	−1	+11	0
March 1933	May 1937	+35	−1	+30	−35	−1	
June 1938	February 1945	+31		+6	−9		
October 1945	November 1948			+8	−1		
October 1949	July 1953	−2	−1	+1	+1		0
August 1954	July 1957	+2	−1	+2	−4	+3	+2
April 1958	May 1960	−2	−5	+25	+7	0	+1
February 1961	November 1969	+15	+2	+25	+13	+27	+5
November 1970	November 1973	+21	+9	+30	+2	+10	+4
March 1975	January 1980	−1	+2	−1	+2	+9	0
July 1980	July 1981	−1	−7	+6	+7	0	+9
November 1982							

Averages

Pre-1945						
1919–29	+4	−3	+6	+2	+4	+2
1919–45	+16	−2	+19	−6	+4	+1
Post-1945						
1945–60	0	−2	+4	−3	+2	+1
1961–82	+6	+2	+17	+6	+10	+4
Pre- and post-1945						
All observations	+9	−1	+14	−2	+7	+3
Omitting 1933–45[d]	+4	−1	+10	+1	+7	+2

Source: Cagan 1971, 23–32. Bill rates are seasonally adjusted through 1969, except 1931–47; bond yields are seasonally adjusted 1948–61 only. From 1969 through 1982, unadjusted data are used.

[a]Discount rate on new issues of ninety-one-day treasury bills (percent).

[b]Moody's Aaa.

[c]Entries in col. 7 are based on matched observations in cols. 3 and 5; entries in col. 8, on matched observations in cols. 4 and 6.

[d]The omitted observations are those in lines 5 and 6 of the table above. They were excluded from the averages in Cagan 1971, table 1-1 through 1-4.

Table 9.15   **Cyclical Timing of Leading and Lagging Indicators, 1885–1982, at Business Cycle Peaks**

Business Cycle Peak	Lead (−) or Lag (+) in Months at Business Cycle Peak			Interval in Months	
	Median Trough, Lagging Group	Median Peak, Leading Group	Median Peak, Lagging Group	Trough in Lagging to Peak in Leading	Peak in Leading to Peak in Lagging
March 1887	−20	−3	+6	17	9
July 1890	−14	−5	+5	9	10
January 1893	−8	−5	+6	3	11
December 1895	−14	−5	+5	9	10
June 1899	−6	−1	+10	5	11
September 1902	−15	−4	+14	11	18
May 1907	−27	−16	+7	9	23
January 1910	−11	−4	+7	7	11
January 1913	−14	−3	+9	11	12
August 1918	−34	−20	+1	14	21
January 1920	−9	−2	+6	7	8
May 1923	−13	−4	+4	9	8
October 1926	−24	−11	−1	13	10
June 1929	−15	−5	+2	10	7
May 1937	−50	−2	+3	48	5
February 6 1945	n.a.	n.a.	n.a.	n.a.	n.a.
November 1948	n.a.	−10	0	n.a.	10
July 1953	−39	−5	+4	34	9
August 1957	−31	−21	+2	10	23
April 1960	−19	−12	+5	7	17
December 1969	−26	−9	+2	17	11
November 1973	−24	−8	+12	16	20
January 1980	−38	−12	+4	26	16
July 1981	−4	−3	+6	1	9
Averages and standard deviations ( )					
All observations	−21 (12)	−7 (6)	+5 (4)	13 (11)	13 (5)
All except 1937	−19 (10)	−8 (6)	+5 (4)	12 (7)	13 (5)

Sources: 1885–1938: Moore 1950, table 11, based on seventy-five leading and thirty lagging series; 1948–82: *Business Conditions Digest*, October 1977, appendix F, and subsequent issues, based on twelve leading and six lagging series.

Note: n.a. = data not available.

Table 9.16   Cyclical Timing of Leading and Lagging Indicators, 1885–1982, at Business Cycle Troughs

Business Cycle Trough	Lead (−) or Lag (+) in Months at Business Cycle Trough			Interval in Months	
	Median Peak, Lagging Group	Median Trough, Leading Group	Median Trough, Lagging Group	Peak in Lagging to Trough in Leading	Trough in Leading to Trough in Lagging
May 1885	n.a.	−6	+2	n.a.	8
April 1888	−7	−2	+13	5	15
May 1891	−5	−4	+12	1	16
June 1894	−11	−4	+4	7	8
June 1897	−13	−9	+18	4	27
December 1900	−8	−5	+6	3	11
August 1904	−9	−9	+6	0	15
June 1908	−6	−6	+8	0	14
January 1912	−17	−13	−2	4	11
December 1914	−14	−1	+10	13	11
April 1919	−7	−3	0	4	3
July 1921	−12	−5	+9	7	14
July 1924	−10	−6	+3	4	9
November 1927	−14	−4	+4	10	8
March 1933	−43	−5	0	38	5
June 1938	−10	−4	+10	6	14
October 1945	n.a.	n.a.	n.a.	n.a.	n.a.
October 1949	−11	−5	+6	6	11
May 1954	−6	−6	+8	0	14
April 1958	−6	−2	+5	4	7
February 1961	−5	−2	+7	3	9
November 1970	−9	−2	+12	7	14
March 1975	−4	−1	+20	3	21
July 1980	−2	−1	+8	1	9
November 1982	−10	−2	n.a.	8	n.a.
Averages and standard deviations ( )					
All observations	−10 (8)	−4 (3)	+7 (5)	6 (8)	12 (5)
All except 1933	−9 (4)	−4 (3)	+8 (5)	5 (3)	12 (5)

Sources: 1885–1938: Moore 1950, table 11, based on seventy-five leading and thirty lagging series; 1948–82: *Business Conditions Digest*, October 1977, appendix F, and subsequent issues, based on twelve leading and six lagging series.

Note: n.a. = data not available.

the *subsequent* record, was quite similar during 1948–75 to the record shown in tables 9.15 and 9.16 (Moore 1983a, chap. 24).

At business cycle peaks the average length of lead of the leading group, 1885–1982, was seven months, with a standard deviation of six months. At troughs the mean and standard deviation were about half as large, four and three months, respectively. There is some evidence in the tables that the leads at peaks have become longer and the leads at troughs shorter since 1948 than before (see below).

The lags of the lagging group average five months at peaks and seven months at troughs, with standard deviations of four and five months, respectively. When the turns in the lagging group are compared with the opposite turns in the business cycle, the leads that emerge are quite long, averaging twenty-one months at peaks and ten months at troughs. They are also quite variable, with standard deviations of twelve months at peaks and eight months at troughs.

What tables 9.15 and 9.16 reveal, then, is an almost unbroken sequence of turning points during successive business cycles over the past hundred years. In view of our finding in section 9.3 that the principal shift in the length of business cycle phases took place after World War II, it is of interest to examine the sequence before and after 1945, as in the following summary:

	Average Interval in Months		
	1885–1938	1948–82	1885–1982
A. Business cycle peak to peak in lagging indicators	6	4	5
B. Peak in lagging indicators to trough in leading indicators	7	4	6
C. Trough in leading indicators to business cycle trough	5	3	4
D. Business cycle trough to trough in lagging indicators	6	10	7
E. Trough in lagging indicators to peak in leading indicators	12	16	13
F. Peak in leading indicators to business cycle peak	6	10	7
A + B + C. Business cycle contraction	18	11	15
D + E + F. Business cycle expansion	24	36	27

Each of the intervals into which the business cycle contraction is broken by these turning points has become shorter, on average, while each of the intervals that constitute the business cycle expansion has become longer. This in itself supports the finding of a major shift in the length of business expansions vis-à-vis contractions, since the intervals between the indicator turning points (though not their sum) are independent of the business cycle chronology.

One other noteworthy feature of tables 9.15 and 9.16 is the evidence that the lengths of the leads or lags at successive turning points are positively correlated. The correlation coefficients (*r*) are as follows:

	All	*Excluding*
At business cycle peaks, 1887–1981	*Observations*	*1933 and 1937*
Trough in lagging and peak in leading	+.46	+.70
Peak in lagging and peak in leading	+.43	+.47
At business cycle troughs, 1885–1982		
Peak in lagging and trough in leading	+.28	+.53
Trough in leading and trough in lagging	+.36	+.36

The correlations are not high, but they are all positive, and they are about as high when opposite turns are compared as when like turns are compared. This gives some support to the hypothesis that cyclical influences run from the lagging to the leading indicators as well as from the leading to the lagging indicators (see Moore 1983a, chap. 23).

Apart from the shift toward shorter recessions and longer expansions and the associated shift in the intervals between turns in the indicators, the most notable feature of the record is the absence of major changes in the timing relationships among the groups of indicators.

9.13   Summary and Conclusions

1. After World War II business cycle expansions in the United States became much longer and recessions much shorter than before. From 1846 to 1945, expansions were one and a half times as long as recessions. From 1945 to 1982, they were four times as long. Recessions also became more uniform in length. Total cycle durations from peak to peak or trough to trough show no significant trend.

2. Historically, expansions have long been relative to recessions when the long-run trend in prices was upward and shorter when the price trend was downward. This is mainly because expansions generate more upward pressure on prices than recessions do. However, we find no association between the rate of inflation during each business cycle and the relative duration of the phases.

3. Business cycle recessions since World War II have been much less severe than before, as indicated by comprehensive measures of employment, production, and real income. Shifts in the industrial composition of employment, changes relating to unemployment and labor force participation, and trends in the distribution of personal income by major sources and types have all contributed to that moderation.

4. Inflation was much higher in 1969–81 than in 1948–69, whereas real growth on the average was lower. In the past, periods of relatively low long-term growth tended to have relatively high variability of annual growth rates. However, the variability of economic change (measured by standard deviations of real GNP growth rates) can be judged low by historical standards in both 1948–69 and 1969–81.

5. The average rates of inflation were very similar in the United States expansions before and after 1945 but much higher in the postwar than in the prewar contractions. The inflation of recent decades can be attributed principally to the (novel) persistence of upward price pressures in contractions, not to an intensification of such pressures in expansions. Wholesale prices have continued to show considerable sensitivity to the degree of severity of business contractions.

6. Short-term interest rates moved with very large relative amplitudes, high positive conformity, and variable timing in the business cycles of 1949–82. Before World War II their movements tended to be smaller relative to the cycle average, and they often had long lags at turning points. Long-term rates continued to lag behind the short rates most of the time and to show much smaller amplitudes of movement and lower conformity to business cycles.

7. The longest available record of the cyclical timing of leading and lagging indicators covers nearly a century. Apart from a shift toward shorter recessions and longer expansions and the associated shift in the intervals between turns in the indicators, the most notable feature of the record is the absence of major changes in the timing relationships among the groups of indicators.

We conclude that various structural, institutional, and policy changes contributed to the evolution of business cycles. The process is continuing. There have been important changes, yet the most basic characteristics and many outward manifestations of the business cycle remain much the same (as illustrated by the timing sequences of the indicators). The cyclical processes are sometimes stretched out and sometimes compressed, depending on long-term trends in growth, inflation, and so forth, as well as on the nature, size, and frequency of outside disturbances.

More intensive research is very much needed on each of the topics we could address only briefly in this overview. In addition, there are other aspects of the changing nature of business cycles that we had to exclude. The most important of these are international. For example, greater conformity of United States exports to business cycles in recent times has been noted by Mintz (1967) and Moore (1983a). Business cycles, and even major fluctuations in positive growth rates, appear to be rather integrated among the industrialized trading countries. The full implications of this fact remain to be analyzed.

Comment   Alan J. Auerbach

Zarnowitz and Moore present a wealth of data on output, employment, prices, and interest rates from the past century, using the business cycle as the unit of time over which these data are broken down, studied, and related. The broad question to which the authors seek an answer is, How has the character of the business cycle changed, both in terms of the behavior of macroeconomic aggregates over the cycle and in terms of the frequency, severity, and longevity of the cycles themselves? The answer is that the post–World War II business cycle has been less severe than before, with expansions lasting longer and contractions just the opposite. Part of this change is associated with a secular shift in output from industries with a strongly cyclical character, such as manufacturing, to those less sensitive to the cycle, such as government. Likewise, the contributions to personal income from such volatile sources as farming and unincorporated business have declined as transfer income, many parts of which are intentionally counter-cyclical, was rising. I use the word "associated" here rather than caused, because without a specific model or explanation for macroeconomic activity itself, it is really impossible to determine causality from these observed correlations. The authors are usually careful to recognize these limitations, although it is difficult to divorce one's view of the way the world works from the way data are presented and analyzed. I do not wish to offer a blanket criticism of "measurement without theory," if for no other reason than that the associated arguments are by now so well known. Basic information on statistical relationships may be useful and relevant for a number of theories. At certain points, however, I believe the data could have been presented in a more helpful way.

The paper begins with a summary of business cycle activity since 1846, based on figures presented in table 9.1. Here it is evident that, according to the NBER dating of cycles preferred by the authors, contractions have occupied successively less time in the overall business cycle. At this point it is probably appropriate to consider the usefulness of the business cycle as the unit of analysis. Why not, for example, give statistics on average annual output changes over successive ten-year periods? The authors do not offer any explicit justification for their approach, but there must be an implicit view that whatever model is appropriate for describing the economy, dynamic relationships change over time according to what is happening within the business cycle. Two specific arguments in this vein are that economic relationships differ during expansions and contractions or that

Alan J. Auerbach is professor of economics at the University of Pennsylvania.

as business cycles change in length the unit of calendar time appropriate for dynamic relationships also changes. Support for this latter view is given in section 9.12, where we see that as the length of contractions has shortened over time, there has been a relatively uniform shortening of the subperiods into which contractions are divided. The same is true in reverse for expansions and their subperiods.

Returning to the paper's presentation of basic trends, we observe in tables 9.2 and 9.3 that from an epoch during which periods of rising and falling prices alternated, we have experienced rising prices during the past half century. As table 9.13 shows us later in the paper, this change in long-run price behavior is associated with the fact that prices no longer fall during contractions rather than with more rapid inflation during expansions. Given the additional fact that expansions now seem to last longer, the mathematics tells us that we are experiencing more inflation than we used to. Here the authors do come a little too close, in my opinion, to an attribution of causality, in saying that this inflation "was due not to an intensification of upward price pressures during business expansions, but to the new persistence of pressures during contractions." This statement may be correct, but table 9.13 reports prices, not pressures.

After presenting the basic facts on output and price variations, the authors seek the reasons for the cycle's changing character. They concentrate on shifts in output and labor force composition, adding that demand management is another possible explanation but that this "topic will not be pursued here." I think they are misleading us a bit. If one looks ahead to the discussion of personal income sources, one finds in table 9.9 that included in the category of personal income that declines least during recessions is "other labor income and transfer payments," which grew from 0.9% of personal income for 1913 to 18.9% in 1981, and "wages and salaries, government," which grew from 4.6% to 11.2% over the same period. Omitting these two sources of growth would leave us with a very different picture of the changing composition of personal income among volatile and nonvolatile sources.

While we are studying table 9.9, let me point out a couple of other problems that make the trend even less obvious. Both relate to the use of personal income rather than a more comprehensive income concept. The third important source of stable income, according to the table, is interest payments. But these are *nominal* interest payments. They may be stable and bigger than they used to be, but the picture would be quite different if real, realized interest payments were included. The same type of correction to include capital gains would be helpful. This problem emphasizes that one cannot divorce statistics from models. Unless consumers are completely myopic, or in some equivalent way constrained, nominal interest income is not an interesting measure.

Turning to another explanation, shifts in output composition have, I believe, clearly contributed to the overall decline in volatility that we have observed. Tables 9.5 and 9.6 show us that nonagricultural employment has been steadily shifting from manufacturing to services, and that cyclical changes in employment are and have always been much smaller in the latter sector than the former.

Finally, the authors turn from their discussion of changes in cycle volatility to the changing behavior of prices and interest rates over the cycle. I have already discussed their findings about prices. I have some difficulty in commenting on their analysis of interest rates, for it is nominal interest rates that they study.

Hence the fact pictured in figure 9.2 that, on average, rates were higher at the end than at the beginning of the trough-to-trough cycles since 1949 is not very surprising, but does not tell us whether the behavior of real rates has changed. The same is true of the generally upward trend in Aaa bond yields pictured in figure 9.3, although here there is also the problem of disentangling the relationship between short and long rates, something that we, as economists, have not done very well as yet. In the study of prices and interest rates, as well as when one looks at sources of personal income, the nose of government policy is clearly observable under their tent, even if Zarnowitz and Moore are struggling to be inhospitable. They do weaken a little in section 9.10 when they present growth rates for the money stock, nominal income, and prices over three periods, but here they do not emphasize cyclical movements.

To conclude, I think that Zarnowitz and Moore have offered us an interesting picture of the changing character of business cycles, organizing and presenting the mass of available data in a very helpful way. They have also presented some evidence for the usefulness of taking the business cycle as a unit of measurement, and about the sources of observed changes in postwar cycles. I would encourage them to present companion statistics on rates of inflation and real interest rates to go along with those already offered on nominal interest rates and price levels. Such additional data, combined with those already presented, could further increase our understanding of how business cycles have changed during the postwar years.

Comment   Solomon Fabricant

Along with Auerbach, I welcome the information Zarnowitz and Moore provide on the changing characteristics of business cycles in the United

Solomon Fabricant is a research associate of the National Bureau of Economic Research.

States over the past century or so—and I would stress, the information on the persistent characteristics of these cycles.

They entitle their paper "Major Changes in Cyclical Behavior," but of course it covers only *some* major changes, as they explicitly recognize. Other data already in their hands (to judge from this paper and their appendix A, to this volume, on the NBER's business cycle chronologies) could be analyzed or analyzed further. I hope they will do so. And perhaps analyses along other lines could also be added.

I was somewhat surprised to find not even a reference—let alone any discussion or analysis—to a hypothesis on cyclical changes in cyclical behavior suggested by Burns and Mitchell almost forty years ago (Burns and Mitchell 1946, 455–64). Though they claimed only that the hypothesis "may turn out to have substance," coming from these two economists, that is enough to make the hypothesis well worth examining—in the light of developments since World War II, and with more data than Burns and Mitchell used in their very preliminary investigation.

You may (and Zarnowitz and Moore will) remember that in their 1946 volume Burns and Mitchell were concerned with the variation of cyclical behavior over time. They wanted to be reasonably confident that the average cyclical patterns they and their colleagues were constructing would yield useful first approximations to the typical features of business cycles—that changes in cyclical behavior, in other words, were not so pronounced as to discredit the use of averages. Among the possible changes in cyclical behavior they considered were changes within long cycles tentatively marked off by severe depressions. In studying the changes within these periods they observed a difference between the cyclical behavior of industrial activity (measured by pig iron production and deflated bank clearings) and of speculative activity (bond yields, call money rates, and shares traded). The difference suggested their hypothesis: "After a severe depression industrial activity rebounds sharply, but speculation does not. The following contraction in business is mild, which leads people to be less cautious. Consequently, in the next two or three cycles, while the cyclical advances become progressively smaller in industrial activity, they become progressively larger in speculative activity. Finally, the speculative boom collapses and a drastic liquidation follows, which ends this cycle of cycles."

Later, in 1955, Moore himself looked a bit further into the question and found recoveries after severe depressions in output, employment, and profits to be usually faster than after mild contractions (Moore 1961b, 88). In contrast, stock prices usually advanced more rapidly after mild recessions than after severe contractions. Also relevant to the Burns/Mitchell hypothesis is Ilse Mintz's study of the deterioration in the quality of foreign bonds issued during the 1920s (Mintz 1951). An analysis of the post–World War II period would, I suspect, turn up some interesting parallels to that experience—and some interesting differences.

Also surprising to me was the short shrift given—in all the conference's papers—to the changing characteristics of business cycles outside the United States. Even if business cycles in the United States were our only concern, what we could learn by studying the other countries surely would be helpful. And so would a discussion of changes, if any, in the interrelations among business cycles in the United States and those in other countries. The brief remarks Zarnowitz and Moore leave for the last paragraph of their paper can only be called tantalizing.

Of course, updating the NBER's business cycle chronologies for other countries could be quite a job. However, it might not be as heavy as it seems. Many of the fluctuations in European countries and Japan during their rapid economic growth following the war look more like growth cycles than business cycles. And Zarnowitz and Moore have already provided us with a chronology of growth cycles for these countries, as well as the United States, in table A.8 of appendix A. But the table is unaccompanied by any serious analysis despite the considerable interest expressed in growth cycles during the past fifteen or twenty years.[1] In 1968, for example, Burns suggested the possibility that the classical business cycle might be gradually merging into a cycle in which the rate of aggregate growth continues to fluctuate but remains positive (Burns 1968). On this, too, the passage of time has provided information that could be put to use.

Apart from the question of any "progress toward economic stability," there are questions about differences between mild and severe business cycles, and also between business cycle contractions and retardations (or slowdowns) that are not severe enough to be designated business cycle contractions. Well before World War I some fluctuations were so mild as to be classified as business cycles only with some doubt. Specifically, Zarnowitz and Moore refer (table 9.1, note d) to such slowdowns in 1869–70, 1887–88, and 1899–1900. Another example might possibly be 1926–27. Further, in appendix A they point to changes during 1951–52, 1962–64, and 1966–67 and definitely characterize them as retardations during expansion rather than as business cycle contractions. A review of the changes during these episodes, with regard to the characteristics on which Zarnowitz and Moore dwell (duration, amplitude, extent of diffusion, dates of turns in leaders, etc.), could

---

1. This gap has been partly filled by a new NBER volume (Moore and Klein 1985) that analyzes growth cycles and cyclical indicators in ten countries (including the United States).

be interesting. And so could a review of the characteristics of the expansion or speedup that followed a slowdown, and of the subsequent "classical" contraction—developments, for example, during 1949–52 and 1952–54, if the period 1949–54 were broken in two. All of this would also contribute further evidence on the question that bothers Auerbach, how useful the business cycle is "as a unit of measurement"—a question that obviously also bothered Burns and Mitchell, and to which they devoted a good deal of space in their 1946 volume.

Three things are obvious, to me at least, viewing Zarnowitz and Moore's paper in the context of the conference as a whole. First, the kind of business cycle research that Zarnowitz and Moore do is not at all "fancy," judged by contemporary econometric standards or practices. Second, it requires a lot of hard and careful digging into historical data, as well as good judgment in putting the data to use. This is a task in which—so far, at any rate—mathematics and computers can be of only limited assistance. And third, as is demonstrated in their papers, it can yield results that, though clearly of limited compass, do throw light on the question before this conference—the question of continuity and change in business cycles.

Discussion Summary

The major part of the discussion focused on the clear methodological difference between this paper and all the other papers presented at this conference. Stanley Fischer first drew attention to the fact that although several other papers had paid homage to Mitchell's reference cycle method, they all had inevitably ended up conducting their investigations in the time domain. Moore noted that Blanchard and Watson stated they had decided against the reference cycle approach because it offered no way to conduct rigorous tests of hypotheses, whereas Moore believed that many hypotheses could be and had been rigorously tested in this way. Examples abound in the business cycle studies of the NBER. Sims responded that calendar time was preferable to reference cycles for a number of reasons. In a vector autoregression system it is possible to use the data explicitly to formulate a distribution over the system's forecasts. One can then test how well the estimated system tracks the economy. In a reference cycle framework such forecasts and tests are more difficult because the researcher does not know what the length of the current cycle will be.

Some participants contended that theoretical justifications for the use of the reference cycle technique are also weak. Sims remarked that it is possible to construct linear models that exhibit stationary random fluctuations. In general, however, the times between peaks and troughs vary widely in such models. He also noted that even when the reference cycle is the true model, the usefulness of time series methods is not ruled out. Lawrence Summers elaborated on this point, stating that results obtained by his graduate students supported this view. He found that VARs were able to capture asymmetries over successive business cycles. (See the DeLong/Summers paper on symmetry in this volume following the Blanchard/Watson paper [chap. 2].) Moore remarked that the cyclical behavior of a series is dependent on the sampling period used and said he understood that VARs were sensitive to the choice of the sampling period. Sims responded that this is less true now, since it appears that monthly VAR systems are often able to track both short- and long-term movements in variables quite well.

As an addendum to this discussion, Zarnowitz notes that the prevailing procedure in applied econometrics is to use discrete-time fixed unit periods on the implicit assumption that the timing interval of the given model coincides with the data sampling interval. The two intervals, however, need not be equal, and where they are not major errors may well result (as shown in recent papers by Christiano and others). In short, the results of empirical analyses can be highly sensitive to the timing specifications of a model, yet the latter are often arbitrary and seldom tested. How stable over time the decision lags are is also generally unknown, but it is clear that some important timing relations vary rather systematically over the business cycle; for example, the average delivery periods ("vendor performance") lengthen in expansions and shorten in contractions. The related problems of the proper choice of the time units and the variability of the lags are both important and in need of much further study: strong claims of knowledge about how to treat them seem to be lacking foundation at present.

References

Baily, Martin N. 1978. Stabilization policy and private economic behavior. *Brookings Papers on Economic Activity* 1:11–60.

Beck, Morris. 1980. The public sector and economic stability. In *The business cycle and public policy, 1929–80*, 105–29. A compendium of papers submitted to the Joint Economic Committee, Congress of the United States. Washington, D.C.: Government Printing Office.

Bednarzik, Robert W., and Deborah P. Klein. 1977. Labor force trends: A synthesis and analysis. *Monthly Labor Review* 100 (October):3–12.

Bowers, Norman. 1981. Have employment patterns in recessions changed? *Monthly Labor Review* 104 (February):15–28.

Burns, Arthur F. 1968. The nature and causes of business cycles. In *International encyclopedia of the social sciences*, 2:226–45. New York: Macmillan.

Burns, Arthur F., and Wesley C. Mitchell. 1946. *Measuring business cycles.* New York: National Bureau of Economic Research.

Cagan, Phillip. 1971. Changes in the cyclical behavior of interest rates. In *Essays on interest rates*, ed. Jack M. Guttentag, 2:3–34. New York: National Bureau of Economic Research.

———. 1975. Changes in the recession behavior of wholesale prices in the 1920s and post–World War II. *Explorations in Economic Research* 2 (Winter):54–104.

Creamer, Daniel. 1956. *Personal income during business cycles.* Princeton: Princeton University Press. Foreword by Geoffrey H. Moore.

Cullity, John P. 1983. The changing structure of personal income and business cycles in the 1980's. Mimeographed. Center for International Business Cycle Research, Columbia University.

Easterlin, Richard A. 1968. *Population, labor force, and long swings in economic growth: The American experience.* New York: Columbia University Press.

Fellner, William. 1980. The valid core of the rationality hypothesis in the theory of expectations. *Journal of Money, Credit and Banking* 12 (November):763–87.

Flaim, Paul O. 1979. The effect of demographic changes on the nation's unemployment rate. *Monthly Labor Review* 102 (March):12–23.

Friedman, Milton, and Anna J. Schwartz. 1963. *A monetary history of the United States, 1867–1960.* Princeton: Princeton University Press.

———. 1982. *Monetary trends in the United States and the United Kingdom: Their relation to income, prices, and interest rates, 1867–1975.* Chicago: University of Chicago Press.

Fuchs, Victor R. 1968. *The service economy.* New York: Columbia University Press.

Gordon, R. A. 1969. The stability of the U.S. economy. In *Is the business cycle obsolete?* ed. Martin Bronfenbrenner, 3–33. New York: Wiley-Interscience.

Haberler, Gottfried. 1964. *Prosperity and depression.* Cambridge: Harvard University Press. Originally published by the League of Nations, 1937.

Heller, Walter W. 1966. *New dimensions of political economy.* Cambridge: Harvard University Press.

Jerome, Harry. 1926. *Migration and business cycles.* New York: National Bureau of Economic Research.

Kendrick, John W. 1961. *Productivity trends in the United States.* Princeton: Princeton University Press.

Keynes, John M. 1936. *The general theory of employment, interest, and money.* London: Macmillan.

Klein, Philip A., and Geoffrey H. Moore. 1985. *Monitoring growth cycles in market-oriented countries.* Cambridge, Mass.: Ballinger.

Kuznets, Simon. 1971. *Economic growth of nations.* Cambridge: Belknap Press of Harvard University Press.

Lilien, David M. 1982. Sectoral shifts and cyclical unemployment. *Journal of Political Economy* 90 (August):777–93.

Macaulay, Frederick R. 1938. *Some theoretical problems suggested by the movements of interest rates, bond yields and stock prices in the United States since 1856.* New York: National Bureau of Economic Research.

Mills, Frederick C. 1926. An hypothesis concerning the duration of business cycles. *Journal of the American Statistical Association* 21 (December):447–57.

Mincer, Jacob. 1966. Labor-force participation and unemployment: A review of recent evidence. In *Prosperity and unemployment*, ed. R. A. Gordon, and M. S. Gordon, 73–112, New York: John Wiley.

———. 1967. Research in labor force and in unemployment. In *Forty-seventh annual report*, 16–22, New York: National Bureau of Economic Research.

Mintz, Ilse. 1951. *Deterioration in the quality of foreign bonds issued in the United States, 1929–1930.* New York: National Bureau of Economic Research.

———. 1967. *Cyclical fluctuations in the exports of the United States since 1879.* New York: National Bureau of Economic Research.

Mitchell, Wesley C. 1927. *Business cycles: The problem and its setting.* New York: National Bureau of Economic Research.

Moore, Geoffrey H. 1950. Statistical indicators of cyclical revivals and recessions. Occasional Paper 31, National Bureau of Economic Research.

———, ed. 1961a. *Business cycle indicators.* 2 vols. Princeton: Princeton University Press.

———. 1961b. Leading and confirming indicators of general business changes. In *Business cycle indicators*, ed. Geoffrey H. Moore, vol. 1. Princeton: Princeton University Press.

———. 1983a. *Business cycles, inflation, and forecasting.* 2d ed. Cambridge, Mass.: Ballinger.

———. 1983b. Some secular changes in business cycles. In *Business cycles, inflation, and forecasting*, 2d ed., by Geoffrey H. Moore, chap. 10. Cambridge, Mass.: Ballinger. Originally published 1974.

Personick, Valerie A. 1983. The job outlook through 1995: Industry output and employment projections. *Monthly Labor Review* 106 (November):24–36.

Sachs, Jeffrey. 1980. The changing cyclical behavior of wages and prices, 1890–1976. *American Economic Review* 70 (March):78–90.

Schultze, Charles L. 1981. Some macro foundations for micro theory. *Brookings Papers on Economic Activity*, 2:521–76.

Schumpeter, Joseph A. 1939. *Business cycles*. 2 vols. New York: McGraw-Hill.

Selden, Richard T. 1963. Trends and cycles in the commercial paper market. Occasional Paper 85, National Bureau of Economic Research.

Thorp, Willard L. 1926. *Business annals*. New York: National Bureau of Economic Research.

———. 1932. The depression as depicted by business annals. News-Bulletin no. 43, National Bureau of Economic Research.

U.S. Department of Commerce, Bureau of Economic Analysis. 1973. *Long term economic growth, 1860–1970*. Washington, D.C.: Government Printing Office.

Warren, George F., and Frank A. Pearson. 1933. *Prices*. New York: John Wiley.

Zarnowitz, Victor. 1981. Business cycles and growth: Some reflections and measures. In *Wirtschaftstheorie und Wirtschaftspolitik: Gedenkschrift für Erich Preiser*, ed. W. J. Mückl and A. E. Ott, 475–508. Passau: Passavia Universitätsverlag.

———. 1985. Recent work on business cycles in historical perspective: A review of theories and evidence. *Journal of Economic Literature* 23 (June): 523–80.

10 The Cyclical Behavior of Industrial Labor Markets: A Comparison of the Prewar and Postwar Eras

Ben S. Bernanke and James L. Powell

10.1 Introduction

This paper compares the cyclical behavior of a number of industrial labor markets of the prewar (1923–39) and postwar (1954–82) eras. The methodology follows that of the traditional Burns and Mitchell (1946) business cycle analysis in at least two ways. First, the data employed are relatively disaggregated (we use monthly data at the two- or three-digit industry level). Second, we have not formulated or tested a specific structural model of labor markets during the cycle but instead concentrate on measuring qualitative features of the data. As did Burns and Mitchell, we see descriptive analysis of the data as a useful prelude to theorizing about business cycles. Thus, although the research reported here permits *no* direct structural inferences, it should be useful in restricting the class of structural models or hypotheses that may subsequently be considered.

The principal questions we study are also two in number. First, what are the means by which labor input is varied over the business cycle? We consider the intensity of utilization (as measured by gross labor productivity), hours of work per week, and number of workers employed. Both the timing and the relative magnitudes of the changes in these quantities over the cycle are examined. Second, what are the relationships over the cycle of output and labor input to measures of

Ben S. Bernanke is professor of economics at the Woodrow Wilson School, Princeton University, and a research associate of the National Bureau of Economic Research. James L. Powell is assistant professor of economics at Massachusetts Institute of Technology.
We thank Frank Brechling, Ken Rogoff, Larry Summers, and our discussants for useful comments.

583

labor compensation? We look at the cyclical behavior of product wages and real weekly earnings as well as of real wages.

As might be expected, many of our findings are not novel; rather, they tend to support and perhaps refine existing perceptions of cyclical labor market behavior. However, we do reveal some interesting differences between the prewar and postwar periods in the relative use of layoffs and short hours in downturns and in cyclical movements of the real wage. Another finding is that labor productivity may behave in an anomalous manner in more severe recessions. Finally, a number of the familiar regularities are documented in a previously little-used data set, over an unusually long sample period, and by means of some alternative methods.

The paper is organized as follows: Section 10.2 reviews previous empirical work on the cyclical behavior of labor market variables. Sections 10.3 and 10.4 introduce and describe the data set used here. The behavior of key variables over the business cycle is analyzed by frequency domain methods in section 10.5 and by a time domain approach in section 10.6. Section 10.7 focuses on labor market phenomena in four particularly severe recessions. Results are summarized and conclusions drawn in section 10.8.

10.2 Previous Work: Some Regularities and Some Puzzles

There has been a great deal of empirical work that relates, sometimes directly and sometimes tangentially, to the cyclical behavior of labor markets. Without attempting an exhaustive survey, in this section we will try to summarize the major empirical findings of the literature. We will also include some brief discussion of how various authors have interpreted these findings. However, because the focus of this paper is description rather than structural analysis, the results we will present later do little to resolve existing disputes about interpretation.

The discussion of this section will be organized around the two questions of interest raised in section 10.1: the means by which labor input is varied over the cycle and the cyclical relationship of labor input and labor compensation. It might be said that by concentrating on these two questions, rather than on such phenomena as the frequency and duration of unemployment spells or cyclical variations in participation rates, we are emphasizing the "demand side" of the labor market at the expense of the "supply side." This imbalance is unfortunate but is dictated by the nature of the available prewar data.[1]

10.2.1 The Cyclical Pattern of Labor Utilization

The earliest empirical work on the variation of labor input over the cycle was done in the context of NBER business cycle research. Among

1. This is not to say that no empirical work on cyclical aspects of labor supply exists for the prewar period; for a fascinating example, see Woytinsky 1942.

the hundreds of data series whose business cycle patterns were pains-takingly analyzed by Wesley Mitchell, and later by Mitchell and Arthur Burns, were a number of labor market variables. For example, Mitchell (1951) documented the high conformity of employment and weekly hours with output. (However, Mitchell was perhaps more interested in labor cost measures; see below.)

An early NBER finding was the strong tendency of weekly hours (that is, the length of the average workweek) to lead output and em-ployment over the cycle (Moore 1955; Bry 1959). Weekly hours sub-sequently became a component of the NBER's well-known index of leading indicators. (For a relatively recent discussion and updating of this index, see Zarnowitz and Boschan 1975.) Other labor market vari-ables identified as leading the cycle by the NBER included accession and layoff rates and initial claims for unemployment insurance (Shiskin 1961). Employment and unemployment were found to be coincident with the cycle.

Arguably the most important contribution of the NBER research program in this area was the classic paper by Hultgren (1960). With the purpose of investigating a hypothesis of Mitchell's about labor cost, Hultgren collected monthly data on output, aggregate hours worked, and payrolls for twenty-three industries. (The sample period was 1932–58.) With these and other data, Hultgren discovered that output per worker-hour is procyclical (or equivalently, that employment and hours worked vary relatively less over the cycle than does output).

The finding of procyclical labor productivity, or "short-run increasing returns to labor" (SRIRL), spawned a voluminous literature. Important early contributions were made by Kuh (1960, 1965), Okun (1962), Eck-stein and Wilson (1964), and Brechling (1965). (Okun's famous "law" is, of course, SRIRL applied to the aggregate economy.) These and numerous other studies (including, notably, Ball and St. Cyr 1966; Masters 1967; Brechling and O'Brien 1967; and Ireland and Smyth 1967) found the SRIRL phenomenon to be ubiquitous: it occurs at both high and low levels of output aggregation, for both production and non-production workers, and in virtually all industrial countries.

Because of the neoclassical presumption of diminishing marginal returns to factors of production, SRIRL originally was perceived (and to some extent still is) as a deep puzzle. One favored explanation was that, because of the existence of specific human capital, firms "hoard" labor during downturns (Oi 1962; Solow 1968; Fair 1969); the hoarded labor is utilized more fully as demand recovers, giving the illusion of increasing returns. For empirical purposes, the labor hoarding model has become closely identified with a model in which increasing marginal costs of adjusting the labor stock induce the firm to move toward the desired level of employment only gradually (Brechling 1965; Coen and Hickman 1970); conceptually, however, the two models are not quite the same. Another popular explanation of SRIRL is that it is a reflection of unobserved (by the econometrician) variations in capital utilization rates that are associated with changes in labor input (Ireland and Smyth 1967; Lucas 1970; Solow 1973; Nadiri and Rosen 1973; Tatom 1980).

What is probably the most general current view is that SRIRL is the outcome of a complex dynamic optimization problem solved by the firm, in which labor is only one of a number of inputs, each with a possibly different degree of quasi-fixity. For example, Nadiri and Rosen (1973) emphasized that the rate at which employment will be varied depends not only on the costs of adjusting labor stocks but also on the costs of adjusting all other inputs (including inventories and rates of utilization); Morrison and Berndt (1981) showed that these interactions could result in the SRIRL phenomenon even if labor itself were a perfectly variable factor.

Overall, the research that followed Hultgren's original paper has made two valuable contributions to knowledge. First, from Brechling (1965) to Nadiri and Rosen (1973) to Sims (1974), there has been generated a wealth of empirical material on the sluggish short-run response of employment to output change and on the relationship over the cycle of employment to hours worked, inventories, and other factors of production. Second, the general dynamic optimization model of firm input utilization developed in this literature has proved to be a most useful and flexible research tool. (For example, it has permitted the incorporation of rational expectations; see Sargent 1978 or Pindyck and Rotemberg 1982.)

We may summarize the received findings on the cyclical behavior of labor inputs as follows: Employment and weekly hours are procyclical. Productivity is also procyclical; that is, employment and worker-hours vary less than output over the cycle. Finally, weekly hours lead output, while employment coincides with or possibly lags output over the cycle.

10.2.2 Labor Compensation over the Cycle

Although the qualitative behavior of labor inputs over the business cycle seems relatively well established, there is very little agreement about how to characterize the cyclical movements of labor compensation, especially of real wages. The debate about real wages began when Keynes (1936) conjectured that, again because of diminishing marginal returns, labor's marginal productivity and hence the real wage should be countercyclical.[2] Empirical studies by Dunlop (1938) and Tarshis (1939) purported to show that this conjecture was false; but these studies were in turn disputed (see Bodkin 1969 for references).

2. Bodkin 1969 notes that the French economist Rueff made the same prediction in 1925.

The debate prompted Keynes (1939) to aver that countercyclical real wages were in fact not an essential implication of his theory.

Postwar research has done little to resolve the question of the cyclical behavior of real wages. One can find papers supporting procyclicality (Bodkin 1969; Stockman 1983), countercyclicality (Neftci 1978; Sargent 1978; Otani 1978; Chirinko 1980), and acyclicality (Geary and Kennan 1982). Altonji and Ashenfelter (1980) have argued that the best statistical model of the real wage is the random walk. It would not be much help for us to present a detailed comparison of these papers here. Instead, we simply list some of the major methodological issues that have arisen in this literature.

First, researchers have typically found that these results are sensitive to whether the nominal wage is deflated by an index of output prices, such as the wholesale price index or the producer price index or by a cost-of-living index such as the consumer price index. (See Ruggles 1940; Bodkin 1969; or Geary and Kennan 1982.) This does not seem unreasonable, since the wage divided by the output price (henceforth the "product wage") corresponds conceptually to the "demand price" of labor, while the wage deflated by the cost of living (henceforth the "real wage") corresponds to the "supply price"; it is not difficult to think of conditions under which the short-run behaviors of these two variables might differ. Unfortunately, however, the difference in behavior does not seem to vary systematically across studies.

Second, there is some dispute over whether the contemporaneous correlation of the real wage and output (or employment) is an interesting measure of the real wage's cyclical pattern. Neftci (1978) and Sargent (1978) have argued that, because of the complex dynamics of the wage/employment relationship, it is necessary to look at correlations at many leads and lags. (See also Clark and Freeman 1980.)

Finally, it has been founded that empirical results concerning the short-run behavior of wages may be particularly sensitive to aggregation biases, both when the aggregation is over individuals (Stockman 1983) and when it is over industries (Chirinko 1980).

The apparently very weak relationship of real wages and the business cycle has posed a problem for some prominent theories of cyclical fluctuations (or at least for simple versions of those theories; see, for example, Altonji and Ashenfelter 1980 and Ashenfelter and Card 1982). However, attempts to reconcile the low correlation of wages and the cycle with theories of short-run employment fluctuations have also led to a number of interesting lines of research: these include disequilibrium modeling of the cycle (Solow and Stiglitz 1968; Barro and Grossman 1971), contracting approaches that divorce wage payments and short-run labor allocations (see Hall 1980 for a discussion), Lucas's (1970) theory of capacity and overtime, and others.

Real and product wages are not the only measures of labor compensation whose cyclical behavior has been studied, although they have absorbed a large part of the research effort. Mitchell theorized in very early work that unit labor costs might play an important role in the business cycle; Hultgren's (1960, 1965) studies found that, in reasonably close correspondence to Mitchell's prediction, labor costs lag the cycle. Various other compensation measures were studied by the NBER analysts: nominal labor income, for example, was reported by Shiskin (1961) to be coincident with the cycle.

Another variable that has commanded some attention is the nominal wage. In an NBER Occasional Paper, Creamer (1950) studied monthly wage rates in a number of industries for 1919–31. (His aggregate wage rate series extended to 1935.) Creamer's most important conclusion was that nominal wage rates lagged business activity by nine months or more, a finding that some subsequent authors viewed as supporting the "stickiness" of wages. (Creamer also showed that the cyclical behaviors of an index of wage rates and of average hourly earnings were similar, a very useful result given the paucity of direct information on wage rates.) "Stickiness" was also a major issue for later students of the nominal wage: for example, Sachs (1980) has argued that wages became relatively more rigid after World War II, and Gordon (1982) has found United States postwar wages to be stickier than those of the United Kingdom and Japan. Gordon's result is the opposite of earlier characterizations by Sachs (1979) and others.

Overall, the question of how to characterize the cyclical behavior of labor compensation remains rather unsettled. This is unfortunate, given the central role of wages in much of macroeconomic theory.

10.3   The Data

This paper reassesses the qualitative empirical findings described in the previous section, with particular attention to possible differences between the prewar and postwar eras. This section introduces our data set and compares it briefly with what has been employed by others.

The data we use are monthly, roughly at the level of the "industry," and cover the time periods 1923–39 and 1954–82. We felt that the high-frequency data were necessary if short-run relationships were to be distinguished; the industry-level data were used both to reduce aggregation bias and to avoid reliance on the aggregate production indexes, which are poorly constructed for our purpose (see below). In contrast to our approach, few studies since Hultgren have used monthly, industry-level data (Fair 1969 is an important exception). Also, little recent work has used prewar data; the exceptions have typically looked only at annual, highly aggregated numbers.

There were many variables we could have chosen to study. Considerations of data availability and economic relevance led to the following short list (with mnemonic abbreviations):

IP Industry output or production

EMP Employment (number of production workers)

HRS Hours of work per week (per production worker)

PROD Gross labor productivity = $IP/(EMP \times HRS)$

WR Average hourly earnings (nominal) divided by a cost-of-living index; the "real wage."

WP Average hourly earnings divided by the industry wholesale output price; the "product wage"

EARN Real weekly earnings per production worker = $HRS \times WR$.

In the analysis below, we concentrate not on the levels of these variables but on the log differences (roughly, the monthly growth rates). From now on, therefore, the mnemonic names just defined should be understood to denote log differences.

The variables above were collected for eight prewar manufacturing, eight postwar manufacturing, and three postwar nonmanufacturing industries. These industries are listed in table 10.1. Note that the eight prewar and postwar manufacturing industries are approximately a "matched set." This was done to facilitate comparison of the two eras. We did not have com-

Table 10.1 **Industries Included in Data Set**

Prewar Industry Title	Postwar Industry Title (SIC code)
Manufacturing Industries (prewar and postwar data)	
1. Iron and steel (STEEL)	Blast furnaces and steel mills (331)
2. Automobiles (AUTOS)	Motor vehicles and equipment (371)
3. Meat-packing (MEAT)	Meat-packing plants (201)
4. Paper and pulp (PAPER)	Paper and allied products (26)
5. Boots and shoes (SHOES)	Footwear, except rubber (314)
6. Wool textiles (WOOL)	Weaving and finishing mills, wool (223)
7. Leather tanning and finishing (LEATH)	Leather tanning and finishing (311)
8. Lumber and millwork (excluding furniture (LUMBR)	Lumber and wood products (24)
9. All manufacturing industries (ALL MFG)	All manufacturing industries
Nonmanufacturing Industries (postwar data only)	
10. NA (COAL)	Bituminous coal and lignite mining (12)
11. NA (ELECT)	Electric services (491)
12. NA (CONST)	Construction (no code)

parable prewar data for the three nonmanufacturing industries. However, we included these industries because they represent major sectors of the economy (mining, utilities, and construction) and because it seemed to us that nonmanufacturing industries have been slighted somewhat (relative to manufacturing industries) by students of the business cycle.

Some explanation should be given for the rather miscellaneous character of the manufacturing industries chosen. For the prewar period, the eight industries included represent the largest class for which complete and reasonably consistent data were available. In particular, our desire to have series on hours of work restricted us to industries regularly surveyed, beginning in the early 1920s, by the National Industrial Conference Board. The Bureau of Labor Statistics, which surveyed many more industries, did not collect hours data before 1932. Also, we included only industries whose output indexes were based on direct measures of physical output (e.g., number of automobiles) rather than on scaled-up input measures (e.g., man-hours). A wider selection of industries is available for the postwar period, of course, but because of the burden of collecting and entering the data, only those manufacturing industries "matching" the available prewar industries were used. In terms of employment or value added, the industries here studied made up about one-fifth of total manufacturing in the prewar era and about one-sixth of total manufacturing after the war.

A nice fringe benefit of using the Conference Board data rather than that from the Bureau of Labor Statistics (BLS) is that it gives us a prewar data set that has not been previously analyzed, except in a partial and desultory way by some earlier NBER studies. In particular, it is quite different from the data set used by Hultgren (1960).

A potential problem with studying only manufacturing industries that have more or less continuous identities since the 1920s is that it biases the sample toward older, often declining industries at the expense of new and growing fields. However, for the purpose of studying cyclical (as opposed to trend) behavior of labor market variables, this sample bias is probably not important. In particular, our informal comparisons of the declining manufacturing industries with the expanding manufacturing and nonmanufacturing industries did not reveal obvious differences in cyclical behavior.

For the purposes of comparison with the industry-level findings, we also analyzed prewar and postwar monthly data for aggregate manufacturing. Although these data obviously have broader coverage than the industry data, we have less confidence in the results using aggregates, for three reasons: (1) aggregation across industries introduces well-known cyclical biases; (2) the aggregate production indexes are heavily contaminated with input-based measures of output; and (3) the prewar output, price, and labor input series are not perfectly mutually consistent. (See the data appendix to this chapter for an explanation and for a more detailed discussion of all the data and their sources.)

10.4   Some Basic Statistics

Most of the analysis below follows the application of a deseasonalization process and the removal of means from the log-differenced series. As a preliminary step, this section looks at some features of the raw log differences.

Tables 10.2 and 10.3 present the means of the variables for each industry and for the prewar and postwar periods separately. The means are multiplied by 100 and thus can be interpreted approximately as percentage rates of growth *per month*.

Considering first the productivity column in table 10.2, we note that average prewar rates of productivity growth compared well with those of the postwar era. Rates of productivity growth were higher during 1923–39 than during 1954–82 in five of the eight manufacturing industries, as well as in aggregate manufacturing. The prewar rate of pro-

Table 10.2   **Monthly Rates of Growth (%) of Output, Employment, Weekly Hours, and Productivity**

Industry	Period	IP	EMP	HRS	PROD
STEEL	1923–39	0.18	0.07	−0.25	0.35
	1954–82	−0.12	−0.26	−0.01	0.14
AUTOS	1923–39	0.34	0.07	−0.14	0.42
	1954–82	0.16	−0.09	0.00	0.25
MEAT	1923–39	0.04	0.05	−0.08	0.07
	1954–82	0.18	0.02	−0.01	0.17
PAPER	1923–39	0.33	0.06	−0.12	0.39
	1954–82	0.33	0.03	0.00	0.29
SHOES	1923–39	0.01	−0.07	−0.14	0.22
	1954–82	−0.13	−0.22	−0.01	0.10
WOOL	1923–39	0.04	−0.08	−0.12	0.24
	1958–82	−0.14	−0.43	0.01	0.28
LEATH	1923–39	−0.09	−0.14	−0.10	0.15
	1954–82	−0.17	−0.29	0.00	0.12
LUMBR	1923–39	−0.07	−0.14	−0.10	0.17
	1954–82	0.18	−0.06	0.01	0.23
ALL	1923–39	0.22	−0.01	−0.12	0.34
MFG	1954–82	0.27	−0.02	0.00	0.29
COAL	1954–82	0.18	−0.13	0.06	0.26
ELECT	1954–82	0.48	0.11	0.00	0.36
CONST	1954–82	0.13	0.11	0.02	0.00

ductivity growth reached rather exceptional levels in automobiles, paper and pulp, and iron and steel. The rapid expansion of prewar productivity observed in these data supports the view that the period between the world wars (particularly the 1920s) was a time of transformation of industrial technologies, leading to sharp reductions in costs; see Jerome (1934) and Bernstein (1960). In the postwar period, the best productivity performance among our manufacturing industries was by paper and allied products; best overall in the postwar sample was by electric services.

Productivity growth is, of course, definitionally equal to output growth minus the sum of employment and hours growth. Examining these constituents of productivity, we note first that the fastest prewar growth in output was experienced by automobiles and by paper and pulp; in the postwar period, paper took the output growth honors for manufacturing, with electric services again doing best overall. It appears that the high-output industries were also the high-productivity industries; the rank correlation between output growth and productivity growth is .945 for the eight prewar industries, .913 for the eleven postwar industries.

Despite the depression of the 1930s, employment growth in the prewar manufacturing industries studied tended to exceed that in their post-war counterparts (seven of eight cases); this was also true for the aggregates. This difference largely reflects serious long-term declines by a number of the postwar industries: in wool textiles, leather tanning and finishing, and footwear, prewar tendencies toward decline accelerated after the war; in iron and steel, prewar growth in employment changed to postwar shrinkage. The strongest employment growth in the sample took place in two postwar nonmanufacturing industries (electric services and construction). As a whole, the employment column of table 10.2 is consistent with the often-noted secular fall in the fraction of total employment absorbed by manufacturing.

The behavior of the last component of productivity, hours of work, was quite different in the two sample periods. Weekly hours declined steadily during the prewar period in all industries, most precipitously in iron and steel (a notorious "long-hours" industry during the early 1920s, in which eighty-four-hour workweeks were not uncommon). This fall reflected changes in work organization during the 1920s (in a few cases as a response to the pressure of public opinion against long hours) and the "work sharing" of the depressed 1930s (sometimes initiated by employers, sometimes the result of New Deal legislation or union demands); see Zeisel (1958) for further discussion. In contrast, the postwar workweek was almost perfectly stable.

Finally, we may consider the mean rates of growth of the alternative measures of production worker compensation (table 10.3). It is inter-

Table 10.3   **Monthly Rates of Growth (%) of Real Wages, Product Wages, and Real Weekly Earnings**

Industry	Period	WR	WP	EARN
STEEL	1923–39	0.31	0.29	0.06
	1954–82	0.16	0.10	0.15
AUTOS	1923–39	0.31	0.30	0.17
	1954–82	0.11	0.16	0.11
MEAT	1923–39	0.29	0.29	0.21
	1954–82	0.06	0.15	0.04
PAPER	1923–39	0.24	0.24	0.12
	1954–82	0.13	0.15	0.13
SHOES	1923–39	0.11	−0.01	−0.03
	1954–82	0.03	0.05	0.02
WOOL	1923–39	0.21	0.20	0.08
	1958–82	0.05	0.31[a]	0.06
LEATH	1923–39	0.27	0.25	0.17
	1954–82	0.05	0.03	0.05
LUMBR	1923–39	0.28	0.27	0.17
	1954–82	0.09	0.13	0.10
ALL MFG	1923–39	0.26	0.27	0.14
	1954–82	0.09	0.10	0.09
COAL	1954–82	0.12	−0.04	0.18
ELECT	1958–82	0.13	0.05[b]	0.13
CONST	1954–82	0.09	0.03	0.11

[a]Sample period is 1958–75.

[b]Sample period is 1958–82.

esting that, though productivity gains during the prewar period were larger than during the postwar period in only five of the eight manufacturing industries studied, real wage growth was significantly larger during the prewar in *all* eight industries, as well as in the aggregate. Prewar product wages also rose sharply, except in boots and shoes. Within the major sample periods, the rank correlation of real wage growth with productivity growth was .815 for the eight prewar industries, .864 for the eleven postwar industries. (Although these correlations are high, note that they are somewhat lower than the correlations of productivity and output growth reported above.) The large prewar growth in real wages was not fully reflected in increases in worker buying power, as the last column of table 10.3 shows; because of the sharp declines in hours of work, real weekly earnings rose much more slowly than real wages.

Turning from the first to the second moments, tables 10.4 and 10.5 contain the standard deviations of the raw log differences, multiplied by 100 so they can be interpreted as percentages. We will not comment on these figures except to note, first, how surprisingly large the vari-

Table 10.4   **Standard Deviations (%) of Monthly Growth Rates of Output, Employment, Weekly Hours, and Productivity**

Industry	Period	IP	EMP	HRS	PROD
STEEL	1923–39	13.40	4.70	6.85	8.00
	1954–82	16.09	11.53	2.25	7.06
AUTOS	1923–39	30.12	10.37	8.13	22.47
	1954–82	7.80	9.69	4.14	8.69
MEAT	1923–39	9.91	4.03	3.16	7.95
	1954–82	2.82	1.80	1.84	3.87
PAPER	1923–39	5.71	1.83	2.47	5.15
	1954–82	1.83	1.06	0.98	2.06
SHOES	1923–39	11.87	3.18	5.39	10.08
	1954–82	4.05	2.86	2.58	5.63
WOOL	1923–39	12.04	6.09	4.93	8.64
	1958–82	9.30	2.71	2.01	10.17
LEATH	1923–39	5.52	2.93	3.52	5.46
	1954–82	3.39	2.32	1.71	4.82
LUMBR	1923–39	6.80	5.63	4.88	6.79
	1954–82	2.85	2.47	1.87	3.62
ALL MFG	1923–39	4.70	2.36	2.59	2.92
	1954–82	3.28	1.36	1.17	2.58
COAL	1954–82	14.00	16.05	8.18	11.74
ELECT	1954–82	1.45	0.91	0.91	1.94
CONST	1954–82	7.88	6.17	2.87	5.25

ability of the industry data often is and, second, that aggregation seems to reduce measured variability somewhat. To see how much of total variability was attributable to business cycles, we used a frequency domain technique to wipe out the variance associated with the high-frequency (seasonal) and the low-frequency (trending or long-wave) bands. The resulting standard deviations for five key variables are in table 10.6. Three facts are obvious from the table. First, the share of total variability of the data to be associated with business cycles is relatively small in both the prewar and postwar periods. Second, the business cycle has dampened considerably during the postwar period. Third, in most industries the cyclical variance of hours of work per week has, between the prewar and postwar periods, been reduced relatively more than that of employment.

This last observation, which is also confirmed in the raw data (table 10.4) and in section 10.7 below, is worth remarking on a bit further. Why have postwar employers relied relatively more heavily on layoffs, rather than on short workweeks, to reduce labor input in downturns? Two possible sources of the change are the greater postwar importance of unions and the advent of unemployment insurance programs. Union objective functions might be such that layoffs of a relatively small

Table 10.5   **Standard Deviations (%) of Monthly Growth Rates of Real Wages, Product Wages, and Real Weekly Earnings**

Industry	Period	WR	WP	EARN
STEEL	1923–39	2.14	2.24	7.02
	1954–82	1.32	1.50	2.96
AUTOS	1923–39	1.90	2.24	8.32
	1954–82	1.69	1.87	5.21
MEAT	1923–39	2.24	4.81	3.25
	1954–82	1.29	4.05	2.43
PAPER	1923–39	1.30	2.14	2.43
	1954–82	0.83	3.61	1.36
SHOES	1923–39	2.70	2.47	5.41
	1954–82	0.95	1.80	2.60
WOOL	1923–39	2.14	2.97	4.79
	1958–82	1.06	1.48[a]	2.37
LEATH	1923–39	1.47	3.03	3.37
	1954–82	0.92	2.96	2.12
LUMBR	1923–39	4.14	4.74	5.25
	1954–82	1.32	1.99	2.37
ALL MFG	1923–39	1.24	1.48	2.55
	1954–82	2.30	2.34	2.69
COAL	1954–82	1.95	2.19	9.04
ELECT	1954–82	0.90	1.11[b]	1.44
CONST	1954–82	1.05	1.02	2.80

[a]Sample period is 1958–75.
[b]Sample period is 1958–82.

number of junior workers are preferred to a general reduction of hours. (Cross-sectional evidence that unions prefer layoffs was presented in Medoff 1979. Medoff also cited a study by Slichter, Healy, and Livernash 1960 claiming that unions, which initially approved of some work sharing, moved toward a preference for layoffs in the early postwar period.) Perhaps more important than unionism is the fact that in the United States, fully unemployed workers can receive government compensation but the partially unemployed cannot. See Baily (1977) for a formal analysis.

10.5   Analysis in the Frequency Domain

We turn now to the study of these variables over the business cycle. To obtain characterizations of "typical" cyclical patterns, we subjected the data to both frequency domain and time domain analysis. In the frequency domain work we followed the approach suggested by Granger and Hatanaka (1964); in the time domain our analysis is in the spirit of Sims (1980). (There are, of course, close formal connections between

Table 10.6		Standard Deviations (%) of Monthly Growth Rates of Five Variables: Business Cycle Frequencies (Twelve to Ninety-Six Months) Only				
Industry	Period	IP	EMP	HRS	PROD	WR
STEEL	1923–39	3.96	1.59	1.73	1.53	0.59
	1954–82	2.28	1.05	0.48	1.15	0.27
AUTOS	1923–39	4.54	2.72	1.46	2.93	0.36
	1954–82	1.85	1.43	0.47	0.77	0.31
MEAT	1923–39	1.66	1.05	0.49	1.01	0.49
	1954–82	0.46	0.27	0.19	0.36	0.21
PAPER	1923–39	1.33	0.60	0.65	0.76	0.36
	1954–82	0.56	0.30	0.16	0.27	0.14
SHOES	1923–39	1.26	0.47	0.94	0.78	0.68
	1954–82	0.71	0.39	0.38	0.60	0.17
WOOL	1923–39	3.16	1.69	1.06	0.99	0.67
	1954–82	1.56	1.01	0.61	1.74	0.22
LEATH	1923–39	1.19	0.97	0.77	0.82	0.47
	1954–82	0.59	0.49	0.22	0.52	0.14
LUMBR	1923–39	1.75	1.48	0.85	1.19	0.70
	1954–82	0.87	0.61	0.21	0.44	0.23
ALL MFG	1923–39	1.53	0.97	0.67	0.48	0.33
	1954–82	0.60	0.39	0.15	0.21	0.20
COAL	1954–82	0.92	0.71	0.61	0.84	0.25
ELECT	1954–82	0.22	0.16	0.10	0.28	0.13
CONST	1954–82	0.69	0.75	0.21	0.77	0.15

these two approaches; this is evidenced by the similarity of the results obtained.) The results from the frequency domain will be discussed here. Those from the time domain are presented in section 10.6.

The data used in the frequency domain work (as well as in the time domain) were the deseasonalized log differences of the basic series. (Deseasonalization was done by the use of seasonal dummies; see our data appendix.) Each variable was analyzed separately by industry and for the prewar and postwar sample periods.

Spectra of these data showed power in the business cycle frequency range, but rarely were clear peaks apparent in that range. (Sargent 1979, 254, warns that this is to be expected.) We decided to investigate the properties of cycles with periods exceeding one year (so as to exclude remaining seasonal and other high-frequency influences) but shorter than eight years. (According to the NBER chronology, the longest business cycle in our sample—the one extending from 1929 to 1937—was eight years long.) For each industry/sample period, we calculated the coherences and phase relationships of the variables over the one- to eight-year band.

The coherences of six variables (the rates of growth of employment, weekly hours, productivity, real wages, product wages, and real weekly earnings) with the rate of growth of industry output over the business cycle range are reported in table 10.7. (Standard errors of the coherence estimates are also included. See the appendix for a description of how these were calculated.) Coherence is a measure of the degree of association of a pair of variables over a prescribed set of frequencies; a coherence of zero indicates the minimum association, a coherence of one the maximum. The table suggests that employment and hours bear the strongest relation to output over the business cycle. Productivity and earnings also are strongly related to output for most industries. The connection between the two wage measures and output is erratic across industries and, on the whole, is weaker; this is especially true in the postwar period. Note, however, that the coherences of wages and output appear to be statistically significant in both periods.

A particularly informative exercise in the frequency domain is the calculation of phase relationships. For a given frequency, think of variables as tracing out sine curves over time. Then the "phase lead" of variable A with respect to variable B is the number of months after A reaches a given point on its sinusoidal path that B reaches the corresponding point. We shall say a variable that has a phase lead with respect to output of near zero is "procyclical"; a variable whose phase lead with respect to output is approximately half the period of the full cycle is "countercyclical." (There are, however, some caveats to this interpretation of phase leads; see Hause 1971.)

The phase leads of six variables with respect to output growth, plus standard errors, are given in table 10.8. The phase leads are evaluated at the frequency with period of fifty-four months, the period at the center of the range considered. (See the appendix for more discussion.) We find that employment, hours, and earnings are roughly procyclical. Productivity is procyclical but slightly leading in the postwar period; its lead over output is greater in the prewar period. Hours typically leads, though by less than productivity, while employment consistently lags a few months behind output. Earnings is approximately coincident.

The interrelation of productivity, hours, output, and employment is essentially stable between the prewar and postwar periods and, except for the introduction of some subtleties in timing, is consistent with earlier findings. In conjunction with the dynamic model of the firm discussed in section 10.2, this interrelation suggests a simple economic interpretation: cycles are dominated by demand changes. Firms anticipating an increase in demand respond first by increasing nonlabor inputs and asking for more work effort; this increases productivity. As demand strengthens, hours of work expand. Finally, as the increase in demand assumes greater permanence, firms make the hiring and training investments needed to add to the work force. This story is hardly original (see, for example, Baily 1977), and we emphasize again that

Table 10.7   **Coherences of Growth Rates of Six Variables with Growth Rate of Output**

Industry	EMP	HRS	PROD	WR	WP	EARN
			Prewar Data			
STEEL	.828	.883	.915	.272	.230	.854
	(.060)	(.042)	(.031)	(.175)	(.179)	(.051)
AUTOS	.854	.583	.692	.252	.271	.568
	(.051)	(.125)	(.099)	(.177)	(.175)	(.128)
MEAT	.773	.657	.836	.541	.330	.292
	(.076)	(.107)	(.057)	(.134)	(.168)	(.173)
PAPER	.661	.870	.721	.610	.507	.836
	(.106)	(.046)	(.091)	(.119)	(.140)	(.057)
SHOES	.717	.836	.651	.098	.142	.794
	(.092)	(.057)	(.109)	(.187)	(.185)	(.070)
WOOL	.934	.878	.783	.449	.429	.797
	(.024)	(.043)	(.073)	(.151)	(.154)	(.069)
LEATH	.754	.742	.341	.473	.634	.823
	(.082)	(.085)	(.167)	(.147)	(.113)	(.061)
LUMBR	.749	.784	.276	.354	.659	.638
	(.083)	(.073)	(.175)	(.165)	(.107)	(.112)
ALL MFG	.935	.916	.567	.567	.607	.902
	(.024)	(.031)	(.128)	(.128)	(.119)	(.035)
			Postwar Data			
STEEL	.898	.895	.863	.527	.180	.829
	(.027)	(.028)	(.036)	(.102)	(.137)	(.044)
AUTOS	.912	.724	.479	.733	.578	.809
	(.024)	(.067)	(.109)	(.065)	(.094)	(.049)
MEAT	.592	.585	.618	.430	.706	.648
	(.092)	(.093)	(.087)	(.115)	(.071)	(.082)
PAPER	.911	.771	.856	.360	.735	.672
	(.024)	(.057)	(.038)	(.123)	(.065)	(.078)
SHOES	.714	.594	.503	.159	.094	.590
	(.069)	(.092)	(.106)	(.138)	(.140)	(.092)
WOOL	.418	.295	.586	.252	.573	.294
	(.127)	(.141)	(.101)	(.144)	(.123)	(.141)
LEATH	.620	.412	.416	.164	.368	.385
	(.087)	(.117)	(.117)	(.138)	(.122)	(.120)
LUMBR	.881	.845	.658	.378	.489	.779
	(.032)	(.040)	(.080)	(.121)	(.108)	(.056)
ALL MFG	.941	.839	.684	.378	.314	.693
	(.016)	(.042)	(.075)	(.121)	(.128)	(.073)
COAL	.603	.710	.331	.371	.063	.676
	(.090)	(.070)	(.126)	(.122)	(.141)	(.077)
ELECT	.290	.359	.734	.287	.203	.413
	(.129)	(.123)	(.065)	(.130)	(.148)	(.117)
CONST	.568	.344	.384	.274	.507	.397
	(.096)	(.125)	(.121)	(.131)	(.105)	(.119)

Note: Bandwidth is twelve to ninety-six months. Standard errors are given in parentheses.

Table 10.8   **Phase Leads of Growth Rates of Six Variables with Respect to Growth Rate of Output, in Months**

Industry	EMP	HRS	PROD	WR	WP	EARN
			Prewar Data			
STEEL	−4.7	1.8	2.3	−5.3	−0.3	1.2
	(1.11)	(0.9)	(0.7)	(5.7)	(6.9)	(1.0)
AUTOS	−0.5	10.4	−2.9	−10.6	−6.0	9.8
	(1.0)	(2.3)	(1.7)	(6.2)	(5.8)	(2.4)
MEAT	−6.0	2.2	4.6	−22.2	−7.6	−5.1
	(1.3)	(1.9)	(1.1)	(2.5)	(4.7)	(5.3)
PAPER	−7.3	2.4	2.3	−19.3	26.5	−0.5
	(1.8)	(0.9)	(1.6)	(2.1)	(2.8)	(1.1)
SHOES	−6.3	−2.4	9.0	−11.5	9.0	−3.0
	(1.6)	(1.1)	(1.9)	(16.6)	(11.3)	(1.2)
WOOL	−2.6	2.1	2.7	−15.8	24.7	−0.6
	(0.6)	(0.9)	(1.3)	(3.2)	(3.4)	(1.2)
LEATH	−5.7	2.8	11.1	−14.6	26.5	−0.7
	(1.4)	(1.5)	(4.5)	(3.0)	(1.9)	(1.1)
LUMBR	−3.8	2.0	11.2	−19.1	27.0	−0.7
	(1.4)	(1.3)	(5.7)	(4.3)	(1.9)	(2.0)
ALL MFG	−3.9	2.3	9.3	−11.6	−19.5	−0.3
	(0.6)	(0.7)	(2.4)	(2.4)	(2.1)	(0.8)
			Postwar Data			
STEEL	−2.8	1.1	2.2	3.1	9.3	1.6
	(0.6)	(0.6)	(0.7)	(2.0)	(6.6)	(0.8)
AUTOS	−2.5	4.5	5.0	3.6	3.9	4.1
	(0.5)	(1.2)	(2.2)	(1.1)	(1.7)	(0.9)
MEAT	−4.1	2.3	1.8	0.1	−1.6	1.3
	(1.7)	(1.7)	(1.6)	(2.6)	(1.2)	(1.4)
PAPER	−4.4	2.1	3.9	7.2	10.0	3.5
	(0.6)	(1.0)	(0.7)	(3.2)	(1.1)	(1.3)
SHOES	−5.9	1.6	3.8	−7.6	11.9	0.8
	(1.2)	(1.7)	(2.1)	(7.6)	(12.9)	(1.7)
WOOL	−3.4	−1.0	1.5	4.9	24.3	0.5
	(2.8)	(4.1)	(1.8)	(4.9)	(2.0)	(4.1)
LEATH	−2.3	3.5	1.7	−5.4	12.4	1.8
	(1.5)	(2.7)	(2.7)	(7.3)	(3.1)	(2.9)
LUMBR	−3.9	2.0	6.4	−1.2	25.7	1.0
	(0.7)	(0.8)	(1.4)	(3.0)	(2.2)	(1.0)
ALL MFG	−2.4	2.1	4.4	0.7	8.4	1.6
	(0.5)	(0.8)	(1.3)	(3.0)	(3.7)	(1.3)
COAL	−5.1	−0.1	9.1	−10.4	−21.3	−1.7
	(1.6)	(1.2)	(3.5)	(3.0)	(19.2)	(1.3)
ELECT	−16.0	−0.3	1.9	2.8	−5.4	1.3
	(4.0)	(3.2)	(1.1)	(4.1)	(4.9)	(2.7)
CONST	−4.2	4.2	5.0	11.6	12.3	6.7
	(1.8)	(3.3)	(2.9)	(4.3)	(2.0)	(2.8)

Note: Bandwidth is twelve to ninety-six months. Standard errors are given in parentheses.

we have done no explicitly structural test. Still, it is interesting that this interpretation seems at least to be consistent with the facts for so many disparate industries, and for both the prewar and postwar eras.

This stability across industries and sample periods is not shared by the relationship of wages and output. There seems to be a definite difference between the prewar and postwar behavior of wages. Let us concentrate on real, rather than product, wages. During the prewar period, real wages lagged output significantly—not quite enough to be called countercyclical, but still "half out of phase."[3] (A well-known example of this is the positive growth of real wages in 1931–32, even as output and employment plunged.) In contrast, during the postwar period real wages were nearly in phase (procyclical), even leading the cycle in some industries.

Why did the cyclical behavior of real wages change between the prewar and postwar periods? A satisfactory answer to this question would require an explicit structural model, which we do not attempt in this paper. However, we do present a simple heuristic example suggesting that this change may be related to one of our earlier findings, that layoffs have become relatively more important than work sharing in the postwar period.

Suppose that, because of fixed costs, workers can hold only one job at a time. (This example will generalize as long as an individual's work effort is not infinitely divisible among employers.) Then the labor market is cleared not by the hourly wage, but by the total utility available to the worker in a job. Assume that workers get utility from total real compensation Y and disutility from hours of work per week H. If, for simplicity, the marginal utilities of income and leisure are taken to be constant, then instantaneous utility at time t, U_t, can be written as

$$(1) \qquad U_t = Y_t - \alpha H_t,$$

where α is a parameter.

To retain their labor forces, firms must provide workers with (Y_t, H_t) combinations such that workers' utility equals or exceeds $\bar{U}$, the (exogenous) utility level obtainable elsewhere in the economy. Assuming for purposes of this example that business cycles are regular sine waves and that $\bar{U}$ is procyclical, we can write

$$(2) \qquad \bar{U}_t = \bar{U}_0 (1 + a \sin t),$$

where $\bar{U}_0$ is average obtainable utility and a is a positive parameter measuring the cyclical sensitivity of $\bar{U}$.

---

3. This is reminiscent of Creamer's (1950) result for nominal wage rates. See section 10.2.

Firms' choices about which (Y_t, H_t) combinations to offer (from among those combinations that satisfy the external utility constraint) will arise from a maximization calculation that takes into account the nature of the production function, the existence of specific human capital or adjustment costs, and so forth. For this heuristic example we do not explicitly specify the firm's maximization problem but simply assume (realistically) that its outcome will imply a procyclical workweek:

$$(3) \qquad\qquad H_t = H_0 (1 + b \sin t),$$

where H_O is the average workweek over the cycle and b measures the workweek's cyclical sensitivity. Equation (3) is to be interpreted as a reduced form; the parameter b may well depend on the other parameters in the problem.

The three equations just given, plus the assumption that real earnings are just high enough to meet the external utility constraint, imply that the cyclical behavior of real earnings per worker is

$$(4) \qquad\qquad Y_t = (\bar{U}_0 + \alpha H_0) + (a + \alpha b) \sin t.$$

Average earnings Y_0 equal $\bar{U}_0 + \alpha H_0$.

In this example, the measured "real wage" W_t is just Y_t/H_t. Under what conditions will the measured wage be procyclical (i.e., have a positive sensitivity to the exogenous cycle)? It is easy to show that the necessary and sufficient condition for real wage procyclicality is

$$(5) \qquad\qquad a > b.$$

That is, wages are procyclical if reservation utility has a greater sensitivity to the cycle than do hours of work.

It is difficult to say what has happened over time to the cyclical sensitivity of reservation utility; perhaps reservation utility has become less cyclical in the postwar period, which would work against the present argument. However, in section 10.4 we introduced evidence that b, the cyclical sensitivity of hours, has fallen in the postwar era. The example shows that, everything else being equal, reduced cyclical sensitivity of hours tends to be associated with greater observed procyclicality in real wages. Thus, two of the novel findings of this paper—that hours have become less procyclical and that real wages more procyclical in the postwar period—may be related.

An important question is whether the cyclical relationships described in tables 10.7 and 10.8 are the same in long and short business cycles. Closely related is whether it is useful to study "reference cycles." Burns and Mitchell frequently measured timing relationships in terms of "stages" of a standard "reference cycle" instead of in calendar times. For this to be worthwhile, it must be the case that cyclical lead/

lag relationships are roughly constant fractions of the cycle length rather than constant when measured in calendar time; that is to say, phase angles must be constant across business cycle frequencies.

Some insight on this question is provided by table 10.9. That table gives the estimates of the phase leads of the six variables for the deseasonalized high-frequency band (two to twelve months); for short cycles (one to two years); and for long cycles (two to eight years). (The business cycle band was broken up in that particular way because there are approximately as many frequencies with periods between twelve and twenty-four months as there are with periods between twenty-four and ninety-six months.) Also reported for each variable are the results of a statistical test for constancy of phase angles between short and long business cycles. Inspection of table 10.9 suggests two observations.

First, while not much systematic emerges in the high-frequency band, the qualitative pattern of leads and lags is the same in the short and long business cycles ranges (the b and c rows in the table). For example, productivity still leads the cycle, employment still lags.

Second, there appears to be a bit of support for the "reference cycle" construction (and, by implication, for the "time deformation" approach to cycles recently suggested by Stock 1983). The hypothesis of constant phase angles between short and long business cycles, which is implied by the reference cycle approach, is not usually rejected by the data. (Exceptions are the prewar meat-packing industry and, to some extent, aggregate manufacturing in both the prewar and postwar periods.) Thus, assuming that leads and lags are proportional to cycle length does not seem unreasonable. On the other hand, it should be noted that this evidence in favor of reference cycles may possibly be spurious: as an example in Hause (1971) shows, two variables with a fixed distributed lag relationship in the time domain may also exhibit a phase relationship that is roughly proportional to the period of the cycle.

The observations we have made so far apply to more or less all the industries in the sample, with a few distinctions drawn between the patterns visible in the prewar period and those in the postwar era. We had hoped to be able to make more cross-sectional distinctions (e.g., like the finding of Nadiri and Rosen 1973 that input responses are much more rapid in durable goods industries). Unfortunately, much less cross-sectional variation than we expected was evident when we grouped the industries in the obvious ways.

To see if the industries might be grouped by the nature of their cyclical behavior, we estimated the coherences and phases between industry outputs and the aggregate index of output, for the prewar and postwar periods separately. These are presented in table 10.10. An odd result is that almost all the phase leads are positive; this may be due to the inclusion of input-based measures of output in the aggregate index.

Table 10.9   **Phase Leads of Growth Rates of Six Variables with Respect to Growth Rate of Output, in Months**

Industry		EMP	HRS	PROD	WR	WP	EARN
				Prewar Data			
	(a)	−0.4	0.0	0.2	−1.9	2.5	−0.1
STEEL	(b)	−1.6	0.6	0.8	2.2	2.4	0.8
	(c)	−5.0	2.1	2.5	−13.8***	−13.5***	−0.4
	(a)	0.3	0.5	−0.2	−1.4	−1.2	0.4
AUTOS	(b)	−0.3	4.1	−0.9	−2.2	−1.2	4.0
	(c)	0.1	6.6	−3.6	−15.3	−9.4	5.0*
	(a)	−1.0	−0.1	0.2	−2.0	−1.2	−0.2
MEAT	(b)	−2.2	0.6	1.1	−8.2	−5.5	0.2
	(c)	−5.8	23.9***	10.4***	−16.1	0.3***	−18.9***
	(a)	−1.4	−0.6	0.3	−3.0	−2.4	−0.9
PAPER	(b)	−3.1	0.7	0.8	−7.1	−8.9	0.1
	(c)	−4.5	3.4	2.7	−18.1	27.8	−2.7
	(a)	−0.3	−0.1	0.1	2.8	2.6	0.1
SHOES	(b)	−1.9	−0.9	3.0	−7.4	4.4	−1.1
	(c)	−8.6	−1.1	9.8	−5.0	0.6	−2.3
	(a)	−0.6	−0.1	0.4	−2.6	−3.4	−0.3
WOOL	(b)	−0.6	0.6	0.6	−5.3	−8.9	0.2
	(c)	−4.4	2.9	5.3	−17.5	25.6	−3.5
	(a)	0.0	−0.1	0.0	1.9	−3.3	0.2
LEATH	(b)	−2.4	0.8	3.5	−4.9	8.8	0.1
	(c)	−3.2	4.0	18.7	−15.9	29.5	−4.0
	(a)	−0.4	0.6	−0.1	−2.6	−3.0	0.4
LUMBR	(b)	−1.8	0.4	4.6	−7.4	−8.8	−0.5
	(c)	−1.3***	5.7	−0.9*	−5.7	28.8	0.8
	(a)	−0.5	−0.1	0.6	3.4	−3.2	−0.1
ALL MFG	(b)	−1.7	0.6	2.3	−3.9	−7.2	0.0
	(c)	−3.3*	3.4	19.9***	−12.8	−20.0	−0.7
				Postwar Data			
	(a)	−0.4	0.0	0.1	0.7	0.9	0.1
STEEL	(b)	−0.9	0.1	0.5	0.8	0.8	0.3
	(c)	−3.3	2.9***	4.4*	4.7	17.6	3.4
	(a)	−0.2	−0.1	1.7	−0.2	−0.1	−0.1
AUTOS	(b)	−0.8	1.5	1.6	1.2	2.0	1.4
	(c)	−2.7	4.6	6.1	3.9	−0.7*	4.3
	(a)	−1.3	0.1	0.0	−0.6	−0.4	−0.1
MEAT	(b)	−1.3	0.9	0.5	1.0	−0.2	0.9
	(c)	−4.9	1.9	2.4	−5.6*	−2.4	−1.5
	(a)	0.4	−0.6	0.0	2.7	−2.0	−0.4
PAPER	(b)	−1.2	0.3	1.0	−2.8	3.1	0.1
	(c)	−5.5	3.6	5.8*	8.7	12.0	5.8*
	(a)	0.3	0.5	0.1	1.0	1.2	0.5
SHOES	(b)	−1.9	0.9	0.6	−3.5	5.3	0.5
	(c)	−6.7	0.8	8.3	−5.6	10.9	0.1

Table 10.9   (continued)

Industry		*EMP*	*HRS*	*PROD*	*WR*	*WP*	*EARN*
	(a)	0.0	0.1	0.0	0.5	2.5	0.1
WOOL	(b)	−1.9	−1.9	0.5	1.0	−5.2	0.5
	(c)	−2.2	3.7	0.8	7.1	25.2**	4.6
	(a)	0.7	0.7	−0.1	0.7	1.8	0.7
LEATH	(b)	−0.4	1.5	−0.1	−3.3	−8.5	0.7
	(c)	−3.2	3.0	4.2	−2.6	13.3	1.7
	(a)	−0.2	0.1	0.0	0.4	1.2	0.3
LUMBR	(b)	−1.4	0.7	1.3	−2.6	−7.7	0.2
	(c)	−6.2	0.8	18.7***	−8.5	29.1	0.2
	(a)	−0.0	0.2	0.1	0.6	0.7	0.1
ALL MFG	(b)	−0.7	0.0	1.0	−1.8	2.8	−0.7
	(c)	−2.9	4.7***	9.5**	5.7**	9.3	9.5**
	(a)	−0.2	−0.2	0.1	−2.7	−1.6	−0.2
COAL	(b)	−1.1	−0.3	0.7	−3.7	−3.2	−1.1
	(c)	−6.2	0.8	18.7***	−8.5	29.0	0.2
	(a)	2.1	0.7	−0.1	−2.2	0.6	0.3
ELECT	(b)	−5.7	1.1	0.3	−3.3	−4.4	−0.8
	(c)	−16.5	−9.0*	3.1	8.5***	−0.1	5.2
	(a)	0.0	0.2	0.0	−3.4	−3.1	0.2
CONST	(b)	−0.8	1.6	0.6	7.0	5.6	3.2
	(c)	−6.7	1.5	8.5	4.9***	10.3**	4.0

Note: Asterisks denote significance of *t*-tests of difference of phase angles between frequency bands (b) and (c), at marginal significance levels of .10 (*), .05 (**), and .01 (***).

(a) Bandwidth: two to twelve months.

(b) Bandwidth: twelve to twenty-four months.

(c) Bandwidth: twenty four to ninety-six months.

The coherence estimates suggest that cyclical influences became relatively less important for the industries in the postwar period. There is also a tendency in the postwar sample for durable goods industries to exhibit a relatively higher coherence with the cycle than nondurable goods industries. However, except for meat-packing, there is surprisingly little evidence of this pattern in the prewar period. Overall, cross-sectional differences still seem less significant than cross-sectional similarities.

10.6   Analysis in the Time Domain

To complement the frequency domain analysis of the data, we employed time domain methods, primarily vector autoregressions (VARs). Separate VARs, using twelve monthly lags of four variables (output, hours, employment, and real wages), were estimated for each of the

Table 10.10   **Coherences and Phase Leads of Growth Rates of Output in Each Industry with Respect to Growth Rate of "All Manufacturing" Output**

Industry	Period	Coherence (SE)	Phase Lead (SE)
STEEL	1923–39	94.7 (2.0)	1.3 (0.6)
	1954–82	64.6 (8.2)	0.2 (1.4)
AUTOS	1923–39	78.0 (7.4)	−4.1 (1.3)
	1954–82	78.6 (5.4)	0.2 (1.0)
MEAT	1923–39	19.5 (18.2)	1.2 (8.2)
	1954–82	26.2 (13.2)	4.8 (4.5)
PAPER	1923–39	86.7 (4.7)	2.3 (0.9)
	1954–82	79.7 (5.2)	1.2 (0.9)
SHOES	1923–39	73.9 (8.6)	6.7 (1.5)
	1954–82	46.4 (11.1)	4.9 (2.3)
WOOL	1923–39	80.1 (6.8)	3.5 (1.2)
	1954–82	31.9 (13.9)	1.4 (3.9)
LEATH	1923–39	75.0 (8.3)	0.6 (1.4)
	1954–82	38.8 (12.0)	3.7 (2.9)
LUMBR	1923–39	88.0 (4.3)	1.0 (0.9)
	1954–82	73.9 (6.4)	5.3 (1.1)
COAL	1954–82	28.4 (13.0)	−5.4 (4.1)
ELECT	1954–82	44.7 (11.3)	−2.1 (2.4)
CONST	1954–82	57.4 (9.5)	6.3 (1.7)

Note: Bandwidth is twelve to ninety-six months.

prewar and postwar industries and for the aggregates. The data were the same centered and seasonalized log differences described in section 10.5. As in Sims (1980), the estimated VARs were used to do three things. First, we looked at the statistical significance of blocks of coefficients in order to search for patterns of causality (in the Granger sense). Second, we calculated the percentages of the forecast errors attributable to (triangularized) innovations in the right-hand-side variables, for four forecast horizons. Finally, the implied impulse/response diagrams were examined for systematic timing relationships among the variables. We briefly discuss each of these exercises.

Table 10.11 summarizes the results of the Granger-causality F-tests. There is one matrix for each dependent variable. In each matrix, the rows designate the industry to which the VAR applies, the columns give the block of independent variables being tested. One, two, or three asterisks in a given cell of a matrix implies that the twelve monthly lags of the independent variable jointly "explain" the dependent variable (for the given industry and period) at the .10, .05, or .01 level of significance. No asterisks in a cell implies that the joint contribution of all lags of the given regressor is not significant at the .10 level.

Table 10.11   **VAR *F*-Tests**

Dependent Variables	Industry	Independent Variables			
		IP	*HRS*	*EMP*	*WR*
	Prewar Data				
IP					
	STEEL	**	*		***
	AUTOS	***		***	
	MEAT		**		**
	PAPER			**	
	SHOES	***	**		*
	WOOL	*		***	
	LEATH		*		
	LUMBR	***	***		***
	ALL MFG	***			
HRS					
	STEEL	***	***	***	***
	AUTOS		***		
	MEAT		**	*	*
	PAPER	***	*		*
	SHOES	***	***	***	
	WOOL	***	**	***	
	LEATH	***	***	***	
	LUMBR	**	***		
	ALL MFG	***	*	***	
EMP					
	STEEL	*			
	AUTOS	***	***	**	*
	MEAT	**	**		
	PAPER	**		**	
	SHOES	**	**	***	
	WOOL	***		***	
	LEATH	***		**	
	LUMBR	**		**	
	ALL MFG	**	*		
WR					
	STEEL				
	AUTOS		**		
	MEAT				
	PAPER			**	
	SHOES	**	**		
	WOOL				
	LEATH	**			
	LUMBR	***	*	*	***
	ALL MFG			*	
	Postwar Data				
IP					
	STEEL	*			
	AUTOS	*		***	
	MEAT	***	**		*
	PAPER	***		**	***
	SHOES	***	***	**	
	WOOL	***	***		
	LEATH	***	**		
	LUMBR	***		***	***

Table 10.11   (continued)

Dependent Variables	Industry	Independent Variables			
		IP	HRS	EMP	WR
	ALL MFG	***	**	***	
	COAL	***		*	
	ELECT	***			***
	CONST	***			**
HRS					
	STEEL	**	***	**	
	AUTOS		***		
	MEAT	**	***		**
	PAPER	***	***	*	
	SHOES	***	***	***	
	WOOL	*	***	***	***
	LEATH		***	**	*
	LUMBR		***		
	ALL MFG	***	***	**	
	COAL	***	***	*	**
	ELECT		***		
	CONST		***		
EMP					
	STEEL	***	**		
	AUTOS	***	**	***	
	MEAT	***		**	
	PAPER	***	***	***	
	SHOES	**	***	***	
	WOOL	***	***	***	***
	LEATH		***	***	
	LUMBR	***		***	**
	ALL MFG	***		**	
	COAL	*		***	
	ELECT		**	***	
	CONST			***	
WR					
	STEEL				***
	AUTOS	***		***	***
	MEAT	*			**
	PAPER				***
	SHOES		**		***
	WOOL		*		***
	LEATH				***
	LUMBR			**	
	ALL MFG				***
	COAL				***
	ELECT	**		***	***
	CONST				***

Note: F-tests whose outcomes are reported are tests of the joint significance of all twelve lags of the independent variable in the explanation of the dependent variable. (All variables are in growth rates.)

*F-test significant at .10 level.

**F-test significant at .05 level.

***F-test significant at .01 level.

Table 10.11 suggests that, for all industries taken together:

1. Output growth tends to be relatively exogenous (in the Granger sense), at least in comparison with the growth rates of employment and hours. (Thus hours may be a "leading indicator" without having incremental predictive value for output. See Neftci 1979.) Output seemed to be much more "persistent" in the postwar period, in the sense that lagged growth rates of output became much stronger predictors of the current growth rate.

2. Hours and employment are rarely found to be Granger exogenous; they respond both to each other and to output. The two variables are also found to be persistent, in the sense just defined, in both the prewar and postwar samples. The persistence of employment will be an appealing finding for supporters of the view that there are "adjustment costs" to changing employment. Are there also adjustment costs to changing hours of work? The data seem consistent with this.

3. The real wage seems to vary nearly independently of the three other variables, neither consistently predicting nor being predictable by them. A remarkably strong finding about the real wage is that, like output, its persistence significantly increased between the prewar and postwar periods.

The results of the forecast error decomposition exercise are given in Table 10.12. To save space, we report results for three industries only: iron and steel (a durable goods industry), paper and pulp (nondurables), and leather tanning and finishing (semidurables). Results for the manufacturing aggregates are also reported. The prewar and postwar forecast error decompositions are placed side by side in the table, for easier comparison. Also note that, since the growth in productivity is just a linear combination of the growth in output, hours, and employment (all of which were included in the VARs), it is possible to report decompositions for this variable as well.

As the reader familiar with these methods is aware, the attribution of forecast error at different horizons to the (triangularized) innovations in the regressors is not invariant to the ordering of the variables. The ordering used here (and for the construction of the impulse/response diagrams below) is as follows: (log differences of) output, hours, employment, real wages. Given that the data are monthly and that forecast horizons up to forty-eight months are studied, the choice of ordering is not likely to be crucial to the results.

The pattern of relationships suggested by table 10.12 is, perhaps not surprisingly, very similar to that revealed by the F-tests reported in table 10.11. Note, for example, that the relatively exogenous output variable (IP) is shown in table 10.12 to be largely "self-caused," even at the four-year forecast horizon. (This tendency seems to be even

Table 10.12   **Percentages of Forecast Error _k_ Months Ahead Produced by Each Innovation (Prewar/Postwar)**

Forecast Error		Triangularized Innovation			
	_k_	_IP_	_HRS_	_EMP_	_WR_
		Iron and Steel			
IP	6	89/91	2/3	3/5	6/1
	12	79/87	5.4	4/6	13/2
	24	66/85	8/5	5/8	21/2
	48	63/85	8/5	6/8	23/2
EMP	6	31/55	1/1	63/41	5/3
	12	29/52	4/6	59/39	8/4
	24	29/51	5/7	53/38	12/4
	48	29/51	6/7	51/38	15/4
HRS	6	40/43	40/52	19/4	2/1
	12	41/41	34/50	19/7	7/2
	24	40/41	31/49	17/8	12/2
	48	39/41	31/49	17/8	13/2
WR	6	3/4	3/8	6/1	88/86
	12	6/6	5/9	7/4	82/82
	24	8/6	6/9	8/4	78/81
	48	8/6	7/9	8/4	77/81
PROD	6	57/76	29/10	3/12	11/2
	12	49/74	30/10	5/13	16/2
	24	40/73	30/11	7/14	24/3
	48	39/73	30/11	7/14	24/3
		Paper and Pulp			
IP	6	83/92	3/2	10/5	4/0
	12	75/83	6/3	11/7	8/7
	24	71/80	8/3	12/7	10/9
	48	71/80	8/3	12/7	10/9
EMP	6	21/31	1/5	72/62	6/2
	12	19/30	5/6	68/57	8/7
	24	19/30	5/6	65/55	11/10
	48	19/30	5/6	65/54	11/10
HRS	6	30/11	61/86	3/2	6/2
	12	32/14	56/80	4/3	8/3
	24	32/14	54/79	4/4	10/4
	48	32/14	54/79	4/4	10/4
WR	6	9/1	10/2	2/2	80/96
	12	13/2	10/3	8/3	69/93
	24	13/3	10/4	10/3	67/91
	48	13/3	10/4	10/3	66/91
PROD	6	50/64	26/18	19/17	5/1
	12	45/60	27/16	20/18	8/6
	24	43/58	26/17	19/18	12/8
	48	43/58	26/17	19/18	12/8

Table 10.12   (continued)

Forecast Error		Triangularized Innovation			
	k	IP	HRS	EMP	WR
Leather Tanning and Finishing					
IP	6	84/90	5/3	8/5	3/2
	12	80/87	8/5	7/5	4/3
	24	78/85	10/7	8/5	5/4
	48	78/85	10/7	8/5	5/4
EMP	6	21/8	8/9	69/82	2/2
	12	23/8	9/10	65/78	4/4
	24	29/8	9/10	58/78	4/4
	48	29/8	10/10	56/78	5/4
HRS	6	19/3	69/89	7/3	6/5
	12	21/5	65/84	8/6	6/6
	24	23/5	61/82	9/6	7/7
	48	24/5	60/81	9/6	7/7
WR	6	8/3	12/1	7/3	72/92
	12	14/4	14/3	8/5	64/88
	24	16/5	16/3	9/5	59/87
	48	16/5	16/3	9/5	58/87
PROD	6	24/58	36/14	37/26	3/1
	12	33/55	34/17	30/25	4/3
	24	34/54	34/17	28/25	4/4
	48	35/53	34/17	28/25	4/4
All Manufacturing Firms					
IP	6	94/93	1/2	3/4	2/1
	12	77/86	8/4	8/7	7/3
	24	71/82	12/6	10/9	7/3
	48	70/80	12/6	11/10	7/4
EMP	6	64/59	1/2	33/39	2/0
	12	57/57	9/3	31/39	3/2
	24	54/57	11/4	30/38	5/2
	48	53/56	11/4	31/38	5/2
HRS	6	51/22	38/74	9/4	1/1
	12	47/21	38/71	12/5	2/3
	24	46/22	37/68	14/6	4/4
	48	46/22	37/68	14/6	4/4
WR	6	7/2	5/3	11/1	77/94
	12	7/3	9/3	14/2	70/92
	24	13/4	9/3	15/2	62/91
	48	14/4	9/3	16/2	61/91
PROD	6	22/18	41/47	36/34	2/1
	12	22/18	39/44	34/35	5/3
	24	20/19	39/42	35/36	5/3
	48	21/19	39/42	35/36	5/3

greater in the postwar period than in the prewar.) Hours and employment are fairly sensitive to output innovations except, for some reason, in the postwar leather industry. The "persistence" of both hours and employment is apparent; this persistence increases markedly for hours in the postwar era. The productivity variable is largely driven by innovations in output, especially in the postwar period, although productivity's other components (employment and hours) also play a role.

Again, a most striking finding is the relationship (or lack of a relationship) between real wages and the other variables. Innovations in the real wage appear to have virtually no predictive power for output, employment, and weekly hours; and in the other direction, no variable except the real wage itself is of much use in forecasting the real wage. This essential independence of the real wage and the other variables is more pronounced in the postwar period.

The final exercise in the time domain was the use of the estimated VARs to generate impulse/response (IR) diagrams. These diagrams show the movement over time of each variable in the VAR in response to a (triangularized) innovation to one of the regressors. (The response of productivity to innovations in the other variables was also analyzed.) The ordering of the variables was the same as in the forecast error decompositions above. Since the data are in log differences, we printed out cumulative response diagrams; this allowed us to interpret the patterns in terms of log levels. These diagrams were useful for gaining a qualitative appreciation of "typical" short-run patterns in the data.

The number of industries, variables, and sample periods meant that there were potentially hundreds of IR diagrams to study. We chose to look carefully only at the three representative industries (iron and steel, paper, leather); we also looked closely at construction. The reader will be burdened with only a few sample IR diagrams (see figs. 10.1 and 10.2). These show the forty-eight month response pattern of (the log levels of) output, hours, employment, real wages, and productivity to a one standard deviation innovation in output growth in the iron and steel industry. Figure 10.1 *a–d* cover the prewar period; figure 10.2 *a–d* cover the postwar period. The path of output is included in each diagram, for reference.

From our examination of all the IR diagrams, we drew the following conclusions:

1. Generally, the IRs reinforce the characterization of the cycle obtained in the frequency domain. For example, the conclusion of section 10.5 that productivity is highly coherent with output and that it tends to lead the cycle by a few months emerges distinctly from the IR diagrams; this is true no matter which disturbance term provides the initial shock. Similarly, the high coherence and the lead/lag patterns

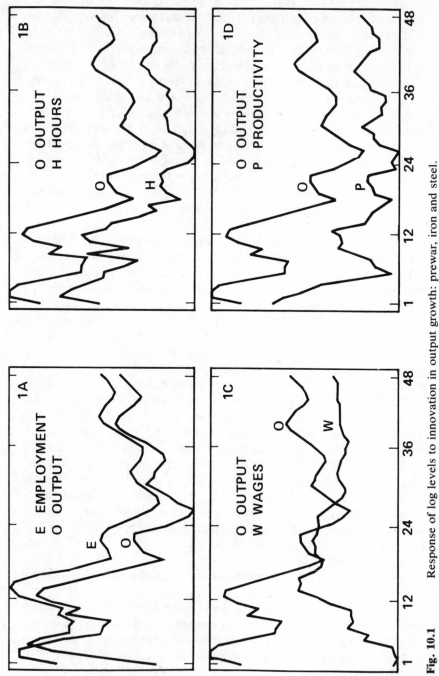

Fig. 10.1 Response of log levels to innovation in output growth: prewar, iron and steel.

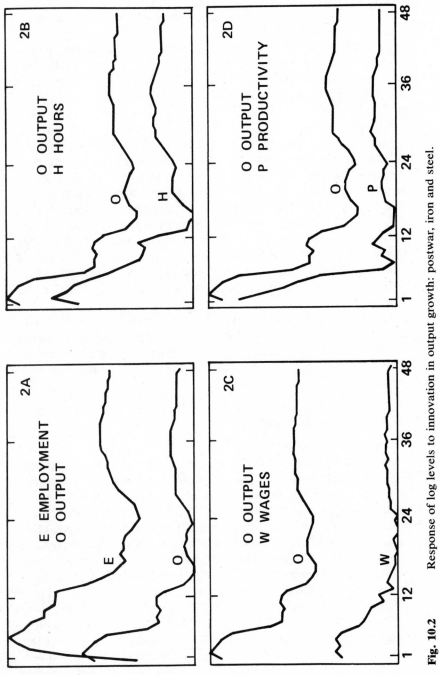

Fig. 10.2 Response of log levels to innovation in output growth: postwar, iron and steel.

for hours and employment found by frequency domain techniques recur almost exactly in the IRs. Figures 10.1*a, b, d* and 10.2*a, b, d* are here perfectly representative.

2. As the frequency domain analysis was less clear about the cyclical characteristics of the real wage, so it is the case in the time domain. The pictures show a real wage behavior that is not very stable across industries and that is also sensitive to the source of the initial shock, especially in the prewar sample. However, as in section 10.4, there still appear to be noticeable differences between prewar and postwar wage movements. (See figs. 10.1*c* and 10.2*c*.) During the postwar period, in the cases when there is a visible relationship between output and wages, the IRs show the real wage to be a roughly coincident, procyclical variable. In the prewar data, the real wage is usually "half out of phase," either lagging (the typical response to output shocks; see fig. 10.1*c*) or leading (when there is an employment shock). There is also an interesting contrast between the prewar and postwar periods with regard to the effect of a wage shock on the rest of the system: a prewar wage shock tends to result in declining output and employment, whereas a wage shock in the postwar sample typically has just the opposite effect.

3. Finally, the diagrams show a postwar decline in cyclical variability (given a "typical" shock), which is consistent with several findings already discussed. Output and real wages in particular (reflecting their increased "persistence"?) are much less prone to gyrations in the postwar sample.

10.7 Four Major Recessions

The analysis so far has been "democratic" in its use of the data, allowing every sample observation equal weight in the calculations. This is consistent with the view that business cycles are realizations of stationary stochastic processes. An alternative view is that serious recessions or depressions are "special" occurrences, governed by different laws of probability than the "normal" parts of the sample. (This idea is investigated more formally by the Blanchard/Watson paper in this volume.) In the spirit of this alternative view, this section looks briefly at the behavior of labor market variables during four major downturns—two prewar and two postwar.

The four downturns studied are 1929:3 to 1933:1, 1937:2 to 1938:2, 1973:4 to 1975:1, and 1981:3 to 1982:4. Note that, except for the first, the recessions are of comparable length. (The peak and trough quarters are from the official NBER chronology.) For each of the four downturns, table 10.13 gives (for each of the seven labor market variables studied) the ratio of the average value of the *level* of the variable in

Table 10.13   **Trough-to-Peak Ratios of Seven Variables for Four Selected Recessions**

Industry	Cycle	IP	EMP	HRS	PROD	WR	WP	EARN
STEEL	I	.17	.50	.56	.62	.91	.84	.50
	II	.36	.72	.65	.77	.95	.92	.62
	III	.87	.96	.95	.95	1.00	.81	.95
	IV	.57	.68	.96	.87	.99	1.05	.94
AUTOS	I	.18	.40	.76	.58	.99	.88	.75
	II	.36	.49	.85	.86	1.02	.90	.87
	III	.60	.74	.93	.88	.95	.92	.88
	IV	.96	.87	1.01	1.10	.97	.97	.97
MEAT	I	.91	.77	.95	1.25	.95	1.50	.90
	II	1.07	.93	1.03	1.12	.99	1.12	1.02
	III	.97	.98	.99	1.00	1.01	1.17	1.00
	IV	.90	.96	1.00	.94	.94	.94	.94
PAPER	I	.59	.74	.79	1.01	.99	.87	.79
	II	.71	.87	.86	.95	1.06	1.13	.91
	III	.74	.88	.95	.89	.96	.82	.91
	IV	.98	.95	.99	1.05	1.02	1.02	1.01
SHOES	I	.79	.89	.92	.96	.99	.95	.91
	II	.82	.93	.73	1.20	1.00	1.02	.73
	III	.81	.87	.91	1.03	.95	.98	.86
	IV	.87	.91	.98	.97	1.00	1.01	.98
WOOL	I	.62	.73	.88	.95	.94	1.23	.83
	II	.44	.68	.80	.80	1.01	1.21	.81
	III	.47	.57	.71	1.16	.91	1.23	.65
	IV	.77	.77	.82	1.22	.99	NA	.82
LEATH	I	.76	.80	.91	1.04	.98	1.43	.89
	II	.71	.79	.85	1.06	1.03	1.23	.87
	III	1.03	.99	.99	1.06	.95	1.24	.94
	IV	.88	.90	1.01	.97	1.02	1.07	1.03
LUMBR	I	.32	.42	.74	1.04	.92	1.13	.68
	II	.67	.86	.87	.89	1.02	1.22	.88
	III	.75	.78	.94	1.01	.96	1.21	.91
	IV	1.10	.99	1.02	1.09	1.01	1.06	1.02
ALL MFG	I	.50	.72	.79	.89	.96	1.01	.76
	II	.62	.73	.81	1.05	.97	1.04	.78
	III	.81	.88	.96	.96	.97	.88	.93
	IV	.90	.90	.99	1.01	.99	1.02	.98
COAL	III	1.05	1.20	1.01	.87	.96	.68	.97
	IV	.83	.84	.91	1.09	1.02	1.02	.93
ELECT	III	.96	.98	.97	1.00	.96	.80	.94
	IV	.93	1.00	1.01	.93	1.02	1.00	1.02
CONST	III	.78	.87	.98	.92	.94	.89	.92
	IV	.99	.93	.98	1.09	1.00	1.04	.98

Note: The variables from which the ratios are formed are detrended, deseasonalized, quarterly averages of levels (not growth rates). Peak and trough quarters are from the official NBER chronology.

  I: 1933:1/1929:3.
 II: 1938:2/1937:2.
III: 1975:1/1973:4.
IV: 1982:4/1981:3.

the trough quarter to its average value in the preceding peak quarter. (The data are detrended and deseasonalized.) The purpose of this is to get a rough measure of the behavior of these variables in individual major recessions. (Alternatives would have been to construct multistage Burns/Mitchell "reference cycles" or to look at all quarters of the downturns. We experimented with both of these but did not find them much more informative.)

A preliminary point that should be made is that the designated peaks and troughs are based on aggregate economic variation, which may not coincide exactly with the industry-level cycles. Nevertheless, there is obviously a strong correlation between aggregate and industry output: in table 10.13 the trough-to-peak ratio for (detrended) production exceeds one only four times in thirty-eight cases.

The trough-to-peak ratios for most of the variables displayed in table 10.13 do not seem too far out of line with our findings of previous sections. Employment and hours display their strong procyclicality throughout. As in section 10.4, we see again here that postwar employers seemed to rely more on layoffs than on short workweeks as the means of reducing labor input in the trough, whereas prewar employers relied relatively more heavily on part-time work. Real wages show little systematic peak-to-trough change, which is indicative of the low coherence of real wages and output. Product wages are more variable than real wages; they also show some tendency to countercyclicality. Weekly real earnings, as would be predicted, are clearly procyclical.

A variable that is somewhat puzzling is productivity. The standard finding that productivity is procyclical implies that its trough-to-peak ratio should be less than one. This ratio is actually below one in only about half of the thirty-four cases in which output declines between peak and trough. Productivity is most procyclical in the heavy durable goods industries (iron and steel, automobiles); in the other industries productivity is more likely to rise than fall, peak to trough.

A partial explanation of these results may follow from our earlier finding that productivity, though essentially procyclical, may lead the cycle by a number of months. Thus productivity at the output peak has already fallen from its highest level, while at the output trough it has already begun to recover. (A similar observation is made by Gordon 1980.) The recovery of productivity in the trough may also be particularly strong in very deep recession, in which financial pressure on firms increases the costs of hoarding labor or permitting inefficient production. These considerations serve at least to reduce this new productivity puzzle, though they probably do not eliminate it.

Putting aside the productivity question, table 10.13 does suggest that there are qualitative similarities between major recessions and less dramatic economic fluctuations. This should be encouraging to fore-casters and policymakers, whose tasks would be impossible if every severe fluctuation were essentially a unique event.

10.8   Conclusion

This exercise in "measurement without theory" has supported some existing perceptions about the cyclical behavior of labor markets and has uncovered a few additional facts. To summarize the most important findings:

1. Procyclical labor productivity (SRIRL) appears to be present in every industry, in both the prewar and postwar periods. (This paper is the first to document SRIRL for the pre-1932 period, as far as we know.) However, in confirming this standard empirical result, we have found two qualifications. First, productivity is a leading, rather than coincident, variable. Second, SRIRL may be less pronounced in major recessions.

2. Weekly hours and employment are strongly procyclical. Hours lead output, whereas employment lags. Our evidence that employment is lagging rather than coincident is somewhat novel; otherwise these observations replicate previous results.

3. A new finding is that there has been an increased reliance in the postwar period on layoffs, rather than short workweeks, as a means of reducing labor input.

4. The relationship of the real wage to other variables over the business cycle is weak, and it has been weaker in the postwar period. On the question whether any cyclical sensitivity of the real wage exists at all, the results from the frequency domain analysis are much more affirmative than those for the time domain. The difference between the two approaches probably arises because the frequency domain analysis blocks out some high-frequency interference that the time domain analysis does not; this permits the frequency domain approach to recover a relationship at business cycle frequencies that is less apparent in the time domain. The noisiness of the wage/employment relationship in the time domain may explain the inability of Geary and Kennan (1982) to reject the hypothesis that these two series are independent.

5. To the extent that the real wage is related to the cycle, there seems to be a definite difference between its prewar and its postwar behavior. The real wage was procyclical (essentially coincident) in the postwar period but "half out of phase" (usually lagging) in the prewar. This difference has not been noticed before for real wages, although Creamer (1950) found that nominal wages lagged the cycle in the early prewar period.

6. The relationship of product wages to the cycle is, if anything, weaker and more erratic than that of real wages. Real weekly earnings are strongly procyclical in both major samples.

7. Cyclical variation is a relatively small part of the total variation of the labor market variables. (A similar finding is in Bernanke 1983.) The postwar data exhibit more stability (i.e., less total variance and less business cycle variance). They also are more serially persistent than the data from the earlier period, which may be interpreted either as being consistent with Sach's (1980) finding of greater rigidity or as simply reflecting a more stable economy.

We hope that this and similar analyses will lead to a better understanding of the cyclical behavior of labor markets. However, we emphasize once again that this research is intended to be a complement to, not a substitute for, structural modeling of these phenomena.

Appendix

Sources

The sources of the *prewar* industry data used in this study are as follows:

1. Earnings, hours, and employment data are from Beney (1936) and Sayre (1940). These data are the result of an extensive monthly survey conducted by the National Industrial Conference Board (NICB) from 1920 until 1947.

All the industries in the sample paid at least part of their work force by piece rates (see *Monthly Labor Review* 41 [September 1935]:697–700). No correction was made for this.

2. Industrial production data are from the Federal Reserve Board. See "New Federal Reserve Index of Industrial Production," *Federal Reserve Bulletin* 26 (August 1940):753–69, 825–74.

3. Wholesale price indexes are from the Bureau of Labor Statistics (BLS). See the following publications of the United States Department of Labor: *Handbook of Labor Statistics* (1931 ed., bulletin 541; 1936 ed., bulletin 616; 1941 ed., bulletin 694) and *Wholesale Prices 1913 to 1927* (Washington, D.C.: Government Printing Office, 1929, bulletin 473). For the automobile industry we merged two BLS series of motor vehicle prices. Neither series covered 1935; the price series on all metal products was used to interpolate the automobiles price series for that year.

4. The consumer price series is from Sayre (1948).

All basic data were seasonally unadjusted. The span of the prewar sample is January 1923 to December 1939. Although some of the data exist before 1923, there are two major problems with extending the sample further back: some of the industrial production data are missing, and there is a six-month gap in the NICB survey in 1923. The December 1939 stop date was chosen to avoid considering the many special features of the wartime economy.

The sources of the *postwar* industry data are as follows:

1. Earnings, hours, and employment data are from *Employment and Earnings, United States* (Bureau of Labor Statistics).

2. Industrial production indexes for industries 1–10 are from the Federal Reserve Board (see Board of Governors, Federal Reserve Board, *Industrial Production,* 1976. Updates are from the *Federal Reserve Bulletin,* and some unpublished series were obtained directly from the board.) The output index for construction was obtained by dividing the value of new construction (as reported by the *Survey of Current Business [SCB]*) by the Department of Commerce construction cost index (also available in the *SCB*).

3. Wholesale prices are again from the Bureau of Labor Statistics. See *Wholesale Prices and Price Indexes, 1963* (BLS bulletin 1513), *Producer Price Indexes,* and the *Monthly Labor Review.*

4. The consumer price series used to calculate real wages is the Department of Labor's consumer price index (all items, wage earners and clerical workers, revised).

Again, the basic data are seasonally unadjusted. The span of the postwar sample is 1954–82, except for the wool textile industry, where the data begin in January 1958. Adequate data on output prices (and therefore on product wages) are missing for wool textiles after 1975 and for electric services before 1958.

The *total manufacturing* series were as follows:

1. For the prewar period, output was measured by the industrial production index for manufacturing. Employment, hours, and earnings data come from the National Industrial Conference Board, as reported in Beney (1936) and Sayre (1940). The NICB series are based on twenty-five major manufacturing industries; the coverage is similar but not identical to that of the industrial production index. The manufacturing output price, used only in the construction of the product wage variable, is the BLS wholesale price index for nonagricultural, nonfuel goods. Again the coverage is similar but not identical to that of the IP index.

2. For the postwar period, again the IP index for manufacturing is used to measure output. Employment, hours, and earnings data are for manufacturing production workers; the output price is the wholesale price index for total manufacturers. Those data are from *Business Sta-*

tistics and the *Survey of Current Business* and, as far as we can tell, are mutually consistent.

Stationarity

The log-differenced data series appeared in general to be stationary. We arrived at this conclusion by studying the autocorrelations and partial autocorrelations of the log-differenced data and by testing for the presence of trend shifts and higher-order trend terms in the log levels. Rejections of stationarity were sufficiently infrequent and weak that, for the sake of uniform treatment of the data, we decided to ignore them.

Reduction of High-Frequency Noise

The spectra of most of the series exhibited considerable power in the higher frequencies; high-frequency noise (primarily seasonality) may interfere with the analysis of the data at business cyle frequencies. To reduce this noise, we regressed each log-differenced series against constant, seasonal dummies and (where applicable) dummy variables for strike periods. (There was no pooling of regressions across industries or between the two major sample periods. There also appeared to be no need to allow for shifts of the regression coefficients within subsamples.) The residuals from these regressions, "cleaned" of much of the very high- and low-frequency noise of the original series, were treated as the basic data in the frequency and time domain analyses.

Details of Frequency Domain Calculations

The entries of tables 10.7 through 10.10 were constructed by simple averaging of the finite Fourier transforms, evaluated at evenly spaced intervals on $(0,\pi)$, for each data series. Since the prewar and postwar sample sizes differed, the frequencies corresponding to the "business cycle" varied as well; thus each calculation involved averages of about 7% (that is, $1/12-1/96$) of the number of periodogram ordinates calculated for each variable.

Table 10.6 gives square roots of the cumulated periodogram ordinates (between twelve and ninety-six months) for each variable. These calculations (and those in the remaining tables) will not be affected by the seasonal or strike adjustments made for the log-differenced data.

Standard errors for the sample coherence $\hat{\rho}$ and phase $\hat{\theta}$ between each pair of variables were computed using the following formulas, adapted from Hannan (1970, chap. 7):

$$[SE(\hat{\rho})]^2 = \nu^{-1/2}(1 - \hat{\rho}^2), \quad \text{and}$$

$$[SE(\hat{\theta})]^2 = \nu^{-1/2}\left(\frac{1 - \hat{\rho}^2}{\hat{\rho}^2}\right)^{1/2},$$

where v is twice the number of periodogram ordinates in the 12–96 month range. Since these expressions are derived from the asymptotic behavior of finite Fourier transforms, the resulting confidence intervals are only approximate and will be poorly behaved for $\hat{\rho}$ near zero or one; still, the standard errors are useful guides to the precision of the estimates.

The estimated phase leads of tables 10.8 through 10.10 were expressed in months by dividing the estimated phase angle $\hat{\theta}$ (and its standard error) by the frequency corresponding to the period in the center of the bandwidth considered. That is, the phase leads calculated for the 12–96, 2–12, 12–24, and 24–96 month bandwidths correspond to cycles with period lengths 54, 7, 18, and 60 months, respectively. These period lengths are uniformly higher than the period lengths corresponding to the average frequency in the bandwidth (which is, for example, about $2/(1/12 + 1/96) = 21.33$ months for the 12–96 month bandwidth). Since the coherences and phase angles are implicitly assumed to be constant within each frequency band, the phase lead for any frequency in the interval can be obtained by rescaling; that is, to obtain a phase lead for a "typical" 20 month cycle, the reported phase lead (and its standard error) for the 12–24 month bandwidth can simply be multiplied by 20/18. The tests of equality of phase angles in table 10.9 do not use the "scaled" phase leads above; rather, t-statistics for the difference in phase angles are constructed directly from the standard error formulas reported above (and use the large-sample independence of the phase estimates for the prewar and postwar periods).

All calculations were carried out using the RATS statistical package (see Doan and Litterman 1981). Other, more theoretical references to frequency domain methods are the texts by Hannan (1970) and Anderson (1971).

Comment   Martin N. Baily

This was a very valuable paper, and I wish there were more like it. It simply presents the data, without imposing much structure or bringing in a lot of prior judgments. Of course from a discussant's point of view it is nice if authors go way out on a limb, for then you can knock them off. These authors kept fairly close to what they were observing, so that I have no major criticisms to make.

They start with a review of the literature. It would have been worthwhile in this review to distinguish overhead labor from labor hoarding.

Martin N. Baily is a senior fellow at the Brookings Institution.

They mention only labor hoarding, although they do cite the article by Solow that develops the overhead labor hypothesis. The difference between the two in principle is that with labor hoarding there are workers who could be dispensed with—the same amount of output could be produced with fewer workers. With overhead labor there is a nonconvexity of the production set—in the short run the number of security guards looking after the plant cannot be reduced. The two are also different in practice. Since estimates of firm-specific human capital suggest that it is small, this means that labor hoarding is a short-run phenomenon, whereas overhead labor is likely to be longer term. The relative importance of the two can be judged from the timing of the short-run increasing returns observed in the data.

The main part of the paper is an analysis of data on output, employment, weekly hours, and wages, and the authors have done a fine job of data collection. They distinguish the real wage, defined as the money wage divided by the CPI, from the product wage, defined as the money wage divided by the wholesale price index for the particular industry they are looking at. They emphasize that there are aggregation biases and that we should look at individual industries. They have data for eight individual manufacturing industries and three nonmanufacturing industries, and they do throw in the manufacturing aggregate so that we can see what that looks like too. Since their output numbers are based on Federal Reserve Board indexes, the argument against using aggregate data is very strong, for the aggregate series is heavily contaminated with labor input data. However, there are pitfalls in avoiding the aggregate numbers that I will mention at the end. They say they cannot use high-tech industries because of the continuity problem. That seems sensible, though I think it might have introduced some bias. It is in the nature of the economy that old industries die and new ones come on line, and things that might hold true for a set of industries that have been around for a long time might not be true for new industries.

The first result they get from the raw data is that productivity growth was surprisingly strong in 1923–39 relative to 1954–82. That is consistent with my own view that the Great Depression did not push down the underlying productivity trend. It argues against a view that I encounter quite often, that slack demand since 1973 has been a major influence on the recent productivity slowdown. This first result contrasts with their second finding, that there is a very high correlation between labor productivity and output in the short run. As they indicate, this may be due to errors in the data. Correlating output divided by hours with output is a dangerous exercise. I would have left out some of those correlations. The output data are obtained from shipments adjusted by an estimate of the change in inventories. The inventory numbers are very suspect in the short run, so that the output numbers are somewhat suspect also.

Their next findings are that real wage growth was larger in 1923–39 than in the postwar period for all industries, but that declining hours of work in 1923–39 kept down real weekly earnings. They also find that the variances are very large in the output and employment numbers. They might have made more of this; it is a rather important fact. They observe extremely large variability of monthly employment, variability that is not related to aggregate conditions. Within each industry there is a lot of month-to-month variation. That gives an insight into the size of adjustment costs, an important issue because adjustment costs are used to explain persistence in equilibrium business cycle models. If the month-to-month variations within individual industries are large, this indicates that adjustment costs are not as large as they would have to be to make the persistence story carry through.

Bernanke and Powell's next empirical observation is that in the postwar period employers made greater use of layoffs and less use of hours variations compared with their prewar behavior. They suggest that this was because workers laid off in the postwar period are in a better position financially because of unemployment insurance and possibly other programs than workers who were laid off in the earlier period. Firms respond to the existence of unemployment insurance by putting their work forces on temporary layoff rather than by reducing hours.

Turning to the frequency analysis, they use deseasonalized log differences—that is, rates of growth. Dummies are used to get out the seasonal variation, a procedure I have used myself with monthly employment and output data. I was staggered by the size of the seasonal adjustments, and I thought the authors might tell us more about what they found. I found, for example, that the lowest-productivity month in manufacturing was December, and that April had productivity over 7% higher than that. The high productivity months exceeded December by the equivalent of between one and two working days' output. I found that rather implausible, and I am curious about what Bernanke and Powell found. Some of the seasonal variation comes about because of the way the data are collected. Employment is measured as of the twelfth of the month, so that holidays such as New Year's Day or Christmas reduce a month's apparent productivity.

After they remove the seasonal effects the authors look at the coherences, the phase relationships, among their different variables. Employment had the strongest coherence with output. Productivity and earnings were next, and wages and output are not very coherent. I was not sure how much to make of these results. They suggest that their findings indicate that the cycle is dominated by movements in demand. First, there are productivity gains as firms get people to work harder, then they add extra hours, and finally they add workers. It was not clear to me why this pattern showed that the cycle is demand driven. For wages, they found in the prewar period that real wages lagged output and in the postwar period real wages were more or less coherent; they even were leading in some industries. In other words, there was no consistent lead or lag between wages and output.

The authors turn next to what they call the time domain and use vector autoregressions. They found that output is exogenous and that its movements were more persistent in the postwar period than in the prewar. They found that hours and employment were not exogenous but respond to each other and to output. These results do indicate that output is driven by demand fluctuations, which then lead to hours and employment variations. They suggest that the persistence of hours indicates that there is an adjustment cost to hours variation. I did not see that; the persistence might result from expectations. When a firm decides whether to vary the number of people employed or to vary the number of hours of the people already employed, it looks ahead to see what future output is going to be, not just current output. So the finding of persistence in hours variation indicates persistence in the expectation of future output. Their analysis of wages in the time domain finds that the real wage varies independent of the other variables. This confirms the conventional wisdom that the real wage seems neither to drive nor to be driven by employment and hours. The forecasting decomposition says much the same as the results just described, and so I have no additional comments on those.

The authors then turn to major recessions, using NBER reference cycles, and they do not find that major recessions are very different from minor ones. These results reemphasize the idea that that employers relied more on layoffs in postwar major recessions than in prewar major recessions. They point out that productivity moves somewhat differently when they consider NBER reference cycles rather than correlating productivity with output in the same industry. Using the reference cycles, productivity rises peak to trough, whereas the relation with output is usually the other way. I think this finding is because their industries do not move exactly in phase with the NBER cycle. Manufacturing is typically out of phase with the overall cycle.

That completes my review of the paper and my detailed comments. I will finish with a few general points. First, I may be biased, but it seemed that contract theory did reasonably well out of these numbers. That there was a difference in the prewar versus postwar layoffs and hours decision is consistent with a contract framework. Employers are responding to the income workers receive when they are not at the firm. The lack of relationship between the wage variable and other variables is also consistent with the contract framework.

My second general point is that the authors should have recognized more clearly that there are micro results as opposed to macro results. The argument about aggregation bias is valid, but the problem is that there are results that hold at the aggregate level that would not necessarily hold at the industry level. For example, if there is a smoothly functioning labor market in which workers can move easily from one industry to another, then there is no reason for wages in a particular industry to be related to the productivity or the employment or any variable of that particular industry. Presumably firms pay the market wage, and in a high-productivity growth industry relative price falls. The finding of no relation between employment and the wage for a single industry means something very different from a similar finding for the whole economy. Even if there is not a perfectly mobile labor force, it may be that labor unions will lock up relative wages. This is another reason the wage in a particular industry may not be related to employment, even though these variables could be related in the aggregate.

The mention of labor unions brings me to my next point. The authors might have explored labor market institutions more fully. There were many changes in the organization of the labor market over the period they were looking at. It would have been interesting to track these to see if there was any relation between them and other variables. Labor union influence fell in the early 1920s, then grew very rapidly in the 1930s with the New Deal and was strong in the postwar period. A related institutional change was the growth of three-year wage contracts in the postwar period. Perhaps these changes would have been undetectable in the data, but that would have been worth knowing, too. Another way of checking for the importance of unions is that some of their industries were unionized and some were not. Cross-industry differences might have emerged.

My final point has to do with use of frequency analysis for studying cyclical behavior. The cycle is not regular; different cycles have different durations. Moreover, in the postwar period there have been several abrupt recessions, giving rise to spikes in the data. This means that in a spectral decomposition, it would be better to hang on to the high frequency end of the distribution to capture the spikes. And possibly the low frequency part of the distribution also carries cyclical information. I do not think there is a narrow range of frequencies that can be clearly identified as the cyclical component, such that all the other information can be thrown away. There is a danger of not picking up relationships among variables when information is thrown away. There were virtues to old-fashioned NBER cyclical analysis that recognized that the cycle is not a simple sine wave. Cycles do have different durations, and booms and slumps are not of the same length and do not have quite the same character.

I will stop here and again thank the authors for putting together a very useful set of data and doing a very systematic and helpful analysis of it. I think they themselves will use the data more in the future to set out what salient facts of the labor market are to be explained.

Comment   Edward P. Lazear

Bernanke and Powell have presented us with a very fine piece of work. Their contribution meets two of the necessary conditions for an important paper. First, it is informative, providing valuable data that are summarized in an accessible form. Second, it is provocative. It stimulates others to pick up where they left off.

The major point I would like to make should be regarded as an extension rather than a criticism of what they have done. It is a point I have made in another context,[1] but it seems important to make it here as well.

Bernanke and Powell present detailed data on a few important series for the prewar and postwar periods. The series they are most concerned with are output, employment, productivity, and some measure of real wages. Of obvious importance is the relation of real wages to output. Whether real wages are rigid over the business cycle is of central concern to many macroeconomic theories. Although most of the important biases are discussed, there is one that is likely to be crucial but that has been ignored in the past.

Truncation Bias

The point I want to emphasize is that workers are not homogeneous and that the weights associated with various groups shift over the business cycle. This really can be broken up into two points.

First, workers are not homogeneous. The proportion of the average wage of black males compared with white males is approximately 0.7. Similarly, the proportion for white females compared with white males is about 0.6. Even within a demographic and/or occupational group, there is a great deal of dispersion in wage rates. Among the most important factors is experience, since wage rates tend to rise rapidly during the first few years on the job.

Second, employment decreases are not spread randomly across all worker classes. In particular, blacks, females, and less experienced

Edward P. Lazear is a professor in the Graduate School of Business at the University of Chicago.

1. See the discussion in Lazear 1983 on the widening of union/nonunion wage differentials during recessions.

workers tend to be affected by recessions to a greater extent than other groups.

What this implies is that the reported real wage in a recession refers to a different set of workers than the real wage during an expansion. Since these workers' wages differ, part of the movement in real wages over the business cycle reflects a change in the weights rather than some change in the wage itself.

This factor tends to suppress observed movements in wages over the business cycle. Even though the entire wage distribution may shift left in a downturn, there is a tendency for the lower tail of that distribution to disappear. The observed mean might actually rise if enough selective reduction in employment occurred in the slump.

To illustrate that this point is likely to be important in terms of magnitude, I have used Bernanke and Powell's numbers to examine the importance of this effect. What the next few paragraphs report is that this weight-shifting effect may, and is even likely to, swamp everything else.

Let us concentrate on only one factor. Suppose that workers are homogeneous in all respects other than work experience or, almost equivalently, age. The two facts from labor economics that are of central importance here are that experience/earnings profiles are positively sloped and that layoffs are negatively related to seniority.

Figure C10.1 depicts a typical experience/earnings profile. (There is much documentation of this, the most noted source being Mincer 1974.)

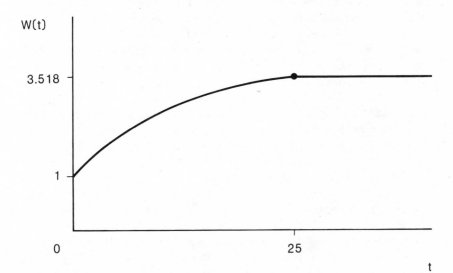

Fig. C10.1   Experience/earnings profile.

The profile is positively sloped and concave. Define $W(t)$ as the wage rate at experience level t and suppose that t goes from zero to thirty-nine years. Normalize by defining $W(0) = 1$. The function shown in figure C10.1 can be approximated by

(1) $$W(t) = [W(t - 1)] [1 + g(t - 1)],$$

where

(2) $$\begin{aligned} g(t) &= .1 - .004t & \text{for } t \leqslant 25 \\ &= 0 & \text{for } t > 25. \end{aligned}$$

Equations (1) and (2) imply that wages grow initially at 10% per year and that the growth rate declines linearly to zero after twenty-five years, at which point it remains zero.

Suppose that workers are distributed uniformly by experience group so that initially, say at a peak, workers are found in equal numbers in each of the experience categories between zero and thirty-nine years. This distribution, coupled with the wage process described in (1) and (2), yields an average wage for all workers taken together at the peak of 2.164. Recall that $W(0) = 1$. (This is derived by computer simulation.)

Now think of moving from a peak to a trough as moving from one standard deviation above the industry employment mean to one standard deviation below it. Further, suppose that layoffs are in reverse order of seniority so that the least experienced workers are released first. If the standard deviation is expressed in percentage terms, then two times the standard deviation times thirty-nine years is removed from the bottom of the distribution. Instead of being uniform between 0 and 39, it is now uniform between, say, 0.9 and 39.

Again, a mean can be calculated for this truncated distribution, which applies during the recession. What is essential here is that the distribution is not shifted at all, but the average wage will rise because the lower tail is removed.

Table C10.1 does exactly this using the Bernanke and Powell figures from their table 10.6. That table reports the seasonally adjusted, business cycle only variation in monthly growth rates of employment and real wage by industry. The first entry for each industry is for the prewar period, and the second entry is for the postwar period. The last three entries are only for the postwar period.

Column 1 merely reproduces the employment figures from table 10.6, and column 2 reproduces the real wage series from table 10.6 of Bernanke and Powell. The most important information is contained in column 3. Recall that the average wage was 2.164 when the entire labor force was employed. What column 3 does is report the average wage corresponding to the recession work force. For example, the first row of table C10.1 reports the information for the prewar period in the steel

Table C10.1

Industry	(1)	(2)	(3)	(4)	(5)
Steel	1.590	0.590	2.230	0.030	2.572
	1.050	0.270	2.214	0.023	4.272
Autos	2.720	0.360	2.259	0.044	6.083
	1.430	0.310	2.227	0.029	4.649
Meat	1.050	0.490	2.214	0.023	2.354
	0.270	0.210	2.197	0.015	3.572
Paper	0.600	0.360	2.204	0.018	2.542
	0.300	0.140	2.197	0.015	5.463
Shoes	0.470	0.680	2.201	0.017	1.249
	0.390	0.170	2.199	0.016	4.760
Wool	0.690	0.670	2.232	0.031	2.337
	1.010	0.220	2.213	0.023	5.143
Leather	0.970	0.470	2.212	0.022	2.361
	0.490	0.140	2.201	0.017	6.138
Lumber	1.480	0.700	2.228	0.029	2.092
	0.610	0.230	2.204	0.018	4.002
Coal	0.710	0.250	2.206	0.019	3.888
Electronics	0.160	0.130	2.194	0.014	5.360
Construction	0.750	0.150	2.207	0.020	6.619

Note: $\overline{WR} = 2.164$.

(1) $= \sigma_{EMP}(\%)$

(2) $= \sigma_{WR}(\%)$

(3) $= W\hat{R}$

(4) $= \dfrac{W\hat{R} - \overline{WR}}{WR}$

(5) $= \dfrac{100\left(\dfrac{W\hat{R} - \overline{WR}}{\overline{WR}}\right)}{2\sigma_{WR}}$

industry. There the standard deviation of monthly growth rates was 1.59%. Under our assumptions, this implies that a recession truncates the lower 3.18% of the distribution and raises the average wage from 2.164 to 2.230.

To get a feel for the magnitude of the effect, columns 4 and 5 are presented. Column 4 reports the proportionate change in the wage that results from this truncation effect. They range from 0.014 to 0.044, and the effect measured this way is invariably smaller after the war than before.

Column 5 compares this percentage change to two standard deviations of the real wage growth rate. Those figures are perhaps the most striking because they reveal that in every case the truncation effect exceeds two standard deviations of wage growth. This is true even though the truncation effect was generated by only two standard deviations of employment reduction. In fact, in some cases it goes as high as six times two real-wage standard deviations.

Additionally, the importance of this effect relative to the change in wage rates has grown over time. For the most part, the postwar numbers in column 5 exceed the prewar numbers. Of course, the standard deviation of postwar wage rates may be low precisely because of this effect.

Although this is only an example, the Bernanke and Powell data show that truncation effects may well swamp everything else that goes on in a time series of real wages. The numbers in table C10.1 imply that it is easy for any given employed worker's real wage to drop during a recession even though the average wage remains constant or even rises. In the case of, say, postwar autos, the underlying wage distribution could shift left by approximately 3%, and as a result of the truncation effect the average wage would be observed to be constant over the business cycle. That shift in wages would correspond to 2 × (1.43%) drop in employment so that the actual, but unobserved, wage movement would equal the employment movement.

This point finds potential support not only in the Bernanke and Powell data, but also in a recent paper by Raisian (1983). Using panel data (the Panel Study of Income Dynamics), he shows that the wage of a given continuously employed worker falls significantly over the business cycle. In fact, Raisian finds that a 1% increase in the unemployment rate of a given worker's industry results in a 0.65% decline in his wage. Obviously, truncation effects are absent in panel data.

There are some findings that might be explained by this. In particular, Bernanke and Powell show that employment adjustments are more important in the postwar period. To the extent that employment adjustments are more likely to involve truncation effects hours reductions (i.e., they are more closely linked to seniority and wage levels), the truncation effect would be more important in the postwar data. This would tend to counteract procyclic movements in real wages. In fact, Bernanke and Powell find that the real wage series is less variable during the postwar period. A similar argument can be made to explain the greater persistence of the real wage in the postwar data.

If the truncation effect is important, then it helps to reconcile some findings but makes others even more difficult to explain. In particular, the procyclicality of productivity, termed SRIRL by Bernanke and Powell, creates even more of a puzzle when we recognize that the workers who retain their jobs during the recession are the higher wage group. Even though there may not be a perfect correlation between wages and productivity, it seems reasonable that the relationship would be positive. This means that SRIRL is even greater than it appears.

The point is that truncation bias is likely to be an important force. It can be dealt with explicitly, and it should be when drawing inferences about the relation of real wages to the business cycle.

Other Points

A few additional points are worthy of mention. They are listed in no particular order:

1. The emphasis in this paper is on the time series within industry. Yet, given the data, there is interesting cross-sectional evidence that might be presented. For example, tables 10.5 and 10.6 report the standard deviation within an industry over time. It would also be useful to know whether industry variables like output, employment, and real wages move in parallel across industries to a greater or lesser extent in the postwar period. Are recessions more or less confined to particular industries than they were in the past? It is conceivable that changes in demand might reflect different relative shares for the various products, leaving the aggregate output unchanged. Alternatively, a fall in employment in one industry might be mirrored in the same percentage fall in another industry. These data are ripe for this type of investigation.

2. Related, an investigation of the sort conducted by Gordon (1982) is feasible, but the analysis would be across industries rather than across countries. In particular, one can imagine that there might be a negative correlation between the effect of a fall in output on employment and on wages. In industries where wages are sensitive to changes in demand for the product, is employment less sensitive?

Some minor points:

3. Since industry definitions are quite broad, it would be useful to present more detail on what four- or five-digit industries make up the aggregate and how this has changed over time. One could argue that some of the results reflect weight shifts.

4. Is the hours figure reported hours worked or hours paid? This might be important if vacation and sick time varies over the business cycle.

5. In addition to reporting the phasing of real wages, and so on, to output, it would be useful to provide some measure of the amplitudes as well. A flat in-phase series has different implications than a highly variable in-phase series.

6. Some reporting on the nominal wage and CPI separately would be useful. One wants to know which of the two variables drives the results. This is especially important when it is recognized that the CPI is an ex post measure of prices and may not be what the worker inserts into his labor supply function.

7. I have argued elsewhere (Lazear 1974) that recessions are a time for rebuilding and for investing in new technologies, including human

capital. My results suggest that this is true to some extent. If so, output is relatively understated during downturns. Again, this may vary by industry.

8. Since output is the numerator of the productivity measure, the positive rank correlation reported in section 10.4 may reflect errors in variables. Some investigation of this might be worthwhile.

The authors are to be applauded for a provocative and useful paper that has already stimulated much thought and discussion.

Discussion Summary

The tone of the discussion was generally favorable toward both the data set and the statistical methods employed in the paper. Most of the comments involved suggestions for extensions or possible explanations of puzzling results. There was general agreement that the truncation example Lazear presented overstated his case. Even during recessions a large proportion of separations come through retirements and quits. As Summers noted, this upper truncation bias offsets the lower truncation bias elaborated by Lazear. Solomon Fabricant suggested that another possible channel for the cyclical behavior of productivity might be the production function. Bottlenecks in the delivery of the amount or quality of materials and capital goods over the business cycle might produce cyclical behavior in measured labor productivity. Robert Gordon felt that Bernanke and Powell's conclusion 5 on the acyclicality of the real wage was an artifact of their technique. If one were to remove the supply shocks of the 1970s, in which the real wage was strongly procyclical, it would be found that over the remaining business cycles the real wage moved countercyclically.

Geweke noted that the presence of a linear relation between the phase length of a variable and the length of the business cycle, investigated in tables 10.9 and 10.10 did not necessarily imply that a reference cycle approach was superior to time domain methods. Christopher Sims issued a caution regarding Bernanke and Powell's results on the lack of feedback from hours and employment to output. His experience suggested that had hours times employment been used instead, more feedback would have been found. Hence the results were sensitive to the way the variables were allowed to enter. Sims also noted that sampling errors in the interwar data might be large enough to cast doubt on the reliability of the results obtained. He suggested this might be a profitable area for further investigation.

References

Altonji, Joseph, and Orley Ashenfelter. 1980. Wage movements and the labour market equilibrium hypothesis. *Economica* 47 (August):217–45.

Anderson, T. W. 1971. *The statistical analysis of time series.* New York: John Wiley.

Ashenfelter, Orley, and David Card. 1982. Time series representations of economic variables and alternative models of the labour market. *Review of Economic Studies* 49 (special issue):261–82.

Baily, Martin Neil. 1977. On the theory of layoffs and unemployment. *Econometrica* 45 (July):1043–63.

Ball, R. J., and E. B. A. St. Cyr. 1966. Short-term employment functions in British manufacturing industry. *Review of Economic Studies* 33 (July):179–207.

Barro, Robert J., and Herschel I. Grossman. 1971. A general disequilibrium model of income and employment. *American Economic Review* 61 (March):82–93.

Beney, M. Ada. 1936. *Wages, hours, and employment in the United States, 1914–1936.* New York: National Industrial Conference Board.

Bernanke, Ben S. 1983. On the sources of labor productivity variation in U.S. manufacturing, 1947–1980. *Review of Economics and Statistics* 65 (May):214–24.

Bernstein, Irving. 1960. *The lean years: A history of the American worker, 1920–1933.* Boston: Houghton-Mifflin.

Bodkin, Ronald G. 1969. Real wages and cyclical variations in employment: A re-examination of the evidence. *Canadian Journal of Economics* 2 (August):353–74.

Brechling, F. P. R. 1965. The relationship between output and employment in British manufacturing industries. *Review of Economic Studies* 32 (July):187–216.

Brechling, F. P. R., and P. O. O'Brien. 1967. Short-run employment functions in manufacturing industries: An international comparison. *Review of Economic Studies* 99 (August):277–87.

Bry, Gerhard. 1959. The average workweek as an economic indicator. Occasional Paper 69, National Bureau of Economic Research.

Burns, Arthur F., and Wesley C. Mitchell. 1946. *Measuring business cycles.* New York: National Bureau of Economic Research.

Chirinko, Robert. 1980. The real wage over the business cycle. *Review of Economics and Statistics* 62 (August):459–61.

Clark, Kim B., and Richard B. Freeman. 1980. How elastic is the demand for labor? *Review of Economics and Statistics* 62 (November):509–20.

Coen, Robert M., and Bert G. Hickman. 1970. Constrained joint estimation of factor demand and production functions. *Review of Economics and Statistics* 52 (August):287–300.

Creamer, Daniel. 1950. Behavior of wage rates during business cycles. Occasional Paper 34, National Bureau of Economic Research.

Doan, T. A., and R. B. Litterman. 1981. *RATS user's manual, version 4.1.* Minneapolis: VAR Econometrics.

Dunlop, John T. 1938. The movement of real and money wage rates. *Economic Journal* 48 (September):413–34.

Eckstein, Otto, and Thomas A. Wilson. 1964. Short-run productivity behavior in U.S. manufacturing. *Review of Economics and Statistics* 46 (February):41–54.

Fair, Ray C. 1969. *The short-run demand for workers and hours.* Amsterdam: North-Holland.

Geary, Patrick T., and John Kennan. 1982. The employment–real wage relationship: An international study. *Journal of Political Economy* 90 (August):854–71.

Gordon, Robert J. 1980. The "end-of-expansion" phenomenon in short-run productivity behavior. Working Paper 427, National Bureau of Economic Research.

———. 1982. Why U.S. wage and employment behavior differs from that in Britain and Japan. *Economic Journal* 92 (March):13–44.

Granger, C. W. J., and M. Hatanaka. 1964. *Spectral analysis of economic time series.* Princeton: Princeton University Press.

Hall, Robert E. 1980. Employment fluctuations and wage rigidity. *Brookings Papers on Economic Activity* 1:91–124.

Hannan, E. J. 1970. *Multiple time series.* New York: John Wiley.

Hause, John C. 1971. Spectral analysis and the detection of lead-lag relations. *American Economic Review* 61 (March):213–17.

Hultgren, Thor. 1960. Changes in labor cost during cycles in production and business. Occasional Paper 74, National Bureau of Economic Research.

———. 1965. *Costs, prices, and profits: Their cyclical relations.* New York: National Bureau of Economic Research.

Ireland, J. J., and D. J. Smyth. 1967. Short-term employment functions in Australian manufacturing. *Review of Economics and Statistics* 49 (November):537–44.

Jerome, Harry. 1934. *Mechanization in industry.* New York: National Bureau of Economic Research.

Keynes, John Maynard. 1936. *The general theory of employment, interest, and money.* London: Macmillan.

———. 1939. Relative movements of real wages and output. *Economic Journal* 49 (March):34–51.

Kuh, Edwin. 1960. Profits, profit markups, and productivity. Joint Economic Committee Paper 15. Washington, D.C.: Government Printing Office.

————. 1965. Cyclical and secular labor productivity in United States manufacturing. *Review of Economics and Statistics* 97 (February):1–12.

Lazear, Edward P. 1974. The timing of technical change: An analysis of cyclical variations in technology production. Ph.D. diss., Harvard University.

————. 1983. A competitive theory of monopoly unionism. *American Economic Review* 73 (September):631–43.

Lucas, Robert E., Jr. 1970. Capacity, overtime, and empirical production functions. *American Economic Review* 60 (May):23–27.

Masters, Stanley H. 1967. The behavior of output per man during recessions: An empirical study of underemployment. *Southern Economic Journal* 33 (January):388–94.

Medoff, James L. 1979. Layoffs and alternatives under trade unions in U.S. manufacturing. *American Economic Review* 69 (June):380–95.

Mincer, Jacob. 1974 *Schooling, experience, and earnings.* New York: Columbia University Press.

Mitchell, Wesley C. 1951. *What happens during business cycles.* Cambridge, Mass.: Riverside Press.

Moore, Geoffrey H. 1955. Business cycles and the labor market. *Monthly Labor Review* 78 (March):288–92.

Morrison, Catherine J., and Ernst R. Berndt. 1981. Short-run labor productivity in a dynamic model. *Journal of Econometrics* 16 (August):339–65.

Nadiri, M. Ishaq, and Sherwin Rosen. 1973. *A disequilibrium model of demand for factors of production.* New York: Columbia University Press.

Neftci, Salih N. 1978. A time-series analysis of the real wages–employment relationship. *Journal of Political Economy* 86 (April):281–91.

————. 1979. Lead-lag relations, exogeneity, and prediction of economic time series. *Econometrica* 47 (January):101–13.

Oi, Walter Y. 1962. Labor as a quasi-fixed factor. *Journal of Political Economy* 70 (December):538–55.

Okun, Arthur M. 1962. Potential GNP: Its measurement and significance. In *Proceedings of the Business and Economics Section,* 98–104. Washington, D.C.: American Statistical Association.

Otani, Ichiro. 1978. Real wages and business cycles revisited. *Review of Economics and Statistics* 60 (May):301–4.

Pindyck, Robert S., and Julio J. Rotemberg. 1982. Dynamic factor demands and the effects of energy price shocks. Research Paper, Massachusetts Institute of Technology.

Raisian, John. 1983. Contracts, job experience, and cyclical labor market adjustment. *Journal of Labor Economics* 1 (April):152–70.

Ruggles, Richard. 1940. The relative movements of real and money wage rates. *Quarterly Journal of Economics* 55 (November):130–49.

Sachs, Jeffrey. 1979. Wages, profits, and macroeconomic adjustment: A comparative study. *Brookings Papers on Economic Activity* 2 (1979):269–319.

———. 1980. The changing cyclical behavior of wages and prices: 1890–1976. *American Economic Review* 70 (March):78–90.

Sargent, Thomas J. 1978. Estimation of dynamic labor demand schedules under rational expectations. *Journal of Political Economy* 86 (December):1009–44.

———. 1979. *Macroeconomic theory.* New York: Academic Press.

Sayre, R. A. 1940. Wages, hours, and employment in the United States, 1934–1939. *Conference Board Economic Record 2* 10 (March):115–37.

———. 1948. *Consumers' prices, 1914–1948.* New York: National Industrial Conference Board.

Shiskin, Julius. 1961. Signals of recession and recovery. Occasional Paper 77, National Bureau of Economic Research.

Sims, Christopher A. 1974. Output and labor input in manufacturing. *Brookings Papers on Economic Activity* 3 (1974):695–728.

———. 1980. Macroeconomics and reality. *Econometrica* 48 (January):1–48.

Slichter, Sumner H., James J. Healy, and E. Robert Livernash. 1960. *The impact of collective bargaining on management.* Washington, D.C.: Brookings Institution.

Solow, Robert M. 1968. Distribution in the long and short run. *Proceedings of a conference held by the International Economics Association at Palermo,* ed. Jean Marchal and Bernard Ducrois. New York: St. Martin's Press.

———. 1973. Some evidence on the short-run productivity puzzle. *Development and planning: Essays in honour of Paul Rosenstein-Rodan,* ed. Jagdish Bhagwati and Richard Eckaus. London: Allen and Unwin.

Solow, Robert M., and Joseph E. Stiglitz. 1968. Output, employment, and wages in the short run. *Quarterly Journal of Economics* 82 (November):537–60.

Stock, James H. 1983. Economic models subject to time deformation. Ph.D. diss., University of California at Berkeley.

Stockman, Alan C. 1983. Aggregation bias and the cyclical behavior of real wages. Research Paper, University of Rochester.

Tarshis, Lorie. 1939. Changes in real and money wages. *Economic Journal* 49 (March):150–54.

Tatom, John A. 1980. The "problem" of procyclical real wages and productivity. *Journal of Political Economy* 88 (April):385–94.

Woytinsky, W. S. 1942. *Three aspects of labor dynamics*. Washington, D.C.: Committee on Social Security–Social Science Research Council.

Zarnowitz, Victor, and Charlotte Boschan. 1975. Cyclical indicators: An evaluation and new leading indexes. *Business Conditions Digest* 15 (May):v–xix.

Zeisel, Joseph S. 1958. The workweek in American industry, 1850–1956. *Monthly Labor Review* 81 (January):23–29.

11 Improvements in Macroeconomic Stability: The Role of Wages and Prices

John B. Taylor

Macroeconomic fluctuations have been less severe in the past thirty years than in the period before World War II. Although the recessions in the 1970s and 1980s have been large and have been associated with big swings in inflation, the average amplitude of cyclical fluctuations is still smaller than in the prewar period.

This improvement in macroeconomic performance was already evident to most economists by the end of the 1950s. It served as the focal point of Arthur Burns's 1959 presidential address before the American Economic Association. Burns contrasted the milder postwar fluctuations with those he studied with Wesley Clair Mitchell at the National Bureau of Economic Research. He attributed the improvement to countercyclical fiscal and monetary policy as well as to structural changes in the economy: more stable corporate dividends, steadier employment practices, better inventory controls, and greater financial stability owing to deposit insurance.

The improvement in economic performance still deserves the attention of macroeconomists. An understanding of the reasons for the improvement is invaluable for recommending what changes in policy should, or should not, be adopted. Moreover, at a time when macroeconomic research is undergoing difficult and fundamental changes, the improvement serves as a useful reminder of the practical importance of continued progress in macrotheory and macroeconometrics. Regardless of one's approach to macroeconomic research, one can, as

John B. Taylor is a professor in the Department of Economics at Stanford University.

This research was supported by the National Science Foundation and was conducted in part at the Federal Reserve Bank of Philadelphia. I am grateful to Phillip Cagan, Otto Eckstein, Steven Fries, Robert Gordon, and Carlos Leal for helpful comments and assistance.

640   John B. Taylor

James Tobin (1980) has urged, "take some encouragement from the economic performance of the advanced democratic capitalist nations since the Second World War."

This paper examines the role of wage and price rigidities in this improvement in macroeconomic performance. Wage and price rigidities are at the center of most modern economic theories of the business cycle. According to these theories, if wages and prices were more flexible the economy would experience shorter and less severe business cycle fluctuations. Many economists have therefore suggested economic reforms—such as synchronized wage and price setting—to make wages and prices more flexible.

I examine changes in wage and price rigidities and in macroeconomic performance by concentrating on two episodes in United States history: the quarter-century before World War I, from 1891 through 1914, and the slightly longer period after World War II, from 1952 through 1983. Each period includes eight economic fluctuations. By ending the earlier period before World War I, we exclude the economic turbulence of both world wars as well as the Great Depression of the 1930s.[1] Even with these exclusions, economic fluctuations in the earlier period were larger than those in the postwar period. The data also indicate that wages and prices were more flexible in the earlier period. This latter finding, which has also been noted by other researchers,[2] presents a puzzle. Less flexibility of wages and prices should lead to a deterioration in economic performance. The comparison suggests that the opposite has occurred. Either other factors—such as those mentioned by Burns—were strong enough to offset the reduced wage/price flexibility, or macrotheory needs some revision if it is to provide a satisfactory explanation for economic fluctuations in both these periods of United States history.

The research reported here makes use of some recently developed econometric time series methodology. The differences in economic fluctuations in the two periods are documented using simple reduced-form vector autoregressions and their moving average representations.

1. The interwar period would also make a useful comparison. In the first draft of this paper I looked at the period 1910–40. To omit the observations from World War I—which would be analogous to the omission of World War II from the later sample—would mean that the period could not begin until 1919 at the earliest; and since some observers interpret the 1920 recession as a direct consequence of demobilization, the same logic would call for starting in 1921 or 1922. The sample size would then be fewer than twenty annual observations, which is already very small for statistical time series analysis. If one worried further that the Great Depression was unique and should not be lumped together with other cycles, then one would be left with the 1920s, a period far too short for statistical analysis. For these reasons I decided to focus on the period before World War I. This period has some other advantages as a contrast with the period 1952–83. These are discussed in the next section.

2. See Cagan 1979, Gordon 1983, and Mitchell 1983, for example.

These give the "facts without theory," much as the Burns/Mitchell NBER reference cycle methods did. This reduced-form evidence is then given an explicit structural interpretation in a simple mathematical form. One advantage of this statistical approach over the earlier NBER methods is that it provides a tight and formal connection between theory and the facts. The connection between theory and the facts revealed through reference cycle charts is necessarily looser and less formal, although these charts can be very useful in the early stages of model development. The methodology used here to compare time periods by looking at both reduced forms and simple structural models is similar to the method I used for an international comparison of different countries (Taylor 1980, 1982).

11.1 A Simple Scorecard for Macroeconomic Performance

It is useful to begin with some simple but objective statistical measures of macroeconomic performance in the different periods. These measures as well as all the statistical analysis in this paper are based on annual data. Output is measured by real GNP, prices are measured by the GNP deflator, and wages are based on average hourly earnings in manufacturing.

The means and standard deviations of the three detrended series are presented in table 11.1. To be specific, let Y be real GNP and let Y^* be potential GNP. Then detrended output given by $y = (Y - Y^*)/Y^*$, and is referred to as the *output gap* in the figures and tables of the paper. Potential GNP is assumed to be growing at a constant, but different, exponential rate in each of the periods. The level of potential is chosen so that the average of y is zero in each period. Experimentation with some alternative assumptions about the growth of Y^* did not affect the results by much. For example, when the trend in Y^* was permitted to change in 1973 to reflect the slowdown in productivity

Table 11.1   Measures of Inflation and Output Stability

	1891–1914	1952–83	1910–40
Standard deviation of			
Output gap	4.8	3.6	10.1
Wage inflation	1.9	2.2	8.9
Price inflation	2.8	2.6	8.1
Average of			
Wage inflation	1.5	5.4	4.1
Price inflation	0.9	4.2	1.5

Note: By definition the average output gap is zero. Prices are measured by the GNP deflator and wages by average hourly earnings in manufacturing.

growth in the United States, the results were similar. I chose to detrend output using a deterministic trend rather than first differences to capture the tendency for output to return to its potential growth path after a disturbance.

On the other hand, wages and prices were detrended by taking first differences of the logarithms; that is, by looking at the rate of price inflation (p) and the rate of wage inflation (w). In the postwar period there is no tendency for the price level to return to a trend path after a disturbance. At best, the *rate of inflation* tends to regress to some mean value; even this tendency was not present in the postwar data before 1982–83. Although the United States was on a gold standard during the period before World War I, the levels of prices and wages show no tendency to regress to a fixed trend or level in that period either, presumably because of changes in the world gold stock and in the relative price of gold.

The statistics reported in table 11.1 refer to the detrended series for output y, wage inflation w, and price inflation p. According to the standard deviation measure, output fluctuations have been about 25% smaller in the period after World War II than in the quarter-century before World War I. The improved output performance does not extend to inflation, however. The standard deviation of the year-over-year inflation rate is about the same in the two periods—up slightly for wage inflation (w) and down slightly for price inflation (p). The average inflation rate is much higher in the postwar period by both measures of inflation.

To provide some perspective, I have also included in column 3 of table 11.1 the same performance measures for the period 1910–40, which includes both World War I and the Great Depression. This period is far worse than the other two by any of the performance measures. Output fluctuations are almost three times as large as in the post–World War II period, and inflation fluctuations are about four times as large. Only the average inflation rate is less in this period than in the postwar period, but since the average is taken over very large positive values and very large negative values, this is not a very meaningful performance measure.

11.2 Output and Inflation Fluctuations

The statistics in table 11.1 are far from sufficient for characterizing the dynamic behavior of two such serially and contemporaneously correlated variables as output and inflation. Time series charts for inflation and output in the two periods are shown in the upper and lower panels of figures 11.1 and 11.2. For additional perspective, the corresponding charts for the 1910–40 time period are shown in the middle panels.

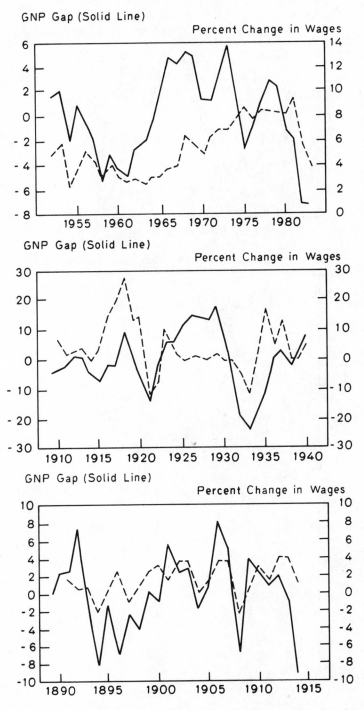

Fig. 11.1   Wage inflation and deviations of real output from trend during
three periods.

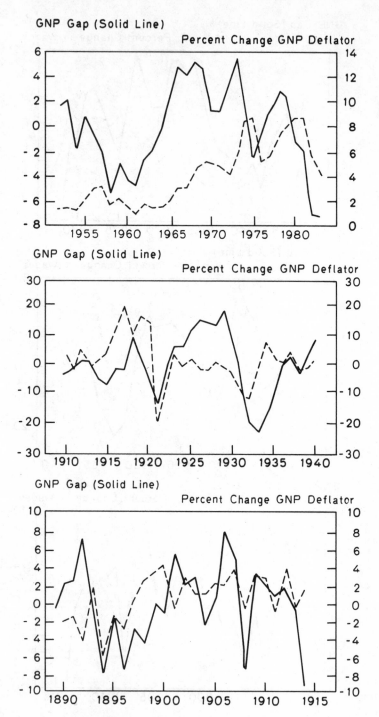

Fig 11.2   Price inflation and the deviation of real output from trend during three periods.

Note that the scales on the charts for the different time periods are different. (The output gap $y = (Y - Y^*)/Y^*$ is superimposed on both the wage inflation charts and the price inflation charts.) Some of the milder recessions in the earlier period are smoothed out by the use of annual data. The severe recession that began early in 1893 and ended in mid-1894 stands out as one of the worst of the period, as does the brief but sharp recession that began with the financial panic in 1907. The period ends with the 1914 recession before the beginning of World War I.

The charts clearly indicate that the tendency for inflation to fall in recessions and rise in booms is not new. Inflation fell during all the more severe downturns between 1891 and 1914. Inflation was negative on average from 1891 to 1907 and positive on average from 1907 until 1914. During this latter subperiod the world gold supply steadily increased.

A comparison of the charts for the earlier period with the charts for the later period reveals in a rough way many of the differences between the two periods that I will focus on. First, the amplitude of the fluctuations in output is smaller in the postwar period, as we have already observed. (Again note the difference in the scales on these figures.) Second, the duration of the fluctuations in inflation is longer in the postwar period; inflation has been much more "persistent." Stated another way, wages and prices have developed more rigidities, in the sense that past values of wages and prices influence their current values. Much of the higher inflation persistence is due to the prolonged period in the 1970s when the inflation rate was abnormally high before it fell sharply in 1982 and 1983. In comparison, during the period before World War I wage inflation fluctuated up and down much more rapidly. Even the persistent negative trend in prices and wages before 1897 is swamped by the fluctuations in the inflation rate; similarly, the positive trend after 1897 is hidden by the larger fluctuations around the trend. The third important difference between the two periods is in the duration of the fluctuations of real output. As with inflation, these are longer since World War II.

The fourth important difference between the two periods is more difficult to see in the charts but is somewhat more evident in figures 11.3 and 11.4. It relates to the timing of the fluctuations of inflation and output. In the postwar period, there is a marked tendency for increases in inflation to bring about a downturn in the economy, although with a lag. After the downturn inflation begins to fall. For example, an increase in inflation in the late 1960s preceded the downturn in the economy in 1969–70. After the downturn, inflation declined. Similarly, an increase in inflation in 1973–74 preceded the downturn in the economy in 1974–75. Inflation then subsided. Finally, an increase

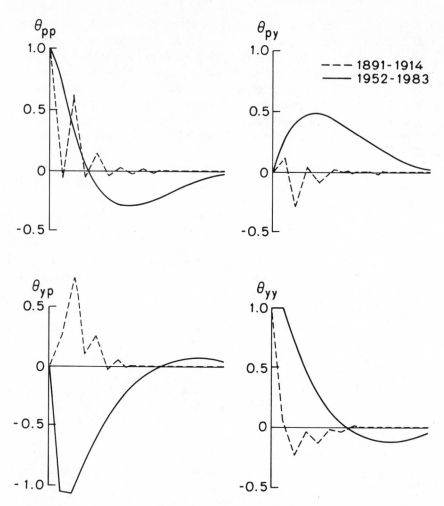

Fig. 11.3   Moving average representation for price inflation and output.

in inflation in 1979–80 preceded the back-to-back recessions in 1980–82. And as usual, inflation then fell. It is very difficult to detect similar patterns in the period 1891–1914. Increases in inflation do not seem to lead the economic downturns, and the declines in inflation seem to occur simultaneously with the declines in the real economy. Although this timing difference can be pried out of the charts, it emerges much more easily in the statistical time series analysis of the next two sections.

The middle panels in figures 11.1 and 11.2 clearly indicate that the amplitude of the fluctuations is much larger in 1910–40 than in either the period before or the period after. The effect of World War I is evident in the boom and the subsequent recession of 1920. But the

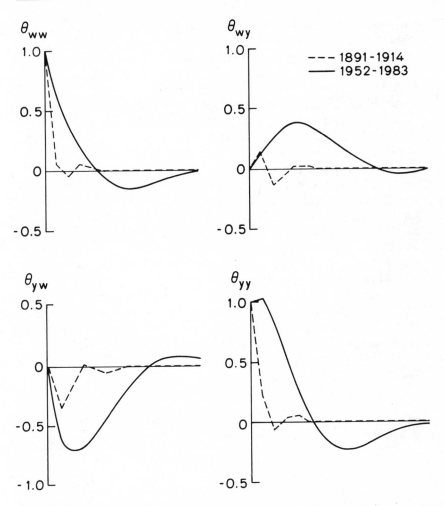

Fig. 11.4   Moving average representation for wage inflation and output.

extended boom in the 1920s and the Great Depression dominate the charts. The wide fluctuations in wages and prices indicate the same type of flexibility that is evident before World War I. The persistence of wage and price inflation—a sign of wage and price rigidities used in macrotheory—definitely seems relatively new.

11.3 Vector Autoregressions

The dynamic properties of output, wages, and prices can be examined more systematically by estimating unconstrained vector autoregressions. Estimates of bivariate autoregressions for wage inflation and output, and for price inflation and output, are reported in tables 11.2 and 11.3 for both 1893–1914 and 1954–83. The lag length is equal to two years for all the regressions. For annual data this choice of lag length seemed to eliminate most of the serial correlation of the residuals to the equations. Higher-order systems with both wage inflation and price inflation together with output were also estimated but are not reported here. At this level of aggregation the movements of wages and prices are very similar, so that including a third variable does not add much to the analysis.

These autoregressions are not necessarily structural equations. They are reduced-form equations that in principle can be derived from a variety of systems of structural equations. The lag coefficients in the autoregressions are in principle functions of parameters in all the structural equations. The shocks to each of the autoregression equations are in principle functions of the shocks to all the structural equations and depend on simultaneity parameters in the structural equations. In this section my aim is simply to describe the autoregressions rather than to give them a structural interpretation.

A quick glance at tables 11.2 and 11.3 reveals that the structure of the autoregressions differs by a large amount in the two periods. Both the structure of the shocks to the equations (the impulses) and the lag coefficients (the propagation mechanism) are much different.

Table 11.2   **Autoregression Estimates for Price Inflation and Output, 1893– 1914 and 1954–83**

Dependent Variable	Lagged Dependent Variables				ρ	σ	R^2
	$p(-1)$	$p(-2)$	$y(-1)$	$y(-2)$			
	Sample Period 1893–1914						
p	−.051	.574	.108	−.281	−.02	1.91	.46
	(−0.3)	(3.3)	(1.0)	(−2.5)			
y	.279	.734	.053	−.260	−.18	4.00	.24
	(0.8)	(2.0)	(0.2)	(−1.1)			
Contemporaneous correlation between residuals = .30							
	Sample Period 1954–83						
p	.721	.084	.257	−.027	−.09	1.03	.82
	(3.5)	(0.4)	(2.7)	(−0.3)			
y	−1.05	.76	1.00	−.004	−0.5	2.07	.66
	(−2.6)	(2.0)	(5.2)	(−0.0)			
Contemporaneous correlation between residuals = .23							

Note: Each equation was estimated with a constant term. The variable p is the annual percentage rate of change in the GNP deflator. The variable y is the percentage deviation of output from linear trend estimated over the sample period. The numbers in parentheses are t-ratios; ρ is the first-order autocorrelation coefficient; σ is the standard error of the residuals.

Table 11.3   **Autoregression Estimates for Wage Inflation and Output, 1893–1914 and 1954–83**

Dependent Variable	Lagged Dependent Variables				ρ	σ	R^2
	$w(-1)$	$w(-2)$	$y(-1)$	$y(-2)$			
	Sample Period 1893–1914						
w	0.52	.007	.147	−.213	.02	1.66	.30
	(0.2)	(0.1)	(1.3)	(−1.8)			
y	−.358	−0.30	.220	−.063	.05	4.49	.04
	(−0.6)	(−0.1)	(0.7)	(−0.2)			

Contemporaneous correlation between residuals = .66

	Sample Period 1954–83						
w	.569	.175	.097	.103	−.03	1.20	.70
	(2.5)	(0.7)	(0.8)	(0.8)			
y	−.650	.336	1.026	−.181	.04	2.21	.62
	(−1.6)	(0.8)	(4.5)	(−0.8)			

Contemporaneous correlation between residuals = .52

Note: The variable *w* is the annual percentage rate of change in average hourly earnings in manufacturing. For the definition of other variables see the note to table 11.2.

11.3.1   The Impulses

The variance of the shocks, or the impulses, to the output equation has decreased sharply from the prewar to the postwar period. To the extent that macroeconomic policy works by changing the dynamics of the economy—as it would with feedback policy, the finding that a reduction in the size of the shocks explains most of the reduced variability suggests that such feedback policy was not responsible for improvements in performance. However, part of the change in policy could affect the variance of the shocks by working "within the period" to offset exogenous disturbances. This would be more likely for the automatic stabilizers that react simultaneously, but with annual data even a feedback policy that reacts to economic disturbances within the year would affect the variance of the shocks rather than the dynamics of the system.

The variance of the shocks to the inflation equations is also much smaller in the postwar period. Since the overall variance of inflation is about the same in the two periods, changes in the propagation mechanism must have had a positive influence on the variance of inflation. The impulses have become weaker. It is perhaps surprising that the variance of the shocks to inflation has become smaller. According to these estimates, an increased importance of price shocks in postwar business cycles is not supported by a comparison with the period before World War I.

The contemporaneous correlation between the shocks to the equations is positive in both the prewar and the postwar periods. However, the correlation is stronger in the prewar period. More of the action seems to come within the annual time interval during the prewar period.

11.3.2   The Propagation Mechanism

The sum of the coefficients of the lagged inflation rates in the inflation equations is much smaller in the earlier period. This change is more marked for wage inflation than for price inflation. This change is consistent with the increased persistence of inflation in the postwar period that is evident in the time series charts. The sum of the coefficients on lagged output in the output equation is also higher in the postwar period, reflecting a corresponding increase in the persistence of output fluctuations.

The difference in the temporal ordering of inflation and output movements that seems to emerge from the time series plots is evident in the cross, or off-diagonal, autoregression coefficients. In the prewar period lagged inflation has either a positive or an insignificant effect on output. In the postwar period the effect of lagged inflation on output is significantly negative. Looking at the other side of the diagonal, in the prewar period lagged output has a negative effect on inflation; in the postwar period it has a positive effect.

11.4   Moving Average Representations

The moving average representations provide a more convenient way to look at the propagation mechanisms in the economy. They can be derived directly from the autoregression equations. The vector autoregressions reported in tables 11.2 and 11.3 can be written in matrix notation as follows:

$$(1) \qquad z_t = A_1 z_{t-1} + A_2 z_{t-2} + e_t,$$

where $z_t = (w_t, y_t)$, in the systems with wage inflation and output, and where $z_t = (p_t, y_t)$, in the systems with price inflation and output. A_1 and A_2 are two-by-two matrixes of lag coefficients. The two-by-one vector e_t is supposed to be serially uncorrelated. The moving average representation is then given by

$$(2) \qquad z_t = \Sigma_{i=0} \Theta_i e_{t-i},$$

where the Θ_1 matrixes are found by successive substitution of lagged zs in equation (1). Alternatively, and perhaps more intuitively, the Θ matrixes can be computed by dynamically simulating the effects of unit shocks to each of the equations in (1). The two elements of the first column of Θ_1 are given by the effects of a unit inflation shock on inflation and output, respectively, in this simulation. The two elements of the second column of Θ_1 are given by the effects of a unit output shock on inflation and output, respectively, in the simulation.

Denote the elements of the first column of Θ by θ_{pp} and θ_{yp}, and the elements of the second column of Θ by θ_{py} and θ_{yy}. These four elements of the Θ_i matrixes are tabulated in tables 11.4 through 11.7 for i equals 0 to a value where the coefficients are negligible in size. The coefficients are also plotted in figures 11.3 and 11.4 for easy comparison of the two time periods.

Table 11.4   **Moving Average Representation for Price Inflation and Output, 1893–1914**

θ_{pp}	θ_{py}	θ_{yp}	θ_{yy}
1.00	.00	.00	1.00
−.05	.11	.28	.05
.61	−.28	.73	−.23
−.06	.04	.10	−.03
.15	−.10	.24	−.14
−.04	.02	−.01	−.00
.02	−.02	.04	−.03
−.02	.01	−.02	.01
.00	−.00	−.00	.00
−.00	.00	−.01	.00
−.00	.00	−.00	.00

Note: Derived from the autoregression coefficients reported in table 11.2.

Table 11.5   **Moving Average Representation for Price Inflation and Output, 1954–83**

θ_{pp}	θ_{py}	θ_{yp}	θ_{yy}
1.00	.00	.00	1.00
.72	.26	−1.05	1.00
.33	.41	−1.06	.72
.06	.48	−.85	.47
−.12	.48	−.65	.27
−.23	.44	−.47	.12
−.28	.38	−.32	.02
−.29	.31	−.20	−.05
−.27	.24	−.10	−.09
−.24	.18	−.03	−.11
−.20	.12	.02	−.12
−.16	.08	.05	−.11
−.12	.04	.07	−.10
−.08	.01	.07	−.08
−.05	−.00	.07	−.06
−.03	−.02	.06	−.05

Note: Derived from the autoregression coefficients reported in table 11.2.

Table 11.6   Moving Average Representation for Wage Inflation and Output, 1893–1914

θ_{ww}	θ_{wy}	θ_{yw}	θ_{yy}
1.00	.00	.00	1.00
.05	.15	−.35	.22
−.04	−.17	−.12	−.07
.06	−.06	.01	.03
.03	.01	−.01	.04
−.00	.00	−.02	.00
−.00	−.01	−.00	−.00
.00	−.00	.00	.00
.00	.00	−.00	.00

Note: Derived from the autoregression coefficients reported in table 11.3.

Table 11.7   Moving Average Representation for Wage Inflation and Output, 1954–83

θ_{ww}	θ_{wy}	θ_{yw}	θ_{yy}
1.00	.00	.00	1.00
.57	.10	−.65	1.03
.44	.26	−.70	.81
.21	.35	−.69	.52
.06	.37	−.58	.25
−.06	.35	−.43	.02
−.12	.29	−.28	−.12
−.15	.22	−.15	−.20
−.15	.14	−.05	−.23
−.13	.08	.03	−.22
−.10	.02	.07	−.18
−.07	−.01	.09	−.13
−.04	−.03	.09	−.09
−.02	−.05	.08	−.05
−.00	−.05	.07	−.01

Note: Derived from the autoregression coefficients reported in table 11.3.

The use of moving average representations in macroeconomics originates with the influential paper by Sims (1980) in which he refers to it as innovation accounting; the approach has since been adopted by many other researchers. There are many moving average representations of a given multivariate process depending on what one assumes about the contemporaneous correlation between the shocks. Sims suggests that a form be chosen so that the covariance matrix of the shocks is diagonal—an orthogonalization of the shocks. This requires a transformation of the Θ_i matrixes. The transformation is a function of the correlation of the shocks and depends on how one wishes to order the way the shocks enter the system. The methodology used here is different from that of Sims in that the Θ_i matrixes have not been transformed to yield orthogonal shocks. I have found that such a transformation makes it difficult to give a direct structural economic interpretation of the Θ_i matrixes. The method used here was also used for very similar purposes in an international comparison of economic performance (Taylor 1980).

Figures 11.3 and 11.4 indicate the enormousness of the change that has taken place in the dynamics of inflation and output since the period before World War I. The charts on the diagonal of figures 11.3 and 11.4 show the persistence of inflation θ_{pp} and output θ_{yy}. Both have increased.

The cross effect of the shocks has changed even more. The θ_{py} coefficients have changed sign; an output shock has a long-delayed effect on inflation in the more recent period. Before World War I this dynamic effect was very small. Recall, however, that a positive *contemporaneous* relation between output and inflation existed before World War I. The θ_{yp} coefficients have changed in the reverse direction. Whereas inflation shocks generated a reduction in output in the more recent period, they generated an increase in output before World War I. This change, which emerges so clearly from the moving average representations, is the same change that was barely visible in the time series charts: when inflation rises in the recent period, output falls; inflation then subsequently subsides.

11.5 Summary of the Facts

The preceding examination of the facts of inflation and output fluctuations in 1891–1914 (the first period) and 1952–83 (the second period) can be summarized as follows:

1. Output fluctuations are smaller in amplitude and more persistent in the second period.

2. Inflation fluctuations are about the same in amplitude in both periods but are more persistent in the second.

3. Inflation shocks have a negative, but lagged, effect on output in the second period; output shocks have a positive, but lagged effect on inflation in the second period. No such timing relation exists in the first period. If there is any intertemporal effect in the first period, it is in the reverse direction.

4. There is a positive contemporaneous correlation between the inflation shocks and the output shocks in both periods. This correlation is larger in the first period.

5. The variances of the shocks to inflation and to output are smaller in the later period.

11.6 Structural Interpretations

The vector autoregression can be viewed as a reduced form of a structural model. Unfortunately the mapping from the reduced form to the structural form is not one-to-one. The traditional identification literature shows formally that there will in principle be many structural models that are consistent with a given reduced form. In practice, however, the situation is not so dismal. There are a relatively small number of theoretically sound or "reasonable" structural models. Moreover, the properties of an estimated reduced form can frequently narrow the range of possible structural models.

11.6.1 The Postwar Period

The third property of the estimated autoregressions listed at the end of the previous section is very useful for nailing down a reasonable structural model. The dynamic interaction between inflation and output in the postwar period is very strong. Inflation "Granger causes" output in a negative direction; and output "Granger causes" inflation in a positive direction. This pattern naturally leads to the following interpretation for the postwar period.

The Federal Reserve, or the "aggregate demand authorities" in general, is concerned with stabilizing inflation as well as unemployment. For aggregate demand shocks this joint aim causes no conflict; the best policy for both price and output stabilization is to offset the shocks. When an inflation shock comes, however, there is a conflict. The Fed must decide how "accommodative" to be. On average during the postwar period the Fed seems to have made a compromise. Policy is described by a policy rule. When an inflation shock occurs, the Fed neither fully "accommodates" the shock by increasing the rate of growth of the money supply point for point with inflation nor tries to eliminate it immediately by sharply reducing money growth. Instead, it lets money growth increase, but by less than the inflation shock. The result is the dynamic pattern observed in the vector autoregressions. When inflation increases the Fed lets real money balances—appropriately defined—fall, and the economy slips into a recession. Hence, inflation "Granger causes" output. The slack demand conditions then gradually work to reduce inflation. Hence, output "Granger causes" inflation.

This structural interpretation is by no means new, and it is gradually being incorporated in standard textbooks. For the data used here the following simple algebraic structural model seems to match the reduced form very well:

$$(3) \qquad P_t = \delta p_{t-1} + \alpha E y_t + u_t,$$

$$(4) \qquad y_t = -\beta_1 p_{t-1} + \beta_2 p_{t-2} + y_{t-1} + v_t.$$

The notation for output y_t and inflation p_t is the same as earlier. The operator E is the conditional expectation based on information through period $t - 1$. The shocks u_t and v_t are assumed to be serially uncorrelated.

The first equation is a simple price adjustment equation. This equation has no simulaneous effects between output and inflation. The second equation is the policy rule described above. It states that the rate of growth of output relative to trend is reduced if inflation has risen. If this system is to match up with the reduced-form evidence, the parameters should all be positive.

The estimated equations (written with the constants explicit and the t-ratios in parentheses) are:

$$(5) \qquad p_t = .89p_{t-1} + .25Ey_t + .55 , \qquad \sigma = 1.0, R^2 = .83$$
$$\qquad\qquad (10.1) \qquad (3.6) \qquad (1.3)$$

$$(6) \qquad y_t = -1.01p_{t-1} + .69p_{t-2} + y_{t-1} + 1.17, \qquad \sigma = 2.0, R^2 = .67$$
$$\qquad\quad (-3.5) \qquad\quad (2.5) \qquad\qquad (1.6)$$

These equations were estimated using the full information maximum likelihood method. This method takes account of the cross-equation restrictions that occur when the second equation is used to forecast output in the first equation. The output equation is already in reduced form and is clearly not much different from the estimated equation in table 11.2. The reduced form for inflation can easily be derived by substituting the expectation of equation (6) into equation (5). It also matches up well with the reduced-form equation in table 11.2.

Equation (6) indicates that there is much less accommodation of inflation in the short run than in the long run. The short-run reaction coefficient is about -1, whereas the long-run reaction is about -0.3. Equation (5) indicates that inflation responds to slack demand with a lag.[3] The coefficient on lagged inflation depends on the structure of contracts in the economy as well as on expectations of inflation; the parameter would change with a change in the policy rule that changed expectations, and in this sense it is incorrect to refer to the equation as structural.

The policy rule can be written in the following interesting form:

$$(7) \qquad y_t - y_{t-1} = -.32p_{t-1} - .69(p_{t-1} - p_{t-2}) + 1.17.$$

In other words, the rate of growth of real GNP (relative to potential) is reduced by 32% of the inflation rate in the last period plus 69% of the change of the inflation rate. The response of the Fed to high inflation is stronger when inflation is increasing than when it is decreasing. A

3. The data cannot discriminate between the assumptions that y_t or E_t appears in equation (5). The contemporaneous correlation is positive and could equally well be due to the correlation between the structural shocks as to a direct simultaneous effect of y_t on p_t.

nominal GNP rule could be interpreted[4] as having an implied coefficient
-1 on the lagged inflation rate, with no adjustment for increasing or
decreasing inflation. The estimated rule is less accommodative than a
nominal GNP rule in the short run and more accommodative than a
nominal GNP rule in the long run.

11.6.2   The Prewar Period

This model of price adjustment and policy is explicitly oriented to
the postwar period in the United States. The wide differences between
the autoregressions in the prewar and the postwar periods indicate
that the same model is unlikely to fit in the prewar period. In fact,
the model does very poorly in the prewar period. The coefficient on
lagged inflation in the inflation equation (3) is negative though small
and insignificant, whereas the coefficients on lagged prices in the
output equation (4) are all positive. As the reduced-form results suggested, the dynamic relation between inflation and output in the prewar period is weak and opposite in sign from that for the postwar
period.

The price adjustment equation without the insignificant lagged inflation rate is

(8) $$p_t = .28y_t + 1.33.$$
$$(2.5)\quad (2.0)$$

Hence, although the lagged inflation rate disappears, the adjustment
coefficient is about the same size as before.

There are two possible implications of this failure of the postwar
model.[5] First, prices and wages appear to be more flexible in the prewar
period in that their correlation with output fluctuations is almost entirely
contemporaneous. Adjustments occur within the annual time interval,
unlike the postwar period, where the adjustments are drawn out for
several years. Second, macroeconomic policy appears to be very accommodative; inflation shocks seemed to have no prior negative effect
on output. Are these implications plausible?

11.6.3   More Flexible Wages and Prices?

The reduced importance of the lagged inflation term could be due
to simple expectations effects as well as to changes in the structure of

---

4. Taken literally, a nominal GNP rule would respond to inflation shocks in the current
period. In practice, however, a lag would probably occur.

5. It should be noted that there are fairly strong dynamic feedback effects from output
and prices two years earlier in the price inflation system (see table 11.2). This is puzzling
since the impact from prices and output one year earlier is weak. This two-year leap is
the reason for the sawtooth moving average representation for this system (see fig. 11.3).

wage and price setting. The inertia effect in the postwar period is a combination of expectations effects and structure. Since inflationary expectations were probably much lower in the prewar period, the effect of lagged inflation would be smaller. Unfortunately, it is difficult to distinguish these two effects with aggregate data.

The problem has been addressed by Cagan (1979) and Mitchell (1983) using microeconomic data. Although neither author looks at data before World War I, their findings are probably relevant for the comparison of this paper. Cagan compares price movements in the business cycles of the 1920s with price movements in the business cycles after World War II. Mitchell compares wage adjustments in the 1930s with wage adjustments in the postwar period. Both find that price and wage adjustments were larger and more frequent in the earlier period. From a microeconomic perspective wages and prices were more flexible.

Two possible reasons for this change have been noted. First, the increased importance of large business enterprises and large unions could have centralized price and wage decisions and made them less subject to short-run market pressures. In the major labor unions, for example, the costs of negotiating a large settlement made it economical to have long three-year contracts in many industries. The overlapping nature of these contracts added to the persistence of wage trends. Second, economic policy changed so as to reduce the severity of recessions and thereby lessen the need to reduce wages and prices quickly in the face of slack demand conditions. This policy effect is different from the expectation of inflation effect mentioned above.

11.6.4   More Accommodative Policy?

Although the United States Treasury took on some central bank functions in the early 1900s, during most of the period 1891–1914 monetary policy was determined solely by the United States commitment to the gold standard. A gold standard is normally thought to generate aggregate demand "discipline." Policy would automatically be non-accommodative. For example, if there was an inflation shock, then a contractionary policy would be necessary in order to bring the price level back to its relative position with gold. Then why do the data suggest the opposite, that policy was accommodative?

One explanation comes from the fact that the United States was a small open economy during this period. Most price shocks probably came from abroad, much as the price shocks in the 1970s came from abroad. An increase in external prices with a fixed exchange rate will make domestically produced goods cheaper. This will lead to a balance of payments surplus until internal prices rise. A balance of payments surplus increases the money supply for a country on a gold standard.

The increase in the money supply will therefore tend to occur just as the domestic price level rises in response to the rise in world prices. Policy will look very accommodative.

A fixed exchange rate gold standard will be less accommodative to price shocks that originate at home. A price shock will raise domestic prices relative to external prices. The resulting balance of payments deficit will reduce the domestic money supply, and the economy will tend to fall into a recession. Internal prices will then fall. Either this type of scenario did not occur in 1891–1914, or it occurred so quickly that the timing cannot be detected with aggregate annual data. It is interesting that accommodation under a gold standard seems to be different for external shocks and internal shocks. According to modern expectations theories this discrimination is appropriate. Internal endogenous price and wage shocks are discouraged, whereas external exogenous price shocks are accommodated. Because the external price and wage behavior is unlikely to be influenced by the monetary policy in a small open economy, accommodation will not do any long-run harm. But internal price and wage behavior is likely to be adversely affected by an accommodative policy.

Another way to describe the prewar policy rule is to say that it was accommodative in the short run, permitting much slippage to accommodate external price shocks, but nonaccommodative in the long run. Prices in the United States could not differ from world prices in the long run. This is in contrast to the characterization in the previous section of policy in the postwar period: in the short run policy is much less accommodative than in the long run.

To summarize, the interpretation that prices and wages adjust quickly and that policy is very accommodative in the short run is plausible from a microeconomic perspective. Unlike the postwar period, where lags in the relation between output and inflation permitted one to narrow down the field of potential models, for the prewar period data are more ambiguous. If all the action occurs within the annual timing interval, it is difficult to distinguish one structural model from another. The lags are not long enough to identify the structure. In fact, the contemporaneous relation between prices and output in equation (8) could have been generated from a mechanism like the Lucas (1972) supply curve. If prices were as flexible as they appear to be during this earlier period, then the Lucas model itself is more plausible.

11.7 Concluding Remarks

Macroeconomic performance in the United States from 1891 through 1914 was much different from the performance after World War II. This difference is apparent in reduced-form autoregressions, in their moving average representations, in simple structural models, and even in simple time series charts of the data. The shocks, or *impulses,* to the economic system were smaller in the second period, mainly because of the policy and structural changes that Arthur Burns mentioned in his 1959 presidential address. Deposit insurance, for example, reduced the shocks to aggregate demand that came from financial panics.

But the dynamics, or *propagation mechanisms,* of the economic system are much slower and more drawn out in the postwar period. This tends to translate the smaller shocks into larger and more prolonged movements in output and inflation than would occur if the prewar dynamics were applicable in the later period. In other words, the change in the dynamics of the system offset some of the gains from the smaller impulses. These postwar dynamics can be given a structural interpretation in terms of the accommodative stance of monetary policy and the speed of wage and price adjustments. These dynamics were not evident in the prewar period.

One interpretation of these developments is that the change in the dynamics was a direct result of the reduction in the importance of the shocks. For example, prices and wages may have became more rigid because of the reduced risks of serious recessions or because movements in the money supply began to do some of the macroeconomic stabilization work that was previously done by wage and price adjustments. The analysis of this paper is not conclusive on this or on the other interpretation that the change in the dynamics was unrelated to the change in policy. But the possibility that a combination of the smaller postwar shocks with the shorter prewar dynamics might improve macroeconomic performance should be sufficient motivation for further study of these historical developments and their alternative interpretations.

Comment   Phillip Cagan

It has long been noted that prices fluctuate less in post–World War II business cycles than they used to, though with the higher rates of inflation in the 1970s the amplitude of fluctuations became larger. One reason was that business cycles were generally less severe in the postwar period; none matched the severity of 1929–33, 1937–38, 1920–21, or 1907. Yet even for cycles of comparable severity in terms of real variables the postwar period appeared to exhibit less price fluctuation. It was generally agreed that prices and wages had become less flexible.

Phillip Cagan is professor of economics at Columbia University.

In Taylor's annual data, these differences between periods are less clear. Compared with the interwar cycles 1910–40, the post–World War II period shows a standard deviation only one-quarter of the earlier value for price inflation and one-third of the earlier value for wage inflation. But compared with the pre-World War I cycles 1891–1914, the post–World War II cycles had about the same standard deviations— only 8% smaller for price inflation and actually 16% larger for wage inflation, even though the standard deviation of real GNP from its trend was 25% smaller in the post–World War II period. Inflation rates in this later period had a greater upward trend until the past few years, however, so that their standard deviations, if measured from trend, would be smaller.

The smaller variation in inflation in the later period becomes clear in the vector autoregression analysis of price and wage inflation and the real GNP gap. The residuals from these regressions represent unexplained movements, which Taylor interprets as "shocks" to the system. These shocks are much smaller in the postwar period. Compared with the pre–World War I period, in the postwar period shocks are reduced by 50% for prices and for the output gap and by 25% for wages.

Taylor uses this comparison of shocks to explain why, if prices and wages are less flexible in the postwar period, the output gap at the same time shows less rather than more variability. The answer is that shocks in the postwar period were sufficiently smaller to overcome the tendency of cyclical fluctuations to show up more in output than in prices and wages.

What are these shocks? Some are supply shocks, best illustrated by the OPEC oil price increases of 1973 and 1979 or by major labor strikes, as in steel in 1953 and automobiles in 1971, but for the most part these are fairly rare events. Shocks can also appear on the demand side, as in the financial panics of 1893 and 1907, which produced sudden contractions in the available money supply. In addition, we should recognize the possibility of mundane but ubiquitous measurement errors, particularly in the earlier period when the data are clearly less accurate. When Simon Kuznets put together his annual GNP data for the pre-1929 period, he was so concerned with the imprecision of the estimates that he was unwilling to publish the annual figures and planned to release only five-year averages. He was subsequently persuaded, I understand, to allow Friedman and Schwartz to use the data in annual form, since the five-year averages would have been useless for cyclical analysis. Kuznets obviously knew something about these data that the rest of us should not ignore. The GNP series from *Historical Statistics* that Taylor used are not much better.

Finally, Taylor's shocks may reflect variations over time in cyclical relationships that cannot be captured by a small number of autoregression lag terms. Cycles vary in duration and amplitude, and such variations may reflect the internal dynamics of the cyclical process as well as different dynamics depending on the type of shock, particularly whether it is viewed as temporary or permanent. I cannot refrain here from expressing my uneasiness with the spreading popularity of vector autoregression analysis. My concern is not with its atheoretical approach, which bothers some critics—that can often be an advantage—but with the fact that relatively simple autoregression and moving average representations do not fit many time series adequately, even though the residuals may pass tests as white noise. In work that I have done, an ARIMA fit to M1 growth produces residuals that have a much smaller variance in the 1960s than in the 1950s and 1970s. There is no simple way to model this pronounced change in variance. I also found that GNP growth in the 1970s cannot be represented by ARIMA functions that fit earlier periods. (Of course, structural econometric models may face the same problem of inadequate fit over different periods.) The NBER used to have a tradition of presenting charts of basic data. I would be less uneasy if the users of vector autoregressions pondered charts of their fits and showed them to the reader.

Having raised these red warning flags, I do not wish to dismiss all such statistical analyses. In many cases, and in Taylor's analysis of prices and wages, I find the vector autoregressions a useful and enlightening supplement to other modes of analysis.

His autoregressions contain three other pieces of information in addition to the variance of the residuals. The first is the contemporaneous correlation of residuals in the paired regressions. These are about the same for the pre–World War I and post–World War II periods but twice as large in the wage as in the price regressions. Although Taylor does not comment on this information, I interpret it as some evidence against greater measurement error in the earlier period. The shocks should be correlated, since most demand and supply shocks will affect prices and wages as well as output in the span of one year. Measurement error would normally be uncorrelated and thus would produce no correlation of residuals.

Another more important piece of information provided by the vector autoregressions is the coefficients on lagged values of the dependent variables. These are a measure of persistence—the degree to which the series is a continuation of its previous values. Based on the size and statistical significance of these coefficients, the postwar period shows much more persistence, as we knew it would from previous studies of the flexibility of prices and wages. Taylor's measure of persistence nicely summarizes this development. The pattern of increasing persistence is broken, however, by a large significant coefficient in the earlier period on the lag of prices two years previous. This coefficient, which is positive and characteristic of "sawtooth" movements, has no obvious interpretation. A feedback mechanism such as existed under the gold standard would produce a negative coefficient. It appears to be a fluke and lends support to the importance of measurement error.

The cross-coefficients in these regressions, those showing the effect of price and wage inflation on output, can be interpreted as the response of the monetary system to inflationary pressures. Positive coefficients indicate accommodation, zero coefficients no accommodation, and negative coefficients a counter response. Here I am surprised by the results, and apparently Taylor was also. In the postwar period these coefficients of prices and wages in the output regressions are negative for the first lag and positive for the second. This has the interesting interpretation that policy since World War II has initially opposed inflationary pressures but then accommodated them, possibly as a reaction to the consequences of the initial anti-inflationary actions or in any event as an inability or unwillingness to carry through with them. Although I am surprised to find this in the autoregressions, it is not implausible. The time series pattern of inflation since World War II can be viewed as supporting this interpretation: inflationary movements have fluctuated but overall have tended to rise from cycle to cycle, except (let us hope!) for the most recent episode, 1979–83.

The indicated degree of such accommodation in the pre–World War I period is quite different. The response to wage inflation is weakly negative in the first lag and then zero in the second, indicating either a partial accommodation over the two years or perhaps an immediate strong opposition to inflation that is completed within one year and so is absent from the first lagged year. For price inflation, however, the response in the pre–World War I period is surprisingly positive, and it is significantly positive in the second lagged year. This implies that price movements were more fully accommodated under the gold standard than later under the Federal Reserve System. This may at first seem counterintuitive, but I believe it correctly depicts the dynamics of the gold standard. The vaunted monetary discipline of the gold standard occurred only in the long run. The gold standard took two to three cycles or more to reverse monetary and price developments if they were moderate and not severely out of line with world trends, and it was quite loose in the short run. I and others have pointed out that United States gold specie flows were much smaller than cyclical movements in the foreign trade balance. Most of the cyclical trade imbalances were financed by capital flows, probably because of a general expectation that gold would remain convertible at a fixed exchange rate. The distribution of growing world gold stocks to maintain fixed exchange rates worked slowly over long periods, except when convertibility was threatened, such as by financial panics or by the United

States silver purchase legislation of the early 1890s. The managed monetary regime under the Federal Reserve System, on the other hand, could and usually did act more quickly at first to counter inflationary pressures, but since World War II, unfortunately, inadequately.

The vector autoregression technique allows a description of the path of the variables when a shock to one of the variables occurs. Taylor shows the paths of the variables for the two periods in his figures 11.3 and 11.4 where the contemporaneous correlation between the error terms has been ignored. He suggests that the two periods are best represented by two quite different model interpretations. For the later period he postulates that changes in output depend on the one-year lagged inflation rate and the change in the inflation rate between the two previous years. This is consistent with the results reported for the autoregression equation. It is intended to represent a one-year lagged effect of monetary policy on output. When fit to the data, this equation suggests that policy actions reduce output by 30% of the previous year's inflation rate and by 70% of the change in the inflation rate in the previous year. This differs from a straightforward rule of keeping nominal GNP constant, by which the coefficient for the inflation rate in this equation on a one-year lag would be -1. The fitted equation for the later period thus differs from the GNP rule in that the response is well under unity, and stronger if inflation is increasing than if decreasing.

In the other equation for the later period, price inflation is made dependent on the one-year lagged inflation rate and the expected output gap. This expectation is based on the output equation. The assumption that expected rather than actual output belongs in this equation follows the literature on rational expectations and staggered contracts. Price inflation is persistent because of contracts but partially responds in any year to expected demand, here represented by expected output.

This model for the later period is an interesting and ingenious interpretation of the empirical results. It is useful for comparison with the earlier period. My main difficulty is with its extreme abstraction from the details of the business cycle. Monetary policy is assumed to respond only to inflation and not to output or other variables, and all the contributions to the business cycle other than policy and price responses are subsumed in the error terms. It is anyone's guess whether the cyclical process that is approximated by this high degree of abstraction is valid or misleading.

In comparing the later with the earlier period, what in summary can be said? First of all, prices in the later period lost much of the flexibility they displayed earlier. Unions and longer wage contracts are a major reason. But I believe the later inflexibility reflects more than this: adjustments have become less flexible on a broader scale than can be attributed to union contracts or their influence on costs. Taylor mentions the growth of large business enterprises centralizing price decisions, but inflexibility is just as true of fabricated products supplied by many small firms. The only broad effect that Taylor or anyone else, including me, has been able to identify that stands up is the lessened severity of cyclical fluctuations since World War II and presumably a general expectation that government policies will oppose severe price movements, thus reducing the likelihood that major price or wage changes will have to be made. This shows up in the time series as autocorrelation and greater persistence.

The second conclusion is that in the short run the monetary system did not accommodate price movements in the later period but did so in the earlier period. Taylor suggests that the earlier period reflected the difference between external and internal price shocks. Under the gold standard external price increases from abroad produced trade surpluses and gold inflows along with direct price increases and thus appeared to accommodate the price shock. On the other hand, domestic price increases not matched abroad led to gold outflows and a subsequent contraction. The effect of internal price shocks in the earlier period either occurred very quickly and so was invisible in the annual data or was dominated by the external shocks. The latter is conceivable, but there is no particular reason to believe that external shocks dominated. Although the United States was somewhat like a small open economy in this period and so was subject to influences from abroad, it also generated major internal shocks such as harvest surpluses, banking panics, and the silver agitation.

In any event, I favor Taylor's other explanation, which in my interpretation is to view the gold standard as accommodative in the short run through variations in the gold reserve and as disciplined to be nonaccommodative only in the long run to maintain convertibility.

Finally, although shocks were smaller in the later period, the dynamics of the system translated the shocks into larger and more prolonged movements in output and inflation. The change in dynamics from the earlier to the later period would have produced *larger* cycles in the later period had the shocks not become smaller.

The lack of conclusiveness of the results here is due to the undefined character of the shocks. Taylor alludes to stabilizing developments listed by Arthur Burns in his 1959 presidential address, which included deposit insurance to prevent panics, less fluctuation in dividend payments, automatic fiscal stabilizers, and so on. Most of these are "shocks" only in the sense that they are not directly specified in Taylor's vector autoregression. Moreover, they may not have been independent of the dynamics. As Taylor suggests, price adjustments may have become slower in response to these other developments that reduced the amplitude of the shocks.

The interpretation of these developments I like is that policy became more responsive to output gaps in the later period and that this allowed prices and wages to become less responsive. The effect was both to reduce cyclical fluctuations and to accommodate a gradually rising inflation rate. At first sight the autoregressions appear to contradict this explanation, which implies that the output gap in the later period should have a negative coefficient on its lagged value when in fact it has a positive value. However, the negative coefficient may occur only for contractions in output, not expansions, if policy has been asymmetrical. The vector autoregressions miss such a distinction.

Taylor's analysis forces us to grapple with an apparent change in the degree of accommodation between the earlier and later periods and a reduction in the amplitude of shocks. I find these results generally plausible. My main reservation is that the shocks may be misleading if their large size in the earlier period reflects an inadequacy of the price and output lags for explaining the dependent variables. It might be that a structural representation of both periods would yield exogenous shocks of equal amplitude. A comparison of these periods will remain incomplete until we can empirically demonstrate whether structural changes or a decline in shocks account for the reduction in amplitude of cycles. But my best guess is that mild cycles in both periods were similar in dynamics and shocks and that the periods differ overall because of selected "severe" cycles owing to monetary disturbances, which were a special breed prevalent before World War II.

Comment   Stephen R. King

John Taylor has written an elegant paper on interpreting the differences in the cyclical behavior of output and inflation between the eight business cycles that preceded World War I and the eight that followed the World War II. The central difference he identifies between the periods is that the postwar fluctuations in inflation and detrended output display lower variance, but higher persistence, than those before World War I. In fact, the mean peak-to-peak period of the postwar output cycles is 4.2 years, ten months longer than in the prewar period.[1] To distinguish the impulses that initiate cycles from the propagation mechanism that extends them, he examines innovations, or shocks to the system, which

Stephen R. King is assistant professor of economics at Stanford University.

1. These calculations are computed from a second-order autoregression for the output gap, using the formula for the mean cyclical period given in Taylor (1980): period $= 2\pi/\cos^{-1}(-0.5(1 - a_1 + a_2))$, where a_i are the coefficients of the ith lags in the autoregression for output.

he finds display much lower variance in the second period, and the degree of serial correlation in the responses of the system to shocks, which he finds increases.

A particular strength of the paper is that Taylor interprets the reduced-form evidence gleaned from vector autoregressions (VARs) of detrended output and inflation in the light of a simple structural model to account for the stylized facts that emerge. The transformation of a mass of data into a few key parameters is very welcome. The model combines "sticky" price setting (with prices unresponsive to contemporaneous demand movements) with a reaction function for aggregate demand policy that implies that the monetary and fiscal authorities respond with some degree of accommodation to output and inflation shocks.

The postwar results, as one might suspect, are quite consistent with the interpretation offered by Taylor's model. The well-known stickiness of wages and prices, combined with partial demand accommodation, leads to a cyclical response of inflation, recession, and eventual return to equilibrium in response to a price shock.

The pre–World War I results do not fit easily with such a model. The shortness of output cycles in the data is consistent with the very low degree of serial correlation of prices (lack of stickiness) in this time period. But the fact that price shocks do not lead to output fluctuations, except contemporaneously, suggests full accommodation by the monetary authority. This is the puzzle Taylor faces us with, since we usually think of policy as being unaccommodative under a gold standard. The resolution of the puzzle is obtained by noting that under a gold standard, imported (but not domestic) price shocks would be accommodated by gold inflows and hence would not necessarily be followed by adverse fluctuations in real output.

Credence is given to this interpretation by adding the growth rate of money to the VAR that Taylor estimates. When this is done, price innovations not only are found to be positively correlated with money shocks, but are also followed by subsequent accommodating monetary movements.[2] For the explanation to be convincing, however, it must

---

2. Exactly the opposite results hold for the postwar period when it appears that positive output shocks leave money unchanged (and are followed by velocity increases), but price shocks are followed by expansionary monetary growth. These observations, too, are in accord with Taylor's conjectures. The actual equations (estimated for 1893–1914 and 1954–83, with m representing the growth rate of M2 prewar and M1 postwar and t ratios in parentheses) are:

$$\text{Prewar: } m_t = .64p_{t-1} + .70p_{t-2} - .52y_{t-1} - .33y_{t-2} \qquad R^2 = 0.51$$
$$\qquad\qquad (2.1) \qquad\quad (2.4) \qquad\quad (2.8) \qquad\quad (1.8)$$

$$\text{Postwar: } m_t = -.59p_{t-1} + 1.25p_{t-2} + .25y_{t-1} + .02y_{t-2} \qquad R^2 = 0.66$$
$$\qquad\qquad (2.1) \qquad\qquad (4.6) \qquad\quad (1.9) \qquad\quad (0.1)$$

also be argued that the price shocks really did originate overseas. In view of the desynchronization of the United States cycle from European fluctuations that Moore and Zarnowitz document for the prewar period, this is by no means self-evident. More doubt arises because Taylor is using a deflator for domestic prices to measure inflation, not one that includes the prices of imports directly. It is true, of course, that the rapid expansion of world gold production after 1896 is consistent with the importation of price rises from abroad. Taylor's other conjecture from looking at the output/inflation results is that output shocks were followed by extinguishing monetary fluctuations. The VAR mentioned above also confirms this supposition.

For whatever reasons, then, prewar policy does appear to have been more accommodating of price shocks and less accommodating of output shocks than it was in the postwar period. What does all this have to do with the role of prices and wages in improving macroeconomic stability? Despite the usefulness of Taylor's interpretive model and reduced-form findings, we learn little about the really fundamental difference between the two time periods. Given that wages and prices do appear stickier in the postwar period, is this increase in stickiness a result of more accommodative demand policy followed since the 1946 Employment Act, or was the accommodative policy itself a reaction to an increase in wage and price stickiness? The answer to this question is absolutely crucial in learning from these two periods.

Many reasons have been advanced for "exogenous" reductions in wage and price flexibility: increased concentration in industry, reduction in the role of primary industries and their replacement by service industry, and increased unionization of the labor force. The growing importance of explicit and implicit contracts is also cited by some. But the increased willingness of the government to accommodate fluctuations, either by automatic stabilizers, by institutions such as deposit insurance, or through discretionary policy, will also increase the incentive of private agents to save on costly negotiations by writing long-term contracts.

Since a problem in interpreting the appearance of high coefficients on the lagged dependent variable in an inflation equation as due to inertia is that they may be in part expectational, it might make sense to estimate inflation equations for the two periods with lagged inflation and anticipated nominal GNP growth (in excess of trend real GNP growth) as explanatory variables. If the lagged dependent variable in Taylor's inflation equation was capturing expectations of inflation ac-

---

The prewar and postwar contemporaneous correlation coefficients of output and money are .61 and .63 respectively, and the corresponding inflation and money correlations are .29 and .36.

commodation, then such an approach might remove the significance of the lags of the dependent variable in the equation. Doing this for the prewar and postwar samples yields an insignificant sum of coefficients on two lags of inflation of .42 ($F(2,19) = 2.81$) for the prewar period, and a highly significant .67 ($F(2,26) = 47.1$) for the postwar.[3] It seems, therefore, that this simple technique has not found evidence that the increased importance of lags represents purely expectational effects. Inertia still characterizes the postwar, more than the prewar, data. Just as in Taylor's paper, however, there is some limited evidence of stickiness in the prewar period at a two-year lag.

One must applaud Taylor's use of the pre–World War I sample. This interesting period deserves study and provides an instructive comparison with the postwar period. At the same time, one runs the risk of treating the prewar period as though it were the "normal" state of affairs and contrasting it with the postwar era with its "exceptional" price stickiness. A slightly broader comparison might be made with some evidence from an earlier period. David Hume, in his justly famous essay on money, reports that in the last year of Louis XIV (1715) in France, prices rose by only one-third the amount by which money grew. That performance is comparable to postwar behavior in the United States. Perhaps, then, the period that requires special explanation is not the recent quarter-century but the twenty-four years that preceded World War I.

Taylor provides results for both price and wage inflation. To measure wages, he uses hourly earnings in manufacturing, which may not reflect economywide wages, especially in view of the hypothesized changes in relative prices of tradable goods. In his empirical results, he consistently finds lower coefficients on wages than on prices, especially in the prewar sample. Because of this, the moving average results give the appearance of a procyclical real wage before the war. Although this may be true, the lower coefficients on nominal wages, and the consequent cyclical pattern of real wages, may simply be due to measurement error in the wage series and hence may be spurious.

A methodological problem with the empirical analysis is the weight put on interpretation of moving average coefficients, whose statistical significance is not given in the paper. The very weak "fit" of the prewar inflation and output equations (for example, none of the coefficients in

3. The actual equations estimated for 1893–1914 and 1954–83 are:

$$\text{Prewar:} \quad p_t = .12p_{t-1} + .30p_{t-2} + .20E(py)_t, \quad R^2 = .41$$
$$(0.6) \qquad (1.5) \qquad (1.6)$$
$$\text{Postwar:} \quad p_t = 1.06p_{t-1} - .39p_{t-2} + .27E(py)_t, \quad R^2 = .85$$
$$(7.0) \qquad (-2.4) \qquad (2.5)$$

where a constant and two lagged values of inflation and growth of nominal output and the money supply are used as instruments for contemporaneous nominal output growth.

the prewar wage/output system is individually significant at the .05 level) must be hiding some "true" stickiness from the observer. It would certainly be surprising if any of the moving average terms from that system were significantly different from zero.

Another obstacle to interpreting the moving average coeffi.ients is Taylor's decision to ignore the contemporaneous correlation of the innovations to the two equations, which in the systems he estimates are always significantly different from zero (and positive). Although there are, as he says, an infinite number of possible decompositions of this correlation, his model specifically implies one. Since prices are modeled as being unresponsive to contemporaneous demand shocks, it seems natural to allow price shocks (assuming they represent something more than pure measurement error) to enter the output gap equation contemporaneously. This might upset the interpretation of the output equation as a policy reaction function. In fact, it would lead to a model with three equations—one for price adjustment, one for real GNP, and a monetary policy rule. In any event, given the size of the contemporaneous correlations involved, such an orthogonalization may well make quite a difference to the results.

In conclusion, John Taylor's paper has made a very useful and provocative contribution to the analysis of price/wage interaction in two disparate periods of United States history. If there are still questions to be answered about the roles of wages and prices in the behavior of the economy between the two periods, then this simply underscores Taylor's concluding statement in the paper: that the policy implications of understanding why the Phillips curve has become flatter with the passage of time are sufficient motivation for further study of the issues.

Comment   J. Bradford DeLong and Lawrence H. Summers

In his contributions to this volume John Taylor reaches exactly the opposite conclusion from that in our paper (chap. 12); he finds that improved macroeconomic performance has taken place in spite of rather than because of the increased rigidity of wages and prices in the postwar period. Our explanation has the virtue of parsimony. We attribute the major change in economic performance to the major change in economic structure rather than telling a complex story involving offsetting effects. Moreover, Taylor provides no explanation of the forces that have accounted for the huge decline in the variance of aggregate demand shocks he claims took place. As we shall argue below, Taylor's

J. Bradford DeLong is a graduate student in the Department of Economics at Harvard University. Lawrence H. Summers is professor of economics at Harvard University.

theory that monetary policy has become less accommodative over time also seems implausible. He rests his conclusions on bivariate time series analysis of prices and output. We begin by showing that his conclusions can be reproduced in a model where increased price flexibility increases macroeconomic instability and then turn to other aspects of his argument.

Begin with an aggregate demand curve similar to that in section 12.3 of our paper:

(1) $$q_{t+1} = \beta_1(m_t - p_t) + \beta_2(E_t p_{t+1} - p_t) + \epsilon_t$$

and assume perfect foresight for investors:

(2) $$E_t p_{t+1} = p_{t+1}.$$

Equation (1) contains q_{t+1} in order to make the timing come out right: think of firms placing orders for investment goods this period, orders that do not show up in output until next period.

For simplicity, specify a simpler aggregate supply equation than in section 12.2;

(3) $$p_{t+1} - p_t = p_t - p_{t-1} + \alpha q_{t+1}.$$

The inflation rate accelerates or decelerates depending on the output gap. This aggregate supply equation is the simplest that both is "superneutral" and exhibits "persistence."

To close the model, a money supply rule is needed. The simple assumption of section 12.2, the assumption of no movement at all in the money stock will not be a satisfactory underpinning for empirical analysis. We assume:

(4) $$m_t = (1 - \lambda)p_t + \lambda p_{t-1}.$$

The money stock accommodates to the price level partially within the period and fully after two periods. A value of one for λ would imply no accommodation within the period; a value of zero would imply complete accommodation within the period.

Denoting $p_t - p_{t-1}$ by $\dot{p}_t$, solving the model, produces:

(5) $$\dot{p}_t = \frac{1 - \lambda\beta_1}{1 - \alpha\beta_2}\dot{p}_{t-1} + \frac{\alpha}{1 - \alpha\beta_2}\epsilon_t$$

(6) $$q_t = \frac{\beta_2 - \lambda\beta_1}{1 - \alpha\beta_2}\dot{p}_{t-1} + \frac{1}{1 - \alpha\beta_2}\epsilon_{t-1}.$$

Stability requires that:

(7) $$\lambda > \beta_2/\beta_1$$

(8) $$\alpha < \frac{2}{\beta_2 + \lambda\beta_1}.$$

If ϵ_t follows a white-noise process with unit variance, then solving for the inverse of the variance of output leads to the equation:

$$(9) \qquad \frac{1}{\sigma_q^2} = 1 - \left(\frac{3}{2}\beta_2 + \frac{1}{2}\beta_1\lambda\right)\alpha + \left(\frac{\beta_2^2}{2} + \frac{\beta_1\beta_2\lambda}{2}\right)\alpha^2.$$

Therefore further increases in the price flexibility parameter α are destabilizing and *increase* the variance of output, so long as

$$(10) \qquad \alpha < \frac{1}{2\beta_2} + \frac{1}{\beta_2 + \beta_1\lambda} \, .$$

But (7) and (8) imply that α must satisfy (10). In this model, the variance of output is least when α equals zero, when there is no flexibility at all in the aggregate price level.

And yet empirical analysis of a system generated by (1) through (4) would produce results that might mimic quite closely those Taylor obtained for the postwar period. An economist who knew the timing of the aggregate supply equation might be able to recover it exactly:

$$(11) \qquad \dot{p}_t = \dot{p}_{t-1} + \alpha q_t \, .$$

And an attempt to estimate a combined aggregate demand/monetary reaction function equation would yield:

$$(12) \qquad \begin{aligned} q_t - q_{t-1} &= \left(-\frac{\lambda\beta_1 - \beta_2}{1 - \alpha\beta_2} - \frac{1}{\alpha}\right)\dot{p}_{t-1} \\ &+ \left(\frac{\lambda\beta_1 - \beta_2}{1 - \alpha\beta_2} + \frac{1 - \alpha\lambda\beta_1}{\alpha(1 - \alpha\beta_2)}\right)\dot{p}_{t-2}\,, \end{aligned}$$

where $\lambda\beta_1 - \beta_2$, $1 - \alpha\beta_2$, and $1 - \alpha\lambda\beta_1$, are all positive.

These coefficients are too large to be taken seriously. However, their size (but not their sign) is clearly an artifact of the model. The coefficients on $\dot{p}_{t-1}$ and $\dot{p}_{t-2}$ are highly correlated, and the introduction of a supply shock or of serial correlation in the demand shock would quickly bring them down to more reasonable values—their large size in (12) is due to the fact that the difference between $\dot{p}_{t-1}$ and $\dot{p}_{t-2}$ carries lots of information about ϵ_{t-1}. It is interesting that (11) and (12) might be rewritten as:

$$(13) \qquad \dot{p}_t = \dot{p}_{t-1} + \alpha q_t$$

$$(14) \qquad q_t = q_{t-1} = -\pi_1\dot{p}_{t-1} + \pi_2\dot{p}_{t-2} + u_t \, ,$$

which bear a close resemblance to Taylor's (5) and (7):

$$(15) \qquad \dot{p}_t = .88\dot{p}_{t-1} + .25q_t$$

$$(16) \qquad q_t - q_{t-1} = -1.03\dot{p}_{t-1} + .73\dot{p}_{t-2}.$$

Therefore we conclude that Taylor's empirical findings are neither evidence for nor evidence against the hypothesis that an increase in persistence has led to an increase in stability. By assuming that the size of the shocks is independent of the structure of the model, he can reach one conclusion. By specifying a different underlying model—one that stresses the role of variations in the real interest rate in producing variations in output—the opposite conclusions emerge.[1]

It is a striking feature of Taylor's structural analysis that in explaining the changes in cyclical patterns between the pre–World War I period and the present one, he finds that all the structural parameters in his model change. Particularly surprising are his conclusions about monetary policy. He finds that it has become less accommodative under the current fiat money regime than it was under the earlier gold standard. He attributes the looseness of short-run monetary policy under the gold standard to the effects of foreign price shocks, which should have led to specie inflows. There are at least two important flaws in this argument. First, it is implausible that, at a time when imports represented only about 6% of GNP, foreign price shocks were the principal source of inflation shocks, especially using the GNP deflator to measure prices. Second, analyses of the gold standard surveyed in Bordo and Schwartz (1984) have made it clear that short-run specie flows in response to price shocks were negligible during the gold standard period. There thus seems to be little evidence for the monetary policy assumptions necessary to drive Taylor's conclusions.

Reply   John B. Taylor

In their comments on my paper DeLong and Summers introduce a simple three-equation macromodel to argue their main point. Using this model, they show that a *decrease* in price flexibility—that is, a reduction of the coefficient of demand in the price adjustment equation—leads to a *decrease* in the variance of real output. They assert that this model is roughly consistent with the empirical findings in my paper. Therefore, they argue, my empirical findings support the view that a decrease in price flexibility unambiguously decreases output variance, contrary to my own stated views.

---

1. Taylor's finding that output is a decreasing function of past inflation is not evidence that the positive effect—through the real interest rate—of inflation on output is small. Taylor's negative coefficient is for an equation that is itself not structural, that is a combination of the aggregate demand equation and the monetary policy reaction function.

Upon closer inspection, however, the model produced by DeLong and Summers is grossly inconsistent with the empirical findings reported in my paper. This inconsistency turns out to be crucial for the question of price flexibility and output variability. The discrepancy between the DeLong/Summers model and the data occurs in their treatment of the stochastic disturbance terms in their equations. These disturbance terms generate the movements in the model that underlie their calculation of the output variance. Although they include a disturbance term in the aggregate demand equation, they put no disturbance terms in the price adjustment equation.

The empirical findings in my paper indicate that disturbances to the price adjustment equation constitute a significant part of the explanation of output fluctuations. Ignoring these shocks could obviously be misleading. Moreover, as I showed in a 1979 *Econometrica* paper, the shocks to the price adjustment equation are what cause the trade-off between output and inflation variance: attempts to stabilize inflation sometimes require increased fluctuations in output, a factor that is ignored throughout the Delong/Summers analysis but that I think is a major factor in the business cycle.

What happens if we add a price shock to the DeLong/Summers price adjustment equation? Suppose that the shock has a variance of 1, and that the shock to the aggregate demand equation has a variance of 4 (these numerical values correspond with the empirical findings in my paper). Suppose also that the coefficient β_1 equals 1, and the coefficient β_2 equals .1. Then for two choices of the policy parameter λ the resulting output variance depends of the coefficient α in the price adjustment equation in the following way:

	Variance of output (q_t)	
α	when $\lambda = .8$	when $\lambda = .9$
.0	00	00
.1	7.87	9.00
.2	6.26	6.91
.3	5.82	6.34
.4	5.69	6.16
.5	5.69	6.16
.6	5.76	6.26
.7	5.89	6.43
.8	6.06	6.68
.9	6.27	7.00

Adding a shock to the price adjustment equation changes the De-Long/Summers results dramatically. Rather than obtaining the minimum value of the output variance when the price adjustment coefficient is zero, we see that the maximum value of the variance (∞) is obtained. The rationale is clear. When demand has no effect on inflation, there is nothing available to stabilize inflation, and the inflation rate takes a random walk with infinite variance. Since inflation appears in the aggregate demand equation, output also has infinite variance. As we increase the price adjustment parameter the variance of output declines, contrary to the DeLong/Summers findings. Only for very large values of the price adjustment term does the variance of output begin to increase again. But such large values are not empirically realistic.

The DeLong/Summers model—appropriately augmented to realistically take account of price shocks—therefore does support the view stated in my paper that an increase in price flexibility would tend to improve macroeconomic performance. In fact their model (with price shocks) is much like the structural model reported and estimated in my 1979 *Econometrica* paper, in which I computed trade-offs between output and inflation fluctuations. In that paper the expected rate of inflation appears in the aggregate demand equation (though with an insignificant negative sign), so that the same possibilities for destabilizing price flexibility, which DeLong and Summers have emphasized, exist in that model. As in this example, such a possibility does not appear to be borne out empirically in the estimated version of that model.

Some of the other criticisms of my analysis that DeLong and Summers raise are irrelevant, in my view. For example, they argue that my explanation of the change in economic performance is too complicated, involving offsetting effects. What is so complex? More stable aggregate demand reduced economic fluctuations more than changes in wage- and price-setting behavior increased them. Many people have investigated the reasons for the increased stability of aggregate demand. That was not the subject of my paper, though I found the revisionist analysis of these issues in the DeLong/Summers paper in this volume fascinating reading. In general, however, how can one defend rejecting a two-step argument that is correct in favor of a one-step argument that is wrong?

DeLong and Summers also question the explanations of my empirical finding that aggregate demand policy appears to be less accommodative under the current fiat money regime than under the gold standard. As the numerical example above shows, the degree of accommodation (as measured by λ) does not change the conclusion that decreased price flexibility increases output variance over the relevant range of parameters. The result also holds for a wide range of values of λ not reported above. In no way is this observed change in the response of aggregate demand policy to inflation "necessary to drive Taylor's conclusions," as DeLong and Summers argue. I found my empirical results on aggregate demand policy surprising and offered some possible explanations, but these results are unrelated to my view of the relation between price flexibility and output variability.

Discussion Summary

Much of the initial discussion focused on the problems involved with Taylor's structural interpretations of his VAR results. Martin N. Baily commented that it seemed impossible to distinguish between aggregate demand and aggregate supply shifts when the reduced- form equations are used. Consequently it was unclear how Taylor's "structure" could be differentiated from a Lucas-type supply function in which price flexibility leads to output fluctuations. Taylor's response was that the dynamics embodied in his VAR results provide evidence for the aggregate demand/supply structure rather than a Lucas supply function. These dynamics show that positive price surprises are associated with negative output movements and hence are identified with aggregate supply shocks. Also, positive output surprises are found, over a longer horizon, to be associated with positive price movements, which is consistent with aggregate demand shocks. Robert Hall remarked that in the classic demand/supply curve estimation problem, Taylor's strategy was equivalent to identifying every price rise with a shift in the demand curve and every price decline with a shift in supply.

Blanchard questioned Taylor's use of a two-variable vector autoregression involving price and output. Since so much of the paper was concerned with the accommodative policies of the government, would not a three-variable VAR including a policy variable like money have been preferable? Taylor replied that he had decided against using a government policy variable for two reasons; first, the problems in finding a satisfactory measure of policy—M1, M2 unborrowed reserves, or such—seemed difficult, and second, the goal of the paper was to place structure on VAR results. This task is difficult enough in a two-variable system. McCallum then noted that the structure Taylor employed essentially involved collapsing the monetary authority's price rule into the aggregate demand curve to arrive at equation (7). McCallum thought that an undesirable feature of the resulting equation was that it implied that the monetary authority could influence the growth rate of real output through its choice of the inflation rate. Taylor agreed with McCallum's interpretation but said he felt equation (7) was justified by the data. In a world of sticky prices, in which the Fed targets nominal GNP growth, its policies can affect real output growth directly.

The final point raised in the discussion was methodological and involved Taylor's procedure for generating the moving average representations shown in tables 11.4–11.7 and figures 11.3 and 11.4. John Geweke declared that VAR techniques can be used for two legitimate purposes: to generate the response of the system to a shock in a particular variable, and to identify how the shocks in each variable feed back from one another over some time period (the "historical decomposition of the series"). Both of these procedures require the researcher to specify how the covariance matrix of the shocks in the system is to be orthogonalized. In constructing his moving average representations Taylor has deliberately avoided specifying such an orthogonalization. He thus ignores the effect of the correlations between the shocks of the two equations on the moving average coefficients. The moving average representations Taylor presents are therefore "partial" in that they ignore the channels for feedback from the other variable. Taylor agreed with Geweke's statements but argued that for the purposes of this paper the "partial" moving average representations facilitated a behavioral interpretation of the results. Transforming the VAR estimates by a sample covariance matrix would only muddle the structural interpretations that could be placed on the resulting moving average representations.

References

Bordo, Michael, and Anna Schwartz, eds. 1984. *A retrospective on the classical gold standard.* Chicago: University of Press.

Burns, Arthur F. 1969. Progress towards economic stability. In *The business cycle in a changing world.* New York: Columbia University Press.

Cagan, Phillip. 1979. Changes in the cyclical behavior of prices. In *Persistent inflation: Historical and policy essays.* New York: Columbia University Press.

Friedman, Milton, and Anna J. Schwartz. 1963. A monetary history of the United States, 1867–1960. Princeton: Princeton University Press.

Gordon, Robert J. 1983. A century of evidence on wage and price stickiness in the United States, the United Kingdom and Japan. In *Macroeconomics, prices and quantities,* ed. James Tobin. Washington, D.C.: Brookings Institution.

Lucas, Robert E., Jr. 1972. Expectations and the neutrality of money. *Journal of Economic Theory* 4:103–24.

Mitchell, Daniel J. B. 1983. Wage flexibility: Then and now. Working Paper 65. Institute of Industrial Relations, University of California at Los Angeles.

Sims, Christopher A. 1980. Macroeconomics and reality. *Econometrica* 48 (January): 1–48.

Taylor, John B. 1980. Output and price stability: An international comparison. *Journal of Economic Dynamics and Control* 2:109–32.

———. 1982. Policy choice and economic structure. Occasional Paper 9, Group of Thirty, New York.

Tobin, James. 1980. *Asset accumulation and economic activity: Reflections on contemporary macroeconomic theory.* Oxford: Basil Blackwell.

12 The Changing Cyclical Variability of Economic Activity in the United States

J. Bradford DeLong and Lawrence H. Summers

Perhaps the most striking feature of business cycles is that their amplitude varies widely from era to era and from country to country. Although there do seem to be striking regularities in the pattern of covariation exhibited by variables connected with the business cycle, there are large changes in the magnitude of the cycle itself. These differences in cyclical variation should properly be a subject of study by economists. The existence of these differences suggests that "universal" models of business cycles—models that neglect institutional determinants of business cycle behavior—will not be adequate to explain the phenomenon of the business cycle.

This paper extends discussions by Burns (1960) and Baily (1978) of the changing extent of cyclical variability in the American economy. We seek to link this changing variability to changing institutional factors. In the process, we are led to a view of the role of price flexibility in cyclical fluctuations that, while consistent with Keynes's own views, diverges sharply from the views characteristic both of modern Keynesians and of classical macroeconomists of the new and old schools.

We begin by examining the extent of cyclical variability over different parts of the period 1893–1982. Using a variety of measures of variability and several different statistical techniques, we find clear evidence that the amplitude of cyclical fluctuations is much lower after World War II than it was before. This result holds even if the Great Depression is excluded from the pre–World War II sample period.

J. Bradford DeLong is a graduate student in the Department of Economics at Harvard University. Lawrence H. Summers is professor of economics at Harvard University.

We wish to thank the National Science Foundation for financial support and Robert Eisner, Stanley Fischer, Richard Freeman, Robert Gordon, Herschel Grossman, Bennett McCallum, Jeffrey Sachs, Andrei Shleifer, and Peter Temin for helpful comments.

There is weak evidence that output shocks have had more persistence in the post–World War II period than in the pre–World War II period. This casts doubt on the hypothesis that the successful application of discretionary stabilization policy is a significant cause of improved macroeconomic performance since World War II. A number of structural explanations for this have been suggested, including the declining role of agriculture, the increasing role of government, and the declining share of investment. Our examination of the data indicates that only the increasing role of government can account for even a small part of the decline in the cyclical variability of output and employment that is observed when we compare the pre– and post–World War II periods.

A clear distinction between the patterns of pre– and post–World War II data is the larger size of aggregate demand shocks during the earlier period. We attribute this to two factors. First, the growth of government between the two eras led to significant changes in the relationship between disposable income and GNP. The existence of a large and progressive tax system after World War II tended to mitigate cyclical fluctuations in disposable income. This effect was accentuated by the growth of countercyclical entitlement programs such as unemployment insurance. But large fluctuations in disposable income do not necessarily have any consequences for the behavior of aggregate demand if all consumers can borrow and lend freely. Hence the importance of the second major factor: a decline in the fraction of consumption accounted for by liquidity-constrained households. Growth in the availability of consumer credit of various types led to a reduction in the number of consumers who were forced to cut back their consumption as a result of transitory declines in disposable income. These two factors combined to substantially reduce the Keynesian multiplier[1] and therefore to enhance stability.

Most of the major institutional changes in the economy during this century have had the effect of making the economy less "Walrasian." Both the size of the government and the extent of government regulations have increased markedly. Labor and product markets have become more concentrated with the growth to significance of unions and conglomerates. The attachment between workers and firms was less and wage flexibility was greater before World War II than it has been since. In sum, the pre–World War II economy was much closer to the perfectly competitive, atomistic ideal of economic theory than the post–World War II economy.

Conventional macroeconomic theory of both the Keynesian and the classical varieties suggests that macroeconomic performance should have been better in the pre–World War II economy because it was

---

1. Blanchard 1981 concludes that in America today there is essentially no multiplier.

relatively free of institutional rigidities and imperfections. Yet this was not the case. We raise the possibility that the increasing institutionalization of the economy may have contributed to macroeconomic stability by preventing destabilizing deflations and by facilitating private arrangements to smooth production and employment. This possibility, noted by Keynes, has been largely ignored by both American Keynesian and classical macroeconomists.[2] The much greater cyclical variance in real interest rates observed in the pre–World War II period is a piece of evidence in favor of this alternative hypothesis. Further evidence on the importance of this Keynes effect in explaining the changing character of the business cycle is provided by an investigation of vector autoregression systems.

The paper is organized as follows: Section 12.1 profiles the changing size of cyclical fluctuations over the period 1893–1982. Section 12.2 discusses the role of stabilization policies in accounting for the decline in output variability in the postwar period. Section 12.3 examines the relation between the "Walrasian" character of the economy, price flexibility, and output flexibility. Section 12.4 discusses a number of sources of evidence suggesting that the increasing institutionalization of the economy may have contributed to economic stability. Section 12.5 offers a short restatement of our conclusions.

12.1 The Changing Cyclical Variability of Output

The sharp reduction in the size of cyclical fluctuations in output and employment between the pre– and post–World War II periods has been noted many times. In his amazingly prescient 1959 presidential address to the American Economic Association, Arthur Burns noted that "its [the business cycle's] impact on the lives and fortunes of individuals has been substantially reduced in our generation. . . . There is no parallel for such a sequence of mild—or such a sequence of brief—contractions, at least during the past hundred years in our own country." Figures 12.1 and 12.2 plot the rate of change of annual GNP and the percentage deviation of GNP from trend over the period 1893–1982. They show clearly the declining variability of real output.

An indication of the magnitude of the decline in cyclical variability is provided by a comparison of the peak-to-trough decline in output between prewar and postwar recessions as defined by the NBER chronology. During the postwar period, the median decline was 0.2%, and the maximum decline was 1.8% during the 1973–75 recession. During the period 1893–1940 the median decline was 3.8%, and the maximum

---

2. A prominent exception is Tobin 1975.

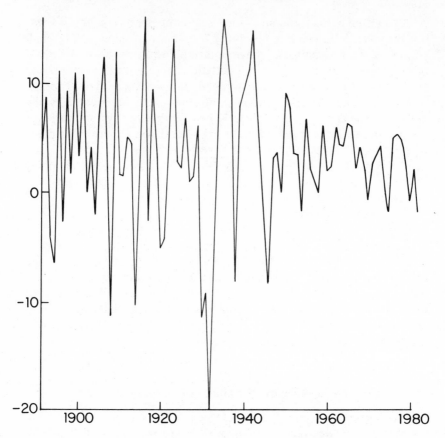

Fig. 12.1   Annual percentage changes in real GNP.

decline was 37% between 1929 and 1933.[3] Similar conclusions are obtained using data on employment or industrial production. For example, the median decline from peak to trough in industrial production was 12% during 1893–1940 compared with a maximum decline in industrial production of 9% during the postwar period.

A somewhat more systematic examination of the changing variability of GNP is presented in table 12.1. Three alternative measures of variability are used. The first is the standard deviation of the growth rate of quarterly GNP as estimated by Gordon (1982a). The second is the standard deviation of the output gap as estimated using Gordon's natural GNP estimates. The third measure is the standard deviation of the residuals when a continuous piecewise exponential trend is fit through the GNP series. Estimates of volatility over a number of subperiods

3. Calculated on an annual basis. Eisner's comment (below) relies on quarterly data.

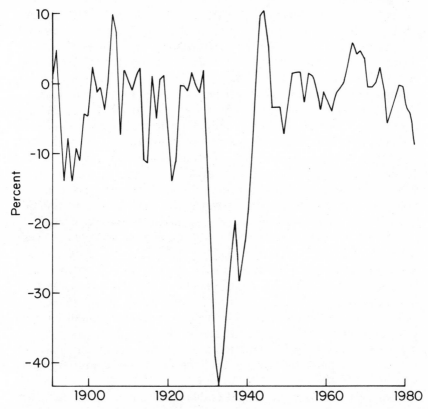

Fig. 12.2   Percentage deviation of real GNP from natural GNP.

Table 12.1   **The Changing Cyclical Variability of Output**

Period	$\sigma^a_{\Delta y}$	σ^b_{y/y_n}	$\sigma^c_{y/y_{\text{trend}}}$
1893–1915	.046	.061	.087
1893–1915/23–40	.044	.118	.138
1923–40	.041	.142	.160
1947–82	.011	.034	.046
1947–70	.011	.036	.037
1971–82	.011	.027	.051

Note: All calculations are based on GNP data described in Gordon 1982a.

[a]Standard deviation of the quarter-to-quarter change in the log of real GNP.

[b]Standard deviation of the difference between the log of real GNP and the log of natural real GNP.

[c]Standard deviation of the difference between the log of real GNP and its piecewise linear trend (breakpoints at 1915, 1922, 1940, 1946, and 1970).

are presented. The periods 1915–18 and 1941–46 are omitted because of the special effects of wars on economic activity. We also omit the four-year aftermath of World War I because rapid inflation and subsequent deflation make this period uncharacteristic of the remaining American economic experience.

Regardless of which volatility measure is used, the conclusion is that output was more variable before World War II than after it. By all three measures, output variability was about three times as great in the earlier period. Surprisingly, the much ballyhooed increase in economic turbulence during the 1970s barely shows up in the data. Apparently the 1970s were turbulent only in comparison with the remarkably placid 1960s. The data on the period 1893–1915 make it clear that the greater volatility of output during the prewar period was not just a reflection of the Great Depression. However, using either measure of volatility in the level of GNP, there is a noticeable increase in volatility between the subperiods 1893–1915 and 1923–40. This is wholly a consequence of the protracted downturn in output represented by the depression. No increase in the standard deviation of GNP changes appears because this measure places more weight on high-frequency fluctuations.

There remain the questions whether the declining variability in real GNP documented in table 12.1 is statistically significant and whether it reflects a decrease in the amount of statistical noise in the GNP figures rather than a real change. Neither possibility seems very likely to us.

It is not clear how one should go about determining the statistical significance of the differences shown in table 12.1. Output movements are serially correlated, and all tests of significance require some explicit model of the process generating output. We will simply note that if successive observations are treated as independent normal random variables, then the hypothesis that the variance in output is constant can be rejected at a level of confidence of less than .1% for annual data and .01% for quarterly data.

It is certainly true that the GNP data—particularly for 1893 to 1915—are somewhat shaky. Gordon's quarterly data series is based on annual estimates originally constructed by Kuznets and Kendrick. Kuznets, at least, did not regard his data for the period before 1919 with confidence. He sought to divert people into studying his estimates in the form of five- or ten-year moving averages, and he was reluctant to publish his annual estimates.[4] It seems likely, however, that the deficiencies in the data lead us to underestimate rather than overestimate the extent of cyclical variation in the pre–World War I economy. The original annual estimates assume that the relation between commodity

4. See the appendixes to Kuznets 1961.

production and GNP before 1909 is the same as the mean relation from 1919 to 1939. The estimates thus damp out independent variation in services and transportation that is uncorrelated with commodity production. Moreover, a recent reworking of the commodity production figures that underlie these estimates suggests that the original annual estimates give too high values to investment during the exceptionally depressed 1890s and thus generate estimates for business cycle variance that are too small.[5] On balance, we are led to conclude that the decline in the size of economic fluctuations between the pre– and post–World War II periods is a real phenomenon, one that economists should be able to explain.

12.1.1   Accounting Explanations

One natural way to start an investigation of the declining volatility of GNP is to look separately at its different components. Perhaps output has become more stable over time because the stable components of GNP have grown relative to the unstable ones. In particular, government—which is acyclic—has grown greatly in importance over the last century. And agriculture, which is notoriously unstable, has shrunk rapidly as a share of GNP.[6] It has also been suggested that the share of durable goods in GNP has declined over time. Since the demand for durable goods is volatile, this is also a potential explanation for the decline in the volatility of GNP.

Table 12.2 presents some evidence on these issues. It does not appear that the changing composition of GNP can account for most of the decline in the magnitude of output fluctuations. The percentage variability in year-to-year changes in our estimate of private nonfarm GNP declined by 56% between 1893–1940 and 1947–82 compared with 67% for total GNP. The variance of nonagricultural GNP is only slightly less than the variance in total GNP, even in the period 1893–1915. This somewhat surprising result occurs because the value of agricultural products demanded is actually slightly *less* variable than all other commodity groups except for nonagricultural nondurables. The increased decline in the relative variability of total GNP is due primarily to the rise of government purchases, which go from approximately 5% of GNP in 1900 to approximately 15% of GNP today. Government purchases exert a stabilizing influence in table 12.2 because the measure of variability used (year-to-year changes) filters out the massive swings in government expenditure in the post–World War II period associated

---

5. See the appendixes to Lewis 1978.

6. This idea is a relatively recent one. In the 1949 conference that was the ancestor of this one, Kuznets referred to the neat coincidence of the simultaneous rise of acyclic services and decline of acyclic agriculture. See Simon Kuznets, "Comment" on Joseph A. Schumpeter, "Historical Approach to Business Cycles," in Anderson 1951.

Table 12.2   The Variance of Alternative Output Measures

Period	$\sigma^a_{\Delta y1}$	$\sigma^b_{\Delta y2}$	$\sigma^c_{\Delta y3}$	$\sigma^d_{\Delta y4}$	$\sigma^e_{\Delta c}$
1893–1915	.069	.076	.065	.070	.040
1893–1915/23–40	.081	.093	.078	.088	.055
1923–40	.098	.115	.094	.110	.077
1947–82	.027	.040	.027	.039	.018

Source: General data from the national income and product accounts and from Kuznets 1961, Shaw 1947, and Goldsmith 1955.

[a]Standard deviation of the year-to-year change in the log of real GNP.

[b]Standard deviation of the year-to-year change in the log of private GNP. For the period before 1929 government transfers were assumed to be equal to zero and data on government expenditures were taken from Goldsmith 1955.

[c]Standard deviation of the year-to-year change in the log of nonfarm GNP. For the period before 1929 the proportion of farm output in GNP was assumed to be the same as the proportion of agricultural commodity production in total commodity production plus construction. Figures on commodity production were taken from Shaw 1947.

[d]Standard deviation of the year-to-year change in the log of private nonfarm GNP. Constructed according to (b) and (c) on the assumption that, before 1929, the government purchased no agricultural products.

[e]Standard deviation of the year-to-year change in the log of consumption. Before 1929, "consumption" is defined according to Kuznets. Thus it includes some government purchases, but fortunately these are small.

with military purchases that occur at longer than business cycle frequencies.

The last column of table 12.2 shows that the standard deviation of annual percentage changes in consumption has declined dramatically from 5.5% in 1893–1940 to 1.8% in the postwar period. This development occurred despite a substantial increase—detailed in the Gordon and Veitch paper in this volume (chap. 5)—in the share of consumer durables in consumption between the two periods. This suggests that the decreasing share of durable goods in GNP cannot account for a large part of the decline in the variance in output fluctuations. Moreover, Gordon and Veitch show that if consumer durables are included, then there has been no secular downward trend in the share of GNP attributable to investment.

We have also examined a number of breakdowns of GNP by component, including its industrial composition and the standard national income accounting breakdown into consumption, investment, government, and net exports. None of these exercises contributed significantly to explaining the declining volatility of output, and so they are not detailed further here.

12.1.2   Financial Panics and Monetarist Explanations

Many economists have argued that a major cause of the superior macroeconomic performance of the United States since World War II has been the smoother path followed by the money stock. According to this line of thought, the Federal Reserve Board has done a good (albeit not perfect) job in the postwar period. It has kept the money stock from exhibiting the substantial year-to-year swings that characterized earlier periods.

The problem with this line of argument is that monetary aggregates are in general endogenous variables. It is very hard to determine whether movements in the money stock are causes or consequences of movements in output. This is particularly true for the period of the gold standard, during which the relation between the monetary base and the money stock was very loose. Therefore, in order to examine monetary liquidity approaches to the business cycle, we concentrate our analysis on a class of events—financial panics—that appear likely to be *exogenous* with respect to output and that are associated with substantial declines in the money stock. We conclude below that, since financial panics cannot account for a significant fraction of output variance before World War I, although they do account for a significant part of the variance in the money stock, fluctuations in monetary aggregates are perhaps best viewed as consequences of output fluctuations. Arguments (like the one above) that regard the smoother growth of aggregates as a cause of reduced variability rely on weak empirical support.

It is also important to study financial panics because a large body of thought from Bagehot (1873) to Bernanke (1983) places stress on the importance of a smoothly running financial system for good macroeconomic performance and on the serious real consequences of collapses in the chain of financial intermediation.

This line of argument has typically run as follows: the financial sector is unstable—subject to sudden sharp increases in the demand for liquidity—in the absence of a lender of last resort. Finance, it is suggested, bears a strong resemblance to musical chairs; the last one to the bank during a panic walks away empty-handed. Therefore a financial system that lacks a lender of last resort will be prone to a collapse, to a sudden reduction in the amount of credit available and a sudden increase in the price of whatever credit is available.

When it occurs, this financial collapse has serious real consequences. The division of labor, the successful functioning of specialized enterprises, depends upon the existence of a credit system: agents must be able to quickly and cheaply acquire the resources to enable them to separate the time of purchase from the time of sale. In the aftermath of a panic there is a lower degree of financial sophistication and there are fewer possible paths of intermediation. This is, in some sense, a reduction in the "natural" level of output. With the financial system paralyzed as a result of the preceding panic, production opportunities that would be profitable if there were a high level of intermediation are not profitable at the lower level of intermediation prevailing.

This point of view is supported by Sprague's narrative history of American financial crises (Sprague 1910, 58–61), where he recounts, to give just one example, how the unwillingness of banks to extend credit for trans-Atlantic shipments during the panic of 1873 threatened the "cessation of commodity exports" and how the news of this financial stringency in New York "partially paralyzed" the movement of crops in the Midwest. This point of view is also supported by Bernanke (1983), who points out the striking correlation between financial crises during the downward slide of the Great Depression and reductions in output in excess of what one would have predicted from the behavior of the money stock alone.

To test the adequacy of this hypothesis about the important role played by financial panics, we examine the effect of removing panic periods on various measures of macroeconomic stability. We focus on the period 1890–1913, before the founding of the Fed, when panics should have had their greatest impact. According to one formulation of the point of view, periods immediately after financial panics have lower levels of "equilibrium" output. Therefore, under this formulation, the variance of real GNP about trend should be significantly lower if the immediate aftermath of panics is excluded from analysis.

According to an alternative formulation, panics occur at the ends of periods of "overtrading," of "speculation." Therefore the periods immediately before panics are periods of abnormally high output, and the aftermath of the panic—which sees the decline of output back to trend and then below trend to its trough—is not necessarily characterized by an excessively high variance of real GNP about trend. But in this case the aftermath of panics should show an excessively large and negative average value for the rate of change of real GNP: if the decline from overfull output to some level of low intermediation equilibrium is to be ascribed to the panic, the decline must take place quickly, before the financial system recovers its ability to provide credit. In the limit, if the economy grew at a constant rate except for panic induced declines, then excluding panic periods would reduce the variance of the rate of growth to zero. In practice, one would still expect the exclusion of the large negative growth rates during panics to reduce the calculated variance of the growth rate.

We considered two possible ways to identify panics. First, there is the list of major panics that Sprague considers important enough to warrant chapters in his book. In the period from 1890 to 1910, from the beginning of the Gordon output series to the publication of Sprague's book, Sprague finds incidents worth a chapter occurring in August 1890, May through July 1893, and October 1907. An alternative, less judgmental definition of a "panic"—as a time in which either there is a (month-to-month) jump of one percentage point in the commercial paper rate or banks cease paying out deposits at par—produces twelve panics in the relevant period: 1890:4, 1893:2, 1893:3, 1896:1, 1896:3, 1898:2, 1899:4, 1901:2, 1903:2, 1905:4, 1907:4, and 1909:4. Note that two of these less judgmentally defined panics, 1893:2 and 1893:3, are really part of a single disturbance according to Sprague.

Given these two lists of panics, we calculated variances for both the logarithm of output and the quarterly rate of change of output for several different sets of periods: first for the entire period 1890–1913, then for the period with the panic quarters and three quarters on each side of them removed, for the period with the panic quarter and one quarter on each side removed, and last with the panic quarter and the two following quarters removed. The results were as shown in table 12.3.

Given the results of this simple exercise, it is hard to argue that there is any way more than 20% of the standard deviation of either output or its rate of change could be ascribed to the influence of financial panics. Since nearly 40% of the variance in nominal monetary growth is attributable to panic periods, this suggests that financial and monetary shocks are less important sources of depression than we had suspected. Note that this exercise places an upper bound on the influence of financial panics: if whatever causes steep recessions also increases the probability of financial panics, the pattern shown in table 12.3 could be generated easily without any direct path of transmission from financial panics to the macroeconomy.

Are the numbers generated by this exercise reasonable? Is there any way to rationalize the apparent lack of strong links between financial uproar and real recession? We believe that the conclusions of the exercise above are reasonable, because the effects of financial panics upon the rest of the real economy are smaller than is usually realized.

12.1.3 The 1907 Panic

We illustrate this by considering in some detail one typical panic. Consider the panic of 1907, which occurred two quarters into a recession that saw a year-over-year decline in output of approximately 6.4%. It was marked by the typical features of Sprague's major panics: nominal interest rates suddenly increase, banks outside New York City attempt to reduce their loan portfolios, everyone scrambles for liquidity, banks refuse to pay out cash on demand at par to depositors, and "business activity" slumps by 26% from the quarter before to two quarters after the panic (see Sprague 1910).

But what is most interesting is the smallness of the movements in the variables that link the financial sector to real businesses. When

Table 12.3   Contribution of Financial Panics to Macroeconomic Instability

Measure of Variability	1890–1910	Sprague Panics Removed			Interest Rate Panics Removed		
		Three-Quarter Window	Seven-Quarter Window	Three-Quarter, One-Sided Window	Three-Quarter Window	Seven-Quarter Window	Three-Quarter, One-Sided Window
Log (y/y^a)	.0661	.0686	.0657	.0619	.0641	.0612	.0548
Δ (log y)	.0526	.0522	.0540	.0455	.0489	.0445	.0438

Note: Numbers are standard deviations of measures of variability on the left for the period 1890–1910 and for various subperiods that have dates associated with financial panics removed as described in the text.

Three-quarter window: preceding, panic, and following quarters removed from sample; Seven-quarter window: three preceding, panic, and three following quarters removed from sample; Three-quarter, One-sided window: panic and two following quarters removed from sample Basic data from Gordon 1982a. Panics calculated as described in the text from Sprague 1910 and from the four- to six-month commercial paper rate.

banks refuse to pay out cash for deposits at par, one dollar in bank deposits suddenly becomes a commodity with a cash price; in the panic of 1907, the "price" of deposits followed the smooth path given in table 12.4. Similarly, with the breakdown of the regular system of intermediation, one thousand dollars in deposits in New York suddenly became a commodity with a price in Philadelphia or Saint Louis.

These deviations from par are all small, taking the values as of 26 October (they are within the normal range) as a basis for comparison. Even at the height of the crisis a bank in Saint Louis could still obtain deposits in New York by paying a premium of less than 1%. Similarly, the premium required on cash to make depositors willing to keep their deposits in banks never rose above 3%.

It is likely that these prices do not give a good idea of the full extent of the panic. Agents may well have attempted to preserve the goodwill of their traditional customers by continuing to trade with them on "normal" terms of trade; "new" customers may have faced prices significantly farther from par than those given above. It is clear that the deviations from par values of bank deposits could have had a decisive effect on the profitability of any enterprise only if it were leveraged to an extraordinary degree. If the quantity of credit were rationed to familiar customers at "normal" prices, the panic could have had significant real effects without these effects' leaving their traces in the numbers of table 12.4.

But the quantity of credit outstanding was not significantly reduced during the panic of 1907, at least according to Sprague. Between 22 August and 3 December, the volume of loans outstanding decreased

Table 12.4   **Financial Disturbances Associated with the Panic of 1907**

Date	Average Discount on Deposits[a] for That week (%)	Price of $1,000 in New York in[b]		
		Boston	Saint Louis	New Orleans
October	0	$999.75	$999.75	$999.00
November	2.6	999.75	1,000.00	998.50
November	3.0	1,000.30	1,003.50	998.50
November	3.0	1,001.50	1,007.00	997.50
November	2.4	1,002.00	1,007.00	997.00
November	1.1	1,00.00	1,004.50	1,000.00
December	1.1	999.75	1,002.50	1,000.00
December	1.5	999.70	1,004.50	1,000.00

Source: Sprague 1910 and Andrew 1908.

[a]Average weekly discount from par of bank deposits priced in currency.

[b]For bank-to-bank transactions.

by only 2%. Sprague concludes that for the crisis of 1907 at least, "it seems fair to assume that positive loan contraction was a comparatively slight disturbing factor." The fall in output from August to December was far greater, proportionately, than the decline in credit outstanding.

Moreover, the New York Clearing House banks, the linchpins of the financial system, increased their loans—from $712 million to $775 million. A reduction in the quantity of credit available on account of the panic could not have had severe repercussions on the level of real output.

How, in the face of the depositors' scramble for liquidity that was one of the major characteristics of the panic, did banks manage to avoid a major contraction in the volume of loans? Two ways. The first was the suspension of cash payments to depositors at par that has already been mentioned. The second way was the creation of new reserves by the banking system. On the assumption that privately created reserves functioned as the equal of high-powered money, private actions increased the monetary base by 10% during the later months of the panic. Privately created reserves were of limited acceptability, it is true, but within the banking system the $238 million of large-denomination certificates issued by the New York Clearing House and backed by the long-run assets of the clearinghouse banks functioned perfectly well as high-powered money. And these $238 million of extra reserves were also augmented by $23 million of small clearinghouse certificates, by $12 million of clearinghouse checks, by $14 million of cashier's checks, and by $47 million of manufacturers' paychecks—all of which functioned in at least some spheres as substitutes for currency (see Andrew 1908, reprinted in Sprague 1910).

The small changes in the prices of financial resources during the panic of 1907 and the quick action of private agents to take over the function of the nonexistent lender of last resort—the function of providing additional reserves—seem to indicate that the American national banking system had by then developed a pattern of behavior that kept financial stringency from having devastating effects on the real economy.[7]

These considerations lead us to doubt that the reduced volatility of output during the postwar period was primarily the result of the avoidance of financial panics. We do not mean, however, that panics never had real effects. In particular, during the Great Depression, when the presence of the Fed discouraged banks from taking collective action to avoid disastrous consequences but the Fed itself was passive, financial panics may well have played an important role. But the view that financial panics were a principal cause of economic instability before World War II does not seem to be strongly supported. This

7. Cagan 1965 also notes the existence of unauthorized money creation during panics.

finding weakens the monetarist argument linking output variability to erratic monetary growth by showing that relatively little of the variability in output observed before World War II can be linked to exogenous changes in the money stock. We will return to the question of changing monetary policy in section 12.4.

The analysis so far suggests that it is unlikely that either structural or monetary factors can account for the decline in the variability of output since World War II. The one plausible lead we have uncovered is the increasing role of government. We investigate the role of stabilization policy in the next section.

12.2   The Effects of Stabilization Policies

A major difference between the pre– and post–World War II periods was the government's acceptance after World War II of an obligation to stabilize the economy. This obligation was recognized by statute in the Employment Act of 1946 and pragmatically in the speeches and actions of various high officials. It is natural to conjecture that this change in attitudes and policies contributed to the decline in the volatility of output observed after World War II. It is also frequently argued that automatic stabilization in the form of a progressive tax system and countercyclical expenditure measures such as unemployment insurance have enhanced economic stability by reducing the multiplier. Econometric exercises support this hypothesis: Hickman and Coen's (1976) estimates of the real autonomous expenditures impact multiplier drop from 3.23 in the interwar period to 1.88 in the postwar period. This section examines the contribution of both automatic fiscal stabilizers and discretionary policies in explaining the postwar improvement in economic performance.

12.2.1   Automatic Stabilizers

The traditional argument that automatic stabilization has improved macroeconomic performance emphasizes the role of taxes and transfers in mitigating the effects of changes in GNP on disposable income.[8]

This account is less satisfactory than it first appears. Modern theories of the consumption function assume consumers' ability to smooth out fluctuations in disposable income by borrowing and lending. If consumers in fact possess this ability, it is not clear why the government's smoothing the path of disposable income through fiscal actions should have real effects. Automatic stabilization policies will have important real effects only if a sizable fraction of consumption represents purchases by liquidity-constrained consumers. Thus, establishing the ex-

8. See, for example, the treatment in Burns 1960, Gordon 1984, or Baily 1978.

istence of liquidity-constrained consumers is necessary to a demonstration of the efficacy of automatic stabilization policy. But this discussion raises another possibility. Perhaps the multiplier has changed over time because the fraction of liquidity-constrained consumers has declined owing to growth in the availability of consumer credit.

This section explores these issues. We begin by documenting the changing relationship between GNP and disposable income fluctuations over time, then we examine the importance of liquidity constraints.

We have already emphasized the importance of the increasing size of government. The extent to which this growth has changed the nexus between GNP and disposable income can be seen in table 12.5, which reports the results of regressions of disposable income on GNP for various subperiods of the period 1898–1982. We use slightly different subperiods here than in the preceding sections because data on disposable income do not go all the way back to 1890. The results indicate a dramatic change in the relation between the prewar and postwar periods. During 1949–82 a marginal dollar of GNP raised disposable income by thirty-nine cents compared with seventy-six cents during the prewar period. There is no strong evidence of any change between the pre–World War I period and the interwar period in the share of GNP changes that falls on disposable income.

The changing relationship between GNP and disposable income is well illustrated by the two recent serious United States recessions. During the 1981–82 recession when GNP fell by 1.8%, disposable income actually rose by 1.0%. During the 1973–75 recession when output fell by a comparable amount, disposable income rose by 1.1%.

Fiscal policies are not the only determinant of the linkage between GNP and disposable income. Other considerations include the cyclical

Table 12.5   Response of Disposable Income to a Change in Total Income

Period	Coefficient of Δy	$\bar{R}^2$	DW
1898–1916	.76 (.16)	.54	0.97
1923–40	.95 (.24)	.61	1.70
1949–82	.39 (.06)	.59	2.07

Source: Annual data taken from Kuznets 1961, Goldsmith 1955, and the National income and product accounts. Before 1929, "disposable income" is approximated by nominal income minus the sum of federal, state, and local government revenues and minus corporate gross internal saving.

Note: Equation estimated in real magnitudes,
   $\Delta Y^d = c_0 + \alpha(\Delta y) + \varepsilon$,
   $E(\varepsilon^2)$ proportional to Y^2.

effects on the distribution of factor incomes, and corporate payout policies also impinge on the relationship. We briefly examined these issues but found little evidence that changes in these other factors have worked to stabilize disposable income in the postwar period. We thus credit fiscal policies with almost all the changes shown in table 12.5. This conclusion runs somewhat counter to Burns's (1960) rather impressionistic discussion, but we do not pursue the issue here.

The foregoing discussion is relevant to the behavior of real economic activity only if liquidity constraints are important in determining aggregate consumption. To identify the extent of liquidity constraints, we model aggregate consumption as a combination of the consumption of unconstrained consumers whose consumption evolves according to a random walk as specified in Hall (1978), and liquidity-constrained consumers whose consumption is assumed to be a constant fraction of disposable income.

For convenience we work with the data in logarithmic form.[9] We postulate that consumption of nondurable goods and services evolves according to:

$$(1) \qquad C_t = C_t^u + m(YD_t),$$

where C_t^u represents unconstrained consumption and m indicates approximately the fraction of disposable income spent by liquidity-constrained consumers. The polar case, where $m = 0$, gives rise to the pure permanent income hypothesis. When $m = 1$, consumption depends just on current disposable income.

The argument of Hall (1978) implies, assuming that the real rate of return can be approximated as a constant, that

$$(2) \qquad C_t^u = b_1 C_{t-1} + U_t,$$

where U_t is uncorrelated with any information available at time $t - 1$.

To estimate m we proceed as follows. First we assume that YD evolves according to a second-order autoregression process. That is,

$$(3) \qquad YD_t = \rho_0 + \rho_1 YD_{t-1} + \rho_2 YD_{t-2} + \rho_3 t + u.$$

Combining (1) and (2) and (3), we obtain the estimable equation:

$$(4) \qquad \begin{aligned} C_t = b_0 &+ b_1 C_{t-1} + m[\rho_0 + (\rho_1 - b_1)YD_{t-1} \\ &+ \rho_2 YD_{t-2} + \rho_3(t)], \end{aligned}$$

where e_t is a residual that is uncorrelated with the variables on the right-hand side of (4). Now (3) and (4) can be estimated jointly to yield

---

9. We also worked with the model in level form, but we found that the overidentifying restrictions present in the model presented below were more frequently rejected.

estimates of m. The overidentifying restrictions implied by the model can be tested by estimating (3) and (4) in unconstrained fashion.

Estimates of both restricted and unrestricted forms of the system (3) and (4) using annual data on the consumption of nondurables and services are presented in table 12.6 for various periods. The results for the prewar periods are striking. For 1899–1916 the data support the hypothesis that essentially all consumption was done by liquidity-constrained consumers. Moreover, the overidentifying restrictions implied by the model are accepted comfortably. The results for the entire prewar period also support this conclusion, though they are less satisfactory. In the constrained equation case the point estimate of m is 1.4, which is implausibly large. The overidentifying restrictions are also less well satisfied. These less satisfactory results probably occur because our autoregression is not a good predictor of future income during the depression. When (in results not shown) the depression years are dropped from the sample but the 1920s are included, the results look very much like those for 1899–1916.

Unfortunately, the extent of liquidity constraints in the postwar process is difficult to gauge because disposable income was not far from following a random walk. However, the point estimates of both the constrained and the unconstrained versions of the model suggest that some but not all consumers were liquidity constrained. Unfortunately, the data have the power to reject neither of the interesting polar hypotheses. Hence nothing definitive can be said.[10]

Taken together these estimates confirm that liquidity constraints matter for aggregate consumption, as already asserted by Flavin (1981).

Table 12.6   **Estimates of the Extent of Liquidity Constraints**

Period	Restricted	Y_{-1}	Y_{-2}	t	C_{-1}	t	m	Log L
1949–82	No	1.02	−.30	.012	.73	.014	.28	192.32
		(.19)	(.18)	(.077)	(.13)	(005)	(.31)	
1949–82	Yes	.77	.06	.056	1.00	—	.50	189.89
		(.15)	(.14)	(.14)	(.02)		(.46)	
1899–1916	No	.35	−.05	.02	−.1	.01	1.1	70.28
		(.22)	(.23)	(.01)	(.3)	(.01)	(1.2)	
1899–1916	Yes	.33	.20	0.14	−.1	—	1.1	69.35
		(.17)	(.12)	(.005)	(.2)		(.1)	
1899–1916	No	1.17	−.35	.003	.43	.013	.54	99.14
1922–40		(.16)	(.15)	(002)	(.14)	(.004)	(.41)	
1899–1916	Yes	1.07	−.31	.005	.62	—	1.4	97.63
1922–40		(.12)	(.10)	(.002)	(.09)		(.2)	

Note: The left-hand columns are estimates of equation (3) while estimates of (4) are on the right-hand side. Numbers in parentheses are standard errors.

10. We also examined quarterly data for this interval but did not find that they shed much light, so no results are reported here.

This suggests a role for automatic stabilizers in explaining why output was less volatile in the postwar period. They also indicate, however, that progress in financial intermediation may have contributed to stability by enhancing the consumer's ability to smooth fluctuations in income by borrowing. Certainly households have had much easier access to liquidity in the postwar than in the prewar period. The most striking rise is in the volume of consumer credit outstanding: from $6 billion in 1945, or 5% of consumption, to $380 billion or 23% of consumption in 1982. The growth of nonfarm mortgage debt has also been remarkable: from $27 billion or 54% of consumption in 1934 to $1,548 billion or 82% of consumption in 1982. By and large, before World War II American households had (except for some mortgages and loans intended to support the leveraged purchase of securities) little access to credit markets. According to Robert A. Gordon's paper in Anderson (1951), the post–World War I construction boom was primarily in apartments, not single-family houses. Since World War II households have had a great deal of access. It would be surprising if this structural shift had had no macroeconomic effects.

12.2.2   Discretionary Stabilization Policy

The most direct way to assess the efficacy of discretionary stabilization policies would be to examine whether discretionary policy was countercyclical in the postwar period and to estimate its effects. This is much easier said than done. Distinguishing the discretionary from the automatic component of policy is difficult. Moreover, given uncertainties about lags, gauging the effects of policies is also a problem. Exercises such as the one performed by Eckstein and Sinai in this volume (chap. 1) tend to suggest that monetary policy caused at least as many recessions as it prevented, and they do not find much evidence for the success of discretionary fiscal policies. We do not attempt such an exercise here. Rather, we turn to a less direct test of the possible efficacy of discretionary stabilization policies.

The essential idea of our test is as follows. The variance in real GNP depends on both the size of initial shocks to it and the extent to which they persist. Discretionary stabilization policies presumably work by reducing the persistence of shocks to GNP, not by limiting the size of initial shocks. Thus if discretionary stabilization policies became more efficacious in the postwar period, one would expect to see a decline in the persistence of output shocks during this time.

Table 12.7 presents estimated impulse response functions for GNP for various intervals. The variance of shocks is also presented. All calculations are based on autoregressions of annual GNP data.[11] The

---

11. The data are taken from Friedman and Schwartz 1983, who try to construct consistent annual time series back to 1867.

Table 12.7   Persistence of Output Shocks

Period	0	1	2	3	4	Standard Deviation of Shocks
1893–1915						
AR 1	1.00	.39	.15	.06	.03	.062
		(.19)	(.14)	(.09)	(.06)	
AR 2	1.00	.42	.11	.02	.00	.063
		(.22)	(.18)	(.11)	(.09)	
AR 3	1.00	.42	.08	.08	.06	.064
		(.23)	(.19)	(.18)	(.19)	
1923–40						
AR 1	1.00	.87	.76	.66	.57	.095
		(.12)	(.21)	(.28)	(.32)	
AR 2	1.00	1.33	1.25	.97	.64	.083
		(.21)	(.25)	(.24)	(.25)	
AR 3	1.00	1.37	1.26	.95	.62	.086
		(.26)	(.29)	(.30)	(.28)	
1949–82						
AR 1	1.00	.70	.49	.35	.22	.026
		(.15)	(.21)	(.22)	(.21)	
AR 2	1.00	.81	.47	.22	.09	.026
		(.19)	(.23)	(.32)	(.27)	
AR 3	1.00	.82	.46	.24	.12	.027
		(.20)	(.27)	(.35)	(.33)	

Note: Annual GNP data from Friedman and Schwartz 1983. Standard errors—generated by stochastic simulation—in parentheses.

calculations reveal that if anything the persistence of output fluctuations increased between the pre–World War I and post–World War II periods. Concomitantly, the decline in the variance of output shocks between the two periods exceeds the decline in the variance of real GNP. Thus the data provide little support for the discretionary stabilization policy argument.

A more subtle form of the discretionary policy argument, noted in Baily (1978), runs as follows. Whether or not stabilization policy is actually efficacious, it is perceived as effective. Because they expect recessions to be short, consumers and investors do not cut back on spending plans as much as they otherwise would. The prophecy is therefore self-fulfilling and the economy is more stable. This argument is also put forth to explain greater wage and price rigidity in the postwar period. It is suggested that because the economy is expected to return to equilibrium more quickly, workers and producers feel less pressure to cut wages and prices in the face of shortfalls in demand. This argument, like the more direct one, predicts that serial correlation in output should have declined in the postwar period. As just noted, this prediction is refuted by the data.

The pattern followed by stock market prices provides a further way to test arguments about confidence in the face of economic downturns if one is willing to accept two assumptions: First, that the expectations implicit in the stock market's guesses about the discounted value of the future profitability of American enterprise are the same as the expectations of those who decide on investment. We recognize the weakness of this support of our argument, but we see no way to avoid making it that will allow us to use the information found in the pattern of stock prices. Second, that the relation between the profitability of those companies counted in stock market averages and the macroeconomic performance of the economy has remained constant. As a test of this second assumption, we examined the cyclical variability of dividends paid by companies listed in the Standard and Poor's 500 index; we cannot find any significant changes in the cyclical flexibility of dividends, and so we are led to tentatively accept this second assumption.

The stock market is a leading indicator. It typically reaches its real peak several quarters before output. The agents whose expectations set prices in the stock market know a recession is coming. The magnitude of the decline in profitability that they expect can be seen in the magnitude of the decline in profitability that they expect can be seen in the magnitude of the decline in the stock market. And so the elasticity of the level of the stock market with respect to future values of the GNP gap is a measure of the "sanguinity" of stock market investors, a measure of the subjective probability assigned to the possibility that the recession may be the beginning of a deep, long period of subnormal output rather than a short, shallow correction to the economy.

Accordingly, we regressed the log of the real value of two stock market indexes (the Dow-Jones industrial and Standard and Poor's composite) on a quadratic in time and on five, six, and nine leads (for quarterly data) of the difference between the log of GNP and the log of natural GNP. We also corrected for (substantial) serial correlation. Because the behavior of the two indexes was nearly identical, only the Standard and Poor's results are reported here. The parameter of interest is ΣB_i.

Interpretations of these results, which are displayed in table 12.8, are dubious, because the exceptionally large degree of serial correlation in the residuals tells us that whatever is moving stock prices does not follow a simple trend and dominates those movements induced by the near term (within two years) cyclical outlook. There is also an errors in variables problem here: the value of the independent GNP gap used is the ex post realized value rather than the ex ante expected value. To the degree that agents do not correctly forecast the near-term cyclical outlook, the estimates of the sum of the lag coefficients are not consistent.

Nevertheless, simple inspection of the various sums of the lead coefficients does not lend support to the hypothesis of the increasing "sanguinity" of investors. A given cyclical movement in the GNP gap over

Table 12.8   Stock Market Elasticities

Period	n = 5			n = 6			n = 9		
	$\Sigma\beta_i^a$	ρ	$\bar{R}^2$	$\Sigma\beta_i$	ρ	$\bar{R}^2$	$\Sigma\beta_i$	ρ	$\bar{R}^2$
1893–1915	1.75	.73	.975	2.12	.73	.975	2.20	.76	.977
	(.50)	(.08)		(.57)	(.08)		(.79)	(.08)	
1922–40	1.81	.82	.905	1.69	.81	.905	1.56	.75	.912
	(.59)	(.07)		(.61)	(.07)		(.56)	(.08)	
1947–70	3.51	.95	.945	.233	.94	.953	1.05	.93	.965
	(.92)	(.03)		(.99)	(.03)		(1.07)	(.04)	
1947–80	2.90	.92	.929	2.32	.92	.934	1.13	.90	.944
	(.83)	(.03)		(.90)	(.03)		(1.06)	(.04)	
1970–80	3.52	.78	.987	3.59	.78	.987	3.17	.78	.987
	(1.47)	(.10)		(1.57)	(.10)		(1.98)	(.11)	

Note: Estimation procedure described in text.
ᵃSum of leads.

the two years to come seems to be preceded by a relative decline in the stock market that is, if anything, larger since World War II than it was before. A given expected decline in real GNP relative to trend seems to be associated with a slightly greater decline in the discounted value of future profits—as measured by the stock market—than before World War II. This simple exercise seems to indicate that those investing in the stock market do not expect the same initial decline in GNP to be recouped more quickly—owing to government stabilization policies—after World War II than before.

The analysis in this section suggests that automatic stabilizers have contributed to the reduction in variance of GNP that has been observed since World War II. There is little evidence that discretionary policies have played an important role. Indeed, the persistence of output shocks has actually increased. But it seems unlikely that automatic stabilization can account for the whole of the decline in the variance of output. The declines in the volatility of investment that have been observed since the war exceed the declines in the volatility of consumption. Moreover, quantitative estimates of the change in the Keynesian multiplier such as those provided by Hickman and Coen (1976) are not large enough to account for a threefold decline in the variance of output shocks reported in table 12.7. We therefore turn in the next section to an examination of other structural changes that may contribute to explaining the declining variance of output.

12.3 Price and Output Flexibility

Some common contemporary explanations of business cycles focus on the role of institutional factors that lead to deviations from the atomistic competitive model of classical economic theory. For example, long-term nominal labor contracts are sometimes invoked to explain how nominal shocks can have real effects on economic activity. Alternatively, long-term attachments between workers and firms combined with asymmetrical information—in a phrase, implicit contracts—are sometimes invoked to account for involuntary unemployment and cyclical fluctuations.

The evidence presented in this section suggests that this focus may well be misplaced. We show in the first part of this section that in a variety of ways the American economy has become much less "Walrasian" over the same century that has also seen a pronounced trend toward greater macroeconomic stability. This suggests that the sources of economic instability do not lie in the non-Walrasian character of certain economic institutions.[12] We then demonstrate that plausible macroeconomic models imply that increased price rigidity will increase rather than reduce macroeconomic stability. Finally, we suggest that price flexibility, by raising real interest rates, may have exacerbated the 1929–33 economic downturn.

The extent to which the economy was "Walrasian" in the past is obviously impossible to gauge precisely. Market power depends not only on the extent of concentration in product and labor markets, but also on factors such as costs of search and the extent of information asymmetries. All these factors share the characteristic of being very hard to quantify. However, the available evidence suggests that the American economy was significantly more competitive before World War II than it has been since.

One indicator is the increased role of government after World War II. The share of GNP passing through the public sector rose from approximately 4% about 1900 to approximately 10% in 1929–37 and to about 16% by 1970. Of potentially greater importance is the greatly increased scope of government regulation: by the estimates of Nutter and Einhorn (1969), close to 22% of GNP produced in 1958 came from sectors of the economy where government was a predominant presence. And this estimate predates the rise in the 1960s and 1970s of what is termed the "regulatory state."

A similar conclusion is suggested by the available data on industrial concentration. The percentage of national income originating in proprietorships dropped from 28% in 1929 to 18% in 1969. In 1918, 35% of total manufacturing assets were held by the nation's one hundred

---

12. Of course, it is possible that, as John Taylor argued in his paper in this volume (chap. 11), increasing price rigidity did exacerbate cyclical fluctuations, but that this influence was more than offset by other factors. We further discuss Taylor's analysis in our comment on his contribution, chapter 11.

largest manufacturing corporations. By 1970 their share had reached 49%.

Perhaps the most dramatic changes have occurred in the character of the labor market. Some information on the changing character of labor markets is presented in table 12.9. A clear pattern emerges. Long-term contracts were essentially nonexistent before passage of the Wagner Act. A small proportion of workers were in unions, and the prevailing political climate offered unions few of the sources of institutionalized strength that legal procedures gave them in the postwar period. The share of unionized nonfarm workers was only 9% in 1930 compared with 29% in 1950. Likewise, the fraction of workers in institutionalized settings has increased dramatically. The fraction working on farms has fallen from 38% in 1900 to 3% in 1970, and in 1900 close to half of all farmers were owner-operators. And the fraction of workers in white-collar jobs increased from 17% in 1900 to 48% in 1970. This is an interesting statistic in light of the fact that a substantial proportion of white-collar workers are engaged in what one might call non-market-oriented coordination of production.

Perhaps the strongest evidence of the changng character of labor markets comes from information on separations. Ross (1958) examines the argument that a new industrial feudalism developed in the United States after World War II. As table 12.10 indicates, the monthly quit rate per hundred employees in manufacturing (the only sector on which data are available) declines from over 6% before World War I to close by 2% recently. The total separation rate declined by about 42% between 1920–23 and 1973–79, implying an equal percentage increase in average manufacturing job tenure. Even though most turnover involves

Table 12.9   **Unionization and Occupational Structure**

| | Union Members as | | Percentage of Workers Holding | | |
| | | | | | |
Year	Percentage of Labor Force	Percentage of Nonfarm Labor Force	White Collar Jobs	Blue-Collar Jobs	Farm Jobs
1900	3	4	17	36	38
1910	5	8	21	38	31
1920[a]	12	16	25	41	26
1930	7	9	29	39	21
1940	14	17	31	40	17
1950	24	29	36	41	12
1960	26	29	42	39	6
1970	26	27	48	37	3

Source: *Historical Statistics*.

[a]More than one-third of these unions were broken during the deflation that followed 1920.

Table 12.10   **Peacetime Business Cycle Averages of Quit and Separation Rates**

Cycle	Manufacturing Quit Rate	Manufacturing Layoff Rate
1910–13	6.8	–
1920–23	4.2	1.5
1923–26	2.9	1.0
1928–29	2.5	1.0
1929–37	1.3	3.4
1948–53	2.5	1.7
1953–57	1.7	1.9
1957–60	1.3	2.3
1960–89	1.9	1.5
1969–73	2.2	1.5
1973–79	1.9	1.5

Source: Historical Statistics and Ross 1958.

the young, these data still indicate a substantial increase over time in the importance of something that might be called job-specific human capital, and therefore in implicit long-term labor contracts.

Quantifying the extent of deviation from the Walrasian ideal owing to more subtle factors such as increased labor market specialization and increased product differentiation is obviously not possible. However, a number of things suggest those factors have increased in importance. Expenditures on advertising and promotion have surely increased faster than the GNP, suggesting a greater role in firms facing downward sloping product demand areas. The educational level of the work force has risen greatly, as has the number of different occupations. To gauge the extent of imperfections in today's economy, one need only ask how many firms are indifferent to selling more output at prevailing prices. Or how many workers are indifferent to losing their jobs.

It seems very likely that increased economic stability has been a by-product of these developments. Permanent attachments between workers and firms, for example, slow the response of employment to fluctuations in demand. This in turn reduces the extent to which demand shocks are propagated by increasing the stability of disposable income. More formally, it is possible to demonstrate in a variety of implicit contracting models that because of workers' desire for insurance, employment is more stable than it would be if a Walrasian equilibrium were attained in every period. Likewise, increasing conglomeration of firms, and the resulting increased reliance on internal finance, reduces the liquidity effects of economic downturns. It is also natural to conjecture that regulatory policies are likely to keep the output of regulated firms relatively stable.

It is unquestionably true that price volatility in the American economy declined in conjunction with the changes discussed above. The standard deviation of annual rates of inflation from trend was 1.5% for 1949–82, compared with 2.4% for 1893–1915 and 4.8% for 1923–40. It is less clear whether wages and prices have become more flexible in response to output shocks of a given size. Cagan (1975) and Sachs (1980) report that wholesale prices have been less sensitive to movements in aggregate demand during the postwar period. However, Schultze (1981) argues that there was little change in the sensitivity of prices—measured by the nonfarm GNP deflator—between the prewar and postwar periods. Gordon (1980) finds that the initial response of prices to nominal demand has not changed but notes the increasing persistence of inflation in the postwar period.[13]

It is not easy to make a coherent interpretation of these findings. We suspect there has been a small decline in short-run price flexibility (a decline in the slope of the short-run aggregate supply curve) but that this decline has been so small that it is not apparent in the less sensitive GNP deflator and can be seen only in measures of producer prices. We do conclude that there has been an increase in the persistence of price movements. Below, we present a simple model to analyze the effect of an increase in such persistence on macroeconomic performance. Before examining this issue, it is important to emphasize that the evidence presented in the preceding section suggests that greater price rigidity in the postwar period cannot be attributed to greater certainty that downturns would be temporary. This possibility is refuted by the evidence suggesting that output shocks have become *more*, not less, persistent and that the sensitivity of the stock market to output shocks has if anything declined.

12.3.1   Is Price Flexibility Destabilizing?

In the remainder of this section, we entertain the hypothesis that greater price flexibility in the pre–World War II period was a cause of greater instability in output. This is, of course, the exact opposite of the canonical Keynesian nominal rigidities point of view, which leads, in John Taylor's words, to the assertion that "less flexible wages and prices should lead to a deterioration of macroeconomic performance." But John Maynard Keynes disagreed, and in *The General Theory* (1936) he argued against this very proposition, claiming instead that

> it would be much better that wages should be rigidly fixed and deemed incapable of material changes, than that depression should be accompanied by a gradual downward tendency of money-wages, a

13. And Schultze also finds increasing persistence after 1967, which he interprets as a shift in the inflation norm.

further moderate wage reduction being expected to signalize each increase of, say, one percent in the amount of unemployment. For example, the effect of an expectation that wages are going to sag by, say, two percent in the coming year will be roughly equivalent to the effect of a rise of two percent in the amount of interest payable for the same period. (Quoted in Tobin 1975)

Keynes seeks to argue that the simple solution to involuntary unemployment—lowering the nominal wage—will not work. For the economy is not a static object converging to a stationary equilibrium. The lowering of wages (and prices) required to get the quantity of real balances up to its full employment equilibrium value itself creates an additional intertemporal disequilibrium. For changes in the aggregate price level disturb what is perhaps the single most important price in the whole economy—the real interest rate.

This point of view deserves a more formal examination, which we provide within the framework of a simple macroeconomic model. The model highlights the fact that it is the ex ante real—not the nominal—interest rate that should enter into the determination of investment. It also provides for the distinction between price *flexibility* and price *persistence* stressed by Gordon (1980).

We treat all variables (except interest and inflation rates) as log deviations from trends. Solving out an IS-LM system, where the nominal interest rate enters the LM equation and the real interest rate enters the IS equation, yields an aggregate demand curve of the form:

(5) $$q_t - \beta_1(m_t - p_t) + \beta_2(E_t p_{t+1} - p_t) + \epsilon_t.$$

We model expectations by assuming perfect foresight on the part of investors:

(6) $$E_t p_{t+1} = p_{t+1}.$$

The aggregate supply side of the model is somewhat more complex. An easy way to model the independent dimensions of short-run price flexibility and of price persistence is to adopt a multiperiod nominal contract framework. Workers are divided into $n + 1$ equal groups. Group j negotiates an $n + 1$ period contract, with a fixed nominal wage, in all periods for which $(t)_{\text{mod } n + 1} = j$. That is, using superscripts to denote worker groups:

(7) $$W_{t+1}^j = W_t^j, j \neq (t)_{\text{mod } n+1}$$

(8) $$W_{t+1}^j = W_t^j + \frac{1}{n} \sum_{i=1}^{n} (W_{t+1-i}^{(j-i)\text{mod } n+1} - W_{t-i}^{(j-i)\text{mod } n+1}) + \alpha q_t.$$

In the contract period, group j's nominal wage is renegotiated for the next $n + 1$ periods. The wage rise won by group j in these negotiations is the average of the wage rise won by the other n groups in their negotiations plus or minus a term (αq_t) which is supposed to capture the effect of labor market tightness. In their negotiations, workers are backward looking. Since we are working within the Keynesian tradition, we do not think this is an important defect in the model.[14] Moreover, any attempt to model the wage determination process fully within an optimizing framework would be hopelessly complex.

To close the model, the price level is taken to be a simple average of the prevailing wage levels:

(9)
$$p_t = \sum_{i=1}^{n+1} W_t^i$$

(10)
$$(1 + n)(p_{t+1} - p_t) = \frac{1}{n}((n + 1)[(p_t - p_{t-1})$$
$$+ \ldots + (p_{t-n+1} - p_{t-n})]) + \alpha q_t$$

(11)
$$p_{t+1} - p_t = \frac{1}{n}(p_t - p_{t-n}) + \frac{\alpha}{n+1} q_t ,$$

which, with (5) and (6), results in workable solutions for p_t and q_t

(12)
$$q_t = \frac{(\beta_2 - n\beta_1)p_t - \beta_2 p_{t-n} + n\beta_1 m_t + n\epsilon_t}{n - \beta_2\alpha\left(\dfrac{n}{n-1}\right)}$$

(13)
$$p_t = \left(1 + \frac{1}{n} + \frac{\frac{\alpha}{n}(\beta_2 - n\beta_1)}{n + 1 - \beta_2\alpha}\right)p_{t-1} - \frac{1}{n - \beta_2\alpha\left(\dfrac{n}{n+1}\right)}$$
$$p_{t-1-n} + \frac{\alpha\beta_1}{n + 1 - \beta_2\alpha} m_{t-1} + \frac{\alpha}{n + 1 - \beta_2\alpha} \epsilon_{t-1} .$$

In this framework, increases in the contract period—$n + 1$—can be interpreted as increases in price persistence. Increases in the labor market conditions coefficients—increases in α—can be interpreted as increases in short-run aggregate price flexibility. Because the model is designed to highlight the effects of inflation on output, it has no role for discretionary fiscal policy and no source of shocks other than ϵ_t, the shock to aggregate demand. We take monetary policy to be completely nonaccommodative: m_t is equal to its trend value (zero) always.

---

14. In subsequent work, we hope to examine the issues here within a model like that of Taylor 1979, where contracts are partly forward and partly backward looking. It seems unlikely that this will alter qualitative conclusions.

This rules out the possibility that the driving force behind economic instability is inappropriate government policy (a bad monetary reaction function) rather than the internal dynamics of the model itself. We wish to use this model to show *only* that the conventional wisdom holding that an increase in nominal rigidities (either in the form of a smaller response of wages to labor market conditions or in the form of a longer contract period—more "persistence") is harmful to macroeconomic stability rests on shaky theoretical foundations.

We assume a white noise, unit variance generating process for the demand shock ϵ_t and simulate the model for various parameter values. Recall that a high value of β_1 implies either that the direct ("liquidity") effect of a decline in real balances is large or that the effect of a decline in real balances on the interest rate is large—that is, that the elasticity of money demand with respect to the interest rate is small. A high value for β_2 implies that the expected inflation effects on aggregate demand are large, owing either to real interest effects or to redistributions between debtors and creditors. The parameter estimates are chosen to be reasonable. For example, if $\beta_1 = 1.0$ and $\beta_2 = 1.6$, the standard IS-LM Keynesian multiplier is 1.5.[15] Experimenting with parameter values outside the range displayed frequently resulted in instability but did not alter the qualitative conclusions.

Three conclusions emerge from table 12.11, where the variance of output is calculated for various parameter values. First, in many cases the economy is unstable under the assumption that monetary policy is nonaccommodative with respect to output shocks. This result parallels that of Tobin (1975). Second, in the cases where stability is attained, the variance of output *decreases* with increases in the contract length.[16] When the length of the period over which wages remain fixed increases, the volatility of output declines. This result implies that increasing wage flexibility by reducing the length of the contract period might well worsen macroeconomic performance. This inference is strengthened by noting that increasing the length of the contract period increases the likelihood that the economy will be stable at all. Third, increases in the sensitivity of current wages to output have an ambiguous effect on the volatility of output.

These results are entirely attributable to the fact that the real interest rate—and so $E_t p_{t+1}$—enters into the determination of aggregate demand.

The model considered here obviously is highly stylized. No role is allowed for lagged responses of output or money demand to changes

---

15. Assuming that the constant interest rate multiplier is 3.0.
16. Except for cases in which a high adjustment parameter combined with a long contract length leads to negative feedback so strong that it is destabilizing.

Table 12.11   Output Variance Generated by a Unit Variance White Noise Demand Shock

| | | $\beta_1 = 1.0$ | $\beta_2 = 1.6$ | | | | | $\beta_1 = 1.0$ | $\beta_2 = 2.4$ | | |
| | | | Contract Length | | | | | | Contract Length | | |
		2	3	4	5	6		2	3	4	5	6
$\alpha =$	.25	*	*	*	2.1	1.2	$\alpha =$	*	*	*	14.4	1.4
	.5	*	*	*	1.5	1.4		*	*	*	6.2	1.6
	1.0	*	*	3.9	2.3	1.9		*	*	*	4.2	2.9

| | | $\beta_1 = 2.0$ | $\beta_2 = 1.0$ | | | | | $\beta_1 = 2.0$ | $\beta_2 = 0.5$ | | |
| | | | Contract Length | | | | | | Contract Length | | |
		2	3	4	5	6		2	3	4	5	6
$\alpha =$	.25	*	*	1.3	1.1	1.1	$\alpha =$	*	*	1.2	1.1	1.1
	.5	*	2.9	1.4	1.3	1.2		*	1.6	1.3	1.2	1.1
	1.0	*	*	*	13.1	*		*	*	*	2.4	*

*Model unstable for these parameter values.

in real interest rates. Deflation has no direct effect on aggregate demand, operating only through its impact on real interest rates. Thus the distributional effects emphasized by Tobin (1975) are suppressed entirely. Perhaps most important, we assume no response of monetary or fiscal policy variables to demand shocks. This exercise hardly proves that price flexibility increased the volatility of economic activity before World War II. But it does strongly suggest that deviations of the real interest rates from its general equilibrium value caused by the process of equilibration in product and labor markets may contribute as much to economic instability as deviations in product prices or wages from their static equilibrium values, if not more.

It might be objected that our analysis here misses the point, since we assume an aggregate supply mechanism implying that a change in the monetary rule could have a long-run effect on output. Such an objection is made by McCallum (1983) to analyses similar to the one presented here. This objection is misplaced. At one level the criticism is irrelevant, since we do not use our model to consider alternative monetary rules. At a more fundamental level, it ignores the need for economic theory to provide a theory of how prices move to clear markets. As Fisher (1983) and others have eloquently argued, it is insufficient to assert that economies will always reach their Walrasian equilibriums without describing how they get there. Some sort of price adjustment equation like (11) is an indispensable part of any fully articulated economic model.

A macroeconomic view that stresses the dangerous potential for destabilizing deflation present under a regime of flexible prices can avoid some of the problems that economists have traditionally encountered while trying to analyze the origins of the Great Depression in the United States. Economists like Temin (1974), who attempt to account for the Great Depression by a decline in exogenous spending induced by falling "animal spirits," have a difficult time explaining why those who make investment decisions suddenly become more pessimistic. Without making reference to the destabilizing effects of deflation, it is also difficult to account for rising real interest rates in the face of an autonomous decline in spending.

Economists like Friedman and Schwartz (1963), who attempt to account for the Great Depression in terms of an inappropriately contractionary monetary policy, have a difficult time explaining the behavior of the real money supply. As figure 12.3 shows, the real money supply actually increased slightly between 1929 and 1933 while output was falling by close to 50%. Since aggregate demand should be closely linked to the real money supply, it is hard to see how a monetary impulse could have caused the depression without ever reducing real money balances. Moreover, without making reference to the effects of defla-

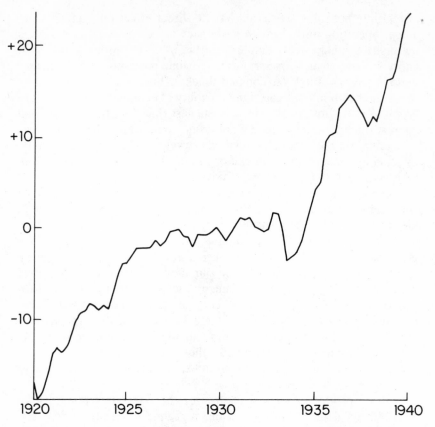

Fig. 12.3   Percentage deviation of the real money supply (M1) from its
average 1926–29 value.

tion, it is hard to explain why nominal interest rates fell in the face of
a monetary shock.

More generally, evidence for the view that increased price flexibility
is destabilizing comes from an examination of the changing behavior
of real interest rates plotted in figure 12.4. The standard deviation of
ex post real rates on an annual basis was 3.10% in the period 1893–
1915, compared with 0.57% in 1949–70 and 1.37% in 1971–82.[17] Before
1979, the highest real interest rate observed on a quarterly basis was
6% in 1974, and in only five quarters in the pre-1979 post–World War
II period were real rates greater than 4% observed. On the other hand,

17. The behavior of real rates since 1979 is, in the context of the rest of the post–
World War II period, anomalous. A glance at recent real rates seems to suggest that
American economic policymakers are attempting to restore the pattern of real rates
characteristic of the 1890s.

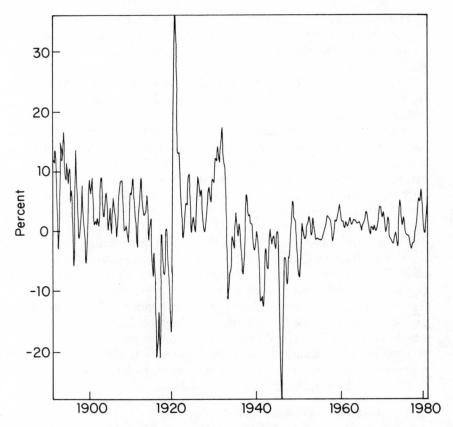

Fig. 12.4   Ex post short-term real interest rates.

real rates greater than 6% occurred in every single reference cycle recession (except 1903–04) during the pre–World War I period. It seems clear that these variations in real rates should have contributed greatly to economic instability.

12.4 Is Aggregate Price Flexibility Destabilizing?

In section 12.3 we argued that in the standard aggregate demand/ aggregate supply framework there are no strong theoretical reasons for believing that a small increase in aggregate price flexibility—defined either as an increase in the responsiveness of wages to labor market conditions or as a decrease in "persistence"—would reduce the variance of output. We also expressed our suspicion that in the United States the relation between price and output flexibility goes the other way from that typically assumed. We suggested that some of the relative macroeconomic good fortune of the United States since World War II can be traced to the possibility that a flatter short-run aggregate supply curve dampens fluctuations in the real interest rate and so dampens fluctuations in output.

We put forth this potential explanation because the other mechanisms we have identified cannot account for all of the decline in the variability of output from the prewar to the postwar period. The rising share of government expenditures can account for a small fraction of the decline in variance, and the smoothing of purchases of consumer nondurables and services as a result of automatic stabilizers and commercial credit can account for a significant portion. But there remains a substantial decline in the relative variance of "long-term" expenditures—construction, business investment, and consumer durable purchases—that is documented in Robert Gordon and John Veitch's paper in this volume. The standard explanation is that this decline in the variability of "long-term" expenditures is due to the expectation of successful stabilization policy. But since we cannot find the traces in other economic variables that we expected to find if this were indeed correct, we believe that the decline in the variance of "long-term" expenditures needs further explanation. And since "long-term" expenditures are in theory very much dependent on the real interest rate, we advance the hypothesis that the primary channel through which price flexibility affects macroeconomic performance is the instability induced by aggregate price flexibility in the real interest rate.

12.4.1   Reduced-Form Evidence: Theory

In this section we present some empirical evidence to back up the hypothesis that price rigidity has contributed to macroeconomic stability. We had hoped to estimate a simple structural model and thus to see if the data supported our hypothesis by testing whether the parameters of the structural model fell in a region where aggregate price flexibility was destabilizing on the margin. But we are unable to do so. Attempts at estimation repeatedly failed to converge or converged to unstable parameter values. We appear to have been unable to nest our hypothesis in a structural model that is both tractable, in the sense of being simple enough for us to gain some analytic understanding of its properties, and believable, in the sense of not being rejected out of hand by the data.

Since the restrictions we found necessary if we were to formulate a model that we could understand and interpret also destroyed the fit of the model with the data, we shifted to nonstructural estimation. The current practice among economists seeking to draw conclusions that are not highly sensitive to minor changes in the underlying model is to use vector autoregressions and to plot the resulting impulse response functions. In such an analysis, a positive response of output to an inflation shock might be taken as evidence in favor of our approach.

We have run analyses along these lines, but we find problems in interpreting the impulse response functions as evidence for any position, since we have no good idea of what an "inflation shock" is or what actual economic processes it represents. Therefore we also present (quasi-) reduced forms for output and argue that the pattern of coefficients that emerges is hard to justify with any underlying theoretical model other than our hypothesis.

According to the mainstream Keynesian macroeconomic approaches, the primary determinants of output are three: lagged output, (lagged) real money balances—operating through wealth and liquidity effects—and the nominal interest rate. Lower real money balances choke off aggregate demand in general, and higher nominal interest rates reduce the demand for investment goods in particular. Whether one believes that real balances are only a passive indicator of nominal interest rates, credit conditions, and animal spirits or that interest rates are only an index of the underlying determinant, real balances, it remains true that output should be, in any kind of reduced form, a positive function of (present and) lagged real balances and a negative function of (present and) lagged interest rates.

Implicit in the mainstream view is a "Keynesian" picture of price adjustment. Changes in real balances or nominal interest rates cause disturbances in aggregate demand. Because in the aggregate quantity adjusts more quickly than price, the changes in the movement of the price level associated with changes in real balances and in interest rates show up—in the time period relevant to the study of business cycles—only after the movement in output. In the mainstream view, the price level responds to its own lagged values and to the level of nominal demand. The mainstream view cannot account for a significant positive link running from prices to output without abandoning the "Keynesian" interpretation of the relative speeds of price and quantity adjustment that is its foundation. There is one set of events that, according to the mainstream view, should generate a correlation between present price movements and future output. This is the case of the "supply shock," in which present jumps in prices are associated with declines in future output. But this produces a correlation with the opposite sign from that expected according to a theory centered on the real interest rate.

The explanation for output fluctuations usually given by classical economists follow these lines: some agents (workers, not firms) misperceive relative prices. They believe that the real wage is higher (or lower) than it really is and so work more (or less) than is optimal. If there are intermediate goods in the production process, it is possible to claim that output depends both on the degree of relative price misperception and on lagged production of intermediate goods—on lagged output. This line of though produces a Lucas aggregate supply function:

(14) $$q_t = \alpha_1(p_t - E_{t-1}p_t) + \alpha_2 q_{t-1}.$$

Note that the new classical approach predicts that, in a reduced form of output on lagged output, present and lagged prices, and other variables, the only variables that can enter with positive coefficients are lagged output. Lagged prices are useless as predictors of $p_t - E_{t-1}p_t$ and should, in the new classical framework, not enter into the reduced form at all.[18] Therefore we conclude that a significant positive effect of lagged prices on present output fits easily into neither the mainstream nor the new classical view of the macroeconomy. And we believe that the existence of such a positive effect is evidence in favor of an older view of business cycles, a view that places special stress on the role of the real interest rate.

With these theoretical observations in mind, we estimated vector autoregressions for a variety of periods and specifications on quarterly data taken from Gordon (1982a) and annual data taken from Friedman and Schwartz (1983). The results provide some evidence in favor of our hypothesis. A price innovation has, looking at the impulse response functions, a positive effect on future output. And in the reduced form for output, lagged price enters with a generally positive coefficient.

We find this significant. According to the view that stresses the importance of nominal rigidities in causing business cycles, price innovations have to (when nominal balances are held constant) have a negative effect on future output. Deflation should raise the real money stock and thus increase output. But the equations indicate, in support of our more dynamic view, that deflation may itself lower output.

12.4.2   Reduced-Form Evidence: Empirical Results

The first set of vector autoregressions estimates the following three-equation system:

$$
\begin{bmatrix} \dot{p} \\ q \\ i \end{bmatrix} =
\begin{bmatrix} 0 & \alpha_{012} & \alpha_{013} \\ 0 & 0 & \alpha_{023} \\ 0 & 0 & 0 \end{bmatrix}
\begin{bmatrix} \dot{p} \\ q \\ i \end{bmatrix} + A(L)
\begin{bmatrix} \dot{p} \\ q \\ i \end{bmatrix} +
\begin{bmatrix} \epsilon_{\dot{p}} \\ \epsilon_q \\ \epsilon_i \end{bmatrix},
$$

where $A(L)$ is a three-by-three matrix polynomial of order five in the lag operator. The variables in this autoregression are:

q the output ratio, real GNP/natural real GNP

18. According to the new classical view of things, shocks have persistent effects even though lagged prices are not in the equation for q_t. Past prices affect past output, and past output enters the equation that determines present output.

$\dot{p}$ the quarter-to-quarter inflation rate
i the commercial paper rate.
(All data are taken from Gordon 1982a.)

Note that the arrangement of the variables in the VAR is such as to minimize the potential impact of any innovation in p. Only that part of

$$\dot{p}_t - E_{t-1}\dot{p}_t$$

that is uncorrelated with $q_t - E_{t-1}q_t$ and $i_t - E_{t-1}i_t$ will be counted as an inflation innovation. Thus the risk that our interpretation of the results is in error, that the VAR is reading correlations between $\dot{p}$ and q that are really driven by causal links from q to $\dot{p}$ and from lagged q to q as evidence in favor of our hypothesis, is minimized.

The VAR was initially estimated for time periods 1893:1 to 1915:4, 1923:1 to 1940:4, and 1949:1 to 1982:4. This particular three-variable system was chosen because no quarterly data on the money stock are available before 1907. Thus there are not enough data to estimate a VAR including the money stock for any pre–World War I period. We are reluctant to base any arguments on a comparison of the post–World War II period with the interwar period alone. The Great Depression represents an extraordinary cumulation of shocks and so is probably not well studied using the VAR method.

An objection to estimating this particular system might be made along the following lines: the choice of variables—output, inflation, and interest rates—implies that the effects attributed to the inflation variable are *only* the effects of movements in accommodated inflation. Unaccommodated movements in inflation will, because the interest rate is an index of the real money stock, also appear as movements in interest rates. And so some of the depressing effect of price rises on output will appear as an effect of interest rate movements on output.

Two facts militate against this argument. First, it implies that the contemporaneous correlation between inflation and interest rates should be positive, that α_{013} should be greater than zero. Instead, α_{013} is less than zero (though not significantly so).

Second, the equations were also estimated for the four-equation system consisting of inflation, the commercial paper rate, the output ratio, and the detrended nominal money stock. The variables were so ordered as to give the maximum potential scope to the monetary innovation, the second place to the output innovation, the third place to the interest rate innovation, and the least potential scope to the inflation innovation.

Quasi-reduced-form equations for output are shown in table 12.12. Impulse responses of output to an inflation innovation are plotted in figures 12.5 and 12.6. We note two things from these empirical results. First, this method is not suited to the interwar period. The interwar

Table 12.12   **Quasi-Reduced-Form Equations for Output**

Period	R^2	SEE	Interest Rate				Inflation Rate				Lagged Output				Nominal Money			
			Cont.	−1	−2	S(5)	Cont.	−1	−2	S(5)	Cont.	−1	−2	S(5)	Cont.	−1	−2	S(5)
1893–1915	.63	.038	−.06 (.65)	−1.5 (.76)	.87 (.80)	−2.6 (.99)	—	.44 (.34)	−.27 (.27)	.32 (.70)	—	.89 (.12)	.12 (.16)	.75 (.15)	—	—	—	—
1923–40	.95	.039	.05 (.46)	2.22 (2.38)	−2.35 (2.53)	−.07 (1.37)	—	.53 (.46)	−.47 (.49)	.92 (.59)	—	.93 (.14)	.03 (.18)	.96 (.06)	—	—	—	—
1949–82	.94	.008	.19 (.10)	−.23 (.15)	−.30 (.16)	−.27 (.11)	—	.31 (.14)	−.02 (.14)	.21 (.19)	—	1.10 (.09)	−.01 (.14)	.93 (.03)	—	—	—	—
1923–40	.96	.034	—	3.43 (1.52)	−3.24 (2.50)	1.32 (.74)	—	.22 (.43)	−.64 (.45)	−.48 (.66)	—	.83 (.15)	−.06 (.19)	.83 (.10)	.90 (.27)	1.33 (.18)	−.16 (.33)	.97 (.03)
1949–82	.95	.008	—	−.09 (.10)	−.34 (.14)	−.09 (.04)	—	.33 (.14)	.00 (.15)	.15 (.18)	—	1.23 (.09)	−.15 (.13)	.96 (.03)	−.01 (.02)	.02 (.05)	.04 (.03)	.90 (.03)

Source: Data from Gordon 1982a.
Note: Cont. = contemporaneous coefficient of variable; S(5) = sum of coefficients on five lags.

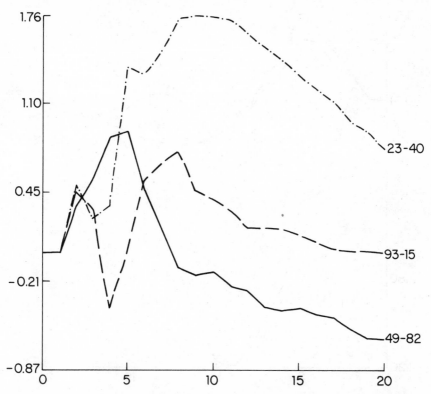

Fig. 12.5   Output response to inflation innovations, three-variable system, 1949–82, 1923–40, 1893–1915.

period is so strongly dominated by the Great Depression that all correlations are warped: the decline of the nominal interest rate during the onset of the depression is the only variable the model can latch on to in accounting for the depression, hence the excessively large difference in the coefficients on the first and second lag of the interest rate. If one turns back to figure 12.2, this should come as no surprise. The Great Depression was a unique event, and attempts to analyze the entire interwar period are, in essence, attempts to generalize from a sample of one.

Second, both the coefficients on lagged inflation in the output equation and the impulse responses of output to an inflation shock are positive and, in general, significant at at least the .10% level. This correlation is not easy to explain within either the new classical framework or the mainstream framework. The hypothesis urged here, with its emphasis on real interest rate effects, does provide a natural explanation.

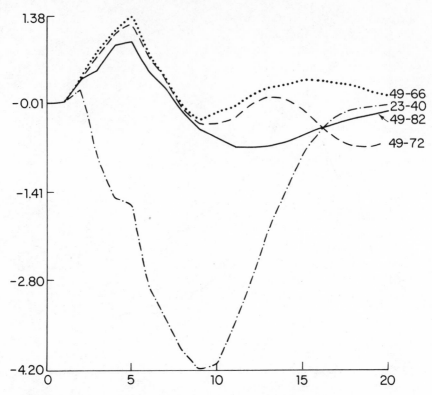

Fig. 12.6   Output response to inflation innovations, four-variable system, 1949–82, 1949–72, 1923–40.

This belief is bolstered by additional equations run (but not reported). For various combinations of interest rates, inflation rates, output ratios, real and nominal money stocks, the only equation that failed to generate a positive correlation between inflation innovations and future output and positive terms on lagged prices in the output equation was a VAR that included no interest rate variable—only the output ratio, inflation, and the nominal money stock. Furthermore, the effect of lagged inflation innovations on output is significantly greater for the four-variable system for those two post–World War II periods that do not include the supply shock ridden 1970s. This tends to support our hypothesis. The 1970s were dominated by supply shocks, by disturbances that first raised $\dot{p}$ and then reduced q. These shifts in the short-run aggregate supply schedule should mask the effects we are looking for in the post–World War II period. That these supply shocks do reduce the positive effect for the period 1949:1 to 1982:4, and that this masking is only partial, encourages us to think that we are correctly interpreting our

VARs and that the effect of price innovations is, in the United States today, strongly procyclical.

To sum up: an unstructured analysis of the correlations between macroeconomic variables carried out by means of VARs produces a finding—inflation innovations have a positive effect on future output—that is hard to interpret from either an equilibrium business cycle or a nominal rigidities perspective. We can think of no other convincing reasons for this association besides the one we advocate: changes in the aggregate price level produce changes in the real cost of capital that have effects on the level of expenditures on items having a high interest elasticity of present value. Thus deflation at the beginning of a recession would deepen the recession by causing a further cutback in investment. This correlation suggests that reducing nominal price rigidity would not diminish the seriousness of business cycles.

12.5 Conclusions

We began by suggesting that the large change in the variance of output between the prewar and postwar periods was a fact that should be explicable within a satisfactory business cycle theory. We then argued that a number of factors frequently alleged to have led to greater stability, including structural changes in the economy, discretionary stabilization policy, and the avoidance of financial panics, probably did relatively little to enhance stability. We conclude that the two principal factors promoting economic stability have been greater public and private efforts to smooth consumption and the increasing rigidity of prices. We attribute the latter development to the increasing institutionalization of the economy.

Comment   Robert Eisner

I am glad to find Keynes rediscovered, if only in part.

DeLong and Summers see the amplitude of cyclical fluctuations as less in the postwar period and attribute this principally to "greater public and private efforts to smooth consumption and the increasing rigidity of prices." The public efforts are related to a greater government component in aggregate demand and automatic, but not discretionary, countercyclical fiscal instruments. The easing of liquidity constraints, which DeLong and Summers relate to greater amounts and

Robert Eisner is the William R. Kenan Professor of Economics at Northwestern University.

ease of household borrowing, has further encouraged a divorce of consumption from fluctuations in current income and hence reduced the multiplier of exogenous shocks.

DeLong and Summers reject the argument attributed to unnamed "Keynesians" that rigid wages and prices contribute to fluctuations in employment and output. They suggest rather, going back to Keynes (via Tobin), that less rigid prices magnify fluctuations. A fall in prices, for example, generates an expectation of falling prices. This contributes to higher *real* rates of interest and thus aggravates the real decline that initiated the price movement.

DeLong and Summers might well have recalled the rigorous development of the argument by Oscar Lange (1952) that flexible prices could not be relied upon to eliminate excess supply of goods or labor (unemployment). This is not to claim, as DeLong and Summers do (sect. 12.3), that rigidities can make employment "more stable than it would be if a Walrasian equilibrium were attained in every period." Walrasian equilibrium presumably means zero excess supply in all markets and hence no unemployment at all. But as Lange pointed out, if price expectations were relatively elastic, flexible prices might not correct a situation of excess supply in commodity markets, or excess demand for money; Walrasian equilibrium would not be attained. Simply enough, lower prices would then generate an expectation of still lower future prices, raising the current-to-future price ratio and hence reducing current demand for commodities and raising the real demand for money.[1]

But this is not to say that, under these conditions of relatively elastic price expectations, less flexible prices are necessarily better than more flexible prices. Keynes argued, indeed in the lines quoted by DeLong and Summers, that "it would be much better that wages should be rigidly fixed and deemed incapable of material changes, than that depression should be accompanied by a gradual downward tendency of money-wages." Complete rigidity would be better, but a more gradual fall—greater rigidity—may well generate more in the way of expectations of further declines than the quicker and more rapid decline that might be associated with less rigidity.

DeLong and Summers's discussion of this issue seems at times to be caught in the misunderstandings among Keynes, neoclassicists, and new macroeconomists. To the neoclassicists and the new macroeconomists, it is presumably the real wage that matters. Excess supply of labor—or unemployment—would be eliminated if workers would allow their wages to fall. This would increase employers' demand for labor

---

1. A "positive monetary effect," to offset this and generate a net increase in the demand for commodities, would require action by the monetary authority to ensure that the supply of real cash balances increased *more* than the demand for them.

and decrease workers' supply of labor and hence restore equilibrium in the labor market.

To Keynes, however, this was nonsense. He insisted that workers had no means of lowering the *real* wage. If they agreed to lower nominal wages, since prices under conditions of perfect competition equal marginal costs and marginal costs depend overwhelmingly, if not exclusively, on variable labor costs, the reduction in wages could be expected to bring about an equal reduction in prices. Hence, for Keynes, flexible wages entailed equally flexible prices and a real balance effect that would lower nominal and (if the elasticity of expectations were unity) real interest rates. The neoclassical Pigou/Haberler argument could readily be appended to this so that increasing real money balances would raise aggregate demand via a direct wealth effect as well as by lowering the rate of interest.

But if this is the argument that DeLong and Summers think to test, they could not expect much empirical evidence, as Pigou and Patinkin long ago acknowledged. It is hardly plausible that a fall of 1% or 2% in prices, let alone a mere slowing in the rate of increase of prices, would have enough of a real balance or wealth effect to make much difference in consumption or in the amount of recession fall in aggregate demand. As Patinkin (1951) pointed out, even the major fall in prices in the Great Depression of the thirties could not have made much difference.

But the suggestions DeLong and Summers make about the role of lesser price flexibility, developed more rigorously, point further to a serious contradiction of another of their major arguments: that higher government expenditures and automatic stabilizers have probably contributed to lesser cyclical amplitude but that discretionary countercyclical policy has not. I should make clear that I am not disposed to argue very enthusiastically that discretionary policy has made much difference. My own view is that discretionary fiscal policy had been so rarely and fitfully—if ever—applied that nothing of a stabilizing nature is likely to show up in the data on its account. Monetary policy has been, understandably, generally so much more accommodative than countercyclical that, given the intrinsic limitations of the powers of the monetary authority, I do not look for much in the way of results of discretionary policy there.

That said, though, I find seriously suspect the authors' argument that the lesser magnitude of cyclical fluctuations may be attributed to automatic stabilizers but that allegedly greater persistence of fluctuations is evidence that discretionary countercyclical policies have not been effective.

To begin with, I have serious trouble with a number of DeLong and Summers's measures. It is not clear to me that the magnitude of cyclical fluctuations can be well grasped by the standard deviation of either quarter-to-quarter changes in the log of real GNP or the difference between the log of real GNP and the log of "natural" or "trend" real GNP. I would measure the amplitude of cyclical fluctuations in terms of movements from trough to peak and peak to trough or, adjusting for trend, as the movement in the differences from trend as the economy progresses from trough to peak and peak to trough. The DeLong and Summers measures will tell us more about how abruptly movements are made or how long the economy is markedly above or below its trend or "natural" positions than about the total amplitude of fluctuations. The corollary of this is that something that slows a decline, or curbs a boom and hence stretches it out, will be viewed by DeLong and Summers as reducing "cyclical variability" but increasing persistence.

Yet there is no reason to assume that what discretionary counter-cyclical actions may have been implemented functioned to hasten turning points rather than merely to reduce rates of change. And classical views of the business cycle suggest that a slower decline might well delay a turning point by slowing the "cleansing" via working off of excess stocks of inventory and fixed capital. Similarly, the very purpose of slowing a boom (not a Keynesian recommendation) would be to prolong it.

The authors' argument about greater price rigidity suggests that declines would have been slowed (and upturns as well) by reduction of the destabilizing expectations factor that would otherwise tend to raise real interest rates in a recession and lower them in a boom. But then this factor also would tend to increase the persistence of fluctuations. We appear to be left with no grounds at all for the argument that greater (or at least no lesser) persistence of recessions and booms in the post-war period must imply a failure of discretionary countercyclical policy (whatever it may have been).

But that leads to another problem with DeLong and Summers's measures. They all are apparently addressed to the cycle as a whole, with no distinction between recessions and booms. In the prewar days, it was customary to think of Western economies as victims of chronic unemployment, recessions or depressions driving unemployment well below its chronic levels, and "sick recoveries which die in their infancy," in the words of Alvin Hansen (1944, 370) and which rarely if ever brought us even briefly to periods of full capacity, full employment boom. As J. R. Hicks (1950, chap. 6) put it neatly, the economy could well struggle along a floor, with recovery never reaching the full employment ceiling, as I illustrate in figure C12.1. If it did, it would be aborted abruptly by a shortage of accelerated-induced investment when growth became limited by the slope of the ceiling at full capacity. But this view of the cycle, which I find appealing, suggests a rather different

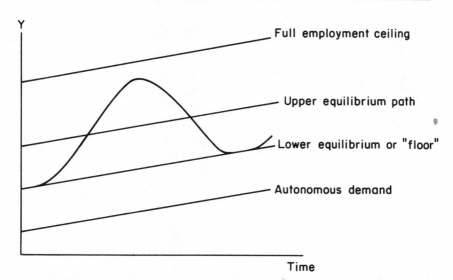

Fig. C12.1 Hicksian trade cycle: low autonomous (or government) demand.

interpretation of the data on which DeLong and Summers have focused. In the Hicksian treatment, the increase in the proportion of gross national product purchased by government as well as the increased cushion of exogenous consumption provided by government guarantees of income, current and (via social insurance) future, results in a higher floor, a higher equilibrium path, and, most important, much longer periods during which the economy can remain at or close to its ceiling, as shown in figure C12.2. The higher floor would mean that the amplitude of fluctuations is reduced, since the economy can fluctuate only between its floor and its ceiling. But the longer periods at the ceiling— witness the relatively full employment for five years from 1965 through 1969, for example—would turn up as greater "persistence" in the DeLong and Summers measures. Such persistence would not necessarily imply that recessions have been longer than in the prewar period.[2]

The explanation of alleged greater stability DeLong and Summers offer turns to lessened "liquidity constraints" on consumers in the postwar period. These are presumed to supplement the countercyclical tax and transfer payments that tend to divorce personal income from

2. Keynes, it may be recalled, was highly critical—very correctly, I would insist—of policies to stabilize the economy by lopping off the booms. He wanted, rather, to fill in the troughs. The Kennedy/Johnson tax cut may be viewed as a discretionary policy designed to do just that, and the Vietnam War, whatever its intent, served economically to prolong a boom.

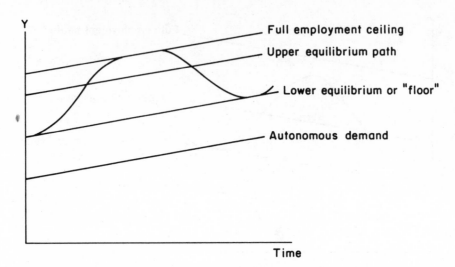

Fig. C12.2   Hicksian trade cycle: high autonomous (or government) demand.

gross national product. As DeLong and Summers point out, if there were no constraints that tied current consumption to current income, consumers optimizing in terms of a life cycle or permanent income consumption function would not even need countercyclical taxes and transfer payments to maintain consumption relatively constant despite loss of jobs and income.

Here DeLong and Summers seem to get some of their numbers wrong and ignore others that are relevant. For one thing, the evidence of greater postwar stability is somewhat marred by the actual facts of the 1973–75 and 1981–82 recessions. First, the maximum decline in real GNP, which did occur during the 1973–75 recession, was not 1.8%, as DeLong and Summers report in section 12.1, but 4.88% (from $1,266.06 billion in the fourth quarter of 1973 to $1,204.258 billion in the first quarter of 1975). And the most recent decline was not the 1.8% that they report in section 12.2.1 but 2.96% (from $1,522.105 billion in the third quarter of 1981 to $1,477.061 billion in the third quarter of 1982).[3]

What is more, real disposable income did not rise by the 1.1% and 1.0% that they report (sect. 12.2.1) but fell, by 3.24% in the earlier period (from $874.1 billion in 1973:4 to $845.8 billion in 1975:1) and by 0.50% in the most recent recession (from $1,058.091 billion in 1981:3 to $1,052.847 billion in 1982:1).[4]

3. See table 1.2 of the national income and product accounts, as revised in July 1984.
4. Ibid., table 2.1.

But none of us should take these disposable income figures that seriously without careful adjustment. It should be well known that disposable personal income includes nominal interest payments, which have of course recently become enormous, now surpassing $400 billion, rather than real interest payments. Another way of putting this is that in periods of inflation, holders of debt suffer losses in real value that should be netted against their interest receipts in calculating their income. With such inflation adjustments, real disposable income may be seen to have nose-dived considerably more than GNP in the sharp supply side, inflation shock recession of 1973–75 as well as during the onslaught of the 1981–82 recession. Although higher marginal rates of taxes and transfer payments probably did contribute to the sharply lower regression coefficient of changes in disposable income on changes in GNP in the postwar period noted in DeLong and Summers's table 12.5, I would not infer much from that without viewing movements of an appropriately adjusted disposable income in particular cycles.

I also find their associated argument about the changes in liquidity constraints suspect. In particular, in a number of places they equate the easing of liquidity constraints with greater amounts and hence, to them, greater ease of consumer borrowing. In fact, of course, consumer debt has increased greatly and is now vastly more than in the prewar period. But what is relevant in its impact on the smoothing of consumption is not the amount of consumer borrowing per se, but net *movements* in consumer debt during cycles.

My cursory examination of the data confirms my a priori notion that net changes in consumer debt varied procyclically. For example, net increases in total consumer credit (*Economic Report,* 1984, table B–69, p. 301) moved down from $25.6 billion in 1973 to $9.7 billion in 1974 and $9.1 billion in 1975, and then up again to $25.2 billion in 1976 and $39.7 billion in 1977. $48.2 billion in 1978, and $44.6 billion in 1979. But then they declined to $4.2 billion in 1980 and rose to $24.0 billion in 1981, only to fall again to $18.2 billion in 1982. These changes were in nominal dollars. There must certainly have been substantial declines in the real value of consumer credit outstanding during recession years.

Perhaps of even more moment were sharp declines in rates of increase in mortgage debt outstanding during recession years. For aside from the relation of this to residential investment, it seems apparent that substantial amounts of mortgage debt were used to finance consumption expenditures. We may note, for example, that mortgage debt outstanding on one- to four-family houses increased by $96 billion in 1980, by $78 billion in 1981, and by $49 billion in 1982 (*Economic Report,* table B–71, p. 303). Since these figures are derived from mortgage debt outstanding in nominal dollars, the results of conversion to changes in real debt suggest that these forms of liquidity contributed to magnifying rather than reducing downward pressures on consumption.

I find various of DeLong and Summers's analyses and tests imaginative and ingenious but less than fully convincing. On the whole question of lesser competitiveness in the postwar economy, it is difficult to get any clear measure, particularly as it may relate to price flexibility, and DeLong and Summers offer little more than intuitive judgments. One of their points, that union membership increased among nonfarm workers from 9% in 1930 to 29% in 1950, is hardly persuasive in view of the substantial subsequent decline in union membership since.

Relying on future stock market movements as measures of anticipated persistence of declines or rises in economic activity strikes me as particularly frail. I doubt that DeLong and Summers would risk much money investing on the basis of such a presumed relation. Indeed, one may wonder that they did not consider real interest rate movements, on which they had focused in their theoretical discussion. I should think that in at least some instances economic declines have been associated with increases in real interest rates and booms have correlated with declines, and these might well have contributed to greater "persistence" in economic movements as well as movements of stock prices.

And I must confess I am left somewhat cold by the variety of VARs DeLong and Summers (and many of our colleagues) display. I am not sure they know quite what to do with their results; they accept some of the equations reported (acknowledged to be only some of the many equations run) while they reject others with statements such as, "this methodology is not suited to the interwar period . . . so strongly dominated by the Great Depression that all correlations are warped" (sect. 12.4.2). "The Great Depression," we are told, "was a unique event." But how many other unique events might have accounted for the various coefficients and their movements, with relevant differences in coefficients rarely very statistically significant?

My own view of the story on cyclical fluctuations is fairly simple. There *has* been a change that relates essentially to a much larger role of government, perhaps facilitated by rationalizations stemming from the Keynesian revolution. The huge surge in aggregate demand stemming from government expenditures in World War II propelled the economies of the United States and much of the industrial world close to full utilization of capacity. Shortages of capital as a consequence of the war stimulated an investment boom. The increase in public debt, at least in the United States, contributed both a perception of wealth and, directly or indirectly, liquidity. These brought on higher levels of consumption demand and, possibly also, a greater independence of consumption from current income. Consumption demand was increased further by the great growth in social insurance that raised individual perceptions of permanent income and reduced some of the risk and uncertainty with which it was anticipated.

Increased government expenditures and consumption did not, however, reduce investment demand. Even narrowly defined business nonresidential investment in plant and equipment was far above its depression levels, while more broadly defined investment, including government and household expenditures for tangible capital as well as investment in intangible capital, boomed.

As a consequence of the secular upward movement in aggregate demand—the inverse of the secular stagnation of the prewar period—employment and output, aided by the particular stimuli of the Korean and Vietnam wars and generally high military spending (certainly high compared with prewar periods), were generally much closer to full employment and full capacity. With "autonomous" demand from government and government support programs generally higher and with substantial anticipations of continued long-term growth and prosperity, recessions were generally shallower; in some cases it was hard to find more than temporary retardations in the rate of growth, or recessions that did not show up in annual data. And booms were flatter and longer as persistent, high, government-generated demand, at least where it became excess, tended to generate inflation rather than quickly unstable peaks of output. Employment did not really become "overfull" or rise above its "natural" rate. In a relatively free economy and society, workers are not "tricked" into working more than they want, anybody's parables to the contrary notwithstanding.

Hence, the postwar period does evidence generally lesser amplitude of fluctuations and, perhaps, greater persistence stemming from longer periods of relative prosperity. Some jarring exceptions must be noted, though: the severe 1973–75 dip stemming from the interaction of supply shocks and the resultant inadvertent (and apparently not greatly understood) contribution of inflation to effectively tight fiscal and monetary policy, and the also severe 1981–82 recession, again the result of the impact of inflation in creating largely unrecognized fiscal as well as monetary tightness.[5]

When you shake down the facts DeLong and Summers present and discount some of their imaginative but uncertain inferences, you may find their story not that inconsistent with mine.

5. See Eisner and Pieper 1984.

Comment   Herschel I. Grossman

In the forty years since World War II, fluctuations in aggregate economic activity on average have been strikingly smaller than during the preceding fifty years. DeLong and Summers calculate various measures of this change, critically evaluate a variety of previously suggested explanations, and propose the unconventional hypothesis that nominal wage stickiness mitigates aggregate real fluctuations.

The only standard explanation to which DeLong and Summers give credence is the effect of fiscal arrangements—especially increases in both income tax rates and income maintenance expenditures—in reducing the aggregate marginal propensity to consume out of income and the demand multiplier. DeLong and Summers usefully stress that this effect results from the importance of liquidity-constrained consumers in determining the aggregate marginal propensity to consume and that the reduction in the multiplier probably has involved both a reduction in the aggregate response of disposable income to income and a reduction in the proportion of liquidity-constrained consumers.

DeLong and Summers reject, with good reason, explanations for the decreased magnitude of fluctuations based on changes in the composition of economic activity and on the absence of financial panics. They also reject the explanation that "discretionary stabilization policies" have been more efficacious, but here their argument seems largely semantic. They implicitly define discretionary stabilization policies as attempts to reduce the persistence of disturbances to aggregate activity, and they observe, interestingly, that persistence actually has not decreased in the post–World War II period. This observation, however, has no apparent relevance for determining whether aspects of policy other than the fiscal arrangements mentioned above have contributed to the reduced magnitude of aggregate fluctuations. The analysis they present leaves this general question largely unanswered.

In this regard, one of the weaker arguments in the paper is the attempt to dismiss the importance of decreased volatility of monetary aggregates in the post–World War II period. The distinctions DeLong and Summers stress between exogenous and endogenous changes in monetary aggregates and between monetary policy as a cause and an effect of fluctuations in real aggregates are both false and irrelevant. Monetary policy, like all purposeful human action, depends on prior events, but at the same time both the form of this dependence and the policy actions themselves can influence other events—past, present, and future. The relevant question is whether in the post–World War II period the re-

Herschel I. Grossman is professor of economics at Brown University.

lation of monetary policy to the factors that influence it has changed in such a way as to produce both a reduction in fluctuations in monetary aggregates and a consequent reduction in the magnitude of fluctuations in real aggregates.

Much existing theoretical and empirical analysis suggests a positive answer to this question. DeLong and Summers do not pose this question directly or address the standard arguments. Their suggestion that the demonstrated unimportance of financial panics implies the unimportance of monetary policy hardly deals with the critical issue of the importance of the process generating monetary policy and does not even follow from their own analysis, which suggests that the unimportance of financial panics resulted from arrangements that stabilized monetary aggregates.

The most unusual idea DeLong and Summers present is that the magnitude of aggregate real fluctuations is inversely related to the degree of wage flexibility. To derive this hypothesis, they begin by pointing out that in the textbook IS-LM model aggregate output depends positively on both real money balances and inflationary expectations. Thus, assuming that the price level is positively related to the nominal wage level, a smaller decline in the nominal wage level in response to a negative demand disturbance would mean a smaller real money balance, which by itself would cause a larger decline in aggregate output. The net change in aggregate output, however, would also depend on the effect of a smaller decline in the nominal wage level on inflationary expectations.

DeLong and Summers append to this model a wage setting mechanism according to which a decrease in the fraction of workers whose nominal wages are adjusted each period—a presumed consequence of the apparent lengthening since World War II of the average duration of wage agreements—causes both the current nominal wage level and rationally expected future inflation to decrease less in response to a negative demand disturbance. DeLong and Summers argue that, for certain parameter values, the effect of the smaller decrease in expected inflation would more than offset the effect of the smaller increase in real money balances and yield a smaller decline in aggregate output. Although their illustrative parameter values are plausible for small changes, they probably would not remain constant as money balances became large. The combination of Pigou and Keynes effects associated with real balances should dominate in the limit.

DeLong and Summers point out that an essential characteristic of their wage mechanism is that it is backward looking. One implication of this mechanism is that workers are universally concerned not with their wages relative to the prices or other wages that will materialize over the term of their wage agreements, but with their wages over this term relative to the history of other wages at the time of their wage negotiation. DeLong and Summers do not attempt to rationalize this aspect of their model.

Their setup, moreover, involves the even stronger assumption, which is critical but which they do not recognize explicitly, that current nominal wage changes depend as much on wages that were set in the distant past as on wages set in the recent past. This assumption implies that the importance of recent nominal wage changes for current nominal wage changes is negatively related to the average length of wage agreements. This effect creates the positive relation between the fraction of workers who negotiate lower nominal wages now and the expected future change in the nominal wage level.

DeLong and Summers judiciously regard the implications of this analysis as merely suggestive. Perhaps not surprisingly, they report no success in fitting the data to a structural representation of their model. As an alternative, they try to interpret the results of a vector autoregression involving aggregate output, the price level, and a nominal interest rate as supporting their hypothesis. The main empirical findings to which they appeal are positive effects of price level innovations and lags of the price level on current aggregate output. Contrary to their interpretation, however, we can take these results, together with the positive relation between current output and past output, merely to be indicative of the importance and persistent effects of demand disturbances.

The position DeLong and Summers take regarding the data suggests the following analogous argument: The amount of damage from a storm is positively correlated with the amount of swaying of buildings during a storm; therefore we could reduce storm damage by making buildings more rigid.

Although DeLong and Summers focus on the decreased post–World War II magnitude of fluctuations in aggregate economic activity, other notable characteristics of macroeconomic fluctuations also have changed since World War II. As DeLong and Summers also point out, fluctuations seem to have become more persistent. Another difference that possibly reflects a fundamental change in the economic structure involves the cyclical pattern of aggregate activity and inflation. For example, before World War II, inflation and unemployment almost always moved in opposite directions. Moreover, for a given inflation rate, unemployment tended to be higher when unemployment was decreasing than when it was increasing. In contrast, since World War II, this tendency has been dramatically reversed. In addition, inflation and unemployment have moved in the same direction for extended periods. The question naturally arises of the relations among all these changes. The characteristics of convincing explanations for what we observe may become clearer if we try to keep the entire factual picture in mind.

Discussion Summary

Martin N. Baily commented on the relation between his own work and the DeLong/Summers paper. In 1978 he had argued that stabilization policy not only had a direct effect on the economy, but also induced a reinforcing response from the private sector, making consumption and investment less volatile in response to cyclical output movements. Contrary to a statement by DeLong and Summers, he had stressed the importance not only of discretionary policy, but also of the automatic stabilizers and the commitment by the Federal Reserve to avoid wild swings in the money supply. In the same paper he had also pointed out the destabilizing effect of price flexibility through its impact on real interest rates—a major feature of the current DeLong and Summers paper. Baily also argued that the existence of high serial correlation in output data is not evidence against the hypothesis of reinforcing response from the private sector. For example, the long sustained recovery after 1961 must have resulted in very high serial correlation in output data, but this was just the kind of period that strengthened the belief of the private sector in the stability of the economy and reduced the volatility of private expenditure decisions.

Robert Barro took exception to the paper's assertion that the multiplier had fallen. He claimed that the military spending multiplier had always been less than one and had not changed in the postwar era. Robert Hall agreed with Barro that the point estimate of the multiplier may have remained constant, but he noted that the standard error of the multiplier estimate was very large.

Moses Abramovitz observed that the most striking contrast between the prewar and postwar periods was that there had been no one really large depression. He hypothesized that the lingering memories of the Great Depression were an important factor in changing the character of the business cycle in the postwar period. Phillip Cagan recalled the 1949 NBER conference findings of Robert A. Gordon, that severe and moderate cycles differed in character. He maintained that since we have had no severe cycles since the war—owing to the lack of monetary panics—the character of the remaining postwar cycles may not differ from comparable prewar cycles.

John Taylor contrasted the role of prices in the model with his own paper, in which he avers that inflation control by the government is responsible for the increased persistence of output fluctuations. He felt that the omission of policy endogeneity from the analysis lost the main reason for the deterioration of economic performance.

Robert Gordon noted that the observation of the role of disposable income in business fluctuations was not new; it had reached the level of textbooks some years ago and had been discussed by Hickman and Coen in 1976 (See the reference in this volume's Introduction). He also pointed out that whereas the paper had enumerated three channels of influence of price changes on demand, the Keynes, Pigou, and expectations effects, there was one more—the redistribution effect (discussed in Fisher's 1933 article on debt and deflation).

Lawrence Summers doubted that the effects of the Great Depression would have lasted the entire postwar period. He also felt that comparing mild prewar cycles with all postwar cycles was not very meaningful, since one could always select *some* prewar cycles that were similar to postwar cycles.

References

Anderson, Martha, ed. 1951. *Conference on Business Cycles.* New York: National Bureau of Economic Research.

Andrew, A. Piatt. 1908. Substitutes for cash in the panic of 1907. *Quarterly Journal of Economics* 22 (August): 497–542.

Bagehot, Walter. 1873. *Lombard Street.* New York: Charles Scribner's Sons.

Baily, Martin. 1978. Stabilization policy and private economic behavior. *Brookings Papers on Economic Activity* 1:11–60.

Bernanke, Benjamin. 1983. Nonmonetary influences of the financial crisis in the propagation of the Great Depression. *American Economic Review* 73:257–76.

Blanchard, Olivier. 1981. What is left of the multiplier accelerator? *American Economic Review* 71:150–54.

Bordo, Michael, and Anna J. Schwartz, eds. 1984. *A retrospective on the classical gold standard.* Chicago: University of Chicago Press.

Burns, Arthur. 1960. Progress toward economic stability. *American Economic Review* 50:1–19.

Cagan, Phillip. 1965. *Determinants and effects of changes in the stock of money.* New York: National Bureau of Economic Research.

———. 1975. Changes in the recession behavior of wholesale prices. *Explorations in Economic Research* 2:54–104.

Eisner, Robert, and Paul J. Pieper. 1984. A new view of the public debt and budget deficits. *American Economic Review* 74:11–29.

Fisher, Franklin. 1983. *Disequilibrium foundations of equilibrium economics.* Cambridge: Cambridge University Press.

Flavin, Marjorie. 1981. The adjustment of consumption to changing expectations about future income. *Journal of Political Economy* 89:974–1009.

Friedman, Milton, and Anna J. Schwartz. 1963. *A monetary history of the United States, 1867–1960.* Princeton: Princeton University Press.

———. 1983. *Monetary Trends in the United States and the United Kingdom: Their Relation to Income, Prices, and Interest Rates, 1867–1975.* Chicago: University of Chicago Press.

Goldsmith, Raymond. 1955. *A study of saving in the United States.* Princeton: Princeton University Press.

Gordon, Robert J. 1980. A consistent characterization of a near century of price behavior. *American Economic Review* 70:243–49.

———. 1982a. Price inertia and policy ineffectiveness in the United States, 1890–1980. *Journal of Political Economy* 90:1087–1117.

———. 1982b. Why U.S. wage and employment behaviour differs from that in Britain and Japan. *Economic Journal* 92:13–44.

———. 1984. *Macroeconomics.* 3d ed. Boston: Little, Brown.

Hall, Robert. 1978. Stochastic implications of the life cycle–permanent income hypothesis. *Journal of Political Economy* 86:971–88.

Hansen, Alvin H. 1944. Economic progress and declining population growth. In *Readings in business cycle theory,* ed. American Economic Association, 366–84. Philadelphia: Blakiston. Originally published 1939.

Hickman, Bert, and Robert Coen. 1976. *An annual growth model of the U.S. economy.* Amsterdam: North-Holland.

Hicks, J. R. 1950. *A contribution to the theory of the trade cycle.* Oxford: Oxford University Press.

James, John. 1978. *Money and capital markets in post-bellum America.* Princeton: Princeton University Press.

Keynes, John Maynard. 1936. *The general theory of employment, interest and money.* London: Macmillan.

Kuznets, Simon. 1961. *Capital in the American economy.* Princeton: Princeton University Press.

Lange, Oscar. 1952. *Price flexibility and employment.* Bloomington, Ind.: Principia Press. Originally published 1944.

Lewis, W. Arthur. 1978. *Growth and fluctuations, 1870–1913.* London: Allen and Unwin.

McCallum, Bennett T. 1983. The liquidity trap and the Pigou effect. *Economica* 48 (November):395–406.

Nutter, G. Warren, and Henry Einhorn. 1969. *Enterprise monopoly in the United States.* New York: Columbia University Press.

Patinkin, Don. 1951. Price flexibility and employment. In *Readings in monetary theory,* ed. F. P. Lutz and L. W. Mint, 252–83. Homewood, Ill.: Richard Irwin. Originally published 1949.

Ross, Arthur. 1958. Do we have a new industrial feudalism? *American Economic Review* 48:747–71.

Sachs, Jeffrey. 1980. The changing cyclical behavior of wages and prices, 1890–1976. *American Economic Review* 70:78–90.

Schultze, Charles. 1981. Some macro foundations for micro theory. *Brookings Papers on Economic Activity* 2:521–92.

Shaw, William. 1947. *Value of commodity output since 1869.* New York: National Bureau of Economic Research.

Sprague, O. M. W. 1910. *History of crises under the national banking system.* Washington, D.C.: Government Printing Office.

———. 1915. The crisis of 1914 in the United States. *American Economic Review* 5:499–533.

John B. Taylor. 1979. Staggered wage setting in a macro model. *American Economic Review, Papers and Proceedings* (May), 108–13.

Temin, Peter. 1974. *Did monetary forces cause the Great Depression?* New York: W. W. Norton.

Tobin, James. 1975. Keynesian models of recession and depression. *American Economic Review* 65:195–202.

United States Council of Economic Advisers. 1984. *Economic report of the president.* Washington, D.C.: Government Printing Office.

Appendix A
The Development and Role of the National Bureau of Economic Research's Business Cycle Chronologies

Geoffrey H. Moore and Victor Zarnowitz

1. Defining Business Cycles

Business cycles consist of recurrent sequences of expansions, downturns, contractions, and upturns in a great number of diverse economic activities. These movements are both sufficiently diffused and sufficiently synchronized to create major fluctuations in comprehensive aggregates of employment, production, real income, and real sales. They are as a rule asymmetric in that expansions typically exceed contractions in size and duration. (In earlier history, however, the differences in duration were relatively small and irregular, as we will show below.) Of course, in any secularly growing economy, expansions must necessarily be on the average larger than contractions. It is a rare business cycle that does not contain a visible element of growth.

Persistent and pervasive fluctuations of this type are characteristic of the course of industrial economies with large sectors of private enterprise and markets relatively unconstrained by government. They have accompanied the development of modern capitalism in the Western world. The first systematic accounts are over a hundred years old (Juglar 1862). Authoritative studies date the phenomenon back at least to the late eighteenth century.

As a rule, several years are required for the cumulative processes of business expansion and contraction to complete a round from peak to peak or from trough to trough. But business cycles, though recurrent, are in their directly observable manifestations nonperiodic, unlike the

Geoffrey H. Moore is head of the Center for International Business Cycle Research of the Graduate School of Business at Columbia University. Victor Zarnowitz is a professor in the Graduate School of Business at the University of Chicago.

cycles of the seasons.[1] Indeed, they vary considerably in duration and as well as in intensity and scope, and they do so in ways that appear to be largely unsystematic and unpredictable.

Seasonal movements, which are periodic but often quite variable in amplitude and incidence over the calendar year, may obscure the cyclical developments to an observer of current changes in individual time series. In addition, short erratic movements are likewise continually present in most economic indicators, and they too frequently impede the contemporaneous reading of business cycle signals. Historically, however, and looking across data representing many different variables, business cycles can be clearly distinguished from the other fluctuations in that they are usually *larger, longer,* and *more widely diffused.* Seasonal movements typically run their course within a year; most isolated random events also have repercussions of similar or shorter duration. Thus it is business cycles that usually dominate changes in the economy over spans of several years, just as seasonal and other shorter variations dominate many changes over spans of a few weeks or a few months. The developments across decades are, to be sure, primarily the work of forces of secular growth—rising population, labor force, and physical capital, as well as gains in productivity attributable to technological, educational, and organizational improvements. However, business cycles and long trends can and do interact in varied and subtle ways (about which more later).

A succinct definition of business cycles, first formulated in the 1920s and revised in the 1940s, runs as follows:

> Business cycles are a type of fluctuation found in the aggregate economic activity of nations that organize their work mainly in business enterprises: a cycle consists of expansions occurring at about the same time in many economic activities, followed by similarly general recessions, contractions, and revivals which merge into the expansion phase of the next cycle; the sequence of changes is recurrent but not periodic; in duration business cycles vary from more than one year to ten or twelve years; they are not divisible into shorter cycles of similar character with amplitudes approximating their own.[2]

This working definition, in substantially its present form, has been in use at the National Bureau of Economic Research for over fifty years and is currently employed by the NBER to identify and date the United States business cycle. These dates are widely accepted by government,

1. The term "cycles" is often applied to measurable and recurrent but nonperiodic fluctuations in sciences other than economics, as noted by Wesley Mitchell, who refers to sunspot cycles that "varied in length from 7 to 17 years since 1788" (see his introduction to Thorp 1926, 32–33).

2. Burns and Mitchell 1946, 1; for the earlier version, see Mitchell 1927, 468.

academic, and business analysts. The definition served as the basis for the NBER's pre–World War II business cycle chronologies for England, France, and Germany as well as the United States. With a modest adjustment to allow activity to be measured relative to its long-run trend, the definition has been used to develop "growth cycle" chronologies for many countries. It has surely passed a severe test of time, considering all the far-reaching changes in the structure of modern industrialized economies and the character of contemporary business cycles.

The concept of "aggregate economic activity" is purposely vague, yielding to the recognition that what matters is the evolution over time of a vector of many diverse activities that are not readily reducible to any single aggregate.[3] The reasons are in part economic: for example, in times past when prices fluctuated cyclically around a relatively stable level, GNP in current dollars was often a more sensitive indicator than GNP in constant dollars; but in the recent era of long-persisting inflation the opposite is generally the case. Business cycles involve multidimensional processes, in which quantities and prices, stocks and flows, outputs and inputs, real, monetary, and financial variables all tend to participate, albeit with many timing and amplitude differentials and at varying rates. The definition properly stresses that the expansions and contractions occur with rough synchronism in "many economic activities" (and, we would add, in a fair number of activities generally regarded as "noneconomic" as well). The high cyclical conformity or coherence of numerous variables, that is, the wide diffusion or pervasiveness of business cycles, was and remains their common and most salient characteristic.

Statistical considerations are also important in this context. It is simply a fact that no single comprehensive measure of the nation's economic activity is available monthly or quarterly for a long historical period. Whether the aggregates refer to output, income, expenditures, or employment, they individually lack sufficient comparability of coverage and sufficient solidity of estimation over long stretches of time. It seems best therefore to rely on the evidence from a number of comprehensive indicators rather than any single one. Particular attention needs to be paid to the comovement of the economic variables, taking account of any systematic timing differences among them. This

---

3. The term itself entered the definition in 1946; in Mitchell 1913 and 1927 there is less apparent emphasis on overall aggregates and more on the collective concept of "a species of fluctuations in the economic activities of organized communities" or in "activities which are systematically conducted on a commercial basis" (1927, 488). The development of the national income and product accounts between 1927 and 1946 is of course highly relevant here.

also helps to reduce the risk of drawing erroneous inferences from data containing measurement errors and biases owing to changes in the quality of the information.

In addition to being pervasive, business cycles are also persistent; that is, the expansions and contractions are congeries of serially correlated as well as cross-correlated movements in many activities. The requirement that business cycles not be "divided into shorter cycles of similar character with amplitudes approximating their own" has in practice meant that no rise or decline in aggregate output, employment, and such is recognized as a cyclical movement unless it is at least as large as the smallest expansion or contraction in the historical record. Beyond that, no quantitative specifications are imposed upon either the amplitude or the scope of the cycles.

The only numerical limits mentioned refer to the duration of a full cycle (expansion and contraction), and they are broad: from more than a year to ten or twelve years. Thus the range of admissible fluctuations is wide, accommodating short and long, weak and strong cycles. There is no recognition of any systematic distinctions in these respects: unlike some other contemporary scholars (Schumpeter 1939; Hansen 1941, 1951; R. A. Gordon 1952), Burns and Mitchell (1946, chaps. 10 and 11) found no cogent reasons to differentiate a priori between "minor" and "major" or between "Kitchin" and "Juglar" cycles. However, this is a case of suspended judgment, not a definitive conclusion. Important differences clearly exist. For example, inventory investment plays a central role in the short "Kitchin" cycles, whereas fixed capital investment is more instrumental in the longer "Juglar" cycles. But such distinctions, and more generally all considerations of causality, are viewed as matters to be treated in further research, not as parts of a tentatively accepted definition. The long waves of fifty to sixty years hypothesized by Kondratieff in 1926 are quite different phenomena whose precise nature, and even existence, has not yet been widely accepted. Schumpeter's 1935 hypothesis that each such long wave contains six Juglar cycles of from nine to ten years' duration, while every Juglar is divisible into three Kitchin cycles of roughly forty months each, has also failed to be validated.

Burns and Mitchell make it clear that by their definition a mere slowing down or cessation of growth is not enough to qualify as a business cycle contraction: what is required is an absolute fall in "aggregate economic activity." Note, however, that this requirement has been modified in the recent work on "growth cycles." The rise and fall is not restricted to some limited measure of economic activity, for example, production in manufacturing or corporate profits, sufficient to define a business cycle: the latter must be clearly reflected in economywide aggregates of output and employment. Moreover, contractions as well as expansions are taken to be *cumulative* movements, which implies that they cannot be very short. Historical evidence indicates, for example, that a decline of less than six months could not reach the dimensions that would qualify it as a cyclical contraction, in particular a state in which a majority of industries experience falling demand (new orders or sales), production, and employment.

2. Early Views and Developments

Business cycles must be strictly distinguished from the various "crises" associated with foreign and civil wars, epidemics, bad harvests, earthquakes, isolated and transient monetary disorders, speculative "manias," and other episodic or random disturbances. Such events, whether due to acts of nature or of man, can disrupt the ordinary rhythm of economic life and cause much distress at any time, and they did so for ages under all forms of social organization. In contrast, business cycles, as defined above, "are found only in modern nations where economic activities are organized mainly through business enterprises and where individuals enjoy considerable freedom in producing, pricing, trading, and saving or investing" (Burns 1968, 228).

In the early literature on the subject, business cycles were often viewed as the natural way growth takes in modern capitalist economies. The latter have achieved historically unprecedented records of long-term development, for example, approximately fivefold gains in output per capita in the United States, France, and Germany.[4] Private enterprise thrived on and fostered advances in science and technology by seeking higher profits in surges of innovative investment. There was increasing division and specialization of labor as new techniques were introduced, new markets opened, new products discovered. Inevitably, this was associated with various frictions, difficult adjustments, and costly resource transfers in response to the (in large part unanticipated) shifts in demands and supplies.

Over decades, fairly smooth rising trends in population and labor force and much faster growth in the stock of reproducible capital can be broadly documented.[5] Improvements from the progress of knowl-

4. In the periods 1834–43 to 1963–67, 1831–40 to 1963–66, and 1850–59 to 1963–67, respectively. In the older developed countries of Europe and in Japan, population almost tripled and total output increased by a factor of at least fifteen over a century. These growth rates are far greater than those that can reasonably be assigned to earlier eras. See Kuznets 1971, 10–33 and 303–5; also, U.S. Department of Commerce, Bureau of the Census 1973.

5. For the United States between 1869 and 1955, for example, the net capital stock per member of the labor force is estimated to have grown at least 14% per decade, according to Kuznets 1971, 64–67. (This covers not only the very large component of business plant and equipment, but also housing, inventories, and claims against foreign countries.)

edge, new technologies, and new skills kept raising the *quality* and marginal productivity of human and tangible capital. This was sufficient to prevent a downward trend in the profitability of new investment that would otherwise have resulted, under the law of diminishing marginal returns, from the growing abundance of physical capital relative to labor and the nonreproducible natural resources.[6] Over shorter periods, however, profit totals, margins, and rates were continually undergoing large fluctuations induced by movements in sales, in product prices relative to wages and costs of materials and finance, in investment, and in the demand for and supply of credit. In turn, the rise and fall of profits, cash flow, and rates of return caused parallel movements in expectations of future profitability and hence in business decisions concerning production, employment, and investment. Changes in money and credit interacted with these general changes in economic expectations and activity.

To be sure, this is merely a brief, rough sketch of some trends in the classic era of industrialization, economic growth, and business cycles that originated about two hundred years ago in Britain and spread worldwide in the past century. Some observers placed more stress on real factors: cyclical innovations and growth spurts, recurrent overinvestment, imbalances between production of capital and consumer goods, intersectoral shifts. Others emphasized monetary processes: changes in the supply of bank credit, discrepancies between market and equilibrium interest rates. Still others paid special attention to the role of uncertainty and failure of foresight, interdependent expectations, and waves of errors of optimism and pessimism. Finally, the focus on cyclical changes in relative prices and profits is also compatible with important roles being played by other real forces as well as monetary and expectational variables. But it is generally correct to see the early theories of business cycles as mainly endogenous, that is, concentrating on the internal relations of the economic system rather than on the effects of external shocks; as multicausal, that is, concerned with interactions of the real, monetary, and expectational factors; and as dynamic, that is, incorporating elements of long-term growth into the analysis of short-term instability.[7]

The historical setting of business cycle phenomena suggests that they developed gradually along with the growing interdependence within

---

6. For a discerning discussion of the nature and working of this process, see Fellner 1956, esp. chaps. 4 and 8.

7. The characterizations above apply broadly to most of the principal contributors to the literature on business cycles in the period between the 1890s and the 1930s: Tugan-Baranovskii, Bouniatian, Aftalion, Pigou, Hawtrey, Robertson, Mitchell, Spiethoff, Schumpeter, and Hayek. For a review and references, see Haberler 1964 (originally published 1937).

and among the modern capitalist economies. The processes and institutions that mark this evolution include the buildup of fixed capital in progressively mechanized production requiring new sources of labor, energy, and materials; lessening of barriers to trade through advances in transportation and communications; and the spread of money transactions, banking and credit, and investment finance. As these factors moved the market economies of the Western world onto higher levels of economic interdependence, strongly diffused and persistent business fluctuations emerged where disjointed acts of nature and man-made disturbances had previously held sway. Since Juglar (1862) it has been widely recognized that the acute financial crises that happened from time to time are merely transitory events that cannot be well understood in isolation from the major problem of recurrent sequences of general expansions and contractions. Between 1894 and 1927, most of the leading scholars in the field (Tugan-Baranovskii, Aftalion, Mitchell, Spiethoff, Schumpeter) strongly endorsed and elaborated the conception of business cycles as a characteristic motion of the development of modern capital creating, money exchange, market oriented economies.

The dating of the earliest business cycles is imprecise and impeded by severe limitations of the available data. Schumpeter (1939, vol. 1, chap. 6.B, esp. pp. 223–24, 248–52) argued that capitalism goes "as far back as the element of credit creation" and that "there must have been also prosperities and depressions of the cyclical type" in the seventeenth and eighteenth centuries. But he concedes to the critics of this view that wars, poor harvests, and other "noncyclical catastrophies" played a much greater role in the preindustrialization era than in the cycles of the later period.[8]

A reference chronology of cyclical turning points for eighteenth-century England has been compiled from fragmentary but carefully assembled and explained chronicles and data by T. S. Ashton (1959), and some of his results are summed up in table A.1. Bad harvests occurred frequently, causing shortages for small farmers who produced grain mainly for themselves and their livestock and depressing real wages of industrial workers, the demand for textiles and other manufactured products, and output of commodities subject to excise duties. Government revenue would fall at the same time as the costs of provisions for the navy and army rose. The resulting deficits tended to raise the costs of borrowing and to decrease public confidence. More grain had to be imported at high prices, adversely affecting the balance of payments and the domestic supply of credit. Large farmers may

---

8. Schumpeter 1939, 1:224–25, refers to Mitchell and Spiethoff as having a "strong aversion to admitting that we may speak of cycles . . . before the end of the eighteenth century," while others, historians among them, do not hesitate to go far beyond that."

Table A.1   Economic Fluctuations in England, 1700–1802

Trough	Peak	Financial Crisis	Poor Harvest, Short Supplies of Grain	War
1700	1701	February–March 1701		War of the Spanish Succession since 1701
1702	1704	October–December 1704		
1706	1708	August–December 1710	1708–9	Victories in 1703–4, reverses in 1705
1712	1714	July–December 1715		Peace 1714
1716	1717–18	March 1719; August–December 1720		War with Spain, August 1718–20
1722	1724–25	October–December 1726	1725–26	Abolition of duties on British exports, 1722
1727	1728		1728–29	New War with Spain, 1727–29
1730	1733	October–December 1733		
1734	1738		1740–41	
1742	1743			
1746	1746	September 1745–April 1746		War with France, 1744–48
1748	1751			
1755	1761	June–December 1761	1757–58	Seven Years War, 1756–63
1763	1764	July–October 1763	1767–68	
1769	1771–72	June 1772–January 1773	1773–75	
1775	1777	January–April 1778		United States War of Independence 1776
1781	1783	September 1783–January 1784	1782–84	Franco-Spanish cooperation against British 1778–81; peace 1783
1784	1787	May–June 1788	1788–90	
1789	1792	November 1792–April 1793		
1794	1796	February–June 1797	1796–98	War with France, 1793–1802
1798	1799	August–November 1799	1799–1800	
1800	1802			

Source: Ashton 1959; see pp. 172–73 for cols. 1–3, chap. 2 for col. 4, and chap. 3 for col. 5.

have benefited from higher grain prices, but overall the bad consequences prevailed.

Although Britain fought her wars on the seas or on alien soil, they were recurrent, protracted, and often associated with other disasters such as epidemics and famines. They had large but mixed effects on overall economic activity, since the extent to which they curtailed civilian consumption or increased production varied greatly, as did the extent to which they were financed by taxation versus loans. The periods of decline, as dated by Ashton, lasted longer on average than the periods of growth.

In sum, weather and wars seem to account for much of the fluctuation in economic fortunes before the industrial revolution of the 1780s in Britain. But endogenous economic and financial processes played an increasingly important role as well. Bank notes and commercial paper provided an elastic supply of means of payment. Speculation in commodities and securities spread in prosperous times, and financial crises accompanied or followed most of the peak dates (Ashton 1959, chap. 5). Longer building cycles also persisted (ibid., chap. 4, and Lewis 1965). Rostow (1980, 37–38) compares the effects of bad harvests on real incomes and the balance of payments to the effects of oil price rises in 1973–74 and 1979 and the associated "supply side recessions" in the United States and elsewhere. It is interesting that the Ashton dates suggest a sequence of sixteen "cycles" with durations concentrated heavily between three and six years and averaging about five years (whether measured from trough to trough or from peak to peak). This is very close to the average length of the twenty-eight cycles identified in Great Britain in the NBER chronology for 1792–1932 (fifty-nine or sixty months; see Burns and Mitchell 1946, 371).

3.   Business Annals, Historical Statistics, and Reference Dates

The first step the National Bureau of Economic Research took toward identifying historical business cycles shortly after its founding in 1920 was to compile comprehensive chronological records of changes in general economic conditions in the United States and England (1790–1925), France (1840–1925), Germany (1853–1925), Austria (1867–1925), and twelve other countries (1890–1925). These "business annals" were based on detailed studies of a large collection of official documents, reports by contemporary observers and students of economic history, periodicals, pamphlets, and books. The resulting volume by Willard Thorp (1926) lists several hundred sources. This was a major effort to extract year-by-year information on the spread, timing, duration, and intensity of past business fluctuations in the "great commercial nations," both old and new.

A second NBER project, also started in the early 1920s, was to collect statistical time series data on a variety of pertinent aspects of modern economies and subject them to a systematic analysis. These materials are more massive yet, and they are obviously necessary as a basis for more precise quantitative results as well as to check the inferences from the business annals. However, it is also useful to check the inferences from the statistical data with the aid of the reports of contemporary observers and other documents underlying the annals. In short, the two collections of materials provide evidence that is to a large extent complementary.

The time series cover shorter periods than the annals and are limited to four countries: the United States, England, France, and Germany. The available statistical record shrinks rapidly as one goes back into the 1800s, and the series extending to the earliest decades covered by the British and United States business annals are very scanty. The early data are predominantly annual, and their coverage and quality leave much to be desired. This makes the business annals indispensable for the study of the more distant past. Their materials enabled Thorp and the NBER staff to characterize each successive year covered according to the business conditions that prevailed. They called the generally good and bad times "prosperity" and "depression," respectively, and the generally shorter upper and lower transition periods "recessions" and "revivals," often attaching to these terms such adjectives as "brief," "slow," "rapid," "mild," "moderate," or "severe." Frequently the recessions and revivals were dated more closely within a year by such designations as "early" or "late," or even by months or seasons. Thus a single year would occasionally be classified into more than one of the four basic cycle phases.[9]

Although business annals and indexes of general economic activity may differ with respect to the mix of the processes covered, measurement errors, and so on, Mitchell (1927, 20–31) presents evidence of a generally close agreement between the two approaches on the fluctuations in the United States, 1875–1925, and in England, 1855–1914. Even for the earlier cycles, back to 1796, there is a fairly good correspondence between the recession dates based on the annals and those based on statistical series (mainly wholesale commodity prices).[10]

Table A.2 compares the annual reference dates for the British and United States business cycles between 1790 and 1858, as estimated by Thorp from annals (United States through 1833) and by Burns and Mitchell from annals and time series studies. A close correspondence

9. In addition to these aggregate characteristics, the annals also provide brief references to conditions in the main industries, markets, or sectors of each economy in year.

10. For a compilation of early data on United States business cycles, see Smith and Cole 1935, 3–84.

between the cycles in the two countries is indicated. Eight of the peak and three of the trough dates coincide. The degree of synchronization is particularly high for the (more precisely determined) dates of financial crises, in 1815, 1825, 1836–37, 1847, and 1857. The business annals for other countries available for the later period reinforce the finding that many cycles had an international sweep, as do the more recent and statistically firmer NBER chronologies for the United States, England, France, and Germany (see below). This again applies especially to the major cycles, which were often accompanied by financial crises or panics, as in 1873, 1893, 1907, and 1929.

According to the annual chronologies in table A.2, the durations of business cycles in this era comprising seven decades of the rise of modern capitalism and industrialization averaged about four and a half years in both Great Britain and the United States, whether measured from trough to trough or from peak to peak. The standard deviations of these estimates are close to two years. Most contractions did not exceed one or two years. Five of the fourteen identified cycles in either country fall into the early turbulent period of almost continuous wars that ended in 1815.

4. Monthly Business Cycle Chronologies: Problems and Procedures

For the United States and Britain since 1854, for France since 1865, and for Germany since 1879, sufficient evidence could be assembled by the NBER to permit estimation of monthly, as well as quarterly and annual, reference chronologies of business cycles. The work involved a painstaking collective effort. Burns and Mitchell (1946, 80) credit Kuznets for taking "a leading part in the preparation of the original set of reference dates" and Abramovitz, Moore, Shiskin, Garvy, and Walt Rostow, among others, for help in extending, revising, or criticizing the dates.

Before presenting and discussing the results (in the next section), we need to consider the main problems encountered in this research and the methods adopted to overcome them. The lack of a single sufficiently long and consistent measure of aggregate economic activity has already been noted. There is no doubt that no time series exists to fill this role for any country. This applies even to the recent periods covered by the quarterly data on national income and product accounts, as we will argue later. In any case, for the years before World War II these series are fragmentary and not very dependable.

In constructing their "reference scales" of business cycles after World War I, the NBER team could draw on monthly series of production in manufacturing and mining and of the number of factory employees. Before World War I, however, these data have a slender sampling basis

Table A.2   **Annual Reference Dates and Duration of Business Cycles in Great Britain and the United States, 1790–1858**

Dates of Peaks and Troughs by Years		Duration in Years			
		Contraction	Expansion	Full Cycle	
Trough (T)	Peak (P)	(P to T)	(T to P)	(T to T)	(P to P)
(1)	(2)	(3)	(4)	(5)	(6)
Great Britain					
	1792				
1793	1796	1	3		4
1797	1802	1	5	4	6
1803	1806	1	3	6	4
1808	1810	2	2	5	4
1811	1815	1	4	3	5
1816	1818	1	2	5	3
1819	1825	1	6	3	7
1826	1828	1	2	7	3
1829	1831	1	2	3	3
1832	1836	1	4	3	5
1837	1839	1	2	5	3
1842	1845	3	3	5	6
1848	1854	3	6	6	9
1855	1857	1	2	7	3
1858		1		3	
Mean duration (years)		1.3	3.3	4.6	4.6
Standard deviation (years)		0.7	1.5	1.5	1.8
United States					
1790	1796		6		
1799	1802	3	3	9	6
1804	1807	2	3	5	5
1810	1812[a]	3	1.5	6	4.5
1812[a]	1815	0.5	3	2	3.5
1821	1822	6	1	9	7
1823	1825	1	2	2	3
1826	1828	1	2	3	3
1829	1833	1	4	3	5
1834	1836	1	2	5	3
1838	1839	2	1	4	3
1843	1845	4	2	5	6
1846	1847	1	1	3	2
1848	1853	1	5	2	6
1855		2		7	
Mean duration (years)		2	2.6	4.6	4.4
Standard deviation (years)		1.5	1.5	2.4	1.6

Source: Great Britain: Burns and Mitchell 1946, table 16, p. 79; United States: 1790–1833, Thorp 1926, 113–26; 1834–55, Burns and Mitchell 1946, table 16, p. 78.

[a]In 1812 there is first a "brief recession," then a revival. The corresponding duration measures are based on the assumption that the recession occurred in the first half of the year, before the outbreak of the war with England (for evidence, see Thorp 1926, 42, 117).

and leave much to be desired. The series on bank clearings, wholesale prices, and interest rates are much longer. Historically, their cyclical sensitivity tended to be high, and the researchers found them on the whole very useful. Much reliance was placed, too, on a variety of indexes of business conditions, mostly in physical terms.

In sum, the historical records decrease in both volume and reliability when pushed back into the past. In general they are more satisfactory for the United States than for the foreign countries, but the reverse is true in a few cases involving the data for unemployment and interest rates (Burns and Mitchell 1946, 73–76).

Given the limitations of the individual indicators, the task of identifying and dating the historical business cycles required the analysis of both the voluminous business annals and numerous time series covering diverse activities. Before deciding *when* a peak (trough) occurred, it is necessary to determine *whether* the expansion (contraction) is of cyclical dimensions. To ascertain the critical characteristics of the scope and size of the economy's movement, there was no alternative to the laborious procedure of extracting common signals from the noisy indications of fallible data on a whole range of economic processes. This remains true even today when much better and more comprehensive cyclical indicator statistics are available, because the diffusion aspect of business cycles is as important as ever. It is still true as well, despite the great improvement in the data, that measurement errors are mostly unknown but often large. A careful comparative analysis of interrelated but independently derived time series can help reduce the effects of such errors on a business cycle chronology.

The working definition of business cycles cited above implies that peaks and troughs of time series representing a broad array of economic processes are not randomly interspersed but form alternating clusters. The clusters of peaks and troughs typically extend over many months, but it is also true that as a rule they show rather definite points of concentration (see, e.g., Moore 1961, chart 7-3 and pp. 196–202). These dates, around which most of the series reach their highest (lowest) local levels, indicate roughly the timing of the peaks (troughs) in the otherwise not observable "aggregate economic activity."

Of course, some series deserve more attention than others because they are more comprehensive, more significant economically, more adequate statistically, or more reliable with respect to their cyclical timing and conformity characteristics. Some series such as unemployment tend to rise in contractions and fall in expansions, hence they must be used in inverted form. Some series such as new orders for capital goods and construction contracts rise and fall early; others such as the volumes of business inventories and loans typically move late; still others move early at peaks and late at troughs, or vice versa. These systematic differences in behavior, once known, can and should be taken into account in identifying and dating the generalized expansions and contractions—often by excluding them from the sample of series used in the procedure.

It should be clear that the monthly or quarterly dates of business cycle turns are of necessity uncertain estimates. No high degree of precision is generally possible here; the best achievable result is a chronology that is well supported by the most pertinent evidence one can obtain. But this is also a major result and worth much effort. A well-designed and well-tested chronology is a valuable tool in the analysis and understanding of business cycle phenomena, some of which at least are of prime interest to macroeconomic theory and policy. A common reference scale has many practical uses, one of them being to confer the advantage of economies of scale on the handling of large numbers of contemporaneous time series. As Burns and Mitchell said (1946, 70–71), "If our analysis were restricted to a few time series, it would be simple to compare their specific cycles directly. But when the analysis covers hundreds of series, it is clumsy and wasteful to compare the timing of each series with every other; indeed, as clumsy and wasteful as it would be to express the exchange value of each commodity in terms of every other commodity." Other analytical uses of the business cycle chronologies, for international comparisons and the measurement of relative durations, amplitudes, and spread of cyclical movements, are illustrated below (fig. A.1 and tables A.4, A.6, and A.7).

5. The NBER Business Cycle Chronologies for 1854–1938

Table A.3 shows the monthly, quarterly, and annual lists of reference dates compiled by the NBER for the periods before World War II. The bulk of this information comes from Burns and Mitchell, as cited. Only a few of the dates, all referring to the United States cycles in 1919–38, were subsequently changed in light of additional and revised data. The resulting shifts were small: two dates were shifted by one month, and two were shifted by two months.

The quarterly and annual dates are necessary for working with time series cast in the corresponding time units, in particular where monthly data are not available, but the monthly dates are basic since only they permit observation of cyclical behavior in the essential detail (Burns and Mitchell 1946, 80–81). Hence the monthly dates control the others and should be given preference and used wherever possible.

If the monthly choice falls in the middle month of the quarter, that quarter is always taken as the quarterly reference date. If it falls on the first or third month, the quarterly turn is placed either in the quarter containing the reference month or in the quarter adjacent to that month, according to the indications of a sample of important economic series measured by quarters (including monthly data converted to quarterly).

Annual records alone are a poor guide to dating, since they obscure some mild and short business cycles. Phases of twelve months or less that overlap two calendar years (mostly contractions) have been frequent, particularly in the United States since the 1870s. Independent annual dating can miss the short business cycles and combine two or even three of them into one, while producing only a rough one-to-one correspondence with the longer cycles in the monthly chronology. There is ample statistical evidence that this is a serious measurement problem (Burns and Mitchell 1946, chap. 6, esp. 262). Hence the adopted procedure is to set monthly reference dates first and then make the annual ones match them as well as possible. However, the annual turns are intended to identify the years in which the overall activity in the economy reached a high or a low point, and these years need not always coincide with those in which the corresponding *monthly* peaks or troughs fall. When the monthly date occurs early in the year t, the annual date may well be the year $t - 1$; similarly, when the monthly turn is late, the annual one will often be the year $t + 1$.

According to these chronologies, business cycles have indeed been recurrent but not periodic in each of the countries covered. Contractions ranged from 7 to 65 months in the United States, 6 to 81 months in Britain, 8 to 68 months in France, and 12 to 61 months in Germany. The corresponding ranges for expansion are 10 to 50, 8 to 64, 8 to 62, and 16 to 61 months. The shortest full-cycle durations (measured from peak to peak or from trough to trough) are 17 months for the United States and Great Britain, 24 months for France, and 34 months for Germany; the longest are 101, 135, 110, and 122 months, respectively.

However, these measures are based on rare outliers; there is considerably more of a central tendency among business cycles than they suggest. For example, declines lasting from 10 months to 2 years account for 67% (43 out of 64) of the business contractions recorded in table A.3. Expansions lasting 1½ to 3½ years represent 66% (42 out of 64) of all observations in this category. Full cycles lasting 2½ to 5½ years account for 64% (41 out of 64) of all cycles measured from trough to trough. These ranges contain half or more of the corresponding listings for each of the four countries covered.

It is important to note that business cycles have tended to be shorter in the United States than in the foreign countries. Thus the period 1854–1938 witnessed twenty-one United States cycles averaging four years and only sixteen British cycles averaging 5⅓ years. For 1879–1938, the comparison is as follows:

Table A.3   Business Cycle Chronologies and Durations to 1938

| | Dates of Peaks and Troughs | | | | Duration in Months | | | |
| | By Months and Quarters | | By Calendar Years | | | | Full Cycle | |
Trough (T) (1)	Peak (P) (2)	Trough (T) (3)	Peak (P) (4)	Contraction (P to T) (5)	Expansion (T to P) (6)	T to T (7)	P to P (8)
		United States, 1854–1938					
December 1854:4	June 1857:2	1855	1856	18	30		
December 1858:4	October 1860:2	1858	1860	8	22	48	40
June 1861:3	April 1865:1	1861	1864	32	46	30	54
December 1867:1	June 1869:2	1867	1869	18	18	78	50
December 1870:4	October 1873:3	1870	1873	18	34	36	52
March 1879:1	March 1882:1	1878	1882	65	36	99	101
May 1885:2	March 1887:2	1885	1887	38	22	74	60
April 1888:1	July 1890:3	1888	1890	13	27	35	40
May 1891:2	January 1893:1	1891	1892	10	20	37	30
June 1894:2	December 1895:4	1894	1895	17	18	37	35
June 1897:2	June 1899:3	1896	1899	18	24	36	42
December 1900:4	September 1902:4	1900	1903	18	21	42	39
August 1904:3	May 1907:2	1904	1907	23	33	44	56
June 1908:2	January 1910:1	1908	1910	13	19	46	32
January 1912:4	January 1913:1	1911	1913	24	12	43	32
December 1914:4	August 1918:3	1914	1918	23	44	35	67
March 1919:1	January 1920:1	1919	1920	7	10	51	17
July 1921:3	May 1923:2	1921	1923	18	22	28	40
July 1924:3	October 1926:3	1924	1926	14	27	36	41
November 1927:4	August 1929:3	1927	1929	13	21	40	34
March 1933:1	May 1937:2	1932	1937	43	50	64	93
June 1938:2		1938		13		63	
		Averages					
Twenty-one cycles, 1854–1938							
Mean duration (months)				21	26	48	48
Standard deviation (months)				14	11	18	20
Thirty-five cycles, 1790–1938[a]							
Mean duration (months)				23	28	50	50
Standard deviation (months)				16	14	24	20

Great Britain, 1854–1938

December 1854/55:1	September 1857:4	1855	1857	6	33	39	36
March 1858:1	September 1860:4	1858	1860	27	30	57	66
December 1862:4	March 1866:2	1862	1866	24	39	63	78
March 1868:2	September 1872:4	1868	1873	81	54	135	123
June 1879:2	December 1882:1	1879	1883	42	42	84	93
June 1886:2	September 1890:3	1886	1890	53	51	104	117
February 1895:1	June 1900:3	1894	1900	15	64	79	36
September 1901:4	June 1903:2	1901	1903	17	21	38	48
November 1904:4	June 1907:2	1904	1907	17	31	48	66
November 1908:4	December 1912:1	1908	1913	21	49	70	70
September 1914:3	October 1918:2	1914	1917	6	49	55	17
April 1919:2	March 1920:2	1919	1920	15	11	26	56
June 1921:2	November 1924:4	1921	1924	20	41	61	28
July 1926:3	March 1927:2	1926	1927	18	8	26	28
September 1928:3	July 1929:3	1928	1929	37	10	47	98
August 1932:3	September 1937:3	1932	1937	12	61	73	
September 1938:3		1938					

Averages

Sixteen cycles, 1854–1938
Mean duration (months)				26	37	63	64
Standard deviation (months)				19	18	29	33

Twenty-nine cycles, 1790–1938[a]
Mean Duration (months)				22	39	60	62
Standard deviation (months)				16	18	24	28

Table A.3 (continued)

	Dates of Peaks and Troughs				Duration in Months			
By Months and Quarters		By Calendar Years			Contraction	Expansion	Full Cycle	
Trough (T)	Peak (P)	Trough (T)	Peak (P)		(P to T)	(T to P)	T to T	P to P
(1)	(2)	(3)	(4)		(5)	(6)	(7)	(8)

France, 1865–1938

Trough (T)	Peak (P)	Trough (T)	Peak (P)	Contraction (P to T)	Expansion (T to P)	T to T	P to P
December 1865	November 1867	1865	1866		23		33
October 1868	August 1870	1868	1869	11	22	34	37
February 1872	September 1873	1871	1873	18	19	40	55
August 1876	April 1878	1876	1878	35	20	54	44
September 1879	December 1881	1879	1882	17	27	37	109
August 1887	January 1891	1887	1890	68	41	95	110
January 1895:1	March 1900:1	1894	1900	48	62	89	38
September 1902:3	May 1903:2	1902	1903	30	8	92	50
October 1904:3	July 1907:3	1904	1907	17	33	25	71
February 1909:1	June 1913:3	1908	1913	19	52	52	60
August 1914:3	June 1918:2	1914	1917	14	46	66	27
April 1919:2	September 1920:3	1918	1920	10	17	56	49
July 1921:3	October 1924:3	1921	1924	10	39	27	24
June 1925:3	October 1926:3	1925	1926	8	16	47	41
June 1927:3	March 1930:1	1927	1930	8	33	24	40
July 1932:3	July 1933:3	1932	1933	28	12	61	47
April 1935:1	June 1937:2	1935	1937	21	26	33	
August 1938:3		1938		14		40	
Averages							
Mean duration (months)				22	29	51	52
Standard deviation (months)				16	15	23	25

Germany, 1879–1932

February 1879:1	January 1882:1	1878	1882		35		
August 1886:3	January 1890:1	1886	1890	55	41	90	96
February 1895:1	March 1900:2	1894	1900	61	61	102	122
March 1902:1	August 1903:3	1902	1903	24	17	85	41
February 1905:1	July 1907:2	1904	1907	18	29	35	47
December 1908:4	April 1913:1	1908	1913	17	52	46	69
August 1914:3	June 1918:2	1914	1917	16	46	68	62
June 1919:2	May 1922:2	1919	1922	12	35	58	47
November 1923:4	March 1925:2	1923	1925	18	16	53	34
March 1926:2	April 1929:2	1926	1929	12	37	28	49
August 1932:3		1932		40		77	
Averages							
Mean duration (months)				27	37	64	63
Standard deviation (months)				18	14	24	29

Source: National Bureau of Economic Research.

Note: For a basic statement of the method of determining business cycle peaks and troughs, see Burns and Mitchell 1946, chap. 4. Some of the dates shown there (p. 78) have been revised.

aCombines the observations in table A.2 for 1790–1855 (converted from annual to monthly durations) with observations in this table for the subsequent cycles through 1938.

	United States	Great Britain	France	Germany
Number of cycles (trough to trough)	17	13	14	10
Mean duration (months)	48	65	53	64

Figure A.1 uses a schematic form to compare the timing of business cycle peaks and troughs in the four countries. It suggests a fairly high overall degree of correspondence between the chronologies, as shown by the following summary.

	Peaks		Troughs	
	Number	Percent	Number	Percent
Matched turns				
All four countries	44	62	48	64
Three countries	18	25	18	24
Two countries	2	3	2	3
Unmatched turns	7	10	7	9
Total	71	100	75	100

A closer look at the diagram makes it clear that much of the time, notably during the four decades 1879–1919, the conformity between the business cycles in the three European countries was very close, while the United States followed a different pattern of shorter and more frequent fluctuations. In the earlier years the movements were generally less synchronized, in part because of the annual dating for France and Germany. In the 1920s and 1930s, the European countries were much less in phase with each other than in the preceding forty years, but the degree of conformity between their cycles and those in the United States increased.[11]

6. On the Dependability of Historical Reference Dates

In the early United States business cycles, the average length of contractions was close to that of expansions, whereas more recently expansions have become much longer. This is clearly so according to the following measures of mean duration of the cyclical phases dated by the NBER.

11. Cf. Morgenstern 1959, chap. 2, for a discussion of the international timing of business cycles, 1879–1938.

	1834–55	1857–82	1885–99	1900–1918	1919–37	1948–82
Number of cycles	5	5	5	5	5	8
Expansion, months ($\bar{E}$)	26	31	22	26	26	45
Contraction, months ($\bar{C}$)	24	28	19	20	19	11
Ratio, $\bar{E}/\bar{C}$	1.1	1.1	1.2	1.3	1.4	4.1

Fluctuations of trend-adjusted aggregates in the post–World War II period show alternating phases of high and low growth that have similar durations (e.g., in 1948–75 for the United States, these phases lasted on the average twenty and eighteen months, respectively). In such "growth cycles" (see section 8 below) the near symmetry is persistent and understandable because the fluctuations are measured from a long-run upward trend laid flat, as it were; that is, the growth element is eliminated. In contrast, the secular trend is retained in the measurement of business cycles as defined by the NBER, so that stages of less than average but positive growth are included in expansions and only the periods of sufficiently large and broad *absolute declines* qualify as contractions.

Accordingly, one might expect business cycle expansions to be significantly longer than contractions on the average over long periods of economic development. If so, one might also be somewhat surprised by, and suspicious of, the near equality of the early $\bar{E}$ and $\bar{C}$ measures listed above.

These views are not compelling: conceivably, the averages could reflect the dominance of lengthy periods of slow decline among the contractions and of short periods of rapid growth among the expansions. But it is also possible that some of the historical reference dates refer to growth cycles rather than business cycles, that is, that some of the phases designated as actual declines in the overall economic activity represent merely phases of low (less than the trend) growth rates. The limitations of data available for the identification of the early cycles, and the consequent reliance on business annals and selected indexes of business conditions, might well have produced a certain bias in this direction. This applies in particular to the period 1834–52, the segment of the NBER reference cycle chronology for which there are no comprehensive measures or indexes of economic activity without trend adjustments.

A partial reappraisal of the evidence for the United States confirms that generally the contractions in NBER chronology do represent cyclical declines in either real income and output, or money income and spending, or both the real and the nominal aggregates (Zarnowitz 1981). It is important to note that, historically, both groups of variables deserve a thorough consideration. In the recent era of inflation, the cycles

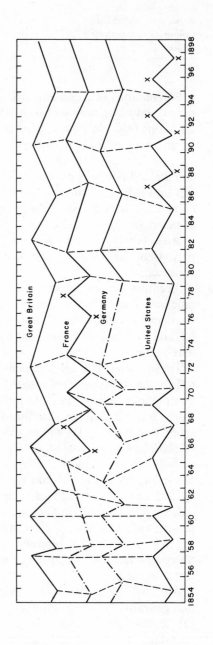

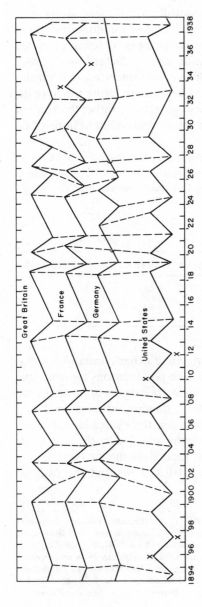

Fig. A.1 Timing of reference cycles for four countries and matched turning points, 1854–1938. For each country, the lines connect the dates of business cycle peaks (upper turning points) and troughs (lower turning points). Thus the upward-sloping segments of each country line represent expansions; the downward-sloping segments, contractions. The dashed links between the country lines connect the matched peaks or troughs for two or more countries. The sign x denotes an unmatched turn. For France before 1865 and for Germany before 1879, the reference dates are annual. They are plotted at midpoint of the given calendar year and connected with dashed and dotted lines. All other reference dates are monthly and are connected with solid lines. German annual turning points 1855–1963 estimated from Hoffman 1965 by Rostow 1980, 38–39. All other dates are from Burns and Mitchell 1946, 78–79.

are mainly in the real aggregates, but in the past, when the price level fluctuated and long periods of deflation occurred, the cycles were often more pronounced in the nominal aggregates.

Nevertheless, a few episodes are doubtful. All of these go back to the nineteenth century. (The 1918–19 and 1926–27 contractions have been questioned by some investigators, but there is sufficient evidence in favor of their inclusion.)[12] The most dubious is the 1845–46 phase, but 1869–70, 1887–97, and 1899–1900 are also uncertain. Given the limited information on hand, it seems impossible to refute the hypothesis that these were periods of below-average growth rather than actual delines. Fewer doubts attach to some other minor contractions (Zarnowitz 1981, 494–505).

If the four periods just listed were treated as growth cycle slowdowns instead of business cycle contractions, the differences between the $\bar{E}$ and $\bar{C}$ duration measures would be substantially increased. The tabulation below illustrates these effects.

	1834–55		1854–1919	
	Five Cycles	Four Cycles	Sixteen Cycles	Thirteen Cycles
Expansion, months ($\bar{E}$)	26	36	27	37
Contraction, months ($\bar{C}$)	24	27	22	23
Ratio, $\bar{E}/\bar{C}$	1.1	1.3	1.2	1.6

Comparisons of the NBER chronology and other chronologies disclose very few discrepancies and provide no good reasons for revisions (see references in note 12). Comparisons with indexes of business activity (both trend adjusted and, after 1882, unadjusted) also point to a very high degree of correspondence between the cycles identified by the NBER and the consensus of fluctuations revealed by the best available information from time series data. Indeed, in most cases there is a one-to-one agreement between the NBER dates and the cyclical turning points in these indexes.[13]

12. Eckler 1933 and Gilbert 1933 omit the 1918–19 contraction; Axe and Houghton 1931, Hubbard 1936, and Ayres 1939 omit the 1926–27 contraction. See Burns and Mitchell 1946, table 27 and pp. 107–10, for a comparison of the NBER chronology with these and two other independently compiled chronologies (Kitchin 1923 and Persons 1931). The available data indicate that 1918–19 is appropriately viewed as a sui generis end of the war recession along with the similar short 1945 episode. The 1926–27 recession is marginal but also supported by the preponderance of the evidence. See also Zarnowitz 1981, 504.

13. See Burns and Mitchell 1946, chart 10 and pp. 111–13, for the check provided by the "standard pattern of short-term fluctuations in American business activity" from Frickey 1942. Also see Zarnowitz 1981, tables 3 and 4 and pp. 494–504, for comparisons with several indexes of trade and industrial activity and deflated bank clearings.

Table A.4 provides some evidence on how well the United States chronology fits the cyclical movements in business activities phase by phase. It shows the percentages of series rising during each expansion and falling during each contraction for eighteen indicators of commercial and industrial activity (production, trade, orders, bank clearings) and twenty-eight indicators of prices and financial activity (commodity and security prices, interest rates, bonds and shares traded, business failures). The series that tend to move countercyclically are inverted, and allowance is made for fixed leads or lags—the timing characteristics of the indicators. The diffusion measures are predominantly high: about half of the phase percentages in columns 1–3 exceed 90, three-quarters exceed 80, and practically all exceed 50. However, the percentages tend to be higher for the series that rise during expansions than for those that decline during contractions (compare the entries in lines 1–20 and 30–49). The overall averages range from 80% to 97% (lines 25 and 54). Thus the represented variables are shown to have participated with substantial regularity in the successive business cycle expansions and contractions dated by the NBER, exhibiting a generally high level of cyclical conformity.

The diffusion ought to be positively correlated with the amplitude of cyclical fluctuations, that is, those movements that are more widely spread among the various sectors, industries, and processes of the economy would also be expected to be larger in terms of the most comprehensive measures of economic activity that are available. Table A.4 provides some evidence that this is indeed so. Here amplitudes are measured by the average of three trend-adjusted indexes of business activity that cover the entire period 1854–1933 (col. 4) and by the average of four indexes without trend adjustments that begin in the 1870s or later (col. 5). For either set of measures, the phases that rank higher according to the amplitudes tend to have larger diffusion, that is, higher proportions of series conforming with respect to the direction of the economy's movement (see the sections on "Averages," lines 21–29 and 50–58, in the table).

We conclude that the NBER historical reference dates of United States business cycles receive strong support from the phase-by-phase behavior of both the individual indicators and the weighted combinations of various time series (indexes of business activity). However, it is important to keep in mind the obvious fact that the chronologies cannot be made more reliable than the available information permits. The true cyclical movements in the economy at large cannot be observed directly without comprehensive, nonduplicative measures of aggregate economic activity, but it is only for the most recent decades that the required statistical data exist. The series used as proxies for such measures could either underestimate or overestimate the true

Table A.4   Measures of Diffusion and Amplitude of Business Cycles, United States, 1854–1933

Line Number	Business Cycle Expansion[a]	Percentage of Series Rising			Average Percentage Rise (Rank)	
		Commercial and Industrial Activity[b] (1)	Prices and Financial Activity[c] (2)	All Series Covered[d] (3)	Three Trend Adjusted Indexes[e] (4)	Four Indexes Not Adjusted for Trend[f] (5)
1	1854–57	100	67	75	12.3 (2)	
2	1858–60	100	86	88	16.8 (8)	
3	1861–65	100	89	90	18.1 (11)	
4	1867–69	100	67	79	6.9 (1)	
5	1870–73	88	60	72	18.4 (12)	
6	1879–82	100	93	97	27.6 (18)	58.1 (15)
7	1885–87	94	92	93	22.7 (14)	49.6 (11)
8	1888–90	100	55	76	16.6 (6)	34.2 (5)
9	1891–93	89	54	67	16.3 (5)	20.8 (1)
10	1894–95	100	75	85	25.3 (15)	37.6 (8)
11	1897–99	94	96	96	26.6 (17)	54.4 (13)
12	1900–1902	100	82	89	14.2 (4)	36.8 (7)
13	1904–7	100	96	98	20.2 (13)	45.8 (9)
14	1908–10	94	96	96	25.6 (16)	47.5 (10)
15	1912–13	100	86	91	13.6 (3)	24.0 (2)
16	1914–18	94	89	91	29.8 (19)	54.4 (12)
17	1919–20	100	89	93	17.9 (10)	30.9 (3)
18	1921–23	100	82	89	38.0 (20)	54.5 (14)
19	1924–26	100	71	83	17.8 (9)	34.5 (6)
20	1927–29	94	75	83	16.7 (7)	31.6 (4)

Averages

Line Number	Business Cycle Contraction[a]	Percentage of Series Declining			Average Percentage Decline (Rank)	
		Commercial and Industrial Activity[b] (1)	Prices and Financial Activity[c] (2)	All Series Covered[d] (3)	Three Trend Adjusted Indexes[e] (4)	Four Indexes Not Adjusted for Trend[f] (5)
1854–1929[g]						
21	Smallest (ranks 1–5)	98	71	80	12.7	
22	Ranks 6–10	99	75	85	17.2	
23	Ranks 11–15	96	82	88	20.9	
24	Largest (ranks 16–20)	96	91	94	29.5	
25	All	97	80	87	20.1	
1879–1929[h]						
26	Smallest (ranks 1–5)	97	71	82		28.3
27	Ranks 6–10	99	84	90		40.4
28	Largest (ranks 11–15)	96	90	93		54.2
29	All	97	82	88	21.9	41.0
30	1857–58	100	100	100	21.0 (10)	
31	1860–61	100	100	100	14.1 (6)	
32	1865–67	100	83	85	11.4 (4)	
33	1869–70	40	89	71	7.9 (1)	
34	1873–79	50	100	79	26.9 (15)	
35	1882–85	88	100	94	27.9 (16)	21.1 (11)
36	1887–88	89	68	78	11.2 (3)	10.2 (4)
37	1890–91	83	79	80	17.0 (9)	11.0 (5)
38	1893–94	94	100	98	30.7 (18)	28.8 (14)
39	1895–97	89	79	83	24.3 (14)	17.4 (8)
40	1899–1900	67	64	65	14.4 (7.5)	9.9 (3)

Table A.4 (continued)

		Percentage of Series Declining			Average Percentage Decline (Rank)	
Line Number	Business Cycle Contraction[a]	Commercial and Industrial Activity[b] (1)	Prices and Financial Activity[c] (2)	All Series Covered[d] (3)	Three Trend Adjusted Indexes[e] (4)	Four Indexes Not Adjusted for Trend[f] (5)
41	1902–4	94	79	85	14.4 (7.5)	14.8 (6)
42	1907–8	94	100	98	29.5 (17)	27.0 (12)
43	1910–12	78	82	80	12.0 (5)	8.4 (2)
44	1913–14	94	88	90	23.2 (13)	18.3 (9)
45	1918–19	83	57	67	22.0 (12)	18.6 (10)
46	1920–21	100	100	100	34.7 (19)	27.1 (13)
47	1923–24	83	94	89	21.8 (11)	17.0 (7)
48	1926–27	67	68	67	9.3 (2)	8.4 (1)
49	1929–33	100	100	100	75.1 (20)	
			Averages			
1857–1933[g]						
50	Smallest (ranks 1–5)	75	78	76	10.4	
51	Ranks 6–10	89	84	86	16.2	
52	Ranks 11–15	80	83	82	23.6	
53	Largest (ranks 16–20)	95	100	98	39.6	
54	All	85	86	85	22.4	
1882–1927[h]						
55	Smallest (ranks 1–5)	77	72	74		9.6
56	Ranks 6–10	89	87	83		17.2
57	Largest (ranks 11–14)	94	84	98		26.0
58	All	86	83	84	20.9	17.0

Sources: Cols. 1–3: Burns and Mitchell 1946, tables 23 and 24, pp. 102–3; cols. 4 and 8: Moore 1961, vol. 1, table 3.6, pp. 104–5; col. 5: Zarnowitz 1981, table 4, p. 500, based on NBER files. Number of series covered: col. 1, 17–18 (before 1879, eight or fewer); col. 2, 15–28 (before 1879, eleven or fewer); col. 3, 32–46 (before 1879, nineteen or fewer).

[a]Identified by years of turning points in the NBER monthly reference chronology (table 3).

[b]Includes ten indexes of general business activity, four series on orders for investment goods, two on production, and two on foreign trade. For details, see Burns and Mitchell 1946, table 21, pp. 98–99.

[c]Includes nine indexes of general or wholesale prices, six series on wholesale prices for individual commodities, nine series on volume of trade, prices, and yields in money and security markets, and four series on business failures. See Burns and Mitchell 1946, table 21, pp. 98–99.

[d]Includes the forty-six series in the groups in notes b and c.

[e]Since 1879, the figures are averages based on three seasonally and trend adjusted indexes: American Telephone and Telegraph Company index of business activity, index of industrial production and trade constructed by Warren M. Persons and continued by the Barron's Publishing Company, and Ayres's index of business activity compiled by the Cleveland Trust Company. Before 1879, the entries are for Ayres's index alone. The rise from the specific cycle trough to specific cycle peak in each index is taken as a percentage of the average level of the index during the full specific cycle (trough to trough), and the fall from specific peak to specific trough is taken as a percentage of the same base. The amplitude measures are ranked from smallest (1) to largest (20). Because the indexes are trend adjusted, the contraction amplitudes are approximately the same, on average, as the expansion amplitudes.

[f]The indexes, adjusted for seasonal variations but not for trends, are: (1) Bank clearings (1875–1918) and bank debits (1919–30). NBER data (Macaulay 1938, table 30, pp. A289–96) deflated by Carl Snyder's index of general price level; (2) Axe/Houghton index of trade and industrial activity (1879–1929) furnished by A. W. Axe and Company, New York; (3) Babson index of physical volume of business activity (1889–1929) furnished by Babson's Reports, Inc.; (4) American Telephone and Telegraph Company (1899–1929), Chief Statistician's Division (a confidential release, 6 September 1944). For details, see Zarnowitz 1981, 499–502.

[g]These expansions and contractions are divided into four groups according to the ranks recorded in col. 4: the mildest ones (ranks 1–5), the most vigorous or severe (ranks 16–20), and two intermediate groups. The entries are simple arithmetic means of the corresponding figures in the columns above.

[h]These expansions and contractions are divided into three groups according to the ranks recorded in col. 5: the mildest ones (ranks 1–5), the intermediate (ranks 6–10), and the most vigorous or severe (ranks 11–15 for expansions, 11–14 for contractions). The entries are simple arithmetic means of the corresponding figures in the columns above.

movements. Perhaps the greater risk is that of overestimation because the data appear to represent the cyclically sensitive sectors of the economy, notably manufacturing, better than they do the other sectors. Still, the NBER-designated phases provide about as good approximations to the historical incidence of business expansions and contractions as the data allow. On the other hand, considerable uncertainty attaches to the precise dates of some of the early reference turns.

In comparison with the United States dates, Burns and Mitchell (1946, 113) assessed the NBER chronologies for the foreign countries as being "at least tolerable, if not equally good, approximations," while listing a few particular doubts and difficulties.[14] Independent compilations of turning points show on the whole good agreement on the identification of the cycles; some more serious discrepancies arise because of differences in how the cycles are defined and divided into phases.[15]

7. The United States Business Cycle Chronology since 1933

Since World War II the NBER's work in this field has been directed toward maintaining the United States business cycle chronology along the lines previously established and developing the concept of a growth cycle chronology and applying it to the United States and other major industrial countries. In this section we discuss the chronology of the recent United States business cycles, and the following section is devoted to growth cycles in fourteen countries.

Table A.5 gives the monthly, quarterly, and annual business cycle dates for the United States from 1933 to 1982, together with the durations of contractions, expansions, and full cycles.[16] Ten cycles have occurred in the past 49 years, or about one every five years. In the preceding 143 years, from 1790 to 1933, there were thirty-four cycles, or about one every four years. Hence the frequency of cycles has diminished somewhat. But the biggest change that the chronology re-

14. The German contraction 8/1903 to 2/1905 is acknowledged to be "dubious," and the French dates in the 1860s and 1870s, and also after 1932, are in need of careful reexamination.

15. Matthews 1959, 215–26 stresses the longer cycles of seven to ten years' duration, especially for Great Britain. Friedman and Schwartz 1982, 74, omit the 1901 trough and the 1903 peak recognized in the NBER chronology for Britain. In his German chronology published in 1955, Spiethoff 1955 skips the contraction of 1903–4 about which Burns and Mitchell had some doubts of their own (on German chronologies, see Bry 1960, app. B, 474–80). These authors concentrate on the characterization of annual data.

16. The pre–World War II monthly NBER chronologies presented in table A.3 include the cycles through the 1938 troughs, for the United States and other countries. But a new epoch in the United States economic history and policy opened after the traumatic experience of the Great Contraction in 1929–33, and we find it instructive to cover in table A.5 all subsequent reference dates and durations. (Note that, therefore, the individual dates for the 1933–37–38 cycle are included in both tables.)

Table A.5   **Business Cycle Chronologies and Durations, United States, 1933–82**

| | Dates of Peaks and Troughs | | | | Duration in Months[a] | | | |
| | By Months and Quarters | | By Calendar Years | | Contraction | Expansion | Full Cycle | |
Trough (T) (1)	Peak (P) (2)	Trough (T) (3)	Peak (P) (4)	(P to T) (5)	(T to P) (6)	T to T (7)	P to P (8)
March 1933:1	May 1937:2	1932	1937		50		93
June 1938:2	February 1945:1	1938	1944	13	80W	63	45
October 1945:4	November 1948:4	1946	1948	8W	37	88	56
October 1949:4	July 1953:2	1949	1953	11	45W	48	49
May 1954:2	August 1957:3	1954	1957	10W	39	55	32
April 1958:2	April 1960:2	1958	1960	8	24	47	116
February 1961:1	December 1969:4	1961	1969	10	106W	34	47
November 1970:4	November 1973:4	1970	1973	11W	36	117	74
March 1975:1	January 1980:1	1975	1979	16	58	52	18
July 1980:3	July 1981:3	1980	1981	6	12	64	
November 1982:4		1982		16		28	
		Averages					
Ten cycles, 1933–82							
Mean duration (months)				11	49	60	59
Standard deviation (months)				3	27	26	31
Thirty cycles, 1854–1982							
Mean duration (months)				18	33	51	50
Standard deviation (months)				12	20	21	23
Forty-four cycles, 1790–1982							
Mean duration (months)				20	33	52	51
Standard deviation (months)				15	20	24	22

Source: National Bureau of Economic Research.

[a] W = wartime expansion and following contraction.

veals is the shift in the length of contractions compared with expansions. In the period for which only annual dates are available, 1790 to 1855, contractions averaged about twenty-four months, expansions thirty-one months. Then from 1854 to 1933, when monthly dates are available, the average durations are twenty-two and twenty-five months respectively. But since 1933 the average contraction has lasted only eleven months, while expansions have averaged forty-nine months (twenty-seven months when the wartime expansions are excluded).

In other words, since the depression of the early 1930s, the contraction phase of the business cycle has been reduced by about a year, while the expansion phase has been extended by two years. Before 1933, recessions lasted almost as long as expansions. Since then, expansions have been more than four times as long as recessions: the economy has been in recession less than 20% of the time.

Recessions have become not only shorter but also much more uniform in length. Using the standard deviation as a measure, the variability among contractions in 1790–1855 was eighteen months; in 1854–1933, fourteen months; and in 1933–82, only three months. In this sense, recessions have become more predictable. On the other hand, expansions have become less uniform in length. Between 1790 and 1855 the standard deviation of durations of expansions was eighteen months, the same as for the contractions. From 1854 to 1933, the standard deviation of expansions was nine months. But from 1933 to 1983, it was twenty-seven months. Expansions have become nine times as variable as contractions.

It is not our purpose here to investigate the reasons for this shift in variability, or for the shift in the length of expansions relative to contractions. The latter appears to be connected with the rising trend of prices since the 1930s, which in turn may be related to the stronger effort of government to control recessions (See Moore 1983, chap. 15). But this is a worthy subject for further study.

The length of a period of rise or fall in aggregate economic activity is one of the criteria considered in establishing the business cycle chronology. The size and scope of the movement are also considered. Measures of these dimensions for all the expansions between 1949 and 1982 are given in table A.6, and all the contractions since 1920 are covered in table A.7. Measures similar to these, but somewhat more extensive, have been used by the NBER staff in deciding what intervals should be classified as expansions or as contractions and what the peak and trough dates should be.[17]

17. The NBER sources for the successive United States reference dates in the post–World War II period are Moore 1961, 1:104–5 (through 1958); NBER *Annual Reports* for 1961 (Moore, 38–41) and 1962 (Moore, 65–66); supplement to *National Bureau Report 8*, May 1971 (Fabricant); NBER *Annual Reports* for 1975 (Moore, 23–26; Zarnowitz and

Study of the tables will reveal one development that led to a shift in this procedure during the 1960s. During the three expansions 1949–60 and during the five recessions 1923–38 and 1948–49, GNP in current dollars moved in wider swings than did GNP in constant dollars. Prices moved up and down with the business cycle, enhancing the current dollar swings. Since 1960, apart from a small one-quarter decline in 1982, current dollar GNP has not declined at all. Whereas before 1960 the current dollar aggregates for GNP, sales, and income had figured importantly in the determination of the business cycle chronology, since the 1960s they have played no role at all. As long as the rate of inflation remains persistently positive, this is likely to continue.

The tables make it clear that not only have recessions become shorter, they have become milder as well. None of the recessions since 1948 have approached the Great Depression in depth, nor have they come close to the major depressions of 1920–21 or 1937–38. All have been in a class either with the fairly sharp recession of 1923–24 or the mild recession of 1926–27. The tables record considerable "progress toward economic stability" (Burns 1960).

A word should be said about the problem of identifying business cycles contemporaneously. How soon a peak or trough can be recognized depends partly upon how rapidly the economy descends from the peak or rises from the trough. It also depends upon one's ability and willingness to make forecasts—for example, that a decline in the several measures of aggregate activity will last as long and go as deep as in previously recognized recessions, and that the declines will be widespread. Since the NBER's decisions on dates have not depended on forecasts, turns in the business cycle have been recognized only with a lag. For example, the trough date for the most recent recession, November 1982, was determined by the National Bureau of Economic Research in July 1983. Even that involved a presumption that the recovery then under way would continue and ultimately develop the characteristics of a business cycle expansion.

We have recently developed one way to reduce this recognition lag in a paper on sequential signals of recession and recovery (Zarnowitz and Moore 1982). The signals are based upon smoothed short-run growth rates in the composite leading and coincident indexes published by the

---

Boschan, 26–29) and 1977 (Zarnowitz and Boschan, 34–38). A comprehensive report on the 1973–76 developments, which shows in detail how the chronology for this period was derived, is Zarnowitz and Moore 1977. Since 1980, the turning points for the United States are identified by the NBER's Committee on Business Cycle Dating; on the composition and work of the committee and the analysis behind its decisions concerning the recession and recovery of 1980, see Zarnowitz and Moore 1981. The NBER United States chronology is published in the United States Commerce Department's monthly report on cyclical indicators entitled *Business Conditions Digest* (*BCD*).

Table A.6   Measures of the Duration, Vigor, and Diffusion of Expansions, 1949–82

	Business Cycle Trough/Peak							Average, Seven Expansions
	Oct. 1949 Jul. 1953	May 1954 Aug. 1957	Apr. 1958 Apr. 1960	Feb. 1961 Dec. 1969	Nov. 1970 Nov. 1973	Mar. 1975 Jan. 1980	Jul. 1980 Jul. 1981	
Duration (months)								
Business cycle	45	39	24	106	36	58	12	46
GNP, current dollars	42	39	30	—[a]	—[a]	—[a]	—[a]	n.a.
GNP, constant dollars	48	39	24	105	45	60	15	48
Industrial production	45	35	21	104	43	48	12	44
Nonfarm employment	44	31	23	109	47	59	12	46
Increase (percent)[b]								
GNP, current dollars	43.8	24.0	16.3	—[a]	—[a]	—[a]	—[a]	n.a.
GNP, constant dollars	28.1	13.2	11.3	49.2	17.1	24.3	4.4	21.1
Industrial production	50.1	23.7	26.0	78.9	25.9	37.4	9.6	35.9
Nonfarm employment	17.7	9.1	7.5	33.7	11.9	19.1	1.9	14.4
Unemployment rate								
Minimum	2.5	3.6	4.9	3.3	4.5	5.5	7.1	4.5
Decrease	−5.3	−2.3	−2.4	−3.6	−1.4	−3.3	−0.6	−2.7

	Jul. 1950	May 1955	Jan. 1959	Dec. 1965	Mar. 1972	Feb. 1977	Oct. 1980	
Rate of increase (percent per year)								
GNP, current dollars	10.9	6.9	6.2	—[a]	—[a]	—[a]	—[a]	n.a.
GNP, constant dollars	6.4	3.9	5.5	4.7	4.3	4.4	3.5	4.7
Industrial production	11.4	7.6	14.1	6.9	6.6	8.3	9.6	9.2
Nonfarm employment	4.5	3.4	3.8	3.2	2.9	3.6	1.9	3.3
Diffusion (percent)								
Nonfarm industries, maximum percentage with rising employment, with date when maximum was reached[c]	100	95	92	91	86	85	73	89

Source: U.S. Department of Commerce, U.S. Department of Labor, Board of Governors of the Federal Reserve System, National Bureau of Economic Research.

Note: n.a. = not available.

[a]No cycle.

[b]Percentage change from trough month or quarter in the series to the peak month or quarter, over the periods shown. For the unemployment rate the minimum figure is the lowest for any month during the expansion, and the decreases are from the highest month to the lowest, in percentage points.

[c]Based on changes in employment over six-month spans, centered on the fourth month of the span, in 30 nonagricultural industries, 1948–59; 172 industries, 1960–71; 186 industries, 1972–81.

Table A.7 **Measures of Duration, Depth, and Diffusion of Recessions, 1920–82**

	Business Cycle Peak/Trough					
	January 1920 / July 1921	May 1923 / July 1924	October 1926 / November 1927	August 1929 / March 1933	May 1937 / June 1938	February 1945 / October 1945
Duration (months)						
Business cycle	18	14	13	43	13	8
GNP, current dollars	n.a.	6	12	42	9	6
GNP, constant dollars	n.a.	3	3	36	6	n.a.
Industrial production	14	14	8	36	12	27
Nonfarm employment	n.a.	n.a.	n.a.	43	11	22
Depth (percent)[b]						
GNP, current dollars	n.a.	−4.9	−3.0	−49.6	−16.2	−11.9
GNP, constant dollars	n.a.	−4.1	−2.0	−32.6	−13.2	n.a.
Industrial production	−32.4	−17.9	−7.0	−53.4	−32.4	−38.3
Nonfarm employment	n.a.	n.a.	n.a.	−31.6	−10.8	−10.1
Unemployment rate						
Maximum	11.9[c]	5.5[c]	4.4[c]	24.9[c]	20.0	4.3
Increase	+10.3[c]	+2.6[c]	+2.4[c]	+21.7[c]	+9.0	+3.4
Diffusion (percent)						
Nonfarm industries, maximum percentage with declining employment, and date when maximum was reached[d]	97	95	71	100	97	n.a.
	September 1920	April 1924	November 1927	June 1933	December 1937	

Business Cycle Peak/Trough

	November 1948 October 1949	July 1953 May 1954	August 1957 April 1958	April 1960 February 1961	December 1969 November 1970	November 1973 March 1975	January 1980 July 1980	July 1981 November 1982
Duration (months)								
Business cycle	11	10	8	10	11	16	6	16
GNP, current dollars	12	12	6	3	—a	—a	—a	3
GNP, constant dollars	6	12	6	9	6	15	3	6
Industrial production	15	9	13	13	13	9	16	16
Nonfarm employment	13	14	14	10	8	6	4	17
Depth (percent)b								
GNP, current dollars	−3.4	−1.9	−2.8	−0.6	—a	—a	—a	−0.4
GNP, constant dollars	−1.5	−3.2	−3.3	−1.2	−1.0	−4.9	−2.3	−3.0
Industrial production	−10.1	−9.4	−13.5	−8.6	−6.8	−15.3	−8.5	−12.3
Nonfarm employment	−5.2	−3.5	−4.3	−2.2	−1.5	−2.9	−1.4	−3.1
Unemployment rate								
Maximum	7.8	5.9	7.3	6.9	5.9	8.8	7.7	10.7
Increase	+4.5	+3.4	+3.7	+2.0	+2.6	+4.3	+2.2	+3.6
Diffusion (percent)								
Nonfarm industries, maximum percentage with declining employment, with date when maximum was reachedd	90	87	88	80	80	88	77	79
	February 1949	March 1954	September 1957	October 1960	May 1970	January 1975	April 1980	August 1982

Source: U.S. Department of Commerce, U.S. Department of Labor, Board of Governors of the Federal Reserve System, National Bureau of Economic Research. For a fuller version of this table, see Fabricant 1972, 100–110.

Note: n.a. = not available.

aNo decline.

bPercentage change from the peak month or quarter in the series to the trough month or quarter, over the invervals shown. For the unemployment rate the maximum figure is the highest for any month during the contraction, and the increases are from the lowest month to the highest, in percentage points.

cThe maximum figures are annual averages for 1921, 1924, 1928, and 1933 (monthly data not available). Increases, in percentage points, are for 1919–21, 1923–24, 1926–28, and 1929–33.

dSince 1948 based on changes in employment over six-month spans, centered on the fourth month of the span, in 30 nonagricultural industries, 1948–59; 172 industries, 1960–71; 186 industries, 1972–82. Before 1948 based on cyclical changes in employment in 41 industries.

Department of Commerce. When these growth rates reach certain pre-determined levels, a preliminary signal of a peak or trough occurs. If they reach another set of levels, a second signal is passed, and so on with a third and final signal. Safeguards against false signals are built into the system. Historical tests have shown that the signals would have identified each of the United States business cycle peaks and troughs since 1949 without undue delays or false signals. One of the potential uses for the system is to activate or deactivate countercyclical policies.

8. Growth Cycle Chronologies

A modification of the concept of business cycles employed in the chronologies discussed above was developed by Mintz at the NBER in the 1960s (Mintz 1969, 1974). The growth cycle represents a fluctuation around the long-run growth trend of a nation's economy, that is, a trend adjusted business cycle. Chronologies based upon this concept, using the classical business cycle definition cited above but applying it to data from which long-run trends have been eliminated, are shown in figure A.2 and table A.8. The dates mark the approximate time when aggregate economic activity was farthest above its long-run trend level (peak) or farthest below its long-run trend level (trough).

The specific procedures used to establish these chronologies, initiated by Moore and Klein at the NBER in 1973, are as follows:

1. Measures of aggregate economic activity such as industrial production, gross national product, personal income, employment, unemployment, and sales of goods and services are expressed in physical units or in constant prices, seasonally adjusted, with their long-run trend removed. The trend fitting procedure, called the phase average trend, provides a fairly flexible growth trend that is substantially free of the shorter-term cyclical movements in the series (Boschan and Ebanks 1978).

2. For each of the series above, computer selected peaks and troughs are derived from the deviations of the seasonally adjusted data from the growth trend. The program for turning point selection is described in Bry and Boschan (1971).

3. These turning points are visually inspected and sometimes altered by shifting the date, omitting the turn, or adding another turn. These changes are relatively rare, affecting perhaps 5% of the turning points.

4. Median dates in the clusters of peaks and troughs formed by all the series mentioned above are computed.

5. A composite index based on the series above before their adjustment for trend is constructed, the growth trend is removed from

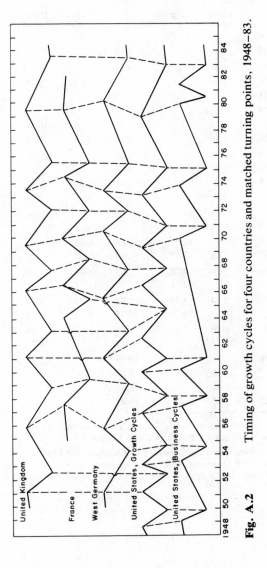

Fig. A.2   Timing of growth cycles for four countries and matched turning points, 1948–83.

Table A.8   Growth Cycle Peak and Trough Dates, Fourteen Countries,
                   1948–83

Peak or Trough	United States	Australia	Belgium	Canada	France	Italy	Japan	South Korea
P	7/48							
T	10/49			5/50				
P	3/51	4/51		4/51				
T	7/52	11/52		12/51				
P	3/53			3/53			12/53	
T	8/54			10/54			6/55	
P	2/57	8/55		11/56	8/57	10/56	5/57	
T	4/58	1/58		8/58	8/59	7/59	1/59	
P	2/60	8/60		10/59				
T	2/61	9/61		3/61				
P	5/62			3/62	2/64	9/63	1/62	
T	10/64			5/63	6/65	3/65	1/63	
P							7/64	
T							2/66	
P	6/66	4/65	10/64	3/66	6/66			
T	10/67	1/68	7/68	2/68	5/68			8/66
P	3/69	5/70	9/70	2/69	11/69	8/69	6/70	1/69
T	11/70	3/72	7/71	12/70	11/71	9/72	1/72	3/72
P	3/73	2/74	7/74	2/74	5/74	4/74	11/73	2/74
T	3/75	10/75	10/75	10/75	6/75	5/75	3/75	6/75
P		8/76		5/76		12/76		7/76
T		10/77		12/77		10/77		
P	12/78		6/79	10/79	8/79	2/80	2/80	
T				5/80				
P		6/81		6/81				
T	12/82	5/83		11/82			6/83	

Source: For the United States, National Bureau of Economic Research. For other countries, Center for International Business Cycle Research.

Note: The four-, seven-, and eight-country chronologies are based on composite indexes of output, income, employment, and trade, weighted by each country's GNP in 1970, expressed in United States dollars. The four countries are the United Kingdom, West

Nether-lands	Sweden	Switzer-land	Taiwan	United Kingdom	West Ger-many	Countries		
						Four	Seven	Eight
		2/50						
7/50		3/51		3/51	2/51			
6/52		2/53		8/52				
					2/54			
10/56		6/57		12/55	10/55	5/57	5/57	2/57
5/58		9/58		11/58	4/59	2/59	2/59	5/58
								2/60
								2/61
3/61		4/64		3/61	2/61	3/61	3/61	2/62
2/63			6/63	2/63	2/63	2/63	2/63	2/63
							11/64	
11/65	2/65		4/65	2/66	5/65	3/66		3/66
8/67	7/67	5/68	8/67	8/67	8/67	5/68	5/68	10/67
11/70	7/70	5/70	11/68	6/69	5/70	5/70	6/70	8/69
8/72	7/72	1/71	1/71	2/72	12/71	2/72	2/72	8/71
8/74	6/74	4/74	12/73	6/73	8/73	7/74	11/73	10/73
7/75		8/75	2/75	8/75	5/75	8/75	11/75	5/75
9/76			6/76					
11/77	7/78		7/77					
12/79			8/78	6/79	2/80	2/80	2/80	2/80
			10/82	6/83	7/83		4/83	2/83

Germany, France, and Italy. The seven countries include these four plus Canada, Japan, and Australia, and the eight countries include the United States as well. The chronologies begin at different dates because appropriate data are not available earlier. The absence of a recent date does not necessarily mean that a turn has not occurred.

the index, and turning points are selected in the deviations from trend.

6. The clusters of dates, the median dates, and the composite index dates are inspected, and a decision is made on which monthly date best represents the consensus. These dates are the growth cycle peaks and troughs.

Comparisons of growth cycle and business cycle chronologies show that the number of growth cycles during a given period usually exceeds the number of business cycles, because slowdowns that sometimes occur during long business cycle expansions become actual contractions in the trend-adjusted figures. In the United States, for example, such slowdowns occurred in 1951–52, 1962–64, and 1966–67, interrupting the long business cycle expansions from 1949 to 1953 and from 1961 to 1969. Hence growth cycles are, on average, shorter than business cycles. Another difference is that peaks in the growth cycle usually occur some months before the corresponding peaks in the business cycle, because activity usually slows before a business cycle peak is reached. Growth cycle and business cycle troughs tend to be more nearly simultaneous. As a result of these differences, expansions and contractions are more nearly symmetrical, in both duration and amplitude, in growth cycles than in business cycles. Also, the variability in duration and in amplitude is more nearly uniform between expansions and contractions of growth cycles. The international connections among growth cycles since World War II seem to be about as pervasive as those among business cycles before the war (compare figs. A.1 and A.2).

The continuing public concern with slowdowns in growth, some of which turn into declines in aggregate economic activity and some of which do not, justifies further attention to this concept of the business cycle. So also does the growing concern with the international spread of economic fluctuations, since slowdowns in one country may become substantial declines in another. The widening use of both business cycle and growth cycle chronologies in many countries testifies to the value of this well-tested tool for research and public understanding (see Klein and Moore 1985).

References

Ashton, T. S. 1959. *Economic fluctuations in England, 1700–1800*. Oxford: Clarendon Press.

Axe, E. W., and R. Houghton. 1931. Financial and business cycles, manufacturing growth and analysis of individual indicators, 1883–1930. *Annalist,* 16 January, 150–51.

Ayres, Leonard P. 1939. *Turning points in business cycles*. New York: Macmillan.

Boschan, Charlotte, and Walter W. Ebanks. 1978. The phase-average trend: A new way of measuring growth. In *Proceedings of the Business and Economic Statistics Section*. Washington, D.C.: American Statistical Association.

Bry, Gerhard. 1960. *Wages in Germany, 1871–1945*. New York: National Bureau of Economic Research.

Bry, Gerhard, and Charlotte Boschan. 1971. *Cyclical analysis of time series: Selected procedures and computer programs*. New York: Columbia University Press.

Burns, Arthur F. 1960. Progress towards economic stability. *American Economic Review* 50 (March): 1–19.

———. 1968. Business cycles. In *International Encyclopedia of the Social Sciences* 2:226–45. New York: Macmillan.

Burns, Arthur F., and Wesley C. Mitchell. 1946. *Measuring business cycles*. New York: National Bureau of Economic Research.

Cloos, George W. 1963a. How good are the National Bureau's reference dates? *Journal of Business* 36 (January): 14–32.

———. 1963b. More on reference dates and leading indicators. *Journal of Business* 36 (July): 352–64.

Eckler, A. Ross. 1933. A measure of the severity of depressions, 1873–1932. *Review of Economic Statistics* 15 (February): 75–81.

Fabricant, Solomon. 1972. The recession of 1969–1970. In *The business cycle today*, ed. Victor Zarnowitz. New York: National Bureau of Economic Research.

Fellner, William. 1956. *Trends and cycles in economic activity*. New York: Henry Holt.

Frickey, Edwin. 1942. *Economic fluctuations in the United States*. Cambridge: Harvard University Press.

Friedman, Milton, and Anna J. Schwartz. 1982. *Monetary trends in the United States and the United Kingdom: Their relation to income, prices, and interest rates, 1867–1975*. Chicago: University of Chicago Press.

Gilbert, Donald W. 1933. Business cycles and municipal expenditures. *Review of Economic Statistics* 15 (August): 140–41.

Gordon, Robert Aaron. 1952. *Business fluctuations*. New York: Harper.

Haberler, Gottfried. 1964. *Prosperity and depression*. Cambridge: Harvard University Press. Originally published 1937.

Hansen, Alvin H. 1941. *Fiscal policy and business cycles*. New York: W. W. Norton.

———. 1951. *Business cycles and national income*. New York: W. W. Norton.

Hoffman, Walther G. 1965. *Das Wachstum der deutschen Wirschaft seit der Mitte des 19. Jahrhunderts*. Berlin: Springer-Verlag.

Hubbard, Joseph B. 1936. Business declines and recoveries. *Review of Economic Statistics* 18 (February): 16–23.

Juglar, Clément. 1862. *Des crises commerciales et de leur retour périodique en France, en Angleterre et aux Etats Unis*. Paris: Guillaumin.

Kitchin, Joseph. 1923. Cycles and trends in economic factors. *Review of Economic Statistics* 5 (January): 10–16.

Klein, Philip A., and Geoffrey H. Moore. 1985. *Monitoring growth cycles in market-oriented countries*. Cambridge, Mass.: Ballinger.

Kuznets, Simon. 1971. *Economic growth of nations*. Cambridge: Belknap Press of Harvard University Press.

Lewis, John P. 1965. *Building cycles and Britain's growth*. London: Macmillan; New York: St. Martin's Press.

Matthews, R. C. O. 1959. *The trade cycle*. Cambridge: Cambridge University Press.

Mintz, Ilse. 1969. *Dating postwar business cycles: Methods and their application to Western Germany, 1950–67*. New York: Columbia University Press.

———. 1974. Dating United States growth cycles. *Explorations in Economic Research* 1, no. 1:1–113.

Mitchell, Wesley C. 1913. *Business cycles*. Berkeley: University of California Press.

———. 1927. *Business cycles: The problem and its setting*. New York: National Bureau of Economic Research.

Moore, Geoffrey H., ed. 1961. *Business cycle indicators*. Princeton: Princeton University Press.

———. 1967. What is a recession? *American Statistician* 21 (October) 16–19. (Reprinted, with more recent figures and references added, in Moore 1983.)

———. 1983. *Business cycles, inflation, and forecasting*. 2d ed. Cambridge, Mass.: Ballinger.

Morgenstern, Oskar. 1959. *International financial transactions and business cycles*. New York: National Bureau of Economic Research.

Persons, Warren M. 1931. *Forecasting business cycles*. New York: John Wiley.

Rostow, W. W. 1980. Cycles in the fifth Kondratieff upswing. In *The business cycle and public policy, 1929–80*, 34–66. A compendium of papers submitted to the Joint Economic Committee, Congress of the United States. Washington, D.C.: Government Printing Office.

Schumpeter, Joseph A. 1939. *Business cycles: A theoretical, historical, and statistical analysis of the capitalist process*. 2 vols. New York: McGraw-Hill.

Smith, Walter B., and Arthur H. Cole. 1935. *Fluctuations in American business, 1790–1860*. Cambridge: Harvard University Press.

Spiethoff, Arthur. 1955. *Die wirtschaftlichen Wechsellagen: Aufschwung, Krise, Stockung*. 2 vols. Zurich: Polygraphischer Verlag.

Trueblood, Lorman C. 1961. The dating of postwar business cycles. In *Proceedings of the Business and Economic Statistics Section.* Washington, D.C.: American Statistical Association.

U.S. Department of Commerce, Bureau of the Census. 1973. *Long term Economic Growth, 1860–1970.* Washington, D.C.: Government Printing Office.

Zarnowitz, Victor. 1963a. On the dating of business cycles. *Journal of Business* 36 (April): 179–99.

———. 1963b. Cloos on reference dates and leading indicators: A comment. *Journal of Business* 36 (October): 461–63.

———. 1981. Business cycles and growth: Some reflections and measures. In *Wirtschaftstheorie und Wirtschaftspolitik: Gedenkschrift für Erich Preiser,* ed. W. J. Mückl and A. E. Ott, 475–508. Passau: Passavia Universitätsverlag.

Zarnowitz, Victor, and Geoffrey H. Moore. 1977. The recession and recovery of 1973–76. *Explorations in Economic Research* 4, (Fall): 472–557.

———. 1981. The timing and the severity of the recession of 1980. [NBER] *Economic Reporter* (Spring), 19–21.

———. 1982. Sequential signals of recession and recovery. *Journal of Business* 55 (January): 57–85. (Reprinted and updated in Moore 1983.)

Appendix B
Historical Data

Nathan S. Balke and Robert J. Gordon

1. Annual Data from 1869 to 1983

Year	Nominal GNP	Real GNP (1972 dollars)	GNP Deflator (1972 = 100)	Trend Real GNP	Commercial Paper Rate	Yield on Corporate Bonds
1869	8.06	34.93	23.07	34.93	10.95	9.11
1870	7.83	35.96	21.78	36.78	8.54	8.99
1871	7.80	35.25	22.13	38.72	8.27	8.93
1872	9.02	42.94	21.01	40.76	9.92	8.77
1873	9.00	43.36	20.76	42.91	11.60	8.80
1874	8.79	42.78	20.54	45.17	7.27	8.49
1875	8.74	43.57	20.06	47.56	6.73	7.93
1876	8.84	46.19	19.14	50.07	6.42	7.64
1877	9.13	49.54	18.45	52.71	6.47	7.65
1878	9.04	52.95	17.08	55.49	6.09	7.58
1879	9.65	58.44	16.48	58.44	6.35	7.24
1880	12.14	66.74	18.19	60.50	6.52	6.94
1881	12.13	67.97	17.84	62.04	6.49	6.62
1882	13.10	71.12	18.41	63.94	6.93	6.67
1883	12.79	70.28	18.19	65.89	6.91	6.69
1884	12.44	72.18	17.24	67.90	6.49	6.64
1885	11.66	72.44	16.10	69.98	5.35	6.44
1886	12.06	75.96	15.88	72.12	6.05	6.17
1887	12.56	78.30	16.04	74.32	7.04	6.23
1888	12.48	76.44	16.32	76.59	6.18	6.16
1889	12.96	78.93	16.42	78.93	6.15	6.02
1890	13.65	84.82	16.09	82.44	6.91	6.14
1891	14.02	88.65	15.83	86.62	6.48	6.31
1892	14.82	97.19	15.24	90.74	5.40	6.19

Nathan S. Balke is a graduate student at Northwestern University. Robert J. Gordon is professor of economics at Northwestern University.

Annual Data from 1869 to 1983   (continued)

Year	Nominal GNP	Real GNP (1972 dollars)	GNP Deflator (1972 = 100)	Trend Real GNP	Commercial Paper Rate	Yield on Corporate Bonds
1893	14.40	92.36	15.57	95.06	7.64	6.29
1894	13.12	89.92	14.59	99.58	5.22	6.08
1895	14.47	100.55	14.39	104.32	5.80	5.95
1896	13.78	98.44	14.00	109.28	7.02	5.99
1897	15.18	107.86	14.06	114.48	4.72	5.80
1898	16.00	110.20	14.52	119.92	5.34	5.74
1899	18.05	120.40	14.98	125.62	5.50	5.60
1900	19.40	123.55	15.70	131.60	5.71	5.66
1901	21.47	137.87	15.57	137.87	5.40	5.66
1902	22.39	139.13	16.09	142.96	5.81	5.73
1903	23.80	146.10	16.29	147.71	6.16	5.97
1904	23.78	144.21	16.48	152.89	5.14	5.99
1905	26.07	155.04	16.81	158.26	5.18	5.94
1906	29.88	172.97	17.27	163.82	6.25	6.03
1907	31.59	175.61	17.99	169.57	6.66	6.25
1908	28.80	161.22	17.86	175.52	5.00	6.22
1909	33.39	180.93	18.44	181.69	4.67	6.13
1910	35.26	185.98	18.96	188.06	5.72	6.28
1911	35.98	191.90	18.74	194.67	4.75	6.32
1912	39.34	201.51	19.52	201.50	5.41	6.36
1913	39.54	203.38	19.44	206.31	6.20	6.53
1914	38.84	195.96	19.83	210.18	5.47	6.52
1915	40.14	193.63	20.73	214.66	4.01	6.65
1916	48.30	208.19	23.20	219.23	3.84	6.51
1917	60.54	211.43	28.61	223.90	5.07	6.77
1918	76.56	244.33	31.30	228.68	6.02	7.14
1919	84.29	228.99	36.80	233.55	5.37	7.19
1920	91.54	214.22	42.70	238.52	7.50	8.12
1921	69.52	199.94	34.80	243.61	6.62	8.46
1922	74.16	229.54	32.30	248.80	4.52	7.13
1923	83.38	254.09	33.60	254.10	5.07	7.24
1924	84.88	256.39	33.10	262.73	3.98	6.89
1925	93.30	276.03	33.80	273.17	4.02	6.31
1926	97.17	291.81	33.30	283.23	4.34	5.92
1927	95.01	293.27	32.40	293.66	4.11	5.51
1928	97.17	296.22	32.80	304.48	4.85	5.46
1929	103.42	315.69	32.76	315.70	5.85	5.87
1930	90.73	285.52	31.75	323.86	3.59	5.83
1931	76.12	263.46	28.87	330.61	2.64	7.31
1932	58.33	227.04	25.67	338.32	2.73	9.56
1933	55.84	222.13	25.13	346.22	1.73	7.81
1934	65.27	239.09	27.30	354.30	1.02	6.39
1935	72.50	260.04	27.88	362.57	0.76	5.83
1936	82.79	295.54	28.00	371.03	0.75	4.82
1937	90.89	310.16	29.30	379.69	0.94	4.94
1938	85.05	296.75	28.66	388.55	0.81	5.84

Annual Data from 1869 to 1983 (continued)

Year	Nominal GNP	Real GNP (1972 dollars)	GNP Deflator (1972 = 100)	Trend Real GNP	Commercial Paper Rate	Yield on Corporate Bonds
1939	90.95	319.83	28.43	397.61	0.59	5.00
1940	100.04	344.16	29.06	406.89	0.56	4.74
1941	125.30	400.40	31.23	416.39	0.53	4.32
1942	158.59	461.80	34.32	426.11	0.66	4.27
1943	192.20	531.66	36.14	436.05	0.69	3.94
1944	210.64	569.13	37.01	446.23	0.73	3.64
1945	212.11	560.17	37.91	456.64	0.75	3.32
1946	209.89	478.28	43.88	467.30	0.81	3.04
1947	233.00	470.39	49.53	478.20	1.03	3.21
1948	259.48	489.74	52.98	489.36	1.44	3.47
1949	258.30	492.24	52.48	500.78	1.49	3.43
1950	286.45	534.57	53.55	523.73	1.45	3.25
1951	330.73	579.17	57.10	547.68	2.16	3.39
1952	347.95	600.63	57.93	572.83	2.33	3.51
1953	366.75	623.46	58.83	599.00	2.52	3.71
1954	366.78	615.64	59.58	621.18	1.59	3.54
1955	400.05	657.37	60.85	639.33	2.19	3.51
1956	421.70	671.72	62.78	659.03	3.31	3.81
1957	443.98	683.57	64.95	680.18	3.82	4.66
1958	449.60	680.88	66.03	705.03	2.47	4.74
1959	487.90	721.72	67.60	724.20	3.96	5.02
1960	506.50	737.01	68.73	749.65	3.85	5.22
1961	524.55	756.59	69.33	778.45	2.96	5.08
1962	565.03	800.29	70.60	806.65	3.26	5.04
1963	596.73	832.20	71.70	834.15	3.56	4.86
1964	637.73	875.96	72.80	865.70	3.96	4.76
1965	691.03	929.00	74.38	895.48	4.38	4.85
1966	756.00	984.62	76.78	936.48	5.55	5.56
1967	799.58	1011.38	79.05	977.83	5.11	6.15
1968	873.40	1058.06	82.54	1012.43	5.90	6.91
1969	943.98	1087.58	86.80	1048.43	7.83	7.70
1970	992.73	1085.58	91.45	1087.60	7.71	9.07
1971	1077.65	1122.42	96.00	1131.85	5.11	8.61
1972	1185.93	1185.92	99.98	1173.63	4.73	8.19
1973	1326.38	1254.20	105.74	1217.20	8.15	8.16
1974	1434.23	1246.30	115.10	1257.08	9.84	9.36
1975	1549.20	1231.61	125.75	1298.98	6.32	10.42
1976	1718.03	1298.20	132.33	1345.10	5.34	9.75
1977	1918.30	1369.71	140.02	1391.38	5.61	8.98
1978	2163.83	1438.55	150.35	1436.63	7.99	9.42
1979	2417.78	1479.44	163.41	1480.75	10.91	10.54
1980	2631.70	1474.98	178.44	1525.18	12.29	13.38
1981	2957.75	1512.15	195.61	1570.95	14.76	15.97
1982	3069.23	1479.98	207.39	1618.10	11.89	16.35
1983	3304.78	1534.68	215.30	1667.00	8.81	13.52

Annual Data from 1869 to 1983   (continued)

	Money Supply			Disposable Income	Disposable Income NIPA
Year	M1	M2	Base	(1929 dollars)	(1972 dollars)
1869	—	1.73	0.62	—	—
1870	—	1.83	0.63	—	—
1871	—	2.03	0.64	—	—
1872	—	2.18	0.64	—	—
1873	—	2.19	0.65	—	—
1874	—	2.23	0.66	—	—
1875	—	2.33	0.63	—	—
1876	—	2.28	0.62	—	—
1877	—	2.24	0.62	—	—
1878	—	2.14	0.62	—	—
1879	—	2.26	0.66	—	—
1880	—	2.76	0.78	—	—
1881	—	3.31	0.89	—	—
1882	—	3.57	0.94	—	—
1883	—	3.79	0.97	—	—
1884	—	3.79	0.99	—	—
1885	—	3.89	1.01	—	—
1886	—	4.21	0.99	—	—
1887	—	4.49	1.04	—	—
1888	—	4.61	1.08	—	—
1889	—	4.88	1.10	—	—
1890	—	5.31	1.14	—	—
1891	—	5.54	1.20	—	—
1892	—	6.00	1.26	—	—
1893	—	5.78	1.28	—	—
1894	—	5.80	1.29	—	—
1895	—	6.01	1.23	—	—
1896	—	5.90	1.19	—	—
1897	—	6.29	1.27	24.43	—
1898	—	7.13	1.38	25.39	—
1899	—	8.26	1.49	26.97	—
1900	—	8.96	1.61	28.37	—
1901	—	10.14	1.72	31.46	—
1902	—	11.08	1.78	31.51	—
1903	—	11.77	1.87	33.56	—
1904	—	12.54	1.99	34.27	—
1905	—	13.89	2.04	36.01	—
1906	—	15.02	2.17	40.64	—
1907	—	15.73	2.33	41.77	—
1908	—	15.55	2.53	38.18	—
1909	—	17.25	2.56	43.55	—
1910	—	18.12	2.60	42.38	—
1911	—	19.21	2.69	42.88	—
1912	—	20.54	2.52	43.36	—
1913	—	21.34	2.79	45.71	—
1914	—	22.21	2.89	44.60	—

Annual Data from 1869 to 1983   (continued)

	Money Supply			Disposable Income	Disposable Income NIPA
Year	M1	M2	Base	(1929 dollars)	(1972 dollars)
1915	12.21	23.93	2.99	47.60	—
1916	14.38	28.39	3.40	50.42	—
1917	16.71	32.68	4.07	52.21	—
1918	18.57	36.37	4.91	47.50	—
1919	21.40	42.32	5.46	59.14	—
1920	23.01	47.37	5.92	51.19	—
1921	20.70	44.58	5.38	50.05	—
1922	21.24	46.14	5.18	54.37	—
1923	22.28	49.93	5.51	62.09	—
1024	23.32	52.67	5.67	64.64	—
1925	25.19	57.44	5.80	65.20	—
1926	25.38	59.49	5.86	68.71	—
1927	25.49	61.02	5.89	70.72	—
1928	25.69	63.32	5.88	71.12	—
1929	25.79	63.44	5.87	76.10	229.53
1930	24.77	62.04	5.73	68.15	210.89
1931	22.78	57.24	5.98	62.78	202.10
1932	20.10	47.79	6.40	51.55	174.66
1933	19.06	42.21	6.77	—	169.41
1934	21.59	45.77	7.55	—	179.93
1935	25.52	52.66	8.88	—	196.90
1936	29.03	58.91	10.16	—	220.23
1937	29.57	61.72	11.03	—	227.37
1938	29.76	61.67	12.04	—	212.41
1939	33.63	66.83	14.49	—	229.57
1940	39.01	74.80	17.50	—	243.79
1941	45.82	84.84	19.30	—	277.59
1942	56.13	97.44	20.97	—	317.79
1943	72.65	123.60	24.77	—	331.75
1944	85.72	146.75	29.47	—	343.42
1945	98.29	174.01	34.52	—	338.14
1946	104.79	189.90	36.12	—	332.51
1947	109.83	200.40	36.84	—	318.88
1948	110.10	203.32	37.71	—	335.70
1949	109.07	202.39	37.17	—	336.68
1950	112.21	206.99	35.65	—	363.08
1951	117.23	214.74	38.14	—	372.97
1952	123.01	226.38	39.89	—	383.45
1953	125.99	234.96	41.03	—	399.08
1954	127.95	243.19	41.34	—	403.61
1955	132.00	252.18	41.68	—	426.96
1956	133.51	256.51	42.18	—	446.54
1957	134.10	263.30	42.52	—	455.22
1958	136.02	276.10	43.20	—	461.00
1959	141.38	292.15	43.90	—	479.39
1960	141.41	303.05	43.98	—	489.55

Annual Data from 1869 to 1983   (continued)

Year	Money Supply			Disposable Income (1929 dollars)	Disposable Income NIPA (1972 dollars)
	M1	M2	Base		
1961	144.45	323.38	45.08	—	503.79
1962	147.99	348.63	46.74	—	524.82
1963	152.64	377.93	48.87	—	542.62
1964	158.61	407.55	51.62	—	580.49
1965	165.49	440.58	54.51	—	616.30
1966	172.76	469.58	57.68	—	646.96
1967	180.00	502.33	60.73	—	673.11
1968	192.66	544.55	64.75	—	701.44
1969	203.79	578.30	68.32	—	722.77
1970	211.63	600.75	72.05	—	751.66
1971	226.17	673.63	77.75	—	779.02
1972	242.56	757.85	83.49	—	810.32
1973	259.73	833.40	90.79	—	865.18
1974	272.61	885.18	98.50	—	858.43
1975	285.39	969.38	106.30	—	875.46
1976	301.85	1097.00	115.18	—	906.88
1977	325.19	1239.00	123.03	—	943.30
1978	351.66	1349.25	133.85	—	988.59
1979	379.03	1468.08	144.93	—	1015.48
1980	401.48	1567.10	157.00	—	1021.70
1981	430.08	1715.28	167.10	—	1049.73
1982	458.50	1879.08	178.58	—	1058.51
1983	509.18	2116.30	195.53	—	1095.54

Year	Real Consumption			Year	Real Consumption		
	DeLong and Summers (1929) dollars	Kendrick (1929) dollars	NIPA (1972) dollars		DeLong and Summers (1929) dollars	Kendrick (1929) dollars	NIPA (1972) dollars
1869	—	—	—	1879	—	—	—
1870	—	—	—	1880	—	—	—
1871	—	—	—	1881	—	—	—
1872	—	—	—	1882	—	—	—
1873	—	—	—	1883	—	—	—
1874	—	—	—	1884	—	—	—
1875	—	—	—	1885	—	—	—
1876	—	—	—	1886	—	—	—
1877	—	—	—	1887	—	—	—
1878	—	—	—	1888	—	—	—

Annual Data from 1869 to 1983   (continued)

	Real Consumption				Real Consumption		
Year	DeLong and Summers (1929) dollars	Kendrick (1929) dollars	NIPA (1972) dollars	Year	DeLong and Summers (1929) dollars	Kendrick (1929) dollars	NIPA (1972) dollars
1889	—	18.00	—	1932	63.13	66.03	173.90
1890	—	17.96	—	1933	—	64.57	170.50
1891	—	19.25	—	1934	—	67.97	176.90
1892	—	20.16	—	1935	—	72.29	187.70
1893	—	20.26	—	1936	—	79.65	206.20
1894	—	19.66	—	1937	—	82.62	213.80
1895	—	22.12	—	1938	—	81.33	208.80
1896	—	22.06	—	1939	—	85.88	219.80
1897	23.98	23.79	—	1940	—	90.47	229.90
1898	24.96	24.19	—	1941	—	96.42	243.60
1899	26.76	27.05	—	1942	—	94.67	241.10
1900	27.57	27.30	—	1943	—	97.30	248.20
1901	30.25	30.65	—	1944	—	101.23	255.20
1902	30.73	30.91	—	1945	—	108.60	270.90
1903	32.59	32.76	—	1946	—	120.94	301.00
1904	33.31	33.19	—	1947	—	122.57	305.80
1905	34.89	35.09	—	1948	—	125.13	312.20
1906	37.71	38.97	—	1949	—	128.47	319.30
1907	39.30	39.70	—	1950	—	136.30	337.30
1908	38.18	37.20	—	1951	—	137.18	341.60
1909	41.17	41.27	—	1952	—	141.36	350.10
1910	42.05	42.03	—	1953	—	147.55	363.40
1911	43.04	44.06	—	1954	—	—	370.00
1912	42.72	45.21	—	1955	—	—	394.10
1913	44.59	46.70	—	1956	—	—	405.40
1914	47.12	46.12	—	1957	—	—	413.80
1915	48.21	45.32	—	1958	—	—	418.00
1916	48.80	49.41	—	1959	—	—	440.40
1917	50.02	48.34	—	1960	—	—	452.00
1918	48.45	48.12	—	1961	—	—	461.40
1919	49.85	50.25	—	1962	—	—	482.00
1920	50.86	52.71	—	1963	—	—	500.50
1921	54.78	56.08	—	1964	—	—	528.00
1922	57.10	58.15	—	1965	—	—	557.50
1923	61.99	63.43	—	1966	—	—	585.70
1924	66.55	68.13	—	1967	—	—	602.70
1925	64.81	66.14	—	1968	—	—	634.40
1926	69.78	71.55	—	1969	—	—	657.90
1927	71.63	73.16	—	1970	—	—	672.10
1928	72.41	74.81	—	1971	—	—	696.80
1929	77.30	78.95	215.10	1972	—	—	737.10
1930	72.54	74.67	199.50	1973	—	—	768.50
1931	71.36	72.52	191.80	1974	—	—	763.60

Annual Data from 1869 to 1983 (continued)

	Real Consumption				Real Consumption		
	DeLong and Summers (1929)	Kendrick (1929)	NIPA (1972)		DeLong and Summers (1929)	Kendrick (1929)	NIPA (1972)
Year	dollars	dollars	dollars	Year	dollars	dollars	dollars
1975	—	—	780.20	1980	—	—	931.80
1976	—	—	823.10	1981	—	—	950.50
1977	—	—	864.30	1982	—	—	963.30
1978	—	—	903.20	1983	—	—	1009.20
1979	—	—	927.60				

Section 1 Source Notes

Nominal GNP

(Billions of dollars) 1869–88: nominal income (net national product) from Milton Friedman and Anna J. Schwartz, *Monetary Trends in the United States and the United Kingdom: Their Relation to Income, Prices, and Interest Rates, 1867–1975* (Chicago: University of Chicago Press, 1982), 122–29, added to capital consumption from Simon Kuznets, *Capital in the American Economy; Its Formation and Financing* (Princeton: University of Princeton Press, 1961), table R8, 499, and unraveled five-year moving average table R29, 572–73. Linked in 1889 to

1889–1908: series A7 from *Long Term Economic Growth, 1860–1970* (Washington, D.C.: Department of Commerce, 1973). Linked in 1909 to

1909–28: *National Income and Product Accounts of the United States, 1929–76 Statistical Tables* (Washington, D.C.: Department of Commerce, 1981), table 1.22.

1929–83: national income and product accounts, table 1.1.

Real GNP

(Billions of dollars) 1869–88: real income (real net national product) from Friedman and Schwartz, *Monetary Trends,* 122–29, added to capital consumption from Kuznets (1961), table R8, 499, and unraveled five-year moving average table R29, 572–73. Linked in 1889 to

1889–1908: series A1 from *Long Term Economic Growth, 1860–1970*. Linked in 1909 to

1909–28: *National Income and Product Accounts of the United States, 1929–76 Statistical Tables,* table 1.22.

1929–83: national income and product accounts, table 1.2.

GNP deflator

1869–1983: nominal GNP divided by real GNP, then multiplied by 100.

Trend real GNP

1869–1948: geometric interpolation between the benchmark years 1869, 1879, 1889, 1901, 1912, 1923, 1929, and 1949.

1950–82: Robert J. Gordon, *Macroeconomics,* 3d ed. (Boston: Little, Brown, 1984), app. B.

1983: extrapolation from 1982 using an annual growth rate of 3%.

Commercial paper rate

1869–89: Friedman and Schwartz, *Monetary Trends,* 122–29. Linked in 1890 to

1890–1941: 4–6-month prime commercial paper from *Banking and Monetary Statistics, 1919–1941,* 448.

1942–46: 4–6-month prime commercial paper from *Banking and Monetary Statistics, 1942–1970,* 674.

1947–83: 6-month commercial paper—bank discount basis from *CITIBASE.*

Yield on corporate bonds
  1869–1918: yields on railroad bonds adjusted for drift from Frederick R. Macaulay, *The Movements of Interest Rates, Bond Yields and Stock Prices in the United States since 1856* (New York: National Bureau of Economic Research, 1938), A141–61. Linked in 1919 to
  1919–46: yield on corporate bonds, Moody's Baa rating, *Banking and Monetary Statistics.*
  1947–83: yield on corporate bonds, Moody's Baa rating, *Business Statistics.*
Money supply, M1
  1915–83: average of quarterly M1 series described in section 2 source notes.
Money supply, M2
  1869–74: money stock from Friedman and Schwartz, *Monetary Trends,* 122–29. Linked in 1875 to
  1875–1983: averaged from the quarterly M2 series described in section 2 source notes.
Money supply, Base
  1869–74: high-powered money from Friedman and Schwartz, *Monetary Trends,* 122–29.
  1875–1983: averaged from the quarterly money base series described in section 2 source notes.
Disposable income
  1897–1932: J. Bradford DeLong and Lawrence H. Summers, "The Changing Cyclical Variability of Economic Activity," in this volume.
Disposable income, NIPA
  1929–83: Disposable income from national income and product accounts, table 2.1, divided by the implicit price deflator for personal consumption expenditures from national income and product accounts, table 7.1.
Consumption, Kendrick
  1890–1953: series A23 from *Long Term Economic Growth, 1860–1970.*
Consumption, derived from Kuznets
  1897–1932: DeLong and Summers, this volume.
Consumption, NIPA
  1929–83: national income and product accounts, table 1.2.

2. Quarterly Data from 1875 to 1983

Quarter	Nominal GNP	Real GNP (1972 dollars)	GNP Deflator (1972 = 100)	Trend Real GNP	Commercial Paper Rate	Yield on Corporate Bonds
1875:1	8.83	43.44	20.44	46.64	6.74	8.07
2	8.88	44.03	20.16	47.25	6.14	7.95
3	8.62	43.27	19.92	47.86	6.34	7.88
4	8.60	43.55	19.74	48.48	7.73	7.83
1876:1	9.08	46.09	19.69	49.11	7.01	7.67
2	8.78	46.11	19.04	49.74	6.39	7.66
3	8.58	45.98	18.66	50.38	5.34	7.60
4	8.94	46.57	19.20	51.04	6.95	7.64
1877:1	9.18	48.17	19.06	51.70	6.12	7.66
2	9.21	48.58	18.95	52.36	5.44	7.69
3	9.10	50.59	17.99	53.04	6.68	7.61
4	9.04	50.82	17.78	53.73	7.64	7.65

Quarterly Data from 1875 to 1983   (continued)

Quarter	Nominal GNP	Real GNP (1972 dollars)	GNP Deflator (1972 = 100)	Trend Real GNP	Commercial Paper Rate	Yield on Corporate Bonds
1878:1	9.15	51.99	17.61	54.42	6.72	7.63
2	8.92	52.20	17.09	55.13	5.86	7.59
3	9.17	53.90	17.02	55.84	5.30	7.57
4	8.93	53.71	16.62	56.56	6.50	7.52
1879:1	8.95	54.83	16.32	57.29	5.69	7.33
2	8.97	56.59	15.85	58.04	6.00	7.26
3	9.41	58.74	16.02	58.79	6.37	7.17
4	11.29	63.61	17.75	59.55	7.34	7.19
1880:1	12.59	66.18	19.02	59.90	6.69	7.07
2	12.14	66.91	18.15	60.26	6.37	7.04
3	11.85	66.52	17.81	60.62	6.20	6.93
4	11.98	67.34	17.79	60.98	6.81	6.73
1881:1	11.84	66.57	17.78	61.34	6.68	6.66
2	11.84	67.48	17.54	61.81	5.54	6.59
3	12.24	68.58	17.85	62.27	6.17	6.56
4	12.61	69.27	18.20	62.74	7.56	6.66
1882:1	12.68	69.86	18.15	63.22	6.83	6.69
2	13.11	70.82	18.51	63.69	6.30	6.65
3	13.37	71.78	18.63	64.18	6.96	6.66
4	13.24	72.03	18.38	64.66	7.64	6.69
1883:1	13.12	70.48	18.62	65.15	7.04	6.69
2	12.91	69.90	18.47	65.64	6.84	6.69
3	12.56	70.32	17.86	66.14	6.75	6.71
4	12.55	70.44	17.82	66.64	7.02	6.69
1884:1	12.78	71.34	17.91	67.14	6.04	6.60
2	12.72	73.06	17.40	67.64	6.47	6.62
3	12.40	72.53	17.10	68.16	6.94	6.69
4	11.89	71.78	16.56	68.67	6.52	6.66
1885:1	11.74	71.76	16.36	69.19	5.84	6.55
2	11.59	72.13	16.07	69.71	5.02	6.48
3	11.48	72.54	15.83	70.24	4.93	6.40
4	11.84	73.35	16.15	70.77	5.60	6.33
1886:1	12.05	74.19	16.24	71.31	5.32	6.19
2	11.87	75.37	15.75	71.84	5.34	6.16
3	12.15	77.07	15.76	72.39	6.27	6.14
4	12.18	77.23	15.77	72.94	7.27	6.18
1887:1	12.67	78.17	16.21	73.49	6.51	6.19
2	12.61	78.62	16.04	74.04	6.53	6.20
3	12.29	77.67	15.83	74.60	7.78	6.25
4	12.65	78.73	16.07	75.16	7.33	6.30
1888:1	12.37	75.67	16.35	75.73	6.51	6.20
2	12.21	75.72	16.12	76.30	6.11	6.19
3	12.41	76.64	16.19	76.88	5.86	6.12
4	12.93	77.71	16.64	77.46	6.22	6.13
1889:1	12.96	78.39	16.53	78.05	5.76	6.05
2	12.74	77.93	16.35	78.64	5.30	5.99

Quarterly Data from 1875 to 1983   (continued)

Quarter	Nominal GNP	Real GNP (1972 dollars)	GNP Deflator (1972 = 100)	Trend Real GNP	Commercial Paper Rate	Yield on Corporate Bonds
1889:3	12.89	78.93	16.33	79.23	6.24	5.98
4	13.25	80.49	16.47	79.83	7.32	6.05
1890:1	13.15	82.17	16.00	80.86	6.44	6.07
2	13.47	84.45	15.95	81.90	6.44	6.09
3	13.94	85.80	16.25	82.96	6.50	6.15
4	14.04	86.86	16.16	84.03	8.25	6.26
1891:1	13.63	84.77	16.08	85.12	6.72	6.24
2	13.64	84.90	16.07	86.11	6.42	6.33
3	14.28	91.17	15.67	87.12	6.65	6.37
4	14.54	93.78	15.51	88.14	6.14	6.29
1892:1	14.64	96.55	15.17	89.17	5.25	6.21
2	14.42	96.85	14.89	90.21	4.59	6.18
3	14.83	97.16	15.27	91.26	5.49	6.17
4	15.36	98.21	15.64	92.33	6.27	6.21
1893:1	15.88	98.04	16.19	93.41	6.29	6.19
2	15.26	96.85	15.75	94.50	8.08	6.26
3	13.41	88.73	15.11	95.60	9.86	6.46
4	13.06	85.82	15.22	96.72	6.33	6.28
1894:1	12.76	86.72	14.71	97.85	5.16	6.16
2	12.60	87.17	14.46	98.99	4.83	6.08
3	13.35	90.76	14.71	100.15	5.14	6.07
4	13.75	95.03	14.47	101.32	5.75	6.00
1895:1	13.66	96.88	14.11	102.51	6.39	6.02
2	14.44	98.73	14.62	103.70	5.14	5.99
3	14.81	102.28	14.48	104.92	5.43	5.88
4	14.98	104.33	14.35	106.41	6.25	5.90
1896:1	14.13	99.97	14.14	107.38	7.59	5.96
2	13.76	99.00	13.90	108.64	5.94	5.93
3	13.42	97.73	13.73	109.91	7.94	6.08
4	13.81	97.06	14.23	111.19	6.62	5.99
1897:1	14.44	103.28	13.99	112.49	4.56	5.86
2	14.56	105.80	13.77	113.80	4.56	5.81
3	15.59	110.46	14.12	115.13	4.80	5.77
4	16.10	111.92	14.39	116.48	4.96	5.75
1898:1	16.19	111.32	14.55	117.84	5.10	5.73
2	16.25	109.69	14.82	119.22	6.23	5.82
3	15.66	108.74	14.40	121.61	5.23	5.73
4	15.91	110.07	14.32	122.02	4.79	5.67
1899:1	17.06	117.78	14.49	123.44	4.73	5.61
2	17.42	118.69	14.68	124.89	4.85	5.56
3	18.37	121.64	15.10	126.34	5.68	5.59
4	19.34	123.48	15.66	127.82	6.73	5.67
1900:1	19.51	122.63	15.91	129.32	6.24	5.65
2	19.42	123.63	15.71	130.83	5.31	5.65
3	19.35	123.75	15.64	132.36	5.47	5.67
4	19.30	124.20	15.54	133.90	5.80	5.66

Quarterly Data from 1875 to 1983   (continued)

Quarter	Nominal GNP	Real GNP (1972 dollars)	GNP Deflator (1972 = 100)	Trend Real GNP	Commercial Paper Rate	Yield on Corporate Bonds
1901:1	20.55	132.71	15.49	135.57	5.09	5.62
2	21.33	138.79	15.37	137.05	5.40	5.64
3	21.79	139.80	15.59	138.65	5.65	5.68
4	22.20	140.91	15.84	140.27	5.45	5.68
1902:1	21.62	137.71	15.70	141.14	5.43	5.67
2	22.01	137.93	15.96	142.46	5.37	5.69
3	22.51	140.61	16.01	143.56	5.86	5.75
4	23.42	140.27	16.70	144.66	6.57	5.82
1903:1	24.14	144.64	16.69	145.80	5.80	5.86
2	23.95	147.68	16.22	147.07	5.79	5.94
3	23.98	148.31	16.17	148.34	6.50	6.04
4	23.12	143.78	16.08	149.63	6.54	6.02
1904:1	23.70	143.33	16.54	150.92	5.61	6.03
2	23.24	143.05	16.25	152.23	4.71	6.01
3	23.48	143.20	16.39	153.55	4.92	5.96
4	24.68	147.26	16.76	154.58	5.32	5.95
1905:1	25.15	149.33	16.84	156.22	4.72	5.92
2	25.51	152.80	16.70	157.57	4.75	5.94
3	26.11	155.81	16.76	158.94	5.08	5.93
4	27.49	162.22	16.95	160.32	6.17	5.95
1906:1	28.89	168.88	17.10	161.71	5.85	5.98
2	29.38	170.74	17.21	163.11	5.83	6.02
3	29.76	173.90	17.11	164.52	6.55	6.05
4	31.49	178.38	17.65	165.94	6.76	6.06
1907:1	31.72	178.52	17.77	167.38	6.67	6.11
2	32.18	179.22	17.95	168.83	6.14	6.18
3	32.25	177.26	18.19	170.29	6.71	6.27
4	30.20	167.44	18.04	171.77	7.16	6.45
1908:1	27.72	157.63	17.59	173.26	6.01	6.30
2	28.13	158.04	17.80	174.76	4.71	6.26
3	29.09	161.87	17.97	176.27	4.59	6.20
4	30.26	167.37	18.08	177.80	4.71	6.14
1909:1	31.41	174.23	18.03	179.34	4.30	6.09
2	32.77	178.71	18.34	180.89	4.25	6.11
3	33.92	183.58	18.48	182.46	4.49	6.14
4	35.46	187.20	18.94	184.04	5.64	6.19
1910:1	35.82	187.60	19.09	185.64	5.22	6.22
2	35.64	185.72	19.19	187.25	5.51	6.30
3	35.14	184.69	19.03	188.87	6.26	6.32
4	34.45	185.91	18.53	190.50	5.88	6.29
1911:1	35.03	188.97	18.54	192.15	4.64	6.31
2	35.11	191.02	18.38	193.82	4.41	6.31
3	36.64	193.26	18.96	195.50	4.99	6.33
4	37.13	194.37	19.10	197.19	4.97	6.33
1912:1	37.88	197.52	19.18	198.90	4.68	6.32
2	39.44	200.43	19.68	200.62	4.83	6.34

Quarterly Data from 1875 to 1983   (continued)

Quarter	Nominal GNP	Real GNP (1972 dollars)	GNP Deflator (1972 = 100)	Trend Real GNP	Commercial Paper Rate	Yield on Corporate Bonds
1912:3	39.75	202.84	19.60	202.36	5.63	6.38
4	40.30	205.25	19.63	204.12	6.50	6.40
1913:1	39.68	204.12	19.44	204.99	5.75	6.42
2	39.07	202.99	19.25	205.90	6.15	6.56
3	39.81	204.51	19.47	206.75	6.58	6.56
4	39.59	201.90	19.61	207.63	6.31	6.59
1914:1	39.07	200.19	19.52	208.52	4.64	6.50
2	39.24	200.54	19.57	209.62	4.43	6.48
3	39.47	195.97	20.14	210.73	6.54	0.00
4	37.55	187.11	20.07	211.84	6.28	0.00
1915:1	38.63	188.71	20.47	212.96	4.23	6.64
2	39.09	189.26	20.66	214.09	4.31	6.63
3	39.97	193.74	20.63	215.22	3.90	6.74
4	42.88	202.81	21.14	216.36	3.62	6.58
1916:1	46.31	208.15	22.25	217.50	3.50	6.50
2	47.14	207.53	22.71	218.65	3.67	6.53
3	47.84	208.43	22.95	219.81	4.17	6.55
4	51.92	208.64	24.89	220.97	4.03	6.47
1917:1	53.20	203.40	26.16	222.14	4.32	6.45
2	60.90	210.64	28.91	223.31	5.03	6.69
3	63.17	211.98	29.80	224.49	5.26	6.85
4	64.89	219.70	29.54	225.68	5.69	7.07
1918:1	67.24	229.84	29.26	226.87	5.90	7.12
2	75.37	248.53	30.33	228.07	6.08	7.18
3	81.82	254.60	32.14	229.29	6.11	7.26
4	81.81	244.35	33.48	230.49	6.00	7.00
1919:1	77.97	229.01	34.05	231.70	5.29	7.12
2	81.42	228.00	35.71	232.93	5.34	7.23
3	87.29	229.53	38.03	234.16	5.38	7.06
4	90.43	229.43	39.41	235.40	5.46	7.34
1920:1	95.98	227.51	42.19	236.64	6.42	7.78
2	95.95	216.09	44.40	237.89	7.38	8.17
3	93.84	212.44	44.17	239.15	8.13	8.52
4	80.40	200.82	40.04	240.41	8.09	7.99
1921:1	69.78	191.68	36.40	241.68	7.71	8.50
2	68.56	196.63	34.87	242.96	7.09	8.53
3	69.35	202.42	34.26	244.25	6.17	8.48
4	70.37	209.02	33.67	245.54	5.50	8.34
1922:1	69.65	216.05	32.24	246.84	4.88	7.70
2	72.44	226.51	31.98	248.14	4.42	7.14
3	75.49	233.41	32.34	249.45	4.13	6.89
4	79.07	242.27	32.64	250.77	4.67	6.78
1923:1	84.71	251.51	33.68	252.09	4.75	6.98
2	87.17	257.75	33.82	253.43	5.13	7.17
3	84.68	253.39	33.42	254.77	5.21	7.34
4	84.93	253.71	33.48	256.11	5.17	7.46

Quarterly Data from 1875 to 1983   (continued)

Quarter	Nominal GNP	Real GNP (1972 dollars)	GNP Deflator (1972 = 100)	Trend Real GNP	Commercial Paper Rate	Yield on Corporate Bonds
1924:1	87.30	260.65	33.49	258.73	4.88	7.24
2	82.86	252.46	32.82	261.38	4.42	7.03
3	82.00	249.84	32.82	264.05	3.29	6.67
4	87.35	262.60	33.26	266.75	3.34	6.62
1925:1	91.08	268.68	33.90	269.47	3.75	6.44
2	91.27	271.89	33.57	271.92	3.92	6.41
3	94.41	278.86	33.86	274.39	4.04	6.20
4	96.44	284.70	33.88	276.88	4.38	6.17
1926:1	96.60	287.33	33.62	279.40	4.34	6.09
2	96.15	288.21	33.36	281.94	4.13	5.98
3	97.93	295.01	33.19	284.50	4.34	5.79
4	97.98	296.71	33.02	287.08	4.54	5.81
1927:1	95.94	295.63	32.45	289.69	4.17	5.61
2	95.44	297.42	32.09	292.32	4.17	5.48
3	94.77	292.78	32.37	294.98	4.08	5.55
4	93.88	287.20	32.69	297.66	4.00	5.38
1928:1	94.31	289.40	32.59	300.37	4.04	5.35
2	96.18	292.98	32.83	303.09	4.54	5.33
3	99.01	299.71	33.04	305.85	5.38	5.58
4	99.16	302.80	32.75	308.63	5.42	5.58
1929:1	101.03	308.94	32.70	311.43	5.59	5.63
2	105.02	321.65	32.65	314.26	6.00	5.80
3	106.72	323.69	32.97	317.12	6.13	5.95
4	100.92	308.45	32.72	319.99	5.67	6.11
1930:1	96.53	297.27	32.47	321.53	4.63	5.92
2	95.25	295.58	32.22	323.08	3.71	5.70
3	88.35	281.13	31.43	324.69	3.08	5.77
4	82.77	268.10	30.87	326.19	2.92	5.94
1931:1	80.66	268.66	30.02	327.75	2.67	6.41
2	79.74	273.35	29.17	329.65	2.21	6.72
3	74.99	262.62	28.55	331.56	2.00	7.08
4	69.09	249.14	27.73	333.47	3.67	9.04
1932:1	63.84	240.16	26.58	335.40	3.80	9.13
2	58.83	228.43	25.75	337.34	3.13	10.46
3	56.08	220.46	25.44	339.29	2.29	10.79
4	54.57	219.12	24.90	341.26	1.71	7.87
1933:1	49.78	206.38	24.11	343.23	1.92	8.01
2	54.13	221.26	24.47	345.21	2.21	9.12
3	61.55	238.85	25.77	347.21	1.50	6.62
4	58.11	222.05	26.17	349.22	1.29	7.49
1934:1	62.88	234.29	26.84	351.24	1.38	7.01
2	67.22	247.72	27.14	353.27	0.96	6.01
3	65.50	237.19	27.61	355.31	0.88	6.13
4	65.49	237.16	27.61	357.37	0.88	6.40
1935:1	70.36	252.31	27.89	359.44	0.79	5.98
2	70.62	253.14	27.90	361.51	0.75	6.13

Quarterly Data from 1875 to 1983   (continued)

Quarter	Nominal GNP	Real GNP (1972 dollars)	GNP Deflator (1972 = 100)	Natural Real GNP	Commercial Paper Rate	Yield on Corporate Bonds
1935:3	72.43	260.14	27.84	363.61	0.75	5.67
4	76.58	274.58	27.89	365.71	0.75	5.54
1936:1	76.81	275.90	27.84	367.82	0.75	5.00
2	81.14	293.20	27.67	369.95	0.75	4.91
3	84.71	301.59	28.09	372.09	0.75	4.84
4	88.49	311.58	28.40	374.24	0.75	4.54
1937:1	90.60	310.53	29.17	376.41	0.75	4.49
2	93.75	318.41	29.44	378.58	1.00	4.84
3	93.94	317.21	29.62	380.77	1.00	4.91
4	85.30	294.46	28.97	382.98	1.00	5.52
1938:1	81.08	282.02	28.75	385.19	0.96	5.89
2	81.96	286.48	28.61	387.42	0.88	6.47
3	87.03	303.22	28.70	389.66	0.73	5.63
4	90.13	315.35	28.58	391.91	0.67	5.36
1939:1	88.59	312.34	28.36	394.18	0.56	5.12
2	86.76	307.79	28.19	396.46	0.56	5.15
3	90.37	319.32	28.30	398.75	0.60	4.84
4	98.15	339.96	28.87	401.06	0.63	4.88
1940:1	95.49	330.14	28.92	403.38	0.56	4.86
2	96.82	334.66	28.93	405.71	0.56	4.74
3	100.92	348.32	28.97	408.06	0.56	4.80
4	106.92	363.54	29.41	410.42	0.56	4.56
1941:1	110.65	371.18	29.81	412.79	0.56	4.38
2	120.35	391.93	30.71	415.18	0.56	4.33
3	131.40	412.57	31.85	417.58	0.50	4.28
4	138.80	426.38	32.55	420.00	0.52	4.28
1942:1	148.12	441.54	33.55	422.43	0.62	4.29
2	152.57	446.44	34.18	424.87	0.64	4.26
3	161.11	466.52	34.53	427.33	0.69	4.30
4	172.57	492.72	35.02	429.80	0.69	4.24
1943:1	182.22	510.87	35.67	432.28	0.69	4.16
2	188.69	522.00	36.15	434.78	0.69	3.96
3	195.56	539.31	36.26	437.30	0.69	3.81
4	202.31	554.55	36.48	439.83	0.69	3.82
1944:1	205.77	559.06	36.81	442.37	0.69	3.76
2	208.28	562.33	37.04	444.93	0.74	3.68
3	211.90	571.49	37.08	447.50	0.75	3.57
4	216.63	583.66	37.12	450.09	0.75	3.55
1945:1	220.99	595.55	37.11	452.70	0.75	3.46
2	220.85	588.95	37.50	455.31	0.75	3.36
3	207.80	546.93	37.99	457.95	0.75	3.26
4	198.81	509.24	39.04	460.60	0.75	3.20
1946:1	198.18	488.02	40.53	463.26	0.75	3.01
2	198.43	471.71	42.06	465.94	0.75	2.96
3	217.12	479.68	45.26	468.64	0.80	3.03
4	225.82	473.73	47.66	471.35	0.94	3.15

Quarterly Data from 1875 to 1983   (continued)

Quarter	Nominal GNP	Real GNP (1972 dollars)	GNP Deflator (1972 = 100)	Natural Real GNP	Commercial Paper Rate	Yield on Corporate Bonds
1947:1	225.10	466.05	48.30	474.07	1.00	3.13
2	229.30	469.88	48.80	476.81	1.00	3.16
3	233.60	470.02	49.70	479.57	1.01	3.18
4	244.00	475.63	51.30	482.34	1.13	3.35
1948:1	250.00	479.85	52.10	484.43	1.35	3.52
2	257.50	488.62	52.70	487.14	1.38	3.47
3	264.50	492.55	53.70	490.76	1.46	3.37
4	265.90	497.94	53.40	492.10	1.56	3.50
1949:1	260.50	492.44	52.90	493.90	1.56	3.46
2	257.00	490.46	52.40	497.40	1.56	3.45
3	258.90	495.03	52.30	503.10	1.46	3.46
4	256.80	491.01	52.30	508.70	1.36	3.36
1950:1	267.60	512.64	52.20	515.00	1.31	3.24
2	277.10	525.81	52.70	520.80	1.31	3.23
3	294.80	543.91	54.20	526.60	1.46	3.32
4	306.30	555.90	55.10	532.50	1.71	3.22
1951:1	320.40	564.09	56.80	538.50	1.95	3.17
2	328.30	575.97	57.00	544.60	2.19	3.35
3	335.00	587.72	57.00	550.70	2.25	3.53
4	339.20	588.89	57.60	556.90	2.26	3.50
1952:1	341.90	593.58	57.60	563.30	2.38	3.50
2	342.10	593.92	57.60	569.60	2.32	3.50
3	347.80	600.69	57.90	576.00	2.31	3.50
4	360.00	614.33	58.60	582.40	2.31	3.54
1953:1	366.10	622.62	58.80	589.00	2.33	3.51
2	369.40	628.23	58.80	595.60	2.62	3.65
3	368.40	624.41	59.00	602.30	2.75	3.86
4	363.10	618.57	58.70	609.10	2.37	3.82
1954:1	362.50	610.27	59.40	616.00	2.04	3.71
2	362.30	607.89	59.60	618.30	1.63	3.47
3	366.70	616.30	59.50	622.90	1.36	3.50
4	375.60	628.09	59.80	627.50	1.31	3.46
1955:1	388.20	643.78	60.30	632.20	1.61	3.45
2	396.20	652.72	60.70	636.90	1.97	3.49
3	404.80	663.61	61.00	641.70	2.33	3.52
4	411.00	669.38	61.40	646.50	2.83	3.59
1956:1	412.80	666.88	61.90	651.30	3.00	3.60
2	418.40	670.51	62.40	656.20	3.26	3.68
3	423.50	671.16	63.10	661.60	3.35	3.80
4	432.10	678.34	63.70	667.00	3.63	4.17
1957:1	440.20	683.54	64.40	672.60	3.63	4.49
2	442.30	683.62	64.70	677.00	3.68	4.44
3	449.40	688.21	65.30	684.20	3.95	4.73
4	444.00	678.90	65.40	686.90	3.99	4.99
1958:1	436.80	665.85	65.60	691.10	2.82	4.83
2	440.70	669.76	65.80	700.60	1.72	4.67

Quarterly Data from 1875 to 1983   (continued)

Quarter	Nominal GNP	Real GNP (1972 dollars)	GNP Deflator (1972 = 100)	Natural Real GNP	Commercial Paper Rate	Yield on Corporate Bonds
1958:3	453.90	685.65	66.20	711.30	2.13	4.53
4	467.00	702.26	66.50	717.10	3.21	4.92
1959:1	477.00	711.94	67.00	716.10	3.30	4.87
2	490.60	725.74	67.60	721.00	3.60	4.86
3	489.00	721.24	67.80	723.70	4.19	5.08
4	495.00	727.94	68.00	736.00	4.76	5.28
1960:1	506.90	741.08	68.40	740.80	4.69	5.34
2	506.30	738.05	68.60	747.20	4.07	5.20
3	508.00	737.30	68.90	752.10	3.37	5.22
4	504.80	731.59	69.00	758.50	3.27	5.11
1961:1	508.20	737.59	68.90	767.90	3.01	5.10
2	519.20	750.29	69.20	775.00	2.86	5.01
3	528.20	760.00	69.50	781.70	2.90	5.09
4	542.60	778.48	69.70	789.20	3.06	5.13
1962:1	554.20	789.46	70.20	797.70	3.24	5.08
2	562.70	798.16	70.50	805.60	3.20	5.02
3	568.90	805.81	70.60	810.00	3.33	5.05
4	574.30	807.74	71.10	813.30	3.26	4.99
1963:1	582.00	815.13	71.40	821.00	3.31	4.91
2	590.70	826.15	71.50	828.20	3.32	4.87
3	601.80	839.33	71.70	839.80	3.70	4.84
4	612.40	848.20	72.20	847.60	3.91	4.83
1964:1	625.30	863.67	72.40	857.40	3.95	4.83
2	634.00	873.28	72.60	864.70	3.93	4.85
3	642.80	880.55	73.00	869.00	3.91	4.83
4	648.80	886.34	73.20	871.70	4.06	4.53
1965:1	668.80	906.23	73.80	880.80	4.30	4.80
2	681.70	919.97	74.10	888.60	4.38	4.80
3	696.40	933.51	74.60	901.80	4.38	4.88
4	717.20	956.27	75.00	910.70	4.47	4.93
1966:1	738.50	975.56	75.70	923.00	4.97	5.06
2	750.00	979.11	76.60	931.00	5.43	5.41
3	760.60	987.79	77.00	940.10	5.79	5.68
4	774.90	996.01	77.80	951.80	6.00	6.10
1967:1	780.70	997.06	78.30	963.70	5.45	5.97
2	788.60	1004.59	78.50	971.40	4.72	5.83
3	805.70	1016.02	79.30	985.00	4.97	6.26
4	823.30	1027.84	80.10	991.20	5.30	6.52
1968:1	841.20	1036.22	81.18	997.20	5.58	6.84
2	867.20	1056.02	82.12	1010.10	6.08	6.97
3	884.90	1068.72	82.80	1018.70	5.96	6.98
4	900.30	1071.28	84.04	1023.70	5.96	6.84
1969:1	921.20	1084.15	84.97	1035.70	6.66	7.32
2	937.40	1088.73	86.10	1043.60	7.54	7.54
3	955.30	1091.90	87.49	1053.80	8.49	7.70
4	962.00	1085.53	88.62	1060.60	8.62	8.22

Quarterly Data from 1875 to 1983   (continued)

Quarter	Nominal GNP	Real GNP (1972 dollars)	GNP Deflator (1972 = 100)	Natural Real GNP	Commercial Paper Rate	Yield on Corporate Bonds
1970:1	972.00	1081.32	89.89	1071.20	8.55	8.86
2	986.30	1083.01	91.07	1082.40	8.17	8.70
3	1003.60	1093.37	91.79	1091.60	7.84	9.40
4	1009.00	1084.60	93.03	1105.20	6.29	9.33
1971:1	1049.30	1111.55	94.40	1119.20	4.59	8.74
2	1068.90	1116.93	95.70	1130.90	5.04	8.45
3	1086.60	1125.78	96.52	1136.90	5.74	8.76
4	1105.80	1135.43	97.39	1140.40	5.07	8.48
1972:1	1142.40	1157.21	98.72	1155.90	4.06	8.23
2	1171.70	1178.54	99.42	1170.20	4.58	8.24
3	1196.10	1193.12	100.25	1177.40	4.94	8.23
4	1233.50	1214.79	101.54	1191.00	5.33	8.06
1973:1	1283.50	1246.72	102.95	1202.50	6.28	7.90
2	1307.60	1248.31	104.75	1210.80	7.47	8.09
3	1337.70	1255.70	106.53	1221.00	9.87	8.24
4	1376.70	1266.05	108.74	1234.50	8.98	8.41
1974:1	1387.70	1253.34	110.72	1237.50	8.30	8.58
2	1423.80	1254.67	113.48	1252.80	10.46	8.88
3	1451.60	1246.86	116.42	1264.70	11.53	9.55
4	1473.80	1230.32	119.79	1273.30	9.05	10.41
1975:1	1479.80	1204.26	122.88	1279.90	6.56	10.62
2	1516.70	1218.82	124.44	1291.60	5.92	10.34
3	1578.50	1246.05	126.68	1307.90	6.67	10.33
4	1621.80	1257.31	128.99	1316.50	6.12	10.37
1976:1	1672.00	1284.97	130.12	1327.30	5.29	10.24
2	1698.60	1293.68	131.30	1336.70	5.57	9.83
3	1729.00	1301.08	132.89	1353.60	5.53	9.63
4	1772.50	1313.06	134.99	1362.80	4.99	9.29
1977:1	1834.80	1341.23	136.80	1374.60	4.81	9.08
2	1895.10	1363.28	139.01	1384.70	5.24	9.07
3	1954.40	1385.80	141.03	1398.80	5.81	8.87
4	1988.90	1388.51	143.24	1407.40	6.59	8.89
1978:1	2031.70	1400.01	145.12	1419.00	6.80	9.17
2	2139.50	1436.97	148.89	1430.70	7.20	9.32
3	2202.50	1448.82	152.02	1442.40	8.08	9.60
4	2281.60	1468.40	155.38	1454.40	9.90	9.59
1979:1	2335.50	1472.57	158.60	1464.40	10.10	10.13
2	2377.90	1469.20	161.85	1475.20	10.03	10.33
3	2454.80	1486.59	165.13	1486.20	10.60	10.29
4	2502.90	1489.38	168.05	1497.20	13.10	11.40
1980:1	2572.90	1496.40	171.94	1508.30	14.25	12.42
2	2578.80	1461.40	176.46	1519.50	10.62	14.19
3	2639.10	1464.20	180.24	1530.80	9.65	12.67
4	2736.00	1477.90	185.13	1542.10	14.51	14.23
1981:1	2875.80	1513.50	190.01	1553.60	14.52	15.03
2	2918.00	1511.70	193.03	1565.10	15.35	15.56

Quarterly Data from 1875 to 1983   (continued)

Quarter	Nominal GNP	Real GNP (1972 dollars)	GNP Deflator (1972 = 100)	Natural Real GNP	Commercial Paper Rate	Yield on Corporate Bonds
1981:3	3009.30	1522.10	197.71	1576.70	16.27	16.17
4	3027.90	1501.30	201.69	1588.40	12.94	17.11
1982:1	3026.00	1483.50	203.98	1600.20	13.70	17.10
2	3061.20	1480.50	206.77	1612.10	13.48	16.78
3	3080.10	1477.10	208.52	1624.00	11.53	16.80
4	3109.60	1478.80	210.28	1636.10	8.81	14.73
1983:1	3173.80	1491.00	212.86	1648.40	8.34	13.94
2	3267.00	1524.80	214.26	1660.70	8.61	13.29
3	3346.60	1550.20	215.88	1673.20	9.44	13.39
4	3431.70	1572.70	218.20	1685.70	9.19	13.46

Quarter	Money Supply			Index of All Common Stocks (41–43 = 10)	Index of Wholesale Prices, All Commodities (67 = 100)
	M1	M2	Base		
1875:1	—	2.33	0.64	—	42.83
2	—	2.33	0.63	—	42.14
3	—	2.33	0.63	—	41.45
4	—	2.31	0.62	—	40.76
1876:1	—	2.29	0.62	—	40.25
2	—	2.28	0.62	—	38.53
3	—	2.28	0.61	—	37.67
4	—	2.28	0.62	—	39.22
1877:1	—	2.28	0.62	—	39.39
2	—	2.26	0.62	—	39.22
3	—	2.24	0.62	—	36.64
4	—	2.18	0.62	—	35.43
1878:1	—	2.17	0.62	—	33.88
2	—	2.14	0.63	—	31.99
3	—	2.13	0.63	—	31.65
4	—	2.10	0.62	—	30.96
1879:1	—	2.12	0.63	—	30.96
2	—	2.18	0.64	—	30.27
3	—	2.28	0.67	—	30.79
4	—	2.45	0.71	—	34.74
1880:1	—	2.62	0.74	—	37.32
2	—	2.69	0.77	—	35.09
3	—	2.78	0.79	—	34.40
4	—	2.94	0.82	—	34.74

Quarterly Data from 1875 to 1983   (continued)

Quarter	Money Supply			Index of All Common Stocks (41 − 43 = 10)	Index of Wholesale Prices, All Commodities (67 = 100)
	M1	M2	Base		
1881:1	—	3.09	0.84	—	35.43
2	—	3.25	0.88	—	35.43
3	—	3.42	0.90	—	36.64
4	—	3.46	0.92	—	37.84
1882:1	—	3.50	0.93	—	38.01
2	—	3.53	0.93	—	38.87
3	—	3.59	0.94	—	38.87
4	—	3.65	0.95	—	37.67
1883:1	—	3.70	0.96	—	37.32
2	—	3.80	0.98	—	36.29
3	—	3.84	0.98	—	34.40
4	—	3.84	0.98	—	34.06
1884:1	—	3.85	0.98	—	34.23
2	—	3.78	0.97	—	33.02
3	—	3.76	0.99	—	32.34
4	—	3.77	1.00	—	31.13
1885:1	—	3.80	1.01	—	30.79
2	—	3.84	1.02	—	30.10
3	—	3.93	1.01	—	29.41
4	—	4.00	1.00	—	29.93
1886:1	—	4.12	0.99	—	29.76
2	—	4.18	0.99	—	28.38
3	—	4.24	0.99	—	28.38
4	—	4.30	1.01	—	28.55
1887:1	—	4.41	1.02	—	29.93
2	—	4.49	1.04	—	29.76
3	—	4.52	1.05	—	29.41
4	—	4.53	1.06	—	30.10
1888:1	—	4.57	1.07	—	30.79
2	—	4.57	1.08	—	30.10
3	—	4.64	1.08	—	29.93
4	—	4.68	1.09	—	30.44
1889:1	—	4.76	1.09	—	29.41
2	—	4.83	1.10	—	28.55
3	—	4.94	1.10	—	28.38
4	—	5.00	1.10	—	28.90
1890:1	—	5.15	1.11	—	28.29
2	—	5.29	1.13	—	28.57
3	—	5.38	1.15	—	29.57
4	—	5.41	1.17	—	29.55
1891:1	—	5.44	1.19	—	29.50
2	—	5.48	1.19	—	29.50
3	—	5.55	1.19	—	28.50
4	—	5.70	1.22	—	27.98
1892:1	—	5.87	1.25	—	26.95
2	—	6.03	1.27	—	26.14

Quarterly Data from 1875 to 1983   (continued)

Quarter	Money Supply			Index of All Common Stocks (41 − 43 = 10)	Index of Wholesale Prices, All Commodities (67 = 100)
	M1	M2	Base		
1892:3	—	6.09	1.26	—	26.97
4	—	6.02	1.25	—	27.86
1893:1	—	5.97	1.24	—	29.24
2	—	5.82	1.25	—	28.17
3	—	5.67	1.30	—	26.52
4	—	5.65	1.33	—	26.57
1894:1	—	5.72	1.32	—	25.06
2	—	5.74	1.31	—	24.34
3	—	5.83	1.28	—	25.01
4	—	5.91	1.25	—	24.70
1895:1	—	5.91	1.22	—	24.30
2	—	6.02	1.24	—	25.82
3	—	6.10	1.24	—	25.59
4	—	6.01	1.20	—	25.23
1896:1	—	5.89	1.18	—	24.49
2	—	5.80	1.16	—	23.77
3	—	5.91	1.18	—	23.31
4	—	5.99	1.24	—	24.48
1897:1	—	6.08	1.27	—	23.96
2	—	6.14	1.26	—	23.44
3	—	6.36	1.27	—	24.23
4	—	6.59	1.29	—	24.79
1898:1	—	6.78	1.32	—	25.01
2	—	6.98	1.39	—	25.63
3	—	7.21	1.39	—	24.73
4	—	7.53	1.43	—	24.77
1899:1	—	7.89	1.47	—	25.52
2	—	8.20	1.48	—	26.25
3	—	8.44	1.50	—	27.43
4	—	8.52	1.50	—	28.88
1900:1	—	8.61	1.53	6.19	29.52
2	—	8.72	1.59	6.08	29.03
3	—	9.09	1.64	5.87	28.83
4	—	9.41	1.67	6.45	28.52
1901:1	—	9.78	1.70	7.28	28.28
2	—	10.02	1.71	8.12	27.97
3	—	10.27	1.73	7.99	28.55
4	—	10.51	1.74	7.98	29.31
1902:1	—	10.78	1.75	8.17	29.24
2	—	10.96	1.76	8.45	30.01
3	—	11.17	1.78	8.76	30.24
4	—	11.39	1.82	8.29	31.89
1903:1	—	11.58	1.84	8.32	31.80
2	—	11.69	1.86	7.51	30.62
3	—	11.83	1.88	6.65	30.43
4	—	11.99	1.90	6.37	30.13

Quarterly Data from 1875 to 1983   (continued)

| Quarter | Money Supply | | | Index of All Common Stocks (41 − 43 = 10) | Index of Wholesale Prices, All Commodities (67 = 100) |
	M1	M2	Base		
1904:1	—	12.15	1.96	6.55	31.11
2	—	12.30	1.98	6.55	30.31
3	—	12.65	2.01	7.04	30.53
4	—	13.05	2.01	8.06	31.25
1905:1	—	13.40	2.01	8.76	31.29
2	—	13.74	2.03	8.68	30.79
3	—	14.04	2.05	9.10	30.81
4	—	14.37	2.08	9.40	31.13
1906:1	—	14.56	2.11	9.74	31.39
2	—	14.81	2.15	9.30	31.60
3	—	15.15	2.19	9.61	31.41
4	—	15.55	2.25	9.91	32.80
1907:1	—	15.81	2.28	9.39	33.28
2	—	16.00	2.31	8.78	33.75
3	—	15.80	2.31	7.71	34.18
4	—	15.32	2.41	6.49	33.49
1908:1	—	14.92	2.53	6.77	31.91
2	—	15.24	2.52	7.50	32.16
3	—	15.74	2.54	8.12	32.58
4	—	16.31	2.54	8.71	33.09
1909:1	—	16.68	2.53	8.93	33.49
2	—	17.09	2.56	9.58	34.62
3	—	17.49	2.57	10.10	35.26
4	—	17.75	2.57	10.24	36.58
1910:1	—	17.94	2.58	9.92	37.08
2	—	17.99	2.58	9.46	37.19
3	—	18.09	2.62	8.80	36.41
4	—	18.46	2.63	9.23	34.55
1911:1	—	18.68	2.67	9.34	33.57
2	—	19.11	2.69	9.48	32.56
3	—	19.31	2.68	9.16	33.63
4	—	19.74	2.70	8.97	33.95
1912:1	—	20.12	2.72	9.15	34.43
2	—	20.34	2.74	9.58	35.90
3	—	20.71	2.65	9.75	35.97
4	—	21.00	1.96	9.65	36.31
1913:1	—	21.17	2.77	9.02	36.12
2	—	21.19	2.77	8.49	35.71
3	—	21.32	2.80	8.40	36.09
4	—	21.67	2.83	8.12	36.05
1914:1	—	21.85	2.85	8.39	35.24
2	—	22.11	2.85	8.14	34.81
3	—	22.35	2.86	0.00	35.62
4	—	22.52	3.01	0.00	34.88
1915:1	11.59	22.79	2.86	7.48	35.24
2	11.83	23.31	2.94	8.04	35.43

Quarterly Data from 1875 to 1983   (continued)

Quarter	Money Supply			Index of All Common Stocks (41 − 43 = 10)	Index of Wholesale Prices, All Commodities (67 = 100)
	M1	M2	Base		
1915:3	12.31	23.97	3.02	8.14	35.47
4	13.10	25.67	3.13	9.36	37.13
1916:1	13.66	26.82	3.25	9.23	40.57
2	14.03	27.73	3.33	9.23	42.50
3	14.57	28.71	3.44	9.40	43.93
4	15.27	30.28	3.58	10.00	49.48
1917:1	15.99	30.44	3.80	9.30	54.06
2	16.54	32.75	4.01	9.02	61.37
3	16.92	33.68	4.15	8.48	63.86
4	17.37	33.85	4.33	7.17	63.28
1918:1	17.87	35.14	4.58	7.31	64.35
2	17.97	35.37	4.79	7.37	66.29
3	18.77	36.72	4.94	7.54	69.45
4	19.65	38.24	5.33	7.94	70.33
1919:1	20.18	39.64	5.30	8.30	68.03
2	20.90	41.11	5.41	9.24	69.47
3	21.81	43.11	5.47	9.53	73.36
4	22.72	45.43	5.67	9.60	75.10
1920:1	23.22	46.86	5.82	8.90	81.42
2	23.23	47.63	5.93	8.55	85.86
3	23.05	47.70	6.02	8.13	82.97
4	22.54	47.30	5.92	7.72	68.51
1921:1	21.57	46.05	5.68	7.32	55.26
2	20.72	44.66	5.47	7.16	49.62
3	20.29	43.76	5.26	6.82	48.21
4	20.22	43.84	5.12	7.33	48.37
1922:1	20.36	43.87	5.06	7.83	47.66
2	21.08	45.60	5.16	8.76	49.12
3	21.49	47.00	5.19	8.98	51.14
4	22.01	48.11	5.29	9.34	51.74
1923:1	22.21	49.07	5.39	9.60	53.29
2	22.21	49.91	5.51	9.08	52.65
3	22.31	50.05	5.55	8.46	50.89
4	22.38	50.68	5.61	8.65	50.89
1924:1	22.38	50.86	5.58	9.18	51.22
2	22.96	51.72	5.63	8.90	49.55
3	23.74	53.37	5.70	9.61	49.83
4	24.20	54.74	5.78	10.06	51.39
1925:1	24.47	55.81	5.83	11.01	53.51
2	24.99	56.72	5.76	11.03	52.72
3	25.64	58.20	5.78	11.78	53.60
4	25.64	59.02	5.81	12.74	53.58
1926:1	25.58	59.39	5.88	12.94	52.65
2	25.52	59.56	5.87	12.24	51.79
3	25.33	59.67	5.88	13.28	51.29
4	25.11	59.34	5.82	13.41	50.86

Quarterly Data from 1875 to 1983   (continued)

Quarter	Money Supply			Index of All Common Stocks (41 − 43 = 10)	Index of Wholesale Prices, All Commodities (67 = 100)
	M1	M2	Base		
1927:1	25.36	60.00	5.84	13.94	49.36
2	25.45	60.86	5.93	14.73	48.37
3	25.54	61.26	5.90	15.86	49.16
4	25.63	61.95	5.89	16.83	49.97
1028:1	25.85	62.95	5.86	17.49	49.48
2	25.49	63.54	5.90	19.16	50.02
3	25.62	63.03	5.84	19.42	50.50
4	25.80	63.76	5.92	21.68	49.59
1929:1	25.74	63.46	5.88	24.24	49.43
2	25.85	63.07	5.81	24.43	49.09
3	26.16	63.61	5.90	28.12	49.69
4	25.40	63.62	5.90	21.90	48.49
1930:1	25.39	62.65	5.77	21.36	47.15
2	24.79	62.28	5.69	21.80	46.03
3	24.56	62.00	5.73	19.27	43.53
4	24.35	61.25	5.72	15.29	41.95
1931:1	23.94	60.16	5.83	15.29	39.73
2	23.30	59.01	5.88	13.07	37.86
3	22.53	57.11	6.08	11.90	37.03
4	21.35	52.68	6.15	8.61	35.97
1932:1	20.56	49.62	6.21	7.41	34.33
2	19.95	47.95	6.36	5.08	33.33
3	19.92	46.72	6.47	6.37	33.54
4	19.99	46.87	6.58	6.26	32.83
1933:1	19.01	44.25	7.26	5.93	31.13
2	18.86	41.15	6.52	8.01	32.35
3	18.92	41.45	6.56	9.96	35.98
4	19.46	41.99	6.73	9.03	36.65
1934:1	20.34	43.37	6.93	10.08	37.75
2	21.03	45.04	7.55	9.72	38.12
3	22.01	46.63	7.82	8.91	39.35
4	23.00	48.03	7.89	8.90	39.54
1935:1	24.03	50.16	8.37	8.72	40.88
2	25.07	51.71	8.63	9.37	41.30
3	26.29	53.67	9.01	10.71	41.38
4	26.71	55.11	9.50	11.93	41.62
1936:1	27.52	55.93	9.71	13.70	41.42
2	28.96	58.45	9.75	13.58	40.85
3	29.55	60.13	10.36	14.57	41.92
4	30.11	61.14	10.82	15.87	42.67
1937:1	30.30	62.04	10.96	16.65	44.72
2	29.93	62.11	11.12	15.19	45.17
3	29.28	62.01	11.00	14.91	45.20
4	28.76	60.72	11.05	10.95	42.72
1938:1	28.84	60.97	11.39	10.31	41.35
2	28.93	60.57	11.77	9.59	40.44

Quarterly Data from 1875 to 1983   (continued)

Quarter	Money Supply			Index of All Common Stocks (41 − 43 = 10)	Index of Wholesale Prices, All Commodities (67 = 100)
	M1	M2	Base		
1938:3	30.24	61.68	12.19	11.35	40.45
4	31.02	63.44	12.81	12.08	40.08
1939:1	31.48	64.09	13.11	11.79	39.65
2	32.59	65.23	14.10	10.78	39.22
3	34.65	67.81	15.11	11.55	39.47
4	35.81	70.18	15.66	12.14	40.90
1940:1	36.84	71.94	16.17	11.91	40.68
2	38.15	73.57	17.06	10.70	40.33
3	39.49	75.62	18.04	10.15	40.09
4	41.57	78.09	18.73	10.55	40.99
1941:1	43.78	81.68	19.28	10.05	41.78
2	45.18	83.96	19.25	9.60	43.89
3	46.35	86.25	19.18	10.23	46.59
4	47.97	87.48	19.50	9.40	47.90
1942:1	50.50	90.14	19.90	8.59	49.93
2	53.55	93.76	20.42	8.03	50.93
3	57.84	99.51	21.30	8.64	51.17
4	62.62	106.34	22.25	9.44	51.82
1943:1	67.12	114.83	23.82	10.62	52.94
2	72.80	119.90	23.74	11.81	53.60
3	73.72	128.78	25.55	12.03	53.22
4	76.98	130.91	25.96	11.56	53.17
1944:1	80.19	136.24	27.04	11.91	53.44
2	83.03	143.16	28.93	12.22	53.70
3	88.13	149.06	29.92	12.80	53.66
4	91.52	158.54	31.98	12.94	53.87
1945:1	95.45	165.67	32.89	13.79	54.20
2	97.00	171.30	34.29	14.73	54.70
3	100.00	177.07	35.11	15.15	54.50
4	100.69	182.01	35.77	16.96	54.90
1946:1	102.28	183.38	35.94	17.87	55.60
2	104.85	189.42	36.02	18.65	57.40
3	105.66	192.71	36.35	16.95	65.00
4	106.38	194.09	36.19	14.86	71.30
1947:1	108.07	196.69	36.52	15.39	74.30
2	109.66	199.58	36.76	14.59	74.90
3	110.54	201.77	37.01	15.43	76.80
4	111.04	203.56	37.09	15.25	80.10
1948:1	110.74	204.11	37.01	14.41	81.80
2	110.03	203.01	37.09	16.12	82.50
3	110.08	203.28	37.67	16.04	84.10
4	109.54	202.87	39.07	15.56	83.00
1949:1	109.13	202.18	38.82	15.01	80.70
2	109.22	202.73	37.83	14.55	78.60
3	108.90	202.32	36.52	15.18	77.90
4	109.05	202.32	35.53	16.18	77.70

Quarterly Data from 1875 to 1983   (continued)

Quarter	Money Supply			Index of All Common Stocks (41 − 43 = 10)	Index of Wholesale Prices, All Commodities (67 = 100)
	M1	M2	Base		
1950:1	110.20	203.97	35.44	17.15	77.90
2	111.75	206.58	35.61	18.34	78.90
3	112.95	208.09	35.69	18.30	83.40
4	113.93	209.32	35.86	19.82	87.10
1951:1	115.08	211.11	37.17	21.61	92.10
2	116.19	212.75	38.00	21.80	91.90
3	117.76	215.64	38.49	22.77	90.30
4	119.89	219.48	38.91	23.16	90.20
1952:1	121.31	222.64	39.40	23.92	89.40
2	122.37	224.83	39.63	23.95	88.50
3	123.64	227.58	40.03	25.01	88.80
4	124.72	230.46	40.50	25.11	87.70
1953:1	125.33	232.24	40.73	26.01	87.20
2	126.05	234.44	40.93	24.50	87.00
3	126.22	235.81	41.27	23.98	87.90
4	126.37	237.32	41.17	24.43	87.40
1954:1	126.54	239.25	41.27	26.02	87.80
2	127.18	241.44	41.27	28.44	87.80
3	128.38	244.74	41.27	30.77	87.60
4	129.72	247.34	41.53	33.53	87.10
1955:1	131.07	250.09	41.53	36.30	87.50
2	131.88	251.74	41.67	38.38	87.80
3	132.40	252.97	41.70	43.15	88.10
4	132.64	253.93	41.83	44.14	88.40
1956:1	133.11	254.62	42.07	45.36	89.20
2	133.38	255.85	42.10	46.95	90.60
3	133.48	256.95	42.13	48.04	91.10
4	134.09	258.60	42.40	46.15	92.00
1957:1	134.29	260.80	42.47	44.31	92.70
2	134.36	262.72	42.53	46.46	93.00
3	134.26	264.50	42.53	46.11	93.80
4	133.48	265.19	42.53	40.64	93.80
1958:1	133.72	267.93	42.70	41.50	94.60
2	135.22	274.52	43.20	43.60	94.70
3	136.64	279.33	43.37	47.55	94.50
4	138.48	282.62	43.53	52.31	94.50
1959:1	140.35	286.60	43.70	55.51	94.80
2	141.75	291.00	43.90	57.51	95.10
3	142.23	294.90	44.07	58.73	94.80
4	141.20	296.10	43.93	57.76	94.40
1960:1	140.83	297.20	43.87	56.28	94.90
2	140.83	299.90	43.93	56.07	95.00
3	142.00	305.30	44.03	55.72	94.70
4	141.98	309.80	44.07	55.33	94.90
1961:1	142.85	314.80	44.70	62.00	95.20
2	143.88	320.70	44.67	65.98	94.30

Quarterly Data from 1875 to 1983   (continued)

Quarter	Money Supply			Index of All Common Stocks $(41 - 43 = 10)$	Index of Wholesale Prices, All Commodities $(67 = 100)$
	M1	M2	Base		
1961:3	144.90	326.20	45.13	66.83	94.30
4	146.18	331.80	45.80	70.27	94.40
1962:1	147.18	338.90	46.10	69.86	94.90
2	147.95	345.90	46.57	62.22	94.40
3	147.90	351.30	46.90	57.83	94.90
4	148.93	358.40	47.40	59.62	94.80
1963:1	150.45	366.30	47.93	65.55	94.40
2	151.93	374.20	48.50	69.67	94.30
3	153.38	381.90	49.17	70.97	94.60
4	154.80	389.30	49.87	73.27	94.70
1964:1	155.85	395.80	50.57	77.55	94.80
2	157.20	402.50	51.17	80.30	94.40
3	159.75	411.70	52.00	82.88	94.70
4	161.63	420.20	52.73	84.75	94.90
1965:1	162.90	428.50	53.40	86.57	95.40
2	163.90	435.70	54.03	87.43	96.30
3	166.05	444.10	54.77	86.93	97.00
4	169.10	454.00	55.83	91.76	97.60
1966:1	171.95	462.50	56.63	91.63	99.10
2	172.98	468.30	57.47	88.15	99.50
3	172.80	471.30	58.13	81.43	100.60
4	173.33	476.20	58.47	79.82	99.90
1967:1	175.25	484.00	59.33	87.08	99.90
2	178.10	495.50	60.20	91.66	90.70
3	181.93	509.50	61.17	94.44	100.10
4	184.73	520.30	62.23	94.54	100.30
1968:1	187.15	529.30	63.27	91.63	101.70
2	190.63	538.10	64.10	98.02	102.30
3	194.30	549.00	65.17	99.92	102.70
4	198.55	561.80	66.47	105.21	103.30
1969:1	201.73	571.20	67.40	100.93	104.80
2	203.18	576.50	67.93	101.67	106.20
3	204.18	580.30	68.50	94.47	107.00
4	206.10	585.20	69.43	94.28	108.00
1970:1	207.90	587.30	70.20	88.71	109.60
2	209.78	593.10	71.33	79.20	110.10
3	212.78	603.50	72.67	78.74	110.80
4	216.08	619.10	74.00	86.23	110.90
1971:1	220.28	640.40	75.63	96.73	112.60
2	225.25	666.60	77.10	101.47	113.90
3	228.45	684.60	78.67	98.55	114.80
4	230.70	702.90	79.60	96.41	114.90
1972:1	235.60	725.20	81.00	105.41	117.00
2	239.38	744.30	82.63	108.16	118.20
3	244.55	768.50	84.10	109.20	119.90
4	250.70	793.40	86.23	114.04	121.20

Quarterly Data from 1875 to 1983   (continued)

Quarter	Money Supply			Index of All Common Stocks (41 − 43 = 10)	Index of Wholesale Prices, All Commodities (67 = 100)
	M1	M2	Base		
1973:1	254.80	813.80	88.23	115.00	127.10
2	258.40	827.90	89.97	107.41	133.20
3	261.03	840.30	91.73	105.08	138.70
4	264.68	851.60	93.23	102.22	139.90
1974:1	268.77	868.70	95.37	95.67	149.20
2	271.23	880.00	97.57	90.64	154.50
3	273.73	889.60	99.47	75.66	165.40
4	276.73	902.40	101.60	69.42	171.20
1975:1	278.75	920.10	103.20	78.81	171.20
2	283.80	954.30	105.20	89.07	173.00
3	288.13	989.10	107.40	87.62	176.70
4	290.88	1014.00	109.40	89.11	178.60
1976:1	295.18	1046.00	111.50	99.53	179.50
2	299.53	1080.00	114.30	101.62	182.10
3	303.35	1110.00	116.30	104.31	184.30
4	309.35	1152.00	118.60	102.58	186.00
1977:1	316.55	1192.00	120.80	101.78	190.10
2	321.80	1225.00	121.00	99.03	194.70
3	327.60	1254.00	123.80	98.05	194.90
4	334.80	1285.00	126.50	93.95	197.20
1978:1	341.13	1309.00	129.50	89.35	202.00
2	348.70	1334.00	132.50	95.93	208.00
3	355.45	1361.00	135.30	101.66	211.20
4	361.38	1393.00	138.10	97.13	216.00
1979:1	367.08	1415.00	140.60	99.35	223.90
2	376.10	1451.00	143.30	101.18	231.80
3	384.58	1489.00	146.40	106.22	239.10
4	388.38	1517.30	149.40	105.30	247.50
1980:1	394.30	1518.90	152.30	110.30	259.00
2	390.00	1535.70	154.60	108.40	264.20
3	405.50	1588.00	158.50	123.28	272.90
4	416.10	1625.80	162.60	133.12	279.20
1981:1	420.90	1654.50	163.80	131.52	287.60
2	429.30	1697.70	166.40	132.81	294.10
3	432.60	1731.70	168.30	125.68	296.10
4	437.50	1777.20	169.90	122.17	295.80
1982:1	448.80	1819.80	173.50	114.21	298.30
2	451.30	1853.20	177.00	114.12	298.60
3	458.20	1896.60	180.00	113.82	300.00
4	475.70	1946.70	183.80	136.71	300.30
1983:1	490.90	2046.30	189.00	147.65	300.50
2	505.20	2100.40	194.10	162.73	301.50
3	517.20	2136.60	197.60	165.51	304.40
4	523.40	2181.90	201.40	165.75	305.90

Section 2 Source Notes

Nominal GNP
1875–1918: interpolated by the Chow-Lin method using the algorithm described in Gordon and Veitch, this volume. Dependent variable: annual real GNP described in section 1 source notes. Quarterly interpolators: constant, linear time trend, and index of industrial production and trade from Warren M. Persons, *Forecasting Business Cycles* (New York: Wiley, 1931). Notes on the interpolation—Persons's index does not contain a secular trend, only a cyclical component (it is similar to the output ratio concept used by Robert J. Gordon). Rather than trying to introduce a trend into Persons's index, real GNP was detrended using benchmarks 1876, 1888, 1901, 1913, 1929. These years correspond to years when Persons's index is close to 100. Once the quarterly detrended real GNP series was interpolated, the secular trend in GNP was introduced using the benchmarks above.
1919–46: interpolated by Chow-Lin method. Dependent variable: annual real GNP. Quarterly interpolators: constant, linear time trend, and index of industrial production and trade from Persons, *Forecasting Business Cycles,* for 1919–30 linked to detrended index of industrial production total, seasonally adjusted, from *Industrial Production, 1976 Revision* (Washington, D.C.: Board of Governors of the Federal Reserve System, 1979). GNP and industrial production were detrended using the benchmarks 1876, 1888, 1901, 1913, 1929, and 1949.
1947–83: national income and product accounts, table 1.2.
GNP deflator
1875–1946: interpolated by Chow-Lin method. Dependent variable: annual GNP deflator described in section 1 source notes. Quarterly interpolators: constant, linear time trend, and wholesale price index, all commodities. The interpolation was divided into two subsamples: 1875–1918 and 1919–46.
1947–83: national income and product accounts, table 7.1.
Trend real GNP
1875–1948: secular trend in real GNP calculated using the benchmarks 1869, 1879, 1889, 1901, 1912, 1923, 1929, and 1949.
1949–83: Gordon, *Macroeconomics,* app. C.
Commercial paper rate
1875–89: Commercial paper rate in New York City from Macaulay, *Movements of Interest Rates,* A141–61. Linked in 1890Q1 to
1890–1980: 4–6 -month prime commercial paper from Gordon, "Price Inertia."
1981–83: 6-month commercial paper from various issues of the *Federal Reserve Bulletin.*
Yields on corporate bonds
1875–1918: yields on railroad bonds adjusted for drift from Macaulay, *Movements of Interest Rates,* A141–61. Linked in 1919 to
1919–46: yield on corporate bonds, Moody's Baa rating.
1947–83: yield on corporate bonds, Moody's Baa rating. *Business Statistics.*
Money supply, M1
1915–46: Gordon and Veitch, this volume.
1947–58: old M1 from various issues of *Federal Reserve Bulletin.* Linked in 1959Q1 to
1959–83: new M1 from various issues of *Federal Reserve Bulletin.*
Money supply, M2
1875 to 1907:2: Milton Friedman and Anna J. Schwartz, *Monetary Statistics of the United States* (New York: National Bureau of Economic Research, 1970), 61–65, col. 5. Linked in 1907:3 to
1907:3 to 1980: Gordon, "Price Inertia."
1981–83: various issues of *Federal Reserve Bulletin.*
Money supply, base
1875 to 1907:2: Friedman and Schwartz, *Monetary Statistics,* 344–80, col. 6.
1907:3 to 1918: high-powered money from Milton Freidman and Anna J. Schwartz, *A Monetary History of the United States, 1867–1960* (Princeton: Princeton University Press, 1963), 800–801. Linked in 1919:1 to
1919–83: Gordon and Veitch, this volume.

Wholesale price index, all commodities
   1875–89: Bureau of Labor Statistics, bulletin 572, 111–14.
   1890–1912: Bureau of Labor Statistics, bulletin 521, 13–17.
   1913–46: Bureau of Labor Statistics, bulletins 473, 572, 616, 694, and 916.
   1947–83: series 330 from various issues of *Business Conditions Digest.*
Index of all common stocks
   1900–1918: *Banking and Monetary Statistics, 1942–1970,* 764–65.
   1919–83: NBER tape, dataset 11A.
   Security Markets: data originally collected by Standard and Poor's.

3. Quarterly Data from 1919 to 1941 and from 1947 to 1983

	Producers' Durable Equipment			Nonresidential Structures		
Quarter	Nominal	Real (1972 dollars)	Deflator (1972 = 100)	Nominal	Real (1972 dollars)	Deflator (1972 = 100)
1919:1	3.39	12.51	27.09	1.73	7.66	22.63
2	3.48	12.30	28.28	1.73	7.39	23.38
3	4.45	15.26	29.12	2.01	8.16	24.65
4	4.29	14.22	30.15	1.93	7.42	26.00
1920:1	5.16	16.46	31.35	2.44	8.54	28.59
2	5.01	15.72	31.89	2.28	7.66	29.72
3	4.78	14.74	32.46	1.70	5.71	29.71
4	4.00	12.01	33.27	1.64	5.75	28.51
1921:1	3.19	9.66	33.02	1.62	6.23	25.96
2	2.99	9.32	32.07	2.04	8.55	23.86
3	2.88	9.14	31.54	2.21	9.63	22.90
4	2.75	8.99	30.55	2.48	10.79	22.99
1922:1	2.67	8.82	30.24	2.81	12.15	23.11
2	3.05	10.11	30.18	3.43	14.81	23.16
3	3.29	10.88	30.24	3.46	14.91	23.23
4	3.88	12.64	30.69	3.75	15.81	23.72
1923:1	4.27	13.96	30.60	4.02	16.60	24.19
2	4.89	15.43	31.67	4.60	18.56	24.80
3	4.76	14.73	32.33	4.28	17.31	24.70
4	4.40	13.45	32.69	4.71	19.12	24.65
1924:1	4.55	13.99	32.57	4.95	19.89	24.88
2	3.98	12.23	32.56	5.08	20.60	24.68
3	3.94	12.01	32.80	5.13	21.08	24.35
4	4.64	14.20	32.70	5.07	20.90	24.26
1925:1	4.74	14.61	32.43	5.14	20.90	24.58
2	4.34	13.35	32.49	5.54	22.56	24.55
1925:3	4.56	14.07	32.37	5.83	23.71	24.59
4	4.97	15.32	32.43	5.55	22.52	24.66
1926:1	5.10	15.71	32.47	5.77	23.52	24.54
2	4.96	15.19	32.66	5.70	23.19	24.56
3	5.06	15.48	32.67	5.60	22.72	24.64
4	5.08	15.47	32.83	5.33	21.65	24.64

Quarterly Data from 1919 to 1941 and from 1947 to 1983   (continued)

	Producers' Durable Equipment			Nonresidential Structures		
Quarter	Nominal	Real (1972 dollars)	Deflator (1972 = 100)	Nominal	Real (1972 dollars)	Deflator (1972 = 100)
1927:1	4.96	15.04	32.99	4.93	20.23	24.38
2	4.74	14.29	33.19	5.28	21.97	24.01
3	4.56	13.75	33.18	5.17	21.39	24.16
4	4.37	13.26	32.99	5.26	21.80	24.13
1928:1	4.64	14.06	33.01	4.59	19.06	24.06
2	4.80	14.55	33.02	4.85	20.11	24.11
3	5.03	15.24	33.04	4.72	19.51	24.19
4	5.36	16.31	32.85	4.92	20.27	24.30
1929:1	5.54	16.47	33.63	5.64	23.04	24.50
2	5.64	16.79	33.58	5.65	23.08	24.47
3	5.84	17.40	33.54	5.10	20.87	24.45
4	5.26	15.52	33.92	4.78	19.71	24.26
1930:1	4.75	14.67	32.39	4.80	20.14	23.83
2	4.59	14.06	32.67	4.95	21.03	23.53
3	4.16	12.83	32.45	4.02	17.30	23.22
4	3.49	10.87	32.08	3.37	14.87	22.69
1931:1	3.09	9.67	31.95	3.03	13.74	22.03
2	3.01	9.50	31.73	2.82	13.16	21.46
3	2.65	8.43	31.41	2.20	10.45	21.05
4	2.08	6.95	29.95	1.86	9.04	20.52
1932:1	1.93	6.10	31.71	1.40	7.00	20.02
2	1.30	4.34	30.01	1.36	7.09	19.24
3	1.33	4.56	29.20	1.27	6.78	18.81
4	1.44	4.98	28.84	1.10	6.01	18.32
1933:1	.95	3.66	25.86	0.89	4.86	18.26
2	1.47	5.70	25.85	0.94	5.15	18.18
3	1.94	7.20	26.97	0.97	4.87	19.82
4	1.56	5.64	27.72	1.21	5.87	20.60
1934:1	2.18	7.34	29.69	1.20	6.01	20.01
2	2.42	8.12	29.82	1.09	5.41	20.08
3	1.86	6.19	30.12	1.14	5.66	20.14
4	2.13	7.03	30.23	1.17	5.79	20.17
1935:1	2.59	8.75	29.65	1.12	5.30	21.09
2	2.60	8.63	30.15	1.41	6.60	21.43
3	2.90	9.72	29.78	1.20	5.65	21.30
4	3.48	11.59	30.04	1.65	7.77	21.26
1936:1	3.44	11.72	29.32	1.65	7.91	20.89
2	3.72	12.62	29.49	1.56	7.49	20.84
1936:3	4.16	14.11	29.49	1.82	8.69	20.96
4	4.50	15.19	29.60	2.10	9.79	21.42
1937:1	4.90	16.23	30.21	2.35	10.34	22.74
2	5.10	16.25	31.37	3.27	13.68	23.89
3	5.28	16.41	32.18	2.60	10.76	24.17
4	4.09	12.59	32.52	2.26	9.39	24.11

Quarterly Data from 1919 to 1941 and from 1947 to 1983   (continued)

		Producers' Durable Equipment			Nonresidential Structures	
Quarter	Nominal	Real (1972 dollars)	Deflator (1972 = 100)	Nominal	Real (1972 dollars)	Deflator (1972 = 100)
1938:1	3.43	10.49	32.74	2.21	9.31	23.76
2	3.05	9.37	32.61	1.84	7.79	23.60
3	3.49	10.80	32.28	2.01	8.65	23.28
4	3.90	12.04	32.44	2.13	9.12	23.30
1939:1	3.68	11.37	32.41	2.21	9.65	22.95
2	3.42	10.56	32.39	2.15	9.42	22.84
3	3.92	12.16	32.24	1.99	8.72	22.86
4	4.81	14.95	32.16	2.23	9.49	23.46
1940:1	4.91	14.86	33.04	1.74	7.43	23.38
2	4.97	15.01	33.08	2.02	8.64	23.35
3	5.39	16.30	33.06	2.56	10.99	23.28
4	5.75	17.42	33.00	3.82	16.13	23.65
1941:1	5.95	17.56	33.88	3.42	14.37	23.83
2	6.27	18.06	34.69	3.06	12.41	24.63
3	6.68	18.83	35.47	4.19	16.55	25.35
4	7.37	20.09	36.67	2.15	8.18	26.25
1947:1	15.20	32.40	46.91	8.10	19.03	42.56
2	15.50	31.76	48.81	8.20	18.75	43.74
3	15.30	30.77	49.72	8.50	18.79	45.25
4	16.40	32.22	50.90	8.70	18.62	46.74
1948:1	17.60	34.40	51.17	9.00	18.69	48.17
2	17.00	32.45	52.39	9.70	19.77	49.06
3	17.40	31.76	54.79	10.30	20.57	50.07
4	18.40	33.08	55.62	10.50	20.83	50.42
1949:1	17.10	30.82	55.49	10.10	20.31	49.73
2	16.40	28.77	57.00	9.70	19.81	48.96
3	15.50	27.23	56.92	9.20	18.84	48.84
4	15.20	26.84	56.62	9.00	18.41	48.88
1950:1	15.40	27.11	56.81	9.40	19.30	48.70
2	17.50	30.49	57.41	9.80	20.11	48.74
3	19.80	33.76	58.65	10.50	21.04	49.90
4	20.00	33.30	60.06	11.30	21.67	52.14
1951:1	19.80	31.74	62.38	11.70	21.56	54.26
2	20.10	32.28	62.28	12.40	22.40	55.37
3	20.60	33.19	62.06	12.50	22.22	56.26
4	20.60	32.98	62.46	12.10	21.34	56.69
1952:1	20.70	33.16	62.42	12.20	21.35	57.14
2	21.20	33.52	63.24	12.30	21.61	56.92
1952:3	18.00	28.58	62.98	12.40	21.81	56.86
4	20.30	31.79	63.86	12.80	22.63	56.57
1953:1	21.70	34.05	63.72	13.30	23.32	57.04
2	21.70	33.68	64.42	13.70	23.71	57.77
3	22.50	34.72	64.80	13.90	23.84	58.30
4	21.80	33.89	64.32	14.10	24.23	58.18

Quarterly Data from 1919 to 1941 and from 1947 to 1983   (continued)

	Producers' Durable Equipment			Nonresidential Structures		
Quarter	Nominal	Real (1972 dollars)	Deflator (1972 = 100)	Nominal	Real (1972 dollars)	Deflator (1972 = 100)
1954:1	21.00	32.24	65.14	14.00	24.44	57.29
2	20.80	31.45	66.13	14.00	24.67	56.75
3	21.50	32.57	66.01	14.10	24.80	56.85
4	21.50	32.19	66.80	14.10	24.81	56.83
1955:1	21.50	32.43	66.29	14.50	25.44	57.00
2	23.50	35.47	66.25	14.90	25.98	57.35
3	25.40	37.68	67.41	15.50	26.67	58.12
4	26.70	39.22	68.08	16.20	27.30	59.33
1956:1	25.90	37.39	69.27	17.50	28.30	61.83
2	26.40	37.32	70.74	18.10	29.38	61.61
3	27.30	37.81	72.21	18.80	29.75	63.19
4	27.60	37.35	73.90	19.00	29.79	63.77
1957:1	28.70	38.09	75.34	19.00	29.48	64.45
2	28.60	37.91	75.44	19.20	29.44	65.23
3	29.70	39.25	75.67	19.20	29.33	65.47
4	29.10	37.80	76.99	19.10	29.32	65.15
1958:1	25.80	33.89	76.13	18.40	28.87	63.74
2	24.80	32.33	76.71	17.80	27.76	64.11
3	24.60	31.83	77.29	17.30	26.94	64.21
4	26.10	33.54	77.83	17.70	27.42	64.54
1959:1	27.60	35.29	78.20	17.50	27.21	64.31
2	28.70	36.43	78.78	18.20	28.20	64.53
3	29.60	37.51	78.90	18.70	29.03	64.42
4	29.60	37.66	78.61	18.60	28.87	64.43
1960:1	30.60	38.64	79.19	19.60	30.29	64.71
2	31.30	39.33	79.58	19.00	29.70	63.98
3	30.00	37.56	79.88	19.20	30.13	63.72
4	28.90	36.18	79.88	19.90	31.43	63.31
1961:1	27.90	35.05	79.59	20.00	31.58	63.34
2	29.20	36.65	79.67	19.60	30.91	63.41
3	29.40	37.00	79.47	19.60	30.88	63.47
4	31.10	39.19	79.35	20.00	31.34	63.83
1962:1	31.90	40.11	79.54	19.90	31.28	63.61
2	32.70	41.12	79.52	20.70	32.44	63.80
3	32.90	41.25	79.75	21.50	33.69	63.82
4	32.90	41.15	79.95	21.10	32.96	64.02
1963:1	33.50	41.86	80.04	20.30	31.61	64.23
2	34.10	42.72	79.83	21.20	32.97	64.30
1963:3	35.50	44.47	79.82	21.20	33.06	64.13
4	36.80	46.05	79.91	21.80	33.76	64.57
1964:1	37.80	47.19	80.10	22.00	34.02	64.67
2	38.60	48.02	80.39	22.80	35.16	64.85
3	39.80	49.45	80.48	23.40	35.86	65.25
4	40.90	51.01	80.17	23.90	36.51	65.46

Quarterly Data from 1919 to 1941 and from
1947 to 1983   (continued)

Quarter	Producers' Durable Equipment			Nonresidential Structures		
	Nominal	Real (1972 dollars)	Deflator (1972 = 100)	Nominal	Real (1972 dollars)	Deflator (1972 = 100)
1965:1	44.20	54.85	80.58	25.50	38.77	65.78
2	45.00	55.72	80.76	27.20	41.22	65.98
3	47.50	58.83	80.74	28.00	41.90	66.83
4	49.20	60.79	80.93	29.70	44.14	67.29
1966:1	51.80	63.70	81.32	30.50	44.84	68.01
2	53.70	65.56	81.90	30.30	43.74	69.28
3	54.10	65.65	82.40	31.40	45.05	69.70
4	55.20	66.35	83.19	30.80	43.73	70.43
1967:1	53.30	63.69	83.68	31.20	43.87	71.12
2	54.30	64.58	84.08	30.50	42.43	71.89
3	53.90	63.73	84.58	31.00	42.71	72.59
4	56.00	65.74	85.19	31.20	42.45	73.49
1968:1	58.20	67.69	85.98	32.70	43.78	74.68
2	57.30	65.95	86.88	32.60	43.08	75.68
3	59.10	67.32	87.79	32.70	42.92	76.18
4	61.70	69.65	88.58	34.20	44.35	77.11
1969:1	64.10	72.04	88.98	35.50	45.08	78.75
2	65.20	72.78	89.59	36.30	45.05	80.59
3	66.50	73.58	90.38	39.00	47.18	82.66
4	66.60	73.12	91.08	38.80	45.99	84.37
1970:1	66.50	72.22	92.08	38.50	44.89	85.76
2	66.70	71.81	92.88	39.10	44.72	87.44
3	67.30	71.92	93.57	39.60	44.48	89.02
4	64.60	68.17	94.76	40.10	44.16	90.80
1971:1	66.20	68.85	96.15	40.30	43.75	92.11
2	68.40	70.48	97.04	40.80	43.49	93.81
3	68.90	70.57	97.64	41.70	43.80	95.20
4	71.30	72.66	98.13	41.80	43.05	97.10
1972:1	74.70	75.36	99.12	43.50	44.17	98.49
2	76.60	76.60	100.00	44.30	44.66	99.20
3	78.30	77.92	100.49	45.00	44.87	100.30
4	84.00	83.75	100.29	46.70	45.82	101.92
1973:1	88.90	88.55	100.39	48.30	46.57	103.71
2	93.90	92.62	101.38	50.80	47.74	106.42
3	96.00	93.78	102.37	53.20	48.89	108.83
4	97.50	94.15	103.56	54.30	48.65	111.62
1974:1	99.50	95.43	104.26	55.50	47.69	116.38
2	101.10	94.78	106.66	57.80	46.37	124.65
3	105.20	95.23	110.47	57.20	42.87	133.42
4	104.20	89.80	116.04	58.50	41.99	139.33
1975:1	101.60	83.71	121.38	55.80	39.01	143.03
2	102.60	81.68	125.62	55.10	38.21	144.20
3	105.20	82.51	127.50	56.70	39.13	144.91
4	107.30	82.67	129.79	58.00	39.74	145.93

Quarterly Data from 1919 to 1941 and from 1947 to 1983   (continued)

Quarter	Producers' Durable Equipment			Nonresidential Structures		
	Nominal	Real (1972 dollars)	Deflator (1972 = 100)	Nominal	Real (1972 dollars)	Deflator (1972 = 100)
1976:1	111.10	84.43	131.58	58.80	40.15	146.44
2	114.40	86.27	132.61	59.30	40.02	148.18
3	120.10	89.37	134.39	60.30	40.34	149.47
4	123.70	91.10	135.78	61.10	40.42	151.18
1977:1	133.80	97.40	137.37	61.60	39.97	154.11
2	140.70	101.25	138.96	65.30	41.32	158.05
3	144.20	101.81	141.64	68.20	42.61	160.06
4	154.10	106.86	144.21	69.50	42.14	164.93
1978:1	154.70	105.39	146.79	72.10	43.21	166.85
2	164.60	110.77	148.60	78.70	45.43	173.25
3	168.40	111.60	150.90	83.30	46.39	179.57
4	175.70	115.06	152.71	87.60	47.31	185.17
1979:1	182.60	117.57	155.32	88.90	46.64	190.63
2	182.50	115.24	158.37	94.80	48.84	194.09
3	191.90	119.09	161.14	101.60	50.43	201.48
4	188.10	115.53	162.82	107.40	51.78	207.41
1980:1	203.60	123.00	165.53	113.60	52.30	217.21
2	193.90	115.70	167.59	110.00	49.10	224.03
3	200.20	118.10	169.52	111.20	47.90	232.15
4	205.80	119.40	172.36	116.00	48.90	237.22
1981:1	215.30	123.30	174.62	123.40	50.80	242.91
2	220.60	123.10	179.20	131.90	52.80	249.81
3	226.00	125.20	180.51	143.60	55.60	258.27
4	225.30	123.80	181.99	147.40	55.70	264.63
1982:1	220.10	121.70	180.86	149.80	55.80	268.46
2	211.80	115.10	184.01	144.40	54.40	265.44
3	207.10	113.40	182.63	139.70	52.90	264.08
4	204.30	111.60	183.07	140.50	52.70	266.60
1983:1	207.60	114.50	181.31	131.40	49.40	265.99
2	217.10	119.30	181.98	126.50	48.50	260.83
3	231.50	126.40	183.15	127.10	48.70	260.99
4	251.10	135.30	185.59	137.50	51.80	265.44

Quarterly Data from 1919 to 1941 and from 1947 to 1983   (continued)

	Investment				
	Residential Structures			Change in Business Inventories	
Quarter	Nominal	Real (1972 dollars)	Deflator (1972 = 100)	Nominal	Real (1972 dollars)
1919:1	1.62	7.32	22.16	−4.44	−15.40
2	2.35	9.96	23.58	−7.52	−25.42
3	2.99	11.88	25.15	−7.30	−23.79
4	3.03	11.25	26.90	−8.52	−26.19
1920:1	3.55	11.96	29.72	−1.77	−4.99
2	3.75	12.12	30.95	0.81	2.15
3	3.32	10.60	31.35	2.94	7.88
4	2.89	9.30	31.03	−1.02	−2.76
1921:1	2.39	8.26	28.93	−1.54	−4.49
2	2.34	8.78	26.66	−4.41	−13.53
3	2.30	8.99	25.55	−5.38	−16.80
4	2.29	9.20	24.90	−3.34	−10.62
1922:1	2.31	9.33	24.76	−3.08	−10.13
2	2.70	10.89	24.75	−4.36	−14.37
3	2.64	10.60	24.85	−4.20	−13.86
4	2.77	10.86	25.53	−2.62	−8.57
1923:1	3.14	12.16	25.82	−2.38	−7.76
2	3.38	12.49	27.05	−0.96	−3.08
3	3.27	11.92	27.45	0.36	1.14
4	3.45	12.47	27.67	−2.01	−6.31
1924:1	3.72	13.42	27.75	−3.04	−9.51
2	3.58	12.99	27.59	−4.10	−12.99
3	3.28	11.91	27.52	−3.86	−12.23
4	3.20	11.69	27.38	−2.80	−8.79
1925:1	3.16	11.55	27.41	−0.67	−2.09
2	3.67	13.38	27.44	−0.35	−1.09
3	4.18	15.29	27.37	−1.68	−5.20
4	4.12	15.02	27.46	0.49	1.49
1926:1	4.18	15.26	27.40	−0.67	−2.06
2	4.36	15.83	27.55	−0.14	−0.44
3	4.44	16.08	27.61	−0.31	−0.96
4	4.37	15.76	27.73	0.63	1.92
1927:1	4.25	15.37	27.65	1.46	4.50
2	4.57	16.62	27.51	−1.16	−3.60
3	4.49	16.27	27.60	−0.10	−0.32
4	4.54	16.57	27.43	−1.33	−4.12
1928:1	4.55	16.66	27.34	−1.89	−5.85
2	4.63	16.91	27.41	−2.23	−6.93
3	4.27	15.55	27.48	−0.81	−2.51
4	4.08	14.79	27.59	−1.44	−4.43
1929:1	4.17	15.04	27.71	−0.22	−0.67
2	4.10	14.73	27.82	1.12	3.45

Quarterly Data from 1919 to 1941 and from 1947 to 1983 (continued)

	Investment				
	Residential Structures			Change in Business Inventories	
Quarter	Nominal	Real (1972 dollars)	Deflator (1972 = 100)	Nominal	Real (1972 dollars)
1929:3	3.57	12.82	27.87	2.74	8.35
4	2.64	9.50	27.80	2.41	7.29
1930:1	2.34	8.43	27.75	1.33	4.16
2	2.43	8.83	27.48	−0.71	−2.19
3	1.88	6.92	27.13	−0.94	−3.03
4	1.69	6.38	26.45	−0.42	−1.32
1931:1	1.85	7.14	25.85	−0.54	−1.86
2	1.87	7.40	25.23	−0.69	−2.31
3	1.50	6.13	24.46	−1.01	−3.54
4	1.23	5.27	23.26	−1.19	−4.16
1932:1	0.78	3.56	21.85	−0.48	−1.78
2	0.71	3.47	20.36	−1.49	−5.68
3	0.64	3.27	19.54	−2.98	−11.43
4	0.55	2.97	18.66	−2.28	−9.25
1933:1	0.38	2.03	18.64	−2.82	−11.02
2	0.43	2.33	18.29	−1.88	−7.93
3	0.48	2.35	20.44	0.84	3.10
4	0.73	3.33	21.82	−1.26	−5.13
1934:1	0.78	3.53	22.02	−0.75	−2.66
2	0.77	3.44	22.24	0.63	2.40
3	0.78	3.52	22.14	−1.88	−6.77
4	0.81	3.74	21.60	−1.59	−5.90
1935:1	0.86	3.95	21.66	1.33	4.79
2	1.05	4.83	21.79	0.80	2.89
3	1.10	5.09	21.51	0.95	3.47
4	1.35	6.16	21.84	0.43	1.54
1936:1	1.29	5.76	22.40	−0.80	−2.93
2	1.31	5.77	22.71	1.95	6.95
3	1.67	7.28	22.90	1.17	4.25
4	1.62	7.00	23.19	1.69	5.89
1937:1	1.72	7.28	23.55	2.45	8.77
2	2.00	7.97	25.09	2.58	8.76
3	1.76	6.80	25.86	3.37	11.62
4	1.53	5.80	26.30	−0.81	−2.71
1938:1	1.52	5.80	26.14	−1.43	−5.04
2	1.57	6.00	26.23	−0.97	−3.32
3	2.06	7.98	25.89	−0.69	−2.44
4	2.34	8.94	26.14	0.25	0.86
1939:1	2.60	9.91	26.20	−0.08	−0.28
2	2.69	10.29	26.18	−0.76	−2.68
3	2.80	10.73	26.13	−0.04	−0.14
4	2.84	10.64	26.69	2.52	8.75

Quarterly Data from 1919 to 1941 and from 1947 to 1983   (continued)

	Investment				
	Residential Structures			Change in Business Inventories	
Quarter	Nominal	Real (1972 dollars)	Deflator (1972 = 100)	Nominal	Real (1972 dollars)
1940:1	2.51	9.28	27.04	1.64	5.65
2	2.77	10.16	27.21	1.50	5.20
3	3.46	12.75	27.12	3.20	10.93
4	3.92	14.27	27.44	1.18	4.12
1941:1	3.50	12.52	27.93	0.69	2.31
2	3.54	12.14	29.14	2.70	8.92
3	4.81	15.92	30.20	3.69	11.71
4	2.67	8.46	31.53	8.44	25.96
1947:1	8.90	17.94	49.60	0.50	0.10
2	9.00	17.11	52.60	−1.10	−0.90
3	10.60	19.70	53.80	−2.60	−2.90
4	13.20	23.87	55.30	1.40	2.70
1948:1	13.30	23.71	56.10	3.40	4.10
2	14.30	25.09	57.00	5.10	5.60
3	14.10	24.14	58.40	6.10	6.90
4	13.00	22.15	58.70	4.20	5.30
1949:1	12.10	20.47	59.10	0.00	−0.30
2	11.90	20.17	59.00	−5.30	−7.10
3	12.70	22.16	57.30	−1.70	−2.50
4	14.40	25.17	57.20	−5.20	−7.70
1950:1	16.40	28.72	57.10	2.40	4.40
2	18.50	31.57	58.60	4.70	7.70
3	20.40	33.44	61.00	4.70	8.00
4	19.20	31.58	60.80	15.10	22.10
1951:1	18.70	29.73	62.90	10.50	13.40
2	16.30	25.55	63.80	15.10	19.90
3	15.20	23.71	64.10	10.40	14.60
4	15.50	23.92	64.80	5.20	7.00
1952:1	16.00	24.58	65.10	5.20	7.30
2	16.40	24.96	65.70	−2.40	−2.70
3	16.50	24.89	66.30	4.20	5.40
4	17.20	25.98	66.20	5.40	7.20
1953:1	17.50	26.52	66.00	2.30	3.90
2	17.60	26.63	66.10	3.10	5.10
3	17.10	25.64	66.70	0.70	1.90
4	16.90	25.45	66.40	−4.60	−5.00
1954:1	17.00	25.76	66.00	−2.50	−3.40
2	18.30	27.64	66.20	−2.70	−4.10
3	19.70	29.40	67.00	−2.20	−2.70
4	21.00	31.34	67.00	1.20	1.50
1955:1	22.80	33.83	67.40	4.70	5.90
2	23.40	34.36	68.10	6.10	8.00

Quarterly Data from 1919 to 1941 and from 1947 to 1983   (continued)

	Investment				
	Residential Structures			Change in Business Inventories	
Quarter	Nominal	Real (1972 dollars)	Deflator (1972 = 100)	Nominal	Real (1972 dollars)
1955:3	23.10	33.62	68.70	6.10	7.80
4	22.00	31.98	68.80	7.10	9.20
1956:1	21.30	30.60	69.60	6.10	7.50
2	21.50	30.41	70.70	4.40	5.50
3	21.10	29.76	70.90	4.10	4.90
4	20.70	29.28	70.70	4.30	5.40
1957:1	20.10	28.43	70.70	2.00	2.50
2	19.70	27.79	70.90	2.30	2.90
3	19.60	27.49	71.30	3.30	3.70
4	19.50	27.62	70.60	−2.30	−3.00
1958:1	19.00	26.91	70.60	−5.40	−6.80
2	19.00	26.87	70.70	−5.10	−6.20
3	20.40	28.81	70.80	0.20	0.30
4	22.60	31.92	70.80	4.00	5.30
1959:1	25.10	35.60	70.50	4.30	5.50
2	26.00	36.88	70.50	10.10	12.60
3	25.50	36.12	70.60	1.40	1.40
4	24.70	34.94	70.70	6.80	8.70
1960:1	25.40	35.88	70.80	10.40	12.70
2	23.30	32.86	70.90	2.80	3.30
3	22.40	31.50	71.10	2.60	3.40
4	22.30	31.45	70.90	−4.20	−5.30
1961:1	22.20	31.31	70.90	−3.20	−4.10
2	22.50	31.73	70.90	1.60	1.80
3	23.90	33.71	70.90	5.10	6.50
4	24.40	34.41	70.90	5.80	7.70
1962:1	24.90	34.97	71.20	8.20	10.40
2	26.10	36.66	71.20	6.40	8.10
3	26.20	36.85	71.10	5.80	7.50
4	26.10	36.71	71.10	4.40	5.30
1963:1	27.00	37.87	71.30	5.60	7.40
2	28.90	40.82	70.80	6.20	7.90
3	29.20	41.83	69.80	6.40	8.00
4	30.30	43.10	70.30	5.60	6.70
1964:1	30.40	43.74	69.50	5.40	6.90
2	29.50	41.84	70.50	5.80	7.40
3	29.00	40.56	71.50	4.60	5.50
4	28.70	39.97	71.80	6.70	8.60
1965:1	29.50	41.03	71.90	12.30	14.80
2	30.10	42.33	71.10	9.50	11.30
3	29.60	40.88	72.40	9.10	11.00
4	29.30	40.41	72.50	8.50	10.00

Quarterly Data from 1919 to 1941 and from 1947 to 1983   (continued)

	Investment				
	Residential Structures			Change in Business Inventories	
Quarter	Nominal	Real (1972 dollars)	Deflator (1972 = 100)	Nominal	Real (1972 dollars)
1966:1	29.40	40.50	72.60	13.10	15.60
2	28.80	38.45	74.90	14.60	17.10
3	26.80	36.07	74.30	11.20	13.60
4	23.60	31.22	75.60	17.50	20.80
1967:1	23.30	30.54	76.30	12.40	14.50
2	26.30	34.47	76.30	6.00	7.30
3	28.40	36.84	77.10	10.20	11.80
4	30.50	39.51	77.20	12.90	15.20
1968:1	31.50	40.08	78.60	4.70	5.40
2	33.00	41.35	79.80	10.70	12.20
3	33.50	41.56	80.60	8.50	9.80
4	35.00	42.27	82.80	7.70	8.60
1969:1	37.10	43.60	85.10	10.40	11.70
2	37.50	43.30	86.60	10.40	11.80
3	36.30	40.92	88.70	12.30	13.70
4	34.90	38.86	89.80	6.20	7.00
1970:1	34.70	38.68	89.70	1.60	2.10
2	33.40	36.78	90.80	4.40	5.00
3	34.90	38.69	90.20	6.00	6.50
4	38.50	42.45	90.70	0.90	1.40
1971:1	42.30	45.98	92.00	10.60	11.20
2	47.80	50.69	94.30	9.90	10.40
3	51.30	53.83	95.30	6.80	7.00
4	54.30	56.10	96.80	3.20	3.60
1972:1	58.90	60.29	97.70	6.20	6.30
2	60.30	61.22	98.50	12.00	12.10
3	61.40	61.28	100.20	12.80	12.80
4	65.60	63.38	103.50	9.80	9.70
1973:1	68.10	64.55	105.50	16.30	16.00
2	66.90	61.60	108.60	15.40	15.20
3	65.20	58.84	110.80	15.20	13.80
4	62.10	54.86	113.20	27.00	23.70
1974:1	58.20	50.00	116.40	12.60	13.20
2	56.20	46.99	119.60	17.80	12.60
3	54.80	44.59	122.90	10.70	7.70
4	49.90	39.70	125.70	15.40	12.90
1975:1	48.20	37.36	129.00	− 14.20	− 14.30
2	49.90	38.15	130.80	− 14.60	− 11.30
3	53.50	40.62	131.70	2.10	1.00
4	57.90	43.08	134.40	− .80	− 2.30

Quarterly Data from 1919 to 1941 and from 1947 to 1983   (continued)

		Investment			
		Residential Structures		Change in Business Inventories	
Quarter	Nominal	Real (1972 dollars)	Deflator (1972 = 100)	Nominal	Real (1972 dollars)
1976:1	63.60	46.76	136.00	15.30	10.00
2	67.30	48.14	139.80	17.30	11.30
3	67.80	47.61	142.40	11.40	7.30
4	76.60	52.29	146.50	3.30	2.40
1977:1	r 81.00	53.57	151.20	22.40	10.50
2	91.90	58.61	156.80	20.80	13.80
3	95.30	59.90	159.10	27.60	18.70
4	99.60	59.29	168.00	13.00	10.10
1978:1	98.90	58.52	169.00	25.00	17.30
2	107.40	60.64	177.10	27.00	18.40
3	109.60	59.79	183.30	19.10	13.30
4	111.60	58.86	189.60	17.70	15.20
1979:1	112.50	58.08	193.70	24.30	12.90
2	112.90	56.34	200.40	33.00	13.70
3	114.90	55.51	207.00	13.30	4.80
4	115.40	54.93	210.10	− 0.90	− 2.30
1980:1	106.40	49.47	215.10	− 1.60	− 0.50
2	87.40	39.62	220.60	3.00	− 2.10
3	93.50	41.52	225.20	− 25.40	− 10.10
4	105.00	46.40	226.29	− 15.10	− 4.70
1981:1	107.60	46.40	231.90	21.90	8.10
2	104.90	44.50	235.73	23.70	12.40
3	96.90	40.20	241.05	39.70	17.50
4	90.00	36.80	244.57	18.90	7.20
1982:1	83.40	33.90	246.02	− 17.00	− 6.70
2	85.90	35.00	245.43	− 10.90	− 4.00
3	84.50	34.40	245.64	− 15.30	− 6.40
4	92.50	38.10	242.78	− 61.10	− 24.60
1983:1	108.90	43.80	248.63	− 42.90	− 16.50
2	125.30	51.00	245.69	− 19.40	− 6.10
3	137.70	54.70	251.74	− 4.30	0.90
4	138.70	55.20	251.27	12.70	7.20

Quarterly Data from 1919 to 1941 and from 1947 to 1983   (continued)

	Consumption					
	Durable Goods			Nondurable Goods and Services		
Quarter	Nominal	Real (1972 dollars)	Deflator (1972 = 100)	Nominal	Real (1972 dollars)	Deflator (1972 = 100)
1919:1	4.21	12.71	33.13	43.91	141.43	31.05
2	4.69	13.54	34.63	45.77	142.58	32.10
3	6.26	16.56	37.81	48.59	143.47	33.87
4	8.07	19.17	42.09	52.26	145.98	35.80
1920:1	7.42	16.44	45.11	54.76	144.14	37.99
2	6.55	13.79	47.53	57.74	142.90	40.41
3	6.53	13.35	48.94	57.27	143.43	39.93
4	5.74	11.53	49.75	55.01	142.76	38.54
1921:1	4.81	9.83	48.98	53.20	146.86	36.22
2	5.50	11.60	47.39	52.90	152.86	34.60
3	5.64	12.53	45.03	53.23	155.24	34.29
4	5.29	12.05	43.94	52.55	155.33	33.83
1922:1	5.17	12.01	43.03	50.42	154.09	32.72
2	5.81	13.73	42.30	50.60	155.83	32.47
3	6.01	14.23	42.22	51.65	159.20	32.44
4	6.24	14.71	42.44	53.98	164.68	32.78
1923:1	7.10	16.56	42.89	54.89	167.16	32.83
2	7.41	17.14	43.24	56.31	169.44	33.23
3	7.37	16.92	43.56	56.36	166.87	33.78
4	7.68	17.45	44.04	58.71	172.51	34.03
1924:1	8.24	18.56	44.39	60.80	179.55	33.86
2	7.38	16.69	44.25	60.39	179.80	33.59
3	6.99	15.80	44.23	60.00	177.91	33.72
4	7.03	15.86	44.32	60.17	176.45	34.10
1925:1	7.71	17.40	44.31	58.81	171.66	34.26
2	8.23	18.62	44.20	57.37	166.52	34.45
3	8.30	18.76	44.25	58.55	165.95	35.28
4	9.44	21.26	44.40	60.74	169.78	35.78
1926:1	9.24	20.88	44.27	62.48	174.81	35.74
2	8.72	19.83	43.95	64.16	179.84	35.68
3	8.60	19.58	43.92	64.78	184.72	35.07
4	8.56	19.44	44.04	65.74	185.64	35.41
1927:1	8.66	19.69	43.96	64.10	183.27	34.98
2	8.72	19.92	43.76	64.72	184.44	35.09
3	8.25	18.86	43.74	64.07	184.53	34.72
4	7.90	18.19	43.45	64.71	184.97	34.99
1928:1	8.35	19.14	43.63	65.75	189.52	34.69
2	8.30	19.29	43.00	65.06	187.62	34.68
3	8.74	20.05	43.57	67.08	192.72	34.81
4	9.01	21.19	42.50	68.12	195.45	34.85
1929:1	9.71	21.58	44.98	67.48	194.56	34.68
2	9.25	21.16	43.72	67.22	193.40	34.76

Quarterly Data from 1919 to 1941 and from 1947 to 1983   (continued)

		Consumption				
		Durable Goods			Nondurable Goods and Services	
Quarter	Nominal	Real (1972 dollars)	Deflator (1972 = 100)	Nominal	Real (1972 dollars)	Deflator (1972 = 100)
1929:3	9.37	21.35	43.87	69.00	196.20	35.17
4	8.65	19.56	44.23	68.33	192.23	35.54
1930:1	7.69	17.96	42.79	64.42	186.93	34.46
2	7.40	16.91	43.73	65.25	185.83	35.11
3	6.61	15.74	42.00	60.47	181.06	33.40
4	6.97	15.74	44.28	60.90	178.03	34.21
1931:1	5.76	15.19	37.93	56.13	179.01	31.36
2	5.92	14.87	39.83	57.56	180.97	31.81
3	5.34	14.24	37.47	53.48	176.74	30.26
4	4.92	12.96	37.98	52.88	172.83	30.60
1932:1	4.21	12.00	35.07	48.07	168.82	28.47
2	3.78	11.01	34.34	45.54	163.18	27.91
3	3.46	10.18	33.94	44.54	159.66	27.90
4	3.15	10.28	30.65	41.73	160.06	26.07
1933:1	3.35	9.61	34.85	41.62	153.06	27.19
2	3.14	10.13	31.04	40.51	164.41	24.64
3	3.82	11.55	33.12	47.92	166.82	28.73
4	3.52	11.35	31.00	39.40	155.80	25.29
1934:1	4.06	11.29	35.99	48.37	161.43	29.96
2	4.12	12.18	33.81	43.95	163.19	26.93
3	4.20	12.15	34.55	48.53	165.35	29.35
4	4.49	12.87	34.85	47.62	168.54	28.25
1935:1	4.74	14.09	33.62	49.28	169.12	29.14
2	4.85	14.09	34.44	49.73	169.25	29.38
3	5.12	15.19	33.71	50.05	173.32	28.88
4	5.79	16.53	35.03	53.55	178.86	29.94
1936:1	5.72	17.31	33.03	51.61	179.96	28.68
2	6.23	18.11	34.44	55.41	184.93	29.96
3	6.46	19.11	33.78	55.35	189.86	29.15
4	6.91	19.67	35.15	60.47	196.66	30.75
1937:1	6.85	20.06	34.15	57.72	196.48	29.38
2	7.01	19.69	35.60	61.68	196.31	31.42
3	7.24	20.23	35.80	58.45	192.50	30.36
4	6.62	17.97	36.85	60.84	191.30	31.80
1938:1	5.51	15.25	36.15	56.22	190.01	29.59
2	5.31	14.60	36.36	57.97	187.69	30.88
3	5.62	15.57	36.10	58.15	195.28	29.78
4	6.29	17.38	36.18	61.06	199.06	30.67
1939:1	6.60	18.36	35.94	58.33	197.87	29.48
2	6.46	18.06	35.76	59.95	199.21	30.09
3	6.71	18.60	36.10	60.25	201.77	29.86
4	6.96	19.45	35.81	62.65	206.47	30.34

Quarterly Data from 1919 to 1941 and from 1947 to 1983   (continued)

	Consumption					
	Durable Goods			Nondurable Goods and Services		
Quarter	Nominal	Real (1972 dollars)	Deflator (1972 = 100)	Nominal	Real (1972 dollars)	Deflator (1972 = 100)
1940:1	7.63	20.54	37.13	62.10	205.00	30.29
2	7.46	20.57	36.28	62.23	206.34	30.16
3	7.84	21.07	37.24	64.38	208.67	30.85
4	8.16	22.56	36.15	64.09	214.26	29.91
1941:1	9.36	23.89	39.17	67.70	214.07	31.62
2	9.63	24.97	38.58	69.05	220.69	31.29
3	9.99	25.06	39.87	74.37	224.83	33.08
4	9.65	22.77	42.38	73.31	217.36	33.73
1947:1	19.40	28.91	67.10	136.50	273.25	49.95
2	20.00	29.59	67.60	140.00	277.59	50.43
3	20.30	29.81	68.10	143.20	277.46	51.61
4	22.00	32.16	68.40	145.60	274.60	53.02
1948:1	22.00	32.12	68.50	148.30	276.71	53.59
2	22.40	32.09	69.80	151.60	280.07	54.13
3	23.70	32.96	71.90	153.20	279.66	54.78
4	23.30	32.77	71.10	154.50	282.70	54.65
1949:1	22.80	32.25	70.70	153.80	283.47	54.26
2	24.80	35.43	70.00	153.40	284.38	53.94
3	25.80	36.80	70.10	151.80	282.55	53.73
4	26.80	37.69	71.10	153.30	284.83	53.82
1950:1	27.70	38.85	71.30	155.10	288.71	53.72
2	28.10	39.19	71.70	158.60	294.41	53.87
3	35.60	48.97	72.70	164.80	298.86	55.14
4	31.50	43.21	72.90	166.30	296.61	56.07
1951:1	33.80	44.30	76.30	174.50	301.31	57.91
2	28.90	38.08	75.90	175.00	299.94	58.35
3	28.30	37.14	76.20	178.00	303.88	58.58
4	28.30	36.85	76.80	184.50	309.74	59.57
1952:1	28.90	37.58	76.90	182.30	305.18	59.73
2	29.00	38.26	75.80	186.10	310.48	59.94
3	27.30	35.78	76.30	189.90	314.52	60.38
4	31.40	40.46	77.60	193.60	318.36	60.81
1953:1	32.90	42.34	77.70	195.40	320.59	60.95
2	32.80	41.94	78.20	197.10	322.67	61.08
3	32.50	41.77	77.80	198.00	321.86	61.52
4	31.90	42.53	75.00	198.10	320.27	61.85
1954:1	31.20	40.94	76.20	200.70	322.75	62.18
2	31.80	41.35	76.90	202.40	324.69	62.34
3	31.30	42.41	73.80	205.10	329.43	62.26
4	33.00	45.14	73.10	207.80	333.27	62.35
1955:1	36.20	48.07	75.30	210.60	337.09	62.48
2	38.60	51.26	75.30	213.30	340.84	62.58

Quarterly Data from 1919 to 1941 and from 1947 to 1983 (continued)

		Consumption				
		Durable Goods		Nondurable Goods and Services		
Quarter	Nominal	Real (1972 dollars)	Deflator (1972 = 100)	Nominal	Real (1972 dollars)	Deflator (1972 = 100)
1955:3	40.30	52.68	76.50	215.70	343.65	62.77
4	39.40	52.25	75.40	220.60	350.45	62.95
1956:1	37.60	49.28	76.30	223.70	353.75	63.24
2	37.60	48.83	77.00	226.20	354.97	63.72
3	37.30	48.07	77.60	229.50	356.58	64.36
4	38.90	48.75	79.80	232.90	360.28	64.64
1957:1	40.00	49.94	80.10	236.10	361.88	65.24
2	39.50	48.77	81.00	238.80	363.80	65.64
3	39.10	47.98	81.50	243.70	366.96	66.41
4	38.80	47.96	80.90	245.60	367.84	66.77
1958:1	36.80	45.15	81.50	247.20	365.86	67.57
2	36.00	44.50	80.90	250.80	370.48	67.70
3	36.70	45.09	81.40	255.00	375.92	67.83
4	38.00	46.68	81.40	257.40	378.66	67.98
1959:1	41.20	49.40	83.40	262.20	384.62	68.17
2	43.00	51.25	83.90	266.10	388.46	68.50
3	43.90	52.14	84.20	270.30	390.99	69.13
4	41.60	49.70	83.70	274.60	395.01	69.52
1960:1	43.00	51.07	84.20	276.80	397.15	69.70
2	43.90	52.32	83.90	282.00	401.99	70.15
3	43.40	51.79	83.80	282.60	400.91	70.49
4	42.20	50.54	83.50	285.80	402.65	70.98
1961:1	39.70	47.72	83.20	288.90	406.47	71.08
2	40.70	48.34	84.20	292.30	411.63	71.01
3	41.90	49.41	84.80	293.80	412.02	71.31
4	44.00	51.83	84.90	298.80	418.48	71.40
1962:1	45.00	52.88	85.10	302.50	421.60	71.75
2	46.30	54.22	85.40	306.70	425.44	72.09
3	46.80	54.67	85.60	310.20	428.82	72.34
4	48.80	57.08	85.50	314.60	433.13	72.63
1963:1	49.80	58.11	85.70	317.30	434.77	72.98
2	51.10	59.35	86.10	320.00	437.91	73.07
3	51.90	60.14	86.30	326.00	443.74	73.47
4	52.90	61.02	86.70	329.20	446.64	73.71
1964:1	55.00	63.15	87.10	335.60	453.45	74.01
2	56.40	64.75	87.10	341.40	460.65	74.11
3	58.20	66.74	87.20	347.60	467.42	74.37
4	56.10	64.56	86.90	351.50	470.82	74.66
1965:1	61.60	70.48	87.40	356.30	475.65	74.91
2	61.50	70.69	87.00	362.90	480.31	75.56
3	63.30	73.09	86.60	369.60	486.27	76.01
4	65.60	76.10	86.20	380.80	497.98	76.47

Quarterly Data from 1919 to 1941 and from 1947 to 1983   (continued)

	Consumption					
	Durable Goods			Nondurable Goods and Services		
Quarter	Nominal	Real (1972 dollars)	Deflator (1972 = 100)	Nominal	Real (1972 dollars)	Deflator (1972 = 100)
1966:1	68.70	79.79	86.10	387.50	501.49	77.27
2	66.00	76.30	86.50	394.50	505.65	78.02
3	68.50	78.83	86.90	400.90	509.95	78.62
4	68.80	78.72	87.40	405.40	511.55	79.25
1967:1	67.30	77.27	87.10	411.50	517.63	79.50
2	70.60	80.69	87.50	416.90	521.83	79.89
3	70.80	80.00	88.50	423.20	525.18	80.58
4	71.60	80.00	89.50	429.20	528.05	81.28
1968:1	76.80	85.24	90.10	441.00	535.59	82.34
2	78.70	86.87	90.60	451.40	542.97	83.14
3	83.00	90.81	91.40	462.60	551.46	83.89
4	83.30	90.45	92.10	470.70	554.25	84.93
1969:1	85.30	92.32	92.40	480.50	559.52	85.88
2	85.70	92.05	93.10	491.20	564.15	87.07
3	85.90	91.77	93.60	500.80	567.72	88.21
4	86.00	91.20	94.30	511.70	572.37	89.40
1970:1	84.90	89.75	94.60	523.00	577.58	90.55
2	86.30	90.75	95.10	530.60	579.86	91.50
3	87.30	91.13	95.80	540.90	585.32	92.41
4	82.40	84.77	97.20	551.60	588.89	93.67
1971:1	93.00	93.94	99.00	559.80	592.83	94.43
2	95.90	96.38	99.50	570.10	596.79	95.53
3	98.20	99.09	99.10	579.40	598.94	96.74
4	102.00	103.55	98.50	590.60	604.88	97.64
1972:1	105.60	106.24	99.40	604.00	612.31	98.64
2	109.00	109.00	100.00	618.40	622.11	99.40
3	112.20	111.64	100.50	632.00	629.76	100.36
4	117.60	117.60	100.00	649.40	639.50	101.55
1973:1	125.50	124.75	100.60	664.60	644.43	103.13
2	124.30	122.46	101.50	678.60	644.24	105.33
3	123.40	120.86	102.10	697.30	649.91	107.29
4	120.20	117.15	102.60	714.10	650.22	109.82
1974:1	118.50	114.49	103.50	735.00	647.99	113.43
2	121.70	114.70	106.10	756.90	650.20	116.41
3	127.40	115.82	110.00	779.30	654.05	119.15
4	118.50	104.50	113.40	795.60	652.85	121.87
1975:1	122.40	106.53	114.90	812.70	657.52	123.60
2	127.10	109.01	116.60	834.50	667.23	125.07
3	136.70	115.95	117.90	855.40	670.49	127.58
4	142.60	119.23	119.60	874.30	675.17	129.49

Quarterly Data from 1919 to 1941 and from 1947 to 1983   (continued)

	Consumption					
	Durable Goods			Nondurable Goods and Services		
Quarter	Nominal	Real (1972 dollars)	Deflator (1972 = 100)	Nominal	Real (1972 dollars)	Deflator (1972 = 100)
1976:1	152.00	125.10	121.50	895.80	685.59	130.66
2	154.60	125.59	123.10	912.60	692.05	131.87
3	158.10	126.89	124.60	936.10	700.22	133.69
4	162.60	128.54	126.50	965.30	710.67	135.83
1977:1	173.70	135.70	128.00	990.10	715.89	138.30
2	175.70	136.84	128.40	1010.50	719.02	140.54
3	179.40	138.64	129.40	1038.00	727.99	142.59
4	186.40	142.29	131.00	1068.00	738.80	144.56
1978:1	185.00	139.52	132.60	1093.30	744.59	146.83
2	200.10	148.11	135.10	1129.90	752.53	150.15
3	202.00	147.02	137.40	1167.90	764.29	152.81
4	210.20	150.79	139.40	1206.40	772.79	156.11
1979:1	212.50	149.65	142.00	1241.70	775.81	160.05
2	207.40	144.13	143.90	1270.60	778.40	163.23
3	213.30	146.70	145.40	1315.80	786.61	167.28
4	216.10	146.01	148.00	1366.20	795.62	171.71
1980:1	220.70	145.20	152.00	1399.70	793.00	176.51
2	200.80	129.97	154.50	1425.70	789.60	180.56
3	213.80	135.57	157.70	1469.50	793.80	185.12
4	223.60	139.00	160.86	1518.30	800.90	189.57
1981:1	237.80	146.10	162.77	1560.20	804.10	194.03
2	232.40	140.00	166.00	1596.90	809.10	197.37
3	242.50	143.50	168.99	1634.80	812.10	201.31
4	228.90	134.00	170.82	1662.90	812.90	204.56
1982:1	239.40	138.50	172.85	1691.80	815.20	207.53
2	241.60	138.80	174.06	1717.20	820.10	209.63
3	244.50	139.30	175.52	1756.70	824.90	212.96
4	255.00	145.20	175.62	1791.20	831.10	215.52
1983:1	259.40	146.80	176.70	1811.00	835.60	216.73
2	276.10	156.20	176.76	1865.50	850.00	219.47
3	284.10	159.60	178.01	1897.40	856.10	221.63
4	299.80	167.20	179.31	1930.50	865.20	223.13

Quarterly Data from 1919 to 1941 and from
1947 to 1983   (continued)

Quarter	Exports			Imports		
	Nominal	Real (1972 dollars)	Deflator (1972 = 100)	Nominal	Real (1972 dollars)	Deflator (1972 = 100)
1919:1	10.29	15.54	66.22	4.13	6.87	60.08
2	11.58	18.41	62.91	4.57	7.64	59.85
3	10.76	16.22	66.30	5.73	8.88	64.55
4	9.55	12.63	75.60	6.60	9.56	69.01
1920:1	11.85	16.88	70.21	7.73	9.55	80.95
2	10.71	13.35	80.24	7.63	8.86	86.03
3	9.91	12.93	76.70	7.59	9.11	83.33
4	11.44	17.60	64.99	5.40	7.52	71.85
1921:1	7.09	12.25	57.87	3.74	6.71	55.79
2	6.14	13.06	47.05	3.23	7.13	45.24
3	5.82	13.49	43.14	2.97	7.43	39.98
4	4.88	9.78	49.85	3.40	7.88	43.09
1922:1	4.72	10.89	43.36	3.64	8.42	43.20
2	5.33	11.41	46.66	3.84	8.94	42.93
3	5.22	11.32	46.06	4.26	9.80	43.45
4	5.28	11.41	46.31	4.92	10.65	46.15
1923:1	5.34	10.20	52.37	5.20	9.96	52.17
2	5.63	11.17	50.43	5.40	10.09	53.53
3	5.61	11.58	48.51	4.81	9.37	51.34
4	5.85	13.11	44.66	4.79	9.58	50.05
1924:1	5.95	11.52	51.63	4.79	9.20	51.99
2	5.91	12.20	48.41	4.72	9.25	50.99
3	5.99	12.95	46.24	4.71	9.71	48.50
4	6.85	14.95	45.80	4.96	10.04	49.35
1925:1	7.01	14.52	48.31	5.33	9.87	54.03
2	6.24	13.00	48.05	5.33	9.79	54.43
3	6.71	13.98	47.96	5.81	10.46	55.56
4	6.29	12.65	49.70	6.03	10.84	55.63
1926:1	6.44	14.54	44.33	6.24	11.57	53.95
2	6.22	13.77	45.18	5.69	10.75	52.96
3	6.75	14.93	45.23	5.76	10.78	53.42
4	6.55	14.96	43.76	5.85	11.02	53.06
1927:1	6.52	14.76	44.14	5.36	10.44	51.35
2	6.81	16.97	40.15	5.68	11.73	48.43
3	6.42	15.45	41.57	5.64	11.43	49.37
4	6.38	15.56	41.00	5.41	10.92	49.57
1928:1	6.55	15.25	42.98	5.44	11.19	48.56
2	6.91	16.40	42.12	5.39	11.21	48.06
3	6.79	15.79	42.97	5.51	11.48	48.02
4	7.40	17.34	42.67	5.46	11.42	47.82
1929:1	7.52	17.25	43.59	5.91	12.49	47.34
2	7.06	16.72	42.22	6.07	13.22	45.91
3	6.90	16.32	42.28	5.93	13.13	45.14
4	6.72	16.51	40.70	5.57	12.77	43.60

Quarterly Data from 1919 to 1941 and from 1947 to 1983 (continued)

Quarter	Exports			Imports		
	Nominal	Real (1972 dollars)	Deflator (1972 = 100)	Nominal	Real (1972 dollars)	Deflator (1972 = 100)
1930:1	6.17	15.19	40.60	5.02	12.20	41.17
2	5.80	14.91	38.92	4.71	11.93	39.48
3	5.24	13.93	37.60	4.10	10.80	37.94
4	4.71	12.77	36.88	3.86	10.67	36.21
1931:1	4.00	12.25	32.68	3.46	10.08	34.30
2	3.92	12.57	31.16	3.17	10.11	31.31
3	3.36	11.34	29.64	3.11	10.31	30.13
4	3.25	10.63	30.52	2.76	9.49	29.06
1932:1	2.65	10.11	26.20	2.43	9.02	26.98
2	2.57	9.61	26.76	2.14	8.53	25.16
3	2.31	8.90	25.89	1.85	7.60	24.38
4	2.36	8.58	27.56	1.89	8.06	23.48
1933:1	1.97	9.11	21.60	1.65	8.18	20.18
2	2.17	8.90	24.39	1.77	8.50	20.80
3	2.67	9.22	28.98	2.40	9.22	26.00
4	2.84	9.17	31.04	2.33	8.51	27.42
1934:1	3.01	9.66	31.16	2.33	8.47	27.53
2	2.99	9.66	30.97	2.37	8.76	27.05
3	3.17	10.34	30.65	2.30	8.76	26.31
4	2.67	9.14	29.21	2.49	9.61	25.91
1935:1	3.32	10.52	31.57	2.94	11.27	26.08
2	2.97	9.68	30.63	3.10	11.69	26.49
3	3.42	11.03	31.02	3.25	12.06	26.92
4	3.31	10.76	30.79	3.32	12.17	27.30
1936:1	3.64	11.71	31.07	3.30	11.86	27.86
2	3.34	10.70	31.19	3.31	11.69	28.31
3	3.74	11.89	31.46	3.43	11.90	28.85
4	3.43	10.51	32.68	3.62	12.14	29.78
1937:1	4.50	13.14	34.28	4.40	13.54	32.49
2	4.67	13.24	35.28	4.63	13.78	33.62
3	4.84	14.06	34.46	4.27	13.23	32.26
4	4.67	15.57	29.98	3.73	12.25	30.43
1938:1	4.70	13.47	34.87	3.20	10.66	30.00
2	4.47	14.15	31.59	2.94	9.92	29.62
3	4.27	13.44	31.75	3.01	10.23	29.45
4	4.11	12.94	31.79	3.09	10.39	29.73
1939:1	4.27	13.84	30.87	3.16	10.70	29.58
2	4.27	13.78	30.99	3.28	11.10	29.51
3	4.45	13.92	31.99	3.25	10.66	30.52
4	5.41	15.66	34.56	3.83	11.14	34.38
1940:1	5.45	15.38	35.42	3.65	11.00	33.16
2	5.64	16.64	33.92	3.51	10.89	32.21
3	5.06	14.95	33.86	3.65	11.43	31.91
4	5.47	15.03	36.40	3.76	11.09	33.91

Quarterly Data from 1919 to 1941 and from 1947 to 1983   (continued)

		Exports			Imports	
Quarter	Nominal	Real (1972 dollars)	Deflator (1972 = 100)	Nominal	Real (1972 dollars)	Deflator (1972 = 100)
1941:1	4.92	14.05	34.99	4.20	12.45	33.71
2	5.65	15.24	37.08	4.71	13.47	34.95
3	6.19	16.48	37.59	4.83	13.44	35.94
4	7.84	19.84	39.53	4.97	13.44	37.01
1947:1	20.63	32.80	62.90	7.90	13.81	57.20
2	22.01	33.50	65.70	8.60	13.87	62.00
3	21.88	32.80	66.70	8.00	13.11	61.00
4	20.26	29.80	68.00	8.80	14.10	62.40
1948:1	19.68	28.20	69.80	10.10	15.59	64.80
2	18.09	25.80	70.10	10.50	15.86	66.20
3	18.28	26.00	70.30	11.00	16.47	66.80
4	17.32	25.10	69.00	10.60	15.92	66.60
1949:1	18.73	27.70	67.60	10.10	15.56	64.90
2	18.10	27.30	66.30	9.90	15.76	62.80
3	16.49	25.60	64.40	9.50	15.40	61.70
4	14.26	22.60	63.10	9.60	15.64	61.40
1950:1	14.03	22.60	62.10	10.10	16.21	62.30
2	14.38	23.30	61.70	10.80	16.77	64.40
3	15.26	23.80	64.10	13.60	19.77	68.80
4	16.68	24.60	67.80	14.30	19.27	74.20
1951:1	18.32	25.80	71.00	15.60	19.65	79.40
2	21.04	28.20	74.60	15.90	18.91	84.10
3	22.08	30.00	73.60	15.00	18.03	83.20
4	22.30	30.50	73.10	14.70	18.26	80.50
1952:1	22.58	30.80	73.30	15.60	19.33	80.70
2	20.61	28.00	73.60	15.30	19.17	79.80
3	19.13	26.20	73.00	15.90	20.33	78.20
4	19.18	26.60	72.10	17.00	21.85	77.80
1953:1	18.91	26.30	71.90	16.50	21.60	76.40
2	19.16	26.80	71.50	17.10	22.65	75.50
3	19.47	27.00	72.10	17.00	22.43	75.80
4	18.96	26.30	72.10	16.30	21.59	75.50
1954:1	18.32	25.70	71.30	15.50	20.53	75.50
2	20.31	28.40	71.50	16.90	21.81	77.50
3	19.78	27.90	70.90	16.00	20.67	77.40
4	20.86	29.30	71.20	16.20	20.98	77.20
1955:1	21.51	30.30	71.00	16.90	22.01	76.80
2	21.24	29.70	71.50	17.90	23.43	76.40
3	22.46	31.20	72.00	18.30	23.95	76.40
4	22.80	31.40	72.60	18.90	24.42	77.40
1956:1	24.29	33.00	73.60	19.80	25.35	78.10
2	25.68	34.80	73.80	19.80	25.29	78.30
3	26.75	36.20	73.90	20.10	25.74	78.10
4	27.53	37.10	74.20	19.40	24.65	78.70

Quarterly Data from 1919 to 1941 and from 1947 to 1983   (continued)

		Exports			Imports	
Quarter	Nominal	Real (1972 dollars)	Deflator (1972 = 100)	Nominal	Real (1972 dollars)	Deflator (1972 = 100)
1957:1	30.06	39.40	76.30	21.00	26.32	79.80
2	29.87	39.10	76.40	21.10	26.44	79.80
3	29.07	37.70	77.10	20.60	25.81	79.80
4	27.52	35.60	77.30	20.50	26.05	78.70
1958:1	25.15	33.00	76.20	20.40	26.36	77.40
2	25.13	33.20	75.70	21.00	27.42	76.60
3	25.07	33.20	75.50	20.70	27.17	76.20
4	25.07	33.20	75.50	21.80	28.76	75.80
1959:1	24.17	32.10	75.30	22.40	29.79	75.20
2	24.62	32.70	75.30	23.60	31.09	75.90
3	26.66	35.40	75.30	24.00	31.79	75.50
4	26.45	34.90	75.80	23.60	30.93	76.30
1960:1	28.50	37.30	76.40	23.90	31.12	76.80
2	29.45	38.20	77.10	24.00	31.13	77.10
3	30.30	38.90	77.90	23.40	30.47	76.80
4	30.22	39.20	77.10	22.30	29.30	76.10
1961:1	30.80	39.90	77.20	22.30	29.30	76.10
2	29.64	37.80	78.40	22.50	29.53	76.20
3	30.77	39.40	78.10	24.00	31.54	76.10
4	31.51	40.30	78.20	24.50	32.24	76.00
1962:1	31.08	40.00	77.70	24.80	33.16	74.80
2	32.93	42.60	77.30	25.40	33.96	74.80
3	32.84	42.60	77.10	25.60	34.45	74.30
4	32.49	42.20	77.00	26.00	35.04	74.20
1963:1	32.35	41.90	77.20	25.60	34.32	74.60
2	34.72	44.80	77.50	26.40	35.11	75.20
3	35.08	45.20	77.60	27.20	35.79	76.00
4	36.70	47.30	77.60	27.30	35.78	76.30
1964:1	38.85	50.00	77.70	27.60	35.84	77.00
2	38.38	49.20	78.00	28.40	36.74	77.30
3	39.72	50.60	78.50	29.10	37.74	77.10
4	40.55	51.40	78.90	30.00	38.86	77.20
1965:1	37.59	46.70	80.50	29.10	37.50	77.60
2	43.20	53.60	80.60	32.70	42.19	77.50
3	42.85	53.10	80.70	33.00	42.25	78.10
4	43.04	53.60	80.30	34.40	43.65	78.80
1966:1	43.93	54.10	81.20	36.00	45.69	78.80
2	44.33	53.80	82.40	37.00	46.42	79.70
3	45.54	54.60	83.40	39.40	49.31	79.90
4	46.45	55.10	84.30	39.80	49.44	80.50
1967:1	47.80	56.90	84.00	40.60	50.50	80.40
2	47.01	56.10	83.80	40.10	50.13	80.00
3	47.29	56.30	84.00	40.60	50.56	80.30
4	48.27	57.40	84.10	42.80	53.70	79.70

Quarterly Data from 1919 to 1941 and from 1947 to 1983   (continued)

		Exports			Imports	
		Real (1972	Deflator (1972 =		Real (1972	Deflator (1972 =
Quarter	Nominal	dollars)	100)	Nominal	dollars)	100)
1968:1	49.44	59.00	83.80	45.70	56.98	80.20
2	51.63	60.10	85.90	46.90	57.76	81.20
3	54.57	63.60	85.80	49.90	61.68	80.90
4	53.52	62.30	85.90	49.80	61.18	81.40
1969:1	49.73	57.10	87.10	45.90	55.84	82.20
2	58.98	67.40	87.50	55.30	67.03	82.50
3	59.54	67.20	88.60	55.60	66.91	83.10
4	61.81	68.30	90.50	56.60	66.51	85.10
1970:1	63.64	69.40	91.70	57.10	66.16	86.30
2	66.71	71.50	93.30	58.60	66.97	87.50
3	66.08	70.60	93.60	59.60	66.37	89.80
4	66.32	70.40	94.20	60.70	66.78	90.90
1971:1	68.37	70.70	96.70	61.00	66.02	92.40
2	69.14	71.20	97.10	65.60	70.92	92.50
3	71.75	74.20	96.70	67.90	72.54	93.60
4	66.01	67.70	97.50	64.30	67.90	94.70
1972:1	74.00	74.90	98.80	74.30	76.92	96.60
2	73.75	74.20	99.40	74.00	74.60	99.20
3	77.97	78.20	99.70	76.50	75.74	101.00
4	84.07	82.50	101.90	82.10	79.63	103.10
1973:1	95.82	91.00	105.30	88.80	83.38	106.50
2	105.01	95.90	109.50	93.50	82.09	113.90
3	114.07	99.80	114.30	95.60	80.47	118.80
4	123.49	102.40	120.60	103.60	81.13	127.70
1974:1	136.85	108.10	126.60	114.70	79.82	143.70
2	146.40	111.50	131.30	134.60	93.60	143.80
3	147.49	107.50	137.20	139.80	81.37	171.80
4	154.15	106.90	144.20	142.10	80.33	176.90
1975:1	156.00	104.00	150.00	130.30	71.83	181.40
2	149.15	100.30	148.70	120.70	66.80	180.70
3	152.73	102.50	149.00	127.80	71.72	178.20
4	161.96	107.40	150.80	133.80	75.08	178.20
1976:1	163.98	107.60	152.40	145.60	80.89	180.00
2	170.18	109.30	155.70	153.40	83.32	184.10
3	173.65	111.60	155.60	161.40	85.94	187.80
4	177.47	111.90	158.60	168.10	88.52	189.90
1977:1	177.82	111.00	160.20	180.00	88.76	202.80
2	184.97	113.90	162.40	186.80	91.30	204.60
3	186.85	115.20	162.20	187.20	90.26	207.40
4	181.25	111.40	162.70	192.90	93.19	207.00
1978:1	195.46	118.10	165.50	207.20	99.04	209.20
2	213.17	124.30	171.50	217.20	101.92	213.10
3	223.98	128.80	173.90	222.90	103.53	215.30
4	242.18	135.60	178.60	232.00	106.23	218.40

Quarterly Data from 1919 to 1941 and from 1947 to 1983   (continued)

| | | Exports | | | | Imports | |
| | | Real (1972 | Deflator (1972 = | | | Real (1972 | Deflator (1972 = |
Quarter	Nominal	dollars)	100)	Nominal		dollars)	100)
1979:1	256.22	138.80	184.60	238.90	105.38	226.70
2	268.16	140.40	191.00	259.10	108.96	237.80
3	290.64	149.20	194.80	274.50	109.36	251.00
4	310.61	156.40	198.60	300.00	112.15	267.50
1980:1	335.38	164.40	204.00	322.50	114.52	281.60
2	336.65	161.00	209.10	314.20	108.42	289.80
3	337.67	156.40	215.90	300.50	102.91	292.00
4	345.40	154.70	223.27	322.00	109.30	294.60
1981:1	368.40	161.20	228.54	335.30	112.50	298.04
2	369.80	161.00	229.69	347.50	116.30	298.80
3	368.70	159.30	231.45	343.90	118.70	289.72
4	372.80	159.40	233.88	341.10	118.20	288.58
1982:1	359.40	152.20	236.14	331.70	117.30	282.78
2	366.30	155.10	236.17	330.80	121.00	273.39
3	346.30	146.60	236.22	339.70	120.90	280.98
4	321.70	136.70	235.33	315.40	112.60	280.11
1983:1	328.50	138.20	237.70	308.90	115.30	267.91
2	328.10	137.00	239.49	334.50	123.40	271.07
3	342.00	141.60	241.53	358.40	129.70	276.33
4	346.10	141.00	245.46	375.90	139.10	270.24

| | | Government Purchases | | | | Government Purchases | |
| | | Real (1972 | Deflator (1972 = | | | Real (1972 | Deflator (1972 = |
Quarter	Nominal	dollars)	100)	Quarter	Nominal	dollars)	100)
1919:1	8.48	50.95	16.64	1922:1	5.89	32.38	18.20
2	9.62	55.60	17.30	2	5.89	32.34	18.21
3	10.05	55.92	17.96	3	5.96	32.61	18.26
4	9.70	51.64	18.79	4	6.07	32.76	18.51
1920:1	6.43	31.89	20.15	1923:1	5.93	32.15	18.45
2	5.68	27.40	20.74	2	6.13	32.34	18.95
3	5.63	26.84	20.98	3	6.28	32.73	19.20
4	5.84	27.89	20.93	4	6.42	33.20	19.34
1921:1	6.37	31.95	19.93	1924:1	6.54	33.78	19.35
2	6.33	33.26	19.03	2	6.63	34.26	19.35
3	6.30	33.81	18.62	3	6.75	34.70	19.46
4	6.19	33.84	18.29	4	6.88	35.11	19.60

Quarterly Data from 1919 to 1941 and from 1947 to 1983   (continued)

	Government Purchases				Government Purchases		
Quarter	Nominal	Real (1972 dollars)	Deflator (1972 = 100)	Quarter	Nominal	Real (1972 dollars)	Deflator (1972 = 100)
1925:1	7.09	35.40	20.02	1936:1	11.81	56.53	20.89
2	7.24	35.79	20.23	2	12.20	58.14	20.99
3	7.33	36.12	20.30	3	12.35	58.69	21.04
4	7.38	36.12	20.44	4	12.31	58.39	21.09
1926:1	7.17	34.80	20.60	1937:1	11.65	55.55	20.96
2	7.23	34.82	20.76	2	11.90	55.22	21.54
3	7.33	35.20	20.82	3	12.16	55.61	21.87
4	7.48	35.79	20.89	4	12.46	56.60	22.02
1927:1	7.69	36.94	20.82	1938:1	12.96	59.40	21.81
2	7.82	37.56	20.81	2	13.16	60.44	21.78
3	7.94	38.01	20.88	3	13.18	61.05	21.59
4	8.00	38.34	20.86	4	13.33	61.63	21.62
1928:1	8.01	38.27	20.92	1939:1	13.41	62.49	21.46
2	8.11	38.60	21.01	2	13.48	63.01	21.39
3	8.23	39.02	21.09	3	13.52	63.40	21.32
4	8.38	39.52	21.20	4	13.61	63.50	21.43
1929:1	8.60	40.18	21.40	1940:1	13.36	62.52	21.36
2	8.76	40.70	21.52	2	13.50	62.94	21.45
3	8.89	41.24	21.56	3	13.99	64.70	21.63
4	9.05	42.03	21.52	4	15.83	70.81	22.36
1930:1	9.38	43.86	21.39	1941:1	22.90	94.27	24.29
2	9.50	44.65	21.28	2	25.42	100.09	25.39
3	9.57	45.17	21.18	3	26.14	100.63	25.98
4	9.56	45.62	20.96	4	25.30	96.08	26.34
1931:1	9.53	45.96	20.74	1947:1	24.60	74.77	32.90
2	9.54	46.35	20.58	2	25.40	75.82	33.50
3	9.49	46.63	20.35	3	25.50	76.35	33.40
4	9.26	46.45	19.94	4	26.10	75.43	34.60
1932:1	8.62	44.35	19.43	1948:1	27.70	76.52	36.20
2	8.33	44.14	18.88	2	30.70	83.20	36.90
3	8.23	44.30	18.58	3	33.20	86.91	38.20
4	8.08	44.17	18.30	4	36.00	91.60	39.30
1933:1	7.91	42.45	18.63	1949:1	36.70	93.15	39.40
2	7.87	42.40	18.56	2	38.40	96.73	39.70
3	8.35	42.89	19.46	3	39.10	98.99	39.50
4	8.86	43.99	20.15	4	39.20	98.00	40.00
1934:1	9.66	47.22	20.46	1950:1	37.70	98.69	38.20
2	10.03	48.34	20.75	2	36.90	96.34	38.30
3	10.20	48.89	20.87	3	38.00	95.48	39.80
4	10.18	49.13	20.72	4	41.40	101.97	40.60
1935:1	10.00	48.57	20.59	1951:1	49.60	115.62	42.90
2	10.08	48.84	20.64	2	56.70	128.57	44.10
3	10.16	49.52	20.53	3	64.40	141.23	45.60
4	10.57	51.17	20.65	4	69.60	149.04	46.70

Quarterly Data from 1919 to 1941 and from 1947 to 1983   (continued)

	Government Purchases				Government Purchases		
Quarter	Nominal	Real (1972 dollars)	Deflator (1972 = 100)	Quarter	Nominal	Real (1972 dollars)	Deflator (1972 = 100)
1952:1	70.90	152.80	46.40	1963:1	122.10	195.67	62.40
2	75.50	159.28	47.40	2	121.30	195.02	62.20
3	77.50	163.85	47.30	3	124.30	199.20	62.40
4	78.30	163.13	48.00	4	127.00	200.00	63.50
1953:1	81.70	167.76	48.70	1964:1	128.30	201.73	63.60
2	82.60	170.31	48.50	2	130.00	203.44	63.90
3	82.40	169.90	48.50	3	130.00	202.18	64.30
4	83.40	171.96	48.50	4	130.90	202.95	64.50
1954:1	79.50	162.58	48.90	1965:1	131.60	202.15	65.10
2	75.40	155.79	48.40	2	135.60	207.34	65.40
3	74.60	153.81	48.50	3	140.10	211.63	66.20
4	73.40	151.65	48.40	4	146.10	217.74	67.10
1955:1	74.30	152.88	48.60	1966:1	150.00	221.24	67.80
2	74.10	150.92	49.10	2	155.30	224.75	69.10
3	75.40	153.56	49.10	3	162.00	233.77	69.30
4	76.20	152.10	50.10	4	167.30	238.66	70.10
1956:1	77.20	151.97	50.80	1967:1	174.90	244.27	71.60
2	79.30	153.98	51.50	2	177.50	246.94	71.88
3	79.70	152.98	52.10	3	182.00	250.69	72.60
4	81.30	154.86	52.50	4	186.50	252.37	73.90
1957:1	86.20	160.22	53.80	1968:1	192.40	256.53	75.00
2	86.60	161.27	53.70	2	198.60	260.97	76.10
3	87.50	161.44	54.20	3	201.00	262.40	76.60
4	88.10	161.95	54.40	4	204.00	261.20	78.10
1958:1	91.20	165.22	55.20	1969:1	204.50	258.53	79.10
2	94.20	168.82	55.80	2	207.40	259.25	80.00
3	96.10	171.00	56.20	3	210.70	256.95	82.00
4	98.70	174.69	56.50	4	212.40	254.98	83.30
1959:1	97.80	171.58	57.00	1970:1	216.40	252.80	85.60
2	98.00	171.03	57.30	2	217.70	249.66	87.20
3	97.50	170.16	57.30	3	221.10	250.97	88.10
4	97.00	169.28	57.30	4	225.30	250.89	89.80
1960:1	97.30	169.22	57.50	1971:1	229.70	249.95	91.90
2	99.30	172.40	57.60	2	232.40	248.29	93.60
3	101.80	174.32	58.40	3	236.40	250.42	94.40
4	102.70	175.56	58.50	4	240.90	251.46	95.80
1961:1	105.00	179.49	58.50	1972:1	249.70	254.54	98.10
2	106.80	181.02	59.00	2	251.50	253.27	99.30
3	108.40	182.80	59.30	3	252.90	252.40	100.20
4	112.30	188.42	59.60	4	258.30	252.00	102.50
1962:1	116.10	191.27	60.70	1973:1	264.90	254.71	104.00
2	116.80	191.79	60.90	2	266.30	251.23	106.00
3	118.80	194.75	61.00	3	268.90	251.31	107.00
4	120.40	194.82	61.80	4	281.60	256.47	109.80

Quarterly Data from 1919 to 1941 and from 1947 to 1983   (continued)

	Government Purchases				Government Purchases		
Quarter	Nominal	Real (1972 dollars)	Deflator (1972 = 100)	Quarter	Nominal	Real (1972 dollars)	Deflator (1972 = 100)
1974:1	286.80	258.15	111.10	1979:1	456.90	280.59	162.84
2	300.60	261.62	114.90	2	464.50	280.18	165.79
3	309.20	262.03	118.00	3	478.50	280.97	170.30
4	319.70	262.91	121.60	4	497.60	285.29	174.42
1975:1	327.70	264.27	124.00	1980:1	517.60	283.93	182.30
2	333.60	264.34	126.20	2	535.50	286.82	186.70
3	344.00	268.12	128.30	3	539.10	284.04	189.80
4	354.30	269.84	131.30	4	559.00	282.50	197.88
1976:1	357.00	268.42	133.00	1981:1	576.60	286.00	201.61
2	358.10	266.44	134.40	2	585.30	285.10	205.30
3	362.80	265.98	136.40	3	601.30	287.40	209.22
4	370.40	266.09	139.20	4	622.70	289.60	215.02
1977:1	377.90	268.51	140.74	1982:1	630.90	290.20	217.40
2	390.70	271.34	143.99	2	633.70	287.00	220.80
3	398.70	273.66	145.69	3	656.30	292.80	224.15
4	408.00	275.81	147.93	4	681.00	300.60	226.55
1978:1	412.80	274.57	150.34	1983:1	678.80	294.30	230.65
2	424.40	276.40	153.55	2	682.20	292.40	233.31
3	439.30	280.06	156.86	3	689.80	292.00	236.23
4	451.10	280.14	161.03	4	691.40	288.80	239.40

	Real Net Capital Stock (1972 dollars)			Cost of Capital Services	
Quarter	Producers' Durable Equipment	Business Structures	Consumers' Durable Goods	Producers' Durable Equipment	Business Structures
1919:1	91.99	207.46	55.62	21.62	11.32
2	91.64	205.99	56.17	22.05	11.45
3	92.05	204.74	57.45	21.70	11.48
4	92.18	203.32	59.31	21.49	11.68
1920:1	92.86	202.20	60.39	20.98	12.21
2	93.33	200.89	60.76	20.52	12.33
3	93.54	199.10	61.00	21.34	12.70
4	93.07	197.36	60.77	21.51	11.82
1921:1	92.02	195.76	60.13	23.53	12.01
2	90.92	194.76	59.96	24.15	11.69
3	89.82	194.06	60.04	24.12	11.38
4	88.73	193.65	59.99	23.70	11.56

Quarterly Data from 1919 to 1941 and from 1947 to 1983   (continued)

	Real Net Capital Stock (1972 dollars)			Cost of Capital Services	
Quarter	Producers' Durable Equipment	Business Structures	Consumers' Durable Goods	Producers' Durable Equipment	Business Structures
1922:1	87.63	193.59	59.93	23.69	11.57
2	86.90	194.20	60.31	23.09	11.16
3	86.38	194.82	60.79	22.96	11.04
4	86.33	195.66	61.37	22.97	11.07
1923:1	86.61	196.68	62.38	22.97	11.39
2	87.24	198.17	63.48	23.71	11.71
3	87.68	199.33	64.47	23.98	11.61
4	87.78	200.92	65.55	24.30	11.65
1924:1	88.01	202.68	66.84	23.81	11.50
2	87.79	204.59	67.60	23.83	11.34
3	87.52	206.59	68.11	23.60	10.89
4	87.82	208.51	68.60	23.27	10.71
1925:1	88.20	210.40	69.45	21.89	9.96
2	88.27	212.68	70.60	20.40	8.75
3	88.53	215.20	71.73	20.25	8.79
4	89.08	217.39	73.43	19.54	8.35
1926:1	89.71	219.79	74.94	19.57	8.28
2	90.19	222.08	76.12	19.95	8.51
3	90.72	224.21	77.17	20.75	9.09
4	91.23	226.03	78.14	21.37	9.53
1927:1	91.61	227.47	79.12	20.99	9.02
2	91.80	229.33	80.11	21.60	9.22
3	91.84	231.01	80.78	21.44	9.11
4	91.75	232.77	81.25	21.31	9.12
1928:1	91.87	233.81	81.94	21.83	9.50
2	92.11	235.10	82.63	21.95	9.59
3	92.51	236.22	83.47	21.73	9.50
4	93.16	237.51	84.56	21.87	9.75
1929:1	93.83	239.47	85.69	22.62	10.02
2	94.56	241.41	86.65	23.02	10.31
3	95.41	242.77	87.62	22.83	10.25
4	95.76	243.81	88.09	22.16	9.53
1930:1	95.88	244.95	88.14	22.27	10.00
2	95.85	246.29	87.92	22.07	9.64
3	95.51	246.68	87.42	23.10	10.13
4	94.69	246.45	86.94	22.95	10.10
1931:1	93.60	245.94	86.35	26.02	11.51
2	92.51	245.30	85.72	27.99	12.77
3	91.20	243.99	84.95	30.28	14.00
4	89.56	242.35	83.90	32.31	16.05
1932:1	87.77	240.22	82.67	38.23	17.84
2	85.61	238.16	81.25	40.60	19.88
3	83.58	236.04	79.70	41.90	20.96
4	81.73	233.77	78.25	40.99	19.88

Quarterly Data from 1919 to 1941 and from 1947 to 1983 (continued)

Quarter	Real Net Capital Stock (1972 dollars)			Cost of Capital Services	
	Producers' Durable Equipment	Business Structures	Consumers' Durable Goods	Producers' Durable Equipment	Business Structures
1933:1	79.62	231.24	76.70	35.95	19.45
2	78.10	228.84	75.37	40.64	22.23
3	77.01	226.40	74.45	33.44	18.47
4	75.57	224.24	73.53	35.79	19.58
1934:1	74.61	222.16	72.64	31.91	15.51
2	73.87	219.96	72.02	30.15	13.75
3	72.69	217.86	71.43	26.94	11.82
4	71.76	215.82	71.04	27.37	11.87
1935:1	71.29	213.69	70.98	24.07	10.60
2	70.81	211.93	70.92	22.33	9.24
3	70.62	209.95	71.14	20.33	7.81
4	70.90	208.53	71.69	19.90	7.42
1936:1	71.21	207.18	72.40	19.89	7.05
2	71.73	205.74	73.27	18.94	6.23
3	72.60	204.62	74.35	20.10	6.85
4	73.71	203.80	75.52	20.88	7.95
1937:1	75.04	203.12	76.72	22.12	8.86
2	76.33	203.29	77.78	22.30	9.29
3	77.61	202.73	78.91	23.35	9.74
4	77.88	201.84	79.42	21.90	8.76
1938:1	77.62	200.94	79.23	23.39	9.55
2	77.09	199.67	78.88	24.30	10.51
3	76.94	198.64	78.79	23.88	10.09
4	77.10	197.74	79.16	22.84	9.42
1939:1	77.09	196.99	79.76	23.44	9.50
2	76.88	196.20	80.25	24.04	9.98
3	77.07	195.24	80.85	23.73	9.83
4	77.96	194.49	81.63	23.93	10.37
1940:1	78.79	193.24	82.65	23.76	9.77
2	79.62	192.31	83.62	24.72	10.38
3	80.75	191.98	84.67	24.91	10.60
4	82.12	192.95	86.04	26.14	11.55
1941:1	83.47	193.45	87.67	24.48	10.22
2	84.90	193.46	89.49	23.71	9.57
3	86.46	194.50	91.24	21.34	7.98
4	88.29	193.44	92.33	20.31	7.19
1947:1	118.50	188.50	91.10	15.67	6.73
2	122.38	190.34	93.80	16.24	6.90
3	125.88	192.17	96.41	16.31	7.05
4	129.62	193.92	99.48	16.36	7.24
1948:1	133.78	195.67	102.38	16.32	7.50
2	137.30	197.66	105.12	16.46	7.50
3	140.54	199.82	107.94	16.80	7.41
4	143.99	202.01	110.57	17.31	7.65

Quarterly Data from 1919 to 1941 and from 1947 to 1983   (continued)

	Real Net Capital Stock (1972 dollars)			Cost of Capital Services	
Quarter	Producers' Durable Equipment	Business Structures	Consumers' Durable Goods	Producers' Durable Equipment	Business Structures
1949:1	146.76	204.04	112.93	17.37	7.57
2	148.92	205.91	115.96	17.94	7.49
3	150.63	207.51	119.18	18.00	7.52
4	152.18	208.98	122.46	17.85	7.45
1950:1	153.74	210.66	125.85	17.88	7.35
2	156.09	212.50	129.16	17.98	7.32
3	159.18	214.56	134.74	18.08	7.47
4	162.05	216.74	138.59	17.99	7.33
1951:1	164.43	218.86	142.52	19.38	8.24
2	166.87	221.15	144.69	19.11	8.14
3	169.45	223.37	146.51	19.90	8.95
4	171.89	225.34	148.17	20.58	9.69
1952:1	174.29	227.27	149.92	19.85	9.04
2	176.69	229.25	151.75	19.77	8.63
3	177.78	231.24	152.87	19.11	8.19
4	179.64	233.41	155.10	19.05	7.89
1953:1	182.00	235.71	157.69	18.42	7.49
2	184.18	238.09	160.04	18.71	7.62
3	186.55	240.45	162.23	19.35	8.35
4	188.63	242.88	164.50	20.26	9.37
1954:1	190.22	245.33	166.25	20.50	9.63
2	191.57	247.79	168.01	20.93	9.85
3	193.14	250.26	169.95	20.95	9.90
4	194.57	252.68	172.47	21.03	9.84
1955:1	196.01	255.23	175.60	21.05	10.02
2	198.16	257.87	179.36	20.57	9.73
3	200.79	260.65	183.27	20.56	9.61
4	203.71	263.54	186.89	20.93	9.94
1956:1	206.08	266.64	189.57	21.47	10.62
2	208.35	269.96	192.00	21.68	10.46
3	210.66	273.32	194.11	21.72	10.47
4	212.78	276.65	196.29	22.24	10.67
1957:1	215.01	279.84	198.65	22.50	10.60
2	217.12	282.98	200.59	22.45	10.70
3	219.49	286.04	202.24	22.68	11.00
4	221.42	289.05	203.80	22.90	10.80
1958:1	222.30	291.91	204.58	22.52	10.47
2	222.76	294.44	205.15	22.64	10.51
3	223.09	296.74	205.84	22.61	10.43
4	223.83	299.11	206.90	23.12	10.88
1959:1	224.98	301.40	208.58	22.97	10.71
2	226.38	303.91	210.63	22.89	10.64
3	228.00	306.58	212.80	23.07	10.84
4	229.60	309.17	214.25	23.52	11.42

Quarterly Data from 1919 to 1941 and from 1947 to 1983   (continued)

Quarter	Real Net Capital Stock (1972 dollars)			Cost of Capital Services	
	Producers' Durable Equipment	Business Structures	Consumers' Durable Goods	Producers' Durable Equipment	Business Structures
1960:1	231.39	312.08	215.97	23.84	11.78
2	233.29	314.79	217.91	23.87	11.67
3	234.69	317.57	219.62	23.93	11.68
4	235.69	320.64	220.93	23.92	11.67
1961:1	236.38	323.69	221.46	23.80	11.68
2	237.44	326.54	222.13	23.78	11.73
3	238.55	329.33	223.02	23.66	11.76
4	240.17	332.19	224.48	23.51	11.86
1962:1	242.25	335.00	226.12	21.34	10.70
2	243.54	338.06	228.01	21.51	10.75
3	244.82	341.38	229.92	21.94	11.03
4	246.02	344.47	232.33	21.85	11.01
1963:1	247.35	347.17	234.88	21.20	10.64
2	248.85	350.17	237.60	21.13	10.67
3	250.74	353.15	240.38	21.21	10.69
4	252.94	356.27	243.24	21.23	10.73
1964:1	255.35	359.39	246.48	22.14	10.56
2	257.88	362.76	249.95	21.72	10.29
3	260.68	366.25	253.75	21.77	10.37
4	263.76	369.85	256.80	21.26	10.00
1965:1	267.68	373.96	261.18	21.31	10.14
2	271.68	378.63	265.38	21.30	10.11
3	276.30	383.39	269.97	21.01	10.17
4	281.25	388.64	275.07	21.10	10.21
1966:1	286.74	393.98	280.83	21.58	10.63
2	292.49	398.97	285.42	21.73	10.96
3	298.05	404.21	290.41	21.81	10.97
4	303.57	409.05	295.11	22.03	11.31
1967:1	308.23	413.84	299.20	22.02	11.21
2	312.94	418.20	303.94	21.85	11.05
3	317.26	422.57	308.27	22.22	11.60
4	321.92	426.81	312.37	22.35	11.85
1968:1	326.89	431.31	317.57	22.12	11.99
2	331.25	435.57	322.91	22.33	12.19
3	335.79	439.73	328.96	21.95	11.86
4	340.74	444.18	334.60	21.86	11.75
1969:1	346.10	448.75	340.42	22.05	12.22
2	351.45	453.24	345.88	22.11	12.59
3	356.80	458.20	350.98	22.47	13.09
4	361.84	462.78	355.68	22.48	13.38
1970:1	366.47	467.02	359.77	23.19	14.21
2	370.82	471.15	363.90	22.53	13.71
3	375.04	475.16	367.92	22.81	14.31
4	378.17	479.03	370.14	22.72	14.45

Quarterly Data from 1919 to 1941 and from 1947 to 1983 (continued)

	Real Net Capital Stock (1972 dollars)			Cost of Capital Services	
Quarter	Producers' Durable Equipment	Business Structures	Consumers' Durable Goods	Producers' Durable Equipment	Business Structures
1971:1	381.35	482.74	374.53	21.26	13.30
2	384.82	486.33	379.31	20.42	12.80
3	388.18	489.94	384.52	20.42	13.14
4	391.94	493.31	390.58	19.88	12.83
1972:1	396.23	496.91	396.99	19.94	12.88
2	400.68	500.58	403.77	19.85	12.75
3	405.29	504.24	410.85	19.94	13.00
4	411.19	508.09	419.06	19.75	13.12
1973:1	418.06	512.06	428.64	19.43	12.88
2	425.70	516.27	437.15	19.54	13.24
3	433.35	520.70	444.82	19.42	13.32
4	440.81	525.01	451.16	19.16	13.25
1974:1	448.31	529.01	456.52	18.99	13.58
2	455.37	532.62	461.65	19.00	14.33
3	462.28	535.30	466.79	19.30	15.22
4	467.57	537.72	468.84	19.60	15.45
1975:1	471.14	539.36	471.29	18.78	13.97
2	474.08	540.77	474.24	18.21	12.67
3	477.11	542.39	478.77	17.83	12.14
4	480.08	544.14	483.88	17.64	11.85
1976:1	483.37	545.97	490.20	17.77	11.95
2	487.00	547.74	496.32	17.64	11.87
3	491.27	549.56	502.44	17.89	12.11
4	495.81	551.37	508.66	17.37	11.59
1977:1	501.76	553.04	516.35	17.37	11.49
2	508.45	555.02	523.93	17.57	11.83
3	515.04	557.30	531.57	17.80	11.93
4	522.64	559.43	539.73	18.50	12.87
1978:1	529.59	561.79	546.77	19.36	14.00
2	537.63	564.67	555.60	19.99	15.29
3	545.58	567.74	563.70	19.80	15.31
4	554.10	571.00	572.32	19.40	15.23
1979:1	562.93	574.05	580.22	19.78	15.94
2	570.84	577.59	586.32	19.34	15.40
3	579.43	581.49	592.76	19.02	15.12
4	586.81	585.66	598.69	19.82	16.68
1980:1	595.78	589.89	604.11	20.57	18.64
2	602.60	593.27	605.45	21.85	21.22
3	609.76	596.29	608.11	19.59	18.21
4	616.98	599.52	611.51	20.98	20.64
1981:1	624.81	603.10	616.33	21.02	21.19
2	632.55	607.02	619.67	21.53	21.91
3	640.45	611.39	623.67	22.07	23.47
4	647.63	615.98	625.21	22.45	25.23

Quarterly Data from 1919 to 1941 and from
1947 to 1983   (continued)

| | Real Net Capital Stock (1972 dollars) | | | Cost of Capital Services | |
Quarter	Producers' Durable Equipment	Business Structures	Consumers' Durable Goods	Producers' Durable Equipment	Business Structures
1981:1	653.78	620.36	627.58	22.43	25.24
2	658.26	624.68	630.07	22.24	24.79
3	661.88	628.63	632.13	22.32	24.90
4	664.87	632.42	635.32	20.39	21.81
1983:1	668.10	635.57	639.00	19.35	20.45
2	672.51	638.21	645.16	19.23	20.07
3	678.20	641.13	651.36	19.37	20.34
4	685.79	644.30	658.66	20.81	21.27

Section 3 Source Notes
Investment in producers' durable equipment: nonresidential and residential, investment
in nonresidential structures: nonresidential and farm structures, investment in residential structures, consumption of durable goods, consumption of nondurable goods
and services, exports, imports, and government purchases—
   Nominal: 1919–41, interpolated series from Gordon and Veitch, this volume. 1947–
   83, national income and product accounts, table 1.1.
   Real: 1919–41, interpolated series from Gordon and Veitch, this volume. 1947–83,
   national income and products accounts, table 1.2.
   Deflator: 1919–83, nominal series divided by the real series, then multiplied by 100.
Investment, change in business inventories
   Nominal: 1919–41, interpolated series from Gordon and Veitch, this volume. 1947–
   83, national income and product accounts, table 1.1.
   Real: 1919–41, interpolated series from Gordon and Veitch, this volume. 1947–83,
   national income and product accounts, table 1.2.
Real net capital stock, producers' durable equipment
   1919–83: constructed series described in Gordon and Veitch, this volume.
Real net capital stock, business structures
   1919–83: constructed series described in Gordon and Veitch, this volume.
Real net capital stock, consumers' durable goods
   1919–83: constructed series described in Gordon and Veitch, this volume.
Cost of capital services, producers' durable equipment
   1919–83: constructed series described in Gordon and Veitch, this volume.
Cost of capital services, business structures
   1919–83: constructed series described in Gordon and Veitch, this volume.

4.   Total Manufacturing: Real Production, Shipments, and Inventories (Millions of 1929 Dollars)

Year	Month	Production	Shipments	Inventories at End of Month
1929	January	13525.8		12884.3
1929	February	13429.0	13248.3	13065.0
1929	March	13630.5	13794.3	12901.2

Total Manufacturing: Real Production, Shipments, and Inventories   (continued)

Year	Month	Production	Shipments	Inventories at End of Month
1929	April	13763.7	13676.4	12988.5
1929	May	13902.4	13620.7	13270.2
1929	June	14096.8	14197.8	13169.2
1929	July	14187.1	13982.3	13374.0
1929	August	14047.6	13846.6	13575.0
1929	September	13827.0	13572.6	13829.4
1929	October	13811.7	13704.0	13937.0
1929	November	13218.5	12966.6	14188.9
1929	December	13584.8	13770.5	14003.2
1930	January	12576.7	12347.2	14232.7
1930	February	12479.1	12553.7	14158.2
1930	March	12197.5	12068.8	14286.9
1930	April	12151.1	12192.8	14245.3
1930	May	11807.6	11754.4	14298.5
1930	June	11390.0	11130.0	14558.6
1930	July	10899.1	10517.6	14940.1
1930	August	10556.5	10416.5	15080.1
1930	September	10457.3	10687.2	14850.2
1930	October	10216.2	10474.0	14592.3
1930	November	9994.4	9988.9	14597.8
1930	December	9883.9	11226.1	13255.6
1931	January	9773.5	9157.0	13872.1
1931	February	9881.4	10038.6	13715.0
1931	March	9900.9	10018.8	13597.1
1931	April	9867.2	10010.7	13453.6
1931	May	9704.1	9582.5	13575.2
1931	June	9327.3	9273.2	13629.3
1931	July	9312.4	9395.6	13546.2
1931	August	8935.5	9070.8	13410.8
1931	September	8579.6	8642.9	13347.6
1931	October	8304.0	8517.8	13133.8
1931	November	8204.4	8350.6	12987.6
1931	December	8111.5	8946.8	12152.3
1932	January	8018.5	7611.6	12559.2
1932	February	7751.0	7761.0	12549.2
1932	March	7300.2	7309.0	12540.4
1932	April	6882.2	6913.3	12509.3
1932	May	6692.3	6688.5	12513.2
1932	June	6494.1	6709.3	12297.9
1932	July	6315.9	6563.2	12050.7
1932	August	6390.7	6511.1	11930.2
1932	September	6970.3	7159.0	11741.5
1932	October	7347.9	7608.7	11480.7
1932	November	7243.4	7342.2	11381.9
1932	December	7187.7	7882.2	10687.5
1933	January	7106.3	6738.0	11055.8
1933	February	6923.9	6889.2	11090.4

Total Manufacturing: Real Production, Shipments, and Inventories   (continued)

Year	Month	Production	Shipments	Inventories at End of Month
1933	March	6257.9	6251.0	11097.4
1933	April	6955.1	7123.8	10928.7
1933	May	8087.7	8421.3	10595.1
1933	June	9463.9	9676.3	10382.8
1933	July	9614.9	9872.3	10125.4
1933	August	9766.0	9491.8	10399.6
1933	September	9386.6	9289.2	10497.1
1933	October	8947.2	8879.1	10565.2
1933	November	8343.0	8070.2	10837.9
1933	December	8685.3	7671.0	11852.2
1934	January	8701.6	9304.3	11249.5
1934	February	9240.0	9334.8	11154.8
1934	March	9605.3	9529.5	11230.5
1934	April	9767.4	9542.6	11455.3
1934	May	9796.1	9753.2	11498.2
1934	June	9616.1	9550.3	11564.1
1934	July	8949.7	8812.8	11701.0
1934	August	8755.4	8905.0	11551.4
1934	September	8383.2	8622.2	11312.4
1934	October	8681.2	8898.9	11094.6
1934	November	8625.7	8725.7	10994.6
1934	December	9660.2	9621.7	11033.1
1935	January	10230.5	10530.8	10732.8
1935	February	10584.7	10639.4	10678.2
1935	March	10401.1	10375.3	10704.0
1935	April	10195.3	10265.9	10633.5
1935	May	10032.4	10086.1	10579.8
1935	June	10011.7	10033.5	10557.9
1935	July	10417.3	10352.0	10623.2
1935	August	10646.2	10692.8	10576.5
1935	September	10972.3	10893.2	10655.7
1935	October	11486.6	11415.3	10727.0
1935	November	11634.8	11630.1	10731.7
1935	December	11496.0	11320.0	10907.6
1936	January	11498.9	11443.2	10963.4
1936	February	11204.8	11075.8	11092.4
1936	March	11530.8	11437.0	11186.2
1936	April	12156.5	12076.3	11266.4
1936	May	12491.6	12255.8	11502.2
1936	June	12731.9	12611.0	11623.2
1936	July	12955.3	12939.6	11638.9
1936	August	12968.1	12754.3	11852.7
1936	September	13185.9	13007.8	12030.8
1936	October	13632.4	13493.4	12169.7
1936	November	13843.1	13814.4	12198.4
1936	December	13764.9	13167.7	12795.6
1937	January	14139.5	14228.4	12706.7

Total Manufacturing: Real Production, Shipments, and Inventories   (continued)

Year	Month	Production	Shipments	Inventories at End of Month
1937	February	14583.1	14518.8	12771.0
1937	March	15036.1	14796.3	13010.8
1937	April	15130.6	14900.0	13241.3
1937	May	15247.9	14952.7	13536.6
1937	June	14890.4	14641.2	13785.7
1937	July	14837.0	14832.9	13789.9
1937	August	14448.9	14271.6	13967.2
1937	September	13820.0	13446.9	14340.2
1937	October	12899.8	12849.0	14391.0
1937	November	11307.2	11322.4	14375.8
1937	December	10529.3	11401.3	13503.9
1938	January	9751.3	9346.9	13908.3
1938	February	9964.9	9982.9	13890.3
1938	March	10155.8	10423.5	13622.6
1938	April	9902.5	9969.3	13555.8
1938	May	9845.8	9986.5	13415.1
1938	June	9827.7	10059.3	13183.5
1938	July	10388.4	10566.6	13005.3
1938	August	10868.2	10858.9	13014.5
1938	September	11316.6	11311.2	13019.9
1938	October	11584.4	11617.1	12987.2
1938	November	11968.5	11815.3	13140.3
1938	December	11616.6	12055.0	12701.9
1939	January	12040.9	11554.9	13187.9
1939	February	12316.7	12460.9	13043.8
1939	March	12549.6	12579.5	13013.9
1939	April	12465.9	12402.1	13077.7
1939	May	12292.4	12263.2	13106.9
1939	June	12670.0	12693.7	13083.2
1939	July	12731.8	12521.3	13293.6
1939	August	12694.4	12645.1	13342.9
1939	September	13556.1	13986.6	12912.4
1939	October	14657.9	14532.6	13037.8
1939	November	14968.8	14477.9	13528.7
1939	December	14462.0	13916.9	14073.9
1940	January	14621.2	14265.4	14429.8
1940	February	14269.7	14151.8	14547.7
1940	March	14104.0	14050.2	14601.4
1940	April	14129.1	14148.2	14582.3
1940	May	14590.4	14500.4	14672.3
1940	June	15123.6	14914.7	14881.2
1940	July	15046.2	14848.7	15078.7
1940	August	15340.8	15364.7	15054.7
1940	September	15809.7	15616.5	15248.0
1940	October	16371.9	16560.8	15059.1
1940	November	16717.9	16468.6	15308.4
1940	December	16684.5	16474.7	15518.2

Total Manufacturing: Real Production, Shipments, and Inventories   (continued)

Year	Month	Production	Shipments	Inventories at End of Month
1941	January	17589.8	17540.9	15567.1
1941	February	18382.9	18025.8	15924.3
1941	March	19085.5	19050.3	15959.5
1941	April	19522.1	19469.8	16011.7
1941	May	20372.8	20391.0	15993.6
1941	June	20815.3	20771.1	16037.7
1941	July	21095.9	20867.0	16266.7
1941	August	21089.8	20959.5	16397.0
1941	September	21210.0	21037.0	16570.0
1941	October	21397.6	21170.3	16797.0
1941	November	21576.7	20988.7	17385.3
1941	December	22168.8	20901.1	18653.1
1942	January	22665.0	23526.5	17791.6
1942	February	23161.2	23192.2	17760.6
1942	March	23707.0	23620.3	17847.4
1942	April	24281.1	24192.7	17935.8
1942	May	24611.4	24330.6	18216.7
1942	June	24894.8	24577.8	18533.7
1942	July	25748.8	25545.9	18736.5
1942	August	26238.8	26165.7	18809.7
1942	September	26705.4	26620.4	18894.6
1942	October	27353.1	27325.3	18922.4
1942	November	27963.5	27969.1	18916.8
1942	December	27658.1	27522.0	19052.9

5.   Total Manufacturing: Nominal Production, Shipments, and Inventories (Millions of Current Dollars)

Year	Month	Production	Shipments	Inventories at End of Month
1929	January	13591.5		12946.9
1929	February	13499.4	13317.8	13133.5
1929	March	13770.8	13936.3	13034.0
1929	April	13904.2	13816.0	13121.0
1929	May	13980.6	13697.4	13344.9
1929	June	14244.9	14347.0	13307.6
1929	July	14327.7	14120.9	13506.6
1929	August	14054.0	13853.0	13581.2
1929	September	13777.8	13524.3	13780.2
1929	October	13656.3	13549.9	13780.2
1929	November	12942.0	12695.3	13892.1
1929	December	13501.2	13685.8	13917.0
1930	January	12319.7	12094.9	13941.9
1930	February	12197.0	12269.8	13838.0

Total Manufacturing: Nominal Production, Shipments, and Inventories   (continued)

Year	Month	Production	Shipments	Inventories at End of Month
1930	March	11821.1	11696.3	13846.0
1930	April	11722.3	11762.4	13742.5
1930	May	11334.6	11283.5	13725.7
1930	June	10725.2	10480.3	13708.8
1930	July	9961.6	9612.9	13655.1
1930	August	9538.5	9412.0	13625.9
1930	September	9454.1	9662.0	13425.6
1930	October	9157.1	9388.2	13079.6
1930	November	8844.0	8839.1	12917.5
1930	December	9140.1	10381.3	12258.0
1931	January	8482.3	7947.2	12039.3
1931	February	8486.8	8621.7	11779.3
1931	March	8406.3	8506.4	11544.5
1931	April	8224.9	8344.5	11214.3
1931	May	7962.1	7862.3	11138.2
1931	June	7554.2	7510.3	11038.4
1931	July	7478.9	7545.7	10879.1
1931	August	7142.9	7251.1	10720.4
1931	September	6797.0	6847.1	10574.3
1931	October	6548.6	6717.3	10357.5
1931	November	6451.5	6566.5	10212.8
1931	December	6578.7	7256.2	9856.0
1932	January	6156.8	5844.4	9643.3
1932	February	5921.5	5929.1	9587.1
1932	March	5568.9	5575.6	9566.3
1932	April	5212.4	5235.9	9474.2
1932	May	5023.9	5021.1	9393.6
1932	June	4842.2	5002.7	9169.8
1932	July	4700.9	4884.9	8969.1
1932	August	4722.3	4811.3	8815.6
1932	September	5113.5	5251.9	8613.7
1932	October	5375.7	5566.5	8399.2
1932	November	5277.0	5348.9	8292.0
1932	December	5242.6	5858.8	7944.0
1933	January	5044.4	4782.9	7847.9
1933	February	4862.6	4838.3	7788.8
1933	March	4386.0	4381.1	7777.8
1933	April	4866.3	4984.3	7646.5
1933	May	5801.0	6040.2	7599.4
1933	June	6949.7	7105.6	7624.5
1933	July	7332.4	7528.7	7721.7
1933	August	7489.4	7279.1	7975.3
1933	September	7315.4	7239.5	8180.9
1933	October	7102.1	7048.1	8386.5
1933	November	6604.9	6389.0	8580.1
1933	December	6482.3	5725.3	8846.0
1934	January	7028.7	7515.5	9086.7

Total Manufacturing: Nominal Production, Shipments, and Inventories   (continued)

Year	Month	Production	Shipments	Inventories at End of Month
1934	February	7592.0	7669.9	9165.3
1934	March	7905.5	7843.1	9243.2
1934	April	8008.0	7823.7	9391.8
1934	May	8127.2	8091.6	9539.3
1934	June	7995.1	7940.3	9614.7
1934	July	7393.0	7279.9	9665.6
1934	August	7248.5	7372.3	9563.2
1934	September	7002.7	7202.3	9449.5
1934	October	7250.5	7432.4	9266.2
1934	November	7218.1	7301.8	9200.4
1934	December	8018.4	7986.4	9158.0
1935	January	8773.6	9031.1	9204.4
1935	February	9187.0	9234.4	9268.1
1935	March	9044.4	9022.0	9307.8
1935	April	8906.8	8968.5	9289.6
1935	May	8802.2	8849.3	9282.5
1935	June	8741.5	8750.6	9218.4
1935	July	9021.4	8964.9	9199.7
1935	August	9252.5	9293.1	9192.0
1935	September	9526.2	9457.5	9251.3
1935	October	10028.5	9966.2	9365.3
1935	November	10179.3	10175.2	9389.2
1935	December	10059.8	9905.9	9545.0
1936	January	10046.0	9997.3	9578.1
1936	February	9789.9	9677.2	9691.7
1936	March	9959.0	9878.0	9661.4
1936	April	10511.8	10442.4	9742.1
1936	May	10692.3	10490.5	9845.4
1936	June	10910.5	10806.9	9960.4
1936	July	11165.4	11151.9	10030.9
1936	August	11212.2	11027.4	10247.9
1936	September	11359.4	11206.0	10364.3
1936	October	11804.2	11683.9	10537.8
1936	November	12104.7	12079.6	10666.6
1936	December	12017.2	11495.9	11171.0
1937	January	12721.5	12801.5	11432.4
1937	February	13222.4	13164.1	11579.4
1937	March	13780.2	13560.5	11924.0
1937	April	13998.5	13785.2	12250.6
1937	May	14172.0	13897.6	12581.4
1937	June	13868.6	13636.5	12839.8
1937	July	13911.6	13907.7	12929.8
1937	August	13521.1	13355.2	13070.3
1937	September	12912.3	12563.8	13398.4
1937	October	11994.6	11947.5	13381.3
1937	November	10370.1	10384.0	13184.5
1937	December	9787.9	10598.4	12553.0

Total Manufacturing: Nominal Production, Shipments, and Inventories   (continued)

Year	Month	Production	Shipments	Inventories at End of Month
1938	January	8706.4	8345.4	12418.0
1938	February	8810.0	8825.9	12280.5
1938	March	8980.9	9217.7	12046.6
1938	April	8665.7	8724.1	11862.6
1938	May	8577.4	8700.0	11686.9
1938	June	8579.4	8781.6	11508.9
1938	July	9049.1	9204.4	11328.7
1938	August	9361.8	9353.8	11210.6
1938	September	9715.1	9710.5	11177.3
1938	October	9910.5	9938.5	11110.6
1938	November	10177.1	10046.8	11173.5
1938	December	10196.3	10581.1	11149.0
1939	January	10199.3	9787.6	11170.9
1939	February	10486.6	10609.3	11105.7
1939	March	10667.6	10693.0	11062.3
1939	April	10566.1	10512.0	11084.6
1939	May	10406.5	10381.8	11096.0
1939	June	10703.7	10723.7	11052.7
1939	July	10648.8	10472.8	11118.8
1939	August	10589.2	10548.0	11130.1
1939	September	11662.4	12032.8	11108.7
1939	October	12723.4	12614.7	11317.1
1939	November	12958.2	12533.2	11711.6
1939	December	12451.2	11981.9	12117.0
1940	January	12643.8	12336.0	12478.2
1940	February	12326.7	12224.9	12566.9
1940	March	12118.6	12072.5	12546.1
1940	April	12136.0	12152.4	12525.3
1940	May	12542.8	12465.4	12613.2
1940	June	12907.7	12729.4	12700.8
1940	July	12868.5	12699.6	12896.3
1940	August	13119.5	13139.9	12874.8
1940	September	13550.8	13385.1	13069.3
1940	October	14184.9	14348.5	13047.4
1940	November	14577.5	14360.2	13348.5
1940	December	14558.7	14375.6	13541.0
1941	January	15543.3	15500.0	13755.9
1941	February	16276.5	15960.3	14099.6
1941	March	17015.6	16984.2	14228.6
1941	April	17637.4	17590.2	14465.9
1941	May	18730.0	18746.7	14703.9
1941	June	19534.3	19492.8	15050.8
1941	July	20110.7	19892.5	15507.1
1941	August	20394.0	20268.1	15856.0
1941	September	20744.1	20575.0	16206.0
1941	October	21230.2	21004.7	16665.9
1941	November	21391.6	20808.6	17236.1

Total Manufacturing: Nominal Production, Shipments, and Inventories   (continued)

Year	Month	Production	Shipments	Inventories at End of Month
1941	December	21164.5	19954.2	17808.0
1942	January	23103.5	23981.6	18135.8
1942	February	23792.9	23824.7	18245.0
1942	March	24525.4	24435.7	18463.5
1942	April	25291.3	25199.3	18682.0
1942	May	25682.9	25389.8	19009.8
1942	June	25974.5	25643.8	19337.5
1942	July	26875.0	26663.3	19556.0
1942	August	27432.4	27355.9	19665.3
1942	September	27949.1	27860.1	19774.5
1942	October	28742.8	18713.6	19883.8
1942	November	29392.9	29398.8	19883.8
1942	December	29181.4	29037.8	20102.3

Contributors

Moses Abramovitz
Department of Economics
Stanford University
Stanford, California 94305

Alan J. Auerbach
Department of Economics
University of Pennsylvania
160 McNeil Building/CR
Philadelphia, Pennsylvania 19104

Martin J. Bailey
Department of Economics
University of Maryland
College Park, Maryland 20742

Martin N. Baily
The Brookings Institution
1775 Massachusetts Avenue
Washington, D.C. 20036

Robert J. Barro
Department of Economics
University of Rochester
Rochester, New York 14627

Ben S. Bernanke
Graduate School of Business
Stanford University
Stanford, California 94305

Stanley W. Black
Department of Economics
University of North Carolina
Gardner Hall, 017A
Chapel Hill, North Carolina 27514

Olivier J. Blanchard
Department of Economics, E52-
    271B
Massachusetts Institute of
    Technology
Cambridge, Massachusetts 02139

Alan S. Blinder
Department of Economics
Princeton University
Princeton, New Jersey 08544

Phillip Cagan
Department of Economics
Columbia University
New York, New York 10027

Angus Deaton
Department of Economics
Princeton University
Princeton, New Jersey 08544

J. Bradford DeLong
Department of Economics
Harvard University
Cambridge, Massachusetts 02138

851

Rudiger Dornbusch
Department of Economics, E52-357
Massachusetts Institute of
    Technology
Cambridge, Massachusetts 02139

Robert Eisner
Department of Economics
Northwestern University
Evanston, Illinois 60201

Solomon Fabricant
National Bureau of Economic
    Research
269 Mercer Street, Eighth Floor
New York, New York 10003

Stanley Fischer
Department of Economics, E52-
    280A
Massachusetts Institute of
    Technology
Cambridge, Massachusetts 02139

Benjamin M. Friedman
Department of Economics
Littauer Center 127
Harvard University
Cambridge, Massachusetts 02138

John Geweke
Department of Economics
Duke University
Durham, North Carolina 27706

Stephen M. Goldfeld
Department of Economics
Princeton University
Princeton, New Jersey 08540

Robert J. Gordon
Department of Economics
Northwestern University
Evanston, Illinois 60201

Herschel I. Grossman
Department of Economics
Brown University
Providence, Rhode Island 02912

Robert E. Hall
Herbert Hoover Memorial Building
Stanford University
Stanford, California 94305

Douglas Holtz-Eakin
Department of Economics
Columbia University
New York, New York 10027

Robert G. King
Department of Economics
University of Rochester
Rochester, New York 14627

Stephen R. King
Department of Economics
Stanford University
Stanford, California 94305

Edward P. Lazear
Graduate School of Business
University of Chicago
1101 East 58th Street
Chicago, Illinois 60637

Michael C. Lovell
Department of Economics
Wesleyan University
Middletown, Connecticut 06457

Bennett T. McCallum
Graduate School of Industrial
    Administration
Carnegie-Mellon University
Pittsburgh, Pennsylvania 15213

Allan H. Meltzer
Graduate School of Industrial
    Administration
Carnegie-Mellon University
Pittsburgh, Pennsylvania 15213

Geoffrey H. Moore
Center for International Business
    Cycle Research
808 Uris Hall
Graduate School of Business
Columbia University
New York, New York 10027

James L. Powell
Department of Economics
Massachusetts Institute of
  Technology
Cambridge, Massachusetts 02139

Anna J. Schwartz
National Bureau of Economic
  Research
269 Mercer Street, Eighth Floor
New York, New York 10003

Robert J. Shiller
Department of Economics
Yale University
New Haven, Connecticut 06520

John B. Shoven
Department of Economics
Encina Hall, Fourth Floor
Stanford University
Stanford, California 94305

Christopher A. Sims
Department of Economics
University of Minnesota
1035 Business Administration
  Building
Minneapolis, Minnesota 55455

Allen Sinai
Shearson Lehman/American Express, Incorporated
55 Water Street
New York, New York 10041

Kenneth J. Singleton
Department of Economics
Carnegie-Mellon University
Pittsburgh, Pennsylvania 15213

Lawrence H. Summers
Department of Economics
Harvard University
Cambridge, Massachusetts 02138

John B. Taylor
Department of Economics
Stanford University
Stanford, California 94305

Peter Temin
Department of Economics, E52-
  274C
Massachusetts Institute of
  Technology
Cambridge, Massachusetts 02139

John M. Veitch
Department of Economics
University of Southern California
Los Angeles, California 90089

Mark W. Watson
Department of Economics
Harvard University
Cambridge, Massachusetts 02138

Victor Zarnowitz
Graduate School of Business
University of Chicago
1101 East 58th Street
Chicago, Illinois 60637

Participants

Moses Abramovitz	Stanford University
Alan J. Auerbach	University of Pennsylvania
Martin J. Bailey	University of Maryland
Martin N. Baily	The Brookings Institution
Robert J. Barro	University of Rochester
Ben S. Bernanke	Stanford University
Stanley W. Black	University of North Carolina
Olivier J. Blanchard	Massachusetts Institute of Technology
Alan S. Blinder	Princeton University
Phillip Cagan	Columbia University
Lindley Clark	Wall Street Journal
Rosanne Cole	IBM Corporation
Angus Deaton	Princeton University
J. Bradford DeLong	Harvard University
Rudiger Dornbusch	Massachusetts Institute of Technology
Robert Eisner	Northwestern University
Solomon Fabricant	National Bureau of Economic Research
Stanley Fischer	Massachusetts Institute of Technology
Benjamin M. Friedman	Harvard University
John Geweke	Duke University
Stephen M. Goldfeld	Princeton University
Robert J. Gordon	Northwestern University
Herschel I. Grossman	Brown University
Robert E. Hall	Stanford University
James W. Hanson	Exxon Corporation
David Hartman	National Bureau of Economic Research
Douglas Holtz-Eakin	Columbia University
Robert G. King	University of Rochester
Stephen R. King	Stanford University
Edward P. Lazear	University of Chicago
Michael C. Lovell	Wesleyan University
Bennett T. McCallum	Carnegie-Mellon University
Allan H. Meltzer	Carnegie-Mellon University

Kenneth Militzer	American Telephone and Telegraph
Geoffrey H. Moore	Columbia University
Joel Popkin	Joel Popkin and Company
James L. Powell	Massachusetts Institute of Technology
Joan Robinson	Northwestern University
Anna J. Schwartz	National Bureau of Economic Research
Eli Shapiro	National Bureau of Economic Research
Robert J. Shiller	Yale University
John B. Shoven	Stanford University
Christopher A. Sims	University of Minnesota
Allen Sinai	Shearson Lehman/American Express, Incorporated
Kenneth J. Singleton	Carnegie-Mellon University
Lawrence H. Summers	Harvard University
John B. Taylor	Stanford University
Peter Temin	Massachusetts Institute of Technology
John M. Veitch	University of Southern California
Mark W. Watson	Harvard University
Victor Zarnowitz	University of Chicago
Seymour Zucker	Business Week

Author Index

Abel, Andrew B., 275, 277, 278, 301
Abramovitz, Moses, 183, 190, 206
Ackley, Gardner, 221
Altonji, Joseph, 240, 242, 587
Anderson, Barry, 240
Anderson, Leonall A., 7
Andrew, A. Piatt, 692
Ashenfelter, Orley, 587
Ashton, T. S., 741, 743

Bach, G. L., 442
Bagehot, Walter, 687
Baily, Martin, 595, 597, 679, 698
Ball, R. J., 585
Barro, Robert J., 240, 261, 361, 366, 370, 371, 381, 388, 390, 444, 587
Becker, Gary, 239
Bednarzik, Robert W., 546
Bernanke, Benjamin, 287, 618, 687, 688
Berndt, Ernst R., 586
Bischoff, Charles W., 274
Black, Stanley W., 503
Blanchard, Olivier J., 149, 227, 275, 277, 301, 325
Blank, David M., 328
Blinder, Alan S., 184, 186, 187, 188, 189, 206, 224, 225, 227, 229, 232
Bodkin, Ronald G., 586, 587
Boschan, Charlotte, 775
Bosworth, Barry, 280
Brechling, F. P. R., 585, 586
Breeden, D. T., 114

Brennan, Michael J., 225
Brimmer, Andrew F., 113
Bronfenbrenner, Martin, 105
Brunner, Karl, 397, 442, 444, 446
Bruno, Michael, 477
Bry, Gerhard, 585, 775
Burns, Arthur F., 1, 3, 25, 125, 520, 522, 523, 526, 576, 583, 679, 695, 738, 739, 745, 747, 748, 749, 764, 767
Butkiewicz, James, 240, 367, 369

Cagan, Phillip, 442, 556, 558, 563, 704
Card, David, 587
Chirinko, Robert S., 272, 274, 278, 587
Chow, Gregory C., 287, 329
Christ, Carl, 108
Clarida, Richard H., 426
Clark, J. M., 6, 301
Clark, Kim B., 587
Clark, Peter K., 325
Coen, Robert M., 585
Cohn, Richard A., 280
Creamer, Daniel, 547, 551, 588, 617
Cukierman, A., 446

de Leeuw, F., 151, 152
DeLong, J. Bradford, 558
Dornbusch, Rudiger, 503
Dunlop, John T., 586

Subject Index